FEDERAL INCOME TAXATION
OF CORPORATIONS AND PARTNERSHIPS

FEDERAL INCOME TAXATION OF CORPORATIONS AND PARTNERSHIPS

Third Edition

RICHARD L. DOERNBERG
K. H. Gyr Professor of Law
Emory University

HOWARD E. ABRAMS
Professor of Law
Emory University

ASPEN LAW & BUSINESS
A Division of Aspen Publishers, Inc.
Gaithersburg   New York

Permissions
Aspen Law & Business
1185 Avenue of the Americas
New York, NY 10036

Printed in the United States of America

ISBN 0-7355-1211-6

1 2 3 4 5 6 7 8 9 0

Library of Congress Cataloging-in-Publication Data

Federal income taxation of corporations and partnerships / Richard L. Doernberg ... [et al.].
    p. cm.
    Includes index.
    ISBN 0-7355-1211-6 (alk. paper)
    1. Corporations—Taxation—Law and legislation—United States—Cases. 2. Partner-
ship—Taxation—United States—Cases. I. Doernberg, Richard L.

KF6463.F43 2000
343.7305'267—dc21

                                                                    99-056001

About Aspen Law & Business
Legal Education Division

With a dedication to preserving and strengthening the long-standing tradition of publishing excellence in legal education, Aspen Law & Business continues to provide the highest quality teaching and learning resources for today's law school community. Careful development, meticulous editing, and an unmatched responsiveness to the evolving needs of today's discerning educators combine in the creation of our outstanding casebooks, coursebooks, textbooks, and study aids.

ASPEN LAW & BUSINESS
A Division of Aspen Publishers, Inc.
A Wolters Kluwer Company
www.aspenpublishers.com

To Nancy, Alison, and Sarah

RLD

To my parents, Leonard and Diana. And to Jan

HEA

SUMMARY OF CONTENTS

I

SUBCHAPTER C CORPORATIONS   1

II

SUBCHAPTER S CORPORATIONS   587

III

SUBCHAPTER K PARTNERSHIPS   649

CONTENTS

5

Redemptions and Partial Liquidations 177

6

Distributions of Stock   249

7

Liquidations   291

8

Integration of the Corporate and Individual Income
Taxes   331

9

10

11

Divisive Reorganizations   451

12

One-Party Reorganizations   493

13

Combining Tax Attributes: Net Operating Losses and Affiliated Corporations   503

14

Penalty Provisions   535

15

The Corporation as a Separate Taxable Entity   559

II

SUBCHAPTER S CORPORATIONS

16

S Corporations: Overview

17

S Corporations: Selected Topics   615

18

Transition Issues   637

III

SUBCHAPTER K PARTNERSHIPS   649

19

The Structure of Partnership Taxation   651

20

Determining Distributive Shares 671

21

22

23

A Partner's Transactions with the Partnership

24

Acquisitions of Partnership Interests

25

Dispositions of Partnership Interests   827

28

Partnership-Level Issues   899

PREFACE

This book traces its ancestry back to Professor Bittker's one-volume Federal Income Taxation casebook, published in 1955. Over the years, virtually every section of the Internal Revenue Code has been amended, almost always in the direction of greater complexity. Professor Bittker's original work has split three-for-one with separate volumes on individual, transfer, and corporate taxation. This book is the third edition of the volume on corporate taxation. With the increasing importance of partnership taxation in the world of commerce, this third edition combines both corporate and partnership taxation in a single volume that can be used to teach corporate taxation, partnership taxation, or a course that combines both areas.

Ironically, increasing complexity in the world of tax demands a more principled and straightforward treatment of teaching materials than ever before. It is no longer possible (and certainly not desirable) in an introductory business taxation course to tame the sea of minutiae that now comprise subchapters C, K, and S. Instead, it is our hope that through a thoughtful and orderly presentation of the themes that permeate the taxation of business entities, readers will develop the sophistication and expertise necessary to confront new challenges in the practice of law.

We have tried to listen to recommendations of past users in writing the third edition. To that end, we have updated every chapter of the book, interspersing new examples and problems throughout. Recent legislative and administrative developments have been integrated into the discussion. New cases and rulings have been added where helpful, and outdated cases and rulings have been removed. The materials selected for the book are deliberately noncomprehensive. We have tried to choose illustrative cases that not only describe typical commercial transactions but also emphasize major themes that run through the provisions dealing with entity taxation. It is our belief that the book can be covered in a three- or four-hour course, but it can easily be adapted to a two-hour course as well.

The taxation of business entities is a difficult subject even under the best of circumstances. We have tried not to "hide the ball." Our approach is to make liberal use of examples and to simplify some of the intricacies. We have no doubt that, notwithstanding our approach, students will be left with plenty to ponder. We have tried to clear away some of the underbrush so that students can contemplate the forest. In addition to the cases and note materials, the book features problems in almost every chapter. They can be used to lead students through the fundamentals of the tax provisions and can form a centerpiece for discussion of the cases and notes.

In exploring the tax consequences of business entities, the third edition is divided into three parts. Part I deals with the classical double tax system: tax at the corporate level, and tax at the shareholder level, embodied in subchapter C. Bridging Parts I and III is Part II's discussion of subchapter S, which contains elements of both subchapters C and K. Part III addresses the pass-through paradigm of partnership taxation laid out in subchapter K, where partners are taxed directly as the partnership earns income.

Each part unfolds in a manner calculated to help students master the concepts within. Part I uses a "cradle-to-grave" approach to reveal the mysteries of subchapter C. Starting with the formation of a corporation, including the capital structure, this part discusses the tax implications of corporate operation at the corporate level. Then nonliquidating distributions are considered, followed by liquidating distributions. Part I considers the world of corporate acquisitions and other reorganizations, both taxable and nontaxable. Several chapters on important aspects of corporate operation such as penalty provisions wrap up Part I.

Part II first looks at the operation of S corporations with no subchapter C history, then turns to the treatment of S corporations that had previously been C corporations and have elements of both subchapters C and S.

Part III explains the taxation of partnerships. Starting with the structure of partnership taxation, this part turns to the seminal issue in partnership taxation—determining distributive shares. It then proceeds to discuss the treatment of distributions, a partner's transactions with the partnership, acquisition and disposition of partnership interests, and a variety of partnership-level issues.

Students of taxation must possess an eye-hand coordination not required of other students. Not only must they read and study the casebook, but at the same time they must consume the Internal Revenue Code and corresponding regulations. The ability to read two or more things at the same time is a residual benefit one receives from the study of taxation. The book refers to the Code constantly. Rather than reproducing its splendor, the authors rely on students to study the Code as they study the book.

Students should not hesitate to consult additional references when interested. Bittker and Eustice's *Federal Income Taxation of Corporations and*

Shareholders (6th ed. 1998) with supplementation is a student's ready companion, offering lucid and more detailed explanations of all areas of corporate taxation. For partnership taxation issues, students may want to consult McKee, Nelson, and Whitmire, *Federal Taxation of Partnerships and Partners* (3d ed. 1997) with supplementation.

A few ministerial comments are in order at this point. First, the book makes ample use of cross-references because corporate tax provisions do not operate in a vacuum. As students learn more and more pieces of the subchapter C puzzle, the pieces will begin to interrelate and form a pattern. Second, the cases have been edited to feature the salient points. We have endeavored to indicate the omissions, but readers should be aware that citations and footnotes in the cases have often been omitted or abridged. Third, we have tried to incorporate some of the themes developed in the individual tax course. Assignment of income, the value of deferral, the interplay of the original issue discount rules with the installment sales rules, and the concepts of recapture are often invoked in the context of corporate transactions. Fourth, while we hope the book has a certain timeless quality to it, we would be remiss if we did not note that it is current through July of 1999.

The authors are greatly indebted to Professor Boris Bittker and Lawrence Stone who were co-authors on previous editions of this book. We express our gratitude to Mr. Fred T. Witt for his insights into the complex issues surrounding cancellation of indebtedness generally as well as his great help in the section on bankruptcy reorganizations more particularly. Lori Brenner, Seth Finkell, Allison Myers, and David Voss provided able research assistance. Finally, we would like to thank the American Law Institute for permission to reprint an excerpt from the Reporter's Study of Corporate Tax Integration (Federal Income Tax Project 1993). Copyright © 1993 by the American Law Institute. Reprinted by permission.

Howard E. Abrams
Richard L. Doernberg

August 1999

FEDERAL INCOME TAXATION
OF CORPORATIONS AND PARTNERSHIPS

I

SUBCHAPTER C CORPORATIONS

1

Introduction to the Corporate Income Tax

You may recall that the Supreme Court struck down the 1894 federal individual income tax in Pollack v. Farmers' Loan & Trust Co., 158 U.S. 601 (1895), as a direct tax requiring apportionment pursuant to article I, §9, clause 4, of the Constitution. In Flint v. Stone Tracy Co., 220 U.S. 107 (1911), the Supreme Court upheld a corporate income tax antedating the enactment of the sixteenth amendment as an indirect or "excise" tax imposed on corporations exercising the privilege of engaging in business as a corporation. In *Pollack* the Court also invalidated a corporate income tax too intertwined with the individual income tax to stand on its own. Congress has taxed corporate profit continuously since the 1909 statute upheld in Flint v. Stone Tracy Co. With the enactment of the sixteenth amendment in 1913, the constitutional validity of the federal corporate income tax was made doubly secure.

The 1909 act imposed a tax of 1 percent on corporate net income in excess of $5,000. Some 262,500 corporations filed returns for 1909, paying an aggregate amount of about $21 million. As of 1993, the highest corporate tax rate became 35 percent (see I.R.C. §11(b)), and as of 1996 the number of annual corporate returns exceeded 4.6 million.[1] These 4.6 million returns reported income of about $639 billion and produced about $170 billion in revenue. For comparison, in 1996 more than 120 million individual returns were filed, generating more than $658 billion in revenue. Thus, the corporate income tax produces about one-quarter of the

---

1. The Internal Revenue Service publishes in its quarterly Statistics of Income (SOI) bulletins various reports analyzing statistical data distilled from filed tax returns. Unfortunately, but understandably, these reports appear several years after the underlying data are generated. The figures in the text were taken from the Winter of 1998/1999 SOI bulletin.

revenue generated by the individual income tax. Combined, the corporate and individual income taxes account for more than half of all federal revenues and represent in excess of 10 percent of the gross national product (GNP).

The United States imposes an income tax on every citizen and resident alien. Dividends received, as well as most other accessions to wealth, form the base of that tax. Together, the corporate and individual income taxes form what is often called a double tax on corporate income. It is called a double tax because under this system the earnings of a corporation are taxed once when earned by the corporation and a second time when distributed to its shareholders as dividends.

For example, suppose corporate earnings are taxed at a flat rate of 35 percent while dividends are taxed to shareholders at a flat rate of 40 percent. The combined tax burden imposed by the corporate double tax is 61 percent, computed as follows. If the corporation earns $100, it must remit $35 in taxes, given the rates assumed in this example. That leaves $65 available for distribution, and if that entire amount is distributed, the shareholder receiving this $65 will in turn owe $26 in taxes. Thus, the shareholder will have only $65 − $26, or $39, to spend, and that means $61 of the $100 in earnings was paid in taxes.

Because a double tax is imposed on corporate earnings while only a single tax is imposed on unincorporated profits, you might suspect that businesses would eschew the corporate form in favor of some less heavily taxed enterprise such as a partnership. There are several nontax reasons why taxpayers might prefer the corporate form even at the cost of higher taxes. Traditionally, limited liability is one obvious reason for preferring a corporation to a partnership. However as noted at pages 562-565, taxpayers can now elect to have a limited liability company treated for tax purposes as if it were a partnership, thereby resulting in a single level of taxation while retaining limited liability. This development has changed the calculus for deciding whether to incorporate or to "check-the-box" to have a limited liability company treated as a partnership.

Nevertheless, the corporation is the most common form of business organization, and using such a familiar form may result in significant economies. Surprisingly, though, use of the corporate form can be tax advantageous, depending on the relative rates of the individual and corporate taxes. For example, assume that the individual tax is imposed at a 50 percent rate while the corporate tax is imposed at a 10 percent effective rate (the low rate may result from available deductions). If $100 of corporate earnings are distributed in the year earned, they will be subject to a combined tax of $55, $10 at the corporate level and an additional $45 (50 percent of the remaining $90) at the shareholder level. This of course compares unfavorably with profits earned directly by a shareholder, taxed (under our assumptions) at a flat 50 percent.

But now suppose that the corporation delays for three years distributing its after-tax $90 of earnings. The shareholder-level tax remains $45, but because the distribution has been delayed for three years, the present value of that tax burden as of the year in which earned is only about $34, assuming a 10 percent annual discount rate.[2] Thus, the total effective tax burden is only about $44 (the $10 corporate-level tax plus the present value of the shareholder-level tax), which compares favorably with a single, immediate tax of $50. In other words, if the shareholder-level income tax can be deferred and the corporate-level income tax is sufficiently low, the combined burden of the double tax on corporate earnings can be less than the single tax imposed on unincorporated profits. Similarly, if distributed corporate earnings are taxed to the shareholders at a preferential rate as compared with unincorporated profits, the combined burden of the corporate double tax may be less than the burden of the single, individual income tax.

Historically, the highest corporate tax rate was well below that of the highest individual tax rate. Accordingly, taxpayers often structured their transactions to deflect income away from themselves and their family members and to their controlled and family corporations. Between 1986 and 1992, however, the highest corporate individual tax rate exceeded the highest individual income tax rate. During this period, taxpayers shifted their strategy, trying instead to deflect income away from corporations and to individual taxpayers. As a result, some existing businesses were disincorporated, some new businesses were started in unincorporated form, and presumably many transactions were structured to minimize or wholly avoid the corporate income tax.

Starting in 1993, the highest marginal corporate tax rate became 35 percent while the highest individual rate became 39.6 percent.[3] Thus, we are back where we began, with taxpayers once again able to reduce their tax liabilities by sheltering taxable income within the corporate form. To be sure, a second tax may be due if corporate earnings are eventually distributed as dividends, but that second tax often can be postponed, minimized, or avoided by astute tax planners.

For example, when corporate earnings must be reported by shareholders, they sometimes can be reported as capital gain if the taxpayer sells or exchanges shares of stock. Currently, most capital gains are taxed at a 20 percent rate. §1(h). Recall that if a shareholder's estate or beneficiary sells shares of stock, §1014 provides a date-of-death fair market value basis,

---

2. That is, $34 invested for three years at 10 percent annual interest will grow to about $45.

3. While 39.6 percent is the highest nominal tax rate, the effective tax rate on individual income may be significantly higher because personal exemptions as well as itemized deductions are phased out for high-bracket individuals. Thus, the highest marginal rate for individual taxpayers in some cases is closer to 45 to 50 percent.

which may mean no taxation upon a sale of the shares. Depending on the length of deferral and the anticipated effective tax rate on a sale of shares, tax planners may see the corporate form as a tax haven or as a tax pitfall. This issue is explored in Chapter 8.

If a corporation could deduct the dividends it pays, the corporate double tax would be eliminated because the shareholder-level taxation would always be accompanied by a corporate-level deduction. While corporations cannot, in general, deduct their dividends, they can, like other taxpayers, deduct interest paid or accrued. §163. Interest and dividends are to some extent substitutes for each other because each is the price paid by a corporation to its investors for the use of their funds. For example, a corporation using debt to finance a continuing or new project will be entitled to deduct interest payments made to its lenders for the use of their money. On the other hand, if equity is used instead of debt, what would have been deductible interest payments becomes nondeductible dividends. It should come as no surprise that the use of corporate debt is widespread, due in part to the deductibility of payments on debt (interest) versus the nondeductibility of payments on equity (dividends).

For most of the income and deduction provisions with which you are already familiar, a corporation is a taxpayer like any other. Subchapter C addresses those issues peculiar to corporate taxpayers: In particular, it addresses corporate formations, corporate terminations (called *liquidations* in tax parlance), corporate rearrangements (*reorganizations*), and the complex set of problems incidental to corporate distributions made to shareholders as part of a corporation's ongoing operations. Subchapter C is divided into seven parts, the first three of which form the primary concern of this course. Take a moment to examine subchapter C, particularly part I, §§301-318 (distributions by corporations), part II, §§331-346 (corporate liquidations), and part III, §§351-368 (corporate organizations and reorganizations). Examination of these and other provisions of the Code begins in Chapter 2.

2

Corporate Formation

A. INTRODUCTION

1. The §351 Philosophy

Normally, when a taxpayer exchanges property for other property, any gain or loss realized on the exchange must be recognized by the transferor. §1001(c). The propriety of taxation is weakened, though, if the exchange does not significantly alter the nature of the taxpayer's investment. For example, §1031 provides for the nonrecognition of a taxpayer's gain or loss on the exchange property for other property of like kind. Consider *T,* an individual who owns an office building with an adjusted basis of $30,000 and a fair market value of $100,000. If *T* sells the building for $100,000, *T* has realized and must recognize a gain of $70,000. If instead *T* exchanges the office building for another office building also worth $100,000, *T*'s realized gain is again $70,000, but none of this gain is currently recognized. §1031(a). Because *T*'s basis in the old building becomes the basis in the new building, the $70,000 unrecognized gain is deferred until disposition of the new building.

Section 1031 reflects the congressional belief that taxation is inappropriate when there is substantial continuity of investment after the exchange. Reconsider the example above, but assume that now *T* exchanges the office building for all the stock of newly created *X* Corp. While §1031 does not apply to this exchange, *T* has hardly altered the substance of the original investment even though the form has changed: *X* Corp. owns the building, and *T* owns *X* Corp.

Since 1921 Congress has provided that this type of property-for-stock exchange should not be a taxable event. At the same time, it has never been the case that all transfers of property to corporations have been tax free. For example, a taxpayer who sells property to a corporation for cash is, and properly should be, subject to the general recognition rule of §1001(a).

Current §351 permits a taxpayer to defer taxation only if the taxpayer-transferor (1) transfers property to a corporation, (2) receives stock of the transferee corporation in exchange, and (3) is in control of the corporation immediately after the transaction (along with other transferors of property, if any). Through these requirements, §351 seeks to differentiate those exchanges more closely resembling mere changes in the form of investment from those exchanges resembling sales. Note that §351 can apply both to the formation of new corporations and to transfers to existing corporations (sometimes called "midstream" contributions).

Underlying all three requirements is the notion of continuity of investment. While the form of a taxpayer's investment may have changed from unincorporated to incorporated, the nature of the investment remains the same. These considerations apply only to a transfer of property. For example, suppose T and three other transferors form X Corp., with T contributing services while the other transferors contribute property. Although all transferors receive back X Corp. stock, the stock received by T is merely compensation for services rendered. Regardless of the form it takes, compensation will be immediately taxable on receipt. By its own terms, §351 does not apply to the exchange of services for stock. See §351(d)(1). Because such an exchange radically alters the form of a taxpayer's investment from human to corporate capital, immediate taxation seems appropriate. Moreover, the failure of T to qualify under §351 may render the provision inapplicable to the other three transferors (i.e., the transferors of property), whose stock interest in the corporation may be insufficient to satisfy the "control" requirement.

Under the second requirement of §351, the transferors must receive stock of the transferee corporation. Suppose T and three other joint owners of an office building that has appreciated in value transfer the property to X Corp. If T receives cash back while the other transferors receive X Corp. stock, will nonrecognition be appropriate? For T, who is not an X Corp. shareholder, nonrecognition under §351 is not available. There is no continuity; T simply has sold his share of the building. If T were to receive stock, however, nonrecognition seems appropriate since T would continue to enjoy the financial benefits of an interest in the property indirectly through stock ownership. If T receives both stock and cash for T's interest in the building, gain will be recognized to the extent of the cash since pro tanto T has terminated (i.e., sold) the investment.

What happens if T receives an interest in the corporation that carries less continuity than stock but more continuity than cash? Historically, a transferor receiving a long-term debt instrument (i.e., a security) from the transferee corporation could qualify for nonrecognition under §351. Now debt instruments are not qualifying property under §351.

Even if *T* transfers property in exchange for corporate stock, the third requirement — sufficient control over the corporate entity — may not be met. Suppose *T* and the other transferors exchange their interests in the building to General Motors for General Motors stock. The transferors' relationship to the original property is now far more attenuated than if they had incorporated the building into a newly formed, closely held corporation. This transaction would be treated like an all-cash transaction, substantially as if the transferors had sold the building to General Motors and then used the proceeds to purchase General Motors stock. To qualify for nonrecognition, the transferors of property must collectively satisfy §368(c), which requires that the transferors of property own at least 80 percent of the total combined voting power of all classes of stock entitled to vote and at least 80 percent of the total number of shares of all other classes of stock. See pages 47-63 infra.

Somewhere between the transfer of property to a wholly owned corporation and a transfer to General Motors is the transfer by a group of taxpayers, including *T*, of a variety of assets to *X* Corp. Suppose *T* transfers a building, *A* transfers machinery and equipment, and *B* transfers a truck, each receiving stock in exchange from *X* Corp. Now *T* has a stock interest in more than his original asset. At the same time, *T* no longer has the sole interest in his transferred property. Is the continuity sufficient in this type of transfer? Nonrecognition under §351 does envision incorporation by multiple transferors of property if together they meet the control requirement. But see the discussion of "swap funds" at page 10 infra.

2. The Statutory Terrain

When a corporation is formed, we are concerned with tax consequences both to the transferors and to the transferee corporation:

Transferors
§351 and §357 determine whether any gain or loss realized on the exchange is recognized;
§358 determines the transferor's basis in stock and property received from the corporation; and
§1223(1) determines the holding period of stock received from the corporation.

Transferee Corporation
§1032 provides nonrecognition for the corporation issuing stock in exchange for money or other property;
§362(a) determines the corporation's basis in property received; and
§1223(2) determines the holding period of the property received.

To illustrate: *B* owns a building with a basis of $30,000 and a fair market value of $75,000. *C* owns undeveloped real estate with a basis of $60,000 and a fair market value of $25,000. Together they form *X* Corp. in exchange for their assets. *B* receives $75,000 of *X* Corp. stock, and *C* receives $25,000 of *X* Corp. stock. Section 351 prevents *B* and *C* from recognizing gain and loss, respectively, on the exchange. One "price" *B* pays for nonrecognition of his gain is the transfer of *B*'s $30,000 basis in the building to the stock received. §358(a). When and if *B* sells his stock, the previously realized but unrecognized $45,000 gain attributable to the building will be taken into account. The "consolation" *C* gets for the nonrecognition of her loss is the transfer of her $60,000 basis to the stock. When and if *C* sells her stock, the $35,000 loss that went unrecognized on the formation of the corporation will be taken into account. On a sale or exchange of their stock, both *B* and *C* must "tack" the holding period of their respective capital or §1231 assets on to the holding period of their stock. Thus, if the total period of time during which *B* held his capital asset and stock is more than one year, the sale of stock will produce long-term capital gain, assuming the stock is a capital asset in the hands of *B*.

X Corp., which exchanges its own stock for assets, receives nonrecognition treatment under §1032. The basis of the assets received carries over from the transferors to *X* Corp., resulting in a $30,000 basis in the building and a $60,000 basis in the undeveloped real estate pursuant to §362(a). Upon a sale or exchange of the assets, *X* Corp. must tack the holding period of the transferors in those assets. §1223(2).

Note that if *B* immediately sells his stock for $75,000, he will recognize a $45,000 gain, and if *X* Corp. sells the building for $75,000, it will also recognize a $45,000 gain. This double gain may seem an unfair product of the corporate income tax. See discussion at page 331 infra. The same double counting can occur with losses as well. A sale by *C* of stock and by *X* Corp. of the undeveloped real estate results in a double loss deduction. Can you think of a way to avoid this double gain or loss? Indeed, if both the stock and the asset basis did not preserve the previously unrealized gain, then indefinite postponement of gain might be possible. If the asset's basis were increased on incorporation, the asset could be converted to cash with no further gain. If the stock basis were increased, however, a shareholder could sell at no gain the stock whose value reflects the property's appreciation.

Suppose a dozen independent business people transfer their separate businesses to a newly organized corporation, each receiving stock equal to the value of the assets given up. Does §351 apply even though the nature of each transferor's investment has changed, or must there be a showing (although no statutory provision explicitly requires it) that the transferors have not drastically altered their economic status? The cases and the rulings do not require any such showing in general, but Congress has focused on this issue in a specific area.

Section 351(e)(1) deals with so-called swap funds. These were invest-ment pools organized by stockbrokers to enable investors holding appreci-ated securities (ordinarily in a single company or in a few companies) to transfer these undiversified investments to a holding company in exchange for stock in a newly organized company that would obtain a wide range of investments (because the transferors as a group held a variety of securities, even though each individual might not). Note how such an exchange would satisfy the three requirements of §351 set out at page 8 supra. The result was diversification on a tax-free basis, assuming the applicability of §351. After a few favorable rulings, the IRS announced that it would no longer accede to §351 treatment for swap fund exchanges. See Treas. Regs. §1.351-1(c)(1). Congress thereafter enacted §351(e) to settle the question.

With these general principles in mind, we turn to the specific require-ments of §351.

B.   PROPERTY

Not surprisingly, when a person transfers services for stock, that person does not fall under §351 and normally will recognize gain on the exchange. But can that transaction affect the tax treatment of others who are transfer-ring property to a corporation in exchange for stock?

James v. Commissioner
53 T.C. 63 (1969)

SIMPSON, Judge. . . .

The issue for decision is whether the transaction by which Mr. James and Mr. Talbot acquired stock in a corporation was taxable or whether such transaction was tax free under section 351 of the Internal Revenue Code of 1954. The answer to the question thus posed with respect to each person depends on the determination of whether Mr. James received his stock in exchange for a transfer of property or as compensation for services.

FINDINGS OF FACT

For many years, Mr. James was a builder, real estate promoter, and devel-oper with offices in Myrtle Beach, S.C. He has held the office of vice president of the National Association of Home Builders and was chairman of the association's Senior Citizens Housing Committee. During 1963, the James Construction Co. was licensed by the State of South Carolina to engage in the business of general contracting.

On January 12, 1963, Mr. and Mrs. Talbot entered into an agreement with Mr. James for the promotion and construction of a rental apartment project, consisting of not less than 50 apartments, the project to conform to Federal Housing Administration (FHA) standards. The agreement provided that on completion of the project the parties would form a corporation to take title to the project. The voting stock in such corporation was to be distributed one-half to the Talbots and one-half to Mr. James, and nonvoting stock was to be issued to the parties "as the equity of each party in the corporation shall be," with the proviso that Mr. James should have the right to purchase up to 50 percent of such stock over a period of years. The Talbots agreed to transfer to the corporation the land on which the apartment project was to be built, such land to be the only asset contributed by the Talbots to the venture. Mr. James agreed "to promote the project . . . and . . . [to] be responsible for the planning, architectural work, construction, landscaping, legal fees, and loan processing of the entire project." . . .

After the execution of the January 12 agreement, Mr. James began negotiations to fulfill his part of the contract. He made arrangements with an attorney and an architectural firm to perform the work necessary to meet FHA requirements — development of legal documents, preparation of architectural plans, and the like; and he obtained from United Mortgagee Service Corp. (United Mortgagee), a lender, its agreement to finance the project and a commitment by FHA to insure the financing. Mr. James personally met with the FHA only twice — once in connection with the amount of the commitment and again at the final closing of the loan, after construction of the project was completed in the late summer of 1964. Most of the arrangements necessary to the securing of the loan and the FHA commitment were handled by the attorney, the architectural firm, and United Mortgagee. The attorney's and architect's fees were not paid by Mr. James but were paid out of the proceeds of the construction loan by the corporation subsequently established.

On August 8, 1963, the FHA issued to United Mortgagee a commitment for the insurance of advances in the amount of $850,700 to Chicora Apartments, Inc., for the apartment project sponsored by Mr. James and the Talbots. On August 27, 1963, United Mortgagee sent Mr. James a draft of a proposed agreement to make a first mortgage loan of $850,700 on the Chicora Apartment project in accordance with Mr. James' application for such loan. . . .

On November 5, 1963, Chicora Apartments, Inc. (Chicora), was granted, upon application of Messrs. Talbot and James, a corporate charter, stating its authorized capital stock to consist of 20 no-par common shares. On the same date, the land on which the apartment project was to be constructed was conveyed to Chicora by Mrs. Talbot in consideration for 10 shares of stock. Nine of these shares were issued to Mrs. Talbot, and one share was issued to Mr. Talbot. . . . Also on November 5, 1963, 10 shares of stock were issued to Mr. James. The minutes of a meeting of Chicora's board of directors held on that date state that those 10 shares were issued to Mr. James in consideration of his "transfer" to the corporation of the "following described property":

> 1. FHA Commitment issued pursuant to Title 2, Section 207 of the National Housing Act, whereby the FHA agrees to insure a mortgage loan in the amount of $850,700.00, on a parcel of land in Myrtle Beach, South Carolina. . . .
>
> 2. Commitment from United Mortgagee Servicing Corp., agreeing to make a mortgage loan on said property in the amount of $850,700.00 and also commitment from said mortgagee to make an interim construction loan in an identical amount.
>
> 3. Certain contracts and agreement which W. A. James over the past two years have [sic] worked out and developed in connection with the architectural and construction services required for said project.
>
> 4. The use of the finances and credit of W. A. James during the past two years (and including the construction period) in order to make it possible to proceed with the project.

Thus, as a result of these transactions, Chicora had outstanding all 20 of its authorized shares of stock. . . .

Both Mr. and Mrs. James and Mr. and Mrs. Talbot deemed their receipt of Chicora common stock to be in return for a transfer of property to a controlled corporation under section 351. Accordingly, neither family reported any income from such receipt on their respective income tax returns for 1963. In his statutory notice of deficiency, the respondent determined that Mr. James received such stock, with a value of $22,000, for services rendered and not in exchange for property, and thus received taxable income in that amount. He further determined that the Talbot's [sic] transfer of property to Chicora did not meet the requirements of section 351, with the result that they should have recognized a long-term capital gain of $14,675 — the difference between $7,325, the basis of the land transferred, and $22,000, the value of the stock received.

OPINION

The first, and critical, issue for our determination is whether Mr. James received his Chicora stock in exchange for the transfer of property or as compensation for services. The petitioners argue that he received such stock in consideration of his transfer to Chicora of the FHA and United Mortgagee commitments and that such commitments constituted "property" within the meaning of section 351. . . . The respondent does not appear to challenge the petitioners' implicit assertion that Mr. James was not expected to render future services to the corporation in exchange for the issuance of stock to him. Although the accuracy of this assertion is subject to some question, the state of the record is such that we must decide the issues as the parties have presented them. Thus, the sole question on this issue is whether Mr. James' personal services, which the petitioners freely admit were rendered, resulted in the development of a property right which was transferred to Chicora, within the meaning of section 351. . . .

[The predecessor to §351(d)(1)] was first included in the statute as a part of the 1954 Code, although it is said merely to restate the case law. See Bittker & Eustice, Federal Income Taxation of Corporations and Shareholders 70 (2d ed. 1966). In explaining the [provision], the House Ways and Means Committee stated:

> In accordance with this provision, such stock or securities received by a person who has rendered or will render services to the transferee corporation would be fully taxable as compensation upon receipt. Your committee does not intend, however, to vitiate the remaining portion of the transaction, through application of this provision.

(H. Rept. No. 1337, to accompany H.R. 8300 (Pub. L. 591), 83d Cong., 2d Sess., p. A117 (1954).)

According to the petitioners' argument, Mr. James, as a result of the services performed by him, acquired certain contract rights which constituted property and which he transferred to Chicora. The fact that such rights resulted from the performance of personal services does not, in their view, disqualify them from being treated as property for purposes of section 351. In support of this position, the petitioners refer to situations involving the transfer of patents and secret processes. . . .

It is altogether clear that for purposes of section 351, not every right is to be treated as property. . . . [Section 351(d)(1)] indicates that, whatever may be considered as property for purposes of local law, the performance of services, or the agreement to perform services, is not to be treated as a transfer of property for purposes of section 351. Thus, if in this case we have merely an agreement to perform services in exchange for stock of the corporation to be created, the performance of such services does not constitute the transfer of property within the meaning of section 351.

Although patents and secret processes — the product of services — are treated as property for purposes of section 351, we have carefully analyzed the arrangement in this case and have concluded that Mr. James did not transfer any property essentially like a patent or secret process; he merely performed services for Chicora. In January of 1963, he entered into an agreement to perform services for the corporation to be created. He was to secure the necessary legal and architectural work and to arrange for the financing of the project, and these were the services performed by him. Although he secured the services of the lawyer and the architect, they were paid for by the corporation. He put in motion the wheels that led to the FHA commitment, but it was not a commitment to him — it was a commitment to United Mortgagee to insure a loan to Chicora, a project sponsored by Mr. James. It was stipulated that under the FHA regulations, a commitment would not be issued to an individual, but only to a corporation. Throughout these arrangements, it was contemplated that a corporation would be created and that the commitment would run to the corporation. The petitioners rely heavily on the claim that Mr. James had a right to the commitment, that such right constituted property, and that such right was transferred to the corporation in return for his stock. However, the commitment was not his to transfer; he never acquired ownership of the commitment — he could not and did not undertake to acquire such ownership. The evidence as to the commitment by United Mortgagee to make a loan for the construction of the project is somewhat incomplete, but since all the parties knew that a corporation was to be formed and that the FHA commitment would be made to that corporation, it seems clear that there was no commitment to loan to Mr. James the funds necessary for the construction of the project. Thus, throughout these arrangements, Mr. James never undertook to acquire anything for himself; he was, in accordance with his agreement with the Talbots, making the preliminary arrangements for the construction of the apartment project. The enterprise would be operated, once the initial steps were completed, by a corporation, Chicora, and everything that was done by him was done on behalf of the contemplated corporation. In these circumstances, it seems clear that Mr. James received his share of the stock in the corporation in return for the services performed by him and that he did not transfer any property, within the meaning of section 351, to the corporation. . . .

The facts of this case are substantially similar to those in United States v. Frazell, 335 F.2d 487 (C.A.5, 1964), . . . certiorari denied 380 U.S. 961 (1964). In that case, the taxpayer, a geologist, investigated certain oil and gas properties to be acquired by a joint venture, and he was to receive an interest in the joint venture. However, before any transfer was made to him, a corporation was formed to take over the assets of the joint venture, and part of the stock was transferred to the taxpayer. It was not clear whether the taxpayer acquired an interest in the joint venture which was then exchanged for his share of the stock or whether he acquired the stock directly in exchange for the services performed by him. The court found that, in either event, the taxpayer received compensation for his services. If he received the stock in return for the services performed by him, such stock was taxable as compensation; and he did not transfer any property to the corporation within the meaning of section 351. See also Mailloux v. Commissioner, 320 F.2d 60 (C.A.5, 1963), affirming on this issue a Memorandum Opinion of this Court.

The next question is whether the Talbots are taxable on the gain realized from the exchange of their land for Chicora stock. Section 351(a) applies only if immediately after the transfer those who transferred property in exchange for stock owned at least 80 percent of Chicora's stock. Sec. 368(c). Since Mr. James is not to be treated as a transferor of property, he cannot be included among those in control for purposes of this test. Fahs v. Florida Machine & Foundry Co., 168 F.2d 957 (C.A.5, 1948); . . . Bittker & Eustice, supra. The transferors of property, the Talbots, did not have the required 80-percent control of Chicora immediately after the transfer, and therefore, their gain must be recognized. This result is inconsistent with the apparent meaning of the second sentence from the committee report, but the statutory scheme does not permit any other conclusion.

Decisions will be entered for the respondent.

NOTES

1. *Services*. Services transferred to a corporation do not qualify as property for purposes of §351. §351(d)(1). One reason for this restriction is to prevent conversion of ordinary income from services into capital gains when the worker sells the stock received. Note the inconsistency between the treatment of services that do not qualify as property under §351 and inventory that does qualify even though its sale would produce ordinary income. If a transferor of appreciated inventory receives stock in a §351 transaction, does the sale of stock produce a capital gain? See §341, discussed at page 551 infra, which seeks to curb attempts through the use of collapsible corporations to convert ordinary income to capital gains.

As *James* indicates, the consequences that flow from a transfer of services can be devastating both to the transferor of services as well as to the transferors of property. James, unable to avail himself of the nonrecognition provisions of §351, was forced to treat the stock received as compensation. What effect did James's failure to satisfy §351 have on the Talbots? After all, they did transfer property in receipt for stock. Since *the transferors of property* were not in "control" of Chicora, however, they too failed to satisfy the requirements of §351. In accordance with §1001, they were taxed on the difference between the adjusted basis of the property transferred and the fair market value of the stock received. Given §351's purpose, is this an appropriate outcome? Note that the consequences of a transfer of services may be welcome, rather than devastating, to transferors of property who wish to recognize gain because of the availability of offsetting losses from other transactions and to those who wish to recognize losses on the exchange. See page 71 infra.

Suppose James had transferred property as well as services in exchange for stock. Would he have gain to recognize? Would the Talbots? One who transfers both property and personal services is considered a transferor for purposes of satisfying the 80 percent control group requirement. Gain or loss attributable to the property transferred for stock will not be recognized under §351, and *all* the stock received can be counted toward the 80 percent control test. Treas. Regs. §1.351-1(a)(2) (example 3). What if James had transferred $1 of cash and $21,999 of services in exchange for his $22,000 stock interest? See Treas. Regs. §1.351-1(a)(1)(ii) and Rev. Proc. 77-37, 1977-2 C.B. 568 (for ruling purposes, property transferred must be equal at least to 10 percent of the stock received).

Note that the Talbots and James had some tax counseling before forming the corporation. The Chicora corporate minutes stated that the transfer of stock to James was in exchange for property. What property? The line between services and property is fuzzy at best. In United States v. Frazell, discussed in *James*, the taxpayer-geologist was to locate certain properties for a group of unincorporated investors in return for an interest in the properties. When the taxpayer received stock in a corporation organized to hold the acquired properties, he did not report the fair market value of the stock as income, arguing instead that he had transferred a partnership interest to the corporation. The Fifth Circuit ruled against the taxpayer without having to decide whether the taxpayer transferred a property interest. Either the taxpayer received stock for services, in which case §351 would be inapplicable, or if property (that is, a partnership interest) was transferred, the taxpayer was taxable on the receipt of the partnership interest for services rendered. In the latter case, the transfer of the partnership interest would qualify under §351. For a collection of cases on the property versus services question, see Stafford v. United States, 727 F.2d 1043 (11th Cir. 1984).

For a full discussion of the what constitutes property for purposes of §351, see IRS Field Service Advice 1999-1154.

2.   *Intellectual property. James* and *Frazell* illustrate the tension between services and service-flavored property. Nowhere is the line more blurred than in cases involving industrial "know how," secret processes and formulas, etc. In Rev. Rul. 64-56, 1964-1 C.B. (pt. 1) 133, and Rev. Rul. 71-564, 1971-2 C.B. 179, amplifying it, the Service set forth guidelines for distinguishing between industrial know-how and services. Did the court in *James* adequately address this issue?

Section 351 requires that property be "transferred." What constitutes a transfer? The issue arises most often when intangibles are assigned to corporations. The Service takes the position that there must be a sale or exchange within the meaning of the capital gains provisions of §1222 in order to qualify under §351 or else the transaction will be considered a license resulting in income to the licensor in the amount of the stock or securities received. The Service's requirement means that an exclusive, unqualified right in perpetuity must be given to the transferee. See Rev. Rul. 71-564, 1971-2 C.B. 179; Rev. Rul. 69-156, 1969-1 C.B. 101; Rev. Rul.

64-56, 1964-1 C.B. (pt. 1) 133. In E.I. DuPont de Nemours & Co. v. United
States, 471 F.2d 1211 (Ct. Cl. 1973), however, the court held that the sale
or exchange requirement of §1221 is not embodied in §351. The court
determined that a nonexclusive, royalty-free license in exchange for stock
was a sufficient transfer to qualify under §351. See IRS Field Service Advice
1999-1154 for a full discussion of intellectual property and §351.

  3. *Accounts receivable.* Suppose a cash basis transferor has performed
services for a third party prior to incorporation in exchange for an account
receivable. What treatment is appropriate if the receivable is transferred
to a newly formed corporation as part of a §351 transaction? In Hempt
Bros., Inc. v. United States, 490 F.2d 1172 (3d Cir. 1974), the court held
that accounts receivable constituted property for purposes of §351. Does
the assignment of income doctrine render the transferor or the corporation taxable when the receivable is paid? See page 79 infra. Suppose a cash
basis taxpayer performs services for the transferee corporation in exchange
for an account receivable. If the taxpayer exchanges the receivable for
stock, does the receivable constitute property? Is this more or less what
happened in *James*?

  4. *Miscellaneous property interests.* Money constitutes property for purposes of §351. See Rev. Rul. 69-357, 1969-1 C.B. 101. An equitable interest
in property constitutes property for purposes of §351. In Roberts Co. v.
Commissioner, 5 T.C. 1 (1945), attorneys who had a contingent fee interest
in the proceeds from an eventual sale of land were, along with the land-
owners, considered transferors of property.

  Section 351(d)(2) and (3) excludes debt of the transferee not evidenced by a security as well as accrued interest, which in effect is treated
as paid with stock. Presumably, this exclusion from property status will
allow the creditor to claim a bad debt deduction under §166 if the debt
is only partially satisfied with the transferee's stock, but the creditor must
recognize gain to the extent that the fair market value of the stock exceeds
the basis in the debt. For the treatment of the debtor corporation, see
§108(e)(10).

C. STOCK

1. Boot

Before considering what constitutes stock, consider why it matters. Section
351(a) mandates nonrecognition on an exchange only if it is *solely* for
stock of the transferee corporation. Receipt of stock carries a continuity
of investment in the assets transferred. Yet §351(b) tells us that "solely"
does not mean solely. If a transfer would be covered by §351(a) but for
the fact that nonqualifying property ("boot") is received in addition to

stock, §351 protection is still available. The fair market value of the non-qualifying property will, however, be taxable to the extent of any gain realized on the transfer. For example, suppose *T* transfers an asset with a basis of $10 and fair market value of $50 to *X* Corp. in exchange for $20 of *X* Corp. stock and $30 of cash in a transaction that would otherwise qualify under §351. In accordance with §351(b), *T* would include in income the $30 of boot since it does not exceed the $40 realized gain.

The character — capital gain or ordinary income — of any recognized gain will be determined by looking at the nature of the property transferred. Any taxable gain is treated as ordinary income to the extent the transferred property is subject to depreciation recapture. Note that in the absence of boot, depreciable property transferred in a §351 exchange will not be subject to recapture. §§1245(b)(3) and 1250(d)(3).

It should be noted that when property whose basis exceeds its fair market value (i.e., loss property) is transferred to a corporation, the receipt of boot does not remove the transaction from the reach of §351, thereby permitting a loss to be recognized. §351(b)(2).

In a transaction that otherwise qualifies under §351, the receipt of boot is taxable to a transferor exchanging appreciated property for stock. If a transferor transfers more than one piece of property to a transferee corporation, how is boot allocated?

Rev. Rul. 68-55
1968-1 C.B. 140

In determining the amount of gain recognized under section 351(b) . . . where several assets were transferred to a corporation, each asset must be considered transferred separately in exchange for a portion of each category of consideration received. The fair market value of each category of consideration received is separately allocated to the transferred assets in proportion to the relative fair market values of the transferred assets. Where as a result of such allocation there is a realized loss with respect to any asset, such loss is not recognized under section 351(b)(2) of the Code.

Advice has been requested as to the correct method of determining the amount and character of the gain to be recognized by Corporation *X* under section 351(b) . . . under the circumstances described below.

Corporation *Y* was organized by *X* and *A*, an individual who owned no stock in *X*. *A* transferred 20*x* dollars to *Y* in exchange for stock of *Y* having a fair market value of 20*x* dollars and *X* transferred to *Y* three separate assets and received in exchange stock of *Y* having a fair market value of 100*x* dollars plus cash of 10*x* dollars.

In accordance with the facts set forth in the table below if *X* had sold at fair market value each of the three assets it transferred to *Y*, the result would have been as follows:

Character of asset	Asset I	Asset II	Asset III
	Capital asset held more than [one year]	Capital asset held not more than [one year]	Section 1245 property.
Fair market value	$22x	$33x	$55x
Adjusted basis	40x	20x	25x
Gain (loss)	($18x)	$13x	$30x
Character of gain or loss	Long-term capital loss.	Short-term capital gain.	Ordinary income.

The facts in the instant case disclose that with respect to the section 1245 property the depreciation subject to recapture exceeds the amount of gain that would be recognized on a sale at fair market value. Therefore, all of such gain would be treated as ordinary income under section 1245(a)(1) of the Code.

Under section 351(a) of the Code, no gain or loss is recognized if property is transferred to a corporation solely in exchange for its stock and immediately after the exchange the transferor is in control of the corporation. If section 351(a) of the Code would apply to an exchange but for the fact that there is received, in addition to the property permitted to be received without recognition of gain, other property or money, then under section 351(b) of the Code gain (if any) to the recipient will be recognized, but in an amount not in excess of the sum of such money and the fair market value of such other property received, and no loss to the recipient will be recognized.

The first question presented is how to determine the amount of gain to be recognized under section 351(b) of the Code. The general rule is that each asset transferred must be considered to have been separately exchanged. See the authorities cited in Revenue Ruling 67-192, C.B. 1967-2, 140, and in Revenue Ruling 68-23, [1968-1 C.B. 144], which hold that there is no netting of gains and losses for purposes of applying sections 367 and 356(c) of the Code. Thus, for purposes of making computations under section 351(b) of the Code, it is not proper to total the bases of the various assets transferred and to subtract this total from the fair market value of the total consideration received in the exchange. Moreover, any treatment other than an asset-by-asset approach would have the effect of allowing losses that are specifically disallowed by section 351(b)(2) of the Code.

The second question presented is how, for purposes of making computations under section 351(b) of the Code, to allocate the cash and stock received to the amount realized as to each asset transferred in the exchange. The asset-by-asset approach for computing the amount of gain realized in the exchange requires that for this purpose the fair market value of each category of consideration received must be separately allocated to the transferred assets in proportion to the relative fair market values of the transferred assets. See section 1.1245-4(c)(1) of the Income Tax Regulations, which, for the same reasons, requires that for purposes of computing the amount of gain to which section 1245 of the Code applies each category of consideration received must be allocated to the properties transferred in proportion to their relative fair market values.

Accordingly, the amount and character of the gain recognized in the exchange should be computed as follows:

	Total	Asset I	Asset II	Asset III
Fair market value of asset transferred	$110x	$22x	$33x	$55x
Percent of total fair market value		20%	30%	50%
Fair market value of Y stock received in exchange	$100x	$20x	$30x	$50x
Cash received in exchange	10x	2x	3x	5x
Amount realized	$110x	$22x	$33x	$55x
Adjusted basis		40x	20x	25x
Gain (loss) realized		($18x)	$13x	$30x

Under section 351(b)(2) of the Code the loss of 18x dollars realized on the exchange of Asset Number I is not recognized. Such loss may not be used to offset the gains realized on the exchanges of the other assets. Under section 351(b)(1) of the Code, the gain of 13x dollars realized on the exchange of Asset Number II will be recognized as short-term capital gain in the amount of 3x dollars, the amount of cash received. Under sections 351(b)(1) and 1245(b)(3) of the Code, the gain of 30x dollars realized on the exchange of Asset Number III will be recognized as ordinary income in the amount of 5x dollars, the amount of cash received.

NOTES

Y's basis in the assets received under §362 is equal to A's basis plus any gain recognized to A. Accordingly, for Asset I, Y's basis is $40x; for Asset II, Y's basis is $23x (transferred basis of $20x plus $3x of recognized gain); for Asset III, Y's basis is $30x (transferred basis of $25x plus $5x gain recognized). Notice that the basis Y takes in the transferred assets preserves the gain (or loss) that went unrecognized by X on the §351 transfer.

Next consider the basis X takes in the stock it receives from Y under §358. Is the basis (and holding period) of the stock received determined in the aggregate (i.e., by looking at the aggregate bases of the property transferred by X and the aggregate gain recognized)? Or does that portion of the stock received by X in exchange for each asset derive its basis (and holding period) from that asset?

Rev. Rul. 85-164 _____
1985-2 C.B. 117

ISSUE

May a transferor determine the bases and holding periods of stock . . . received in a transfer under section 351 of the Internal Revenue Code by designating the specific property to be exchanged for particular stock. . . ?

FACTS

A, an individual, was engaged in a business as a sole proprietor. The assets of the sole proprietorship consisted of trade accounts receivable with an adjusted basis of zero and a fair market value of $60x$ dollars, machinery with an adjusted basis of $5x$ dollars and a fair market value of $10x$ dollars, and real estate (land and building) with an adjusted basis of $25x$ dollars and a fair market value of $30x$ dollars. A had held the real estate and machinery for over one year. Both the real estate and machinery were property described in section 1231 of the Code.

In order to limit personal liability, A transferred all of the assets associated with the sole proprietorship to a new corporation, Y, in exchange for all of Y's stock. . . . A transferred the accounts receivable to Y in exchange for 100 shares of common stock, the fair market value of which was $60x$ dollars. A transferred the machinery and real estate to Y in exchange for [100 shares of preferred stock],* which had a principal amount and a fair market value of $40x$ dollars. The selection of specific items for exchange was made to allocate assets with a high basis and long-term holding period to the [preferred stock].

LAW AND ANALYSIS

Section 351(a) of the Code provides that no gain or loss will be recognized if property is transferred to a corporation by a person solely in exchange

---

* In the ruling, A receives common stock and securities that under the law then in effect were qualifying property under §351. Because securities are no longer qualifying property under §351, the ruling will apply to allocate basis to any stock received (e.g., common and preferred stock). — EDS.

for stock . . . in such corporation and immediately after the exchange such person is in control (as defined in section 368(c)) of the corporation.

Section 358(a)(1) of the Code and section 1.358-1 of the Income Tax Regulations provide that in the case of an exchange to which section 351 applies in which only nonrecognition property is received, the basis of all of the stock . . . received in the exchange shall be the same as the basis of all property exchanged therefor. Section 358(b)(1) directs that, under regulations prescribed by the Secretary, the basis determined under subsection (a)(1) shall be allocated among the properties permitted to be received without the recognition of gain or loss.

Section 1.358-2(a) of the regulations prescribes rules for the allocation of basis among nonrecognition property received in corporate reorganization exchanges governed by sections 354, 355, 356. . . . In general, these rules allow limited tracing of the basis of old stock . . . into new only with respect to (i) persons who owned stock . . . of more than one class . . . before the exchange and (ii) corporate recapitalizations under section 368(a)(1)(E). In all other cases, including exchanges under section 351, section 1.358-2(b)(2) provides that the basis of property transferred shall be allocated among all the stock . . . received in proportion to the fair market values of the stock of each class. . . .

Section 1223(1) and section 1.1223-1(a) of the regulations require that, in determining the period for which a taxpayer has held property received in an exchange, there shall be included the period for which he held the property exchanged if (i) in the taxpayer's hands the property received has the same basis in whole or in part as the property exchanged and (ii) for exchanges after March 1, 1954, the property exchanged was at the time of exchange a capital asset as defined in section 1221 or property used in a trade or business as described in section 1231.

Rev. Rul. 62-140, 1962-2 C.B. 181, holds that a share of stock received in exchange for a debenture and a cash payment had a split holding period. The portion of each share received attributable to ownership of the debenture was treated as including the period for which the taxpayer held the debenture and the portion of each share received attributable to the cash payment was treated as held beginning with the date following the date of acquisition.

Rev. Rul. 68-55, 1968-1 C.B. 140, holds that when property is transferred to a corporation under section 351(a) of the Code each asset must be considered transferred separately in exchange for a proportionate share of each of the various categories of the total consideration received.

In the instant case, A formed Y by transferring all of the business assets of the sole proprietorship to Y in exchange solely for all of Y's stock. . . . Y will continue to carry on the business that A conducted, and A will remain in control of Y. The transfer, therefore, is subject to section 351 of the Code, with the bases and holding periods of the Y stock . . . in

the hands of *A* determined under sections 358 and 1223 of the Code,
respectively.

A may not determine the bases and holding periods of the *Y* stock
. . . received by designating specific property to be exchanged for particular
stock. . . . Under sections 1.358-1 and 1.358-2(b)(2) of the regulations, the
aggregate basis of the property transferred is allocated among the stock
. . . received in proportion to the fair market values of each class. The
holding period of the *Y* stock . . . received by *A* is determined by referring
to the assets deemed exchanged for each portion of the stock. . . . The
aggregate basis of the property transferred was $30x$ dollars. Since the [com-
mon and preferred] stock . . . *A* received had fair market values of $60x$
dollars and $40x$ dollars, respectively, a basis of $18x$ dollars ($60x/100x \times
30x$) is allocated to the *Y* [common] stock received by *A*, and a basis of
$12x$ dollars ($40x/100x \times 30x$) is allocated to the *Y* [preferred stock] received. In addition, each share of *Y* stock . . . received by *A* has a split
holding period and a split basis for purposes of determining long-term or
short-term capital gain or loss. That fraction of each share of *Y* stock . . .
attributable to the real estate and machinery ($40x/100x$) is treated as
including the period (over one year) for which *A* held the real estate and
machinery and has a basis solely attributable to the real estate and machinery (e.g., the $40x/100x$ of each share of stock attributable to the real estate
and machinery will have a basis of $.18x$ dollars ($18x/100$ shares)). The
fraction of each share of *Y* stock . . . attributable to the accounts receivable
($60x/100x$) has a holding period beginning on the day after the exchange
and has a zero basis. If part or all of the stock . . . received in the exchange
is disposed of at a time when the split holding period is relevant in determining tax liability, the same fractions will be applied to apportion the
amount realized among the above components of the stock. . . .

This holding would be unaffected if *A* were to make a transfer in
exchange for stock at separate times, and the transfers were part of a single
integrated transaction.

2. *Assumption of Liabilities*

If the transferee corporation assumes an indebtedness of the transferor
on the exchange, that benefit may be the equivalent of boot. The parallel
is particularly pronounced if the transferor mortgages the property immediately before the exchange, keeps the cash thus raised, and then transfers
the property for stock plus an assumption of the mortgage. The economic
consequences to the transferor are substantially similar to a transfer of the
unencumbered property for stock plus cash. In United States v. Hendler,
303 U.S. 564 (1938), the court held that an assumption of the transferor's
indebtedness constituted boot under somewhat parallel reorganization sections. The "victory" by the Service threatened the federal coffers since

transferee corporations would probably be entitled to a stepped-up basis under §362(a) for gain that should have been recognized by the transferors — even if that gain was unreachable because the statute of limitations had run on the year of the exchange. Consider the mitigation provisions of §§1311-1314. The Treasury hastened to relinquish its victory, culminating in the enactment of §357.

The general rule of §357(a) provides that the assumption of a liability or the acquisition of property subject to a liability by the transferee corporation is not to be treated as money or other property exchanged and does not prevent the exchange from qualifying as a tax-free transaction under §351. Section 357(b) provides an exception, treating the assumption as boot if the principal purpose of the assumption was not a "bona fide business purpose" or was to avoid federal income tax on the exchange. For example, it might cover the case of a mortgage placed on property on the eve of incorporation. See Thompson v. Campbell, 353 F.2d 787 (5th Cir. 1965).

Section 357(c) is another exception to the rule of §357(a). If the liabilities assumed by the transferee corporation exceed the adjusted bases of all the property transferred by the transferor, the excess is treated as gain on the sale or exchange of such property. To the extent of the excess, the taxpayer has cashed in the gain inherent in the property transferred. For example, suppose T transfers property with a basis of $1,000 and a fair market value of $15,000 to X Corp. in a transaction that qualifies under §351. In exchange, T receives $12,000 of X Corp. stock and X Corp. assumes T's $3,000 mortgage obligation. Sections 357(c) and 351 cause T to recognize the $2,000 gain on the transfer of property — the amount by which the assumed indebtedness exceeds the adjusted basis. Section 357(c) applies even when the transferor remains legally responsible for the liabilities assumed by the corporate transferee. See Owen v. Commissioner, 881 F.2d 832 (9th Cir. 1989). However, if the transferee does not agree to or is not expected to satisfy a recourse liability, then the liability is ignored for purposes of §357. §357(d)(1)(A). For example, if the transferor transfers property with a basis of $40 and and a fair market value of $100, securing a $70 recourse loan to a corporation in a transaction qualifying under §351, the transferor will have no gain if it is clear that the transferor rather than the transferee will satisfy the $70 obligation. Otherwise, the transferor might have a $30 gain under §357(c) or a $70 gain if §357(b) applied.

In general, a nonrecourse liability is treated as having been assumed by the transferee of any asset encumbered by the laibility. But there is an important exception discussed in connection with the basis of the transferee infra at 45.

Suppose T transfers to X Corp. equipment with a basis of $30 and a fair market value of $50 and a building with a basis of $10 and a fair market value of $100 in exchange for stock and X's assumption of a $40 liability encumbering the building. Does T experience a $30 gain under §357(c), or can the basis of *all* assets be aggregated to produce $0 gain? See Treas. Regs. §1.357-2(a). The theory seems to be that *T* has cashed in gain only to the extent that debt relief exceeds the basis of all transferred assets. What if *B* transfers the equipment and *T* the building? Can *T* use the basis of *B*'s asset to avoid §357(c) gain? Compare the language of §357(c) with Rev. Rul. 66-142, 1966-2 C.B. 66 (using a person-by-person approach).

Suppose *T* conducts a business as a sole proprietor with assets having combined bases of $60,000 and a fair market value of $100,000. The assets are subject to a $75,000 mortgage incurred for business reasons. If *T* transfers the assets to newly formed *X* Corp. in a transaction qualifying under §351, *T* faces a $15,000 recognition of gain under §357(c).

Suppose instead that in addition to the assets, *T* transfers $15,000 of cash to *X* Corp. Under §357(c), *T* would not recognize gain on the §351 transaction because the liabilities do not exceed the "total of adjusted basis of the property transferred." Would it matter whether *T* contributed his own money or money borrowed from a bank? Suppose *T* had borrowed $15,000 from *X* Corp. years ago. What is the result if *T* transfers a promise (i.e., *T*'s own note) to pay $15,000 to *X* Corp. in five years, bearing appropriate interest? This raises the issue of determining whether *T*'s own note is "property" for purposes of §351, and, if so, *T*'s basis in that note.

Peracchi v. Commissioner
143 F.3d 487 (9th Cir. 1998)

KOZINSKI, Circuit Judge:

We must unscramble a Rubik's Cube of corporate tax law to determine the basis of a note contributed by a taxpayer to his wholly owned corporation.

THE TRANSACTION

The taxpayer, Donald Peracchi, needed to contribute additional capital to his closely held corporation (NAC) to comply with Nevada's minimum premium-to-asset ratio for insurance companies. Peracchi contributed two parcels of real estate. The parcels were encumbered with liabilities which together exceeded Peracchi's total basis in the properties by more than half a million dollars. As we discuss in detail below, under section 357(c), contributing property with liabilities in excess of basis can trigger immediate recognition of gain in the amount of the excess. In an effort to avoid this, Peracchi also executed a promissory note, promising to pay NAC $1,060,000 over a term of ten years at 11 percent interest. Peracchi maintains that the note has a basis equal to its face amount, thereby making his total basis in the property contributed greater than the total liabilities.

If this is so, he will have extracted himself from the quicksand of section 357(c) and owe no immediate tax on the transfer of property to NAC. The IRS, though, maintains that (1) the note is not genuine indebtedness and should be treated as an unenforceable gift; and (2) even if the note is genuine, it does not increase Peracchi's basis in the property contributed.

The parties are not splitting hairs: Peracchi claims the basis of the note is $1,060,000, its face value, while the IRS argues that the note has a basis of zero. If Peracchi is right, he pays no immediate tax on the half a million dollars by which the debts on the land he contributed exceed his basis in the land; if the IRS is right, the note becomes irrelevant for tax purposes and Peracchi must recognize an immediate gain on the half million. The fact that the IRS and Peracchi are so far apart suggests they are looking at the transaction through different colored lenses. To figure out whether Peracchi's lens is rose-tinted or clear, it is useful to take a guided tour of sections 351 and 357 and the tax law principles undergirding them.

INTO THE LOBSTER POT: SECTION 351

The Code tries to make organizing a corporation pain-free from a tax point of view. A capital contribution is, in tax lingo, a "nonrecognition" event: A shareholder can generally contribute capital without recognizing gain on the exchange. It's merely a change in the form of ownership, like moving a billfold from one pocket to another. See I.R.C. section 351. So long as the shareholders contributing the property remain in control of the corporation after the exchange, section 351 applies: It doesn't matter if the capital contribution occurs at the creation of the corporation or if — as here — the company is already up and running. The baseline is that Peracchi may contribute property to NAC without recognizing gain on the exchange.

GAIN DEFERRAL: SECTION 358(A)

Peracchi contributed capital to NAC in the form of real property and a promissory note. Corporations may be funded with any kind of asset, such as equipment, real estate, intellectual property, contracts, leaseholds, securities or letters of credit. The tax consequences can get a little complicated because a shareholder's basis in the property contributed often differs from its fair market value. The general rule is that an asset's basis is equal to its "cost." See I.R.C. section 1012. But when a shareholder like Peracchi contributes property to a corporation in a nonrecognition transaction, a cost basis does not preserve the unrecognized gain. Rather than take a basis equal to the fair market value of the property exchanged, the shareholder must substitute the basis of that property for what would otherwise be the cost basis of the stock. This preserves the gain for recognition at a later day: The gain is built into the shareholder's new basis in the stock, and he will recognize income when he disposes of the stock.

The fact that gain is deferred rather than extinguished doesn't diminish the importance of questions relating to basis and the timing of recognition. In tax, as in comedy, timing matters. Most taxpayers would much prefer to pay tax on contributed property years later — when they sell their stock — rather than when they contribute the property.[1] Thus what Peracchi is seeking here is gain deferral: He wants the gain to be recognized only when he disposes of some or all of this stock.

CONTINUITY OF INVESTMENT: BOOT AND SECTION 351(b)

Continuity of investment is the cornerstone of nonrecognition under section 351. Nonrecognition assumes that a capital contribution amounts to nothing more than a nominal change in the form of ownership; in substance the shareholder's investment in the property continues. But a capital contribution can sometimes allow a shareholder to partially terminate his investment in an asset or group of assets. For example, when a shareholder receives cash or other property in addition to stock, receipt of that property reflects a partial termination of investment in the business. The shareholder may invest that money in a wholly unrelated business, or spend it just like any other form of personal income. To the extent a section 351 transaction resembles an ordinary sale, the nonrecognition rationale falls apart.

Thus the central exception to nonrecognition for section 351 transactions comes into play when the taxpayer receives "boot" — money or property other than stock in the corporation — in exchange for the property contributed. See I.R.C. section 351(b). Boot is recognized as taxable income because it represents a partial cashing out. It's as if the taxpayer contributed part of the property to the corporation in exchange for stock, and sold part of the property for cash. Only the part exchanged for stock represents a continuation of investment; the part sold for cash is properly recognized as yielding income, just as if the taxpayer had sold the property to a third party.

Peracchi did not receive boot in return for the property he contributed. But that doesn't end the inquiry: We must consider whether Peracchi has cashed out in some other way which would warrant treating part of the transaction as taxable boot.

---

1. Of course, should the taxpayers be lucky enough to die before disposing of the stock, their heirs would take a stepped-up basis in the stock equal to its fair market value as of the date of death. See I.R.C. section 1014.

ASSUMPTION OF LIABILITIES: SECTION 357(A)

The property Peracchi contributed to NAC was encumbered by liabilities. Contribution of leveraged property makes things trickier from a tax perspective. When a shareholder contributes property encumbered by debt, the corporation usually assumes the debt. And the Code normally treats discharging a liability the same as receiving money: The taxpayer improves his economic position by the same amount either way. See I.R.C. section 61(a)(12). NAC's assumption of the liabilities attached to Peracchi's property therefore could theoretically be viewed as the receipt of money, which would be taxable boot. See United States v. Hendler, 303 U.S. 564 (1938).

The Code takes a different tack. Requiring shareholders like Peracchi to recognize gain any time a corporation assumes a liability in connection with a capital contribution would greatly diminish the nonrecognition benefit section 351 is meant to confer. Section 357(a) thus takes a lenient view of the assumption of liability: A shareholder engaging in a section 351 transaction does not have to treat the assumption of liability as boot, even if the corporation assumes his obligation to pay. See I.R.C. section 357(a).

This nonrecognition does not mean that the potential gain disappears. Once again, the basis provisions kick in to reflect the transfer of gain from the shareholder to the corporation: The shareholder's substitute basis in the stock received is decreased by the amount of the liability assumed by the corporation. See I.R.C. section 358(d), (a). The adjustment preserves the gain for recognition when the shareholder sells his stock in the company, since his taxable gain will be the difference between the (new lower) basis and the sale price of the stock.

SASQUATCH AND THE NEGATIVE BASIS PROBLEM: SECTION 357(C)

Highly leveraged property presents a peculiar problem in the section 351 context. Suppose a shareholder organizes a corporation and contributes as its only asset a building with a basis of $50, a fair market value of $100, and mortgage debt of $90. Section 351 says that the shareholder does not recognize any gain on the transaction. Under section 358, the shareholder takes a substitute basis of $50 in the stock, then adjusts it downward under section 357 by $90 to reflect the assumption of liability. This leaves him with a basis of minus $40. A negative basis properly preserves the gain built into the property: If the shareholder turns around and sells the stock the next day for $10 (the difference between the fair market value and the debt), he would face $50 in gain, the same amount as if he sold the property without first encasing it in a corporate shell.[2]

---

2. If the taxpayer sells the property outright, his amount realized includes the full amount of the mortgage debt, see Crane v. Commissioner, 331 U.S. 1, 14 (1947), and the result is as follows: Amount realized ($10 cash + $90 debt) − $50 basis = $50 gain.

But skeptics say that negative basis, like Bigfoot, doesn't exist. Compare Easson v. Commissioner, 33 T.C. 963, 970 (1960) (there's no such thing as a negative basis) with Easson v. Commissioner, 294 F.2d 653, 657-658 (9th Cir. 1961) (yes, Virginia, there is a negative basis). Basis normally operates as a cost recovery system: Depreciation deductions reduce basis, and when basis hits zero, the property cannot be depreciated further. At a more basic level, it seems incongruous to attribute a negative value to a figure that normally represents one's investment in an asset. Some commentators nevertheless argue that when basis operates merely to measure potential gain (as it does here), allowing negative basis may be perfectly appropriate and consistent with the tax policy underlying nonrecognition transactions. See, e.g., J. Clifton Fleming, Jr., The Highly Avoidable Section 357(c): A Case Study in Traps for the Unwary and Some Positive Thoughts About Negative Basis, 16 J. Corp. L. 1, 27-30 (1990). Whatever the merits of this debate, it seems that section 357(c) was enacted to eliminate the possibility of negative basis. See George Cooper, Negative Basis, 75 Harv. L. Rev. 1352, 1360 (1962).

Section 357(c) prevents negative basis by forcing a shareholder to recognize gain to the extent liabilities exceed basis. Thus, if a shareholder contributes a building with a basis of $50 and liabilities of $90, he does not receive stock with a basis of minus $40. Instead, he takes a basis of zero and must recognize a $40 gain.

Peracchi sought to contribute two parcels of real property to NAC in a section 351 transaction. Standing alone the contribution would have run afoul of section 357(c): The property he wanted to contribute had liabilities in excess of basis, and Peracchi would have had to recognize gain to the extent of the excess, or $566,807:[3]

	Liabilities	Basis
Property #1	1,386,655	349,774
Property #2	161,558	631,632
	1,548,213	981,406

Liabilities	1,548,213
Basis	981,406
Excess (357(c))	566,807

3. Peracchi remained personally liable on the debts encumbering the property transferred to NAC. NAC took the property subject to the debts, however, which is enough to trigger gain under the plain language of section 357(c). See Owen v. Commissioner, 881 F.2d 832, 835-836 (9th Cir. 1989).

THE GRIFT: BOOSTING BASIS WITH A PROMISSORY NOTE

Peracchi tried to dig himself out of this tax hole by contributing a personal note with a face amount of $1,060,000 along with the real property. Peracchi maintains that the note has a basis in his hands equal to its face value. If he's right, we must add the basis of the note to the basis of the real property. Taken together, the aggregate basis in the property contributed would exceed the aggregate liabilities:

	Liabilities	Basis
Property #1	1,386,655	349,774
Property #2	161,558	631,632
Note	0	1,060,000
	1,548,213	2,041,406

Under Peracchi's theory, then, the aggregate liabilities no longer exceed the aggregate basis, and section 357(c) no longer triggers any gain. The government argues, however, that the note has a zero basis. If so, the note would not affect the tax consequences of the transaction, and Peracchi's $566,807 in gain would be taxable immediately.

ARE PROMISES TRULY FREE?

Which brings us (phew!) to the issue before us: Does Peracchi's note have a basis in Peracchi's hands for purposes of section 357(c)?[4] The language of the Code gives us little to work with. The logical place to start is with the definition of basis. Section 1012 provides that "[t]he basis of property shall be the cost of such property. . . ." But "cost" is nowhere defined. What does it cost Peracchi to write the note and contribute it to his corporation? The IRS argues tersely that the "taxpayers in the instant case incurred no cost in issuing their own note to NAC, so their basis in the note was zero." Brief for Appellee at 41. See Alderman v. Commissioner, 55 T.C.

---

4. Peracchi owned all the voting stock of NAC both before and after the exchange, so the control requirement of section 351 is satisfied. Peracchi received no boot (such as cash or securities) which would qualify as "money or other property" and trigger recognition under 351(b) alone. Peracchi did not receive any stock in return for the property contributed, so it could be argued that the exchange was not "solely in exchange for stock" as required by section 351. Courts have consistently recognized, however, that issuing stock in this situation would be a meaningless gesture: Because Peracchi is the sole shareholder of NAC, issuing additional stock would not affect his economic position relative to other shareholders. See, e.g., Jackson v. Commissioner, 708 F.2d 1402, 1405 (9th Cir. 1983).

662, 665 (1971); Rev. Rul. 68-629, 1968-2 C.B. 154, 155.[5] Building on this premise, the IRS makes Peracchi out to be a grifter: He holds an unenforceable promise to pay himself money, since the corporation will not collect on it unless he says so.

It's true that all Peracchi did was make out a promise to pay on a piece of paper, mark it in the corporate minutes and enter it on the corporate books. It is also true that nothing will cause the corporation to enforce the note against Peracchi so long as Peracchi remains in control. But the IRS ignores the possibility that NAC may go bankrupt, an event that would suddenly make the note highly significant. Peracchi and NAC are separated by the corporate form, and this gossamer curtain makes a difference in the shell game of a C Corp. organization and reorganization. Contributing the note puts a million dollar nut within the corporate shell, exposing Peracchi to the cruel nutcracker of corporate creditors in the event NAC goes bankrupt. And it does so to the tune of $1,060,000, the full face amount of the note. Without the note, no matter how deeply the corporation went into debt, creditors could not reach Peracchi's personal assets. With the note on the books, however, creditors can reach into Peracchi's pocket by enforcing the note as an unliquidated asset of the corporation.

The key to solving this puzzle, then, is to ask whether bankruptcy is significant enough a contingency to confer substantial economic effect on this transaction. If the risk of bankruptcy is important enough to be recognized, Peracchi should get basis in the note: He will have increased his exposure to the risks of the business — and thus his economic investment in NAC — by $1,060,000. If bankruptcy is so remote that there is no realistic possibility it will ever occur, we can ignore the potential economic effect of the note as speculative and treat it as merely an unenforceable promise to contribute capital in the future.

When the question is posed this way, the answer is clear. Peracchi's obligation on the note was not conditioned on NAC's remaining solvent. It represents a new and substantial increase in Peracchi's investment in the corporation.[6] The Code seems to recognize that economic exposure of the shareholder is the ultimate measuring rod of a shareholder's investment. Cf. I.R.C. section 465 (at-risk rules for partnership investments). Peracchi therefore is entitled to a step-up in basis to the extent he will be

5. We would face a different case had the Treasury promulgated a regulation interpreting section 357(c). A revenue ruling is entitled to some deference as the stated litigating position of the agency which enforces the tax code, but not nearly as much as a regulation. Ruling 68-629 offers no rationale, let alone a reasonable one, for its holding that it costs a taxpayer nothing to write a promissory note, and thus deserves little weight.

6. We confine our holding to a case such as this where the note is contributed to an operating business which is subject to a non-trivial risk of bankruptcy or receivership. NAC is not, for example, a shell corporation or a passive investment company; Peracchi got into this mess in the first place because NAC was in financial trouble and needed more assets to meet Nevada's minimum premium-to-asset ratio for insurance companies.

subjected to economic loss if the underlying investment turns unprofitable. Cf. HGA Cinema Trust v. Commissioner, 950 F.2d 1357, 1363 (7th Cir. 1991) (examining effect of bankruptcy to determine whether long-term note contributed by partner could be included in basis). See also Treas. Reg. section 1.704-1(b)(2)(ii)(c)(1) (recognizing economic effect of promissory note contributed by partner for purposes of partner's obligation to restore deficit capital account).

The economics of the transaction also support Peracchi's view of the matter. The transaction here does not differ substantively from others that would certainly give Peracchi a boost in basis. For example, Peracchi could have borrowed $1 million from a bank and contributed the cash to NAC along with the properties. Because cash has a basis equal to face value, Peracchi would not have faced any section 357(c) gain. NAC could then have purchased the note from the bank for $1 million which, assuming the bank's original assessment of Peracchi's creditworthiness was accurate, would be the fair market value of the note. In the end the corporation would hold a million dollar note from Peracchi — just like it does now — and Peracchi would face no section 357(c) gain.[7]

The only economic difference between the transaction just described and the transaction Peracchi actually engaged in is the additional costs that would accompany getting a loan from the bank. Peracchi incurs a "cost" of $1 million when he promises to pay the note to the bank; the cost is not diminished here by the fact that the transferor controls the initial transferee. The experts seem to agree: "Section 357(c) can be avoided by a transfer of enough cash to eliminate any excess of liabilities over basis; and since a note given by a solvent obligor in purchasing property is routinely treated as the equivalent of cash in determining the basis of the property, it seems reasonable to give it the same treatment in determining the basis of the property transferred in a section 351 exchange." Bittker & Eustice paragraph 3.06[4][b].

We are aware of the mischief that can result when taxpayers are permitted to calculate basis in excess of their true economic investment. See Commissioner v. Tufts, 461 U.S. 300 (1983). For two reasons, however, we do not believe our holding will have such pernicious effects. First, and most significantly, by increasing the taxpayer's personal exposure, the contribution of a valid, unconditional promissory note has substantial economic effects which reflect his true economic investment in the enterprise. The main problem with attributing basis to nonrecourse debt financing is

---

7. In a similar vein, Peracchi could have first swapped promissory notes with a third party. Assuming the bona fides of each note, Peracchi would take a cost basis in the third party note equal to the face value of the note he gave up. Peracchi could then contribute the third party note to NAC, and (thanks to the added basis) avoid any section 357(c) gain. NAC could then close the circle by giving the third party note back to the third party in exchange for Peracchi's note, leaving Peracchi and NAC in exactly the same position they occupy now.

that the tax benefits enjoyed as a result of increased basis do not reflect the true economic risk. Here Peracchi will have to pay the full amount of the note with after-tax dollars if NAC's economic situation heads south. Second, the tax treatment of nonrecourse debt primarily creates problems in the partnership context, where the entity's loss deductions (resulting from depreciation based on basis inflated above and beyond the taxpayer's true economic investment) can be passed through to the taxpayer. It is the pass-through of losses that makes artificial increases in equity interests of particular concern. See, e.g., Levy v. Commissioner, 732 F.2d 1435, 1437 (9th Cir. 1984). We don't have to tread quite so lightly in the C Corp. context, since a C Corp. doesn't funnel losses to the shareholder.[8]

We find further support for Peracchi's view by looking at the alternative: What would happen if the note had a zero basis? The IRS points out that the basis of the note in the hands of the corporation is the same as it was in the hands of the taxpayer. Accordingly, if the note has a zero basis for Peracchi, so too for NAC. See I.R.C. section 362(a).[9] But what happens if NAC — perhaps facing the threat of an involuntary petition for bankruptcy — turns around and sells Peracchi's note to a third party for its fair market value? According to the IRS's theory, NAC would take a carryover basis of zero in the note and would have to recognize $1,060,000 in phantom gain on the subsequent exchange, even though the note did not appreciate in value one bit. That can't be the right result.

Accordingly, we hold that Peracchi has a basis of $1,060,000 in the note he wrote to NAC. The aggregate basis exceeds the liabilities of the properties transferred to NAC under section 351, and Peracchi need not recognize any section 357(c) gain.

GENUINE INDEBTEDNESS OR SHAM?

The Tax Court never reached the issue of Peracchi's basis in the note. Instead, it ruled for the Commissioner on the ground that the note is not genuine indebtedness. The court emphasized two facts which it believed

---

8. Our holding therefore does not extend to the partnership or S Corp. context.

9. But see Lessinger v. Commissioner, 872 F.2d 519 (2d Cir. 1989). In *Lessinger*, the Second Circuit analyzed a similar transaction. It agreed with the IRS's (faulty) premise that the note had a zero basis in the taxpayer's hands. But then, brushing aside the language of section 362(a), the court concluded that the note had a basis in the *corporation's* hands equal to its face value. The court held that this was enough to dispel any section 357(c) gain to the taxpayer, proving that two wrongs sometimes do add up to a right.

We agree with the IRS that *Lessinger's* approach is untenable. Section 357(c) contemplates measuring basis of the property contributed in the hands of the taxpayer, not the corporation. Section 357 appears in the midst of the Code sections dealing with the effect of capital contributions on the shareholder; sections 361 et seq., on the other hand, deal with the effect on a corporation, and section 362 defines the basis of property contributed in the hands of the corporation. Because we hold that the note has a face value basis to the shareholder for purposes of section 357(c), however, we reach the same result as *Lessinger*.

supported the view that the note is a sham: (1) NAC's decision whether to collect on the note is wholly controlled by Peracchi and (2) Peracchi missed the first two years of payments, yet NAC did not accelerate the debt. These facts certainly do suggest that Peracchi paid imperfect attention to his obligations under the note, as frequently happens when debtor and creditor are under common control. But we believe the proper way to approach the genuine indebtedness question is to look at the face of the note and consider whether Peracchi's legal obligation is illusory. And it is not. First, the note's bona fides are adequate: The IRS has stipulated that Peracchi is creditworthy and likely to have the funds to pay the note; the note bears a market rate of interest commensurate with his creditworthiness; the note has a fixed term. Second, the IRS does not argue that the value of the note is anything other than its face value; nothing in the record suggests NAC couldn't borrow against the note to raise cash. Lastly, the note is fully transferable and enforceable by third parties, such as hostile creditors. On the basis of these facts we hold that the note is an ordinary, negotiable, recourse obligation which must be treated as genuine debt for tax purposes. See Sacks v. Commissioner, 69 F.3d 982, 989 (9th Cir. 1995).

The IRS argues that the note is nevertheless a sham because it was executed simply to avoid tax. Tax avoidance is a valid concern in this context; section 357(a) does provide the opportunity for a bailout transaction of sorts. For example, a taxpayer with an unencumbered building he wants to sell could take out a nonrecourse mortgage, pocket the proceeds, and contribute the property to a newly organized corporation. Although the gain would be preserved for later recognition, the taxpayer would have partially cashed out his economic investment in the property: By taking out a nonrecourse mortgage, the economic risk of loss would be transferred to the lender. Section 357(b) addresses this sort of bailout by requiring the recognition of gain if the transaction lacks a business purpose.

Peracchi's capital contribution is not a bailout. Peracchi contributed the buildings to NAC because the company needed additional capital, and the contribution of the note was part of that transaction. The IRS, in fact, stipulated that the contribution had a business purpose. Bailout potential exists regardless of whether the taxpayer contributes a note along with the property; section 357(b), not 357(c), is the sword the Service must use to attack bailout transactions.

Is the Note a Gift?

The IRS also offers a more refined version of the sham transaction argument: The note was really a gift to NAC because Peracchi did not receive any consideration from the exchange. The IRS admits that the tax deferral resulting from avoiding section 357(c) gain is a benefit to Peracchi. It argues, nonetheless, that this is not enough to make the bargain enforceable because it works no detriment to NAC. This argument would classify all contributions of capital as gifts. A corporation never gives up anything explicitly when it accepts a capital contribution. Instead, the corporation implicitly promises to put the money to good use, and its directors and officers undertake the fiduciary duty to generate the highest possible return on the investment. The contribution of the note was no more a gift than the contribution of $1 million in cash to the corporation would have been; it does not reflect the "detached and disinterested generosity" which characterizes a gift for purposes of federal income taxation. See Commissioner v. Duberstein, 363 U.S. 278, 285 (1960).

THE AFTERMATH

We take a final look at the result to make sure we have not placed our stamp of approval on some sort of exotic tax shelter. We hold that Peracchi is entitled to a step up in basis for the face value of the note, just as if he contributed cash to the corporation. See I.R.C. section 358. If Peracchi does in fact keep his promise and pay off the note with after tax dollars, the tax result is perfectly appropriate: NAC receives cash, and the increase in basis Peracchi took for the original contribution is justified. Peracchi has less potential gain, but he paid for it in real dollars.

But what if, as the IRS fears, NAC never does enforce the note? If NAC goes bankrupt, the note will be an asset of the estate enforceable for the benefit of creditors, and Peracchi will eventually be forced to pay in after tax dollars. Peracchi will undoubtedly have worked the deferral mechanism of section 351 to his advantage, but this is not inappropriate where the taxpayer is on the hook in both form and substance for enough cash to offset the excess of liabilities over basis. By increasing his personal exposure to the creditors of NAC, Peracchi has increased his economic investment in the corporation, and a corresponding increase in basis is wholly justified.[10]

CONCLUSION

We hold that Peracchi has a basis of $1,060,000 in the note, its face value. As such, the aggregate liabilities of the property contributed to NAC do

10. What happens if NAC does not go bankrupt, but merely writes off the note instead? Peracchi would then face discharge of indebtedness income to the tune of $1,060,000. This would put Peracchi in a worse position than when he started, since discharge of indebtedness is normally treated as ordinary income. Peracchi, having increased his basis in the stock of the corporation by $1,060,000 would receive a capital loss (or less capital gain) to that extent. But the shift in character of the income will normally work to the disadvantage of a taxpayer in Peracchi's situation.

not exceed its basis, and Peracchi does not recognize any section 357(c) gain. The decision of the Tax Court is REVERSED. The case is remanded for entry of judgment in favor of Peracchi.

FERNANDEZ, Circuit Judge, Dissenting:

Is there something that a taxpayer, who has borrowed hundreds of thousands of dollars more than his basis in his property, can do to avoid taxation when he transfers the property? Yes, says Peracchi, because by using a very clever argument he can avoid the strictures of 26 U.S.C. section 357(c). He need only make a promise to pay by giving a "good," though unsecured, promissory note to his corporation when he transfers the property to it. That is true even though the property remains subject to the encumbrances. How can that be? Well, by preparing a promissory note the taxpayer simply creates basis without cost to himself. But see 26 U.S.C. section 1012; Rev. Rul. 68-629, 1968-2 C.B. 154; Alderman v. Commissioner, 55 T.C. 662, 665 (1971). Thus he can extract a large part of the value of the property, pocket the funds, use them, divest himself of the property, and pay the tax another day, if ever at all.

But as with all magical solutions, the taxpayer must know the proper incantations and make the correct movements. He cannot just transfer the property to the corporation and promise, or be obligated, to pay off the encumbrances. That would not change the fact that the property was still subject to those encumbrances. According to Peracchi, the thaumaturgy that will save him from taxes proceeds in two simple steps. He must first prepare a ritualistic writing — an unsecured promissory note in an amount equal to or more than the excess of the encumbrances over the basis. He must then give that writing to his corporation. That is all. But is not that just a "promise to pay," which "does not represent the paying out or reduction of assets?" Don E. Williams Co. v. Commissioner, 429 U.S. 569, 583, 97 S. Ct. 850, 858, 51 L. Ed. 2d 48 (1977). Never mind, he says. He has nonetheless increased the total basis of the property transferred and avoided the tax. I understand the temptation to embrace that argument, but I see no real support for it in the law.

Peracchi says a lot about economic realities. I see nothing real about that maneuver. I see, rather, a bit of sortilege that would have made Merlin envious. The taxpayer has created something — basis — out of nothing.

Thus, I respectfully dissent.

NOTES

1. *Basis in a taxpayer's own note.* The court in *Peracchi* reached the right conclusion that for purposes of §357(c) a taxpayer has a basis in the taxpayer's own note equal to its fair market value. Basis in an asset under U.S. tax law is the amount that can be received tax free on a sale of that

asset. If a taxpayer makes a promissory note for $5,000 bearing a market rate of interest, the taxpayer is not taxed on a "sale" of that note by the maker in exchange for $5,000. In effect, a taxpayer must be deemed to have a $5,000 basis in his own note.

Nevertheless, the Ninth Circuit decision in *Peracchi* is contrary to the result in Alderman v. Commissioner, 55 T.C. 662 (1971). If *Alderman* was correctly decided (i.e., a taxpayer has no basis in his own note), then what basis does the transferee corporation take in the note following §351 transaction? Suppose *T* transfers her own $5,000 note bearing a market rate of interest to *X* Corp. in exchange for $5,000 of *X* Corp. stock in a §351 transaction. If *T* has a basis of $0 in her own note, then under §362, *X* Corp. would take a $0 basis in *T*'s note. What happens when *T* pays off the note? Should *X* Corp. have $5,000 of income? That would be an odd result. If *T* had originally transferred $5,000 in cash to *X* Corp., *X* Corp. would have had no income; there is no reason why a different result should occur if the $5,000 is paid at a later date. *X* Corp. should have no income when *T* pays off the note. To achieve that result, *X* Corp. must have a $5,000 basis in the note. Because *X* Corp.'s basis derives from *T*'s basis under §362, *T* must have a $5,000 basis in her own note.

If Peracchi had borrowed the $1,060,000 from a bank and then contributed the borrowed funds along with his other assets and liabilities, there would have been no liability under §357(c) because the liabilities assumed by the corporation did not exceed the total bases of the assets transferred. After such a transfer, the bank would have been Peracchi's creditor. Should there be a different result if the transferee corporation is Peracchi's creditor?

Note that the result in *Peracchi* is consistent with the result in Crane v. Commissioner, 331 U.S. 1 (1947), that borrowed funds used to acquire property are included in basis. In a sense, Peracchi borrowed funds from the transferee corporation in making the promise to repay the transferee corporation in the future. Whether Peracchi transfers cash or the promise to pay that cash in the future, Peracchi's basis in the asset transferred should be the same. See generally Manning, "The Issuer's Paper: Property or What? Zero Basis and Other Income Tax Mysteries," 39 Tax L. Rev. 159 (1984).

2. *Deductible liabilities.* Prior its amendment in 1978, §357(c) generated considerable litigation regarding the treatment of a cash basis taxpayer who transfers accounts receivable with zero basis (e.g., the right to be paid for goods or services provided to customers on credit) in exchange for stock and the assumption by the corporation of the transferor's accounts payable (e.g., a liability to pay a supplier of raw materials). Since the liability necessarily exceeds the basis of the transferred receivable, assumption of that liability by the corporation triggers the recognition of gain. For example, suppose *T* transfers a receivable with a basis of $0 and a fair market value of $100 for $70 of *X* Corp. stock and the assumption

by X of T's \$30 account payable. We might recharacterize the transaction in the following manner: X Corp. borrows \$30 from the creditor of the account payable and distributes that \$30 along with \$70 of stock to T, who then uses the \$30 to pay off her obligation to the creditor. Viewed in this manner, the transaction would produce income to T equal to the \$30 boot received, but T would have an offsetting deduction for the payment of an expense deductible under §162(a). Accordingly, when X Corp. assumes responsibility for an account payable or any other deductible obligation, the transferor should not be taxed.

Courts reached this conclusion by employing a variety of rationales. In Bongiovanni v. Commissioner, 470 F.2d 921 (2d Cir. 1972), the court held that the term "liability" for purposes of §357(c) does not include accounts payable. In Thatcher v. Commissioner, 533 F.2d 1114 (9th Cir. 1976), the court allowed a constructive deduction against §357(c) income. Finally, in Focht v. Commissioner, 66 T.C. 233 (1977), the court, following *Bongiovanni,* held that an obligation of a cash basis taxpayer should not be treated as a liability under §357(c) to the extent that its payment would have been deductible if made by the transferor. See Rev. Rul. 80-199, 1980-2 C.B. 122 (following *Focht* for transactions occurring prior to 1978).

Section 357(c)(3) now codifies the result reached in *Focht.* Does §357(c)(3) imply that the transferee will be able to deduct the liabilities when paid even though they were incurred by another taxpayer (i.e., the transferor) who received "credit" for the deduction by offsetting §357(c) gain? Apparently it does. Rev. Rul. 80-198, 1980-2 C.B. 113. This is contrary to the usual rule that one cannot get a deduction for paying the expenses of another. It is another manifestation of the double taxation, and sometimes double benefit, created by the corporate income tax. Does the treatment of payables imply that the transferred receivables will be taxable to the corporation and not to the transferor contrary to the assignment of income rules? See Hempt Bros. v. United States, 490 F.2d 1172 (3d Cir. 1974) (assignment of income doctrine not applicable). See also page 79 infra.

In Orr v. Commissioner, 78 T.C. 1059 (1982), a cash basis taxpayer arranged vacation packages for clients as a sole proprietor. When he incorporated, he transferred all the operating assets to the corporation in exchange for stock and the corporation's assumption of his liabilities. The liabilities consisted of refundable customer deposits for tours. He did not transfer the cash deposits. The Service argued that §357(c) required the recognition of gain to the extent that the assumed liabilities exceeded the taxpayer's basis. The taxpayer countered that §357(c) was inapplicable because *Focht,* now codified as §357(c)(3), dictates that the deposits not be considered liabilities for purposes of §357(c). The court sided with the Service, noting that the customer deposits were not included in income when received and would not be deductible when refunded.

In Rev. Rul. 95-74, 1975-2 C.B. 36, Corporation P operated a manufacturing plant on land that was contaminated. For bona fide business purposes, *P* engaged in a §351 transaction in which it transferred all assets of that business including the contaminated land to a newly formed corporation *S* in exchange for all of *S*'s stock and *S*'s assumption of all liabilities associated with the business. Two years later, *S* undertook soil and water remediation efforts the cost of which would have been partly deductible if there had been no §351 transaction and if the remediation costs had been incurred by *P*. The IRS ruled that (1) the liabilities assumed by *S* were not liabilities for purposes of §357(c)(1) because the liabilities assumed by *S* were not taken into account by *P* as a deduction or as an increase in basis before the transfer; (2) the liabilities assumed by *S* in the §351 exchange were deductible by *S* under its method of accounting (determined as if *S* has owned the land for the period and in the same manner as it was owned by *P*).

In Lessinger v. Commissioner, 872 F.2d 519 (2d Cir. 1989), the taxpayer transferred accounts payable that arose when the business was conducted as a sole proprietorship. In light of §357(c)(3), why was there any tax issue under §357(c)(1)? Notice that for §357(c)(3) to apply, the liabilities must be deductible when paid. For Lessinger, an accrual basis taxpayer, the accounts payable would not be deductible when paid.

3. *Relationship between §357(b) and (c)*. If transferred property is subject both to §357(b) (because of the taxpayer's improper purpose) and to §357(c), does the taxpayer recognize the entire liability as boot under §357(b), or only the excess of basis under §357(c)? See §357(c)(2)(A).

3. Stock

With the treatment of boot in mind, consider the thorny question of what property constitutes boot and what constitutes stock.

The term "stock" is defined neither in the Code nor in the regulations. Stock unquestionably is qualifying property under §351 whether common or preferred, voting or nonvoting. Stock rights, options, warrants, or other rights to purchase stock at a fixed price are not treated as stock for purposes of §351. Treas. Regs. §1.351-1(a)(1); cf. Helvering v. Southwest Consolidated Corp., 315 U.S. 194 (1942) (warrants issued as part of a reorganization are not voting stock). What are the tax consequences if *T* transfers property to *X* Corp. in exchange for some stock and a certificate for additional shares to be issued later, contingent on valuation of *T*'s property? Contingent stock interests have been distinguished from stock rights because no additional payment is required from the transferor. See Carlberg v. United States, 281 F.2d 507, 517-518 (8th Cir. 1960), and Hamrick v. Commissioner, 43 T.C. 21, 32-33 (1964). Is this a distinction without a difference? Why should stock rights and warrants not be treated in the same manner as stock?

Suppose a taxpayer transfers an asset to a preexisting corporation that is wholly owned. The asset is encumbered by a nondeductible liability that exceeds the adjusted basis but is less than the fair market value of the asset. For example, the basis might be $100, the fair market value $500, and the liability $300. The transferor receives no stock in exchange for the asset. Does §351 apply, or is the transfer a contribution to capital? Why does it matter? Consider §357(c), which applies only if §351 applies. In *Peracchi*, the court applied §351 even though no stock was received by the transferor.

Under §351(g), certain "nonqualified preferred stock" is treated as boot if received in a §351 transaction. Such nonqualified preferred stock must first be "preferred stock" within the meaning of §351(g)(3)(A) and then must be nonqualified as specified in §351(g)(2)(A), subject to the limitations in §351(g)(2)(B)–(C). In general, such nonqualified preferred stock is subject to a redemption right or obligation within 20 years or has a dividend rate that references interest rates or an equivalent index.

A corporation's common stock represents a residual interest in the entity, which means that the holders of the common stock are paid last but in a potentially unlimited amount. A corporation's bonds and debentures, on the other hand, represent an investment that is both preferred and limited: Debt holders are preferred in the sense that they are paid before equity holders, and their interests are limited in the sense that they receive only a specified interest rate (albeit one that may vary over time) and a fixed return of their principal regardless of the success of the venture. Thus, common shareholders take a large risk (because they are paid last) for a bigger potential gain (because their return is unlimited).

For purposes of §351(g), stock is "preferred" only if it is both preferred *and* limited. §351(g)(3)(A). Further, stock is not "preferred" in this sense if it can share in future growth of the corporation by being converted into some other class of stock. Thus, taxpayers wishing to avoid application of §351(g) should be able to do so by using a class of stock that either is not preferred (i.e., does not come ahead of common stock as to the payment of dividends or upon liquidation) or is not limited (i.e., that participates to some significant extent in the growth of the company). This definition of "preferred" is much more restrictive than that used in the context of §§305 and 306.

Even if stock is both preferred and limited, it is not "disqualified" preferred stock unless it contains a feature described in §351(g)(2). If the preferred stock must be redeemed, it is disqualified. §351(g)(2)(A)(ii). If redemption is not mandatory but merely optional, the test is more complex. If the holder of the preferred stock can demand redemption, the stock is disqualified, §351(g)(2)(A)(i), but if it is the corporation that can insist on redemption, then the stock is disqualified only if (as of the issue date) it is more likely than not that the redemption will occur,

§351(g)(2)(A)(iii). However, these redemption provisions are relevant only if they can be exercised within 20 years of issuance of the stock and the redemption is not subject to a contingency which makes the likelihood of redemption remote. §351(g)(2)(B). In addition, special provision is made for redemptions related to death, disability, or change of employment status. §351(g)(2)(C).

Finally, preferred stock is disqualified if the dividend rate on the stock varies with interest rates, commodity prices, or similar measures. Such preferred stock, by paying a periodic payment tied to interest rates or some similar measure and offering no share in the growth of the corporate venture, is considerably closer to straight debt than to common stock on the debt/equity spectrum.

4. Securities

Suppose *T* transfers property to *X* Corp. in exchange for an *X* Corp. debt instrument as part of a transaction that otherwise qualifies under §351. Certainly the debt instrument provides *T* with more continuity with the property transferred than an outright sale of the property for cash. If the transferee corporation is productive, *T* is more likely to be paid. Indeed, in some circumstances, a debt instrument may provide more continuity than stock. For financially disabled corporations, for example, debt ownership may provide greater ownership rights than stock ownership.

Until 1990, §351 granted nonrecognition upon the receipt of stock or securities (generally long-term debt instruments). The distinction between securities (i.e., qualifying property) and short-term debt (i.e., nonqualifying property) proved troublesome. Section 351 now draws a sharper line, providing that only the receipt of stock may qualify a transferor for nonrecognition treatment. Even so, it may not always be easy to determine whether a financial instrument constitutes stock or debt. See Bradshaw v. United States, page 64 infra.

Although §351 does not provide nonrecognition to a transferor who receives a debt instrument in exchange for appreciated property, it does not follow that the transferor is immediately taxable on the fair market value of the debt instrument received. See the discussion of installment reporting below.

The distinction between short-term debt and long-term securities is still important in the reorganization area. See page 441 infra.

5. Boot and Installment Reporting

In a §351 transaction, if a transferor exchanges appreciated property for a combination of debt and stock, the debt constitutes boot. If, however, the transferor simply sells the property in exchange for a debt instrument, gain from the sale might be recognized not when the sale takes place but when the debt is paid off in accordance with the installment reporting provisions. §453. Because §351 taxes the receipt of boot only to the extent of the transferor's gain, installment reporting under §453 is also available to a transferor in a §351 transaction. See Prop. Treas. Regs. §1.453-1(f)(3)(ii). For example, suppose T transfers appreciated land with a basis of $120 and a fair market value of $200 to X Corp. in a transaction that qualifies under §351. In exchange T receives $100 of stock and $100 of debt. Although the debt constitutes boot, the transferor normally is taxable on $80 of gain under §351(b) when the debtor pays off the debt rather than when the debt instrument is received. For the allocation of basis between the stock and debt, see page 45 infra.

A transferor is not always entitled to report under the installment method when property is exchanged for debt in a transaction qualifying under §351. For example, §453(g) restricts the use of the installment method if depreciable property is transferred to a corporation by a transferor owning more than 50 percent of the stock of the corporation. Also, §453 does not apply to transfers of inventory or property held for sale to customers or to publicly traded debt instruments received by the transferor. Even if installment reporting is available, §453(i) requires immediate recognition of any gain subject to depreciation recapture under §§1245 or 1250. Finally, a transferor may elect out of installment reporting (if, for example, the transferor has an expiring loss deduction that will offset the gain).

6. Transferor's Basis

To restate our exploration to this point: Section 351 can confer nonrecognition of gain or loss on a transferor who exchanges property for stock. A transferor will, however, recognize gain on the exchange to the extent of boot received; the receipt of boot does not result in the recognition of any loss that may be realized in the exchange. Nonrecognition under §351 postpones but does not forgive realized gain. Rather, the basis provisions of §358 preserve the unrecognized gain or loss for a later date. For example, suppose T transfers property to X Corp. with a basis of $30 and a fair market value of $100 in exchange for $100 of X Corp. stock. Section 358 preserves the $70 unrecognized gain by giving T a basis of $30 in the stock received. If T sells the stock for $120, T would recognize a $90 gain, not merely the $20 appreciation in the value of the stock. If the stock is sold for $20, T would recognize a $10 loss, not the $80 loss representing the loss in stock value.

Suppose T receives a mixture of different classes of stock for the property transferred. How does T allocate basis? See §358(b) and Treas.

Regs. §1.358-2(b). Not surprisingly, basis is allocated in accordance with the fair market value of the stock received. In the example above, if T receives $50 of common stock and $50 of preferred stock, T will take a basis of $15 in the common stock and $15 in the preferred stock.

Suppose in exchange for the property T receives $20 of X Corp. stock and $80 of boot in the form of cash or other property. Since T will recognize the $70 gain because it is fully covered by the boot, the basis in the stock received should and does reflect that fact. Section 358(a)(1) requires two adjustments to the taxpayer's original $30 basis. It is adjusted up to reflect the $70 gain recognized on the transfer. §358(a)(1)(B). It is adjusted down by $80 because the boot received takes a fair market value basis under §358(a)(2). §358(a)(1)(A). The result is that the taxpayer holds the stock with a fair market value of $20 and a basis of $20, reflecting the fact that the taxpayer's gain was fully recognized. If T sells the stock, the holding period includes the period during which T held the transferred property. §1223(1).

Suppose T transfers property to X Corp. with a basis of $30 and a fair market value of $100 in exchange for $20 of stock and $80 of debt in a transaction that qualifies under §351. As indicated at page 42 supra, T does not recognize gain until the notes are paid. Does this nonrecognition pose basis problems for T under §358(a)(1)(B)(ii)? See Prop. Treas. Regs. §1.453-1(f)(3)(ii) (treating the gain as recognized solely for purposes of applying §358). The $80 of debt is boot and will be taxed to the extent of T's $70 gain. But that gain can be reported under the installment method when the debt is paid. T's $30 basis is allocated to any stock received in an amount not in excess of the fair market value of the stock (here, $20). Any remaining basis ($10) is allocated to the debt, paving the way for a $70 gain when the $80 debt instrument is paid. Prop. Treas. Regs. §1.453-1(f)(3)(ii).

In the example above, suppose T receives $70 in stock and X Corp. assumes T's $30 mortgage obligation. While the assumption does not create boot under §357(a), it is treated as cash received for purposes of the basis calculation. §358(d)(1). Therefore, T's basis in the $70 stock would be the original $30 basis minus the deemed cash received (debt assumed) of $30. The $0 basis preserves the $70 gain that goes unrecognized under §351. For purposes of §358, the debt assumed is determined under §357(d).

Suppose instead that the assumed obligation is a deductible account payable in the amount of $50 and that T received back $50 in stock in exchange for the property transferred. Section 357(c)(3) protects T from recognizing gain on the assumption and §358(d)(2) provides that the assumption is not treated as cash for purposes of calculating basis. T, then, would take a basis of $30 in stock. The $20 gain preserved is equivalent to the $70 gain, lurking in T's original property minus the $50 deduction T would have received for satisfaction of the account payable.

7. Treatment of Transferee Corporation

What happens to the transferee corporation when it issues its stock for the property of the transferor? Section 1032 provides that the corporation does not recognize gain or loss on the receipt of property (including cash) in exchange for stock it distributes. (Section 1032 can apply ouside of the §351 context as well.) What happens if the corporation issues stock in exchange for services? See Treas. Regs. §1.1032-1(a). Can the corporation not only avoid recognition of gain but also take a deduction for compensation under §162? See Rev. Rul. 62-217, 1962-2 C.B. 59, modified by Rev. Rul. 74-503, 1974-2 C.B. 117 (deduction appropriate).

When the transferee corporation receives property in exchange for stock in a §351 transaction, §362(a) provides that the transferor's basis for the transferred property carries over to the transferee corporation. If the transferee corporation receives multiple assets, the transferor's basis in each transferred asset carries over to the corporation. See P.A. Birren & Son v. Commissioner, 116 F.2d 718 (7th Cir. 1940).

If the transferor recognized any gain on the §351 exchange, that gain increases the corporation's bases in the assets acquired. Just how the increase is allocated if the corporation receives multiple assets on the transfer is not clear. Arguments can be made for allocation using basis, fair market value, or increase in value above basis as the determining factor when looking at the transferred assets. See B. Bittker and J. Eustice, Federal Income Taxation of Corporations and Shareholders ¶3.11 (6th ed. 1998). Consistency with Rev. Rul. 68-55, page 19 supra, suggests that any gain recognized by a transferor with respect to a particular asset is allocated to that asset in the hands of the transferee corporation under §362.

Suppose that a transferor transfers property with a basis of $50 and a fair market value of $100, securing a loan of $120 to a U.S. corporation in a transaction that qualifies under §351. Section 362(d)(1) in this context clarifies that the transferee's basis cannot exceed the fair market value of the transferred property — $100. This is consistent with similar treatment by some courts involving a sale of an asset where the fair market value of the transferred property is less than the accompanying mortgage. See Pleasant Summit Land Corp. v. Commissioner, 863 F. 2d 263 (3d Cir. 1988). Presumably, if later it turns out that the transferee does satisfy the entire $120 liability, there will be an appropriate basis adjustment. In this example, even if the transferor is a nonresident, not subject to U.S. tax under §357(c) on the transfer, the transferee still would take a basis that reflects the liability (not in excess of the fair market value of the transferred property). §362(d)(2).

Suppose that the $120 liability is nonrecourse and is secured by the transferred property and additional property with a fair market value of $100 that the transferor does not transfer. What is the basis of the transferee in the transferred asset? Under §362, the basis is equal to the $50 basis of the transferred property plus $10 of gain that the transferor recognizes in accordance with §357(c). That is, the $120 liability secured by two pieces of property each with a fair market value of $100 must be allocated $60 to each piece of property. The property transferred is therefore deemed to be subject to $60 liability, which results in $10 of gain to the transferor under §357(c). The basis to the transferee under §362 is the same whether the transferor is subject to tax under §357 or, perhaps because the transferor is a nonresident, no tax results.

If the corporation sells an asset received in a §351 transaction, it can tack on the transferor's holding period in accordance with §1223(2). If the transferred asset was subject to recapture that was not recognized on the §351 exchange, the recapture taint follows the property into the corporation (but the transferor's stock is not tainted). See Treas. Regs. §1.1245-2(c)(2).

Section 362(a) provides the transferee with the transferor's basis in the transferred property increased by gain recognized to the transferor on the exchange. If the transferor receives a debt instrument from the corporation in a §351 transaction, gain may not be recognized by the transferor until payment on the note. See discussion of §453 at page 42 supra. Does the transferee corporation increase its basis in the transferred assets by the gain *to be* recognized? Should the transferee increase its basis as gain is recognized by the transferor? Does the language of §362(a) preclude any increase in basis? See Jacobs, Something Simple: A Tax-Free Incorporation, 37 Tax L. Rev. 133, 148-153 (1983), and Prop. Treas. Regs. §1.453-1(f)(3)(ii) (transferee's basis increases as transferor recognizes gain).

Suppose that as part of a transaction qualifying under §351 the transferee corporation distributes nonqualifying property (e.g., real property) with a fair market value in excess of its basis. Under §351(f), the transferee corporation must recognize gain on the §351 transfer as if the property had been sold to the shareholders. A transferee corporation may not recognize a loss if the property has a basis that is greater than its fair market value. See the discussion of §311 at page 136 infra.

PROBLEMS

2-1.   *A, B, C,* and *D* organize *X* Corp. by transferring the following:

	Transfers to X		Receives from X	
	Basis	*FMV*	*Shares*	*Cash*
A — cash	—	$10,000	10,000	$ 0
B — land/building	$50,000	$80,000	80,000	$ 0
C — inventory	$ 1,000	$10,000	5,000	$5,000
D — machinery	$15,000	$10,000	5,000	$5,000

With regard to *A, B, C, D,* and *X,* determine (1) the amount of realized and recognized gain or loss and (2) the applicable basis and holding period. How does your answer change as a result of the following alternatives (each considered independently)?

a. Suppose that *B* received 80,000 shares of preferred stock.
b. Suppose *B* transferred services worth $80,000.
c. Suppose *B* transferred services worth $60,000 and property with a basis of $12,000 and a fair market value of $20,000.
d. Suppose *B* received from *X* Corp. $40,000 of stock and a debt instrument in the amount of $40,000 bearing an appropriate interest rate.
e. Suppose *B*'s transfer took place a year after the transfers of *A, C,* and *D.*
f. Suppose *D*'s transfer took place a year after those of *A, B,* and *C.*
g. Suppose *C*'s transfer took place three years after those of *A, B,* and *D* and that *B* purchased an additional 2,000 shares for $2,000 at that time.

D. CONTROL

Sections 351 and 368(c) require transferors to satisfy a control test in order for nonrecognition under §351 to apply. The cases below explore two of the issues that arise in applying the control test — (1) which shareholders do we look at in determining whether the control test is satisfied and (2) how long must these shareholders hold the stock received?

Kamborian v. Commissioner _____
56 T.C. 847 (1971)

... **FINDINGS OF FACT**

1. International Shoe Machine Corp. (International) was incorporated in Massachusetts in 1938 and at the time of the trial herein was engaged in the business of manufacturing and leasing shoe machinery and the sale of related supplies. . . .

On September 1, 1965, prior to the transaction here in question, International's capital stock was held as follows:

	Shares of International	
Name	*Class A* *common*	*Class B* *[nonvoting]* *common*
Jacob Kamborian Revocable Trust	20,324	182,916
Jacob Kamborian, Jr.	4,220	37,980
Lisabeth (Kamborian) Godley	3,620	32,580
Michael Becka	60	540
Elizabeth Kamborian Trust	5,000	45,000
Others	3,916	35,244
Total	37,140	334,260

Jacob S. Kamborian (Jacob) founded International and served as its president at all times relevant herein. Jacob S. Kamborian, Jr., and Lisabeth Kamborian Godley are the children of Jacob and his wife, Elizabeth. Michael Becka (Becka) is not related to the members of the Kamborian family. At the time of the trial herein he had been employed by International or an affiliate since at least 1943 and had served as International's executive vice president and general manager since approximately 1960. . . .

The Elizabeth Kamborian Trust (Elizabeth's trust) was established by Jacob in 1949. At about that time Jacob and Elizabeth experienced domestic difficulties; they separated for a time, and the trust was established on their reconciliation in order to provide financial security for Mrs. Kamborian. . . .

As of September 1, 1965, Becka and Lisabeth K. Godley were the trustees. Jacob had appointed them as successor trustees in 1963 and 1964, respectively. At all times relevant herein, Becka served as the managing trustee; Mrs. Godley did not live in Boston during this period, and periodically Becka informed her of the trust's activities. As of September 1, 1965, the only assets of the trust were 5,000 shares of International's class A common stock and 45,000 shares of its class B common stock.

As of September 1, 1965, International's board of directors consisted of Jacob, Jacob, Jr., Albert Kamborian (Jacob's brother), Becka, Paul Hirsch II, Harold V. Daniels, and Roy S. Flewelling.

Campex Research & Trading Corp. (Campex), a Swiss corporation with its principal place of business in Zug, Switzerland, was a patent holding and licensing company. It held primarily foreign shoe machine patents (i.e., patents not issued by the United States) and granted and administered licenses under them in a number of European countries and in Mexico. On September 1, 1965, and prior to the transaction here in question, the outstanding stock of Campex was held as follows:

Name	*Shares of Campex*
Jacob Kamborian Revocable Trust	39
Jacob Kamborian, Jr.	4
Lisabeth (Kamborian) Godley	4
Michael Becka	3

On September 1, 1965, the board of directors of International author-ized Jacob to enter into an agreement under which (a) the owners of all of the issued and outstanding shares of Campex would exchange their stock for common stock of International and (b) "certain stockholders" of International would purchase for cash additional shares of International's common stock.

As part of the transaction it was contemplated that the Elizabeth Kamb-orian Trust would purchase additional shares of theretofore unissued Inter-national stock for about $5,000, so that the former owners of the Campex stock and the Elizabeth Kamborian Trust, when considered collectively and treated as transferors under section 351(a) . . . would own at least 80 percent of International's stock immediately after the transaction in an attempt to comply with the requirements of section 368(c). . . . If the Elizabeth Kamborian Trust were not taken into account, the International stock held by the former owners of Campex immediately after the transac-tion amounted to 77.3 percent of each class of outstanding stock of Interna-tional — an amount that was insufficient to satisfy the requirements of section 368(c). . . .

International acquired Campex stock as part of its program of prepar-ing for a public issue of its stock. On the advice of underwriters and other specialists, it was thought that ownership of foreign patents would enable International to display worldwide activities which would be of value in establishing the price of the public issue. . . . As of September 1, 1965, no date had been set for the offering and at the time of the trial herein the public offering had not yet been made. . . .

As trustee of Elizabeth's trust, Becka borrowed approximately $5,000 at an interest rate of 6 percent in order to finance the trust's purchase of the total of 418 shares of International stock on September 1, 1965. The corpus of the trust consisted exclusively of International stock, and Becka anticipated that the loan would be repaid out of dividends paid on the stock. In deciding to acquire additional International stock, Becka also anticipated that International would make a public offering which might enhance the value of the stock. Prior to the purchase of the International stock on behalf of the trust, Becka discussed his plans with both Jacob and Elizabeth. Jacob, personally and as grantor of the Jacob S. Kamborian Revocable Trust, held a sufficient number of International shares to con-trol the corporation and thus to determine whether it would issue addi-tional shares. In his discussions with Elizabeth, Becka explained that because the $5,000 loan would have to be repaid out of dividends paid on the International stock held by the trust, her income from the trust would be diminished until the loan was repaid. Elizabeth told Becka to go ahead with the transaction. . . .

On their respective Federal income tax returns for 1965, petitioners reported no gain or loss stemming from the exchange of their Campex stock for International stock. . . .

OPINION

RAUM, Judge.

1. EXCHANGE OF CAMPEX STOCK FOR INTERNATIONAL STOCK

Petitioners contend that the gain they realized on their transfer of Campex stock to International in return for International's common stock qualifies for nonrecognition under section 351(a). . . . That section provides for nonrecognition of gain or loss on the transfer of property to a corporation in exchange for the corporation's stock or securities — if immediately after the exchange the transferor or transferors are "in control" of the corporation. . . .

Immediately after the exchange here in issue the stock of International was held as follows:

| Name | Shares of — | | |
	Class A (voting common)	Class B (nonvoting common)	Percent of total of each class
Jacob S. Kamborian Revocable Trust	22,108	198,971	56.01
Jacob S. Kamborian, Jr.	4,403	39,627	11.16
Lisabeth (Kamborian) Godley	3,803	34,227	9.64
Michael Becka	197	1,775	.50
Elizabeth Kamborian Trust	5,042	45,376	12.77
Others	3,916	35,244	9.92
Total	39,469	355,220	

Petitioners contend that the transferors of property for purposes of section 351(a) were the five named stockholders listed above and that their percentage stockholdings after the transfer satisfy the 80-percent control requirement imposed by sections 351(a) and 368(c).

The Commissioner's position is that only the first four stockholders listed above — i.e., the former owners of Campex — may be considered as transferors of property here, that the fifth (the Elizabeth Kamborian Trust) may not be taken into account in this connection, and that since there would thus be a failure to satisfy the control requirement, all gain realized on the exchange must be recognized. In particular, he urges that International stock issued to the Elizabeth Kamborian Trust in return for $5,016 does not qualify as stock issued for property within the meaning of section 351(a) and that consequently the persons making qualified transfers of property to International in return for its stock held only 77.3

percent of its stock after the exchange. The Commissioner relies on regulations section 1.351-1(a)(1)(ii). . . .

The Commissioner contends that since the Elizabeth Kamborian Trust purchased only 42 shares of class A common and 376 shares of class B common, the securities issued were "of relatively small value" in relation to the 5,000 shares of class A common and 45,000 shares of class B common which is already held and that the primary purpose of the transfer was to qualify the exchange of Campex stock by the other stockholders for nonrecognition treatment under section 351(a).

Petitioners attack the Commissioner's position on a variety of grounds. They urge (a) that regulations section 1.351-1(a)(1)(ii) is invalid; (b) that even if valid it is inapplicable to the transaction in issue. . . .

(a) *Validity of the regulation.* Initially we note the well-settled principle that "Treasury regulations must be sustained unless unreasonable and plainly inconsistent with the revenue statutes and that they constitute contemporaneous constructions by those charged with administration of these statutes which should not be overruled except for weighty reasons." Commissioner v. South Texas Lumber Co., 333 U.S. 496, 501. . . .

Petitioners . . . contend that the regulation's reference to "property which is relatively small value in comparison to the value of stock . . . already owned" and its reliance upon the taxpayer's motive find support nowhere in the language of section 351 and that the regulation is for that reason invalid as beyond the scope of the statute. Again, we must disagree. By disqualifying certain token exchanges, the regulation is reasonably designed to exclude from the scope of section 351 transactions which comply with its requirements in form but not in substance. Far from being unreasonable or inconsistent with the statute, the regulation promotes its purpose by helping to ensure substantial compliance with the control requirement before the nonrecognition provisions become operative. In this light the absence of direct support for the regulation in the language of the statute is of minimal significance. . . . We conclude that the regulation is valid.

(b) *Applicability of the regulation.* Petitioners contend that even if it is valid, the regulation is inapplicable to the transaction here in issue. They argue first that even if Elizabeth's trust had not purchased shares of International stock, the control requirement would have been satisfied, that therefore the purchase was not necessary to meet the control requirement, and that consequently the regulation is by its own terms inapplicable. Petitioners reach this conclusion by asserting that the shares held by Becka and Lisabeth Godley as trustees of Elizabeth's trust should be attributed to them as individuals . . . and added to the shares they held personally in nonfiduciary capacities. On the basis of this premise, petitioners conclude that the 80-percent-control requirement would have been satisfied even if Elizabeth's trust had not participated in the September 1, 1965, transaction. . . . Petitioners' argument is ingenious but unacceptable, for it falters on petitioners' premise that the trust's shares may be attributed to the individual trustees. While legal title to the shares may have been in the names of the trustees, they had no beneficial interest in such shares. The distinction is not one of form but of plain economic reality. . . . In these circumstances we think the trustees' interests in the trust's shares were far too remote to justify attributing the shares to them for purposes of section 351. . . .

Petitioners also contend that the primary purpose for the trust's acquisition of International's stock was not to qualify the other stockholders' exchanges under section 351 and that for this reason the regulation is inapplicable. We note at the outset that the regulation does not make it entirely clear whose purpose is to be taken into account. However, both parties have assumed that the purpose of the transferor of property is critical. The language of the regulation (which appears to distinguish between a "transfer" of property and the issuance of stock) supports their assumption, and we shall therefore proceed on this basis. Although Elizabeth's trust was technically the transferor herein, the parties have also assumed that Becka's purpose is critical in this respect — apparently on the ground that as the managing trustee he was primarily responsible for the decision to make the purchase of International stock. We shall proceed on the basis of this assumption as well.

The question of Becka's primary purpose is one of fact, cf. Malat v. Riddell, 383 U.S. 569, and after a review of all the evidence we conclude that his primary purpose was to qualify the other stockholders' exchanges under section 351. We note in particular that at about the time of the transaction, Jacob was ill and Becka was in charge of International's affairs, that in planning the acquisition Becka participated in lengthy discussions with regard to planning the transaction as a tax-free exchange, and that both the vote of International's board of directors and the agreement of September 1, 1965, treated the purchase by Elizabeth's trust and the exchange of Campex stock by the other stockholders as component parts of an integrated transaction avowedly designed to meet the 80-percent-control requirement and thereby qualify for nonrecognition treatment under section 351.

At the trial herein, Becka testified that if the trust had not participated in the transaction, the issue of International stock to the other major stockholders would have diluted the trust's percentage interest in International and that he authorized the purchase of International stock in order to minimize such dilution. In particular he testified that the total percentage stock interest held by the trust and the two Kamborian children exceeded 33 1/3 percent and that preservation of that interest protected Mrs. Kamborian against the making of certain corporate decisions (requiring a two-thirds majority) without her consent. . . . We do not give his testimony very much weight, however. The record does not establish whether or why the children were regarded as allies of Mrs. Kamborian rather than as allies of her husband. Moreover, the trust's participation in the transaction left them with an aggregate stock interest of 33.57 percent — only 0.08 of 1 percent more than they would have held if the trust had not purchased any additional shares.

Becka also testified that he authorized the purchase of the stock because it was a "good investment." While he may well have taken this into account in making his decision, the record leaves us convinced that the purchase was made primarily to qualify the exchanges by the other stockholders (one of whom was Becka himself) . . . under section 351. We conclude that section 1.351-1(a)(1)(ii) is applicable. . . .

Decisions will be entered under Rule 50.

Intermountain Lumber Co. v. Commissioner
65 T.C. 1025 (1976)

WILES, Judge. . . .

The only issue for decision is whether a certain corporate formation was nontaxable under section 351(a). . . . This depends solely upon whether the primary incorporator had "control" of the requisite percentage of stock immediately after the exchange within the meaning of section 368(c).

FINDINGS OF FACT

From 1948 until March of 1964, Mr. Dee Shook (hereinafter Shook) individually owned a sawmill at Conner, Mont. During that time Mr. Milo Wilson (hereinafter Wilson) had logs processed there into rough lumber for a fee. Shook owned the remaining logs processed at the sawmill, which constituted about half of all the logs processed there.

From 1954 until March of 1964, rough lumber from the sawmill was processed into finished lumber at a separate finishing plant which Shook and Wilson owned as equal shareholders.

In March of 1964, fire damaged the sawmill. Shook and Wilson wanted to replace it with a larger one so that the finishing plant could operate at full capacity. Shook was financially unable, however, to do so. He accordingly induced Wilson to personally coguarantee a $200,000 loan to provide financing. In return, Wilson insisted upon an equal voice in rebuilding the sawmill and upon an opportunity to become an equal shareholder with Shook in the new sawmill.

On May 28, 1964, Shook, Wilson, and two other individuals, all acting as incorporators, executed articles of incorporation for S&W Sawmill, Inc. (hereinafter S&W). . . .

Minutes of the first stockholders meeting on July 7, 1964, stated in part that "Mr. Shook informed the meeting that a separate agreement was being prepared between he and Mr. Wilson providing for the sale of one-half of his stock to Mr. Wilson." Also on that date, 1 share was issued to each of the other two incorporators.

Shook executed a bill of sale for his sawmill equipment and deeded his sawmill site to S&W on July 15 and 16, 1964, respectively. In exchange, Shook received 364 S&W shares on July 15, 1964. Shook and Wilson also received 1 share each as incorporators. The 364 shares and the 4 incorporation shares constituted all outstanding capital stock of S&W on July 15, 1964.

Also on that date, minutes of a special meeting stated in part that "The President, Dee Shook, announced that he and Milo E. Wilson had entered into an agreement whereby Mr. Wilson was to purchase 182 shares of Mr. Shook's stock." That agreement, dated July 15, 1964, and entitled "Agreement for Sale and Purchase of Stock" (hereinafter agreement for sale) provided in part as follows:

> [I]t is the intention of all the incorporators that Shook and Wilson are to be the owners of the majority of the stock of said corporation;
>
> AND WHEREAS, it is the desire and plan of both parties hereto that a sufficient number of shares of stock be sold by Shook to Wilson so that eventually the stock ownership would be equal;
>
> AND WHEREAS, the purchase of said shares of stock by Wilson from Shook is to be financed by a series of payments;
>
> IT IS THEREFORE AGREED, that for and in consideration of the covenants to be performed and the payments to be made as hereinafter set forth, the sale and purchase of said stock is to be as follows:
>
> 1. Dee Shook is to sell to Milo E. Wilson 182 shares of stock in S&W SAWMILL, INC. for the agreed price of $500.00 per share.
>
> 2. Wilson is to pay Shook for said stock as follows:
>
> Interest on unpaid balance due is to be paid annually at 3% per annum from August 1, 1964 to July 31, 1968.
>
> Interest on unpaid balance due is to be paid annually at 4% per annum from August 1, 1968, to July 31, 1970.
>
> Interest on unpaid balance due is to be paid annually at 5% per annum from August 1, 1970, until entire balance is paid in full.
>
> In addition to interest $6,000.00 on the principal is due November 1, 1969.
>
> In addition to interest, $15,000.00 on the principal is due annually, beginning Nov. 1, 1970, and continuing until the entire purchase price is paid. The payments may be made in advance at any time and in any amount.
>
> 3. As each principal payment is made the proportionate number of shares of stock are to be transferred on the corporate records and delivered to Wilson.
>
> 4. In the event any payment of principal is not made on the due date, or within 90 days thereafter, Wilson thereby forfeits and loses his right to

purchase that proportionate number of shares of stock; PROVIDED HOW-
EVER, that nevertheless any subsequent, or later payment of principal may
be made according to the above payment schedule, and thereupon Wilson
will be entitled to the proportionate number of shares of stock as represented
by such payment. Interest payment must always be kept current before any
delivery of stock is to be made resulting from a payment of principal.

5. For the period of one year from the date hereof Wilson is to have
the full power to vote all of the stock herein agreed to be sold to him by
Shook. Thereafter the voting rights of the stock is (sic) to be determined by
the stock ownership records of the corporation.

On July 15, 1964, Shook also executed an irrevocable proxy granting to
Wilson voting rights in 182 shares until September 10, 1965. Two other
documents also executed on that date related to share ownership between
Shook and Wilson. One, entitled "S&W Sawmill, Inc. Stockholders' Restrictive Agreement," provided in part as follows:

[S]uch provisions (against stock transferability) do not apply to the presently
existing Agreement for Sale and Purchase of Stock entered into between Dee
Shook and Milo E. Wilson, dated the 15th day of July, 1964, and providing for
the purchase by Milo E. Wilson of 182 shares of stock in the company.

IT IS THE INTENTION AND PURPOSE of the incorporators that the
majority of the ownership of the corporation is to be held by Dee Shook
and Milo E. Wilson on an equal share basis when Milo E. Wilson completes
the purchase of the stock certificates which are the subject of said purchase
agreement. The other, entitled "Option to Buy Stock Forming Part Of Stockholders' Restrictive Agreement," provided in part that "the ownership of
shares in S&W Sawmill, Inc., as the same now stands, to-wit: Dee Shook 365
shares, Milo E. Wilson 1 shares (sic) . . . shall continue."

In connection with the agreement for sale, Shook deposited stock
certificates representing 182 shares with an escrow agent on July 17, 1964.

On August 19, 1964, S&W borrowed $200,000, in part upon the per-
sonal guarantees of Shook, Wilson, and their wives. The loan agreement
referred to Shook and Wilson as "the principal officers and stockholders"
of S&W. S&W agreed therein to insure the lives of Shook and Wilson for
$100,000 each.

On March 19, 1965, Shook and Wilson agreed to purchase additional
shares from S&W in an agreement which provided in part as follows:

Witnesseth

THAT WHEREAS, Prior to this date stock in the Corporation had been
purchased by the Stockholders and a number of said shares are subject to
an escrow agreement at Citizens State Bank, Hamilton, Montana, providing
for the purchase by Milo E. Wilson of a certain number of shares of such
stock from Dee Shook; that the purpose of said escrow arrangement is to

provide for an equal ownership of the stock of said Corporation by Milo E. Wilson and Dee Shook;

THAT WHEREAS, it is the desire of all parties at this time that each of the Stockholders purchase an additional One Hundred Shares of Stock at Five Hundred Dollars ($500.00) per share, and payment for the same having been made to the Corporation;

NOW, THEREFORE, for and in consideration of the mutual benefits to be derived by all parties hereto, IT IS HEREBY AGREED AS FOLLOWS:

That each of the Stockholders are to purchase One Hundred Shares of stock of the Corporation at Five Hundred Dollars ($500.00) per share;

That, as well as with other stock purchases, it is the desire of the Stockholders that stock ownership held by Dee Shook and Milo E. Wilson are to remain equal; that any stock purchased or issued as a result of this agreement is to be regulated accordingly. . . .

Wilson made all payments in 1965 and 1966 specified in the agreement for sale and accordingly claimed interest deductions on his Federal income tax returns for those years.

On July 1, 1967, before principal payments were required by the agreement for sale, petitioner purchased all outstanding S&W stock. In anticipation of this purchase, a letter to petitioner dated May 3, 1967, and signed by Shook and Wilson stated as follows:

> To have it in the record, Milo E. Wilson owes Dee Shook $91,000 for 182 shares of S&W Sawmill Inc. stock in escrow at Citizens State Bank Hamilton Montana. On the purchase contract, Intermountain Lumber Co. would pay Dee Shook $91,000.00 more over the 14 yrs. than Milo E. Wilson.

OPINION . . .

In this case, respondent is in the unusual posture of arguing that a transfer to a corporation in return for stock was nontaxable under section 351, and Intermountain is in the equally unusual posture of arguing that the transfer was taxable because section 351 was inapplicable. The explanation is simply that Intermountain purchased all stock of the corporation, S& W, from its incorporators, and that Intermountain and S&W have filed consolidated income tax returns for years in issue. Accordingly, if section 351 was applicable to the incorporators when S&W was formed, S&W and Intermountain must depreciate the assets of S&W on their consolidated returns on the incorporators' basis. Sec. 362(a). If section 351 was inapplicable, and the transfer of assets to S&W was accordingly to be treated as a sale, S&W and Intermountain could base depreciation on those returns on the fair market value of those assets at the time of incorporation, which was higher than the incorporators' cost and which would accordingly provide larger depreciation deductions. . . .

Petitioner thus maintains that the transfer to S&W of all of S&W's property at the time of incorporation by the primary incorporator, one Dee Shook, was a taxable sale. It asserts that section 351 was inapplicable because an agreement for sale required Shook, as part of the incorporation transaction, to sell almost half of the S&W shares outstanding to one Milo Wilson over a period of time, thereby depriving Shook of the requisite percentage of stock necessary for "control" of S&W immediately after the exchange.

Respondent, on the other hand, maintains that the agreement between Shook and Wilson did not deprive Shook of ownership of the shares immediately after the exchange, as the stock purchase agreement merely gave Wilson an option to purchase the shares. Shook accordingly was in "control" of the corporation and the exchange was thus nontaxable under section 351.

Respondent has abandoned on brief his contention that Wilson was a transferor of property and therefore a person to also be counted for purposes of control under section 351. Respondent is correct in doing so, since Wilson did not transfer any property to S&W upon its initial formation in July of 1964. Wilson's agreement to transfer cash for corporate stock in March of 1965 cannot be considered part of the same transaction.

Since Wilson was not a transferor of property and therefore cannot be counted for control under section 351, William A. James, 53 T.C. 63, 69 (1969), we must determine if Shook alone owned the requisite percentage of shares for control. This determination depends upon whether, under all facts and circumstances surrounding the agreement for sale of 182 shares between Shook and Wilson, ownership of those shares was in Shook or Wilson.

A determination of "ownership," as that term is used in section 368(c) and for purposes of control under section 351, depends upon the obligations and freedom of action of the transferee with respect to the stock when he acquired it from the corporation. Such traditional ownership attributes as legal title, voting rights, and possession of stock certificates are not conclusive. If the transferee, as part of the transaction by which the shares were acquired, has irrevocably foregone or relinquished at that time the legal right to determine whether to keep the shares, ownership in such shares is lacking for purposes of section 351. By contrast, if there are no restrictions upon freedom of action at the time he acquired the shares, it is immaterial how soon thereafter the transferee elects to dispose of his stock or whether such disposition is in accord with a preconceived plan not amounting to a binding obligation. Stephens, Inc. v. United States, 464 F.2d 53, 66-67 (8th Cir. 1972), cert. denied 409 U.S. 1118 (1973). . . . After considering the entire record, we have concluded that Shook and Wilson intended to consummate a sale of the S&W stock, that they never doubted that the sale would be completed, that the sale was an integral part of the incorporation transaction, and that they considered themselves to be co-owners of S&W upon execution of the stock purchase agreement in 1964. These conclusions are supported by minutes of the first stockholders meeting on July 7, 1964, at which Shook characterized the agreement for sale as a "sale"; minutes of a special meeting on July 15, 1964, at which Shook stated Wilson was to "purchase" half of Shook's stock; the "Agreement for Sale and Purchase of Stock" itself, dated July 15, 1964, which is drawn as an installment sale and which provides for payment of interest on unpaid principal; Wilson's deduction of interest expenses in connection with the agreement for sale, which would be inconsistent with an option; the S&W loan agreement, in which Shook and Wilson held themselves out as the "principal stockholders" of S&W and in which S&W covenanted to equally insure Shook and Wilson for $100,000; the March 1965 stock purchase agreement with S&W, which indicated that Shook and Wilson "are to remain equal" shareholders in S&W; the letter of May 1967 from Shook and Wilson to Intermountain, which indicated that Wilson owed Shook the principal balance due on the shares as an unpaid obligation; and all surrounding facts and circumstances leading to corporate formation and execution of the above documents. Inconsistent and self-serving testimony of Shook and Wilson regarding their intent and understanding of the documents in evidence is unpersuasive in view of the record as a whole to alter interpretation of the transaction as a sale of stock by Shook to Wilson.

We accordingly cannot accept respondent's contention that the substance varied from the form of this transaction, which was, of course, labeled a "sale." The parties executed an "option" agreement on the same day that the "agreement for sale" was executed, and we have no doubt that they could and indeed did correctly distinguish between a sale and an option.

The agreement for sale's forfeiture clause, which provided that Wilson forfeited the right to purchase a proportionate number of shares for which timely principal payments were not made, did not convert it into an option agreement. Furthermore, the agreement for sale made no provision for forgiving interest payments on the remaining principal due should principal payments not be made on earlier dates; indeed, it specifically provided that "Interest payment must always be kept current before any delivery of stock is to be made resulting from a payment of principal."

We thus believe that Shook, as part of the same transaction by which the shares were acquired (indeed, the agreement for sale was executed before the sawmill was deeded to S&W), had relinquished when he acquired those shares the legal right to determine whether to keep them. Shook was under an obligation, upon receipt of the shares, to transfer the stock as he received Wilson's principal payments. Cf. S. Klein on the Square, Inc., 14 T.C. 786, 790 (1950), aff'd 188 F.2d 127 (2d Cir. 1951), cert. denied 342 U.S. 824 (1951). We note also that the agreement for sale gave Wilson the right to prepay principal and receive all 182 shares at any time in advance. Shook therefore did not own, within the meaning of section 368(c), the requisite percentage of stock immediately after the exchange to control the corporation as required for nontaxable treatment under section 351.

We note also that the basic premise of section 351 is to avoid recognition of gain or loss resulting from transfer of property to a corporation which works a change of form only. . . . Accordingly, if the transferor sells his stock as part of the same transaction, the transaction is taxable because there has been more than a mere change in form. In this case, the transferor agreed to sell and did sell 50 percent of the stock to be received, placed the certificates in the possession of an escrow agent, and granted a binding proxy to the purchaser to vote the stock being sold. Far more than a mere change in form was effected.

We accordingly hold for petitioner. Because of concessions of other issues, decisions will be entered under Rule 155.

NOTES

1. *Definition of "control."* Nonrecognition under §351 is available only if the transferors of property are in control of the transferee immediately after the transfer. Section 368(c) provides two 80 percent tests in determining control: the ownership of at least 80 percent of the total combined voting power of all classes of stock entitled to vote and 80 percent of all other classes of stock. The determination of control is made by looking at the number of shares rather than the value of the corporation's shares. Suppose after a purported §351 transfer, the transferors own 90 percent of the voting stock, 70 percent of the class A nonvoting preferred and 90 percent of the class B nonvoting preferred, for an overall 83 percent interest in the total preferred outstanding. Do they have control? Compare the language of §368(c) with Rev. Rul. 59-259, 1959-2 C.B. 115 (voting stock classes combined in applying 80 percent test, but 80 percent test applies separately to *each* class of nonvoting stock).

Suppose T transfers property to X Corp. in exchange for stock in a transaction that appears to qualify under §351 because T receives back 80 percent of the X Corp. stock. As part of a prearranged plan, X Corp. then transfers the assets to its subsidiary, Sub Corp., in a §351 transaction that results in X Corp.'s owning 80 percent of the stock of Sub Corp.; 20 percent is owned by outside shareholders. The result is that T owns 64 percent (80 percent of an 80 percent interest) of Sub Corp., which holds T's original assets. In Rev. Rul. 83-34, 1983-1 C.B. 79, the Service ruled that §351 does apply to a taxpayer in T's position.

2. *Who is in the "control" group?* As *Kamborian* indicates, an exchange can qualify under §351 even though the transferors do not *acquire* control in the exchange itself. Rather, the transferors can include previously owned

stock in satisfying the 80 percent requirement. The problem in *Kamborian* was the amount being transferred by the Elizabeth Kamborian Trust relative to its existing holdings. The trust transferred $5,000 for new stock while it owned almost $600,000 in preexisting stock. If the receipt of stock in an amount less than 1 percent of the value of existing stock is not enough for an accommodation transferor, what *is* the magical amount? In Rev. Proc. 77-37, 1977-2 C.B. 568, the Service stated that for advance ruling purposes, property will not be considered "of relatively small value" within the meaning of Treas. Regs. §1.351-1(a)(1)(ii) if it equals at least 10 percent of the value of stock or securities already owned by the transferor, or to be received for services by the transferor. In *Kamborian*, if the Elizabeth Kamborian trust had purchased $60,000 of additional stock, could the transferor group have included all the trust's stock in the 80 percent calculations?

3.   *Unbalanced exchanges*. In *Kamborian* the taxpayer also argued that Treas. Regs. §1.351-1(a)(1)(ii) was invalid because it supposedly adopted a "proportionate interest" test repudiated by Congress in 1954. Section 351 dropped the requirement contained in its predecessor, §112(b)(5) of the 1939 Code, that "in the case of an exchange by two or more persons this paragraph shall apply only if the amount of the stock . . . received by each is substantially in proportion to his interest in the property prior to the exchange." This clause gave rise to difficult questions of valuation as well as to conflicting opinions on how the proportion of change was to be calculated and on what constituted a "substantial" change. Moreover, the purpose of the requirement was obscure.

Though abandoning the proportionate interest requirement, the Code points out that an exchange may have the effect of a gift or of the payment of compensation. §351(g)(3) and (g)(4); Treas. Regs. §1.351-1(b). See also Rev. Rul. 76-454, 1976-2 C.B. 102, in which *T* and his wholly owned subsidiary, *X* Corp., formed *Y* Corp. with *T* receiving a disproportionate amount of stock for the property transferred; held, recharacterized to give *T* and *X* each a proportionate number of shares, followed by a taxable dividend by *X* of the "excess" *Y* stock. What would be the result if *X* had received and retained more than its share of the *Y* stock?

4.   *Immediately after*. Section 351 requires that the transferors be in control of the corporation "immediately after the exchange." See Treas. Regs. §1.351-1(a)(1). *Intermountain* typifies much of the litigation over this term. Most of the cases involve situations where the transferors are momentarily in control of the transferee but thereafter dispose of enough shares to bring the transferor group below the 80 percent requirement.

Notice the litigation posture in *Intermountain*. The taxpayer argued that §351 did not apply, while the Service argued that the nonrecognition provision did apply. Why? Why did the Service care who won the case? If §351 was inapplicable, then Shook should have been taxed on the formation of the corporation. (Presumably, he already had paid a tax on the gain associated with his sale of stock to Wilson.) Can't the Service send him a notice of deficiency for the tax on the gain associated with the stock not sold to Wilson? Is there a statute of limitations problem with the original transfer by Shook that doesn't exist when the Service challenges Intermountain's current depreciation deductions? Consider §§1311-1314, particularly §1312(7). Why else might the Service have litigated *Intermountain*? A disparity in tax rates applicable to Intermountain and Shook? Perhaps Shook's gain would have produced a capital gain, while Intermountain's stepped-up basis produces larger depreciation deductions to offset ordinary income? But see §1239.

The court ruled in favor of the taxpayer because of the preconceived plan for Shook to sell stock to Wilson. But why don't Shook and Wilson together satisfy the control test? Suppose Wilson purchased 20 shares from the corporation when it was first incorporated and then purchased the remainder of his half interest from Shook? Would Wilson be considered a transferor? See page 59 supra, discussing accommodation transferors. Suppose Wilson had transferred his personal note to the corporation in exchange for half of the stock when it was first incorporated. See Peracchi v. Commissioner, page 26 supra.

In Rev. Rul. 79-194, 1979-1 C.B. 145, *B* and *C* transfer property to Newco in exchange for 80 percent and 20 percent of the Newco stock, respectively. Pursuant to a prearranged plan, *B* sells 31 percent of the outstanding stock to *C*, leaving *B* with 49 percent and *C* with 51 percent. Under this fact pattern, the Service ruled that *C* would be considered a transferor and that *B* and *C* as a transferor group would satisfy the control requirement of §351(a) and §368(c). Suppose instead that on the original transfer, *B* received 99 percent of the outstanding stock and *C*, 1 percent, both amounts determined in accordance with value of the property transferred. Pursuant to a prearranged plan, *B* sells 50 percent of the outstanding Newco stock to *C*, leaving *B* with 49 percent and *C* with 51 percent. Relying on Treas. Regs. §1.351-1(a)(1)(ii), the Service ruled that *C* would not qualify as a transferor. Because *B* did not own the requisite 80 percent immediately after the exchange, §351 was inapplicable.

The "immediately after" problem arises in the context of the pervasive step transaction doctrine, examined in more detail on page 319 infra. That doctrine will sometimes be applied to integrate more than one transaction into a single, unified transaction. *T*'s receipt of control in a purported §351 exchange will sometimes be integrated with a postacquisition sale of stock to spoil nonrecognition treatment. The test most often applied to integrate two transactions is the "mutual interdependence" test. (*Query:* Can there be nonmutual interdependence?) One court stated the test: "Were the steps so interdependent that the legal relations created by one transaction would have been fruitless without a completion of the series?" American Bantam Car Co. v. Commissioner, 11 T.C. 397, 405 (1948), aff'd, 177 F.2d 513 (3d Cir. 1949). The Tax Court, while articulating the mutual interdependence test, refused to integrate steps in the absence of a preexisting binding commitment by the transferors to sell the stock received in McDonald's of Zion, Ill., Inc. v. Commissioner, 76 T.C. 972 (1981), rev'd sub nom. McDonald's Restaurants of Ill., Inc. v. Commissioner, 688 F.2d 520 (7th Cir. 1982). Consider the implication of Reg. §1.368-1(e).

In ascertaining whether steps are interdependent, the amount of time between transactions can be important. If the steps are contemporaneous or separated by short time intervals, courts are more likely to integrate the steps. See American Bantam Car v. Commissioner, supra. But compare Commissioner v. Ashland Oil & Refining Co., 99 F.2d 588 (6th Cir. 1938), cert. denied, 306 U.S. 661 (1939) (steps that occurred six years apart integrated), with Henricksen v. Braicks, 137 F.2d 632 (9th Cir. 1943) (transactions one half-hour apart treated as separate).

In a special statutory rule, Congress has determined that fleeting control is insignificant. Section 351(c) specifically allows corporate transferors to distribute the stock received to their shareholders without violating the control requirement. See Martin Ice Cream Co. v. Commissioner, 110 T.C. 189 (1998). Does this restricted exception suggest that fleeting control is insufficient where the special rule is inapplicable?

In the context of a corporate reorganization, the Treasury has issued Treas. Reg. §1.368-1(e), which finds a suffcient continuity of interest, regardless of the length of time a shareholder holds qualified property. For example, suppose *A* is a shareholder of *T* Corp. *T* Corp. merges into *P* Corp. with *A* receiving *P* Corp. stock in exchange for *A*'s *T* Corp. stock. Immediately after the merger, *A* sells the *P* Corp. stock to *B*, a purchaser unrelated to *P* Corp. This transaction will qualify as a tax-free merger so that *P* Corp. takes a carryover basis under §362 in the assets acquired from *T* Corp. There is sufficient continuity of interest even where *A*'s sale of the *P* Corp. stock is prearranged prior to the merger.

The continuity of interest regulations on their face only apply to reorganizations, but should the reasoning also apply to corporate formations as well? Suppose that *A* forms *X* Corp. in a purported §351 transaction and immediately after the formation, *A* sells half of the *X* Corp. stock to *B*. In *Intermountain*, page 53 supra, the court ruled that §351 did not apply because of the prearranged sale to B who was not a "transferor." Has the result in *Intermountain* (i.e., §351 not applicable) been effectively eviscerated by the continuity of interest regulations?

Suppose instead of a transfer followed by a sale, there is a transfer followed by a gift. Is the time factor important? Wilgard Realty Co. v. Commissioner, 127 F.2d 514 (2d Cir. 1942), involved a transfer of appreciated property by an individual to a corporation in exchange for all its stock. Immediately after the stock was issued to him, he transferred more than 20 percent of it by gift to members of his family. On a later sale of the transferred property, the corporation claimed a stepped-up basis on the ground that the incorporation failed the control test and therefore that §351 was inapplicable. The court held that §351 was applicable since the transferor was not legally bound to make a gift. In contrast, the court in Florida Machine & Foundry Co. v. Fahs, 168 F.2d 957 (5th Cir. 1948), ruled that §351 did not apply when more than 20 percent of the shares were issued directly to the transferor's son even though the transferor may have been under an obligation to make the gift. See also Mojonnier & Sons v. Commissioner, 12 T.C. 837 (1949). But see Stanton v. United States, 512 F.2d 13 (3d Cir. 1975), and D'Angelo Associates v. Commissioner, 70 T.C. 121 (1978), rejecting a distinction in gift cases based on whether the donee receives stock directly from the transferee or from the transferor.

Until this point the focus has been on an attempted §351 transaction followed by a sale or gift of the stock received. The "immediately after" issue also arises when soon after the exchange, the transferee corporation issues additional stock. In American Bantam Car Co. v. Commissioner, supra, the transferors transferred assets to the corporation in exchange for common stock. The plan also called for a sale of preferred shares to the public through underwriters who were to get more than 20 percent of the common shares if they sold the preferred. Four months later, the underwriters sold the preferred and received the common shares. The court held §351 applicable by ruling that control existed after the exchange and that a later loss of control was not an integral part of the transaction since the exchange itself would have taken place even if the plan for the public sale of the preferred had failed.

The Service has clarified the area somewhat in Rev. Rul. 78-294, 1978-2 C.B. 141, in which two situations were presented. In each a sole proprietor who needed additional capital decided to incorporate and increase capital by a public offering of stock. In the first situation, the incorporator, the corporation, and the underwriter agreed that the underwriter would use its best efforts to sell 50 percent of the stock directly to the public, and, in fact, it did so within two weeks after the offering. The Service ruled that for the control test of §368(c) the public investors who purchased the shares should be treated along with the incorporator as transferors. In the second situation, the corporation's contract for the sale of 50 percent of the shares with the underwriter was a "firm commitment" underwriting, so that if the underwriter was not successful in selling the shares the underwriter was obliged to retain them. The Service ruled that the underwriter and the incorporator were the transferors who together had all the shares, therefore satisfying the control test and §351.

PROBLEMS

2-2. In the following, *A* starts out with a parcel of land held for investment worth $1,000 with an adjusted basis of $300 and ends up with $500 cash and a 50 percent interest in *X* Corp., a newly formed corporation that obtains the property. *B* starts out with $500 and ends up with a 50 percent interest in *X* Corp. Determine the tax consequences to all the parties of the following:

a.   *A* transfers the property to *X* Corp. for all of *X*'s stock. Shortly thereafter, *A* sells half of his *X* stock to *B* for $500.
b.   Prior to incorporation *A* sells a half interest in the property to *B* for $500, and then both *A* and *B* form *X* Corp.
c.   *A* and *B* both form *X* Corp., with *A* contributing his property in exchange for $500 cash (borrowed by *X*) and a 50 percent stock interest and *B* receiving a 50 percent stock interest for her cash.
d.   *A* borrows $500 from a lender, using his property as security. *A* then transfers the property (subject to the debt) to *X* Corp. in exchange for a 50 percent stock interest, while *B* receives a 50 percent interest in return for her $500 cash.

2-3.   Suppose in 2-2(c) that *A* transfers two parcels, one with a basis of $200 and a value of $700 and the other with a basis of $800 and a value of $300. What are the tax consequences?

2-4.   Suppose in 2-2(c) that *X* also issued $100 of nonvoting preferred stock to *C*, *X* Corp.'s lawyer for organizing the corporation. What are the tax consequences?

E.   INTERACTION OF §351 WITH OTHER CODE SECTIONS AND LEGAL DOCTRINES

Section 351 does not operate in a vacuum. Other code provisions and legal doctrines may affect the application of the provision. Indeed, there are a variety of situations where a taxpayer envisions more favorable treatment by seeking to avoid §351. In the first two cases that follow, the taxpayers tried to avoid the nonrecognition of §351. Why? As you read, try to determine why one taxpayer was successful while the other was not. The third case in this section, *Hempt Bros.*, focuses on the relationship of §351 to assignment of income principles.

Bradshaw v. United States* _____
683 F.2d 365 (Ct. Cl. 1982)

OPINION

BENNETT, Judge.
    Both parties agree that there are only two questions for decision. The first is whether the transfer of real property to Castlewood, a [wholly

---

* Bradshaw, a party to the consolidated action, is not affected by this part of the court's opinion. — EDS.

owned] corporation, in exchange for installment obligations was a sale of the property to that corporation or, instead, was either a transfer of property to a controlled corporation solely in exchange for stock . . . of that corporation within the meaning of section 351 or a capital contribution to that corporation. [Discussion of second question omitted.]

We find that the transfer of real property to Castlewood in exchange for installment obligations was a sale rather than a transfer governed by section 351 or a capital contribution. . . . Accordingly, we hold for the plaintiffs and against the defendant for the reasons hereafter stated.

I

On January 6, 1961, Thomas E. Swift (Thomas) purchased a tract of land, consisting of approximately 200 acres, in Dalton, Whitfield County, Georgia, for $60,000. Two dispositions of property out of this 200 acres were made by Thomas in the summer of 1968. The consolidated cases herein concern one of these dispositions, the transfer of 40.427 acres, subsequently known as Castlewood Subdivision (the subdivision), to Castlewood [Inc.] on July 29, 1968. The conservative fair market value of the subdivision on the date of transfer was $250,000. Thomas' adjusted basis in this portion of the property was $8,538. In exchange for the transfer, Thomas received from Castlewood five promissory notes (the Castlewood notes), each in the principal amount of $50,000 and bearing interest at the rate of 4 percent per annum. The first note matured on January 29, 1971, with each successive note maturing at 1-year intervals. Thomas received no down payment for the transfer, and no security or other collateral was taken for the purchase price. He elected to report his gain from the transaction on the installment method pursuant to section 453(b).

At the time of transfer, various opportunities were available to Thomas to dispose of the subdivision, including sale to third parties. While he had not developed property himself, Thomas was highly expert in real estate matters in the Dalton area. Based upon this knowledge, including knowledge of sales of other real estate in the vicinity of the subdivision, Thomas evaluated the prospects for the development of the subdivision to be bright, whether such development was undertaken by himself, by a corporation that he might organize, or by a third party. He considered the alternative opportunities available to him to dispose of the property and decided to develop the property himself through a corporation rather than sell it to a third party.

Consequently, Castlewood was organized and incorporated on July 29, 1968, under the laws of the State of Georgia, to obtain, subdivide, develop and sell lots in the subdivision. On July 29, 1968, Castlewood issued its Certificate No. 1, representing 50 shares of common stock, to Thomas in exchange for the transfer to the corporation of an automobile valued at $4,500. At all times relevant herein, Thomas was the sole shareholder of Castlewood and was responsible for conducting its business affairs. His expertise was available to and utilized by the corporation in its development of the subdivision, enabling it to minimize development costs and thus increase profits. . . .

Castlewood subdivided the subdivision into two tracts. . . . From August 1970 to April 1973, Castlewood sold 16 lots in Tract I and two lots in Tract II for an aggregate sales price of $239,880. It did not advertise the sale of these lots, use realtors, or pay sales commissions. The property sold had an allocated land cost (of the $250,000 purchase price) and development cost of $159,378.39, yielding a net return to the corporation of $80,501.11. Castlewood reported sales of lots on its federal income tax returns for the fiscal years ended July 31, 1971, July 31, 1972, and July 31, 1973. . . .

By statutory notice of deficiency dated September 20, 1976, the Commissioner determined that additional income tax was due from Castlewood for its 1971 and 1972 tax years, for the reason that the transfer of the subdivision to that corporation by Thomas was not a sale, as treated by the corporation on its tax returns, but rather a transfer of property solely in exchange for stock . . . within the meaning of section 351. Thus, he concluded that, pursuant to section 362, Castlewood's predevelopment basis in the property was equal to that of the transferor immediately before the transfer, or $8,538. This, in turn, increased Castlewood's taxable income on sales of lots. Additionally, the Commissioner concluded that no debtor-creditor relationship was established between Castlewood and Thomas, thereby disallowing certain deductions of interest paid . . . on the notes taken for the purchase price of the property. . . .

II

The first question concerns the proper tax treatment of Thomas' transfer of the subdivision to Castlewood in exchange for the five $50,000 promissory notes. If the transfer is treated as a sale, as plaintiff contends, then Castlewood's adjusted basis for its sales of the lots from the subdivision property would include the $250,000 purchase price (a cost basis), it would be allowed deductions of the interest paid on the notes and its taxable income would be generally as shown on its returns for the years in issue. However, if, as defendant claims, the transfer was not a sale but was either a transfer under section 351 or a contribution to the corporation's capital, then Castlewood's adjusted basis in the lots sold would be reduced to Thomas' original basis (a carryover basis) pursuant to section 362, it would be denied deductions of the interest paid on the notes and its taxable income would be generally as shown on the notice of deficiency issued with respect to it. The sale versus capital contribution problem arises from a situation which often confronts taxpayers with holdings in undeveloped real estate. It is not uncommon for a landowner with a large tract of land suitable for development to want to freeze as capital gain the appreciation in the value of the property that has accrued during its ownership. While an outright sale of the property achieves this result, it also deprives the landowner of any participation in the profits to be reaped from its ultimate development. On the other hand, if the landowner develops and sells the property himself, he runs the risk of being treated as a dealer of the property and any gain generated through sales, including the gain associated with the land's appreciation in value while undeveloped, is taxable to him at ordinary income rates. See, e.g., . . . Suburban Realty Co. v. United States, 615 F.2d 171 (5th Cir.), cert. denied, 449 U.S. 920 (1980).

In the face of such a dilemma, taxpayers have devised an apparently viable solution. By selling the real property to a controlled corporation, they can realize their capital gain on the appreciation which has accrued during their ownership and, at the same time, preserve their opportunity to later participate in the developmental profits as shareholders of the development corporation. Moreover, the corporation obtains a cost basis in the real property, thereby reducing the amount of ordinary income to be received from subsequent sales.

Not unexpectedly, the Commissioner has repeatedly challenged the characterization of such a transaction as a sale, instead maintaining that the transfer is, in reality, a capital contribution and that the transferee corporation is only entitled to a carryover basis for the property. See, e.g., Burr Oaks Corp. v. Commissioner, 365 F.2d 24 (7th Cir. 1966), cert. denied, 385 U.S. 1007 (1967); Aqualane Shores, Inc. v. Commissioner, 269 F.2d 116 (5th Cir. 1959). The two principal reasons asserted for denying the desired tax treatment to the corporation have their origin in the dual subparts of section 362(a). While the main thesis is that section 351 governs such a transaction and that the corporation's basis for the property is to be determined pursuant to section 362(a)(1), it is also maintained that, regardless of the applicability of section 351, the transfer to the corporation is, in substance, a contribution to capital and that the adjusted basis for the property is to be determined under section 362(a)(2). . . .

The proper characterization of a transaction, as a "sale" or a "capital contribution," is a question of fact to be decided as of the time of the transfer on the basis of all of the objective evidence. Gooding Amusement Co. v. Commissioner, 236 F.2d 159, 165 (6th Cir. 1956), cert. denied, 352 U.S. 1031 (1957). While the form of the transaction is relevant, we are required to examine all of the pertinent factors in order to determine whether the substance of the transaction complies with its form. Gregory v. Helvering, 293 U.S. 465, 469-70 (1935). The essential nature of the transaction is to be determined from a consideration of all of the surrounding circumstances. Piedmont Corp. v. Commissioner, 388 F.2d 886, 889 (4th Cir. 1968).

In this case, the objective evidence points to a sale. First, and foremost, the price paid for the subdivision reflected its actual fair market value. Since it has been stipulated that the value of the subdivision was $250,000, the very amount for which it was sold to Castlewood, the transfer cannot be considered a "pretextuous device" to divert the earnings and profits of the corporation, otherwise taxable as ordinary income, into sales proceeds taxable as capital gain. Piedmont Corp. v. Commissioner, 388 F.2d 886, 889 (4th Cir. 1968). The sales price did not constitute an inflated value for the property, and, thus, did not represent an attempt to transfer to Thomas any subsequent capital increment in the value of the property, nor any of the gain from its development. In this respect, the transfer was clearly a sale.

Additionally, the various formalities of a sale were strictly observed. The five instruments involved constituted negotiable instruments in the form of "notes" under Georgia law . . . , contained an unqualified obligation to pay the principal amount, with fixed maturity dates ranging from two and one-half to six and one-half years after the date of sale and bore a reasonable rate of interest. The notes were not subordinated to general corporate creditors and contained a means for collection at maturity, which was never utilized as the principal and interest were always paid as due until the Commissioner challenged the tax treatment of those payments. On these bases, the notes contained all of the traditional elements of sales-generated debt.

Even so, defendant asks that upon consideration of the economic substance of the transfer, the transaction be recast as a capital contribution. This is so, we are told, because Congress has dictated that no tax consequences shall attach to a transaction where direct ownership of property is changed into indirect ownership through a proprietary interest in a corporation. Thus, where the circumstances of a purported sale demonstrate that the transferor, in fact, retained a continuing interest in the property transferred, the transaction is more appropriately characterized as a capital contribution.

Defendant calls our attention to an alleged factual pattern to be discerned in those instances where it has been determined that the economic substance of a purported sale was actually a contribution to capital. In such cases, it is claimed, a newly formed, inadequately capitalized corporation received assets which were essential to its purpose, and which required at the outset substantial improvements to convert them into income-producing property. Whereas, in those cases holding that the transaction resulted in a sale, the transfer involved proven, income-producing assets. Defendant submits that the distinction drawn in these cases turns on the nature and degree of risk inherent in the transfer of unproven assets and that in such instances, because of the high degree of risk, the transferor is likely to have retained a continuing interest in the property transferred.

In the present case, defendant maintains, unproven real property was transferred to an untried, undercapitalized business in return for notes, which were to be satisfied from the proceeds expected to be generated through the sale of lots. From this, defendant urges that we conclude that the notes represented a continuing interest in the corporate business, for repayment was totally dependent upon the success of the enterprise.

We cannot quarrel with the policies underlying section 351, nor with its intended scope. However, even accepting defendant's premise that the prior cases can be meaningfully differentiated along the lines suggested, we are unable to agree with the conclusion defendant draws in this case. Rephrasing defendant's position, we are asked to find that the degree of risk herein was of the type normally associated with a capital contribution. Thus stated, the salient inquiry is whether the notes occupied the position of equity, the assets and prospects of the business being unable to assure payment of the debt according to its terms.

Admittedly, the stipulated facts show Castlewood to have been a "thin" corporation. Its initial capitalization consisted entirely of an automobile valued at $4,500. The corporation then issued five notes, each in the face amount of $50,000, in consideration for the subdivision property. While an additional $3,200 was contributed to Castlewood 4 months later, in practical terms it had no funds of its own with which to conduct business. . . . It cannot be refuted that Castlewood had a very high ratio of debt to equity. But the mere fact that a corporation is or is not thinly capitalized does not, per se, control the character of the transaction. See Gyro Eng. Corp. v. United States, 417 F.2d 437, 439 (9th Cir. 1969). . . . As these cases demonstrate, if the corporation is adequately capitalized for its intended purpose, then we are not prevented from treating the notes as valid debt.

The facts reveal that in addition to its formal capitalization, Castlewood anticipated having access to, did have access to, and utilized funds in the form of loans from C&S, the partnership owned by Thomas and his family, which served as Thomas' personal bank account. Castlewood also had access to an important resource in the expertise Thomas brought to the business, which allowed the corporation to minimize its development expenses. See Murphy Logging Co. v. United States, 378 F.2d 222, 224 (9th Cir. 1967). Given these resources, which were certainly adequate to finance the level of development activities undertaken, and the absence of any need to employ advertising or to use realtors, there was little reason for the corporation to maintain a large surplus of liquid capital. Under the circumstances, we cannot say that undercapitalization is fatal to plaintiff's position.

Integrally related to this discussion, as defendant recognizes, is the nature or quality of the risk assumed by the transferor. However, unlike defendant, we do not find the fact that what was sold to Castlewood was unimproved real estate to be necessarily indicative of a high degree of risk. Concomitantly, nor do we view repayment of the Castlewood notes to have been dependent upon the success of the business. Under the stipulated facts of this case, at the time of transfer, because of the character and location of the subdivision, there was a reasonable anticipation that the development of the property would succeed and yield a profit. And, as planned, the subdivision was developed, a cash flow generated and the notes paid, with interest, as due. . . . Moreover, at all times the value of the property was increasing, irrespective of its development, and, if necessary, the corporation could have borrowed the money against the property to pay off the notes. Clearly, it was always within Castlewood's ability to make payment as required. To be sure, as with any new venture, there was some risk of loss; but the evidence manifests that such risk was significantly reduced in this case. From the beginning, there existed a reasonable assurance of repayment of the notes regardless of the success of the business. To us, this is further indicia that the notes were debt, not equity. The facts just do not support the inference that, in holding the Castlewood notes, Thomas was assuming the risk of loss normally associated with equity participation.

We are referred by defendant to, among others, Burr Oaks Corp. v. Commissioner, 365 F.2d 24 (7th Cir. 1966), cert. denied, 385 U.S. 1007 (1967), and Aqualane Shores, Inc. v. Commissioner, 269 F.2d 116 (5th Cir. 1959), two of the leading decisions to hold a purported sale to be a contribution to capital. In *Burr Oaks,* undeveloped land, intended for subdivision, was transferred to a newly formed corporation for more than twice its fair market value. In exchange therefor, the transferors received back 2-year promissory notes. Development costs ran extremely high and sales of lots were, at best, slow. Consequently, the notes were only partially paid at maturity and new notes were given for the unpaid balance. Moreover, some of the property was eventually retransferred to the noteholders at little or no cost. On these facts, the Seventh Circuit had no difficulty affirming the decision of the Tax Court, finding a strong inference that the transfer was an equity contribution where "payment to the transferors [was] dependent on the success of an untried undercapitalized business with uncertain prospects." 365 F.2d at 27. In *Aqualane Shores,* the land transferred to the development corporation was mangrove swamp. Thus, vast improvements were essential to its successful development, which, even then, was highly speculative. With its only source of revenue being the sale of lots, the corporation was forced to borrow substantial amounts of money in order to put the land in marketable condition. No payments on the notes taken back for the land were made for 4 years after maturity. On this basis, payment of the obligations to the transferors was deemed to be dependent upon and at the risk of the success of the venture, and the transfer subject to . . . the predecessor to section 351. 269 F.2d at 119-20.

The evidentiary basis of the present case, as previously set forth, contrasts sharply with these decisions. Unlike either case, the prospects for financial success were bright, such success was realized, and the corporation was always able to meet its obligations as they matured. Moreover, the promise of repayment was never in jeopardy, for the properties' self-liquidating potential guaranteed that repayment of the notes would not be subject to the fortunes of the business. In all major respects, the present case is more analogous to Piedmont Corp. v. Commissioner, 388 F.2d 886 (4th Cir. 1968), than to either *Burr Oaks* or *Aqualane Shores. Piedmont* involved successive transfers of options to purchase real property to a controlled corporation in exchange for unsecured promissory notes. The Fourth Circuit considered *Burr Oaks* and *Aqualane Shores,* but found both to be distinguishable. In reversing the decision of the Tax Court that the transfers were in effect a contribution to capital, the following were held to be determinative: (1) the facts indicated "some degree of certainty to the financial success of the venture"; (2) "a fair purchase price was paid"; (3) the corporation "paid the interest and installments of principal when due, promptly and regularly"; and (4) the corporation "did not retransfer any portion of any option, or any land which it acquired by exercise of an option" to the noteholders. Thereupon, the court concluded that "an evidentiary basis to disregard the purported sales as bona fide sales [was] lacking." 388 F.2d at 890-91.

These same factors appear in this case and, accordingly, we choose to be guided in our deliberations by *Piedmont,* rather than by *Burr Oaks* or *Aqualane Shores.* As supported by the record and confirmed by *Piedmont,* the transfer was in substance, as well as in form, a sale and not a capital contribution.

Defendant's remaining contention is that, notwithstanding a determination that the Castlewood notes were valid debt, the subject transaction falls within the literal provisions of section 351. . . .

We have already given our reasons as to why the Castlewood notes did not constitute a continuing proprietary interest in Castlewood and we will not repeat them here.

[The court's discussion of other issues including whether the notes constituted "securities" under then existing law is omitted.]

C-lec Plastics v. Commissioner
76 T.C. 601 (1981)

DRENNEN, Judge. . . .

The only issue for our decision is, for purposes of section 165(a), . . . to determine petitioner's adjusted basis in certain plastic molds and rings which were destroyed by fire.

FINDINGS OF FACT . . .

Edward D. Walsh (hereinafter Walsh) was the president and sole shareholder of petitioner at all times relevant herein.

Prior to May 31, 1970, petitioner, through the individual efforts of Walsh, created certain property which was used or sold to perform a contract with Physics International. The property consisted of 1 pattern mold, 3 master molds, 50 molds, 48 lite rings, and 1 plastic ring. (Hereinafter, this property will be referred to collectively as the molds.) The cost involved in creating the molds was deducted on petitioner's income tax return for its taxable year ended May 31, 1970.

On or about February 29, 1972, petitioner terminated the lease of its business premises and abandoned the molds along with various other properties. On or about the same date, Walsh took possession and acquired ownership of the abandoned molds. Walsh's basis in the molds for Federal income tax purposes and for purposes of this proceeding was at all times zero.

As of May 31, 1973, petitioner's bank account was overdrawn and it was in a cash-poor financial position. As of that date, petitioner's books and records showed that it owed $53,785.16 to Walsh. . . .

In early 1973, events occurred which indicated that a new market could emerge for products made with the molds and, thus, it became advantageous for petitioner to reacquire the molds.

On June 1, 1973, a special meeting of petitioner's board of directors was held. The corporate minutes of that meeting provide in pertinent part: . . .

> The Corporation in exchange for the molds and rings would issue common stock at the rate of $80.00 per share. If this proposal is accepted, Edward Walsh will purchase additional common stock to round the issuance to 500 shares and permit the Corporation to reduce the officers' loan account liability by $2,982.23. . . .

On or about June 1, 1973, Walsh reconveyed possession and ownership of the molds. At the same time, petitioner issued an additional 500 shares of common stock to Walsh. Additionally, a net reduction of $2,982.23 was made in the loan account. Walsh did not receive any cash or monetary consideration, nor any note or evidence of indebtedness from petitioner at the time he reconveyed the molds to petitioner; nor did petitioner pay Walsh any interest.

By journal entry in petitioner's books dated December 31, 1973, petitioner's acquisition of the molds was recorded by: (1) A debit of $37,017.77 in the research and development account; (2) a debit of $2,982.23 in the loan account; and (3) a credit of $40,000 in the common stock issued account. . . .

The molds were destroyed by fire on December 1, 1973. . . .

In the statutory notice of deficiency, respondent determined that petitioner had an adjusted basis of zero in the molds and, thus, was not entitled to any casualty loss deduction for the molds.

Walsh did not report any income arising out of his reconveyance of the molds to petitioner on his individual income tax returns for 1973, or any subsequent year.

OPINION

Section 165(a) allows a deduction for any loss sustained during the taxable year which is not compensated for by insurance or otherwise. There is no dispute that the molds were destroyed by fire, that no compensation was received or receivable therefor, and that any loss thereon is properly deductible under section 165(a). The only issue to be decided is the amount of that loss. Section 165(b) provides that the amount of the deductible loss is measured by the taxpayer's adjusted basis in the property as provided for in section 1011. See also sec. 1.165-7(b), Income Tax Regs. Thus, a determination of petitioner's adjusted basis in the molds is required. . . .

Petitioner argues that the general rule of sections 1011 and 1012 applies, resulting in an adjusted basis of $37,017.77 in the molds, because petitioner did not exchange its common stock for the molds but rather purchased the molds in an arm's-length transaction.

Based on the testimony of its only witness, Robert E. Williams (hereinafter Williams), petitioner's accountant, petitioner contends that on or about June 1, 1973, there were two separate transactions which were entered into for separate and different reasons. One transaction involved petitioner's issuance of $40,000 in common stock to Walsh in consideration for a like-amount debit to the loan account. This was done, petitioner contends, to improve its capital structure and preclude any allegation that it was thinly capitalized.

The second transaction was the purchase of the molds for the cash equivalent of a $37,017.77 credit to the loan account, which amount was in fact paid to Walsh by the conclusion of petitioner's taxable year ended May 31, 1976, at which time the loan account was zero. This purchase, petitioner contends, brings into operation the general rule of sections 1011 and 1012.

Petitioner explains the seemingly inconsistent December 31, 1973, journal entry concerning the acquisition of the molds, as an example of the "common practice" in recordkeeping, whereby the two transactions were "compounded" in one book entry and only the "net effect" thereof was shown. Similarly, petitioner explains the seemingly inconsistent corporate minutes of the special board of directors' meeting as the work of an unsophisticated corporate secretary who also only recorded the "net effect" of the two transactions.

In opposition to petitioner's contentions, respondent argues that the corporate minutes and books and records indicate that the only transaction was an exchange of the common stock for the molds and an incidental amount of cash (in the form of a debit to the loan account) and that such a transaction falls within the purview of section 351. Accordingly, since Walsh recognized no gain on the transfer, petitioner took Walsh's zero basis in the molds pursuant to section 362(a).

It has long been a principle of Federal income tax law that a transaction's substance rather than its form controls. See, e.g., Commissioner v. Court Holding Co., 324 U.S. 331 (1945); Minnesota Tea Co. v. Helvering, 302 U.S. 609 (1938); Gregory v. Helvering, 293 U.S. 465 (1935). . . .

Williams testified that Walsh approached him seeking advice as to effecting petitioner's acquisition of the molds from Walsh. Petitioner's cash-poor financial position precluded an outright cash purchase. Given petitioner's then-existing debt to Walsh in the amount of $53,785.16, Williams also considered it inadvisable for petitioner to purchase the molds solely on credit by increasing the amount it owed to Walsh. Williams testified that he accordingly recommended that petitioner issue $40,000 of common stock to Walsh in exchange for a $40,000 reduction in the loan account and that the petitioner then "purchase" the molds for $37,017.77 by increasing the loan account in an equal amount.

The only possible conclusion that can be drawn from Williams' testimony is that the two transactions were not separable but were two steps of an integrated whole. The impetus for both transactions was the need for petitioner to acquire the molds and there is nothing to suggest that one transaction would have been effected without the other. In substance, petitioner acquired the molds, and reduced its loan account in the amount of $2,982.23, and Walsh received an additional $40,000 in common stock. Despite the accountant's explanation of his "compounded" book entries, the book entries reflect precisely the action taken by the board of directors as reflected in the minutes of their meeting on June 1, 1973. Under these circumstances, to view the acquisition of the molds as a purchase for cash would be to ignore the best evidence of what was actually intended and what took place. That the transaction was "arm's length" in the sense that $37,017.77 may have been a reasonable price for the molds does not alter the basic substance of the transaction as an exchange of common stock for the molds. Moreover, it is of no import that petitioner did not intend for the transaction to qualify under section 351; that provision applies regardless of petitioner's intent. . . .

In this case, the evidence shows that both the substance and the form of the transaction support our conclusion that the molds were exchanged solely for petitioner's common stock and that the transaction falls within the purview of section 351. Thus, section 362 would apply and petitioner's adjusted basis in the molds would be the same as Walsh's, increased by any gain recognized by Walsh.

Furthermore, we do not believe it is necessary in resolving the issue presented to determine whether there were two transactions or one. Even if there were two transactions, it is clear that they were integrated components of a single whole, the substance of which was that petitioner acquired the molds and Walsh only received common stock. . . .

In summary, the carryover basis provision of section 362 results in petitioner's having an adjusted basis of zero in the molds, thereby precluding any casualty loss deduction under section 165.

Decision will be entered for the respondent.

NOTES

1. *Section 351 versus sale*. Section 351 by its terms is not an elective provision. Taxpayers, however, sometimes deliberately fail to comply with the formalities of §351 when noncompliance is to their benefit. Notice in *Bradshaw* that the formation of the corporation and the purported sale took place on the same day. In *C-lec Plastics* the issuance of stock and the purported sale also took place on the same day. Why was one taxpayer successful and the other unsuccessful in the quest to avoid §351 and its carryover basis provisions? Are formalities important?

Could the taxpayer in *C-lec Plastics* have argued that the tangible property transferred (i.e., the molds) embodied the transferor's services and must be so treated for §351 purposes? See the discussion of *James* at page 11 supra. If the molds were not considered property for §351 purposes, how would that determination have helped the taxpayer?

In Kolkey v. Commissioner, 27 T.C. 37 (1956), aff'd, 254 F.2d 51 (7th Cir. 1958), the Tax Court established criteria for making the sale/§351 distinction:

> Was the capital and credit structure of the new corporation realistic? What was the business purpose, if any, of organizing the new corporation? Were the noteholders the actual promoters and entrepreneurs of the new adventure? Did the noteholders bear the principal risks of loss attendant upon the adventure? Were payments of "principal and interest" on the notes subordinated to dividends and to the claims of creditors? Did the noteholders have substantial control over the business operations; and, if so, was such control reserved to them as an integral part of the plan under which the notes were issued? Was the "price" of the properties, for which the notes were issued disproportionate to the fair market value of such properties? Did the noteholders, when default of the notes occurred, attempt to enforce the obligations?

In the following cases the court ruled that an attempted sale was a §351 transfer, thereby denying a stepped-up basis to the transferee for the reasons indicated: Hayutin v. Commissioner, 508 F.2d 462 (10th Cir. 1974) (undercapitalization, subordinated debt, excessive purchase price); Burr Oaks Corp. v. Commissioner, 365 F.2d 24 (7th Cir. 1966) (undercapitalization, speculative repayment of purported indebtedness); Nye v. Commissioner, 50 T.C. 203 (1968) (no business reason for separating attempted sale from §351 transfer).

Sale characterization was respected in the following: Murphy Logging Co. v. Commissioner, 378 F.2d 222 (9th Cir. 1967) (despite unfavorable capitalization and a tax avoidance purpose); Piedmont v. Commissioner, 388 F.2d 886 (4th Cir. 1968) (notes bore reasonable interest, were not subordinated, and were paid).

Under §1239, any gain recognized by a transferor on the sale or exchange of property between certain related persons constitutes ordinary income if such property is depreciable in the hands of the transferee. For purposes of §1239, a person is deemed related to a corporation if the transferor owns, directly or indirectly, 50 percent or more of the value of the corporation's outstanding stock. Why didn't §1239 foil the taxpayer's attempt in *Bradshaw* to lock in a capital gain on the transfer of the real property to the transferee corporation? Consider whether the property was depreciable in the hands of the transferee corporation. See §§1221(1) and 167(a).

Receipt of a stepped-up basis by the transferee is only one reason to prefer a sale over §351. A transferor of property with an unrealized loss may seek recognition unavailable through §351. Even if a sale transaction is respected, the transferor must navigate §267, which prevents a loss deduction on a sale by an individual to a corporation, where the transferor directly or indirectly owns more than 50 percent in value of the outstanding stock of the enterprise. See also Higgins v. Smith, 308 U.S. 473 (1940), which may support a judicial expansion of §267.

One reason for a transfer like that in *Bradshaw* is that the tax rate at the corporate level may be less than the rate at the individual level. But even if the applicable corporate tax rate is higher than the tax rate that would apply to an individual, will we still observe transactions like that in *Bradshaw*? Tax rates are not the only consideration. The corporate form offers nontax advantages such as limited liability and perhaps easier access to financial markets. The use of a subchapter S corporation might provide use of the corporate form with individual tax rates. See Chapter 16.

From a tax standpoint, when would a sale to a corporation be preferable to a §351 transaction? There are a host of reasons why a sale may be more advantageous, aside from a lower tax rate at the corporate level. First, if the taxpayer has capital losses, those losses can offset only up to $3,000 of ordinary income. §1211(a). By selling appreciated property to a corporation, a taxpayer can generate a capital gain that will be fully absorbed by the capital losses. Even if the capital gain is not fully offset with corporate losses, an individual taxpayer may prefer the preferential capital gains tax rate to the higher ordinary income rates that would apply if the taxpayer developed and sold the property in parcels. See §1201. Another reason for a *Bradshaw*-type transaction might be an expectation of increased ordinary income rates in the future. A taxpayer might want to lock in a capital gain now rather than risk a higher ordinary income tax at a later point. Or a taxpayer might be willing to recognize gain on a sale in order to provide the purchasing corporation with a stepped-up basis under §1012, particularly if the taxpayer can postpone recognition through installment reporting.

2. *Contributions to capital by shareholders.* In *Bradshaw* the Service argued that the attempted sale was a contribution to capital. Had the Service

prevailed, what would the consequences have been? Section 118 shields a corporation from recognition of income for contributions to the corporation's capital. The corporation's basis for the new capital is determined under §362(a) for transfers by shareholders. As explained in the following Note, §362(c) provides a special rule for contributions "not contributed by a shareholder as such."

The shareholder who contributes capital does not recognize gain or loss on the contribution and can increase stock basis by the property contributed. Treas. Regs. §1.118-1. Should the basis increase be measured by the basis or fair market value of the property contributed?

Notice what would happen in *Bradshaw* and similar cases if the notes received by the "seller" are ignored because they are too speculative. Payments of what would otherwise be interest will be reclassified as dividends. What difference would this make to the recipient? How about the payor? What happens when the corporation "retires the debt"? Normally, the recipient would have no income or perhaps a capital gain. §1271(a). Now the recipient faces the possibility of ordinary income treatment on a failed redemption. See §302(d), discussed at page 178 infra.

The same consequences may befall a transferor and transferee on any occasion where debt is reclassified as stock. See discussion of the debt-equity issue at pages 98-116 infra.

3.   *"Contributions" to the capital of a corporation by nonshareholders.* Over the years, there has been confusion over the treatment to be accorded contributions by governmental agencies, community groups, and private persons to business to encourage or assist the business in providing or expanding a service. The cases involve two basic issues for the recipient: (1) Is the contribution income? (2) Does the use of the contribution give rise to any tax benefits, such as a deduction for current expenses or a depreciation deduction? The payment also creates tax issues for the contributor. If the contributor is a business and it subsidizes a railroad to extend service to a new area, is the grant a current business deduction or a capital expenditure? If a capital item, it would ordinarily be recovered through a series of deductions over time — that is, depreciation deductions — unless it will last indefinitely (like land). In the latter event there would be no deduction until the recipient sells the land. If the grantor is a charity, grants to private businesses to accomplish the aims of the charity, such as the prevention of community deterioration or providing new employment opportunities, might endanger its exemption.

The exclusion from income of nonshareholder contributions to capital derives from Edwards v. Cuba Railroad Co., 268 U.S. 628 (1925), in which the Court held that government subsidies to a railroad to induce the construction of railroad facilities were not taxable income within the meaning of the sixteenth amendment.

Since 1954 the Code has provided in §118 that gross income does not include any "contribution to capital," thus implicitly recognizing that contributions to capital can be received from nonshareholders. The general rule of §362(a) is that the corporation takes as its tax basis for the property given to it the same basis that the transferor had. Section 362(c), however, provides that contributions by nonshareholders take a zero basis.

Prior to the enactment of §362(c), it was possible under the 1939 Code for the recipient of funds from nonshareholders to receive a double tax benefit. First, the amounts received were not recognized as income; second, the taxpayer was allowed to claim depreciation deductions on the contributor's basis. See Detroit Edison Co. v. Commissioner, 318 U.S. 98 (1943), and United States v. Chicago, Burlington & Quincy Railroad, 339 U.S. 583 (1950), permitting the depreciation. Section 362(c) laid to rest the depreciation issue by providing a zero basis for nonshareholder contributions to capital, but the issue still remains of what is a receipt of taxable income versus a nontaxable contribution to capital by a nonshareholder.

The 1954 codification, via §118, intended as an incorporation of existing decisional law relating to contributions to capital of corporations, was designed to deal with those transfers to a corporation that fall in the gray area between genuine gifts, on the one hand, and payments clearly for direct future services, on the other hand. The legislative history speaks of contributions to capital, as in the case where "the contributor expects to derive indirect benefits, the contribution cannot be called a gift; yet the anticipated future benefits may also be so intangible as to not warrant treating the contributions as a payment for future services." S. Rep. No. 1622, to accompany H.R. 8300 (Pub. L. No. 591), 83d Cong., 2d Sess. 18-19 (1954). See also Treas. Regs. §1.118-1.

The inquiry into the transferor's anticipated benefits was made in Federated Department Stores v. Commissioner, 51 T.C. 500 (1968), aff'd, 426 F.2d 417 (6th Cir. 1970), where it was found that the contribution of money and land by a developer to induce a department store to move into a new shopping center provided only indirect and intangible benefits to the developer; therefore, a tax-free contribution of capital was found. Accord, May Department Stores Co. v. Commissioner, 33 T.C.M. (CCH) 1128 (1974), aff'd per curiam, 519 F.2d 1154 (8th Cir. 1975). But when payments have a reasonable connection with services that are the recipient corporation's business to provide, amounts received are treated as taxable income. John B. White, Inc. v. Commissioner, 55 T.C. 729 (1971), aff'd per curiam, 458 F.2d 989 (3d Cir. 1972) (subsidies from Ford Motor Co. to Ford automobile dealer to induce dealer to move showroom to new location were taxable income). The cases are not easily reconcilable. See Teleservice of Wyoming Valley v. Commissioner, 27 T.C. 722 (1957), aff'd, 254 F.2d 105 (3d Cir. 1958) (payments from prospective customers to finance construction costs to corporation operating community television antenna system were taxable income).

Sometimes receipts can be eliminated from income under what has been known as the conduit theory. In Seven Up Co. v. Commissioner, 14 T.C. 965 (1950), a soft-drink manufacturer received funds from bottlers who voluntarily contributed for an advertising campaign. The manufacturer was held to be a mere conduit for the funds, holding them solely as a trustee and required to disburse them for a specific purpose to benefit the bottlers. Therefore, the funds were not income to the manufacturer under §61. Accord, Ford Dealers Advertising Fund v. Commissioner, 55 T.C. 761 (1971), aff'd per curiam, 456 F.2d 255 (5th Cir. 1972). If the history of these cases seems confusing, see the concluding sentence of Judge Tannenwald's opinion in State Farm Road Corp., 65 T.C. 217 (1975), that in this area "a page of logic is worth a volume of history," taking note of Justice Holmes's statement that normally "a page of history is worth a volume of logic," New York Trust Co. v. Eisner, 256 U.S. 345, 349 (1921).

Section 118(b) provides no exclusion for contributions "in aid of construction or any other contribution as a customer or potential customer." The new provision reverses some of the prior cases, including Edwards v. Cuba Railroad Co., supra, which gave birth to §118.

Hempt Bros., Inc. v. United States
490 F.2d 1172 (3d Cir. 1974)

ALDISERT, Circuit Judge.

[A cash basis partnership transferred its assets to a newly formed corporation in exchange for all the corporation's stock in a transaction qualifying under §351. Among the transferred assets were $662,820 in accounts receivable with a $0 basis. The Service argued that the corporation, whose basis was $0 under §362, should recognize gain when the receivables were paid off. The taxpayer argued that the transferor partnership should have been taxed, a result that was precluded by the applicable statute of limitations.]

I

Taxpayer argues here, as it did in the district court, that because the term "property" as used in Section 351 does not embrace accounts receivable, the Commissioner lacked statutory authority to apply principles associated with Section 351. The district court properly rejected the legal interpretation urged by the taxpayer.

The definition of Section 351 "property" has been extensively treated by the Court of Claims in E. I. DuPont de Nemours and Co. v. United States, 471 F.2d 1211, 1218-19 (Ct. Cl. 1973), describing the transfer of a non-exclusive license to make, use and sell area herbicides under French patents:

Unless there is some special reason intrinsic to [Section 351] the general word "property" has a broad reach in tax law. . . . For section 351, in particular, courts have advocated a generous definition of "property," . . . and it has been suggested in one capital gains case that nonexclusive licenses can be viewed as property though not as capital assets. . . .

We see no adequate reason for refusing to follow these leads.

We fail to perceive any special reason why a restrictive meaning should be applied to accounts receivable so as to exclude them from the general meaning of "property." Receivables possess the usual capabilities and attributes associated with jurisprudential concepts of property law. They may be identified, valued, and transferred. Moreover, their role in an ongoing business must be viewed in the context of Section 351 application. The presence of accounts receivable is a normal, rather than an exceptional accoutrement of the type of business included by Congress in the transfer to a corporate form. . . .

The taxpayer next makes a strenuous argument that "[the] government is seeking to tax the wrong person." It contends that the assignment of income doctrine as developed by the Supreme Court applies to a Section 351 transfer of accounts receivable so that the transferor, not the transferee-corporation, bears the corresponding tax liability. It argues that the assignment of income doctrine dictates that where the right to receive income is transferred to another person in a transaction not giving rise to tax at the time of transfer, the transferor is taxed on the income when it is collected by the transferee; that the only requirement for its application is a transfer of a right to receive ordinary income; and that since the transferred accounts receivable are a present right to future income, the sole requirement for the application of the doctrine is squarely met. In essence, this is a contention that the nonrecognition provision of Section 351 is in conflict with the assignment of income doctrine and that Section 351 should be subordinated thereto. Taxpayer relies on the seminal case of Lucas v. Earl, 281 U.S. 111 (1930), and its progeny for support of its proposition that the application of the doctrine is mandated whenever one transfers a right to receive ordinary income.

On its part, the government concedes that a taxpayer may sell for value a claim to income otherwise his own and he will be taxable upon the proceeds of the sale. Such was the case in Commissioner v. P. G. Lake, Inc., 356 U.S. 260 (1958), in which the taxpayer-corporation assigned its oil payment right to its president in consideration for his cancellation of a $600,000 loan. Viewing the oil payment right as a right to receive future income, the Court applied the reasoning of the assignment of income doctrine, normally applicable to a gratuitous assignment, and held that the consideration received by the taxpayer-corporation was taxable as ordinary income since it essentially was a substitute for that which would otherwise be received at a future time as ordinary income.

Turning to the facts of this case, we note that here there was the transfer of accounts receivable from the partnership to the corporation pursuant to Section 351. We view these accounts receivable as a present right to receive future income. In consideration of the transfer of this right, the members of the partnership received stock — a valid consideration. The consideration, therefore, was essentially a substitute for that which would otherwise be received at a future time as ordinary income to the cash basis partnership. Consequently, the holding in *Lake* would normally apply, and income would ordinarily be realized, and thereby taxable, by the cash basis partnership-transferor at the time of receipt of the stock.

But the terms and purpose of Section 351 have to be reckoned with. By its explicit terms Section 351 expresses the Congressional intent that transfers of property for stock or securities will not result in recognition. It therefore becomes apparent that this case vividly illustrates how Section 351 sometimes comes into conflict with another provision of the Internal Revenue Code or a judicial doctrine, and requires a determination of which of two conflicting doctrines will control. . . .

While we cannot fault the general principle "that income be taxed to him who earns it," to adopt taxpayer's argument would be to hamper the incorporation of ongoing businesses; additionally it would impose technical constructions which are economically and practically unsound. None of the cases cited by taxpayer, including *Lake* itself, persuades us otherwise. In *Lake* the Court was required to decide whether the proceeds from the assignment of the oil payment right were taxable as ordinary income or as long term capital gains. Observing that the provision for long term capital gains treatment "has always been narrowly construed so as to protect the revenue against artful devices," 356 U.S. at 265, the Court predicated its holding upon an emphatic distinction between a conversion of a capital investment — "income-producing property" — and an assignment of income per se. "The substance of what was assigned was the right to receive future income. The substance of what was received was the present value of income which the recipient would otherwise obtain in the future." Ibid., at 266. A Section 351 issue was not presented in *Lake*. Therefore the case does not control in weighing the conflict between the general rule of assignment of income and the Congressional purpose of nonrecognition upon the incorporation of an ongoing business.

We are persuaded that, on balance, the teachings of *Lake* must give way in this case to the broad Congressional interest in facilitating the incorporation of ongoing businesses. As desirable as it is to afford symmetry in revenue law, we do not intend to promulgate a hard and fast rule. We believe that the problems posed by the clash of conflicting internal revenue doctrines are more properly determined by the circumstances of each case. Here we are influenced by the fact that the subject of the assignment was accounts receivable for partnership's goods and services sold in the regular course of business, that the change of business form from partnership to corporation had a basic business purpose and was not designed for the purpose of deliberate tax avoidance, and by the conviction that the totality of circumstances here presented fit the mold of the Congressional intent to give nonrecognition to a transfer of a total business from a noncorporate to a corporate form.

But this too must be said. Even though Section 351(a) immunizes the transferor from immediate tax consequences, Section 358 retains for the transferors a potential income tax liability to be realized and recognized upon a subsequent sale or exchange of the stock certificates received. As to the transferee-corporation, the tax basis of the receivables will be governed by Section 362. . . .

NOTES

1. *Assignment of income.* Nonrecognition under §351 can clash with the well-entrenched assignment of income doctrine developed through a series of Supreme Court cases. See, e.g., Lucas v. Earl, 281 U.S. 111 (1930); Helvering v. Horst, 311 U.S. 112 (1940). We have already seen that the transfer by a cash basis transferor of accounts receivable to a corporation will not trigger recognition at the time of the exchange if the standards of §351 are met. See page 11 supra. A decision reached on this point does not necessarily foreclose the recognition of income by the transferor *when the transferee collects*. Nevertheless, in transactions in which the assets of a going business are incorporated, courts have generally declined to invoke the assignment of income doctrine on collection by the transferee.

In contrast to *Hempt Bros., Inc.,* consider Brown v. Commissioner, 115 F.2d 337 (2d Cir. 1940). There, an attorney brought a lawsuit to collect fees for services rendered. A few months before settling the suit, he transferred the claim to a wholly owned corporation whose only asset was the claim and whose only purpose was to facilitate collection. Under these circumstances the court ruled that the transferor was taxable on the collection of the claim by the transferee. See also Weinberg v. Commissioner, 44 T.C. 233 (1965), aff'd per curiam, 386 F.2d 836 (9th Cir. 1967), where the court treated a sale of growing crops by a newly formed corporation as a sale by the shareholder-transferors who had made the transfer shortly before harvest.

In Rev. Rul. 80-198, 1980-2 C.B. 113, the Service approved of the results in both *Hempt* and *Brown,* citing a business purpose for incorporation, or lack thereof, as determinative.

Notice that in the usual assignment of income situation, a taxpayer who assigns away income from the performance of services avoids taxation of that income. However, when the transferors in *Hempt* transfer the receivables to the transferee corporation, the assignment is not complete. Not only is the transferee corporation taxable when the receivables are collected, but the transferors will also be taxed when the transferee corporation distributes the proceeds (or when the transferors sell their stock, the basis of which reflects the $0 basis in a cash basis taxpayer's accounts receivable). Perhaps it is the corporate double tax that underlies the court's willingness to sidestep the application of Lucas v. Earl in a §351 transaction.

2.   *Tax benefit rule*. In Nash v. United States, 398 U.S. 1 (1970), accrual basis transferors exchanged receivables for stock. The Supreme Court held that there had been no "recovery" of a previously deducted bad debt reserve sufficient to trigger recognition by the transferors. In *Nash* the value of the stock received equaled the value of the receivables minus the bad debt reserve. If the value of the stock received exceeds the value of the property exchanged, the *Nash* rationale may not save the transferor from recognition under the tax benefit doctrine. See United States v. Bliss Dairy, 460 U.S. 370 (1983).

3.   *Business purpose*. This ubiquitous doctrine will sometimes be invoked to ignore a purported §351 transfer. For example, in Rev. Rul. 60-331, 1960-2 C.B. 189, the Service disregarded an attempted transfer of stock in one corporation on which a dividend was due to a second corporation to try to qualify for the dividends-received deduction of §243. See also West Coast Marketing Corp. v. Commissioner, 46 T.C. 32 (1966), in which the court disregarded the formation of a corporation solely for the purpose of qualifying the subsequent exchange of stock for nonrecognition under the reorganization provisions when the direct exchange of property would have subjected the transferor to capital gains treatment.

4.   *Clear reflection of income*. In addition to judicially created doctrines, the Service has several statutory weapons in its arsenal. In Palmer v. Commissioner, 267 F.2d 434 (9th Cir. 1959), an individual taxpayer in the construction business, who had been reporting income on the completed contract method, transferred the business to a corporation shortly after a large payment was due for work done prior to the transfer. The court upheld the Commissioner's adjustment under §446(b), putting the transferor on the percentage of completion method of accounting, thereby allocating a large part of the income back to the taxpayer. See also Shore v. Commissioner, 631 F.2d 624 (9th Cir. 1980) (incorporation triggered §481 recognition).

In Rooney v. United States, 305 F.2d 681 (9th Cir. 1962), a husband and wife's farming business was incorporated under §351 after the transferors had taken deductions pertaining to the crop transferred. Employing §482, the court held that the deductions for business expenses could be denied to the transferors and allocated to the corporation, to be matched with the subsequently realized income to which the expenses related. For further discussion of §482, see page 572 infra.

5.   *Organizational expenses*. Besides issuing stock, a new corporation must contend with a host of expenditures incident to its formation, such as legal fees for drafting the charter, bylaws, and stock certificates; account-

ing fees; expenses for the organizational meeting of directors or stockholders; and fees paid to the state of incorporation. Section 248 permits a corporation to elect to amortize such "organizational expenses" over a period of 60 months or more. For a definition of "organizational expenditures," see §248(b) and Treas. Regs. §1.248-1(b)(2). Expenditures incurred in the process of raising capital — such as commissions and printing costs — are excluded from the reach of §248. Why? If the corporation does not elect to amortize under §248, presumably organizational expenses can be deducted in the year the corporation dissolves. See Bryant Heater Co. v. Commissioner, 231 F.2d 938 (6th Cir. 1956).

6. *Section 351 and redemptions.* For the interplay among §§351, 302, and 304, see page 240 infra.

7. *Section 351 and reorganizations.* There is an overlap between §351 and the provisions governing reorganizations. For example, suppose *T* wants to transfer appreciated property to *X* Corp. without recognizing gain. *T* is not a shareholder of *X* Corp. A direct attempt at a §351 transfer would leave *T* short of the control requirement. Suppose, though, that *T* and *X* Corp. together form Sub Corp., with *T* contributing the appreciated property and *X* Corp. all its assets. Together the transferors hold 100 percent of the Sub Corp. stock. The final step is that the *X* Corp. shareholders receive Sub Corp. stock in exchange for their *X* Corp. stock. Assume that the *X* Corp. stock has not appreciated so that no gain is recognized by the shareholders on the exchange. Has *T* made an end run around the control requirements of §351? See Rev. Rul. 68-349, 1968-2 C.B. 143 (transaction treated as reorganization; §351 nonrecognition unavailable to *T*).

8. *Section 351 and passive activity losses.* Suppose *B*, a transferor in a §351 transaction, transfers rental real estate that has been subject to the passive loss limitations under §469. Does the §351 transfer trigger suspended passive losses, thereby allowing *B* to use those losses to offset nonpassive income (such as portfolio income or income from services)? A taxable disposition of a passive activity triggers the use of any suspended losses against any type of income. §469(g).

The Senate Finance Committee report accompanying the Tax Reform Act of 1986 makes clear that a §351 transfer does not trigger the suspended losses because *B* retains an interest in the property. To the extent there is taxable boot in the §351 transaction, the suspended passive losses can be used to offset that income. The suspended losses will be fully deductible when *B* disposes of her entire interest in the corporation.

PROBLEMS

2-5. *T,* a cash basis taxpayer, transfers real property and IBM stock to *X* Corp. in exchange for *X* stock in a transaction that qualifies under §351. Discuss the tax consequences to *T* and *X* Corp. in the following.

a. The real property has a basis of $200,000 and a fair market value of $900,000. It is subject to a liability of $500,000, which X will assume. The IBM stock has a basis of $100,000 and a fair market value of $70,000.

b. Suppose in (a) that X takes the property subject to the liability so that T remains liable on the underlying note. Suppose instead that T guarantees X's payment of the liability.

c. Suppose in (a) that T borrows $200,000 from a bank and contributes the cash as part of the §351 transaction.

d. Suppose in (c) that T had borrowed $200,000 from X in an unrelated transaction. The loan bears a market rate of interest and the loan is due in 10 years. T transfers the loan proceeds as part of the §351 transaction.

e. Suppose in (a) that T makes a promissory note to X in the amount of $200,000 bearing a market rate of interest and transfers the note as part of the §351 transaction. The note is due in 10 years.

2-6. T, a cash basis taxpayer who operates a sole proprietorship, transfers $1,000 in uncollected accounts receivable (with a basis of $0) to X, a wholly owned corporation. In exchange, T receives $700 of X stock and X's assumption of $300 of T's accounts payable.

a. What are the tax consequences to T and X?

b. Suppose T is an accrual basis taxpayer transferring property with a basis of $0 and a fair market value of $1,000 in exchange for $700 of X stock and X's assumption of $300 of T's account payables. What are the tax consequences?

c. In (a), what are the tax consequences when X collects on the accounts receivable and pays off the accounts payable?

2-7. T owns all the stock of X Corp. T transfers to X Corp. a parcel of real estate with a basis of $100,000 and a fair market value of $500,000. In exchange T receives an interest-bearing debt instrument due in five years. Following the transfer, X Corp. developed the property into 10 single-family dwellings, each of which was sold for $100,000. Ignoring the development costs, discuss the tax consequences of these transactions to T and X Corp.

3

Corporate Operation

A. CORPORATE TAX RATES AND BASE

1. Taxable Entity

For a discussion of when a corporation is treated as a separate taxable entity, see Chapter 15.

2. Tax Rate

Section 11 imposes graduated tax rates ranging from 15 percent to 35 percent on corporate taxpayers. The graduation is steep: Corporations with taxable income of more than $75,000 find themselves in the 34 percent bracket. The 35 percent bracket applies to corporate taxable income over $10 million. The little graduation that exists is eliminated for corporations with taxable income greater than $18,333,333. Those corporations are taxed at a flat 35 percent rate because Congress wanted to restrict the benefits of the lower rates to smaller businesses.

Section 11 implements this congressional policy in a somewhat convoluted manner. First, an additional tax is imposed on taxable income in excess of $100,000. The additional tax is equal to 5 percent of a corporation's income in excess of $100,000 up to a maximum additional tax of $11,750, which occurs at $335,000 of taxable income. The $11,750 figure represents the difference between taxing the first $75,000 of taxable income at a flat 34 percent ($25,500) and taxing it at the graduated rates ($13,750). As a corporation's taxable income increases from $100,000 to $335,000, the benefits of the reduced tax rates on the first $75,000 vanish.

Note also that for taxable income in the range of $100,000 to $335,000, the marginal tax rate on the next dollar earned is not 34 percent but equals 34 percent plus the 5 percent surtax, or 39 percent.

A second provision of the same type phases out the 34 percent bracket for corporate taxpayers with taxable income exceeding $15 million. These taxpayers must pay 3 percent of taxable income in excess of $15 million or $100,000, whichever is less. Accordingly for taxpayers with taxable income between $15,000,000 and $18,333,333, a 38 percent rate applies. For taxpayers with taxable income exceeding $18,333,333, there is a flat 35 percent rate.

All of the above result in marginal rates as follow:

Taxable Income	Rate
Up to $50,000	15%
Over $50,000 but not over $75,000	25
Over $75,000 but not over $100,000	34
Over $100,000 but not over $335,000	39
Over $335,000 but not over $10,000,000	34
Over $10,000,000 but not over $15,000,000	35
Over $15,000,000 but not over $18,333,333	38
Over $18,333,333	35

While §11(a) contains only slightly graduated tax rates, even that slight graduation is denied to "qualified personal service corporations," which are taxed at a flat 35 percent rate. A corporation is a qualified personal service corporation if it meets a function test and an ownership test. See §448(d). Under the function test, substantially all of the activities of the corporation must involve the performance of services in the fields of health, law, engineering, architecture, accounting, actuarial science, performing arts, or consulting. Under the ownership test, substantially all of the stock (by value) of the corporation must be held directly or indirectly by employees performing the services, by retired employees who performed the services in the past, by their estates, or by persons who hold stock in the corporation by reason of the death of an employee or retired· employee within the past two years.

Notice that the denial of graduated rates applies only to "qualified" personal service corporations. Such corporations are "qualified" to be treated more harshly than other corporations. The definition of qualified personal service corporations used in §§11(b) and 448(d) is quite narrow. Indeed §448 prohibits the use of the cash method of accounting by corporations except for the narrow category of qualified professional corporations. Why would Congress use this narrow category to impose higher tax rates? Notice how Congress both giveth and taketh away. Qualified personal service corporations can use the cash method of accounting but cannot have the advantages of graduated rates. Why are qualified personal service corporations subject to a higher rate schedule than manufacturing or sales corporations? What policy reason, if any, justifies this discrimination?

While it is easy to categorize some businesses as qualified personal service corporations, such as incorporated doctors, dentists, lawyers, and accountants, the treatment of other businesses is not so clear. Are incorporated health clubs, nutritionists, and weight control clinics considered in the health field? Treas. Regs. §1.448-1T provides that health services do not include services not directly related to a medical field even if the services purportedly relate to the health of the recipient. Health clubs and spas are specifically excluded from coverage. Similar questions arise with respect to the performing arts. Under the regulation, performing arts services do not include services of managers or promoters or the activities of broadcasters. Athletes are not considered performing artists.

Perhaps the most uncertain area is consulting. According to the regulations, consulting is the giving of advice and counsel; sales and brokerage activities are not consulting. If compensation is contingent on the consummation of a transaction, any services performed in the transaction are not consulting services. For example, financial planners who are paid on the basis of advice are engaged in consulting and are subject to the flat 35 percent rate while financial planners who are paid on the basis of trade orders in securities or commodities are not consulting.

3. Taxation of Capital Gains and Losses

For noncorporate taxpayers, §1(j) currently provides a rate ceiling of 20 percent on capital gains. Section 1201 accomplishes a similar (but less rewarding) function for corporations by providing an alternative tax for corporations with net capital gains in lieu of the tax imposed by §11 if the §1201 tax is less. This tax is the sum of (1) the §11 tax on the corporation's taxable income minus the net capital gains and (2) 35 percent of the net capital gains. That is, the maximum tax on corporate net capital gains is 35 percent — the same maximum rate for ordinary income. However, if the tax rate for ordinary income goes up, capital gains may only be taxed at a 35 percent rate.

Section 1201 is triggered if the rate of tax under §11 exceeds 35 percent. Suppose a corporation with $15 million of ordinary income earns a $500,000 capital gain. Does §1201 provide a top rate on the capital gain of 35 percent since the effective rate under §11 is 35 percent plus the 3 percent additional tax on the $500,000 gain?

There are also some differences in the treatment of capital losses for corporations vis-à-vis other taxpayers. A corporation can deduct capital losses only to the extent of capital gains. §1211(a). No ordinary income can be offset by capital losses. Cf. §1211(b) (individuals can offset up to

$3,000 of ordinary income with capital losses). Although individuals can carry unused capital losses forward indefinitely, corporations are generally given a three-year carryback period and a five-year carryforward period. The unused loss is carried back to the earliest year and then carried forward chronologically until the balance is used up or the carryforward period expires.

4. Corporate Tax Base

The §11 tax (or the §1201 tax) is applied to "taxable income." While in most respects a corporation's taxable income is determined in the same manner as an individual's, there are some differences aside from the capital loss carryover provision discussed above. For individual taxpayers, "adjusted gross income" serves as a halfway house in moving from the calculation of gross income to taxable income. An individual's charitable, medical, and casualty loss deductions are all based on adjusted gross income. A corporation does not have an adjusted gross income. Instead, all appropriate corporate deductions are subtracted directly from gross income in arriving at taxable income.

Some deductions that are treated differently by individual and corporate taxpayers include the following:

1. The standard deduction allowed under §63(c) for individuals is not available for corporations, which instead must itemize their deductions;
2. the personal exemption deduction under §151 is not available for corporations;
3. personal deductions authorized under §§211-220 (including items such as medical expenses and alimony) do not apply to corporations, although §162 permits a corporation to deduct expenses incurred for the production of income not in a trade or business that for individuals are deductible under §212; and
4. charitable contribution deductions are allowed to corporations up to 10 percent of taxable income under §170(b)(2).

A number of provisions were enacted specifically to apply to corporate taxpayers. For example, Congress has shown concern over corporations' making large compensation payments to corporate officers in the event of a corporate takeover. These "golden parachutes" appear to some as a raid on the corporate treasury by the officers. To others the payments ensure that the officers will do what is best for the corporation in the event of a takeover attempt without worrying about personal consequences (e.g., the loss of a well-paying job).

Through the use of the tax system, Congress has raised the cost of making golden parachute payments. Section 280G denies a deduction for payments of "excessive" compensation to corporate officers triggered by changes in corporate control. Excessive payments are determined by comparing the payments with a designated base period. In addition, §4999 imposes an excise tax on the recipient.

A publicly held corporation cannot deduct compensation paid to a "covered employee" in excess of $1 million if the compensation is "applicable employee remuneration." §162(m). The term "covered employee" refers to any employee who (1) as of the close of the taxable year is the chief executive officer of the corporation or (2) is one of the corporation's four highest compensated officers (other than the CEO) for the tax year. The term "applicable employee remuneration" refers to a covered employee's aggregate remuneration for services performed. The term does not apply, however, to commission payments or other performance-based compensation if (1) the performance goals are established by a compensation committee of the board of directors that has two or more outside directors, (2) the material terms of the compensation are approved by a majority vote of the shareholders before compensation is paid, and (3) the compensation committee certifies that the performance goals were satisfied. For example, compensation based on increases in stock price, market share, or earnings per share are not counted in determining the $1 million limit if the specified procedural requirements are satisfied. Notice that the limited deduction imposed by §162(m) applies to publicly held corporations, where there is accountability to outside directors and to the shareholders, but does not apply to privately held corporations, where there is more room for manipulation.

With the increase of corporate takeover activity in the 1980s and 1990s, members of Congress voiced concern that regulation was needed to stem the tide. While many commentators argue that takeovers are one of the free market's means of disciplining inefficient management and deploying corporate assets in the most efficient manner, others decry the dislocations to workers and communities caused by some takeovers and lament the amount of debt (i.e., leverage) used in some acquisitions.

There is no dispute, however, that Congress has looked to the tax laws as a means of regulating the market for corporate control. Section 279, enacted in 1969, disallows a deduction for corporate interest in excess of $5 million per year on specified "corporate acquisition indebtedness," defined to include certain convertible, subordinated debt. The effect of this provision is to make debt-financed takeovers less attractive. See page 369 infra.

More recent provisions have focused on all aspects of corporate acquisitions. Section 162(k) denies a deduction for any amount paid or incurred by a corporation to redeem its own stock. This provision is aimed at "greenmail" payments made by a corporation to a potential corporate "raider" to repurchase the "raider's" stock. Furthermore, §5881 imposes an excise tax of 50 percent on any gain or other income realized by the greenmail recipient. "Greenmail" is defined in §5881 as consideration paid by a corporation in redemption of its stock held for less than two years if the holder threatened a public tender offer. It is not clear that greenmail payments are "bad," but it is clear that the Code discourages such payments. See Macey and McChesney, A Theoretical Analysis of Corporate Greenmail, 95 Yale L.J. 133 (1985).

Section 382, discussed in more detail in Chapter 13, does not attempt to increase the direct cost of corporate acquisitions. Instead, these provisions limit the ability of acquiring corporations to use net operating losses of the acquired corporation to offset future income, thereby decreasing the attraction of some corporate takeovers.

In addition to the deductions discussed above, a corporation is entitled to a variety of tax credits. Perhaps the most significant one is the foreign tax credit. §§27 and 901. A corporation can offset any applicable U.S. federal income tax on income from foreign sources with foreign income taxes paid on that income. Credits are also available for research (§41), targeted jobs expenditures (§51), and rehabilitation and energy expenditures (§§46-48).

The preceding discussion of the corporate tax rate and base is aimed at domestic corporations (corporations incorporated in any state in the United States). Foreign corporations (corporations incorporated abroad) are subject to U.S. taxation on income that is connected in designated ways to the United States. See generally §§881 and 882. For example, a foreign corporation engaged in a trade or business in the United States is taxed in the same manner as a U.S. corporation on income that is "effectively connected" with the conduct of that U.S. trade or business (i.e., trade or business income). §882. The rules governing tax rates and base apply to such business income. A foreign corporation that has investment income from interest, dividends, rents, royalties, and so on is generally taxed at a flat rate of 30 percent (or in some cases, a lower treaty rate) on the gross amount of the payments. §881. No deductions are permitted. A foreign corporation can elect, however, to have rental payments for the use of U.S. real property taxed as business income that can be offset by appropriate deductions rather than being taxed at the flat 30 percent rate. §882(d).

5. Passive Loss Limitations

In an effort to curtail investment solely or primarily for the purpose of securing tax benefits, Congress enacted §469, a provision that limits the deduction of passive activity expenses against other income (i.e., active business income or portfolio income). Any losses suspended as a result of the limitation can be carried forward and treated as deductions in the following year or can be taken when the taxpayer disposes of the entire interest in the passive activity. §469(b) and (g). In general, an activity is passive if it involves the conduct of a trade or business and if the taxpayer does not "materially participate" in the activity. By definition, rental activity (e.g., ownership of an apartment building) is considered a passive activity regardless of the level of activity. An important exception, however, applies for taxpayers in the real estate business. See discussion below.

Although an exhaustive discussion of the passive loss provisions is beyond the scope of a corporate tax course, the provisions do apply to certain personal service corporations and closely held corporations. Accordingly, a personal service corporation that also rents real estate may not be able to offset any active income from the performance of services with deductions from the real estate rental activity. A personal service corporation is defined as a corporation whose principal activity is the performance of personal services when such services are performed by an employee who owns any stock of the corporation. See §§469(j)(2) and 269A(b)(2).

In the case of a closely held corporation (other than a personal service corporation) the passive loss rules apply in modified form. §469(e)(2). Passive losses may be used to offset active business income but not portfolio income (e.g., interest, dividends, and royalties). A closely held corporation is defined as a corporation that has more than 50 percent in value of its outstanding stock owned by not more than five individuals. §§469(j)(1), 465(a)(1)(B), 542(a)(2).

Material participation for a corporation that is subject to §469 is achieved if one or more shareholders owning in the aggregate more than 50 percent of the outstanding stock of the corporation materially participate. §469(h)(4). Shareholders materially participate if they spend more than 500 hours on the activity or if they meet one of the other tests specified under the regulations. Treas. Regs. §§1.469-1T(g), -5T.

If more than 50 percent of a closely held corporation's gross receipts for the taxable year are derived from real property trades or businesses in which the corporation materially participates, the rental activities are not considered passive. Accordingly, losses can be used to offset nonpassive income. A real property trade or business is any real property development, redevelopment, construction, reconstruction, acquisition, conversion, rental, operation, management, leasing, or brokerage trade or business. §469(c)(7).

If passive losses are suspended, those losses can be taken in full when the taxpayer disposes (in a taxable transaction) of the entire interest in the passive activity. §469(g)(1). The reason for the rule is that prior to the disposition, it is difficult to determine whether there has actually been gain or loss with respect to the activity. For example, allowable deductions may or may not exceed unrealized appreciation. On a taxable disposition, a final accounting can be made for the activity.

Suppose a personal services corporation is also engaged in a rental real estate activity and that the deductions for the rental activity exceed the passive income from that activity by $20,000. Those excess deductions would not be allowed under §469. If the corporation then disposes of the rental real estate in a taxable transaction that produces a $15,000 gain, the suspended losses first apply against that gain. The remaining $5,000 of suspended loss can then reduce any other passive income. Finally, any unused suspended losses then reduce any other income or gain. §469(g). Suspended passive losses are not triggered when the passive activity interest is transferred to a related party. §469(g)(1)(B). On an installment sale, suspended losses can be recognized in proportion to the ratio of recognized gain on the sale for the taxable year to the overall gain from the sale of the property. §469(g)(3).

In general, suspended losses are not triggered by a nontaxable transfer such as a like-kind exchange (except to the extent of any gain recognized on the transaction) but instead are triggered on disposition of the received property. If an activity ceases to be passive (for example, the corporation no longer rents the property but uses it as part of its active service trade or business), any suspended losses can offset net income from the formerly passive but now nonpassive activity or income from other passive activities. §469(f).

6. Taxable Year and Accounting Methods

In general, a corporation can choose any taxable year. §441(b). This flexibility has been exploited by taxpayers seeking to defer recognition of income for tax purposes. For example, prior to the enactment of §441(i), a personal service corporation was free to adopt any taxable year on its federal income tax return that conformed with its annual accounting period. A popular strategy was to adopt a January 31 business year. A doctor earning $200,000 a year might take a $10,000 monthly salary from the personal service corporation and take the remaining $80,000 as a January bonus. As a calendar year taxpayer, the doctor could defer the taxes on the bonus to the following year.

Under §441(i) a personal service corporation must adopt a calendar year unless the taxpayer receives approval from the Treasury Secretary for use of a different taxable year. An exception allows the use of a fiscal year if the deferral period is not more than three months (i.e., fiscal years ending in September through December). §444. See also §280H requiring certain minimum distributions. For purposes of these provisions, a personal service corporation is a corporation whose principal activity is the performance of services if those services are substantially performed by owner-employees who together own more than 10 percent (by value) of the corporation's stock. §269A(b)(1) and (b)(2).

Most corporations are prohibited from using the cash method of accounting. §448. Accordingly, installment reporting is not available. In general, the accrual method of reporting more accurately reflects the economic results of a taxpayer's trade or business over a taxable year. Congress has, however, excepted certain entities, including qualified farming businesses, personal service corporations, and entities with average annual gross receipts of $5 million or less for a three-year testing period from the prohibition against the cash basis accounting method. §448(b).

A qualified personal service corporation is one that meets a function test and an ownership test. The function test is met if substantially all of the activities of the corporation are the performance of services in the fields of health, law, engineering, architecture, accounting, actuarial science, performing arts, or consulting. §448(d)(2)(A). Can you think of any policy reason to limit the cash basis method to these enterprises? The ownership test is met if substantially all the value of the outstanding stock of the corporation is owned by employees (present or retired). §448(d)(2)(B).

In some situations a corporation's method of accounting is modified to conform with the accounting method of shareholders. For example, §267(a)(1) prevents the deduction of losses on the sale or exchange of property between a corporation and a shareholder owning 50 percent (or more) in value of the corporation's stock. Section 267(a)(2) requires an accrual basis corporation to deduct compensation, interest, and other deductible payments made to a cash basis owner-employee when such payment is made rather than when the payment accrues. The purpose of this provision is to prevent a mismatching of deduction and income when the liability for payment accrues in one year but actual payment is deferred to a subsequent year.

7. Corporate Alternative Minimum Tax

As you have already discovered, the Code is littered with provisions that provide tax incentives to engage in or abstain from various activities. Although Congress presumably has tailored these provisions to provide the desired level of activity in the aggregate, it also has shown a desire to prevent any particular taxpayer from benefiting too much from an induced tax incentive. If 10 taxpayers engage in a particular tax-favored activity, each may be able to take a deduction because the activity is one that Congress has purposefully encouraged, but if one taxpayer engages in the activity tenfold, there may be limitations on the deduction even though in the aggregate the level of activity may be precisely what Congress intended. Rather than limit the deduction directly, in general Congress has opted for a minimum tax mechanism.

The alternative minimum tax (AMT) under §55 operates mechanically as a tax added on to the regular tax under §11. Conceptually, it is more accurate to think of the AMT as a shadow tax so that a corporation pays whichever is greater, the regular tax or the AMT. As compared with the regular tax under §11, the AMT has a broader tax base and a lower tax rate. In general, the tax base is the corporation's regular taxable income increased by the taxpayer's tax preferences and by certain other adjustments. §55(b)(2). The resulting amount is "alternative minimum taxable income" (AMTI), a term that seeks to identify the corporation's economic income before it behaves in a tax-induced manner. The AMTI is then reduced by an exemption amount and is subject to a 20 percent tax. §55(b)(1)(A). The exemption amount for corporations is $40,000, reduced by 25 percent of the amount by which AMTI exceeds $150,000. §55(d). Therefore, for a corporation with AMTI of $310,000 or more, no exemption is available.

The alternative minimum tax does not apply to corporation with average annual gross receipts of $5 million or less for a three-year period. §55(e)(1). A corporation that meets this test continues to be exempt from the AMT as long as its average annual gross receipts for the previous three-year period do not exceed $7.5 million.

The adjustments that must be made to the taxpayer's taxable income to arrive at AMTI are set out in §§56-58. For example, to the extent that a corporation's depreciation deductions exceed depreciation calculated under an alternative method, the excess will be treated as a tax preference that must be added to taxable income. §56(a)(1). The reason for the adjustment is Congress's concern that depreciation permitted under §168 as an investment incentive exceeds actual economic depreciation. The alternative method for real property is defined as straight line depreciation over a specified life that is longer than the period permitted for figuring depreciation deductions under §168(b) (e.g., 40 years for residential real property under the AMT compared with 27.5 under §168). §§56(a)(1), 168(g).

A significant preference affecting corporations is the adjustment for "adjusted current earnings" (ACE). §56(g). Congress was concerned that corporations such as General Electric Co. and W.R. Grace that reported substantial earnings to their shareholders for financial purposes (either through public reporting requirements or through voluntary disclosure) were able to report little or no earnings for tax purposes because of available deductions or credits (e.g., the foreign tax credit). Presumably, Congress regarded this phenomenon as a threat to taxpayer morale because appearances suggested that profitable corporations were escaping appropriate taxation.

Although adding back specific preferences to taxable income in arriving at AMTI addresses the problem somewhat, Congress has backstopped the process by requiring a corporation to add to its AMTI an amount equal to 75 percent of the excess of the corporation's ACE over its AMTI (computed without this ACE adjustment). "Adjusted current earnings" is defined as AMTI with a variety of adjustments intended to reflect a corporation's economic income available for distribution. §56(g)(4). For example, tax-exempt interest that increases a corporation's wealth is not included in the AMTI calculation but is added back for purposes of calculating the ACE. For a better understanding of the ACE adjustments, see the discussion of earnings and profits at page 129 infra.

Other adjustments that must be made to taxable income in determining AMTI include using the percentage of completion method of accounting rather than the completed contract method, adding accelerated depletion in connection with mineral exploration, and ignoring the deferral of installment reporting in the case of certain property. §56(a).

In attempting to reconstruct an economic tax base for purposes of determining minimum tax liability, an adjustment must be made to net operating losses (NOLs). §56(a)(4). For AMT purposes, NOLs tend to be overstated because they may reflect the tax preferences the AMT is trying to address. Consequently, for purposes of the AMT, net operating loss is determined by adding to taxable income any tax preferences or adjustments. For example, if in year 1 a taxpayer has $20,000 of income and $35,000 of deductions, of which $10,000 is a preference item (such as accelerated depreciation), the AMT net operating loss for the year would be $5,000. §56(d). Thus, in any subsequent (or prior) year to which the loss may be carried, a $5,000 net operating loss deduction is allowed to reduce income subject to the AMT. Assume that in year 2 the taxpayer has $20,000 of AMTI before accounting for the AMT net operating loss. The taxpayer reduces AMTI to $15,000 by the AMT net operating loss deduction. §56(a)(4). The net operating loss deduction for the regular tax is not affected by this computation (that is, the taxpayer has a $15,000 loss carryover from year 1 for use against the regular tax). Moreover, the alternative tax net operating loss deduction cannot exceed 90 percent of AMTI. §56(d)(1)(A). Suppose that for the year in question a taxpayer has $10 million of AMTI and an AMT net operating loss of $11 million. The net operating loss reduces AMTI to $1 million, giving rise to $200,000 of AMT liability. The taxpayer may then carry forward $2 million of AMT net operating loss.

Once AMTI is determined, the tentative minimum tax equals 20 percent of the excess of AMTI over the exemption. §55(b)(1)(A). A taxpayer can in some cases then offset the tax with a specially computed foreign tax credit. §55(b)(1)(B). First, the credit is recomputed to account for any preferences that decreased U.S. source income and thereby increased the foreign tax credit. Second, no more than 90 percent of tentative minimum tax liability can be offset by foreign tax credits. §59(a). Although conceptually the AMT applies if it is higher than the regular tax, under §55(a) the excess of the alternative minimum tax over the regular tax under §11 is added to the regular tax to determine total tax liability.

Section 53 introduces a credit for a prior year's AMT liability. The credit can be taken against a taxpayer's regular tax, not the AMT. The purpose of the credit is to reflect the fact that some of the tax preferences added to taxable income in determining AMTI reflect deferral preferences (such as accelerated depreciation) rather than permanent avoidance (such as percentage depletion). For example, taxpayers paying the AMT as a result of taking accelerated depreciation deductions potentially face a double penalty. First, the AMT must be paid. Then in a later year, the taxpayer loses a part of the deduction that would have been available if no accelerated depreciation had been taken (instead, that part was taken in the earlier year, giving rise to the AMT liability). The result is a higher regular tax in the later year.

The AMT credit is intended to allow the taxpayer in the later year to offset the regular tax liability with a prior year's AMT liability. The AMT credit can be carried forward indefinitely. The credit is allowed only with respect to liability arising as a result of deferral preferences (that is, preferences other than those that result in permanent exclusion of certain income for regular tax purposes). Accordingly, the amount of the AMT liability that can be credited is reduced by the AMT liability that would have arisen if the only applicable preferences were exclusion preferences.

PROBLEMS

3-1.   How might a profitable U.S. corporation pay no U.S. taxes?

3-2.   Suppose X Corp., a construction company engaged in a major project, in year 1 has no regular tax liability under its regular completed contract method of accounting. It does have $100,000 of AMT liability, principally because of §56(a)(3) which mandates the percentage of completion method of accounting for AMT purposes. In year 2, when the project is completed, X Corp.'s regular tax liability is $400,000 (there is no AMT liability in year 2). Why might X Corp. complain about this result? Does the Code offer any relief?

B. CAPITAL STRUCTURE

A corporation can raise capital either by issuing stock (equity) or by issuing a debt instrument in exchange for cash or property. In either case, an investor holds a financial instrument with a claim on corporate assets. The nature of those claims can be very different. A prototypical debt instrument provides that the borrower (i.e., the corporation) will repay the debt after a fixed term. Moreover, while the loan is outstanding, the borrower promises to pay the investor a fixed rate of interest regardless of the corporation's performance. Whether the corporation performs well or poorly, the return to the lender is fixed and, in the prototypical case, subject to little risk.

In contrast, the prototypical common stock instrument is riskier because it entitles the holder to no guarantees. Unlike the prototypical loan, there is no fixed date of repayment. While interest is paid with respect to a debt instrument, stock ownership does not guarantee the receipt of dividends. Under state corporate law, creditors must be paid before any dividend distributions are made to shareholders. In many cases, the payment of dividends depends on the corporation's performance. The value of an investor's stock also depends on the performance of the corporation. If the corporation does well and is expected to do well in the future, typically the fair market value of the outstanding common stock increases. Conversely, if the corporation does poorly, the fair market value of the stock usually declines. At the extremes, prototypical debt has little risk and a limited upside potential; stock has more risk and an unlimited upside potential. Between these extremes is a bewildering assortment of financial instruments bearing various risk levels and expected profit levels.

In deciding whether to issue debt or equity, a corporation must consider both nontax and tax factors. Many financial theorists believe that, taxes aside, the value of a corporation is independent of financial structure. See Modigliani and Miller, The Cost of Capital, Corporation Finance, and the Theory of Investment, Am. Econ. Rev. 261-267 (June 1958). Nevertheless, a corporation with a high ratio of outstanding debt to equity may find difficulty in obtaining additional bank financing and in attracting future investors. Conversely, a corporation with little or no debt may be viewed as underperforming and may be a takeover candidate.

The following excerpt considers the effect of federal taxes on a corporation's financial structure.

Joint Committee on Taxation, Federal Income Tax Aspects of Corporate Financial Structures* _____

101st Cong., 1st Sess. (Jan. 18, 1989)

IV.   POLICY ISSUES

A.   TAX ADVANTAGE OF DEBT VERSUS EQUITY

The total effect of the tax system on the incentives for corporations to use debt or equity depends on the interaction between the tax treatment at the shareholder and corporate levels.

_____
* Footnotes omitted. — EDS.

The case of no income taxes. — In a simple world without taxes or additional costs in times of financial distress, economic theory suggests that the value of a corporation, as measured by the total value of the outstanding debt and equity, would be unchanged by the degree of leverage of the firm. This conclusion explicitly recognizes that debt issued by the corporation represents an ownership right to future income of the corporation in a fashion similar to that of equity. In this simple world there would be no advantage to debt or to equity and the debt-equity ratio of the firm would not affect the cost of financing investment.

Effect of Corporate Income Tax

Tax Advantages

Taxes greatly complicate this analysis. Since the interest expense on debt is deductible for computing the corporate income tax while the return to equity is not, the tax at the corporate level provides a strong incentive for debt rather than equity finance.

The advantages of debt financing can be illustrated by comparing two corporations with $1,000 of assets that are identical except for financial structure: the first is entirely equity financed; while the second is 50-percent debt financed. Both corporations earn $150 of operating income. The all-equity corporation pays $51 in corporate tax and retains or distributes $99 of after-tax income ($150 less $51). Thus, as shown in Table IV-A, the return on equity is 9.9 percent ($99 divided by $1,000).

The leveraged corporation is financed by $500 of debt and $500 of stock. If the interest rate is 10 percent, then interest expense is $50 (10 percent times $500). Taxable income is $100 after deducting interest expense. The leveraged corporation is liable for $34 in corporate tax (34 percent times $100) and distributes or retains $66 of after-tax income ($100 less $34). Consequently, the return on equity is 13.2 percent ($66 divided by $500). Thus, as shown in Table IV-A, increasing the debt ratio from zero to 50 percent increases the rate of return on equity from 9.9 to 13.2 percent.

This arithmetic demonstrates that a leveraged corporation can generate a higher return on equity (net of corporate income tax) than an unleveraged company or, equivalently, that an unleveraged company needs to earn a higher profit before corporate tax to provide investors the same return net of corporate tax as could be obtained with an unleveraged company. More generally, the return on equity rises with increasing debt capitalization so long as the interest rate is less than the pre-tax rate of return on corporate assets. This suggests that the Code creates an incentive to raise the debt-equity ratio to the point where the corporate income tax (or outstanding equity) is eliminated.

Table IV-A _____

Effect of Debt Financing on Returns to Equity Investment

Item	All-equity corporation	50-percent debt-financed corporation
Beginning Balance Sheet:		
Total assets	$1,000	$1,000
Debt	0	500
Shareholders' equity	1,000	500
Income Statement:		
Operating income	150	150
Interest expense	0	150
Taxable income	150	100
Income tax	51	34
Income after corporate tax	99	66
Return on Equity[1] (percent)	9.9	13.2

1. Return on equity is computed as income after corporate tax divided by beginning shareholders' equity.

Costs of Financial Distress

With higher levels of debt the possibility of financial distress increases, as do expected costs to the firm which occur with such distress. These additional costs include such items as the increase in the costs of debt funds; constraints on credit, expenditure or operating decisions; and the direct costs of being in bankruptcy. These expected costs of financial distress may, at sufficiently high debt-equity ratios, offset the corporate tax advantage to additional debt finance.

Effect of Shareholder Income Tax

The above analysis focuses solely on the effect of interest deductibility at the corporate level. Shareholder-level income taxation may offset to some degree the corporate tax incentive for corporate debt relative to equity.

Shareholder Treatment of Debt and Equity

The conclusion that debt is tax favored relative to equity remains unchanged if interest on corporate debt and returns on equity are taxed at the same effective rate to investors. In this case, the returns to investors on both debt and equity are reduced proportionately by the income tax; the advantage to debt presented by corporate tax deductibility remains. One noteworthy exception exists if the marginal investments on both debt and equity are effectively tax-exempt. Given the previously documented importance of tax-exempt pension funds in the bond and equity markets, this case may be of some importance.

Shareholder-Level Tax Treatment of Equity

In general, returns to shareholders and debtholders are not taxed the same. Although dividends, like interest income, are taxed currently, equity income in other forms may reduce the effective investor-level tax on equity below that on debt. First, the firm may retain earnings and not pay dividends currently. In general, the accumulation of earnings by the firm will cause the value of the firm's shares to rise. Rather than being taxed currently on corporate earnings, a shareholder will be able to defer the taxation on the value of the retained earnings reflected in the price of the stock until the shareholder sells the stock.*

Other aspects of capital gain taxation serve to reduce further the individual income tax on equity. Since tax on capital gain is normally triggered after a voluntary recognition event (e.g., the sale of stock), the taxpayer can time the realization of capital gain income when the effective rate of tax is low. The rate of tax could be low if the taxpayer is in a low or zero tax bracket because other income is abnormally low, if other capital losses shelter the capital gain, or if changes in the tax law cause the statutory rate on capital gains to be low. Perhaps most important, the step up in the adjusted tax basis of the stock upon the death of the shareholder may permit the shareholder's heirs to avoid tax completely on capital gains. For all these reasons, the effective rate of tax on undistributed earnings may be already quite low.

Corporations can distribute their earnings to owners of equity in forms that generally result in less tax to shareholders than do dividend distributions. Share repurchases have become an important method of distributing corporate earnings to equity holders. When employed by large publicly traded firms, repurchases of the corporation's own shares permit the shareholders to treat the distribution as a sale of stock (i.e., to obtain capital gain treatment, and recover the basis in the stock without tax). The remaining shareholders may benefit because they have rights to a larger fraction of the firm and may see a corresponding increase in the value of their shares. Thus, less individual tax will generally be imposed on a $100 repurchase of stock than on $100 of dividends. In addition, share repurchases allow shareholders to choose whether to receive corporate distributions by choosing whether to sell or retain shares, so as to minimize tax liability.

Acquisitions of the stock of one corporation for cash or property of another corporation provides a similar method for distributing corporate earnings out of corporate solution with less shareholder tax than through

---

* For individuals, a capital gain is generally taxed at a maximum 20 percent rate compared with a maximum 39.6 percent for dividends. — EDS.

a dividend. The target shareholders generally treat the acquisition as a sale and recover their basis free of tax. For purposes of analyzing the individual tax effect of corporate earnings disbursements, this transaction can be thought of as equivalent to a stock merger of the target with the acquiror followed by the repurchase of the target shareholders' shares by the resulting merged firm. The result is similar to the case of a share repurchase in that cash is distributed to shareholders with less than the full dividend tax, except that two firms are involved instead of one.

Since dividends typically are subject to more tax than other methods for providing returns to shareholders, the puzzle of why firms pay dividends remains. Because dividends are paid at the discretion of the firm, it appears that firms cause their shareholders to pay more tax on equity income than is strictly necessary. Until a better understanding of corporate distribution policy exists, the role of dividend taxation on equity financing decisions remain uncertain.

To summarize, although the current taxation of dividends to investors is clearly significant, there are numerous reasons why the overall individual tax on equity investments may be less than that on interest income from debt. Since the effective shareholder tax on returns from equity may be less than that on debt holdings, the shareholder tax may offset some or all of the advantage to debt at the corporate level. . . .

This excerpt points out that at the corporate level, the payment of interest generates a deduction while the payment of dividends does not. At the shareholder level, while both interest and dividends received are taxable to the recipients in the same manner, shareholders holding equity can lessen, or in some cases eliminate, shareholder-level tax. The mere appreciation of a shareholder's stock is not a taxable event. By allowing accumulation at the corporate level, shareholders can defer any shareholder-level taxation. When shareholders eventually sell or exchange their stock, any gain is taxed at a capital gains rate, entitled to any capital gains preference that might exist. Moreover, upon the death of a shareholder, any appreciated stock takes a fair market value basis, permitting disposition without any recognition of gain.

Notwithstanding the advantages of equity at the shareholder level, the deductibility of interest payments at the corporate level may create a corporate bias in favor of debt over equity. But whether a financial instrument is treated as debt or equity is an issue that haunts our federal income tax system. Much may ride on the distinction, and yet the distinction is often difficult to make. After all, debt and equity are each paper representations of an interest in corporate assets. Although a debt instrument signifies a contractual relationship for repayment while stock provides residual rights for shareholders once creditors have been paid, the price of each kind of instrument reflects the associated risks. Is there a justification for treating debt differently from equity for tax purposes?

Whatever the theoretical answer to the previous question, the practical answer is that the two types of financial instruments are treated very differently. The characterization often determines (1) the gain to a transferor and the basis to the corporate transferee during the formation of a corporation, see Bradshaw v. United States, page 64 supra; (2) the treatment of the borrower (or issuer) as periodic payments are made to the instrument holder; and (3) the treatment of the instrument holder on surrender of the obligation.

The most significant difference in the treatment of debt and equity involves the second category above. The return on borrowed money (debt) typically is deductible as interest. §163. The return on stock (equity) constitutes a nondeductible dividend payment. To an instrument holder, both interest and dividends are includible as ordinary income. For corporate instrument holders, §243 provides a deduction to the recipient of from 70 to 100 percent, depending on the degree of ownership. See discussion at pages 134-135 infra.

Because interest is deductible by the corporation while dividends are not, there is a tax incentive for a corporation to raise needed capital through the issuance of debt rather than stock. Moreover, certain personal tax advantages will accrue to the organizers or principal owners of the corporation if they become creditors as well as stockholders. If the corporation prospers, it may pay off its debt, and the creditor-stockholders will realize income only to the extent that the payment exceeds the adjusted basis of the debt instruments paid off. The income, if any, will be capital gain. §1271. If the organizers hold only stock, however, amounts distributed to them by the corporation as shareholders (including amounts paid for a pro rata reacquisition of stock) may be taxed as dividends. See the discussion of §302 in Chapter 5. For the use of debt in connection with corporate acquisitions, see page 369 infra.

In light of the advantages that debt can offer to corporate issuers, not surprisingly taxpayers often like to label financial instruments as debt. Notwithstanding the label, the Service will attempt to recharacterize an instrument if it resembles equity more than debt. The following case illustrates a typical situation.

Bauer v. Commissioner
748 F.2d 1365 (9th Cir. 1984)

Before Chambers, Hug, and Boochever, Circuit Judges.
    Hug, Circuit Judge.
    This case concerns a determination of whether cash payments by two stockholders to their wholly-owned corporation were loans or contribu-

tions to capital. The Commissioner of Internal Revenue contended that the payments by the stockholders were contributions to capital and not loans, as the stockholders and the corporation maintained. The documentation between the parties and the books of the corporation reflected the cash payments as loans and the periodic payments by the corporation as principal and interest payments to the stockholders. The corporation deducted the interest payments and the stockholders declared the interest payments as income and treated the principal payments as a return of capital. The Commissioner contended that because the stockholders' cash advances to the corporation were contributions to capital and not loans, the corporation could not deduct the claimed interest and the stockholders were required to treat the payments made to them as taxable dividends. The Commissioner assessed deficiencies accordingly. The stockholders and the corporation contested the assessments in the Tax Court and the cases were consolidated for trial. The Tax Court held for the Commissioner in each instance. On appeal, the sole issue is whether the Tax Court was clearly erroneous in holding that the stockholders' cash advances to the corporation were capital contributions rather than loans. We reverse.

FACTS

The parties entered into a stipulation of facts, which we summarize here.

Philip Bauer and his father-in-law, Phillip Himmelfarb, are officers and sole stockholders of the Federal Meat Company ("Federal"). They formed Federal in 1958 with paid-in capital of $20,000. The initial and only stock issuance was 2,000 shares, of which Bauer owns 25 percent and Himmelfarb 75 percent. Federal is a custom slaughterer in the business of selling dressed meat to chain store buyers, retailers, and wholesalers. It buys live animals and has them custom slaughtered for fixed fees. Federal does not own a packing house, and it leases its premises and delivery equipment.

Since Federal's incorporation, and continuing throughout the years at issue, Bauer and Himmelfarb advanced various amounts of money to Federal. By the end of the calendar year 1958, a total of $102,650 had been advanced by Bauer and Himmelfarb. Numerous advances and repayments then occurred so that as of December 31, 1972, the net balance advanced by Bauer and Himmelfarb totaled $810,068. . . .

The parties treated all of the transactions as loans and repayments. Each advance to Federal was evidenced by a negotiable promissory note that was unsecured and was payable on demand. The notes carried a seven percent interest rate during 1972-1974 and a ten percent interest rate in 1976. The notes were not convertible into stock, nor were they subordinated to any other obligation. For each advance made to Federal, an amount representing "accrued interest payable" was entered in the corporate ledger at the end of each month as an addition to liabilities in the form of "outstanding loans payable-officers." Each year's total of accrued interest was paid within two and one-half months of the close of Federal's fiscal year. On its financial statements, Federal included the outstanding balances as a current liability labeled "loan payable-officers."

On its corporate federal income tax returns for the years at issue, Federal claimed interest expense deductions in the amounts of $79,638, $103,506, and $103,007, for its fiscal years ending April 30 of 1974, 1975, and 1976, respectively, for the amounts paid as interest to Bauer and Himmelfarb. These amounts, in turn, were reported by Bauer and Himmelfarb as interest income in the calendar year in which they were received. The amounts received from Federal characterized as loan principal repayments were not reported as income. These amounts for Bauer were: $65,000 in 1973, $25,000 in 1974, and $35,000 in 1975; for Himmelfarb, the amount was $75,000 in 1975. Bauer and Himmelfarb each received a yearly salary of $70,000 or $80,000. Federal has never paid dividends; the earnings of the corporation from its inception in 1958 were retained and reinvested to meet the continued growth of the corporation. By the end of the fiscal years in issue, the retained earnings were: 1974, $634,107; 1975, $657,973; and 1976, $486,092. (In the 1976 fiscal year, Federal suffered a net loss.)

The Tax Court concluded that the advances by Bauer and Himmelfarb to Federal were capital contributions and disallowed the interest deductions claimed by Federal on the ground that no debtor-creditor relationship was established to support treatment of the payments as interest. In addition, the principal payments made by Federal to Bauer and Himmelfarb were held to be taxable dividends. . . .

ANALYSIS

The determination of whether an advance is debt or equity depends on the distinction between a creditor who seeks a definite obligation that is payable in any event, and a shareholder who seeks to make an investment and to share in the profits and risks of loss in the venture. . . . The outward form of the transaction is not controlling; rather, characterization depends on the taxpayer's actual intent, as evidenced by the circumstances and conditions of the advance. . . .

In 1969, Congress authorized the Secretary of the Treasury to prescribe regulations setting forth the factors to be considered in determining whether an advance is debt or equity. 26 U.S.C. §385. The Secretary did not issue such regulations until 1982. . . .* Here we must still be guided

---

* The regulations under §385 were withdrawn in 1984. See page 110 infra. In addition, they were not applicable to the years in controversy. — EDS.

by the case law and by the five factors that Congress suggested, as part of the 1969 statute, might be included in the regulations. This court has identified eleven factors:

> (1) the names given to the certificates evidencing the indebtedness; (2) the presence or absence of a maturity date; (3) the source of the payments; (4) the right to enforce the payment of principal and interest; (5) participation in management; (6) a status equal to or inferior to that of regular corporate creditors; (7) the intent of the parties; (8) "thin" or adequate capitalization; (9) identity of interest between creditor and stockholder; (10) payment of interest only out of "dividend" money; and (11) the ability of the corporation to obtain loans from outside lending institutions.

A. R. Lantz Co., 424 F.2d at 1333. No one factor is controlling or decisive, and the court must look to the particular circumstances of each case. Id. "The object of the inquiry is not to count factors, but to evaluate them." Tyler v. Tomlinson, 414 F.2d 844, 848 (5th Cir. 1969). The burden of establishing that the advances were loans rather than capital contributions rests with the taxpayer. O. H. Kruse Grain & Milling v. Commissioner, 279 F.2d 123, 125 (9th Cir. 1960).

A.   RATIO OF DEBT TO EQUITY

In the present case, the Tax Court gave great weight to the eighth factor: whether Federal was adequately capitalized. The court found that Federal's debt-to-equity ratio was as high as 92 to 1 during the years in question and that Federal was seriously undercapitalized. The Tax Court found this to be a strong indication that the advances were capital contributions rather than loans. The Tax Court apparently based its finding of a debt-to-equity ratio of 92 to 1 on a paragraph of the Stipulation of Facts signed by the parties. That paragraph states:

> The ratio of stockholder debt to corporate stock was approximately 92 to 1 for the fiscal year ending April 30, 1976.

This is accurate insofar as it compares the ending debt owed to the stockholders in 1976 of $1,850,067 to their initial stock purchase in 1958 of $20,000. This is not a true or meaningful debt-to-equity ratio. First, it completely ignores the earnings that had been retained in the corporation as it grew over the 18-year period. The stockholders' equity in a corporation is composed not only of the paid-in-capital, but also of the profits that have been generated and retained in the corporation as "retained earnings." Thus, if the debt-to-equity ratio were considered to be a comparison of stockholder loans to the correct calculation of stockholder equity including retained earnings in the corporation, this "debt-to-equity" ratio would be only 1.5 to 1 in 1974-1975 and 3.6 to 1 in 1976, as hereinafter shown.

The more meaningful debt-to-equity ratio compares the total liabilities to the stockholders' equity. The stockholders' equity would include both the initial paid-in capital and the retained earnings. Basically, the stockholders' equity is the difference between the assets and liabilities of the corporation.

Congress recognized this as the appropriate method of calculating the debt-to-equity ratio in enacting section 385.

The debt-equity ratio of the issuing corporation for purposes of this test generally is determined by comparing the corporation's total indebtedness with the excess of its money and other assets over that indebtedness. S. Rep. No. 552, 91st Cong., 1st Sess., *reprinted in* 1969 U.S. Code Cong. & Ad. News 1645, 2027, 2172. The calculation of Federal's debt-to-equity ratio for the years in question would therefore be as follows. In our view, the total debt-to-equity ratio is the appropriate ratio to review in determining whether a corporation is too thinly capitalized; however, we also show the stockholder debt-to-equity ratio for illustrative purposes. . . .

Total Debt-to-Equity Ratio
1974: $1,410,603 divided by $654,107 = 2.15 to 1
1975: $1,952,944 divided by $677,973 = 2.88 to 1
1976: $3,880,642 divided by $506,092 = 7.66 to 1

Stockholder Debt-to-Equity Ratio
1974: $1,025,067 divided by $654,107 = 1.56 to 1
1975: $1,030,067 divided by $657,973 = 1.56 to 1
1976: $1,850,067 divided by $506,092 = 3.65 to 1

Thus, during the years in question, the total debt-to-equity ratio, as reflected on the books of the corporation, was not 92 to 1, but ranged from a little over 2 to 1 to less than 8 to 1. The stockholder debt-to-equity ratio during those years was a minimum of 1.5 to 1 and a maximum of 3.6 to 1.

The purpose of examining the debt-to-equity ratio in characterizing a stockholder advance is to determine whether a corporation is so thinly capitalized that a business loss would result in an inability to repay the advance; such an advance would be indicative of venture capital rather than a loan. Gilbert v. Commissioner, 248 F.2d 399, 407 (2d Cir. 1957). Essentially, we are concerned with the degree of risk the loan presents to the lender and whether an independent lender, such as a bank, would be willing to make the loan. In addition to the numerical debt-to-equity ratio, other factors in the financial picture would also be important to an independent lender in analyzing the risk. Federal's history was that of a successful company whose increasing cash needs arose from growth, not a lack of profits or business reverses. Federal had virtually no fixed assets; its plant and equipment were leased. The assets were principally current assets which could be quickly turned into cash. At all times during the years in question, Federal's current assets exceeded all liabilities by at least $300,000, which presents a strong financial picture.

Federal's financial structure and these other factors indicate that Federal could readily have obtained a loan from a bank or other financial institution for the purpose for which the stockholders' loans were made, which was to finance inventory and accounts receivable. There is specific evidence in this case that one bank would have been willing to make these loans. In a letter from a vice president of Bank of America that was attached to the Stipulated Facts, the officer noted that it had dealt with Federal and was familiar with Federal's financing during the years in question and the bank was "ready to make bank loans for those amounts of officers' loans and/or more if Federal Meat Co. desired to use bank financing." The bank officer also noted that "in the event Federal wanted to liquidate during this period, Federal would have paid off its creditors, the bank, the officers' loans from conversion of its meat inventory, and accounts receivable within a three to four week cycle most likely without any need of selling the small amount of fixed assets."

Neither the numerical debt-to-equity ratio nor other factors in the analysis of the corporation's financial structure justify a conclusion that the advances should be characterized as venture capital rather than loans.

B. PROPORTIONAL HOLDINGS OF DEBT AND EQUITY

The Tax Court also gave weight to the alleged fact that Bauer and Himmelfarb had loaned Federal amounts that were roughly proportional to their respective capital investments. The court found that during the years in question Himmelfarb had advanced a total of $970,000 to Federal while Bauer had advanced $270,000, a ratio of about 3 1/2 to 1 as compared to the 3 to 1 ratio of their stockholdings. We agree that where a stockholder owns "debt" in the same proportion to which he holds stock in a certain corporation, the characterization as "debt" may be suspect. See *Gilbert*, 248 F.2d at 407. However, the Tax Court clearly miscalculated the amounts of Bauer's and Himmelfarb's advances to Federal.

The Tax Court looked only at the gross amount of Bauer and Himmelfarb's advances during the years in question. It failed to consider either the amount of the loans outstanding at the beginning of the three-year period or the effect of the repayments that Federal made during this period. At the beginning of the three-year period, Federal already owed $805,068 to Himmelfarb, but only $5,000 to Bauer. At the end of the period, the figures had grown to $1,700,068 and $150,000, a ratio of about 11 to 1. Even if the three-year period is considered in isolation — an approach that makes little sense given that the stockholders had been making loans to Federal since 1958 — the net amounts advanced by Himmelfarb and Bauer during that period were $895,000 and $145,000, respectively, a ratio of about 6 to 1. These figures simply will not support a finding that Bauer and Himmelfarb made advances to Federal in proportion to their capital investments.

C. OTHER FACTORS

The Tax Court also found it significant that all of Federal's shareholder debt was evidenced by demand notes with no fixed date of maturity. Although some repayments were made during the years in question, repayments never kept up with advances. We agree that lack of a fixed date of maturity on the debt instruments, together with continual growth of the debt, may suggest that there is no intention to make full repayment. But that one factor is not enough to carry the entire weight of this case. Many other factors favor the petitioners, as the Tax Court conceded: the existence of notes; fixed and reasonable interest rates; actual timely payment of interest; corresponding treatment of the interest as income by Bauer and Himmelfarb; the cash-flow demands of the custom slaughter business; and the lack of subordination of shareholder debt to other corporate debt. Additionally, this court concludes that Federal's ratio of debt to equity was within reasonable bounds and that Bauer and Himmelfarb did not own debt in proportion to their stockholdings.

CONCLUSION

The Tax Court erred in the basis of its calculation of Federal's debt-to-equity ratio. In reviewing the actual debt-to-equity ratio and the current assets in relation to the liabilities, and considering the general strength of the corporate financial picture, there is no reason to justify a conclusion that the loans were in fact "venture capital." Also, the record does not support the Tax Court's finding that Bauer and Himmelfarb made advances to Federal in rough proportion to their stockholdings. The documentation and the accounting procedures followed support the taxpayers' contention that the advances were loans. For these reasons and the other reasons above specified, we hold that the Tax Court's recharacterization of Federal's debt as equity is clearly erroneous, and the decision of the Tax Court is therefore reversed.

NOTES

1. *Statutory and regulatory classification of "equity" and "debt."* The House version of the 1954 Code contained definitions designed to indicate

precisely what instruments would qualify for the interest deduction and for other tax privileges. But the Senate dropped these definitions, stating "Your committee believes that any attempt to write into the statute precise definitions which will classify for tax purposes the many types of corporate stocks and securities will be frustrated by the numerous characteristics of an interchangeable nature which can be given to these instruments." S. Rep. No. 1622, 83d Cong., 2d Sess. 42 (1954).

Despite this pessimistic conclusion, the Tax Reform Act of 1969 added §385 to the Code authorizing the Treasury to issue regulations to determine whether an interest in a corporation is to be treated "for purposes of this title as stock or indebtedness." The Treasury may take into account, along with other factors, the existence of a written unconditional promise to pay a sum certain and a fixed rate of interest, the subordination or preference over any indebtedness, the debt-equity ratio, the convertibility into stock, and the relationship between holdings of stock and of the interest in question. The Treasury has made three attempts to promulgate suitable regulations. Each attempt has been heavily criticized and ultimately withdrawn.

In some cases, the IRS has been "whipsawed" by inconsistent treatment of financial instruments by the issuer and the holders. For example, the issuer might prefer to treat a financial instrument as debt in order to deduct the interest. A corporate holder of the instrument, however, may prefer to treat periodic distributions as dividends that may not increase taxable income because of the dividends-received deduction in §243. See page 134 infra. Under §385(c)(1), the characterization by the issuer of an instrument as debt or equity is binding on the holders of the instrument. Section 385(c)(2), however, does permit a holder of an instrument to adopt an inconsistent treatment so long as such treatment is dislocated on the holder's tax return.

For some general guidance on factors that may be used to distinguish debt from equity, see Notice 94-47, 1994-1 C.B. 357.

2. *Judicial classification of "equity" and "debt."* In *Bauer* the court was concerned with the ratio of debt to equity. For those corporations whose outstanding debt far exceeds equity, debtholders would likely regard themselves as stockholders or potential stockholders because of the risk associated with repayment. Their chances of repayment would rise and fall with the success or failure of the corporation. See, e.g., Dobkin v. Commissioner, 15 T.C. 31 (1950), aff'd per curiam, 192 F.2d 392 (2d Cir. 1951); Burr Oaks Corp. v. Commissioner, 365 F.2d 24 (7th Cir. 1966). For well-capitalized corporations, the risk of default on outstanding debt instruments is lower.

There is no mathematical threshold for determining permissible debt-equity ratios. In Briggs Co. v. Commissioner, 1946 T.C.M. ¶46,109, a ratio of 4 to 1 was found excessive in light of surrounding financial considerations, while in Baker Commodities v. Commissioner, 48 T.C. 374 (1967), a ratio of 700 to 1 was upheld as justified since cash flow and earnings power were sufficient to support repayment. A ratio of inside debt to equity that does not exceed 3 to 1 is likely to withstand attack. See B. Bittker and J. Eustice, Federal Income Taxation of Corporations and Shareholders ¶4.04 (7th ed. 1998). The withdrawn §385 Regulations did not consider debt to be excessive if the inside debt-equity ratio did not exceed 3 to 1 and the outside ratio (i.e., debt held by all creditors) did not exceed 10 to 1.

In *Bauer* the outcome hinged on how to measure the value of stock for purposes of determining the debt-equity ratio. Who has the stronger point, the Ninth Circuit, which used the fair market value of the outstanding stock (actually book value plus retained earnings), or the Tax Court, which used the book value of the stock?

Thin capitalization is only one sign pointing toward recharacterizing debt as equity. For closely held corporations, when debt is owned in the same proportions as equity, the courts tend to scrutinize the situation closely. In *Bauer* the ratio of stock held by the two shareholders was 3 to 1, while the ratio of new loans to the corporation incurred by the shareholders during the years in question was 3 1/2 to 1. Why did the Ninth Circuit find that the holdings were not roughly proportionate?

Under the withdrawn §385 regulations, proportionality was deemed a key factor. Straight debt with no equity features held disproportionately would be respected as debt; proportionately held debt was subject to much stricter scrutiny. Disproportionality was helpful to the taxpayer in Green Bay Steel v. Commissioner, 53 T.C. 451 (1969). Proportionality alone would not necessarily cause recharacterization. See, e.g., Litton Business Systems v. Commissioner, 61 T.C. 367 (1973), in which a parent corporation's advances to subsidiaries were held valid debt despite an absence of formalities. Interest was charged, the parent expected repayment, outside funding was available, and the subsidiary was not thinly capitalized. Cf. United States v. Uneco, Inc., 532 F.2d 1204 (8th Cir. 1976).

Other factors considered by some courts when characterizing financial instruments include whether repayment in fact took place, whether formalities were observed when the "loan" was made, and whether the proceeds were used for "essential" assets. See Laidlaw Transportation, Inc. v. Commissioner, 98 T.C.M. 232 (1998) (equity found where related creditor corporation did not intend to request repayment on maturity dates, continually postponed maturity dates, and borrowed funds were used to purchase essential assets). In *Bauer* the Tax Court found that the loans were made during the formative stages of the corporation for essential operating assets and were therefore equity contributions. Should the timing of the loans be a factor?

3. *Hybrid securities: bifurcation*. When a corporation is unable to issue ordinary evidences of indebtedness, usually because of a fear of damaging its credit position, there have been attempts to get the same tax effect by

issuing "hybrid" securities. These instruments often look like preferred stock to creditors, but it is hoped that they will be treated as bonds, debentures, or notes by the IRS. Among the characteristics of such "hybrid" securities are the following: (a) They are often held only by shareholders and in the same proportions as the stock; (b) they may be transferable only with stock; (c) they have long maturities or no maturity dates; (d) the "interest" is geared to corporate income or is discretionary with the directors; (e) payment of the "interest" or "principal" (or both) is subordinated to the claims of general creditors; and (f) they are sometimes issued only to present stockholders and not for new consideration. If too many of these features are found, the instruments will be treated as preferred stock rather than as evidences of indebtedness.

The leading case on the subject is John Kelley Co. v. Commissioner, 326 U.S. 521 (1946). In that case, the nominal debt instruments provided for 8 percent interest, which was noncumulative, and payment was contingent on sufficient corporate earnings. The instruments matured in 20 years and were subordinate to all creditors. In determining that the hybrid instruments constituted debt, the Supreme Court reasoned that the corporation had a lot of outstanding stock and was not thinly capitalized.

In Farley Realty Corp. v. Commissioner, 279 F.2d 701 (2d Cir. 1960), a nonshareholder lent money to a corporation for the acquisition of a building. The obligation provided for a fixed payment of interest and a fixed maturity date. Furthermore, the lender was entitled to 50 percent of any appreciation on the sale of the building even if the sale took place after the maturity date. The court permitted a deduction for the fixed interest but not for the lender's share of the realized appreciation. But see Rev. Rul. 83-51, 1983-1 C.B. 48 (allowing a deduction for shared appreciation paid by a borrower to a lender on a home residence loan (i.e., a noncommercial context) with payment due upon sale of the residence or at the end of the 10-year loan term).

In Helvering v. Richmond, F & P.R.R., 90 F.2d 971 (4th Cir. 1937), the court permitted an interest deduction for guaranteed 7 percent dividend payments on preferred stock when the guaranteed dividends were a first lien on corporate assets ahead of all creditors. Payments in excess of the guaranteed amount were treated as nondeductible dividends.

Notwithstanding these cases, in general courts have resisted bifurcation. See generally Hariton, "Distinguishing Between Equity and Debt in the New Financial Environment," 49 Tax L. Rev. 499 (1994). Several Code provisions, however, permit or mandate bifurcation. Section 385(a) authorizes regulations permitting the bifurcation of a corporate obligation as part equity and part debt. The legislative history of this provision explains: "[S]uch treatment may be appropriate in circumstances where a debt instrument provides for payments that are dependent to a significant extent (whether in whole or in part) on corporate performance, whether through equity kickers, contingent interest, significant deferral of payment, subordination, or an interest rate sufficiently high to suggest a significant risk of default." H.R. Rep. No. 247, 101st Cong., 1st Sess. 1235-1236 (1989).

Congress has also clamped down on the availability of a corporate interest deduction in connection with certain corporate takeovers by bifurcating certain high-yield discount obligations. See page 379 infra.

Another form of bifurcation is found in §163(j), the "earnings stripping" provision. If an interest expense is deductible but the recipient is not taxable upon receipt, there is a loss to the U.S. tax system as a whole and an incentive to borrow from tax-exempt lenders such as related foreign corporations and certain U.S. pension funds. Congress has addressed the practice of stripping away earnings of a taxable U.S. corporation through an interest payment to a tax-exempt related party by denying an interest deduction under specified circumstances.

Section 163(j) essentially disallows an interest deduction on "excess interest expense" of a payor corporation with a ratio of debt to equity in excess of 1.5 to 1 at the end of the tax year. "Excess interest expense" is defined as the amount by which the corporation's net interest expense exceeds 50 percent of its adjusted taxable income. Any interest deduction disallowed under §163(j) may be carried over to a subsequent year, when it may be deductible if there is no excess interest expense.

On the regulatory front, the Treasury has issued a proposed regulation that bifurcates payments made on certain original issue discount debt instruments that provide for both noncontingent and contingent payments. Prop. Treas. Regs. §1.1275-4(g). In general, the noncontingent payments are deductible but the contingent payments are not.

Can a financial instrument ever be bifurcated over time? That is, can an instrument that is considered equity when it is issued (e.g., because a corporation is thinly capitalized) be considered a debt instrument at a later time (e.g., when the corporation's debt-equity ratio improves)? For the possibility that an instrument may be a chameleon, see Edwards v. Commissioner, 50 T.C. 220 (1968) (notes that constituted bona fide debt in hands of original owners must be treated as equity in hands of purchasers, who had simultaneously purchased the stock of the obligor corporation when it was in a deficit position), rev'd, 415 F.2d 578 (10th Cir. 1969) (purchasers "took the capital financial structure as they found it," including valid debt); Cuyuna Realty Co. v. United States, 382 F.2d 298 (Cl. Ct. 1967) (debtor-creditor relationship changed with passage of time to equity-investor relationship).

4. *Hybrid securities: convertibility.* A debt instrument that is convertible into corporate stock contains both debt and equity features. A holder of the instrument may enjoy a fixed rate of return with relatively little risk, but the holder also has the right to share in future corporate growth by exercising the conversion privilege. As a general rule, a conversion feature by itself does not automatically result in the treatment of a financial instrument as equity. In Rev. Rul. 85-119, 1985-2 C.B. 60, a publicly traded debt

instrument contained a conversion feature that was mandated by banking regulations. At maturity, the note was convertible into stock of the issuing corporation equal to the face value of the note. A holder could also elect to receive cash instead of stock. In determining that the note was a debt instrument (and that interest payments were deductible), the ruling highlighted the following factors: The note was publicly traded and not held in proportion to stock ownership; the issuing corporation was not thinly capitalized; the instrument had a fixed maturity date; interest payments were not contingent on earnings; and instrument holders did not participate in corporate governance. The convertibility feature was not controlling because the amount of stock to be received was equal to the face value of the note.

In contrast, Rev. Rul. 83-98, 1983-2 C.B. 40, ruled that a nominal debt instrument was really an equity instrument, in part because the instrument contained a conversion feature. Under the conversion feature, a holder could convert the note to 50 shares of the issuer's stock (worth $1,000 at the time the instrument was issued) or receive $600 when the instrument matured. The issuer also had the right to call the instrument for $600 at any time. These conversion characteristics made it highly likely that holders would convert to stock. Section 163(l) disallows a deduction for interest on a "disqualified debt instrument," which is a corporate debt instrument payable (i.e., a substantial amount of either interest or principal) in equity of the issuer or a related party.

5. *Preferred stock versus debt.* If common stock and straight debt are the endpoints on the debt-equity spectrum, preferred stock is right in the middle. Typically, preferred stockholders receive fixed payments (like debtholders) and do not share in the growth of the issuing corporations (like debtholders). But preferred shareholders do not receive dividends until creditors have been paid (like common shareholders) and stand in line behind creditors in the event of liquidation (like common shareholders).

In Rev. Rul. 90-27, 1990-1 C.B. 50, the issue was whether a financial instrument was preferred stock or really a debt instrument (although labeled preferred stock). Typically, an issuer wants the instrument to be characterized as debt because of the interest deduction. But in contrast to *Bauer,* here the taxpayer (i.e., the shareholder, Corporation *Y*) wanted the financial instrument to be treated as preferred stock and the distributions to be treated as dividends. A corporation that receives dividends must include them in income but then can deduct a percentage of the dividends received. See §243, discussed at page 134 infra. In contrast, interest received on debt instruments is fully includible.

The ruling points out that the financial instruments are very much like short-term debt to the holders. The principal amount of the obligation is always $100,000, and the rate of return is adjusted every 49 days in accordance with the market to keep the fair market value of the instrument at $100,000. Nevertheless, the ruling points out that the equity features of the instruments outweigh the debt features. The holders are not entitled to receive a sum certain either on demand or on a specified date, and distributions can be made only in accordance with state law dividend requirements.

6. *Retirement, redemption, and worthlessness*. The decision whether to issue debt or equity affects not only the characterization of the payments made on the obligation — whether such payments constitute interest or dividends — but also the treatment of the obligation itself on retirement or redemption. Generally, any gain (or loss) on the retirement of a debt instrument because of postpurchase fluctuation in the market interest rate will produce capital gain or loss. See §1271, but see §1276, which treats gain from prepurchase fluctuation in the market interest rate as ordinary income. Gain (or loss) on the redemption of stock by a corporation may result in ordinary or capital gain (or loss), depending on the successful navigation of the safe harbors of §302, which offer exchange treatment. See Chapter 5.

If retirement or redemption is unavailable because a corporation fails, then worthless stock, bonds, and other evidence of debt that are "securities" under §165(g)(2) ordinarily give rise to long- or short-term capital loss under §165(g)(1). Debt instruments that are not "securities" under §165(g)(2) are nonbusiness bad debts and produce short-term capital losses under §166(d). See, e.g., Litwin v. United States, 983 F.2d 997 (10th Cir. 1993) (bad debt deduction allowed for advances by taxpayer with respect to his closely held business when taxpayer convinced the court that the corporation was formed to allow him to earn a salary).

In light of the attendant restrictions on capital losses imposed by §§1211 and 1212, Congress enacted §1244 in 1958, under which an individual's loss on "§1244 stock" can be deducted from ordinary income with certain limitations. The principal features of §1244 include the following: (1) Section 1244 stock must be issued by a corporation whose capital does not exceed $1 million; (2) only common stock qualifies; (3) the corporation must have been active for a period of time prior to the stock's worthlessness; (4) the stock must be issued to an individual for money or other property; (5) the aggregate amount that can be treated as an ordinary loss for any taxable year may not exceed $50,000 ($100,000 per joint return). See also §165(g)(3), which affords corporations ordinary losses for worthless securities in certain subsidiaries. This ordinary loss treatment strangely does not apply if the corporation sells the securities.

PROBLEMS

3-3. *X* Corp., with only one class of stock outstanding, issues adjustable rate convertible notes with the following characteristics. The instruments are offered in exchange for either $1,000 or 50 shares of X Corp. stock (trading at $20 per share). The investor will receive annual payments equal to the dividends payable on 50 shares of X Corp. stock plus 2 percent of the $1,000 issue price ($20). The annual payment was guaranteed to be at least $60 and no more than $175 in all years. Stated differently, the investor was guaranteed a return of between 6 percent and 17.5 percent of face value. The notes were convertible at any time by the investor into 50 shares of X Corp. stock. If the investor chooses not to convert, the instrument will be redeemed for $600 at the end of 20 years. X Corp. retains an option to call the note for $600 at any time more than two years after issuance, although the investor can elect to convert if X Corp. exercises its option. X Corp. consults you about the tax treatment of the annual payments made on the instruments. See Rev. Rul. 83-98, 1983-2 C.B. 40.

3-4.   X Corp., a U.S. corporation, borrows $10 million from Y Corp., its Dutch parent. Pursuant to an income tax treaty between the Netherlands and the United States, Y Corp. is not subject to U.S. taxation on its interest income. The loan has a 10-year term and bears a 10 percent rate, the market rate when the loan was made. Discuss the tax treatment of the interest payments made from X Corp. to Y Corp.

4

Distributions of Cash and Property

In Chapter 2 we looked at the formation of a corporation. Once in existence, a corporation reports income and takes deductions in much the same way as individuals. See pages 90-92 supra. At some point, however, the shareholders may want the corporation to distribute some or all of what it has earned or even part of their capital contributions.

Section 61(a)(7) includes "dividends" in a taxpayer's gross income. But what are dividends? Certainly not every distribution by a corporation is a taxable dividend. Suppose T forms X Corp. with $100. At the end of its first year, X Corp. has lost $10 and holds $90 in assets. T, in need of cash, causes X Corp. to distribute $20. Is the distribution a dividend, subjecting T to tax? If not, what is it?

The labyrinth of statutory provisions governing this subject begins with §301(a), referring to distributions of "property," as defined by §317(a). This provision excludes the corporation's own stock from the term "property." Such distributions are governed by §305, discussed in Chapter 6. In Rev. Rul. 90-11, 1990-1 C.B. 10, the Service ruled that the adoption by a corporation of a "poison pill" plan, which provides for the issuance of a separately tradable right to purchase a fractional share of preferred stock for every share of common stock in the event of an unfriendly takeover attempt, is not a distribution of "property" to shareholders even though the adoption of the plan was a dividend under state law.

Returning from §317(a) to §301(a), note that there must be a distribution of property by a corporation to a shareholder *with respect to its stock* in order for §301 to apply. Transfers such as salaries or debt repayment, even if the recipient is a shareholder, are not covered by §301(a) because they are not made "with respect to [the paying corporation's] stock." The amount of a distribution made with respect to a shareholder's stock is computed under §301(b). While the amount of a cash distribution is self-evident, distributions of property create some complexity. Is the amount distributed equal to the fair market value of the property, its basis to the corporation, or some other measure? How do liabilities encumbering the property affect the amount distributed? These issues are addressed at page 139 infra.

Once the "amount" of a distribution is determined, its tax treatment is governed by §301(c), which consists of three tiers: §301(c)(1), (c)(2), and (c)(3). Section 301(c)(1) states that dividends are to be included in gross income, a rule already announced in §61(a)(7). For the definition of "dividend," §301(c)(1) refers us to §316. Section 316(a) informs us that distributions out of certain "earnings and profits" will be treated as dividends. Section 316(a)(1) specifies "accumulated" earnings and profits and §316(a)(2) addresses "current" earnings and profits, but nowhere does the Code provide a definition of earnings and profits. Section 312 instructs us to increase or decrease earnings and profits to take account of various transactions but fails to tell us just what we are adjusting. See discussion at page 142 infra.

Returning to §301(c), distributions that are not dividends are applied to reduce the adjusted basis of the taxpayer's stock. §301(c)(2). If the stock basis is reduced to zero, further distributions will be given sale or exchange treatment, resulting in capital gains if the stock is a capital asset. §301(c)(3)(A).

Section 301 and the related sections summarized above govern the tax treatment of the distributee shareholder. Distributions may also cause tax consequences to the distributing corporation. Is the distributing corporation taxable on a distribution of cash? On a distribution of appreciated property? Can it deduct a loss if the distributed property is worth less than its basis? Section 311 controls the tax consequences to the distributing corporation. Historically, a distributing corporation was generally not taxed on a distribution of appreciated property. §311(a). The Tax Reform Act of 1986, however, radically altered this area by providing that a distributing corporation will recognize gain on the distribution of appreciated property. Moreover, distributions require adjustments to the corporation's earnings and profits account that will affect the tax consequences to the shareholders of *future* distributions. §312.

This quick trip through the distributions maze becomes slightly more bewildering when one realizes that we have encountered only some types of distributions, albeit the ones that are most frequently encountered. See §301(f). Stock distributions are governed by §305. Distributions in redemption or partial liquidation are governed by §302. Liquidations are governed by §§331-338. Distributions in connection with reorganizations are discussed in §§354-368. In Chapter 2 we already considered distributions in connection with the formation of a corporation. §351(b).

This chapter is divided into four parts, each focusing on a different type of distribution: (1) cash distributions, (2) property distributions other than cash, (3) disguised or constructive dividends, and (4) intercorporate dividends. All these subjects require an understanding of the concept of "earnings and profits," which is examined at the outset, in the context of a cash distribution.

A.   CASH DISTRIBUTIONS

The Revenue Ruling that follows illustrates how the earnings and profits, once calculated, determine the amount of a dividend. The *Divine* case shows the importance and the uncertainty involved in the calculation of earnings and profits.

Rev. Rul. 74-164
1974-1 C.B. 74

Advice has been requested concerning the taxable status of corporate distributions under the circumstances described below.

X corporation and Y corporation each using the calendar year for Federal income tax purposes made distributions of $15,000 to their respective shareholders on July 1, 1971, and made no other distributions to their shareholders during the taxable year. The distributions were taxable as provided by section 301(c) of the Internal Revenue Code of 1954.

SITUATION 1

At the beginning of its taxable year 1971, X corporation had earnings and profits accumulated after February 28, 1913, of $40,000. It had an operating loss for the period January 1, 1971 through June 30, 1971, of $50,000 but had earnings and profits for the entire year 1971 of $5,000.

SITUATION 2

At the beginning of its taxable year 1971, Y corporation had a deficit in earnings and profits accumulated after February 28, 1913, of $60,000. Its net profits for the period January 1, 1971 through June 30, 1971, were $75,000 but its earnings and profits for the entire taxable year 1971 were only $5,000.

SITUATION 3

Assume the same facts as in Situation 1 except that X had a deficit in earnings and profits of $5,000 for the entire taxable year 1971.

SITUATION 4

Assume the same facts as in Situation 1 except that X had a deficit in earnings and profits of $55,000 for the entire taxable year 1971.

Sections 301(a) and 301(c) of the Code provide, in part, that: (1) the portion of a distribution of property made by a corporation to a shareholder with respect to its stock which is a dividend (as defined in section 316), shall be included in the shareholder's gross income; (2) the portion of the distribution which is not a dividend shall be applied against and reduce the adjusted basis of the stock; and (3) the portion which is not a dividend to the extent that it exceeds the adjusted basis of the stock and is not out of increase in value accrued before March 1, 1913, shall be treated as gain from the sale or exchange of property.

Section 316(a) of the Code provides that the term "dividend" means any distribution of property made by a corporation to its shareholders out of its earnings and profits accumulated after February 28, 1913, or out of its earnings and profits of the taxable year computed as of the close of the taxable year without diminution by reason of any distribution made during the year, and without regard to the amount of earnings and profits at the time the distribution was made.

Section 1.316-2(a) of the Income Tax Regulations provides, in part, that in determining the source of a distribution, consideration should be given first, to the earnings and profits of the taxable year; and second, to the earnings and profits accumulated since February 28, 1913, only in the case where, and to the extent that, the distributions made during the taxable year are not regarded as out of the earnings and profits of that year.

Applying the foregoing principles, in Situation 1, the earnings and profits of X corporation for the taxable year 1971 of $5,000 and the earnings and profits accumulated since February 28, 1913, and prior to the taxable year 1971, of $40,000 were applicable to the distribution paid by it on July 1, 1971. Thus, $5,000 of the distribution of $15,000 was paid from the earnings and profits of the taxable year 1971 and the balance of $10,000 was paid from the earnings and profits accumulated since February 28, 1913. Therefore, the entire distribution of $15,000 was a dividend within the meaning of section 316 of the Code.

In Situation 2 the earnings and profits of Y corporation for the taxable year 1971 of $5,000 were applicable to the distribution paid by Y corporation on July 1, 1971. Y corporation had no earnings and profits accumulated after February 28, 1913, available at the time of the distribution. Thus, only $5,000 of the distribution by Y corporation of $15,000 was a dividend within the meaning of section 316 of the Code. The balance of such distribution, $10,000 which was not a dividend, applied against and reduced the adjusted basis of the stock in the hands of the shareholders, and to the extent that it exceeded the adjusted basis of the stock was gain from the sale or exchange of property.

In the case of a deficit in earnings and profits for the taxable year in which distributions are made, the taxable status of distributions is dependent upon the amount of earnings and profits accumulated since February 28, 1913, and available at the dates of distribution. In determining the amount of such earnings and profits, section 1.316-2(b) of the regulations provides, in effect, that the deficit in earnings and profits of the taxable year will be prorated to the dates of distribution.

Applying the foregoing to Situations 3 and 4 the distribution paid by X corporation on July 1, 1971, in each situation was a dividend within the meaning of section 316 of the Code to the extent indicated as follows:

Situation #3

Accumulated Earnings and Profits (E&P) [Jan. 1]	$ 40,000
E&P deficit for entire taxable year ($5,000) Prorate to date of distribution [July 1] (½ of $5,000)	(2,500)
E&P available [July 1]	$ 37,500
Distribution [July 1] ($15,000)	(15,000) taxable as a dividend
E&P deficit from [July 1-Dec. 31]	(2,500)
[Accumulated E&P at end of year]	$ 20,000

Situation #4

Accumulated E&P [Jan. 1]	$ 40,000
E&P deficit for entire taxable year ($55,000) Prorate to date of distribution [July 1] (½ of $55,000)	(27,500)
E&P available [July 1]	$ 12,500
Distribution [July 1] ($15,000)	(12,500) taxable as a dividend
E&P deficit from [July 1-Dec. 31]	(27,500)
Accumulated E&P balance [Dec. 31]	$(27,500)

Divine v. Commissioner
500 F.2d 1041 (2d Cir. 1974)

WATERMAN, Circuit Judge.

I . . .

The outcome of this case depends on our resolution of two legal issues. [The first issue, involving collateral estoppel, is omitted.] Second, when, pursuant to the terms of statutory restricted stock options granted by a corporation to its employees, those employees, in exercising the options, purchased the stock for less than the stock's fair market value, should the corporation's "earnings and profits" under 316 of the Internal Revenue Code ("IRC" or "Code") be reduced by the difference between the fair market value of the stock so purchased and the prices paid by the employees? . . .

Rapid American Corporation (hereinafter "Rapid" or the "Corporation") is a publicly owned corporation. Its common stock during the years 1961 and 1962 was listed on the American Stock Exchange. As of January 31, 1963, Rapid had over 2,000 shareholders who held in the aggregate more than 2,000,000 shares of Rapid's common stock. Appellant Divine was one of those shareholders; his approximate holdings amounted to 37,000 shares in 1961 and rose to 40,000 in 1962.

During the years 1961 and 1962, Rapid made certain cash distributions, totaling some $840,840.53 in 1961, and $1,024,836.93 in 1962, to its shareholders. Appellant's portions of these disbursements were $18,501.40 in 1961 and $20,572.04 in 1962. Rapid advised the shareholders that the distributions did not have to be included by them in their individual personal income tax returns. This advice was predicated on the belief that Rapid's "earnings and profits" were insufficient to render these distributions dividends taxable as ordinary income to the recipients, but, rather, the recipients should consider the payments to be returns of capital and hence non-taxable.

At issue in this case is the manner in which Rapid's "current earnings and profits" and "accumulated earnings and profits" for its taxable years 1961 and 1962 should be computed. Specifically at issue is the correctness of a reduction of earnings and profits to account for purported "compensation expenses" measured by the "loss" Rapid absorbed in making "bargain" sales of its common stock to certain of its employees who possessed restricted stock options to purchase the stock.* Pursuant to the terms of these restricted stock options, during the period from January 1, 1957 to January 31, 1962, Rapid sold 174,395 shares of its common stock to some of its employees. Although these shares had a fair market value of $5,307,206, the corporation received only $1,889,360 from the employees who exercised their options. Rapid thus received $3,417,846 less for its stock than it could have received if the shares had been sold on the open market. In the period from February 1, 1962 to January 31, 1963 corporation employees purchased an additional 12,163 shares pursuant to the terms of options they held. Again, the prices paid by the employees, $155,388 in the aggregate, were substantially below the fair market value of the shares of stock, $363,914. It is argued that these differences of $3,417,846 and $208,526 represent compensation expense which should reduce corporate earnings and profits. . . .

* Pursuant to the restricted stock option at issue, the amount of the "spread" was neither includible by the employees nor deductible by the corporate employer. — EDS.

II

[The collateral estoppel issue is omitted.]

III . . .

In this case the Commissioner claims that the cash distributions made to appellant by Rapid constitute "dividend" income which under §61(a)(7) of the IRC is taxable to appellant as ordinary income. The word "dividend" is a term of art, the definition of which is found in §316 IRC: A "dividend" is "any distribution of property made by a corporation to its shareholders — (1) out of its earnings and profits accumulated after February 28, 1913, or (2) out of its earnings and profits of the [current] taxable year." Much to our chagrin, and that of many of our judicial ancestors, however, the Internal Revenue Code does not define the operative phrase "earnings and profits" or describe the manner in which that elusive quantity should be calculated. Congress could, and certainly should, rectify this deficiency by promulgating guidelines to assist the courts which must control the evolution of the concept. Be that as it may, such legislative guidelines do not now exist, so we must treat the problem as adequately as we can with the resources at our disposal.

Most of the commentators have experienced no difficulty in explaining what "earnings and profits" are not. For example, the term is synonymous with neither "corporate surplus," nor with "taxable income." Notably less successful have been the copious attempts to establish a coherent and workable scheme for determining when particular corporate transactions should reduce or increase a corporation's "earnings and profits." One of the most traditional approaches explains:

> Earnings and profits, on the other hand, are not defined by act; but they have a settled and well defined meaning in accounting. Generally speaking, they are computed by deducting from gross receipts the expense of producing them. Thus, under the ordinary method of accounting, in computing earnings and profits there will be deducted, not only the items shown above, but others which are not, under the statute, deductible in computing taxable net income. In this classification may be listed such items as extraordinary expenses, charitable contributions, taxes paid the Federal Government, and taxes assessed against local benefits tending to increase the value of the property. Again, many items, such as interest upon the obligations of a state or political subdivision, tax-free Federal securities, and dividends from other corporations, must necessarily be considered in computing earnings and profits, though forming no part of taxable net income.

R. M. Weyerhaeuser, 33 B.T.A. 594, 597 (1935). . . . We propose . . . to determine whether . . . the option spread "loss" suffered by a corporation upon an employee's exercise of a stock option is an "expense of producing gross receipts," resulting in a reduction of "earnings and profits." . . .

Compensation paid to and received by the employees of a business are, of course, business "expenses of producing gross receipts" and therefore reduce earnings and profits. We must therefore ascertain whether the "bargain spread" existing when an employee exercises a stock option is a "compensation expense." Compensation of employees for past, present and future services represents one of the most fundamental and necessary expenses of operating a business. Payment may be made in myriad modes; it need not always be by way of cash disbursement. For instance, an employee may be paid in stock. In lieu of such an immediate transfer of stock to an employee the employee may instead be granted an option to purchase the employer corporation's stock at a fixed price per share from the company at some future date. Employees find the stock option to be a particularly attractive compensation device; in a rising market it gives the employee the opportunity to make a "bargain purchase." The question of whether the "bargain or option spread" (i.e., the difference between the option price and the fair market value of the stock at the time of the exercise of the option) existing at the time the option is exercised is compensatory in nature has been well settled for nearly twenty years. In Commissioner of Internal Revenue v. LoBue, 351 U.S. 243 (1956), the Supreme Court, noting that "it seems impossible to say that (the bargain transfer) was not compensation," id. at 247, commented upon this point:

When assets are transferred by an employer to an employee to secure better services they are plainly compensation. It makes no difference that the compensation is paid in stock rather than in money.

Id. at 246-247.

When compensation is paid in its conventional form, cash, the magnitude of the expense (and, consequently, the reduction in earnings and profits) is easily visualized because there is an actual outflow of liquid corporate assets. When a bargain sale of stock to employees is made, however, both the existence and the extent of the corporate efflux are not as readily discernible. The same conceptual problems are presented when a corporation incurs an economic detriment when compensating employees by making awards of bonus stock to employees for the receipt of which the employees pay nothing into the corporate treasury. Yet the Service has twice ruled that the transfer of an employer's corporate stock to an employee as compensation produces for the transferor corporation a business expense deduction measured by the fair market value of the transferred stock, irrespective of whether that value exceeds the corporation's cost basis, if any, in the stock. Inasmuch as this deduction is allowed under §162, . . . these rulings appear to recognize that grants of bonus stock are expenses and have caused or should be considered as causing actual depletion of the corporate assets. Furthermore, these rulings demonstrate that the Service itself chooses to regard the *fair market value,* and not the cost basis, as one of the indices to be used in gauging the extent of the corporate expense incurred in compensating an employee by means of a direct award of stock. But the economic impact upon the corporation of the transfer of stock to employees pursuant to the exercise of employee stock options is in all important respects indistinguishable from the transfer of bonus corporation stock to employees. The only distinguishing feature of the option arrangement is that the employee pays something rather than nothing, but, it remains that in both instances, "at the end of these transactions, [the corporate] employer [is] worth . . . less to its stockholders." Commissioner of Internal Revenue v. LoBue, supra at 245. Accordingly, we would expect that the "bargain spread" would be considered to constitute a cognizable expense which would necessarily reduce earnings and profits. . . .

As a concluding comment, we reiterate our belief that the holding which we reach today is one which comports with economic reality and with the mechanics of operating a business. As the Seventh Circuit noted in Luckman v. Commissioner, [418 F.2d 381 (7th Cir. 1969)], if, instead of stock options, the corporation's employees had received cash there obviously would have been a cognizable corporate "expense." These stock options so granted were presumably the product of careful and deliberate negotiations between the corporation and the employees involved, and were apparently considered by the employees to be an acceptable, indeed, probably a superior, alternative to cash. In turn, the corporation undoubtedly expected to profit, and probably did profit, in precisely the same way it would have profited if it had awarded cash to those key employees, for, of course, this supplemental compensation to employees would normally cause the recipients to produce increased earnings and profits for the corporation.

In approaching a proper resolution of the tax issue here it is inequitable and unreasonable not to weigh the tangible corporate detriment resulting from the corporation's lost opportunity to sell the optioned stock to the public at its Fair Market Value, a detriment incurred in the hope that the grant of the options would result in producing added revenues. Moreover, in measuring the extent of the compensation, and the corresponding expense, by the amount of the excess of the Fair Market Value over the option price, realistic account is taken of the relationship between the employer and the employee. A company's revenues and profitability have a strong influence on the value of its stock and thus on the potential compensation accruing to the employee by virtue of the spread existing when the option he holds is exercised. Yet, typically, the employees who hold options are capable of increasing corporate revenues through their intensified labor and, insofar as such employees can affect corporate profitability, these same employees can indirectly influence the magnitude of their own compensation. Thus, the "bargain spread" does, in the form of increased employee compensation to the employees holding options, accurately reflect the economic detriment which the corporation has incurred in order, hopefully, to produce more revenue just like any other "development expense."

FRIENDLY, Circuit Judge (concurring and dissenting).

[Concurrence on collateral estoppel issue is omitted.]

The question in this case reduces to whether the "opportunity cost" incurred by Rapid in issuing the stock to the employees at less than its current market value rather than selling it to others is cognizable for purposes of reducing earnings and profits. There can be no claim that Rapid incurred out-of-pocket costs such as to reduce the earnings and profits available for distribution to shareholders. . . .

With all deference, I think the question can only be answered in the negative. Apart from the absence of evidence that Rapid could have sold the optioned stock at the market prices on the respective days of issuance, or would have done so, precisely the same sort of "cost" is incurred on the exercise of a warrant at a price below current market value, where no one suggests that this spread can be deducted from earnings and profits. The fact that here the options were issued to provide "incentive" to employees is not sufficient to support a different result. Selling stock at less than current market value does not impair the corporation's ability to make distributions without invading capital or paid-in surplus, which is what "earnings and profits" are mainly about. The effect of the exercise of an option, whether issued to an employee or to an outsider, at a "bargain spread" is to decrease the market price and, in some but not all instances, the book value of the shares of other stockholders. It has no adverse effect on the corporate accounts.

The petitioner's principal reliance is on two revenue rulings that, despite the general provision of §1032(a) prohibiting recognition of gain or loss on a corporation's receipt of money or property in exchange for stock (including treasury stock), a corporation may deduct as a business expense under §162 the fair market value of stock issued as compensation, whether the stock be treasury or theretofore unissued stock, Rev. Rul. 62-217, 1962-2 Cum. Bull. 59; Rev. Rul. 69-75, 1969-1 Cum. Bull. 52, with the presumable consequence that the same amount may be deducted from earnings and profits. Not only were these payments clearly compensation and nothing more, but the rulings can be rationalized on the basis that since the employee was subject to tax on the fair market value of the stock issued, allowing the deduction to the corporation was necessary to avoid unfairness. . . . By contrast, in the case of restricted stock options such as that before us, the employee escapes regular income taxation both when the option is issued and when it is exercised. There is therefore no reason to disregard the general principle of allowing no deduction, either from income or from earnings and profits, for mere loss of "opportunity costs." In substance [the restricted stock option] represented a trade-off. In return for the eagerly sought privilege of tax-free receipt and exercise of stock options by executives, the corporation would forego any deduction under §162 for the excess of the market value of the stock, when issued, over the option price. . . . There can be no fair doubt that the Congress that expressly ruled out use of the "bargain spread" to employees as a deduction would also have forbidden its use to reduce earnings and profits if it had ever considered the problem whether the "bargain spread" should enable the corporation to make a later distribution to stockholders as out of capital rather than from earnings and profits in the unusual case where this possibility might exist. . . .

I would affirm the judgment of the Tax Court.

NOTES

1. *"Earnings and profits."* It is a curious fact that the Code, ordinarily so prodigal in its use of words, does not define the term "earnings and profits" even though it is not a term that has a clear independent meaning outside of the Code. The term is partly explained by Treas. Regs. §1.312-6, and the effect of a number of transactions on earnings and profits is prescribed by the Code. See §§312 and 381(c)(2). The concept of earnings and profits is not the same as earned surplus for state law or financial reporting purposes. For example, a distribution of common stock by a corporation decreases earned surplus but has no effect on earnings and profits. Otherwise, nontaxable stock dividends under Eisner v. Macomber, 252 U.S. 189 (1920), would clear away the corporation's earnings and profits account, allowing it to make nontaxable subsequent distributions of cash and property.

Similarly, the term "dividend" as defined for income tax purposes by §316(a) may not correspond with the term "dividend" under state law, with the result that a distribution may be a dividend under §316(a) although it impairs capital under state law. Conversely, it is possible for a distribution to constitute a dividend under state law without qualifying as a dividend under §316(a). In the former instance, the dividend will ordinarily be taxable to the stockholder under the "claim of right" doctrine, notwithstanding a potential liability to creditors under state law. See United States v. Lesoine, 203 F.2d 123 (9th Cir. 1953), holding that the claim of right doctrine requires that dividends be taxed in year of receipt even if the distribution may have been illegal under state law.

The determination of the earnings and profits account is often no simple feat, especially when the account must be traced through a series of corporate reorganizations or similar transactions. It may be necessary to go back many years to decide how a transaction should have been taxed under a now-interred income tax provision because of its effect on earnings and profits. See, e.g., Union Pacific Railroad v. United States, 524 F.2d 1343 (Cl. Ct. 1975), claiming that an accounting error affected earnings and profits between 1900 and 1907.

If a corporation is initially organized for cash, the reason for gearing the taxability of its distributions to its record of earnings and profits is clear enough. Until the corporation has engaged in profitable operations, any distribution to its original stockholders is a return of their investment rather than income. Once the corporation has realized profits, its distributions may pro tanto be fairly regarded as income to the stockholders.

The equity and logic of §§316 and 301(c) may be less clear if we assume that after a period of corporate profits, the stock changes hands, and that before additional earnings arise (the next day, if you will), there is a distribution to the new stockholder. Should the distribution be treated as a return of capital? Sections 316 and 301(c) are inescapable: To the extent of earnings and profits, the surprised shareholder has realized income. This "miracle of income without gain" — the phrase is from Powell, Income from Corporate Dividends, 35 Harv. L. Rev. 363 (1922) — long ago was attested and explained by the Supreme Court in United States v. Phellis, 257 U.S. 156, 171-172 (1921):

> Where, as in this case, the dividend constitutes a distribution of profits accumulated during an extended period and bears a large proportion to the par value of the stock, if an investor happened to buy stock shortly before the dividend, paying a price enhanced by an estimate of the capital plus the surplus of the company, and after distribution of the surplus, with corresponding reduction in the intrinsic and market value of the shares, he was called upon to pay a tax upon the dividend received, it might look in his case like a tax upon his capital. But it is only apparently so. In buying at a price that reflected the accumulated profits, he of course acquired as a part of the valuable rights purchased the prospect of a dividend from the accumulation — bought "dividend on," as the phrase goes — and necessarily took subject to the burden of the income tax proper to be assessed against him by reason of the dividend if and when made. He simply stepped into the shoes, in this as in other respects, of the stockholder whose shares he acquired, and presumably the prospect of a dividend influenced the price paid, and was discounted by the prospect of an income tax to be paid thereon.

2. *Source of distributions.* If a corporation has earnings and profits in a taxable year, any distribution in that year subject to §301 will be taxable pro tanto even though the corporation has a deficit from prior years equal to or exceeding the current year's profits. §316(a)(2). See Situation 2 of Rev. Rul. 74-164 at page 121 supra. This provision has a curious ancestry. It was enacted in 1936 as a relief measure when the undistributed profits

tax was in effect. That tax was imposed on the undistributed part of corporate income, computed by deducting "dividends" from total income. Unless a deficit corporation could treat distributions out of current earnings as "dividends" for this purpose, it would be unable to avoid the undistributed profits tax no matter how large its distributions to stockholders. To enable such corporations to obtain a credit for "dividends" paid out of current earnings, §316(a) was enacted. Apparently, no thought was given to the effect of the new subsection apart from the undistributed profits tax. Nor was §316(a)(2) repealed when the short-lived undistributed profits tax was repealed.

Treas. Regs. §1.316-2 sets forth hierarchical rules for classifying distributions. Distributions are first deemed to come out of the corporation's current earnings and profits account. If the account is exhausted, accumulated earnings and profits are tapped. If there is a deficit in the current earnings and profits account, distributions are deemed to be out of accumulated earnings and profits decreased by the current deficit prorated to the date of distribution unless the actual current deficit as of the transaction date can be ascertained. Rev. Rul. 74-164, above, illustrates these source rules. Note, though, that in Situation 3 of the ruling the current deficit in the earnings and profits account is prorated even though the actual current deficit as of July 1, the distribution date, is known. Doesn't this treatment in the ruling conflict with Treas. Regs. §1.316-2? See also Rev. Rul. 69-440, 1969-2 C.B. 46, discussing priorities among distributions.

If there is more than one distribution during a taxable year, the current earnings and profits are prorated among the distributions for purposes of determining whether a distribution is a dividend. Accumulated earnings and profits, however, are allocated to distributions chronologically on a first come, first served basis. Treas. Regs. §1.316-2(b), (c).

As earnings and profits are distributed, the corporation decreases its earnings and profits account in accordance with §312(a). Note that a corporation cannot create an earnings and profits deficit through distributions. See §312(a) and Estate of Uris v. Commissioner, 605 F.2d 1258 (2d Cir. 1979). How then can there be a deficit in the earnings and profits account?

3. *Relationship of earnings and profits to taxable income.* A determination of earnings and profits most often starts with an analysis of taxable income. To convert taxable income into earnings and profits, three types of adjustments are necessary. First, some items excludible from taxable income are included in earnings and profits. They are included because they represent an accretion to the corporation that can be distributed without impairing the corporation's original capital. The items include proceeds from life insurance contracts under §101(a), interest on certain government obligations under §103, and amounts received through accident or health insurance for personal injuries to or sickness of insured employees under §104(a). See Treas. Regs. §1.312-6(b).

Section 312(n) contains some upwards adjustments to earnings and profits to ensure that earnings and profits conform more closely to economic income. For example, if a corporation sells property at a gain on the installment method, the entire gain goes into earnings and profits immediately even though there is deferred recognition of some or all of the gain. Similarly, a corporation that reports income and expenses attributable to a long-term contract on the completed contract method must use the percentage-of-completion method for earnings and profits purposes. Corporations using "last in, first out" (LIFO) accounting for inventory must adjust earnings and profits by the LIFO recapture amount.

Second, some items that are deductible in computing taxable income may not be deducted in computing earnings and profits. Often, these are "artificial" deductions in that no cash outlay is required that would deplete the earnings available for distribution. These items include the dividends-received deduction under §243 (which allows qualifying corporations to deduct from 70 percent to 100 percent of the amount of intercorporate dividends received) and the excess of accelerated over straight-line depreciation using recovery periods specified in §312(k). In addition, net operating losses under §172 and capital loss carrybacks under §1212 do not reduce earnings and profits since they represent a carryback or carryover of losses that reduced earnings and profits in the year in which they occurred.

Several provisions require a slower rate of deduction for earnings and profits purposes than for the purpose of computing gain or loss. For example, intangible drilling costs and mineral and development costs to the extent deductible must be capitalized for earnings and profits purposes. §312(n)(2). Similar rules are provided for expenses amortizable under §§173, 177, and 248, see §312(n)(3), and for construction period carrying charges. §312(n)(1).

Third, some items that cannot be deducted in determining taxable income are deducted in computing earnings and profits because they represent a real drain on earnings available for distribution to shareholders. Included in this category are dividend distributions in prior years (but see §312(a)); federal income taxes;[1] excess charitable contributions (not deductible because of the 10 percent limitation of §170(b)); nondeductible expenses under §265; unreasonable compensation; and deductions disallowed on public policy grounds under §162(c), (e), (f), or (g). See Rev. Rul. 77-442, 1977-2 C.B. 264.

In *Divine* the court faced an issue involving the third category — whether an item not deductible in computing taxable income (the difference between the cost of the stock and the fair market value of the stock)

---

1. Treas. Regs. §1.312-6(a) provides that the method of accounting used to compute earnings and profits should be the same as that used for determining taxable income. Accordingly, a cash basis taxpayer cannot accrue a tax liability; for a cash basis taxpayer, earnings and profits are reduced only when taxes are paid. Mazzocchi Bus Co., Inc. v. Commissioner, 14 F.2d 923 (3d Cir. 1994).

is deductible in computing earnings and profits.[2] The Tax Court tried its view twice and was reversed both times — once by the Seventh Circuit in Luckman v. Commissioner, 418 F.2d 381 (7th Cir. 1969), and once by the Second Circuit in *Divine,* although the Tax Court did convince Judge Friendly. Who is right, the majority or Judge Friendly? It is true that the purchase of stock by Divine did not deplete the cash or other property available for distribution to shareholders. The same is true, however, if an employee is compensated with stock, a transaction that unquestionably reduces taxable income and therefore earnings and profits. See Rev. Rul. 62-217, 1962-2 C.B. 59. If Divine had been compensated in cash for the "spread" between the option price and fair market value and had then reinvested the cash plus his own cash in the corporation by purchasing some of its stock, would doubts still exist about the transaction's effect on earnings and profits?

While *Divine* involves the effect on earnings and profits of a nondeductible item, in Bangor & Aroostook Railroad v. Commissioner, 193 F.2d 827 (1st Cir. 1951), the court confronted a discharge of indebtedness that went unrecognized — and hence was excluded from gross income — because of the taxpayer's election under the predecessors of §§108 and 1017. Since a reduction in basis accompanied the nonrecognition, the court ruled that there should be no increase in earnings and profits until the assets with the reduced basis were sold. See §312(f), relied on by the court, and §312(l)(1), which codified this result.

4. *The future of earnings and profits.* You may not need much convincing at this point that the concept of earnings and profits adds complexity to the Code. Moreover, if the purpose of the concept is to ensure that shareholders will not be taxed on the return of their capital, curious results abound for a stock purchaser receiving a distribution shortly after purchase and before the accumulation of any additional earnings. See page 130 supra. If there are accumulated earnings and profits, the distribution will be a dividend even though there have been no subsequent earnings following purchase. Finally, there is room for manipulation. For example, the impact of current earnings and profits where the corporation has an accumulated earnings and profits deficit sometimes can be avoided by postponing the distribution until the following year. If the corporation has no earnings in that year and still has an accumulated earnings and profits deficit, the distribution will be received tax free since it will fall under neither §316(a)(1) nor §316(a)(2). If a corporation can deplete its earnings and profits account, it may be able to borrow against appreciated property to make tax-free distributions to shareholders and then use the property's earnings to repay the loan.

---

2. *Divine* serves as a nice reminder of the *Golsen* rule — that the Tax Court by its own rules is not bound to follow a court of appeals decision unless appellate jurisdiction is in that circuit. See Golsen v. Commissioner, 54 T.C. 742, 757 (1970), aff'd without discussion of this issue, 445 F.2d 985 (10th Cir. 1971).

This combination of complexity, failure of purpose, and potential abuse has led some commentators, as well as some members of Congress from time to time, to consider a repeal of the earnings and profits concept, with relief for obvious distributions of capital. See Blum, The Earnings and Profits Limitation on Dividend Income: A Reappraisal, 53 Taxes 68 (1975); Colby, Blackburn, and Trier, Elimination of "Earnings and Profits" from the Internal Revenue Code, 39 Tax Law. 285 (1986). See also Staff of Senate Comm. on Finance, 99th Cong., 1st Sess., The Reform and Simplification of the Income Taxation of Corporations (1985). No change in this regard appears imminent.

5. *Relief from taxation of dividends.* Earnings and profits serve as the benchmark for measuring dividend income, thereby producing the "double tax" — taxation to the corporation earning income and taxation to shareholders on dividend distributions. See discussion of the double tax in Chapter 8.

There is a special allowance for dividends received by corporate shareholders to mitigate the multiple taxation of corporate earnings. This relief provision can be illustrated by considering the tax results that would prevail in its absence. If, for example, individual A owns all the stock in P Corp., which owns all the stock in Q Corp., earnings of Q Corp. might be subject to a triple tax by the time the earnings reach A. Q Corp. would be taxed when it earns income; P Corp. and then A face taxation on the dividend. Since 1935, however, §243 has provided for a deduction by a corporation that is a shareholder in another corporation. Although §243 is a "deduction" provision, it provides, in effect, an exclusion for the shareholder-corporation (i.e., the corporation can deduct some portion of the dividend that has been received).

Currently, §243 permits a shareholder-corporation to deduct 70 percent of the dividend received from a distributing corporation. This provision at current rates makes the effective maximum tax rate on dividends received by a corporation 10.5 percent — that is, the highest corporate rate of 35 percent imposed on 30 percent of dividends received. If the recipient corporation owns 20 percent or more (by vote and value) of the stock of the distributing corporation, the deduction is increased to 80 percent. Notice that dividends paid on "portfolio stock" (i.e., when the receiving corporation owns less than 20 perent) are subject to a higher effective rate of tax.

The lowest rate on intercorporate dividends is available with respect to distributions from affiliated corporations. An affiliated group of corporations can eliminate intragroup dividends from gross income entirely by electing to file consolidated returns under the relevant Code provisions. §§1501 et seq. Moreover, §243(a)(3) permits a 100 percent deduction for certain dividends for electing members of an affiliated group, as defined in §1504(a), who are willing to abide by certain restrictions. See §243(b)(3).

For a discussion of problems raised by the dividends-received deduction, see pages 165-175 infra.

PROBLEMS

4-1. Determine the tax consequences in the following situations:

a. On July 1, 1999, *X* Corp., a calendar year taxpayer, made distributions of $20,000 to *A*, its sole shareholder, whose stock had a $5,000 basis. No other distributions were made in 1999. As of December 31, 1998, *X* Corp. had no earnings and profits. In 1993 *X* Corp. had earnings and profits of $15,000 as of July 1 but only $5,000 for the entire year.

b. Suppose in (a) that *X* Corp. had an accumulated earnings and profits deficit of $15,000 as of December 31, 1998.

c. Suppose in (a) that *X* Corp. had accumulated earnings and profits of $15,000 as of December 31, 1998, and that in 1999 *X* Corp. had a $15,000 earnings and profits deficit on July 1 but a $5,000 earnings and profits account for the entire year.

d. Suppose in (c) that *X* Corp. had $15,000 of current earnings and profits as of July 1, 1999, but a deficit of $20,000 for the entire year.

4-2. *X* Corp. is an accrual basis taxpayer. Compute its current earnings and profits from the following information. Assume that *X* Corp. is taxed at a flat 30 percent rate.

Gross income from business	$27,000
Dividend income	20,000
Interest on municipal bonds	9,000
Long-term capital gain	5,000
Contribution to capital	2,000
	$63,000
Wages, rent, office supplies	$15,000
Fines and kickbacks	7,000
Depreciation (excess over §168(g)(2) amount = $4,000)	6,000
Interest incurred to purchase municipal bonds	2,000
Dividends-received deduction	14,000
Capital losses	6,000
	$50,000
"Net"	$13,000

B. PROPERTY DISTRIBUTIONS

1. *The Effect of a Distribution of Property on the Distributing Corporation's Income*

The United States employs a classic double tax system. When a corporation earns income from operations, there is a corporate-level tax. When those earnings are distributed to the shareholders as dividends, there is a shareholder-level tax under §301. Similarly, if the corporation sells appreciated property and distributes the sales proceeds, there will typically be a corporate-level tax on the sale and a dividend on the distribution of the sales proceeds. Note that the gain recognized by the corporation on the sale increases the corporation's earnings and profits, making it more likely that the distribution will be taxed as a dividend.

Suppose instead that the corporation distributes the appreciated property to its shareholders, who then sell the property. We know that the shareholders will have dividends equal to the fair market value of the property distributed if the corporation has sufficient earnings and profits. §301(b). If there are insufficient earnings and profits, the shareholders may escape dividend treatment, instead reducing their bases in the distributing corporation's stock. §301(c)(2). In any case, the distributed property will have a basis in the hands of the shareholders equal to its fair market value. §301(d). If the property is then sold, the shareholders will recognize no additional gain. To summarize, the shareholders will recognize, at most, one level of taxation (dividend treatment), and if there are insufficient earnings and profits, the shareholders may have no income as a result of the distribution and sale.

Contrast this treatment with the corresponding tax results when the corporation sells the property and then distributes the proceeds, resulting in both a corporate-level and shareholder-level tax. To prevent the form of the transaction from dictating the tax consequences, it is necessary that there be a corporate-level tax if the appreciated property is distributed and then sold, just as there is if the property is sold and the proceeds distributed. This conclusion is not an endorsement of the system of double taxation. Rather, it takes the double taxation feature as a given, emphasizing the need for consistency. For a consideration of the double tax system, see Chapter 8.

The seminal case considering the tax consequences to a corporation distributing appreciated property is General Utilities & Operating Co. v. Helvering, 296 U.S. 200 (1935). In that case, General Utilities corporation located a purchaser for Islands Edison common stock that it owned. The stock had a value of approximately $1 million and an adjusted basis of $20,000. If General Utilities had completed the sale, there would have been a corporate-level tax followed by a shareholder-level tax if the sales proceeds were distributed to the shareholders as dividends.

To minimize these potential tax consequences, General Utilities distributed the Islands Edison stock to its shareholders with an understanding that they would sell the distributed stock to the purchaser. Four days after the distribution, the shareholders sold the Islands Edison stock to the purchaser on the same terms as negotiated by General Utilities. No gain was reported on the sale because the shareholders took a fair market value basis in the distributed stock. §301(d).

The Service claimed that the distribution by General Utilities was a taxable event at the corporate level because it used appreciated property to discharge the indebtedness it created by declaring a dividend. Before the Board of Tax Appeals, the government relied on the theory that the corporation had (1) by declaring a dividend of $1 million, created a debt of $1 million, and then (2) satisfied the indebtedness by distributing the securities. Before the court of appeals, the government added a second argument — that a sale of the property that occurred immediately after the distribution should be attributed to the corporation, although made in form by the shareholders. (This rationale, commonly known as the *Court Holding Co.* doctrine, has often been accepted if the corporation negotiates the sale and then makes a last-minute effort to avoid recognizing gain by distributing the property to its shareholders before the sale. See page 308 infra.) On this point the court of appeals agreed with the Treasury. In its Supreme Court brief, the Treasury added a third argument — that a corporation must recognize taxable income on a distribution of appreciated property to its stockholders since the transfer is a "sale or other disposition" under §1001.

The Supreme Court agrees with the Board of Tax Appeals that the distributed assets were not used to discharge a corporate debt. As to the second point, the Court held that it should have been raised at the trial level and could not be belatedly argued in the appellate court; the government's third argument was not mentioned. Although the commentators could not agree on whether the theory of realization-by-distribution was rejected on the merits by implication or passed over because it was advanced too late in the proceeding, the former explanation of its fate became popular with the courts, and the *General Utilities* doctrine was born.

From the beginning there were exceptions to the *General Utilities* doctrine. For example, in Commissioner v. First State Bank of Stratford, 168 F.2d 1004 (5th Cir. 1948), a distributing corporation was taxed on a distribution of debt instruments (not its own) to its shareholders when the distributing corporation had taken bad debt deductions with respect to the notes, although payments on the notes were made to the shareholders. Using assignment of income principles, the court taxed the distributing corporation on the collection of the notes.

In 1954 Congress enacted the "general rule" of §311(a), which codified the *General Utilities* rule that no gain or loss shall be recognized to a corporation on a distribution of property with respect to its stock. In recommending the enactment of §311, however, the Senate Finance Committee Report stated: "[Y]our committee does not intend to change existing law with respect to attribution of income of shareholders to their corporation as exemplified for example in the case of Commr. v. First State Bank of Stratford."

Following the enactment of §311(a), courts began to chip away at *General Utilities*. For example, in First Wisconsin Bankshares Corp. v. United States, 369 F. Supp. 1034 (E.D. Wis. 1973), the taxpayer donated to a charity certain notes that had been previously determined worthless by the national banking examiner and had been deducted as bad debts. Relying heavily on *Stratford Bank*, the court found first that the charitable deduction claimed by the taypayer constituted a recovery that offset the prior bad debt deduction and, second, that when the charitable donee received repayment of the notes, the taxpayer realized income under the anticipatory assignment of income principle to the extent that the portion of the note repayments constituted interest. Contra, Continental Illinois National Bank & Trust Co. v. Commissioner, 69 T.C. 357 (1977), in which the court held that no tax benefit was recovered when the taxpayer wrote off a bad debt for which it received virtually worthless stock from the debtors' trustee in bankruptcy. When the common stock increased in value it was donated to charity, and a charitable deduction for its fair market value was claimed. The court viewed the receipt of stock and later donation as two separate transactions and refused to treat the appreciation as a further recovery of the bad debt.

In Bush Brothers & Co. v. Commissioner, 668 F.2d 252 (6th Cir. 1982), the corporation, a food processor, purported to distribute contracts to buy beans at a specified price to its shareholders, who then sold the contracts. The court of appeals attributed the sale to the corporation in light of its extensive involvement in the transactions. At the trial court level, the Tax Court reached the same result because of an improper tax avoidance motive. The approach taken by the Tax Court majority draws strength from United States v. Lynch, 192 F.2d 718 (9th Cir. 1952). There, a corporation in the fruit business distributed a dividend of 22,000 boxes of apples to its shareholders. The fruit remained in the corporation's warehouse and was sold by the corporation two months later on behalf of the shareholders. The Ninth Circuit attributed the sale to the corporation, not so much because of corporate involvement but because of an improper tax reduction motive. The court relied on Commissioner v. Transport Trading & Terminal Corp., 176 F.2d 570 (2d Cir. 1949), in which the Second Circuit determined that a distribution of appreciated securities from a subsidiary corporation to its parent, followed by a sale, produced a tax at the subsidiary level. The holding was broad, indicating that a tax-motivated distribution in the face of an anticipated shareholder sale would result in a tax to the distributing corporation. Accord, ABCD Lands, Inc. v. Commissioner, 41 T.C. 840 (1964).

Congress also began to chip away at the codification of *General Utilities* under §311(a). By 1984 the exceptions to §311(a) all but swallowed up the nonrecognition rule for appreciated property. The Tax Reform Act of 1986 overturned most of the remaining vestiges of *General Utilities*. Section 311(b) now provides that if a corporation distributes property (other than the distributing corporation's own obligation) in which the fair market value exceeds the distributing corporation's adjusted basis, the distributing corporation will recognize gain as if it had sold the property to the shareholder at fair market value.

Note that the appreciation recognized by the distributing corporation is not limited to post-incorporation appreciation. For example, suppose *B* forms *X* Corp. in a §351 transaction by exchanging property including one item with a basis of $100 and a fair market value of $500 for all the *X* Corp. stock. Before *X* Corp. earns any income, it distributes that item to *B*. Under §311(b), *X* Corp. must recognize the $400 of appreciation. The gain will be ordinary or capital, depending on the nature of the asset. The holding period may be long or short term, but recall that *X* Corp. tacks on *B*'s holding period under §1223(2). Moreover, *X* Corp.'s earnings and profits account will increase from $0 to $400 (minus taxes paid by *X* Corp.) because *X* Corp.'s taxable income reflects the §311(b) gain. The increase in earnings and profits will cause *B* to recognize a dividend of about $400 under §301(c)(1). This phenomenon will doubtless precipitate some careful planning as indicated below.

If a corporation distributes property subject to a liability, the fair market value of the property distributed for purposes of §311(b)(1)(B) is not less than the amount of the liability. See §§311(b)(2) and 336(b). For example, suppose *X* Corp. distributes property with a basis of $700 and a fair market value of $400 to *B*, a shareholder. The property is subject to a liability of $900. Under §311(b), *X* Corp. must recognize gain as if the property had been sold to *B*. Had there been a sale, *X* Corp. would have recognized a $200 gain under Tufts v. Commissioner, 461 U.S. 300 (1983).

A true repeal of the *General Utilities* doctrine would allow a distributing corporation to deduct a loss on the distribution of property with an adjusted basis that exceeds its fair market value. Suppose *X* Corp. held property with a basis of $700 and a fair market value of $200. If *X* Corp. sells the property, it will recognize a $500 loss. The distribution of the proceeds to the shareholders will be taxable to the shareholders under §301(c)(1) if there are sufficient earnings and profits after reducing taxable income by the amount of the loss. If, however, *X* Corp. distributes the property to its shareholders, §311(b) provides no loss deduction. Moreover, there is no decrease in *X* Corp.'s earnings and profits as a result of distributing the loss property. The shareholders will have a $200 dividend if there are sufficient earnings and profits. Finally, the shareholders will take the property with a basis of $200, its fair market value under §301(d). Notice that by mandating a fair market value basis, the Code forever eliminates the loss deduction.

Why does §311(b) disallow recognition of losses to the distributing corporation? Perhaps Congress was concerned that shareholders would have it in their power to cause their corporations to distribute "loss property" while not distributing "gain property." In this way corporations could exploit the realization doctrine by recognizing losses but not unrealized gains. If this was the concern, there are several responses. A corporation always has the power to exploit the realization doctrine by selling loss rather than gain property. Indeed, the limitation on capital loss deductions in §§1211 and 1212 is a response to that problem.

But it could be argued that the capital gains limitation is not sufficient when the loss property is transferred to a related party. Congress has addressed that problem as well by enacting §267, which prohibits the deduction of losses with respect to exchanges between related parties. A corporation is considered related to any shareholder who owns, directly or indirectly, more than 50 percent in value of the corporation's stock. For a discussion of the attribution rules, see page 189 infra. A sale of loss property to a 25 percent shareholder, for example, will produce a deductible loss. Why didn't Congress treat all nonliquidating distributions as if the corporation had sold the property to the shareholders and allow §267 to determine the deductibility of losses?

A side effect of not using §267 in connection with distributions of loss property is the basis consequence to the shareholders. Under §267 a purchaser takes a basis equal to cost — generally fair market value. But if the purchaser sells the property at a gain, the loss that went unrecognized to the seller is available to the purchaser to offset the gain. §267(d). There is no equivalent provision in §311.

Suppose X Corp. distributes two pieces of property to B, its shareholder. One has a basis of $200 and a fair market value of $900; the other has a basis of $900 and a fair market value of $200. Has X Corp. made a distribution of appreciated property? Suppose X Corp., a partner in the XY partnership, wants to distribute the appreciated partnership interest to its shareholders. To decrease the amount of gain it has to recognize under §311(b), X transfers loss property to the partnership. The effect of the transfer is to increase the corporation's basis in the partnership interest by the basis of the contributed property under §722 in a manner comparable to §358 in a §351 transaction, while the fair market value of the partnership interest increases by the fair market value of the contributed property. The overall effect, if successful, would be to use the loss property to decrease gain that would otherwise be recognized on the distribution. Section 311(b)(3) allows the Service to promulgate regulations that disregard the contribution of the loss property in determining the basis and fair market value of the distributed partnership interest.

Given the treatment to a distributing corporation of both gain and loss property, what strategies would you expect taxpayers to pursue? Suppose X Corp., with sufficient earnings and profits, wants to get a piece of property with a basis of $200 and a fair market value of $900 into the hands of B, its shareholder. A distribution will trigger gain at both the corporate and shareholder level. Suppose instead that X Corp. sells the property to B, who pays with a note bearing appropriate interest and payable in 10 years. If the transaction is respected, X Corp. will recognize no immediate gain on the sale because of installment reporting. §453. But consider the application of both §§267 and 1239. B, the purchaser, will have no gain on the acquisition of the property and will take a cost basis under §1012 of $900.

Later, if the shareholder defaults on the note, presumably the shareholder will recognize $900 of income as a discharge of indebtedness. §61(a)(12). The distributing corporation should be allowed to take a bad debt deduction under §166 for the $200 basis of the note. Consider first that this treatment is less onerous in absolute income terms than dividend characterization in the year of the property's distribution because there is no corporate-level income (indeed there is a corporate-level loss) in the year of default. Moreover, B has had the benefit of deferral on the $900 of income that would be recognized at the shareholder level. Undoubtedly the Service may try to recharacterize the transaction as a distribution of the appreciated property followed years later by B's contribution to capital when the note is paid.

If X Corp. wants to distribute property to B with a basis of $900 and a fair market value of $200, a similar strategy may be employed. X Corp. could declare a cash dividend and then satisfy the dividend with a distribution of the loss property. See, e.g., Kenan v. Commissioner, 114 F.2d 217 (2d Cir. 1940) (satisfaction of a cash legacy with appreciated stock treated as a sale or disposition). Indeed, this technique is precisely what the Service accused the taxpayer of doing at the trial court in *General Utilities*. The Service presumably would argue that there never was an intention to pay a cash dividend and that the distribution of property cannot generate a loss under §311(b). Again consider the application of §267.

Suppose X Corp. had decided to distribute property with a basis of $900 and fair market value of $200 to shareholder B, who would then sell it to P. Immediately prior to the transaction, X Corp. decides to make the sale itself to P and to distribute the proceeds to B. This fact pattern is the converse of that presented in *General Utilities*. There, the distributing corporations made distributions before the sale took place. Here, the corporation sold the property and distributed the proceeds. One can expect that in appropriate circumstances the Service will reverse the argument that it relied on in these cases, claiming that actually the corporation distributed the property before the sale transpired. Such a recharacterization would deny the loss deduction to the distributing corporation. §311(b).

Taxpayers and their advisors have developed all manner of intricate ways of trying to avoid the repeal of *General Utilities*. See Notice 94-93, 1994-2 C.B. 563, and Land, Strange Loops and Tangled Hierarchies, 49 Tax L. Rev. 53 (1993).

2. The Effect of a Distribution of Property on the Distributing Corporation's Earnings and Profits

Although we have looked at what goes into earnings and profits in general, we need to consider the effect of a distribution on the earnings and profits account. Until the repeal of the *General Utilities* doctrine, distributing corporations did not normally recognize gain on the distribution of appreciated property. Consequently, §312(a)(3) required earnings and profits to be decreased only by the adjusted basis of any property distributed because the appreciation never was taken into income by the corporation. With the repeal of the *General Utilities* doctrine, a corporation that appreciated property must include the appreciation as income. The increase in taxable income results in an increase in earnings and profits. Therefore, it is appropriate to decrease the earnings and profits account after the distribution by the fair market value of the property distributed. Section 312(b)(2) accomplishes that result by substituting fair market value for adjusted basis in §312(a)(3) when appreciated property is distributed.

You may ask why Congress did not simply amend §312(a)(3) to read "fair market value" instead of "adjusted basis." The answer lies in the treatment of loss property. Because a distributing corporation does not take a loss into account for tax purposes when distributing property with a basis that exceeds its fair market value, it would be inappropriate to decrease earnings and profits only by the fair market value of the property distributed. Accordingly, §312(a)(3) allows the distributing corporation to decrease earnings and profits by the higher adjusted basis.

Section 312(b)(1) does not work smoothly with §311(b). Because §311(b) now requires a distributing corporation to recognize gain on the distribution of appreciated property, that gain will go into taxable income and then automatically into earnings and profits (because computation of taxable income is the first step in computing earnings and profits) for purposes of evaluating the tax consequences to the distributees. Read literally, §312(b)(1) would require the appreciation to increase earnings and profits again. But such a reading cannot be justified.

To illustrate the workings of §312(b), suppose *X* Corp., with no earnings and profits, distributes property with a basis of $0 and a fair market value of $400 to its shareholders. *X* Corp. will have $400 of taxable income on the distribution under §311(b). For purposes of evaluating the tax consequences to the shareholders, X Corp.'s earnings and profits will increase by the $400 gain recognized. Therefore, the shareholders will have dividend treatment under §301(c)(1). Following the distribution, X Corp.'s earnings and profits will be reduced from $400 to $0 under §312(b)(2) and (a)(3) because X Corp.'s earnings were fully distributed. Notice that §312(b)(1) increases earnings and profits, then the tax consequences to the shareholders are evaluated, then the earnings and profits account is decreased by the fair market value of the property distributed.

Finally, consider the effect of §312(a) on distributions of a specific type of property — a corporation's own note. For example, suppose X Corp., with $100,000 of accumulated earnings and profits, distributes its own notes with a $100,000 principal amount maturing in 10 years and bearing no interest. Assume further that the notes have a present value of $20,000. X is not permitted to reduce its earnings and profits by the $100,000 principal amount in order to pave the way for future cash distributions. Instead, §312(a)(2) now mandates a reduction by the $20,000 issue price. Each year, the corporation can reduce its taxable income and its earnings and profits by a portion of the original issue discount. §163(e).

3.   The Effect of a Distribution of Property on Shareholders

For both corporate and noncorporate distributees, §301(b)(1) specifies that the fair market value of property is the amount distributed for purposes of determining what constitutes a dividend under §§301(c) and 316. If a corporation distributes an asset to T with a basis of $40 and a fair market value of $100, subject to a $70 mortgage, what is the amount distributed? See §301(b)(2). The basis of property received by noncorporate distributees is determined under §301(d). What is T's basis in the asset received? Why isn't it reduced by the mortgage?

PROBLEMS

4-3.   Discuss the tax consequences in the following, ignoring the quantitative effect of any corporate-level taxes on earnings and profits:

a.   X Corp., a cash basis taxpayer with no earnings and profits, makes a distribution of property that has a basis of $3,000 and that X Corp. values at $3,000. The recipient is B, a shareholder whose basis in the X Corp. stock is $5,000. If the Service determines the property has a value of $7,000, what are the tax consequences?

b.   Suppose in (a) that the property has a fair market value of $7,000 but is subject to a mortgage of $8,000.

c. Suppose in (a) that X Corp. transfers the property to B in exchange for B's $7,000 note.
d. Suppose in (a) that X Corp. has earnings and profits of $4,000 and that the property X Corp. distributes has a basis of $7,000 and a fair market value of $3,000. What happens if the property increases in value after the distribution and then B sells the property for $7,000?
e. Suppose in (d) that X Corp. distributes the loss property and another piece of property with a basis of $3,000 and a fair market value of $7,000.
f. Suppose in (d) that X Corp. declares a $3,000 cash dividend and then distributes the loss property in satisfaction of the dividend.
g. Suppose in (d) that P, an unrelated purchaser, wants to buy the property. X Corp. prepares to declare a dividend of the loss property so that B can execute the sale, but at the last moment, X Corp. decides to sell directly to P and to distribute the proceeds.

C. DISGUISED OR CONSTRUCTIVE DIVIDENDS

Dividend treatment is often an unattractive tax outcome for individual shareholders and their controlled corporations. Not only is the dividend taxable to the recipient as ordinary income, but the distributing corporation does not get a deduction. Moreover, high-bracket shareholders who wish to transfer corporate funds to low-bracket relatives pay the income tax on the dividend and perhaps a gift tax on the transfer to the relative.

To avoid such unpleasantries, taxpayers often try to avoid dividend treatment while still pulling money out of corporate solution. Such attempts by taxpayers generally fall into two categories: (1) a distribution disguised as a deductible item to the distributing corporation even though it is taxable to the recipient and (2) a distribution disguised as a nontaxable receipt for the recipient even though the corporation gets no deduction. Either category may be preferable to dividend characterization, which offers no deduction to the corporation and requires inclusion by the recipient. In a third category, which combines the first two, the corporation tries to deduct an expenditure while the shareholder excludes it.

The most common illustration of the first category is the excessive compensation situation. If successful, characterizing a corporate payment as salary generates a corporate deduction, even if the payment happens to be made to shareholders, since the payment is not a distribution "with respect to [the corporation's] stock" within the meaning of §301(a). (The same is true for interest and rental payments.) Section 162(a)(1) limits the compensation deduction to a "reasonable" allowance. In determining what is reasonable, courts generally have looked at a variety of factors, including the role of the recipient in the company, the comparative compensation of similarly situated employees of other companies, the character and condition of the company, the power of the recipient to control compensation levels, and internal consistency by the company (e.g., bonuses that are not part of a consistent program or that track the percentage of stock ownership may be suspect). For a discussion of these and other factors, see Elliots, Inc. v. Commissioner, 716 F.2d 1241 (9th Cir. 1983) (mere absence of dividend payments not conclusive as to whether compensation was "reasonable").

Corporate loans offer a common version of the second category. Loans produce no corporate deduction, but there is no shareholder inclusion. Predictably, the use of these and other techniques is limited only by the bounds of a taxpayer's imagination. Predictably too, the Service will scrutinize transactions between shareholders and their closely held corporations to determine if the payment constitutes a "disguised" or "constructive" dividend.

The third category is illustrated by a corporation's payment of a shareholder's legal expenses in contesting a divorce that also threatened control of the business. See Dolese v. United States, 605 F.2d 1146 (10th Cir. 1979).

The cases and notes that follow offer a sampling of the litigation in the area of constructive dividends. The recharacterization of a payment as a disguised dividend is by its nature a finding of fact, and examples abound in a wide variety of transactions. Both cases that follow — one involving a bargain purchase and the other involving a transaction between related corporations — occasion the finding of a constructive dividend in situations where the shareholder does not directly receive a corporate distribution.

Baumer v. United States
580 F.2d 863 (5th Cir. 1978)

Before Wisdom, Goldberg, and Rubin, Circuit Judges.
GOLDBERG, Circuit Judge.

This appeal presents a novel variation of the recurrent problem of determining the tax consequences of transactions between closely held corporations and their shareholders. Here a corporation granted an option to purchase a one-half interest in a parcel of real estate to the son of the corporation's sole shareholder for nominal consideration. In the proceedings below, the district court held that the grant of this option resulted in a constructive dividend from the corporation to the father, measured by the ascertainable value of the option. . . .

I.   THE TRANSACTION

[The following fact statement appears in a later disposition of *Baumer* at 685 F.2d 1319-1320:

On January 30, 1966, the Seven Eighty-Eight Greenwood Avenue Corporation (Corporation) contracted to purchase a parcel of residential property for $175,000. Erwin G. Baumer (Father) was the sole shareholder of Corporation. When Erwin H. Baumer (Son) learned of this transaction, he asked for an interest in the property and, in May, 1966, was given an option to purchase a one-half interest in the property. The term during which the option was exercisable was one year from its effective date and the exercise price was $88,000 plus five and one-half percent interest calculated from the effective date. In August, 1966, Corporation entered into a contract for the purchase of an adjacent piece of property for $25,000. Son was granted an amended option in January, 1967, which encompassed both properties. The exercise price for the new option was $100,000. The stated consideration for both options was $10, which Son did not recall having paid. Also in January, 1967, Corporation granted Pope & Carter Company, Inc. an option to purchase the properties for $500,000. In early December, 1968, Son exercised his option, giving a note to Corporation for $114,501.23, the entire option price [plus interest]. On December 27, 1968, Pope & Carter exercised its option. The sale by Son and Corporation to an assignee of Pope & Carter was closed on July 1, 1969. Son received $252,700 for his one-half interest in the properties.

The Commissioner determined that upon Son's exercise of his option in 1968, Father received a constructive dividend taxable to Father based on the difference between the exercise price of the option and the fair market value of the property. The Commissioner also determined that Son's gain on the sale of his one-half interest should be imputed to Corporation. The District Court ruled that imputation was not warranted.

The District Court determined that the option and its amendment were distributions of corporate property resulting in a constructive dividend to Father. The court assumed, without deciding, that the constructive dividend occurred when Son was granted the option in 1966 and at the time of its amendment in 1967, years not in issue in the proceedings. The District Court, however, found that the option had no ascertainable value at the time of its grant or its amendment. Therefore, under the open transaction doctrine of Burnet v. Logan 283 U.S. 404 (1931), the District Court ruled that tax liability attached at the time the option was exercised in 1968. The court's valuation of the option was based on the consideration paid by Pope & Carter for [exercising] its option.]

II.   IMPUTING SON'S INCOME TO CORPORATION

We first examine the government's contention that the sale by Corporation to Son of a one-half interest in the property immediately prior to the exercise of the Pope & Carter option was a sham transaction designed to shift half of Corporation's gain on that impending sale to Son. The government maintains that under the doctrine of Commissioner v. Court Holding Co., 324 U.S. 331 (1945), the district court should have taxed the Corporation on the entire gain from the sale to Pope & Carter. . . .

In the instant case, the district court concluded that the government's *Court Holding* theory was "inapplicable to the factual situation presented in this case," finding that the distribution of the option to Son occurred before a sale of the property was even contemplated, that Son was personally involved to a substantial extent in the development activity which led to the increased value of the Piedmont-Old Ivy properties, and that Son negotiated with Pope & Carter in his own behalf with respect to his interest in the properties. . . . Our review of the record convinces us that there is ample evidence to support the court's factual determinations. We therefore affirm the court's judgment that this transaction was not stricken by *Court Holding*'s selling virus.

In so holding we are not unaware of certain doubts raised by the government concerning the economic reality of the transactions between Corporation and Son. The government correctly notes that the corporation bore all the risks with respect to the zoning action, which was necessary to make the purchase a profitable venture. Son did not actually exercise his option and acquire title to the property until favorable zoning was obtained and the sale to Pope & Carter became a virtual certainty. Furthermore, Corporation actively participated in the negotiations with Pope & Carter which led to the sale of the Piedmont-Old Ivy properties. Son never expended a single cent on the transaction, either in acquiring the option or in exercising it. Indeed, the note Son gave Corporation as payment for the properties was modified shortly after its execution to allow a pass through to Corporation of Pope & Carter's payments to Son. The government further argues that, as a matter of law, the options granted by Corporation to Son were merely continuing offers to sell which did not transfer a present property interest to Son. Were this the case, no property interest would have been transferred from Corporation to Son until after the agreement with Pope & Carter was negotiated and virtually consummated by Corporation. To the extent Son participated in the negotiations before the sale from Father to Son, his activities would have been on behalf of Corporation since Son would have had no interest of his own. In such circumstances, a finding that the sale of Son's interest to Pope & Carter's assignee was made by Son, rather than by Corporation, would be difficult, if not impossible, to support. . . .

Nonetheless, there is other evidence in the record which supports the district court's findings and conclusions. . . . It is absurd to suggest that income may be imputed to the Corporation simply because it negotiated with third parties concerning this disposition *of its own interest* in the property. Instead, the crucial question becomes whether the Corporation "actively participated" in the sale of Son's share of the property. . . .

The court found that at the time the option was granted, Father and Son intended to use the property themselves "for a motel." This finding, supported by evidence in the record, indicates that no sale of the property was contemplated when Son received the property interest reflected by the option. This, in turn, supports the conclusion that the option was not merely a subterfuge designed to conceal Corporation's subsequent sale of the entire property, but instead was intended to pass an interest to Son which Son, and not Corporation, later disposed of in the sale to Pope & Carter.

The court's determination that Son, rather than Corporation, negotiated with respect to Son's interest in the property is further supported by evidence that Son was personally involved to a substantial extent in the development activity which led to the increased value of the properties. The district court found that these efforts were attributable to Son's belief that he had an interest in the property. The fact that Son had previously treated the option as constituting a personal property interest and had relied on this personal interest in developing the Piedmont-Old Ivy tracts strongly suggests that when Son later participated in the negotiations with Pope & Carter, he also did so in his own behalf. The prior treatment of a transaction by the parties is a relevant consideration, which in this case, supports the finding that Son, and not Corporation, negotiated with Pope & Carter with respect to Son's interest in the property.

In sum, we are not persuaded that the transactions at issue must necessarily be characterized as a sham, as less than bona fide, or as, "in substance," a sale by Corporation. . . . Accordingly, we affirm the court's decision not to impute income from that sale to Corporation under the *Court Holding* rationale.

III. The Option: Arm's-Length Transaction or Constructive Dividend?

Our conclusion that income from the sale of Son's interest in the Piedmont-Old Ivy property is not imputable to Corporation under *Court Holding* requires us to examine the government's alternative theory that the ascertainable value of property conferred by Corporation on Son without adequate consideration is taxable to Father as a constructive dividend. The district court substantially agreed with this theory and held that Father received a constructive dividend when Corporation granted the option to Son in 1966 and amended it in 1967. However, finding that the value of the option was not ascertainable in 1966 or 1967, the court deferred recognition of the dividend and liability for the tax until Son exercised his option in 1968. The court then valued the option with reference to the consideration paid by Pope & Carter for monthly extensions of its option.

Our review of the court's holding involves several distinct inquiries. In subsection III(A) we discuss why, as a general matter, the district court was correct in refusing to assume at once that a transaction between a corporation and the sole shareholder's son was an arm's-length transaction. We then consider in subsection III(B) whether constructive dividend treatment was warranted in this case. Finally, in subsection III(C) we examine the district court's valuation of the constructive dividend. . . .

A. JUDICIAL SCRUTINY OF TRANSACTIONS BETWEEN CLOSELY HELD CORPORATIONS AND THEIR SHAREHOLDERS: A GENERAL DISCUSSION

We begin by considering taxpayers' contention that the option to Son was granted by Corporation at a fair price in an arm's-length transaction. According to taxpayers, no tax consequences should attach either to the grant or to the exercise of the option. In taxpayers' view, Son's option should be treated no differently than the option granted to Pope & Carter. We conclude that this argument is untenable. In order to elucidate our views on the oft-perplexing problem of the conferral of benefits on a controlling shareholder by a closely held corporation, we begin with first principles.

Distributions of "property" made by a corporation to a shareholder with respect to its stock are dividends to the extent of the corporation's current and accumulated earnings and profits, . . . and must be included by the shareholder in gross income. [§§301(a), 301(c)(1), and 316.]

In accordance with [the] broad definition of property, dividends may be "in cash or in kind, and may also result when the corporation makes a 'bargain sale' of its property to the shareholder at less than fair market value. When there is a 'bargain sale,' the shareholder receives a dividend in the amount of the difference between the fair market value and the price paid for the corporate property. . . ." Green v. United States, 460 F.2d 412, 419 (5th Cir. 1972). As the Supreme Court has recognized, "a sale, if for substantially less than the value of the property sold, may be as effective a means of distributing profits among stockholders as the formal declaration of a dividend." Palmer v. Commissioner, 302 U.S. 63 (1937). No such formal declaration is required for a shareholder to be charged with a constructive dividend. Crosby v. United States, 496 F.2d 1384 (5th Cir. 1974).

Two other guiding principles require mention at this stage. It is clear that the intent of the parties does not govern the characterization of a distribution. Instead, courts have looked to the economic *effect* of the transaction at issue in determining the existence of a dividend. It is also well settled that a dividend does not escape taxation "simply because it fails to pass through the hands of the particular taxpayer when . . . the dividend is diverted at the behest of the shareholder into the hands of others." Green v. United States, supra, 460 F.2d at 419, quoting Sammons v. United States, 433 F.2d 728, 730 (5th Cir. 1970), cert. denied, 402 U.S. 945 (1971). . . .

These expansive principles governing the treatment of constructive dividends reflect an awareness by Congress and the courts of the ingenious methods which have been devised by owners of closely held corporations trying to escape taxes at the corporate or shareholder level. . . . As a consequence, courts have generally examined dealings between a closely held corporation and its shareholders or relatives of shareholders with a jaundiced eye and microscopic vision. Such transactions are simply not entitled to the presumption that they are conducted at arm's length. Indeed, they call for special scrutiny. We suggest that the metaphor of a corporation and its sole shareholder walking arm-in-arm is more descriptive of reality than the vision of the corporation and shareholder holding each other apart at arm's length. . . .

B. THE GRANT OF THE OPTION AS A CONSTRUCTIVE DIVIDEND

Our inquiry is in two parts. First, we must focus on whether, in fact, the grant of the option conferred a benefit on Son by distributing valuable rights without consideration. If we determine that the option conferred such a benefit, we must then examine whether the resulting corporate distribution constituted a constructive dividend to Father. . . .

1. The Option: Valuable Rights or Fair Bargain?

Our initial task of valuing the option to determine whether the corporation distributed valuable rights to Son is greatly complicated by the unsettled state of the law in this area. Neither the Code nor the applicable case law provides clear guidance. Taxpayers maintain that under the Supreme Court's decision in Palmer v. Commissioner, 302 U.S. 63 (1937), there is no dividend if the exercise price of the option represents the fair market value of the underlying property at the time the option is issued, even if the value of the underlying property has appreciated greatly by the time the option is exercised. Taxpayers argue that the $100,000 exercise price of the option on the combined properties was a reasonable valuation of the fair market value of those properties at the time the option was granted to Son. Thus, according to taxpayers, no valuable rights constituting a dividend were distributed by Corporation.

The government responds first that taxpayer's argument rests on an erroneous reading of *Palmer*, and, second, that the 1954 Code has modified this aspect of the *Palmer* decision in any event. We agree with the government that the position contended for by taxpayers is justified neither by good sense nor by the applicable case law.

The Supreme Court's decision in *Palmer* has been a controversial one. In that case, a corporation distributed options, exercisable for 15 days, to its shareholders, entitling those shareholders to purchase from the corporation portfolio shares in a second corporation. On the date distribution of the option was authorized, the exercise price of the options equaled the market value of the portfolio shares. By the time the options were issued, eight days later, the market value of the portfolio shares had increased considerably.

The Court held first that under the Revenue Act of 1928, a shareholder who is granted an option to purchase portfolio shares is not subject to income tax on the receipt of the option, even though the option itself is valuable. "The mere issue of rights to subscribe and their receipt by stockholders, is not a dividend. No distribution of corporate assets or diminution of the net worth of the corporation results in any practical sense." 58 S. Ct. at 70. The Court then considered whether the shareholders would be taxable upon exercise of their option rights when a spread developed between the option price and the market value of the shares. The Court held that the exercise of these rights does not result in a dividend if the circumstances demonstrate "that distribution of corporate assets, effected by the sale, was not intended to be a means of distributing earnings, and that the price when fixed represented the fair market value of the property to be distributed." Id. at 71. Such a distribution "is not converted into a dividend by the mere circumstance that later, at the time of their delivery to the stockholders, [the assets] have a higher value." Id.

We recognize that this language appears to support taxpayers' contention that because the exercise price of Son's option equaled the fair market value of the property when the option was granted. . . , no dividend should result from either the grant or exercise of the option. The continuing vitality of this aspect of the *Palmer* decision under the 1954 Code, however, is far from self-evident. . . .

The 1954 Code . . . specifies the method for determining the value of a distribution. Under section 301(b)(1)(A), the amount of the distribution is measured by the *fair market value* of the property received. Thus, in the case at bar the amount of the distribution should be measured by the *fair market value* of the option, rather than by the spread between the exercise price and the value of the underlying property at the time of grant. . . . While that spread in some cases may approximate the fair market value of the option, here the duration of the option period and the likelihood of obtaining favorable rezoning must also be considered in determining the option's fair market value. . . . Thus the determination of whether the grant of the option conferred a benefit on Son is governed by the value of the option, rather than by the spread between the exercise price and the value of the underlying property.

Applying this standard, we are in complete agreement with the district court's finding that the rights granted under the option were of great value to Son. The option entitled Son to reap the benefits of the contemplated rezoning without incurring any of the risks associated with the real estate venture. He paid no consideration for his rights. If, during the two and one half year option period the properties appreciated in value, Son would realize a gain. If the value of the property decreased or remained the same, Son would be no worse off. Son was truly in a "heads I win, tails I don't lose" position. This "option privilege" represented valuable property to Son. . . .

Any doubts that Corporation distributed valuable rights to Son when it granted the option are dispelled by comparing Son's option with that received by Pope & Carter. Pope & Carter agreed to pay substantial amounts to keep its option open and, in addition, obligated itself to devote reasonable time and effort to obtaining favorable rezoning. In return it received the right to acquire the property for $500,000, a price far in excess of the fair market value of the property at the time the option was granted. Son's option, on the other hand, remained in effect for a longer period, imposed no obligations on Son, and allowed him to purchase a one-half interest in the property for only $100,000 plus 5 1/2 percent interest. Even if we ignore the fact that the amendment to Son's option, which extended the exercise period for an additional two years without increasing the exercise price, was granted a mere thirteen days before the grant of the Pope & Carter option . . . , it is apparent that in granting the option, Corporation conferred a benefit on Son by distributing valuable rights.

2. The Corporate Distribution: A Constructive Dividend?

Having concluded that Corporation distributed valuable rights to Son, we can easily dispose of taxpayers' contention that the grant of the option should not result in a constructive dividend to Father. . . .

Taxpayers maintain that the option was granted because of Corporation's interest in obtaining the benefit of Son's services. The evidence, however, more than adequately supports the conclusion that the grant of the option primarily served the personal interests of Father in his shareholder capacity. Indeed, taxpayers admit that the option was granted to satisfy the moral obligation of Father to compensate Son for taking advantage of a business opportunity Father had personally discouraged Son from pursuing. . . .

Since we hold that there is no clear error in the findings of the district court, we affirm the district court's conclusion that Father received a constructive dividend from the grant by Corporation to Son of the option on the Piedmont-Old Ivy property.

C. VALUING THE DIVIDEND

The final issue presented by this appeal is whether the district court properly valued Father's constructive dividend. In particular, questions have been raised concerning the district court's use of the consideration paid by Pope & Carter in valuing Son's option. To resolve this issue, we must first examine whether the dividend occurred upon the grant of the option or upon its exercise by Son. If we determine that *grant* of the option constituted a dividend, we must then consider both the district court's finding that the option had no ascertainable value at the time of grant and the Court's subsequent valuation of the option at the time of exercise in 1968. If, on the other hand, the dividend arose only upon Son's *exercise* of the option, we need only consider the proper valuation of the option at that time.

[The court ruled that the taxable event was the grant of the option but that since valuation was impossible at that time, the "open transaction" doctrine was appropriate. See Burnet v. Logan, 283 U.S. 404 (1931). However, the court rejected the district court's reliance on the value of the Pope & Carter option as evidence of the value of Son's option, since the options were different in duration, price and required activity by the optionee.]

Thus in the instant case the option should be valued by subtracting the exercise price of approximately $100,000 from the fair market value of the underlying property when the option was exercised on December 6, 1968. . . . We therefore remand the case to the district court for a redetermination of the value of the constructive dividend taxable to Father.

IV. CONCLUSION

The concepts of imputed income and constructive dividend have been developed to prevent taxpayers from clothing their activities in tax-repellant garb. Both doctrines require courts to look behind the superficial or formal nature of a transaction. Application of these concepts in complicated tax cases involves the difficult task of characterizing elusive transactions. . . .

Here the district court found that Son, rather than Corporation, negotiated and consummated the sale of Son's interest in the Piedmont-Old Ivy property to Pope & Carter and therefore concluded that income from this sale should not be imputed to Corporation. The court also found that valuable rights were distributed by Corporation to Son without business purposes because of Father's position as the controlling shareholder of Corporation and therefore concluded that Father received a constructive dividend from Corporation. These factual determinations are supported by the record, and the court's ultimate conclusions rest on a correct application of the controlling law. These determinations are therefore affirmed. The court, however, failed to apply the proper standard for determining the value of Son's option at the time of exercise and therefore improperly computed the amount of Father's constructive dividend. Accordingly, this portion of the case must be remanded for further proceedings consistent with this opinion. The judgment of the district court is affirmed in part, reversed in part, and remanded in part.

Gilbert v. Commissioner
74 T.C. 60 (1980)

TANNENWALD, Judge.

Respondent determined a deficiency in petitioners' income tax for the year 1975 in the amount of $7,483. The issue for decision is whether a transfer of $20,000 by Jetrol, Inc., to G & H Realty Corp. constituted a constructive dividend to petitioner Gilbert L. Gilbert, the common shareholder of each corporation.

FINDINGS OF FACT . . .

During the years 1974 and 1975, Gilbert was the president and sole shareholder of Jetrol, Inc. (Jetrol), a manufacturing company. He was also, during the first part of 1975, a 50-percent shareholder of G & H Realty Corp. His brother, Henry Gilbert (Henry), was the other 50-percent shareholder. G & H Realty Corp. (Realty) owned the building at 27 Lois Street, Rochester, N.Y., in which Jetrol conducted its business as a tenant. Jet Rochester, Inc., another manufacturing company, occupied the balance of the premises. Henry was the sole shareholder of Jet Rochester, Inc., until February 1975, at which time he sold all his stock to two former employees unrelated to Gilbert.

During 1975, Henry and Gilbert decided to redeem Henry's stock in Realty because Henry wanted to retire. Henry had no legal restrictions as to whom he could sell his stock nor was there ever a contractual relationship between Gilbert and Henry obligating Gilbert to purchase the stock. The parties have stipulated that Realty did not have sufficient funds to redeem the stock.

Realty attempted to borrow $20,000 from Central Trust Co. (the bank) in Rochester, N.Y., but the bank was unwilling to loan the funds to Realty. The bank might have considered refinancing the mortgage on Realty's property, but that would have involved an appraisal, a higher interest rate, and related problems which would have delayed the redemption, and

Henry was in a hurry. The bank was willing to loan, and did loan, $20,000 to Jetrol on April 9, 1975, with Gilbert personally guaranteeing the loan.

On April 17, 1975, Jetrol transferred the same $20,000 to Realty, which forthwith used the money to redeem all of its stock owned by Henry. The check from Jetrol to Realty had the words "Loan to G & H Realty" typed on its face. The $20,000 was recorded on the books of account of Jetrol as a loan receivable and on the books of Realty as a loan payable. No note or other indicia of indebtedness was executed by Realty. No rate of interest was stated on the "loan" between Jetrol and Realty to Jetrol. The $20,000 was carried on the books of account of the two corporations until Realty furnished the $20,000 to Jetrol in 1977. . . .

Jetrol's business was growing in 1975 and subsequently. It needed room to expand its facilities, preferably at 27 Lois Street. Jet Rochester operated in the building on annual leases with Realty, effective February 1, 1975, and February 1, 1976. In December 1976, Gilbert sent Jet Rochester a letter stating that he would not renew the lease in 1977 because Jetrol needed the space. Jet Rochester vacated the building around April 1977, at which time Jetrol began to occupy the entire building.

Later in 1977, Gilbert contracted to sell all of the capital stock of Jetrol to the Pantasote Co. (Pantasote). As part of the purchase agreement, Gilbert guaranteed payment of the obligations owed by Realty to Jetrol. Pantasote would not close the sale until the Realty "loan" was off the books. On August 12, 1977, Gilbert borrowed money from the bank and "loaned" it to Realty. Realty used the money to repay Jetrol, without interest, on August 15, 1977. Thereafter, Jetrol repaid its bank loan. Following the sale of Jetrol to Pantasote, Gilbert repaid his note at the bank.

As of December 31, 1975, Jetrol had accumulated earnings and profits of $127,310.

OPINION

It is well established that transfer between related corporations can result in constructive dividends to their common shareholder if they were made primarily for his benefit and if he received a direct or tangible benefit therefrom. Schwartz v. Commissioner, 69 T.C. 877, 884 (1978); Rapid Electric Co. v. Commissioner, 61 T.C. 232, 239 (1973). However, if the transfer represents a bona fide loan or, even though not a loan, if the benefit to the shareholder is indirect or derivative in nature, there is no constructive dividend. Joseph Lupowitz Sons, Inc. v. Commissioner, 497 F.2d 862, 868 (3d Cir. 1974). . . . The issues of existence of a loan or the nature of the benefit to the shareholder are issues of fact and turn upon the circumstances of the particular case. See Schwartz v. Commissioner, supra at 884. The burden of proof is on the petitioners. Welch v. Helvering, 290 U.S. 111 (1933); Rule 142(a), Tax Court Rules of Practice and Procedure.

Petitioners argue that the transfer at issue constituted a bona fide loan, thereby negating respondent's determination of a dividend. The critical question in resolving this issue is whether there was a genuine intention to create a debt, which, in turn, depends upon weighing such objective factors as reasonable expectation of repayment and the economic reality of the claimed debtor-creditor relationship. Litton Business Systems, Inc. v. Commissioner, 61 T.C. 367, 377 (1973).

Petitioners rely on Gilbert's testimony that a loan was intended. They further point to the facts that the transfer was consistently treated as a loan on the books of account and balance sheets of both corporations and that the check issued by Jetrol to Realty included a notation that it was a loan. More importantly, they contend that the subsequent repayment of the amount transferred demonstrates that it was a valid debt of Realty. Finally, they claim that since Pantasote treated the transfer as a debt (after examining Jetrol's books), so should we. Respondent replies that, since there was no note, no stated interest nor interest paid, no security given, no repayment schedule nor a fixed repayment date, it was not a bona fide debt.

We agree with respondent that, on the facts revealed by the record . . . , no real indebtedness was created. The factors that petitioners argue establish an intent to repay are not convincing. "Such allegedly objective economic indicia of debt such as consistent bookkeeping and consistent financial reporting on balance sheets are in our opinion little more than additional declarations of intent, without any accompanying objective economic indicia of debt." Alterman Foods, Inc. v. United States, 505 F.2d 873, 879 (5th Cir. 1974). See also Dean v. Commissioner, 57 T.C. 32, 44 (1971). These declarations of intent must be viewed with some diffidence unless supported by objective factors demonstrating economic reality.

The fact that the advance was repaid, at Pantasote's insistence, prior to the closing of the sale of Gilbert's stock in Jetrol, is also not determinative of the parties' intent at the time the initial transfer was made. The lapse of some 2 1/2 years between the transfer and the sale diminishes any inference which might be drawn from repayment. The repayment demand may merely have been a negotiating tactic which affected Pantasote's net purchase price by extinguishing Jetrol's very real debt to the bank. Moreover, the manner in which repayment occurred, with Gilbert effectively taking Jetrol's place by borrowing the money to enable funds to be applied for the repayment of Jetrol's debt to the bank, tends to indicate that Realty was never really expected to repay Jetrol.

It is true that, in other contexts, we have minimized the importance of some of the factors relied on by respondent. For example, it is clear that a valid debt may exist even where no formal debt instrument exists. Joseph Lupowitz Sons, Inc. v. Commissioner, supra. In fact, the existence of a debt instrument in this context would be of little weight without the accompaniment of other factors. Litton Business Systems, Inc. v. Commissioner, 61 T.C. at 378. Similarly, the absence of interest on such a debt is not determinative. Joseph Lupowitz Sons, Inc. v. Commissioner, supra. We think the absence of interest significant in the instant case, however, because Jetrol borrowed the same money at interest and we see no business purpose for it to have subsidized Realty by "loaning" the same funds without requiring the payment of at least an equivalent rate of interest. Moreover, Realty did not have funds of its own to accomplish the redemption, and the record is devoid of any evidence of the likelihood that it would have funds available to repay at a later date funds "borrowed" for this purpose. Finally, although the other factors relied upon by respondent have not been considered significant in other cases where different fact situations existed, we are not disposed to treat them so lightly here. In short, petitioners have failed to convince us that at the time Realty received the money from Jetrol it intended to repay it. Thus, they have not carried their burden of proving the transfer gave rise to a bona fide debt.

We now turn to the question whether, since no valid indebtedness was created, Gilbert realized a constructive dividend from the transfer. It is clear that neither the finding of an indebtedness nor the mere existence of common ownership is per se determinative that the common shareholder realized a dividend. See Joseph Lupowitz Sons, Inc. v. Commissioner, 497 F.2d 868; Rushing v. Commissioner, 52 T.C. at 893-894. The test is usually the existence of a direct versus indirect benefit (see Rapid Electric Co. v. Commissioner, 61 T.C. at 239) which in turn usually depends upon the existence of a business purpose on the part of the corporate transferor. See and compare Kuper v. Commissioner, 533 F.2d 152 (5th Cir. 1976), rev'g 61 T.C. 624 (1974). Petitioners' argument that it was in Jetrol's interest to consolidate ownership of its landlord in friendly hands (due to planned expansion) does not withstand scrutiny. There is no evidence that the relationship between Gilbert and his brother, Henry, was unfriendly or that Jetrol would have encountered any difficulties if Henry had remained as a 50-percent shareholder of Realty. Moreover, we note that Gilbert testified that it would only have cost Jetrol $10,000 to $12,000 to move, including the costs of reinstallation. To have obligated itself for $20,000 (as it is claimed Realty did) to save such expense seems, to put it mildly, a lack of economic sense. Thus, any business purpose which may have been involved is simply too tenuous to be recognized. See Sammons v. Commissioner, 472 F.2d 449, 452 (5th Cir. 1972). . . .

But the absence of business purpose is not necessarily determinative that a constructive dividend occurred. Such a purpose merely refutes, or relegates to the status of incidental or indirect, any benefit to the common shareholder of the two corporations. Obviously, the primary purpose of the transfer in question herein was to redeem Henry's Realty stock, thus making Gilbert the sole shareholder of Realty. Since the funds with which such redemption was made represented fresh funds to Realty, they clearly enhanced the value of Gilbert's Realty stock (even though they were paid

out) if not offset by an equivalent liability, and such enhancement could
be considered a constructive dividend. Since we have found that no valid
indebtedness from Realty to Jetrol was created, there was no such offsetting
liability at the corporate level.

Gilbert, however, personally guaranteed the loan of Jetrol and thus
had a contingent liability to the bank. Under the circumstances of this
case, we think that this potential offset should not be taken into account.
According to Gilbert, the bank was unwilling to make the loan to Realty
unless the mortgage was refinanced. There is nothing in the record to
indicate that the possibility of an unsecured loan to Realty with a personal
guaranty by Gilbert would have been acceptable. On the other hand, the
bank was willing to make the loan to Jetrol, albeit with the requirement
of a personal guaranty by Gilbert. Gilbert testified that Jetrol was an expanding and fast growing business, and the balance sheets of Jetrol, as well
as its subsequent acquisition of additional space, confirm this evaluation.
From the foregoing, we infer that the bank looked to the primary obligor
(Jetrol) for repayment and that Gilbert's guaranty was in effect simply a
means of protecting the bank if its expectations were not capable of being
realized. The fact that Gilbert personally borrowed the funds utilized to
repay the bank at the time of the Pantasote transaction, some 2 1/2 years
later, has little significance. . . . The reasons for handling the repayment
in the manner set forth in our findings of fact are not revealed in the
record. Based upon the foregoing, we are of the opinion that Gilbert's
contingent liability as a guarantor, as of February 1975, lacked sufficient
substance to warrant taking it into account determining whether Gilbert
received a constructive dividend from Jetrol at that time; at the very least,
petitioners have not carried their burden of proving otherwise. . . .

In sum, the benefits to Gilbert in 1975 were straightforward. He was
able to obtain sole ownership of Realty without reducing the value of his
interest in Realty's assets . . . and without investing additional personal
funds which would have been subordinated to Realty's mortgage debt.
Moreover, he was able to use Jetrol's borrowing power to obtain control
of Realty. See Rapid Electric Co. v. Commissioner, 61 T.C. at 239. Realty
was unable to accomplish the redemption itself. It is Gilbert's use of Jetrol's
earnings and profits for a primarily personal and noncorporate motive of
Jetrol that is critical and causes such use to be a constructive dividend to
him.

Decision will be entered for the respondent.

NOTES

1. *Shareholders' loans that may not be bona fide.* In Jacques v. Commissioner, 935 F.2d 104 (6th Cir. 1991), the taxpayer claimed that the proceeds received from the corporation were a loan which he intended to

repay. The Tax Court found a dividend for federal tax purposes even though under state law no dividend distribution was permitted. Conversely, in Rev. Rul. 90-11, 1990-1 C.B. 10, the Service ruled that the adoption of a "poison pill" plan did not constitute a dividend for federal tax purposes even though the adoption of a plan was a dividend under state law.

In *Jacques,* the taxpayer did not repay the purported loans. Would repayment be conclusive proof that a loan was made? See *Crowley v. Commissioner,* 962 F.2d 1077 (1st Cir. 1992) (withdrawals by a minority shareholder treated as constructive dividend rather than a loan, even though some repayments were made because of unrestricted withdrawal privilige).

In Alterman Foods v. United States, 611 F.2d 866 (Cl. Ct. 1979), a corporate parent was saddled with dividend treatment on "advances" from its subsidiaries. Under the then applicable version of §243, the taxpayer was taxable on 15 percent of the constructive dividends. Among the factors relied on by the court were the paucity of historical dividends despite strong earnings and profits; the lack of a specified interest rate, promissory note, limit on the advances, or collateral; and a pattern of "advances" with no repayment from 57 subsidiaries. Compare Tollefsen v. Commissioner, 431 F.2d 511 (2d Cir. 1970), in which advances by a subsidiary to the controlling shareholder of the parent were treated as a dividend by the parent to the shareholder and not as a bona fide loan, with Gilbert v. Commissioner, 552 F.2d 478 (2d Cir. 1977), in which a bona fide loan was found because of clear intent to repay and because the prompt assignment of assets given were sufficient to secure the amounts owed.

2. *Shareholders' loans with below-market interest rates.* Suppose a corporation makes a bona fide loan to its shareholder but charges no interest.[3] In Dean v. Commisisoner, 35 T.C. 1083 (1961), the court found no income to the borrower since any imputed income would be offset with an interest deduction. Section 7872 substantially alters the *Dean* rule. When the loan is a demand loan, the shareholder-borrower is deemed to have received a dividend of imputed interest, which in turn is repaid to the corporation-lender. For the borrower, there may be a wash if the interest is deductible. But see §265. Also consider §163(h), which denies a deduction in many instances for interest incurred for personal rather than business or investment purposes. For the lender, the dividend is not deductible, but the deemed interest received must be included in income each year the loan is outstanding.

If the loan is a term loan, the shareholder-borrower will be deemed to have received the difference between the loan principal and the present value of the payments due under the loan as a dividend. In accordance with the original issue discount rules of §§1271-1273, the borrower is entitled to deduct the imputed interest over the term of the loan. The mirror image

---

3. The fact that there is no interest may count against "loan" characterization, but it is not conclusive. Thus, a "no-interest loan" is not a self-contradictory phenomenon.

governs the corporation-lender. It is deemed to have made a dividend payment in the first year and to receive taxable interest payments over the life of the loan.

3. *Bargain sale or purchase between corporation and shareholder.* The bargain purchase in *Baumer* was the purchase for $10 (which may never have been paid) for an option worth more than $10. How much more?

Suppose someone offers to sell you an option to buy property that has a fair market value of $100. The option has an exercise price of $70 and has a duration of five minutes. Chances are you will pay up to $30 for the option. Suppose, instead, the exercise price is $100. You would probably pay nothing for this option since it will cost you $100 if you choose to exercise it. In Palmer v. Commissioner, 302 U.S. 63, 71 (1937), the Supreme Court broadly stated: "The mere issue of rights to subscribe and their receipt by stockholders, is not a dividend." The court also ruled that the later exercise of the option when the property had appreciated in value was not a dividend. In *Palmer* there was no spread between exercise price and fair market value of the property at the time the option was issued. Moreover, the option period was only 15 days. *Palmer* was limited to its facts by Commissioner v. Gordon, 391 U.S. 83, 90 n.4 (1968), in which the Court stated: "It has not . . . been authoritively settled whether an issue of rights to purchase at less than fair market value itself constitutes a dividend, or the dividend occurs on the actual purchase." In Redding v. Commissioner, 630 F.2d 1169, 1182 (7th Cir. 1980), the court ruled that *Palmer* had been overruled by the enactment in 1954 of the "corporate distribution provisions as a whole" in circumstances in which there was a spread when the option was granted.

Suppose instead that there is no spread between the exercise price and the fair market value of the property, but the duration of the option is two years — the *Baumer* situation. Now is the option worth something? Suppose you pay $20 for the option. If the property decreases in value, you will not exercise the option and will not recoup your $20. If the property increases in value — say, to $200 — you will pay the $100 exercise price, ending up with an $80 profit. The longer the option period, the more valuable the option is. Is anything left of *Palmer* after *Redding* and *Baumer*?

In *Baumer* why wasn't the option taxable to the shareholder when issued rather than when exercised? On remand the district court did conclude that the option should be taxed in the year of receipt. This conclusion meant victory for the taxpayer since that year was not before the court. 518 F. Supp. 813 (N.D. Ga. 1981). The taxpayer's celebration was short-lived as the court of appeals again reversed, holding the law of the case dictated the use of the open transaction method. The district court was directed to find a dividend in the amount by which the fair market value at the time of exercise exceeded the exercise price. 685 F.2d 1318 (11th Cir. 1982). This reversal by the Eleventh Circuit is limited to the law of

the case and does not suggest that in future cases the dividend consequences won't be determined in the year in which the option is granted
if valuation is possible. See generally Jassy, Dividend Treatment of Distributions of Options to Acquire Assets of the Distributing Corporation, 34 Tax
L. Rev. 607 (1979).

If *Baumer* had been decided under current law, would the distributing
corporation have been taxed on the distribution of the option? See
§311(b). If the distributing corporation should be taxed, when should it
be taxed? How and when should the earnings and profits account be
adjusted? In light of §311(b), would the Service need to rely on the *Court
Holding Co.* doctrine?

In Martin Ice Cream Co. v. Commissioner, 110 T.C. 189 (1998), the
court refused to attribute a shareholder sale of property received as a
dividend to the distributing corporation under the *Court Holding Co.* doctrine, but found the corporation taxable under §311(b) on the distribution
of the appreciated property to the shareholder.

Note that in *Baumer* the father was taxed even though the option was
granted to the son. In Green v. United States, 460 F.2d 412 (5th Cir. 1972),
a bargain element in a sale to the children of a shareholder-officer was
held taxable to him even though he was a minority shareholder because
he exerted substantial influence over the transaction.

Honigman v. Commissioner, 466 F.2d 412 (5th Cir. 1972), serves as a
reminder that shareholders dealing with closely held corporations tread
on dangerous ground. There, the shareholder was taxed on the difference
between the actual purchase price and the court-determined fair market
value on the corporation's distribution of a deteriorating hotel. At trial
evidence was introduced that there was no other buyer, the purchasing
shareholder was not in control of the corporation and there was a valid
business reason for the sale.

The flip side of the bargain purchase is the inflated sale to a controlled
corporation. In Pizzarelli v. Commissioner, 40 T.C.M. 156 (1980), the
shareholder was taxed on a dividend when he purchased property for
$20,000 in 1969 and sold it in 1970 to the corporation for $70,000 with
no apparent reason for the sudden appreciation.

4. *Transfers between commonly controlled corporations.* Suppose *A* owns
all the stock of *X* Corp. and *Y* Corp. If *X* Corp. makes a purported loan
to *Y* Corp. in circumstances suggesting that the funds are not to be repaid,
how should the transaction be treated? Since *X* Corp. owns no stock of *Y*
Corp., the transfer does not seem to be a distribution by *X* Corp. "with
respect to its stock" to *Y* Corp. When transfers between commonly controlled corporations are recharacterized, there is a deemed distribution to
the shareholder from one corporation followed by a deemed contribution
of the property or cash by the shareholder to the other corporation. The
analysis in *Gilbert* is typical of these cases. Often the court will first deter-

mine whether there was a bona fide intercorporate loan. If not, did the intercorporate contribution to capital have a business purpose, or did it promote the taxpayer's personal goals?

Compare Sammons v. Commissioner, 472 F.2d 449 (5th Cir. 1972) (a transfer by a parent corporation of funds to its nearly insolvent subsidiary so that the subsidiary could pay off the debt owed to the parent's controlling shareholder was a dividend to the shareholder since the purpose was to benefit the shareholder rather than the transferor), with Rapid Electric Co. v. Commissioner, 61 T.C. 232 (1974) (the extension of credit between two commonly owned corporations was held not a dividend to the sole shareholder because the transfer was beneficial for the transferor corporation's purposes).

In Stinnett's Pontiac Service v. Commissioner, 730 F.2d 634 (11th Cir. 1984), the court found that a purported intercorporate loan from an automobile dealership to a Bahamian corporation constituted a constructive dividend to the common shareholder. The loan was unsecured and subordinated and had no terms of repayment. Furthermore the court could discern no corporate purpose behind the loan. See also Sparks Nugget, Inc. v. Commissioner, 458 F.2d 631 (9th Cir. 1972) (excessive rent paid between commonly controlled corporations taxable to controlling shareholder).

5.   *Unreasonable salaries or fees.* The allowance for a reasonable salary deduction under §162 has been interpreted by the IRS and the courts to disallow, by inference, a deduction for any portion of salaries deemed excessive. Such excessive salaries may be reclassified as dividends if, as is often the case, the employee is also a shareholder and there are sufficient earnings and profits. What happens if there are insufficient earnings and profits? See Note 8 infra. In Charles McCandless Tile Service v. United States, 422 F.2d 1336 (Cl. Ct. 1970), the Court of Claims found that even reasonable salaries could be reclassified as dividends if the distributing corporation was profitable and had not made dividend distributions. In Laure v. Commissioner, 70 T.C. 1087 (1978), the Tax Court rejected the *McCandless* reasoning and upheld a large salary deduction even in the absence of dividends for an 18-year period. See also Rev. Rul. 79-8, 1979-1 C.B. 92 (insubstantial dividends alone do not cause denial of §162 deduction); Elliots, Inc. v. Commissioner, 716 F.2d 1241 (9th Cir. 1983) (*McCandless* rejected).

Shareholders sometimes contractually commit themselves to repay amounts deemed excessive by the IRS. Their hope is that if the salary is held to be a dividend, the repayment of such amounts to the corporation will be a business expense deduction covered by §162. In Oswald v. Commissioner, 49 T.C. 645 (1976), under a corporate by-law a shareholder-officer was so obligated and was permitted a deduction. But in Pahl v. Commissioner, 67 T.C. 286 (1976), there was no *Oswald* contract provision requiring repayment; the excess salary was deemed a disguised dividend, and the repayment was labeled a capital contribution increasing basis.

Sometimes corporations try to use fee payments, rather than salaries, in lieu of dividends to distribute earnings in a manner that provides a §162 deduction. In Tulia Feedlot v. United States, 513 F.2d 800 (5th Cir. 1975), a corporation paid its directors a fee for guaranteeing a corporate loan; the guarantees were made by the director-shareholders in proportion to their stock ownership. The Court held this to be a constructive dividend, nondeductible by the corporation because no evidence was presented to show guarantors' fees were customary in the trade or that the fees were reasonable in amount. See also Olton Feed Yard v. United States, 592 F.2d 272 (5th Cir. 1979) (same result). In a later year and in a different jurisdiction, however, the same company prevailed when the fees were shown to be customary and were paid in proportion to the guarantees rather than the amount of stock owned. Tulia Feedlot v. United States, 52 A.F.T.R.2d 5702 (Cl. Ct. 1983).

6. *Corporate payment of expenses incurred to benefit the stockholder rather than the corporation.* Sometimes a controlling shareholder will cause a corporation to pay his personal expenses in the hope that the corporation can deduct what the shareholder cannot. In these situations, the courts look to see if the payment benefits "primarily" the corporation or the taxpayer. In American Properties v. Commissioner, 262 F.2d 150 (9th Cir. 1958), it was held that the expenses of designing, constructing, and racing speed boats, paid by a one-person corporation, were not deductible under §162(a) by the corporation and constituted disguised dividends to the sole shareholder, who "had an insatiable desire for speed." In Magnon v. Commissioner, 73 T.C. 980 (1980), the sole shareholder received a constructive dividend when the corporation performed electrical contracting services on the shareholder's personal property.

In Dolese v. United States, 605 F.2d 1146 (10th Cir. 1979), payments by a corporation for legal fees and expenses in connection with a divorce of its sole shareholder were deemed constructive dividends. Those payments incurred to fight divorce proceedings that interrupted corporate business were, however, treated as a deductible expense by the corporation with no dividend treatment to the shareholder. But see Jack's Maintenance Contractors v. Commissioner, 703 F.2d 154 (5th Cir. 1983) (dividend to shareholder where corporation incurred legal expenses in defending shareholder against criminal tax evasion charges; benefit to shareholder far outweighed benefit to corporation).

When a court finds a constructive dividend, what is the measure of inclusion? See Ireland v. United States, 621 F.2d 731 (5th Cir. 1980) (amount of dividend from personal use of company plane based on private charter fare, not cost of operation).

7. *Excessive compensation paid to the relatives of shareholders.* Section 162(a)(2) allows a corporation to deduct "a reasonable allowance for sala-

ries or other compensation for personal services actually rendered." Suppose X Corp. is a family-owned corporation whose shareholders are Mom and Pop. Suppose X Corp. compensates Son and Daughter as though they were full-time employees when in fact they perform only minor services for the corporation during vacations. Why might the family choose to distribute corporate earnings in this fashion? How should the payments be treated? In this and similar cases, the transaction will be recharacterized as a dividend payment to Mom or Pop or both, followed by a gift from the shareholder(s) to Son and Daughter. See, e.g., Duffey v. Lethert, 316 F.2d 473 (D. Minn. 1963) (corporate "compensation" to sister of shareholder treated as dividend to shareholder when sister performed only occasional services). Note that in addition to possible dividend treatment, shareholders may have gift tax treatment on the deemed gift.

Should the corporation or shareholders that participate in the diversion of corporate assets to nonworking employees be subject to civil or criminal fraud penalties? Does it matter if the corporation is wholly owned by the shareholders causing the diversion or whether there are outside shareholders?

8. *Constructive dividends and earnings and profits.* Suppose a taxpayer diverts corporate funds for personal use. Normally, there would be dividend consequences to the shareholder. But what is the result if the corporation has no current or accumulated earnings and profits? In Truesdell v. Commissioner, 89 T.C. 1280 (1987), the taxpayer's withdrawals from the corporation were treated by the Tax Court as constructive distributions. But in the absence of earnings and profits, the distributions were not taxable to the taxpayer. The court in *Truesdell* distinguished a nontaxable diversion from an *unlawful* diversion that is taxable regardless of the earnings and profits account. See, e.g., Leaf v. Commissioner, 33 T.C. 1093 (1960), aff'd per curiam, 295 F.2d 503 (6th Cir. 1961).

In Di Zenzo v. Commissioner, 348 F.2d 122 (2d Cir. 1965), the court ruled that the taxpayer (the sole shareholder) had no dividend and no §61 income in the absence of earnings and profits. See also Simon v. Commissioner, 248 F.2d 869 (8th Cir. 1957). For a holding to the contrary, see United States v. Miller, 545 F.2d 1204 (9th Cir 1976), in which the existence of earnings and profits was held not necessary in criminal fraud proceedings against taxpayer (not the sole shareholder) diverting corporate monies to himself. Can the cases be distinguished on the basis of whether funds were unlawfully diverted from another person, either another shareholder or a creditor? When a sole shareholder diverts funds from a corporation with no earnings and profits, who is the victim so long as no obligation to a creditor is breached? How is the shareholder enriched?

In Hagaman v. Commissioner, 958 F.2d 684 (6th Cir. 1992), the court affirmed the tax court's determination that a corporation should reduce its accumulated earnings and profits by the amount of constructive dividends deemed paid to the shareholders. The constructive dividends consisted of the fraudulent diversion of vending-machine receipts and rental payments.

PROBLEMS

4-4. *T* is a shareholder of *X* Corp., a "start-up" company producing computer software. In its early years, *X* Corp. has experienced large research and development expenses. *X* Corp. makes an interest-free loan of $100,000 to *A*, its sole shareholder, payable on demand by *X* Corp. Discuss the tax consequences to both *X* Corp. and *T*.

4-5. *X* Corp., with a $5,000 earnings and profits deficit in year 1, issues to *B*, a shareholder, an option to buy a parcel of real estate at a price of $1,000, the property's fair market value and basis. The option has a three-year duration. In year 3, *B* exercises the option. At the time of exercise, the real estate had a fair market value of $3,000. *X* Corp. has no accumulated earnings and profits at the end of year 2 and no current earnings and profits in year 3. Discuss the tax consequences.

4-6. *A* owns all the stock in *X* Corp. and *Y* Corp. Each corporation runs a restaurant. *X* Corp. makes a $100,000 loan to *Y* Corp. Discuss the tax consequences.

4-7. *X* Corp. rents land from *A*, its sole shareholder, at an annual rental of $2,400, the fair rental value. The lease has a 10-year duration, and there are no renewal options. In year 5, *X* Corp. constructs a building on the property at a cost to *X* Corp. of $50,000. The building has a 20-year useful life, and the lease provides that all improvements made by the lessee revert to the lessor at the termination of the lease. At the end of the lease term, *A* enters into another lease with *X* Corp. at an annual rental of $3,600, the fair rental value for land and building. Is there a constructive dividend? When? Consider the applicability of §§109 and 1019. See Safeway Steel Scaffolds Co. v. United States, 590 F.2d 1360 (5th Cir. 1979).

D. INTERCORPORATE DIVIDENDS

Litton Industries, Inc. v. Commissioner _____
89 T.C. 1086 (1987)

CLAPP, Judge. Respondent determined a deficiency in petitioner's Federal corporate income tax for the year ended July 29, 1973 in the amount of $11,583,054. After concessions, the issue for decision is whether Litton Industries received a $30,000,000 dividend from Stouffer Corporation, its wholly owned subsidiary, or whether that sum represented proceeds from the sale of Stouffer stock to Nestle Corporation.

FINDINGS OF FACT

. . . On October 4, 1967, petitioner acquired all the outstanding stock of Stouffer Corporation (Stouffer), a corporation whose common stock was listed and traded on the New York stock exchange. Stouffer manufactured and sold frozen prepared food and operated hotels and food management services and restaurants. . . .

In early 1972, Charles B. Thornton (Thornton), the chairman of Litton's board of directors, Joseph Imirie, president of Stouffer, and James Biggar, an executive of Stouffer, discussed project "T.I.B.," i.e., the sale of Stouffer. In July 1972, Litton's board of directors discussed the mechanics and problems of selling Stouffer. As of August 1, 1972 Stouffer's accumulated earnings and profits exceeded $30,000,000. On August 23, 1972, Stouffer declared a $30,000,000 dividend which it paid to Litton in the form of a $30,000,000 negotiable promissory note, and at that time, Thornton believed that Litton would have no difficulty in receiving an adequate offer for Stouffer. Two weeks later, on September 7, 1972, petitioner announced publicly its interest in disposing of Stouffer. Subsequent to said announcement, Litton received inquiries from a number of interested sources, including TWA, Green Giant, investment banking houses, and business brokers about the possible purchase of all or part of the Stouffer business.

Beginning in mid-September 1972, Litton and several underwriters discussed the feasibility of a public offering of Stouffer Stock. In early September 1972, Litton negotiated with Lehman Brothers for a public offering of Stouffer stock, but Lehman Brothers decided not to participate in the offering. During October 1972, Litton, Stouffer and Merrill Lynch, a brokerage firm that thought Stouffer had an excellent outlook, prepared a public offering of Stouffer stock. During November 1972, petitioner, Stouffer, and Hornblower and Weeks prepared a partial public offering of Stouffer stock. Merrill Lynch had a policy of not effecting partial distributions of corporate subsidiaries and thus did not participate in the negotiations with Hornblower and Weeks. In mid-December 1972, Litton decided that a complete public offering was preferable and abandoned the idea of a partial public offering. The S-1 Registration Statement, which Stouffer filed with the Securities and Exchange Commission, stated that $30,000,000 of the proceeds would be used to pay the promissory note which Litton received as a dividend.

On March 1, 1973, Nestle Alimentana S.A. Corporation (Nestle), a Swiss corporation, offered to buy all of Stouffer's stock for $105,000,000. On March 5, 1973, Nestle paid Litton $74,962,518 in cash for all the outstanding stock of Stouffer and $30,000,000 in cash for the promissory note. Because Litton sold Stouffer to Nestle, the underwriters stopped work on the scheduled public offering.

OPINION

The issue for decision is whether the $30,000,000 dividend declared by
Stouffer on August 23, 1972, and paid to its parent, Litton, by means of a
negotiable promissory note was truly a dividend for tax purposes or
whether it should be considered part of the proceeds received by Litton
from the sale of all of Stouffer's stock on March 1, 1973. If, as petitioner
contends, the $30,000,000 constitutes a dividend, petitioner may deduct
85 percent of that amount as a dividend received credit pursuant to section
243(a), as that section read during the year at issue. However, if the
$30,000,000 represents part of the selling price of the Stouffer stock, as
contended by respondent, the entire amount will be added to the proceeds
of the sale and taxed to Litton as additional capital gain. Respondent's
approach, of course produces the larger amount of tax dollars.

The instant case is substantially governed by Waterman Steamship
Corp. v. Commissioner, 50 T.C. 650 (1968), revd. 430 F.2d 1185 (5th Cir.
1970), cert. denied 401 U.S. 939 (1971). Respondent urges us to follow
the opinion of the Fifth Circuit, which in substance adopted the position
of Judge Tannenwald's dissent (concurred in by three other judges) from
our Court-reviewed opinion. If we hold for respondent, we must overrule
our majority opinion in *Waterman Steamship*. Petitioner contends that the
reasoning of the Fifth Circuit in *Waterman Steamship* should not apply since
the facts here are more favorable to petitioner. Additionally, petitioner
points out that several business purposes were served by the distribution
here which provide additional support for recognition of the distribution
as a dividend. For the reasons set forth below, we conclude that the
$30,000,000 distribution constituted a dividend which should be recog-
nized as such for tax purposes. We believe that the facts in the instant case
lead even more strongly than did the facts in *Waterman Steamship* to the
conclusion that the $30,000,000 was a dividend. Accordingly, we hold that
the Stouffer distribution to Litton was a dividend within the meaning of
section 243(a).

In many respects, the facts of this case and those of *Waterman Steamship*
are parallel. The principal difference, and the one which we find to be most
significant, is the timing of the dividend action. In *Waterman Steamship*, the
taxpayer corporation received an offer to purchase the stock of two of its
wholly-owned subsidiary corporations, Pan-Atlantic and Gulf Florida, for
$3,500,000 cash. The board of directors of Waterman Steamship rejected
that offer but countered with an offer to sell the two subsidiaries for
$700,000 after the subsidiaries declared and arranged for payments of
dividends to Waterman Steamship amounting in the aggregate to
$2,800,000. Negotiations between the parties ensued, and the agreements
which resulted therefrom included, in specific detail, provisions for the
declaration of a dividend by Pan-Atlantic to Waterman Steamship prior to

the signing of the sales agreement and the closing of that transaction. Furthermore, the agreements called for the purchaser to loan or otherwise advance funds to Pan-Atlantic promptly in order to pay off the promissory note by which the dividend had been paid. Once the agreement was reached, the entire transaction was carried out by a series of meetings commencing at 12 noon on January 21, 1955, and ending at 1:30 P.M. the same day. At the first meeting the board of directors of Pan-Atlantic met and declared a dividend in the form of a promissory note in the amount of $2,799,820. The dividend was paid by execution and delivery of the promissory note. At 12:30 P.M., the board of directors of the purchaser's nominee corporation ("Securities") met and authorized the purchase and financing of Pan-Atlantic and Gulf Florida. At 1 P.M., the directors of Waterman authorized the sale of all outstanding stock of Pan-Atlantic and Gulf Florida to Securities. Immediately following that meeting, the sales agreement was executed by the parties. The agreement provided that the purchaser guaranteed prompt payment of the liabilities of Pan-Atlantic and Gulf Florida including payment of any notes given by either corporation as a dividend.

Finally at 1:30 P.M., the new board of directors of Pan-Atlantic authorized the borrowing of sufficient funds from the purchaser personally and from his nominee corporation to pay off the promissory note to Waterman Steamship, which was done forthwith. As the Fifth Circuit pointed out, "By the end of the day and within a ninety minute period, the financial cycle had been completed. Waterman had $3,500,000, hopefully tax-free, all of which came from Securities and McLean, the buyers of the stock." 430 F.2d at 1190. This Court concluded that the distribution from Pan-Atlantic to Waterman was a dividend. The Fifth Circuit reversed, concluding that the dividend and sale were one transaction. 430 F.2d at 1192.

The timing in the instant case was markedly different. The dividend was declared by Stouffer on August 23, 1972, at which time the promissory note in payment of the dividend was issued to Litton. There had been some general preliminary discussions about the sale of Stouffer, and it was expected that Stouffer would be a very marketable company which would sell quickly. However, at the time the dividend was declared, no formal action had been taken to initiate the sale of Stouffer. It was not until 2 weeks later that Litton publicly announced that Stouffer was for sale. There ensued over the next 6 months many discussions with various corporations, investment banking houses, business brokers, and underwriters regarding Litton's disposition of Stouffer through sale of all or part of the business to a particular buyer, or through full or partial public offerings of the Stouffer stock. All of this culminated on March 1, 1973, over 6 months after the dividend was declared, with the purchase by Nestle of all of Stouffer's stock. Nestle also purchased the outstanding promissory note for $30,000,000 in cash.

In the instant case, the declaration of the dividend and the sale of the stock were substantially separated in time in contrast to *Waterman Steamship* where the different transactions occurred essentially simultaneously. In *Waterman Steamship*, it seems quite clear that no dividend would have been declared if all of the remaining steps in the transaction had not been lined up in order on the closing table and did not in fact take place. Here, however, Stouffer declared the dividend, issued the promissory note and definitely committed itself to the dividend before even making a public announcement that Stouffer was for sale. Respondent argues that the only way petitioner could ever receive the dividend was by raising revenue through a sale of Stouffer. Therefore, respondent asserts the two events (the declaration of the dividend and then the sale of the company) were inextricably tied together and should be treated as one transaction for tax purposes. In our view, respondent ignores the fact that Stouffer could have raised sufficient revenue for the dividend from other avenues, such as a partial public offering or borrowing. Admittedly, there had been discussions at Litton about the sale of Stouffer which was considered to be a very saleable company. However, there are many slips between the cup and the lip, and it does not take much of a stretch of the imagination to picture a variety of circumstances under which Stouffer might have been taken off the market and no sale consummated. Under these circumstances it is unlikely that respondent would have considered the dividend to be a nullity. On the contrary, it would seem quite clear that petitioner would be charged with a dividend on which it would have to pay a substantial tax. Petitioner committed itself to the dividend and, thereby, accepted the consequences regardless of the outcome of the proposed sale of Stouffer stock. See Crellin v. Commissioner, 17 T.C. 781, 785 (1951), aff'd 203 F.2d 812 (9th Cir. 1953), cert. denied 346 U.S. 873 (1953).

Since the facts here are distinguishable in important respects and are so much stronger in petitioner's favor, we do not consider it necessary to consider further the opinion of the Fifth Circuit in *Waterman Steamship*.

The term "dividend" is defined in section 316(a) as a distribution by a corporation to its shareholders out of earnings and profits. The parties have stipulated that Stouffer had earnings and profits exceeding $30,000,000 at the time the dividend was declared. This Court has recognized that a dividend may be paid by a note. T. R. Miller Mill Co. v. Commissioner, 37 B.T.A. 43, 49 (1938), affd. 102 F.2d 599 (5th Cir. 1939). Based on these criteria, the $30,000,000 distribution by Stouffer would clearly constitute a dividend if the sale of Stouffer had not occurred. We are not persuaded that the subsequent sale of Stouffer to Nestle changes that result merely because it was more advantageous to Litton from a tax perspective.

It is well established that a taxpayer is entitled to structure his affairs and transactions in order to minimize his taxes. This proposition does not give a taxpayer carte blanche to set up a transaction in any form which will avoid tax consequences regardless of whether the transaction has substance. Gregory v. Helvering, 293 U.S. 465 (1935). A variety of factors present here preclude a finding of sham or subterfuge. Although the record in this case clearly shows that Litton intended at the time the dividend was declared to sell Stouffer, no formal action had been taken and no announcement had been made. There was no definite purchaser waiting in the wings with the terms and conditions of sale already agreed upon. At that time, Litton had not even decided upon the form of sale of Stouffer. Nothing in the record here suggests that there was any prearranged sale agreement, formal or informal, at the time the dividend was declared.

Petitioner further supports its argument that the transaction was not a sham by pointing out Litton's legitimate business purposes in declaring the dividend. Although the code and case law do not require a dividend to have a business purpose, it is a factor to be considered in determining whether the overall transaction was a sham. TSN Liquidating Corp. v. United States, 624 F.2d 1328 (5th Cir. 1980). Petitioner argues that the distribution allowed Litton to maximize the gross after-tax amount it could receive from its investment in Stouffer. From the viewpoint of a private purchaser of Stouffer, it is difficult to see how the declaration of a dividend would improve the value of the stock since creating a liability in the form of a promissory note for $30,000,000 would reduce the value of Stouffer by approximately that amount. However, since Litton was considering disposing of all or part of Stouffer through a public or private offering, the payment of a dividend by a promissory note prior to any sale had two advantages. First, Litton hoped to avoid materially diminishing the market value of the Stouffer stock. At that time, one of the factors considered in valuing a stock, and in determining the market value of a stock was the "multiple of earnings" criterion. Payment of the dividend by issuance of a promissory note would not substantially alter Stouffer's earnings. Since many investors were relatively unsophisticated, Litton may have been quite right that it could increase its investment in Stouffer by at least some portion of the $30,000,000 dividend. Second, by declaring a dividend and paying it by a promissory note prior to an anticipated public offering, Litton could avoid sharing the earnings with future additional shareholders while not diminishing to the full extent of the pro rata dividend, the amount received for the stock. Whether Litton could have come out ahead after Stouffer paid the promissory note is at this point merely speculation about a public offering which never occurred. The point, however, is that Litton hoped to achieve some business purpose and not just tax benefits in structuring the transaction as it did.

Under these facts, where the dividend was declared 6 months prior to the sale of Stouffer, where the sale was not prearranged, and since Stouffer had earnings and profits exceeding $30,000,000 at the time the dividend was declared, we cannot conclude that the distribution was merely a device designed to give the appearance of a dividend to a part of the sales proceeds. In this case the form and substance of the transaction coincide; it was not a transaction entered into solely for tax reasons, and it should be recognized as structured by petitioner.

On this record, we hold that for Federal tax purposes Stouffer declared a dividend to petitioner on August 23, 1972, and, subsequently, petitioner sold all of its stock in Stouffer to Nestle for $75,000,000.

Decision will be entered under Rule 155.

NOTES

1. *Impact of dividends-received deduction on corporate shareholders*. In the discussion of disguised dividends at page 134 supra, the taxpayer was trying to disguise a dividend as some other type of transaction. Sometimes the tables are turned, and the taxpayer tries to hide some other transaction as a dividend. In Waterman Steamship Corp. v. Commissioner, 430 F.2d 1185 (5th Cir. 1970), the taxpayer found a purchaser willing to pay $3.5 million for the stock of its subsidiary. The taxpayer, with a basis of $700,000 in the subsidiary's stock, was not thrilled with the prospect of a $2.8 million capital gain. Consequently, the transaction was restructured to have the subsidiary distribute a $2.8 million note as a dividend to taxpayer, followed by a sale of the subsidiary's stock to the purchaser for $700,000. The purchaser was to provide funds to the subsidiary in order to discharge the note. Because of the consolidated return provisions, the dividend, if respected, would have been tax free. See page 525 infra for a discussion of consolidated return provisions.

What were the anticipated tax consequences on the sale and later payment on the note? The Service argued successfully that the purported dividend should be ignored and that the purchaser should be deemed to have paid the full $3.5 million purchase price. Accord, Basic, Inc. v. United States, 549 F.2d 740 (Cl. Ct. 1977). But see TSN Liquidating Co. v. United States, 624 F.2d 1328 (5th Cir. 1980), in which the court refused to recharacterize a dividend of unwanted assets by a subsidiary to its parent even though the purchaser of the subsidiary's stock reinfused the subsidiary with cash following the purchase. Accord, Dynamics Corp. of America v. United States, 449 F.2d 402 (Cl. Ct. 1971) (distribution and sale were unconnected events).

In *Litton Industries*, how did the court distinguish *Waterman Steamship?* Is the distinction convincing if the reason Litton declared the dividend was to decrease its tax liability on its intended sale of stock? What were the so-called business reasons that justified dividend treatment in the court's view?

2. *Debt-financed portfolio stock*. The availability of the dividends-received deduction under §243 presents some tax arbitrage possibilities. For

example, a shareholder-corporation could finance an investment in stock with borrowed funds, thereby enabling it to receive tax-favored dividend income while deducting the interest on the indebtedness. Suppose that stock of Blue Chip Corp. regularly pays dividends of $8 per year on its common stock selling for $100 per share, an 8 percent return. If Investment Corp. can borrow funds at 10 percent interest, should it borrow money to purchase stock of Blue Chip? Suppose Investment Corp. is in the 34 percent bracket and borrows $100 to buy one share of Blue Chip stock. The after-tax cost of borrowing $100 at 10 percent is $6.60 because of the interest deduction. The after-tax return on the $8 dividend is $7.18, assuming a 70 percent dividends-received deduction, thereby resulting in an $.82 tax on the $2.40 that enters taxable income. The pretax losing proposition becomes a $.58 post-tax winner (i.e., $7.18 minus $6.60). Do we want a tax system that encourages purchases that would not be made in the absence of taxes?

In principle, Congress's response to the problem resembles §265, which prohibits an interest deduction for debt incurred to purchase tax-exempt securities. The primary mechanism employed by §246A (primary rather than exclusive because of the Treasury's power under §246A(f)), however, does not limit the interest deduction. Instead, the provision reduces the dividends-received deduction otherwise available under §§243-246 by a percentage related to the amount of debt used to purchase the stock. Thus, if a taxpayer purchases stock with some cash and some debt such that the "average indebtedness percentage" is 50 percent, then the §243 deduction in the example above will be 35 percent rather than 70 percent. See §246A(a) and (d). Section 246A applies to "portfolio stock" only. Stock will not be considered portfolio stock if the corporate shareholder owns a sufficient interest in the subsidiary (e.g., 50 percent of the voting power or value). §246A(c)(2). Presumably, a substantial ownership interest in the subsidiary suggests that the parent is interested in more than the subsidiary's dividends: The corporations are likely to be part of a multicorporate structure. The enforcement difficulties that plague §265 are likely to dog §246A. In particular, it will be very difficult to ascertain "portfolio indebtedness," indebtedness directly attributable to investment in portfolio stock. §246A(d)(3). In general, portfolio indebtedness refers to debt incurred to finance the stock purchase or to debt incurred after the stock purchase if secured by the stock.

3. *Dividend-related losses.* Even if the purchase of stock is not financed with debt, tax arbitrage opportunities may still be present. For example, suppose X Corp. purchases 100 shares of Y Corp. stock for $10,000 immediately before the dividend "record date." Y distributes a $1,000 dividend, which, after a 70 percent dividends-received deduction, results in $300 of taxable income to X and after-tax income of $898 (i.e., $1,000 minus $102 tax liability). X then sells the stock for $9,000 (i.e., the value of the stock reflects the dividend paid), reporting a $1,000 capital loss. In sum, X,

which started with $10,000, ends up with $10,238 (i.e., $898 from the dividend, $9,000 from the stock sale, and $340 in taxes saved as a result of the $1,000 capital loss deduction).

Under §246(c), no dividends-received deduction is available unless the stock is held for more than 45 days (90 days for certain preferred stock). This holding period is tolled if the shareholder-corporation diminishes its risk of loss in specified ways. §246(c)(4). See Rev. Rul. 90-27, page 115 supra, and Progressive Corp. v. United States, 970 F.2d 188 (6th Cir. 1992) (purchase of stock and sale of a call option tolled the holding period). If the dividend to be received is extraordinarily large relative to the price of the stock, a shareholder-corporation may be able to satisfy the holding period of §246(c) with a minimal risk of loss. Accordingly, Congress enacted §1059, mandating a basis reduction for corporate shareholders in their stock on the receipt of "extraordinary dividends," as defined in §1059(c), if the stock on which the dividends are paid is sold before it has been held for two years.

For example, suppose X Corp. purchases the stock of Y Corp. for $10,000 on January 1, receives an "extraordinary dividend" of $2,000 on February 1, and sells the stock on March 1 for $8,000, the January 1 value reduced by the amount of the dividend. X Corp. includes only $600 of the dividend in taxable income ($1,400 deducted under §243), and in the absence of §1059 would claim a $2,000 loss on the sale of the stock. See, e.g., Silco, Inc. v. United States, 779 F.2d 282 (5th Cir. 1986). Under §1059, X Corp. must reduce its stock basis by the $1,400 deducted under §243. On the sale, X Corp. will recognize a loss of $600 ($8,000 realized less basis of $8,600). This matches the gain reported on the dividend, an appropriate result since X Corp. ends up with $10,000, the amount with which it started.

Section 1059(c) defines an "extraordinary dividend" as a dividend that equals or exceeds 10 percent of the taxpayer's adjusted basis in the underlying stock. Under §1059(c)(4), a taxpayer can use the fair market value of the stock on the day before the ex-dividend day if the value can be established to the satisfaction of the Secretary. For example, if a taxpayer has a stock basis of $100 and the fair market value of the stock is $900, a $50 dividend exceeds 10 percent of the adjusted basis, but the alternative fair market value test would save the taxpayer from basis reduction under §1059. Dividends paid within an 85-day period are aggregated for purposes of the 10 percent test.

For distributions on preferred stock, a dividend is extraordinary if it exceeds 5 percent of the underlying stock's adjusted basis (or fair market value). An exception for certain preferred stock, however, pays fixed dividends not exceeding 15 percent of the lesser of adjusted basis or liquidation preference. §1059(e)(3).

Section 1059 can apply to any transaction taxed as a dividend including distributions in redemption of stock, see §302(d), as well as redemptions through related corporations, see §304(a). If a sale of stock in one corporation (called the issuing corporation) to another corporation (called the acquiring corporation) is taxed as a distribution under §304(a)(1), the sale is recast as (1) a transfer of the stock sold for stock of the acquiring corporation, (2) which is then redeemed by the acquiring corporation in a transaction described in §302(d). If the shareholder engaging in this §304 transaction is itself a corporation (call it the "selling" corporation), then the effect of this hypothetical stock acquisition and redemption is to ensure that if the selling corporation excludes more than its basis in the shares sold by reason of the §243 dividends-received deduction, that excess will be taxable immediately as gain under §1059(a)(2).

For example, assume Parent Corp. owns all the outstanding stock of Brother Corp. with an adjusted basis of $5,000 as well as all the outstanding stock of Sister Corp. with an adjusted basis of $50,000, and assume that the fair market value of each subsidiary corporation equals $50,000. If Parent Corp. sells the stock of Brother Corp. to Sister Corp. for cash of $50,000, this transaction is a redemption by related corporations as described in §304(a)(1), and because Parent Corp. retains complete control of Brother Corp. after the transaction, it is taxable as a distribution pursuant to §304(a)(1) and §301.

Suppose that the combined earnings and profits of Brother and Sister exceed $50,000, so that the entire distribution is taxed as a dividend. See §§304(b)(2), 301(c)(1). If this is treated as an extraordinary distribution, Parent Corp. is deemed to contribute its stock of Brother Corp. to Sister Corp. for Sister Corp. stock which is then redeemed and taxed as a dividend. The Sister Corp. stock hypothetically received by Parent has a substituted basis of only $5,000 under §358(a)(1), so that the subsequent hypothetical $50,000 redemption produces not only a $50,000 dividend and a $50,000 dividends-received deduction but also a taxable gain of $45,000 under § 1059(a)(2). Note in particular that Parent Corp. was unable to offset that gain with its pre-existing basis in the stock of Sister Corp. that it actually owns.

4. *Dividends-received deduction and earnings and profits.* Cases like *Litton Industries* and *Waterman Steamship* illustrate that shareholders that are corporations may prefer dividend treatment for distributions while individual shareholders may try to avoid dividend treatment. As part of this tax schizophrenia, the earnings and profits concept has been broadened so that distributions to individual shareholders are more likely to be treated as dividends. For example, §312(n), discussed on page 131 supra, requires that certain items that are deferred for purposes of computing taxable income (e.g., installment sale gains) be taken into account for purposes of computing earnings and profits. Any increase in earnings and profits resulting from such an adjustment means that a distribution to a shareholder that is a corporation is more likely to be treated as a dividend.

To illustrate the perceived abuse, suppose that in *Litton Industries,* Stouffer had no earnings and profits. If Stouffer had sold an asset on the installment method, thereby deferring any gain, the immediate increase in earnings and profits would permit the distribution of a dividend to Litton, thereby decreasing the capital gain that Litton would have to recognize on the sale of the Stouffer stock to Nestle.

Section 301(e) prevents this result by providing that adjustments to earnings and profits mandated by §312(k) and (n) are not made for purposes of determining the taxable income (and adjusted basis) of any "20 percent corporate shareholder." This term refers to any corporation, entitled to a dividends-received deduction with respect to a distribution, that owns, directly or indirectly, stock possessing at least 20 perent of the total combined voting power or value (excluding nonvoting preferred stock) of the distributing corporation. The effect of §301(e) is that a distribution that might have been a dividend generating a dividends-received deduction now will reduce the shareholder's basis in the distributing corporation's stock. In the example above, if the distribution to Litton was not a dividend but was treated as a return of basis under §301(c)(2), Litton would recognize the same gain on a sale to Nestle that would have been recognized had the distribution not taken place. That is, Nestle would pay less because of the distribution but Litton's basis would be decreased by precisely the amount of the distribution.

PROBLEM

4-8.   *X* Corp. has owned all the stock of *Y* Corp. since its formation. The stock has a basis of $2 million and a fair market value of $5 million. *P* Corp. wants to purchase the stock of *Y* Corp. for $5 million. Prior to the sale, *Y* Corp. distributes a note to *X* Corp. in the amount of $3 million payable in one year. The note bears a market rate of interest. In light of *Y* Corp.'s debt obligation, *P* Corp. pays $2 million to *X* Corp. for the *Y* Corp. stock. Within a year of *P* Corp.'s purchase, *Y* Corp. pays *X* Corp. $3 million on the note.

5

Redemptions and Partial Liquidations

A. TREATMENT OF SHAREHOLDERS

Corporate profit can become shareholder cash in a variety of ways. One possibility is for the corporation to distribute some of its profits to its shareholders as a dividend. Assuming the corporation has adequate earnings and profits, the shareholders must include the full amount of the distribution in gross income. §301.

Alternatively, a shareholder can sell some or all of her shares without waiting for a distribution. Here, too, the shareholder will turn some of her corporate investment into cash. But note that the tax consequences of a dividend distribution — no recovery of basis and ordinary income rather than capital gain — are the opposite of the tax consequences of a sale of stock — the shareholder receives an amount equal to her basis tax free and reports any excess as capital gain. These differences result from the conflicting congressional desires to tax distributed corporate profits as ordinary income while treating corporate shares as capital assets.

How should a shareholder be taxed if she sells some or all of her shares *to the corporation*? On one hand, funds will come out of corporate solution just as if there had been a dividend declaration; in this respect, a sale of stock to the issuing corporation (a "redemption") differs from a sale of the stock to a third party. On the other hand, the shareholder's percentage ownership of the corporation may decrease as a result of the transaction; if so, the transaction can be likened to a sale of stock to a third party. Note, though, that if stock is redeemed pro rata from all the shareholders, their proportionate interests in the corporation remain unchanged — as is the case when ordinary dividends are paid. Congress

177

has in §302 sought to distinguish redemptions resembling sales from those resembling dividends.

Before turning to §302, note the definition of a "redemption" in §317(b). A redemption in this context is the distribution of property by a corporation *in exchange for* its own stock. Certain redemptions are taxed to the selling shareholder under §302(a) as sales of stock, allowing the shareholder to be taxed under §§1001 et seq. Other redemptions are taxed to the selling shareholder under §302(d) as distributions subject to the rules of §301, yielding dividend income if the corporation has sufficient earnings and profits. If the property distributed to the selling shareholder includes noncash property, the corporation may recognize taxable gain as on any nonliquidating distribution.

Consider the case of X Corp., having 10,000 shares of common stock outstanding, owned half by P and half by Q. Suppose X Corp. has a fair market value of $100,000, and that P's 5,000 shares are redeemed for $50,000 in cash. Assuming that X Corp. has at least $50,000 of accumulated earnings and profits, how should P be taxed? Since P no longer has any interest in the corporation, the effect of the redemption on P is the same as if he had sold his stock to Q. A redemption resulting in a complete termination of the shareholder's interest in the corporation is a compelling case for sale or exchange treatment, and Congress has recognized this in §302(b)(3). Note, though, that Q becomes the sole shareholder of the corporation without having paid out any additional personal funds; in effect, the corporation's payment to P has transformed Q from a 50 percent to a 100 percent owner (albeit in a company only half its former size). We will return (at pages 215-224, 266-268 infra) to the possible tax consequences to Q of this change in status.

At the opposite end of the spectrum is a redemption of part of the stock of a sole shareholder. Suppose Q, after the redemption of P's stock, has X Corp. redeem half of his stock for $25,000. Has Q's interest in X Corp. been changed? While the number of shares that Q owns decreases from 5,000 to 2,500, his percentage ownership remains at 100. Under state law, the fact that Q surrendered half of his shares would cause some of the distribution to be charged to the corporation's capital or paid-in surplus account — if no shares had been surrendered, presumably the charge would be only to the corporation's earned surplus account. Should Q's taxation turn on this distinction? In §302(b) (excluding the partial liquidation provision of §302(b)(4), discussed at pages 208-213 infra), Congress has elected to focus on the effect of a redemption on the recipient shareholder rather than on the distributing corporation. Accordingly, the redemption of Q's stock will be taxed as a distribution subject to the rules of §301, and, if X Corp. has at least $25,000 in earnings and profits, Q will have a dividend in the entire amount.

Between these two extremes lies a morass; the courts have struggled with an endless variety of factual patterns, in each case attempting to distinguish redemptions taxable as exchanges from redemptions taxable as distributions. Particularly troublesome have been cases in which the shareholder whose stock is redeemed is related to the remaining shareholders. For example, what are the consequences if P and Q in the example above are husband and wife, mother and daughter, or brother and sister? As you read the following cases, keep in mind this distinction (between redemptions more closely resembling the sale of stock to a third party from those resembling receipt of a nonliquidating distribution from the corporation) that §302 and the courts are trying to draw. If you come away with the sense that no line can be found, reconsider whether nonliquidating corporate distributions should be taxed so much more harshly than sales of corporate shares.

As you study §302, keep in mind that even if capital gains were not taxed at a favorable rate, exchange treatment under §302(a) is more favorable than distribution treatment under §301. Exchange treatment allows the shareholders to offset the amount of the distribution by the basis of the stock surrendered, while (generally) no such offset is permitted against distributions taxable under §301.

1. Complete Terminations under §302(b)(3)

Seda v. Commissioner
82 T.C. 484 (1984)

OPINION

FAY, Judge. . . .

On October 15, 1957, petitioners [Mr. and Mrs. Seda] organized B & B Supply Company (herein the company), and, within two years after incorporation, they had acquired all of the company's stock. Mr. Seda was the company's president and chairman of the board and owned 22,910 shares of the company's stock. Mrs. Seda was a director, vice-president, and secretary and owned 1,010 shares of the company's stock.

The company was engaged in the business of selling garage doors as a wholesaler in Colorado and Wyoming. It purchased most of the garage doors from Frantz Manufacturing Co. (herein Frantz Co.). In addition to working for the company from approximately 1952 until April 1981, Mr. Seda also worked as a manufacturer's representative for Frantz Co., earning a three percent commission on all garage door sales he made to the company on behalf of Frantz Co.

Because of their declining health, in 1979 petitioners decided to terminate their ownership of the company. Their son James L. Seda (James) had worked for the company since 1973 and was ready to assume ownership and control of the company. On June 30, 1979, petitioners entered into a redemption agreement wherein the company redeemed all of petitioners' stock for $299,000 ($12.50 per share). Pursuant to the redemption agreement, the company also issued 1,000 shares of stock to James for $1,000. Thus, James was the sole shareholder of the company after the redemption. Petitioners resigned from their positions as officers and directors of the company on June 30, 1979.

Prior to signing the redemption agreement, petitioners hired an accountant to advise them with respect to the tax consequences of the redemption. The accountant advised them that in order to achieve long-term capital gain treatment they would have to terminate their relationship with the company completely. Because of James' insistence, however, Mr. Seda continued to work for the company after the redemption, and he continued to receive a salary of $1,000 per month. Neither petitioners nor James believed such employment would prevent petitioners from achieving long-term capital gain treatment in connection with the redemption of their stock. In June 1981, immediately after learning that his employment relationship could result in the gain from the redemption of his stock being taxed as ordinary income, Mr. Seda terminated his employment relationship with the company. Mrs. Seda never served as an employee, officer, or director of the company after the redemption.

The company has never paid a dividend, and its retained earnings as of June 30, 1978 were $202,455. . . .

The first issue is whether the redemption of all petitioners' stock in the company is taxable as a dividend distribution under section 301 or as long-term capital gain under section 302(a). Section 302(a) provides that a distribution of property to a shareholder by a corporation in redemption of stock will be treated as a sale or exchange of such stock if the redemption falls within one of four categories enumerated in section 302(b). If the redemption fails to so qualify, it is treated as a dividend distribution to the extent of the corporation's earnings and profits. See secs. 301 and 302(a).

Section 302(b)(3) provides that a shareholder is entitled to sale or exchange treatment if all his stock in the corporation is redeemed. For purposes of determining whether there has been a complete termination within the meaning of section 302(b)(3), the constructive stock ownership rules of section 318(a) will apply unless the requirements set out in section 302(c)(2)(A) are satisfied. Sec. 302(c)(1). Respondent contends that petitioners failed to effect a complete termination within the meaning of section 302(b)(3) because James' interest in the company after the redemption is attributable to petitioners pursuant to section 318(a)(1). Petitioners counter that James' interest is not attributable to them because they satisfied the requirements of section 302(c)(2)(A).

Section 302(c)(2)(A) provides in relevant part as follows:

(A)   In the case of a distribution described in subsection (b)(3), section 318(a)(1) shall not apply if —

(i)   immediately after the distribution the distributee has no interest in the corporation (*including an interest as officer, director, or employee*), other than an interest as a creditor,

(ii)   the distributee does not acquire any such interest (other than stock acquired by bequest or inheritance) within 10 years from the date of such distribution, and

(iii)   the distributee, at such time and in such manner as the Secretary by regulations prescribes, files an agreement to notify the Secretary of any acquisition described in clause (ii) and to retain such records as may be necessary for the application of this paragraph.

(Emphasis added.)

Focusing on the parenthetical language in section 302(c)(2)(A)(i), respondent's first argument is that petitioners are not entitled to the relief provided by section 302(c)(2)(A) because Mr. Seda remained an employee of the company after the redemption. Petitioners argue, however, that section 302(c)(2)(A)(i) does not prohibit all employment relationships. Thus, they contend that Mr. Seda's employment after the redemption was not the retention of a prohibited interest in the company. For the following reasons, we agree with respondent.

Congress' purpose in enacting section 302(c)(2) was to ensure that the family attribution rules would not prevent a bona fide severance of a shareholder's interest in a corporation from resulting in capital gains treatment. H. Rept. No. 1337, 83d Cong. 2d Sess., p. 36 (1954); S. Rept. No. 1622, 83d Cong., 2d Sess., p. 45 (1954). This Court has previously stated that it is reasonable to infer from the legislative history that in enacting section 302(c)(2)(A) Congress was primarily concerned with a situation where a redeeming shareholder retained a financial stake in the corporation or continued to control the corporation and benefit by its operations after making only a nominal transfer of his stock. Estate of Lennard v. Commissioner, 61 T.C. 554, 561 (1974).

Although section 302(c)(2)(A)(i) may not prohibit the retention of all employment relationships, it is clear that the level of employment engaged in by Mr. Seda herein is prohibited. After the redemption, Mr. Seda continued to work for the company for almost two years and received a salary of $1,000 per month. By receiving that salary Mr. Seda did retain a financial stake in the company. Moreover, petitioners have failed to show that Mr. Seda ceased to be involved in the management of the company after the redemption. The fact that petitioners did not know that Mr. Seda's continued employment would prevent them from achieving long-term capital gain treatment is unfortunate, but not controlling. Thus, we find that petitioners failed to satisfy section 302(c)(2)(A)(i).

Accordingly, James' interest in the company is attributable to petitioners and, therefore, petitioners failed to effect a complete redemption of all of their stock within the meaning of section 302(b)(3). Thus, the proceeds from the redemption are taxable under section 302(d) as a dividend distribution to the extent of the company's earnings and profits. . . .

Reviewed by the Court.

Simpson, Wiles, Wilbur, Chabot, Korner, Shields, Cohen and Swift, JJ., agree with the majority opinion.

WHITAKER, J., concurring.

While I concur in the result reached, the majority fails to apply the per se rule which, in my opinion, is mandated by the statute. Section 302(c)(1) and (2)(A)(i) prescribes that the family attribution rules may not be waived if after a redemption the former shareholder performs any services for, or receives any remuneration from, the redeeming corporation as an officer, director or employee. The parenthetical language of section 302(c)(2)(A)(i) — "(including an interest as officer, director, or employee)" — is neither ambiguous nor equivocal; it contains no qualification such as that suggested by the majority. Nothing in the statutory language or legislative history suggests that an "interest as officer, director, or employee" must be substantial to be prohibited. Rather, it contains a flat rule.

While Congress did not address directly the issue of whether a per se rule was to be applied in interpreting the parenthetical language of section 302(c)(2)(A)(i), it is clear that section 302(c) was intended to bring an element of certainty to an area that had become a confusing morass under prior law. Congress recognized that it was necessary to replace the difficult detailed factual inquiries that had become commonplace. With regard to corporate redemptions, the House Report states:

> . . . Redemptions of stock. — Under present law it is not clear when a stock redemption results in capital gain or ordinary income. . . .
>
> Your committee's bill sets forth definite conditions under which stock may be redeemed at capital-gain rates. . . .
>
> . . . At the present time a possible opportunity for tax avoidance results where redemptions are effected in the case of family-owned corporations. To prevent tax avoidance, but at the same time to provide definitive rules for the guidance of taxpayers, your committee has provided precise standards whereby under specific circumstances, a shareholder may be considered as owning stock held by members of his immediate family (or by partnerships, corporations, or trusts which he controls).

[H. Rept. 1337, 83d Cong., 2d Sess. 35-36 (1954).]

Section 302(c) thus was enacted as something of a "safe haven." Facts and circumstances must be considered in the application of some of the section 302(b) and (c) rules, such as the determination under section 302(b)(1) as to dividend equivalency, but we should not judicially modify the mechanical rules where they can be applied mechanically. Contrary to the majority's view, Congress did intend to "prohibit the retention of all employment relationships." In the context of Lewis v. Commissioner, 47 T.C. 129 (1966), I do agree with Judge Simpson that "Congress did not intend us to hold that an officer or director who performs no duties, receives no compensation, and exercises no influence has retained an interest in the corporation." 47 T.C. at 137 (Simpson, J., concurring). The principle of substance over form prevents us from applying the per se rule where no duties are performed and no compensation received by reason of status as an officer, director or employee. But where, as here, the facts are otherwise, the congressional attempt to achieve certainty should be allowed to operate. . . .

Dawson, Sterrett, Goffe, Nims, Parker, Hamblen, and Clapp, JJ., agree with this concurring opinion.

NOTES

1. *Constructive ownership of stock under §302(b)(3).* Although all the stock owned by Mr. Seda was redeemed, he failed to qualify under §302(b)(3) for exchange treatment on the redemption.[1] The complete termination provision of §302(b)(3) was inapplicable in this case solely because Mr. Seda's son owned stock in the corporation after the redemption and this stock was attributed to Mr. Seda under §302(c)(1). Because of §302(c)(1), the constructive attribution rules of §318 generally apply to determinations of stock ownership under §302. The constructive attribution rules of §318 are discussed further at pages 189-190 infra.

One distinctive feature of the complete termination of interest provision in §302(b)(3) is the ability of the redeemed shareholder to waive application of the family attribution rules of §318(a)(1). See §302(c)(2). For such a waiver to be effective, however, the taxpayer must not retain, and agree not to acquire for 10 years, any interest in the corporation other than as a creditor. If a taxpayer whose stock is redeemed fails to make the election provided by §302(c)(2), then the attribution rules will apply in full in determining whether the redemption qualifies under §302(b)(3). In *Seda,* the taxpayers filed a §302(c) election, but the retention of an interest in the corporation by Mr. Seda eviscerated the election's effect.

As part of electing out of the family attribution rules, a taxpayer must file an agreement under §302(c)(2)(A)(iii) that extends the statute of limitations with respect to his redemption. This agreement allows the Commissioner to reopen the redemption year and collect a deficiency if the taxpayer acquires a tainted interest in the corporation within 10 years.

---

1. The opinion does not consider why Mrs. Seda failed to qualify under §302(b)(3). Is Mr. Seda's employment imputed to his wife?

Under §302(c)(2)(B), a taxpayer may not waive the family attribution rules if any of the redeemed stock was acquired within 10 years from a related person, "related" being defined by reference to §318(a). In addition, a taxpayer may not waive the family attribution rules if he transferred any stock within 10 years to such a related person. These two limitations do not apply, however, if the transfer of stock "did not have as one of its principal purposes the avoidance of Federal income tax."

Suppose X Corp. has 100 shares outstanding, all of which are owned by H. If H gives 10 shares to W, his wife, and then W's 10 shares are immediately redeemed, §302(c)(2)(B)(i) operates to prevent W from avoiding application of the family attribution rules. Thus, W will be deemed to own 100 percent of X Corp.'s shares both before and after the redemption, and the redemption will be subject to the distribution rules of §301.

Suppose instead that H gives W all but 10 shares and then has his stock completely redeemed. Now H will seek to waive application of the family attribution rules, but §302(c)(2)(B)(ii) prevents him from doing so. H will thus be deemed to own 100 percent of the X Corp. stock both before and after the redemption and so will be taxed under the distribution rules of §301. Note, however, that §302(c)(2)(B) applies only to transfers that have "the avoidance of Federal income tax" as one of their principal purposes. In Rev. Rul. 77-293, 1977-2 C.B. 91, the Service ruled that a transfer of appreciated stock to the taxpayer's son was not subject to §302(c)(2)(B) when made "solely for the purpose of enabling [the taxpayer] to retire while leaving the business to [his son]." See also Rev. Rul. 85-19, 1985-1 C.B. 94, in which the father gifted stock to his son and subsequently reacquired some of the gifted stock by purchase. The son's remaining stock was redeemed by the corporation, and he filed an election under §302(c)(2)(A)(iii) to waive the family attribution rules. The Service ruled that the waiver was valid because the resale of stock by the son to his father merely returned the stock to its original owner and was not undertaken to avoid tax.

2. *Retention or reacquisition of a tainted interest.* As *Seda* illustrates, a taxpayer desiring to waive the family attribution rules pursuant to §302(c)(2) must not retain (or acquire within 10 years) an interest in the corporation "other than an interest as a creditor." The concurring opinion of Judge Whitaker emphasizes that Congress seemingly drew a bright line in §302(c)(2)(A)(i) by specifically providing that an interest as an "officer, director, or employee" is proscribed. The majority opinion does not specifically embrace that reading of the statute. Judge Whitaker agrees that a nominal directorship entailing no duties and without compensation, the situation litigated in *Lewis,* is not a prohibited interest under §302(c)(2)(A)(i), and the majority in *Seda* condemn the minimal activity engaged in by the taxpayer in that case. What fact pattern might fall between *Lewis* and *Seda* to justify Judge Whitaker's concerns?

In Lynch v. Commissioner, 83 T.C. 597 (1984), the father was the sole shareholder of *X* Corp. He transferred some of the stock to his son, and thereafter *X* Corp. redeemed all the father's remaining stock. The father continued, as an independent contractor, to render services to *X* Corp. under a consulting agreement. The father sought capital gain treatment on the redemption via §302(b)(3) and a waiver of the family attribution rules. Held, exchange treatment allowed because (1) an independent contractor is not an "employee" within the meaning of §302(c)(2)(A)(i), and (2) the father's transfer to his son did not have as one of its principal purposes the avoidance of federal income tax. What would the Tax Court's opinion in *Lynch* leave of *Seda* (other than a trap for the ill advised)? The court of appeals reversed the Tax Court in *Lynch,* saying that Congress sought certainty in this area of the law by enacting §302(c)(2)(A). 801 F.2d 1176 (9th Cir. 1986). Compare Cerone v. Commissioner, 87 T.C. 1 (1986), in which the Tax Court rejected a bright-line reading of §302(c)(2)(A), saying instead that a taxpayer who continues to perform services for his corporation after a redemption will fail §302(c)(2)(A) only if the taxpayer has a significant financial stake in, or continues to control, the corporation.

How should "creditor" status be defined in the context of §302(c)(2)(A)(i)? Under Treas. Regs. §1.302-4(d), a permissible creditor must have rights neither broader in scope than is necessary for the enforcement of her claim nor subordinate to the claims of general creditors. See Dunn v. Commissioner, 615 F.2d 578 (2d Cir. 1980). See also Lynch v. Commissioner, supra, in which a note was held not to run afoul of Treas. Regs. §1.302-4(d) even though the noteholder agreed, subsequent to the redemption, to subordinate his note to a new debt acquired by the corporation. Would a retiring shareholder be beyond the bounds of §302(c)(2)(A)(i) if he received a note of the corporation secured by corporate stock? What if the retiring shareholder could vote the stock upon default of the note?

In Rev. Rul. 77-467, 1977-2 C.B. 92, the Service ruled that a taxpayer could waive the family attribution rules under §302(c)(2) despite retaining his interest as lessor of the corporation's office building pursuant to a 10-year lease entered into five years before the taxpayer's redemption. The taxpayer's status was not a prohibited interest within the meaning of §302(c)(2)(A)(i) because "[t]he payments under the lease will not be dependent on [the corporation's] future earnings and will not be subordinate to the claims of [the corporation's] general creditors." Was Mr. Seda's salary as an employee any more dependent on future corporate earnings than the lease payments in Rev. Rul. 77-467? Remaining an employee of the corporation after the redemption plainly fails the congressionally delineated test of §302(c)(2)(A)(i). Does this suggest that the reasoning in Rev. Rul. 77-467 is flawed?

Can the family attribution rules be waived if the exiting shareholder retains the right to a lifetime pension from the corporation? If the pension is unfunded, the payments are unrelated to the corporation's future earnings, and the rights of the exiting shareholder are unsubordinated to the claims of general creditors of the corporation, the answer is yes. Rev. Rul. 84-135, 1984-2 C.B. 80.

In a series of rulings, the Service has held that retention of the legal right to vote shares violates a §302(c)(2)(A) waiver even if the taxpayer has no equitable interest in the stock. See Rev. Rul. 81-233, 1981-2 C.B. 83 (custodian of stock under Uniform Gift to Minors Act); Rev. Rul. 71-426, 1971-2 C.B. 173 (retention of interest as trustee of voting trust). But see Rev. Rul. 79-334, 1979-2 C.B. 127 (appointment by will as trustee of trust holding stock not a forbidden "interest"); Rev. Rul. 72-380, 1972-2 C.B. 201 (executor of estate holding stock not a forbidden "interest").

3. *Corporate shareholders and §302.* When a corporate shareholder's stock is redeemed, the taxpayer and the Service often switch sides; the corporation usually prefers dividend treatment because of the generous dividends-received deduction pursuant to §243, and the Service prefers capital gains treatment. To avoid §302(b)(3), a corporate shareholder might arrange to have its stock redeemed in a series of redemptions, arguing that only the final redemption in the series should be taxable as a complete termination. In Bleily & Collishaw v. Commissioner, 72 T.C. 751 (1979), however, the Commissioner successfully argued that a series of redemptions should be combined and taxed as a single, complete termination of the corporate shareholder's interest. See also Rev. Rul. 77-226, 1977-2 C.B. 90, in which the Service found that a corporate shareholder had transacted a §302(b)(3) redemption by combining various steps in a complicated transaction. Can a noncorporate taxpayer "step" a series of redemptions together to qualify for exchange treatment under §302(b)(3)? See Benjamin v. Commissioner, 592 F.2d 1259 (5th Cir. 1979), in which the court refused to treat a partial redemption as part of a complete redemption since (1) there was no time frame in which the "plan for total redemption" was to be completed and (2) the shareholder had wide discretion as to when the redemption would be completed.

PROBLEMS

5-1. *X* Corp. has a net value of $1 million and earnings and profits of $800,000. Of the 1,000 outstanding shares of *X*, 500 are owned by Father with a basis of $600 per share, and 500 are owned by Son with a basis of $700 per share. Father would like to transfer the value of his interest to Son, and he contemplates the following four transactions: (a) Have the corporation redeem Father's stock and then give the proceeds to Son; (b) have the corporation redeem the stock from Father's estate after Father's death and devise the proceeds to Son; (c) give Father's stock to Son and then cause the corporation to redeem the stock gifted to Son; (d) devise the stock to Son and have the corporation redeem it after Father's death.

What are the tax consequences to Father and Son of each of these transactions?

5-2. In Problem 5-1, suppose Father wants to pass the value of his stock on to Mother, his wife. Reconsider the tax consequences of each of the four transactions, assuming that Mother, rather than Son, will receive the value of Father's stock and that Mother, rather than Son, is a beneficiary of the estate.

2. Substantially Disproportionate Redemptions under §302(b)(2)

A less compelling case for exchange treatment than a complete redemption is a disproportionate redemption in which a shareholder's relative equity interest in the corporation is reduced significantly, though not to zero. Under §302(b)(2), a disproportionate redemption will qualify for exchange treatment under §302(a) if it satisfies the following three-part test: (1) The redeemed shareholder must own less than 50 percent of the total combined voting power of the corporation immediately after the redemption, (2) the shareholder's voting power after the redemption must be less than 80 percent of his former voting power, and (3) the shareholder's percentage ownership of all common stock (nonvoting as well as voting) must also be less than 80 percent of his former percentage ownership.

Consider the following example. Assume E Corp. has 300 shares of common stock outstanding, owned 70 percent (210 shares) by P and 30 percent (90 shares) by Q. If E Corp. redeems 20 shares of Q's stock, will the redemption qualify under §302(b)(2)? The following table sets forth the relevant data.

	Total Shares Outstanding	Q's Shares	Q's Percentage
Preredemption	300	90	30
Postredemption	280	70	25

Here, more than 20 percent of Q's stock has been redeemed (20 of 90 shares), and Q's percentage of ownership drops from 30 to 25. To qualify for sale or exchange treatment under §302(b)(2), Q's ownership would have had to fall below 24 percent (since 80 percent of her prior 30 percent is 24 percent). Accordingly, Q does not meet the safe harbor test of §302(b)(2). This example displays the often-overlooked fact that a redemption will not qualify under §302(b)(2) if only 20 percent of a shareholder's stock is redeemed: Because a redemption reduces the total number of shares outstanding as well as the number of shares held by the redeemed shareholder, the percentage of a taxpayer's shares that must be redeemed to qualify under §302(b)(2) always exceeds 20 percent and turns on the redeemed shareholder's preredemption percentage ownership of the corporation.

Now consider a more abstract example. X Corp. has 200 shares of voting stock outstanding, owned half by K and half by L. What is the least number of shares that K must have redeemed if he is to qualify under §302(b)(2)? Before the redemption, K owns 100 of the 200 shares outstanding, or 50 percent. After the redemption, K must own less than 0.80 times 50 percent, or less than 40 percent. If K has x shares redeemed, then his postredemption percentage of ownership will be $(100 - x)/(200 - x) \times 100$ percent. To satisfy §302(b)(2), then, K must choose an x such that $(100 - x)/(200 - x) < .4$, and the smallest x satisfying this condition is 33.34. Accordingly, K must have at least 33.34 of his shares redeemed (and not merely a fraction more than 20 shares!) to qualify under §302(b)(3).[2]

Note the requirement imposed by the concluding paragraph of §302(b)(2)(C): Not only must the 80 percent test be satisfied as to all voting stock, but it also must be satisfied with respect to the shareholder's common stock taken alone. The Service has ruled that this test will not disqualify a corporation redeeming voting preferred stock of a shareholder who owns (actually and constructively) no common stock before the redemption. Rev. Rul. 81-41, 1981-1 C.B. 121. In addition, the Service has ruled that if multiple classes of common stock are outstanding, the test of §302(b)(2)(C) is applied to a shareholder's aggregate ownership of common stock rather than on a class-by-class basis. If the test were applied class by class, no redemption could qualify as substantially disproportionate unless shares of each class of stock were redeemed. Rev. Rul 87-88, 1987-2 C.B. 81.

Suppose a corporation is equally owned by two shareholders. While a pro rata redemption of the two shareholders' stock will fail to qualify for exchange treatment under §302(a), can they obtain capital gain treatment if the corporation redeems a substantial portion of one shareholder's stock in one redemption and then redeems an equal portion of the other shareholder's stock in a second transaction? Under §302(b)(2)(D), a redemption that is part of a series of redemptions will not qualify under §302(b)(2) unless the series in total is "substantially disproportionate." Treas. Regs. §1.302-1(a)(3).

Suppose individual A, the controlling shareholder of X Corp., knows that X Corp. will in one month repurchase all the shares of individual B,

---

2. If T is the total number of shares outstanding just prior to the redemption, and if N is the number of those shares held by the shareholder, then the number of shares needed to be redeemed to meet the 80 percent test under §302(b)(2) is any amount above $NT/(5T - 4N)$.

a minority shareholder. How should A be taxed on a redemption that, viewed in isolation, satisfies the tests of §302(b)(2) but that would fail those tests had the distribution to A come after the complete termination of B? For the Service's position that the distributions to A and to B must be treated as a single transaction, see Rev. Rul. 85-14, 1985-4 C.B. 92.

NOTES

1. *Constructive ownership of stock under §302.* By virtue of §302(c)(1), the constructive attribution rules of §318(a) apply to determinations under §302. The explicit reference in §302(c)(1) to §318(a) is important, for §318 does not apply except when "expressly made applicable." §318(a).

The constructive ownership rules of §318 consist of three main parts: attribution between family members, §318(a)(1); attribution *from* entities to their beneficial owners, §318(a)(2); and attribution *to* entities from their beneficial owners, §318(a)(3). In addition, holders of stock options are treated as owners of the optioned stock even though they have not yet exercised (and may never exercise) the option. §318(a)(4). Finally, §318(a)(5)(A) permits two or more attribution rules of §318 to be applied in sequence, resulting in a chain of links.

The mechanics of §318 can best be gleaned from a number of examples. Assume X Corp. has 100 shares of common stock outstanding, owned 25 by E, 25 by F, 25 by the T trust, and 25 by the P partnership. While E, F, T, and P each actually own 25 percent of X Corp., their constructive (or deemed) ownership will depend on the relationships among them. For example, suppose E is a 60 percent partner in the P partnership. Now, E will have a total constructive ownership of 40 shares, 25 actually owned and 60 percent of the 25 shares owned by P. §318(a)(2)(A). P, however, will be deemed to own 50 shares, for all of E's shares will be imputed to P under §318(a)(3)(A).

If E is also a beneficiary of the T trust, the matter becomes more complicated. Suppose E's actuarially determined interest in the T trust is 80 percent of the trust's value. Then E's total constructive ownership jumps by 20 shares to 60, for he must add 80 percent of the trust's holdings to his own under §318(a)(2)(B)(i). Further, P's constructive ownership also increases by 20 shares, for under §318(a)(5)(A), E's constructive ownership can be imputed to a related party such as P, as is actual ownership.

Now assume F has the other 40 percent interest in the P partnership. P's total constructive ownership will increase by 25 shares under §318(a)(3)(A). F's total constructive ownership will increase to 35 shares, 25 actually owned and 10 constructively owned through attribution of 40 percent of P's *actual* ownership. Why is F not deemed to own 40 percent of P's actually *and constructively* owned shares? Under §318(a)(5)(C), stock attributed *into* an entity under §318(a)(3) cannot then be reattributed *out of* the entity under §318(a)(2). A similar rule limits reattribution through family members so that, for example, there is no attribution between siblings via the chain: child 1 to parent to child 2. See §318(a)(5)(B). Note also that attribution to and from corporations is limited to its 50 percent shareholders. §318(a)(2)(C), (a)(3)(C).

Recall §302(c)(2), which allows a taxpayer to waive application of the family attribution rules to qualify under the complete termination safe harbor of §302(b)(3). Note that this waiver applies only to the attribution rules in §318(a)(1) — the *family* attribution rules — and that it applies only to determinations under §302(b)(3). In Rickey v. United States, 592 F.2d 1251 (5th Cir. 1979), it was held that an estate could waive the entity attribution rules of §318(a)(3) for purposes of §302(b)(3). In the legislative reports discussing §228 of the Tax Equity and Fiscal Responsibility Act of 1982, Congress indicated that the holding of *Rickey* was specifically disapproved.

Entities as well as individuals can waive the family attribution rules to qualify under §302(b)(3). See §302(c)(2)(C). Such a waiver might be appropriate when a trust completely terminates its interest in a corporation but the parent of a trust beneficiary continues to be a shareholder of the corporation. Note that the restrictions of §302(c)(2)(A) — a 10-year prohibition from acquiring a tainted interest in the corporation and the filing of an extension of the statute of limitations — are imposed on the entity and on all persons related to the entity (related by virtue of the family attribution rules of §318(a)(3). See §302(c)(2)(C).

2. *The case of the disappearing basis.* When a taxpayer receives an ordinary dividend, the basis of her shares is unaffected by the receipt, and gain or loss on a subsequent disposition of the shares, computed under §1001(a), will be the difference between the amount realized and the basis of the shares. A redemption of some or all of the taxpayer's shares that fails to qualify for exchange treatment under §302(a) similarly leaves the taxpayer's stock basis unaffected, but she no longer has the redeemed shares for a later sale or other disposition. What happens to her basis in the redeemed shares? If it is lost, a §302(d) distribution is not the equivalent of an ordinary dividend; it is worse than one. See Treas. Regs. §1.302-2(c), stating that when a redemption of stock is treated as dividend, "proper adjustment of the basis *of the remaining stock* will be made with respect to the stock redeemed" (emphasis added), and note examples 1 to 3. Note that the shareholder may not own any shares after the redemption, as was true in *Seda*. What is the "proper adjustment" in *Seda*? See Levin v. Commissioner, 385 F.2d 521 (2d Cir. 1967) (transfer of basis to related shareholder).

PROBLEMS

5-3. *X* Corp. is owned by two unrelated individuals, *P* and *Q*. *P* owns 60 shares with a basis of $60 per share, and *Q* owns 40 shares with a basis of $70 per share. *X* has earnings and profits of $2,000, and the fair market value of each share is $100. What tax consequences does each of the following transactions have for *P*, *Q*, and *X*?

    a.   *P* sells 10 shares to *Q* for $1,000.
    b.   *P* sells 10 shares to *X* Corp. for $1,000.
    c.   *P* sells 21 shares to *X* Corp. for $2,100.
    d.   *P* sells 50 shares to *X* Corp. for $5,000.
    e.   Suppose in (d) that —
        i.   *P* is *Q*'s sister.
       ii.   *P* is *Q*'s mother.
      iii.   *P* and *Q* are each 50 percent partners in the *PQ* Partnership.
      iv.   *Q* is a corporation, and *P* owns 50 percent of the stock of *Q*. Unrelated shareholders own the other 50 percent.
       v.   *Q* is a corporation and P's father owns 50 perent of the stock of *Q*. Unrelated shareholders own the other 50 percent.

3. *Redemptions Not Essentially Equivalent to a Dividend*

United States v. Davis
397 U.S. 301 (1970)

Justice MARSHALL delivered the opinion of the Court.

    In 1945, taxpayer and E. B. Bradley organized a corporation. In exchange for property transferred to the new company, Bradley received 500 shares of common stock, and taxpayer and his wife similarly each received 250 such shares. Shortly thereafter, taxpayer made an additional contribution to the corporation, purchasing 1,000 shares of preferred stock at a par value of $25 per share.

    The purpose of this latter transaction was to increase the company's working capital and thereby to qualify for a loan previously negotiated through the Reconstruction Finance Corporation. It was understood that the corporation would redeem the preferred stock when the RFC loan had been repaid. Although in the interim taxpayer bought Bradley's 500 shares and divided them between his son and daughter, the total capitalization of the company remained the same until 1963. That year, after the loan was fully repaid and in accordance with the original understanding, the company redeemed taxpayer's preferred stock. . . .

    [T]axpayer considered the redemption as a sale of his preferred stock to the company — a capital gains transaction under §302 of the Internal Revenue Code of 1954 resulting in no tax since taxpayer's basis in the stock equaled the amount he received for it. . . . According to the Commissioner, the redemption of taxpayer's stock was essentially equivalent to a dividend and was thus taxable as ordinary income under §§301 and 316 of the Code. Taxpayer paid the resulting deficiency and brought this suit for a refund. The District Court ruled in his favor. . . .

The Court of Appeals held that the $25,000 received by taxpayer was "not essentially equivalent to a dividend" within the meaning of that phrase in §302(b)(1) of the Code because the redemption was the final step in a course of action that had a legitimate business (as opposed to a tax avoidance) purpose. . . . We reverse.

The Internal Revenue Code of 1954 provides generally in §§301 and 316 for the tax treatment of distributions by a corporation to its shareholders; under those provisions, a distribution is includible in a taxpayer's gross income as a dividend out of earnings and profits to the extent such earnings exist. There are exceptions to the application of these general provisions, however, and among them are those found in §302 involving certain distributions for redeemed stock. . . .

Under subsection (a) of §302, a distribution is treated as "payment in exchange for the stock," thus qualifying for capital gains rather than ordinary income treatment, if the conditions contained in any one of the four paragraphs of subsection (b) are met. In addition to paragraph (1)'s "not essentially equivalent to a dividend" test, capital gains treatment is available where (2) the taxpayer's voting strength is substantially diminished, (3) his interest in the company is completely terminated. . . . Paragraph (4) is not involved here, and taxpayer admits that paragraphs (2) and (3) do not apply. Moreover, taxpayer agrees that for the purposes of §§302(b)(2) and (3) the attribution rules of §318(a) apply and he is considered to own the 750 outstanding shares of common stock held by his wife and children in addition to the 250 shares in his own name.

Taxpayer, however, argues that the attribution rules do not apply in considering whether a distribution is essentially equivalent to a dividend under §302(b)(1). According to taxpayer, he should thus be considered to own only 25 percent of the corporation's common stock, and the distribution would then qualify under §302(b)(1) since it was not pro rata or proportionate to his stock interest, the fundamental test of dividend equivalency. See Treas. Reg. §1.302-2(b). However, the plain language of the statute compels rejection of the argument. In subsection (c) of §302, the attribution rules are made specifically applicable "in determining the ownership of stock for purposes of this section." Applying this language, both courts below held that §318(a) applies to all of §302, including §302(b)(1) — a view in accord with the decisions of the other courts of appeals, a long-standing treasury regulation, and the opinion of the leading commentators.

Against this weight of authority, taxpayer argues that the result under paragraph (1) should be different because there is no explicit reference to stock ownership as there is in paragraphs (2) and (3). Neither that fact, however, nor the purpose and history of §302(b)(1) support taxpayer's argument. . . .

Indeed, it was necessary that the attribution rules apply to §302(b)(1) unless they were to be effectively eliminated from consideration with regard to §§302(b)(2) and (3) also. For if a transaction failed to qualify under one of those sections solely because of the attribution rules, it would according to taxpayer's argument nonetheless qualify under §302(b)(1). We cannot agree that Congress intended so to nullify its explicit directive. We conclude, therefore, that the attribution rules of §318(a) do apply; and, for the purposes of deciding whether a distribution is "not essentially equivalent to a dividend" under §302(b)(1), taxpayer must be deemed the owner of all 1,000 shares of the company's common stock.

II

After application of the stock ownership attribution rules, this case viewed most simply involves a sole stockholder who causes part of his shares to be redeemed by the corporation. We conclude that such a redemption is always "essentially equivalent to a dividend" within the meaning of that phrase in §302(b)(1) and therefore do not reach the Government's alternative argument that in any event the distribution should not on the facts of this case qualify for capital gains treatment.[8]

The predecessor of §302(b)(1) came into the tax law as §201(d) of the Revenue Act of 1921. . . . Enacted in response to this Court's decision that pro rata stock dividends do not constitute taxable income, Eisner v. Macomber, 252 U.S. 189 (1920), the provision had the obvious purpose of preventing a corporation from avoiding dividend tax treatment by distributing earnings to its shareholders in two transactions — a pro rata stock dividend followed by a pro rata redemption — that would have the same economic consequences as a simple dividend. Congress, however, soon recognized that even without a prior stock dividend essentially the same result could be effected whereby any corporation, "especially one which has only a few stockholders, might be able to make a distribution to its stockholders which would have the same effect as a taxable dividend." H.R. Rep. No. 1, 69th Cong., 1st Sess., 5. In order to cover this situation, the law was amended to apply "(whether or not such stock was issued as a stock dividend)" whenever a distribution in redemption of stock was made "at such time and in such manner" that it was essentially equivalent to a taxable dividend. Revenue Act of 1926, §201(g), 44 Stat. 11. . . .

Unfortunately, however, the policies encompassed within the general language of §115(g)(1) and its predecessors were not clear, and there resulted much confusion in the tax law. . . .

---

8. Of course, this just means that a distribution in redemption to a sole shareholder will be treated under the general provisions of §301, and it will only be taxed as a dividend under §316 to the extent that there are earnings and profits.

By the time of the general revision resulting in the Internal Revenue Code of 1954, the draftsmen were faced with what has aptly been described as "the morass created by the decisions." Balenger v. United States, 301 F.2d 192, 196 (C.A.4 1962). In an effort to eliminate "the considerable confusion which exists in this area" and thereby to facilitate tax planning, H.R. Rep. No. 1337, 83d Cong., 2d Sess., 35, the authors of the new Code sought to provide objective tests to govern the tax consequences of stock redemptions. Thus, the tax bill passed by the House of Representatives contained no "essentially equivalent" language. Rather, it provided for "safe harbors" where capital gains treatment would be accorded to corporate redemptions that met the conditions now found in §§302(b)(2) and (3) of the Code.

It was in the Senate Finance Committee's consideration of the tax bill that §302(b)(1) was added, and Congress thereby provided that capital gains treatment should be available "if the redemption is not essentially equivalent to a dividend." . . . However . . . we find from the history of the 1954 revisions and the purpose of §302(b)(1) that Congress intended more than merely to re-enact the prior law.

In explaining the reason for adding the "essentially equivalent" test, the Senate Committee stated that the House provisions "appeared unnecessarily restrictive, particularly, in the case of redemptions of preferred stock which might be called by the corporation without the shareholder having any control over when the redemption may take place." S. Rep. No. 1622, 83d Cong., 2d Sess., 44. This explanation gives no indication that the purpose behind the redemption should affect the result. . . .

The intended scope of §302(b)(1) as revealed by this legislative history is certainly not free from doubt. However, we agree with the Government that by making the sole inquiry relevant for the future the narrow one whether the redemption could be. characterized as a sale, Congress was apparently rejecting past court decisions that had also considered factors indicating the presence or absence of a tax-avoidance motive.[11] At least that is the implication of the example given. Congress clearly mandated that pro rata distributions be treated under the general rules laid down in §§301 and 316 rather than under §302 and nothing suggests that there

---

11. This rejection is confirmed by the Committee's acceptance of the House treatment of distributions involving corporate contractions — a factor present in many of the earlier "business purpose" redemptions. In describing its action, the Committee stated as follows:

Your committee, as did the House bill, separates into their significant elements the kind of transactions now incoherently aggregated in the definition of a partial liquidation. Those distributions which may have capital-gain characteristics *because they are not made pro rata* among the various shareholders would be subjected, at the shareholder level, to the separate tests described in [§§301 to 318]. On the other hand, those distributions characterized by what happens solely at the corporate level by reason of the assets distributed would be included as within the concept of a partial liquidation.S. Rep. No. 1622, supra, at 49. (Emphasis added.)

should be a different result if there were a "business purpose" for the redemption. . . .

Taxpayer strongly argues that to treat the redemption involved here as essentially equivalent to a dividend is to elevate form over substance. Thus, taxpayer argues, had he not bought Bradley's shares or had he made a subordinated loan to the company instead of buying preferred stock, he could have gotten back his $25,000 with favorable tax treatment. However, the difference between form and substance in the tax law is largely problematical, and taxpayer's complaints have little to do with whether a business purpose is relevant under §302(b)(1). It was clearly proper for Congress to treat distributions generally as taxable dividends when made out of earnings and profits and then to prevent avoidance of that result without regard to motivation where the distribution is in exchange for redeemed stock.

We conclude that that is what Congress did when enacting §302(b)(1). If a corporation distributes property as a simple dividend, the effect is to transfer the property from the company to its shareholders without a change in the relative economic interests or rights of the stockholders. Where a redemption has that same effect, it cannot be said to have satisfied the "not essentially equivalent to a dividend" requirement of §302(b)(1). Rather, to qualify for preferred treatment under that section, a redemption must result in a meaningful reduction of the shareholder's proportionate interest in the corporation. Clearly, taxpayer here, who (after application of the attribution rules) was the sole shareholder of the corporation both before and after the redemption, did not qualify under this test. The decision of the Court of Appeals must therefore be reversed and the case remanded to the District Court for dismissal of the complaint.

It is so ordered.

Reversed and remanded.

Mr. Justice DOUGLAS, with whom Mr. Justice BRENNAN concurs, dissenting. . . .

[R]espondent's contribution of working capital in the amount of $25,000 in exchange for 1,000 shares of preferred stock with a par value of $25 was made in order for the corporation to obtain a loan from the RFC and that the preferred stock was to be redeemed when the loan was repaid. For the reasons stated by the two lower courts, this redemption was not "essentially equivalent to a dividend," for the bona fide business purpose of the redemption belies the payment of a dividend. . . .

When the Court holds it was a dividend, it effectively cancels §302(b)(1) from the Code. This result is not a matter of conjecture, for the Court says that in the case of closely held or one-man corporations a redemption of stock is "always" equivalent to a dividend. I would leave such revision to the Congress.

Henry T. Patterson Trust v. United States _____
729 F.2d 1089 (6th Cir. 1984)

Before Edwards and Krupansky, Circuit Judges, and Peck, Senior Circuit Judge.

KRUPANSKY, Circuit Judge. . . .

Prior to 1969, Henry Patterson, Sr. was the sole shareholder and chief executive officer of Puritan [Laundry and Dry Cleaning Company]. In 1969, he gave forty shares of Puritan stock to each of his children — John, Hank and Ellen. At the time, Ellen was married to Bill Hicks (Hicks), who, along with Hank, was employed by Puritan. Henry Patterson retained 200 shares of Puritan stock.

Bill Hicks was apparently a skilled business manager, while Hank Patterson (Hank) lacked effectiveness. Through the years, a bitter tension between Hicks and Hank developed, resulting in numerous altercations, one of which ended with Hank's hospitalization. At one point, John Patterson (John) participated in the management of the business but, because of the Hank-Hicks rivalry, John resigned and pursued a teaching career.

At trial, there was testimony that Henry Patterson desired that Hicks operate the company after Patterson's retirement. In early 1970, Patterson suffered a broken hip which forced him to remain away from the company. He designated Hicks to act as Puritan's president and general manager in his absence. Patterson's health continued to deteriorate and he died in November 1971.

In June 1971, Hicks presented the Puritan directors with a demand for an increase in salary and a proposal that they place all of the Puritan shares in a voting trust which Hicks would then control. The directors demurred and Hicks resigned. He immediately staged a slowdown of Puritan employees and persuaded the company's most substantial commercial accounts to demand that Puritan rehire him. Within ten days of Hicks' resignation, Puritan was on the verge of collapse. John, who had since returned to the business, contacted Hicks and negotiated a five-year employment contract with him.

Hicks' contract provided an increased salary, a profit sharing arrangement, and a five-year option to acquire eighty shares of Puritan stock. Hicks acquired five of those shares and his option on the remaining seventy-five shares remained open. At the same time, Hank also received a five-year contract.

During the ensuing five years, Puritan performed well but problems between Hank and Hicks became increasingly aggravated; Hank, John, and Ella Patterson, their mother, often were at odds with Hicks and his wife, Ellen.

In the spring of 1976, the Patterson estate was closed. Henry Patterson had placed his 200 shares of Puritan stock in the Henry T. Patterson Trust (Trust) with his widow, Ella, as the beneficiary with the power to appoint the corpus at her death. Following the closing of the estate, the Puritan stock was thus distributed:

Henry T. Patterson Trust	200 shares
Ella Patterson	25 shares
Hank Patterson	40 shares
John Patterson	40 shares
Ellen (Patterson) Hicks	40 shares
Bill Hicks	5 shares
Lester Winkler	6 shares

Hicks devised a two-step plan whereby he and his wife could obtain control of Puritan. First, Puritan would redeem the Trust shares and, following the redemption, Hicks would exercise his option and acquire an additional seventy-five shares. As a result, Hicks and his spouse would own 120 shares and the remaining shareholders would control only 111 shares, thus Hicks would acquire a controlling interest in Puritan.

The Reeves Bank, as Trustee, determined that if it refused to redeem the shares, Hicks would leave the company and eventually the Trust corpus would be worthless. Thus, acting in what it perceived as the best interests of the Trust and the beneficiary, the Reeves Bank determined to accept the proposed redemption.

On April 2, 1976, the directors were presented with the proposal. The Trustee reported that it would be in Ella's best interest to redeem the shares and invest the proceeds. . . .

The Trust reported the transaction as a capital gains sale. Upon review, the Commissioner determined that the amount received by the Trust in the redemption, $190,000.00, was a dividend taxable as ordinary income under §301 of the Internal Revenue Code of 1954. . . .

[A]t issue here is the propriety, as a matter of law, of the district court's determination that the Trust's redemption was not essentially a dividend, as defined by §302(b)(1).

In United States v. Davis, 397 U.S. 301 (1970), the Supreme Court evaluated the intended scope of §302(b)(1). In that case, a sole shareholder caused part of his shares to be redeemed by the corporation; the Court concluded that such a redemption is always equivalent to a dividend and thus subject to ordinary income tax. However, the Court's examination of §302(b)(1)'s history is germane to the analysis of this appeal:

> It was clearly proper for Congress to treat distributions generally as taxable dividends when made out of earnings and profits and then to prevent avoidance of that result without regard to motivation where the distribution is in exchange for redeemed stock.
> We conclude that that is what Congress did when enacting §302(b)(1). If a corporation distributes property as a simple dividend, the effect is to

transfer the property from the company to its shareholders without a change in the relative economic interests or rights of the stockholders. Where a redemption has that same effect, it cannot be said to have satisfied the "not essentially equivalent to a dividend" requirement of §302(b)(1). Rather, to qualify for preferred treatment under that section, a redemption must result in a meaningful reduction of the shareholder's proportionate interest in the corporation. Clearly, taxpayer here, who (after application of the attribution rules) was the sole shareholder both before and after the redemption, did not qualify under this test.

397 U.S. at 313.

As explicated by the Supreme Court, §302(b)(1) provides that corporate distributions which do not alter the shareholder's "relative economic interests or rights" will be taxed as a dividend, regardless of the form or nomenclature given the transactions. The test is to examine the change in the taxpayer's relationship to the corporation; §302(b)(1) is satisfied, under this test, if the examination establishes a "meaningful reduction" of the taxpayer's relative interests or rights in the company.

Whether a distribution by redemption of stock was "essentially equivalent to a dividend" for the purposes of the 1954 Code is a question of fact. The district court's factual determinations must be upheld on appeal if they are supported by substantial evidence within the record considered as a whole. . . .

To determine if the district court properly discerned a meaningful reduction in the Trust's interest and rights in Puritan, the starting point must be a comparison of the Trust's relative holdings prior to and after the redemption. As in United States v. Davis, supra, this comparison requires application of the attribution statutes.

Briefly stated, the 1954 Code provided that a trust constructively owned its shares plus the shares held by the beneficiary, including those shares which §318 attributed to the beneficiary. §§302(c), 318.

Applying this statute, it is readily apparent that prior to the redemption, the Trust constructively owned 345 shares of the Puritan company, computed from its own shares (200), Ella's holdings (25), and the shares owned by Ella's children (John — 40, Hank — 40, Ellen Hicks — 40). Following the redemption, the Trust's constructive holdings were reduced to 145 shares (25 owned by Ella, 120 held by her children). Only 11 other shares remained actually outstanding (Hicks — 5, Winkler — 6); therefore, the Trust held 345/356 shares, or 97%, before and 145/156 shares, or 93%, immediately after the redemption.

When the district court made this comparison it included the seventy-five option shares held by Hicks. Accordingly, the district court determined that the Trust held 80% of the company before redemption (345/431), and 62.8% after redemption (145/231). Because the Trust no longer controlled the company after the redemption (holding less than two-thirds of the stock), the district court concluded that the "meaningful reduction" test had been satisfied. The district court included the Hicks option in its calculations pursuant to the plain language of the attribution statute, §318(a)(4), which stated (emphasis added): "If *any* person has an option to acquire stock, such stock shall be considered as owned by such person."

On appeal, the Government urges that §318(a)(4) actually applies only to the taxpayer or to individuals whose shares are otherwise attributable to the taxpayer. The Government would therefore greatly narrow the scope of §318(a)(4). Under the Government's view of the statute, the Trust's ownership interest in Puritan was reduced only 4% as a result of the redemption, from 97 to 93%, which, it contends, was not meaningful as a matter of law.

"[I]n determining the scope of a statute, one is to look first at its language." Dickerson v. New Banner Institute, Inc., [460 U.S. 103, 100] (1983). . . . "Absent a clearly expressed legislative intention to the contrary, that language must ordinarily be regarded as conclusive." Consumer Product Safety Comm'n v. GTE Sylvania, Inc., 447 U.S. 102, 108 (1980). Further, "[i]t is axiomatic that where a statute is clear and unambiguous on its face, a court will not look to legislative history to alter the application of the statute except in rare and exceptional circumstances." Pope v. Rollins Protective Services Co., 703 F.2d 197, 206 (5th Cir. 1983). . . . Finally, "Congress is presumed to use words in their ordinary sense unless it expressly indicates the contrary." Davis Bros., Inc. v. Donovan, 700 F.2d 1368, 1370 (11th Cir. 1983). . . .

Nevertheless, the Government invites this court to examine the legislative history of §318(a)(4) and conclude that "any person" actually means only those "parties in the line of attribution." . . . The Government relies on the commentary in the "Detailed Discussion of Bill" portion of the Senate Report relative to §318(a)(3) (currently effective as §318(a)(4)). The commentary describes the operation of the relevant portions of the attributive statute in the following manner:

§318. Constructive Ownership of Stock

This section describes the area in which although in fact transactions related to stock ownership are in connection with a specific individual, ownership of stock is deemed to be in the hands of persons other than the person directly involved. Thus, for the purpose of determining whether a redemption of stock qualifies as a disproportionate redemption . . . consideration is given not only to the stock held by such person but also to stock owned by members of his family. . . .

The area of constructive ownership includes members of the family, persons having interests in . . . trusts, . . . such . . . trusts, . . . and stock held under an option.

In the family area (sec. 318(a)(1)) an individual is deemed to own stock owned by his parents, his children, and his grandchildren. . . . In the case of trusts, . . . the beneficiary or grantor is deemed to own his proportionate interest in the stock owned by the trust or estate and the trust or estate is deemed to own all of the stock owned by its beneficiaries or grantors. In any of the cases *above described* where stock, though not owned, is subject to an option, the holder of such option is deemed to own such stock (sec. 318(a)(3)).

S. Rep. No. 1622, 83d Cong., 2d Sess. 45 (emphasis added).

The Government urges that as a result of the commentary's apparent limitation of the option attribution rule to "the cases above described," "the Senate indicated its intent that §318(a)(3) (now §318(a)(4)) should be limited to parties in the line of attribution." The Internal Revenue Service has consistently followed the reasoning herein argued by the Government, see, e.g., Rev. Rul. 68-601, and the tax court has adopted the Service's view as well. However, only two appeals courts have addressed the issue and they, without analysis, adopted diverse positions.

In Friend v. United States, 345 F.2d 761 (1st Cir. 1965), the First Circuit's dictum indicated that that court believed that "Congress intended that section to apply only where options are held by the person whose shares are being redeemed." 345 F.2d at 764. In Sorem v. C.I.R., 334 F.2d 275, 280 (10th Cir. 1964), the court, again without analysis, applied the plain language of the options attribution provision of §318(a), and rejected the Government's view.

The Government argues that this court should defer to the Service's consistently-applied interpretation of the Code. However, while it is axiomatic that where statutory language remains vague even when illuminated by the legislative history, the construction offered by the agency charged with the enforcement of the statute will often be accorded dispositive weight, it is an equal principle that the agency may not so interpret the statute as to controvert its plain and unambiguous language. Except in "rare and exceptional circumstances," Rubin v. United States, supra, such as where Congress "expressly indicates" its intent that the plain meaning of the statutory language be avoided, Davis Bros., Inc. v. Donovan, supra, unambiguous statutory language "is to be regarded as conclusive." Dickerson v. New Banner Institute, supra.

Instantly, the Government asserts only the commentary of the Senate Report, reprinted above, as support for its construction of "any person" in §318(a)(4). The commentary falls short of a clear indication by Congress that the natural impact of the statutory language under review should be restrained. Accordingly, the district court appropriately included the option shares held by Hicks in determining the Trust's relative holdings prior to and following redemption.

It should be noted that, even if the Hicks shares were excluded, on the instant record the district court would have been entitled to enter the factual finding that the transaction under review was not essentially equivalent to a dividend and was therefore properly claimed as a capital gain. "The question whether a distribution in redemption of stock . . . is not essentially equivalent to a dividend . . . depends upon the facts and circumstances of each case." 26 C.F.R. §1.302-3(b) (1983 Treasury Regulations); United States v. Davis, supra. Obviously, one of the pertinent facts would be the relative holdings of the taxpayer as computed under §318's constructive stock ownership provisions, 26 C.F.R. §1.302(b). United States v. Davis. However, neither statutory enactment nor judicial construction would support the proposition that the resulting comparative calculation would become the exclusive and dispositive fact. In this case, the redemption effected "a change in the relative economic interests or rights" of all the stockholders of the Puritan company. Therefore, despite the fact that — excluding operation of §318(a)(4) — the Trust's relative holdings fell only 4% after redemption, under the unique facts and circumstances of this case, such was a "meaningful reduction" and the distribution was therefore not a dividend.

Accordingly, because substantial evidence supports the district court's factual determination that the transaction was not essentially equivalent to a dividend, the judgment below is affirmed.

NOTES

1. *The chain of attribution in* Patterson Trust. At issue in *Patterson Trust* was the taxation of the distribution in redemption of all of the shares owned by the trust. The trust could not qualify for exchange treatment under the complete termination safe harbor of §302(b)(3) because it constructively owned shares in the corporation after the redemption. Which shares did it constructively own?

Because Ella was a beneficiary of the trust, all her shares were attributed to the trust under §318(a)(3)(B)(i). Note that there is complete attribution from Ella to the trust regardless of her actuarial interest in the trust corpus. If, however, Ella had had only a remote contingent interest in the trust corpus, then there would have been *no* attribution under §318(a)(3)(B)(i).

Could the trust have filed an election under §302(c)(2)(C) and thereby have avoided all attribution from Ella? Recall that the §302(c)(2) waiver applies only to the *family* attribution rules of §318(a)(1). Since attribution from Ella to the trust arises under §318(a)(3), a §302(c) waiver would have had no effect on the attribution to the trust of the shares actually owned by Ella.

Not only are the shares actually owned by Ella attributed to the trust, but shares constructively owned by Ella may also be attributed to the trust under §318(a)(5)(A). Thus, the shares actually owned by Ella's children — Hank, John, and Ellen — are attributed to Ella and then to the trust under

§318(a)(1)(A)(ii), (a)(3)(B)(ii), and (a)(5)(A). While a §302(c)(2) waiver would avoid the attribution from Hank, John, and Ellen to Ella, that waiver applies only to determinations under §302(b)(3).

Are the shares actually owned by Hicks attributed to the trust? No. There can be attribution from Hicks to his wife, Ellen, see §318(a)(1)(A)(i), but those shares cannot be further attributed from Ellen to her mother because of the antisidewise attribution limitation in §318(a)(5)(B). Similarly, in computing Hicks's constructive ownership, there will be attribution of those shares actually owned by Ellen, see §318(a)(1)(A)(i), but he will not be attributed any shares Ellen only constructively owns (i.e., stock actually owned by family members) because of §318(a)(5)(B).

The number of shares owned by Hicks was relevant in *Patterson Trust* because, for making determinations under §302(b)(2), a shareholder's percentage ownership is a function of the number of shares owned (actually and constructively) by the shareholder relative to the total number of shares outstanding. For computing the total number of shares outstanding, should shares attributed from one shareholder to another be counted twice? Did the court in *Patterson Trust* count any shares twice?

Under §318(a)(4), shares subject to an option are treated as owned by the person having the option. The Service argued in *Patterson Trust* that this provision was intended to ensure that a taxpayer could not qualify for exchange treatment on a redemption while possessing the ability to reacquire a substantial interest in the corporation by exercise of an option. Thus, according to the Service, §318(a)(4) is applicable only in determining the constructive ownership of the taxpayer receiving a distribution in redemption of some of his shares.

The court, however, refused to read §318(a)(4) as limited in this way. Accordingly, the court treated the option given to Hicks as shares constructively owned by him, thereby increasing the total number of shares outstanding. The effect of the court's interpretation of §318(a)(4) was to reduce the trust's pre- and postredemption percentage of ownership of the corporation. Can the test of §302(b)(2) be manipulated through the strategic use of options as part of redemption transactions? See Bloom and Willens, How to Treat Option Shares Held by Third Parties in Planning for a Redemption, 62 J. Taxn. 80 (1985).

Suppose the option in *Patterson Trust* had been exercisable only after a specified period of time. Would §318(a)(4) still apply to the option? In Rev. Rul. 89-64, 1989-1 C.B. 91, the Service ruled that §318(a)(4) continues to apply. This ruling does not address the length of the specified period. If an option was exercisable only after 50 years, should the option fall under §318(a)(4)?

2. *The limited role of §302(b)(1).* As *Davis* indicates, the courts have given §302(b)(1) a narrow scope. In Levin v. Commissioner, 385 F.2d 521 (2d Cir. 1967), the court reviewed the legislative history of §302(b)(1)

before concluding that "it was intended to play a modest role in the statutory scheme." The court agreed with the observation that the "major function" of §302(b)(1) was to immunize redemptions of minority holdings of (nonvoting) preferred stock, citing B. Bittker and J. Eustice, Federal Income Taxation of Corporations and Shareholders 291 (2d ed. 1966). But see Rev. Rul. 85-106, 1985-2 C.B. 116, in which the Service ruled that §302(b)(1) is inapplicable to the redemption of six of nine shares of preferred stock held by a trust when the trust owns, with attribution, 18 percent of the corporation's voting common stock both before and after the redemption.

What role should §302(b)(1) play? In *Wright v. United States*, 482 F.2d 600 (8th Cir. 1973), the court held that a redemption reducing a shareholder's ownership from 85 percent to 61.7 percent was not essentially equivalent to a dividend when state law imposed a two-thirds voting requirement on certain corporate actions. Compare Rev. Rul. 78-401, 1978-2 C.B. 127, in which the Service ruled that a reduction in ownership from 90 percent to 60 percent was essentially equivalent to a dividend when no action requiring a supermajority was contemplated. See also Rev. Rul. 75-502, 1975-2 C.B. 111, in which the Service ruled that a reduction from 57 percent to 50 percent could be meaningful when the remaining 50 percent was held by a single other shareholder.

The Supreme Court wrote in *Davis* that "to qualify for preferred treatment under [§302(b)(1)], a redemption must result in a meaningful reduction of the shareholder's proportionate interest in the corporation." How great must a reduction be to be "meaningful"? In Rev. Rul. 76-385, 1976-2 C.B. 92, the Service ruled that a reduction in proportionate interest from 0.0001118 to 0.0001081 was "meaningful." The Service has also ruled, however, that a reduction in interest from 100 percent to 81 percent is not "meaningful." Rev. Rul. 73-2, 1973-1 C.B. 171. Was the court right in *Patterson Trust* when it said that a reduction of the trust's interest from 97 percent to 93 percent could be "meaningful"? Indeed, the court in *Patterson Trust* simply assumed that a reduction from 80 percent to 60 percent is "meaningful." Is this assumption subject to challenge?

In a pre-*Davis* case, the Second Circuit looked to the effect of a redemption on three aspects of stock ownership: (1) the right to vote, (2) the right to participate in nonliquidating distributions, and (3) the right to share in net assets on liquidation. Himmel v. Commissioner, 338 F.2d 815 (2d Cir. 1964). The Service has ruled that a redemption resulting in a reduction of these rights may satisfy the *Davis* "meaningful reduction" standard. Rev. Rul. 75-502, 1975-2 C.B. 111. A redemption of nonvoting preferred stock might reduce rights (2) and (3) but not (1), while a redemption of common stock with preferred stock outstanding might reduce (1) yet have little effect on (2) and (3). How should these different aspects of stock ownership be combined? Would it be appropriate to look to the relative change in fair market value of the redeemed shareholder's stock?

3.   *Constructive ownership after* Davis. While the narrow issue before the Supreme Court in *Davis* was whether the attribution rules apply to determinations under §302(b)(1), language in the Court's opinion seems to speak to how those attribution rules should be applied to the whole of §302(b). Would it be proper, after *Davis,* to take into account evidence of a shareholder's estrangement from, or independence of, the persons whose shares would be imputed to him under §302(c)(1)? Compare David Metzger Trust v. Commissioner, 693 F.2d 459 (5th Cir. 1982) (family hostility cannot override attribution rules), aff'g 76 T.C. 42 (1981) (court reviewed), with Haft v. Commissioner, 510 F.2d 43 (1st Cir. 1975) (remand to consider whether family hostility might mitigate attribution rules), and David Metzger Trust v. Commissioner, 76 T.C. 42, 80-84 (1981) (Tannenwald, J., concurring); see also Cerone v. Commissioner, 87 T.C. 1 (1986).

4.   *Redemptions by publicly held corporations.* The development of both the statutory and judicial law of redemptions has focused on closely held corporations, which traditionally were the only corporations, that customarily redeemed their shares. In recent years, however, some publicly held corporations have embarked on large-scale programs of repurchasing their own shares. This practice and its tax implications have been described as follows:

> Thus, suppose that *X* Corporation, with one million shares of common stock outstanding, is a stable, non-growth company which annually generates $1 million of earnings after tax, or $1 per share. Unable to reinvest its earnings at a profitable rate of return, *X* decides to distribute the $1 million to its shareholders. The stock of *X,* which normally sells at 10 times earnings, is currently quoted at $11, i.e., normal value of $10 plus $1 per share available for distribution.
>
> If *X* distributes the $1 million as a dividend, and if the shareholders of *X* pay tax at an average rate of 30 percent, then the net wealth per share of an average shareholder following the distribution will be $10.70, i.e., normal value of *X* stock ($10) plus the after-tax value of the dividend ($0.70). In the alternative, if *X* uses the $1 million to repurchase its own shares at $11 per share, it will be able to retire approximately 90,909 shares at that price. Earnings per share will then rise to about $1.10 on the 909,991 shares that remain outstanding, and, with no change in the multiplier of 10, the value of the stock held by non-selling shareholders will be $11, as compared with an average net wealth per share of $10.70 if a dividend is paid. Shareholders who have chosen to resell their stock will hold $11 in cash for each share sold less any capital gain tax resulting from the sale, with the net proceeds varying from individual to individual depending on original cost.
>
> Without detriment to those who prefer to sell, but provided always that the only tax imposed is a capital gain tax on sellers disposing of appreciated shares, *X* Corporation can benefit non-selling shareholders by applying its "unwanted" cash assets to the retirement of outstanding stock instead of paying dividends. Aside from tax effects, though possibly bearing some relation thereto, share repurchase has the further advantage of providing an

option to shareholders, since those who desire current income can obtain it by selling a portion of their shares, while those who do not can avoid it by retaining all of theirs.

The critical assumptions that underlie the tax results just described are, first, that repurchase produces capital gain (or loss) for shareholders who choose to surrender their shares to the company, and second, that repurchase has no present tax consequences (other than the postponement of gain or loss) for those who do not. The Internal Revenue Service has thus far raised no question about the legitimacy of these results as a matter of law. They are also either ignored or taken for granted by the tax bar, presumably for the reason, mentioned above, that dividend equivalency problems are rarely associated with publicly held corporations.

Chirelstein, Optional Redemptions and Optional Dividends: Taxing the Repurchase of Common Shares, 78 Yale L.J. 739 (1969).

What is the statutory foundation for the first "critical assumption" (that capital gain treatment will be available to the tendering shareholder) identified by Professor Chirelstein in the final paragraph of the extract? Is it necessarily the case that any redemption by a publicly held corporation is "substantially disproportionate" (or at least not essentially equivalent to a dividend)? Should the attribution rules be applicable to the redemption of publicly held stock? See Bacon, Share Redemptions by Publicly Held Companies: A New Look at Dividend Equivalency, 26 Tax L. Rev. 283 (1971). As to the second "critical assumption" (that nontendering shareholders are unaffected by the redemption) identified by Professor Chirelstein, you should suspend your judgment until §305 is examined. In general, though, little attention has been focused on the tax consequences of a redemption to a nontendering shareholder. What alternatives are there? See Doernberg, The Taxation of Reinvested Corporate Earnings, 24 Wm. & Mary L. Rev. 1 (1982).

5. *Redemption of stock versus retirement of bonds.* Section 302 speaks of a redemption of "stock." On the repayment of corporate debt, the creditor has no gain or loss unless she receives more than her basis for the debt instrument. Even if there is a gain, the retirement of corporate bonds and other evidences of indebtedness is ordinarily a capital gain or loss transaction by virtue of §1271(a)(1), and there is no counterpart of §302 in the Code to treat the retirement of such creditor instruments as a distribution of earnings and profits. Once more (recall the discussion of equity and debt in Chapter 3), we find the Code smiling on the issuance of debt instruments instead of stock by the newly organized corporation and the ongoing, closely held corporation. Note the radically different treatment Davis would have received had the monies advanced for the preferred stock instead been contributed for bonds. See the penultimate paragraph in the *Davis* opinion. But the same criteria that turn ostensible bonds or debentures into stock so as to deny an interest deduction may also require the bonds to be treated as stock under §302.

6. *Redemption of §306 stock.* A possible end-run around §§302 and 301 takes the form of a sale of a shareholder's stock to an unrelated third party from whom the stock is later redeemed by the corporation. For example, how should a shareholder be taxed if he sells some of his shares in a closely held corporation to a third party subject to the understanding that the shares will be redeemed immediately? How definite must such an "understanding" be for the Commissioner to attribute the redemption to the selling shareholder? In any event, is the Commissioner likely to be able to discern the presence of a prearranged plan of redemption from the facts disclosed on the parties' tax returns?

A shareholder who tries this route to avoid §§302 and 301 may well find himself out of the frying pan and into the fire if he uses common stock as the bailout mechanism. What happens if, for example, the third party refuses to accede to the redemption? The tax-avoiding shareholder might end up with a stranger owning (and voting) a significant portion of the stock of his corporation. For this reason, sales of stock subject to prearranged redemptions will most often involve nonvoting preferred stock.

Section 306, dealing with the redemption or sale of certain classes of stock (primarily preferred stock issued as a stock dividend), is examined at page 269 infra. Consider also in this context the tax advantages of the gift of stock to a charitable organization in anticipation of redemption.

7. *Redemptions to pay death taxes.* Section 303, relating to distributions in redemption of stock to pay death taxes as well as funeral and administration expenses, first entered the Code in 1950. The general purpose of §303 is to protect against forced sales of family businesses. Consider, for example, the case of a taxpayer who at death leaves a substantial estate composed predominantly of the stock of a closely held corporation. The decedent's executor will need cash for the payment of administrative expenses, funeral costs, the federal estate tax, and possibly a state inheritance tax. With such an illiquid estate, the executor may have no choice but to cause the corporation to redeem some of the estate's stock to raise the needed funds. Although the estate will have a fair market value adjusted basis in the stock pursuant to §1014, in the absence of §303 the estate might incur a tax liability on the redemption pursuant to §§301 and 302. Application of §303, though, will give exchange treatment to the estate on the redemption, thereby eliminating all tax liability by virtue of the basis step-up at death under §1014.

While the simple example above describes the situation to which §303 was intended to speak, the benefits of §303 are available without any showing that the estate lacks sufficient liquid assets to cover its expenses. The benefit of §303, however, is available only to an estate in which stock of the redeeming corporation constitutes more than 35 percent of its gross value less the deduction provided by §§2053 and 2054 for taxes, expenses, debts, and losses, although the stock of two or more corporations can qualify under certain circumstances, §303(b)(2)(B). Section 303 can apply to taxpayers other than an estate, although it can only apply to owners of stock actually chargeable for debts, expenses, or taxes of the estate and only to the extent thereof.

In Rev. Rul. 87-132, 1987-2 C.B. 82, the Service adopted an expansive interpretation of the transactions covered by §303. An estate and an unrelated individual each owned 50 percent of the outstanding stock of a corporation. The estate wanted the benefits of §303 without diminishing its voting control over the corporation. Accordingly, the corporation declared a stock dividend of new nonvoting stock and then promptly redeemed two-thirds of the nonvoting stock issued to the estate. The Service ruled that this redemption was protected by §303, emphasizing that "the basis of the stock redeemed [was] determined by reference to the basis of the 'old stock' included in the estate."

Because the benefits of §303 are available only to substantial owners of a corporation, shareholders will sometimes seek to inflate their stock ownership beyond their actual holdings. For example, the taxpayer in Estate of Byrd v. Commissioner, 388 F.2d 223 (5th Cir. 1967), argued that the attribution rules of §318 could be applied to determinations under §303. Because §303 does not explicitly reference §318, however, the court held that application of the attribution rules to §303 determinations would be improper, relying on the first clause of §318(a).

In Rev. Rul. 84-76, 1984-1 C.B. 91, the Service ruled that §303 does not apply to redemptions of stock not actually owned by the decedent but includible in his gross estate under §2035(a) (transfers made within three years of death). The Service did rule, however, that such stock can be used to satisfy the 35 percent test of §303(b)(2)(A), thereby allowing stock actually owned by the decedent to qualify for §303 treatment.

Section 303 historically has played a minor role in the drama of subchapter C. Nonetheless, exchange treatment is important not only because of a preferential rate of tax but also because of the recovery of basis obtained prior to the recognition of any income, however taxed. Because of the fair market value basis rule of §1014 applicable to property passing through the estate of a decedent, exchange treatment of postdeath redemptions will avoid recognition of income altogether.

8. *Constructive redemptions.* Suppose a controlling shareholder sells stock at a gain to employees pursuant to a corporate stock bonus plan. Because the corporation had an obligation to sell stock to the employees under the stock bonus plan, the transaction presumably should be recharacterized as a transfer from the controlling shareholder to the corporation and then from the corporation to the employees. In fact, the Seventh Circuit adopted this approach, recharacterizing the transaction as if the corporation redeemed the controlling shareholder's shares (producing

ordinary income under §§302(d) and 301) followed by an issuance of stock by the corporation to the employees. Schneider v. Commissioner, 855 F.2d 435 (7th Cir. 1988).

PROBLEMS

5-4. Reconsider Problem 5-1(b) on page 186, but assume that Father's estate consists of the X Corp. stock as well as cash of $800,000 and that the federal estate tax imposed on Father's estate is $400,000. What are the tax consequences? Does your answer change if Father's estate consisted only of the X Corp. stock and $2 million of stock in a variety of other corporations? Assume Father's estate incurs no expenses described in §§2053 or 2054.

4. Partial Liquidations under §302(b)(4)

A corporate redemption of stock, if it is a "partial liquidation" within the meaning of §302(b)(4), will be taxed to the tendering shareholders as a sale or exchange. Until 1982, the definition of a "partial liquidation" was in §346. The Tax Equity and Fiscal Responsibility Act of 1982 (TEFRA) repealed that section and moved the definition to §302(e); while the language of §302(e) is not identical to old §346, the changes are not substantive. Accordingly, the case law that developed under old §346 as well as the Treasury regulations promulgated under that section should be considered fully applicable to §302(b)(4).

The definition of a partial liquidation is in §302(e)(1). While the language of subsection (e)(1)(A) mirrors the "not essentially equivalent to a dividend" language of §302(b)(1), the thrust of §302(e)(1)(A) is very different from that of §302(b)(1). Determinations under §302(b)(1) are made by looking to the effect of the redemption on the tendering shareholder and her interest in the redeeming corporation. Determinations under §302(e)(1)(A), in contrast, are made solely by reference to the effect of (and reasons for) the redemption at the corporate level. Compare this with the Supreme Court's holding in Davis that corporate purpose is irrelevant to determinations under §302(b)(1). Note also §302(e)(4), which allows a partial liquidation to qualify for exchange treatment under §302(a) even if made pro rata to the distributing corporation's shareholders.

Subsection (e)(1)(B) adds the dual requirement that a partial liquidation be made "pursuant to a plan" and occur "within the taxable year in which the plan is adopted or within the next succeeding taxable year." Note that the "not essentially equivalent to a dividend" language in

§302(e)(1)(A) is unlikely to have much impact because §302(e)(2) sets forth a two-part test which, if passed, is deemed to satisfy §302(e)(1)(A).

Rev. Rul. 60-322
1960-2 C.B. 118

Advice has been requested relative to the tax consequences of a proposed distribution by a corporation of cash, realized from the sale of United States Government bonds and excess inventories, to its stockholders under the circumstances described below.

M corporation has 3,800 shares of common stock, par value of $10x$ dollars per share, of which 200 shares are held in the treasury. The balance sheet indicates accumulated earnings of $1,500x$ dollars.

The corporation was engaged in the business of buying raw skins and tanning and selling the leather to a certain segment of the leather trade. It showed consistent profits until two years ago when the demand therefor suffered a serious, if not a permanent, decline. In an effort to revitalize the business, the corporation changed over to buying raw skins of another kind and tanning and selling the leather to another segment of the leather trade. However, the situation did not improve with the result that continuing losses were incurred and a large inventory of $5,000x$ dollars was accumulated.

Early in the year under consideration, M corporation determined that further purchases should be curtailed and inventories liquidated. Pursuant to this policy, the inventory was reduced to $3,000x$ dollars. In doing so, the corporation had sustained substantial operating losses. However, in view of the depressed state of the market and the grim future prospects, the process of liquidating its inventory is expected to be continued and the operations will be carried on at a modified basis with purchases kept at a minimum. In this manner, it is felt that the operating losses can be minimized and if the business decline continues, then a complete liquidation will eventually be voted by the stockholders. Accordingly, the M corporation proposes to redeem a portion of its stock with cash from the sale of United States Series G bonds and from the proceeds of the inventories being liquidated in the ordinary course of business. . . .

Where a corporation has earnings available, in order for the distribution of assets by it to its shareholders to be treated as a partial liquidation, the distribution must result from a genuine contraction of the business of the corporation. See Joseph W. Imler v. Commissioner, 11 T.C. 836. . . . In the instant case, the earnings and profits of prior years were retained in the corporation and resulted in building up a large inventory and investment of funds in Government bonds.

Under the foregoing set of facts, it is held that neither the sale of investments nor the sale of a large part of the inventory in the ordinary course of business constitutes a genuine contraction of the business of the corporation. Accordingly, the proposed distribution of cash for the portion of the stock of *M* corporation to be redeemed will not constitute a distribution in partial liquidation within the purview of section [302(b)(4)] of the code. The provisions of section 301 will apply to this distribution and, accordingly, the distribution will be taxed as a dividend to the extent provided in section 316.

NOTES

1. *Corporate contractions.* While §302(e) does not explicitly use the term "corporate contraction," that phrase has been the touchstone of a "partial liquidation" since before the first statutory treatment of partial liquidations. *Imler,* cited in Rev. Rul. 60-322, is the classic example of a contraction of a business.

> The principal building owned by the company had been damaged by fire in 1941. When the company undertook to repair the building it was found that, because of war conditions, the shortage of building materials, and high costs, it was advisable to abandon 2 damaged floors and reduce the 7-story building to one of 5 stories. The consequence was that the company found its facilities inadequate to carry on the retinning and soldering operations formerly engaged in. Moreover, these operations had proved unprofitable in recent experience because of the war conditions and shortage of necessary materials. For these reasons the company discontinued the retinning and soldering operations. This reduction in operations likewise reduced the amount of capital necessary for carrying on the business activities of the company. This was a bona fide contraction of the business operations and consequent reduction in capital used. The company thus had a real and legitimate purpose for reducing its outstanding capital stock.
>
> The motives of the corporation were all related to the above business purpose and were, therefore, legitimate and properly conceived. If the excess of insurance proceeds be set to one side, the surplus of the company had remained almost constant for 10 years. The company had followed a conservative dividend policy throughout its history and had not paid a dividend since 1934. The original issuance of the stock had occurred many years before and there was no connection between the issuance and the redemption of the same. There was no special circumstance or condition relating to the distribution excepting the fact that the company had in its hands the excess insurance proceeds, which formed the basis of the distribution. We are convinced that, except for the fire and excess insurance proceeds, there would have been no distribution.

11 T.C. 836, 840-841.

See Rev. Rul. 74-296, 1974-1 C.B. 80, distinguishing Rev. Rul. 60-322 and finding a genuine contraction in a change of business from a department store to a discount store. Here the taxpayer discontinued most of its operations and then changed the remaining business. Compare Estate of Chandler v. Commissioner, 22 T.C. 1158 (1954), aff'd, 228 F.2d 909 (6th Cir. 1955), in which a corporation distributed substantial cash in a pro rata partial redemption of its shares shortly after selling its general department store and opening a ladies' ready-to-wear store. Held, no valid partial liquidation because the distributed cash came from surplus rather than a reduction in working capital; the new store required as much working capital as did the prior department store.

In an effort to lend a degree of certainty to the concept of "corporate contraction," Congress as part of the 1954 Code enacted the predecessor of §302(e)(2) and (3). Unlike the "not essentially equivalent to a dividend" test of §302(b)(1) and §302(e)(1)(A), the "termination of a business" test in §302(e)(2) is intended to be objectively determinable. To meet the "termination" requirement, the corporation must distribute the assets, *or the proceeds,* of a business that was actively conducted for the five-year period immediately preceding the distribution, and immediately after the distribution it must continue to be engaged in a second trade or business with a similar five-year history. The concepts used by §302(e), and some of its problems, overlap those of §355. Section 355 concerns the so-called divisive reorganizations in which a corporation distributes to its shareholders the stock of a subsidiary corporation operating a going business while the parent corporation continues to operate another trade or business. See Chapter 11 infra.

Regulations under old §346 specify that an "active trade or business" be defined by reference to §355 and Treas. Regs. §1.355-1. New regulations have been promulgated under §355 defining an active trade or business since §364 was repealed, see Treas. Regs. §1.355-3. The examples in Treas. Regs. §1.355-3(c) are especially helpful in determining what activities rise to the level of an active trade or business.

Note that a qualified trade or business must have been conducted for at least five years prior to the partial liquidation. §302(e)(3)(A). If the distributing corporation did not conduct it for that entire period, some other taxpayer must have done so *and* the distributing corporation must have acquired the business in a tax-free transaction. See §302(e)(3)(B). Suppose *X* Corp. purchases all the stock of *Y* Corp. and then liquidates *Y* Corp. in a tax-free §332 liquidation. Has *X* acquired the business formerly conducted by *Y* in a transaction qualifying as tax free under §302(e)(3)(B)? See Treas. Regs. §1.355-3(b)(4)(i).

2. *Distributions of working capital.* The Service has ruled that on a genuine corporate contraction a distribution in partial liquidation may include not only the net proceeds from a sale of the operating assets but also an amount of capital equal to the working capital attributable to the terminated business activity. Rev. Rul. 60-232, 1960-2 C.B. 115. At the same time, if a corporation reinvests the working capital of a ceased business in

its other business, a subsequent distribution of cash will not be related back to the business cessation. Rev. Rul. 67-299, 1967-2 C.B. 138. See also Gordon v. Commissioner, 424 F.2d 378 (2d Cir. 1970), holding that a distribution of less than the entire proceeds received from the sale of an active trade or business cannot qualify as a partial liquidation.

3. *Surrender of shares.* If no shares are surrendered, as is true in an informal pro rata partial liquidation of a closely held corporation, the transaction may nevertheless qualify as a redemption. See Fowler Hosiery v. Commissioner, 301 F.2d 394 (7th Cir. 1962). See also Joint Comm. on Taxn., General Explanation of the Tax Equity and Fiscal Responsibility Act of 1982, at 126 (1982). What portion of the shareholders' basis will be applied against the amount realized? See Rev. Rul. 57-334, 1957-2 C.B. 240. Is a distribution likely to qualify as a redemption described in §302(b)(1)-(3) if no shares are surrendered?

If the recipient of a distribution in partial liquidation is itself a corporation, §302(b)(4)(A) renders §302(a) inapplicable. Why this difference in treatment between individual and corporate shareholders of a distributing corporation? Note that because of the dividends-received deduction of §243 this rule will most often work in favor of corporate shareholders. The discontinuance of a subsidiary's business and distribution of its assets (or the proceeds) to the shareholders of its parent may work a partial liquidation of the *parent* corporation. See Rev. Rul. 75-223, 1975-1 C.B. 109, clarified, Rev. Rul. 77-376, 1977-2 C.B. 107. But see Rev. Rul. 79-184, 1979-1 C.B. 143. Until 1982, exchange treatment for partial liquidations was available to corporate and noncorporate shareholders alike.

Consider, for example, the case of *ABC*, Inc., which operates a business and also owns all the stock of *XYZ*, Inc., which operates a second business. Suppose *XYZ* sells its business and distributes the proceeds to *ABC* in a liquidating distribution, which then distributes those proceeds to its own shareholders, all of whom are individuals. How will the distribution to *ABC* be taxed? How should the distribution to the shareholders of *ABC* be taxed?

4. *Corporate distributees.* Corporate shareholders cannot qualify for sale or exchange treatment under the partial liquidation provision of §302(b)(4). See §302(b)(4)(A). For the most part, this limitation works in favor of corporate shareholders because of the dividends-received deduction provided by §243. Under §1059(e)(1)(A), however, a corporate shareholder receiving a distribution in redemption of stock that would qualify as a partial liquidation to a noncorporate shareholder must treat the distribution as an extraordinary dividend. Recall that, under §1059(a), a corporation must reduce its basis in stock held for less than two years by any extraordinary dividends received with respect to such stock. Thus, a partial liquidation to a corporate distributee eventually will produce the equivalent of sale or exchange treatment if the corporate distributee does not

hold its remaining stock in the distributing corporation for two years. See the discussion of §1059 at page 173 supra.

PROBLEMS

5-5. Consider whether T qualifies for exchange treatment under §302(b)(4) on each of the following distributions.

a. X Corp. has operated a steel mill for many years. Because business has declined, X Corp. shuts down one of its furnaces, lays off 25 percent of its employees, and reduces production to 60 percent of its former capacity. X sells approximately 40 percent of its inventory as well as small machinery used with the closed furnace. The sale proceeds, as well as approximately 40 percent of X's working capital, is distributed to T and to the other X shareholders pro rata. Is it relevant whether T is an individual or a corporation? Must the shareholders turn in a portion of their shares?

b. Y Corp. has operated a log mill and a lumberyard for 10 years. The fair market value of the log mill is $250,000. The entire output of the log mill is sent to the lumberyard, although that output accounts for only 25 percent of the lumberyard's inventory. Y sells the log mill and distributes the proceeds to T, its 60 percent shareholder, in redemption of stock worth $200,000. Would it make a difference if Y had operated the lumberyard for only four years? If it had acquired the lumberyard four years ago?

c. Z Corp. has operated an ice cream parlor for 15 years. Seven years ago a small food menu was added, and the seating capacity was expanded. The food operation now accounts for more than half of Z's gross receipts and profits. Z Corp. distributes the ice cream equipment, ice cream trademark, and associated goodwill to T, its major shareholder in complete redemption of all of T's stock. T will continue to run the ice cream business at a new location.

B. TREATMENT OF THE CORPORATION

As discussed at pages 136-142 supra, a corporation, as a general rule, recognizes gain but not loss on a nonliquidating distribution of property. §311(b). See Martin Ice Cream Co. v. Commissioner, 110 T.C. 189 (1998), where the Tax Court found a corporation taxable under §311(b) on the distribution of appreciated property to the shareholder in a redemption.

Because redemptions under §302 are a subclass of the more general term "distributions," the redemption of stock with appreciated property ordinarily will result in recognition of gain to the distributing corporation.

A corporation redeeming some of its shares must consider the earnings and profits implication of the transaction. To the extent that gain is recognized by the distributing corporation (because appreciated property is distributed), earnings and profits will be increased pursuant to §312(b). Also, because the transaction involves a distribution of corporate assets, a decrease to the earnings and profits account also might be in order. How should a redemption affect the distributing corporation's earnings and profits? If the redemption is taxed under §301, then presumably the usual rule of §312(a) ought to apply. But what if the redemption is taxed to the shareholder as an exchange pursuant to §302(a)?

A difficulty arises when the corporation has appreciated assets, for in such cases the amount distributed in redemption may exceed each redeemed share's allocable proportion of capital plus retained earnings, the excess being an allocable proportion of unrealized appreciation not yet reflected in the corporation's books or its earnings and profits account. Should this excess be charged, in whole or in part, to the corporation's earnings and profits account? See §312(n)(7). To understand the workings of that section, consider the following example taken from the Conference Report accompanying the 1984 Deficit Reduction Act.

X Corp. has outstanding 1,000 shares of class A common stock and 1,000 shares of class B common stock. Both classes are $10 par stock, and both were issued for $20 per share (for a total of $40,000). The class A stock has a preference as to dividends and on liquidation in a ratio of 2 to 1 over the class B stock, while only the class B stock votes. If X Corp. distributes $140,000 in cash in redemption of all the class A stock at a time when it has $120,000 in current and accumulated earnings and profits and assets with net value of $210,000, (i.e., with $50,000 of unrealized appreciation), how much of the distribution should be charged to X Corp.'s earnings and profits?

The committee report specifically states that $80,000 should be charged to the corporation's earnings and profits, leaving only $60,000 to be applied against the corporation's capital account. The amount reducing the earnings and profits account is two-thirds of the corporation's total earnings and profits, a fraction determined by reference to the redeemed stock's preferential claim on the corporation's assets. The effect of §312(n)(7) is to allocate part of the corporation's earnings and profits account to each outstanding share, taking into account not only the total number of shares outstanding but also the legal priorities of each class of stock.

How should a corporation's earnings and profits be allocated between common stock and stock that is preferred and limited as to dividends and on liquidation (i.e., preferred stock)? According to the Conference Report,

[N]o earnings and profits generally should be allocable to preferred stock which is not convertible [into common stock] or participating to any significant extent in corporate growth. Therefore, a redemption of such preferred stock should result in a reduction of the capital account only, unless the distribution includes dividend arrearages, which will reduce earnings and profits.

H.R. Rep. No. 861, 98th Cong., 2d Sess. 840, 1984-3 C.B. (vol. 2) 94.

What are the tax consequences if a corporation redeems a share of stock for less than the share's allocable portion of earnings and profits? For example, suppose a corporation has 100 shares of common stock outstanding and earnings and profits of $1,000. How should the redemption of one share for $7 affect the corporation's earnings and profits? Note the "not in excess of" language in §312(n)(7). According to the Senate Report accompanying the Deficit Reduction Act of 1984, "the committee does not intend that earnings and profits be reduced by more than the amount of a redemption." S. Rep. No. 169, 98th Cong., 2d Sess. 202 (1984).

C. REDEMPTIONS RELATED TO OTHER TRANSACTIONS

1. Redemptions in Lieu of Buy-Sell Agreements

In Old Colony Trust Co. v. Commissioner, 279 U.S. 716 (1929), the Supreme Court ruled that an employee had income when his employer paid the employee's federal income tax obligation pursuant to the employment contract. In another context, suppose that A and B, both shareholders of X Corp., agree that upon the death of either shareholder, the survivor agrees to purchase the shares from the estate of the deceased. But what happens if B dies and instead of A purchasing the shares, X Corp. redeems the shares from B's estate? Do *Old Colony* principles result in taxation to A when X Corp. fulfills A's obligation? Consider the following two cases.

Holsey v. Commissioner _____
258 F.2d 865 (3d Cir. 1958)

Before Maris, Goodrich and McLaughlin, Circuit Judges.
MARIS, Circuit Judge. . . .
J.R. Holsey Sales Company, a New Jersey corporation, was organized on April 28, 1936, as an Oldsmobile dealership. Taxpayer has been president and a director of the company since its organization. Only 20 shares

were issued out of the 2,500 shares of no par value stock authorized; these 20 shares were issued to Greenville Auto Sales Company, a Chevrolet dealership, in exchange for all of the latter's right, title, and interest to the Oldsmobile franchise and other assets with respect to the franchise which had been owned and operated by the Greenville Company. The 20 shares issued were assigned a value of $11,000. Taxpayer's father, Charles V. Holsey, in 1936, owned more than two-thirds of the outstanding stock of the Greenville Company, and taxpayer was vice-president and a director of that corporation.

On April 30, 1936, taxpayer acquired from the Greenville Company an option to purchase 50% of the outstanding shares of the Holsey Company for $11,000, and a further option to purchase, within ten years after the exercise of the first option, all the remaining shares for a sum to be agreed upon. The Greenville Company owned all of the outstanding stock of the Holsey Company from its organization in 1936 until November, 1939, when taxpayer exercised his first option and purchased 50% of the outstanding stock of the Holsey Company for $11,000.

On June 28, 1946, the further option in favor of taxpayer was revised. Under the terms of the revised option, taxpayer was granted the right to purchase the remaining outstanding shares of the Holsey Company at any time up to and including June 28, 1951, for $80,000. The revised option was in favor of taxpayer individually and was not assignable by him to anyone other than a corporation in which he owned not less than 50% of the voting stock. On the date of the revision of this option, taxpayer's father owned 76% of the stock of the Greenville Company and taxpayer was a vice-president and director of that corporation. . . .

On January 19, 1951, taxpayer assigned his revised option to the Holsey Company; on the same date the Holsey Company exercised the option and paid the Greenville Company $80,000 for the stock held by it. This transaction resulted in taxpayer becoming the owner of 100% of the outstanding stock of the Holsey Company. In his income tax return for the year 1951, taxpayer gave no effect to this transaction.

The principal officers and only directors of the Holsey Company from April 28, 1936, to December 31, 1951, were taxpayer, his brother, Charles D. Holsey, and their father, Charles V. Holsey. On January 19, 1951, when the revised option was exercised, the earned surplus of the Holsey Company was in excess of $300,000.

The Oldsmobile franchise, under which the Holsey Company operated, was a yearly contract entered into by the Corporation and the manufacturer in reliance upon the personal qualifications and representations of taxpayer as an individual. It was the manufacturer's policy to have its dealers own all of the stock in dealership organizations.

The Commissioner determined that the effect of the transaction of January 19, 1951, wherein the Holsey Company paid $80,000 to the Greenville Company for 50% of the outstanding stock of the Holsey Company, constituted a dividend to taxpayer, the remaining stockholder. The Commissioner therefore asserted a deficiency against taxpayer in the sum of $41,385.34. The Tax Court sustained the Commissioner. 28 T.C. 962.

The question presented for decision in this case is whether the Tax Court erred in holding that the payment by the Holsey Company of $80,000 to the Greenville Company for the purchase from that company of its stock in the Holsey Company was essentially equivalent to the distribution of a taxable dividend to the taxpayer, the remaining stockholder of the Holsey Company. . . .

It will be observed that section [316(a)] defines a dividend as a distribution made by a corporation "to its shareholders." Accordingly unless a distribution which is sought to be taxed to a stockholder as a dividend is made to him or for his benefit it may not be regarded as either a dividend or the legal equivalent of a dividend. Here the distribution was made to the Greenville Company, not to the taxpayer. This the Government, of course, concedes but urges that it was made for the benefit of the taxpayer. It is true that it has been held that a distribution by a corporation in redemption of stock which the taxpayer stockholder has a contractual obligation to purchase is essentially the equivalent of a dividend to him since it operates to discharge his obligation. But where, as here, the taxpayer was never under any legal obligation to purchase the stock held by the other stockholder, the Greenville Company, having merely an option to purchase which he did not exercise but instead assigned to the Holsey Company, the distribution did not discharge any obligation of his and did not benefit him in any direct sense.

It is, of course, true that the taxpayer was benefited indirectly by the distribution. The value of his own stock was increased, since the redemption was for less than book value, and he became sole stockholder. But these benefits operated only to increase the value of the taxpayer's stock holdings; they could not give rise to taxable income within the meaning of the Sixteenth Amendment until the corporation makes a distribution to the taxpayer or his stock is sold. Eisner v. Macomber, 1920, 252 U.S. 189; Schmitt v. Commissioner of Internal Revenue, 3 Cir., 1954, 208 F.2d 819. In the latter case in a somewhat similar connection this court said (at page 821):

> During these years when Wolverine was buying its own shares it, of course, was subject to income tax as a corporation. Mrs. Green was subject to tax on whatever profit she made by the sale of these shares to the corporation. But what happened to warrant imposing a tax upon Schmitt and Lehren? If one owns a piece of real estate and, because of its favorable location in a city, the land becomes increasingly valuable over a period of years, the owner is not subject to income taxation upon the annual increase in value. In the same way, if a man owns shares in a corporation which gradually become more valuable through the years he is not taxed because of the increase in

value even though he is richer at the end of each year than he was at the end of the year before. If he disposes of that which has increased, of course he must pay tax upon his profit. All of this is hornbook law of taxation; nobody denies it.

We think that the principle thus stated is equally applicable here. Indeed the Tax Court itself has so held in essentially similar cases.

The question whether payments made by a corporation in the acquisition and redemption of its stock are essentially equivalent to the distribution of a taxable dividend has been often before the courts and certain criteria have been enunciated. The most significant of these is said to be whether the distribution leaves the proportionate interests of the stockholders unchanged as occurs when a true dividend is paid. Ferro v. Commissioner of Internal Revenue, 3 Cir., 1957, 242 F.2d 838, 841. The application of that criterion to the facts of this case compels the conclusion that in the absence of a direct pecuniary benefit to the taxpayer the Tax Court erred in holding the distribution in question taxable to him. For in his case prior to the distribution the taxpayer and the Greenville Company each had a 50% interest in the Holsey Company whereas after it was over the taxpayer had 100% of the outstanding stock and the Greenville Company none.

The Government urges the lack of a corporate purpose for the distribution and the taxpayer seeks to establish one. But we do not consider this point for, as we have recently held, "It is the effect of the redemption, rather than the purpose which actuated it, which controls the determination of dividend equivalence." Kessner v. Commissioner of Internal Revenue, 3 Cir., 1957, 248 F.2d 943, 944. Nor need we discuss the present position of the Government that the transaction must be treated as a sham and the purchase of the stock as having been made by the taxpayer through his alter ego, the Holsey Company. For the Tax Court made no such finding, doubtless in view of the fact that at the time the taxpayer owned only 50% of the stock and was in a minority on the board of directors. On the contrary that court based its decision on the benefit which the distribution by the corporation to the Greenville Company conferred upon the taxpayer, which it thought gave rise to taxable income in his hands.

For the reasons stated we think that the Tax Court erred in its decision. The decision will accordingly be reversed and the cause remanded for further proceedings not inconsistent with this opinion.

McLAUGHLIN, Circuit Judge (dissenting).

I think that the net effect of the facile operation disclosed in this case amounts to the distribution of a taxable dividend to the taxpayer. I do not think that the *Schmitt* decision controls here. Quite the contrary to the *Schmitt* facts, this taxpayer himself acquired a valuable option to buy the shares and solely on the theory of a gift of the option rights would make the corporation the true purchaser. I agree with the Tax Court that "The assignment of the option contract to J.R. Holsey Sales Co. was clearly for the purpose of having that company pay the $80,000 in exercise of the option that was executed for petitioner's personal benefit. The payment was intended to secure and did secure for petitioner exactly what it was always intended he should get if he made the payment personally, namely, all of the stock in J.R. Holsey Sales Co."

I would affirm the Tax Court decision.

Sullivan v. United States
363 F.2d 724 (8th Cir. 1966)

Before Vogel, Chief Judge, Blackmun, Circuit Judge, and Stephenson, District Judge.

STEPHENSON, District Judge.

[T]he taxpayer Sullivan purchased the assets of an automobile dealership in Blytheville, Arkansas in 1941. He then formed a corporation to operate the dealership. The individual who became resident manager of the dealership, Loy Eich, eventually acquired 120 shares of the 300 shares of stock outstanding — the rest being owned by taxpayer Sullivan. When Eich terminated his management of the dealership in February 1948, Sullivan purchased his 120 shares of stock. Thereafter, in September, 1948, Frank Nelson became the resident manager of the dealership under an arrangement which included an agreement permitting Nelson to acquire up to forty (40) per cent of the stock and further providing for taxpayer's repurchase of said stock upon Nelson's termination of his employment. After acquiring approximately 38% of the corporation's outstanding stock, Nelson announced his intention to depart from his position in 1956 and offered to sell his stock to taxpayer Sullivan. The corporation's Board of Directors then authorized the redemption of Nelson's stock by the corporation.

The ultimate question before the District Court involved a determination of whether the payment by the corporation in redemption of Nelson's stock constituted a taxable distribution to taxpayer Sullivan, the sole remaining stockholder of the corporation. The District Court found that taxpayer Sullivan was unconditionally and primarily obligated to purchase Nelson's stock in 1956 and that said stock was purchased by the Corporation out of profits distributable as a dividend and therefore held that the taxpayer constructively received income equivalent to a dividend in the amount paid by the Corporation for said stock, ($198,334.58). Initially, an interpretation of the memorandum agreement entered into by Sullivan and Nelson at the time the latter assumed his managerial functions is necessary. The agreement contained the following provisions:

6.   TRANSFER OF SHARES OF STOCK. It is understood and agreed that Sullivan is permitting Nelson to buy stock in said corporation for the purpose of giving him a working interest only, and said Nelson agrees that said shares of stock cannot and will not be mortgaged, hypothecated or transferred by him, his heirs, executor, administrator or trustee to any person other than William J. Sullivan or such person as said Sullivan directs in writing. Any such sale, delivery or transfer to any other person, firm or corporation shall be null and void. Said Sullivan agrees that he will, within thirty (30) days after such shares have been offered for sale to him, accept the offer to sell, provided always that such shares shall be offered for sale at a price to be determined according to this contract.

7.   TERMINATION OF CONTRACT. Said Nelson agrees that if he should terminate his employment or relationship with William J. Sullivan or employment by the said corporation, and if his connection and association with the corporation should cease or be terminated by Sullivan or the major-ity owners of the stock of the corporation, then said Nelson agrees to sell and transfer and deliver to Sullivan at the then book value all shares of stock owned by him in the Sullivan-Nelson Chevrolet Co. . . . If said contract is terminated by Nelson or Sullivan as herein provided or by the death of Nelson, the value of the stock owned by Nelson shall be fixed and determined as set up in paragraphs four and five of this agreement. If said Nelson should die or become so disabled by injury or sickness as to become incapable of managing and operating the business, then said Sullivan shall have the immediate and exclusive rights to purchase the stock owned by Nelson or by his heirs, administrators or executors in accordance with the terms of this contract. Title so (sic) said shares of stock shall automatically rest in Sullivan upon Nelson's death and said Sullivan shall be obligated to Nelson's personal representative or representatives for the value thereof as fixed by this agree-ment.

On the face of the agreement it would appear that Sullivan obligated himself to purchase Nelson's stock when it was offered to him for sale. The petitioner contends, however, that such an interpretation is contrary to the intention of the parties to the agreement and is not in conformity with the circumstances existing at the time the parties entered into the agreement. . . .[5]

At this juncture, the payment by the corporation to Nelson presents two basic questions: (1) Was that payment in actuality a dividend and therefore includable in Sullivan's gross income under §§61(a)(7), 316(a) and 301(c)(1) of the Internal Revenue Code? (2) If the payment is consid-ered as a corporate redemption of stock, was the payment includable in

5. The taxpayer makes an alternative argument to the effect that, even if he was uncondi-tionally obligated to purchase Sullivan's stock, subsequent events constituted a modification or novation of that agreement. Even if this contention is accepted, the court is at a loss as to how the taxpayer is aided. The novation or modification itself would be considered as resulting in an economic benefit and possible constructive dividend taxable against Sullivan. The taxpayer would be left in essentially the same position with respect to his possible tax liability.

Sullivan's gross income as being essentially equivalent to a dividend within the meaning of §302(b)(1)? This court has recognized that both questions are to be resolved as fact issues. Idol v. Commissioner of Internal Revenue, 319 F.2d 647 (8th Cir. 1963). If a finding is supported by substantial evidence on the record as a whole and is not against or induced by an erroneous view of the law, it will not be disturbed on appeal.

When an individual shareholder receives an economic benefit through a diversion of corporate earnings and profits, such a receipt may be taxed as a constructive dividend. This court set forth a criteria for determining whether a payment constitutes a constructive dividend in Sachs v. Commissioner of Internal Revenue, 277 F.2d 879, 882-883 (8th Cir. 1960):

> The motive, or expressed intent of the corporation is not determinative, and constructive dividends have been found contrary to the expressed intent of the corporation. The courts, as arbiters of the true nature of corporate payments, have consistently used as a standard the measure of receipt of economic benefit as the proper occasion for taxation. (footnote omitted)

This court has also adopted criteria for determining whether a redemption of stock is essentially equivalent to a dividend. See Heman v. Commissioner of Internal Revenue, 283 F.2d 227, 230-231 (8th Cir. 1960); United States v. Carey, 289 F.2d 531, 537 (8th Cir. 1961). While there is no sole decisive test in this connection, the several guidelines for the determination include "whether there is a bona fide corporate business purpose, whether the action was initiated by the corporation or by the shareholders, whether there was a contraction of the business, and whether there was a substantial change in proportionate stock ownership." Idol v. Commissioner of Internal Revenue, 319 F.2d 647, 651 (8th Cir. 1963). In addition, the Court has observed that the "net effect of the transaction is at least an important consideration in determining dividend equivalency." . . .

The general net effect and the purpose of and circumstances surrounding the transaction involved herein must be carefully scrutinized to ascertain whether Sullivan received a taxable dividend. Prior to the transaction, Sullivan held approximately 62% of the shares outstanding while Nelson owned the remaining shares. As previously discussed, Sullivan was unconditionally obligated to purchase Nelson's stock if it was offered to him for sale. After the transaction was completed, the relevant facts were essentially as follows: (1) Sullivan's personal obligation had been discharged (2) Sullivan owned all of the outstanding shares of stock of the corporation (3) the corporation's assets were decreased by the amount paid to Nelson for his stock (4) Nelson's stock was held by the corporation as treasury stock. It is true that in terms of the financial worth of Sullivan's interest in the corporation, it was the same after the transaction as it was before.[7] The transaction still resulted in an economic benefit to Sullivan, however, because he was relieved of his personal obligation to purchase Nelson's stock. After careful consideration this court concludes that there was no corporate business purpose or other factor which justifies the taxpayer's position that as to him the payment must be considered a stock redemption and not the equivalent of a dividend.[8] On the facts of this case, Sullivan received a taxable dividend as the result of the corporation's purchase of Nelson's stock.

This court is aware that it is often difficult to distinguish true substance from mere form. Tax law places some weight and significance on form and the choice of one alternative rather than another for achieving a desired end is often critical and may be determinative of the tax effect of a transaction. Judge Becker's opinion comprehensively deals with the evidence and the applicable law of this case. The taxpayer has failed to establish grounds for reversal. The judgment of the District Court is affirmed.

NOTES

1.   *Form and substance.* Are the facts of *Sullivan* so different from *Holsey* as to justify such diametric tax results? In each case, shares that the taxpayer might have purchased were in fact bought by the corporation. In *Sullivan,* the taxpayer had an obligation to purchase the shares while in *Holsey* the taxpayer had only an option. These two cases should make clear that buy-sell agreements ought never require one shareholder to purchase the shares of another but instead should only require one shareholder *or the corporation* to purchase the shares. Since the pitfall of *Sullivan* can be avoided so easily, should the courts allow it to exist at all? One experienced jurist remarked in this context that he would "leave for another day [the possibility of creating] an exception to the now concretized standard of form over substance in [this area]." Jacobs v. Commissioner, 41 T.C.M. (CCH) 951 (1981) (Tannenwald, J.).

Suppose the shareholders of *X* Corp. agree that upon the death of any one shareholder, the remaining shareholders will purchase the decedent's

7. Prior to the transfer of Nelson's stock Sullivan owned 186 shares of the 300 shares outstanding. His stock at this time was worth approximately $323,597.00. After the transfer, his 186 shares were the only outstanding stock of the corporation. Due to the corporate purchase of Nelson's stock, however, the value of the taxpayer's shares remained at approximately $323,597.00.

8. The taxpayer has strongly urged that there was a corporate business purpose motivating the purchase of Nelson's stock because of the valuable services received from him as resident manager of the corporation. The services had already been performed, however, when the stock was purchased. Moreover, it was Sullivan, not the corporation, who was obligated to purchase the stock. Under these circumstances, the District Court properly found that the purchase was not induced by a business purpose. The net effect of the transaction further indicates that a dividend was received by the taxpayer.

stock from her estate. If the shareholders cancel this agreement and replace it with a provision that the corporation will purchase the shares of any deceased shareholder, will they have successfully overcome the *Sullivan* trap? Apparently so, at least if the novation occurs prior to the death of all shareholders. See Rev. Rul. 69-608, 1969-2 C.B. 42.

The *Sullivan-Holsey* distinction remains good law. In Arnes v. Commissioner, 102 T.C. 29 (1994), the Tax Court ruled that the redemption of shares of stock from the wife would result in a constructive dividend to the husband only if the husband was primarily and unconditionally obligated to buy the stock. In a divided opinion, it found no such obligation.

PROBLEMS

5-6.   *X* Corp. has 120 shares of stock outstanding, 40 owned by *B*, 40 by *C*, and 40 by *D*, with each shareholder having an adjusted basis of $40 per share. *B* and *C* have agreed that upon *C*'s demise, *B* will purchase *C*'s shares for their then current fair market value. Subsequent to the signing of this agreement but prior to *C*'s death, *C* purchases the 40 shares owned by *D* for $100 per share. Upon *C*'s death, *C*'s estate tenders all 80 shares to *B* for their current value of $125 per share. *B* desires to purchase only 40 of those shares, although the estate argues that the agreement between *B* and *C* should be understood to require a purchase of all the shares *C* owned at death. To settle their differences, *B* agrees to purchase 40 of the shares owned by *C*'s estate and *X* Corp. agrees to redeem the other 40 shares. What are the tax consequences of these transactions to *B*, *C*, and *X* Corp., assuming *B* is an individual? How does the analysis change if *B* is a corporation? What steps could *B* take to increase the likelihood that a court would uphold a form of the transaction advantageous to *B*?

2.   *Redemptions as Part of Bootstrap Acquisitions*

Redemptions are sometimes utilized to effect "shoestring" purchases of closely held corporations. For example, suppose *A*, who owns all the stock of a corporation, wishes to sell out to *B*, but *B* cannot finance the entire purchase. The corporation's assets include a substantial amount of cash and marketable securities. *A* sells part of his stock to *B*, and the corporation redeems the rest of *A*'s stock, using its cash and securities to make payment. Note that if part of *A*'s stock had been redeemed while *A* was the sole shareholder, the redemption would have been essentially equivalent to a dividend. Despite this fact, it was held under the 1939 Code's predecessor to §302(b)(1) that a redemption following a sale, as described above, is a sale by *A* of his stock, not a dividend. Zenz v. Quinlivan, 213 F.2d 914 (6th Cir. 1954); Edenfield v. Commissioner, 19 T.C. 13 (1952).

The IRS acquiesced in these cases, although it announced that such transactions "will be closely scrutinized to determine whether the selling stockholder 'ceases to be interested in the affairs of the corporation' immediately after redemption." Rev. Rul. 54-458, 1954-2 C.B. 167. See Rev. Rul. 75-447, 1975-2 C.B. 113, concerning *Zenz* and a §302(b)(2) "substantially disproportionate" redemption, ruling that the sequence of redemption and sale is irrelevant. Do not overlook the fact that a bootstrap acquisition using appreciated corporate property can produce taxable gain to the corporation under §311(b).

What is the result if seller *A* does not wholly sever his relationship with the corporation? For example, he might continue to perform services under a profit-sharing agreement, or he might receive a percentage of the future profits as partial payment for his shares. Would the shareholder in either case have retained a forbidden "interest" in the corporation? Recall Seda v. Commissioner and the notes thereafter at pages 179-186 supra. And what about *B*? When the Service announced in Rev. Rul. 54-458, supra, that it would follow the *Zenz* case as to the seller, it went on to say that such redemptions "will . . . be examined to determine whether any payment by the corporation for stock has the effect of a dividend to the stockholders who remain interested in the corporation." Recall the *Holsey* and *Sullivan* cases, above.

When a redemption of stock owned by a corporation is taxed as a dividend, the 70 percent to 100 percent dividends-received deduction of §243 applies. See pages 134-135 supra. But see Waterman Steamship Corp. v. Commissioner, 430 F.2d 1185 (5th Cir. 1970), discussed at page 167 supra, where an ostensible dividend paid by a subsidiary to its parent, coupled with a sale by the parent of its stock in the subsidiary to a third party, was viewed as an integrated transaction so that the "dividend" was recharacterized as part of the purchase price and not a dividend. As a result of the recharacterization, the parent had additional capital gain (or less capital loss) on the sale of the subsidiary stock.

PROBLEMS

5-7.   *A* owns all the outstanding *X* Corp. stock — 100 shares with an aggregate basis of $40,000. The stock has a $100,000 fair market value. *P* wants to purchase *A*'s stock but has only $50,000. Assuming ample earnings and profits for *X* Corp., describe the tax consequences of each of the following situations:

   a.   *X* Corp. distributes $50,000 to *A,* who then sells her stock to *P* for $50,000.

     b.   *A* sells her stock to *P* for $100,000 (payable half in cash, half with a note). *P* then causes *X* Corp. to distribute $50,000 to her, using the cash to pay off the note. Would it matter if *X* Corp. redeemed some of *P*'s stock?

     c.   *A* sells 50 shares to *P* for $50,000, and then *X* Corp. redeems *A*'s remaining 50 shares for $50,000. What happens if the redemption precedes the sale?

     d.   If *A* were a corporation, how would *A* Corp. want to structure this transaction?

5-8.   *B* owns 10 of the 100 outstanding shares of *X* Corp. with adjusted basis of $50 per share and fair market value of $550 per share. While attending the *X* Corp.'s annual meeting, *B* slips and falls. *B* agrees not to sue *X* Corp. in exchange for a payment of $15,000. As part of that agreement, *B* agrees to sell all his stock back to *X* Corp. for $50 per share. What are the tax consequences of these transactions to *B* and to *X* Corp.? What is the result if *B* agreed to sell his shares not to *X* Corp. but to individual *C,* an individual owning 45 of the outstanding shares of *X* Corp.?

3.   Redemptions for More or Less Than Stock Value

Under some circumstances a corporation may repurchase its shares for more than those shares are worth. If the excess reflects a difference of opinion over valuation or a simple misjudgment, the entire amount paid should be treated as the cost of the shares and neither deducted nor capitalized. But what happens if the excess is paid because the corporation receives something from the tendering shareholder in addition to the shares? For example, the shareholder might agree not to purchase additional stock in the future (called a "standstill" agreement), or the shareholder, especially if she is an employee as well as a shareholder, might provide a covenant not to compete with the business of the company.

    Under §162(k),[3] a corporation may not deduct any amount paid or incurred in connection with the redemption of its stock except for those items specified in §162(k)(2). See Fort Howard Corp. v. Commissioner, 103 T.C. 345 (1994). This provision was enacted in response to Five Star Manufacturing Co. v. Commissioner, 355 F.2d 224 (5th Cir. 1966), in which the corporation was permitted to deduct the full amount distributed in redemption of 50 percent of its outstanding stock on the theory that elimination of the shareholder-director whose stock was redeemed was essential for the corporation's survival. The decision in *Five Star Manufacturing* cer-

---

3. Originally enacted by the Tax Reform Act of 1986 as §162(*l*).

tainly seems wrong — in measuring a corporation's profit or loss, amounts paid in redemption of stock should be irrelevant — but the legislative response may be overbroad.

The legislative history of §162(k) provides that the phrase "in connection with" should be construed broadly to include legal, accounting, brokerage, transfer agent, appraisal, and similar fees incurred in connection with the redemption. After INDOPCO, Inc. v. Commissioner, 503 U.S. 79 (1992), might some part of the president's or comptroller's salary fall within the ambit of §162(k)?

The legislative history of §162(k) further provides that §162(k) should apply to amounts paid by the corporation for standstill agreements, whether lasting for a specified or indefinite time. Such amounts, often called "greenmail," might increase the value of the corporation's outstanding stock. If so, should the corporation be entitled to capitalize the greenmail, recovering it when the company is sold or liquidated? While §162(k) does not speak to this issue, courts are unlikely to allow recovery of redemption premiums falling within §162(k) at *any* time. For an intriguing analysis of greenmail, see Macey and McChesney, A Theoretical Analysis of Greenmail, 95 Yale L.J. 13 (1985).

How should a redemption premium be treated under §162(k) if the corporation receives not only shares but also a noncompetition agreement from the tendering shareholder? In the absence of §162(k), an amount paid for a noncompetition agreement is amortized over 15 years, see §197, unless the covenant is not related to the acquisition of a business, see §197(d)(1)(E). If, though, the redemption and noncompetition agreement are parts of a single effort to eliminate an unhappy or uncooperative shareholder-employee, might not a court hold that the entire payment received by the departing shareholder-employee was made "in connection with" the redemption? In other contexts, courts have been willing to interpret the phrase "in connection with" surprisingly broadly. See Alves v. Commissioner, 79 T.C. 864 (1982), aff'd, 734 F.2d 478 (9th Cir. 1984). Note that §162(k) cannot apply if there is no redemption, so the tax treatment of payments for standstill agreements and similar arrangements not connected to a redemption is left open by §162(k).

A corporation might also pay less than full value for redeemed stock. Why might a tendering shareholder accept less than fair market value? The effect of receiving less than full value for redeemed shares is an increase in value of all postredemption outstanding shares, so a shareholder who accepts less than full value for redeemed shares transfers some of her stock value to the other shareholders. To determine how such a transfer should be taxed, we must understand why such a transfer might be made. The following case concerns the most extreme situation, namely, a contribution of stock to the corporation by one shareholder without any return distribution.

Commissioner v. Fink
483 U.S. 89 (1987)

Justice POWELL delivered the opinion of the Court.

The question in this case is whether a dominant shareholder who voluntarily surrenders a portion of his shares to the corporation, but retains control, may immediately deduct from taxable income his basis in the surrendered shares.

Respondents Peter and Karla Fink were the principal shareholders of Travco Corporation, a Michigan manufacturer of motor homes. Travco had one class of common stock outstanding and no preferred stock. Mr. Fink owned 52.2 percent, and Mrs. Fink 20.3 percent, of the outstanding shares. Travco urgently needed new capital as a result of financial difficulties it encountered in the mid-1970s. The Finks voluntarily surrendered some of their shares to Travco in an effort to "increase the attractiveness of the corporation to outside investors." Mr. Fink surrendered 116,146 shares in December 1976; Mrs. Fink surrendered 80,000 shares in January 1977. As a result, the Finks' combined percentage ownership of Travco was reduced from 72.5 percent to 68.5 percent. The Finks received no consideration for the surrendered shares, and no other shareholder surrendered any stock. The effort to attract new investors was unsuccessful, and the corporation eventually was liquidated.

On their 1976 and 1977 joint federal income tax returns, the Finks claimed ordinary loss deductions totaling $389,040, the full amount of their adjusted basis in the surrendered shares. The Commissioner of Internal Revenue disallowed the deductions. He concluded that the stock surrendered was a contribution to the corporation's capital. Accordingly, the Commissioner determined that the surrender resulted in no immediate tax consequences, and that the Finks' basis in the surrendered shares should be added to the basis of their remaining shares of Travco stock. . . .

It is settled that a shareholder's voluntary contribution to the capital of the corporation has no immediate tax consequences. §263; [Treas. Regs.] §1.263(a)-2(f) (1986). Instead, the shareholder is entitled to increase the basis of his shares by the amount of his basis in the property transferred to the corporation. See §1016(a)(1). When the shareholder later disposes of his shares, his contribution is reflected as a smaller taxable gain or a larger deductible loss. This rule applies not only to transfers of cash or tangible property, but also to a shareholder's forgiveness of a debt owed to him by the corporation. [Treas. Regs.] §1.61-12(a) (1986). Such transfers are treated as contributions to capital even if the other shareholders make proportionately smaller contributions, or no contribution at all. See, e.g., Sackstein v. Commissioner, 14 T.C. 566, 569 (1950). The rules governing contributions to capital reflect the general principle that a shareholder may not claim an immediate loss for outlays made to benefit the corporation. Deputy v. du Pont, 308 U.S. 488 (1940); Eskimo Pie Corp. v. Commissioner, 4 T.C. 669, 676 (1945), aff'd, 153 F.2d 301 (C.A.3 1946). We must decide whether this principle also applies to a controlling shareholder's non pro rata surrender of portion of his shares. The Finks concede that a pro rata stock surrender, that by definition does not change the percentage ownership of any shareholder, is not a taxable event. Cf. Eisner v. Macomber, 252 U.S. 189 (1920) (pro rata stock dividend does not produce taxable income).

The Finks contend that they sustained an immediate loss upon surrendering some of their shares to the corporation. By parting with the shares, they gave up an ownership interest entitling them to future dividends, future capital appreciation, assets in the event of liquidation, and voting rights.[7] Therefore, the Finks contend, they are entitled to an immediate deduction. See §§165(a) and (c)(2). In addition, the Finks argue that any non pro rata stock transaction "give[s] rise to immediate tax results." For example, a non pro rata stock dividend produces income because it increases the recipient's proportionate ownership of the corporation. Koshland v. Helvering, 298 U.S. 441, 445 (1936). By analogy, the Finks argue that a non pro rata surrender of shares should be recognized as an immediate loss because it reduces the surrendering shareholder's proportionate ownership.

Finally, the Finks contend that their stock surrenders were not contributions to the corporation's capital. They note that a typical contribution to capital, unlike a non pro rata stock surrender, has no effect on the contributing shareholder's proportionate interest in the corporation. Moreover, the Finks argue, a contribution of cash or other property increases the net worth of the corporation. For example, a shareholder's forgiveness of a debt owed to him by the corporation decreases the corporation's liabilities. In contrast, when a shareholder surrenders shares of the corporation's own stock, the corporation's net worth is unchanged. This is because the corporation cannot itself exercise the right to vote, receive dividends, or receive a share of assets in the event of liquidation. . . .

A shareholder who surrenders a portion of his shares to the corporation has parted with an asset, but that alone does not entitle him to an immediate deduction. Indeed, if the shareholder owns less than 100 percent of the corporation's shares, any non pro rata contribution to the corporation's capital will reduce the net worth of the contributing

---

7. As a practical matter, however, the Finks did not give up a great deal. Their percentage interest in the corporation declined by only four percent. Because the Finks retained a majority interest, this reduction in their voting power was inconsequential. Moreover, Travco, like many corporations in financial difficulties, was not paying dividends.

shareholder.[10] A shareholder who surrenders stock thus is similar to one who forgives or surrenders a debt owed to him by the corporation; the latter gives up interest, principal, and also potential voting power in the event of insolvency or bankruptcy. But, as stated above, such forgiveness of corporate debt is treated as a contribution to capital rather than a current deduction. . . . The Finks' voluntary surrender of shares, like a shareholder's voluntary forgiveness of debt owed by the corporation, closely resembles an investment or contribution to capital. See B. Bittker & J. Eustice, Federal Income Taxation of Corporations and Shareholders §3.14, p. 3-59 (4th ed. 1979) ("If the contribution is voluntary, it does not produce gain or loss to the shareholder"). We find the similarity convincing in this case.

The fact that a stock surrender is not recorded as a contribution to capital on the corporation's balance sheet does not compel a different result. Shareholders who forgive a debt owed by the corporation or pay a corporate expense also are denied an immediate deduction, even though neither of these transactions is a contribution to capital in the accounting sense.[11] Nor are we persuaded by the fact that a stock surrender, unlike a typical contribution to capital, reduces the shareholder's proportionate interest in the corporation. This Court has never held that every change in a shareholder's percentage ownership has immediate tax consequences. Of course, a shareholder's receipt of property from the corporation generally is a taxable event. See §§301, 316. In contrast, a shareholder's transfer of property to the corporation usually has no immediate tax consequences.

The Finks concede that the purpose of their stock surrender was to protect or increase the value of their investment in the corporation. . . . They hoped to encourage new investors to provide needed capital and in the long run recover the value of the surrendered shares through increased dividends or appreciation in the value of their remaining shares. If the surrender had achieved its purpose, the Finks would not have suffered an economic loss. . . . In this case, as in many cases involving closely-held corporations whose shares are not traded on an open market, there is no reliable method of determining whether the surrender will result in a loss

10. For example, assume that a shareholder holding an 80 percent interest in a corporation with a total liquidation value of $100,000 makes a non pro rata contribution to the corporation's capital of $20,000 in cash. Assume further that the shareholder has no other assets. Prior to the contribution, the shareholder's net worth was $100,000 ($20,000 plus 80 percent of $100,000). If the corporation were immediately liquidated following the contribution, the shareholder would receive only $96,000 (80 percent of $120,000). Of course, such a non pro rata contribution is rare in practice. Typically a shareholder will simply purchase additional shares.

11. It is true that a corporation's stock is not considered an asset of the corporation. A corporation's own shares nevertheless may be as valuable to the corporation as other property contributed by shareholders, as treasury shares may be resold. This is evidenced by the fact that corporations often purchase their own shares on the open market.

until the shareholder disposes of his remaining shares. Thus, the Finks' stock surrender does not meet the requirement that an immediately deductible loss must be "actually sustained during the taxable year." [Treas. Regs.] §1.165-1(b) (1986).

Finally, treating stock surrenders as ordinary losses might encourage shareholders in failing corporations to convert potential capital losses to ordinary losses by voluntarily surrendering their shares before the corporation fails. In this way shareholders might avoid the consequences of §165(g)(1), that provides for capital loss treatment of stock that becomes worthless. Similarly, shareholders may be encouraged to transfer corporate stock rather than other property to the corporation in order to realize a current loss. . . .[14]

We therefore hold that a dominant shareholder who voluntarily surrenders a portion of his shares to the corporation, but retains control, does not sustain an immediate loss deductible from taxable income. Rather, the surrendering shareholder must reallocate his basis in the surrendered shares to the shares he retains.[15] The shareholder's loss, if any, will be recognized when he disposes of his remaining shares. . . . We conclude only that a controlling shareholder's voluntary surrender of shares, like contributions of other forms of property to the corporation, is not an appropriate occasion for the recognition of gain or loss.

In this case we use the term "control" to mean ownership of more than half of a corporation's voting shares. We recognize, of course, that in larger corporations — especially those whose shares are listed on a national exchange — a person or entity may exercise control in fact while owning less than a majority of the voting shares. See Securities Exchange Act of 1934, §13(d), 48 Stat. 894, 15 U.S.C. §78m(d) (requiring persons to report acquisition of more than 5 percent of a registered equity security).

---

14. Our holding today also draws support from two other sections of the Code. First, §83 provides that, if a shareholder makes a "bargain sale" of stock to a corporate officer or employee as compensation, the "bargain" element of the sale must be treated as a contribution to the corporation's capital. . . . Second, if a shareholder's stock is redeemed — that is, surrendered to the corporation in return for cash or other property — the shareholder is not entitled to an immediate deduction unless the redemption results in a substantial reduction in the shareholder's ownership percentage. §§302(a), (b), (d); [Regs.] §1.302-2(c) (1986). Because the Finks' surrenders resulted in only a slight reduction in their ownership percentage, they would not have been entitled to an immediate loss if they had received consideration for the surrendered shares. §302(b). Although the Finks did not receive a direct payment of cash or other property, they hoped to be compensated by an increase in the value of their remaining shares.

15. The Finks remained the controlling shareholders after their surrender. We therefore have no occasion to decide in this case whether a surrender that causes the shareholder to lose control of the corporation is immediately deductible. In related contexts, the Code distinguishes between minimal reductions in a shareholder's ownership percentage and loss of corporate control. See §302(b)(2) (providing "exchange" rather than dividend treatment for a "substantially disproportionate redemption of stock" that brings the shareholder's ownership percentage below 50 percent); §302(b)(3) (providing similar treatment when the redemption terminates the shareholder's interest in the corporation).

For the reasons we have stated, the judgment of the Court of Appeals for the Sixth Circuit is reversed.

It is so ordered.

Justice BLACKMUN concurs in the result.

Justice WHITE, concurring.

Although I join the Court's opinion, I suggest that there is little substance in the reservation in footnote 15 of the question whether a surrender of stock that causes the stockholder to lose control of the corporation is immediately deductible as an ordinary loss. Of course, this case does not involve a loss of control; but as I understand the rationale of the Court's opinion, it would also apply to a surrender that results in loss of control. At least I do not find in the opinion any principled ground for distinguishing a loss-of-control case from this one.

Justice SCALIA, concurring in the judgment.

I do not believe that the Finks' surrender of their shares was, or even closely resembles, a shareholder contribution to corporate capital. Since, however, its purpose was to make the corporation a more valuable investment by giving it a more attractive capital structure, I think that it was, no less than a contribution to capital, an "amount paid out . . . for . . . betterments made to increase the value of . . . property," §263(a)(1), and thus not entitled to treatment as a current deduction.

[Dissenting opinion of Justice Stevens omitted.]

NOTES

1. *Stock surrenders and capital contributions.* The taxpayers in *Fink* argued that their non-pro rata stock surrenders were not capital contributions because nothing of value was added to the corporation's capital. Despite the remarks in footnote 11, surely it is the case that a corporation does not increase its wealth by the reacquisition of some of its shares. Were it otherwise, corporations could increase their wealth at will by coordinating pro rata stock surrenders. Moreover, because there is no significant difference between treasury stock and authorized but unissued stock — both can be sold to outside investors — the Court's comments in footnote 11 suggest authorizing additional stock as a fast way to corporate success. The Court's statement that reacquisition of corporate shares must increase corporate wealth or else corporations would not buy their own shares on the open market is a non sequitur: Many transactions between corporations and their shareholders do not increase corporate capital (e.g., the declaration of dividends) but nevertheless are done for sound business reasons. If a corporation believes its shares are undervalued on the open market, it may purchase (redeem) some of its outstanding stock. This purchase

shifts wealth from the selling shareholders to those who continue to hold stock of the corporation. Of course, no wealth — to the corporation or anyone else — is created by this activity.

2. *Stock surrenders and deductible losses*. While it is true that the corporation gains nothing by reason of a stock surrender, it is equally true that the surrendering shareholder loses something. In *Fink,* the surrender of 80,000 shares resulted in the diminution of the Fink's ownership from 72.5 percent to 68.5 percent. If the corporation were worth $1 million, that would be a dollar loss of $40,000. If the Finks lost value and the corporation did not gain it, where did it go?

To the other shareholders, of course. A non-pro rata stock surrender simultaneously reduces the percentage ownership of the surrendering shareholder and increases the value of all outstanding shares. If the surrendering shareholder continues to hold stock in the corporation, some of the value of the surrendered shares will reappear in the form of an increase in value of the remaining shares held by the surrendering shareholder.

Consider the case of *X* Corp.'s having two shareholders, *A* and *B*. *A* owns 75 shares of *X* with adjusted basis and fair market value of $100 per share, while *B* owns the remaining 25 shares of *X* with the same adjusted basis and fair market value. If *A* surrenders 50 of her shares, and still assuming that some loss deduction is appropriate, should *A* be entitled to a loss of $5,000? Note that the stock surrender reduced *A*'s ownership of a corporation worth $10,000 from 75 percent to 50 percent, for an economic loss of $2,500. That value is thus transferred to *B*, while the remaining value of the surrendered shares (also $2,500) remains with *A* in the form of an increase in value of her remaining shares.

Should §302 apply in *Fink*? A stock surrender is just a redemption for $0; if §302 applies to the transaction, a loss will be allowed only if the shareholder qualifies under §302(a) via §302(b). Does this approach adequately respond to the Supreme Court's concerns articulated in *Fink*? Does it permit too great a loss deduction in some cases? Do you think §302 was intended to apply to stock surrenders?

Suppose a corporation redeems 10 shares for $80 when each share is worth $10. Should this be treated as a redemption of eight shares for full value and a surrender of two shares for no consideration? If so, the redemption portion of the transaction would be tested under §302(b), while the basis of the two surrendered shares would be capitalized under *Fink*.

In Reynolds Metal Co. v. Commissioner, 105 T.C. 304(1995), a parent corporation was denied a current capital loss deduction, and treated instead as making a capital contribution to its subsidiary, upon surrendering shares of stock in that subsidiary to creditors of the subsidiary.

PROBLEMS

5-10.   Individual T owns all 10 outstanding shares of X Corp. with adjusted basis of $100 per share and fair market value of $75 per share. Unrelated individual U agrees to perform some accounting work for X Corp. in exchange for two shares of X Corp. from T. Assume the accounting work is worth $150. What are the tax consequences to X Corp., T, and U of the transfer of stock from T to U? Is it relevant whether X Corp. is authorized to issue more than 10 shares? How would your answers change if the transfer of stock from T to U was not for accounting services but instead for a covenant from U not to compete with X Corp. for a period of three years?

D.   REDEMPTIONS BY RELATED CORPORATIONS — §304

A "redemption" under §317(b) is the sale of corporate stock back to the issuing corporation. A similar transaction, though not falling within the definition of §317(b), is the sale of stock to a corporation *related* to the issuing corporation. For example, suppose individual I owns all the stock of P Corp., which in turn owns all the stock of S Corp. If I causes P to repurchase any of its stock, the transaction will be a "redemption" under §317(b), and, unless §302(b)(4) applies, the entire amount distributed will be taxed under the distribution rules of §301. If I instead sells some of his P stock to S, the transaction does not fall within the definition of a "redemption" even though the effect of the transaction is little different than a redemption of the stock by P.

In Rodman Wanamaker Trust v. Commissioner, 11 T.C. 365 (1948), aff'd, 178 F.2d 10 (3d Cir. 1949), the Tax Court held that such a sale of P stock to S does indeed qualify for exchange treatment because the redemption rules (now incorporated in §302) do not apply. In response, Congress added §115(g)(2) to the 1939 Code in order to close the loophole opened by *Rodman Wanamaker Trust,* and the substance of §115(g)(2) became the basis for current §304.

Section 304 addresses two related situations: (1) the sale of stock of one corporation to another corporation controlled by the taxpayer (i.e., the use of a brother-sister corporate pair), see §304(a)(1), and (2) the sale of parent stock to a subsidiary corporation as present in *Rodman Wanamaker Trust,* see §304(a)(2). In each case, §304(a) provides that the sale is subject to the redemption rules of §302 and, if the taxpayer fails to qualify for exchange treatment under §302(b), that the nominal sale will be recharacterized as a distribution subject to the rules of §301.

The following Ruling illustrates the basic operation of §304, focusing on what happens to the basis of stock surrendered by a shareholder in a §304 transaction that is treated as a distribution under §301.

Rev. Rul. 71-563
1971-2 C.B. 175

Advice has been requested regarding the Federal income tax treatment of the transaction described below.

A, an individual, owns 100 shares of corporation X which is all the outstanding stock of X. B, the son of A, owns all the outstanding stock of Corporation Y. A sold 25 shares of stock of X to Y for cash. The purchase price of the X stock was its fair market value. The earnings and profits of Y exceeded the amount of cash paid by Y to A for the X stock.

Section 304(a)(1) of the Internal Revenue Code of 1954 provides that for purposes of section 302 and section 303 of the Code, if one or more persons are in control of each of two corporations and in return for property, one of the corporations acquires stock in the other corporation from the person so in control, then such property shall be treated as a distribution in redemption of the stock of the corporation acquiring such stock. In any such case, the stock so acquired shall be treated as having been transferred by the person from whom acquired, and having been received by the corporation acquiring it, as a contribution to the capital of such corporation. . . .

Section 304(c)(1) of the Code provides that for purposes of section 304 of the Code control means the ownership of stock possessing at least 50 percent of the total combined voting power of all classes of stock entitled to vote, or at least 50 percent of the total value of shares of all classes of stock.

Section 304(c)(3) of the Code makes section 318(a) of the Code (relating to the constructive ownership of stock) applicable to section 304 of the Code, with certain modifications not here relevant, for the purposes of determining control under section 304(c)(1) of the Code. Section 318(a)(1)(A) of the Code provides, in pertinent part, that an individual is considered as owning the stock owned, directly or indirectly, by his children.

Section 318(a)(2)(C) of the Code provides, in pertinent part, that if 50 percent or more in value of the stock in a corporation is owned, directly or indirectly, by any person, such person is considered as owning the stock owned, directly or indirectly, by such corporation, in that proportion which the value of the stock which such person so owns bears to the value of all the stock in such corporation.

A actually owned 100 percent of the stock of *X* before the transaction and by the application of section 318(a)(1)(A) of the Code *A* is considered to have owned all of the stock of *Y* before the transaction. Accordingly, since *Y* acquired the stock of *X* for cash from a person (*A*) in control of both the issuing corporation (*X*) and the acquiring corporation (*Y*), the transaction is considered to be an acquisition of stock by a related corporation within the meaning of section 304(a)(1) of the Code and thus a redemption of the stock of *Y*, the acquiring corporation. See, in this connection, Coyle v. United States, 415 F.2d 488 (4th Cir. 1968).

Under section 1.304-2(a) of the Income Tax Regulations, the amount received by *A* is treated as a distribution of property under section 302(d) of the Code unless the distribution is to be treated as received in exchange for stock pursuant to section 302(a) or section 303 of the Code. Section 303 of the Code (relating to distributions in redemption of stock to pay death taxes) is not applicable in the instant case. Section 302(a) of the Code is applicable if the requirements of section 302(b) of the Code are satisfied.

Section 304(b)(1) of the Code provides that the applicability of section 302(b) of the Code is determined by reference to the stock of the issuing corporation, *X*. Through the application of section 318(a)(2)(C) of the Code, *B* owns the 25 shares of the stock of *X* held by *Y*. The ownership by *B* of the 25 shares of the stock of *X* is attributed to *A* by reason of application of section 318(a)(1)(A) of the Code. Therefore, after the transaction *A* still owns 100 percent of *X* and there is no complete termination of *A*'s interest in the stock of *X* within the meaning of section 302(b)(3) of the Code nor is there a substantially disproportionate redemption within the meaning of section 302(b)(2) of the Code.

The "not essentially equivalent to a dividend" test of section 302(b)(1) of the Code cannot be met since there has been no meaningful reduction in *A*'s proportionate interest in the stock of *X* as a result of the transaction. In determining the existence of a meaningful reduction, the constructive ownership rules of section 318 of the Code are applied (see United States v. Davis, 397 U.S. 301 (1970)).

The inapplicability of section 303 and section 302(a) of the Code results in the amount received by *A* being treated, pursuant to section 302(d) of the Code, as a distribution to which section 301 of the Code applies. Accordingly, the distribution is treated as a dividend to *A* from *Y* under section 301(c)(1) and section 316 of the Code.

Section 1.304-2(a) of the regulations provides that with respect to transactions to which section 304(a)(1) of the Code applies, the stock received by the acquiring corporation shall be treated as a contribution to the capital of such corporation and that section 362(a) of the Code is applicable in determining the basis of such stock. Section 1.304-2(a) of the regulations further provides that the transferor's basis for his stock in the acquiring corporation shall be increased by the basis of the stock surrendered by him.

Accordingly, the basis of the X stock in the hands of Y is the same as the basis of the X stock in the hands of A. Furthermore, since A owns no stock in Y directly after the transaction, the basis of the X stock surrendered is added to the basis of the 75 shares of X stock which A owns after the transaction.

NOTES

1. *"Control" under §304(c).* Note that a person "controls" a corporation within the meaning of §304(c) if he owns at least 50 percent of the total voting power in the corporation *or* at least 50 percent of the total value of all shares of all classes of stock. Furthermore, the attribution rules of §318 apply in determining such control. See §304(c)(3). Note that, by virtue of §304(c)(3)(B), the reach of the attribution rules is broadened in the context of §304.

Suppose X Corp. has two classes of stock outstanding. Individual T owns all the shares of one class and none of the shares of the other class. The X Corp. stock owned by T gives T 40 percent of the vote but 60 percent of the fair market value of X Corp. If T sells some of the X stock to a corporation T controls, can §304 apply to the sale?

Section 304 will apply only if T controls both corporations, and control for purposes of §304(a) is defined in §304(c) to require "at least 50 percent of the total combined voting power of all classes of stock entitled to vote, or at least 50 percent of the total value of all classes of shares." T quite plainly fails the 50 percent vote test, but does T satisfy the 50 percent value test? If this test is applied separately to each class of stock, T fails the test because T owns none of one of the two classes; if the value test is applied to the aggregate of all outstanding classes, T satisfies it. Note that although Congress specified that all classes of stock are "combined" for determining the vote test, no similar specification appears in the value test. Nevertheless, in Rev. Rul. 89-57, 1989-1 C.B. 90, the Service held that the §304(c)(1) value test is applied to the aggregate value of stock held. Accordingly, T is deemed to be in control of X Corp.

If a taxpayer sells stock of one corporation to a second corporation for stock of the second plus other property, it may be that the taxpayer did not control the purchasing corporation before the transaction but does control it afterward. Does §304 apply to such a transaction? Yes. §304(c)(2). Note, though, that §304 applies only to the "other property" received by the taxpayer, not to the stock of the purchasing corporation she receives. Why? Because §304(a) applies only to the exchange of stock for "property," and "property" does not include stock of the distributing (i.e., acquiring) corporation. §317(a).

Aficionados of the §318 attribution rules will observe that application of §318 to §304 is troublesome. Consider a taxpayer who owns 100 percent of the outstanding stock of two corporations, Brother and Sister. If this taxpayer sells some Brother stock to Sister, it is clear that §304 will apply. But is §304(a)(1) or (a)(2) applicable? While §304(a)(1) seems the obvious candidate, application of §318 causes the taxpayer's stock in Sister to be attributed to Brother (and vice versa), thereby making Brother and Sister into a parent-subsidiary pair (with either (or both?) as the parent (or subsidiary)). By its terms, §304(a)(1) defers to §304(a)(2). Thus, this sale of Brother stock to Sister seems to be taxed under §304(a)(2). Does it matter whether §304(a)(1) or (a)(2) applies? See Notes 2 and 4 infra.

Neither the courts nor the Service has been inclined to rearrange a brother-sister §304 transaction when the taxpayer's actual stock ownership placed him within the confines of §304(a)(1). See, e.g., Coyle v. United States, 415 F.2d 488 (4th Cir. 1968); Rev. Rul. 71-563 above. It appears safe to assume that the attribution rules of §318(a) will not be applied to remove a transaction from §304(a)(1) and place it into §304(a)(2). See also Broadview Lumber v. United States, 561 F.2d 698 (7th Cir. 1977).

2. *Application of §302(b) to a §304 transaction.* Sales of stock described in §304(a) are subject to the redemption rules of §§302 and 303. Assuming the inapplicability of §303 (discussed at pages 206-207 supra), the sale will qualify for exchange treatment under §§1001 et seq. only if one of the tests in §302(b) is met. Otherwise, the proceeds received by the selling shareholder will be taxed according to the distribution rules of §301.

Pursuant to §304(b)(1), the tests of §302(b) are applied to the change (if any) in the shareholder's interest in the "issuing corporation" (i.e., the corporation whose shares are nominally being sold). Do not forget that the attribution rules of §318(a) are applicable to determinations under §302, even those triggered by §304. See Treas. Regs. §1.304-2(a).

Consider a taxpayer, *T*, who owns 60 of the 100 outstanding shares of Brother Corp. and 60 of the 100 outstanding shares of Sister Corp. How will *T* be taxed if she sells 20 shares of Brother stock (with basis of $10 per share) to Sister for $15 per share?

T actually owned 60 percent of the outstanding stock of Brother prior to the sale. After the sale, *T* actually owned 40 shares and constructively owned 12 more through her ownership of Sister. See §318(a)(2)(C). Thus, *T*'s ownership of Brother dropped from 60 percent to 52 percent, so *T* cannot qualify under §302(b)(2) or (3) (*T* neither has gone below 80 percent of her former percentage ownership of Brother nor owns less than 50 percent of Brother after the redemption, thereby failing to qualify under §302(b)(2) on two grounds). Assuming arguendo the inapplicability of §302(b)(1) and (4), *T* will have received a distribution in the amount of $300 taxable under §301.

If *T* had sold 40 shares instead of 20, she would have qualified for exchange treatment under §302(a). A sale of 40 shares would bring *T*'s postsale actual and constructive ownership down to 44 percent (20 percent actual and 24 percent constructive ownership), thereby qualifying her under §302(b)(2). As a consequence, *T* would have taxable gain of $200, that being the difference between her amount realized ($600) and her basis in the shares sold ($400).

The application of §304 to a sale of parent stock to its subsidiary corporation is similar, although the application of §318's attribution rules to the transaction is problematic. Consider the case of taxpayer *T* owning 60 of the 100 outstanding shares of Parent Corp., which in turn owns 100 percent of the stock of Sub Corp. How will *T* be taxed if he sells 30 shares of Parent to Sub?

Section 304(b)(1) requires that the tests of §302(b) be applied to *T*'s interest in Parent. His presale ownership of Parent was 60 percent. His postsale *actual* ownership was 30 shares. Can the shares sold to Sub be imputed back to *T*? The Service might seek to form a chain of attribution from Sub to Parent to *T*, but that would require attributing stock of Parent to itself. Treas. Regs. §1.318-1(b)(1) provides that "[a] corporation shall not be considered to own its own stock by reason of section 318(a)(3)(C) [attribution to corporations]."

Assuming that the Parent stock owned by Sub cannot be attributed to *T* through Parent, does that make *T*'s postsale ownership of Parent only 30 percent? Under Treas. Regs. §1.304-3(a), the transaction is treated "as though the parent corporation had redeemed its own stock." Might not the Service argue that *T* should be treated as owning 30 of the 70 outstanding shares of Parent? If so, *T* would still qualify for exchange treatment under §302(b)(2).

How should §302(b)(4) (applicable to redemptions in partial liquidation) be applied in the context of §304? While §302(b)(4) surely applies to determinations under §§302 and 304, neither section specifies which corporation (the issuing corporation or the acquiring corporation) must engage in a partial liquidation. One court has held that the *acquiring* corporation must pass the test of §302(b)(4) if the shareholder is to obtain exchange treatment. See Blaschka v. United States, 393 F.2d 983 (Cl. Ct. 1968).

Suppose *F* and *F*'s son, *S*, own all the stock of *X* Corp. and *Y* Corp. *X* Corp. redeems all of *F*'s stock, and *F* waives the family attribution rules under §302(c)(2) in reporting the transaction as an exchange under §302(b)(3). Two years later, *F* sells his *Y* Corp. stock to *X* Corp. in a transaction governed by §304. Under §304(a)(1), *X* Corp. is treated as redeeming *F*'s *X* Corp. stock. Does this constructive redemption mean that *F* will be deemed to have acquired *X* Corp. stock in violation of §302(c)(2)(A)(iii)? The Service has ruled that the application of §304 does not cause *F* to run afoul of §302(c)(2)(A)(iii). Rev. Rul. 88-55, 1988-2 C.B. 45.

3. *Dividend income in a §304 transaction.* If a transaction described in § 304 is taxed as a distribution, the transferor is treated as receiving stock

from the acquiring corporation which is then immediately redeemed, and this redemption is then taxed under §301. This peculiar hypothetical redemption (which only arises if the transaction has *already* been determined to be taxable as a distribution, and so the redemption rules of §302(b) are not implicated) is important only if the transferor is itself a corporation; in such circumstances, this hypothetical redemption affects the transferor's tax treatment because the transaction may be taxed as an extraordinary dividend under § 1059. See §1059(e)(1)(A) and page 173 supra.

If a taxpayer subject to the rules of §304 has a sale recharacterized as a distribution pursuant to §302(d), then the amount of that distribution constituting a dividend will be determined by reference to the earnings and profits of both the issuing and the acquiring corporations. §304(b)(2). What is the function of the parenthetical in §304(b)(2)? Recall §312.

4. *Basis consequences of a §304 transaction.* If a taxpayer qualifies for exchange treatment in a §304 transaction, her basis in the redeemed shares will be used to offset the sale proceeds. Further, the acquiring corporation presumably will take a cost basis in those shares. But what happens if the taxpayer fails to qualify for exchange treatment and instead is subject to the distribution rules of §301?

In the case of a brother-sister §304 transaction, §304(a)(1) provides that "the stock so acquired shall be treated as having been transferred . . . as a contribution to the capital of [the acquiring] corporation." Accordingly, the taxpayer's basis in her stock of the acquiring corporation will be increased. See Treas. Regs. §1.304-2(a). What happens if the taxpayer has no *actual* ownership of stock of the acquiring corporation? Rev. Rul. 71-563, above. One possibility would be to transfer the basis to the person whose stock was attributed to the taxpayer under §318. An alternate possibility is to increase the taxpayer's basis in any remaining shares of the issuing corporation. Which do you prefer? See Coyle v. United States, 415 F.2d 488 (4th Cir. 1968).

And what of the acquiring corporation? It now owns stock of the issuing corporation, and since it is treated as having received that stock as a contribution to its capital, it carries over the shareholder's basis. See §362(a)(2).

Once again, the basis consequences attending a parent-subsidiary §304 transaction are more complex than the brother-sister situation. Of course, if the shareholder qualifies for exchange treatment under §302(a), then the shareholder recovers his basis as an offset against the amount realized and the acquiring corporation takes a cost basis. But if the transaction is subject to the distribution rules of §301, what happens to the shareholder's basis in the stock transferred?

In Broadview Lumber Co. v. United States, 561 F.2d 698 (7th Cir. 1977), the Service argued that the transaction should be treated as a contribution to the capital of the subsidiary (acquiring) corporation by the taxpayer. The court observed, however, that Congress specifically limited such treatment to brother-sister transactions. The court then held that the subsidiary corporation takes the stock with a cost basis. What does this imply as to the shareholder's basis consequences? Compare Rev. Rul. 70-496, 1970-2 C.B. 74, in which the Service ruled that a corporate taxpayer having no actual ownership of the acquiring corporation after a §304(a)(1) transaction simply loses its basis in the transferred shares.

5. *The relationship between §304 and §351.* If a taxpayer transfers stock of one corporation to a second corporation in exchange for stock of the acquiring corporation plus boot, it may be that both §351 and §304 apply to the transaction. These sections, however, have differing boot rules. Under §351, boot qualifies for exchange treatment and is taxable, if at all, only to the extent of gain on the transaction. Boot in a §304 exchange may be taxed as a dividend regardless of the amount of gain, if any, on the exchange. Because of the more favorable taxation of boot under §351, taxpayers have argued that §351 should override §304 when both are applicable. See, e.g., Haserot v. Commissioner, 46 T.C. 864 (1966), aff'd sub nom. Commissioner v. Stickney, 399 F.2d 828 (6th Cir. 1968).

Congress responded to this situation by providing that §304 overrides §351 (except with respect to certain acquisition indebtedness). See §304(b)(3). Once again, if the taxpayer receives only stock of the acquiring corporation without any boot, then §351 will be the exclusive taxing provision because stock of the acquiring corporation is not "property" for purposes of §304. See §317(a). Compare Rev. Rul. 78-422, 1978-2 C.B. 129, in which an individual transferred encumbered stock of one controlled corporation to another controlled corporation in exchange for stock of the acquiring corporation. Held, receipt of stock in the acquiring corporation is a §351 transaction but assumption by the acquiring corporation of the transferor's debt is like cash and therefore taxable under §304.

While §351 is supposed to defer to §304 by reason of §304(b)(3), Congress may have accidentally reversed that rule when it enacted the special rules for nonqualified preferred stock in §351(g). For purposes of §351(a) (providing for nonrecognition of gain or loss on the contribution of property to a controlled corporation in exchange for stock), receipt of nonqualified preferred stock is treated as boot rather than as stock. §351(g)(1)(A). However, for all other purposes such nonqualified stock remains its character as stock. In particular, receipt of nonquaified preferred stock in a redemption by a related corporation is not taxable under §304 because for that provision *all* stock is excluded, §317(a), even nonqualified preferred stock. Thus, a taxpayer can transfer stock of Brother Corp. to Sister Corp. for, say, common and nonqualified preferred stock of Sister, and gain will be taxable as capital gain to the extent of the value of the nonqualified preferred stock received. The nonqualified preferred stock can then be sold to a third party (at no additional tax cost), and the taxpayer has avoided application of §304. This assumes, though, that the nonqualified preferred stock stock will not be tainted under §306 as well as taxed under §351(b) upon receipt, a result that is not at all clear from the statute. See §306(c)(3). How would the various statutory provisions apply if the taxpayer received *only* nonqualified preferred stock of Sister in exchange for the Brother stock?

PROBLEMS

5-11. *F* sells 70 shares of *X* Corp. stock to *Y* Corp. for $100 per share. Prior to the sale, *F* owned all 100 outstanding shares of *X* Corp., with a basis of $25 per share. *X* Corp. and *Y* Corp. individually have current and accumulated earnings and profits of $5,000. What are the tax consequences of the sale assuming the following situations?

  a. *F* is the sole shareholder of *Y* Corp. Suppose instead of *F, P* Corp. is the sole shareholder of both X and Y Corp.
  b. *F* owns 50 percent of the stock of *Y* Corp.
  c. *F* owns no stock of *Y* Corp., but his son is the sole shareholder of *Y* Corp.
  d. *F* is the sole shareholder of *Y* Corp.; *Y* Corp. has no current earnings and profits and has a $10,000 deficit accumulated earnings and profits account.
  e. Reconsider your answers to (a) and (b) by assuming that *F* receives only $5,000 in cash and $2,000 in the form of *Y* Corp. stock.

In the following case, the relationship between the *Sullivan-Holsey* doctrine, page 215 supra, and §304 is explored. Suppose that *A*, a shareholder's obligation to purchase shares of stock of *X* Corp. from another shareholder is satisfied by a related corporation, *Y* Corp. Does the shareholder have tax consequences?

Citizens Bank & Trust Co. v. Commissioner _____
580 F.2d 442 (Cl. Ct. 1978)

Before Davis, Kunzig, and Bennett, Judges.

OPINION

PER CURIAM. [T]he court agrees with the trial judge's recommended decision. . . .

OPINION OF TRIAL JUDGE

MILLER, Trial Judge. . . .

Plaintiff, John D. MacArthur (John), has at all pertinent times been the sole shareholder, chairman of the board of directors and chief executive officer of Bankers Life and Casualty Company (Bankers), an insurance company. Telfer MacArthur (Telfer), plaintiff's brother, was experienced in the printing and publishing business and was president of Pioneer Publishing Company (Pioneer).

In its operations Bankers required a considerable amount of printed materials, such as applications, medical forms, advertising circulars, and policies. Up to 1950 it printed some of such materials itself, in the basement of its home office, and purchased others from various printing companies, including companies owned and operated by Telfer. During 1950, Telfer and plaintiff agreed to form a corporation, Brookshore Company, which they would jointly own and which would supply Bankers' printing needs at standard going rates. Telfer agreed to manage, staff and supervise Brookshore, and John agreed to furnish most of its capital and to have Bankers purchase its printing needs from it. Each was entitled to one-half of the outstanding stock. This agreement was effectuated in 1951.

In 1957, after Telfer had suffered a heart attack, he proposed to John that they enter into a mutual buy-out agreement. This agreement, executed June 29, 1957, acknowledged that they equally owned 2,235 of the outstanding 2,455 shares of Brookshore, and also all of the shares of Mackley Realty Company (Mackley), which they contributed to Brookshore. They agreed that upon the death of either, his estate was to sell his interest in Brookshore to the survivor and the survivor agreed to purchase such interest from the estate, at a stated price which increases with the passage of time prior to the date of death, with a maximum of $200,000 in the event death occurred after January 10, 1960.

Telfer died January 29, 1960. On February 10, 1960, John wrote to Telfer's widow, Elizabeth —

> As you undoubtedly know, Telfer insisted that I buy his half of Brookshore in the event of his death. I have every intention of keeping faith with him. When you make your final selection of a lawyer and qualify as executrix, let somebody in my office know and I will arrange to make the payment.

Thereafter, in February and March 1960, John requested Wayne R. Cook, an attorney employed by Bankers, to negotiate with Elizabeth and her attorneys in connection with fulfilling the terms and conditions of the 1957 agreement.

While never expressly repudiating its rights and obligations under the 1957 agreement, the representatives of the estate were not receptive to the $200,000 offer. Their reasons included the following:

(a) They believed that one-half of Brookshore, including its subsidiary, Mackley, was worth a great deal more than $200,000.

(b) They wanted additional indemnity agreements from John against various liabilities which the estate might incur, and they did not want to deal with Bankers because of the belief that an insurance company could not properly enter into an indemnity agreement, and

(c) They also wanted John to purchase from the estate for additional consideration Telfer's stock interest in Pioneer.

On March 24, 1960, an agreement was entered into between Elizabeth, individually and as executrix under Telfer's will, and John. Elizabeth was to deliver all of the shares of Brookshore to John or upon his written direction. In return, John was to pay concurrently to Elizabeth $200,000 and to release, indemnify and hold harmless Elizabeth and Telfer's estate against any loss arising out of any claims by himself, by the various corporations, and by Telfer's former wife. In addition, Elizabeth agreed forthwith to deliver to John or upon his written direction the remaining shares of Pioneer, which the estate owned, in exchange for an additional $175,000. The agreement was also approved by representatives of Bankers, Brookshore, and Mackley to indicate their approval of the releases.

On the same day, pursuant to the agreement, Bankers issued a check in the sum of $375,000 to a bank and the latter in turn issued a cashier's check in the same amount payable to the estate of Telfer. Wayne Cook, on behalf of Bankers, delivered the check to Elizabeth's attorneys, and she deposited it in the estate's account. In return, Elizabeth's attorneys delivered the Brookshore, Mackley, and Pioneer shares to Bankers.

It is stipulated that $200,000 of the $375,000 was for the Brookshore and Mackley shares and that the fair-market-value of such shares was at least $244,000.

The Commissioner of Internal Revenue determined that because the $200,000 payment satisfied John's obligation in the same amount and because Bankers had earnings and profits in excess of $200,000, Bankers' payment in that amount constituted a dividend to John. This is also defendant's primary position in this case.

In support of its position defendant relies on two cases, Sullivan v. United States, 363 F.2d 724 (8th Cir. 1966), cert. denied, 387 U.S. 905 (1967) and Wall v. United States, 164 F.2d 462 (4th Cir. 1947).

In *Sullivan* the taxpayer was the majority stockholder in a corporation in which there was only one other stockholder, Nelson. Sullivan had unconditionally agreed that upon Nelson's termination of his employment he would repurchase the stock from Nelson at book value. When Nelson did leave, instead of repurchasing the stock himself, Sullivan caused the corporation to do so. In agreeing with the Government that Sullivan had received a dividend in the amount of the corporation's payment to Nelson, the court concisely stated its rationale (363 F.2d at 729):

> After the transaction was completed, the relevant facts were essentially as follows: (1) Sullivan's personal obligation had been discharged (2) Sullivan owned all of the outstanding shares of stock of the corporation (3) the corporation's assets were decreased by the amount paid to Nelson for his stock (4) Nelson's stock was held by the corporation as treasury stock. It is true that in terms of the financial worth of Sullivan's interest in the corporation, it was the same after the transaction as it was before. The transaction still resulted in an economic benefit to Sullivan, however, because he was relieved of his personal obligation to purchase Nelson's stock.

(Footnotes omitted.)

In *Wall,* plaintiff was one of two equal shareholders. Plaintiff purchased the shares of the other shareholder for a cash down payment plus promissory notes payable in 10 successive years, with the stock to be held by trustees as security for the notes but otherwise for the benefit of plaintiff. After only a single year, the corporation assumed payment of the annual liability on the notes. Plaintiff transferred to the corporation his equity in the stock held by the trustees and the corporation entered such stock on its books as treasury stock. The court upheld the Government's position that the annual payments represented dividend income to plaintiff because (at 464) —

> [t]he transaction is regarded as the same as if the money had been paid to the taxpayer and transmitted by him to the creditor; and so if a corporation, instead of paying a dividend to a stockholder, pays a debt for him out of its surplus, it is the same for tax purposes as if the corporation pays a dividend to a stockholder, and the stockholder then utilizes it to pay his debt.

Neither of these decisions is authority for the defendant's position herein. They do support the idea that a corporation's satisfaction of its stockholder's debt gives him an economic benefit; but defendant ignores the fact that a payment to or for the benefit of a stockholder is not the only element of dividend. A dividend also necessitates a distribution of corporate earnings and profits. I.R.C. §316. Therefore, an exchange of assets of equal value which does not reduce corporate net worth cannot be a distribution of earnings and profits and hence is not a dividend.

This was made clear in Palmer v. Commissioner of Internal Revenue, 302 U.S. 63, 69-70 (1937), wherein the Court stated:

> While a sale of corporate assets to stockholders is, in a literal sense, a distribution of its property, such a transaction does not necessarily fall within the statutory definition of a dividend. For a sale to stockholders may not result

in any diminution of its net worth and in that case cannot result in any distribution of its profits.

[T]he bare fact that a transaction, on its face a sale, has resulted in a distribution of some of the corporate assets to stockholders, gives rise to no inference that the distribution is a dividend within the meaning of §[316]. To transfer it from one category to the other, it is at least necessary to make some showing that the transaction is in purpose or effect used as an implement for the distribution of corporate earnings to stockholders.

While the issue in *Palmer* was whether or not a sale of corporate property to stockholders resulted in a dividend to them, the principles underlying the decision are equally applicable to an exchange of property arising out of a purchase by a corporation. Both the courts and the Commissioner of Internal Revenue have ruled that a corporate payment of money or property to a stockholder to acquire corporate assets at a fair price does not reduce earnings and profits and is not a dividend.

For the same reasons, a corporation's assumption and payment of its stockholder's obligation to purchase from a third person an asset of equal or greater value cannot be deemed a dividend to the stockholder if the corporation acquires the asset. Just such a case was presented in Easson v. Commissioner of Internal Revenue, 294 F.2d 653 (9th Cir. 1961). There the taxpayer owned real property which was encumbered by a mortgage with respect to which the taxpayer was personally liable on the underlying notes. He transferred the property subject to the mortgage to a corporation in exchange for all its stock, but remained personally liable on the notes. The Commissioner contended that when the corporation made payments on the mortgage notes the taxpayer in effect received dividend income because such payments discharged taxpayer's legal obligation. The court rejected that contention with the following explanation (at 661):

While the corporation may incidentally have benefited taxpayer by reducing the mortgage, it is clear that the corporation did not thereby distribute any assets. The corporation owned the apartment subject to the mortgage and as the mortgage decreased its equity in the apartment house increased. Thus when it took money out of cash and applied that amount to the mortgage, its net worth remained constant. Its total assets were unchanged because the credit to the cash account was offset by a corresponding debit to the fixed assets account.

And see also Stout v. Commissioner of Internal Revenue, 273 F.2d 345 (4th Cir. 1959).

Sullivan and *Wall* are distinguishable from the other cases discussed by the fact that the corporations there received no property in exchange for paying their stockholders' obligations. Because they received only their own stock, their net worth was reduced and they had to deplete their earnings and profits to make the payments. In substance, the transactions were stock redemptions in favor of the plaintiffs which were essentially equivalent to dividends and hence taxable as such. (See I.R.C. §302(b).) In *Sullivan,* as the extract from the opinion previously quoted shows, the court stated that it was a relevant fact that corporation's assets were decreased by its payment. In *Wall,* the taxpayer argued that because the shares acquired by virtue of the payments were kept in the corporate treasury they remained assets, but the court responded that irrespective of whether or not they were kept in the treasury (164 F.2d at 465), "As a practical matter, such shares are redeemed in the sense that they no longer constitute any liability of the corporation but represent nothing more than an opportunity to acquire new assets by a reissuance."

Since in return for the $200,000 payment to Telfer's estate Bankers received shares of Brookshore which had an agreed fair-market-value of at least $244,000, it is concluded that Bankers did not distribute any of its earnings and profits by virtue of having satisfied plaintiff's obligation to make such a purchase. Furthermore, the very fact that the purchase was such a bargain makes it difficult to understand how Bankers benefited plaintiff at all by taking over his opportunity to make the purchase. Indeed, the undisputed testimony was that Telfer's estate, the sellers, maintained in the negotiations that the $200,000 plaintiff offered was less than the fair value of their Brookshore shares and sought to avoid their agreement to sell them to plaintiff at such price. Thus it can hardly be said that plaintiff was benefited by being relieved of an "obligation," "liability" or "debt" in the onerous sense which those terms ordinarily connote.

Defendant argues alternatively that the $200,000 payment to Telfer's estate was a dividend pursuant to I.R.C. §304. . . .

Plaintiff and defendant agree that subsection 304(a)(1) is designed to prevent a stockholder who controls two corporations from drawing off accumulated corporate earnings through the device of selling part of his stock in one corporation to the other. Plaintiff had controlling interests in both corporations. Defendant contends that the 1960 transaction was the constructive equivalent of plaintiff obtaining the remaining 50 percent of Brookshore shares from Telfer's estate and then selling them to Bankers in return for Bankers assuming and paying plaintiff's obligation for the purchase price.

To apply section 304 in this manner would be to distort rather than to further the statutory purpose. The entire focus of the section is on closing a loophole. Sales proceeds received by a stockholder from a controlled corporation should be treated as dividend income rather than return of capital or capital gain if what the corporation acquires is nothing more than the stock of another corporation the same stockholder controls; for, under such circumstances, the sale is only a transfer from one pocket to another.

An obvious prerequisite for invoking subsection 304(a)(1) is that the stockholder must have received the sales proceeds. Here, however, when the transaction was completed the $200,000 sales proceeds were received by a third person, Telfer's estate, and not by plaintiff. The superseding of plaintiff's obligation to buy the stock at less than fair market value was not an assumption of a liability nor a benefit to plaintiff. It was a mere incident to Banker's payment and the estate's receipt of the purchase price.

Another prerequisite for application of the statute is that the stockholder must have owned the stock before the transfer; or else the corporation cannot have acquired it from him, but must have acquired it from a third person. Here, however, plaintiff did not own the additional 50 percent stock interest in Brookshore which was the subject of the acquisition by Bankers. Telfer's estate owned the shares and would not convey them to anyone until it received at least $200,000 in cash for them. Since it was Bankers and not plaintiff which paid the $200,000, there is no basis for imputing to plaintiff acquisition of the shares for himself or ownership at any time. Thus, Bankers necessarily acquired them from a third person and not from plaintiff.

It is concluded, therefore, that plaintiff is entitled to judgment. . . .

NOTES

1. *The constructive dividend under §301.* The court was correct, was it not, when it distinguished *Sullivan* by noting that the corporation did not redeem its own shares but rather purchased the shares of another corporation? A corporation's satisfaction of its shareholder's liability should not be a dividend (more accurately, a distribution subject to the rules of §301) if the shareholder transfers valuable property to the corporation in exchange, except to the extent that the shareholder's liability exceeds the fair market value of the transferred property. Since Bankers received for its $200,000 payment stock of Brookshore worth at least $244,000, there should be no constructive dividend under §301. Focusing on the language of §301, was the distribution in *Citizens Bank* made with respect to the taxpayer's stock or made in exchange for the Banker's stock that the corporation acquired?

2. *The dividend under §304.* Was the court correct when it wrote that "[a]n obvious prerequisite for invoking subsection 304(a)(1) is that the stockholder must have received the sales proceeds"? The effect of Bankers's $200,000 payment was to relieve the taxpayer from an obligation of the same amount; satisfaction of a taxpayer's liability has long been recognized as constructive receipt. Old Colony Trust Co. v. Commissioner, 279 U.S. 716 (1929). While it is true that the corporation received fair value for its payment, that value was in the form of stock of a corporation controlled by the taxpayer. Is not the exchange of stock of a controlled corporation for money or property, *or for the payment of an obligation,* precisely the situation addressed by §304?

6

Distributions of Stock

A. DISTRIBUTIONS OF STOCK AND STOCK RIGHTS UNDER §305

1. The General Rule of Nontaxability under §305(a)

In Eisner v. Macomber, 252 U.S. 189 (1920), a provision treating a stock dividend as taxable in the hands of a shareholder was held unconstitutional as applied to a distribution of common stock on common stock by a corporation having no other class of stock outstanding. Subject to the exceptions contained in §305(b), §305(a) continues the *Macomber* rule that stock dividends are nontaxable on receipt. Furthermore, Congress has extended this rule to include the distribution of stock rights. §305(d)(1). Note, though, that the nonrecognition rule of §305(a) applies only to the distribution of a corporation's own stock (or rights to its stock) *made with respect to a shareholder's stock*. Distributions of stock as compensation to an employee or to pay off a debt of the corporation, for example, are not covered by §305, nor are distributions of stock by one corporation of stock in a second corporation. Such distributions, whether of stock or otherwise, will be taxed to the recipients under other provisions of the Code, usually §61. Cf. §83.

Stock dividends received tax free pursuant to §305(a) may be subject to substantial tax disabilities on disposition. Dividend stock (other than common stock received with respect to common stock) will be subject to the rules of §306 if it is received tax free under §305(a). See §306(c)(1)(A). These rules, discussed at pages 269-290 infra, may tax at ordinary rates the entire amount realized for the stock on disposition. In some cases it may be that taxation under §306 is harsher than would be immediate taxation on receipt under §305(b).

If a shareholder receives stock tax free under §305(a), then the basis in that stock is determined under §307(a). Section 307(a) requires an allocation of the old stock basis to both the old and new shares. This allocation is made in proportion to the relative fair market values of each share. Treas. Regs. §1.307-1(a). Thus, if the underlying rationale for tax-free receipt of dividend stock is that the taxpayer's interest has undergone a change in form but not in substance, see the discussion of *Macomber*, above, then the rule of §307(a) simply continues the identification of the old and new shares: The shareholder's old basis is allocated (without increase or decrease) to all shares constituting the new form of the old holding. How should the shareholder determine the holding period of the dividend stock? See §1223(5) (tacking).

What effect should a distribution by a corporation of its own stock have on the corporation's earnings and profits if the distributed stock is received tax free by the shareholders under §305(a)? See §312(d)(1)(B).

2. Exceptions to the General Rule: §305(b) and (c)

a. Actual Distributions

Section 305(b) contains a number of exceptions to the nonrecognition rule of §305(a). Section 305(b)(1) continues the pre-1969 rule that a distribution payable, at the election of any shareholder, in stock or property will be taxable regardless of the shareholder's choice. If she elects to receive property, the distribution rules of §301 apply directly. If she elects to receive stock, the same distribution rules apply by virtue of §305(b)(1). In these circumstances, Congress has taken the view that the shareholders electing to receive stock should be taxed as if they received cash that was then recontributed to the corporation in exchange for additional stock.

Section 305(b)(2) taxes the receipt of dividend stock if the effect of the stock dividend is to increase the proportionate corporate interests of some shareholders while giving other shareholders cash or property. If a shareholder's right to future dividends is increased, then he has an increase in the earnings and profits of the corporation within the meaning of §305(b)(2)(B). Similarly, if a shareholder's right to participate in the corporation's eventual liquidating distribution is increased, he has had an increase in his share of corporate assets. Because most preferred stock has a preference as to dividends and a limitation on liquidation, distributions *of* or *on* preferred stock often will cause a change in relative shareholder interests in the earnings and profits as well as in the assets of the corporation. The examples in Treas. Regs. §1.305-3(e) help clarify the potential scope of §305(b)(2). In particular, be certain that you understand why the distribution described in example 1 is subject to §305(b)(2) while the distribution described in example 2 is not.

A stock dividend cannot be taxable under §305(b)(2) unless shareholders not receiving the stock dividend receive cash or other property as part of the same transaction. This "companion distribution" requirement is easily satisfied because, under Treas. Regs. §1.305-3(b)(3), "there is no requirement that the shareholders receiving cash or property acquire the cash or property by way of a [formal] corporate distribution with respect to their shares, so long as they receive such cash or property in their capacity as shareholders." Distributions of stock and cash or property separated by more than three years, however, will be presumed unrelated for determinations under §305(b)(2). Treas. Regs. §1.305-3(b)(4). Why might Congress have limited taxation under §305(b)(2) to those disproportionate stock dividends having companion distributions? In what way are such stock dividends similar to those taxable under §305(b)(1)?

Section 305(b)(3) taxes stock dividends when some shareholders of common stock receive common stock while others receive preferred stock. Such distributions often will have the disproportionate effect described in §305(b)(2). Why will they not fall within that subsection? Recall the definition of "property" in §317(a), applicable to §§301-318.

Section 305(b)(4) applies to distributions of stock or stock rights made with respect to preferred stock (in common parlance, stock dividends "on" preferred stock). What is the reason for taxing such dividends? Should preferred on preferred stock dividends be tax free under the reasoning of *Macomber?*

The second clause in §305(b)(4) excludes from the rule of §305(b)(4) certain changes to the conversion ratio of preferred stock. The conversion ratio of convertible preferred stock is most often changed when a stock dividend is declared by the corporation on its common stock since if the conversion ratio is not adjusted, the holders of the convertible preferred stock will have had their conversion rights diluted. Since a change in conversion ratio involves no actual distribution of stock or of stock rights, this final clause is misplaced. To be sure, changes in the conversion ratio of preferred stock can have the effect of a stock dividend, so such changes should, in appropriate circumstances, be treated as the equivalent of actual stock dividends. The taxation of constructive stock dividends, however, is addressed generally in §305(c), and the second clause in §305(b)(4) more appropriately belongs in that subsection. Section 305(c) is discussed at pages 261-269 infra.

Section 305(b)(5) taxes the distribution of convertible preferred stock. Suppose a corporation distributes preferred stock that is convertible into common stock. If some (but not all) of this stock is converted, the effect of the distribution is a disproportionate distribution of common and preferred stock. Since disproportionate distributions of common and preferred stock are taxable under §305(b)(3), distributions of convertible preferred stock must also be taxable unless it is shown that the distribution will not have the effect described in §305(b)(2). Why does §305(b)(5) reference §305(b)(2) rather than §305(b)(3)?

The *Frontier Savings Association* case that follows explores the reach of §305(b)(1). Under what circumstances will a shareholder who has received a common stock dividend be taxable under §§305(b) and 301 because the shareholder is deemed to have elected to receive the stock rather than cash? While *Frontier Savings Association* focuses on §305(b)(1), Revenue Ruling 78-375 considers the impact of a dividend reinvestment plan (i.e., a DRIP) under both §305(b)(1) and (b)(2).

Frontier Savings Association v. Commissioner _____
87 T.C. 665 (1986), aff'd sub nom. Colonial Sav. Assn. v. Commissioner, 854 F.2d 1001 (7th Cir. 1988), acq., 1990-1 C.B. 1

SWIFT, Judge. . . .

Frontier Savings has been a member and stockholder of the Federal Home Loan Bank of Chicago (the "Chicago Bank") at all times since the organization of the Chicago Bank. . . .

The Federal Home Loan Bank system was designed primarily as a reserve credit facility for savings and loan associations and other home mortgage credit institutions. Savings and loan associations (such as Frontier Savings) and mutual savings banks that are members or stockholders in the district banks (hereinafter referred to as "members" or "member banks") are required by Federal law to maintain a certain capital stock ownership in the respective district banks of which they are members. The stock ownership requirements are determined at the end of each calendar year and are calculated with reference to each member bank's net home mortgage loans outstanding and total borrowings of each member from the district bank.

Each member bank generally must maintain a capital stock ownership interest in the district bank in an amount equal to at least one percent of the total outstanding balance of its home mortgage loans and at least equal to one-twelfth of total outstanding borrowings of the member bank from the district bank, as of December 31 of each year. Each share of stock in the district banks is valued by statute at its $100 par value. See 12 U.S.C. sec. 1426(b) and (c) (1978).

Based upon the above year-end calculations, member banks that are required to purchase additional stock of district banks must do so by January 31 of the following year at the par value of $100 per share. Member banks that own stock in district banks in excess of the required number of shares ("excess shares") may request that excess shares be redeemed by the district banks. . . .

At a meeting held on November 20, 1978, the board of directors of the Chicago Bank adopted a resolution to pay a 6.58-percent dividend to its stockholders of record as of December 31, 1978. Subject to the approval of the Federal Home Loan Bank Board, the resolution stated that the dividend would be paid in the form of shares of stock in the Chicago Bank. On December 22, 1978, the Director of the Office of District Banks, Federal Home Loan Bank Board, wrote a letter to the President of the Chicago Bank approving the stock dividend.

On December 22, 1978, the Chicago Bank mailed a bulletin to its member banks, informing them that a 6.58-percent stock dividend would be paid, with fractional shares to be paid in cash. The explanation made in the bulletin for paying a stock dividend, rather than a cash dividend, was as follows:

(1) Providing a stock rather than a cash dividend may enable your association to defer the payment of income taxes on the value of the stock dividend. You may wish to consult your tax adviser for the proper handling of a stock dividend.

(2) A stock dividend can be applied toward satisfying the stock investment requirement for members that experienced a growth in assets during 1978 or that will be required to purchase additional stock due to increased borrowings from the Bank.

The bulletin also explained that most member banks would be required to increase their stock holdings in the Chicago Bank due to that year's general increase in outstanding home mortgage loans. . . .

Enclosed with the December 22, 1978, bulletin mailed by the Chicago Bank to its member banks describing the 1978 stock dividend was a form entitled "Calculation of Bank Stock Requirement as of December 31, 1978." Using that form, each member bank could calculate the number of shares of stock it was required, under 12 U.S.C. sec. 1426(c) (1978), to own in the Chicago Bank as of December 31, 1978. If a member bank was required to purchase additional shares of stock, it could submit the form (reflecting the number of shares to be purchased) along with a check in payment therefor to the Chicago Bank. If the member bank held more shares than it legally was required to own, it could use the form to request the redemption of any excess shares. Although the Chicago Bank had no legal obligation to redeem excess shares, in prior years it routinely had done so.

On January 16, 1979, Frontier Savings completed the form calculating the number of shares of common stock in the Chicago Bank it was required to own based on its December 31, 1978, outstanding balance for home mortgage loans. That calculation indicated that Frontier Savings was required to purchase 678 additional shares of common stock in the Chicago Bank (after taking into account the shares received as part of the common stock dividend on December 29, 1978). Frontier Savings, therefore, sent a check in the amount of $67,800 to the Chicago Bank and 678 shares were credited to its stock account at the Chicago Bank. A new stock certificate was issued reflecting the ownership by Frontier Savings of a total of 10,332 shares of common stock in the Chicago Bank. During 1979, none of the shares of common stock in the Chicago Bank owned by Frontier Savings were redeemed or otherwise transferred.

Exclusive of the December 29, 1978, stock dividend received, on December 31, 1978, 195 of the 497 member banks owned sufficient shares of common stock in the Chicago Bank to meet their stock ownership requirements, and 302 member banks did not own sufficient shares to meet their stock ownership requirements. After receipt of the 1978 stock dividend, 69 member banks requested that the Chicago Bank redeem all or some of their excess shares. All such redemption requests were agreed to by the Chicago Bank and the following number of shares of common stock were redeemed by the Chicago Bank from its member banks in the months indicated:

Time Period	Shares Redeemed
December 1978	1,240
January 1979	62,575
February 1979	8,249
Remainder of 1979	22,256

During December of 1978 and 1979, 45 member banks redeemed a number of shares of stock in the Chicago Bank that was equal to or that exceeded the number of shares they received as their portion of the 1978 stock dividend. [A similar stock dividend and redemption occurred in late 1979 and early 1980.]

None of the shares of stock in the Chicago Bank received by Frontier Savings with respect to the 1978 and 1979 stock dividends were redeemed by the Chicago Bank or otherwise disposed of by Frontier Savings prior to 1982. In January of 1982, the Chicago Bank, at the request of Frontier Savings, redeemed 3,584 shares of its stock owned by Frontier Savings.

OPINION

The receipt of common stock dividends generally is not taxable to stockholders. Sec. 305(a). Where, however, dividends from a corporation are payable, at the election of the stockholders, in stock or property (such as cash), the receipt of dividends will be taxable to the stockholders under the provisions of section 301. Sec. 305(b)(1). In that circumstance the receipt of stock dividends will be taxable under sections 305(b)(1) and 301 regardless of whether the stockholders exercise their election to receive the dividends in cash or other property. Sec. 1.305-2(a), Income Tax Regs.

Respondent argues that by redeeming all of the common stock it was requested to redeem from its member banks in 1979 and 1980 (and apparently doing so in years before 1979), the Chicago Bank established such a policy and practice of redeeming excess stock upon request of the member banks that the member banks should be regarded as having had an "election" to receive the 1978 and 1979 stock dividends in cash. Respondent therefore argues that the stock dividends in question do not qualify for exemption from taxability under section 305(a) and should be taxable to the member banks under sections 305(b)(1) and 301. For the reasons explained below, we disagree. . . .

Congress vested in the district banks and in the Federal Home Loan Bank Board discretionary authority to redeem excess shares of common stock held by member banks. Our careful examination of the record herein satisfies us that the manner in which stock dividends were paid and redeemed in 1978 and 1979 by the Chicago Bank was consistent with that grant of discretionary authority and did not vest in the member banks the unilateral right to elect or to require the Chicago Bank to redeem excess shares upon request.

Respondent concedes that the Chicago Bank did not completely abdicate its discretionary authority to redeem its stock but respondent argues that authority was exercised so consistently in favor of redemption that member banks, as a practical matter, had the option or election to have excess shares redeemed at any time. Respondent contends that the option arose "from the circumstances of the distribution" citing section 1.305-2(a)(4), Income Tax Regs. As indicated, we have carefully examined the circumstances of the stock dividends in question and conclude that the member banks, including Frontier Savings, did not have the option or election to have the Chicago Bank redeem excess shares of common stock in the Chicago Bank.

In addition to the factors explained above, we think it significant that the stock dividends of the Chicago Bank were declared and distributed in late December of 1978 and 1979. Member banks, however, normally would not be able to determine until early in the following year (after actual distribution of the stock dividends) whether they would be able even to request a redemption of some of their common stock in the Chicago Bank. In other words, on the day of distribution of the stock dividends, member banks could not know (other than through estimates and projections) whether they would be required to retain the stock dividends they received as part of their required investments in the district bank or whether the stock dividends would qualify as excess shares, in which case redemption thereof, if requested, might occur depending on the decision of the Chicago Bank. . . .

We recognize that the issuance by the Chicago Bank in 1978 and 1979 of stock dividends instead of or in addition to cash dividends was motivated in part by tax considerations. We cannot conclude, however, on the facts before us that the stock dividends were a mere subterfuge for cash distributions or that the Chicago Bank had relinquished its discretionary authority to decline to grant stock redemption requests.

Respondent refers to Rev. Rul. 76-258, 1976-2 C.B. 95. Revenue Rulings are, of course, not binding on this Court. Estate of Lang v. Commissioner, 64 T.C. 404, 406-407 (1975), aff'd, 613 F.2d 770 (9th Cir. 1980). Respondent's litigating position herein is reflected in Rev. Rul. 83-68, 1983-1 C.B. 75. For the reasons explained above and under the facts of this case, we reject the conclusion reached therein that a history or practice of redemptions by the Chicago Bank makes the stock dividends received by petitioner herein taxable under sections 305(b)(1) and 301. . . .

Decisions will be entered under Rule 155.

Reviewed by the Court.

Sterrett, Goffe, Chabot, Nims, Parker, Whitaker, Korner, Shields, Hamblen, Cohen, Clapp, Jacobs, and Parr, JJ., agree with the majority opinion.

Simpson, J., dissents.

Gerber, Wright, and Williams, JJ., did not participate in the consideration of this case.

HAMBLEN, J., concurring.

I concur in the conclusion of the majority based upon the limited factual circumstances involved. If a discretionary act of the Board of Directors of a shareholder corporation to redeem stock dividends becomes a routine matter, it might, in my opinion, develop into an "option" that arises after the distribution or a distribution pursuant to a "plan." See secs. 1.305-2(a) and 1.305-3(b), Income Tax Regs. In such a situation, it seems the redemptions might be periodic rather than isolated. The broad rules of section 305 could invoke different considerations under other circumstances.

Sterrett, Cohen, and Jacobs, JJ., agree with this concurring opinion.

Rev. Rul. 78-375 _____
1978-2 C.B. 130

Advice has been requested as to the treatment for federal income tax purposes of a "dividend reinvestment plan" where the shareholder may not only elect to receive stock of greater fair market value than the cash dividend such shareholder might have received instead, but also the shareholder may, through the plan, purchase additional stock from the corporation at a discount price which is less than the fair market value of the stock.

X is a corporation engaged in commercial banking whose shares of common stock are widely held and are regularly traded in the over-the-counter market. In order to raise additional equity capital for corporate expansion and to provide holders of X's common stock with a simple and convenient way of investing their cash dividends and optional payments in additional shares of X common stock without payment of any brokerage commission, X established an automatic dividend reinvestment plan. An independent agent will administer the plan and will receive the stock from X in the manner described below on behalf of a participating shareholder.

The plan provides the following:

(1) Shareholders can elect to have all their cash dividends (less a quarterly service charge of $3x$ dollars that is paid to an independent agent of the shareholder) otherwise payable on common stock registered in the name of the shareholder automatically reinvested in shares of X common stock. The service charge is paid to the agent for administering the plan and maintaining the stock certificates for the shareholders. The shareholders who elect to participate in the plan acquire X stock at a price equal to 95 percent of the fair market value of such stock on the dividend payment date. The shareholder's option to receive a dividend in additional common stock in lieu of a cash dividend is not transferable apart from a transfer of the common shares themselves.

(2) A shareholder who participates in the dividend reinvestment aspect of the plan as described in paragraph (1) above, in addition, has the option to invest additional amounts to purchase shares of X common stock at a price equal to 95 percent of the fair market value of such stock on the dividend payment date. Optional investments by a shareholder in any quarterly dividend period must be at least $4x$ dollars and cannot exceed $100x$ dollars. The shareholder's right to invest additional amounts under the plan is not transferable apart from a transfer of the common shares themselves.

There is no requirement to participate in the plan and shareholders who do not participate receive their cash dividend payments in full. Certain shareholders have chosen not to participate; therefore, they receive their regular quarterly cash dividend. While the plan continues in effect, a participant's dividends will continue to be invested without further notice to X.

Prior to the dividend payment date no cash dividend is available to either X's participating or nonparticipating shareholders. On the dividend payment date the participant receives written notification that X is acting to effectuate the participant's option to receive stock on that date. The crediting on the plan account and notification to the participant of the exact number of shares acquired (including fractional shares) takes place shortly after the dividend payment date.

A participant may withdraw from the plan at any time, upon written request. Upon withdrawal, certificates for whole shares credited to the participant's account under the plan will be issued and a cash payment based upon the market value of the participant's fractional share interest will be paid by X, through the participant's agent, to the participant. As an alternative, the shareholder may request that all or part of the whole shares credited to its account in the plan be sold for the shareholder's account. The sale will be made by an independent agent acting on behalf of such participant and the proceeds of the sale (less any brokerage commission and transfer tax) will be forwarded to the participant. With regard to the whole shares, X will neither purchase any shares of a participant nor pay any expense attributable to the sale of such stock. Upon a request for sale of a participant's shares, a cash payment equal to the market value of the participant's fractional share interest will be paid by X, through the participant's agent, to the participant. The purpose of the payment of cash is to save X the trouble, expense, and inconvenience of issuing and transferring fractional shares and is not designed to give any particular group of shareholders an increased interest in the assets or earnings and profits of X. . . .

In the present case, the distributions made by X while the plan is in effect are properly treated as payable either in X's stock or in cash at the election of X's common shareholders within the meaning of section 305(b)(1) of the Code. . . .

The optional investment aspect of the present case results in an increase in the proportionate interests of the shareholders making the purchase at a 5 percent discount, and this event increases their proportionate interests in the assets or earnings and profits of X within the meaning of section 305(b)(2)(B) of the Code. Furthermore, the fact that X shareholders who do not participate in the plan receive cash dividends constitutes a receipt of property by those shareholders within the meaning of section 305(b)(2)(A).

Accordingly, under the circumstances described above, it is held as follows:

(a) A shareholder of X who participates in the dividend reinvestment aspect of the plan will be treated as having received a distribution to which section 301 of the Code applies by reason of the application of section 305(b)(1). Pursuant to section 1.305-1(b) of the regulations, the amount of the distribution to a participating shareholder (including participating corporate shareholders) will be the fair market value of the X stock received on the date of the distribution (sections 1.301-1(b) and (d)), plus, pursuant to section 301, 3x dollars, the service charge subtracted from the amount of the shareholder's distribution.

(b) The basis of the shares credited to the account of a participating shareholder pursuant to the dividend reinvestment aspect of the plan will equal the amount of the dividend distribution, as provided in section 301(c) of the Code, measured by the fair market value of the X common stock as of the date of the distribution both as to noncorporate and corporate shareholders, pursuant to section 301(d). Section 1.301-1(h)(1) and

(2) (i) of the regulations. The quarterly service charge paid by a participant who is an individual for the production of income or for the management, conservation, or maintenance of property held for the production of income, is deductible in the year paid by such participant under section 212, provided the individual itemizes deductions. . . . The quarterly service charge, which is paid in carrying on a trade or business by a participant who is an individual, is deductible in the year paid by such participant under section 162. A participant who is a corporation may deduct the service charge under section 162.

(c) A shareholder of X who participates in the optional payment aspect of the plan will be treated as having received a distribution to which section 301 of the Code applies by reason of the application of section 305(b)(2). Pursuant to section 1.305-3(a) of the regulations, the amount of the distribution to a participating shareholder will be the difference between the fair market value on the dividend payment date of the shares purchased with the optional payment and the amount of the optional payment. Section 1.305-3(b)(2).

(d) The basis to the shareholder who participates in the optional payment aspect of the plan is the excess of fair market value of the shares purchased with the optional payment over the optional payment (provided that this deemed distribution is taxable as a dividend under section 301(c)(1) of the Code) . . . plus the amount of the optional payment, pursuant to section 1012.

(e) A participant in the plan will not realize any taxable income upon receipt of certificates for whole shares that were credited to the participant's account pursuant to the plan. . . . Any cash received by an X shareholder in lieu of a fractional share interest will be treated as a redemption of that fractional share interest, subject to the provisions and limitations of section 302 of the Code. . . .

(f) A participant will recognize gain or loss pursuant to section 1001 of the Code when shares are sold or exchanged on behalf of the participant upon the participant's withdrawal from the plan, or when the participant sells the shares after its withdrawal from the plan. In accordance with section 1001, the amount of such gain or loss will be the difference between the amount that the participant receives for the whole shares and the participant's tax basis. Any cash received by the participants, who withdraw from the plan, in lieu of their fractional share interests will be treated as a redemption of that fractional share interest, subject to the provisions and limitations of section 302. . . .

NOTES

1. *The shareholder's election under §305(b)(1).* What is the effect of the parenthetical expression in §305(b)(1)? See Treas. Regs. §1.305-2(a). Sup-

pose a corporation issues two classes of common stock, class A and class B. The corporation's charter provides that dividends cannot be declared on one class without an equal dividend declaration on the other. Dividends on the class A stock will always be paid in cash, while dividends on the class B stock will always be paid in additional shares of class B. Has a shareholder, by choosing to purchase shares of class B rather than class A, "elected" to receive stock dividends in lieu of property so that §305(b)(1) will apply to all stock dividends he will receive? See Treas. Regs. §1.305-2(a)(4).

In *Frontier Savings Association,* the corporation annually declared a stock dividend and then habitually agreed to redeem shares as requested by its stockholders. The Tax Court did not find the requisite shareholder election in such circumstances, although Judge Hamblen added in the concurring opinion that such a routine could run afoul of §305 if the redemptions were "periodic rather than isolated." Yet §305(b)(1) nowhere limits its application to periodic stock dividends. Judge Hamblen apparently was focusing on the taxation of certain redemptions as constructive stock dividends pursuant to §305(c). See discussion of §305(c) at pages 296-303 infra. Even in the absence of a provision such as §305(c), might not a corporation's habitual practice of declaring a stock dividend, if always followed by an optional redemption, fall within the ambit of §305(b)(1)? Was the transaction in *Frontier* more legitimate because of the statutory obligation of the corporation's shareholders to purchase additional stock as their assets and outstanding loans increased? Is it relevant, under §305(b)(1), whether the corporation and shareholders had no tax avoidance motives for the transaction giving rise to an effective election by the shareholders to receive stock or property?

2. *Amount constituting dividend.* Distributions of stock falling within one of the provisions of §305(b) will be subject to the property distribution rules of §301. To noncorporate and corporate shareholders alike, the "amount" of the distribution under §301(b) is the fair market value of the dividend stock. See Treas. Regs. §1.305-2(b) (example 2). Of that amount, the recipient shareholder will have a dividend to the extent of her pro rata share of the distributing corporation's earnings and profits. §§301(c)(1), 316(a). The excess amount of the distribution, if any, will be applied against the shareholder's old stock basis to the extent thereof, §301(c)(2), with any amount in excess of basis treated as though received "in exchange" for the old stock, §301(c)(3). See pages 119-121 supra.

The rules of §305 generally apply to distributions of stock rights. See §305(d)(1). As indicated by Rev. Rul. 78-375 above, the fair market value of an immediately exercisable right to buy stock equals the difference between the current fair market value of the corporation's stock and the amount the holder of the right must pay to acquire the stock. If a stock right cannot be exercised for a specified time, e.g., three or five years, how should the right be valued? Cf. §83. If stock rights are received tax free under §305(a), then the shareholder must allocate a basis to them under §307. Note the special rule for stock rights received tax free that are worth less than 15 percent of the shareholder's old stock: Such rights have a zero basis unless the shareholder elects to allocate some of her old stock basis to them. §307(b).

3. *The companion distribution requirement of §305(b)(2)(A).* A stock dividend increasing the proportionate share of the recipient shareholder's interest in the assets or earnings and profits of the corporation will not fall within §305(b)(2) unless some other shareholder receives a distribution of property. §305(b)(2)(A). Why should taxation of the dividend stock to the recipient shareholder turn on the existence of a companion distribution of property to another shareholder?

Is it likely that a stock dividend will be made to one shareholder (or to one group of shareholders) while the remaining shareholders receive nothing of value? Might the other shareholder agree to a non-pro rata stock dividend if he will receive, as part of the deal, an increase in his salary as a corporate employee? See Treas. Regs. §1.305-3(b)(3) (companion distribution must be to a shareholder "in his capacity as a shareholder"). Would such a salary increase meet the companion distribution requirement of §305(b)(2)(A)? Recall that in Treas. Regs. §1.305-3(b)(4) stock and property distributions separated by more than 36 months are presumed unrelated.

4. *The definition of preferred stock.* Subsections (3), (4), and (5) of §305 refer to "preferred" stock. The Code does not define "preferred stock," although Treas. Regs. §1.305-5(a) provides, in the context of §305(b)(4), that

> [t]he term "preferred stock" generally refers to stock which, in relation to other classes of stock outstanding enjoys certain limited rights and privileges (generally associated with specified dividend and liquidation priorities) but does not participate in corporate growth to any significant extent. The distinguishing feature of "preferred stock" for the purposes of section 305(b)(4) is not its privileged position as such, but that such privileged position is limited and that such stock does not participate in corporate growth to any significant extent.

Does this definition of "preferred stock" comport with the underlying rationale of §305? Note in particular that nonvoting stock need not be "preferred" stock under this definition.

b. Constructive Distributions

Section 305(c) authorizes the promulgation of regulations subjecting certain transactions that have the effect of a stock dividend to the rules of

§305(b). The Treasury Department responded in 1973 with Treas. Regs. §1.305-7. Under that regulation, "a change in conversion ratio, a change in redemption price, a difference between redemption price and issue price, a redemption which is treated as a distribution to which §301 applies, or any transaction (including a recapitalization) having a similar effect on the interest of any shareholder" may be treated as a constructive distribution of stock taxable under §305.

Suppose a corporation has two classes of stock outstanding, common and convertible preferred. If a common stock dividend is declared on the common stock, then the value of the convertibility feature of the preferred will be reduced unless some provision is made to increase its conversion ratio. For example, if each share of the preferred is convertible into one share of common, and if a one-for-one common stock dividend is declared on the common, then the conversion ratio of the preferred stock must be adjusted so that each share of preferred stock can be converted into two shares of common stock. Such a change in conversion ratio to account for stock dividends is called an "antidilution" provision. Treas. Regs. §1.305-7 has special rules for antidilution provisions. Because of the wording of §305(b)(4), some of the antidilution rules also appear in Treas. Regs. §1.305-3(d). (Recapitalizations are also addressed in Treas. Regs. §1.305-3, but consideration of recapitalizations is deferred until Chapter 12 infra.)

The following Rulings illustrate the reach of §305(c). Revenue Ruling 78-60 concludes that dividend treatment under §§305(b) and 301 can apply to a shareholder who receives no actual distribution of stock. Section 305(c) lists a change in conversion ratio as an event that might constitute a constructive distribution, but §305(b)(4) contains an exception. Revenue Ruling 83-42 considers just how far that exception extends.

Rev. Rul. 78-60
1978-1 C.B. 81

Advice has been requested whether under section 302(a) of the Internal Revenue Code of 1954 the stock redemptions described below qualified for exchange treatment, and whether under section 305(b)(2) and (c) the shareholders who experienced increases in their proportionate interests in the redeeming corporation as a result of the stock redemptions will be treated as having received distributions of property to which section 301 applies.

Corporation Z has only one class of stock outstanding. The Z common stock is held by 24 shareholders, all of whom are descendants, or spouses of descendants, of the founder of Z.

In 1975, when Z had 6,000 shares of common stock outstanding, the board of directors of Z adopted a plan of annual redemption to provide a means for its shareholders to sell their stock. The plan provides that Z will annually redeem up to 40 shares to its outstanding stock at a price established annually by the Z board of directors. Each shareholder of Z is entitled to cause Z to redeem two-thirds of one percent of the shareholder's stock each year. If some shareholders choose not to participate fully in the plan during any year, the other shareholders can cause Z to redeem more than two-thirds of one percent of their stock, up to the maximum of 40 shares.

Pursuant to the plan of annual redemption, Z redeemed 40 shares of its stock in 1976. Eight shareholders participated in the redemptions. [No shareholder owned as much as 13 percent of the corporation's stock before or after the redemption. After the redemption, each shareholder actually and constructively owned at least 97 percent of his preredemption holding.]

ISSUE 1 . . .

None of the redemptions here qualified under section 302(b)(3) of the Code because all of the shareholders who participated in the redemptions continue to own stock of Z. Moreover, none of the redemptions qualified under section 302(b)(2) because none of the shareholders who participated in the redemptions experienced a reduction in interest of more than 20 percent, as section 302(b)(2)(C) requires. Therefore, the first question is whether the redemptions were "not essentially equivalent to a dividend" within the meaning of section 302(b)(1). . . .

In United States v. Davis, 397 U.S. 301 (1970), the Supreme Court of the United States said that for a redemption to qualify as not essentially equivalent to a dividend under section 302(b)(1) of the Code, the redemption must result in a meaningful reduction of the shareholder's proportionate interest in the corporation. The Court held that the business purpose of the redemption is irrelevant to this determination and that the ownership attribution rules of section 318(a) apply. Several of the shareholders of Z experienced reductions in their proportionate interests in Z (taking into account constructive stock ownership under section 318 of the Code) as a result of the 1976 redemptions. If their reductions were "meaningful," they are entitled to exchange treatment for their redemptions under section 302(a). Whether the reductions in proportionate interests were "meaningful" depends on the facts and circumstances.

In this case, an important fact is that the 1976 redemptions were not isolated occurrences but were undertaken pursuant to an ongoing plan for Z to redeem 40 shares of its stock each year. None of the reductions in proportionate interest experienced by Z shareholders as a result of the 1976 redemptions was "meaningful" because the reductions were small and each shareholder has the power to recover the lost interest by electing not to participate in the redemption plan in later years.

Accordingly, none of the 1976 redemptions qualified for exchange treatment under section 302(a) of the Code. All of the redemptions are to be treated as distributions of property to which section 301 applies.

ISSUE 2

Section 305(b)(2) of the Code provides that section 301 will apply to a distribution by a corporation of its stock if the distribution, or a series of distributions that includes the distribution, has the result of the receipt of property by some shareholders, and increases in the proportionate interests of other shareholders in the assets or earnings and profits of the corporation. . . .

Section 1.305-7(a) of the Income Tax Regulations provides that a redemption treated as a section 301 distribution will generally be treated as a distribution to which sections 305(b)(2) and 301 of the Code apply if the proportionate interest of any shareholder in the earnings and profits or assets of the corporation deemed to have made the stock distribution is increased by the redemption, and the distribution has the result described in section 305(b)(2). The distribution is to be deemed made to any shareholder whose interest in the earnings and profits or assets of the distributing corporation is increased by the redemption.

Section 1.305-3(b)(3) of the regulations provides that [a] distribution of property incident to an isolated redemption will not cause section 305(b)(2) to apply even though the redemption distribution is treated as a section 301 distribution.

Section 305 of the Code does not make the constructive stock ownership rules of section 318(a) applicable to its provisions.

The 16 shareholders of Z who did not tender any stock for redemption in 1976 experienced increases in their proportionate interests of the earnings and profits and assets of Z (without taking into account constructive stock ownership under section 318 of the Code) as a result of the redemptions. Shareholders B and X, who surrendered small amounts of their stock for redemption in 1976, also experienced increases in their proportionate interests. The 1976 redemptions were not isolated but were undertaken pursuant to an ongoing plan of annual stock redemptions. Finally, the 1976 redemptions are to be treated as distributions of property to which section 301 of the Code applies.

Accordingly, B, X and the 16 shareholders of Z who did not participate in the 1976 redemptions are deemed to have received stock distributions to which sections 305(b)(2) and 301 of the Code apply. See examples (8) and (9) of section 1.305-3(e) of the regulations for a method of computing the amounts of the deemed distributions.

Rev. Rul. 83-42 _____

1983-1 C.B. 76

ISSUE

Is the distribution of common stock on convertible preferred stock, as described below, treated as the distribution of property to which section 301 of the Internal Revenue Code applies by reason of section 305(b)(4)?

FACTS

_X_ is a corporation that has both common and convertible preferred stock outstanding. The convertible preferred stock had been issued earlier in connection with the acquisition of an unrelated corporation. The convertible preferred stock is convertible into common stock according to a certain conversion ratio. The terms of the convertible preferred stock do not provide for anti-dilution protection by means of an increase in the conversion ratio made solely to take account of a stock dividend or stock split with respect to the stock into which such convertible stock is convertible.

On June 1, 1981, _X_ distributed a 10 percent common stock dividend to the holders of its common stock. In addition, _X_ distributed shares of its common stock to holders of its convertible preferred stock in order to offset the dilution of the holder's conversion rights. Dilution of the conversion rights of the holders of convertible preferred would have occurred but for the distribution of common stock to them because of the lack of a full adjustment in the conversion ratio of the preferred stock to reflect the stock dividend on the common stock.

LAW AND ANALYSIS

Section 305(a) of the Code provides generally that gross income does not include the amount of any distribution of the stock of a corporation made by such corporation to its shareholders with respect to its stock, except as otherwise provided in section 305(b) or (c).

Section 305(b)(4) of the Code provides that section 305(a) will not apply to a distribution by a corporation of its stock, and the distribution will be treated as a distribution of property to which section 301 applies, if the distribution is with respect to preferred stock, other than an increase in the conversion ratio of convertible preferred stock made solely to take account of a stock dividend or stock split with respect to the stock into which such convertible stock is convertible.

Section 1.305-5(a) of the regulations states, in part, that under section 305(b)(4), a distribution by a corporation of its stock made with respect to its preferred stock is treated as a distribution of property to which section 301 applies unless the distribution is made with respect to convertible preferred stock to take into account a stock dividend, stock split, or any similar event which would otherwise result in the dilution of the conversion right.

The exception contained in section 305(b)(4) of the Code would permit X to adjust the conversion ratio of its preferred stock to eliminate the dilution which resulted from the 10 percent common stock dividend on June 1, but it will not permit an actual distribution of stock to the holders of preferred stock, even if undertaken for the same anti-dilution purposes. The "distribution" referred to in section 1.305-5(a) of the regulations is only the deemed distribution which is considered to result when the conversion ratio is adjusted for the purpose described in section 305(b)(4). All other distributions on preferred stock are taxable, as expressly provided by section 305(b)(4).

HOLDING

The distribution of X common stock to holders of its convertible preferred stock is a distribution to which section 301 of the Code applies by reason of section 305(b)(4).

NOTES

1. *Redemptions treated as stock dividends to nonredeemed shareholders.* The effect of any non-pro rata redemption of common stock is to increase the proportionate interests of the nonredeemed shareholders while giving the redeemed shareholders cash or other property. This effect, described in §305(b)(2), causes redemptions to be ideal candidates for constructive stock dividend treatment under §305(c). Two substantial limitations, however, are imposed on the Commissioner's ability to treat a redemption to one shareholder as a stock dividend to others.

First, Congress in §305(c) granted authority to tax redemptions as constructive stock dividends only when the redemptions are taxed to the redeemed shareholder under §301 (e.g., when the redemption fails to qualify for exchange treatment under §302(a) for want of qualification under §302(b)(1)-(4)). Even though redemptions taxed as exchanges may have the effect of increasing the nonredeemed shareholders' corporate interests, such redemptions are not described in §305(c). Indeed, under §302(b)(1)-(3), only those redemptions causing the most significant change in the proportionate interests of the shareholders can qualify for exchange treatment. Yet §305(c) cannot apply to such redemptions.

Second, even redemptions taxed as distributions under §301 will not cause the nonredeemed shareholders difficulty under §305(c) so long as the redemption is "an isolated redemption and is not a part of a periodic redemption plan." Treas. Regs. §1.305-3(e) (example 10). The statute makes no special distinction for "isolated" redemptions. Why has the Treasury Department so limited application of §305(c)? If a corporation distributes cash to shareholder *A* and stock to shareholder *B*, then shareholder *B* will be taxed pursuant to §305(b)(2). If the same result is accomplished by redeeming a part of the stock of shareholder *A*, why should the taxation be different if the transaction is "isolated"?

In Rev. Rul. 77-19, 1977-1 C.B. 83, a corporation redeemed shares in 20 isolated transactions during the three prior years from deceased and retiring shareholders. It also redeemed the interests of minority shareholders. The Service ruled that the corporation was not engaged in a periodic redemption plan under §305(c) so as to trigger taxable constructive dividends to the continuing shareholders. Cf. Rev. Rul. 78-60, page 262 supra, in which the Service ruled that periodic small redemptions of stock pursuant to an ongoing plan of annual redemptions were taxable as dividends to the redeeming shareholders and as taxable distributions under §305(b)(2) and (c) to the continuing shareholders whose proportionate interests were increased thereby. See Dietzsch v. United States, 498 F.2d 1344 (Cl. Ct. 1974), in which an auto dealer, contractually obligated to use cash distributions from his corporation to purchase the stock of a co-shareholder in a program leading to eventual acquisition by the dealer of the entire ownership of the corporation, was held taxable on the distributions as a dividend. The court refused to view the various steps as an integrated transaction constituting a complete redemption of the co-shareholder and culminating in a tax-free stock dividend.

Some redemptions will not be subject to §305(c) because they are part of a transaction akin to a security arrangement. For example, in Rev. Rul. 78-115, 1978-1 C.B. 85, a corporation engaged in mandatory, periodic redemptions of nonparticipating, nonvoting stock that had been issued as partial consideration for a prior stock acquisition by the corporation. The Service ruled that such redemptions would not give rise to income to the nonredeemed shareholders under §305(c) because the redeemed stock was created solely to facilitate the prior acquisition when other forms of financing were unavailable. See also Treas. Regs. §1.305-3(e) (example 14).

Note that when §305(c) does apply to a redemption, it does not automatically trigger the recognition of income to any shareholder: Transactions described in §305(c) are recharacterized by that section as distributions increasing the proportionate interests of one or more shareholders in their corporation. The tax consequences of such a deemed distribution must be determined under §305(a) and (b)(2).

2. *Adjustment in conversion ratio.* As made clear in Rev. Rul. 83-42, above, the only antidilution provision excluded from taxation under §305(b)(4) and (c) is an increase or decrease in the conversion ratio of convertible preferred stock to account for stock distributions on, or stock splits of, the stock into which the preferred may be converted. What are the consequences if the conversion ratio of convertible preferred stock is

adjusted to account for cash dividends paid on the common or on the preferred stock? See Treas. Regs. §1.305-3(e) (example 7). To what possible abuse does this example speak? What is the result if the preferred shareholders exercise their conversion rights shortly after a cash dividend paid on the common? Compare §305(b)(2).

Rev. Rul. 84-141, 1984-2 C.B. 80, discusses the consequences of a right given to holders of cumulative preferred stock to have dividend arrearages paid in common stock if cash dividends are unpaid for two consecutive quarters. The Service ruled that the holders of such cumulative preferred stock are subject to taxation under §305(c) and (b)(2) on the passage of two quarters in which the corporation fails to pay cash dividends. Since the holders of the preferred stock have an unqualified right to receive common stock in lieu of accrued dividends at that time, the Service ruled that they are taxable on the fair market value of the common stock they can elect to receive regardless of whether they elect to accept it.

PROBLEMS

6-1.   In the following, assume *X* Corp. has ample earnings and profits. Determine the tax consequences to *M* and *N* in the following situations:

    a.   *X* Corp. has two classes of stock outstanding. *M* holds 100 shares of common stock, and *N* holds 100 shares of nonconvertible preferred stock. *X* distributes:
        i.   Common on common, but common shareholders can elect to receive cash instead of stock. Does it matter if all shareholders elect to receive stock?
        ii.   Preferred on common and cash on preferred. Does it matter if the cash is distributed 18 months before or after the stock dividend?
        iii.   Common on preferred and preferred on common.
    b.   *X* Corp. has two classes of stock outstanding. *M* owns 100 shares of class A common, and *N* owns 100 shares of class B common. The class A and B shares participate ratably in both current and liquidating distributions. *X* distributes:
        i.   Cash on the class A common and class B common on the class B common. How would your answer change if each class of stock were entitled to 50 percent of current and liquidating distributions?
        ii.   Cash in redemption of one-quarter (25 shares) of the class B common.
        iii.   Class A common on the class A common and preferred stock on the class B common.
    c.   *X* Corp. has two classes of stock outstanding. *M* owns 100 shares

of common, and *N* owns 100 shares of nonconvertible preferred. *X* distributes cash on the preferred and common on common. Would your answer change if the preferred stock were convertible into common stock?

B. TAINTING OF STOCK UNDER §306

While the taxation rules of §305(b) and (c) may seem all-inclusive, they are not: Many stock dividends will be tax free under the general rule of §305(a). In particular, a pro rata distribution of preferred stock to all holders of common stock is tax free. To reinforce comprehension of the last section, see if you can parse through the Code to arrive at this result.

How should the sale or redemption of shares received tax free as a stock dividend be taxed? Suppose a corporation has substantial earnings and profits that its sole shareholder would like to remove from corporate solution in the form of cash. A dividend could be declared, but that would produce ordinary income to the shareholder without any recovery of basis. In the absence of a partial liquidation, capital gain treatment on a redemption will be unavailable under §302(b)(1) under *Davis*. But suppose the shareholder follows a three-step plan: (1) declare a stock dividend of nonvoting preferred stock on her common shares, at the issue price at some point in the future; (2) sell this newly created preferred stock to an outside purchaser for the issue price; and (3) cause the corporation to redeem this preferred stock shortly after the sale. If the preferred stock pays a sufficiently high (and guaranteed) dividend rate until redemption, the shareholder should not have great difficulty in selling it. On that sale, the shareholder will claim capital gains under §1202(a). The purchaser will claim exchange treatment on the redemption pursuant to the complete termination safe harbor of §302(b)(3), and, because the purchaser will have a basis in the preferred stock equal to the issue price, there will be no taxable gain on the redemption under §302(a).

How should this type of end-run around §§301 and 302 be addressed? Should the courts or Congress respond?

Chamberlin v. Commissioner _____
207 F.2d 462 (6th Cir. 1953)

Before Simons, Chief Judge, and McAllister and Miller, Circuit Judges.

MILLER, Circuit Judge.

Petitioner C. P. Chamberlin seeks a review of an income tax deficiency determined by the Respondent for the calendar year 1946, and sustained by the Tax Court. . . .

The Metal Moulding Corporation, hereinafter referred to as the Corporation, is a Michigan corporation engaged in the business of manufacturing metal mouldings and bright work trim used in the manufacture of automobiles. . . . From 1940 until December 20, 1946, the issued and outstanding common stock totaled 1,002 1/2 shares, of which Chamberlin and his wife together owned 83.8%. . . .

The business of the Corporation prospered, and after paying substantial cash dividends over a period of years, its balance sheet at the end of the first six months in 1946 reflected total assets of $2,488,836.53 and included in current assets $722,404.56 cash and $549,950 United States Government Bonds and notes.

On December 16, 1946, the Corporation's authorized capital stock was increased from $150,000 to $650,000, represented by 6,500 shares of $100 par value common stock. On December 20, 1946, a stock dividend was declared and distributed of five shares of common for each share of common outstanding, and the Corporation's accounts were adjusted by transferring $501,250 from earned surplus to capital account.

On December 26, 1946, the articles of incorporation were amended so as to authorize, in addition to the 6,500 shares of common stock, 8,020 shares of 4 1/2% cumulative $100 par value preferred stock. On December 28, 1946, a stock dividend was declared of 1 1/3 shares of the newly authorized preferred stock for each share of common stock outstanding, to be issued pro rata to the holders of common stock as of December 27, 1946, and the Company's accounts were adjusted by transferring $802,000 from earned surplus to capital account. The preferred stock was issued to the stockholders on the same day. Prior to the declaration of the preferred stock dividend, the Corporation at all times had only one class of stock outstanding.

On December 30, 1946, as the result of prior negotiations . . . all of the holders of the preferred stock, except the estate of Edward W. Smith, deceased, which owned 20 shares, signed a "Purchase Agreement," with The Northwestern Mutual Life Insurance Company and The Lincoln National Life Insurance Company, which instrument was also endorsed by the Corporation for the purpose of making certain representations, warranties and agreements. Under the "Purchase Agreement" 4,000 shares of the preferred stock was sold to each of the two insurance companies at a cash price of $100 per share plus accrued dividends from November 1st, 1946 to date of delivery. . . .

In the latter part of 1945, the Corporation's attorney and Chamberlin discussed with an investment firm in Chicago the possibility of selling an issue of preferred stock similar to the stock subsequently issued. The Corporation had such a large accumulated earned surplus it was fearful of being subjected to the surtax provided for by [§531], but at the same time Chamberlin, the majority stockholder, was not willing to have the Corporation distribute any substantial portion of its earned surplus as ordinary dividends because his individual income was taxable at high surtax rates. It was proposed that the issuance of a stock dividend to the stockholders and the sale of it by the stockholders would enable the stockholders to obtain accumulated earnings of the Corporation in the form of capital gains rather than as taxable dividends. . . .

The preferred stock contained the following provisions among others: The holders were entitled to cumulative cash dividends at the rate of $4.50 per annum payable quarterly beginning November 1, 1946; the stock was subject to redemption on any quarterly dividend date in whole or in part at par plus specified premiums and accrued dividends; it was subject to mandatory retirement in amounts not exceeding 2,000 shares on May 1, 1948 and 1,000 on May 1st on each succeeding year, depending upon the Corporation's net earnings for the preceding year, until fully retired on May 1, 1954. . . .

The Tax Court held that the issue of whether the stock dividend constituted income to the stockholders should be determined from a consideration of all the facts and circumstances surrounding the issuance of the dividend and not by a consideration limited to the characteristics of the stock declared as a dividend; that each case involving a stock dividend must be decided upon its own facts and circumstances as establishing whether the receipt of a particular kind of stock dividend was in fact taxable; that such a decision did not rest upon matters of form or nomenclature attending a stock dividend distribution but rather upon the real substance of the transaction involved; . . . but that considering the real substance of the transaction it was of the opinion that the stock dividend was not in good faith for any bona fide corporate business purpose, and that the attending circumstances and conditions under which it was issued made it the equivalent of a cash dividend distribution out of available earnings, thus constituting ordinary taxable income in the amount of the value of the preferred shares received. The Court also said that the real purpose of the issuance of the preferred shares was concurrently to place them in the hands of others not then stockholders of the Corporation, thereby substantially altering the common stockholders' pre-existing proportionate interests in the Corporation's net assets and thereby creating an entirely new relationship amongst all the stockholders and the Corporation. . . .

In our opinion, the declaration and distribution of the preferred stock dividend, considered by itself, falls clearly within the principles established in Towne v. Eisner, [245 U.S. 418 (1918)], and Eisner v. Macomber, [252 U.S. 189 (1920)], and is controlled by the ruling in the *Strassburger* case. Accordingly, as a preliminary matter, we do not agree with the Tax Court's statement that the stock dividend is taxable because as a result of the dividend and immediate sale thereafter it substantially altered the common stockholders' pre-existing proportional interests in the Corporation's net assets. The sale to the insurance companies of course resulted in such a change, but the legal effect of the dividend with respect to rights in the corporate assets is determined at the time of its distribution, not by what the stockholders do with it after its receipt. . . .

But respondent contends that the sale of the stock following immediately upon its receipt resulted in the stockholder acquiring cash instead of stock, thus making it a taxable dividend under Secs. 22(a) and 115(a), [1939] Internal Revenue Code. There are two answers to this contention.

A non-taxable stock dividend does not become a taxable cash dividend upon its sale by the recipient. . . . In none of the Supreme Court cases referred to above, dealing with the taxability of stock dividends, was the length of the holding period considered as a factor. Obviously, if the non-taxability of a stock dividend rests solely upon the principle that it does not alter the pre-existing proportionate interest of any stockholder or increase the intrinsic value of his holdings, the disposition of the stock dividend by the stockholder thereafter is not a factor in the determination.

The foregoing conclusion is supported by [§1223(5)], which provides that for the purpose of determining whether a non-taxable stock dividend which has been sold is a long-term capital gain there shall be included in the holding period the period for which the taxpayer held the stock in the distributing corporation prior to the receipt of the stock dividend. This necessarily recognizes that a stock dividend will often be sold before the expiration of six months after its receipt, and makes no distinction between a stock dividend held one day or for any other period less than six months. . . .

The other answer to the contention is that although the stockholder *acquired* money in the final analysis, he did not *receive* either money or property *from* the corporation. . . . The money he received was received from the insurance companies. It was not a "distribution" by the corporation declaring the dividend, as required by [§115(a), 1939 Code; and §316(a), 1954 Code].

We come then to what in our opinion is the dominant and decisive issue in the case, namely, whether the stock dividend, which, by reason of its redemption feature, enabled the Corporation to ultimately distribute its earnings to its stockholders on a taxable basis materially lower than would have been the case by declaring and paying the usual cash dividend, was a bona fide one, one in substance as well as in form. . . .

It seems clear that it was an issue of stock in substance as well as in form. According to its terms, and in the absence of a finding that it was immediately or shortly thereafter redeemed at a premium, we assume that a large portion of it has remained outstanding over a period of years with some of it still unredeemed after nearly seven years. It has been in the hands of the investing public, free of any control by the corporation over its owners, whose enforceable rights with respect to operations of the corporation would not be waived or neglected. Substantial sums have been paid in dividends. The insurance companies bought it in the regular course of their business and have held it as approved investments. For the Court to now tell them that they have been holding a sham issue of stock would be most startling and disturbing news. . . .

If the transaction lacks the good faith necessary to avoid the assessment it must be because of the redemption feature of the stock, which, in the final analysis, is what ultimately permitted the distribution of the corporate earnings and is the key factor in the overall transaction. Redemption features are well known and often used in corporate financing. If the one in question was a reasonable one, not violative of the general principles of bona fide corporate financing, and acceptable to experienced bona fide investors familiar with investment fundamentals and the opportunities afforded by the investment market we fail to see how a court can properly classify the issue, by reason of the redemption feature, as lacking in good faith or as not being what it purports to be. . . .

Each case necessarily depends upon its own facts. The facts in this case show tax avoidance, and it is so conceded by petitioner. But they also show a series of legal transactions, no one of which is fictitious or so lacking in substance as to be anything different from what it purports to be. Unless we are to adopt the broad policy of holding taxable any series of transactions, the purpose and result of which is the avoidance of taxes which would otherwise accrue if handled in a different way, regardless of the legality and realities of the component parts, the tax assessed by the Commissioner was successfully avoided in the present case. We do not construe the controlling decisions as having adopted that view. . . .

Fireoved v. United States _____
462 F.2d 1281 (3d Cir. 1972)

Before Adams, Rosen, and Hunter, Circuit Judges.
    ADAMS, Circuit Judge.
    This appeal calls into question the application of section 306 . . . and the "first in-first out rule" to a redemption of preferred stock in a corporation by plaintiff, one of its principal shareholders. In particular we are asked to decide whether the transaction here had "as one of its principal purposes the avoidance of federal income tax," whether a prior sale of a portion of the underlying common stock immunized a like proportion of the section 306 stock from treatment as a noncapital asset and whether another block of the redeemed stock should be considered to represent stock not subject to section 306.

I. FACTUAL BACKGROUND

On November 24, 1948, Fireoved and Company, Inc. was incorporated for the purpose of printing and selling business forms. At their first meeting, the incorporators elected Eugene Fireoved, his wife, Marie, the plaintiffs, and a nephew, Robert L. Fireoved, as directors of the corporation. Subsequently, the directors elected Eugene Fireoved as president and treasurer and Marie Fireoved as secretary. . . . On December 31, 1948, in consideration for $100 cash, the corporation issued Eugene Fireoved 100 shares of common stock; for $500 cash, it issued him five shares of preferred stock; and in payment for automotive equipment and furniture and fixtures, valued at $6,000, it issued him an additional 60 shares of preferred stock.

In 1954, when Mr. Fireoved learned that his nephew, Robert, was planning to leave the business, he began discussions with Karl Edelmayer and Kenneth Craver concerning the possibility of combining his business with their partnership, Girard Business Forms, that had been printing and selling business forms for some time prior to 1954. Messrs. Fireoved, Edelmayer and Craver agreed that voting control of the new enterprise should be divided equally among the three of them. Because Mr. Fireoved's contribution to capital would be approximately $60,000 whereas the partnership could contribute only $30,000, it was decided that preferred stock should be issued to Mr. Fireoved to compensate for the disparity. In furtherance of this plan . . . the following corporate changes were accomplished: the name of the company was changed to Girard Business Forms; the authorized common stock was increased from 100 to 300 shares and the authorized preferred stock was increased to 1000 shares; Mr. Fireoved exchanged his 100 shares of common and 65 shares of preferred stock for equal amounts of the new stock; an agreement of purchase was authorized by which the company would buy all the assets of the Edelmayer-Craver partnership in return for 200 shares of common and 298 shares of preferred stock; and Mr. Fireoved was issued 535 shares of the new preferred stock as a dividend[6] on his 100 shares of common stock, thereby bringing his total holding of preferred stock to 600 shares to indicate his $60,000 capital contribution compared to the $29,800 contributed by the former partnership.

As the business progressed, Mr. Edelmayer demanded more control of the company. In response, Mr. Fireoved and Mr. Craver each sold 24 shares of common stock in the corporation to him on February 28, 1958.

On April 30, 1959, the company redeemed 451 of Mr. Fireoved's 600 shares of preferred stock at $105 per share, resulting in net proceeds to him of $47,355.[7] The gain from this transaction was reported by Mr. and Mrs. Fireoved . . . as a long term capital gain. Subsequently, the Commissioner . . . assessed a deficiency against the Fireoveds of $15,337.13 based on the Commissioner's view that the proceeds from the redemption of the 451 shares of preferred stock should have been reported as ordinary income and the tax paid at that rate based on section 306. . . .

6. At the time Mr. Fireoved received his stock dividend, the company had accumulated earnings and profits of $52,993.06.

7. In 1959, the company had accumulated earnings and profits of $48,235.

II. BACKGROUND OF SECTION 306

Because we are the first court of appeals asked to decide questions of law pursuant to section 306, it is appropriate that we first examine the circumstances that led to the inclusion in 1954 of this section in the code.

Generally, a taxpayer will benefit monetarily if he is able to report income as a long term capital gain rather than as ordinary income. Under normal circumstances a cash dividend from a corporation constitutes ordinary income to the shareholder receiving such money. Therefore, it would be to the advantage of a shareholder if a method could be devised by which the money could be distributed to him, that would otherwise be paid out as cash dividends, in a form that would permit the shareholder to report such income as a long term capital gain.

A temporarily successful plan for converting ordinary income to long term capital gain is described by the facts of Chamberlin v. C.I.R., 207 F.2d 462 (6th Cir. 1953). There a close corporation had assets of $2.5 million, approximately half of which were in the form of cash and government securities. To have distributed the cash not required in the operation of the business to the shareholders as a dividend would have subjected them to taxation at ordinary income rates. The corporation therefore amended its charter to authorize 8,020 shares of preferred stock to be issued to the shareholders as a dividend on their common stock. The accounts of the corporation were adjusted by transferring $802,000 from earned surplus to the capital account. While these corporate changes were taking place, negotiations occurred between the shareholders and two insurance companies for the purchase of the newly issued preferred stock. In addition, the corporation constructed a timetable for retirement of the preferred stock, which proved satisfactory to the purchasing companies. When the transaction was completed, the selling shareholders reported the gain they realized from the sale of the preferred stock to the insurance companies as a long term gain from the disposition of a capital asset. The Commissioner contended that the gain should have been reported as ordinary income and accordingly assessed a deficiency against the selling shareholders. The tax court agreed with the Commissioner. On review, the Sixth Circuit reversed, holding for the taxpayer thus giving the approval of a federal court to what has been termed "a preferred stock bail-out."

The legislative reaction to the *Chamberlin* decision was almost immediate, resulting in the addition of section 306 to the 1954 code, in order to prevent shareholders from obtaining the tax advantage of such bail-outs when such shareholders retain their ownership interests in the company. . . .

For tax purposes, Congress created a new type of stock known as section 306 stock. When a corporation having accumulated or retained earnings and profits issues a stock dividend which is not otherwise subject to taxation at the time of issuance (other than common on common), the stock received is section 306 stock. The effect of owning such stock is that on its redemption, if the corporation has sufficient retained earnings at that time, the gain* is taxed at ordinary income rates while any loss resulting may not be recognized for federal tax purposes. Section 306(b) sets forth several exceptions to the general rule which serve to remove the section 306 taint from stock disposed of under those circumstances.

Based on the history of section 306 and its plain meaning evidenced by the provisions, it is not disputed that the 535 shares of preferred stock issued to Mr. Fireoved as a stock dividend in 1954 were section 306 stock. Additionally, it is clear that in 1959, when the company redeemed 451 shares of Mr. Fireoved's preferred stock, the general provisions of section 306 — aside from the exceptions — would require that any amount realized by Mr. Fireoved be taxed at ordinary income rates rather than long term capital gain rates, because the company had earnings at that time of $48,235 — more than the $47,355 required to redeem the stock at $105 per share.

Thus, the questions to be decided on this appeal are (1) whether certain of the exceptions to section 306 apply to permit the Fireoveds' reporting their gain as a long term capital gain, and (2) whether 65 of the 451 shares redeemed are not section 306 stock because of the first in-first out rule of Treasury Regulation §1.1012-1(c).

III. Was the Distribution of the Stock Dividend "in Pursuance of a Plan Having as One of Its Principal Purposes Avoidance of Federal Income Tax"?

Mr. Fireoved asserts that the entire transaction should fall within the exception established by section 306(b)(4)(A). . . .

As a threshold point on this issue, the government maintains that because Mr. Fireoved never attempted to obtain a ruling from the "Secretary or his delegate" the redemption should be covered by section 306(a), and the district court should not have reached the question whether the exception applied to Mr. Fireoved. Mr. Fireoved urges that the district court had the power to consider the matter de novo, even without a request by the taxpayer to the secretary or his delegate. Because the ultimate result we reach would not be altered by whichever of these two courses we choose, we do not resolve this potentially complex procedural problem.

The district court, based on the assumption that it had the power to decide the question, found that although one of the purposes involved in

---

* "Gain" or "amount realized"? — Eds.

the issuance of the preferred stock dividend may have been business related, another principal purpose was the avoidance of Federal income tax.

Mr. Fireoved's analysis of the facts presented in the stipulations would reach the conclusion that the *sole* purpose of the stock dividend was business related. He relies heavily on that portion of the stipulation which describes why the decision was made to combine his business with the Edelmayer-Craver partnership: "the partnership could provide the additional manpower which the expected departure of Robert L. Fireoved from the corporation would require. Additionally, the partnership needed additional working capital which the corporation had and could provide." Based primarily on the latter sentence, Mr. Fireoved asserts that the district court had no choice but to find that the transaction was business related and that it therefore had no avoidance incentive.

In making this argument, however, Mr. Fireoved overlooks the plain import of the language of section 306(b)(4). Whether the section requires the decision to be made by the secretary or the district court, it is clear that "one of [the] principal purposes" of the stock dividend was for "the avoidance of Federal income tax." The stipulation demonstrates no more than that the reorganized company required more capital than could be supplied by the partnership alone. The stipulation is completely in harmony with the following fact situation: after the partnership was combined with the corporation, the business required the $30,000 contributed by the partnership and all of the $60,000 Mr. Fireoved had in the corporation. Mr. Fireoved decided to take the stock dividend rather than to distribute the cash to himself as a dividend, and then to make a loan to the corporation of the necessary money because if he took the cash, he would subject himself to taxation at ordinary income rates. Therefore "one of the principal purposes" of the stock dividend would be for "the avoidance of federal income tax."

In a situation such as the one presented in this case, where the facts necessary to determine the motives for the issuance of a stock dividend are peculiarly within the control of the taxpayer, it is reasonable to require the taxpayer to come forward with the facts that would relieve him of his liability. Here the stipulation was equivocal in determining the purpose of the dividend and is quite compatible with the thought that "one of the principal purposes" was motivated by "tax avoidance." We hold then that the district court did not err in refusing to apply the exception created by section 306(b)(4)(A).[11]

11. It is important to note that apparently both Mr. Fireoved, in prosecuting this action for a refund, and the government, in its defense, assumed that if the distribution and redemption of the preferred stock were not controlled by §306(a), the gain would be subject to taxation as a long term capital gain. This is not necessarily the case at all. Whether or not §306 governs the transaction, it nonetheless involves a redemption of stock by a corporation to which §302 could apply. Under the tests set out in §302(b) — the relevant one of which appears to be §302(b)(1) — Mr. Fireoved, who had the burden of proof, may well have

IV. DID THE PRIOR SALE BY MR. FIREOVED OF 24% OF HIS UNDERLYING COMMON STOCK IMMUNIZE SUCH PORTION OF THE SECTION 306 STOCK HE REDEEMED IN 1959?

The district court construed section 306(b)(4)(B) to mean that any time a taxpayer in Mr. Fireoved's position sells any portion of his underlying common stock and later sells or redeems his section 306 stock, an equivalent proportion of the section 306 stock redeemed will not be subject to the provisions of section 306(a). The government has appealed from this portion of the district court's order and urges that we reverse it, based on the history and purpose of section 306 and the particular facts here.

The stipulations indicate that, "on February 28, 1958, Fireoved and Craver each sold 24 shares of common stock in the corporation to Edelmayer," and that appropriate stock certificates were issued. From this fact, Mr. Fireoved reasons that his sale of 24 of his 100 shares of common stock was undertaken solely for the business purpose of satisfying Mr. Edelmayer's desire for more control of the corporation, and therefore he should be given the benefit of section 306(b)(4)(B). In addition, Mr. Fireoved contends that the disposition of his section 306 stock was related to a business purpose because he used part of the proceeds to pay off a $20,000 loan that the company had made to him.

Mr. Fireoved has the same burden here of showing a lack of a tax avoidance purpose that he had in section III supra. It is clear from the limited facts set forth in the stipulations that he has not established that the disposition of 24% of the 535 shares of the section 306 preferred stock he owned "was not in pursuance of a plan having as one of its principal purposes the avoidance of federal income tax."[12] More important, however, is that an examination of the relevant legislative history indicates that Congress did not intend to give capital gains treatment to a portion of the preferred stock redeemed on the facts presented here.

It is apparent from the reaction evinced by Congress to the *Chamberlin* case, supra, that by enacting section 306 Congress was particularly concerned with the tax advantages available to persons who controlled corpo-

---

been unable to show that the redemption was not "essentially equivalent to a dividend." . . . We hold, however, that it is now too late for the government to raise this issue.

12. Consistent with Mr. Fireoved's sale of 24 shares of common stock in 1958 could have been his knowledge that one year later he would be selling his section 306 stock and a desire on his part to avoid taxation at ordinary income rates. As noted later in the opinion, the sale of just 24 shares was enough so that he retained effective control — in the form of veto power — over the corporation. Moreover, the fact that Mr. Fireoved needed $20,000 of the proceeds to pay off a loan to the corporation would not meet his burden. The proceeds of the redemption totaled $47,355. Thus, although $20,000 of the redemption may not have been to avoid taxes, we can ascribe no purpose other than tax avoidance to the receipt of the additional $27,355. Therefore, since one of the principal purposes of the redemption of 451 shares of preferred stock was "the avoidance of Federal income tax," Mr. Fireoved may not take advantage of §306(b)(4)(B) for any part of the redemption.

rations and who could, without sacrificing their control, convert ordinary income to long term capital gains by the device of the preferred stock bailout. The illustration given in the Senate Report which accompanied section 306(b)(4)(B) is helpful in determining the sort of transactions meant to be exempted by section 306(a):

> Thus if a shareholder received a distribution of 100 shares of section 306 stock on his holdings of 100 shares of voting common stock in a corporation and sells his voting common stock before he disposes of his section 306 stock, the subsequent disposition of his section 306 stock would not ordinarily be considered a tax avoidance disposition *since he has previously parted with the stock which allows him to participate in the ownership of the business*. However, variations of the above example may give rise to tax avoidance possibilities which are not within the exception of subparagraph (b). Thus if a corporation has only one class of common stock outstanding and it issues stock under circumstances that characterize it as section 306 stock, a subsequent issue of a different class of common having greater voting rights than the original common will not permit a simultaneous disposition of the section 306 stock together with the original common to escape the rules of subsection (a) of section 306.

S. Rep. No. 1622, 83d Cong., 2d Sess., 1954 U.S.C.C.A. News, pp. 4621, 4881 (emphasis added).

Thus, it is reasonable to assume that Congress realized the general lack of a tax avoidance purpose when a person sells *all* of his control in a corporation and then either simultaneously or subsequently disposes of his section 306 stock. However, when only a portion of the underlying common stock is sold, and the taxpayer retains essentially all the control he had previously, it would be unrealistic to conclude that Congress meant to give that taxpayer the advantage of section 306(b)(4)(B) when he ultimately sells his section 306 stock. Cf. United States v. Davis, 397 U.S. 301 (1970).

Shortly after Mr. Fireoved's corporation had been combined with the Edelmayer-Craver partnership, significant changes to the by-laws were made. The by-laws provided that corporate action could be taken only with the unanimous consent of all the directors. In addition, the by-laws provided that they could be amended either by a vote of 76% of the outstanding common shares or a unanimous vote of the directors. When the businesses were combined in late 1954, each of the directors held 1/3 of the voting stock, thereby necessitating a unanimous vote for amendment to the by-laws. After Messrs. Fireoved and Craver each sold 24 shares of common stock to Mr. Edelmayer, Mr. Fireoved held 25 1/3% of the common (voting) stock, Mr. Craver 25 1/3% and Mr. Edelmayer 49 1/3%. It is crucial to note that the by-laws provided for a unanimous vote for corporate action, and after the common stock transfer, the by-laws were capable of amendment only by a unanimous vote because no two shareholders could vote more than 74 2/3% of the common stock and 76% of the common stock was necessary for amendment. Thus, although Mr. Fireoved did sell a portion of his voting stock prior to his disposition of the section 306 stock, he retained as much control in the corporation following the sale of his common stock as he had prior to the sale. Under these circumstances it is not consonant with the history of the legislation to conclude that Congress intended such a sale of underlying common stock to exempt the proceeds of the disposition of section 306 stock from treatment as ordinary income. Accordingly, the district court erred when it held that any of the preferred shares Mr. Fireoved redeemed were not subject to section 306(a) by virtue of section 306(b)(4)(B).

V. Does the Rule of First In-First Out Mean That 65 of the 451 Redeemed Shares Were Those Which Mr. Fireoved Acquired When He Incorporated His Business in 1948 and Thus Should Not Be Treated as Section 306 Stock?

The district court held that 65 of 451 shares of preferred stock that Mr. Fireoved redeemed in 1959 represented the original shares issued to him in 1948 and were not, therefore, section 306 stock, and that the proceeds from their sales should be treated as a long term capital gain. The court reached this conclusion by applying Treas. Reg. §1.1012-1(c). This regulation provides that when an individual acquires shares of the same class of stock in the same corporation on different dates and for different prices, sells a portion of those shares, and cannot adequately identify which lots were sold, for the purpose of determining the basis and the holding period, the first shares acquired are deemed to be the first shares sold.

Both the district court and Mr. Fireoved reason that the 65 preferred shares he received in 1948 were the first such shares owned by him. In 1954, when the corporation was recapitalized, Mr. Fireoved surrendered his certificate for 65 shares, received a 535 share stock dividend and was issued a certificate representing 600 shares of preferred stock. When he disposed of 451 shares in 1959, it was impossible to identify which shares of the 600 share certificate were being sold. By applying the convenient tool of section 1.1012-1(c), one might conclude that the 65 original shares were sold first because they were received first.

Superficially, this analysis appears to be correct. However, it overlooks the existence of section 1223(5) of the code and the regulations issued pursuant thereto. This section governs the transaction in question because section 307 required Mr. Fireoved to allocate his investment in the underlying common stock between the stock and the preferred stock issued as a dividend. Section 1223(5) is then clear in that it will apply to all situations in which an allocation of basis has occurred pursuant to section 307. These provisions broadly state that the holding period for stock received as a stock dividend is equal to the period for which the underlying stock was held. Applying this test we discover that the preferred stock dividend of 535 shares was issued with respect to the original 100 shares of common received by Mr. Fireoved. Therefore, the holding period for the 535 shares dividend relates back to the date on which the underlying common was issued. Coincidentally, the original 65 shares of preferred stock were issued on the same date as the common. Because the constructive date of issuance for all of the 600 shares of preferred stock owned by Mr. Fireoved is identical, neither the 65 shares nor the 535 shares are first in, but rather are in at the same time.

Since it is impossible adequately to identify which shares were sold when Mr. Fireoved redeemed 451 shares of preferred stock, we hold that a pro rata portion of the 65 shares were redeemed in 1959. In other words, the percentage of the 600 shares of preferred which were not section 306 stock may be represented by the fraction 65/600. That percentage of the 451 shares redeemed in 1959, therefore, would not be section 306 stock. . . .

The Rulings that follow consider what constitutes preferred stock for purposes of §306. Stock labeled common stock might be treated for tax purposes as preferred stock, and vice versa.

Rev. Rul. 81-91
1981-1 C.B. 123

ISSUE

Is the class B stock described below "section 306 stock" within the meaning of section 306(c) of the Internal Revenue Code?

FACTS

A corporation has outstanding a single class of common stock held by 10 individuals, each of whom owned 20 shares. For valid business reasons the corporation entered into a plan of recapitalization under which each outstanding share of common stock was surrendered to the corporation in exchange for one share of new class A stock plus one share of new class B stock of the corporation.

The recapitalization was a reorganization defined in section 368(a)(1)(E) of the Code and the exchanges were nontaxable under section 354(a)(1).

Each share of the class A and class B stock had a par value of 10x dollars. The class B shares were entitled to an annual cumulative dividend of 6 percent of par value payable before any dividend was payable on the class A shares, and a prior right to repayment up to par value in the event of liquidation. After the satisfaction of the class B stock's preferences, each share of class A and class B stock shared equally as to dividends and on liquidation. Each class of shares carried equal voting rights and neither class was by its terms redeemable.

LAW AND ANALYSIS

Section 306(c)(1)(B) of the Code provides, in part and in effect, that "section 306 stock" is any stock, except common stock, that is received by a shareholder pursuant to a plan of reorganization under section 368 with respect to the receipt of which gain or loss to the shareholder was to any extent not recognized by reason of section 354, but only to the extent that the effect of the transaction is substantially the same as the receipt of a stock dividend.

The term "common stock" as used in section 306 of the Code is not defined in that section or the related regulations. In determining whether newly issued stock is "common stock" for purposes of section 306, the "preferred stock bailout" abuse Congress sought to prevent by enactment of that section provides guidance. . . . A bailout occurs if shareholders, through section 306 stock or some other device, withdraw a corporation's earnings and profits at the more favorable tax rates for capital gains. The potential for a preferred stock bailout exists if the shareholders receive a pro rata distribution of two classes of stock in a recapitalization when the corporation has earnings and profits, and the stock of one class, because of its terms, can be disposed of without a surrender by the shareholders of significant interests in corporate growth. Thus, stock is other than "common stock" for purposes of section 306 not because of its preferred position as such, but because the preferred position is limited and the stock does not participate in corporate growth to any significant extent.

The class B stock enjoys voting rights on an equal basis with the class A stock, the only other class of stock outstanding. After satisfaction of its preference to dividends and as to assets in the event of liquidation, the class B stock shares equally with the class A stock. These rights in the class B stock to participate in corporate growth are significant. Thus, a sale of the class B stock cannot occur without a loss of voting control and interest in the unrestricted growth of the corporation. Therefore, the bailout abuse that Congress sought to prevent by the enactment of section 306 cannot be effected through a sale of the class B stock.

HOLDING

The class B stock is "common stock" and is, therefore, excepted from the definition of section 306 stock under section 306(c)(1)(B) of the Code. . . .

Rev. Rul. 76-387
1976-2 C.B. 96

Advice has been requested whether, under the circumstances set forth below, the class A nonvoting common stock is "common stock" for purposes of section 306(c)(1)(B) of the Internal Revenue Code of 1954.

Corporation X had outstanding class A nonvoting common stock, class B voting common stock, and nonvoting preferred stock. The preferred stock was limited and preferred as to dividends, had no dividends in arrears, had a fixed liquidation preference, and was "section 306 stock" within the meaning of section 306(c) of the Code. Neither the class A nor the class B stock was limited or preferred with respect to dividends or distributions in liquidation and neither had a preference over the other in any respect. The only difference between the two classes of common stock was that the class B stock had voting rights while the class A stock did not. Neither the class A stock nor the class B stock was by its terms redeemable.

X desired to simplify its corporate structure by eliminating the preferred stock. Pursuant to a plan of recapitalization, the holders of the preferred stock exchanged such stock solely for shares of class A stock of equal value. The transaction qualified as a reorganization (recapitalization) under section 368(a)(1)(E) of the Code and no gain or loss was recognized to the exchanging shareholders pursuant to section 354. There was no intent to redeem the class A stock when the exchange was made.

Section 306(c)(1)(B) of the Code provides, in part, that "section 306 stock" is any stock, except common stock, that is received by a shareholder in exchange for other "section 306 stock" in pursuance of a plan of reorganization under section 368 with respect to the receipt of which gain or loss to the shareholder was to any extent not recognized. Therefore, if the class A stock in the instant case is "common stock," it is not "section 306 stock" within the meaning of section 306(c)(1)(B). Neither the Code nor the Income Tax Regulations define "common stock" for purposes of section 306.

In determining whether newly issued stock is "common stock" for purposes of section 306 of the Code, the bailout abuse Congress sought to preclude by enactment of that section provides guidance. . . . A bailout occurs if the stockholders can dispose of their stock in question without a loss of voting control and interest in the unrestricted equitable growth of the corporation.

While the class A nonvoting common stock in the instant case can be disposed of without a loss of voting control in X, it cannot be disposed of without the shareholder parting irretrievably with an interest in the unrestricted equitable growth of X represented by such stock.

Accordingly, the class A nonvoting common stock in the instant case is "common stock" for purposes of section 306(c)(1)(B) of the Code. . . .

NOTES

1. *The legislative response to the "preferred stock" bailout.* Section 306 is aimed squarely at the *Chamberlin* type of preferred stock "bailout" — that is, the conversion of potential dividend income into capital gain without diluting the shareholder's equity or control (other than by the restrictions imposed on the shareholder by the holders of the preferred shares). Note that §306 stock includes more than just preferred stock received tax free as a stock dividend. It includes, for example, preferred stock that is received tax free in a reorganization if the receipt of such stock "was substantially the same as the receipt of a stock dividend." §306(c)(1)(B)(ii). The §306 taint does not, however, attach to stock received in a taxable distribution. §301(c)(1)(A).

Under §306, the price of tax-free receipt of stock is, in general, ordinary income on disposition. In *Chamberlin* the preferred stock was worth $100 per share when issued, and the amount of the distribution was fully covered by earnings and profits. Had §306 been applicable to the sale of that stock, the first $100 per share received by the taxpayers for the preferred stock would have been fully includible in their gross incomes. Only the excess, if any, could qualify for sale or exchange treatment.

Query whether §306 would have been necessary had the reasoning of the Tax Court in *Chamberlin* been followed and the various steps viewed as an integrated transaction. Note also that the Tax Reform Act of 1969 substantially reduced the scope of §306 by enlarging the class of stock dividends subject to taxation at the time of distribution under §305. The pro rata distribution of preferred stock to the common shareholders, however, remains tax free, and such stock dividends generally give rise to §306 stock. See Rev. Proc. 77-37, 1977-2 C.B. 568, on the requirements for issuing ruling letters concerning whether convertible preferred stock is §306 stock.

2. *Definition of "§306 stock."* The definition of "§306 stock" is in

§306(c). Section 306(c)(1)(A) is the anti-*Chamberlin* rule, for it imposes a §306 taint on preferred stock received tax free under §305(a).

Preferred stock received tax free in a reorganization (or in a §355 divisive distribution) will also be §306 stock if it is received tax free and if the transaction substantially has the effect of a stock dividend. §306(c)(1)(B). Discussion of reorganizations is deferred until page 381, but it is important to note at this point that the net of §306 extends to the reorganization area. When preferred stock of an acquired corporation that is not "§306 stock" is exchanged for preferred stock of the acquiring corporation of equal value and with substantially similar terms, the preferred stock of the acquiring corporation is not "§306 stock" within the meaning of §306(c)(1)(B). Rev. Rul. 88-100, 1988-2 C.B. 46.

Under §306(c)(1)(C), a §306 taint is not removed by transferring §306 stock in a carryover basis transaction. For example, §306 stock received as a gift or in a §351 transaction is §306 stock. Stock received from a decedent, however, will not be §306 stock because of the fair market value basis rule of §1014. What is the effect of gifting §306 stock to a tax-exempt charity? See Rev. Rul. 76-396, 1976-2 C.B. 55 (§170(e) limits the deduction to the fair market value of the stock less the ordinary income component).

Section 306(c)(2) provides a long-standing rule that no §306 taint will attach to stock received in a distribution in which, had money been distributed instead of stock, no amount would have been includible in income. Thus, tax-free stock dividends cannot produce §306 stock if, at the time of the stock dividend, the corporation had no current or accumulated earnings and profits. This rule recognizes that it is the preferred stock bailout to which §306 speaks: If cash could have been "bailed out" without dividend treatment, then stock distributed in lieu of cash will work no end-run around the §301 distribution rules.

Section 306(c)(3) prevents an abuse of the §306(c)(2) rule. Suppose a taxpayer transfers stock of one controlled corporation (*X* Corp.) to a second controlled corporation (*Y* Corp.) in exchange for preferred stock of *Y* in a transaction qualifying under §351. Because *Y* stock is not "property" for purposes of §304, see §317(a), this transaction is excluded from the definition of §304. If the stock so received is subsequently sold or redeemed the effect of the acquisition and disposition could be to bail out earnings and profits of the corporations.

Such stock-for-stock exchanges are addressed by §306(c)(3). Stock (other than common stock) received in such an exchange will be §306 stock if, had cash been distributed in lieu of the stock, the shareholder would have received dividend treatment under §304. Thus, positive earnings and profits of either controlled corporation will cause noncommon stock received in such an exchange to be characterized as §306 stock.

If a taxpayer receives both nonqualified preferred stock and other stock (i.e., either common or "qualified" preferred stock), the transaction can be described in §351(b) with the nonqualified preferred stock as boot. §351(g)(1)(B). Can such nonqualified preferred stock that is taxable upon receipt also be tainted under §306(c)(3)? Treasury has in the past been willing to limit application of §306(c) when to do otherwise would be inconsistent with the statutory scheme. See Treas. Reg. §1.306-3(f). Might this be another appropriate occasion in which to limit the reach of §306(c)? And if a taxpayer received *only* nonqualified preferred stock, would the §306(c) taint apply?

Note that common stock distributed on common stock is not §306 stock. §306(c)(1)(A). Why not? What is common stock? According to Rev. Rul. 81-91, page 281 supra, and Rev. Rul. 76-387, page 283 supra, common stock for purposes of §306 is any stock that participates without substantial restrictions in the future growth of the corporation. Does this definition of "common" stock adequately respond to the preferred stock bailout abuse? Is it consistent with the statutory language employed by Congress? Should it be consistent with the definition of "common" stock for purposes of §305? See Treas. Regs. §1.305-5(a), discussed in Note 4, page 261 supra.

Will a bailout using common stock necessarily succeed? The Commissioner will, in such circumstances, be forced to relitigate *Chamberlin*. See Rosenberg v. Commissioner, 36 T.C. 716 (1961) (recharacterizing sale of stock by shareholders as sale of stock by corporation followed by distribution of proceeds to old shareholders). The taxpayer will, however, have a new argument: By enacting the detailed rules of §306, Congress may have preempted the field. Should such a legislative preemption argument be accepted in this context?

3. *Disposition of §306 stock*. Section 306(a) provides one rule for disposition of §306 stock by redemption and another rule for all other dispositions (such as sales and exchanges). The redemption rule is simple: A shareholder redeeming §306 stock is subject to the distribution rules of §301 with respect to the amount realized (*not* gain) on the redemption. §306(a)(2). Thus, if the corporation has sufficient earnings and profits at the time of the redemption, the entire amount received by the shareholder can be fully includible at ordinary rates as a dividend.

If §306 stock is disposed of in a transaction other than a redemption, the rule is more complex. Under §306(a)(1), the amount realized in exchange for the §306 stock is treated as ordinary income, but only to the extent of the stock's ratable share of the corporation's earnings as of the time of the distribution of the §306 stock.

For example, suppose X Corp. has 100 shares of common stock outstanding, equally divided between A and B. Assume that these shares are worth $40 per share, that A's basis in each share is $20, and that X Corp. has earnings and profits of $1,500. What are the tax consequences to A if X Corp. declares a stock dividend payable as one share of $100 preferred stock for each five shares of common stock outstanding?

No gain is recognized on the stock dividend by virtue of §305(a). Under §307(a), A must allocate some of his basis in the common stock to the newly received preferred stock. That allocation is made in proportion to the relative fair market values of the common and preferred stock. Treas. Regs. §1.307-1(a).

Prior to the stock dividend, X Corp. had 100 shares of common stock outstanding with aggregate fair market value of $4,000. After the distribution, an additional 20 shares of $100 par value preferred stock are also outstanding. Assuming that the preferred stock is worth par, then the aggregate value of the outstanding preferred is $2,000, which leaves only $2,000 in value for the common. Accordingly, one consequence of the stock dividend is to reduce the value of X Corp.'s common stock from $40 to $20 per share.

A now has $1,000 in common stock (50 shares at $20 per share) and $1,000 in value in preferred stock (10 shares at $100 per share), so he must allocate basis equally between the common and preferred stock. Since the total to be allocated is $1,000, A takes a basis of $10 per share in the common stock and $50 per share in the preferred stock. Is the preferred stock tainted under §306? Yes. See §306(c)(1)(A).

Suppose A sells his 10 shares of preferred stock for $105 per share. How will he be taxed? Absent §306, A would have a capital gain on each share of $105 minus $50, or $55. Under §306(a)(1), we must compute the difference between (1) A's amount realized on the sale and (2) the amount that would have been a dividend had cash been distributed in lieu of the preferred stock.

The fair market value of the preferred stock was $2,000. If cash of $2,000 had been distributed in lieu of the preferred stock, there would have been a dividend to A and B of $1,500, the amount of X Corp.'s earnings and profits. Since 20 shares of preferred stock were distributed, each share's "ratable share" (see §306(a)(1)(A)(ii)) of the dividend would have been $75.

Under §306(a)(1)(A), A will recognize $75 of the $105 amount realized per share as ordinary income. No further gain is recognized by A because the remaining $30 per share of amount realized is less than his basis in the stock. See §306(a)(1)(B). No loss can be recognized, §306(a)(1)(C), so A may add the unrecovered basis in the preferred stock (viz., $20 per share) to his basis in the common stock. See Treas. Regs. §1.306-1(b)(2) (example 2).

The rules for the redemption of §306 stock differ from those applicable to dispositions of §306 other than in redemption. When §306 stock is redeemed, the earnings and profits of the corporation at the time of redemption are relevant. See §§306(a)(2), 301(c)(1). For other types of dispositions, earnings and profits of the corporation at the time of the issuance of the §306 stock are important. See §306(a)(1)(A)(ii). The corporation's earnings and profits at time of issuance can be important even if the §306 stock is redeemed, for the absence of such earnings and profits can remove the stock from §306 ab initio. See §306(c)(2).

4. *Exceptions to the §306 rules.* The draconian rules just described are modified by the exceptions of §306(b). If the shareholder disposes of her entire stock interest (determined by applying the constructive ownership rules of §318) under circumstances set out in §306(b)(1), she can avoid the automatic ordinary income treatment. A redemption of §306 stock in partial or complete liquidation will also relieve the shareholder of §306 disabilities. §306(b)(2)(B).

An exchange of §306 stock in a nontaxable transaction (such as a tax-free reorganization or a §1036 exchange) is not a taxable disposition subject to the rules §306(a). See §306(b)(3). The stock received on the exchange ordinarily will be §306 stock unless it is common stock issued in a reorganization. See §306(c)(1)(B) and (C). A conversion of §306 stock into common stock will eliminate the §306 taint if the detailed rules of §306(e) are met. Those rules generally remove the taint from §306 stock if it is converted into common stock not further convertible into other stock or property.

Section 306(b)(4) describes two circumstances in which the disposition of §306 stock will not be subject to the rules of §306(a). Section 306(b)(4)(A) absolves a shareholder who establishes to the satisfaction of the Secretary of the Treasury (or the Secretary's delegate) that the distribution as well as the redemption or other disposition did not have, as one of its principal purposes, the avoidance of federal income taxes. If the taxpayer sells (or otherwise disposes of) the non-§306 stock at the same time as, or prior to, disposing of the §306 stock, then the taxpayer need convince the Secretary of the Treasury only that the disposition of the §306 stock did not have tax avoidance as one of its principal purposes. §306(b)(4)(B).

In a series of prior revenue rulings, the Service had ruled that §306 stock is not disposed of in pursuance of a tax avoidance plan whenever the stock is widely held. In Rev. Rul. 89-63, 1989-1 C.B. 90, the Service ruled that a shareholder may encounter liability under §306(a) upon disposition of stock of even a widely held corporation unless the shareholder can establish the absence of a tax avoidance motive.

The court in *Fireoved* was able to avoid a difficult procedural question raised by §306(b)(4): May a taxpayer litigate his qualification for §306(b)(4) characterization, or is an appeal to the Secretary of the Treasury his only avenue of relief under that section? The language of §306(b)(4) supports the latter reading, although the courts traditionally have sought to impose *some* judicial review on every exercise of administrative discretion. See, e.g., Crowell v. Benson, 285 U.S. 22 (1932); Johnson v. Robinson, 415 U.S. 361 (1974). When Congress has deliberately granted broad discretion to an administrative agent, the scope of judicial review is appropriately narrow. Surely a taxpayer would have the right to challenge an administrative adverse determination under §306(b)(4) as arbitrary, capricious, or the result of bias or prejudice. But the taxpayer in *Fireoved* sought a favorable judicial determination under §306(b)(4) despite having failed to seek an administrative ruling under that section. Given the clear statement of administrative discretion in §306(b)(4), should not such a failure on the part of the taxpayer have foreclosed judicial review of the issue?

If a taxpayer disposes of §306 stock in a transaction that qualifies as a complete termination of interest under §306(b)(1), then he automatically avoids the harsh rules of §306(a). To so qualify, though, the taxpayer must terminate his interest in the corporation actually and constructively. See §306(b)(1)(A)(iii) and §§306(b)(1)(B), 302(c)(1). If a taxpayer reduces to zero his actual interest in the corporation but continues to have a constructive interest in the corporation, then he may seek an administrative ruling under §306(b)(4)(B). See Rev. Rul. 77-455, 1977-2 C.B. 93, in which a father owned a majority of the corporation's common stock and all the corporation's preferred stock subject to a §306 taint. The father sold some of his common and preferred stock to his son, who already held part of the common, and some to an unrelated party. The balance of the father's stock was redeemed by the corporation. The Service ruled that §306(b)(1) did not apply (because of the rules of constructive ownership) but that §306(b)(4) did apply because the father terminated his actual interest in the corporation.

In Pescosolido v. Commissioner, 91 T.C. 52 (1988), a graduate of Deerfield Academy and Harvard College gave 1,500 shares of appreciated §306 stock to the two institutions and deducted the fair market value of the stock. The IRS, pursuant to §170(e)(1)(A), limited the deduction to the taxpayer's basis in the stock because the stock would not have produced long-term capital gain if sold. Relying on §306(b)(4), the taxpayer argued that the stock would not have produced "tainted" ordinary income if sold because there was no tax avoidance on the distribution or disposition. The Tax Court ruled for the IRS, concluding that the taxpayer was aware that the consequences of the charitable contribution deduction would be the avoidance of ordinary income on the bailout of corporate earnings.

In *Fireoved*, the taxpayer sold a part of his non-§306 stock prior to the disposition of his §306 stock. His prior sale of common stock did not, however, reduce his voting interest in the corporation below that amount necessary to give him a veto over corporate decisions. The court held that under these circumstances the disposition of some of the voting common did not remove the §306 taint from even a proportionate share of the §306 stock. See Rev. Rul. 75-247, 1975-1 C.B. 104, following *Fireoved* in interpreting §306(b)(4)(B).

5. *A comparison of §305 and §306.* The success of the preferred stock bailout in *Chamberlin* turned on two key facts: (1) that the distribution of the preferred stock dividend was tax free on receipt and (2) that the sale

of the dividend stock produced capital gain. This abuse could have been prevented either by taxing the stock dividend or by tainting the dividend stock. Which method should Congress have adopted? Do you agree with the congressional decision to employ both methods, sometimes taxing the stock dividend under §305(b) and other times tainting the dividend stock under §306? If, as a general rule, a tax liability should be imposed only when funds are available to pay the tax, is taxation of stock dividends ever appropriate?

PROBLEMS

6-2. *X* Corp. has 100 shares of stock outstanding, 80 owned by *B* and 20 by *C*. *B* and *D*, an unrelated party, form *Y* Corp., with *B* contributing his *X* stock to *Y* in exchange for 80 shares of *Y* common and 800 shares of *Y* $10 par-value preferred. *D* contributes $2,000 in cash for 20 shares of *Y* common and 200 shares of *Y* $10 par-value preferred. If the fair market value of the *X* stock is $100 per share and *X* has earnings and profits of $5,000, how much of the *Y* common and preferred stock is §306 stock in the hands of *B* and *D*? How does your answer change if *B* receives only 50 percent of the stock of *Y* Corp.?

6-3. *A* and *B* organize *X* Corp. in 1985, each contributing $10,000 in cash in return for 100 shares of common stock. In July 1986, *X* declared a dividend payable in preferred stock: one share of preferred stock for each share of common stock. At the date of distribution, the preferred stock had a fair market value of $200 per share. Immediately prior to the distribution, the common stock was worth $500 per share. On January 1, 1986, *X* had accumulated earnings and profits of $15,000, and *X* had $5,000 in current earnings and profits for 1986. On January 1, 1990, *X* had accumulated earnings and profits of $45,000, and *X* had $5,000 current earnings and profits for 1990. Determine the tax consequences of each of the following situations:

a. In February 1990, *A* sold all her preferred stock to *P* for $11,000, and in January 1991 she sold her common stock to *Q* for $40,000.

b. In February 1990, *X* redeemed all of *A*'s preferred stock for $11,000.

c. In (b) above, *X* also redeemed 50 shares of *A*'s common stock for $20,000.

d. In (c) above, assume there was neither accumulated nor current earnings and profits for 1986. How would your answer change if there had been $1 of current earnings and profits?

7

Liquidations

When a corporation is formed, a shareholder, in the absence of boot, ordinarily recognizes no gain or loss. §351. The price of this nonrecognition is the carryover of the shareholder's basis in the assets transferred to the corporation. §362(a). One might expect a similar statutory structure governing liquidations — that when the corporation is liquidated, no gain or loss would be recognized, but the shareholders would succeed to the corporation's basis in the assets distributed.

Alas, life is not so simple. A complete liquidation is ordinarily a recognition event for both the distributing corporation and the shareholders. The distributing corporation generally recognizes gain or loss on the distribution of its assets as if those assets were sold to the shareholders, and each shareholder generally recognizes gain or loss on the difference between the fair market value of the property received on the distribution and the shareholder's stock basis.

One reason for the nonrecognition pattern on incorporation and the recognition pattern on liquidation may be that there is a continuity of investment in moving a business from unincorporated to incorporated solution, but the same continuity of investment is ordinarily absent when the taxpayer liquidates the business. Often, the business has come to a halt, and the liquidated assets will either be sold for use in another business or used for personal purposes. A liquidation also represents the last opportunity to tax the shareholders on any earnings and profits accumulated by the corporation. Consequently, since 1924 Congress has provided that most often a liquidation will be a taxable event to shareholders. In many but not all respects a liquidation will be treated as if the shareholders sold the corporation's stock back to the corporation and the corporation sold the assets distributed to the shareholders. Note that the liquidation rules apply even if the shareholders continue the business after liquidation.

This chapter focuses on two common liquidation patterns. The first pattern, governed primarily by §§336 and 331, is embodied in the general rule summarized above (and discussed further at Section A infra). For example, suppose X Corp. has assets with an aggregate basis of $100 and a fair market value of $500. The sole shareholder, A, has a basis in the stock of $200. On liquidation X Corp. recognizes gain of $400 under §336. The gain recognized by A equals the difference between the fair market value of the property received and the basis of the surrendered stock, or in this example $300. A's basis in the assets received is the fair market value of those assets in accordance with §334(a). Note now (although it is discussed in more detail below) that historically a liquidating corporation recognized no gain or loss on a liquidation. The Tax Reform Act of 1986 repealed this application of the *General Utilities* doctrine in the liquidation context.

The second pattern involves the liquidation of a subsidiary by a parent corporation (see Section B infra). The subsidiary's assets remain in corporate solution, but the corporate structure has been simplified. Recognizing the continuity here that may be lacking when individuals receive corporate assets, Congress permits both the distributing corporation and the parent corporation to postpone recognition of gain. To illustrate, assume that A in the example above is a corporation rather than an individual. On liquidation there would be no gain to the liquidating corporation under §337. The liquidation is also a nonrecognition transaction for A, the parent corporation, pursuant to §332. The price for nonrecognition is the carryover of X Corp.'s basis in the assets under §334(b). A Corp. will take a $100 basis in the assets received on liquidation. Note that this pattern of taxation is available only if a parent corporation controls the subsidiary within the meaning of §332(b).

The two liquidation patterns outlined above do not operate in a vacuum. Events before, during, and after a liquidation must be considered in evaluating the tax consequences of the liquidation itself. Historically, statutory responses to events preceding or following a liquidation were found in former §337 and §338. Former §337 addressed the liquidating corporation's sale of assets prior to a liquidation (see page 308 infra). Be sure not to confuse former §337 with current §337. As explained below, the two provisions are unrelated. Section 338, in part, deals with the purchase of stock by a corporate shareholder, in some cases, prior to liquidation (see Section B infra).

What is a "liquidation"? That term is not defined in the Code, although the regulations offer some explanation. See Treas. Regs. §1.332-2(c). A liquidation is not necessarily synonymous with turning assets into cash; a distribution in kind is also within the "liquidation" concept. See Rev. Rul. 63-107, 1963-1 C.B. 71. A series of distributions in cancellation of a corporation's outstanding stock can also qualify as a liquidation. Treas.

Regs. §1.332-2(c). It is not necessary that a liquidating corporation dissolve under state law. Moreover, a formal plan of liquidation need not be adopted. See, e.g., Kennemer v. Commissioner, 96 F.2d 177 (5th Cir. 1938). Nevertheless, failure to observe the corporate formalities of adopting a plan of liquidation may tempt the IRS: The early distributions may be treated as dividends rather than liquidating distributions. See, e.g., Estate of Maguire v. Commissioner, 50 T.C. 130 (1968).

Within what time frame must a liquidating distribution be effected to constitute a "complete liquidation"? What corporate activities will be inconsistent with a state of liquidation? Although there is no formal requirement, the longer the process and the more active the liquidating corporation, the more likely the Service will treat the distributions as dividends to the extent of earnings and profits. See Cleveland v. Commissioner, 335 F.2d 473 (3d Cir. 1964) (conduct of business by corporation after distributions rendered them dividends). But see Estate of Fearon v. Commissioner, 16 T.C. 385 (1951) (liquidating distribution more than 23 years after plan adopted respected; court found corporation had tried to dispose of assets). Regardless of the liquidation pattern, tax lawyers often use the three-year period set forth in §332 as a guide for the liquidation time frame.

Consider the following case, which provides an overview of what constitutes a liquidation and how gain or loss is determined.

Rendina v. Commissioner _____

United States Tax Court, T.C. Memo 1996-392

MEMORANDUM FINDINGS OF FACT AND OPINION

BEGHE, Judge:

FINDINGS OF FACT

. . . In 1986, petitioner and Thomas J. Ackerman (Ackerman), a construction contractor, formed WSAI as a general business corporation under Ohio law, for the purposes of constructing and selling 18 condominium units in Willoughby, Ohio. WSAI was operated as a C corporation. Petitioner and Ackerman each paid WSAI approximately $250 for an equal number of common shares of WSAI.

In 1987 and 1988, WSAI constructed the 18 condominium units, known as "South Wood Condominiums" (South Wood). South Wood consists of two-story townhouses, built in clusters of six units in each of three buildings.

WSAI financed the construction of South Wood primarily with borrowed funds. The funds used by WSAI consisted of a loan from Security

Federal Savings and Loan of approximately $740,000, petitioner's deposits in WSAI's checking account of approximately $41,200, and approximately $68,000 in loans from three of petitioner's accounting clients: William and Mary Foss (the Fosses), Vito and Adella Navar (the Navars), and Frank and Benette Posa (the Posas). The principal amounts of the loans from the Fosses, Navars, and Posas were $53,000, $10,000, and $5,000, respectively. The loan checks were made to WSAI, and deposited in WSAI's checking account at National City Bank. WSAI issued promissory notes to the lenders, providing that interest would be paid at a rate of 12 percent per year. . . .

Toward the end of 1988, two of the 18 units remained unsold. Petitioner and Ackerman orally agreed that WSAI would transfer title to the two remaining condominium units to petitioner in consideration of petitioner's assumption of the Foss, Navar, and Posa notes, and petitioner's discharge of WSAI's "debt" owed to him.

In December 1988, WSAI transferred South Wood's two remaining condominium units to petitioner. Petitioner did not report any income or gain from the receipt of the two condominium units on his 1988 Federal income tax return, but did report a taxable dividend from WSAI in the amount of $90. . . .

With the transfer of the last two condominium units to petitioner in 1988, WSAI no longer held business assets, and ceased to be a going concern. Upon transfer of all 18 condominium units in 1988, WSAI ceased doing business, but did not formally dissolve. Its charter was revoked in 1990 for nonpayment and nonfiling of Ohio franchise tax returns.

In April 1989, petitioner sold one of the units for $67,900.

Following his receipt of the last two South Wood condominium units, petitioner gave the Fosses, Navars, and Posas the option of either having their loans repaid, or of having the loan obligations taken over by Canterbury Construction Co. (Canterbury), an S corporation wholly owned by petitioner that is in the business of real estate construction and development. The note holders chose to have Canterbury take over the loan obligations and to continue receiving interest payments. While petitioner did not, in his individual capacity, issue promissory notes to any of the note holders, Canterbury issued new notes to the Fosses, Navars, and Posas sometime after April 1989, and began making interest payments on the notes.

The loans to the Posas and Navars, in the principal amounts of $15,000 and $10,000, respectively, have been paid. As of the date of filing of the petition, the Fosses still held a note issued by Canterbury on which they were receiving interest payments. . . .

OPINION

The substantive tax question before us is whether petitioner's receipt of two condominium units, during the taxable year 1988, was a taxable distribution from WSAI. Respondent determined that petitioner's receipt of the last two units was a dividend in the amount of $135,800 during the taxable year 1988. Petitioner contended that his receipt of the units was not taxable to him because it was offset by discharge of WSAI's debt to him, and his assumption of the Foss, Navar, and Posa notes. Petitioner also maintained that his receipt of the two units could not be a dividend because WSAI had no earnings and profits.

Petitioner, in his reply brief, raised the alternative argument that he received the condominium units in de facto liquidation of WSAI, which would entitle him to use the basis of his WSAI stock to compute his gain on the distribution, if we should determine that his payments into WSAI represented equity rather than debt. Because it appeared to us that this position might have greater merit than the primary position of either of the parties, we had them address this newly raised issue in supplemental briefs.

I. Lack of Prejudice to Respondent in Addressing Liquidation

[Discussion omitted.]

II. De Facto Liquidation

Applying the three-pronged test of Estate of Maguire v. Commissioner, 50 T.C. 130, 140 (1968): (1) Whether there is a manifest intention to liquidate; (2) whether there is a continuing purpose to terminate corporate affairs; and (3) whether the activities of the corporation and its shareholders are directed toward that objective, we are convinced that WSAI and its shareholders displayed a manifest intention to liquidate and continuing purpose to terminate corporate affairs, and that the activities of WSAI and its shareholders were directed to that end. See Olmsted v. Commissioner, T.C. Memo. 1984-381.

Neither the Code nor the regulations to section 331 define the term "complete liquidation." However, as we noted in Olmsted v. Commissioner, T.C. Memo. 1984-381, the regulations under section 332 (governing subsidiary liquidations) contain a definition of "complete liquidation" under section 332 that applies equally to section 331:

A status of liquidation exists when the corporation ceases to be a going concern and its activities are merely for the purpose of winding up its affairs, paying its debts and distributing any remaining balance to its shareholders. A liquidation may be completed prior to the actual dissolution of the liquidating corporation. However, legal dissolution of the corporation is not required. Nor will the mere retention of a nominal amount of assets for the sole purpose of preserving the corporation's legal existence disqualify the transaction.

[Sec. 1.332-2(c), Income Tax Regs.]

Respondent maintains that petitioner never liquidated WSAI. In support of her position, respondent relies on Haley Bros. Constr. Corp. v. Commissioner, 87 T.C. 498, 515-516 (1986). In *Haley Bros. Construction Corp.*, the corporation at issue, Marywood Corp., was not dissolved formally in accordance with State law, and continued to maintain a checking account. We held that there was no liquidation because there was a business purpose for the continued existence of Marywood, which continued to be operated in accordance with that business purpose, holding and selling real property, maintaining a checking account, paying expenses, and filing tax returns. Moreover, the continued corporate existence of Marywood served the purpose of insulating its parent corporation from liabilities on a mortgage and in pending litigation.

In the case at hand, there was no business purpose for WSAI to continue operating. WSAI did not file a corporate tax return for 1988, and, with the sale or distribution of all of the condominium units, WSAI had no further assets of any consequence.

We are unpersuaded by respondent's assertion that, because WSAI continued some activities through the beginning of 1989, it did not liquidate. Complete liquidation can occur despite an extended liquidation process, and several earlier opinions of this court have upheld liquidations despite protracted time frames. See, e.g., Estate of Maguire v. Commissioner, supra; T. T. Word Supply Co. v. Commissioner, 41 B.T.A. 965 (1940); Olmsted v. Commissioner, supra. In order for complete liquidation treatment to apply, it is not essential that a formal plan of liquidation be adopted or that the corporation dissolve, as long as there is a manifest intention to liquidate that is carried out. Genecov v. United States, 412 F.2d 556 (5th Cir. 1969); Stamler v. Commissioner, 145 F.2d 37 (3d Cir. 1944), affg. 45 B.T.A. 37 (1941); Kennemer v. Commissioner, 96 F.2d 177, 178 (5th Cir. 1938), affg. 35 B.T.A. 415 (1937); Olmsted v. Commissioner, supra; Silverman v. Commissioner, T.C. Memo. 1971-143; see Bittker & Eustice, Federal Income Taxation of Corporations & Shareholders, par. 10.02, at 10-9 (6th ed. 1994); 11 Mertens, Law of Federal Income Taxation, sec. 42.06, at 53 (1992 rev.).

Respondent maintains that petitioner has failed to provide the necessary books and records to support his position regarding the liquidation of WSAI. Although we agree with respondent that there are gaps in the record, we believe that it contains sufficient evidence to sustain our conclusion that WSAI was liquidated in 1988. The intentions of petitioner and Ackerman to liquidate WSAI at the end of 1988 were apparent from the sales of WSAI's assets, its cessation of business, and the agreement of petitioner and Ackerman that WSAI would distribute the last two condominium units to petitioner, in consideration of petitioner's assumption of the corporation's liabilities to its lenders and his recovery of his investment out of the balance. With that final distribution, WSAI held title to no further assets of any substantial consequence. With the exception of interest payments made through the beginning of 1989 WSAI engaged in no further activities.

Finally, respondent argues that petitioners made no disclosure of any kind on their 1988 individual income tax return regarding the receipt of the two condominium units as a liquidating distribution, as required by section 1.331-1(d), Income Tax Regs, which states:

> In every case in which a shareholder transfers stock in exchange for property to the corporation which issued such stock, the facts and circumstances shall be reported on his return unless the property is part of a distribution made pursuant to a corporate resolution reciting that the distribution is made in liquidation of the corporation and the corporation is completely liquidated and dissolved within one year after the distribution. See section 6043 for requirements relating to returns by corporations.

Section 1.331-1(d), Income Tax Regs., does not impair our ultimate conclusion that a de facto liquidation did occur during the taxable year 1988 in the case at hand. Although section 1.331-1(d), Income Tax Regs., appears to complement section 6043 and section 1.6043-1, Income Tax Regs., thereunder, providing for the filing of Form 966 (Corporate Dissolution or Liquidation) by a corporation that adopts any resolution or plan of liquidation, the filing of Form 966 is not a condition of liquidation treatment under any provision of the Internal Revenue Code. Maguire v. Commissioner, 222 F.2d 472, 478 (7th Cir. 1955), revg. 21 T.C. 853 (1954); Murphy v. Commissioner, T.C. Memo. 1996-59; see also Fowler Hosiery Co. v. Commissioner, 36 T.C. 201 (1961), affd. 301 F.2d 394 (7th Cir. 1962). We are satisfied that section 1.331-1(d), Income Tax Regs., like the regulation under section 6043, is directory only. While compliance with these regulations serves the evidentiary function of supporting the conclusion that a distribution was received in a corporate liquidation, and helps to avoid controversies of the sort we now deal with, we regard them as playing only a facilitating role. Petitioner's compliance with section 1.331-1(d), Income Tax Regs., is not a condition precedent to our treating the distribution of the condominium units to petitioner as a liquidating distribution.

We are convinced that the agreement of the WSAI shareholders, petitioner and Ackerman, for the distribution of the last two condominium units to petitioner, in consideration of his taking care of the corporate liabilities and recovering his own investment, manifested WSAI's intention to liquidate, and that that intention was carried out in the informal winding-up of WSAI's affairs that followed.

III. Computation of Gain

Having found that WSAI was liquidated in 1988, we turn to the tax treatment of petitioner's receipt of the condominium units. Section 331(a) provides that amounts received by a shareholder in complete liquidation of a corporation shall be treated as "full payment in exchange for the stock", considering a liquidating distribution, in effect, as a sale by the shareholder of his stock to the corporation. Bittker & Eustice, Federal Income Taxation of Corporations & Shareholders, at 10-4, 10-5 (6th ed. 1994); S. Rept. 398, 68th Cong., 1st Sess. 11 (1924), 1939-1 C.B. (pt. 2) 266, 274. As a result, the shareholder computes gain or loss under section 1001(a) by subtracting the adjusted basis of his stock from the amount realized (the fair market value of the distribution), and reports the difference as capital gain or loss if the stock is a capital asset in his hands.

To compute petitioner's gain, we first look at the value of the condominium units distributed to determine the amount realized. We then look at whether petitioner's deposits into the WSAI checking account were loans or equity investments; concluding that they are equity rather than debt, we add them to petitioner's basis in his WSAI stock, rather than treating them as liability offsets to the amount realized. We also look at whether petitioner assumed, or took subject to, WSAI liabilities, because the amount realized under section 1001 on the liquidation exchange is the net value of the distribution, and that amount must be reduced by the amount of liabilities assumed or taken subject to. See Ford v. United States, 160 Ct. Cl. 417, 311 F.2d 951 (1963). We then subtract the basis of petitioner's shares from the amount realized on the distribution to compute his gain.

A. Value of Condominium Units Distributed

Respondent maintains that petitioner received a taxable distribution of $135,800, or the value of the two condominium units received. Petitioner maintains that he gave value equivalent to that of the condominium units. Petitioner's position throughout this proceeding has been that the value of the condominium units was no more than $109,200 — the sum of what he argues were the amount of the WSAI liabilities that he assumed and his deposits into the WSAI account.

We disagree with petitioner's estimate of the value of the condominium units received. The average selling price of the other 14 condominium units was $66,915. Four months after the distribution, petitioner sold one of his condominium units for $67,900.

Petitioner has not convinced us that the fair market value of his condominium units should be less than the average selling price of the other units sold, or $66,915. Thus, we find the fair market value of the condominiums transferred to petitioner to be $133,830.

B. Basis of WSAI Shares: Debt v. Equity

Respondent maintains that no loan or other value was given by petitioner to WSAI. However, the deposit records of National City Bank, where

WSAI maintained a checking account, indicate that petitioner deposited $41,200 into WSAI's account. Because the books and records of WSAI were not made available, we must look to such documentary evidence as bank statements, as well as the testimony of witnesses, in considering whether petitioner gave value to WSAI. Hagaman v. Commissioner, T.C. Memo. 1987-549. We are satisfied that petitioner's deposits into the WSAI account constitute value that resulted in cost to be taken into account in determining petitioner's gain on the receipt of the condominium units.

While the analysis would vary, depending on whether the investment in the corporation were debt or equity, the net tax effect to petitioner would be the same. If petitioner's investment in the corporation were a loan, WSAI's transfer of property to petitioner in satisfaction of the loan would not be governed by section 331 to that extent. This is because the transfer would not be "in payment for" petitioner's stock. In such a case, the corporation merely would be repaying the loan, receiving equal value in exchange for the transfer, resulting in no taxable event for the transferee. See Citizens Bank & Trust Co. v. United States, 217 Ct. Cl. 606, 580 F.2d 442 (1978); J. Hofert Co. v. United States, 23 AFTR 2d 69-845, 69-1 USTC par. 9220 (C.D. Cal. 1969).

If petitioner's investment were equity, petitioner would be entitled to increase his basis in his WSAI shares by the amount of the investment. Under this scenario, petitioner would subtract his basis from the amount of the distribution; if the distribution should exceed petitioner's basis, the excess would be treated as capital gain from sale of the stock.

In Donisi v. Commissioner, 405 F.2d 481, 483 (6th Cir. 1968), affg. T.C. Memo. 1967-62, the court noted that, although the intention of the parties weighs heavily in determining whether advances are loans, proof of such intent is to be found in "the arrangements concerning the normal security, interest and repayment or efforts to secure the same." In Austin Village, Inc. v. United States, 432 F.2d 741, 745 (6th Cir. 1970), the court relied on the fact that there was no unconditional promise to repay the loans, no fixed schedule of payments, and no security given for issuance of the loans.

In the case at hand, none of the factors are present that would tend to show that petitioner reasonably expected WSAI to repay the "loan" in accordance with terms in line with those generally prevailing in the business community. See Nassau Lens Co. v. Commissioner, 308 F.2d 39 (2d Cir. 1962), remanding 35 T.C. 268 (1960). Moreover, no interest payments to petitioner were made or provided for. See Texas Farm Bureau v. United States, 725 F.2d 307, 313-314 (5th Cir. 1984). If petitioner had been a true lender, he would have provided for interest payments. Curry v. United States, 396 F.2d 630, 634 (5th Cir. 1968).

We find that petitioner's $41,200 of deposits into the WSAI checking account was a contribution to the capital of WSAI. Because petitioner was a shareholder of WSAI, his $41,200 of contributions to capital is reflected in an increased basis for his WSAI stock. Sec. 1.118-1, Income Tax Regs. Thus, petitioner's basis in his WSAI stock was $41,450.

Petitioner's amount realized from the distribution of the condominium units should be reduced by the amount of the corporation's liabilities to the Posas, Fosses, and Navars that petitioner agreed to assume, and for whose discharge he made the necessary arrangements. Thus, after subtracting the assumed liabilities of $68,000 from the $92,380 gain ($133,830 amount realized minus $41,450 adjusted basis), petitioner's realized capital gain is $24,380.

Decision will be entered under Rule 155.

NOTES

The taxpayer's successful litigating position was almost an afterthought. The IRS had claimed that the distribution of the two condominium units was a dividend which would be taxable at ordinary income rates. The taxpayer initially replied that the amount distributed should be reduced by corporate liabilities that were assumed and a corporate "debt" owed to the taxpayer. Alternatively, the taxpayer argued that there were no earnings and profits. The court never got to these issues, ruling instead that even in the absence of a declared intention to liquidate, the distribution was a liquidating distribution.

In computing the shareholder's gain on the liquidation, why did the court state that from a tax perspective it did not matter whether the funds advanced by the shareholder to the corporation constituted debt or equity?

As you read the material that follows, consider whether the liquidating corporation should have reported gain or loss on the distribution. Then again, the corporation apparently never filed a return for the year in question and never reported the gain on the sale of the other 16 units. The IRS apparently was seeking more than $100,000 in unpaid taxes and penalties from WSAI. So the taxpayer in this case as a transferee faces bigger problems that were not resolved in this litigation.

A. SECTION 331 LIQUIDATIONS

1. *Treatment of Shareholders*

a. Exchange Treatment under §331

Section 331(a)(1) provides that on a complete liquidation of a corporation, a shareholder's stock is treated as though it had been exchanged

for the amount received by the shareholder from the liquidating corporation. If the stock is a capital asset in the hands of the stockholder, the
liquidation will result in a capital gain or loss. The stockholder realizes
and recognizes capital gain or loss on the difference between the adjusted
basis of the stock surrendered and the value of what is received. See §1001.
Thus, the earnings and profits account, so critical to the tax status of the
distributions of a going concern, becomes irrelevant when the distribution
is in complete liquidation. The analogy for §331(a)(1) is a sale by the
stockholder of the shares to a third party. Is this analogy valid? Consistent
with the recognition of gain or loss, §334(a) provides that the basis of
property received in complete liquidation is its fair market value at the
time of the distribution.

b. Treatment of Liabilities

The fair market value of property received in a liquidation is reduced
by the liability to which the property is subject or that the shareholder
assumes. See Rev. Rul. 59-228, 1959-2 C.B. 59. For example, suppose X
Corp. holds two assets: depreciable real property with a basis of $4,000
and a fair market value of $11,000, and inventory with a basis of $2,000
and a fair market value of $5,000. The real property is subject to a $7,000
mortgage. T, the sole shareholder, has a basis in her X Corp. stock of
$3,000. If X Corp. liquidates, T would recognize a $6,000 gain, and her
basis in the land and inventory would be $11,000 and $5,000, respectively.
§334(a). What would be T's gain or loss on a sale of these assets at fair
market value? Does T's taxable gain or loss correspond to her economic
gain?

Suppose a liquidating corporation distributes assets with a fair market
value of $10,000 subject to a disputed liability for patent infringement.
What is the amount distributed? If the liability cannot be valued, it will
not be taken into account in valuing the distributed assets. Suppose two
years later the shareholder pays the liability, which turns out to be $3,000.
What is the nature of the deduction? See Arrowsmith v. Commissioner,
344 U.S. 6 (1952).

c. Contingent Assets

In some cases, the assets distributed may themselves be difficult to
value even though there are no disputed liabilities. For example, if X
Corp.'s only asset is a contingent contract right that is not valued on
liquidation, the gain to the shareholders will remain "open" on the authority of Burnet v. Logan, 283 U.S. 404 (1931), until the contracts can be
valued. In Rev. Rul. 58-402, 1958-2 C.B. 15, the Service announced that it

"will continue to require valuation of contracts and claims to receive indefinite amounts of income, such as those acquired with respect to stock in liquidation of a corporation, except in rare and extraordinary cases." See also Treas. Regs. §1.1001-1(a). In Commissioner v. Carter, 170 F.2d 911 (2d Cir. 1948), a shareholder on liquidation received oil brokerage contracts that the parties stipulated had no ascertainable fair market value. In a later year, the shareholder collected commissions of $35,000 under the contracts. Is the gain ordinary or capital? The Second Circuit permitted the taxpayer capital gains treatment. Compare Waring v. Commissioner, 412 F.2d 800 (3d Cir. 1969), where a patent royalty contract was valued on liquidation. Consequently, future payments to shareholder in excess of the §334(a) basis were treated as ordinary income in the absence of a sale or exchange. See also Likins-Foster Honolulu Corp. v. Commissioner, 840 F.2d 642 (9th Cir. 1988) (Commissioner applied the open transaction doctrine to the liquidating corporation's claim for condemnation proceeds).

Code §453(j)(2) and Treas. Regs. §15A.453-1(d)(2)(iii) now attempt to curtail sharply the use of the open transaction doctrine. Can a taxpayer elect out of §453 and the above regulation? See §453(d).

d. Installment Notes

If a cash-basis liquidating corporation distributes installment notes in a §331 liquidation, the liquidating corporation must recognize the difference between the adjusted basis and the fair market value of the notes. §453B. Under some circumstances, the shareholders do not have to treat the distributed notes as part of the amount realized. §453(h). Instead, the former shareholders can treat payments on the notes as payments for the stock, thereby producing capital gain (or loss). This treatment for shareholders applies only if the sale or exchange that resulted in the installment obligation occurred during a 12-month period beginning on the date a plan of liquidating was adopted. Furthermore, the liquidation must take place within the same period. Installment obligations for the sale of inventory are accorded this treatment only if there is a bulk sale to one purchaser in one transaction. Installment sale reporting is not available if the stock of the liquidating corporation is publicly traded. §453(k)(2).

If §453(h) does not apply, then a shareholder of a liquidating corporation must treat the fair market value of any installment note distributed as an amount realized on the exchange of stock in the liquidating corporation.

e. Allocation of Stock Basis to Liquidating Distributions

If a shareholder acquires stock on different dates or at different prices, gain or loss is determined separately for each block. Treas. Regs. §1.331-

1(e). In Rev. Rul. 68-348, 1968-2 C.B. 141, the Service sets forth several rules for calculating gain or loss when the liquidating distributions are made over more than one year. This ruling allows the shareholder to recover basis before reporting gain. For example, if *A* holds stock with a basis of $5,000 and receives $4,000 in year 1 and $4,000 in year 2 as a liquidating distribution, the $3,000 gain will be recognized by *A* in year 2. The same principle applies for losses. Suppose *A*'s basis is $10,000. Assuming that the year 2 distribution is the last, *A*'s $2,000 loss deduction will be deferred until year 2. Note that while §267(a)(1) generally disallows loss deductions on the sale or exchange of property between a shareholder and a corporation in which the shareholder owns directly or indirectly more than 50 percent of the stock, shareholder losses incurred on the complete liquidation of a corporation are exempted.

2. Treatment of Liquidating Corporation

a. Recognition of Gain or Loss at the Corporate Level

Recall that in a nonliquidating distribution, there is a shareholder-level tax if the corporation has earnings and profits and a corporate-level tax if the property distributed has a fair market value that exceeds the property's adjusted basis. See pages 119-121 supra. Similarly, in a liquidating distribution, there are likely to be both corporate-level and shareholder-level tax consequences. For the shareholder-level tax consequences, see page 300 supra.

At the corporate level, §336(a) provides that on a liquidation gain or loss shall be recognized to the liquidating corporation as if the property were sold to the distributee at fair market value. The effect of §336(a) is to ensure a corporate-level tax even on preincorporation appreciation. Suppose *B* forms *X* Corp. by contributing property with a basis of $1,000 and fair market value of $9,000 in exchange for all the *X* Corp. stock in a transaction that qualifies under §351. On the exchange, *X* Corp. takes a basis of $1,000 in the property under §362(a), and *B* takes a $1,000 basis in the stock under §358. If *X* Corp. liquidates, the distributing corporation will recognize an $8,000 gain under §336(a), and *B* will recognize an $8,000 gain under §§331 and 1001. *B* will take a $9,000 basis in the property distributed under §334(a).

Why should §336 require a corporate-level tax on this preincorporation appreciation? Could Congress have written §336(a) in a manner that would exclude preincorporation appreciation? Congress did so in the case of preincorporation losses, as is discussed below.

If the property had a fair market value of $1,000 when *B* formed *X* Corp. and then increased in value to $9,000 prior to the liquidation, there is a stronger argument for a double tax on the liquidation — stronger in the sense that to the extent our corporate taxation system is a double tax system, it is not unreasonable to treat a corporation's built-in gains (and losses) in the same manner as recognized gains (or losses) if those built-in gains (or losses) arose during the corporation's existence.

When §336(a) treats the property as if it were sold to the shareholders, are the provisions generally associated with a sale invoked as well? For example, §1239 provides that in the case of a sale between certain related parties, any gain recognized shall be treated as ordinary if the property would be depreciable in the hands of the transferee. Section 1239(b) and (c)(1)(A) treat a corporation and a 50 percent (by value) shareholder as related. Suppose, for example, that X Corp. makes a liquidating distribution of an apartment building to B, its sole shareholder. The building has a basis of $100,000 and a fair market value of $500,000 and is not subject to depreciation recapture because X Corp. used the straight line method for depreciation. Assume the building is a capital asset in X Corp.'s hands. When X Corp. distributes the property, is the $400,000 gain that X Corp. must recognize a capital gain or ordinary income? There appears to be no language precluding the application of §1239.

Section 336 does not apply to all liquidating distributions. For example, a liquidation in the context of a reorganization is not governed by §336. §336(c). Suppose X Corp. transfers all its assets to Y Corp. and then liquidates in a transaction described in §368(a). If X Corp. distributes the appreciated Y Corp. stock as part of the reorganization, X Corp. does not recognize gain under §336(a). §361.

b. Treatment of Liabilities

Section 336(b) provides that if the property distributed in a complete liquidation is encumbered by a liability, the amount realized is not less than the amount of the liability. In effect, §336(b) codifies the result in Tufts v. Commissioner, 461 U.S. 300 (1983). Accordingly, if X Corp. owns property with a basis of $100,000 and a fair market value of $400,000, which is subject to a $600,000 liability. A distribution of that property will trigger a $500,000 corporate-level gain, which will be capital or ordinary depending on the nature of the property distributed. What will the amount realized be for purposes of evaluating the tax consequences to the shareholders?

c. Treatment of Corporate-level Losses

Unlike §311(b), which deals with nonliquidating distributions, §336(a) permits a distributing corporation to recognize losses if the adjusted basis of a distributed asset exceeds its fair market value. Why should a distributing corporation be treated differently in a liquidating distribution than in a nonliquidating distribution? In a liquidating distribution, the distributing corporation distributes all its property — any "gain" property as well as any "loss" property. In a nonliquidating distribution, however, the distributing corporation can "cherry pick" the assets to be distributed. It may choose to distribute "loss" property to recognize a loss for tax purposes while seeking refuge in the realization doctrine with respect to its undistributed and therefore unrealized "gain" property.

Even in a liquidating distribution, Congress has been concerned that taxpayers would take advantage of the loss allowance by artificially creating corporate-level losses. Suppose B owns all the stock of X Corp., whose assets have a basis of $70,000 and a fair market value of $100,000. Assume B's stock basis is also $70,000. B also holds a piece of property with a basis of $130,000 and a fair market value of $50,000. If X Corp. liquidates, it will recognize a $30,000 gain under §336(a), and B will recognize a $30,000 gain under §331. Suppose instead that B exchanges the loss property for additional X Corp. stock in a transaction that qualifies under §351. (A contribution to capital will achieve the same results.) B's basis in the X Corp. stock under §358 increases from $70,000 to $200,000, and X Corp.'s total basis in the assets increases to $200,000 under §362.

Now when X Corp. liquidates, it is treated as if it sold the property to its shareholder for $150,000, its fair market value. Accordingly, X Corp. would recognize a $50,000 loss under §336, and B would recognize a $50,000 loss under §331. Those losses will allow both X Corp. and B to offset other taxable income. Note that B's basis in the loss property after the liquidation is $50,000, its fair market value under §334(a). But B will gladly surrender a higher basis in exchange for a double loss deduction — once by X Corp. and once by B.

Section 336 addresses this and other perceived abuses through two rules governing the treatment of losses. Under §336(d)(1), the liquidating corporation cannot recognize a loss on a distribution to a "related person" if the distribution is not pro rata or if the property distributed is "disqualified property." A "related person" is defined by reference to §267. Why didn't Congress simply provide that a liquidating distribution will be treated as if the liquidating corporation had sold the property to its shareholders at fair market value and then let §267 apply whenever it is triggered? Instead, Congress has enacted a different loss prevention rule in §336.

If the distributee is a related person, a liquidating corporation cannot recognize a loss unless the loss property is distributed pro rata. Suppose X Corp. has property with a basis of $100,000 and a fair market value of $60,000 and $20,000 in cash. A owns 75 percent of the X Corp. stock; B owns the remaining 25 percent. Under §336(d)(1)(A)(i), if X Corp. distributes the loss property to A and the cash to B, X Corp. cannot recognize the loss. If, however, X Corp. distributes 75 percent of the loss property and 75 percent of the cash to A and the remainder to B, then X Corp. will be able to deduct the $40,000 loss on the property. Following the liquidation, A could buy B's $15,000 interest in the property with the $15,000 of cash that was distributed to A. B would not be taxable on the sale because B would hold the $15,000 interest with a fair market value basis following the liquidation. §334(a). Because A and B can end up with a non-pro rata distribution, what is the purpose of the provision?

Even if there is a pro rata distribution to a related party, the liquidating corporation cannot recognize a loss if the distributed property is "disqualified property." That term is defined in §336(d)(1)(B) to mean property that is acquired by the liquidating corporation during the five-year period preceding liquidation if the property was acquired through a §351 transaction or as a contribution to capital. This "antistuffing" provision addresses the problem noted above, in which a shareholder with an unrealized loss transfers the property to a corporation (i.e., stuffs the corporation with loss property) just prior to liquidation in order to turn the unrealized loss into a double recognized loss — once at the corporate level and once at the shareholder level.

Notice that even if the property declines in value while held by the liquidating corporation, no loss will be permitted. Suppose B owns all the stock of X Corp. In year 4, B contributes to X Corp. additional property with a basis of $30,000 and a fair market value of $50,000. In year 7, B decides to liquidate X Corp. At the time of the liquidating distribution, the property still with a basis of $30,000 now has a fair market value of $10,000. Section 336(d)(1)(B) appears to preclude X Corp. from recognizing a loss under §336(a). Perhaps future regulations will soften the provisions in obvious nonabuse cases.

Section 336(d)(1)(B) also applies if the basis of property is determined by reference to the basis of property acquired in the described transaction. Thus, if a liquidating corporation acquires property in a §351 transaction three years prior to a liquidation, it cannot avoid the impact of §336(d)(1)(B) by exchanging the acquired property for like-kind property under §1031 prior to liquidation because the basis of property acquired in a §1031 transaction is determined in part from the basis of the property exchanged. §1031(d).

The second rule applying to liquidating distributions of loss property under §336 does not focus on the relationship between a liquidating corporation and its shareholders. They need not be related parties within the meaning of §267. This rule too is aimed at shareholders attempting to turn unrealized losses into double deductions — once at the corporate level and once at the shareholder level on the distribution. This rule, however, is triggered by and operates in a slightly different manner than the rule governing liquidating distributions to related persons. It might apply, for example, if each of four unrelated shareholders owns 25 percent of the stock of a corporation, although nothing in the language prevents the rule from operating even when there are related persons within the meaning of §267.

The rule is triggered by a distribution, sale, or exchange of property acquired in a §351 transaction (or as a contribution to capital) if the acquisition "was part of a plan a principal purpose of which was to recognize loss by the liquidating corporation with respect to such property in connection with the liquidation." §336(d)(2)(B). This rule applies to sales and exchanges as well as to distributions. Property acquired by the liquidating corporation "after the date two years before the date a corporation adopts a plan of liquidation" is presumed to be part of a loss recognition plan. Accordingly, a contribution of loss property after a corporation adopts a plan of liquidation will not generate a corporation-level loss on liquidation. Note that the two-year rule of §336(d)(2)(B) is measured by the date of adoption of a plan of liquidation, while the five-year rule of §336(d)(1)(B) is based on the date of distribution. Why didn't Congress use the same reference point in both provisions?

Suppose the §351 transfer occurs one year before a plan of liquidation is adopted but has no tax avoidance motive. The Secretary is given authority to promulgate regulations that will exempt nonabuse transfers occurring within the two-year period. The legislative history suggests that contributions of property to be used in the corporation's trade or business or contributions of property during the first two years of a corporation's existence may present such a nonabuse situation. Suppose the §351 exchange occurs more than two years before a plan of liquidation is adopted but has a loss recognition motive. The conference report states that "[the provision disallowing a loss] will apply only in the most rare and unusual cases under such circumstances." H.R. Rep. No. 841, 99th Cong., 2d Sess. (1986).

If the second rule applies, the liquidating corporation is not denied the entire loss deduction relating to offending property. Instead, for purposes of determining loss, the basis of the property is decreased by the excess of the basis of the asset on the date of contribution over its fair market value at that time. §336(d)(2)(A). Suppose that one year prior to adoption of a plan of liquidation, X Corp. acquires, in a §351 transaction, property that has a basis of $50,000 and a fair market value of $30,000. The property continues to decline in value, and on the date of the liquidating distribution it has a fair market value of $15,000. X Corp. will be able to recognize a loss of $15,000 — the decline that occurred while X Corp. held the property. Why doesn't §336 or §311 adopt a similar rule for preincorporation gain property, thereby limiting recognition to gain that occurred while the property was held by the corporation?

Suppose X Corp. acquires loss property in a §351 transaction. Within two years of the acquisition, X Corp. sells the property at a loss. Three years after the acquisition, X Corp. adopts a plan of liquidation and liquidates. Can X Corp. recognize the loss on the sale of the property?

d.   Costs of a Liquidation

Thus far we have focused on the liquidating corporation's gain or loss resulting from the property distributed. How does the liquidating corporation treat the costs of liquidation? The costs associated with preparing and carrying out a plan of liquidation are deductible by the corporation as ordinary and necessary business expenses. See Connery v. United States, 460 F.2d 1130 (3d Cir. 1972); for the treatment of similar expenses in a reorganization context, see page 436 infra.

3.   The *Court Holding Co.* Doctrine and Former §337

Commissioner v. Court Holding Co. _____
324 U.S. 331 (1945)

Mr. Justice BLACK delivered the opinion of the Court.

An apartment house, which was the sole asset of the respondent corporation, was transferred in the form of a liquidating dividend to the corporation's two shareholders. They in turn formally conveyed it to a purchaser who had originally negotiated for the purchase from the corporation. The question is whether the Circuit Court of Appeals properly reversed the Tax Court's conclusion that the corporation was taxable under [§61] for the gain which accrued from the sale. . . .

The respondent corporation was organized in 1934 solely to buy and hold the apartment building which was the only property ever owned by it. All of its outstanding stock was owned by Minnie Miller and her husband. Between October 1, 1939 and February, 1940, while the corporation still had legal title to the property, negotiations for its sale took place. These negotiations were between the corporation and the lessees of the property, together with a sister and brother-in-law. An oral agreement was reached as to the terms and conditions of sale, and on February 22, 1940, the parties met to reduce the agreement to writing. The purchaser was then advised by the corporation's attorney that the sale could not be consummated because it would result in the imposition of a large income tax on the corporation. The next day, the corporation declared a "liquidating dividend," which involved complete liquidation of its assets, and surrender of all outstanding stock. Mrs. Miller and her husband surrendered their stock, and the building was deeded to them. A sale contract was then drawn, naming the Millers individually as vendors, and the lessees' sister as vendee, which embodied substantially the same terms and conditions previously agreed upon. One thousand dollars, which a month and a half earlier had been paid to the corporation by the lessees, was applied in part payment of the purchase price. Three days later, the property was conveyed to the lessees' sister.

The Tax Court concluded from these facts that, despite the declaration of a "liquidating dividend" followed by the transfers of legal title, the corporation had not abandoned the sales negotiations; that these were mere formalities designed "to make the transaction appear to be other than what it was," in order to avoid tax liability. The Circuit Court of Appeals drawing different inferences from the record, held that the corporation had "called off the sale, and treated the stockholders" sale as unrelated to the prior negotiations.

There was evidence to support the findings of the Tax Court, and its findings must therefore be accepted by the courts. Dobson v. Commr., 320 U.S. 489. . . . On the basis of these findings, the Tax Court was justified in attributing the gain from the sale to respondent corporation. The incidence of taxation depends upon the substance of a transaction. The tax consequences which arise from gains from a sale of property are not finally to be determined solely by the means employed to transfer legal title. Rather, the transaction must be viewed as a whole, and each step, from the commencement of negotiations to the consummation of the sale, is relevant. A sale by one person cannot be transformed for tax purposes into a sale by another by using the latter as a conduit through which to pass title. To permit the true nature of a transaction to be disguised by mere formalisms, which exist solely to alter tax liabilities, would seriously impair the effective administration of the tax policies of Congress. . . .

The decision of the Circuit Court of Appeals is reversed, and that of the Tax Court affirmed.

It is so ordered.

Reversed.

NOTES

1. Court Holding Co. Consider the *Court Holding Co.* situation in which *X* Corp. owns a piece of undeveloped land with a basis of $60 and a fair market value of $100. The sole shareholder, *A*, owns stock with a basis of $30 and a fair market value of $100. If *X* Corp. liquidated, former §336 protected *X* Corp. from gain recognition while *A* recognized a $70 gain under §§61, 1001, and 331. Former §336 embodied the *General Utilities* rule in a liquidation context. *A* took a $100 basis in the property pursuant to §334(a). If *A* then sold the property for $100, no further gain was recognized. What happened if the sale was attributed to the corporation as was the case in *Court Holding Co.*?

Court Holding Co. was limited by United States v. Cumberland Public Service Co., 338 U.S. 451 (1950), in which the shareholders first attempted to sell the stock of their corporation. The buyer refused to buy the stock, perhaps because the buyer did not want to assume any undisclosed liabilities to which the corporation was subject. The shareholders then offered to and did sell the assets that they acquired by liquidating the corporation. The Court of Claims held that the sale was made by the shareholders rather than the corporation. The Supreme Court affirmed, stating that, as in *Court Holding Co.*, it relied on the factual finding made by the lower court. The distinction was a delicate one: In *Court Holding Co.* the decision to liquidate seemed to come at the last moment solely for tax avoidance purposes, while in *Cumberland* the plan for a liquidation came early enough for the lower court to find that a genuine liquidation had in fact taken place.

In 1954, in response to the confusion created by *General Utilities, Court Holding Co.*, and *Cumberland,* former §337 was enacted to eliminate the corporate-level tax, whether the sale of assets was made by the corporation before the liquidation or by the shareholders after the liquidation.

2. *Purpose of former §337.* Before reading another line, note well that what is now §337 has nothing to do with former §337, the anti-*Court Holding Co.* provision. Recall the *Court Holding Co.* fact pattern, in which *X* Corp. held an asset with a basis of $60 and a fair market value of $100 and its sole shareholder, *A*, held stock with a basis of $30. If there was a sale of the asset and a liquidation so that *A* ended up with $100 in cash (ignoring taxes), prior to former §337 the ordering of those two events was crucial in determining whether there was one tax or two. Former §337 was enacted to reduce the effect of the formalities of the transaction. Whether the sale is deemed to be made by the corporation or the shareholder, only one tax resulted — the tax to *A* on the liquidation. See §331.

3. *Repeal of the* General Utilities *doctrine and former §337.* When Congress decided to repeal the *General Utilities* doctrine, the need for the anti-*Court Holding Co.* provision of former §337 disappeared. Suppose *X* Corp. holds assets with a basis of $40,000 and a fair market value of $90,000. If purchaser *P* wants to buy the assets, the tax consequences to *X* Corp. and its shareholders on a liquidation followed by a sale are a tax at the corporate level under §336 and a tax on the shareholder level. §331. If *X* Corp. were to sell the assets and distribute the proceeds, logically there also should be a corporate-level and shareholder-level tax. The need for former §337 protection arose only because former §336 gave the liquidating corporation nonrecognition.

Whether both a corporate- and shareholder-level tax on liquidation is appropriate or not, certainly one of the benefits of the repeal of former §337 is the elimination of some of the contentious areas outlined in the previous Note. No longer does a specially drafted nonrecognition provision apply to a sale in connection with a liquidation. Such a sale will be governed by §1001, producing a gain or loss that will be recognized under §1001(c).

4. Court Holding Co. *after the repeal of* General Utilities. With the repeal of the *General Utilities* doctrine under the Tax Reform Act of 1986, you might wonder what, if anything, is left of the *Court Holding Co.* doctrine. Now that a corporation is taxed whether it sells or distributes property, is

there a need to recharacterize a purported distribution followed by a sale as a sale followed by a distribution, or vice versa?

First, the *Court Holding Co.* rule — that steps in an integrated transaction are stepped together — applies in a variety of tax-motivated transactions. For example, a *Court Holding Co.* analysis may be helpful in determining whether the control requirement is satisfied in §351 transactions in which a shareholder sells the stock received immediately after the transfer of receipt of the stock. See page 59 supra.

Second, even in the liquidation context, the *Court Holding Co.* doctrine endures. Suppose *B* owns all the *X* Corp. stock with a basis of $2,000 and a fair market value of $5,000. Among its assets, *X* Corp. owns and has owned for several years an asset with a basis of $5,000 and a fair market value of $1,000. *P*, an unrelated purchaser, wants to buy the asset and starts to negotiate with *B* for the sale. The original negotiations contemplate the liquidation of *X* Corp. followed by a sale of the asset by *B*. Prior to the liquidation, *X* Corp. sells the asset to *P* and then distributes the proceeds.

If the transaction is respected, *X* Corp. will recognize a $4,000 loss on the sale under §1001 because it is unlikely that §336(d)(2) will apply to property acquired by the liquidating corporation more than two years prior to the adoption of the plan of liquidation. *B* will recognize a $3,000 gain on the liquidation under §§331 and 1001. If the transaction is not respected, the Service might recharacterize the transaction as a liquidation followed by a sale. In that event, *X* Corp. would recognize no loss on the liquidating distribution if the property was acquired by *X* Corp. within the five-year period ending on the date of the distribution. §336(d)(1). *B* would still recognize a $3,000 gain under §§331 and 1001. *B* would take a $1,000 basis in the asset under §334(a) and would not recognize gain or loss on the sale to *P*.

Ordering the transactions as a liquidation followed by a sale deprives *B* (and *B*'s wholly owned corporation) of a loss deduction. The *Court Holding Co.* doctrine will continue to function in this and other situations in which differing tax consequences hinge on which taxpayer sold assets.

The loss restriction rule in §336(d)(2) is intended to operate when the §351 transfer and the adoption of a plan of liquidation occur within a two-year period. §336(d)(2)(B)(ii). No statutory provision seems to prevent a full recognition of loss by a corporation that receives a §351 transfer of loss property and that then sells the property. A double loss will then be created if the corporation liquidates, so long as the liquidation takes place outside the two-year period.

To illustrate, suppose *B* owns all the *X* Corp. stock with a basis and fair market value of $6,000. *X* Corp. holds assets with a basis and fair market value of $6,000. Now suppose *B* contributes to *X* Corp. property with a basis of $8,000 and a fair market value of $2,000. If *X* Corp. sells the property almost immediately and then adopts a plan of liquidation more than two years after the §351 transfer, arguably *X* Corp. will recognize a loss of $6,000 on the sale and *B* will recognize a loss of $6,000 on the liquidation (*B*'s basis having increased by the basis of the contributed property).

Is the Service bound by this result, given the fact that it recognized the general problem and Congress specifically enacted §336(d)(2) to deal with it? Or can the Service rely on judicial principles such as *Court Holding Co.* to deny the loss deduction or to treat *B* as if *B* had made the sale? What if *B* played no part in the negotiation of the sale? If no liquidation had taken place, could the Service have attributed the sale to *B*?

5. *A corporate triple tax?* The U.S. corporate tax system seeks to tax corporate earnings twice — once when earned by the corporation and once when distributed to individual shareholders. To reinforce this double taxation paradigm, Congress has enacted §243 to provide a dividends-received deduction for dividends received by a shareholder-corporation. See page 134 supra.

The repeal of the *General Utilities* doctrine creates the potential for a triple tax in a liquidation context. Suppose *B* owns all the stock of *X* Corp., a holding company whose sole asset is all the stock of *Y* Corp. *P*, an unrelated purchaser, seeks to acquire all of *Y* Corp.'s assets (all of which are appreciated). Suppose *P* buys the *Y* Corp. stock from *X* Corp., and then *B* and *P* liquidate their corporations. *X* Corp. has already recognized gain on the sale of the *Y* Corp. stock (single tax), and *B* will recognize gain on the liquidation under §§331 and 1001 (double tax). *P* will recognize no gain on the liquidation of *Y* Corp. because *P* took a cost basis in the *Y* Corp. stock purchased from *X* Corp. When *P* liquidates *Y* Corp., the liquidating corporation will recognize gain (triple tax).

The triple tax could have been avoided if *Y* Corp. had sold its assets directly to *P*, followed by a liquidation of *X* Corp. and *Y* Corp. On the sale, *Y* Corp. would recognize gain (single tax). When *Y* Corp. liquidates into its parent *X* Corp., no gain is recognized. See the discussion of §§337 and 332 at page 314 infra. *B* recognizes gain on the liquidation of *X* Corp. (double tax).

In both examples above, *P* ends up with the assets having a fair market value basis and *B* ends up with cash. The triple tax possibility puts a premium on form and would undoubtedly precipitate *Court Holding Co.* arguments about who sold what. In §336(e), Congress has authorized the Treasury to promulgate regulations that will treat the sale of *Y* Corp. stock by *X* Corp. as if the *Y* Corp. assets were sold instead. In the example above, *X* Corp.'s gain on the sale would be the difference between the amount realized for the *Y* Corp. stock and the adjusted basis of the *Y* Corp. assets (single tax). The *Y* Corp. assets would then take a fair market value regardless of whether *P* liquidated *Y* Corp. No gain would be recognized on the sale of the *Y* Corp. stock itself, but *B* would recognize gain on the liquidation of *X* Corp. (double tax). This treatment, which reduces the triple tax to a double tax, is available if a corporation meets the substantial ownership tests under §1504(a)(2) (80 percent voting control and 80 percent of total value of outstanding stock). See page 525 infra.

6. *Growth of S corporations and other transparent entities.* The repeal of the *General Utilities* doctrine has upped the ante for operating in corporate form — at least in corporate form under subchapter C. Taxpayers now have several choices in addition to operating through a C corporation. For example, a taxpayer can operate through a partnership that is transparent (i.e., not a tax-paying entity for tax purposes). Alternatively, a taxpayer can operate through a limited liability company or other entity where the taxpayer has "checked-the-box" to have the entity taxed as a transparent entity. See the discussion of the "check-the-box" regulations on pages 562-564. Also, Subchapter S, discussed in Chapter 16, offers qualifying taxpayers the advantages of corporate form with only a single shareholder level of taxation. Generally, there is no corporate-level taxation for an S corporation. This difference in treatment, combined with the repeal of the *General Utilities* rule, heightens the attraction of subchapter S status for a corporation contemplating a liquidation.

Suppose *X* Corp. with appreciated assets is planning to sell its assets and then liquidate. The sale will result in a corporate-level gain, and, assuming the *X* Corp. stock is appreciated, the liquidation will produce a shareholder-level gain under §§331 and 1001. Suppose instead that immediately prior to the sale and liquidation, *X* Corp. elects to be taxed under subchapter S. In the absence of a remedial provision, *X* Corp. would recognize no gain on the sale. The shareholders would recognize gain but, as a result, would recognize correspondingly less gain on the liquidation. The effect of the S election would be avoidance of a corporate-level tax.

Section 1374, discussed further in Chapter 17, now imposes a corporate-level tax equal to the highest rate under §11 (or §1201 if applicable) on any net gain (built-in gain) arising prior to the conversion from a C corporation to an S corporation that is recognized by the corporation through sale or distribution within 10 years after the date on which the S election took place. Any gain will be presumed to be a built-in gain unless the taxpayer can establish that the appreciation accrued after the conversion.

PROBLEMS

7-1. Determine the tax consequences in the following situations.

a. *X* Corp. is owned by unrelated individuals, *A* and *B*, who hold 80 percent and 20 percent, respectively, of the outstanding *X* Corp. stock. *A*'s stock has a basis of $300,000 and a fair market value of $800,000. *B*'s stock has a basis of $600,000 and a fair market value of $200,000. *X* Corp. holds two assets. Asset 1 has a basis of

$200,000 and a fair market value of $500,000. Asset 2 has a basis of $800,000 and a fair market value of $500,000. Both assets were transferred to X Corp. in a §351 transaction two years ago. At that time asset 2 had a basis of $800,000 and a fair market value of $900,000. X Corp. has accumulated earnings and profits of $100,000, but no current earnings and profits. What are the tax consequences if X Corp. liquidates, distributing the assets pro rata (i.e., A gets 80 percent of asset 1 and 80 percent of asset 2)?

b.   In (a), suppose asset 2 had a basis of $800,000 and a fair market value of $700,000 at the time of the §351 transfer.

c.   In (b), suppose the §351 transfer took place six years before the liquidation.

d.   In (c), suppose X Corp. distributes all of asset 2 and a $300,000 interest in asset 1 to A and the remaining $200,000 interest in asset 1 to B.

e.   In (a), suppose A and B are planning to sell the assets after liquidation. Does it matter whether X Corp. makes the sale and then distributes $1 million in cash or A and B make the sale following liquidation? In (b), would it matter?

f.   If A is a corporation, how does your answer to (a) change?

B.   SUBSIDIARY LIQUIDATIONS AND RELATED PROVISIONS

1.   Section 332 Liquidations

Section 332 provides in substance that no gain or loss shall be recognized on the liquidation of a subsidiary corporation. This provision, enacted in an earlier form in 1935, was proposed by the Treasury as a measure to encourage the simplification of elaborate corporate structures. In the absence of such a nonrecognition provision, a parent corporation could eliminate subsidiary corporations only by paying a capital gains tax under §331, assuming appreciation in the value of the subsidiary's stock. Furthermore, if a subsidiary distributed appreciated assets in the liquidation, it would have to recognize gain as well. §336.

Note that §332 by its terms is not optional; moreover, it provides for the nonrecognition of both gain and loss. While the technical requirements of §332 allow taxpayers often to avoid its nonelective nature when they so desire, the *Associated Wholesale Grocers* case that follows shows that the ability to manipulate §332 is not unrestrained.

Section 332's basis provision, §334(b), does not follow the usual practice of giving the property received on a tax-free exchange the same basis as the property given up — here, the stock of the subsidiary. For an example of the general rule, see §358, which applies to an exchanging shareholder in a §351 transaction. Instead, §334(b) ordinarily requires the transferee (the parent corporation) to take over the basis of the transferor — its subsidiary — in the distributed assets. Does this unusual principle seek to treat the parent as though it had operated the business, ab initio, without the intervening subsidiary's corporate veil? Note that the basis rule of §334 is consistent with the carryover basis applied to transferees in §351 transactions and in certain mergers, in which the transferee is considered the successor to the transferor.

Taken together, the nonrecognition principle of §332 and the carryover basis rule of §334(b) in effect remove from tax consideration any gain or loss unrecognized by the parent. Consider the following two situations:

	A	B
Parent's stock basis	$10,000	$10,000
Subsidiary's asset basis	3,000	17,000
Fair market value of subsidiary's assets	8,000	13,000

In situation A the parent has an unrecognized $2,000 loss in the stock of its subsidiary; if the parent liquidates within §332, no loss will be recognized on the liquidation, and the parent will hold the subsidiary's assets with a basis of $3,000, thereby producing a gain if the parent should then sell the assets. Conversely, in situation B the parent has a potential $3,000 gain in the subsidiary's stock. If the parent liquidates, no gain will be recognized, and the parent will take a $17,000 basis in the subsidiary's assets, which will produce a $4,000 loss if the parent sells on liquidation.

Associated Wholesale Grocers, Inc. v. United States
927 F.2d 1517 (10th Cir. 1991)

BRORBY, Circuit Judge. . . .

The material facts are not in dispute. In 1976, Super Market Developers, Inc. ("Super Market Developers") made a tender offer for all of the outstanding stock of Weston Investment Co. ("Weston"), a publicly traded holding company which owned a number of corporate supermarkets. Super Market Developers acquired approximately 99.97 percent of the total outstanding shares of Weston by 1980. The management of Super Market Developers' parent corporation, Associated Wholesale Grocers, Inc. ("Associated Grocers"), subsequently decided it was not in their best interests to own and operate grocery stores through subsidiary corporations. . . .

One of Weston's subsidiaries was Weston Market, Inc. ("Weston Market''), a grocery managed by Thomas Elder. In 1980, Mr. Elder expressed to taxpayer his interest in buying Weston Market. Taxpayer advised Mr. Elder that it was not interested in a transaction solely involving the stock or operating assets of Weston Market, but that it would be willing to continue discussions.

The parties eventually structured a disposition of Weston's stock which, taxpayer hoped, would enable it both to cash out Weston's minority shareholders without paying a premium and to recognize a substantial loss in the value of Weston's assets[1] when it sold Weston Market. The transaction took the form of two agreements between Super Market Developers and Elder Food Mart, Inc. ("Elder, Inc."), a corporation organized by Mr. Elder to facilitate the purchase of Weston Market. Both agreements were signed on December 11, 1980, and consummated on December 23, 1980.

Under the "Agreement and Plan of Merger," Weston was merged into Elder, Inc., with Elder, Inc. as the surviving corporation. Elder, Inc. exchanged $300,000 in cash and a non-interest bearing demand promissory note, with a face value of $9,049,703, for the Weston stock. The minority shareholders were entitled to receive $28.50 per share, or more, depending on their pro rata share of the cash and note exchanged for Weston stock.

Under the "Agreement and Plan of Reorganization," which took effect "immediately following the time of effectiveness of the merger," Super Market Developers bought back all the assets acquired by Elder, Inc. under the merger agreement except for the stock of Weston Market. In exchange for those assets, Super Market Developers paid "an amount equal to the principal amount of the promissory note . . . plus an amount equal to the cash received by the [minority] shareholders."

Taxpayer treated the transaction as a taxable sale of Weston's assets and declared a tax loss under I.R.C. §1001(a). Because the transaction brought Super Market Developers $2,353,258 less than its cost basis in the stock of Weston, the taxpayer reported that amount as a long-term capital loss in its 1980 consolidated federal income tax return and sought to carry back portions of the loss to each of the three prior years. The IRS denied the loss, concluding the transaction was not a sale but rather a complete liquidation of taxpayer's subsidiary, Weston. As such, the IRS concluded, recognition of the loss was barred by I.R.C. §332. The IRS assessed a deficiency which the taxpayer paid.

Upon the IRS's denial of taxpayer's claim for refund, taxpayer filed suit in the United States District Court for the District of Kansas. The

---

1. Taxpayer was concerned by the difference between Super Market Developers' cost basis in the Weston stock — the amount it had paid for the stock, $11,727,716 — and the carryover basis representing the market value of Weston's assets, $9,374,458. Under I.R.C. §334, taxpayer would get the carryover basis for Weston's assets upon a complete liquidation of Weston.

district court applied the step transaction doctrine in holding that §332 bars the recognition of taxpayer's loss. *Grocers*, 720 F. Supp. at 890. The court granted summary judgment in favor of the government. Id. This appeal followed. . . .

ARGUMENTS ON APPEAL

The issue presented is whether, as a matter of law, the transaction of December 23, 1980 constitutes a taxable sale or other disposition of Weston's assets under I.R.C. §1001(a) or a non-taxable complete liquidation of Weston under I.R.C. §332.

Taxpayer argues the district court erred in accepting the government's characterization of the transaction as a non-taxable liquidation under §332, and in applying the step transaction doctrine to reach that conclusion. Taxpayer advances five reasons in support of its argument: (1) the transaction does not meet the enumerated requirements of §332; (2) case law rejects application of the step transaction doctrine in the §332 context; (3) this transaction was supported by business purposes which bar application of the step transaction doctrine; (4) even if it is applicable, the step transaction doctrine was improperly applied by the district court; and (5) application of the step transaction doctrine in this case will produce the harsh result of forever depriving taxpayer of the recognition of its tax loss. We now address those contentions.

I. INTERNAL REVENUE CODE §332

. . . The nonrecognition exception of §332 applies or, in other words, a distribution is considered to be in complete liquidation of a subsidiary, only if:

(1) the asset-receiving or "parent" corporation owns, on the date of the adoption of the plan of liquidation and continuously until the receipt of the assets upon liquidation, at least 80 percent of the total voting power and value of the subsidiary (§332(b)(1)); and

(2) the subsidiary distributes its property in complete cancellation or redemption of its stock (§332(b)(2), (3)); and

(3) the subsidiary transfers all of its property to the parent either:

(a) within the taxable year (in which case the shareholders' adoption of the resolution authorizing the distribution of assets in complete cancellation or redemption of stock is considered an adoption of a plan of liquidation) (§332(b)(2)), or

(b) in a series of distributions in accordance with a plan of liquidation under which all property is distributed within three years from the close of the year in which the first distribution is made. (§332(b)(3).)

See I.R.C. §332(b)(1)-(b)(3); 11 J. Mertens, The Law of Federal Income Taxation, §42.42 at 113-14 (1990); cf. Matter of Chrome Plate, Inc., 614 F.2d 990, 994 (5th Cir. 1980).

The significance of the statute in this dispute is apparent: if §332 applies, taxpayer cannot recognize its loss. If §332 is inapplicable, however, taxpayer is entitled to a substantial tax refund.

Taxpayer argues §332 is inapplicable for three reasons: the 80 percent ownership requirement was not continuously met; all of the assets of the subsidiary were not transferred to the parent; and taxpayer did not adopt a plan of liquidation. We will consider these arguments in turn.

II. 80% STOCK OWNERSHIP REQUIREMENT

The stock ownership requirement is found in §332(b)(1), which specifies an 80 percent voting and value requirement. That requirement is not specifically at issue here, as parties agree that taxpayer owned 99.97 percent of Weston's stock until the transactions occurred on December 23, 1980.

At issue is the continuity requirement of §332(b)(1) — whether taxpayer "has continued to be at all times until the receipt of the property" qualified under the 80 percent voting and value test. As explained by Treasury Regulation:

> The recipient corporation must have been the owner of the specified amount of such stock on the date of the adoption of the plan of liquidation and have continued so to be at all times until the receipt of the property. If the recipient corporation does not continue qualified with respect to the ownership of stock of the liquidating corporation and if the failure to continue qualified occurs at any time prior to the completion of the transfer of all the property, the provisions for the nonrecognition of gain or loss do not apply to any distribution received under the plan.

Treas. Reg. §1.332-2(a). The question, then, is whether taxpayer continued qualified with respect to the ownership of Weston stock until taxpayer received Weston's assets.

Section 332(b)(1) and Treas. Reg. §1.332-2(a) each direct our inquiry to two time periods: "the date of the adoption of the plan of liquidation" and "all times until the receipt of the property." We assume for the purposes of the first inquiry that the adoption of the "Agreement and Plan of Merger" by Weston shareholders on December 20, 1980 was an adoption of a plan of liquidation. Taxpayer undisputedly owned 99.97 percent of Weston's stock at that time.

The key dispute concerns the effect of the merger and reorganization transactions on December 23, 1980 — the date on which taxpayer received the property of its subsidiary. Taxpayer argues that because all of Weston's assets were transferred to Elder, Inc. and all of Weston's stock was cancelled under the merger, taxpayer's ownership of Weston stock was cut off before it received Weston's property. Therefore, taxpayer argues, because taxpayer owned no Weston stock when it subsequently received the property of its subsidiary under the reorganization, it did not continue qualified with respect to stock ownership under §332(b)(1).

The government urges this court to disregard Elder, Inc.'s transitory ownership of Weston by applying the step transaction doctrine in holding that the merger and reorganization "should be collapsed and viewed as a single transaction for tax purposes." The district court agreed and "view(ed) the execution of the two integrated agreements as one transaction which did not effect a bonafide sale of stock and conclude(d), as a matter of law, that Super Market Developers, at all relevant times, owned more than 80 percent of the outstanding shares of Weston. . . ." 720 F. Supp. at 890.

A. The Step Transaction Doctrine

"The step-transaction doctrine developed as part of the broader tax concept that substance should prevail over form." American Potash & Chem. Corp. v. United States, 399 F.2d 194, 207, 185 Ct. Cl. 161; see also Security Indus. Ins. Co. v. United States, 702 F.2d 1234, 1244 (5th Cir. 1983); Rosenberg, Tax Avoidance and Income Measurement, 87 Mich. L. Rev. 365, 400 (1988) [hereinafter Rosenberg]. Under the step transaction doctrine:

> interrelated yet formally distinct steps in an integrated transaction may not be considered independently of the overall transaction. By thus "linking together all interdependent steps with legal or business significance, rather than taking them in isolation," federal tax liability may be based "on a realistic view of the entire transaction."

Commissioner v. Clark, 489 U.S. 726, 738 (1989) (quoting 1 B. Bittker, Federal Taxation of Income, Estates and Gifts ¶4.3.5, p. 4-52 (1981)). . . .

Courts and commentators have identified several tests which are used with varying frequency in determining whether to apply the step transaction doctrine. Most sources identify three tests: see, e.g., Security Indus., 702 F.2d at 1244-45 (identifying the "end result," "interdependence," and "binding commitment" tests); McDonald's Restaurants of Illinois, Inc. v. Commissioner, 688 F.2d 520, 524-25 (7th Cir. 1982) (same); 11 J. Mertens, The Law of Federal Income Taxation, §§43.254-43.256 (1990) (same); Comments, Step Transactions, 24 U. Miami L. Rev. 60, 62-66 (1969) (identifying the "time," "intention," and "interdependency" tests). Others differ: see, e.g., King Enters., Inc. v. United States, 418 F.2d 511, 516 (Ct. Cl. 1969) (identifying "end result" and "interdependence" as the "two basic tests"); Schwartz, Liquidation-Reincorporation: A Sensible Approach

Consistent with Congressional Policy, 38 U. Miami L. Rev. 231, 240 n.33 (1984) (same). The "end result" and "interdependence" tests are the most frequently applied. See *Security Indus.*, 702 F.2d at 1244, and Rosenberg, at 409, respectively.

Under the "end result" test, "purportedly separate transactions will be amalgamated into a single transaction when it appears that they were really component parts of a single transaction intended from the outset to be taken for the purpose of reaching the ultimate result." *King Enters.*, 418 F.2d at 516 (quoting Herwitz, Business Planning, 804 (1966)). The "end result" test, like the substance over form principle, is particularly pertinent to cases involving a series of transactions designed and executed as parts of a unitary plan to achieve an intended result. Such plans will be viewed as a whole regardless of whether the effect of so doing is imposition of or relief from taxation. The series of closely related steps in such a plan are merely the means by which to carry out the plan and will not be separated. . . .

The "interdependence test" requires an inquiry as to "whether on a reasonable interpretation of objective facts the steps were so interdependent that the legal relations created by one transaction would have been fruitless without a completion of the series." Paul & Zimet, "Step Transactions," Selected Studies in Federal Taxation 200, 254 (2d Series 1938), quoted in *King Enters.*, 418 F.2d at 516, and *Security Indus.*, 702 F.2d at 1244. The "interdependence test" focuses on the relationship between the steps, rather than on the "end result." *McDonald's Restaurants,* 688 F.2d at 524. Disregarding the tax effects of individual steps under this test is, therefore, "especially proper where . . . it is unlikely that any one step would have been undertaken except in contemplation of the other integrating acts. . . ." Kuper v. Commissioner, 533 F.2d 152, 156 (5th Cir. 1976).

We now consider taxpayer's claim that relevant case law bars the use of step transaction analysis in the context of §332. Taxpayer most heavily relies on Granite Trust Co. v. United States, 238 F.2d 670 (1st Cir. 1956), a taxpayer refund suit involving the liquidation of a corporate subsidiary. In *Granite Trust,* the First Circuit considered whether to allow the taxpayer to avoid the nonrecognition provisions of I.R.C. §112(b)(6) (1939), the predecessor to modern code section 332.

Taxpayer Granite Trust Company (Granite) expected to realize losses upon the liquidation of its wholly owned subsidiary, Building Corp. Granite therefore took two steps to avoid the nonrecognition provisions of §112(b)(6). First, Granite sold 20.5 percent of Building Corp.'s stock in order to circumvent the 80 percent ownership requirement of §112(b)(6). Id. at 672. Second, after adopting a liquidation plan, Granite sold twenty shares of stock and donated two shares to charity. Id. at 673. The dispositions were intended to circumvent the "second condition" of §112(b)(6), one which was not included in modern code section 332. See id. at 672 n.1, 675. That condition allowed recognition of gains or losses where the parent corporation, within a specified time period, disposed of stock in the subsidiary without making countervailing acquisitions. Id. at 675. The *Granite Trust* court ruled on the merits only as to the second step, and allowed taxpayer to recognize its loss. See id. at 675.

Because *Granite Trust*'s decision in favor of the taxpayer hinged on a provision which is no longer present in the Code, *Granite Trust* is not dispositive in this case. However, to the extent the *Granite Trust* court discussed provisions of §112(b)(6) which are still contained in modern §332, some of its reasoning is persuasive.

Granite prevailed over the government's arguments against its recognition of losses. First, the government advanced the "end-result" test in urging the court to ignore the intermediate steps in Granite Trust's liquidation of Building Corp. Id. at 674. The court rejected that argument, stating "the very terms of §112(b)(6) make it evident that it is not an 'end-result' provision, but rather one which prescribes specific conditions for the nonrecognition of realized gains or losses, conditions which, if not strictly met, make the section inapplicable." Id. at 675. The court found support in the legislative history of both §112(b)(6) (1939) and §332 (1954), and concluded "that taxpayers can, by taking appropriate steps, render the subsection applicable or inapplicable as they choose, rather than be at the mercy of the Commissioner on an 'end-result' theory." Id. at 676. The "interdependence test" was neither argued nor discussed.

Second, the government argued that there were in fact no valid sales made by the taxpayer, "that the sales of stock by [Granite Trust] should be ignored on the ground that they were not bona fide, and that the taxpayer therefore retained 'beneficial ownership.'" Id. at 677. . . .

The court ultimately concluded that because the facts "showed legal transactions not fictitious or so lacking in substance as to be anything different from what they purported to be," the sales must be given effect in the administration of §112(b)(6). Id. at 678. Therefore, the taxpayer was able to recognize the loss and claim a substantial tax refund.

In the present case, taxpayer asserts that *Granite Trust* and the legislative history discussed therein stand as a complete bar to any application of step transaction analysis in the context of §332. We disagree. As an initial matter, the First Circuit considered only the "end result" formulation of the step transaction doctrine. 238 F.2d at 675. As noted, the "interdependence test" was neither argued nor considered in *Granite Trust*.[7] The legislative history discussed in *Granite Trust* is equally silent as to the "interdependence test." Id. at 675-77. Taxpayer fails to appreciate the differences between, and the different functions performed by, the "inter-

7. Taxpayer argues that because the *Granite Trust* transactions "clearly" would have met the interdependence test had it been applied, the court's failure to use that test constitutes proof that it believed all forms of the step transaction doctrine to be inapplicable to §112(b)(6). We decline to indulge in such speculative reasoning.

dependence" and "end result" tests. As the "interdependence" test addresses the relationship between, and therefore the integrity of, intermediate steps in a complex transaction, its application is not precluded by *Granite Trust*'s conclusion that a narrow focus on a transaction's "end result" is inappropriate in the context of §112(b)(6).

Furthermore, although the First Circuit concluded from the legislative history that "taxpayers can, by taking appropriate steps, render the subsection applicable or inapplicable as they choose," id. at 676, we think taxpayer misinterprets that conclusion. The nonrecognition mandated by §332 is not optional at the election of taxpayers within the reach of that section. . . . Steps taken by the taxpayer . . . are not immunized from "the question . . . whether the transaction under scrutiny is in fact what it appears to be in form." Chisholm v. Commissioner, 79 F.2d 14, 15 (2d Cir. 1935). . . .

Appellant also relies on Commissioner v. Day & Zimmermann, Inc., 151 F.2d 517 (3rd Cir. 1945), another case where a taxpayer was able to recognize a loss despite §112(b)(6). Yet the Third Circuit did not address the step transaction doctrine in *Day & Zimmermann*. The court took pains to verify the bona fides of the questioned transaction, and emphasized "there was no understanding of any kind between [the stock purchaser] and Day & Zimmermann by which the latter retained any sort of interest in the securities or proceeds therefrom. . . ." 151 F.2d at 519. After a detailed analysis of the motivations of the actors, the court concluded, "the facts before us so manifestly point to the legitimacy of the . . . purchase of stock that they offer no alternative but to accept that view of the transaction." Id.

Granite Trust discussed the significance of *Day & Zimmermann* in terms which indicate the preferred mode of analysis:

> The significant thing in the case is its ultimate rationale that the purported sales of stock to the treasurer were in fact sales, notwithstanding the tax motive which prompted the corporation to enter into the transaction; from which it would seem to be irrelevant how the transfer was arranged, or whether or not it occurred at a public auction or exchange, so long as the beneficial as well as legal title was intended to pass and did pass.

238 F.2d at 676 (emphasis added). Thus *Day & Zimmermann* reaffirms the necessity of determining whether the substance of a transaction matches its form. . . .

B. Business Purpose

. . . The law is unclear as to the relationship between the step transaction doctrine and the business purpose requirement. Our survey of the relevant cases suggests that no firm line delineates the boundary between the two. Most cases applying the step transaction doctrine, far from identi-fying business purpose as an element whose absence is prerequisite to that application, do not even include discussion of business purpose as a related issue. In some cases, the existence of a business purpose is considered one factor in determining whether form and substance coincide. In others, the lack of business purpose is accepted as reason to apply the step transaction doctrine. We have found no case holding that the existence of a business purpose precludes the application of the step transaction doctrine.

We therefore reject the contention that a valid business purpose bars application of step transaction analysis in this context. "A legitimate busi-ness goal does not grant [a] taxpayer carte blanche to subvert Congressio-nally mandated tax patterns." *Kuper*, 533 F.2d at 158. Moreover, we share the government's skepticism as to the alleged significance of taxpayer's claimed business purpose — that of cashing-out certain minority share-holders who collectively owned no more than 0.03 percent of Super Market Developer's stock. Having thus rejected taxpayer's arguments against the applicability of step transaction analysis, we now apply it to the disputed transaction.

C. Step Transaction Analysis Applied

. . . We are mindful of "the central purpose of the step transaction doctrine: ensuring that the tax consequences of a particular transaction turn on substance rather than form." *Security Indus.*, 702 F.2d at 1245. Under the "interdependence test" we focus primarily on the relationship between the steps, *McDonald's Restaurants*, 688 F.2d at 524, and in so doing inquire whether " 'the steps were so interdependent that the legal relations created by one transaction would have been fruitless without a completion of the series.' " *Security Indus.*, 702 F.2d at 1244 (quoting Paul & Zimet, "Step Transactions," in Selected Studies in Federal Taxation 200, 254 (2d Cir. 1938)). We find sufficient evidence of interdependence in the merger and reorganization agreements to answer that question conclusively.

The "Termination" clause included in the merger agreement is itself a strong indication of interdependence. That clause states:

> *Termination.* If the Agreement and Plan of Reorganization dated as of Decem-ber 11, 1980, which has been entered into between the Surviving Corporation [Elder Food Mart, Inc.] and Weston Investments, Inc., . . . a Missouri corpora-tion, is terminated prior to the Merger Date, then this Agreement of Merger shall simultaneously terminate without further action by the parties hereto.

Under the express terms of the merger agreement, the legal relations it created were entirely contingent on the continuing force of the reorgani-zation agreement. Thus, the merger agreement would bear no fruit unless the two-step series could be completed.

The "Purchase and Sale" clause contained in plan of reorganization is another manifestation of the relationship between the two steps. It provides:

> The Buyer [Super Market Developers] agrees to purchase from the Seller [Elder, Inc.] and the Seller agrees to sell to the Buyer all of the assets of every kind and description acquired by the Seller pursuant to the Agreement of Merger, except for the shares of common stock of Weston. As part of the consideration to the Seller for the purchase described in this paragraph, the Buyer agrees to assume and discharge all of the obligations and liabilities of the Seller which were formerly the obligations and liabilities of the Merging Corporation [Weston] and which became the obligations and liabilities of the Seller pursuant to the Agreement of Merger.

So interdependent were the two steps that the parties who drafted the agreement setting forth the second step did not think it necessary to separately list the assets (valued at over nine million dollars) which were bought and sold, or the obligations and liabilities which were assumed and discharged therein — they simply referenced the first agreement "attached hereto."

We also consider the timing of the steps in assessing their interdependence. Again, that matter was squarely addressed by the parties to the transactions. Under the terms of the reorganization agreement:

> The merger shall become effective at, and the Merger Date shall mean, *for the purpose of this Agreement and the Agreement of Merger,* the close of business on the date when the Agreement of Merger is filed with the Secretary of State of the State of Missouri in accordance with Missouri law. The closing of the transactions provided for herein shall take place on the date (the "Closing Date") which is the same day as the Merger Date *immediately following* the time of effectiveness of the merger.

(Emphasis supplied.) This provision is remarkable for at least two reasons. First, it allows virtually no time to pass between the effectiveness of the two steps which taxpayer vociferously argues are separate transactions. Second, the plan of reorganization actually sets forth the time at which the merger (supposedly a separate transaction controlled by a second agreement) will become effective. . . .

D. Substance Over Form

In giving effect to the substance of the overall transaction, we ignore acts taken in intermediate steps which the taxpayer has itself undone with subsequent steps. We also treat as significant the existence of an understanding between the parties that an interest in the assets transferred would be retained by the taxpayer. See *Granite Trust,* 238 F.2d at 677; *Day,* 151

F.2d at 519. The transaction of December 23, 1980 involved two steps — the "merger" of Weston into Elder, Inc. and the "reorganization" of Super Market Developers and Elder, Inc. Under the first step, Elder, Inc. paid taxpayer $300,000 cash and a promissory note for all of Weston's assets. The shares of minority shareholders were also converted to cash. Under the second step, taxpayer "immediately" bought back the same assets except for Weston Market, paying "an amount equal to the principal amount of the promissory note . . . plus an amount equal to the cash received by the [minority] shareholders." Excepting the exchange of Weston Market for $300,000, all acts were undone: taxpayer got back the other assets; Elder, Inc. got the value of the note back; and taxpayer fully reimbursed Elder, Inc. for cashing out the minority shareholders.

The transparent form of the transaction fails to obscure its obvious substance: Elder, Inc. bought Weston Market for $300,000 cash, and Weston was liquidated. In light of this transactional substance, we reject taxpayer's claim to have disposed of Weston's stock before Weston's assets were distributed. Accordingly, taxpayer did continue qualified with respect to Weston stock ownership in the meaning of §332.

III. ASSET DISTRIBUTION AND LIQUIDATION PLAN

Taxpayer also argues the requirements of §332 were not met because all of Weston's assets were not transferred to Super Market Developers, and because the shareholders of Weston adopted a plan of merger, rather than a plan of liquidation. This argument is, of course, premised on the transactional form which we have rejected in favor of substance. . . .

Taxpayer argues, however, that because some but not all of Weston's assets were distributed to Super Market Developers, there was no transfer of all the property under the statute. Taxpayer further argues "Elder, Inc. kept the Weston Market subsidiary stock and, unlike a liquidation of Weston, [Super Market Developers] and the other individual shareholders of Weston did not receive stock of all of the subsidiaries owned by Weston." Taxpayer cites no authority in support of its argument.

Given our holding that the step whereby Weston stock was briefly transferred to Elder, Inc. must be disregarded, this argument is rejected. First, there was a resolution authorizing the distribution of Weston's assets in complete cancellation or redemption of all its stock — the shareholders of Weston approved the Plan of Merger by majority vote on December 20, 1980. Under the transactions of December 23, 1980, Weston stock was cancelled or redeemed and its shareholders — both Super Market Developers and the minority shareholders — received payment in distribution of Weston's assets. Second, Elder, Inc. did not "keep" the stock of Weston Market, as taxpayer suggests, because when the form of the transaction is ignored, the substance of the transaction is that Elder, Inc. did not buy Weston stock — it bought Weston Market. . . .

Finally, taxpayer's objection to the alleged "harshness" of the nonrecognition of its tax loss is insufficient to sustain its claim. We must apply the tax effects of the tax code to transactional substance, not form.

CONCLUSION

As the substance of the disputed transaction met the requirements of I.R.C. §332, no gain or loss shall be recognized. The district court's Order of September 19, 1989 granting summary judgment in favor of the government and denying taxpayer's motion for summary judgment is hereby affirmed.

NOTES

1. *80 percent stock ownership.* Section 332(b)(1) requires (through §1504(a)(2)) that the parent own stock (a) that possesses at least 80 percent of the total voting power of the stock of the subsidiary and (b) that has a value equal to at least 80 percent of the total value of the stock of the subsidiary, except nonvoting stock limited and preferred as to dividends. See §1504(a)(4). The stock must be held continuously from the date of adoption of a plan of liquidation until the final liquidation. Section 332 references §1504(a)(2), a definitional section pertaining to consolidated returns. See page 525 infra. The cross-reference is an attempt to ensure that the liquidation of a subsidiary not filing a consolidated return with its parent is treated the same as the liquidation of a subsidiary that does file a consolidated return.

If a parent lacks the necessary 80 percent control, can it come within the ambit of §332 by acquiring stock immediately before the liquidation? Compare Rev. Rul. 75-521, 1975-2 C.B. 120 (purchase from other individual shareholders just prior to plan of liquidation upheld), with Rev. Rul. 70-106, 1970-1 C.B. 70 (redemption of minority shareholder in order to boost parent over 80 percent mark failed where redemption was part of the liquidation plan). See also George L. Riggs, Inc. v. Commissioner, 64 T.C. 474 (1975) (acquisition of stock to qualify under §332 permitted). Suppose *S*, an individual, owns all the stock of *X* Corp. and *Y* Corp., each of which in turn owns 50 percent of *Z* Corp. If *Z* Corp. is liquidated, can *X* and *Y* rely on §332? Consider the applicability of §318.

If a parent can acquire stock to avail itself of §332, can it dispose of stock to avoid §332? Suppose a parent corporation has a basis of $10,000 in the stock of its wholly owned subsidiary, which owns a single asset with a basis of $12,000 and a fair market value of $8,000. Can the parent sell 21 percent of the subsidiary's stock to an unrelated purchaser in order to recognize the loss on the subsequent liquidation? In Commissioner v. Day & Zimmermann, Inc., 151 F.2d 517 (3d Cir. 1945), a parent sold enough stock in its subsidiary to reduce its ownership below the 80 percent standard. The shares were sold at a public auction to the parent's treasurer, who paid a fair market value price with his own funds. Even though the parent's sole purpose was to avoid §332, the court upheld the transaction. See also Granite Trust Co. v. United States, 238 F.2d 670 (1st Cir. 1956) (contribution of two shares' worth $130 to charity allowed parent successfully to avoid §332 even though charity surrendered the shares in liquidation four days after receipt); Priv. Ltr. Rul. 9049001 (taxpayer, free to structure liquidation under either §331 or §332, chose §331 to step up the basis of the assets received).

Associated Wholesale Grocers sharply reminds taxpayers, however, that the ability to manipulate §332 is not without limitation. Did the court convince you that the earlier decisions in *Granite Trust* and *Day & Zimmermann* were distinguishable, or should the court simply have refused to follow those decisions? Is it significant that in those earlier cases there really was a disposition by the taxpayer, while in *Associated Wholesale Grocers* there was only a transitory disposition followed by an immediate repurchase?

Could the taxpayer have structured the transaction differently so that it would have been successful? Why didn't Super Market Developers first buy out the minority shareholders in Weston and then sell enough stock in Weston to Elder, Inc., to allow Elder, Inc., to receive the Weston Market stock on a liquidation of Weston while all the other assets were distributed to Super Market Developers? Would the sale of Weston stock to Elder, Inc., have been enough to bring Super Market Developers below the 80 percent ownership threshold for purposes of §332? The court determined that the Weston Market stock had a value of $300,000 and that Super Market Developers sold the Weston assets for $9,349,703 and purchased back all the assets of Weston (except Weston Market) for $9,049,703.

For a checklist of information to be submitted to the IRS in connection with a request for a ruling on the liquidation of a controlled subsidiary, see Rev. Rul. 90-52, 1990-2 C.B. 626.

2. *Timing of distribution*. For §332 to apply, the liquidation must take place within one of two prescribed time periods. Under §332(b)(2), a shareholder's resolution authorizing a distribution but not specifying a time period will qualify if the distribution is completed "within the taxable year." Under §332(b)(3), if the plan of liquidation provides for the transfer of all the subsidiary's property within three years of the close of the year during which the first distribution is made, §332 will apply (if the distributions are, in fact, made). Could the taxpayer in *Associated Wholesale Grocers* have avoided the application of §332 by spreading out the liquidating distributions?

In Cherry-Burrell Corp. v. United States, 367 F.2d 669 (8th Cir. 1966), the court liberally permitted the liquidation to qualify under §332, even though the liquidation was not completed within the time period, since the delay was involuntary. What is the effect of a taxpayer's deliberate effort to avoid the timing requirements? In Service Co. v. Commissioner, 165 F.2d 75 (8th Cir. 1948), the court held that a parent could not intentionally avoid §332 through noncompliance with the recordkeeping requirements of Treas. Regs. §1.332-6. But suppose the parent spreads the subsidiary's distributions out over more than four years. Might the Service try to argue that there was constructive receipt by the parent?

In Priv. Ltr. Rul. 9215016, the IRS ruled that the distribution of property by a subsidiary to its parent corporation under a plan of liquidation qualified under §332 even though the subsidiary retained its corporate charter, state insurance licenses, and sufficient assets to meet the minimum capital requirements of the state. The parent corporation's intention was to sell the charter and the insurance licenses to an unrelated party. The IRS ruled that the parent must complete the sale or dissolution of the subsidiary within twelve months of the final liquidating distribution.

3. *Basis, holding period, and carryovers.* As noted above, the parent's basis in the assets received on liquidation is the subsidiary's basis. §334(b). If a distributing subsidiary recognizes gain on a distribution to a parent corporation in a §332 liquidation (e.g., a distribution to a foreign parent corporation, see §367(e)(2)), a corresponding increase in the distributee's basis occurs under §334(b).

Because a parent corporation normally takes the subsidiary's stock basis in a §332 liquidation, the Code provides that the parent inherits the holding periods for the assets of the subsidiary. See §1223(2). In addition, the parent normally acquires the subsidiary's tax attributes under §381(a), including loss carryovers and earnings and profits account. But see §269(b), discussed at page 518 infra, which can deny the parent a loss carryover under some tax avoidance circumstances.

4. *Minority shareholders.* Since §332 applies only to parent corporations, minority shareholders must look to other provisions — typically, §§331(a) and 1001 — to determine their gain or loss on liquidation.

5. *Treatment of liquidating subsidiary.* Section 332(a) provides tax consequences only to the shareholder-parent on liquidation of a subsidiary. What are the tax consequences to the liquidating subsidiary? Current §337 (not to be confused with former §337) provides that no gain or loss shall be recognized to the liquidating corporation on the distribution to an 80 percent distributee in a §332 liquidation.

In situations in which the parent corporation is not taxable on its income, the nonrecognition rule will not apply. This follows from the fact that in these situations nonrecognition would be tantamount to permanent exclusion. For example, if the parent corporation is tax exempt, the liquidating subsidiary must recognize gain or loss in accordance with §336. §337(b)(2)(A).

There is an exception to this exception when the property distributed will be used in an unrelated trade or business of the tax-exempt organization because the parent would be taxed on gains in connection with such unrelated activities. §§337(b)(2)(B), 511, and 512. If the property ceases to be used in an unrelated trade or business, the tax-exempt organization will be taxed at that time on the lesser of the built-in gain at the time of liquidation or the difference between fair market value and adjusted basis at the time of cessation. Similarly, if the parent-corporation is a foreign corporation beyond the reach of U.S. federal taxation, a liquidating corporation may be taxed in accordance with §336. §367(e)(2).

Suppose the stock of Y Corp. is 80 percent owned by X Corp. and 20 percent by B, an individual. If Y Corp. liquidates, it recognizes no gain or loss on the property distributed to X Corp. But §337 does not apply to a liquidating distribution made to individual shareholders. Strangely enough, §336(a) does not apply in its entirety to the liquidating corporation with respect to the property distributed to minority shareholders. Instead, §336(d)(3) denies any loss to the liquidating corporation on such distributions. Presumably, Congress was concerned that a liquidating corporation would distribute gain property to a corporate parent, thereby avoiding gain under §337 while recognizing a loss on the distribution of loss property to the minority shareholders. But note that §336(d)(3) applies even if the liquidating distribution is pro rata to both the corporate parent and the minority shareholders. Apparently, Congress opted to treat a liquidating distribution to minority shareholders as if it were a nonliquidating distribution under principles similar to those in §311. This is not an unreasonable position since the premise of a §332 nontaxable liquidation is the simplification of a corporate structure in which the former activities of the subsidiary are carried on by the parent corporation and the minority shareholders, in effect, have their stock redeemed.

Section 337(b) contains another provision affecting the treatment of the liquidating subsidiary. Ordinarily, if a taxpayer transfers appreciated property in satisfaction of a debt, gain must be recognized. See, e.g., United States v. Davis, 370 U.S. 65 (1962). But if the transfer occurs in the context of a §332 liquidation, it might be very difficult to distinguish a taxable transfer from a subsidiary to a parent-creditor to satisfy the outstanding indebtedness from a nontaxable transfer in exchange for stock. Accordingly, §337(b) provides for nonrecognition of gain or loss on a distribution of property to a parent-creditor to satisfy an indebtedness. Section 334(b)(2) provides that the parent takes the subsidiary's basis in the assets. Compare §1041 in an unrelated context involving transfers between spouses.

6. *Overlap with reorganization provisions.* For a discussion of the relationship of subsidiary liquidations to reorganizations, see page 397 infra.

PROBLEMS

7-2.   Individuals A and B own all the stock of X Corp., which runs a factory that produces thermostatic devices. X Corp. also owns all the stock of Y Corp., which runs two businesses as separate unincorporated divisions. Division 1 produces and sells electricity from solar heating; division 2 produces air conditioners. The primary asset of division 1 is undeveloped land on which the solar panels are situated. The primary asset of division 2 is a factory that produces air conditioners. P Corp., owned by individuals C and D, wants to acquire the assets of division 2. A and B would like to liquidate Y Corp. and operate both the thermostatic device business and solar panel business as unincorporated divisions of X Corp.

X Corp.'s basis in the Y Corp. stock is $650,000. The division 1 assets of Y Corp. have a combined basis of $700,000 and a fair market value of $400,000. The assets of division 2 have a combined basis of $60,000 and a fair market value of approximately $100,000. Consider the tax consequences of the following alternative methods of satisfying the goals of the parties.

- a. X Corp. liquidates Y Corp. and then sells the division 2 assets to P Corp.
- b. Y Corp. distributes the division 1 assets to X Corp. and sells the division 2 assets to P Corp. Y Corp. then liquidates.
- c. Y Corp. sells all its assets to P Corp. for approximately $500,000. P Corp. pays cash for the division 2 assets and issues a note for $400,000 for the division 1 assets. The note bears interest at the market rate and is due in 10 years. X Corp. then liquidates Y Corp. Sometime after P Corp.'s acquisition and the liquidation, X Corp. purchases the division 1 assets from P Corp. for $400,000, payable by a note.
- d. Y Corp. sells the division 1 assets to X Corp. for $400,000 and sells the division 2 assets to P Corp. Y Corp. then liquidates.
- e. X Corp. sells to P Corp. stock in Y Corp. equal to the fair market value of the division 2 assets held by Y Corp. X Corp. and P Corp. then liquidate Y Corp., with the division 1 assets distributed to X Corp. and the division 2 assets distributed to P Corp.
- f. Y Corp. adopts a plan of liquidation, sells the division 2 assets to P Corp. for cash, and then distributes the division 1 assets and the cash, completing the liquidation in 18 months.

8

Integration of the Corporate and Individual Income Taxes

A. THE INCIDENCE AND EFFECTS OF THE CORPORATE TAX

While corporations are the nominal payors of the corporate income tax, in substance that tax is paid by individuals. We know this must be true because corporations are fictional entities, and when we speak of a "corporation" we really are using that term as a convenient shorthand for a collection of contracts and legal relationships among shareholders, debtholders, employees, suppliers, and customers. Accordingly, when a tax is levied on a corporation, the burden of that levy is shared by these groups of individuals, with some bearing a greater and others a lesser share of that burden.

No theory tells us precisely how the corporate tax is shared among the various possible groups of individuals. On one hand, it might be the case that the wages paid to employees and the costs paid to suppliers would be the same even if there were no corporate tax. If so, then the corporate tax is borne only by the stockholders and bondholders as well as by the corporation's consumers. On the other hand, the incidence of the corporate tax might lie on the employees alone or, possibly, on the shareholders and customers. Ultimately this is an empirical question, and unfortunately it is a very complex one. Accordingly, economists can estimate the incidence of the corporate tax only if they make significantly simplifying assumptions.[1] The true incidence of the corporate tax remains to this day a mystery.

---

1. See, e.g., Klein, The Incidence of the Corporation Income Tax: A Lawyer's View of a Problem in Economics, 1965 Wis. L. Rev. 576.

If we do not know who bears the burden of the corporate tax, why do we have one? After all, the revenue collected by the corporate tax could be replaced with some alternate levy such as an increased estate and gift tax or individual income tax, the incidence of which may be easier to determine. Presumably the burden of taxation in this country should be fair, and while different people may have different notions of fairness in this context, so long as we do not know who bears the corporate tax we cannot with confidence assert that its burden is imposed in accordance with *anyone's* concept of fairness.

A cynic might suggest that we have a corporate tax precisely because its incidence is unknown. Raising taxes is difficult for politicians: While most of us may not mind taxes imposed on other people, few of us willingly accept higher taxes imposed on ourselves. Indeed, because most tax increases are imposed on a well-defined group of individuals while the benefits of those tax revenues are spread among the entire electorate, it is easier for opponents of a tax to band together and lobby against an increase than it is for proponents to lobby in favor.

The incidence of the corporate tax is uncertain, so the possible return to voters who choose to fight it may be slight. Accordingly, the financial incentive to lobby against the corporate tax is diminished. Indeed, so long as voters perceive the corporate tax as imposed only on people other than themselves, it offers politicians the opportunity to raise funds seemingly without taking those funds from anyone.

Even without knowing the precise incidence of the corporate tax, we can make some observations. So long as the corporate tax is paid, it is borne by someone; so long as it is borne by someone, the tax system discourages investment in the corporate form. In addition, because of the way in which the corporate tax is implemented, it may encourage some forms of corporate behavior over others. The following excerpt from a recent Treasury Department report identifies possible distortions in economic behavior caused by imposition of the corporate tax. Latent within this discussion is the assumption that the corporate tax is borne exclusively by corporate shareholders. This assumption undoubtedly is false to some extent, but it also likely true to a great extent. As you read the excerpt you might seek to identify the extent to which its conclusions depend on knowledge of the incidence of the corporate tax.

Integration of the Individual and Corporate Tax Systems: Taxing Business Income Once 3-11 _____
Treasury Department Report 1992

The classical corporate income tax system distorts three economic and financial decisions: (1) whether to invest in noncorporate rather than corporate form, (2) whether to finance investments with debt rather than equity, and (3) whether to retain rather than distribute earnings. Apart from corporate and investor level tax considerations, nontax benefits and costs also influence those decisions. To the extent that the classical tax system distorts the choice of organizational form, financial structure, and dividend policy, economic resources can be misallocated.

. . . In deciding whether to undertake an investment, firms require that the investment provide a sufficient after-tax return to compensate investors. The cost of capital is the pre-tax rate of return that is sufficient to cover operating expenses, taxes, economic depreciation, and the investor's required after-tax rate of return. Thus, the cost of capital depends in part on the return firms must pay to suppliers of debt or equity capital to attract funds. The cost of capital also depends in part on such factors as tax rates, the investment's economic depreciation rate, the capital cost recovery deductions allowed on the investment, the inflation rate, and the source of financing for the investment. Because a higher cost of capital makes certain investments unprofitable, corporate and individual income taxes reduce investment incentives by raising the cost of capital. . . .

ORGANIZATIONAL FORM

A simple example illustrates the effect of the current corporate tax system on investment decisions. Suppose that an investor requires an after-tax rate of return of 8 percent and the investor's effective tax rate is 20 percent. An equity investment in a noncorporate enterprise must earn a return high enough to pay tax at the investor's rate (20 percent) and still yield the required 8 percent after-tax return.[11] The noncorporate investment must therefore earn a 10 percent pre-tax rate of return (net of depreciation) in order to cover the investor's income taxes and meet the required return $(0.10 \times (1 - 0.20) = 0.08)$. However, if the corporate tax rate is 34 percent and the corporation distributes all of its income, the cost of capital of an equity financed investment in the corporate sector in the above example is 15.2 percent. This 15.2 percent pre-tax return yields an 8 percent return after paying both the corporate tax and the investor level tax on dividends $(0.152 \times (1 - 0.34) \times (1 - 0.20) = 0.08)$. Since fewer investments can earn the higher required return (15.2 percent as opposed to 10 percent), the corporate tax discourages investment in the corporate sector by raising the cost of capital.

More complex calculations support this result. For example, a Congressional Research Service report estimates, under realistic assumptions,

---

11. This simple example abstracts from other factors affecting the cost of capital, including: (i) differences between tax and economic depreciation; (ii) differences in tax rates among investors; and (iii) inflation.

the total effective Federal income tax rate on corporate equity (taking into account both corporate level and shareholder level taxes) to be 48 percent, compared to 28 percent for noncorporate equity. Therefore, some corporations fail to undertake investments that would be profitable if the tax burden on corporate and noncorporate investments were the same. . . .

International comparisons add perspective on the effect of the corporate tax on the U.S. corporate sector. One measure is the ratio of corporate investment to investment in housing, which provides a comparison of resource allocation in different economies. . . . Throughout the period [1976-1989], the United States has had a lower ratio [of corporate gross fixed investment relative to private residential housing investment] than the United Kingdom. Although the U.S. ratio exceeded that for Japan and Australia until the early 1980s, corporate investment relative to housing has tended upwards over the whole period for Japan and Australia while the ratio for the United States has remained fairly stable, except for the 2 years following the Economic Recovery Tax Act of 1981 [when the ratio dropped significantly]. Indeed, for the last 4 years for which data are available, the United States has had essentially the lowest corporate investment per dollar of housing investment of any of the four nations. . . .

Another useful international comparison is the spread between the pre-tax return on corporate investment and the cost of funds in the United States and other countries. This spread, or corporate "tax wedge," generally depends upon the type of asset acquired, the corporate tax rate, the capital recovery allowances, the rate of inflation, and various other country specific factors. Table 1.1 presents a listing of preliminary [Organisation for Economic Co-operation and Development] calculations of the 1991 corporate tax wedge based on a standard mix of assets and sources of funding for a manufacturer located in several OECD member countries. According to these data, the corporate tax wedge in the United States is higher than in France or Germany, is approximately the same as in the U.K., and is lower than in Canada and Japan.

CORPORATE CAPITAL STRUCTURE

Corporations have three alternatives for financing new investments: (1) issuing new equity, (2) using retained earnings, or (3) issuing debt. There can be important nontax benefits and costs of alternative corporate financing arrangements, and the tax system should avoid prejudicing financial decisions.

The current classical corporate tax system discriminates against equity financing of new corporate investment. . . . Because of the two levels of taxation of corporate profits, the cost of equity capital generally exceeds the cost of debt capital. The Congressional Research Service estimates, under realistic assumptions, the total effective Federal income tax rate on corporate debt to be 20 percent, compared with 48 percent for corporate equity. Moreover, the total effective tax rate for debt financed corporate than for equity financed corporate investment encourages the use of debt by corporations, assuming nontax factors that affect financing decisions do not change.

If a corporation borrows from an individual to finance an investment, the corporation deducts the interest payments from its taxable income and is therefore not taxed on the investment's pre-tax return to the extent of the interest payments, although the lender is taxable on the interest at the individual tax rate. Consequently, to the extent that corporations finance investment with debt, current law does not distort the choice between investment in the corporate and noncorporate sectors. Using the assumptions in the numerical example set forth under "Organizational Form," above, for a 100 percent debt financed corporate investment, the cost of capital is 10 percent ($0.10 \times (1 - 0.2) = 0.08$, the required rate of return). This cost is well below the 15.2 percent cost of capital for equity financed investments for corporations that distribute income as dividends, and is the same as the cost of capital for a noncorporate investment.

Historical data show U.S. corporate debt to be at relatively high levels by postwar standards, with some, but not all, measures growing at an unusually rapid pace in the 1980s. Because there is no single, universally agreed-upon measure of debt, the discussion below considers trends based on alternative measures.

One group of debt measures focuses on corporate balance sheets: the ratio of debt to total assets. The debt to asset ratio can be computed using either book value (the par value of debt and the historical cost of assets as reported for financial accounting purposes) or market value. . . . This ratio grew from 43 percent in 1948 to 61 percent in 1989. Although the ratio generally increased over the postwar period, it declined sharply beginning in 1975 and continued through the mid 1980s. Following that decrease, the ratio began to rise again and by 1989 had reached a post-war high of 61 percent. In 1989, this book-value debt to asset ratio was more than 17 percentage points higher than in 1980, but only 10 percentage points higher than the pre-1980s peak of 51 percent reached in 1973.

. . . Like the book-value measure, the market-value ratio indicates that corporate debt has generally increased since 1961. . . .

A second measure of leverage focuses on the importance of debt in corporations' sources of additional funds rather than corporations' total outstanding debt. . . . Over the entire postwar period, equity finance was dominant. For nonfinancial corporations, retained earnings and new equity issues accounted for roughly 78 percent of funds raised. Debt provided the balance, divided about equally between private issues (bank loans and private placements) and public issues (bonds). Relative financing patterns changed during the 1980s. While corporations continue to rely heavily on retained earnings, they have sharply adjusted the composition of external finance. Most notably, corporations have undertaken substantial repurchases of equity, financed mainly with debt. . . . The increase in nonfinancial corporate debt during the 1980s was largely matched by a reduction in outstanding equity. [N]onfinancial corporations relied significantly more on internal funds (retained earnings) during the 1980s than was the case for the postwar period as a whole.

Recent evidence suggests that share repurchases have contributed to the increase in corporate debt. Rather than simply replacing dividends, repurchases have been financed primarily by debt, which results in higher interests costs. Increased share repurchases, therefore, accounts for part of the recent increases in net interest payments, and may be viewed as one method that firms have used to reduce their corporate tax liabilities. [B]y 1990, over one quarter of the interest payments of nonfinancial corporations was attributable to increased share repurchases. . . .

Debt finance may have nontax benefits. Analysts most sanguine about high levels of corporate debt and debt-service burdens typically maintain that the discipline of debt is desirable because it gives lenders indirect means to monitor the activities of managers. This need for supervision owes to the separation between ownership and management that is characteristic of the traditional corporate structure.

A disadvantage of higher debt levels is that they can increase nontax costs of debt, including costs associated with financial distress. Even when corporations avoid formal bankruptcy proceedings, they incur costs when they cannot meet their interest obligations or when debt covenants restrict operating flexibility. The costs include extra demands on executives' time, supply disruptions, declines in customers' confidence, and, frequently, significant legal fees. Corporations therefore must evaluate the tax and nontax benefits of additional debt relative to these costs. Tax-induced distortions in capital structure can entail significant efficiency costs.

CORPORATE DIVIDEND DISTRIBUTIONS

The current system of corporate taxation also may distort a corporation's choice between distributing or retaining earnings and, if amounts are distributed, whether they are paid in the form of a nondividend distribution, such as a share repurchase. Differences in effective tax rates on dividends and retained earnings are significant.

Assessing the efficiency costs of such tax differentials requires an analysis of motives for corporate dividend distributions in the presence of relatively high taxes on such dividends compared to capital gains. This Report assumes that corporate dividends offer special nontax benefits to shareholders that offset their tax disadvantage,[26] and, accordingly, that corporations set dividend payments so that the incremental nontax benefit of dividends paid equals their incremental tax cost. Under this assumption, the amount of dividends paid out is expected to decrease as the tax burden on dividends relative to capital gains increases; empirical studies are consistent with this prediction. Investor level taxes on dividends also raise the cost of capital (and thereby reduce investment) to the extent that corporations pay out earnings as dividends. Thus, under the assumption used in this Report, dividend taxes reduce the payout ratio and real investment incentives.

The growth in share repurchases in the last decade supports this view of the linkage between the corporate tax and corporate dividends. Share repurchases provide a means of distributing corporate earnings with, in many cases, more favorable shareholder level tax treatment than dividend distributions. While a shareholder pays tax on the full amount of a dividend at ordinary income rates, the shareholder generally pays tax on the proceeds of a share repurchase only to the extent they exceed share basis and, in some cases, at a preferential capital gains rate. Share repurchases increased substantially from 1970 to 1990, growing from 1.2 billion (or 5.4 of dividends) to 47.9 billion (or 34 percent of dividends), and peaking in 1989 at 65.8 billion (or 47 percent of dividends).

NOTES

1. *Market response to the corporate tax*. One might expect that the imposition of a corporate tax would drive the corporate form out of existence. That is, because the corporate tax can be avoided by operating a business in noncorporate form, all businesses would avoid the corporate tax by a simple change in organization. We see, though, that the corporation thrives. How can this be so?

Even though use of the corporate form increases the income taxes levied on a business enterprise, the corporate form may nonetheless be the most efficient choice. First, it is a *familiar* form of organization, and familiarity in this context may allow the organization to raise capital more

26. This assumption is controversial, since not all economic models of the effects of taxation on dividend payments maintain that nontax benefits are associated with dividend payments. There are two leading explanations why corporations continue to pay dividends in spite of the greater investor level tax burden on dividends than on capital gains attributable to retained earnings or share repurchases: the "traditional view" and the "new view." The "traditional view" asserts that dividends offer nontax benefits to shareholders that offset their tax [dis]advantage. Accordingly, dividend taxes distort payout decisions and raise the cost of capital. The "new view" assumes that dividend payments offer no nontax advantages to shareholders and that corporations have no alternative to dividends for distributing funds to shareholders. Under this assumption, dividend taxes reduce the value of the firm, but do not affect firms' dividend or investment decisions. This Report adopts the framework suggested by the "traditional view." . . .

cheaply than otherwise. For example, one alternative to the corporation is a Massachusetts Business Trust. Because this form of business organization is uncommon outside of the northeast United States, such a trust may need to educate potential investors before they would be willing to provide funds to the enterprise. This education (in the form of advertising, additional solicitation materials, or whatever) represents an additional cost of capital, a cost of capital that use of the more familiar corporate form would have avoided.

Use of the corporate form can offer other benefits. Many state laws offer benefits to corporations unavailable to other business organizations. See, e.g., Commissioner v. Bollinger, page 565 infra, in which state law provides corporations more complete access to capital markets than it does to other potential borrowers. Perhaps most important, corporations offer limited liability for their investors, centralized management, continuity of life for the enterprise without regard to the circumstances (such as death or bankruptcy) of investors, and easy transferability of investment interests (i.e., shares).

2. *Relief from the corporate tax*. Not all corporations are subject to the corporate tax. Certain corporations, called "S corporations," pay no tax but instead pass their items of income and deduction through to their shareholders for inclusion on the shareholders' individuals returns. For these corporations there is no corporate tax (except to the extent they have income attributable to a prior taxable year when they were not S corporations, see §§1374-1375). Not all corporations are eligible for S status. S corporations may not have more than 75 shareholders nor may they have a corporate shareholder or a foreign shareholder. §1361(b)(1). In addition, S corporations may not have more than one class of stock outstanding. §1361(b)(1)(D). These and other restrictions limit the feasibility of S corporations in many circumstances. S corporations are discussed further in Chapter 16.

Another form of business organization is the limited liability company. Limited liability companies are much like corporations in that they offer limited liability to their owners just as corporations offer limited liability to their shareholders. In addition, limited liability companies can have centralized management, as do corporations. In essence, a limited liability company is a corporation chartered under a state law that dispenses with the purely formal step of "incorporation." Thus, the state act authorizing the existence of a limited liability company avoids the terms "incorporation," using instead something like "organization" or "formation." While a limited liability company must file papers equivalent to articles of incorporation, because they are called "articles of organization" or something similar, the company is not in a technical sense a corporation. See page 564 infra.

Under current law, an unincorporated entity can choose to be taxed as either a corporation or a pass-through entity. See Treas. Regs. §301.7701-

3(a). If a limited liability company does not choose to be taxed as a corporation (i.e., as a nontransparent entity subject to an entity-level tax), it will be taxed as a partnership (i.e., treated as a transparent entity). A partnership is not subject to tax at the entity level but instead passes its items of income and deduction through to its owners for inclusion on their individual returns. See Chapter 19 infra. The ability of taxpayers to form limited liability companies under state law which are transparent for federal income tax purposes is a self-help method of integration.

There are additional self-help methods for taxpayers that are operating in corporate form. Even in the absence of formal relief from the corporate tax, the burden of the tax is lessened to the extent a corporation can make deductible interest payments.

B.   METHODS OF INTEGRATION

Is there a simple way to eliminate the double tax burden imposed on profits earned in corporate form? One might think that simple elimination of the corporate tax would be the ideal solution, but in fact the problem is considerably more difficult. Indeed, if the corporate tax were repealed, corporate investments would offer a significant tax advantage over noncorporate investments.

In general, the exchange of one investment for another is a taxable transaction. To be sure, exceptions are made for certain like-kind property, see §1031, and for involuntary conversions, see §1034, but for the most part a taxpayer cannot roll one investment into another without the recognition of gain or loss. If, though, the corporate tax were repealed, investments made through corporations could be exchanged for other investments without the imposition of tax so long as the rollover was done by the corporation and not by the shareholder.

For example, suppose individual B creates X Corp. by contributing $10,000. X Corp. then purchases rental property, and assuming the corporate tax has been repealed, that rental income goes untaxed until distributed by X Corp. Thus, X Corp. might invest its rents in some new investment (say, a bond fund) and no tax will yet be due. Had B purchased the real estate directly, the rents would have been taxable upon receipt as would the bond interest.

To continue this example, X Corp. might eventually sell its rental property at a gain, and if the corporate tax is repealed, no tax on that gain will be due. X Corp. could, for example, take the sale proceeds and invest in some unrelated enterprise, all without the imposition of any tax. Of course, taxes will be imposed on B when X Corp. eventually makes distributions, but until that time B enjoys a deferral opportunity as compared with noncorporate investments. Of course, if B should die while holding the X

Corp. stock, the liquidation of X Corp. into B's estate may escape taxation. See §§1014, 336, and 331.

If we are to make the income tax neutral with respect to the form that an investment takes, simply repealing the corporate income tax will not work. Instead, we need to find some way to integrate the corporate and individual income taxes so that income is taxed once, and only once, and at the proper time, whether earned within or without the corporate structure.

Complete integration of the individual and corporate income taxes is achieved when the taxable events of the corporation are reported directly by the corporation's shareholders are they arise. Taxation of S corporations, discussed more completely in Chapter 16, as well as of partnerships, governed by subchapter K, is an example of such direct reporting. See Ch. 19-26 infra. Implementing a system of complete integration, however, is administratively difficult if the number of investors is large and their relationship to the investment complex, as is the case when a corporation has multiple classes of stock outstanding.[2] Two leading scholars have described the debate concerning integration of the corporate and individual income taxes as a clash between idealists and pragmatists.[3]

In considering ways in which the corporate and individual income taxes can be integrated, it is important to keep in mind that appreciation in corporate assets can be realized either by a corporate sale of the assets or by a shareholder sale of stock. To ensure that corporate investments do not offer deferral opportunities, presumably we should tax such appreciation at the earlier of its realization at the corporate and shareholder levels. To avoid the imposition of a corporate double tax, however, we must not tax that realization a second time when recognized at the other level. In the partnership context, these two concerns are addressed by the optional basis adjustment in §743(b). In any proposal to fully integrate the corporate and individual income taxes, some similar mechanism must be included.

The following excerpt offers two possible means of partial integration, that is, of integrating the corporate and individual income taxes with respect to distributed funds only. Under both proposals, undistributed corporate earnings would be subject to a corporate-level tax much as they are today. For a discussion of the relative merits of full versus partial integration, see C. McLure, Must Corporate Income Be Taxed Twice 2-12 (1979).

2. See, e.g., Sunley, Corporate Integration: An Economic Perspective, 47 Tax L. Rev. 621, 625 (1992).

3. Break and Pechman, Relationship Between the Corporation and Individual Income Taxes, 28 Natl. Tax J. 341, 341 (1975); see also Yin, Corporate Tax Integration and the Search for the Pragmatic Ideal, 47 Tax L. Rev. 431 (1992).

Reporter's Study of Corporate Tax Integration 50-57 _____
American Law Institute (Federal Income Tax Project 1993)

There are three basic methods of accomplishing the results of integration with respect to distributed corporate earnings: shareholder credit, dividend deduction, and split rates.

A.   SHAREHOLDER CREDIT INTEGRATION

Under the most common form of integration abroad, shareholders would treat dividend payments just as wage earners now treat wage payments subject to withholding. Cash dividends received would be increased (or "grossed up") by the amount of federal income tax paid by the corporations on the earnings distributed as dividends, just as cash wages are increased by amounts withheld. An eligible shareholder would compute the tax at his regular rate on the gross dividend, and a tax credit would be available for the amount of the gross-up, just as a credit is now available for withholding on wages. Complete implementation of this system would result in the corporate tax becoming simply a withholding tax on individual income earned through corporate entities.

Consider a corporation that receives $100 in taxable income and pays $30 in corporate taxes (assuming a 30 percent corporate tax rate). Table 4 indicates how distributions of $70 and $20 of after-tax corporate income would be treated by shareholders whose tax rates were 20 percent or 40 percent. The grossed-up dividend is equal to the cash dividend (i.e., the dividend net of corporate taxes) divided by $1 \times c$, where c equals the corporate tax rate. Equivalently, the gross dividend equals the net dividend multiplied by $1/(1 - c)$, which equals 1.429 when the corporate tax rate is 30 percent. If all corporations were taxed at the same rate, a single gross-up rate could be used by all shareholders for all dividends for all corporations. Having included the gross dividend in income, the shareholder applies his personal tax rate (p) and reduces the resulting tax by the shareholder credit attributable to corporate tax payments. The credit is always the cash dividend times c, which would be .429 if c were 30 percent. Once again, if all corporations paid tax at the same rate, shareholder credits on all dividends could be determined by applying the same rate. As a result of the gross-up and credit, distributed after-tax corporate earnings are taxed to shareholders at a rate of $(p - c)/(1 - c)$, eliminating the separate burden of the corporate tax.

The results shown in Table 4 accomplish the goals of integration by applying the shareholder tax rate, and only the shareholder tax rate, to distributed corporate income. With a $70 distribution after corporate taxes, each shareholder is in the position he would be in if he had earned

$100 on individual account; with a $20 cash distribution each shareholder is treated as though $29 of income had been earned on individual account. Achieving those results for the 20 percent taxpayer in our example would require that the credit could be used against taxes generated by other income or, if there were no other such taxes, that the credit be refundable. "Shareholder credit integration" along these lines is often referred to abroad as "imputation" because the corporate tax rate is imputed to the shareholder through the gross-up and credit. . . .

As these examples indicate, the shareholder credit leaves the additional cash flow from integration in the hands of shareholders if the corporation does not adjust its dividend payments in response to the shareholder credit. The credit mechanism is therefore sometimes said to be a superior form of integration because the benefits of integration can be denied foreign and tax-exempt shareholders by making the credit nonrefundable to such shareholders.

B. DIVIDEND DEDUCTION

Integration could also be accomplished by permitting a corporate deduction for amounts paid as dividends, just as a deduction is now permitted for amounts paid as interest. The immediate effect of the deduction would be to increase the corporation's cash flow, although some of that benefit might be passed on to its shareholders in the form of increased dividends. In the example illustrated in Table 4, equivalent results would be achieved under a dividend deduction if the cash distribution were increased by 42.0 percent, from $70 to $100 and from $20 to $29.

As the dividend deduction method initially results in more cash at the corporate level, it is sometimes advocated as a superior form of integration on the ground that one of the purposes of integration is to provide additional incentives for corporate capital formation. On the other hand, one of the method's defects is sometimes said to be its automatic extension of the benefits of integration to tax-exempt and foreign shareholders, as compared with the possibility of denying imputation credits to such investors under shareholder credit integration. Finally, a dividend deduction would be simpler from the perspective of shareholders, because dividends would not be subject to a withholding mechanism, as they would be under imputation.

C. SPLIT RATES

An alternative method of integration is to levy a corporate tax on distributed earnings at a rate below that applied to retained earnings. Complete integration with respect to distributed corporate earnings would require a tax rate of zero on distributions and would be indistinguishable from a full dividend deduction. Less-than-complete integration would involve a tax rate on distributed earnings greater than zero but lower than the rate for retained earnings, making it indistinguishable from a partial deduction for dividends. . . .

D.   EQUIVALENCE OF INTEGRATION METHODS

The differences in cash flow under the shareholder credit and dividend deduction methods depend on the assumption that there will be no change in the amount of cash dividends paid by corporations in response to integration. To the extent cash dividends were reduced under the shareholder credit or increased under the dividend deduction, precisely the same results could obtain under either alternative. A choice between the two methods thus depends, in part, on the effect of imperfections in the capital markets and on whether those imperfections suggest that it would be better to have the initial increase in cash flow at the shareholder or the corporate level.

If, for enforcement purposes, a withholding tax on dividends were desirable under the dividend deduction method, that withholding tax would serve the same function as an equivalent rate corporate tax under the shareholder credit. The two integration methods would then be equivalent not only in their ultimate effect assuming perfect capital markets, but also in their immediate result. Under the dividend deduction the shareholder would include in income not only the cash dividends received, but also the withholding tax collected by the corporation, which is precisely the same process as that involved in grossing up the dividend under the shareholder credit. Likewise, the corporate tax on distributed earnings plus the withholding tax on distributed earnings under the dividend deduction would equal the corporate tax due under the shareholder credit. Table 5 illustrates this equivalence when the corporate tax rate is 30 percent, the withholding rate is 30 percent, and a cash distribution of $25 is made to a 40 percent taxpayer by a corporation that has $100 in taxable income.

Although the substantive results are the same under the two methods, the difference in labels might cause different legal, regulatory, or accounting consequences. For instance, the amount of the "dividend" paid for various purposes might differ. Under the dividend deduction, the dividend is arguably $36 in Table 5 because that is the amount deducted, and from which $11 is withheld, if the shareholder receives $25 in cash. Under the shareholder credit, the dividend paid by the corporation is arguably the cash distribution of $25, which gives rise to a credit of $11 on the grossed-up amount. Because part of the tax is characterized as "withholding" under the dividend deduction, the dividend appears to be the gross amount before withholding; under the shareholder credit, the dividend appears to be the cash distribution, net of corporate taxes. An $11 portion of the tax paid by the corporation might therefore be subject to different treatment by regulatory authorities or under tax treaties because it could be characterized as withholding (and therefore paid on behalf of shareholders) under the dividend deduction, but as a corporate tax under the shareholder credit mechanism.

There may also be differences in public perceptions regarding the two methods of distribution-related integration. One possibility is illustrated by the case of Jacques Chaban-Delmas, who as Prime Minister of France was attacked in the press for paying no personal income taxes for several years in the late 1960s, when no net taxes were due because of offsetting imputation credits. The possibility that high income individuals might appear not to be paying taxes would be less likely under a dividend deduction system, but it would be easier to argue that a corporation paid no or little taxes due to the deduction. . . .

NOTES

1. *The Treasury's proposal.* As the Reporter's study indicates, the shareholder credit method and the dividend deduction method of partially integrating the corporate and individual income taxes are functionally equivalent. And as that study also points out, most of the world currently employs the shareholder credit method of integration. It therefore came as a surprise to many when the Treasury recommended (in a portion of the report not excerpted above) that the United States adopt the dividend deduction method of integration. The reason underlying this recommendation was the Treasury's belief that the shareholder credit method is significantly more complex to implement than the dividend deduction method. This belief seems unusually parochial in light of the substantial international experience to the contrary. Further, adopting a method of integration at odds with what most of the world does presents additional difficulties when a corporation earns profits in one country and then distributes those profits to a shareholder residing in a different country. See generally van Raad, Approaches to Internationally Integrated Taxation of Distributed Corporate Income, 47 Tax L. Rev. 613 (1992).

2. *The role of subchapter S in an integrated tax world.* Professor Martin Ginsburg has suggested that the provisions for S corporations should continue even if Congress adopts a shareholder credit or dividend deduction method of partial integration. Ginsburg, Maintaining Subchapter S in an Integrated Tax World, 47 Tax L. Rev. 665 (1992). The justification for this proposal is best said in Professor Ginsburg's words:

Someone once suggested that the one thing that makes subchapter S look really good is subchapter K, the awesomely complex partnership tax provisions. The notion, to which I am much persuaded, is that subchapter S — setting aside the foolish complexity attracted when the S corporation has a subchapter C history — reflects a sensible and successful balance under which the investor surrenders flexibility, precision, and any claim for deduction in excess of her investment, and in exchange is absolved from ever having to master or to be mastered by anything like the partnership provisions' miserable contributed property rules or, worse, the "hot asset" distribution rules.

I suggest that if subchapter K qualifies as an historic justification for subchapter S, general intergation under any Treasury or ALI [American Law Institute] prototype will qualify as a modern, new justification for subchapter S. The familiar K-S trade off, flexibility and precision for simplicity, and more particularly the way the Code expresses that tradeoff, appears exceedingly attactive when integration is center stage.

47 Tax L. Rev. at 670.

For a contrasting reply to Professor Ginsburg, see Schenk, Complete Integration in a Partial Integration World, 47 Tax L. Rev. 697 (1992).

3. *Corporate tax integration today*. Corporate tax integration proposals continue to make their appearance in tax policy and legislative debates. As noted above, many smaller businesses can help themselves to corporate tax integration by operating as limited liability companies or subchapter S corporations. Some of the "flat tax" reform proposals intoduced in Congress in recent years contain integration proposals. For example, Senator Spector introduced the Flat Tax Act of 1999 in the Senate and Representative Armey has introduced similar legislation in the House. Both bills would achieve integration through a flat rate combined with shareholders excluding dividends from their tax base. See also GAO, Report on Impact of Alternative Tax Systems (January 14, 1998); Polito, Dual-Approach Tax Integration: Issues for Discussion, 73 Tax Notes 1213 (1996); Dodge, A Combined Mark-to-Market and Pass-through Corporate-Shareholder Integration Proposal, 50 Tax L. Rev. 265 (1995).

PROBLEMS

8-1. X Corp. intends to make a $100,000 investment in a new enterprise. X Corp. can raise the funds for this investment by issuing preferred stock or bonds. Assume the investment will yield 12 percent annually for five years and then will be returned to X Corp. Assuming the preferred stock can be sold if it offers a 10 percent annual return while bonds must pay 11 percent annual interest to be marketable, which should X Corp. issue? Assume X Corp. is in the 33.3 percent tax bracket.

8-2. If the corporate and individual income taxes were partially integrated, what effect would you expect to see on interest rates?

9

Taxable Acquisitions

Suppose *X* Corp. holds assets with a basis of $300,000 and a fair market value of $900,000 as well as $204,000 in cash. *B*, an individual, owns all the *X* Corp. stock with a basis of $400,000. *P*, an unrelated purchaser, wants to acquire *X* Corp. and is willing to pay fair market value. Among the acquisition choices available are the following:

1. an asset purchase in which either
   a. *X* Corp. sells its assets to *P* and then liquidates, or
   b. *X* Corp. liquidates and *B* sells the former *X* Corp. assets to *P;*
2. a stock purchase in which *P* buys the stock of *X* Corp. from *B* and either
   a. liquidates *X* Corp., or
   b. continues to operate *X* Corp. as a corporation.

These options are not the only ones for *P* and *B*. The nontaxable reorganization provisions discussed in Chapter 10 may allow *B* to exchange the *X* Corp. stock for stock in *P*, if *P* is a corporation, or stock in a corporation set up by *P* to consummate the acquisition. Alternatively, *X* may be able to merge into *P* or a subsidiary of *P* in a nontaxable reorganization. The advantage of a nontaxable reorganization is, not surprisingly, that it is nontaxable. If a reoganization can be nontaxable, why would taxpayers ever structure a taxable acquisition? The answer lies in the stringent requirements, imposed by the Code, that a transaction must meet to qualify as a nontaxable reorganization. Often taxpayers cannot or choose not to meet the requirements. For example, if *B* insists on receiving cash from *P* rather than stock of *P* if *P* is a corporation or stock of a corporation set up by *P*, the transaction will be treated as a taxable acquisition.

A. ASSET PURCHASE

1. Overall Tax Treatment

In the example above, if *P* acquires the assets from *X* Corp. for $900,000, *X* Corp. must recognize gain on the sale of $600,000. If *X* Corp. is taxable at a 34 percent rate, the tax is $204,000, which is paid by *X* Corp. with its cash. If *X* Corp. then liquidates, *B* is taxable under §§331 and 1001 on $500,000. If *B* is taxable on the gain at a 36 percent rate, *B* pays tax of $180,000 and ends up with $720,000. *P*'s basis in the assets purchased is $900,000. §1012. If *P* is a corporation and *X* merges into *P* in accordance with the state merger laws in a transaction in which *B* receives cash, for tax purposes the transaction is treated as a sale of the *X* assets followed by a liquidation of *X*. See West Shore Fuel, Inc. v. United States, 598 F.2d 1236 (2d Cir. 1979). For a discussion of tax-free mergers, see page 398 infra.

If, instead of selling its assets to *P* or merging into *P*, *X* Corp. first liquidates and then *B* sells the former *X* Corp. assets to *P*, the tax consequences are the same. On the liquidation, *X* Corp. recognizes a gain of $600,000 under §336, which it pays with the available cash.[1] *B* is taxed on the difference between the $900,000 fair market value of the *X* Corp. assets and *B*'s $400,000 stock basis. After paying taxes of $180,000, which *B* has in a bank account, *B* ends up with the former *X* Corp. assets with a fair market value and basis of $900,000. §301(d). When *B* sells those assets to *P*, *B* recognizes no further gain and *P* takes a cost basis of $900,000 in the assets. §1012.

Notice that in both taxable acquisition patterns there are two levels of taxation — corporate-level taxation of *X* Corp. and shareholder-level taxation of *B*. In exchange for these two levels of taxation, *P* acquires the *X* Corp. assets with a stepped-up cost basis. As explained in Section B, it is possible for *P* to acquire *X* Corp. through a stock purchase with only a shareholder-level tax, but if there is no corporate-level tax, *P* does not take a stepped-up basis in the corporate assets.

2. Allocation of Purchase Price

Both the seller and the buyer have an interest in the allocation of the purchase price to the various assets sold. For the seller (whether it is *X* Corp. or *B*), gain or loss and the character of that gain or loss (i.e., capital or ordinary) is determined asset by asset. For the buyer, *P*, the allocation of the $900,000 purchase price determines how much basis is allocated to inventory, depreciable assets, and nondepreciable assets.

---

1. Alternatively, *X* Corp. could liquidate, distributing its assets (including cash) subject to the corporate tax liability.

Historically, the parties to a sale often had adverse interests in allocating the purchase price among assets. Sellers wanted to allocate as much of the purchase price as possible to assets yielding tax-favored capital gain, such as land and goodwill. In contrast, buyers benefited from allocating as much as possible to inventory, depreciable property (e.g., buildings, equipment), and amortizable intangibles (e.g., covenant not to compete) to decrease the amount of ordinary income that the seller would have to recognize in the future. Because of these adverse interests, the Service typically respected negotiated purchase agreements that specifically allocated the purchase price to each asset sold. A buyer and seller were bound by the agreement unless mistake, undue influence, fraud, or distress were shown. See, e.g., Commissioner v. Danielson, 378 F.2d 771 (3d Cir. 1967).

Agreements often contain no specific allocation of purchase price. In these situations the seller and buyer historically have taken inconsistent positions whipsawing the government. For example, a buyer often allocated a portion of the purchase price to a covenant not to compete, which was amortizable over the life of the covenant (but produced ordinary income to the seller), while the seller wanted to allocate a portion of the purchase price to goodwill, which resulted in capital gain to the seller (but was not amortizable by the buyer). Also, if little or no differential existed between the rate of tax on capital gain and ordinary income, a seller often did not care about the allocation of purchase price and, along with the buyer, "ganged up" on the Service.

Code §1060 now requires a specific method of allocation that must be followed by both seller and buyer in the case of "any applicable asset acquisition." An "applicable asset acquisition" is any transfer (direct or indirect) of assets that constitute a trade or business and with respect to which the transferee's basis in the purchased assets is determined wholly by the consideration paid for the assets (i.e., cost basis). §1060(c).

The regulations divide all assets into seven classes. (See Treas. Regs. §1.1060-1, which cross-references Treas. Regs. §1.338-6.) Class I comprises cash, bank deposits, and similar assets. Class II covers certificates of deposits, U.S. government securities, and readily marketable stock or securities. Class III includes accounts receivable, mortgages, and credit card receivables which arise in the ordinary course of business. Class IV applies to stock in trade or inventory of a taxpayer. Class V is reserved for all assents not in classes I-IV or classes VI-VII. Class VI assets include all §197 intangibles, except goodwill and going concern value which make up class VII. A covenant not to compete is a class VI asset for purposes of §338. The purchase price paid is allocated first to class I assets based on aggregate fair market value, then to class II assets, and so on. Within each class, the price is allocated to each asset according to fair market value. Any premium paid by the purchaser above the fair market value of the "hard" assets (e.g., tangible assets and specific intangibles such as patents and trademarks) is allocated to goodwill (and going concern value) rather than allocated proportionately to the "hard" assets.

Some allocation disputes under §1060 may be lessened by the enactment of §197, which generally requires 15-year straight-line amortization for all purchased intangibles. This provision is more favorable than prior law with respect to previously unamortizable intangibles such as goodwill. It is less favorable, however, for intangibles that were previously amortizable over shorter periods of time, such as covenants not to compete. The assets covered by §197 include the following: goodwill and going concern value; workforce in place; customer lists and other customer-based intangibles; favorable contracts with suppliers and other supplier-based intangibles; business books and records and any other information base; patents, copyrights, formulas, processes, know-how, designs, and similar items; computer software; franchises, trademarks, and trade names; licenses, permits, and other governmental rights; and covenants not to compete.

Some assets are specifically excluded from §197. These include the following: off-the-shelf intangibles (e.g., computer software sold in stores), interests in tangible property leases (e.g., a lease premium), interests in debt obligations, certain intangibles requiring contingent payments (e.g., payments for a franchise based on productivity), financial interests, interests in land, and fees for professional services (e.g., INDOPCO-type expenses). Some intangibles are covered by §197 only when there is a related acquisition of the assets or in some cases the stock of a business, including patents or copyrights and covenants not to compete.

Even though both goodwill and a covenant not to compete are amortizable over 15 years under §197, there may be incentives for buyers and sellers of assets to allocate purchase price to goodwill rather than a covenant not to compete. First, the sale of goodwill produces capital gain taxed at a maximum 20 percent rate for an individual; payments for a covenant not to compete may be taxed at a 39.6 percent rate if the seller is in the highest tax bracket. Even for corporations where the current capital gains rate is the same as the rate for ordinary income, the sale of goodwill may produce a capital gain which can absorb a capital loss while an amount received for a covenant not to compete is ordinary income which cannot be offset by a capital loss. Second, for financial reporting purposes, goodwill may be amortizable over 40 years, while a covenant not to compete is amortizable over the life of the agreement. Consequently, allocation to goodwill produces higher earnings for financial reporting purposes.

B. STOCK PURCHASE

1. Individual Purchaser

Suppose that, instead of purchasing the assets of X Corp. either from X Corp. or from B after X Corp. liquidates, P purchases the X Corp. stock from *B* for $900,000.[2] On the sale, *B* recognizes gain of $500,000, pays tax of $180,000, and ends up with $720,000 of cash. Notice that *P* has acquired *X* Corp., and, compared with the asset purchases described above, there has been only a shareholder-level tax rather than both a shareholder-level and corporate-level tax. But also notice that *P* has acquired (indirectly through *X* Corp.) assets (other than the cash) that still have a $300,000 basis. In an asset purchase, *P* acquires the *X* Corp. assets with a basis of $900,000.

If *P*, an individual, wants to step up the basis of the *X* Corp. assets to $900,000, *P* can do so, but only if a corporate-level tax is paid. If, after buying *B*'s *X* Corp. stock, *P* liquidates *X* Corp., under §336 *X* Corp. recognizes a $600,000 gain on the liquidation and a tax liability of $204,000, which is paid with *X* Corp.'s cash. *P* has no gain on the liquidation under §§331 and 1001 because *P*'s basis in the *X* Corp. stock is $900,000, which is equal to the fair market value of the distributed assets. *P*'s basis in those assets is $900,000. §334(a).

Obtaining a higher basis in *X* Corp.'s assets may benefit *P*. If the assets are depreciable, the depreciation deductions will be larger. Even if the assets are not depreciable, *P* will have less gain or a larger loss deduction if the assets are sold. But what price will *P* pay to acquire a stepped-up basis? *P* can acquire a stepped up basis in the *X* Corp. assets only if *X* Corp. recognizes a corporate-level gain on the liquidation. Normally, a taxpayer is not willing to trade immediate taxation for future tax benefits (e.g., larger depreciation deductions). If, however, *X* Corp. has a net operating loss carryover that is about to expire, a liquidation might provide a higher asset basis at no immediate tax cost. Also, if *X* Corp.'s assets have bases that exceed fair market value, liquidation may allow *X* Corp. an immediate loss that *P* may gladly trade for a lower fair market value basis in the assets upon liquidation.

2. Corporate Purchaser: §338

If *P* is a corporation (*P* Corp.) and does not intend to liquidate *X* Corp. after purchasing the *X* Corp. stock from *B*, the tax consequences are the same as if *P* were an individual. If *P* is an individual, however, *P* has a choice of recognizing a corporate-level gain and obtaining a stepped-up basis in the *X* Corp. assets through liquidation or holding the *X* Corp. assets in corporate solution with a basis of $300,000. When *P* is a corporation, if *P* Corp. liquidates *X* Corp., *X* Corp. does not recognize a corporate-level gain and *P* Corp. does not obtain the *X* Corp. assets with a

---

2. Although *X* Corp. has assets worth $1,104,000, if *P* anticipates that *X* Corp. will soon either sell its assets or liquidate (thereby recognizing a gain), *P* would be unwilling to pay more for the *X* Corp. stock than for the purchase of the assets directly. If *P* does not anticipate selling the *X* Corp. assets, *P* may be willing to pay up to $1,104,000 for *X* Corp. The actual purchase price is a function of the demand for *B*'s stock.

stepped-up basis. §§337, 3332, 334(b). See page 326 supra. *P* Corp. can obtain a stepped-up basis in the *X* Corp. assets by purchasing them directly, but can *P* Corp. obtain a stepped-up basis if it purchases *B*'s *X* Corp. stock?

In §338 Congress has provided *P* Corp. with a means of obtaining a stepped-up basis in the *X* Corp. assets if *P* Corp. purchases *B*'s *X* Corp. stock; thus, from a tax standpoint, *P* Corp. is more likely to be indifferent whether it acquires *X* Corp. through an asset or stock purchase. For *P* Corp. to obtain a stepped-up basis, *X* Corp. must recognize the $600,000 gain inherent in its assets.

Before looking at the specifics of §338, it may be helpful to outline the provision. It applies when a corporation purchases within a 12-month period at least 80 percent of the voting stock and at least 80 percent of all other stock (not including nonvoting, preferred stock, limited as to dividends) of a target corporation and makes a timely election. If applicable, §338 deems the target corporation, *X* Corp. in the example above, to have sold all its assets. And who is the deemed purchaser? The purchaser in this deemed sale is also the target corporation, *X* Corp. In other words, *X* Corp. sells the assets to itself. The effect of this circular fiction is recognition of gain to the target corporation combined with a cost basis in the target's assets. In the example above, *X* Corp. would recognize a $600,000 gain and would take a $900,000 basis in the assets.

The application of §338 does not require *P* Corp. to liquidate *X* Corp. to secure a cost basis in *X* Corp.'s assets. If *P* Corp. does decide to liquidate following a §338 election, §§332 and 334 will apply, and *P* Corp. takes *X* Corp.'s $900,000 asset basis. To summarize, §338 represents Congress's effort to render the form of an acquisition (stock or asset) irrelevant to an acquiring corporation.

Note that §338 is unavailable (because it is unnecessary) if *P* is an individual. If *P* purchases *B*'s stock for $900,000, *P* could then liquidate *X* Corp. under §§331 and 336, with *X* Corp. recognizing a $600,000 gain (i.e., a $204,000 tax liability) and *P* receiving a $900,000 basis in *X* Corp. assets under §334(a). The election under §338 is necessary only when §§332 and 337 would otherwise prevent *P* Corp. from taking a fair market value basis in a subsidiary's basis. There does not appear to be a good reason, however, why §338 is not available to an individual who purchases stock of a corporation. The availability of §338 would mean that an individual purchaser would not have to liquidate a corporation in order to step up (or step down) the basis of corporate assets so long as the corporation was willing to recognize gain or loss on the deemed §338 sale.

Section 338 had greater importance prior to the repeal of the *General Utilities* doctrine, when it was possible under §338 to obtain a fair market value basis without any corporate-level recognition of gain. Under current law, *P* Corp. gets a stepped-up basis in the factory only if *X* Corp. recognizes a $600,000 gain. Generally, *P* Corp. will not make a §338 election to recognize gain now in order to obtain a stepped-up basis that may increase tax benefits in the future.

As mentioned above, in some situations a §338 election may still be made. Suppose in the example above that X Corp. has a net operating loss (NOL) of $600,000 or more from previous years. If P Corp. elects under §338, X Corp.'s $600,000 gain will be offset by the net operating loss and X Corp. will take a $900,000 basis in the factory on its deemed purchase. The $900,000 basis, rather than a $300,000 basis, may allow larger depreciation deductions, thereby decreasing X Corp.'s taxable income (or it may decrease gain or increase deductible loss on a sale of the assets). But even if X Corp. has an NOL from previous years, a §338 election may not be advisable: Often P Corp. may be able to use X Corp.'s NOL after P Corp. liquidates its subsidiary, or perhaps X Corp. can use its own NOL against future earnings. See §§381 and 382 at page 506 infra. If X Corp.'s NOL is about to expire, however, a §338 election may provide a tax benefit.

Section 338 is useful when P Corp. purchases a foreign target corporation with appreciated assets. The gain on the deemed §338 sale is not usually taxable in the United States (or abroad) and the stepped-up basis on the deemed purchase may result in lower U.S. taxation on any eventual distribution from the target to P Corp. The higher asset basis may in turn result in greater depreciation deductions, lower earnings and profits, and therefore a smaller dividend upon eventual distribution.

NOTES

1. *Qualified stock purchases.* The 80 percent requirements of §338 discussed above must be satisfied by a "qualified stock purchase." "Purchase," as defined in §338(h)(3), in general includes all acquisitions other than those in which the purchasing corporation carries over the transferor's basis. For example, acquisitions by gift or in a §351 transaction do not qualify. In addition, a "purchase" does not include an acquisition from a related party. §338(h)(3)(A)(iii). The 80 percent ownership must be acquired within a twelve-month acquisition period that begins with the date of the first acquisition by purchase. See §338(h)(1).

2. *Election.* Under §338(g)(1), an acquiring corporation can elect to treat the purchase of stock as a purchase of assets any time before the fifteenth day of the ninth month following the month in which the requisite 80 percent control is acquired. The election is irrevocable. See §338(g)(3). See generally Treas. Regs. §1.338-3 for the §338 election requirements. The gain or loss that is recognized on the §338 election cannot be offset by gains or losses of affiliates in either the selling or purchasing groups. §338(h)(9).

3. *Operation of §338.* The deemed sale by the target corporation to itself, set forth in §338(a)(1), will trigger recognition. In determining gain, the sale is deemed to take place at fair market value. The Regulations use the "aggregate deemed sales price" (ADSP) as the fair market value. Treas. Regs. §1.338-4. The purchasing corporation's price for the qualified stock purchase is used as the major component of the ADSP. Section 338(c)(1) provides an additional exception to the general nonrecognition rule of §338(a)(1). If the purchasing corporation does not purchase all the stock of the target (but acquires the requisite 80 percent), §338 will still apply.

Return to our example fact pattern, in which X Corp. holds assets with a basis of $300,000 and a fair market value of $900,000. If P Corp. acquires all the stock of X Corp. for $900,000 and makes the election, a $600,000 gain is recognized, and X Corp.'s basis in the factory becomes $900,000. Suppose P Corp. purchases 80 percent of the X Corp. stock for $720,000. If the election is made, X Corp. will still get a $900,000 basis because it will still recognize a $600,000 gain.

Turning from the deemed sale to the deemed purchase, we find even more complexity. The rules contained in §338(a)(2) and (b) determine the basis that the target has in its assets on the deemed purchase. The rules are set up to deal with two phenomena: First, a purchasing corporation may not purchase all the target's stock, yet a full step-up in basis is allowed; second, the purchasing corporation may have "nonrecently purchased stock" as defined in §338(b)(6), which is stock not acquired by purchase within the acquisition period and is treated separately from "recently purchased stock" as defined in §338(b)(6).

Section 338(b) uses an adjusted grossed-up basis rule (AGUB) to determine the cost basis of the target's assets on the deemed purchase. Treas. Regs. §1.338(b)-5. The assets of the target are treated as purchased for an amount equal to the grossed-up basis of recently purchased stock plus the basis of nonrecently purchased stock. In our example, we can ignore the nonrecently purchased stock component because all the stock held by P Corp. was acquired by purchase within the acquisition period. If P Corp. acquires all the X Corp. stock for $900,000, §338(b)(1)(A) and (b)(4) provide that the basis of the X Corp. assets is $900,000 (P Corp.'s basis in the X Corp. stock) × 100 percent/100 percent, or $900,000, the same basis as if P Corp. had purchased the assets directly. If P Corp. acquires 80 percent of the X Corp. stock for $720,000, the new basis of the X Corp. assets is equal to $720,000 (P Corp.'s basis in the X Corp. stock) × 100 percent/80 percent, or $900,000. Note that the new basis of the X Corp. assets is the same whether P Corp. purchases 80 or 100 percent because in either case X Corp. will recognize a $600,000 gain.

The complexity worsens when nonrecently purchased stock is introduced since it must be excluded from the gross-up calculation. Suppose in our example that *P* Corp. acquires 80 percent of *X* Corp. stock for $720,000 during the acquisition period and that *P* Corp. held an additional 8 percent of the *X* Corp. stock (acquired before the qualified purchase date) with a basis of $20,000 and a fair market value of $72,000 on the acquisition date. The remaining 12 percent of the stock continues to be held by *B*. If *P* Corp. elects §338 after purchasing 80 percent of the *Y* Corp. stock, *X* Corp.'s basis in its assets will equal $720,000 (purchase price of the stock) × 92 percent/80 percent, or $828,000, plus the $20,000 basis of the nonrecently purchased stock, or a total basis of $848,000. Notice that the basis in the target's assets reflects the fact that $52,000 of appreciation has not been recognized on the nonrecently purchased *X* Corp. stock.

In the previous example, however, *P* Corp. can elect to fully step up the basis of the target's assets to $900,000 by recognizing gain on the nonrecently purchased stock (i.e., the 8 percent holding). In the example, the gain would be the difference between the $20,000 basis and the $72,000 deemed sales price under §338(b)(3) ($828,000 × 8 percent/92 percent). The effect of this election is to increase the §338(b)(1)(B) amount to $72,000, which, when added to the $828,000 grossed-up basis, provides a full $900,000 basis. The cost of this additional corporate-level step-up in asset basis is recognition of what otherwise could eventually be shareholder-level gain.

4. *Adjustments for liabilities*. Suppose in our example that *X* Corp.'s assets have a fair market value of $900,000 but are subject to a liability of $200,000. Further assume that *P* Corp. purchases all the *X* Corp. stock for $700,000 (i.e., the net value of *X* Corp.). Section 338(b)(2) and the regulations promulgated thereunder clarify that if *P* Corp. makes a §338 election, *X* Corp. still recognizes a gain of $600,000 and then takes a $900,000 basis in the assets it is deemed to sell to itself. Prop. Treas. Regs. §1.338-4(d). Any tax liability resulting from the deemed sale by *X* Corp. is treated as a liability that increases *X* Corp.'s basis on its deemed purchase. Prop. Treas. Regs. §1.338-5(e). In effect, the tax liability inherent in *X* Corp.'s appreciated asset probably reduced the cash *P* Corp. was willing to pay for the *X* Corp. stock in the same manner as would a mortgage on the factory.

5. *Relationship of ADSP to AGUB*. The aggregate deemed sales price (ADSP) on the target's sale to itself may not initially be equal to the adjusted grossed-up basis (AGUB) on the deemed purchase. For example, there may be some contingent liabilities that are taken into account in determining gain but cannot be immediately reflected in the purchaser's basis. General tax principles determine when liabilities are taken into account to determine a target's gain and its subsequent basis on the deemed sale. Prop. Treas. Regs. §1.338-5. Some contingent liabilities that may not initially be reflected in the AGUB may later be reflected when under

general tax principles an adjustment is appropriate. Treas. Regs. §1.338-5(b)(2)(ii).

6. *Allocation of basis.* In the example above, if *X* Corp. holds only one asset, the allocation of basis on a deemed §338 sale by *X* Corp. to itself is not a problem. If *X* Corp. holds more than one asset (including intangible assets such as goodwill), allocation of basis is necessary. In general, the regulations promulgated under §338(b)(5) require a residual method of allocation in which the basis determined under §338 is allocated to specified assets to the extent of their fair market values, with any balance allocated to goodwill and going concern value. This is the same method of allocation mandated by §1060 on asset sales. See page 349 supra.

Specifically, the target corporation (e.g., *X* Corp.) first reduces its basis by the amount of any cash and cash equivalents received (referred to as class I assets). Prop. Treas. Regs. §1.338-6(b)(1). Remaining basis then is allocated to liquid assets such as certificates of deposit, U.S. government securities, and other marketable stock or securities (referred to as class II assets) to the extent of their fair market values. Prop. Treas. Regs. §1.338-6(b)(2). Basis still remaining after allocation to class II is allocated to class III, which consists of accounts receivable, mortgages, and credit card receivables to the extent of their fair market values. Any remaining basis is next allocated to stock in trade or inventory (class IV assets). Class V assets consist of anything that is not in classes I-IV or VI-VII. For example, property used in a trade or business is a class V asset. Class VI consists of intangibles (e.g., trademarks, patents, copyrights, covenants not to compete), except goodwill and going concern value which are class VII assets.

There are special rules for allocating basis when the deemed AGUB in insufficient to cover the fair market value of the target's assets. Prop. Treas. Regs. §1.338-6(c)(3).

Suppose *P* Corp. purchases the stock of *X* Corp. from its shareholder, *B*. The stock has a basis of $300,000 and a fair market value of $700,000. *P* Corp. pays $1 million in exchange for the stock and *B*'s covenant not to compete for five years. Under §197, *P* Corp. must amortize the amount paid for the covenant not to compete over the statutory 15-year period rather than the five-year period of the covenant itself. Note that because the *X* Corp. assets carry over their bases when *P* Corp. purchases the *X* Corp. stock from *B*, §197 does not permit *X* Corp. to amortize any amount allocated to goodwill even though *X* Corp.'s assets may be stepped up for accounting purposes. If *P* Corp. makes a §338 election, §197 will apply to *X* Corp.'s deemed sale to itself. Any amount of the purchase price allocated to goodwill or other intangibles will be amortizable over a 15-year period.

7. *Consistency requirements and deemed elections.* Sections 338(e) and

(f) present purchasing corporations with an all-or-nothing choice regarding §338. If a §338 election is made, it applies not only to the target corporation but also to any "target affiliates" (§338(g)(6)) whose stock is purchased during the "consistency" period. §338(f). The consistency period basically is a three-year period that includes a year before the acquisition period, the 12-month acquisition period itself, and a one-year period following the acquisition period. §338(h)(4). Moreover, if a purchasing corporation does not make a §338 election, it will be deemed to have made an election if during the consistency period it acquires any asset of the target or an affiliate. §338(e). This deemed election prevents a purchasing corporation from stepping up the basis of desired assets by purchasing them directly while preserving the basis of other assets (and perhaps avoiding gain) by not electing §338.

The Regulations "interpreting" the §337(f) consistency rules all but eliminate the deemed election. Consequently, if P Corp. makes a §338 election with respect to a qualified stock purchase, it can no longer be deemed to make a §338 election with respect to a subsequent stock purchase of an affiliate within the consistency period. Treas. Regs. §1.338-8.

Suppose that P makes a qualified stock purchase of T and makes a §338 election with respect to T. Suppose that T 's only asset is the appreciated stock of its wholly-owned subsidiary T1. If P makes a §338 election for T1 on T 's deemed purchase of the T1 stock resulting from P's §338 election for T, then no gain or loss is recognized on the deemed sale of the T1 stock by T. However, if no election with respect to T1 is made by P, then T must recognize gain on the deemed sale of the T1 stock. Prop. Treas. Regs. §1.338-4(h)(8) examples 1-2. Also if T1 is a foreign corporation, T must recognize gain on P's §338 election with respect to T. Prop. Treas. Regs. §1.338-4(h)(3).

In some situations the §338 deemed election can produce unwanted results. For example, suppose Target Corp. holds two assets: undeveloped land with a basis of $100,000 and a fair market value of $600,000, and a building with a basis of $300,000 and fair market value of $700,000. Target Corp. is owned by Parent Corp., which has a stock basis of $200,000 in the Target Corp. stock. Purchase Corp. wants to acquire Target Corp. and to step up the basis of the building (to increase the depreciation deductions) but not that of the undeveloped land. Suppose Purchase Corp. buys the building for $700,000 directly from Target Corp.; six months later, after the $700,000 has been distributed to Target Corp.'s shareholders or paid as compensation to Target's employees, Purchase Corp. buys the stock of Target Corp. from Parent Corp. for $600,000. Under §338(e), Purchase Corp. is deemed to have made a §338 election and therefore Target Corp. will be deemed to have sold the land to itself, causing the recognition of a $500,000 gain.

Notwithstanding the statutory requirement of a deemed §338 election, the regulations take a completely different approach. Treas. Regs. §1.338-8(d). Instead, no election is deemed, but rather, Purchase Corp. takes a carryover basis of $100,000 in the land. In fact, the regulations no longer permit the Service to impose a deemed §338 election. Moreover, §338(e) generally only applies when the target is a subsidiary in a consolidated group. Treas. Regs. §1.338-8(a). Although these regulations appear completely inconsistent with the Code, perhaps §338(e)(2)(D) allows for such a ruling.

8. *Acquisition of a subsidiary from a consolidated group.* If, in the example above, Parent Corp. sells the stock of Target Corp. to Purchase Corp. for $1,300,000, there is a potential gain of $1,100,000 to Parent Corp. Additionally, if Purchase Corp. makes a §338 election, Target Corp. would recognize a $900,000 gain on the deemed sale of both assets to itself. Under this scenario, two taxable events have taken place.

If, instead, Purchase Corp. bought the assets from Target Corp. directly, Target Corp. would recognize a $900,000 gain. There would be no further gain under §§332 and 337 if Parent Corp. then liquidated Target Corp. In other words, by purchasing the assets directly, the parties can eliminate one of the taxable events and avoid the $1,100,000 gain to Parent Corp.

In an effort to let substance rather than form control in this area, Congress enacted §338(h)(10). If §338(h)(10) is elected, Parent Corp. does not recognize gain on the sale of stock. Instead, only Target Corp. will recognize gain ($900,000) on the deemed asset sale. Following the deemed asset sale, Target Corp. is treated as if it liquidated into Parent Corp. under §332. Treas. Regs. §1.338(h)(10)-1. For §338(h)(10) to apply, Parent Corp. and Target Corp. must meet specified affiliation requirements, the purchaser of stock must be a corporation, and both Purchase Corp. and the consolidated or affiliated group must make the election.

An election under §338(h)(10) preserves the target's tax attributes (e.g., loss carryovers) to the benefit of the selling parent corporation, which inherits those attributes in the deemed §332 liquidation of the target-subsidiary. Consequently, unlike the §338(g) election, the §338(h)(10) election allows the target corporation to be treated as a member of the selling corporation's consolidated group so that gains or losses within the affiliated group can be used to offset gain or loss resulting from the §338(h)(10) election.

Even if §338 is not elected or the §338(h)(10) election is not made because some of the requirements of that subsection are not met, Parent Corp. can in some cases rely on §336(e) to report a single gain of $900,000. If an individual, rather than Purchase Corp., buys the Target Corp. stock, §336(e) may cause the seller to recognize a $900,000 gain instead of a $1,300,000 gain.

PROBLEMS

T Corp., a profitable corporation, has the following assets and liabilities:

Assets	Basis	FMV
Portfolio of marketable securities	$ 20,000	$ 50,000
Inventory	30,000	200,000
Equipment ($50,000 §1245 recapture)	100,000	150,000
Land	150,000	300,000
Building (no recapture)	175,000	340,000
Patent	25,000	60,000
	500,000	1,100,000
Liabilities		
Bank loan		200,000

A owns 50 shares of T Corp. stock with a basis of $300,000; B owns 40 shares of T Corp. stock with a basis of $200,000; C owns 10 shares of T Corp. stock with a basis of $50,000.

The shareholders of T Corp. have decided to sell the business to P. Ignoring the quantitative effects of the tax consequences, outline the tax considerations in the following alternatives:

9-1.   P, an individual, pays $1.2 million to T Corp. for all its assets and assumes T Corp.'s bank loan. T Corp. then liquidates.

9-2.   In Problem 9-1, suppose P pays $1.2 million to the shareholders to purchase their stock in T Corp., and T Corp. does not liquidate.

9-3.   In Problem 9-2, suppose P decides to liquidate T Corp.

9-4.   In Problem 9-2, suppose P is a corporation (P Corp.). Suppose further that P Corp. borrowed the funds used to purchase the stock, thereby generating interest deductions in excess of the income of P Corp. and T Corp. combined.

9-5.   In Problem 9-4, suppose T Corp. has a $700,000 NOL that is about to expire.

9-6.   In Problem 9-4, suppose that P Corp. decides to liquidate T Corp.

9-7.   Suppose P Corp. purchases the land and building from T Corp. for $700,000. One year later, P Corp. purchases the stock of T Corp. for $1 million.

9-8.   Suppose A, B, and C own the stock of H Corp., the only asset of which is the T Corp. stock. H Corp. and T Corp. file a consolidated return. H Corp.'s basis in the T Corp. stock is $200,000. T Corp. sells its assets to P Corp. (which assumes T Corp.'s liability) for $1.2 million and then liquidates. H Corp. then liquidates.

9-9.   In Problem 9-8, suppose that prior to any asset sale, *T* Corp. liquidates, then *H* Corp. liquidates. *A, B,* and *C* then sell the former *T* Corp. assets to *P* Corp. for $1.2 million.

9-10.   In Problem 9-9, suppose that rather than an asset sale, *P* Corp. purchases the stock of *T* Corp. from *H* Corp. for $1.2 million.

C. BOOTSTRAP ACQUISITIONS

For a discussion of the tax consequences of bootstrap acquisitions in connection with a sale of a business, see page 369 infra.

D. EXPENSES IN CONNECTION WITH AN ACQUISITION

INDOPCO, Inc. v. Commissioner
503 U.S. 79 (1992)

Justice BLACKMUN delivered the opinion of the court.

In this case we must decide whether certain professional expenses incurred by a target corporation in the course of a friendly takeover are deductible by that corporation as "ordinary and necessary" business expenses under section 162(a) of the federal Internal Revenue Code.

I

... Petitioner INDOPCO, Inc., formerly named National Starch and Chemical Corporation and hereinafter referred to as National Starch, is a Delaware corporation that manufactures and sells adhesives, starches, and specialty chemical products. In October 1977, representatives of Unilever United States, Inc., also a Delaware corporation (Unilever), expressed interest in acquiring National Starch, which was one of its suppliers, through a friendly transaction. National Starch at the time had outstanding over 6,563,000 common shares held by approximately 3700 shareholders. The stock was listed on the New York Stock Exchange. Frank and Anna Greenwall were the corporation's largest shareholders and owned approximately 14.5% of the common. The Greenwalls, getting along in years and concerned about their estate plans, indicated that they would transfer their shares to Unilever only if a transaction tax-free for them could be arranged.

Lawyers representing both sides devised a "reverse subsidiary cash merger" that they felt would satisfy the Greenwalls' concerns. Two new entities would be created — National Starch and Chemical Holding Corp. (Holding), a subsidiary of Unilever, and NSC Merger, Inc., a subsidiary of Holding that would have only a transitory existence. In an exchange specifically designed to be tax-free under section 351, Holding would exchange one share of its nonvoting preferred stock for each share of National Starch common that it received from National Starch shareholders. Any National Starch common that was not so exchanged would be converted into cash in a merger of NSC Merger, Inc., into National Starch.

In November 1977, National Starch's directors were formally advised of Unilever's interest and the proposed transaction. At that time, Debevoise, Plimpton, Lyons & Gates, National Starch's counsel, told the directors that under Delaware law they had a fiduciary duty to ensure that the proposed transaction would be fair to the shareholders. National Starch thereupon engaged the investment banking firm of Morgan Stanley & Co., Inc., to evaluate its shares, to render a fairness opinion, and generally to assist in the event of the emergence of a hostile tender offer.

Although Unilever originally had suggested a price between $65 and $70 per share, negotiations resulted in a final offer of $73.50 per share, a figure Morgan Stanley found to be fair. Following approval by National Starch's board and the issuance of a favorable private ruling from the Internal Revenue Service that the transaction would be tax-free under section 351 for those National Starch shareholders who exchanged their stock for Holding preferred, the transaction was consummated in August 1978.[2]

Morgan Stanley charged National Starch a fee of $2,200,000, along with $7,586 for out-of-pocket expenses and $18,000 for legal fees. The Debevoise firm charged National Starch $490,000, along with $15,069 for out-of-pocket expenses. National Starch also incurred expenses aggregating $150,962 for miscellaneous items — such as accounting, printing, proxy solicitation, and Securities and Exchange Commission fees — in connection with the transaction. No issue is raised as to the propriety or reasonableness of these charges.

On its federal income tax return for its short taxable year ended August 15, 1978, National Starch claimed a deduction for the $2,225,586 paid to Morgan Stanley, but did not deduct the $505,069 paid to Debevoise or the other expenses. Upon audit, the Commissioner of Internal Revenue disallowed the claimed deduction and issued a notice of deficiency. Petitioner sought redetermination in the United States Tax Court, asserting,

2. Approximately 21% of National Starch common was exchanged for Holding preferred. The remaining 79% was exchanged for cash.

however, not only the right to deduct the investment banking fees and expenses but, as well, the legal and miscellaneous expenses incurred.

The Tax Court, in an unreviewed decision, ruled that the expenditures were capital in nature and therefore not deductible under section 162(a) in the 1978 return as "ordinary and necessary expenses." National Starch and Chemical Corp. v. Commissioner, 93 T.C. 67 (1989). The court based its holding primarily on the long-term benefits that accrued to National Starch from the Unilever acquisition. Id., at 75. The United States Court of Appeals for the Third Circuit affirmed, upholding the Tax Court's findings that "both Unilever's enormous resources and the possibility of synergy arising from the transaction served the long-term betterment of National Starch." National Starch and Chemical Corp. v. Commissioner, 918 F.2d 426, 432-433 (1990). In so doing, the Court of Appeals rejected National Starch's contention that, because the disputed expenses did not "create or enhance . . . a separate and distinct additional asset," see Commissioner v. Lincoln Savings & Loan Assn., 403 U.S. 345, 354 (1971), they could not be capitalized and therefore were deductible under section 162(a). 918 F.2d, at 428-431. We granted certiorari to resolve a perceived conflict on the issue among the Courts of Appeals.[3]

II

Section 162(a) of the Internal Revenue Code allows the deduction of "all the ordinary and necessary expenses paid or incurred during the taxable year in carrying on any trade or business." In contrast, section 263 of the Code allows no deduction for a capital expenditure — an "amount paid out for new buildings or for permanent improvements or betterments made to increase the value of any property or estate." The primary effect of characterizing a payment as either a business expense or a capital expenditure concerns the timing of the taxpayer's cost recovery: While business expenses are currently deductible, a capital expenditure usually is amortized and depreciated over the life of the relevant asset, or, where no specific asset or useful life can be ascertained, is deducted upon dissolution of the enterprise. Through provisions such as these, the Code endeavors to match expenses with the revenues of the taxable period to which they

3. Compare the Third Circuit's opinion, 918 F.2d, at 430, with NCNB Corp. v. United States, 684 F.2d 285, 293-294 (C.A.4 1982) (bank expenditures for expansion-related planning reports, feasibility studies, and regulatory applications did not "create or enhance separate and identifiable assets," and therefore were ordinary and necessary expenses under section 162(a)), and Briarcliff Candy Corp. v. Commissioner, 475 F.2d 775, 782 (C.A.2 1973) (suggesting that *Lincoln Savings* "brought about a radical shift in emphasis," making capitalization dependent on whether the expenditure creates or enhances a separate and distinct additional asset). See also Central Texas Savings & Loan Assn. v. United States, 731 F.2d 1181, 1184 (C.A.5 1984) (inquiring whether establishment of new branches "creates a separate and distinct additional asset" so that capitalization is the proper tax treatment).

are properly attributable, thereby resulting in a more accurate calculation of net income for tax purposes. See, e.g., Commissioner v. Idaho Power Co., 418 U.S. 1, 16 (1974).

In exploring the relationship between deductions and capital expenditures, this Court has noted the "familiar rule" that "an income tax deduction is a matter of legislative grace and that the burden of clearly showing the right to the claimed deduction is on the taxpayer." Interstate Transit Lines v. Commissioner, 319 U.S. 590, 593 (1943); Deputy v. Du Pont, 308 U.S. 488, 493 (1940); New Colonial Ice Co. v. Helvering, 292 U.S. 435, 440 (1934). The notion that deductions are exceptions to the norm of capitalization finds support in various aspects of the Code. Deductions are specifically enumerated and thus are subject to disallowance in favor of capitalization. See sections 161 and 261. Nondeductible capital expenditures, by contrast, are not exhaustively enumerated in the Code; rather than providing a "complete list of nondeductible expenditures," *Lincoln Savings,* 403 U.S., at 358, section 263 serves as a general means of distinguishing capital expenditures from current expenses. See Commissioner v. Idaho Power Co., 418 U.S., at 16. For these reasons, deductions are strictly construed and allowed only "as there is a clear provision therefor." New Colonial Ice Co. v. Helvering, 292 U.S., at 440; Deputy v. Du Pont, 308 U.S., at 493.

The Court also has examined the interrelationship between the Code's business expense and capital expenditure provisions. In so doing, it has had occasion to parse section 162(a) and explore certain of its requirements. For example, in *Lincoln Savings,* we determined that, to qualify for deduction under section 162(a), "an item must (1) be 'paid or incurred during the taxable year,' (2) be for 'carrying on any trade or business,' (3) be an 'expense,' (4) be a 'necessary' expense, and (5) be an 'ordinary' expense." 403 U.S., at 352. See also Commissioner v. Tellier, 383 U.S. 687, 689 (1966) (the term "necessary" imposes "only the minimal requirement that the expense be 'appropriate and helpful' for 'the development of the taxpayer's business,'" quoting Welch v. Helvering, 290 U.S. 111, 113 (1933)); Deputy v. Du Pont, 308 U.S. 488, 495 (1940) (to qualify as "ordinary," the expense must relate to a transaction "of common or frequent occurrence in the type of business involved"). The Court has recognized, however, that the "decisive distinctions" between current expenses and capital expenditures "are those of degree and not of kind," Welch v. Helvering, 290 U.S., at 114, and that because each case "turns on its special facts," Deputy v. Du Pont, 308 U.S., at 496, the cases sometimes appear difficult to harmonize. See Welch v. Helvering, 290 U.S., at 116.

National Starch contends that the decision in *Lincoln Savings* changed these familiar backdrops and announced an exclusive test for identifying capital expenditures, a test in which "creation or enhancement of an asset" is a prerequisite to capitalization, and deductibility under section

162(a) is the rule rather than the exception. We do not agree, for we conclude that National Starch has overread *Lincoln Savings*.

In *Lincoln Savings*, we were asked to decide whether certain premiums, required by federal statute to be paid by a savings and loan association to the Federal Savings and Loan Insurance Corporation (FSLIC), were ordinary and necessary expenses under section 162(a), as Lincoln Savings argued and the Court of Appeals had held, or capital expenditures under section 263, as the Commissioner contended. We found that the "additional" premiums, the purpose of which was to provide FSLIC with a secondary reserve fund in which each insured institution retained a pro rata interest recoverable in certain situations, "serve to create or enhance for Lincoln what is essentially a separate and distinct additional asset." 403 U.S., at 354. "As an inevitable consequence," we concluded, "the payment is capital in nature and not an expense, let alone an ordinary expense, deductible under section 162(a)." Ibid.

Lincoln Savings stands for the simple proposition that a taxpayer's expenditure that "serves to create or enhance . . . a separate and distinct" asset should be capitalized under section 263. It by no means follows, however, that *only* expenditures that create or enhance separate and distinct assets are to be capitalized under section 263. We had no occasion in *Lincoln Savings* to consider the tax treatment of expenditures that, unlike the additional premiums at issue there, did not create or enhance a specific asset, and thus the case cannot be read to preclude capitalization in other circumstances. In short, *Lincoln Savings* holds that the creation of a separate and distinct asset well may be a sufficient but not a necessary condition to classification as a capital expenditure. See General Bancshares Corp. v. Commissioner, 326 F.2d 712, 716 (C.A.8) (although expenditures may not "result in the acquisition or increase of a corporate asset, . . . these expenditures are not, because of that fact, deductible as ordinary and necessary business expenses"), cert. denied, 379 U.S. 832 (1964).

Nor does our statement in *Lincoln Savings*, 405 U.S., at 354, that "the presence of an ensuing benefit that may have some future aspect is not controlling" prohibit reliance on future benefit as a means of distinguishing an ordinary business expense from a capital expenditure. Although the mere presence of an incidental future benefit — "*some* future aspect" — may not warrant capitalization, a taxpayer's realization of benefits beyond the year in which the expenditure is incurred is undeniably important in determining whether the appropriate tax treatment is immediate deduction or capitalization. See United States v. Mississippi Chemical Corp., 405 U.S. 298, 310 (1972) (expense that "is of value in more than one taxable year" is a nondeductible capital expenditure); Central Texas Savings & Loan Assn. v. United States, 731 F.2d 1181, 1183 (C.A.5 1984) ("While the period of the benefits may not be controlling in all cases, it nonetheless remains a prominent, if not predominant, characteristic of a capital item."). Indeed, the text of the Code's capitalization provision,

section 263(a)(1), which refers to "permanent improvements or betterments," itself envisions an inquiry into the duration and extent of the
benefits realized by the taxpayer.

III

In applying the foregoing principles to the specific expenditures at issue
in this case, we conclude that National Starch has not demonstrated that
the investment banking, legal, and other costs it incurred in connection
with Unilever's acquisition of its shares are deductible as ordinary and
necessary business expenses under section 162(a).

Although petitioner attempts to dismiss the benefits that accrued to
National Starch from the Unilever acquisition as "entirely speculative" or
"merely incidental," the Tax Court's and the Court of Appeals' findings
that the transaction produced significant benefits to National Starch that
extended beyond the tax year in question are amply supported by the
record. For example, in commenting on the merger with Unilever, National Starch's 1978 "Progress Report" observed that the company would
"benefit greatly from the availability of Unilever's enormous resources,
especially in the area of basic technology." App. 43. See also id., at 46
(Unilever "provides new opportunities and resources"). Morgan Stanley's
report to the National Starch board concerning the fairness to shareholders of a possible business combination with Unilever noted that National
Starch management "feels that some synergy may exist with the Unilever
organization given a) the nature of the Unilever chemical, paper, plastics
and packaging operations . . . and b) the strong consumer products orien-
tation of Unilever United States, Inc." Id., at 77-78.

In addition to these anticipated resource-related benefits, National
Starch obtained benefits through its transformation from a publicly held,
freestanding corporation into a wholly owned subsidiary of Unilever. The
Court of Appeals noted that National Starch management viewed the transaction as "swapping approximately 3500 shareholders for one." 918 F.2d,
at 427; see also App. 223. Following Unilever's acquisition of National
Starch's outstanding shares, National Starch was no longer subject to what
even it terms the "substantial" shareholder-relations expenses a publicly
traded corporation incurs, including reporting and disclosure obligations,
proxy battles, and derivative suits. The acquisition also allowed National
Starch, in the interests of administrative convenience and simplicity, to
eliminate previously authorized but unissued shares of preferred and to
reduce the total number of authorized shares of common from 8,000,000
to 1,000. See 93 T.C., at 74.

Courts long have recognized that expenses such as these, " 'incurred
for the purpose of changing the corporate structure for the benefit of
future operations are not ordinary and necessary business expenses.' "

General Bancshares Corp. v. Commissioner, 326 F.2d, at 715 (quoting Farmers Union Corp. v. Commissioner, 300 F.2d 197, 200 (C.A.9), cert. denied, 371 U.S. 861 (1962)). See also B. Bittker & J. Eustice, Federal Income Taxation of Corporations and Shareholders, pp. 5-33 to 5-36 (5th ed. 1987) (describing "well-established rule" that expenses incurred in reorganizing or restructuring corporate entity are not deductible under section 162(a)). Deductions for professional expenses thus have been disallowed in a wide variety of cases concerning changes in corporate structure.[7] Although support for these decisions can be found in the specific terms of section 162(a), which require that deductible expenses be "ordinary and necessary" and incurred "in carrying on any trade or business," courts more frequently have characterized an expenditure as capital in nature because "the purpose for which the expenditure is made has to do with the corporation's operations and betterment, sometimes with a continuing capital asset, for the duration of its existence or for the indefinite future or for a time somewhat longer than the current taxable year." General Bancshares Corp. v. Commissioner, 326 F.2d, at 715. The rationale behind these decisions applies equally to the professional charges at issue in this case.

IV

The expenses that National Starch incurred in Unilever's friendly takeover do not qualify for deduction as "ordinary and necessary" business expenses under section 162(a). The fact that the expenditures do not create or enhance a separate and distinct additional asset is not controlling; the acquisition-related expenses bear the indicia of capital expenditures and are to be treated as such.

The judgment of the Court of Appeals is affirmed.

It is so ordered.

NOTES

1. *Form of the transaction.* This transaction was structured as a taxable reverse subsidiary (or triangular) merger. In some cases, a reverse subsid-

---

7. See, e.g., McCrory Corp. v. United States, 651 F.2d 828 (C.A.2 1981) (statutory merger under 26 U.S.C. section 368(a)(1)(A)); Bilar Tool & Die Corp. v. Commissioner, 530 F.2d 708 (C.A.6 1976) (division of corporation into two parts); E.I. du Pont de Nemours & Co. v. United States, 432 F.2d 1052 (C.A.3 1970) (creation of new subsidiary to hold assets of prior joint venture); General Bancshares Corp. v. Commissioner, 326 F.2d 712, 715 (C.A.8) (stock dividends), cert. denied, 379 U.S. 832 (1964); Mills Estate, Inc. v. Commissioner, 206 F.2d 244 (C.A.2 1953) (recapitalization).

iary merger can be tax free to the participants. See page 429 infra. If this had been a tax-free reverse subsidiary merger, the shareholders of National Starch would have exchanged their stock for stock in Holding while NSC Merger merged into National Starch. The result would be that former National Starch shareholders, along with Unilever, would own stock of Holding, which in turn would own National Starch. Shareholders owning 79 percent of the National Starch stock, however, apparently wanted cash rather than Holding stock. If the parties attempted a tax-free reverse subsidiary merger in which shareholders of 79 percent of the National Starch stock received cash, all the shareholders would be taxable, including those that exchanged 21 percent of the National Starch stock for Holding Stock.

To secure tax-free treatment for the 21 percent exchanging stock for stock, the parties agreed to a two-step transaction. First, Unilever and those National Starch shareholders desiring a stock-for-stock exchange formed Holding, with Unilever receiving voting common stock in exchange for the cash it transferred and National Starch shareholders receiving nonvoting preferred stock in exchange for their National Starch stock. This transaction qualified under §351, thereby providing nonrecognition for those National Starch shareholders making the exchange. Then, the remaining National Starch shareholders received cash for their stock as NSC Merger, Inc. merged into National Stock. This part of the transaction is treated as a redemption of the shareholders of National Starch. Rev. Rul. 78-250, 1978-1 C.B. 83. These shareholders were taxable on the difference between their adjusted bases in the National Starch stock and the cash received. Before undertaking this two-step transaction, the parties requested and received a private letter ruling from the Service. See Priv. Ltr. Rul. 7839060.

2. *Other friendly takeovers*. The result in *INDOPCO* does not necessarily mean that all expenses in friendly takeovers must be capitalized. The *INDOPCO* decision identified two categories of long-term benefits justifying capitalization rather than deductibility of acquisition expenses: (a) benefits generated by the resources of the acquiring company and (b) benefits obtained by a target by being a wholly owned subsidiary instead of a publicly held corporation (e.g., avoiding extensive reporting on disclosure requirements).

Certain types of acquisitions may not give rise to these types of long-term benefits. For example, in a leveraged buyout (LBO) by senior management of the target or outside purchasers, the acquiring group may form a new corporation that borrows the funds necessary to make the acquisition. Typically, repayment is made by the target corporation. In this type of leveraged acquisition, the acquiring corporation often has no resources that provide long-term benefits to the target. Moreover, the acquiring corporation often exchanges publicly traded, high-yield debentures for the existing stock of the target corporation. If so, then the target corporation may realize no future savings from reduced reporting requirements. Accordingly, expenses incurred by a target in this type of leveraged transaction may not create the future benefits that resulted in capitalization treatment under *INDOPCO*.

Even if a takeover results in capitalization of expenses under *INDOPCO*, in some cases a target may be able to eliminate the impact of capitalization by making a §338 election. See page 350 supra. Under the election, the capitalized expenditures should either be added to the basis of the assets sold or reduce the deemed sales price.

3. *Hostile takeovers*. Under *INDOPCO*, capitalization is required if long-term benefits are created by an expense. If the expenses are incurred primarily to protect rather than to acquire property, however, deductibility may be appropriate. For example, expenses incurred by a corporation to defend itself in a proxy contest are deductible. See, e.g., Rev. Rul. 67-1, 1967-1 C.B. 28. But see Treas. Regs. §1.212-1(k) (expenses to defend title to property must be capitalized). In other cases, corporate expenditures to defend the corporation were deductible. See, e.g., Dolese v. United States, 605 F.2d 1146 (10th Cir. 1979) (corporate expenses incurred in a divorce proceeding).

Costs associated with specific defensive strategies, such as negotiating with a "white knight," countertender offers, poison pill plans, and corporate charter amendments, on the other hand, are generally nondeductible capital expenditures if the plans are implemented. If the plans are abandoned, a loss deduction should be permitted under §165(a). See A.E. Staley Manufacturing Co. v. Commissioner, 119 F.3d 482 (7th Cir. 1997) (fees paid in an unsuccessful effort to defeat a hostile tender offer deductible as an abandonment loss). See also Rev. Rul. 73-580, 1973-2 C.B. 86.

4. *Loan fees*. Most acquisitions are financed with debt. For the purchaser, the cost of obtaining debt financing (such as fees for negotiating the loan and drafting loan documents and commitment fees) are amortized over the term of the loan. Rev. Rul. 70-359, 1970-2 C.B. 103; Rev. Rul. 70-360, 1970-2 C.B. 103. If borrowed funds are used to redeem the target's stock in a reverse subsidiary merger like the transaction in *INDOPCO*, the Service may attempt to deny a deduction or even an amortization of the loan fees. The Service bases its position on §162(k), which denies a deduction for any amount (except interest) incurred by a corporation in connection with the redemption of its stock. But see United States v. Kroy (Europe) Ltd., 27 F.3d 367 (9th Cir. 1994) (rejecting the Service's broad view of §162(k)); Fort Howard Corp. v. Commissioner, 107 T.C. 187 (1996) (loan fee deduction allowed under revisions to §162(k)(2)).

5. *Organizational expenses*. The costs of organizing a new corporation as part of an acquisition can be amortized over a period of 60 months from the month in which the corporation begins business. §248.

E. CORPORATE ACQUISITIONS AND THE USE OF DEBT

Joint Committee on Taxation, Federal Income Tax Aspects of Corporate Financial Structures _____
101st Cong., 1st Sess. (Jan. 18, 1989)

III. EXAMPLES OF TRANSACTIONS THAT INCREASE DEBT OR REDUCE EQUITY, AND TAX CONSEQUENCES

There are various transactions which can increase the debt of a corporation or reduce its equity. The discussion below describes broad categories of these transactions and uses examples to illustrate their tax consequences. The examples assume that no restrictions on interest deductions or other tax benefits stemming from interest expenses apply. In many cases, however, such limitations are applicable. . . .

Although there are significant tax reasons which may lead a corporation to engage in these transactions, such transactions may also be motivated by reasons apart from Federal income tax considerations. For example, such transactions may be undertaken to increase the value of a corporation's stock, to enhance earnings per share calculations, to concentrate common stock holdings, to create treasury stock, as a defensive maneuver to ward off a takeover, or for other reasons. . . .

C. ACQUISITIONS INCLUDING LEVERAGED BUYOUTS

The acquisition of one corporation by another corporation may be structured in many different ways. An acquiring corporation may acquire control of the "target" corporation or it may acquire a small interest in the stock of another corporation as an investment. The acquiring corporation may finance the acquisition with debt (either by a new borrowing of the necessary funds or by keeping an old borrowing outstanding), or with its own retained earnings, or with funds contributed as new equity capital by investors.

An acquisition of the control of a target company may be a hostile or friendly transaction. It may be structured as an acquisition of the stock of the target company or an acquisition of the assets of the target company. The target company may continue to operate as an independent company in the same manner as before it was acquired, or it may be absorbed into the acquiring company or other companies owned by the acquiring company, or it may cease operations entirely and its assets be divided and sold.

1. Stock Acquisitions out of Retained Earnings

A corporation may finance the acquisition of the stock of another corporation with internally generated funds (i.e., its retained earnings). The purchase of the stock has no tax consequences to the shareholders of the purchasing corporation. Likewise, there are no tax consequences to the acquired corporation as a result of the acquisition. The taxable shareholders of the acquired corporation recognize any gain or loss on the sale of their shares.

There are generally no immediate tax consequences to the purchasing corporation as a result of the transaction. However, the total amount of funds in corporate solution, the earnings of which are subject to a corporate-level tax, may be reduced by the amount spent for the acquisition to the extent that shares are acquired by the acquiring corporation from noncorporate shareholders. Moreover, no compensating additional corporate tax may arise when earnings of the acquired corporation are distributed to the acquiring corporation. This is because earnings of the target company which are distributed to the acquiring corporation as dividends will either be nontaxable under the consolidated return rules, or, if the corporations do not file a consolidated return, will be eligible for the dividends received deduction.

2. Debt-financed Stock Acquisitions Including Leveraged Buyouts

A corporation may finance the acquisition of another corporation's stock by borrowing. The acquiring corporation may borrow using its own assets as security for the loan or it may borrow using the assets of the target company as security for the loan. In either case, debt has been substituted for equity at the corporate level. When the debt is secured by the acquired corporation's assets, the transaction is more likely to be called a "leveraged buyout."

Description

A leveraged buyout refers to a particular type of debt-financed acquisition of a "target" corporation. The purchasers borrow most of the purchase price of the target company, using the assets of the target company as security for the loan. After the acquisition, the target corporation may be able to service the debt obligation out of its cash flow from operations or the purchaser may sell the assets of the target company and use the proceeds to retire the debt.

A leveraged buyout may occur in many different contexts and may be used by many different types of purchasers. The leveraged buyout, also sometimes called a bootstrap acquisition, has long been used to acquire private (i.e., closely held) corporations. More recently, leveraged buyouts have been used to acquire large public companies. A public company may be "taken private" through a leveraged buyout if the purchasers of the target public corporation are a relatively small group of investors. If the purchasers of the target corporation in a leveraged buyout include the current management of the target company, the transaction is sometimes called a "management buyout." A division or a subsidiary of a company also may be purchased through a leveraged buyout.

A leveraged buyout of a target company is usually accomplished by a debt-financed tender offer by the existing corporation for its outstanding publicly held stock, or, alternatively, by a tender offer for the target corporation's stock by a largely debt-financed shell corporation established for this purpose. The target corporation will repurchase its stock from its shareholders or the shell corporation will buy all the stock of the target corporation.[76] If a shell corporation is used, the target corporation and the shell corporation will typically merge immediately after the acquisition.

As mentioned above, most of the funds for a leveraged buyout transaction are borrowed, with the purchasers contributing only a small amount of their own funds as equity. Lenders for these transactions have been banks, investment banks, insurance companies, pension funds, and pools of investors. Debt terms reflect the degree of leverage and the loan security involved. Some of the debt incurred frequently is below investment grade, i.e., so-called "junk" bonds.

Tax Consequences

A leveraged buyout is generally a taxable transaction with respect to the shareholders of the target corporation.[77] Taxable shareholders selling their stock recognize gain or loss on the sale of their shares.[78] There are no immediate tax consequences of a leveraged buyout at the corporate level since generally neither the repurchase by the target corporation of its own shares nor the purchase of the target corporation's shares by a shell corporation followed by the merger of the target and shell corporation is a taxable transaction.

The primary tax consequences of a leveraged buyout to the target corporation arise from the fact that the equity of the corporation has been replaced by debt. Income of the target corporation once paid to investors as nondeductible dividends on stock is instead paid to creditors as tax-deductible interest on debt. As a result of the interest deductions generated by the borrowing in a leveraged buyout, the target corporation may have little, if any, taxable income in the years following a leveraged buyout and

76. Shareholders of the target company typically receive a premium for their stock above the price at which the stock has been trading on the market.

77. Of course, there will be no tax imposed on those shareholders that are not subject to U.S. income tax on their income, i.e., certain foreign investors and tax-exempt investors such as pension funds.

78. Taxable shareholders will generally recognize gain (i.e., the excess of the amount received over their basis in the stock) because acquirors typically pay a substantial premium for stock in a leveraged buyout transaction.

may claim loss carrybacks producing a refund of taxes paid prior to the acquisition. Because the target corporation pays little, if any, of its operating income as Federal income taxes, the portion of the target corporation's income that was once being paid to the Federal government as Federal income taxes may instead be redirected to increase investor returns. However, to the extent increased investor returns are paid to taxable shareholders or holders of debt, there may be an increase in investor-level Federal income taxes paid.

Example III-C

[Company M, with 99,000 shares of stock outstanding and no debt, has $1.5 million annual income. M's federal income tax is $510,000 ($1.5 million × .34), leaving $990,000 of after-tax income, or earnings of $10 per share. M's stock trades at $80 per share (or 8 × earnings per share).] Company M is acquired in a leveraged buyout. The acquirors pay $120 per share of stock, or 50 percent more than the price at which the stock has been trading on the market, for a total price of $11.88 million. Taxable selling shareholders recognize gain or loss on the sale of their shares.

The acquirors put up $880,000 of their own funds and raise the remaining $11 million of the purchase price by issuing notes paying 12 percent interest to be secured by the assets of Company M. The annual income of Company M after the leveraged buyout is unchanged.

The distribution of the operating income of Company M before and after the leveraged buyout is as follows:

	Before	After
Company M shareholders	$990,000	$0
Bondholders	0	1,320,000
Acquirors	0	118,800
Corporate income taxes	510,000	61,200
Total operating income	1,500,000	1,500,000

The leveraged buyout has redistributed the income stream of Company M. [T]he acquirors of Company M, rather than all the shareholders (in the case of a distribution with respect to stock) or the continuing shareholders of Company M (in the case of a stock redemption) receive the profit of $118,800. Company M shareholders who before the transaction received $990,000 a year in dividends now receive no distributions. New bondholders receive interest of 12 percent on $11 million, or $1.32 million. This is one third more than the entire amount of Company M's after-tax income before the leveraged buyout, even though the operating income of Company M is the same before and after the leveraged buyout.

The taxable income of Company M has, however, been reduced from $1.5 million to $180,000 ($1.5 million minus $1.32 million) because most of the income of the company is paid out to investors as interest rather than dividends. Federal income taxes are thereby reduced from $510,000 to $61,200. Acquirors make an after-tax profit of $118,800 (pre-tax profit of $180,000 reduced by Federal income tax of $61,200), a 13.4 percent return on their $880,000 equity investment. The income tax reduction of $448,800 exactly pays for the increased returns to investors (bondholders and the acquirors) as a result of the leveraged buyout. Depending on whether the increased investor returns are paid to taxable shareholders or holders of debt, there may be an increase in investor-level Federal income taxes paid.*

Actual Transactions

Leveraged buyouts of public companies have greatly increased in recent years, and the amounts involved in such transactions have risen dramatically. The largest leveraged buyout transaction to date is the proposed acquisition of RJR Nabisco by the investment firm of Kohlberg Kravis Roberts & Co. ("KKR") for nearly $25 billion. It is expected that this acquisition will be completed by February 1989. Other large leveraged buyout transactions include the acquisition of Beatrice Companies by KKR for $6.25 billion in April 1986, and the management buyout of R.H. Macy & Co., Inc. for $3.5 billion in July 1986.

Newspaper reports indicate that out of the approximately $25 billion needed for the RJR Nabisco acquisition, more than $22.5 billion will be borrowed. Secured bank debt will account for approximately $17.5 billion of the borrowing, with most of the remainder being provided by investment banking firms. A pool of investors organized by KKR will put up $1.5 billion as an equity investment. It has been reported that KKR will contribute approximately $15 million of its own funds as equity. RJR Nabisco shareholders will be paid $109 for each share of common stock. This is almost twice the price at which the stock was trading immediately prior to the

---

* The engine that drives this example is the assumption that the Company M stock initially sells for $80 per share and can be redeemed for $120 per share. Is this a realistic assumption? The example assumes that M's pretax borrowing cost is 12 percent; presumably its rate of return on investment would be higher than 12 percent. Even assuming that the rate of return on investment is 12 percent, M's assets should be worth $12,500,000 ($1,500,000/.12) to produce the assumed annual pretax profit of $1,500,000. Yet the market seems to value the corporation at only $7,920,000 (99,000 shares × $80 per share).

Why might the market value of M be so much below its asset value? There may be a host of reasons. Perhaps the expected cost of a corporate-level tax is one reason. Also, stock may be undervalued because of information failure in the marketplace, or perhaps the assets are not efficiently deployed and transactions costs prevent a more efficient deployment. In any case, the example not surprisingly shows that if you can borrow at 12 percent to purchase an investment (i.e., M stock) that provides a return of almost 19 percent ($1,500,000 income/ (99,000 shares × $80 per share)), it's a good deal.

Notice that in this example the government receives less in taxes when debt is used. The example assumes that the benefits of this tax reduction are shared by the shareholders and the debt holders. As noted at page 331 supra, however, the reduction in taxes might also inure to employees, suppliers, customers, etc. Regardless of who benefits from the tax reduction, tax liability is lowered through the use of debt. — EDS.

announcement of the possible sale of the company. It has been reported that due to increased interest deductions, RJR Nabisco could save up to $682 million annually in Federal and state income taxes and be able to seek the refund of additional amounts of taxes paid in prior years due to the carryback of net operating losses. Other reports have projected the annual savings at $370 million.

In the Beatrice transaction, each common shareholder received $50 per share ($40 in cash). This price of $50 per share was 45 percent higher than the market value of the stock one month prior to the announcement date of the first offer. Financing for the Beatrice leveraged buyout included $6.5 billion in debt and $1.35 billion in equity capital. Four billion dollars of the debt was lent by banks and $2.5 billion came from a new issue of high yield bonds. The equity came from two sources. Six hundred million came from a buyout fund organized by KKR and subscribed to by institutional investors and $750 million came from converting existing common stock to a new issue of preferred stock.

In the Macy transaction, each common share of stock outstanding received $68 in cash. This price of $68 per share was 55 percent higher than the market value of the stock one month prior to the announcement date of the first offer. On completion of the Macy leveraged buyout, the management group held 20 percent of the new company stock and an additional 20 percent was held by General Electric Co.'s credit union. Financing for the Macy leveraged buyout totalled approximately $3.7 billion. Out of this amount, almost $3.2 billion was debt: $770 million was lent from banks, $1.625 billion came from new issues of high yield bonds, and $800 million came from notes secured by mortgages. The remaining $500 million of the financing consisted of $200 million of excess cash of Macy's and $300 million was equity capital contributed by the acquirors.

D. ROLE OF OVERFUNDED PENSION PLANS AND ESOPS IN LEVERAGED BUYOUTS

1. Overfunded Pension Plans

In the case of a leveraged buyout, the assets in the overfunded pension plan of the target company may represent a source of capital to help finance the acquisition. An overfunded pension plan represents a pool of assets that may make a company a target for a takeover. Conversely, this pool of assets may be used by the company to ward off a hostile takeover. In recent years, some companies with significantly overfunded pension plans have been acquired by other companies. After the acquisition, the acquiring company terminated the overfunded pension plan and used the excess assets partially to finance the takeover. An overfunded plan represents an attractive source of cash even if the value of the assets are included in the purchase price.

Another possibility is that a company will itself terminate an overfunded pension plan to assist its efforts to thwart a hostile takeover attempt.

Consider the following example:

Example III-D

Corporation K is a widely held public corporation. K maintains a qualified defined benefit pension plan for the exclusive benefit of its employees. The trust is currently overfunded by approximately $100 million on a termination basis. That is, if the trust is terminated, its assets would exceed the present value of the benefits accrued under the plan by K employees up to the date of plan termination. LBO Fund (L) wants to acquire K.

Under almost any form of acquisition, L, subject to some limitations, could cause K to terminate its pension plan. The termination would enable L, directly or indirectly, to obtain the $100 million. It could be used to assist L in paying for the acquisition, for general corporate purposes, or for any other purpose. While the $100 million would be included in the gross income of K upon termination of the plan, any net operating losses and loss carryovers of K could be used to offset that income. A nondeductible 15 percent excise tax would also apply to the reversion.

If K's current management wanted to prevent an acquisition, it might terminate the plan itself and make use of the proceeds. K might be a less attractive takeover candidate in that event, for it would not have $100 million in readily available cash as an inducement to a potential acquiror.

This utilization of excess pension assets is not peculiar to a leveraged buyout, but is potentially available in any takeover or merger transaction. In addition, any pool of liquid assets, not just excess pension assets, would be attractive to potential acquirors.

2. Employee Stock Ownership Plans (ESOPs)

A leveraged ESOP can be used by an employer as a technique of finance to obtain funds for working capital or plant expansion, or as a means of financing a leveraged buyout. Use of this financing technique can result in a lower cost of borrowing than would be available if conventional debt or equity financing were used. In a typical transaction, the employer enters into a contract with the ESOP to sell the ESOP a specified number of shares of its stock. The ESOP borrows the funds needed to purchase the shares from a bank or other lender and pays them to the employer in exchange for the stock. In subsequent years, the employer makes tax-deductible cash contributions to the ESOP in the amount necessary to amortize the loan principal and interest payments thereon.

A leveraged ESOP may be used not only to provide the company with working capital but also to finance an acquisition of the stock or assets of another corporation. In a typical case, a leveraged ESOP maintained by the acquiring corporation or its subsidiary borrows funds in an amount equal to the amount needed to acquire the target corporation. The proceeds of the loan are used to purchase employer securities from the employer. The employer (or the subsidiary) then uses the proceeds of the sale to purchase the stock or assets of the target company.

One variation of this leveraged-ESOP financing technique is for the employer to purchase target stock, either directly or through a subsidiary, using funds borrowed from a financial institution or other lender. Once the acquisition has been completed, the newly acquired subsidiary establishes a leveraged ESOP. The ESOP borrows money and purchases stock in the subsidiary from the subsidiary (or from the acquiring corporation). The acquiring corporation then uses the proceeds of this sale to pay off the original acquisition loan. The subsidiary makes annual, deductible contributions sufficient to amortize the ESOP loan and pay interest.

Recently, leveraged ESOPs have been used in some situations to thwart hostile corporate takeover attempts. Leveraged ESOPs have also been used to accomplish leveraged buyouts by persons desiring to take the company private.

The establishment of an employee stock ownership plan (ESOP) may reduce the costs of financing a leveraged buyout, as evidenced by the following example.

Example III-E

Partnership *R* purchases Target Company *X* for $3.0 billion, financed by $2.4 billion of debt and $600 million of equity capital. As part of the buyout agreement, *X* establishes an ESOP for its employees. *X* borrows $250 million from a commercial lender and secures the loan by mortgages and asset pledges. *X* then lends $250 million to the ESOP on substantially the same terms as the terms of *X*'s loan from the commercial lender. The ESOP uses the loan proceeds to purchase $250 million of *X*'s stock.

The ESOP pays off the loan with contributions made by *X* in subsequent years. Such contributions will equal the annual principal and interest payments required by the ESOP on the loan from *X*. As the ESOP makes such loan payments, *X* uses the payments to satisfy its repayment requirements to the commercial lender.

Under present law, the contributions of *X* to the ESOP, which equal the principal and interest payments on *X*'s loan to the ESOP, generally are deductible under the rules governing deductions for contributions to qualified pension plans. Consequently, if an ESOP is established by *X*, *X* may deduct both the principal and interest payments on its loan. This result can be illustrated by comparing the following 2 cases:

Case 1. — *X* borrows $250 million from lender *A*. Only the interest on *X*'s payments to *A* are deductible.

Case 2. — *X* establishes an ESOP, which borrows $250 million from lender *A* and uses the proceeds to purchase capital stock from *X*. *X*'s payments to the ESOP equal the principal and interest payments on the ESOP's loan from A. X's payments are fully deductible.

In case 2, X has, in effect, borrowed $250 million from a lender and gets the benefit of a full deduction for its loan repayments. A further advantage of the use of an ESOP in the buyout of X is the special interest exclusion allowed under present law (sec. 133). The commercial lender who loans $250 million to X is entitled to exclude from gross income 50 percent of the interest it receives on the loan. Typically, this tax benefit is passed on partially to the borrower in the form of a reduced cost of borrowing (i.e., rest rate on the loan).

A potential disadvantage of the use of an ESOP in this case is that the employees of X will receive an equity interest in X. As the ESOP loan is repaid, the stock of X purchased by the ESOP will be allocated to the accounts of the ESOP participants. Thus, the ownership of the shares acquired through the ESOP ultimately will be transferred to the ESOP participants. The advantages of using the ESOP to finance a leveraged buyout or other transaction may not outweigh the disadvantage of transferring equity interests to employees.

Actual Transactions

Leveraged ESOPs have been used in a variety of corporate financing transactions. For example, the Procter and Gamble Company plans to add $1 billion (financed by debt) to its existing ESOP (thereby giving the ESOP a 20-percent interest in the company's common stock) in a transaction designed to provide substantial tax benefits and to offer a shield against a threat of hostile takeover. Similarly, the recent establishment of the J. C. Penney Company ESOP is widely viewed as an effort to deter a hostile takeover.

Leveraged ESOPs have also been used to accomplish leveraged buyouts by persons desiring to take a company private. The leveraged ESOP of Parsons Corporation accomplished such a result.

IV. POLICY ISSUES . . .

C. RISKS OF EXCESSIVE CORPORATE DEBT

1. Implication of Excessive Debt for Financial Stability and Economic Growth

Overview

Increased corporate indebtedness potentially has significant implications for the financial health of investors and issuers of the debt as well as for the economy as a whole. Corporate issuers with increased indebtedness must devote larger proportions of earnings and cash flow to interest payments. If leverage ratios are high, and if sales decline or expenses increase, firms may be forced to sell assets, reduce wage costs, or reduce capital and research expenditures. If such actions are insufficient to restore liquidity, debt restructuring or bankruptcy can result. Furthermore, losses incurred by investors holding the corporate debt of troubled firms could adversely affect their own balance sheets. If bankruptcies and debt restructurings are greater than expected, the negative effects could extend beyond distressed lenders and borrowers and reduce employment, income and growth in the economy as a whole. However, increased corporate indebtedness and even increased risk are not necessarily adverse developments, and there is by no means consensus among experts about the significance of increased debt. Some consider it an impending crisis; others consider it to be just one more aspect of financial innovation; yet others consider it as ultimately improving economic efficiency.

NOTES

1. *Acquisition indebtedness.* In the late 1960s, Congress expressed concern over acquisition activity that involved the use of various types of debt instruments, often convertible into common stock of the acquiring corporation. To discourage the use of debt in such acquisitions, Congress enacted §279, which disallows an interest deduction to an acquiring corporation on specified "corporate acquisition indebtedness." Essentially, "corporate acquisition indebtedness" is a debt obligation issued by an acquiring corporation to acquire a specified amount of stock or assets (i.e., two-thirds of the value of the trade or business assets) of another corporation if the following conditions are met:

1. the obligation is subordinated to trade creditors or unsecured creditors;
2. the obligation is convertible into stock of the issuing corporation;
3. the ratio of debt to equity exceeds 2:1 or the projected earnings of the acquiring corporation (or in some cases the combined corporations) does not exceed three times the interest paid or incurred with respect to the obligation.

If an acquiring corporation can avoid any one of these requirements, then §279 does not apply. For example, if the debt is not subordinated to trade creditors, §279 does not apply. If all three requirements are satisfied, then §279 denies an interest deduction in excess of $5 million paid on such corporate acquisition indebtedness. Accordingly, at a 7 percent interest rate, a corporation could have more than $70 million of debt outstanding without triggering §279.

2. *High-yield discount obligations.* In the aftermath of the stock market plunge of 1987, Congress acted again to curb the perceived misuse of corporate debt to fund major acquisitions, although its actions have a narrow scope. An interest deduction may be denied to issuers of any "applicable high-yield discount obligation." This type of obligation typically has an issue price that is significantly lower than the redemption price. The spread between the issue price and the redemption price is original issue discount (OID). Normally, an issuer of an OID bond accrues and deducts (and the lender includes) the spread over the life of the bond even though payment is not made until maturity. §§1272-1273. A related instrument is the "payment in kind" (PIK) bond, in which instrument payments are in the form of other debt or stock of the issuer rather than cash. Both the high-yield and PIK bonds are attractive to issuers in providing deductions before any cash outlay is required.

Section 163(e)(5) divides the OID amount on these bonds between an interest portion that is deductible only when paid and a disqualified portion for which no deduction is allowed but which may qualify for a dividends received deduction for a corporate lender. This approach is a compromise between treating the instrument as equity (i.e., periodic payments would not be deductible) and treating it as debt. An "applicable high-yield discount obligation" is defined as an instrument with: (a) a maturity date of more than five years, (b) a yield to maturity that is at least 5 percentage points more than a designated federal rate, and (c) "significant original issue discount." §163(i).

3. *Debt-financed net operating losses.* Another focus of Congress in 1989 was the use of tax refunds to finance leveraged buyouts. These tax refunds were generated by the acquiring corporation's current net operating losses (NOLs) being carried back for three taxable years, thereby enabling the acquiring corporation to obtain a tax refund for those years. §172. In debt-financed acquisitions, often the interest deductions generated the NOL that resulted in a tax refund. Congress determined that interest incurred in a takeover was not sufficient to justify an NOL carryback.

Section 172(h) limits the carryback of NOLs if the losses are created by interest deductions attributable to a "corporate equity reduction transaction" (CERT). A CERT is either a "major stock acquisition" or an "excess distribution." A "major stock acquisition" is a planned acquisition by a corporation of 50 percent or more of the voting power or value of stock in another corporation. §172(h)(3)(B). An "excess distribution" is an unusually large distribution relative to the distributing corporation's distribution history or net worth. §172(h)(3)(C).

If the CERT limitation applies, interest attributable to the CERT (which may occur as much as two years after the year in which the CERT occurs) cannot be carried back to a year before the CERT. A de minimis rule provides that the limitation applies only if the interest expense in question exceeds $1 million. §172(h)(2)(D).

4. *Integration*. The limited statutory provisions discussed above may have the effect of limiting the use of debt in acquisition activity in some specific cases, but even taken together the attempts are uneven and certainly are complicated. A more general and principled approach to the debt-equity problem may be the integration of corporate and individual income taxes. Under some integration proposals, the tax differences between debt and equity would be either eliminated or lessened, thereby substantially removing tax incentives for debt-financed acquisitions.

For a discussion of integration, see Chapter 8.

10

Acquisitive Reorganizations

A. INTRODUCTION

In its broadest sense, a corporate reorganization can mean any rearrangement of corporate activity, including the division of a single corporation into two or more entities, the combination of two or more corporations into a single entity, and the continuation of a corporation's business by new shareholders. Sales of corporate shares and sales of corporate assets are thus "reorganizations" in this broad sense.

Consider the following example of an acquisitive corporate reorganization. Acquiring Corp. seeks to obtain the business assets of Target Corp. To this end, Acquiring purchases the productive assets of Target, paying with cash, Acquiring stock and securities, or some combination. Target then distributes the consideration received from Acquiring, along with its remaining assets, if any, to its shareholders in exchange for their shares of Target.

In the absence of any special taxing provisions, this transaction will be taxable at both the corporate and shareholder levels. First, Target Corp. will recognize gain or loss on the assets it sells to Acquiring Corp. as well as on the assets it does not sell but instead distributes as part of its liquidating distribution. See §§1001, 336. Second, the Target shareholders will recognize gain or loss on the exchange of their shares for the distributed assets to the extent the adjusted basis in their shares differs from the fair market value of the assets they receive. §331.

One might question whether one or both levels of taxation is appropriate. For example, suppose the consideration used by Acquiring Corp. consisted exclusively of its own common stock so that, in the liquidating distribution of Target Corp., the Target shareholders exchanged their shares of Target for shares of Acquiring. While this exchange works a change in the form of the shareholders' investment, it may have little real impact on the substance of their investment: They continue to own stock of a corporation conducting the business formerly conducted by Target.

In section 368(a), Congress has defined a set of reorganization patterns by which taxation at one or both levels can be avoided. Congress has in many sections shown its willingness to allow businesses to undergo a change in form without the imposition of tax. Section 351, for example, permits the tax-free incorporation of assets, and §721 performs a similar role in the formation of partnerships. The reorganization provisions reflect a similar congressional attitude in the context of corporate combinations and divisions. In this chapter we will look only at the provisions associated with combining two or more corporations — that is, we will examine the acquisitive reorganization provisions.

As you will soon discover, these reorganization provisions are exceedingly complex. Much of this complexity is a result of the conflicting congressional desires to (1) permit a mere change in the form of a corporate enterprise to be effected without immediate taxation while (2) not allowing the sale of a business to escape taxation simply because the business is incorporated. Although Congress and the courts have sought to develop reasonable criteria that distinguish nontaxable corporate reorganizations from taxable sales of corporate enterprises, the current statutory and judicial framework often seems to exalt form (and early tax advice) over substance.

Section 368(a) merely defines what constitutes a reorganization; the tax consequences following from these definitions are found elsewhere. For shareholders, the cornerstone of reorganization taxation is §354(a)(1). To obtain nonrecognition under §354(a)(1), a shareholder must exchange "stock or securities" for "stock or securities," the exchange must be "in pursuance of a plan of reorganization," and both the transferred and the received stock and securities must be "in a corporation a party to a reorganization."

As you know, stock represents an equity interest in a corporation, and a security is a debt interest. But not all corporate debt interests qualify as "securities" under §354(a)(1), and Congress has failed to define this important term. Transactions that constitute "reorganizations" are defined with specificity in §368(a), and a "party" to a reorganization is defined in §368(b). Congressional attention to these issues has not, unfortunately, minimized litigation over such crucial definitions, and the resulting judicial gloss on the statutory provisions has proved substantial.

Before turning to the cases, it is worthwhile to explore the statutory terrain. The principal definition of a "reorganization" is in §368(a)(1), and the various different forms of reorganizations described in that subsection are usually referred to without the preface "§368(a)(1)." Thus, we have A reorganizations (statutory mergers and consolidations), B reorganizations, and all types down to G reorganizations. The acquisitive reorganizations include the types A through D (although not all Ds are acquisitive reorganizations, as we shall see), and they are discussed in this section.

The A reorganization is a "statutory merger or consolidation." In a merger, one corporation (usually called the "acquiring" or "surviving" corporation) acquires all the assets of another corporation (usually called the "target" corporation), and all outstanding target shares are canceled, with the former target shareholders receiving some form of consideration usually including some combination of cash, stock, and debt of the acquiring corporation, and stock and debt of companies related to the acquiring corporation. Thus, if Target Corp. merges into Acquiring Corp., Target will disappear and Acquiring will end up with the assets of Target.

In a consolidation, two corporations join together to form a new, third corporation. Thus, X Corp. and Y Corp. might consolidate into Z Corp., with Z owning the combined assets of X and Y. All stock of X and Y will be canceled, and the former X and Y shareholders will receive consideration usually including some combination of cash, stock, and debt of Z.

Note that an A reorganization is a *statutory* merger or consolidation. The requirement that a merger or consolidation be "statutory" means that the transaction must satisfy some state or federal merger or consolidation statute. Typically, such a statute requires consent by the shareholders of the corporations involved in the transaction and imposes various procedural requirements to ensure that all affected parties (often including workers) are adequately apprised of the event. The nontax aspects of state or federal merger statutes are irrelevant to the tax consequences of the transaction except that the parties must comply with relevant nontax law to fall within the ambit of §368(a)(1)(A). It is worth mentioning now that not all statutory mergers and consolidations qualify as A reorganizations: The courts have felt free to add additional requirements beyond those imposed by the language of §368(a)(1)(A).

The C reorganization is sometimes called the "de facto merger provision" because a C reorganization accomplishes the same effect as an A reorganization without necessarily satisfying any nontax state or federal merger statute. In a C reorganization, the acquiring corporation acquires "substantially all" the assets of the target corporation and then the target corporation liquidates, distributing any of its assets not transferred to the acquiring corporation as well as whatever consideration was paid by the acquiring corporation for the target's assets. If the acquiring corporation uses its own stock as payment, then the former target shareholders will become shareholders of the acquiring corporation. Depending on the relative values of the acquiring and target corporations, the former target shareholders may end up with an insignificant percentage ownership interest in the acquiring corporation (as when a conglomerate swallows up a mom-and-pop grocery store) or a much more substantial interest in the acquiring corporation (when the acquiring corporation and the target corporation are of approximately equal value).

A B reorganization is very different from the A and C reorganizations. In a B reorganization, the acquiring corporation obtains at least 80 percent of the stock of the target corporation so that the target corporation ends up as a subsidiary of the acquiring corporation. One interesting aspect of the B reorganization is that it involves no corporate-level tax, even in the absence of special taxing provisions, because the corporate assets do not change hands. Thus, the effect of qualifying a transaction as a B reorganization is to allow the former shareholders of the target corporation to avoid recognition of gain (and of loss, although that is no advantage) on the sale of their shares to the acquiring corporation.

Section 368(a)(2) contains several provisions expanding the basic reorganization definitions to allow the use of parent-subsidiary combinations in place of a single corporate enterprise. In addition, and for reasons understood only by reference to the history of the reorganization provisions, part of the definition of a C reorganization is found in §368(a)(2). Section 368(b) defines the term "party to a reorganization," and as provisions have been added to §368(a)(2) that expand the use of parent- subsidiary pairs, so too has §368(b) been amended to expand the concept of a party to the reorganization.

Recall that §368 is a *definitional* section: It contains no provision specifying the taxation of parties to a reorganization. In Chapter 2 you were introduced to §354, the basic shareholder-level taxing provision. Section 356 addresses the shareholder taxation of boot (and §357 specifies the circumstances in which the assumption of a liability is treated as nonqualifying property), while §361 plays both roles at the corporate level. The associated basis rules are in §358 (for shareholders) and §§361 to 362 (for the corporate parties to the reorganization). As with most nonrecognition provisions in the Code, the deferral of gain or loss results in the taxpayer's retaining the adjusted basis of the property given up for the new property.

Although the requirements of the various types of statutory reorganizations differ, and certain transactions may fall under more than one type, several theories and factors are common to all reorganizations. Tax-free treatment is based on a *continuity of proprietary interest* principle: the structure of the acquisition must be such that it is fair to describe the shareholders of the target corporation as having a continuing, entrepreneurial interest in the combined venture. In most of the reorganization forms, continuity of proprietary interest is mandated by statute. The A reorganization, though, has no explicit statutory requirements beyond the "statutory merger or consolidation" language. Early on, the Supreme Court determined that transactions lacking a continuity of proprietary interest on the part of the target shareholders should be denied tax-free reorganization treatment despite satisfying all the requirements of a state or federal merger statute.

Kass v. Commissioner _____

60 T.C. 218 (1973), aff'd without opinion, 491 F.2d 749 (3d Cir. 1974)

DAWSON, Judge. . . .

The only issue for decision is whether petitioner, a minority share-holder of an 84-percent-owned subsidiary, must recognize gain upon the receipt of the parent's stock pursuant to a statutory merger of the subsid-iary into the parent. . . .

For a period greater than 6 months prior to 1965, petitioner had owned 2,000 shares of common stock of Atlantic City Racing Association (herein called ACRA). . . .

ACRA was a New Jersey corporation which was formed in 1943 and which was engaged in the business of operating a racetrack. Its total author-ized and outstanding stock consisted of 506,000 shares of common stock. It has approximately 500 stockholders. Track Associates, Inc. (herein called TRACK), is a New Jersey corporation which was formed on November 19, 1965. The total authorized capital stock of TRACK consisted of 500,000 shares of common stock. Its original capitalization consisted of 202,577 shares. Over 50 percent of the original issue was acquired by the Levy family and 8 percent was acquired by the Casey family. The remaining stock went to 18 other individuals. The Levys and the Caseys were also minority shareholders (whether computed separately or as a group) in ACRA. Their purpose in forming TRACK was to gain control over ACRA's racetrack business. They wanted to do away with ACRA's cumbersome capital structure and institute a new corporate policy with regard to capital improvements and higher purses for the races. Control was to be gained by establishing TRACK and then by (1) having TRACK purchase at least 80 percent of the stock of ACRA and (2) subsequently merging ACRA into TRACK.

The Levys acquired 48,300 shares of TRACK stock (out of the total original capitalization of 202,577 shares) in exchange for stock of ACRA. The Caseys acquired 3,450 shares in exchange for their ACRA stock. To-gether the Levys and Caseys purchased an additional 70,823 shares of TRACK stock as part of the original capitalization.

On December 1, 1965, TRACK offered to purchase the stock of ACRA at $22 per share, subject to the condition that at least 405,000 shares (slightly more than 80 percent of ACRA's outstanding shares) be tendered. As a result of this tender offer, which terminated on February 11, 1966, 424,764 shares of ACRA stock were received and paid for by TRACK. A total of 29,486 shares of ACRA stock were not tendered.

The board of directors of TRACK approved a plan of liquidation providing for the liquidation of ACRA by way of merger into TRACK. . . . At a special meeting of the shareholders of ACRA held on March 8, 1966, the aforementioned plan of liquidation and joint agreement were adopted. A copy of the notice of the meeting was sent to the petitioner, and it notified petitioner of the rights of a dissenting stockholder under New Jersey corporate law.

The merger having taken place, the remaining shares of ACRA that were not sold pursuant to the tender offer or the dissenting shareholder provisions were exchanged for TRACK stock, 1 for 1. The petitioner exchanged 2,000 shares of ACRA stock, with a fair market value at the time of $22 per share, for 2,000 shares of TRACK stock. She did not report any capital gain in connection with this transaction.

Petitioner contends that the merger of ACRA into TRACK, although treated at least in part as a liquidation at the corporate level, is at her level, the shareholder level, (1) a true statutory merger and (2) a section 368(a)(1)(A) reorganization, occasioning no recognition of gain on the ensuing exchange. . . . Respondent, on the other hand, argues that the purchase of stock by TRACK and the liquidation of ACRA into TRACK, which took the form of a merger, must be viewed at all levels as an integrated transaction; that the statutory merger does not qualify as a reorganization because it fails the continuity-of-interest test; and that, as a consequence, petitioner falls outside of section 354(a)(1) and must recognize gain pursuant to section [1001]. . . .

Respondent does not take the position that a statutory merger, such as the one we have here, can never qualify for reorganization-nonrecognition status. . . . Rather, his position is simply that the merger in question fails to meet the time-honored continuity-of-interest test. We agree with this and so hold. . . .

Reorganization treatment is appropriate when the parent's stock ownership in the subsidiary was not acquired as a step in a plan to acquire assets of the subsidiary: the parent's stockholding can be counted as contributing to continuity-of-interest, so that since such holding represented more than 80 percent of the stock of the subsidiary, the continuity-of-interest test would be met. Reorganization treatment is inappropriate when the parent's stock ownership in the subsidiary was purchased as the first step in a plan to acquire the subsidiary's assets in conformance with the provisions of section 334(b)(2).* The parent's stockholding could not be counted towards continuity-of-interest, so . . . there would be a continuity-of-interest of less than 20 percent. (Less than 20-percent continuity would

---

* Under old §334(b)(2), a corporation could purchase 80 percent or more of the stock of a target corporation with appreciated assets and then liquidate the target and obtain a step-up in asset basis without recognition of a corporate-level tax. That provision has been repealed, and old §338 was enacted in its place. One central feature of the former §334(b)(2) was that the step-up in basis could be obtained only by liquidating the target. — Eds.

be significantly less continuity-of-interest than that allowed in John A. Nelson Co. v. Helvering, 296 U.S. 374 (1935).) In short, where the parent's stock interest is "old and cold," it may contribute to continuity-of-interest. Where the parent's interest is not "old and cold," the sale of shares by the majority of shareholders actually detracts from continuity-of-interest.

In petitioner's case, TRACK's stock in ACRA was acquired as part of an integrated plan to obtain control over ACRA's business. The plan called for, first, the purchase of stock and, second, the subsidiary-into-parent merger. Accordingly, continuity-of-interest must be measured by looking to all the pre-tender offer stockholders rather than to the parent (TRACK) and the nontendering stockholders only; and by that measure the merger fails and petitioner must recognize her gain. . . .

Faced with the general rule as to the applicability of the continuity-of-interest test, petitioner makes the following arguments, which we will deal with separately.

One, the continuity-of-interest doctrine should not be applied because TRACK was formed by a few stockholders in ACRA in order to purchase the business and, in the process, to acquire a stepped-up basis for as many of the assets as possible via section 334(b)(2). "In effect, the situation was the same as the sale of stock by some shareholders to other shareholders." The petitioner meets herself coming, so to speak, when making this argument. Confronted with the problem of how to characterize the second event in the present two-event transaction, she contends that the transaction was a true statutory merger in both form and substance, at least insofar as she, a minority shareholder, was concerned. Now, confronted with the continuity-of-interest problem, she would have us treat the transaction in a manner inconsistent with the characterization previously given to the transaction, that of a merger. Furthermore, the parties to these events (the selling shareholders of ACRA, the organizers of TRACK, and the nontendering, nondissenting shareholders such as the petitioner) chose the steps that were followed. To allow one of them in a separate proceeding to characterize the facts as being in substance something else would lay the groundwork for an enormous amount of "whipsawing" by and against both taxpayers and the Government.

Two, in applying the continuity-of-interest test, if it is applied, the purchase of stock by TRACK and the subsequent merger should not be viewed as steps in an integrated transaction because the choice of merger over liquidation as a second step had independent significance to the minority shareholders and either choice would have suited TRACK. By so arguing, the petitioner attempts in effect to avoid the step-transaction doctrine and thus to limit the application of the continuity-of-interest test. If the merger can be separated from the stock purchase, the continuity-of-interest test might be applicable only with regard to ACRA's shareholders at the time of the statutory merger, namely, the parent corporation, TRACK, and the minority shareholders, including petitioner. We note at least one flaw: The choice — liquidation or merger — did make a difference to TRACK. If it had liquidated ACRA, TRACK would not have received all of ACRA's assets. Some of the assets would have gone to the minority shareholders, and it would have had to have purchased them from these shareholders at an additional price. By choosing to merge ACRA into itself, it was able to avoid this and other problems.

Three, if the purchase and merger are to be viewed as parts of a single transaction for continuity and reorganization purposes, then the incorporation of TRACK should also be integrated into the transaction for section 351 purposes; thus the petitioner should be viewed as having participated in a tax-free section 351 transaction along with the Levys and Caseys. Briefly, the answer to this argument is that while the purchase and the merger were interdependent events, petitioner's exchange of ACRA stock for TRACK stock was not "mutually interdependent" with the incorporation transfers made by the Levys, Caseys, and 18 other individuals. American Bantam Car Co., 11 T.C. 397, 405-407 (1948), affirmed per curiam 117 F.2d 513 (C.A.3, 1949). . . .

Four, assuming that the continuity-of-interest test is applied, it is met where all 16 percent of the stockholders of ACRA exchanged their stock for a total of 35 percent of the stock of TRACK. The 16-percent figure (really 16.04 percent) is the sum of the percentage of ACRA stock transferred to TRACK at the time of TRACK's formation (10.22 percent) plus the percentage of ACRA stock exchanged for TRACK stock following the statutory merger (5.82 percent). Fortunately, we need not engage in a game of percentages since the continuity figure argued for by petitioner, 16 percent, is not "tantalizingly" high. . . .

Finally, we emphasize that the petitioner is not any worse off than her fellow shareholders who sold their stock. She could have also received money instead of stock had she chosen to sell or to dissent from the merger. The nonrecognition of a realized gain is always an important matter. We hold that petitioner is not entitled to such favorable treatment in this case.

Reviewed by the Court. . . .

NOTES

1. *Continuity of proprietary interest.* The "continuity of proprietary interest" doctrine goes back more than 60 years. In Pinellas Ice & Cold Storage Co. v. Commissioner, 287 U.S. 462 (1933), the seller corporations, in exchange for their assets, received cash plus well-secured promissory notes payable in less than four months. The Supreme Court, holding that the transaction constituted a taxable sale rather than a tax-free reorganization, wrote: "Certainly, we think that to be within the [definition of a reorganization] the seller must acquire an interest in the affairs of the

purchasing company more definite than that incident to ownership of its short-term purchase-money notes." 287 U.S. at 470.

Two years later, in Helvering v. Minnesota Tea Co., 296 U.S. 378 (1935), the Court upheld the tax-free status of a transfer by a corporation of substantially all its assets for voting trust certificates (worth about $540,000) representing 18,000 shares of common stock of another corporation as well as about $425,000 in cash. The 18,000 shares represented about 7 1/2 percent of the outstanding stock of the transferee, a publicly held corporation. This substantial reduction in the transferor's control over the transferred assets caused the Board of Tax Appeals to deny reorganization treatment to the transaction. In coming to the opposite conclusion, the Supreme Court restated the rule of *Pinellas* and then wrote:

> True it is that the relationship of the taxpayer to the assets conveyed was substantially changed, but this is not inhibited by the statute. Also, a large part of the consideration was cash. This, we think, is permissible so long as the taxpayer received an interest in the affairs of the transferee which represented a material part of the value of the transferred assets.

296 U.S. at 386.

Minnesota Tea left open the questions (1) what constitutes an "interest in the affairs of the transferee" and (2) how much of such an interest is a "material part" of the value transferred. The first of these two questions was answered in large part by John A. Nelson & Co. v. Helvering, 296 U.S. 374 (1935), and LeTulle v. Scofield, 308 U.S. 415 (1940).

In *LeTulle*, all the assets of a corporation were conveyed for $50,000 in cash plus $750,000 in bonds of the transferee payable serially over 11 years. The Supreme Court characterized the transaction as a sale, holding that "[w]here the consideration is wholly in the transferee's bonds, or part cash and part such bonds, we think it cannot be said that the transferor retains any proprietary interest in the enterprise." 308 U.S. at 420-421. In *John A. Nelson & Co.*, however, the Court upheld the reorganization treatment of a transfer by a corporation of substantially all its assets for $2 million plus nonvoting preferred stock of the transferee worth about $1.25 million. The preferred stock was redeemable as well as nonvoting, but the Court held that the statute had no requirement of participation by the transferor in the transferee's management.

The line of cases from *Pinellas* through *LeTulle* stands for the proposition that if a transaction is to qualify as a "reorganization," the transferor must receive some stock (a "material part") of the transferee in the exchange. Does this rule make sense? Is the distinction between nonvoting preferred stock and subordinated debt sufficiently important to warrant so great an emphasis? Compare Roebling v. Commissioner, 143 F.2d 810 (3d Cir. 1944), involving a corporation whose assets had been leased to a second corporation on a 900-year lease calling for annual rent of $480,000.

The lessor corporation was merged into the lessee, and the shareholders of the lessor exchanged their stock for 100-year bonds of the lessee paying in aggregate $480,000 per year of interest. The exchanging shareholders argued that their relationship to the underlying assets was no more distant under the 100-year bonds than it had been under the 900-year lease, but the court, relying on *LeTulle* and related cases, held that no reorganization occurred.

In Paulsen v. Commissioner, 469 U.S. 131 (1985), a state-chartered savings and loan association merged into a federally-chartered savings and loan. Prior to the merger, the state-chartered entity had "guaranty stock" outstanding that gave its owners all rights to the association's assets upon liquidation but no practical rights to dividends. The federally-chartered entity had no capital stock outstanding but instead was owned by its depositors and borrowers. Pursuant to the merger, the guaranty stock of the state-chartered entity was exchanged for passbook interests in the continuing enterprise at a rate of one $12 passbook for every share of guaranty stock owned.

The Supreme Court held that the transaction was not an "A" reorganization because the former guaranty share owners received no proprietary interest in the acquiring entity: While the passbook interests had some equity aspects, the debt aspects predominated. The taxpayer had relied on Revenue Ruling 69-3, 1969-1 C.B. 103, which held that a merger of one federally-chartered savings and loan association into another qualified as an "A" reorganization when the target shareholders exchanged passbook accounts of the target entity for equal-value passbook accounts of the acquiring entity. The Supreme Court distinguished this Ruling as follows:

> When two [federally-chartered] associations merge, the shares [that is, the passbooks] received are essentially identical to the shares given up. As long as the cash value of the shares on each side of the exchange is the same, the equity interest by the shares received — though small — is equivalent to the equity interest represented by the shares given up.

Is the Supreme Court's opinion in *Paulsen* consistent with *Roebling*? If the continuity of proprietary interest doctrine speaks only to the form of consideration *received* in the exchange, then how can it be that the Supreme Court is willing to sanction the tax-free merger of a mutual savings and loan into a mutual savings and loan while refusing the same tax treatment to a stock savings and loan merging into a mutual savings and loan? For a thoughtful criticism of the continuity of proprietary interest doctrine, ending with the suggestion that the doctrine be eliminated, see Wolfman, "Continuity of Interest" and the American Law Institute Study, 57 Taxes 840 (1979).

For ruling purposes, Rev. Proc. 77-37, 1977-2 C.B. 568, sets forth the IRS position on the continuity of interest requirement. According to the revenue procedure, a favorable ruling may be obtained if 50 percent of the value received in a merger (or consolidation) is in the form of an equity interest in the acquiring corporation. There is no requirement that each shareholder receive at least 50 percent equity or even that a substantial percentage of shareholders not receive only cash. See Rev. Rul. 66-224, 1966-2 C.B. 114, in which two 25 percent shareholders were cashed out while the other two 25 percent shareholders received stock of the acquiring corporation. Held, the continuity of proprietary interest requirement was satisfied. See also Reilly Oil Co. v. Commissioner, 189 F.2d 382 (5th Cir. 1951) (31 percent of transferor's shareholders elected to receive cash). Of course, shareholders receiving cash or other boot in the reorganization will recognize some of their gain, if any, on the transaction under §356.

While a shareholder receiving cash will be taxed even though the reorganization as a whole meets the continuity of proprietary interest test, if the transaction fails that test, all shareholders (including those receiving only stock) lose the benefit of tax-free treatment. How is it that Kass is taxed on the merger of ACRA into TRACK when she exchanged her stock of the transferee corporation for nothing but stock of the acquiring corporation? The court in *Kass* ended its opinion with the observation that Kass was "not any worse off than her fellow shareholders who sold their stock." While that observation is true, it fails to recognize the injustice that has been worked on Kass: The other shareholders were appropriately taxed to the extent that they cashed out, but Kass did nothing but continue her corporate investment in equity form and so should be entitled to nonrecognition on the exchange.

In *Kass* and *Paulsen,* the issue before the court was whether a transaction meeting all the statutory requirements of a "reorganization" should nevertheless be taxed as a sale. Given the precision of the definitions in §368, should the courts ask for more? When these cases were decided, the only relevant guidance was Treas. Regs. §1.368-1(b), which then stated:

> In order to exclude transactions not intended to be included, the specifications of the reorganization provisions of the law are precise. Both the terms of the specifications and their underlying assumptions and purposes must be satisfied in order to entitle the taxpayer to the benefit of the exception from the general rule.

Try to identify these "underlying assumptions and purposes." Can they be articulated with sufficient clarity to guide a court through the maze of §368?

While cases such as *Pinellas, Minnesota Tea,* and *LeTulle* spoke to the amount of stock in the continuing enterprise needed to be used in the reorganization, they did not address the impact of pre-reorganization sales of shares of the target corporation or post-reorganization sales of shares of the acquiring corporation, two issues that confused the courts for many years. What caused the confusion was a misplaced focus on the *consideration received by the target shareholders* as opposed to the *consideration furnished by the acquiring corporation*. To appreciate this distinction, suppose that the historic shareholders of the target corporation sell their shares for cash to new buyers immediately prior to the merger. Even if the shareholders at the time of the merger receive nothing but stock of the acquiring corporation, the effect of the sale and merger at the shareholder level is of an all-cash transaction.

Or consider what is essentially the same transaction but with the timing reversed. Target Corp. merges into Acquiring Corp., with the shareholders of Target receiving marketable stock of Acquiring. These shareholders then sell their shares of Acquiring immediately after the reorganization is completed. Once again, the shareholder-level effect of the transaction is equivalent to an all-cash transaction. See McDonald's Restaurants of Illinois v. Commissioner, 688 F.2d 520 (7th Cir. 1982), rev'g 76 T.C. 972 (1981).

These issues are now resolved in the comprehensive continuity of proprietary interest regulations. See Treas. Regs. §1.368-1(e), especially the general rule in subsection (e)(1)(i) as well as example 1 in subsection (e)(6). These regulations make clear that pre-merger sales of target stock and post-merger sales of acquiring stock will be disregarded so long as such sales are not made to the issuing corporation nor to a corporation related to the issuing corporation as defined in Treas. Regs. §1.368-1(e)(3).

Consider a merger in which the target shareholders receive exclusively stock of the acquiring corporation but then have most or all of the that acquiring stock redeemed. In effect, it is the redemption proceeds and not its own transitory stock that is the consideration used by the acquiring corporation, and the regulations properly adopt that view. Treas. Regs. §1.368-1(e)(6) (example 4(i)). Of course, the same result should obtain if the acquiring corporation acquires the target stock for cash immediately prior to the merger. Treas. Regs. §1.368-1(e)(6) (example 4(ii)).

Suppose that A Corp. acquires T Corp. in a stock merger and immediately thereafter B Corp. purchases the A Corp. stock received by the former T shareholders. If A and B have a common parent, P Corp. (so that A and B are a brother-sister pair), the merger will fail to qualify as an "A" reorganization for lack of continuity of proprietary interest. See Treas. Regs. §1.368-1(e)(6) (example 4(iii)). In general, A and B will be related if one has 80% control of the other or they share a common 80% parent. See §1504(a). Note that the same result will obtain even if B is not related to A prior to the transaction if the effect of the transaction is to create a sufficient relationship immediately after the acquisition. See Treas. Regs. §1.368-1(e)(3)(ii); see also example 6 of Treas. Regs. §1.368-1(e)(6).

2. *Continuity of business enterprise.* Since the rationale for tax-free treatment of a reorganization is that the transaction is best viewed as a mere change in form of the business enterprise, can a corporate acquisition be

tax free if the acquiring corporation does not continue the historic business of the acquired corporation? The Service argued against tax-free treatment in such circumstances, although the courts regularly rejected the Service's position. See, e.g., Bentsen v. Phinney, 199 F. Supp. 363 (S.D. Tex. 1961), in which the court determined that the doctrine of business continuity requires only that the assets of the acquired corporation be used in *some* business after the transaction. In Rev. Rul. 63-29, 1963-1 C.B. 77, the Service acquiesced in the reasoning of cases like *Bentsen,* holding that the amalgamation of a toy company and a steel company into a single corporation could qualify as a reorganization.

Now, the regulations require that the acquiring must either continue the historic business of the target corporation *or* use a "significant portion" of the target's historic assets in any trade or business. Treas. Regs. §1.368-1(d)(1). In this context, use of the target's assets by any corporation affiliated with the acquiring corporation is treated as use by the acquiring corporation itself. See Treas. Regs. §1.368-1(d)(4). Thus, if a group of subsidiaries of the acquiring corporation use assets of the target corporation which when combined constitute a "significant portion" of the target's assets, the continuity of business enterprise requirement will be satisfied. Treas. Regs. §1.368-1(d)(5) (example 6). Note also that if the target corporation operated multiple lines of business, continuation of only one line by the acquiring corporation can satisfy the continuity of business enterprise requirement. Treas. Regs. §1.368-1(d)(5) (example 1).

Note that nothing requires that the acquiring corporation continue its own historic business or use its own historic assets in any capacity. Rev. Rul. 81-25, 1981 C.B. 65. In considering the business continuity doctrine, you should recognize that labeling one corporation as the "acquiring" corporation and another as the "acquired" corporation usually is a matter of indifference. For example, if *A* Corp. and *B* Corp. merge, the decision whether to make *A* Corp. or *B* Corp. the survivor often will turn on such factors as which corporation has more goodwill associated with its name or whether either corporation owns an asset (such as a favorable long-term lease) that is difficult to transfer. Should the business continuity doctrine focus only on the continued use of the *acquired corporation's* assets when the reorganization involves a minnow swallowing a shark?

What are the tax consequences if the acquired corporation sells its historic assets prior to and in anticipation of the reorganization? See Rev. Rul. 87-76, 1987-2 C.B. 84 (no continuity of business enterprise). In Rev. Rul. 88-25, 1988-1 C.B. 803, however, the Service ruled that if a corporation having two businesses sold one for cash and transferred its remaining assets (plus the cash) for voting stock of an unrelated corporation, the transaction would qualify as a C reorganization. The Service emphasized that, because the first business was sold to an unrelated party and the proceeds were transferred as part of the C reorganization, the transaction was not divisive in nature.

3. *Business purpose.* The doctrines of continuity of proprietary interest and continuity of business enterprise were developed by the courts to deny tax-free reorganization status to transactions that closely resembled sales. Similarly, the business purpose doctrine was developed early on to deny tax-free status to transactions that meet all the formal requirements of a "reorganization" but lack a valid business purpose for the machinations. For example, in 1928 Gregory owned all the outstanding shares of the United Mortgage Corporation (UMC Corp.), which in turn owned 1,000 appreciated shares of the Monitor Securities Corporation. Gregory sought to effect a sale of the Monitor shares at a tax cost of only a capital gain tax at the shareholder level.

Had UMC Corp. distributed the Monitor shares to Gregory as a simple dividend, she would have recognized ordinary income on the distribution because UMC Corp. had adequate earnings and profits. (UMC Corp. would have recognized no gain on the distribution because in 1928 the Code contained no provision similar to §311(b).) To avoid this ordinary income, Gregory adopted the following strategy.

First, Gregory had UMC Corp. form a new corporation, Averill Corp., by transferring the Monitor shares to Averill in exchange for all the Averill stock. The Averill stock was then immediately distributed to Gregory from UMC Corp. Finally, within one week, the newly formed Averill Corp. was liquidated and the Monitor shares were distributed to Gregory in complete liquidation of Averill.

The reorganization statute at the time provided that a "reorganization" included "a transfer by a corporation of all or a part of its assets to another corporation if immediately after the transferor or its stockholders or both are in control of the corporation to which the assets are transferred." Accordingly, the formation of Averill Corp. met the formal requirements of a "reorganization." In addition, the statute provided that a distribution "in pursuance of a plan of reorganization, to a shareholder in a corporation a party to a reorganization, [of] stock or securities in such corporation or in another corporation a party to the reorganization, without the surrender by such shareholder of stock or securities in such corporation, [results in] no gain to the distributee from the receipt of such stock or securities." Thus, Gregory received the stock of Averill without tax. The final step in the plan, the complete liquidation of Averill, was taxable to Gregory, but since she was taxed at capital gain rates on the property distributed in complete liquidation, she had obtained her goal of stepping up the basis in the Monitor shares to fair market value at the cost of a single, capital gain tax. Gregory was then able to sell the Monitor shares to a third party without realizing or recognizing further gain.

In one of the most famous opinions in the tax law, Gregory v. Helvering, 293 U.S. 465 (1935), the Supreme Court denied reorganization status to the transaction:

[T]he facts speak for themselves and are susceptible of but one interpretation. The whole undertaking, though conducted according to the terms of the [statute], was in fact an elaborate and devious form of conveyance masquerading as a corporate reorganization, and nothing else. The rule which excludes from consideration the motive of tax avoidance is not pertinent to the situation, because the transaction upon its face lies outside the plain intent of the statute. To hold otherwise would be to exalt artifice above reality and to deprive the statutory provision in question of all serious purpose.

Judge Learned Hand, author of the circuit court opinion in the *Gregory* case also denying reorganization status to the transaction, shortly thereafter wrote of the case:

In Gregory v. Helvering . . . , the incorporators adopted the usual form of creating corporations; but their intent, or purpose, was merely to draught the papers, in fact not to create corporations as the court understood that word. That was the purpose which defeated their exemption, not the accompanying purpose to escape taxation; that purpose was legally neutral. Had they really meant to conduct a business by means of the two reorganized companies, they would have escaped whatever other aim they may have had, whether to avoid taxes, or to regenerate the world.

Chisolm v. Commissioner, 79 F.2d 14, 15 (2d Cir. 1935).

Line drawing and analysis in this area are difficult. Compare Judge Hand's later comments:

The doctrine of Gregory v. Helvering . . . means that in construing words of a tax statute which describes commercial or industrial transactions we are to understand them to refer to transactions entered upon for commercial or industrial purposes and not to include transactions entered upon for no other motive but to escape taxation.

Commissioner v. Transport Trading & Terminal Corp., 176 F.2d 570, 572 (2d Cir. 1949).

While *Gregory* involved a divisive corporate reorganization, the business purpose doctrine can play an important role in acquisitive reorganizations as well. For an example of the interplay among the business purpose doctrine, the divisive reorganization provisions, and the acquisitive reorganization provisions, see Helvering v. Elkhorn Coal Co., 95 F.2d 732 (4th Cir. 1937). In *Elkhorn* the taxpayer transferred some of its assets to a newly formed subsidiary, and the subsidiary's stock was then distributed to the taxpayer's shareholders, much as in *Gregory*. By itself, such a transaction qualified as a tax-free divisive D reorganization. Then, however, the taxpayer transferred its remaining assets to an unrelated corporation in exchange for voting stock of this company, a transaction that, standing on its own, would constitute an acquisitive C reorganization. Finally, the taxpayer completely liquidated, distributing the stock of the acquiring corporation. (At the time, the subsequent liquidation was not required as part of the C reorganization. Under current §368(a)(2)(G), the liquidation of the transferor corporation is mandatory.)

The statute then provided, as it does now, that a corporation must transfer "substantially all" its properties to qualify as a C reorganization. By spinning off part of its assets to a newly formed corporation immediately prior to the nominal C reorganization, the taxpayer effectively circumvented the "substantially all" requirement. Since the creation of the subsidiary had no purpose other than to qualify the transaction as a tax-free reorganization, the transaction as a whole lacked the proper "spirit." Accordingly, the taxpayer's transfer of its assets to the acquiring corporation in exchange for voting stock of the acquirer, as well as the subsequent complete liquidation, was held to be a taxable event.

PROBLEMS

10-1.   Would the transaction described in *Kass* now qualify as a reorganization under Treas. Regs. §1.368-1(e)? Would there by a better way to structure the transaction so as to ensure tax-free treatment to Mrs. Kass?

10-2.   Determine whether the following transactions are "reorganizations" within the meaning of §368(a)(1)(A).

a.   *X* Corp. has 100 shares outstanding, 40 owned by *A*, 40 by *B*, and 20 by *C*. The fair market value of *X* Corp. stock is $100 per share. *Y* Corp. is owned by 10 individuals. For every dollar of stock held by the *Y* shareholders, they each hold four dollars in 20-year notes of *Y*. *X* Corp. merges into *Y* Corp., with *A*, *B*, and *C* receiving two shares of *Y* stock (worth $100 per share) and an $800 20-year note of *Y* for every 10 shares of *X* stock tendered. What is the result if *A* and *B* receive only notes and *C* receives only stock? Could there be a "reorganization" as to *C* alone?

b.   *F* owns all the stock of *M* Corp., and *G* owns all the stock of *N* Corp. *M* Corp. is worth $1 million, and *N* Corp. is worth $100,000. *M* and *N* consolidate into newly formed *O* Corp., with *F* receiving 100 shares of class A common and *G* receiving 10 shares of class B common. Both classes have equal rights to dividends and on liquidation and both vote. The corporation, however, can redeem the class B shares at any time. What is the result if the class A shares can be redeemed at any time? If the class B shares can be redeemed for 80 percent of their fair market value?

c.   *L* Corp. has lost money in the computer business for several years, and *P* Corp. is a profitable publisher of children's books. What are the consequences if *L* merges into *P*, with the *L* shareholders receiving stock of *P*, assuming that most of the *L* assets will be sold and *P* Corp. will not enter the computer business? If the merger is structured such that *P* merges into *L*, once again assuming that the *L* assets will be sold and only publishing will continue? If *L* and *P* formally consolidate into new corporation *LP*?

10-3.   T Corp. is acquired by A Corp. pursuant to a statutory merger statute, with the shareholders of T receiving stock in A. Shortly thereafter, X purchases all of the A Corp. stock received by the former T Corp. shareholders. X has at all times owned all the outstanding stock of A Corp. Is this transaction an "A" reorganization. Consider the case in which X is a corporation as well as the case in which X is an individual.

B.   DEFINITIONAL ISSUES

As *Kass* demonstrates, whether a corporate rearrangement qualifies as a statutory "reorganization" is determined on the basis of the transaction as a whole rather than taxpayer by taxpayer. It therefore makes sense to ask whether a particular transaction fits within one of the specific reorganization definitions before considering the tax consequences of the transaction to any party. If you can conclude that a statutory reorganization has occurred, then you must determine the parties' tax consequences by looking first to sections such as §354 that explicitly provide for the tax treatment of exchanges incident to a reorganization. If you conclude that a transaction does not fall within any of the reorganization provisions, then the tax consequences of the transaction will be determined by reference to Code provisions applicable independent of the reorganization provisions. Do not assume that a transaction failing to qualify as a reorganization is necessarily taxable in full. For example, a failed reorganization may be a nontaxable liquidation under §332 or, as is often the case, the failed reorganization may contain within it a transaction protected from immediate taxation by §351. As a last warning, be sure to consider *all* the reorganization provisions before labeling a transaction as failing to qualify for reorganization treatment, for failure to qualify under one provision does not preclude qualification under other provisions. See page 416 infra.

Section 368(a) provides the definitions for the seven types of tax-free reorganizations. Reorganizations falling under §368(a)(1)(A), (B), (C), and some under (D) are acquisitive reorganizations used to combine two or more enterprises. Each type of reorganization has somewhat different criteria, and the form will determine which type has been sought or effected. There is some overlap among the various types, and aside from

§368(a)(2)(A) providing that a reorganization qualifying as both a C and a D be taxed as a D, the Code does not determine which type takes priority. No rule of priority is needed, though, since the applicable taxing provisions generally do not distinguish the various types of reorganizations.

The choice of the proper type of reorganization is often governed by important nontax factors. For example, because of contingent liabilities of the transferor corporation, the acquiring corporation may prefer a C to an A or B; preservation of certain rights or licenses of the acquired corporation may require using a B; state and federal securities law requirements may vary depending on the form chosen; shareholder approval of both the transferor and the acquiring corporation are usually required in an A — expensive and time-consuming procedures in the case of publicly held corporations — whereas only approval by shareholders of the transferor may be required in a B or C; appraisal rights for dissenters are more easily awarded in a B than in an A or C. As the various criteria for the different types of reorganizations are examined, keep in mind that the underlying purpose of the criteria in any reorganization should be to separate a nonrecognition change in form from a taxable sale or exchange.

1.   The A Reorganization: Statutory Mergers and Consolidations

In an A merger, shareholders of the transferor(s) exchange their stock for stock or debt of the acquiring corporation. In addition, they may receive cash or other property in the exchange. The statutory definition of an A reorganization does not limit the type of consideration that may be used, and in this sense the A reorganization provides the greatest flexibility of all the reorganization forms. The judicially created continuity of proprietary interest doctrine does, however, apply to A reorganizations, so a statutory merger or consolidation will fail to qualify as a reorganization under §368(a)(1) unless stock of the acquiring corporation constitutes a "material and substantial part" of the consideration.

2.   The B Reorganization: Stock for Stock

In a B reorganization, the acquiring corporation acquires stock of the target corporation, thereby making the target a controlled (but not necessarily wholly owned) subsidiary of the acquiring corporation. In a B reorganization, the sole consideration that can be used by the acquiring corporation is its voting stock (or the voting stock of its parent). The voting stock may be common, preferred, or a combination of the two, but voting stock of the acquiring corporation cannot be combined with voting stock of the acquiring corporation's parent. See Treas. Regs. §1.368-2(c). Because of the statutory requirement limiting consideration in a B to voting stock, the continuity of proprietary interest doctrine is automatically satisfied.

The acquiring corporation must have control, as defined in §368(c) (that is, 80 percent of the total combined voting power plus at least 80 percent of the total number of shares of all other classes) of the target corporation after the exchange. Such control need not be obtained in one transaction. For example, if 30 percent is obtained in one transaction and 51 percent in a second transaction, the second exchange is a B reorganization; the first transaction, however, if independent of the second, is not a B. See Treas. Regs. §1.368-2(c). In addition to this "creeping acquisition" of control, an increase in ownership by a corporation that already has actual 80 percent control can qualify as a B reorganization.

The main obstacle to a B reorganization is that any boot will destroy the transaction. See, however, Rev. Rul. 77-271, 1977-2 C.B. 116, in which a taxpayer exchanged stock of the target company for voting stock of equal market value of the acquiring company and, as part of the agreement, entered into an employment contract in exchange for additional shares of the acquiring corporation. The transaction was treated as a valid stock-for-stock exchange qualifying as a valid B followed by a stock-for-employment contract taxed as compensation income. A contract for fair cash salary for services to be rendered also is not treated as boot.

Although the acquiring corporation in a B reorganization must use only voting stock as consideration for the stock of the target corporation, no similar limitation is placed on the acquiring corporation's ability to acquire nonstock interests in the target corporation (such as debt instruments and stock options). See Rev. Rul. 70-269, 1970-1 C.B. 82 (stock options); Rev. Rul. 70-41, 1970-1 C.B. 77 (debt securities); Rev. Rul. 69-91, 1969-1 C.B. 106 (convertible debentures). Further, an exchange of securities for securities can be tax-free under §354 as part of the reorganization even though the exchange of securities is ignored for determining whether the transaction qualifies as a "B" reorganization as a stock-for-stock exchange. Rev. Rul. 98-10, 1998-1 C.B. ___.

Payment by the acquiring corporation of the target corporation's share of reorganization expenses (such as legal, accounting, appraisal, printing, and registration fees) is not treated as boot in a B reorganization. At the same time, similar expenses of the target shareholders may not be paid by the acquiring corporation without disqualifying the transaction as a B. Rev. Rul. 73-54, 1973-1 C.B. 187.

Chapman v. Commissioner
618 F.2d 856 (1st Cir. 1980)

Before Coffin, Chief Judge, Campbell and Bownes, Circuit Judges.
 LEVIN H. CAMPBELL, Circuit Judge. . . .

We must decide whether the requirement of Section 368(a)(1)(B) that the acquisition of stock in one corporation by another be solely in exchange for voting stock of the acquiring corporation is met where, in related transactions, the acquiring corporation first acquires 8 percent of the acquiree's stock for cash and then acquires more than 80 percent of the acquiree in an exchange of stock for voting stock. The Tax Court agreed with the taxpayers that the latter exchange constituted a valid tax-free reorganization. Reeves v. Commissioner, 71 T.C. 727 (1979)....

The events giving rise to this dispute began in 1968, when the management of ITT, a large multinational corporation, became interested in acquiring Hartford [Fire Insurance Company] as part of a program of diversification. In October 1968, ITT executives approached Hartford about the possibility of merging the two corporations. This proposal was spurned by Hartford, which at the time was considering acquisitions of its own. In November 1968, ITT learned that approximately 1.3 million shares of Hartford, representing some 6 percent of Hartford's voting stock, were available for purchase from a mutual fund. After assuring Hartford's directors that ITT would not attempt to acquire Hartford against its will, ITT consummated the $63.7 million purchase from the mutual fund with Hartford's blessing. From November 13, 1968 to January 10, 1969, ITT also made a series of purchases on the open market totalling 458,000 shares which it acquired for approximately $24.4 million. A further purchase of 400 shares from an ITT subsidiary in March 1969 brought ITT's holdings to about 8 percent of Hartford's outstanding stock, all of which had been bought for cash.

In the midst of this flurry of stock-buying, ITT submitted a written proposal to the Hartford Board of Directors for the merger of Hartford into an ITT subsidiary.... Received by Hartford in December of 1968, the proposal was rejected in February of 1969. A counterproposal by Hartford's directors led to further negotiations, and on April 9, 1969 a provisional plan and agreement of merger was executed by the two corporations....

Concluding that the entire transaction [did not constitute] a nontaxable reorganization, the Service assessed tax deficiencies against a number of former Hartford shareholders who had accepted the exchange offer. Appellees, along with other taxpayers, contested this action in the Tax Court, where the case was decided on appellees' motion for summary judgment. For purposes of this motion, the taxpayers conceded . . . that the initial cash purchases of Hartford stock had been made for the purpose of furthering ITT's efforts to acquire Hartford. . . .

I

The single issue raised on this appeal is whether "the acquisition" in this case complied with the requirement [of a B reorganization] that it be "solely for . . . voting stock." It is well settled that the "solely" requirement is mandatory; if any part of "the acquisition" includes a form of consideration other than voting stock, the transaction will not qualify as a (B) reorganization. See Helvering v. Southwest Consolidated Corp., 315 U.S. 194, 198 (1942) ("'Solely' leaves no leeway. Voting stock plus some other consideration does not meet the statutory requirement"). The precise issue before us is thus how broadly to read the term "acquisition." The Internal Revenue Service argues that "the acquisition . . . of stock of another corporation" must be understood to encompass the 1968-69 cash purchases as well as the 1970 exchange offer. If the IRS is correct, "the acquisition" here fails as a (B) reorganization. The taxpayers, on the other hand, would limit "the acquisition" to the part of a sequential transaction of this nature which meets the requirements of subsection (B). They argue that the 1970 exchange of stock for stock was itself an "acquisition" by ITT of stock in Hartford solely in exchange for ITT's voting stock, such that after the exchange took place ITT controlled Hartford. Taxpayers contend that the earlier cash purchases of 8 percent, even if conceded to be part of the same acquisitive plan, are essentially irrelevant to the tax-free reorganization otherwise effected.

The Tax Court accepted the taxpayers' reading of the statute, effectively overruling its own prior decision in Howard v. Commissioner, 24 T.C. 792 (1955), rev'd on other grounds, 238 F.2d 943 (7th Cir. 1956). The plurality opinion stated its "narrow" holding as follows:

> We hold that where, as is the case herein, 80 percent or more of the stock of a corporation is acquired in one transaction, in exchange for which only voting stock is furnished as consideration, the "solely for voting stock" requirement of section 368(a)(1)(B) is satisfied.

. . . The plurality treated as "irrelevant" the 8 percent of Hartford's stock purchased for cash, although the opinion left somewhat ambiguous the question whether the 8 percent was irrelevant because of the 14-month time interval separating the transactions or because the statute was not concerned with transactions over and above those mathematically necessary to the acquiring corporation's attainment of control.

II

For reasons set forth extensively in section III of this opinion, we do not accept the position adopted by the Tax Court. . . . As explained below, we find a strong implication in the language of the statute, in the legislative history, in the regulations, and in the decisions of other courts that cash purchases which are concededly "parts of" a stock-for-stock exchange must be considered constituent elements of the "acquisition" for purposes of applying the "solely for . . . voting stock" requirement of Section 368(a)(1)(B). We believe the presence of nonstock consideration in such an acquisition, regardless of whether such consideration is necessary to the gaining of control, is inconsistent with treatment of the acquisition as a nontaxable reorganization. . . .

III

A . . .

We begin with the words of the statute itself. The reorganization definitions contained in Section 368(a)(1) are precise, technical, and comprehensive. They were intended to define the exclusive means by which nontaxable corporate reorganizations could be effected. See Treas. Reg. §1.368-1 (1960); 3 J. Mertens, The Law of Federal Income Taxation §20.86 at 364 (1972). In examining the language of the (B) provision, we discern two possible meanings. On the one hand, the statute could be read to say that a successful reorganization occurs whenever Corporation X exchanges its own voting stock for stock in Corporation Y, and, immediately after the transaction, Corporation X controls more than 80 percent of Y's stock. On this reading, purchases of shares for which any part of the consideration takes the form of "boot" should be ignored, since the definition is only concerned with transactions which meet the statutory requirements as to consideration and control. To take an example, if Corporation X bought 50 percent of the shares of Y, and then almost immediately exchanged part of its voting stock for the remaining 50 percent of Y's stock, the question would arise whether the second transaction was a (B) reorganization. Arguably, the statute can be read to support such a finding. In the second transaction, X exchanged only stock for stock (meeting the "solely" requirement), and after the transaction was completed X owned Y (meeting the "control" requirement).

The alternative reading of the statute — the one which we are persuaded to adopt — treats the (B) definition as prescriptive, rather than merely descriptive. We read the statute to mean that the entire transaction which constitutes "the acquisition" must not contain any nonstock consideration if the transaction is to qualify as a (B) reorganization. In the example given above, where X acquired 100 percent of Y's stock, half for cash and half for voting stock, we would interpret "the acquisition" as referring to the entire transaction, so that the "solely for . . . voting stock" requirement would not be met. We believe if Congress had intended the statute to be read as merely descriptive, this intent would have been more clearly spelled out in the statutory language.

We recognize that the Tax Court adopted neither of these two readings. For reasons to be discussed in connection with the legislative history which follows, the Tax Court purported to limit its holding to cases, such as this one, where more than 80 percent of the stock of Corporation *Y* passes to Corporation *X* in exchange solely for voting stock. The Tax Court presumably would assert that the 50/50 hypothetical posited above can be distinguished from this case, and that its holding implies no view as to the hypothetical. . . . In order to distinguish the 80 percent case from the 50 percent case, it is necessary to read "the acquisition" as referring to at least the amount of stock constituting "control" (80 percent) where related cash purchases are present. Yet the Tax Court recognized that "the acquisition" cannot always refer to the conveyance of an 80 percent bloc of stock in one transaction, since to do so would frustrate the intent of the 1954 amendments to permit so-called "creeping acquisitions."

The Tax Court's interpretation of the statute suffers from a more fundamental defect, as well. In order to justify the limitation of its holding to transactions involving 80 percent or more of the acquiree's stock, the Tax Court focused on the *passage* of control as the primary requirement of the (B) provision. This focus is misplaced. Under the present version of the statute, the *passage* of control is entirely irrelevant; the only material requirement is that the acquiring corporation have control immediately after the acquisition. As the statute explicitly states, it does not matter if the acquiring corporation already has control before the transaction begins, so long as such control exists at the completion of the reorganization. Whatever talismanic quality may have attached to the acquisition of control under previous versions of the Code, see Part III B infra, is altogether absent from the version we must apply to this case. In our view, the statute should be read to mean that the related transactions that constitute "the acquisition," whatever percentage of stock they may represent, must meet both the "solely for voting stock" and the "control immediately after" requirements of Section 368(a)(1)(B). Neither the reading given the statute by the Tax Court, nor that proposed as the first alternative above, adequately corresponds to the careful language Congress employed in this section of the Code.

B

The 1924 Code defined reorganization, in part, as "a merger or consolidation (including the acquisition by one corporation of at least a majority of the voting stock and at least a majority of the total number of shares of all other classes of stock of another corporation, or substantially all the properties of another corporation)." Pub. L. No. 68-176, c. 234, §203(h)(1), 43 Stat. 257. Although the statute did not specifically limit the consideration that could be given in exchange for stock or assets, courts eventually developed the so-called "continuity of interest" doctrine, which held that exchanges that did not include some quantum of stock as consideration were ineligible for reorganization treatment for lack of a continuing property interest on the part of the acquiree's shareholders. See, e.g., Cortland Specialty Co. v. Commissioner, 60 F.2d 937, 939-40 (2d Cir. 1932), cert. denied, 288 U.S. 599 (1933); Pinellas Ice Co. v. Commissioner, 287 U.S. 462, 470 (1933).

Despite this judicial development, sentiment was widespread in Congress that the reorganization provisions lent themselves to abuse, particularly in the form of so-called "disguised sales." . . . The Senate Finance Committee . . . propos[ed] to retain these provisions, but with "restrictions designed to prevent tax avoidance." S. Rep. No. 558, 73d Cong., 2d Sess. 15. . . . One of these restrictions was the requirement that the acquiring corporation obtain at least 80 percent, rather than a bare majority, of the stock of the acquiree. The second requirement was stated in the Senate Report as follows: "the acquisition, whether of stock or of substantially all the properties, must be in exchange solely for the voting stock of the acquiring corporation." Id. at 17. The Senate amendments were enacted as Section 112(g)(1) of the Revenue Act of 1934. . . .

Congress revised this definition in 1939 in response to the Supreme Court's decision in United States v. Hendler, 303 U.S. 564 (1938), which held that an acquiring corporation's assumption of the acquiree's liabilities in an asset-acquisition was equivalent to the receipt of "boot" by the acquiree. Since virtually all asset-acquisition reorganizations necessarily involve the assumption of the acquiree's liabilities, a literal application of the "solely for . . . voting stock" requirement would have effectively abolished this form of tax-free reorganization. In the Revenue Act of 1939, Congress separated the stock-acquisition and asset-acquisition provisions in order to exempt the assumption of liabilities in the latter category of cases from the "solely for . . . voting stock" requirement. . . .

The next major change in this provision occurred in 1954. In that year, the House Bill, H.R. 8300, would have drastically altered the corporate reorganization sections of the Tax Code, permitting, for example, both stock and "boot" as consideration in a corporate acquisition, with gain recognized only to the extent of the "boot." . . . The Senate Finance Committee, in order to preserve the familiar terminology and structure of the 1939 Code, proposed a new version of Section 112(g)(1), which would retain the "solely for . . . voting stock" requirement, but alter the existing control requirement to permit so-called "creeping acquisitions." Under the Senate Bill, it would no longer be necessary for the acquiring corporation to obtain 80 percent or more of the acquiree's stock in one "reorganization." The Senate's proposal permitted an acquisition to occur in stages; a bloc of shares representing less than 80 percent could be added to earlier acquisitions, regardless of the consideration given earlier, to meet the control requirement. The Report of the Senate Finance Committee gave this example of the operation of the creeping acquisition amendment:

[C]orporation A purchased 30 percent of the common stock of corporation W (the only class of stock outstanding) for cash in 1939. On March 1, 1955, corporation A offers to exchange its own voting stock, for all the stock of corporation W tendered within 6 months from the date of the offer. Within the 6 months period corporation A acquires an additional 60 percent of the stock of W for its own voting stock. As a result of the 1955 transactions, corporation A will own 90 percent of all of corporation W's stock, No gain or loss is recognized with respect to the exchanges of the A stock for the W stock.

1954 Senate Report, supra, at 273. . . . See also Treas. Reg. §1.368-2(c) (1960).

At the same time the Senate was revising the (B) provision (while leaving intact the "solely for . . . voting stock" requirement), it was also rewriting the (C) provision to explicitly permit up to 20 percent of the consideration in an asset acquisition to take the form of money or other nonstock property. See . . . §368(a)(2)(B). The Senate revisions of subsections (B) and (C) were ultimately passed, and have remained largely unchanged since 1954. . . . Proposals for altering the (B) provision to allow "boot" as consideration have been made, but none has been enacted.

As this history shows, Congress has had conflicting aims in this complex and difficult area. On the one hand, the 1934 Act evidences a strong intention to limit the reorganization provisions to prevent forms of tax avoidance that had proliferated under the earlier revenue acts. This intention arguably has been carried forward in the current versions through retention of the "solely for . . . voting stock" requirement in (B), even while the (C) provision was being loosened. On the other hand, both the 1939 and 1954 revisions represented attempts to make the reorganization procedures more accessible and practical in both the (B) and (C) areas. In light of the conflicting purposes, we can discern no clear Congressional mandate in the present structure of the (B) provision, either in terms of the abuses sought to be remedied or the beneficial transactions sought to be facilitated. At best, we think Congress has drawn somewhat arbitrary lines separating those transactions that resemble mere changes in form of ownership and those that contain elements of a sale or purchase arrangement. In such circumstances we believe it is more appropriate to examine the specific rules and requirements Congress enacted, rather than some questionably delineated "purpose" or "policy," to determine whether a particular transaction qualifies for favorable tax treatment. . . .

C

Besides finding support for the IRS position both in the design of the statute and in the legislative history, we find support in the regulations adopted by the Treasury Department construing these statutory provisions. We of course give weight to the statutory construction contemporaneously developed by the agency entrusted by Congress with the task of applying these laws. The views of the Treasury on tax matters, while by no means definitive, undoubtedly reflect a familiarity with the intricacies of the tax code that surpasses our own. . . .

D

Finally, we turn to the body of case law that has developed concerning (B) reorganizations to determine how previous courts have dealt with this question. Of the seven prior cases in this area, all to a greater or lesser degree support the result we have reached, and none supports the result reached by the Tax Court. [A]fter carefully reviewing the precedents, we are satisfied that the decision of the Tax Court represents a sharp break with the previous judicial constructions of this statute, and a departure from the usual rule of stare decisis, which applies with special force in the tax field where uncertainty and variety are ordinarily to be avoided.

Of the seven precedents, the most significant would seem to be How-ard v. Commissioner, 238 F.2d 943 (7th Cir. 1956), rev'g, 24 T.C. 792 (1955), which stands out as the one case prior to *Reeves* that specifically addressed the issue raised herein. In *Howard,* the Truax-Traer Coal Company acquired 80.19 percent of the outstanding stock of Binkley Coal Company solely in exchange for Truax-Traer voting stock. At the same time and as part of the same plan of acquisition, Truax-Traer purchased the other 19.81 percent of Binkley's stock for cash. The taxpayers, former shareholders of Binkley who had exchanged their shares solely for voting stock, sold some of the Truax-Traer stock they had received in August 1950, the same year as the exchange. The Commissioner, treating the exchange as a taxable event and not a reorganization, employed a new holding period, beginning with the effective date of the exchange, and treated the taxpayers' gain on their sale of the Truax-Traer stock as a short-term capital gain. The Tax Court sustained the Commissioner, con-cluding the exchange had not been made "solely for . . . voting stock," as required by the 1939 Act, even though the cash purchases were not essential to Truax-Traer's acquisition of control. 24 T.C. at 804.

The Seventh Circuit, after reviewing the legislative history of Section 112(g)(1)(B) of the 1939 Code, agreed with the Tax Court's conclusion that the presence of cash purchases prevented the transaction from meet-ing the "solely" requirement of the statute. . . . The principal linchpin of the Seventh Circuit's decision was Helvering v. Southwest Consolidated Corp., 315 U.S. 194 (1942), in which the Supreme Court denied tax-free treatment to an asset acquisition under the 1934 Act because a substantial amount of the consideration was given in the form of stock warrants and cash. The Court first noted that under the law existing before 1934, this transaction would have been a perfectly valid tax-free reorganization. The revised statute, . . . had made the continuity of interest test much stricter, however:

> Congress has provided that the assets of the transferor corporation must be acquired in exchange "solely" for "voting stock" of the transferee. "Solely" leaves no leeway. Voting stock plus some other consideration does not meet the statutory requirement.

315 U.S. at 198. The Seventh Circuit noted that in the 1934 Act the asset and stock acquisition reorganizations were dealt with in the same clause both in the statutory language and in the legislative history. It therefore seemed reasonable to the Seventh Circuit to conclude that the Supreme Court's "no leeway" rule for asset acquisitions applied with equal force to stock acquisitions.

Appellees argue that *Southwest Consolidated* is distinguishable from the present facts, and, implicitly, that it should not have been relied on by the *Howard* court. This argument rests, in our view, on a strained reading of *Southwest Consolidated*. The taxpayers point out that the nonstock consideration in that case amounted to 37 percent of the total consideration, by the Tax Court's reckoning. Further, they say that the stock and nonstock consideration could not be separated where one bundle of assets was exchanged for one bundle of consideration, so that *Southwest Consolidated* was essentially a mixed consideration case. We disagree. Had the Supreme Court chosen to decide the issue of whether "substantially all" the assets of one corporation were obtained solely for voting stock, it could have allocated the consideration on a proportional basis, much as the Tax Court did in making its calculations. The Supreme Court did not consider, however, whether the voting stock consideration was sufficient to cover "substantially all" the assets, so that Section 112(g)(1)(B) would be satisfied. The Court determined rather that the presence of *any* nonstock consideration in the acquisition negated the possibility of a valid tax-free reorganization. While the facts were such that the Court could have reached the same result on another rationale, this does not detract from the weight of its words. The Seventh Circuit was, in our opinion, justified in resting its holding by analogy on the decision in *Southwest Consolidated*. . . .

Besides questioning its lineage, the Tax Court plurality made three attempts to distinguish the *Howard* case or undercut its holding. First, the Tax Court argued that *Howard* was a case in which "some stockholders involved in the one exchange transaction . . . received cash." 71 T.C. at 737. The impact of this distinction is less than clear. There was no finding in *Howard* that any stockholder received both cash and stock for the same shares. In both *Howard* and this case, more than 80 percent of the shares were exchanged for stock only, and additional shares were purchased for cash. The only possible meaning of the Tax Court's statement is that it did not consider the 1968-69 cash purchases and the 1970 exchange offer part of "one exchange transaction." Yet the taxpayers' specific concession on motion for summary judgment was that the two events should be assumed to constitute "parts of the 1970 exchange offer reorganization." We do not see how *Howard* can be distinguished from the present case other than on a finding that the cash and stock transactions here were unrelated as a matter of law, a finding the Tax Court specifically declined to make. (As we are remanding this latter issue to the Tax Court, we take no position on it now.)

The Tax Court's second attack on *Howard* . . . is equally unpersuasive. The fact that one shareholder of Binkley (the acquiree) received voting stock for some of its shares and cash for other shares, so that the 80 percent necessary for control was not acquired from shareholders receiving only stock, was not relied on by the Seventh Circuit. Furthermore, the focus of the statute is on the consideration furnished in the exchange, not on the consideration received by a particular shareholder. . . . Indeed, in this case there is no proof that some of ITT's earlier market purchases were not made from shareholders of Hartford who later exchanged other shares for ITT's voting stock. . . .

Even were we doubtful as to the correctness of the result reached in *Howard* (and we are not), we would nonetheless be reluctant to see a rule of tax law which has stood virtually unchallenged by courts for 25 years discarded so unceremoniously. As the dissenting judges of the Tax Court noted, much tax planning must proceed on the basis of settled rules. Avoidance of risk and uncertainty are often the keys to a successful transaction. Transactions may have been structured on the basis of *Howard*, with cash intentionally introduced to prevent reorganization treatment. Where a long standing tax rule of this sort is not clearly contrary to Congressional intent or markedly inconsistent with some generally accepted understanding of correct doctrine, we think the proper body to make changes aimed at improving the law is Congress, and not the courts. The complex and delicate judgments as to proper tax policy, and the balancing of interests between corporations, their shareholders, and the public, required to formulate appropriate rules in this area are not the proper province of courts. . . .

Our reading of the statute is reinforced by another more recent circuit decision as well. In Mills v. Commissioner, 331 F.2d 321 (5th Cir. 1964), rev'g, 39 T.C. 393 (1962), the issue was whether cash payments for fractional shares in an exchange prevented a nontaxable reorganization. General Gas Corporation, the acquiror, offered the three taxpayers, sole stockholders in three small gas corporations, shares of General common stock in exchange for all of their stock. The number of General shares to be exchanged at a value of $14 per share was to be determined by measuring the net book value of the three small corporations. In the event the purchase price was not evenly divisible by 14, cash was to be paid in lieu of fractional shares. As a result, each taxpayer received 1,595 shares of General stock and $27.36 in cash. The Tax Court held this transaction invalid as a tax-free reorganization, declining to adopt a de minimis rule. 39 T.C. at 400. The Fifth Circuit agreed that cash could not form any part of the consideration in a (B) reorganization, but concluded in reversing the Tax Court that the fractional-share arrangement was merely a bookkeeping convenience and not an independent part of the consideration. 331 F.2d at 324-25.

Taxpayers, and the Tax Court, argued that *Mills* was distinguishable, despite its sweeping language, because each shareholder of the acquired corporations received both stock and cash in the exchange. We have discussed earlier our reasons for rejecting any rule premised on the consideration received by the acquiree's shareholders. If *Mills* were distinguishable at all, it would be only because the consideration for some of the shares in *Mills* consisted of both stock and cash. But even this distinction evaporates when one notes that the one share in each exchange for which a fractional share would have been necessary never constituted more than 20 percent of the stock of any one of the acquiree corporations (since each shareholder held at least six shares in each corporation). In every exchange it was theoretically possible to identify a bloc of more than 80 percent of the stock of the acquiree which was exchanged solely for the voting stock of the acquiring corporation. Thus, in the only case raising the issue now before us under the 1954 Code, the Tax Court accepted as a premise that no cash was permissible as consideration in a (B) reorganization, even where the facts showed that control had passed solely for voting stock.

IV

We have stated our ruling, and the reasons that support it. In conclusion, we would like to respond briefly to the arguments raised by the Tax Court, the District Court of Delaware, and the taxpayers in this case against the rule we have reaffirmed today. The principal argument, repeated again and again, concerns the supposed lack of policy behind the rule forbidding cash in a (B) reorganization where the control requirement is met solely for voting stock. It is true that the Service has not pointed to tax loopholes that would be opened were the rule to be relaxed as appellees request. We also recognize, as the Tax Court and others have highlighted, that the rule may produce results which some would view as anomalous. For example, if Corporation X acquires 80 percent of Corporation Y's stock solely for voting stock, and is content to leave the remaining 20 percent outstanding, no one would question that a valid (B) reorganization has taken place. If Corporation X then decides to purchase stock from the remaining shareholders, the *Howard* rule might result in loss of nontaxable treatment for the stock acquisition if the two transactions were found to be related. See 71 T.C. at 740-41. The Tax Court asserted that there is no conceivable Congressional policy that would justify such a result. Further, it argued, Congress could not have felt that prior cash purchases would forever ban a later successful (B) reorganization since the 1954 amendments, as the legislative history makes clear, specifically provided that prior cash purchases would not prevent a creeping acquisition.

While not without force, this line of argument does not in the end persuade us. First of all, as already discussed, the language of the statute, and the longstanding interpretation given it by the courts, are persuasive reasons for our holding even in the absence of any clear policy behind Congress' expression of its will. Furthermore, we perceive statutory anomalies of another sort which the Tax Court's rule would only magnify. It is clear from the regulations, for example, that a corporation which already owned as much as 80 percent of another's stock, acquired solely for cash, could in some circumstances acquire all or a part of the remainder solely for voting stock as a valid (B) reorganization. Why, then, could not as little as 10 percent of an acquisition constitute a (B) reorganization, if made solely for voting stock, even though the remaining transactions totaling more than 80 percent were made for nonstock consideration? If it is true that Congress did not view related cash transactions as tainting a stock-acquisition reorganization, why would it enact a "solely for . . . voting stock" requirement at all, except to the extent necessary to prevent mixed consideration of the sort employed in the "disguised sales" of the twenties?

Possibly, Congress' insertion of the "solely for . . . voting stock" requirement into the 1934 Act was, as one commentator has suggested, an overreaction to a problem which could have been dealt with through more precise and discriminating measures. But we do not think it appropriate for a court to tell Congress how to do its job in an area such as this. If a more refined statutory scheme would be appropriate, such changes should be sought from the body empowered to make them. While we adhere to the general practice of construing statutes so as to further their demonstrated policies, we have no license to rework whole statutory schemes in pursuit of policy goals which Congress has nowhere articulated. Appellees have not shown us any reason to believe that reaffirmation of the settled rule in this area will frustrate the Congressional purpose of making the (B) reorganization provision generally available to those who comply with the statutory requirements.

A second major argument, advanced primarily by the district court in Pierson [v. United States, 472 F. Supp. 957 (D. Del. 1979), rev'd sub nom. Heverly v. Commissioner, 621 F.2d 1227 (3d Cir. 1980)], is that the previous cases construing this statute are suspect because they did not give proper weight to the changes wrought by the 1954 amendments. In particular, the court argued the liberalization of the "boot" allowance in (C) reorganizations and the allowance of creeping (B) acquisitions showed that Congress had no intent or desire to forbid "boot" of up to 20 percent in a (B) reorganization. As we have discussed earlier, we draw the opposite conclusion from the legislative history. Liberalization of the (C) provision shows only that Congress, when it wished to do so, could grant explicit leeway in the reorganization rules. . . .

A third argument asserts that reliance on the literal language of the 1954 Code, and in particular a focus on the interpretation of "acquisition," is unjustified because the 1954 Code was not intended to alter the status of (B) reorganizations under the 1934 and 1939 Codes. According to this argument, the acquisition of at least 80 percent of the acquiree's stock solely for voting stock was allowed under the pre-1954 version, and must still be allowed even though the present statute refers only to "the acquisition . . . of stock" with no percentage specified. This argument assumes the answer to the question that is asked. As *Howard* and *Southwest Consolidated* illustrate, it has been the undeviating understanding of courts, until now, that the pre-1954 statutes did not allow cash or other "boot" in a (B) reorganization. It cannot be inferred that Congress left intact a rule which never existed by enacting language inconsistent with such a rule.

Finally, we see no merit at all in the suggestion that we should permit "boot" in a (B) reorganization simply because "boot" is permitted in some instances in (A) and (C) reorganizations. Congress has never indicated that these three distinct categories of transactions are to be interpreted in pari materia. In fact, striking differences in the treatment of the three subsections have been evident in the history of the reorganization statutes. We see no reason to believe a difference in the treatment of "boot" in these transactions is impermissible or irrational. . . .

The case will be remanded to the Tax Court for further proceedings consistent with this opinion. . . .

NOTES

1. *The* Chapman *decision*. Notice how the taxpayer in *Chapman* waged a double-barreled attack against the *Howard* adverse precedent. Not only did the taxpayer seek to distinguish *Howard*, but the case cited for support by the *Howard* court (Helvering v. Southwest Consolidated Corp.) also was distinguished. By this technique, the taxpayer offered the court the opportunity to overrule or distinguish the adverse precedent of *Howard*.

The court stated that it could discern no clear policy argument supporting one side's interpretation over the other. In that light, was the court's decision to adopt a narrow construction of the statute a good one, particularly when a "corporate reorganization" (in the colloquial sense) was effected? The Tax Court seemingly has accepted the *Chapman* construction of §368(a)(1)(B). Clark v. Commissioner, 86 T.C. 138, 142 n.5 (1986).

In fact, the Service argued that there was a good policy reason for rejecting the taxpayer's argument in this case. A voting block of 10 percent to 15 percent of a publicly held corporation often produces effective control. By purchasing about 8 percent of Hartford's stock, ITT was able to force on the Hartford board of directors a merger that it had already rejected on almost the same terms. Counsel for the government argued on appeal that a proper interpretation of the statute should not permit such "gunboat diplomacy." Would such a policy argument have been a proper basis for the court's holding?

The effect of the circuit court's decision in *Chapman* was to remand the case to the Tax Court for trial on the merits. While petitions for certiorari in *Chapman* and a related case were pending, however, the case was settled with ITT's agreement to make a one-time payment of $18.5 million to the U.S. Treasury. Since ITT was not a party to the action, why did ITT agree to pay the settlement? What should the tax consequences of this settlement have been to the former Hartford shareholders? In fact, the settlement included the provisions that ITT would not deduct the settlement payment and that no tax deficiencies would be asserted against the former Hartford shareholders. These shareholders, though, were bound to carry over their Hartford stock basis into their ITT stock.

In Rev. Rul. 85-139, 1985-2 C.B. 123, the Service ruled that the solely-for-voting-stock requirement of a B reorganization is not met when the acquiring corporation exchanges its voting stock for 90 percent of the target corporation's stock and a wholly owned subsidiary of the acquiring corporation acquires 10 percent of the target's stock for cash. Is the emphasis placed by *Chapman* and Rev. Rul. 85-139 on the "transaction" justified? To what extent should motives matter?

In Rev. Rul. 69-294, 1969-1 C.B. 10, *X* Corp. owned all the outstanding stock of *Y* Corp. *Y* owned more than 80 percent of the outstanding stock of *Z* Corp. To obtain direct ownership of 100 percent of *Z*, *X* caused *Y* to liquidate and *X* immediately thereafter acquired the minority stock in *Z* for its own voting stock. The Service ruled that the latter exchange was taxable and did not qualify as a B reorganization since *X*, as part of a single unified transaction, had acquired all the stock of *Z* but not "solely for" *X* voting stock. The reasoning was that more than 80 percent of the *Z* stock was received in exchange for its *Y* stock.

Suppose a corporation adopts a "poison pill" antitakeover provision giving shareholders the right to purchase at a bargain price additional shares of the company (or of any acquiring company) if there is a hostile takeover. Can the corporation now participate as the acquiring corporation in a B reorganization, or will the poison pill attached to its stock constitute impermissible nonstock consideration? The Service has consistently ruled that the poison pill rights do not constitute nonstock consideration. See Priv. Ltr. Rul. 9125013; Priv. Ltr. Rul. 8925087; Priv. Ltr. Rul. 8808081.

2. *Contingent stock.* An acquiring corporation in a merger may, in addition to issuing shares of stock outright to the shareholders of the target company, promise to pay additional shares on the occurrence of certain contingencies. The type of contingencies may be, for example, the earnings performance of the target company over some specified future period or the trading value of its stock. The use of contingent stock allows the parties to exploit differing expectations of the future to strike a deal that otherwise would be unobtainable. See H. Raiffa, The Art and Science of Negotiation 91-107 (1982).

Contingent rights to acquire stock that are issued in connection with a reorganization have been treated as stock rather than boot. See Carlberg v. United States, 281 F.2d 507 (8th Cir. 1960); Hamrick v. Commissioner, 43 T.C. 21 (1964). Rev. Proc. 77-37, 1977-2 C.B. 568, provides guidelines for advanced rulings when contingent or escrowed stock is involved. The most important of these relates to the maximum number of shares whose receipt can be made contingent (50 percent of the total that can be issued) and the time during which the contingencies must be resolved (five years). See also Rev. Proc. 84-42, 1984-1 C.B. 521 (amplifying Rev. Proc. 77-37).

Section 483 creates interest income in the case of contingent stock deferred for more than one year after the exchange unless interest is provided for in the form of additional shares. Solomon v. Commissioner, 570 F.2d 28 (2d Cir. 1977); accord, Jeffers v. United States, 556 F.2d 986 (Cl. Ct. 1977); Catterall v. Commissioner, 68 T.C. 413 (1977), aff'd sub nom. Vorbleski v. Commissioner, 589 F.2d 123 (3d Cir. 1978). But in Rev. Rul. 70-120, 1970-1 C.B. 124, the Service ruled that deferred payments do not exist in a reorganization in which bonus stock is issued in each shareholder's name and then is placed in escrow if the shareholders can vote the shares and receive dividends even though they may later be divested of the bonus shares. The result is that interest income under §483 can be avoided if all the stock is issued initially even though some is in effect made contingent by being placed in an escrow. Why? Note that under the regulations, the interest portion imputed on contingent stock is not treated as boot and will not destroy the tax-free status of the reorganization. Treas. Regs. §§1.483-2(a)(2), 1.483-2(b)(3)(i), and 1.483-1(b)(6) (examples 7 and 8).

3. *Cash in lieu of fractional shares.* In Rev. Rul. 66-365, 1966-2 C.B. 116, the Service ruled that cash paid in lieu of issuing fractional shares will not be regarded as boot consideration in an acquisitive reorganization. This favorable ruling is limited, however, to those cases in which the cash is not a separately bargained-for consideration. In what circumstances might cash in lieu of fractional shares be separately bargained for? See also Rev. Rul. 69-34, 1969-1 C.B. 105, and Rev. Rul. 74-36, 1974-1 C.B. 85, extending this rule to E and F reorganizations.

PROBLEMS

10-4.   Determine whether the following transactions are "reorganizations" within the meaning of §368(a)(1)(B).

a.   To ensure a ready source of newsprint, News Corp. purchases 85 percent of the stock of Paper Co. for cash. One year later, News Corp. acquires the remaining stock of Paper Co. in exchange for its own voting preferred stock. What is the result if News Corp. used voting stock of its parent corporation? Of its wholly owned

subsidiary? Could News Corp. use its own nonvoting common
stock? Can News Corp. pay the cost of registering the stock received by the shareholders of Paper Co.?

b.   *T* owns all 100 outstanding shares of *Z* Corp. The shares have an
aggregate value of $100,000 and are subject to a mortgage of
$15,000 incurred by *T* to remodel her home. Big Corp. acquires
all the stock of *Z* by exchanging 85 shares of its $1,000 par value
voting preferred for the *Z* shares and assumption of the outstanding debt. What is the result if it took the shares subject to the
debt but *T* remained personally liable on it?

3. The C Reorganization: Stock for Assets

In a C reorganization, the transferor corporation exchanges at least "substantially all" its assets for voting stock of the acquiring corporation. In
most circumstances, the transferor corporation must liquidate as part of
the plan of reorganization. §368(a)(2)(G). Accordingly, the C reorganization is practically indistinguishable from a statutory merger. As in a B
reorganization (and in distinction to a statutory merger), however, Congress has limited the allowable consideration in a C reorganization to
voting stock of the acquiring corporation or of the acquiring corporation's
parent. §368(a)(1)(C) (parenthetical language).

In United States v. Hendler, 303 U.S. 564 (1938), the Supreme Court
held that the assumption by the acquiring corporation of a liability of the
transferor corporation constitutes boot consideration. Since most businesses encumber their assets, the practical effect of the *Hendler* decision
was to eliminate the C reorganization as a viable possibility. Congress responded by adding to the definition of a C reorganization that the acquiring corporation's assumption of a liability (or taking property subject to a
liability) will not cause the transaction to lose its reorganization status. See
§368(a)(1)(C). A further anti-*Hendler* rule was enacted in §357, discussed
at pages 24-40 supra in the context of §351 incorporations and at page
444 infra in the context of reorganizations.

The technical traps of the reorganization provisions are vividly illustrated by some problems that have arisen under §368(a)(1)(C)'s requirement that the acquiring corporation acquire "substantially all of the
properties" of another corporation. In Bausch & Lomb Optical Co. v.
Commissioner, 267 F.2d 75 (2d Cir. 1959), the acquiring corporation
owned 79 percent of the transferor corporation. The parent issued its stock
for all the assets of the subsidiary, and the subsidiary then liquidated. The
parent received back 79 percent of the newly issued stock, and the minority
shareholders of the subsidiary became shareholders of the parent. Should
the acquisition have been taxed as a C reorganization?

The court held that the transaction did not qualify as a C reorganization. In the court's view, the parent acquired 79 percent of the subsidiary's

assets in exchange for stock of the subsidiary as part of the liquidation: Only the remaining 21 percent was acquired for voting stock of the parent. Therefore, the parent received less than "substantially all" the subsidiary's properties in exchange for its own stock.

This decision makes little sense: The court held that the transaction failed to satisfy the statutory continuity of proprietary interest regulation of §368(a)(1)(C) even though the acquiring corporation ended up owning all of the target's assets and the minority shareholders of the target ended up with voting stock of the acquiring corporation. Fortunately, *Bausch & Lomb Optical* has been overruled by regulation. Treas. Regs. §1.368-2(d)(4). If the acquisition is effected by merger, it will qualify as an "A" reorganization. Treas. Regs. §1.368-1(e)(6) (example 7).

NOTES

1. *"Substantially all" the properties.* Under Rev. Proc. 77-37, 1977-2 C.B. 568, for advance ruling purposes, the Service will consider the substantially-all requirement to be met by the transfer of at least 70 percent of gross assets and 90 percent of the net assets. For example, if X Corp. owns assets with aggregate fair market value of $1 million subject to liabilities of $200,000, the transfer by X of $720,000 or more of its assets for voting stock of the acquiring corporation will satisfy this test.

The judicial interpretation of the substantially-all requirement may be more relaxed than the Service's ruling guidelines. The transferor corporation in a substitutive D reorganization, discussed infra, must also transfer substantially all its assets in the reorganization. See §354(b)(1)(A). In that context, a transfer of all the operating assets of the transferor has been held to satisfy the substantially-all test even when the value of those assets, as a percentage of the net worth of the corporation, has been low. See Smothers v. United States, page 419 infra (15 percent); Armour, Inc. v. Commissioner, 43 T.C. 295 (1961) (51 percent).

2. *The boot relaxation rule of §368(a)(2)(B).* While the "solely for voting stock" requirement is absolute in a B reorganization, Congress has provided in a C reorganization that property other than stock may be used as consideration if at least 80 percent of the fair market value of the acquired corporation's assets are acquired for voting stock. §368(a)(2)(B). In determining whether 80 percent of all property is acquired for voting stock, any liabilities assumed by the acquiring corporation are treated as money or other property. Thus, if the value of the transferor's properties is $100,000 subject to liabilities of $15,000, the acquiring corporation would be limited to paying $5,000 in money or other property in addition to assuming the liabilities. If the liabilities were $21,000, the only consideration allowed in a C reorganization would be voting stock. Since most businesses have substantial liabilities, the boot possibilities for C reorganizations are limited, if not nonexistent.

Can a failed B reorganization be converted into a successful C reorganization by prompt liquidation of the acquired subsidiary? For example, suppose *A* Corp. acquires all the stock of *T* Corp. in exchange for its voting stock worth $1 million plus cash of $100,000. Because of the cash, the acquisition is not a B reorganization. But suppose *A* promptly liquidates *T* Corp. Can the transaction be viewed as an indirect asset acquisition qualifying as a C reorganization? See American Potash & Chemical Corp. v. United States, 399 F.2d 194 (Cl. Ct.), aff'd, 402 F.2d 1000 (Cl. Ct. 1968) (failed B reorganization followed by liquidation of subsidiary cannot qualify as a C reorganization); Rev. Rul. 67-274, 1967-2 C.B. 141 (B reorganization followed by liquidation of acquired corporation taxed as a C reorganization). Should ITT have attempted to convert its Hartford acquisition into a C reorganization?

3. *Contingent stock.* In Rev. Rul. 78-376, 1978-2 C.B. 149, *X* Corp. acquired substantially all the assets of *Y* Corp. in a C reorganization. *A,* the sole shareholder of *Y,* received shares of *X,* a portion of which were placed in escrow as security pending the resolution of a contingent liability of *Y.* When the amount of the liability was determined, the escrowed shares had doubled in value. The agreement provided that the number of shares to be returned to *X* would be based on the amount of the liability and the value of the escrowed stock on the date of return. The Service ruled that *A* recognized gain on return of the shares equal to the excess of the fair market value of the shares not returned (which was equal to the liability) over their adjusted basis. *A*'s basis in the remaining shares was increased by the amount of the claim satisfied. Cf. Rev. Rul. 76-42, 1976-1 C.B. 102, in which no gain was recognized on the return of escrowed shares because the number of shares returned was based on their initial negotiated value and, therefore, the shareholder could receive no benefit or detriment from any changes in the fair market value of the escrowed stock returned. Are these two rulings consistent even assuming the validity of the rationale of the latter?

While escrowed stock is not treated as boot, stock rights, options, and warrants are not considered to be stock or securities but "other property." See Treas. Regs. §1.354-1(e); Helvering v. Southwest Consolidated Corp., 315 U.S. 194 (1942) (warrants). Why should the use of escrowed stock be permissible in B and C reorganizations while stock rights, options, and warrants are not?

PROBLEMS

10-5. Determine whether the following transaction are "reorganizations" within the meaning of §368(a)(1)(C).

    a. Target Corp. owns assets with a fair market value of $200,000 subject to debts of $50,000. Acquiring Corp. exchanges its voting stock worth $150,000 for the Target assets subject to the debt, and Target promptly liquidates. What are the consequences if Acquiring Corp. paid Target Corp. $50,000 to discharge the debts as part of the acquisition? If Acquiring Corp. uses cash of $25,000 and takes the assets subject to $25,000 of debt? How do your answers change if the debt was only $30,000?

b. Suppose in (a) that Acquiring Corp. exchanges voting stock of its Parent Corp. (rather than its own voting stock) for the Target Corp. assets and that after the exchange Acquiring Corp. transfers the assets acquired from Target Corp. to Holding Corp., a wholly owned subsidiary of Acquiring Corp. Assume Acquiring Corp. is a wholly owned subsidiary of Parent Corp.

4. *The Nondivisive D Reorganization*

The D reorganization at first blush seems peculiar in that it contemplates a *transfer* of assets from one corporation to another rather than an *exchange* of assets for stock or some other valuable consideration. Note, though, that such a transfer will not qualify as a D reorganization unless the transferor corporation (or its shareholders) controls the transferee corporation. By virtue of §368(a)(2)(H), "control" for a D reorganization is defined in §304(c) — a 50 percent test — rather than in §368(c) — an 80 percent test — applicable to the other types of reorganization. Were there no more to it than this, a nondivisive D reorganization would be a transfer of assets between a (broadly defined) brother-sister or parent-subsidiary pair.

But there is more. A transfer of assets to a corporation controlled by the transferor (or its shareholders) will not qualify as a D reorganization unless the asset transfer is accompanied by a distribution of stock or securities described in §354, 355, or 356. The two basic forms of D reorganizations are (1) those qualifying by virtue of a §354 distribution and (2) those qualifying by virtue of a §355 distribution. (D reorganizations qualifying under §356 are simply one of the two basic forms in which the distribution includes some boot as well as stock and securities.) We will consider only the first form of the D reorganization here; the second form — a D reorganization qualifying under §355 — effects a divisive reorganization and is discussed infra.

A D reorganization qualifying with a §354 distribution must satisfy the requirements of §354(b)(1). That section requires that the transferor corporation transfer substantially all its assets and then liquidate. The transferor may, but need not, receive stock, securities, or other property in exchange for its assets; whatever it receives, plus all assets not transferred, must be distributed in a complete liquidation.

The D reorganization qualifying with a §354 distribution is often called a "substitutive" (or "acquisitive") D reorganization because the transferee corporation is controlled by the same shareholders who controlled the transferor, §368(a)(1)(D), and it ends up with at least substantially all the transferor's assets, §354(b)(1). The substantially-all requirement of the substitutive D, as well as the forced liquidation of the transferor corporation, should remind you of the C reorganization. Both C and D reorganizations include the following features: (1) an exchange of substantially all the assets of one corporation for stock of another corporation, and (2) the immediate liquidation of the transferor corporation. The difference between the two is that continuity of proprietary interest is ensured in a C reorganization by requiring that 80 percent of the stock received by the transferor corporation be voting stock in the acquiring corporation (or in its parent), while continuity in a D reorganization is ensured by requiring that the shareholders of the transferor corporation control the acquiring corporation immediately after the transaction. Note that some overlap between C and D reorganizations is contemplated, and when such overlap occurs, the transaction is treated as a type D. §368(a)(2)(A).

Usually it is the taxpayer who argues that a corporate rearrangement qualifies as an A, B, or C reorganization, but often it is the Commissioner who argues in favor of the substitutive D, and the Commissioner may sometimes catch a taxpayer off guard. See *Smothers,* below. Consider individual *T,* who owns all the stock of *X* Corp. *X* Corp. has accumulated substantial amounts of cash and other liquid assets, and *T* would like to remove those assets from corporate solution at capital gain rates. Assuming that *X* Corp. has substantial accumulated earnings and profits, *T* would not want to cause *X* Corp. to declare a dividend, for under §301 *T* would have ordinary income equal to the full fair market value of the dividend distribution. Because *T* is the sole shareholder of *X* Corp., a redemption of some of *T*'s stock will not qualify for exchange treatment under §302(b)(1)-(3), and liquid assets (other than the proceeds from the sale of assets used in a business no longer conducted) cannot qualify for partial liquidation treatment under §302(b)(4).

T could cause *X* Corp. to liquidate, making capital gain treatment available under §331(a). But if *T* wishes to continue using the operating assets of *X* Corp. in corporate form, the complete liquidation of *X* might be considered too high a price to pay. One technique for *T* to try is to cause *X* Corp. to create a new subsidiary, *Y* Corp., and transfer to that subsidiary all the *X* Corp. operating assets. Such a transfer would be tax free under §351, and if *X* Corp. then liquidated, *T* would have removed the liquid assets from corporate solution without recognizing any ordinary income. Indeed, *T* would have the added benefit that *Y* Corp. would not be burdened by the prior earnings and profits account of *X*.

Unfortunately for *T,* the creation of *Y* and liquidation of *X* will be taxed as a nondivisive D reorganization. Assuming that the operating assets of *X* constitute substantially all its assets (a point to be examined in Note 2 infra), *X* has transferred substantially all its assets to a corporation (*Y*) controlled by it or its shareholders immediately after the transaction. The

distribution requirement of §354(b)(1) is satisfied by the complete liquidation of X. Thus, T will be taxed under §§354 and 356 on T's exchange
of X stock for the X liquid assets accompanied by the new Y stock. Under §356(a)(2), T may recognize ordinary income on the exchange, limited only by the amount of gain realized by T and by X's earnings and
profits.

The substitutive D reorganization is also used by the Commissioner
to attack liquidation-reincorporations. For example, were T to liquidate X
Corp. and then reincorporate the operating assets, the Commissioner
would argue that the effect of the liquidation-reincorporation was a substitutive D reorganization in which the liquid assets were distributed as boot.
In such a case, however, the Commissioner faces the preliminary difficulty
of identifying the requisite distribution of stock or securities by the transferor. What argument would you advise the Commissioner to make?

Smothers v. United States
642 F.2d 894 (5th Cir. 1981)

Before Wisdom, Garza and Reavley, Circuit Judges.

WISDOM, Circuit Judge. . . .

This dispute arises from the dissolution of one of [the Smothers']
wholly-owned business corporations. The taxpayers contend that the assets
distributed to them by that corporation should be taxed at the capital gain
rate applicable to liquidating distributions. The Internal Revenue Service
(IRS) counters by characterizing the dissolution as part of a reorganization,
thereby rendering the taxpayers' receipt of the distributed assets taxable
at ordinary income rates. The district court viewed the transaction as a
reorganization and ruled for the IRS. We affirm.

I

In 1956, [the Smothers] and an unrelated third party organized Texas
Industrial Laundries of San Antonio, Inc. (TIL). The Smothers owned all
of its outstanding stock from 1956 through the tax year in issue, 1969. TIL
engaged in the business of renting industrial uniforms and other industrial
cleaning equipment, such as wiping cloths, dust control devices, and continuous toweling. It owned its own laundry equipment as well.

Shortly after the incorporation of TIL, the taxpayers organized another corporation, Industrial Uniform Services, Inc. (IUS), specifically to
oppose a particular competitor in the San Antonio industrial laundry market. The taxpayers owned all of the stock of IUS from the time of its
organization until its dissolution. Unlike TIL, IUS did not own laundry
equipment; it had to contract with an unrelated company to launder the

uniforms it rented to customers. J. E. Smothers personally managed IUS, as well as TIL, but chose not to pay himself a salary from IUS in any of the years of its existence.

IUS evidently succeeded in drawing business away from competing firms, for TIL purchased its main competitor in 1965. IUS continued in business, however, until 1969. On the advice of their accountant, the taxpayers then decided to dissolve IUS and sell all of its non-liquid assets to TIL. On November 1, 1969, IUS adopted a plan of liquidation in compliance with I.R.C. §337, and on November 30, it sold the following assets to TIL for cash at their fair market value (stipulated to be the same as their book value):

Assets	Amount
Noncompetitive covenant	$ 3,894.60
Fixed assets	491.25
Rental property	18,000.00
Prepaid insurance	240.21
Water deposit	7.50
Total	$22,637.56[3]

The noncompetitive covenant constituted part of the consideration received by IUS from its purchase of a small competitor. The fixed assets consisted of incidental equipment (baskets, shelves, and a sewing machine), two depreciated delivery vehicles, and IUS's part interest in an airplane. The rental property was an old apartment building in Corpus Christi on land with business potential. These assets collectively represented about 15% of IUS's net value. The parties stipulated that none of these assets were necessary to carry out IUS's business.

After this sale, IUS promptly distributed its remaining assets to its shareholders, the taxpayers, and then dissolved under Texas law:

Assets	Amount
Cash (received from TIL)	$ 22,637.56
Cash (of IUS)	2,003.05
Notes receivable	138,000.00
Accrued interest receivable	35.42
Claim against the State of Texas	889.67
Liabilities assumed	(14,403.35)
Total	$149,162.35

3. The parties stipulated that the purchase price was $22,637.56, and the district court found that as a fact. The items listed add to $22,633.56, however. We ignore the discrepancy and accept the stipulation.

TIL hired all three of IUS's employees immediately after the dissolution, and TIL continued to serve most of IUS's customers.

In computing their federal income tax liability for 1969, the taxpayers treated this distribution by IUS as a distribution in complete liquidation within §331(a)(1). Accordingly, they reported the difference between the value of the assets they received in that distribution, $149,162.35, and the basis of their IUS stock, $1,000, as long-term capital gain. Upon audit, the IRS recharacterized the transaction between TIL and IUS as a reorganization within §368(a)(1)(D), and therefore treated the distribution to the taxpayers as equivalent to a dividend under §356(a)(2). Because IUS had sufficient earnings and profits to cover that distribution, the entire distribution was therefore taxable to the Smothers at ordinary income rates. The IRS timely assessed a $71,840.84 deficiency against the Smothers. They paid that amount and filed this suit for a refund.

The district court held that the transaction constituted a reorganization and rendered judgment for the IRS. . . .

II

Subchapter C of the Internal Revenue Code broadly contemplates that the retained earnings of a continuing business carried on in corporate form can be placed in the hands of its shareholders only after they pay a tax on those earnings at ordinary income rates. That general rule is, of course, primarily a consequence of §301, which taxes dividend distributions as ordinary income. The Code provides for capital gain treatment of corporate distributions in a few limited circumstances, but only when there is either a significant change in relative ownership of the corporation, as in certain redemption transactions, or when the shareholders no longer conduct the business themselves in corporate form, as in true liquidation transactions. The history of Subchapter C in large part has been the story of how Congress, the courts, and the IRS have been called upon to foil attempts by taxpayers to abuse these exceptional provisions. Ingenious taxpayers have repeatedly devised transactions which formally come within these provisions, yet which have the effect of permitting shareholders to withdraw profits at capital gain rates while carrying on a continuing business enterprise in corporate form without substantial change in ownership. This is just such a case.

The transaction in issue here is of the genus known as liquidation-reincorporation, or reincorporation. The common denominator of such transactions is their use of the liquidation provisions of the Code, which permit liquidating distributions to be received at capital gain rates, as a device through which the dividend provisions may be circumvented. Reincorporations come in two basic patterns. In one, the corporation is dissolved and its assets are distributed to its shareholders in liquidation.

The shareholders then promptly reincorporate all the assets necessary to the operation of the business, while retaining accumulated cash or other surplus assets. The transaction in this case is of the alternate form. In it, the corporation transfers the assets necessary to its business to another corporation owned by the same shareholders in exchange for securities or, as here, for cash, and then liquidates. . . . If formal compliance with the liquidation provisions were the only necessity, both patterns would enable shareholders to withdraw profits from a continuing corporate business enterprise at capital gain rates by paper-shuffling. Unchecked, these reincorporation techniques would eviscerate the dividend provisions of the Code.

That result can be avoided by recharacterizing such transactions, in accordance with their true nature, as reorganizations. A reorganization is, in essence, a transaction between corporations that results merely in "a continuance of the proprietary interests in the continuing enterprise under modified corporate form" — a phrase that precisely describes the effect of a reincorporation. Lewis v. Commissioner, 1 Cir. 1949, 176 F.2d 646, 648. Congress specifically recognized that the throw-off of surplus assets to shareholders in the course of a reorganization can be equivalent to a dividend, and if so, should be taxed as such. §§356(a)(1)-(2). The reincorporation transactions described above result in a dividend payment to the shareholders in every meaningful financial sense. The assets retained by the shareholders therefore should be taxed as dividends as long as the transaction can be fitted within the technical requirements of one of the six classes of reorganizations recognized by §368(a)(1).

In general, reincorporation transactions are most easily assimilated into §368(a)(1)(D) ("D reorganization"), as the IRS attempted to do in this case. A transaction qualifies as a D reorganization only if it meets six statutory requirements:

(1)   There must be a transfer by a corporation (§368(a)(1)(D));
(2)   of substantially all of its assets (§354(b)(1)(A));
(3)   to a corporation controlled by the shareholders of the transferor corporation, or by the transferor corporation itself (§368(a)(1)(D));
(4)   in exchange for stock or securities of the transferee corporation (§354(a)(1));
(5)   followed by a distribution of the stock or securities of the transferee corporation to the transferor's shareholders (§354(b)(1)(B));
(6)   pursuant to a plan of reorganization (§368(a)(1)(D)).

On this appeal, the taxpayers concede that the transaction in issue meets every technical prerequisite for characterization as a D reorganization, except for one. They argue that since the assets sold by IUS to TIL amounted to only 15% of IUS's net worth, TIL did not acquire "substantially all of the assets" of IUS within the meaning of §354(b)(1)(A).

We hold to the contrary. The words "substantially all assets" are not self-defining. What proportion of a corporation's assets is "substantially all" in this context, and less obviously, what "assets" are to be counted in making this determination, cannot be answered without reference to the structure of Subchapter C. To maintain the integrity of the dividend provisions of the Code, "substantially all assets" in this context must be interpreted as an inartistic way of expressing the concept of "transfer of a continuing business." [I]t is in a sense simply a limited codification of the general nonstatutory "continuity of business enterprise" requirement applicable to all reorganizations.

This interpretation finds support in the history of §368(a)(1)(D) and §354(b)(1)(A). The Internal Revenue Code of 1939 had no provision equivalent to the "substantially all assets" requirement, and courts almost uniformly approved attempts by the IRS to treat reincorporation transactions as reorganizations within the predecessor of §368(a)(1)(D) in the 1939 Code. The "substantially all assets" requirement of §354(b)(1)(A) and the amendment of §368(a)(1)(D) incorporating that requirement were added during the 1954 recodification as part of a package of amendments aimed at plugging a different loophole — the bail-out of corporate earnings and profits at capital gains rates through divisive reorganizations. There is no indication that Congress wished to relax the application of the reorganization provisions to reincorporation transactions. Indeed, the committee reports indicate the contrary. The Senate report accompanying the bill that contained the "substantially all assets" requirement of §354(b)(1)(A) and the parallel amendment to §368(a)(1)(D) stated that the purpose of those changes was only "to insure that the tax consequences of the distribution of stocks or securities to shareholders or security holders in connection with divisive reorganizations will be governed by the requirements of section 355." The report expressly noted that except with respect to divisive reorganizations, the reorganization provisions "are the same as under existing law and are stated in substantially the same form." Even more significantly, the original House version of the 1954 Code contained a provision specifically dealing with reincorporation transactions. That provision was dropped in conference because the conferees felt that such transactions "can appropriately be disposed of by judicial decision or by regulation within the framework of the other provisions of the bill." As the court said in Pridemark, Inc. v. Commissioner, 4 Cir. 1965, 345 F.2d 35, 40, this response shows that "the committee was aware of the problem and thought the present statutory scheme adequate to deal with it." By implication, this passage approved the IRS's use of the predecessor of §368(a)(1)(D) to meet the problem, and shows that the "substantially all assets" amendment was not thought to restrict its use.

Courts have almost unanimously so interpreted the "substantially all assets" language. Moreover, they have also interpreted the other technical conditions for a D reorganization in ways that accomplish the congressional intent to reach reincorporation transactions. For example, the literal language of §368(a)(1)(D) and §§354(a), 354(b)(1)(B) requires that the transferee corporation "exchange" some of its "stock or securities" for the assets of the transferor, and that those items be "distributed" to the shareholders of the transferor, before a D reorganization can be found. Yet both of those requirements have uniformly been ignored as "meaningless gestures" in the reincorporation context, in which the same shareholders own all the stock of both corporations. Smothers does not even challenge the applicability of that principle here.

Properly interpreted, therefore, the assets looked to when making the "substantially all assets" determination should be all the assets, and only the assets, necessary to operate the corporate business — whether or not those assets would appear on a corporate balance sheet constructed according to generally accepted accounting principles. Two errors in particular should be avoided. Inclusion of assets unnecessary to the operation of the business in the "substantially all assets" assessment would open the way for the shareholders of any enterprise to turn dividends into capital gain at will. For example, if we assume that "substantially all" means greater than 90%, then a corporation need only cease declaring dividends and accumulate surplus liquid assets until their value exceeds 10% of the total value of all corporate assets. The shareholders could then transfer the assets actively used in the business to a second corporation owned by them and liquidate the old corporation. Such a liquidating distribution would be a dividend in any meaningful sense, but an interpretation of "substantially all assets" that took surplus assets into account would permit the shareholders to treat it as capital gain. Indeed, such an interpretation would perversely treat a merely nominal distribution of retained earnings as a dividend, but would permit substantial distributions to be made at capital gain rates. Courts therefore have invariably ignored all surplus assets and have focused on the operating assets of the business — the tangible assets actively used in the business — when making the "substantially all assets" assessment.

Second, exclusion of assets not shown on a balance sheet constructed according to generally accepted accounting principles from the "substantially all assets" assessment would offer an unjustified windfall to the owners of service businesses conducted in corporate form. The most important assets of such a business may be its reputation and the availability of skilled management and trained employees, none of which show up on a standard balance sheet. Other courts have correctly recognized that in appropriate cases those intangible assets alone may constitute substantially all of the corporate assets. Otherwise, for example, a sole legal practitioner who owns nothing but a desk and chair could incorporate himself, accumulate earnings, and then set up a new corporation and liquidate the old at capital gain rates — as long as he is careful to buy a new desk and chair for the new corporation, rather than transferring the old.

When these principles are applied to this case, it is plain that "substantially all of the assets" of IUS were transferred to TIL, and that the transaction as a whole constituted a reorganization. TIL and IUS were both managed and wholly owned by Smothers. By the nature of its business, IUS was wholly a service enterprise; indeed, the parties stipulated that none of the tangible assets of IUS were necessary to the operation of its business. The extent to which those tangible assets were transferred to TIL is therefore entirely irrelevant. IUS's most important assets — its reputation, sales staff, and the managerial services of Smothers — were all transferred to TIL. TIL rehired all three of IUS's employees immediately after IUS's liquidation, and continued to serve IUS's old customers. The same business enterprise was conducted by the same people under the same ownership, and the only assets removed from corporate solution were accumulated liquid assets unnecessary to the operation of the business. To treat this transaction as other than a reorganization would deny economic reality; to permit Smothers to extract the retained earnings of IUS at capital gain rates would make a mockery of the dividend provisions of the Internal Revenue Code.

We do not perceive ordinary income treatment here to be particularly harsh, or a "tax trap for the unwary." It places the Smothers only in the position they would have been in if they had extracted the retained earnings of IUS as the Code contemplates they should have by periodically declaring dividends.

Affirmed.

GARZA, Circuit Judge, dissenting.

After carefully reading the majority's opinion, I find that I must respectfully dissent. Unlike my Brothers, who apparently feel that it is their duty to "plug loopholes," I would remain content in applying the tax law as it reads leaving the United States Congress to deal with the consequences of the tax law as it has been drafted. The only issue before this Court on appeal is whether or not IUS transferred "substantially all of its assets" to TIL. Instead of dealing with this straightforward question, the majority has made a case of evil against liquidation-reincorporation abuses and, in an attempt to remedy every such perceived abuse, they have relieved the Congress of its burden to change the law heretofore requiring that "substantially all" of a corporation's assets be transferred to now read that "only those assets necessary to operate the corporate business" be transferred in order to meet the "D reorganization" requirements. Essentially, the majority has changed the definition of "substantially all assets" to mean only "necessary operating assets." I believe if Congress had meant "necessary operating assets" it would have said so instead of specifically requiring that "substantially all" of the assets be transferred. In my mind "substantially all" plainly means *all* of the assets except for an *insubstantial* amount. Under such a definition, the sale of 15% of IUS's assets to TIL could hardly be defined as "substantially all" of IUS's assets.

However, even after having redefined "substantially all" to mean "necessary operating assets," the IUS liquidation still falls short of the "D reorganization" requirements because the stipulated facts are that absolutely none of the assets sold from IUS to TIL were necessary operating assets for either corporation. Faced with an absence of a proper factual setting, the majority goes on to define necessary operating assets as including a corporation's intangible assets. Now while a sale of intangible assets might be an appropriate consideration in determining whether or not "substantially all" assets of a corporation have been transferred, such a consideration simply has no bearing in this case. All of the assets transferred to TIL were depreciated tangible objects sold at book value after which IUS completely ceased all business operations. There simply was no other transfer of IUS's intangible assets as a continuing business.

The majority has placed great emphasis on the fact that three of IUS's route salesmen were subsequently employed by TIL and that Mr. Smothers' managerial services were available to TIL. Regardless of whether or not these facts enhanced TIL's business, the fact remains that neither the route salesmen or Mr. Smothers' services were *transferred* as assets from one corporation to another. After IUS ceased business its route salesmen were free to seek any employment they desired. Likewise, Mr. Smothers was never obligated to perform services for TIL. From these facts I cannot agree that there was a transfer of a continuing business. The majority imputes adverse tax consequences to IUS's stockholders simply because TIL offered new employment to the route salesmen who were unemployed upon cessation of IUS's business operations. The majority places future stockholders, in Mr. Smothers' position, of choosing between unfavorable tax consequences and helping secure future employment to loyal and deserving employees whom otherwise would be unemployed.

Although the Internal Revenue Service has never questioned the bona fides of IUS's liquidation, the majority has gone beyond the stipulated facts by characterizing the liquidation as a tax avoidance scam. I simply cannot agree. After starting from scratch, Mr. Smothers worked for over a dozen years refraining from drawing salary in order that IUS could pay its taxes, employees and other operating expenses and in order for IUS to become a successful self-sustaining business enterprise. Mr. Smothers was successful but, now that he no longer could devote his service to IUS, his years of labor are now labeled by the majority as a mere "paper shuffle." I do not share the majority's attitude.

The reasons for my position can be more easily understood by a simple review of the bottom-line facts. After IUS began showing a profit and started accumulating a cash surplus, instead of immediately investing in a building or in other equipment for its operations, it continued its operations as before. Now, if IUS had purchased real property or depreciable personal property for its operations (instead of leasing as it had been) and had sold these properties pursuant to its plan of liquidation, certainly no argument would be made that the money initially invested in those properties should have been declared by IUS as dividends. However, instead of investing its accumulations, IUS simply put them in its bank account as the tax laws allow and presumably faced any tax consequences posed by such an accumulation.

After IUS ceased operations, was liquidated, and its assets distributed to its stockholders in exchange for their stock, the I.R.S. issued a deficiency, not because IUS was reorganized within the meaning of . . . §368(a)(1)(D), but rather because the I.R.S. felt the accumulated earnings of IUS coupled with long-term capital gains rates applicable to the stock exchange provided an undesirable windfall to IUS's stockholders. In essence, the I.R.S. sought to expand the "D reorganization" provisions, lessen the availability of long-term capital gains treatment to corporate stockholders, and totally ignore the purpose of the tax upon improperly accumulated surplus as provided in . . . §531. The majority seeks to do equity for the I.R.S. position by "treating" the IUS liquidation as a "D reorganization." I do not believe the taxpayers or the tax laws are served by upholding an I.R.S. deficiency for the sole purpose of "plugging loopholes." The lesson to be learned from the majority's opinion is clear — future corporations faced with similar circumstances need only invest their otherwise accumulated surplus in some method other than savings. In the process of liquidation they need sell whatever assets exist to third parties unrelated to their stockholders and their stockholders should make no effort to find future employment for the corporation's employees.

It seems to me that in its attempt to "plug" a perceived "loophole," the majority is giving this Court's imprimatur to a variation of the same so-called "mockery" of the tax laws sought to be prevented by its opinion.

For these reasons, I respectfully dissent.

NOTES

1. *The control requirement.* A substitutive D reorganization requires, under §368(a)(2)(H), that shareholders of the transferor corporation meet the §304(c) control test in the transferee corporation so that when more than 50 percent of the transferred stock is owned by others, the courts will not find a D reorganization. See, e.g., Gallagher v. Commissioner, 39 T.C. 144 (1962) (decided under prior 80 percent control test). The Service has argued for application of the §318 attribution rules in testing for control, but this position has been generally rejected. See, e.g., Breech v. United States, 439 F.2d 409 (9th Cir. 1971). Without relying on

the attribution rules, however, the court in Stanton v. United States, 512 F.2d 13 (3d Cir. 1975), attributed a wife's 49 percent interest in a new corporation to her husband when she had not transferred any assets to the new corporation for its stock. The court viewed the wife's interest as first held by the husband and then transferred to her as a gift.

Should the continuity of proprietary interest doctrine be part of the gloss on substitutive D reorganizations, given that the transferor's assets will in all events be continued in corporate form controlled by proprietary owners of the transferor? From another perspective, should this doctrine apply not only to limit the entrance of new owners but also to prohibit the elimination of some of the old owners?

2. *Substantially all the assets.* The court in *Smothers* was willing to treat 15 percent of the transferor corporation's assets as "substantially all" because the 15 percent at issue included all the corporation's operating assets. To the same effect, see Moffatt v. Commissioner, 363 F.2d 262 (9th Cir. 1966) (64.52 percent); Armour, Inc. v. Commissioner, 43 T.C. 295 (1964) (51 percent). Are these courts, as Judge Garza argued in dissent in *Smothers,* giving insufficient deference to the words used by Congress in §354(b)(1)?

Liquidation of the transferor corporation was not required as part of a C reorganization until 1984. Until then, the C reorganization did not so closely resemble the nondivisive D reorganization. Given the current similarity of the C and nondivisive D reorganizations, should the interpretation of "substantially all" in §368(a)(1)(C) be informed by these judicial decisions explicating the terms of a substitutive D reorganization? If some but not all of the assets of T Corp. are transferred to A Corp. in exchange for voting stock of A, and T then liquidates, is the transaction more like a sale than a continuation of T's business? If the shareholders of T lack control of A (so that the transaction is not a substitutive D), is the transfer of all the operating assets of T more like a sale than a reorganization? Recall Rev. Proc. 77-37, discussed at page 415 supra, in which "substantially all" means 70 percent of a corporation's gross assets and 90 percent of its net assets.

3. *The transfer requirement.* A service-intensive business may have few or no operating assets. Suppose such a business operating in corporate form is completely liquidated, followed by the formation of a corporation engaged in a similar business employing the same workers and servicing the same clients or customers. Can the Commissioner attack such an arrangement as a nondivisive D reorganization? Under the definition of a D reorganization in §368(a)(1)(D), the transferor corporation must "transfer" substantially all its assets to the acquiring corporation. In the example posed above, have the employees or customers been "transferred" within the meaning of §368(a)(1)(D)?

It has been suggested that employees cannot be "transferred" in this sense. Warsaw Photographic Associates, Inc. v. Commissioner, 84 T.C. 21

(1985). But in Moffatt v. Commissioner, 363 F.2d 262 (9th Cir. 1966), it was held employees could be so "transferred." See also Simon v. Commissioner, 644 F.2d 339 (5th Cir. 1981), in which a nonassignable franchise right was "transferred" within the meaning of §368(a)(1)(D) when the franchise liquidated and the franchise reissued to a corporation controlled by shareholders of the liquidated corporation.

Note also the willingness of the court in *Smothers* to excuse the absence of a distribution. Should the ability to look through form be limited to the government? Compare Commissioner v. Danielson, 378 F.2d 771 (3d Cir. 1967).

PROBLEMS

10-6. *P* Corp. owns operating assets worth $300,000 as well as investment real estate worth $700,000. *F* owns all the stock of *P* Corp. *P* transfers all its assets to *Q* Corp. in exchange for common stock of *Q* worth $800,000 and cash of $200,000. *P* then liquidates, distributing the *Q* stock and cash to *F*. Prior to the transaction, *Q* was wholly owned by individual *S*. After the transaction, *F* owns 40 percent of *Q* and *S* owns 60 percent. Is this transaction a "reorganization" within the meaning of §368? What is the result if *P* did not transfer the real estate, receiving in exchange for the operating assets stock of *Q* worth $300,000 and representing a 20 percent interest? Is it relevant whether *F* and *S* are father and son?

5. Triangular Reorganizations

Before 1954, the acquiring corporation in a B or C reorganization could issue only its own stock as consideration for the stock or assets of the other corporation. See Groman v. Commissioner, 302 U.S. 82 (1937). In 1954, the definition of a C reorganization was amended — by adding the parenthetical phrase of §368(a)(1)(C) — to permit use of stock of the parent of the acquiring corporation. A similar statutory change subsequently was made to permit the use of the stock of a parent corporation in a B reorganization. A B or C reorganization using voting stock of the parent of the acquiring corporation is called a parenthetical B or C reorganization.

One reason for the widespread use of subsidiaries in the reorganization context is that state law may require the shareholders of the acquiring corporation as well as the shareholders of the transferor corporation to vote their approval of the reorganization. This is especially likely in the case of an A reorganization. If the acquiring corporation is publicly held, then the cost of obtaining shareholder consent might be prohibitive. By using a subsidiary as the nominal acquiring corporation, only the vote of

Figure 10-1

the subsidiary's shareholders — usually the board of directors of the parent company — is needed.

While there is no parenthetical A reorganization, §368(a)(2)(D) plays that role. Under this provision, a statutory merger using stock of the acquiring corporation's parent will qualify as a reorganization so long as the transaction would have qualified as an A reorganization had stock of the acquiring corporation been used. Thus, because the continuity of proprietary interest doctrine restricts the consideration that may be used in an A reorganization, it applies to limit the allowable consideration in a §368(a)(2)(D) reorganization. Note also that no stock of the subsidiary may be used. See Figure 10-1.

It may be that the acquisition can be structured more easily as a merger of the acquiring corporation into the target corporation. For example, the target corporation might be the lessee on a favorable long-term lease. In such a case, the acquiring corporation will cause a controlled subsidiary to merge into the target company. As part of the plan, shareholders of the target will exchange their target stock for stock of the acquiring corporation. Such a transaction constitutes a reorganization so long as the only consideration used is voting stock of the parent. §368(a)(2)(E). See Figure 10-2.

Reorganizations described in §368(a)(2)(D) are called "forward triangular (or subsidiary) mergers," while reorganizations described in §368(a)(2)(E) are called "reverse triangular (or subsidiary) mergers." One requirement imposed on both forms of triangular mergers is that substantially all the properties be continued in the surviving company. An alternate route to similar results is afforded by §368(a)(2)(C), which per-

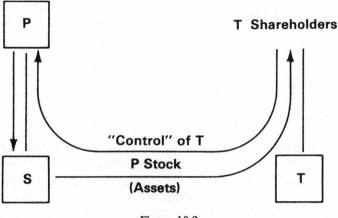

Figure 10-2

mits a corporation to acquire stock or assets in exchange for its own stock and then to transfer the acquired stock or assets to a subsidiary.

PROBLEMS

10-7. Determine whether the following transactions are "reorganizations" within the meaning of §368.

a. Corner Grocery Corp. is acquired by the *BQ* National Chain in the following steps. *BQ* forms a wholly owned subsidiary Sub Corp. Corner Grocery then merges into Sub Corp., with the shareholders of Corner Grocery receiving their consideration half in the form of *BQ* voting preferred stock and half in debentures of *BQ*. What are the consequences if the debentures were debt of the subsidiary? If the stock had been nonvoting?

b. Suppose in (a) that Corner Grocery owns a favorable lease that cannot be transferred. Accordingly, the transaction is structured as follows. *BQ* forms Sub Corp. by contributing *BQ* preferred stock. Sub Corp. is then merged into Corner Grocery, with *BQ* receiving 1,000 shares of Corner Grocery voting stock in exchange for its shares of Sub Corp. At the same time, the former shareholders of Corner Grocery exchange all their common stock of Corner Grocery for the *BQ* preferred owned by Sub Corp. How does your answer change if the former owners of Corner Grocery also owned nonvoting preferred stock in Corner Grocery and those preferred share remain outstanding after the merger?

C. TAXATION

1. *Overview*

Once it is determined that a reorganization has occurred, the tax consequences to all affected corporations and shareholders must be considered. The provisions applicable to the reorganizing corporations are §§357, 361, and 362, while the provisions applicable to their shareholders include §§354, 356, and 358. Other sections implicated by a tax-free reorganization include §§269, 381, and 382, discussed in Chapter 13.

In general, these rules provide that gain or loss is not recognized and that basis is continued unchanged. At the corporate level, this means that the acquiring corporation takes the acquired assets with a carryover basis and that no gain or loss is recognized by either corporation. At the shareholder level, the effect of a corporate reorganization usually is an exchange of stock of the transferor corporation for stock of the acquiring corporation. In the absence of boot, shareholders will not recognize gain or loss on such an exchange and will transfer their basis from the stock given up to the stock received.

Receipt of boot may, at the corporate or shareholder level, trigger the recognition of gain. The definition of a B reorganization precludes the use of boot, while A, C, and D reorganizations allow it. Do not confuse the notion of boot as used in the provisions taxing reorganizations — boot here meaning property other than that permitted to be received without the recognition of gain — with allowable consideration in the definitions of the various types of reorganizations in §368(a)(1). For example, if the acquiring corporation in a C reorganization uses its own securities as well as voting stock consideration to acquire all the assets of a corporation, the securities will constitute boot and will disqualify the reorganization if the total boot exceeds 20 percent of the total consideration. If the boot is less than 20 percent of the consideration, however, the transaction will qualify as a C reorganization. In this case, will distribution of the securities by the acquired company cause recognition to its shareholders? Not necessarily, for, at the shareholder level, securities of the acquiring corporation are not treated as boot unless a shareholder receives securities in excess of those given up. See §354(a)(2).

Do not forget the importance of §368(b)'s definition of the "parties" to a reorganization. At the corporate level, the reorganization provisions apply only to corporations that are parties to the reorganization. See §361(a). At the shareholder level, nonrecognition will apply only to exchanges of stock and securities of corporations that are, once again, parties to the reorganization.

The corporate parties to a reorganization are specified in §368(b). When the 1954 Code was enacted, §368(b) contained only the first sentence of the current provision. As Congress expanded the definition of a reorganization, it also expanded the definition of parties to a reorganization in §368(b).

In a statutory merger qualifying as an A reorganization, the parties to the reorganization are the two merging corporations. In a statutory consolidation, the parties are the consolidating corporations and the newly formed survivor. In the simple B and C reorganizations (in which stock of the acquiring corporation is used rather than stock of its parent), the parties are only the transferor corporation and the acquiring corporation. If a parenthetical B or C reorganization is effected, then the parties include the transferor corporation, the acquiring corporation, and the parent of the acquiring corporation.

In the case of forward triangular reorganizations under §368(a) (2)(D), the parties include both merging corporations and the acquiring corporation's parent. In the case of reverse triangular reorganizations under §368(a)(2)(E), the parties include both merging corporations and the transferor's parent. Lastly, when acquired assets are dropped down to a controlled subsidiary of the acquiring corporation pursuant to §368(a)(2)(C), the controlled subsidiary as well as the transferor and acquiring corporations are parties to the reorganization. In each case, then, the parties to a reorganization include those corporations *and only those corporations* playing a role in the definition of the reorganization.

2. *Corporate-level Taxation*

Five main issues arise in the corporate-level taxation of reorganizations: (1) recognition of gain or loss by the transferor corporation; (2) recognition of gain or loss by the acquiring corporation; (3) the basis of the assets acquired by the acquiring corporation; (4) the impact of the reorganization on net operating losses, earnings and profits accounts, and other tax attributes of corporations; and (5) the tax treatment of expenses incurred by the corporate parties incidental to the reorganization.

Turn first to the taxation of the transferor corporation. Recognition of gain and loss by the transferor corporation is governed by §361. Under §361(a), the transferor corporation recognizes no gain or loss on the exchange of its property for the stock and securities of another corporate party to the reorganization. Further, if the transferor corporation receives other property (boot) in addition to qualifying stock and securities, again no gain or loss is recognized so long as the boot is distributed as part of the reorganization. §361(b)(1)(A). Note that a distribution to a creditor *does* satisfy this requirement. §361(b)(3). Because the transferor corporation will almost always liquidate as part of the reorganization (see §368(a)(2)(G)(ii) for the possible exception), recognition by the transferor corporation is unlikely.

In some circumstances, however, assumption by the acquiring corporation of debts of the transferor corporation is treated as the transfer of money (i.e., as boot, see §357(b) (liability assumed or acquired for tax avoidance), §357(c)(1) (nondeductible liability in excess of basis)). Here the transferor corporation will recognize gain because there is no possibility of distributing the boot. Note that the transferor corporation will never recognize loss on the exchange. §361(b)(2).

Will the transferor corporation recognize gain or loss on its liquidating distribution pursuant to the reorganization? Loss will not be recognized, but gain might be. The transferor corporation's liquidating distribution might include three classes of property: (1) stock or securities of a corporate party acquired from the acquiring corporation, (2) property other than stock or securities (i.e., boot) from the acquiring corporation, and (3) property held by it and not transferred to the acquiring corporation as part of the reorganization.

As to class (1), such stock and securities constitute "qualified property" within the meaning of §361(c)(2)(B) and so will not trigger recognition on the distribution. §361(c). As to class (2), there is no gain to be recognized because the property should not be appreciated: The transferor corporation's basis in boot acquired from the acquiring corporation is fair market value under §358(a)(2). As to class (3), gain will be recognized to the extent the distributed property is appreciated. §361(c)(2)(A). Note that the usual rules applicable to complete liquidations do not apply in this context. §361(c)(4).

What of the acquiring corporation? Before examining the various types of reorganizations individually, recall that §1032 broadly provides that a corporation does not recognize gain or loss on the receipt of property in exchange for its own stock. Since this general provision can apply to exchanges pursuant to a plan of reorganization, it usually will protect the acquiring corporation from the recognition of all gain or loss on the issuance of its stock. Indeed, it has precisely this effect on the acquiring corporation in a nonparenthetical B reorganization.

The acquiring corporation in an A or C or substitutive D reorganization (or in a forward triangular reorganization) may use nonstock consideration. To the extent it does so, gain or loss can be recognized by the acquiring corporation. The use of its own securities ordinarily will not give rise to gain since the acquisition of property for debt is not a taxable event to the acquiring taxpayer. Cash boot also will avoid recognition of gain or loss to the acquiring corporation. The use of appreciated or loss property, however, will cause the acquiring corporation to recognize gain or loss. See §1001.

Use of stock of the acquiring corporation's parent in a parenthetical B or C reorganization presents one of the few gaps in the reorganization provisions: No section specifically provides that the acquiring corporation does not recognize gain or loss on the exchange. In Rev. Rul. 57-278, 1957-1 C.B. 124, the Service ruled without discussion that the acquiring corporation does not recognize gain or loss in these circumstances, and that rule has been endorsed by Treas. Regs. §1.1032-2. Because the parenthetical B and C reorganizations closely resemble the nonparenthetical B and C reorganizations followed by a drop-down of assets under §368(a)(2)(C) — transactions fully protected by §1032 — nonrecognition of gain or loss to the acquiring corporation is appropriate in parenthetical B and C reorganizations.

So much for the recognition of gain or loss at the corporate level. In A, C, and substitutive D reorganizations, the acquiring corporation acquires assets of the transferor. The basis of those assets, determined under §362(b), will be carried over from the transferor corporation, increased by the amount of gain, if any, recognized to the transferor on the exchange. The same basis rule applies, by virtue of the last sentence of §362(b), to the stock of the target corporation acquired in a B reorganization. As to the applicability of §362(b) to a parenthetical B reorganization, see Treas. Regs. §§1.358-4, 1.362-1. The basis of the stock of the acquired subsidiary in the hands of the acquiring corporation in a reverse triangular reorganization has been a sore spot in the reorganization provisions for many years. Prop. Treas. Regs. §1.358-6(c)(2) addresses this issue.

Until 1984, the transferor corporation in a C reorganization was not required to liquidate as part of the reorganization. If it did not liquidate, its basis in the stock (and boot) received in the transaction was determined under §358. Now that the definition of a C includes the requirement that the transferor liquidate, see §368(a)(2)(G), that issue becomes moot. In some circumstances, however, the liquidation requirement can be waived, see §368(a)(2)(G)(ii), and then basis becomes important. In such cases the transferor corporation's basis is determined under §361(b)(2).

It may seem as though these reorganization provisions are exceedingly complex. They are. It may also seem as if you must constantly refer back and forth among the various taxing sections to determine the consequences of a reorganization to all the corporate parties. You must. The only way to become confident in your ability to parse through the complexity of the reorganization provisions is to practice. An example of the technique used to analyze the corporate-level tax effects of a reorganization follows. Remember that a similar exercise should be performed with respect to the shareholder-level tax effects.

X Corp. and T Corp. agree to the following plan. T will transfer most of its assets to X in exchange for (1) voting stock of X worth $80,000, (2) securities of X worth $8,000, (3) real estate worth $5,000, and (4) the assumption by X of a $5,000 liability of T. The fair market value of the assets X will receive is $98,000, and X's adjusted basis in the real estate is $3,500. Immediately after the exchange, T will liquidate, distributing the stock and securities of X, the real estate, and its remaining assets (worth

$2,000 and with adjusted basis of $1,000) to its shareholders in complete liquidation. Assume that T's basis in the transferred assets totals $60,000 and that T's shareholders do not own a significant amount of X stock before or after the transaction.

Is this transaction a reorganization? It would fall under §368(a)(1)(C) but for X's transfer of the securities and the real estate. The boot relaxation rule of §368(a)(2)(B) permits boot in a C reorganization, and because the amount of the stock is equal to or greater than 80 percent of the value of the acquired corporation (it is exactly 80 percent), this is in fact a C reorganization pursuant to §368(a)(1)(C), (a)(2)(B). Note that one additional dollar of boot in lieu of stock would have destroyed the reorganization.

How is T taxed? T has a *realized* gain of $38,000 (amount realized of $98,000 less adjusted basis of $60,000 in the assets transferred). None of that gain, however, will be recognized by virtue of §361(b)(1)(A). T will be taxed on $1,000 of gain on its liquidating distribution because it did not transfer all its appreciated property to X: distribution of the retained assets is taxable in full under §361(c)(2). Distribution of the stock and securities received on the exchange is protected from recognition by §361(c)(2)(B), while distribution of the acquired real estate is protected from recognition by the basis rule of §358(a)(2).

How is X taxed? Section 1032 protects X from the recognition of gain with respect to the T assets acquired for its stock. Further, since gain is not recognized to a taxpayer who purchases assets, X is also absolved from recognition with respect to the T assets acquired for X's securities or for the assumption of T's liability. As to the assets acquired for the real estate, X is subject to taxation under §1001(a). Thus, X recognizes a gain of $1,500 on the exchange.

What is X's basis in the assets acquired from T? Under §362(b), X takes a basis equal to T's basis in those assets ($60,000), increased by any gain recognized by the transferor corporation, namely T. Since T recognized no gain on the exchange, X's basis in the assets is $60,000.

Lastly, consider the tax treatment of any expenses incurred by the corporate parties to a reorganization. Such expenses might include attorney and accountant fees as well as printing costs of a prospectus and related documents. Similar expenses often are incurred in connection with an initial incorporation, and, by virtue of §248, they can be amortized over a period not less than 60 months. No similar provision, however, authorizes the amortization of reorganization expenses. See the discussion of *INDOPCO* at page 360 supra.

PROBLEMS

10-8.   *T* Corp. has 1,000 shares of common stock outstanding, owned 60 percent by *A* and 40 percent by *B*. *A* and *B* each has a basis of $100 per share in their *T* Corp. stock. *T* owns a factory with fair market value of $800,000 and adjusted basis of $300,000, subject to a mortgage of $500,000. *T* also owns inventory with adjusted basis of $100,000 and fair market value of $200,000. *P* Corp., a widely held public corporation, wishes to acquire all the *T* Corp. assets in a tax-free reorganization. Discuss the tax consequences to *P* and to *T* of each of the following.

   a. *P* transfers $500,000 of its voting preferred stock to *T* in exchange for all the assets subject to the mortgage, followed by the complete liquidation of *T*.
   b. *P* transfers $400,000 of its voting common stock to *T* Corp. in exchange for the factory subject to the mortgage as well as half the inventory. *T* then completely liquidates, distributing both the *P* stock and the remaining inventory to its shareholders pro rata.
   c. *P* transfers $400,000 of its voting common stock and $100,000 of its long-term bonds to *T* in exchange for all its assets subject to the mortgage, followed by a complete liquidation of *T*.
   d. How do your answers to (c) change if there had been no mortgage on the factory and *P* had transferred $900,000 of its voting stock as well as $100,000 of securities? If *P* had transferred voting stock worth $900,000 plus land with fair market value of $100,000 and adjusted basis of $50,000?

3. Shareholder-level Taxation

Shareholder-level taxation of a reorganization is governed by §§354, 356, 358, and 1001(a). To some shareholders — notably the shareholders of the transferor corporation — the effect of a reorganization is an exchange of their shares in one corporation for stock and securities of another corporation, sometimes accompanied by other property, or "boot." Such an exchange is fully taxable under the general rule of §1001(a) governing dispositions of property unless some more particular provision, usually §354 or §356, applies. §1001(c). Other shareholders will not be parties to any exchange as a result of the reorganization. Shareholders of the acquiring corporation, for example, usually have no change in their stock and debt interests as a result of a reorganization. For such shareholders, no special taxing provision is needed since the absence of an exchange ensures that they will recognize no gain or loss as a consequence of the reorganization (unless §305(c) applies).

   If, as part of a plan of reorganization, a shareholder exchanges stock and securities in one "party" to the reorganization for stock and securities of another "party" to the reorganization, no gain or loss is recognized on the exchange, §354(a), subject to an exception for the excess principal amount of securities received, §354(a)(2). This nonrecognition rule will fully cover, for example, shareholders of the transferor (i.e., nonsurviving) corporation in an A statutory merger if all they received in the reorganization was stock of the acquiring (i.e., surviving) corporation. Section 354(a) will also ensure nonrecognition for the shareholders of the target corporation in a B reorganization.

If a shareholder receives property in addition to stock and securities of a party to the reorganization (or if excess securities are received), then the boot rule of §356(a) is implicated. Under that section, gain (if any) on the exchange will be recognized, but only to the extent of the boot received.[1] Suppose, for example, that N Corp. merges into O Corp. in a statutory merger qualifying as an A reorganization. The terms of the merger provide that each shareholder of N will receive one share of O common stock, one share of O $10 par value preferred stock, and $5 in cash for each share of N surrendered.

If taxpayer T owns one share of N stock prior to the merger, how will T be taxed when exchanging that share for one share of O common, one share of O preferred, and cash of $5? To compute T's realized gain, we must know T's adjusted basis in the N share and the fair market value of the O shares. Assume that T bought the N share for $20, that the O common is worth $40, and that the O preferred is worth $10. Given these values, T has realized a gain of $35 on the exchange.

T's exchange does not fall within the terms of §354(a) because of the receipt of the cash. The exchange is described, however, in §356(a). By the terms of that section, T will recognize gain on the exchange, but in an amount limited to the value of the boot. Thus, T will recognize a gain of $5 on the exchange. The character of that gain is discussed at pages 441-442 infra.

T's basis in the O common and preferred stock is determined under §358. Under the rule of §358(a), T's combined basis in the two shares equals $20 − $0 (other property) − $5 (cash) − $0 (loss) + $5 (dividend or gain), or $20. That amount is allocated to the stock in proportion to fair market values, so that 40/50th's (80 percent, or $16) is allocated to the O common, and 10/50th's (20 percent, or $4) is allocated to the O preferred. See §358(b)(1); Treas. Regs. §1.358-1, -2. Note that if T had received noncash boot, it would be given a basis equal to fair market value. §358(a)(2).

Shareholders of the transferor corporation in a C reorganization will also fall within the ambit of §354 because, when the transferor corporation liquidates as part of the plan of reorganization, such shareholders will exchange their stock in the transferor for the assets it holds at liquidation,

---

1. If the boot includes corporate debt, then recognition of gain will be subject to the installment sale provisions. See §453(f)(6). In particular, if the gain is taxed under §356(a)(1) as capital gain rather than under §356(a)(2) as a dividend, recognition can be deferred until payment on the debt is received. The characterization of boot under §356(a)(1) and (2) is discussed at pages 441-442 infra.

and those assets will include voting stock of the acquiring corporation. The same is true of shareholders of the transferor corporation in a substitutive *D* reorganization to the extent that they receive stock and securities of the acquiring corporation in the exchange.

NOTES

1. *Receipt of nonqualified preferred stock.* "Nonqualified preferred stock" is defined in section 351(g)(2) as preferred stock that does not participate in the growth of the corporation to any significant extent. Further, to be "nonqualified" such preferred stock must include a redemption feature making it only a short-term in the corporate enterprise or have a dividend rate tied to interest rates or some equivalent index, thereby making the stock little more than debt. Nonqualified preferred stock received as part of an acquisitive reorganization will be tax-free to the extent is is received in exchange for other nonqualified preferred stock or for securities. However, to the extent that nonqualified stock is received in exchange for stock other than nonqualified preferred sock (which includes all common stock and much preferred stock), it is taxed as boot under §354(a)(2)(C). Note, though, that whether stock is "nonqualified preferred stock" or not is relevant only to shareholder-level taxation: at the corporate-level, no distinction is drawn between nonqualified preferred stock and other forms of equity. Thus, an acquiring corporation could use exclusively voting nonqualified preferred stock in a "B" or "C" reorganization with the result that the acquisition would be fully tax-free at the corporate level despite being fully taxable at the shareholder level.

2. *Securities as qualifying property.* Section 354 provides for the tax-free receipt of stock *or securities* by a shareholder in connection with a reorganization. A security is a debt instrument, but not all debt instruments are "securities" for this purpose. If nonrecognition is granted on the theory that the taxpayer has changed an investment in form only, why shouldn't all debt be treated as boot? The answer seems to be that some corporate debt gives the holder as much or more of an interest in the future performance of the assets transferred as a stock interest. Debt obligations that qualify for nonrecognition treatment are referred to as "securities." The leading case on the definition of a security is Camp Wolters Enterprises v. Commissioner, 22 T.C. 737, 751 (1954), aff'd, 230 F.2d 555 (5th Cir. 1956), in which the Tax Court stated:

> The test as to whether notes are securities is not a mechanical determination of the time period of the note. Though time is an important factor, the controlling consideration is an overall evaluation of the nature of the debt, degree of participation and continuing interest compared with similarity of the note to a cash payment.

Prior to the Installment Sales Revision Act of 1980, the distinction between a security and a note could be very significant. The receipt of a note was immediately taxable to the transferor whereas the receipt of a security was not. As indicated at page 42 supra, this distinction in tax treatment has been removed, although other differences in tax treatment remain.

The most important factor separating securities from nonqualifying debt is the length of maturity of the obligation. If taxpayer *T* transfers property to *X* Corp. in exchange for some stock and six-month notes, the notes will be treated as boot, falling on the cash end of the spectrum. If the mix were stock and 30-year debentures, full nonrecognition would be available. Between these extremes lies a bog. Notes with a five-year term or less rarely will qualify as securities, while obligations with a term of 10 years or more seem likely to qualify. In the following cases, obligations were classified as securities: Parkland Place Co. v. United States, 354 F.2d 916 (5th Cir. 1966) (10-year 6 percent interest-bearing note where no interest paid); Nye v. Commissioner, 50 T.C. 203 (1968) (10-year note); Camp Wolters Enterprises v. Commissioner, supra (five- and nine-year subordinated notes). Notes were not treated as securities in the following cases: Bradshaw v. United States, 683 F.2d 365 (5th Cir. 1982) (notes maturing annually for five years); Adams v. Commissioner, 58 T.C. 41 (1972) (2 1/4-year note); Raich v. Commissioner, 46 T.C. 604 (1966) (demand note retired within four years).

As the court in *Camp Wolters* points out, the maturity date is not the only consideration. Consider D'Angelo Associates v. Commissioner, 70 T.C. 121 (1978), in which a demand note was held a security. No interest and only half of the principal of the note had been paid after 16 years. In addition, the corporation did not have sufficient liquid assets to retire the debt. Rental income was to provide funds for repayment. Finally, the note was subordinated to another liability encumbering the transferred assets. The open-ended maturity date of the note in combination with the other features gave the transferor "a continuing participation in the affairs of the debtor corporation." See also United States v. Mills, 399 F.2d 944 (5th Cir. 1968) (one-year unsecured notes where renewal expected; jury decision).

While securities do qualify under §354 for nonrecognition treatment when a taxpayer receives a combination of stock and securities, what happens if a taxpayer receives only securities in exchange for property? Historically, securities could be received tax free under §351 just as they still can be received under §354. The Service addressed the possibility of receiving only securities in that context. In Rev. Rul. 73-472, 1973-2 C.B. 114, four individuals transferred property to a new corporation; three received back stock, and the fourth individual, *D*, received securities in amounts equal to the value of the property transferred. The Service held that *D* would not qualify under §351:

Although *D* is one of the transferors, the ownership of securities provides him with no proprietary interest in the corporation, but rather an interest only as a creditor. In LeTulle v. Scofield, 308 U.S. 415, 420 (1940) . . . , it was stated:

Where the consideration is wholly in the transferee's bonds, or part cash and part such bonds we think it cannot be said that the transferor retains any proprietary interest in the enterprise. On the contrary, he becomes a creditor of the transferee. . . .

Id. Consequently, the Service ruled that *D* would recognize gain or loss in accordance with §§1001 and 453.

3. *Securities as boot.* Although §354(a)(1) classifies the exchange of stock and securities for stock and securities as an event of nonrecognition, it is not the case that receipt of securities of a "party" to the reorganization always will be tax free. By virtue of the limitation in §354(a)(2), the nonrecognition rule of §354(a)(1) is unavailable to a taxpayer who receives securities as part of the exchange if the principal amount of the securities received is greater than the principal amount of securities surrendered.

If a taxpayer receives excess securities in a reorganization exchange, gain (if any) will be recognized under the boot rule of §356. Consistent with §354(a)(2), only the excess principal amount of the securities received will be treated as boot under §356. See §356(d). In one of the more bizarre rules of the Code, it is the fair market value of the excess principal amount, and not the excess principal amount itself, that is treated as boot.

Consider example 4 of Treas. Regs. §1.356-3(b). Pursuant to a plan of reorganization, *D* exchanges a security with principal amount of $1,000 for 100 shares of stock plus a security with principal amount of $1,200 and fair market value of $1,100. The excess principal amount of the security received is $200, and the fair market value of that amount is $200 × (1,100/1,200), or $183.33. Accordingly, *D* can recognize gain of up to $183.33 on the exchange.

4. *Characterization of gain.* Does a shareholder who receives boot as part of a reorganization recognize capital gain or ordinary income? Usually, the character of gain recognized on an exchange described by §356(a)(1) is determined by reference to the property given up. For example, if the stock and securities surrendered were all capital assets held longer than six months, any gain recognized would be long-term capital gain. This general rule, however, is limited by §356(a)(2).

Under §356(a)(2), if some gain must be recognized and the exchange has the effect of a distribution of a dividend, then the taxpayer must treat any gain recognized as dividend income, limited only by the taxpayer's ratable share of the earnings and profits of the corporation. This section poses two difficult questions: When does an exchange have the effect of a "distribution of a dividend"? In computing the earnings and profits limitation, which corporation's earnings and profits should be used?

In Clark v. Commissioner, 489 U.S. 726 (1989), the Supreme Court held that when a shareholder of the target corporation in an acquisitive reorganization receives boot in addition to qualifying property, the shareholder should be taxed as if she received additional stock in place of the boot and then this additional stock was redeemed with the boot actually received by the shareholder. The character of the shareholder's gain will then be determined by reference to the redemption rules of §302 as applied to this hypothetical redemption.

Suppose T Corp. merges into A Corp. when each share of T Corp. stock and of A Corp. stock is worth $50. Assume that individuals P, Q and R own stock in T Corp. and A Corp. as follows:

	Number of Shares	
	T Corp.	A Corp.
P	60	0
Q	60	90
R	0	30
	120	120

The merger gives P $1,500 in cash and 30 shares of A Corp. stock, while Q receives $2,500 in cash and 10 shares of Y Corp. stock. Accordingly, after the merger A Corp. has 160 shares of stock outstanding, of which P owns 30, Q owns 100, and R owns 30.

Following the approach adopted by the Supreme Court in *Clark*, we treat the transaction as if P and Q received only stock in the reorganization and then some of that stock was redeemed. Because each share of A Corp. is worth $50, the $1,500 boot received by P corresponds to 30 shares of A Corp. and the $2,500 boot received by Q corresponds to 50 shares of A Corp. Accordingly, we treat the transaction as if P and Q each received 60 shares of A Corp. stock in the reorganization and then 30 of P's shares and 50 of Q shares were redeemed.

Thus, A Corp. is treated as having 240 shares outstanding, 60 owned by P, 150 owned by Q, and 30 owned by R. The effect of the hypothetical redemption is to reduce P's ownership of A Corp. from 25 percent (60 of 240 shares) to 18.75 percent (30 of 160 shares) and to leave Q's ownership of A Corp. at 62.50 percent (from 150 of 240 shares to 100 of 160 shares). On this redemption, P will qualify for exchange treatment under §§302 (b)(2) and 302(a) while Q will receive dividend income (assuming adequate earnings and profits).

5. *Measuring earnings and profits.* If a taxpayer is determined under the *Clark* test to have received boot that has the effect of a distribution of a dividend, should the amount of the dividend be determined by reference to the earnings and profits of the target corporation, the acquiring corpora-

tion, or both? In Wright v. United States, 483 F.2d 600 (8th Cir. 1973), the court held that only the earnings and profits of the target could be used, a view that the Service has rejected. Rev. Rul. 75-83, 1975-1 C.B. 112. The Supreme Court in *Clark* did not have occasion to determine the proper measure of earnings and profits because in that case the distribution of boot did not have the effect of a dividend, but the Tax Court had the following to say on this issue: "There is no reason why the redemption cannot be considered as having been made by one corporation with the consequences to be measured by the earnings and profits of another corporation." Clark v. Commissioner, 86 T.C. 138 (1986), aff'd, 828 F.2d 221 (4th Cir. 1987), aff'd, 489 U.S. 726 (1989); see also American Manufacturing Co. v. Commissioner, 55 T.C. 204 (1970) (no combination allowed); Atlas Tool Co. v. Commissioner, 614 F.2d 860 (3d Cir. 1980) (same); Davant v. Commissioner, 366 F.2d 874 (5th Cir. 1966) (combination allowed); Rev. Rul. 70-274, 1970-1 C.B. 81 (same). Indeed, because the approach adopted by the Supreme Court in *Clark* treats the redemption as part of the full reorganization, it would seem appropriate to make the earnings and profits of *both* corporations available for dividend income. Compare the earnings and profits computation in §304(b)(2).

6. *Dividend income versus dividend gain.* Section 356(a)(2) has one structural aspect that is difficult to justify. While the receipt of boot will give rise to gain taxable at ordinary rates if the effect of the boot is dividend equivalency, it is still *gain*, rather than the amount of the boot, that is taxable under §356(a)(2). If the effect of the boot is the receipt of a dividend, why is the taxpayer allowed basis recovery before recognizing income? Indeed, if there is no gain on the exchange, then the taxpayer will not recognize any income under §356(a)(2) regardless of the amount of the boot or dividend equivalency.

PROBLEMS

10-9. Discuss the shareholder-level tax consequences of the transactions described in problem 10-8 at page 436 supra.

10-10. *X* Corp. has 100 shares outstanding, 50 owned by individual *A* and 50 by individual *B*. *Y* Corp. also has 100 shares outstanding, 80 owned by *B* and 20 by individual *C*. *X* Corp. has earnings and profits of $1,000, and *Y* Corp. has earnings and profits of $1,500. *A*'s basis in the *X* Corp. stock is $20 per share; *B*'s basis in the *X* Corp. stock is $10 per share; *B*'s basis in the *Y* Corp. stock is $10 per share; *C*'s basis in the *Y* Corp. stock is $30 per share. The shares of *X* and *Y* are worth $50 per share.

X Corp. merges into *Y* Corp. under applicable state law. As part of the merger, *A* receives $1,000 in cash and 30 shares of *Y*. *B* receives $1,500 in cash and 20 shares of *Y*. Accordingly, the ownership of *Y* Corp. after the merger is as follows: *A* owns 30 shares, *B* owns 100 shares, and *C* owns 20 shares.

What are the tax consequences to *A* and *B* of this merger? Assume that *A, B,* and *C* are unrelated to one another.

D. THE STATUS OF CREDITORS IN CORPORATE REORGANIZATIONS

The materials in this chapter focus primarily on the consequences of a corporate reorganization to the shareholders of the corporation whose assets are transferred. Almost always, however, the corporation will have creditors. How are they affected by the reorganization? Do they recognize gain or loss if they surrender their claims and in exchange receive stock or securities of the reorganized corporation or other claims against it?

At the outset it should be noted that the creditors will not necessarily participate in the reorganization exchange. For example, in a B reorganization, the creditors of the acquired corporation may simply ride through the reorganization, preserving intact their claims against their respective debtors.

Alternatively, the acquiring corporation may assume the transferor corporation's liabilities or take the properties subject to those liabilities, still without any exchange by the creditors. Ordinarily, this will not constitute boot to the transferee. §357. Nor will creditors recognize gain or loss since their claims have not been paid, retired, or exchanged. Moreover, §368(a)(1)(C) states explicitly that the requirement that the acquisition be solely for the acquiring corporation's voting stock in a C reorganization is not breached by the corporation's assuming liabilities or taking property subject to liabilities.

Frequently, however, there will be an exchange. The creditors may surrender bonds, debentures, or notes of one corporation and receive stock or securities of another corporation. In general, the exchange will qualify under §354. One difficulty that may arise is that short-term notes (whether given up or received) may not qualify as "securities." See pages 439-441 supra.

There may be other problems as well. If in conjunction with a B reorganization (stock for stock) the acquiring corporation issues bonds in exchange for bonds of the acquired corporation, will the transaction fall outside of §368(a)(1)(B) on the ground that it is not "solely" for voting stock? If the stock-for-stock exchange qualifies, will the bondholders' exchange be "in pursuance of a plan of reorganization" under §354(a)(1)? See Rev. Rul. 70-41, 1970-1 C.B. 77 (exchange of debt of the acquired corporation for stock of the acquiring corporation incident to B reorganization is taxable). Similarly in a C reorganization, if the acquiring corporation issues its own evidences of indebtedness to creditors of the transferee corporation instead of merely assuming the liabilities, should the transaction lose its status as a reorganization?

E.   REORGANIZATIONS OF INSOLVENT OR FINANCIALLY DISTRESSED CORPORATIONS

Under prior law, a transfer of all or part of a corporation's assets to another corporation pursuant to a court-approved plan under the Bankruptcy Act could qualify for tax-free treatment under separate rules applicable to "insolvency reorganizations." In the Bankruptcy Tax Act of 1980, Congress ended the separate regime for debtor corporations in a title 11 (bankruptcy) case by adding a new category of tax-free corporate reorganization under §368(a)(1): the G reorganization. Congress made this change to encourage and facilitate the rehabilitation of bankrupt debtor corporations. As a consequence, many prior law requirements for tax-free treatment were removed, parties were given additional flexibility in structuring the acquisition, and, most importantly, the acquiring corporation was permitted to succeed to the tax attributes of the acquired corporation (such as its net operating loss carryovers). S. Rep. No. 1035, 96th Cong., 2d Sess. 34-25 (1980).

As is often the case, change is not without its problems. While there are benefits to the G reorganization, qualifying transactions must also conform to certain statutory and judicial requirements imposed on all tax-free reorganizations. It is apparent that many of these regular tax reorganization requirements cannot be easily adapted and applied to the unique circumstances faced by a bankrupt corporation.

Difficulties aside, the G reorganization is the most flexible of the acquisitive tax-free reorganization provisions. It is a hybrid provision that borrows most of its characteristics from the other acquisitive reorganization provisions. It is similar to an A reorganization (a state law merger) in that it requires two corporations, and the only limit on the nature of consideration used by the acquiring corporation is the judicial continuity of proprietary interest doctrine discussed at the beginning of this chapter. State law merger requirements, however, need not be met. It is similar to a C reorganization in that it contemplates an acquisition of assets of one corporation by another corporation, but it does not require an exchange of assets solely (as relaxed by statute) for voting stock of the acquiring corporation. It is most like an acquisitive D reorganization, except that it does not require that the shareholders of the acquired corporation also be "in control" of the acquiring corporation.

A G reorganization is defined as (1) a transfer of assets (2) by one corporation to another corporation in a title 11 (bankruptcy) or similar case (3) followed by a distribution as described in §354, §355, or §356 of the consideration received in the transaction. Each of these three requirements is discussed below.

A G reorganization requires that a corporation transfer all or a part of its assets to another corporation, provided one of the corporations is in a bankruptcy (or similar) case and provided the transfer occurs pursuant to a plan of reorganization approved by the bankruptcy court. §368(a)(3)(B). Thus, the transfer of stock of the debtor corporation to its creditors in satisfaction of their claims will not qualify as a G reorganization (although such a transaction may have no adverse tax consequences). Similarly, out-of-court transactions, chapter 7 liquidating cases, and foreign reorganizations are ineligible.

For example, suppose Loss Corp. is hopelessly insolvent. Immediately prior to filing a bankruptcy petition, Loss Corp. agrees to transfer all its assets to Public Corp. in exchange for Public Corp. common stock; Loss Corp. will then distribute the stock received to its creditors in satisfaction of their claims. This acquisition will not qualify as a G reorganization because it did not occur within a title 11 or similar case. Accordingly, the transaction will be tax free only if it meets the standards of one of the other acquisitive reorganization provisions such as the A, C, or D.

As a second example, suppose Loss Corp. is in a chapter 11 bankruptcy case. Loss Corp.'s plan of reorganization provides for a transfer of cash and certain nonoperating assets to secured creditors and of all newly authorized common stock to its unsecured creditors. All previously authorized outstanding common stock is canceled. Loss Corp.'s plan will not qualify as a G reorganization because Loss Corp. has not transferred its assets to another corporation. Although not qualifying as a G reorganization, this transaction likely qualifies for tax-free treatment as an E recapitalization, a form of tax-free reorganization discussed in Chapter 12. See S. Rep. No. 1035, 96th Cong., 2d Sess. 36 (1980).

Distribution of stock or securities of the acquiring corporation in a transaction that qualifies under §354 raises some difficult obstacles. Section 354(b) requires that substantially all the assets of the acquired corporation be transferred to the acquiring corporation. In the context of the C reorganization, the Service requires (for advanced rulings) that at least 90 percent of the net assets and 70 percent of the gross assets be transferred in the reorganization. Rev. Proc. 77-37 (§3.01), 1977-2 C.B. 568. Congress has indicated that the substantially-all requirement be interpreted liberally in the context of the G reorganization in view of the underlying purpose of the provision to facilitate the rehabilitation of financially troubled corporations. Accordingly, substantially all the assets of the debtor corporation should be acquired even if the debtor sells assets to pay creditors or to rearrange its business affairs so as to obtain creditor approval of its plan of reorganization. S. Rep. No. 1035, 96th Cong., 2d Sess. 36-36 (1980). In private rulings, the Service has relaxed its definition of "substantially all" in the context of a G reorganization. See Priv. Ltr. Rul. 8726055; Priv. Ltr. Rul. 8521083.

In addition to the substantially-all requirement, §354(a) requires that stock or securities of the acquiring corporation be distributed to a holder of stock or securities of the acquired corporation. If holders of securities in the acquired corporation actually receive stock or securities (or if shareholders in the acquired corporation actually receive stock) in the acquiring corporation pursuant to the plan of reorganization, the transaction should qualify as a G reorganization even if the value of the stock or securities received represents a small percentage of the value of the total equity consideration given in the transaction. Thus, the threshold exchange requirement of §354(a) should be satisfied if one securityholder receives stock or securities (or if one shareholder receives stock) pursuant to the plan of reorganization. The threshold exchange requirement of §354(a) will not be satisfied, however, if (as is often true in the typical corporate bankruptcy) all the old stock of the debtor corporation is canceled (because there is no equity left) and the acquiring corporation's stock is distributed to short-term creditors whose debt instruments do not rise to the dignity of a tax security.

For example, suppose Loss Corp. is in a chapter 11 bankruptcy case. Loss Corp.'s plan of reorganization provides for the transfer of substantially all its assets to Public Corp. in exchange for Public Corp. common stock with fair market value of $450 and cash of $550. The plan calls for the transfer of cash and certain nonoperating assets to secured creditors and for the distribution of all the Public Corp. common stock to Loss Corp.'s unsecured creditors. One unsecured creditor holds a 10-year bond with a locomotive printed on the face of the certificate. Assume that a locomotive is clear evidence that the bond is a "security" for tax purposes. The old Loss Corp. common stock is canceled, and the shareholders receive nothing under the plan. Because substantially all the assets were acquired by Public Corp. in exchange for an amount of common stock that should satisfy the continuity of proprietary interest doctrine, and because at least one Loss Corp. securityholder received stock pursuant to the plan, the transaction should qualify as a tax-free G reorganization.

The transaction in this example would not qualify as a G reorganization if all of Loss Corp.'s unsecured creditors held only short-term debt. One possible way to avoid this technical trap in the statute is to convert the claims of the creditors into stock of the acquired debtor corporation before the G reorganization is consummated, relying on Helvering v. Alabama Asphaltic Limestone Co., 315 U.S. 179 (1942). In that case, the Supreme Court held that creditors of an insolvent corporation who received stock of a reorganized corporation had a "continuing interest" because, under the full priority rule of bankruptcy proceedings, they had "effective command over the disposition of the properties" of the old corporation.

In Neville Coke & Chemical Co. v. Commissioner, 148 F.2d 599 (3d Cir. 1945), however, the court held that noteholders of a reorganized corporation who exchanged their notes for debentures and common stock could not claim nonrecognition of their gain under what is now §354. The court relied on *Pinellas* and *LeTulle* as establishing that notes received on an exchange do not evidence a continuing interest in the enterprise and are not "securities." It then held that the notes are equally deficient if given up in the exchange. The debtor was in financial difficulties at the time of the exchange, but the court was unwilling to find that the creditors already owned the entire equity, and in fact the old stockholders did participate in the exchange. If, however, the creditors of a distressed corporation in reorganization received stock or securities evidencing a proprietary interest in the enterprise, is it not probable that the claims they gave up, whatever their form, already represented in economic reality a proprietary interest in the assets? For a forceful statement of this view, see Griswold, "Securities" and "Continuity of Interest," 58 Harv. L. Rev. 705 (1945).

In addition to the statutory requirements, a G reorganization must meet judicial requirements imposed on all tax-free corporate reorganizations. Principally, these include continuity of proprietary interest, continuity of business enterprise, and business purpose. These are discussed at pages 388-396 supra. Finally, if a transaction qualifies as both a G reorganization and a different reorganization under another provision (or under §332 or §351), the transaction is treated as qualifying only as a G reorganization. §368(a)(3)(C).

PROBLEMS

10-11.   *L* Corp. is involved in a bankruptcy proceeding. In 1999 and as part of the court-supervised plan of reorganization, Big Corp. transfers its preferred stock worth $50,000 to *L* Corp. in exchange for *L*'s fully depreciated operating assets. *L* Corp. then liquidates, distributing the Big Corp. preferred stock and its nonoperating assets (short-term certificates of deposit with adjusted basis of $22,000 and fair market value of $25,000) to its sole debtholder, *H*, in complete satisfaction of *L*'s $100,000 debt to *H*. The shareholders of *L* Corp. receive nothing, and their stock in *L* Corp. is canceled. What are the tax consequences of this transaction to Big Corp., to *H*, to *L*, and to the former shareholders of *L*?

F. POLICY

Recall that the initial justification for the reorganization provisions was that a corporate rearrangement should be taxable if it resembles a sale but should be tax free if it more closely appears to be a mere change in form of the business enterprise. From that relatively simple notion has grown the complexity you have just discovered.

The simple fact is that most corporate acquisitions can be structured either as reorganizations or as taxable transactions. While not formally elective, reorganization status is practically a matter of choice. The detailed rules of the Code seeking to distinguish tax-free reorganizations from taxable sales have little effect beyond increasing the transaction and uncertainty costs to taxpayers contemplating acquisitive transactions.

Those corporate rearrangements qualifying as reorganizations under §368 are, in general, tax free at both the corporate and shareholder level. Nonqualifying transactions will be taxable at one or both levels, depending on the form selected by the parties. On one hand, a corporate acquisition structured as the sale of shares by the acquired corporation's shareholders will be taxed at the shareholder level only: Because the corporate assets are not formally transferred, no corporate-level tax is imposed. On the other hand, sale by the target of its assets will produce a corporate-level tax, but the shareholders of the target corporation will be safe from taxation until the sale proceeds are distributed.

At the corporate level, this distinction makes little sense. Any bulk transfer of corporate assets is a rearrangement of the business enterprise. Tax-free treatment of any such transaction, *however effected,* is an appropriate incident to the change in form of a business. So long as asset basis is preserved, no corporate-level tax will be avoided. If the corporate parties desire a step-up in basis and are willing to be taxed on the transaction as the price for that step-up, that result should also be acceptable to the Treasury. Section 338 has adopted this elective approach to rearrangements of corporate control effected by sale of the target corporation's stock. Should Congress permit the bulk sale of corporate assets to go untaxed with an accompanying carryover basis rule, the tax treatment of corporate reorganizations will become fully elective.

At the shareholder level, the appropriate taxation seems to turn on what each shareholder receives in the reorganization. That is, the exchange of stock and securities for stock and securities incident to a corporate acquisition ought to be tax free regardless of what other shareholders receive. Kass, for example, should have been entitled to nonrecognition even though most of her co-shareholders properly were taxed.

Accordingly, shareholder-level taxation should be independent of corporate-level taxation: Whether the corporate parties elect nonrecognition or taxable exchange is a matter of indifference to the shareholders. Further, the taxation of each shareholder should be independent of the taxation of all other shareholders: In particular, the continuity of proprietary interest should be abolished. These basic reforms, along with several others, have been proposed by the American Law Institute. See ALI, Federal Income Tax Project: Subchapter C — Proposals on Corporate Acquisitions and Dispositions (1982). In turn, the ALI reforms largely have been embraced by the Senate Finance Committee. See Staff of the Senate Finance Committee, The Subchapter C Revision Act of 1985, 99th Cong., 1st Sess. (Comm. Print 1985).

11

Divisive Reorganizations

A. TAXATION UNDER §355

Coady v. Commissioner
33 T.C. 771 (1960), aff'd per curiam, 289 F.2d 490 (6th Cir. 1961)

TIETJENS, Judge: . . .

The issue for decision is whether the transfer by the Christopher Construction Company of a portion of its assets to E. P. Coady and Co. in exchange for all of the Coady Company's stock, and the subsequent distribution by the Christopher Company of such Coady stock to petitioner in exchange for his Christopher stock, constituted a distribution of stock qualifying for tax-free treatment on the shareholder level under the provisions of section 355 of the 1954 Internal Revenue Code.

All of the facts were stipulated, are so found, and are incorporated herein by this reference. . . .

Christopher Construction Co., an Ohio corporation, is now engaged, and for more than 5 years prior to November 15, 1954, was engaged, in the active conduct of a construction business primarily in and around Columbus, Ohio. In an average year the Christopher Company undertook approximately 6 construction contracts, no one of which lasted for more than 2 years. Its gross receipts varied between $1,500,000 and $2,000,000 per year.

At its central office, located at 16 East Broad Street in Columbus, the Christopher Company kept its books of account, paid its employees, prepared bids for its jobs, and, excepting minor amounts of tools and supplies, made its purchases. In addition, it maintained temporary field offices at each jobsite. It also maintained a central repair and storage depot for its equipment. Equipment in use on particular jobs was kept at the jobsite until work was terminated. Then, it would either be returned to the central depot or moved to another jobsite.

At all times material hereto, the stock of the Christopher Company was owned by M. Christopher and the petitioner. For a number of years, petitioner owned 35 per cent of that stock and Christopher owned 65 per cent. However, on April 19, 1954, petitioner purchased 15 per cent of the total stock from Christopher. From that date until November 15, 1954, each owned 50 per cent of the company's stock.

Sometime prior to November 15, 1954, differences arose between the petitioner and Christopher. As a result, they entered into an agreement for the division of the Christopher Company into two separate enterprises. Pursuant to that agreement, the Christopher Company, on November 15, 1954, organized E. P. Coady and Co., to which it transferred the following assets, approximating one-half the Christopher Company's total assets:

A contract for the construction of a sewage disposal plant at Columbus, Ohio, dated June 1, 1954.
A part of its equipment.
A part of its cash, and certain other items.

In consideration for the receipt of these assets, E. P. Coady and Co. transferred all of its stock to the Christopher Company. The Christopher Company retained the following assets, which were of the same type as those transferred to E. P. Coady and Co.:

A contract for a sewage treatment plant in Charleston, West Virginia.
A part of its equipment.
A part of its cash.

Immediately thereafter, the Christopher Company distributed to the petitioner all of the stock of E. P. Coady and Co. held by it in exchange for all of the stock of the Christopher Company held by petitioner. The fair market value of the stock of E. P. Coady and Co. received by petitioner was $140,000. His basis in the Christopher Company stock surrendered was $72,500.

Since the distribution, both E. P. Coady and Co. and the Christopher Company have been actively engaged in the construction business.

On their 1954 Federal income tax return, petitioner and his wife reported no gain or loss on the exchange of the Christopher Company stock for the stock of E. P. Coady and Co.

Respondent determined that petitioner realized a capital gain on that exchange in the amount of $67,500, 50 per cent of which was taxable in 1954.

Petitioner contends that the distribution to him of the E. P. Coady and Co. stock qualified for tax-free treatment under the provisions of section 355 of the 1954 Code, arguing that it was received pursuant to a distribution of a controlled corporation's stock within the meaning of that section.

Respondent on the other hand maintains petitioner's receipt of the Coady stock did not fall within those distributions favored by section 355, inasmuch as the 5-year active business requirements of 355(b) were not met. More particularly he argues that section 355 does not apply to the separation of a "single business"; and, inasmuch as the Christopher Company was engaged in only one trade or business (construction contracting), the gain realized by petitioner upon receipt of the Coady stock was taxable. As authority for his position respondent points to that portion of his regulations which expressly provides that section 355 does not apply to the division of a single business.[2]

Thus, the issue is narrowed to the question of whether the challenged portion of the regulations constitutes a valid construction of the statute, or whether it is unreasonable and plainly inconsistent therewith. Though this appears to be a case of first impression, the question has not gone without comment. . . .

Section 355 of the 1954 Code represents the latest of a series of legislative enactments designed to deal with the tax effect upon shareholders of various corporate separations. Where the 1939 Code contained three sections, 112(b)(3), 112(b)(11), and 112(g)(1)(D), which controlled the tax impact of these exchanges, present law groups the statutory requirements into two sections, 355 and 368(c). A careful reading of section 355, as well as the Finance Committee report which accompanied its enactment, reveals no language, express or implied, denying tax-free treatment at the shareholder level to a transaction, otherwise qualifying under section 355, on the grounds that it represents the division or separation of a "single" trade or business. . . .

The active business requirements of 355(b)(1) prohibit the tax-free separation of a corporation into active and inactive entities. Section 355(b)(1)(A) extends the provisions of §355(a) only to those divisive distributions where the distributing corporation and the controlled corporation are engaged immediately after the distribution in the active conduct of a trade or business. In the case of those distributions which involve liquidation of the transferor, 355(b)(1)(B) requires that immediately before the distribution the transferor have no assets other than stock or securities in the controlled corporations, and that immediately thereafter each of the controlled corporations is engaged in the active conduct of a trade or business. Neither 355(b)(1)(A) nor (B) concerns itself with the existence of a plurality of businesses per se; rather both speak in terms of a plurality

2. This regulation has been repealed. — Eds.

of corporate entities engaged in the active conduct of a trade or business, a distinction we believe to be vital in light of provisions of 355(b)(2). . . .

Respondent maintains that a reading of 355(b)(2)(B) in conjunction with the requirement of 355(b)(1) that both "the distributing corporation, *and* the controlled corporation . . . , [be] engaged immediately after the distribution in the active conduct of a trade or business" (emphasis supplied) indicates Congress intended the provisions of the statute to apply only where, immediately after the distribution, there exist two separate and distinct businesses, one operated by the distributing corporation and one operated by the controlled corporation, both of which were actively conducted for the 5-year period immediately preceding the distribution. In our judgment the statute does not support this construction.

[T]he only reference to plurality appears in section 355(b)(1), and deals with corporate entities, not businesses. Recognizing the divisive nature of the transaction, subsection (b)(1) contemplates that where there was only one corporate entity prior to the various transfers, immediately subsequent thereto, there will be two or more *corporations*. In order to insure that a tax-free separation will involve the separation only of those assets attributable to the carrying on of an active trade or business, and further to prevent the tax-free division of an active corporation into active and inactive entities, subsection (b)(1) further provides that each of the surviving corporations must be engaged in the active conduct of a trade or business.

A careful reading of the definition of the active conduct of a trade or business contained in subsection (b)(2) indicates that its function is also to prevent the tax-free separation of *active* and *inactive* assets into *active* and *inactive* corporate entities. This is apparent from the use of the adjective "such," meaning beforementioned, to modify "trade or business" in subsection (b)(2)(B), thus providing that the trade or business, required by (b)(2)(B) to have had a 5-year active history prior to the distribution, is the same trade or business which (b)(2)(A) requires to be actively conducted immediately after the distribution. Nowhere in (b)(2) do we find, as respondent suggests we should, language denying the benefits of section 355 to the division of a single trade or business.

Nor can respondent derive support for his position by reading subsections (b)(1) and (b)(2) together, inasmuch as the plurality resulting therefrom is occasioned, not by any requirement that there be a multiplicity of businesses, but rather by the divisive nature of the transaction itself: i.e., one corporation becoming two or more corporations. Moreover, from the fact that the statute requires, immediately after the distribution, that the surviving corporations each be engaged in the conduct of a trade or business with an active 5-year history, we do not think it inevitably follows that each such trade or business necessarily must have been conducted on an individual basis throughout that 5-year period. As long as the trade or business which has been divided has been actively conducted for 5 years preceding the distribution, and the resulting businesses (each of which in this case, happens to be half of the original whole) are actively conducted after the division, we are of the opinion that the active business requirements of the statute have been complied with.

Respondent argues his construction of section 355 is confirmed by the report of the Senate Committee on Finance which accompanied the 1954 Internal Revenue Code. He refers us to that portion of the report which provides:

> Present law contemplates that a tax-free separation shall involve only the separation of assets attributable to the carrying on of an active business. Under the House bill, it is immaterial whether the assets are those used in an active business but if investment assets, for example, are separated into a new corporation, any amount received in respect of such an inactive corporation, whether by a distribution from it or by a sale of its stock, would be treated as ordinary income for a period of 10 years from the date of its creation. Your committee returns to existing law in not permitting the tax free separation of an existing corporation into active and inactive entities. It is not believed that the business need for this kind of transaction is sufficiently great to permit a person in a position to afford a 10-year delay in receiving income to do so at capital gain rather than dividend rates. Your committee requires that *both* the business retained by the distributing company and the business of the corporation the stock of which is distributed must have been actively conducted for the 5 years preceding the distribution, a safeguard against avoidance not contained in existing law. [Emphasis supplied.]

He argues that use of the term "both," with reference to the business retained by the distributing corporation and that operated by the controlled corporation, indicates that Congress intended there be in operation and existence during the 5 years preceding the distribution two or more separate and distinct businesses. We do not agree.

A reading of the quoted section of the report in its entirety reveals that the committee was addressing itself to the nature and the use of the particular assets which were transferred (active v. inactive), rather than to any distinction between one or more businesses. This is obvious when the entire paragraph is considered in the light of its topic sentence. The committee notes that under present law only assets attributable to the carrying on of an active trade or business may be separated tax free. After acknowledging a departure from this requirement in the House bill, the committee disapproves of the position taken by the House, and indicates it is returning to existing law by not permitting the tax-free separation of a corporation into active and inactive entities, and strengthens this provision by requiring that both the business retained by the distributing corporation and that of the controlled corporation must have been actively conducted for 5 years preceding the distribution. The excerpt makes no mention of trades or businesses per se.

Respondent next argues the regulations upon which he relies are entitled to additional stature due to the fact that the Technical Amendments Act of 1958 (72 Stat. 160), which was intended to eliminate unintended benefits and hardships contained in the 1954 Code, was enacted subsequent to their promulgation, and, while making extensive changes in many sections of the statute, made no change in section 355. He relies upon the rule which attributes congressional approval to long-standing regulations under a section of the Internal Revenue Code where the section has been often amended without a revision of its administrative interpretation. See Lykes v. United States, 343 U.S. 118 (1952), rehearing denied 343 U.S. 937 (1952).

We note that the final regulations under subchapter C of the 1954 Code became effective on December 2, 1955, and that the Technical Amendments Act of 1958 was enacted on September 2, 1958. Further we note that section 355 has not been amended since its enactment in August of 1954. Thus, it is apparent that the challenged regulations have neither the longevity nor the congressional approval alluded to in Lykes v. United States, supra.

There being no language, either in the statute or committee report, which denies tax-free treatment under section 355 to a transaction solely on the grounds that it represents an attempt to divide a single trade or business, the Commissioner's regulations which impose such a restriction are invalid, and cannot be sustained. Commissioner v. Acker, 361 U.S. 87 (1959).

Finally, respondent argues that there is presently pending in Congress legislation (H.R. 4459) which would revise section 355(a)(1)(B) so as to permit a nontaxable distribution if either: (1) The active business requirements of 355(b) are met; or (2) it is established to the satisfaction of the Secretary or his delegate that the distribution is not made for the purpose of avoiding tax. As interpretative of this pending legislation, respondent directs our attention to a report dated December 11, 1958, of The Advisory Group on Subchapter C of the Internal Revenue Code of 1954, appointed by the House Subcommittee on Internal Revenue Taxation, wherein it is stated at page 65:

It is further provided in section 355(a)(1)(B)(ii) of the proposed revision that even though the transaction does not otherwise qualify under section 355 because of failure to satisfy the active business requirements or the 20 percent distribution requirement, it will nevertheless qualify under section 355 if it is established to the satisfaction of the Secretary or his delegate that the distribution is not in pursuance of a plan having as one of its principal purposes the avoidance of Federal income tax. *For example, even if the controlled corporation and the distributing corporation are not engaged in separate businesses, the Secretary or his delegate might find that a division of a single business qualifies under section 355, particularly where after the division certain stockholders will own stock in only one of the corporations and the remaining stockholders will own only stock in the other corporation.* Permitting some latitude in administration of the section should serve to prevent a rigid interpretation of the requirements of clause (i). [Emphasis supplied.]

Relying on the italicized language, respondent argues that under the law as presently written, the division of a single trade or business does not qualify for tax-free treatment under section 355.

The short answer to this argument is that *pending* legislation in no way is binding on this Court. Until enacted, H.R. 4459 represents a course of action Congress may or may not take. Moreover, the cited report was not prepared by any congressional committee, but rather by an advisory group appointed to assist in a study of subchapter C of the 1954 Code. Quite possibly, the proposed revision of section 355 was occasioned by the restrictive nature of the Commissioner's regulations, rather than by any interpretation of the nature of existing law. In any event, respondent's reliance upon either the bill or the report as indicative of existing law is misplaced.

Inasmuch as the parties treat the distribution as otherwise qualifying under section 355 for tax-free treatment, and inasmuch as we have found that portion of the regulations denying application of section 355 to the division of a single business to be invalid, we conclude that petitioner properly treated the distribution to him of the stock of E. P. Coady and Co. as a nontaxable transaction.

No evidence having been introduced with respect to the addition to tax under section 294(d)(2) of the 1939 Code, it is sustained subject to our holding on the above issue.

Reviewed by the Court.

Decision will be entered under Rule 50.

Pierce, J., dissents.

[Dissents by Judges Harron and Atkins omitted.]

Rev. Rul. 59-400

1959-2 C.B. 114

Advice has been requested whether a distribution of stock by a corporation engaged in the hotel and real estate business qualifies under the nontaxable provisions of section 355 of the Internal Revenue Code of 1954.

M corporation was engaged in two businesses, operating a hotel and renting improved real estate (both commercial and residential). The hotel business was started upon organization in 1920 and has been actively conducted up to the present time. In 1934, *M* corporation also entered into the rental real estate business when it purchased property, constructed a garage and automobile agency facilities thereon and rented it to a dealer.

In the intervening years, it acquired other rental properties which it has continued to operate. In 1954, the hotel had a fair market value of 550x dollars and a net book value of 350x dollars. The rental properties had a fair market value of 305x dollars and a net book value of 167x dollars.

During the five-year period commencing with 1954, the operation of the hotel business resulted in earnings, after taxes, of 240x dollars, and the operation of the real estate business resulted in earnings of approximately 75x dollars. In 1958, a new rental office building was built for 400x dollars, some 175x dollars thereof being provided by loans from banks. At the beginning of 1959, the hotel business was placed in a new corporation N, and the stock thereof distributed to the shareholders of M on a pro rata basis. N corporation received the hotel, plus certain receivables and other hotel business assets. M corporation retained the real estate liabilities and assets, which at that time had a net book value of 372x dollars and a fair market value of 705x dollars.

Section 355 of the Code states, in part, that in order for a distribution of stock to qualify under the nontaxable provisions of such section, each of the corporations involved must be engaged in a trade or business which has been actively conducted throughout the five-year period ending on the date of distribution, and that the transaction must not be used principally as a device to distribute the earnings and profits of either corporation.

The purpose behind the five-year limitation of section 355 is to prevent the corporate earnings of one business from being drawn off for such a period and put into a new business and thereby, through the creation of a marketable enterprise, convert what would normally have been dividends into capital assets that are readily saleable by the shareholders.

It is the position of the Internal Revenue Service that where a corporation which is devoted to one type of business also engages in the rental business, and substantial acquisitions of new rental property are made within the five-year period preceding the separation of these businesses, a "spin-off" transaction will not qualify under section 355 unless it can be shown that the property acquisitions were substantially financed out of the earnings of the rental business and not out of the earnings of the other business.

From the facts presented herein, it is readily apparent that there has been a very substantial increase in the rental properties subsequent to 1954, primarily as a result of the addition of the large office building in 1958. Further, it is also apparent that, viewing the transaction most favorably to the taxpayer, earnings properly attributable to the hotel business, in the amount of approximately 150x dollars, have been employed in increasing the real estate business. In view of this substantial financing out of the earnings of the hotel business, it is held that the distribution of the stock of N corporation to the shareholders of M corporation will not qualify as a nontaxable distribution under section 355 of the Code.

NOTES

1. *An introduction to §355.* To understand §355, you need to understand the abuse it is intended to forestall. Suppose *X* Corp. has been successful for many years so that it has substantial earnings and profits as well as substantial cash and liquid assets. The shareholders of *X* Corp. would like to get some of its profits into their hands without recognizing dividend income. Of course, a shareholder could sell stock at capital gain rates or redemptions could be structured to obtain the same effect, but in either case the favorable capital gain treatment is obtained only at the cost of giving up some control of the corporation and its future profit-making capability.

Consider the following plan. *X* Corp. creates new Sub Co. in a §351 transaction, transferring its cash and liquid investments to Sub Co. in exchange for all of Sub Co.'s stock. The Sub Co. stock is then distributed by *X* Corp. to its shareholders, and, if that distribution were tax free to *X* Corp. and to its shareholders, Sub Co. could then liquidate; by this mechanism the cash and liquid assets of *X* Corp. would be removed from corporate solution as capital gain. Or, instead of liquidating Sub Co., the shareholders could sell their stock in Sub Co. to obtain capital gains, and the purchasers would have a cost basis in the Sub Co. stock so that its assets could be bailed out in the future without difficulty.

Note that the effect of placing the *X* Corp. assets in a separate corporation (Sub Co.) allows the *X* Corp. shareholders to part with their Sub Co. stock without relinquishing any control over the operating assets of *X* Corp. As we saw when we looked at redemptions,[1] and again at stock dividends,[2] a shareholder should be able to avoid dividend treatment only by reducing ownership of the ongoing profit-making ability of the corporation. If divisive reorganizations permitted the tax-free separation of operating assets from investment assets, earnings and profits could be bailed out with abandon.

To ensure that corporate divisions do not become bailouts, §355 imposes three distinct hurdles. First, the active trade or business requirement of §355(a)(1)(C) mandates that each of the corporations after the division be engaged in a long-standing active trade or business. Thus, the transaction cannot simply separate operating assets from investment assets. Second, the device limitation of §355(a)(1)(B) provides that the transaction cannot be used "principally as a device for the distribution of earnings and profits." This broadly worded provision allows the courts to police divisive transactions with an eye toward the underlying policy of §355; in addition, it has allowed Treasury to promulgate a business purpose test in

---

1. See Chapter 5 supra.
2. See Chapter 6 supra.

the regulations. Third, the distribution requirement of §355(a)(1)(D) limits tax-free treatment to divisive transactions in which the corporations separate completely: With limited exceptions, the distributing corporation cannot retain any ownership of the corporation whose stock it is distributing. These three requirements are discussed in the Notes that follow.

In all §355 transactions, one corporation distributes stock and securities of one or more other corporations, thereby converting a parent-subsidiary structure into a brother-sister structure. In the language of §355, the corporation distributing the stock and securities is called the "distributing" corporation, and the corporations whose stock and securities are distributed are called the "controlled" corporations. In a §355 transaction, there is only one distributing corporation and there can be one or more controlled corporations.

2. *The active trade or business requirement.* Section 355(a)(1)(C), by incorporating §355(b), requires that both the distributing corporation and the controlled corporation be engaged immediately after the transaction in the active conduct of trades or businesses that have been conducted for at least five years. As *Coady* illustrates, this requirement can be met by dividing one active trade or business into two, sometimes called a vertical division. See also Treas. Regs. §1.355-3(c) (example 4), expressly allowing a vertical division.

Note that while the businesses must have been conducted for five years prior to the transaction, they need not have been conducted by the distributing corporation or by the controlled corporation during that entire period. That is, the requirement can be met if one or both of the businesses were acquired during the five-year period. Both businesses must, however, have been actively conducted by *someone* during the preceding five years, and acquisition of the businesses by the distributing corporation or by the controlled corporation must not have occurred within the five-year period unless the acquisition was tax free, see §355(b)(2)(C).

For example, suppose *X* Corp. has actively engaged in the toy manufacturing business for more than five years. Three years ago it acquired a software distributing company, Sub Co., in a tax-free B reorganization; Sub Co. had been actively conducting the software distributing business for more than two years prior to the reorganization. The distribution by *X* Corp. of the Sub Co. stock will satisfy the active trade or business requirement of §§355(a)(1)(C) and 355(b), although if *X* Corp. had purchased the Sub Co. stock in a taxable transaction, the requirement of §355(b)(2)(C) would not be met.

Consider the following variation on this example. Once again, suppose *X* Corp. acquired the Sub Co. stock in a tax-free B reorganization, but now assume Sub Co. acquired the software distributing business one year before in a taxable transaction. Now the distribution of Sub Co. stock by *X* Corp. will fail the active trade or business test by reason of §355(b)(2)(D). See also the example in Treas. Regs. §1.355-3(b)(4)(ii). The effect of

§355(b)(2)(D) is to require that all transfers of the trades or businesses used by the taxpayer to satisfy the requirements of §355(a)(1)(C) occurring during the five-year testing period be by way of tax-free transactions, including §351 formations and §368(a)(1) reorganizations.

Note that the limitation of §355(b) applies to the acquisition of a *business*, not to the acquisition of particular *assets*. For example, suppose again that *X* Corp. has actively engaged in the business of manufacturing toys for more than five years. Suppose further that one year ago *X* Corp. purchased for cash in a fully taxable transaction all the assets of one of its competitors in the toy manufacturing business and that these assets were then used to form a wholly owned subsidiary, Sub Co., in a §351 transaction. *X* Corp. can distribute the stock of Sub Co. without violating the active trade or business requirement because both the distributing corporation (*X* Corp.) and the controlled corporation (Sub Co.) are actively conducting the toy manufacturing business immediately after the transaction and *X* Corp. had been actively conducting this business for more than five years. That is, §355(b) does not prohibit the distribution of a part of a business representing a recent expansion, even if the expansion was by purchase, so long as the expansion continues the historic business of the distributing company. See Treas. Regs. §1.355-3(c) (examples 7 and 8).

Let us consider one more variation on this theme. Suppose *X* Corp. does not acquire the assets of one of its competitors but instead acquires the stock of one of its competitors (Sub Co.). Now the distribution of the Sub Co. stock will fail to satisfy §355(b) because of the language in §355(b)(2)(D). See also Nelson v. Commissioner, 61 T.C. 311 (1973); Boettger v. Commissioner, 51 T.C. 324 (1968). Thus, expansion by purchase of assets will not violate §355(b), although the functionally equivalent expansion by purchase of a company will. To the same effect, in Burke v. Commissioner, 42 T.C. 1021 (1965), it was held that establishing a new branch located in a different city was an extension of the same business and not a new business. In Lockwood's Estate v. Commissioner, 350 F.2d 712 (8th Cir. 1965), the court found that a business that spun off part of its activities by the establishment of a new manufacturing and sales corporation for the same products in a different state was merely the continuation of a single business and that the spun-off subsidiary could use the length of time its parent had been in business to qualify under the five-year test.

If the distributing corporation or the controlled corporation is liquidated, the effect of the §355 distribution and subsequent liquidation is the same as a partial liquidation. It should come as no surprise, then, that both divisive distributions and partial liquidations include an active trade or business requirement. Compare §355(b) with §302(e)(2). Unfortunately, the terms of these two provisions are not precisely the same — there is nothing like §355(b)(2)(D) in §302(e).

In a functional division, two different facets of one business are separated into two corporations. A valid functional division satisfies the technical tests of §355, provided that after the division both companies remain operating entities engaged in the active conduct of a business. If the division creates a passive corporation, the active business requirement is not met and the division will not be tax free under §355. In Rafferty v. Commissioner, 452 F.2d 767 (1st Cir. 1971), no active business was found when the spun-off corporation's activity after the division involved leasing back real estate to its parent. The court found the economic activities were an investment rather than an active trade or business. But cf. King v. Commissioner, 458 F.2d 245 (6th Cir. 1972), finding an active business when the corporation's only source of income was a long-term net lease of realty to the parent; there the real property was fit only for a single use, was needed in the business, and, therefore, was not suitable for a bailout.

Treas. Regs. §1.355-3(b)(2)(iii) states that whether a trade or business is actively conducted is a question of fact but that generally the corporation must perform active and substantial management and operational functions. See also Rev. Rul. 86-125, 1986-2 C.B. 57, in which the Service ruled that the rental of an office building does not constitute an active trade or business when the property is managed by an independent contractor rather than by employees of the corporation.

Suppose a coal mine sells coal only to its owner, a steel mill, which in turn sells steel only to its owner, a manufacturer of automobiles. May the coal mine be spun off to the shareholders of the automobile manufacturer? May the steel mill be spun off? While there was doubt under the old regulations, the current regulations contain examples of such horizontal divisions of an integrated business that meet the active conduct test. See examples 10-12 of Treas. Regs. §1.355-3(c). In the vertical division, there was the question as to whether the statute permitted a division of a single business into two businesses, which has been answered affirmatively by *Coady*. In a functional division (e.g., the company sells machinery and its subsidiary services such machinery), there is first the question as to whether after the division both entities are engaged in an active trade or business as in *Rafferty* and *King*. Even if the answer is affirmative, the second question is whether each business is properly "aged." In *Burke* and *Lockwood* the spun-off business could tack on the parent's history to meet the aging requirement while in *Boettger* it could not. The integrated business division asks whether there can be an active conduct of a trade or business if there are no outside customers. Cf. Groetzinger v. Commissioner, 480 U.S. 23 (1987) (full-time gambler betting on his own account was engaged in a trader business for purposes of §§62(1) and 162).

Note that under Treas. Regs. §1.355-2(d)(2)(iv)(C), the division of an integrated business may be considered a "device" for the distribution of earnings and profits if one of the postseparation corporations engages in a business that has as its principal function the service of the other postseparation corporation, if this captive business can be sold without adversely affecting the primary business. What is the rationale behind this limitation?

3. *The device limitation: in general.* The "device" language of §355(a)(1)(B) stems from congressional recognition that the existence of the active conduct of a trade or business is not sufficient assurance that the division of an existing corporation will not be used as a bailout. The most active trade or business can be sold. In addition to objective tests, Congress included the catchall subjective "device" test as another weapon against a division serving as a vehicle for a bailout. The Service considers several primary indicia in finding a device. Prearranged sales of the stock of either the distributing or controlled corporation have been viewed with suspicion, §355(a)(1)(B) and Treas. Regs. §1.355-2(d)(2)(iii). Treas. Regs. §1.355-2(d)(2)(iii)(B)-(D) states that a sale reasonably anticipated by the parties shall be considered as agreed on before the distribution and that, regardless of whether a sale is negotiated before the distribution, a postdistribution sale will be taken into evidence in determining a device.

Under §355(a)(2)(A), a corporate distribution may be tax free whether the distribution is or is not pro rata. Treas. Regs. §1.355-2(d)(2)(ii), however, suggests that a pro rata distribution presents the greatest potential for the withdrawal of earnings and profits and is more likely to be a device. Compare the policy behind §302. Another indicator of a device is the nature of the assets divided between the two corporations; Treas. Regs. §1.355-2(d)(2)(iv) states that the transfer or retention of cash or liquid assets (including securities and accounts receivable) not related to the reasonable needs of the business will be evidence of a device.

Did the transaction described in Rev. Rul. 59-400 above fail to qualify under §355 because it was a "device" for the distribution of earnings and profits? Note that no postdistribution sale was involved in the ruling. If the driving force behind §355 is that a taxpayer should be unable to obtain the earnings of a corporation as capital gains without relinquishing an interest in the ongoing profit-making capability of the corporation, then the division involved in Rev. Rul. 59-400 offered the potential of cashing out the earnings of both businesses by selling only one.

4. *The device limitation: business purpose.* In Commissioner v. Wilson, 353 F.2d 184 (9th Cir. 1965), the court was unable to discern a business or a nonbusiness motive for the division and refused to upset the Commissioner's determination that the corporate division was a "device" because of the absence of a discernible motive for the transaction. Had there been a finding of a tax avoidance motive, of course, the taxpayer would have been no better off. But what would be the outcome if the trial court had found that the motive behind the division was wholly nontax related? In Rafferty v. Commissioner, 452 F.2d 767 (1st Cir. 1971), a closely held corporation was divided to facilitate nontax estate planning. The court upheld the Commissioner's characterization of the transaction as a device

on the theory that nontax personal motives of a taxpayer cannot protect a transaction that has a considerable potential for bailing out earnings and profits at capital gain rates.

Note that in *Wilson* the Court required a business purpose notwithstanding the arguably more specific device language of §355. Is the requirement of a business purpose redundant? Not if the device language is limited to facts that constitute evidence of a bailout, e.g., a prearranged sale. The business purpose requirement can preclude from §355 those divisions that have a potential bailout in the future and that are not explained by nontax reasons. The ambiguity of such divisions is resolved in the proposed regulations by assuming that their underlying purpose is a bailout. Is *Wilson* clear support for such an across-the-board approach? One might raise the question why putting oneself in the position for a future bailout should be allowed even with a valid purpose. But note that the business activities separated in *Wilson* could originally have been put into two corporations separately owned by the shareholders; these problems would never have arisen in such an arrangement. This is the perplexing question in the corporate division area mentioned at the outset. Regulations have explicitly incorporated the *Wilson* rule that the absence of a business purpose, even if there is no tax avoidance purpose, will be fatal to the reorganization. See Treas. Regs. §1.355-2(b)(1).

Examples of valid business purposes are now found in Treas. Regs. §1.355-2(b)(5) (examples 1, 2, 5, and 8). The relationship between a corporate business purpose and a "device" is now found in Treas. Regs. §1.355-2(d)(3)(ii). The regulations now impose a best-fit requirement: The transaction will fail §355 if the business purpose could be accomplished in a tax-free manner without involving the distribution of stock, unless the alternative transactions are impractical or unduly expensive. Treas. Regs. §1.355-2(b)(3).

The regulations provide that a valid corporate purpose is not the reduction of federal taxes even if that reduction would come about other than from a bailout or similar transaction to which §355 speaks. Treas. Regs. §1.355-2(b)(2). In particular, the regulations provide that a distribution made to facilitate an election under subchapter S is not protected by §355 for want of a valid business purpose. Treas. Regs. §1.355-2(d)(5) (example 6).

This aspect of the regulations should be subject to challenge. Note that the statute fails to include an explicit "business purpose" requirement. Accordingly, such a requirement can be defended only as an attempt to further the purpose of §355. Is there any suggestion that §355 was intended to limit the number of subchapter S elections? Surely the ghost of *Gregory v. Helvering* has reappeared once too often if the Treasury feels secure in promulgating regulations exorcising all divisive transactions motivated by any attempt to minimize federal taxes even without the dangers to which §355 speaks.

In Rev. Rul. 85-122, 1985-2 C.B. 118, the Service ruled that the business purpose requirement of §355 is met if an unprofitable ski resort is separated from a profitable golf and tennis resort to meet the recommendation of the securities underwriter advising the corporation on marketing of debentures of the golf and tennis resort. And in Rev. Rul. 85-127, 1985-2 C.B. 119, the Service ruled that the business purpose requirement is met when two active businesses are split apart to retain the services of a key employee of one of the two businesses.

5. *Shareholder versus corporate business purpose.* The regulations state that a transaction does not qualify under §355 if carried out for purposes not germane to the business of the corporations. Treas. Regs. §1.355-2(b)(2) states that when the business purpose serves the shareholder as well as the corporation, there may be no problem, but if the transaction is undertaken solely for the personal reasons of the shareholder, the distribution will not qualify under §355. Note Parshelsky's Estate v. Commissioner, 303 F.2d 14 (2d Cir. 1962), suggesting the business purpose could be a shareholder purpose rather than a corporate business purpose, but the Court in *Rafferty,* Note 2 supra, rejected the suggestion that a shareholder investment purpose was sufficient. This issue pervades the entire reorganization area.

In Rev. Rul. 88-34, 1988-1 C.B. 115, X Corp. owned all the stock of Y Corp. The president of Y Corp. had recently retired, and individual A was identified as a prospective new president. A insisted that he receive an equity interest in Y Corp. as part of his compensation without acquiring any interest in X. To facilitate the transfer of Y stock to A, X Corp. spun off Y by distributing the Y stock pro rata to the X shareholders. The Service ruled that the spin-off of Y Corp. satisfied the business purpose test of former Treas. Regs. §1.355-2(c) because "the distribution enables the subsidiary corporation [Y Corp.] to hire the key employee it believes is necessary to the continued success of the business." Without knowing more about A's reasons for insisting on acquiring an interest in Y but not in X, has a shareholder purpose been transmuted into a corporate purpose? The current regulations take a more skeptical view of these transactions. See Treas. Regs. §1.355-2(b)(5) (example 8).

6. *The distribution requirement.* By virtue of §355(a)(1)(D), the distributing corporation must either distribute all the stock and securities that it holds in the controlled corporation or distribute an amount of stock constituting "control" (as defined by §368 (c)) *and* must satisfy the Treasury that the retention of stock in the controlled corporation was not in pursuance of a tax avoidance plan. Why this emphasis on a complete, or nearly complete, separation of the two corporations?

Consider individual T, who owns all the outstanding stock of X Corp. X has actively conducted two distinct businesses for more than five years. X transfers one of its two businesses to newly formed Y Corp. in exchange for common and callable preferred stock of Y, and the Y common stock is then distributed to *T*. If this transaction qualified as a tax-free divisive D reorganization, *T* would be in a position to bail out earnings and profits of *Y* Corp. by selling the stock of *X*. To see this, observe that *X* Corp.'s assets include preferred stock of *Y* Corp., so a sale of *X* would include a sale of the *Y* preferred. A purchaser of *X* would pay *T* not only for the value of the *X* operating assets but also for the value of the *Y* preferred stock, and *T* would have only a capital gain on this sale. When the *Y* preferred stock is then redeemed, the bailout is complete. To avoid this type of transaction, Congress placed the "control" requirement in §355(a)(1)(D). Why doesn't §306 handle this abuse?

In Commissioner v. Gordon, 391 U.S. 83 (1968), the distribution of the requisite 80 percent control of the distributed corporation took place in two steps (occurring in 1961 and 1963), and the court held that §355 was not satisfied; the first distribution (of less than 80 percent) was independent in the sense that a further distribution, though contemplated, was not promised or required by the plan. Another issue in the case — whether a distribution of stock pursuant to the exercise of stock rights qualifies under §355 — was left unanswered by the court. On remand it was held that the stock rights did not constitute stock within §354(a), 424 F.2d 378 (2d Cir. 1970). Treas. Regs. §1.355-1(b) states that stock rights or stock warrants are not included in the term "stock or securities."

7. *The forms a divisive transaction can take.* Corporate divisions have generated a lexicon of colorful labels, namely, the "spin-off," the "split-off," and the "split-up." In a *spin-off,* the existing corporation, *X,* transfers some of its assets to *Y* Corp., newly organized for the purpose, in exchange for *Y*'s stock, which *X* then distributes to its shareholders. In a *split-off, X* also transfers some of its assets to *Y* for *Y*'s stock, but *X* distributes the *Y* stock in exchange for part of its own stock. In a *split-up, X* transfers part of its assets to *Y* Corp. and the rest to *Z* Corp., both newly organized for the purpose, and then completely liquidates, distributing the *Y* and *Z* stock in exchange for its own. The economic consequences to *X*'s stockholders of all three methods are practically identical.

Both the split-off and the split-up can be useful when feuding shareholders seek to go their separate ways. For example, suppose *X* Corp. is owned equally by individuals *A* and *B*. If *A* and *B* often disagree on important corporate questions, they may decide to sever their business relationship by dividing their business between two companies. On one hand, if *X* Corp. transfers half of its assets to newly formed *Y* Corp., whose stock is distributed to *B* in exchange for his stock in *X*, then a split-off has been used to divide *X*. On the other hand, if *X* Corp. transfers half of its assets to *Y* Corp. and half to *Z* Corp. and then distributes the *Y* stock to *A* and the *Z* stock to *B* in complete liquidation, a split-up has been used to accomplish the same end.

With one exception, §355 treats all divisive reorganizations the same way. It is applicable both to distributions (spin-offs) and to exchanges (split-ups and split-offs). Moreover, the old corporation can distribute (a term that is defined to include exchanges) the stock and securities of a controlled corporation that it already owns or one created expressly to effect the corporate division. The requirements of §355 that are of particular interest are those in §355(a)(1)(B) and §355(b). Note that §354(b) prevents divisive reorganizations from avoiding the more restrictive provisions of §355 by qualifying under §354.

Not all corporate divisions will be "reorganizations" within the meaning of §368(a)(1). If the division is effected by transferring assets to a newly created subsidiary and then distributing the subsidiary's stock, the transaction is a D reorganization qualifying by virtue of a distribution described in §355. If the division is effected by distributing stock of an existing subsidiary without transferring assets as part of the plan, then §355 is applicable to the distribution of the subsidiary's stock without application of §368(a)(1)(D). While all forms of divisive rearrangements are referred to as "divisive reorganizations," the touchstone of such a transaction is not qualification under §368(a)(1)(D) but application of §355. The tax treatment of a §355 distribution, however, can turn on whether the transaction is a "reorganization" under §368(a)(1)(D).

8. *Taxation of divisive transactions.* Section 355(a)(1) permits a shareholder exchanging stock or securities for stock or securities in a divisive transaction to defer recognition of gain (and loss) realized on the exchange. It plays the same role with respect to divisive transactions as §354(a)(1) plays with respect to acquisitive reorganizations. And like §354, gain (but not loss) will be recognized by a shareholder receiving boot or excess securities. See §§356(a), 356(b), 355(a)(3).

Under some circumstances, boot in a divisive transaction will be taxed under the same rule governing boot in an acquisitive reorganization. In particular, dividend income is limited to the amount of gain realized on the transaction. See §356(a)(2). If the divisive transaction is structured as a *distribution* rather than as an *exchange*, however, the rule of §356(b) applies, subjecting not the gain but the value of the boot received to taxation as a dividend. In light of §355(a)(2) permitting pro rata exchanges in a divisive transaction, an astute taxpayer should always be able to avoid the harsh rule of §356(b).

How is the corporation taxed in a §355 transaction? One would expect that the distribution of stock and securities would be tax free and that gain (but not loss) would be recognized on the distribution of other property. If the divisive transaction happens to be a D reorganization (that is, if a newly formed subsidiary was created and spun off), current law produces these results under §361(b)(3) (nonrecognition on distribution of stock or securities) and §361(c) (recognition of gain but not loss on distribution of other property). If the transaction is not a "reorganization" because the controlled corporation is preexisting, the same taxation results from §355(c).

Suppose *X* Corp. has for many years owned 90 percent of the stock of *Y* Corp., which engages in an active trade or business. The remaining 10 percent of the *Y* Corp. stock was acquired by *X* one year ago in a taxable transaction. If *X* distributes all the *Y* stock to its shareholders, is the distribution tax free under §355? Under §355(a)(3)(B), stock acquired within five years of the distribution in a taxable transaction is treated as boot rather than as qualifying property.

Section 355 imposes no restriction on the type of stock or securities that can be distributed in a divisive reorganization. If debt securities are distributed, however, they will constitute boot under §356(d) to the extent their principal amount exceeds the principal amount of any securities that are surrendered; if preferred stock is distributed, it may be tainted by §306(c)(1)(B). See §356(e). See, e.g., Rev. Rul. 77-335, 1977-2 C.B. 95, where in a §355 spin-off by a parent of the subsidiary's common and preferred stock, the preferred was §306 stock. The ruling stated that §306 status is determined by reference to the earnings and profits of the distributing corporation — i.e., the parent. Section 355(a)(4) refers to §356 for the treatment of boot; §356(a) determines the amount of gain to be recognized and how it is to be taxed; §356(c) prohibits recognition of loss. See Rev. Rul. 74-516, 1974-2 C.B. 121, abandoning the automatic dividend rule in reorganization boot distributions and adopting instead a dividend equivalence test under the principles of §302(b)(1).

How should earnings and profits be allocated between the distributing and the controlled corporation? See §312(h). When the controlled corporation is newly formed, Treas. Regs. §1.312-10 provides that the earnings and profits "generally" should be made in proportion to the fair market value of the business or businesses retained by the distributing corporation as compared with the value of the business or businesses transferred to the controlled corporation.

9. *Pre-distribution purchases.* Suppose *P* Corp. owns 100 percent of the outstanding stock of Sub Corp., and assume the Sub Corp. stock constitutes 25 percent of the value of *P* Corp. Further, assume the Sub Corp. stock is worth $250,000 and *P* Corp.'s adjusted basis in the Sub Corp. stock equals $100,000. *T* Corp. would like to acquire Sub Corp. without the imposition of a corporate-level tax.

If a distribution by *P* Corp. of the Sub Corp. stock will qualify under §355, *P* and *T* can adopt the following plan. First, *T* Corp. will purchase 25 percent of the outstanding shares of *P* Corp. Second, after waiting a sufficient time to satisfy the continuity of interest requirement of Treas. Regs. §1.355-2(c), *P* Corp. will distribute its Sub Corp. stock to *T* in redemption of *T*'s stock of *P*. If §355 applied without limitation, *T* would acquire Sub Corp. from *P* without the imposition of a corporate-level tax, yet *T*'s basis in the Sub Corp. stock will equal its fair market value of $250,000 (because that is what *T* Corp. paid for the *P* Corp. stock it purchased, which was then redeemed). Prior to the transaction, the Sub Corp. stock had a basis of only $100,000 in the hands of *P* Corp. Thus, *T* Corp. has effectively purchased a corporate asset (the Sub Corp. stock) without the selling corporation (*P* Corp.) recognizing any gain.

Section 355(d) responds to this type of transaction not by disqualifying the transaction under §355 but instead by forcing the distributing corporation (here, *P* Corp.) to recognize gain on the distribution of the stock of the controlled corporation (here, Sub Corp.). Note that §355(d) will apply if, immediately after the transaction, a shareholder holds 50 percent or more of the distributing corporation *or* of the controlled corporation if that interest was acquired within five years and was acquired by "purchase," which is defined quite broadly in §355(d)(5).

What is the abuse to which §355(d) speaks? In general, one corporation cannot transfer an appreciated asset to a second corporation without the imposition of a corporate-level tax. To be sure, there are exceptions to this rule for tax-free reorganizations, as discussed in Chapter 10, and for affiliated corporations filing a consolidated return, as discussed in Chapter 13. Aside from these exceptional cases, the transfer of an asset from one corporation to another is a taxable event for the transferor corporation.

In the example above, the Sub Corp. stock initially held by *P* Corp. ended up in the hands of *T* Corp. Yet, were §355 to apply to the transaction, there would be no taxation to *P* Corp. Although application of §355 to this transaction would not permit any assets to be removed from corporate solution, the legislative history of §355(d) indicates that this type of transaction is inconsistent with the repeal of the *General Utilities* doctrine, discussed at pages 136 supra.

The broad reach of §355(d) has been cut back substantially by regulations. Under Prop. Treas. Regs. §1.355-6(b)(3)(i), a transaction described in §355(d)(2) will not be subject to §355(d)(1) if the effect of the transaction is not to "increase direct or indirect ownership in the distributing corporation or any controlled corporation by a disqualified person" nor to "provide a disqualified person with a purchased basis in the stock of any controlled corporation." In this context a "disqualified person" is anyone who holds, directly or indirectly, disqualified stock constituting a 50% or greater interest in the corporation. Prop. Treas. Regs. §1.355-6(b)(3)(ii). For a thorough discussion of this complex regulation, see Cummings, Section 355(d) Proposed Regulations Provide Meaningful Safe Harbors, 91 J. Tax. 5 (1999).

10. *Nonqualifying transactions.* If a spin-off does not qualify under §355, and if the fair market value of the distributed stock exceeds its adjusted basis, gain will be recognized by the distributing corporation. §311(b). In addition, the distribution falls under §301 and will be taxed as a dividend to the extent of the distributing corporation's earnings and profits. But suppose the nonqualifying distribution takes the form of a split-up. Such a transaction amounts to a complete liquidation of the dis-

tributing corporation and presumably will be taxed as any other corporate liquidation. Can a taxpayer argue that a *successful* split-up be taxed as a complete liquidation rather than as a §355 division, particularly if the distribution includes boot? See Telephone Answering Service Co. v. Commissioner, 63 T.C. 423 (1974), aff 'd, 546 F.2d 423 (4th Cir. 1976), especially footnote 14. See also Rev. Rul. 84-71, 1984-1 C.B. 106, in which the Service ruled that §351 could apply to a transfer that was part of a larger acquisitive transaction failing to qualify for reorganization treatment.

11.   *Criss-cross transactions.* If *A* owns 50 percent of the stock of *X* Corp. and of *Y* Corp. and *B* owns the other 50 percent of *X* and *Y,* can they employ §355 to effect a rearrangement of their investments so that *A* will become the sole owner of *X* and *B* the sole owner of *Y?* What might be the mechanics of such a division? Treas. Regs. §1.355-4 holds such a transaction taxable, and the cases have generally integrated the various steps and found such a transaction taxable. See Portland Manufacturing Co. v. Commissioner, 56 T.C. 58 (1971), aff 'd, 75-1 U.S.T.C. (CCH) ¶9449; Kuper v. Commissioner, 61 T.C. 624 (1974), aff'd, 533 F.2d 152 (5th Cir. 1976); Atlee v. Commissioner, 67 T.C. 395 (1976), following Portland. Contra, Badanes v. Commissioner, 39 T.C. 410 (1962), allowing such a division. Can §355 be used to accomplish an exchange under which *A,* owning all the stock of *X* Corp., and *B,* owning all the stock of *Y* Corp., each succeed in becoming the sole owner of the other's corporation? Rev. Rul. 71-336, 1971-2 C.B. 299, prohibits a somewhat similar plan. But see Rev. Rul. 77-11, 1977-1 C.B. 93, for a successful way of dividing two 50 percent-owned brother-sister corporations of differing size, *X* and *Y,* owned equally by *A* and *B,* by a non-pro rata split-off. *X* Corp. transferred $1,850x$ dollars in assets representing half of its net worth to *Z,* a newly formed corporation, for 1,850 shares of *Z*'s voting common stock. *Y* Corp. transferred $350x$ dollars in assets representing half of its net worth to *Z* for 350 shares of *Z*'s voting common stock. Section 351 covered these exchanges. *X* then distributed all the *Z* stock to *B* in exchange for all of *B*'s stock in *X.* Since this is a controlling interest and since the other requirements of §355 were met, this exchange was tax free. *Y* then distributed all the *Z* stock to *B* in exchange for all of *B*'s stock in *Y.* A capital gains tax on *B*'s gain was payable on this exchange since *Y* could not distribute a controlling interest in *Z.* As a result, *A* owned all the stock of *X* and *Y* without tax, and *B* owned all the stock of *Z* at the cost of the capital gain incurred on the exchange with *Y* Corp.

PROBLEMS

11-1.   For the past 15 years, *X* Corp. has engaged in the business of heavy construction. *X* Corp. transfers half of the company's heavy machinery and other operating assets along with one long-term contract to newly formed *Y* Corp. in exchange for all of *Y* Corp.'s stock, and this stock is promptly distributed pro rata to the shareholders of *X* Corp. Immediately after the transaction, both corporations actively conduct the business formerly conducted by *X* Corp. It is anticipated that *Y* Corp. will be liquidated within the taxable year.

  a. Does the distribution of *Y* Corp. stock qualify as a tax-free divisive reorganization under §368(a)(1)(D) and §355?
  b. Does the analysis change if it is *X* Corp. that will be liquidated and its assets distributed in the near future?

11-2. *A* and *B* each owns 50 percent of the stock of *X* Corp. *A*'s basis in the *X* stock is $600, and *B*'s stock basis is $1,400. *X* Corp. carries on (and has carried on for more than five years) two lines of business: (a) the manufacture and sale of computer games (Gameco division) and (b) the manufacture and sale of denim sleepwear (Denco division). The assets of each division have a value of $2,000 and adjusted basis of $800. No liabilities exist, and there are joint earnings and profits of $1,000.

  a. On January 1, 1998, *X* transfers all the Gameco assets to newly formed *Y* Corp. in exchange for all of *Y*'s stock. *X* also transfers all its Denco assets to newly formed *Z* Corp. in exchange for all of *Z*'s stock. *X* then liquidates and distributes the *Y* and *Z* stock ratably to *A* and *B*. What are the tax consequences to *A* and *B*?
  b. Suppose instead that *X* transferred the Gameco assets to *Y* Corp. and retained the Denco assets. Immediately thereafter, *X* distributes the *Y* stock to *A* in exchange for all of *A*'s stock in *X*.
  c. What are the results if *X* transfers the Gameco assets to *Y* and then distributes the *Y* stock equally to *A* and *B*?
  d. How do your answers to (b) change if most of the assets of Gameco consist of appreciated securities traded on the New York stock exchange?
  e. How do your answers to (b) change if Denco was purchased three years before with profits from Gameco? If *X* had purchased the stock of Holding Corp. three years before with profits from Gameco, Holding Corp.'s only asset then being stock of Denco, and, shortly after *X*'s acquisition of the Holding Corp. stock, Holding Corp. liquidated under §332 so that *X* acquired the stock of Denco under §332?

11-3. Parent Corp. owns the entire outstanding stock of Sub-1 Corp., Sub-2 Corp., and Sub-3 Corp. *X*, *Y*, and *Z* each purchase one-third of the outstanding shares of Parent Corp. and Parent Corp. subsequently distributes the stock of Sub-1 to *X*, the stock of Sub-2 to *Y*, and the stock of Sub-3 to *Z*. What are the tax consequences of the distributions to Parent

Corp., *X, Y,* and *Z*? How would your answers change if the distributions had been pro rata so that *X, Y,* and *Z* each ended up with a one-third interest in Sub-1, Sub-2, and Sub-3? Assume each corporation has actively conducted a trade or business for more than five years.

11-4. *X* Corp. purchases all the outstanding stock of *Y* Corp. for $200,000. *Y* Corp.'s assets include all the outstanding stock of *Z* Corp. with adjusted basis of $60,000 and fair market value of $100,000. Three years later, *P* Corp. acquires all the outstanding stock of *Y* Corp. from *X* Corp. in exchange for its own voting preferred stock in a transaction described in §368(a)(1)(B). How are *P* Corp. and *Y* Corp. taxed if *Y* Corp. distributes all its stock in *Z* Corp. one year after the *P-X* B reorganization, assuming the active business requirement of §355(c) is met?

B. VARIATIONS

Bhada v. Commissioner _____

89 T.C. 959 (1987), aff'd, 892 F.2d 39 (6th Cir. 1989)

NIMS, Judge: . . .

McDermott, Inc. (McDermott), was a Delaware corporation at all relevant times. From 1959 until December 10, 1982, McDermott was the parent corporation to a group of corporations hereinafter referred to as the McDermott Group. From 1959 until December 10, 1982, McDermott International, Inc. (International), was a wholly-owned subsidiary of McDermott and a controlled foreign corporation within the meaning of section 957.

Pursuant to a plan of reorganization adopted on October 28, 1982, by the boards of directors of McDermott and International, International made an offer to exchange cash and shares of its own stock (International Common) for shares of the common stock of McDermott (McDermott Common). . . .

Under the terms of the offer, International was to exchange one share of International Common plus $0.35 for each outstanding share of McDermott Common. The offer was conditioned upon the tendering of a minimum of 22 million shares of McDermott Common. International also retained the right to refuse to accept more than 30 million shares of McDermott Common.

On December 10, 1982, International accepted, pursuant to the terms of the Offer, all shares of McDermott Common tendered by each shareholder holding 99 or fewer of such shares and accepted a portion of all the shares of McDermott Common tendered by each shareholder holding 100 or more of such shares, as was determined on the terms concerning proration stated in the Prospectus. International acquired 30 million shares of McDermott Common for which it gave $10,500,000 and 30 million shares of International Common. As a result of the exchange, International held approximately 68 percent of the voting power in Mc-Dermott, and former holders of McDermott Common who participated in the exchange held approximately 90 percent of the voting power in International.

Petitioners participated in the December, 1982, transactions. In response to the Offer, petitioners Rohinton and Patricia Bhada tendered to International 26 shares of McDermott Common and received in return 26 shares of International Common and $9.10 in cash. . . . On December 10, 1982, the fair market value of one share of International Common was $19. . . .

Section 304(c) provides, in part, that control, for purposes of section 304, means ownership of stock possessing at least 50 percent of the total combined voting power of all classes of stock entitled to vote, or at least 50 percent of the total value of shares of all classes of stock.

If section 304(a)(2) applies to the December, 1982, transaction, the International Common and cash received by petitioners must be treated as a distribution in redemption of their stock in McDermott, and it will be necessary to apply section 302 to determine the character of the amounts received by petitioners in International Common and cash. The parties have agreed that the cash received by petitioners is property for purposes of section 304(a)(2) and that if section 304 does not apply to the International Common received by petitioners, the tax consequences of the receipt of that stock will then be governed by section 1001.[2]

Section 304 does not apply to the International Common received by petitioners unless this stock was "property" for purposes of section 304(a)(2). The term "property" is defined in section 317(a), which provides: "For purposes of this part, the term 'property' means money, securities, and any other property; except that such term does not include stock in the corporation making the distribution (or rights to acquire such stock)."

Respondent argues that the true nature of the transaction between International and petitioners was an exchange of International Common for McDermott Common rather than a distribution by International of its stock in exchange for McDermott Common. It is respondent's position that the term "distribution" in section 317(a) refers only to a distribution

---

2. Section 351 does not apply in this case because of the failure to meet the 80 percent control requirement of section 351. Although the former McDermott shareholders owned 90 percent of the total voting power in International after the December, 1982, exchange, they did not own at least 80 percent of the total of all other classes of stock of International. McDermott at all relevant times owned all of the shares of a class of voting preferred stock of International. Respondent speculates that if section 304 does not apply to the December, 1982, transaction, the former shareholders of McDermott will suffer no adverse tax consequences and will in many cases recognize a loss for tax purposes.

by a corporation with respect to its stock to its shareholders in their capacity as shareholders. Because International gave its stock to McDermott's shareholders and not to its own shareholders, respondent maintains that there was no distribution as defined in section 317(a). We disagree.

. . . Respondent finds support for his definition of the term "distribution" by asserting that the term "distribution" as it appears in every section in Part I of Subchapter C refers to a distribution by a corporation to its shareholders in relation to its stock. However, in section 304 itself Congress has used the term "distribution" in its generic sense. Section 304(b)(3)(A), provides, "Except as otherwise provided in this paragraph, subsection (a) (and not section 351 and not so much of sections 357 and 358 as relates to section 351) shall apply to any property received in a distribution described in subsection (a)."

At first glance, it is difficult to determine whether the term distribution in section 304(b)(3)(A) refers to the distribution of property by the acquiring corporation to shareholders of the parent corporation that triggers the application of section 304 or to the hypothetical redemption distribution by the parent to its own shareholders that follows when section 304(a)(2) applies. This ambiguity is resolved, however, by section 304(b)(3)(B), which provides in pertinent part:

> (B)   Certain assumptions of liability, etc. —
> (i)   In general. — In the case of an acquisition described in section 351, subsection (a) shall not apply to any liability —
> (I)   assumed by the acquiring corporation, or
> (II) to which the stock is subject, if such liability was incurred by the transferor to acquire the stock. For purposes of the preceding sentence, the term "stock" means stock referred to in paragraph (1)(B) or (2)(A) of subsection (a).

Section 304(b)(3)(B) provides that in a transaction described in both sections 304(a) and 351, section 304(a) does not apply to certain liabilities assumed by the acquiring corporation or to which the stock is subject. The reference to the assumption of liabilities by the acquiring corporation indicates that section 304(b)(3)(B) refers to the actual transaction, i.e., the distribution of property by the acquiring corporation to shareholders of another corporation rather than the hypothetical redemption under section 304(a). Because section 304(b)(3)(B) refers to the actual transaction that triggers section 304, we can only conclude that section 304(b)(3)(A) also refers to the actual transactions when it uses the term distribution. Accordingly, the term distribution in section 317(a) does not exclusively refer to a distribution by a corporation to its shareholders with respect to its stock.

From this it follows that International "distributed" its own stock to petitioners in the December, 1982, exchange and that such stock is not to be deemed property. This is because the International Common was the stock of the corporation making the distribution, it was not property, and section 304 does not apply.[3]

Respondent contends, however, that section 304(b)(3)(B) refers to actual transactions but that section 304(b)(3)(A) refers to the hypothetical redemption that occurs when section 304 applies. Respondent reasons that section 304(b)(3)(B) concerns liabilities assumed (a much more difficult matter to express in terms of the hypothetical transaction), whereas the conflict between sections 304 and 351 does not arise until after the hypothetical redemption distribution comes into play. We decline to adopt respondent's reading of the statute. Neither section 304(b)(3)(B) nor section 304(b)(3)(A) applies unless there is a conflict between sections 304 and 351. Respondent's analysis assumes that there is no relationship between sections 304(b)(3)(B) and 304(b)(3)(A). The language of the statute does not support respondent's position nor does anything in the legislative history suggest such a contorted reading of the statute. . . .

Before section 304(b)(3) was enacted, it was possible for taxpayers to avoid the application of section 304 to property received in addition to stock in an exchange of stock for stock of a related corporation if they met the 80 percent control requirement of section 351.

To prevent such a circumvention of section 304, Congress enacted section 304(b)(3). The Conference Report explains:

> The conference agreement extends the anti-bailout rules of sections 304 and 306 of present law to the use of corporations, including holding companies, formed or availed of to avoid such rules. Such rules are made applicable to a transaction that, under present law, otherwise qualifies as a tax-free incorporation under section 351.
>
> Section 351 generally will not apply to transactions described in section 304. Thus, section 351, if otherwise applicable, will generally apply only to the extent such transaction consists of an exchange of stock for stock in the acquiring corporation. . . .

[H. Rept. 97-760 (Conf.), to accompany H.R. 4961 (Pub. L. 97248) (1982), 1982-2 C.B. 600, 635.]

Thus, it appears from the Conference Report that Congress was concerned only with the treatment of property received in a transaction that fell under the provisions of both sections 304 and 351. Congress must have assumed that section 304 would not apply to the stock of the acquiring corporation received by the shareholders of the related corporation because the stock of the acquiring corporation in a section 304(a) transaction is not property.

---

3. Because we hold for petitioners in this case, we need not address their other arguments.

Respondent maintains that section 304(b)(3) was directed only at brother-sister transactions described in section 304(a)(1) rather than parent-subsidiary transactions described in section 304(a)(2). Therefore, respondent explains, the stock of a sister corporation received in a 304(a)(1) transaction is not property for purposes of section 304, but the stock of the acquiring subsidiary corporation in a section 304(a)(2) transaction is property. We disagree. Section 304(b)(3) specifically mentions that it applies to both sections 304(a)(1) (brother-sister transactions) and 304(a)(2) (parent-subsidiary transactions). Section 304(b)(3)(B)(i). . . .

Our conclusion comports with the purpose of section 304(a)(2). Section 115(g)(2) of the Internal Revenue Code of 1939, from which section 304 is derived, was enacted in response to the decision in Rodman Wanamaker Trust v. Commissioner, 11 T.C. 365 (1948), affd. 178 F.2d 10 (3d Cir. 1949), in which the Court treated the cash received by the taxpayer from a subsidiary in return for shares of its parent's stock as proceeds of a sale rather than a dividend. . . .

In this case, the cash received by petitioners constitutes assets withdrawn from International in exchange for stock of its parent, McDermott, and the parties agree that section 304 applies to the cash. However, in receiving International Common in return for McDermott Common, petitioners did not withdraw assets from International or McDermott. The transaction resulted in a change in the ownership structure of the two corporations. Congress did not intend to prevent such a change in corporate ownership by enacting section 304. . . .

Finally, respondent maintains that if section 304 does not apply in this case, petitioners will be able to avoid the provisions of section 355. Respondent characterizes the transaction in this case as an indirect redemption by a parent corporation (McDermott) of its own stock in return for the stock of its subsidiary (International). Had McDermott distributed the International stock to its shareholders in this way, section 355 would have required dividend treatment of the stock International received by petitioners. We have already rejected respondent's argument that section 355 was meant to prevent indirect redemptions. Dunn Trust v. Commissioner, 86 T.C. 745 (1986). . . .

Moreover, the transaction in this case differs from the exchange envisioned by respondent.

Had McDermott redeemed its stock and issued 30 million shares of International to petitioners, the corporations would have split up. As a result of the redemption, petitioners would have held an equity interest in International and would have given up most of their interest in McDermott.

In this case, however, petitioners exchanged their McDermott stock with International for stock in International. After this transaction, International became the parent of McDermott, and petitioners became the owners of a direct equity interest in the operations of International and an indirect equity interest in the operations of McDermott.

A transaction in which a parent redeems its own stock by distributing the stock of a subsidiary divides the corporations, and assets are withdrawn from the parent. The redeeming shareholders can bail out corporate assets in such a transaction by selling off the stock of the subsidiary. The result can be equivalent to a distribution of a dividend. Accordingly, a division actually effected by such a transaction is generally tested for dividend equivalence under section 302.

The transaction in this case, however, was not divisive, and, therefore, the anti-bailout provisions of section 355 are not relevant. After the December, 1982, exchange, a holder of International Common could not dispose of his interest in International without disposing of his interest in McDermott at the same time. Thus, no bailout was possible in this case.

Respondent maintains, however, that a holding for petitioners in this case will permit other taxpayers to bail out assets from corporate solution. In support of his argument, respondent presents two hypothetical examples. Respondent's first example involves an exchange of stock as follows:

> Assume that P Corp. owns all the stock of its subsidiary, S Corp. S Corp. has no other class of stock. The value of P is ten times greater than the value of S. The P shareholders desire to cash in on the stock of S at capital gains rates. To this end, S Corp. offers to exchange newly created shares of itself (the same class of stock) representing 80% of the voting power in S Corp. to P's shareholders for shares of P on a value-for-value basis. The P shareholders participate in the exchange with the intent of later disposing of the stock of S at capital gains rates. A direct distribution would have been taxed under I.R.C. §§301 or 302. Respondent's position in this case would treat this indirect distribution in the above transaction just as a direct distribution would have been treated. Petitioners' position would undermine I.R.C. §355 by treating the transaction as a nontaxable exchange under I.R.C. §351 followed by a sale under I.R.C. §1001 at capital gains rates.

Respondent's second example involves the receipt of preferred stock of the subsidiary by shareholder of the parent, as follows:

> Suppose P corporation owns all the stock of S corporation and that P and S each have substantial earnings and profits. P's shareholders want to receive the economic benefit of these earnings but . . . want to avoid dividend treatment. To this end, they cause S to acquire from each of them 10% of their respective P shareholdings in exchange solely for nonvoting limited preferred stock of S. . . . Sometime after the exchange, the P shareholders sell all of their S preferred stock for cash to unrelated third parties. Absent the application of section 304(a)(2), the above example results in the following tax consequences. The exchange of P stock for preferred stock will result

in capital gain to the *P* shareholders. They will thus take a fair market value basis in the *S* preferred stock. Their subsequent sale of the preferred stock will result in no taxation to them assuming its value remains constant. . . . The *S* preferred stock will not be section 306 stock in the hands of the *P* shareholders since, even assuming arguendo that §306(c)(3) applies to parent-subsidiary transactions, the requirements of §306(C)(3) are not met in that the *P* stock/*S* preferred stock exchange was not a transaction described in §351. Since the *S* preferred stock is not section 306 stock, its sale by the *P* shareholders will not result in ordinary income to them under §306.

Respondent may have discovered a potential for bailout under the provisions of section 304.[12] However, the examples presented by respondent are not before us, and we decline to adopt an interpretation of section 304 in contravention of the language of that statute and its legislative history.

Moreover, it seems apparent that the bailout potential perceived by respondent in his examples can be achieved by a value-for-value exchange of stock or an exchange of common stock for preferred between brother and sister corporations, and respondent has conceded that section 304 does not apply to the stock of the acquiring corporation received in a brother-sister transaction described in section 304(a)(1).

To reflect the foregoing, an appropriate order will be issued.

NOTES

1. *Corporate divisions effected without §355.* Although Congress intended §355 to be the exclusive vehicle granting tax-preferred treatment to divisive transactions, taxpayers wishing to avoid the strict limitations of §355 have sought to fit their corporate divisions within the umbrella of less restrictive provisions. In *Bhada,* a stock-for-stock exchange turned the parent-subsidiary pair into a brother-sister pair (albeit with cross-ownership between the brother and sister) and so had the effect of a divisive reorganization. Had the Tax Court held that stock of the distributing corporation constituted "property" for the application of §304(a), the transaction might have been taxed as a distribution, just as a failed §355 transaction is taxed. Unfortunately, the court ruled that §304(a) does not cover the stock of the subsidiary corporation because such stock is stock of the distributing corporation within the meaning of §317(a). Thus, the transaction effected a tax-free divisive reorganization without having to satisfy the hurdles imposed by §355. The Tax Court, while acknowledging that its holding might create an end-run around §355, wrote: "[W]e decline to adopt an

---

12. Bittker and Eustice recognize this potential for bailout as a weakness in section 304 as it is presently written. See Bittker & Eustice, Federal Income Taxation of Corporations and Shareholders, par. 9.32, pp. 9-53 to 9-54 (4th ed. 1979).

interpretation of section 304 in contravention of the language of the statute and its legislative history." 89 T.C. at 977.

PROBLEMS

11-5. *X* Corp., a successful corporation with substantial earnings and profits, has 100 shares of stock outstanding, wholly owned by individual *B*. *B* owns 50 of these shares with adjusted basis of $10 per share and the other 50 shares with adjusted basis of $1,000 per share. Assume each share of *X* Corp. is worth $1,000. *X* Corp. transfers cash of $50,000 to newly formed *Y* Corp. in exchange for 100 shares of *Y* Corp. stock. One year later, *B* transfers the 50 shares of *X* Corp. stock having adjusted basis of $1,000 per share to *Y* Corp. in exchange for 100 shares of *Y* Corp. common stock. What are the tax consequences of this exchange to individual *B*? How will *B* be taxed if her stock of *Y* Corp. is subsequently redeemed?

Commissioner v. Morris Trust
367 F.2d 794 (4th Cir. 1966)

Before Haynsworth, Chief Judge, J. Spencer Bell, Circuit Judge, and Stanley, District Judge.

HAYNSWORTH, Chief Judge.

Its nubility impaired by the existence of an insurance department it had operated for many years, a state bank divested itself of that business before merging with a national bank. The divestiture was in the form of a traditional "spin-off," but, because it was a preliminary step to the merger of the banks, the Commissioner treated their receipt of stock of the insurance company as ordinary income to the stockholders of the state bank. We agree with the Tax Court, that gain to the stockholders of the state bank was not recognizable under §355 of the 1954 Code.

In 1960, a merger agreement was negotiated by the directors of American Commercial Bank, a North Carolina corporation with its principal office in Charlotte, and Security National Bank of Greensboro, a national bank. [T]hough American was slightly larger than Security, it was found desirable to operate the merged institutions under Security's national charter, after changing the name to North Carolina National Bank. . . .

For many years, American had operated an insurance department. This was a substantial impediment to the accomplishment of the merger, for a national bank is prohibited from operating an insurance department except in towns having a population of not more than 5000 inhabitants. To avoid a violation of the national banking laws, therefore, and to accomplish the merger under Security's national charter, it was prerequisite that American rid itself of its insurance business.

The required step to make it nubile was accomplished by American's organization of a new corporation, American Commercial Agency, Inc., to which American transferred its insurance business assets in exchange for Agency's stock which was immediately distributed to American's stockholders. At the same time, American paid a cash dividend fully taxable to its stockholders. The merger of the two banks was then accomplished.

Though American's spin-off of its insurance business was a "D" reorganization, as defined in §368(a)(1), provided the distribution of Agency's stock qualified for nonrecognition of gain under §355, the Commissioner contends that the active business requirements of §355(b)(1)(A) were not met, since American's banking business was not continued in unaltered corporate form. He also finds an inherent incompatibility in substantially simultaneous divisive and amalgamating reorganizations.

Section 355(b)(1)(A) requires that both the distributing corporation and the controlled corporation be "engaged immediately after the distribution in the active conduct of a trade or business." There was literal compliance with that requirement, for the spin-off, including the distribution of Agency's stock to American's stockholders, preceded the merger. The Commissioner asks that we look at both steps together, contending that North Carolina National Bank was not the distributing corporation and that its subsequent conduct of American's banking business does not satisfy the requirement.

A brief look at an earlier history may clarify the problem. . . .

Nonrecognition of gain in "spin-offs" was introduced by the Revenue Act of 1924. Its §203(b)(3), as earlier Revenue Acts, provided for nonrecognition of gain at the corporate level when one corporate party to a reorganization exchanged property solely for stock or securities of another, but it added a provision in subsection (c) extending the nonrecognition of gain to a stockholder of a corporate party to a reorganization who received stock of another party without surrendering any of his old stock. Thus, with respect to the nonrecognition of gain, treatment previously extended to "split-offs" was extended to the economically indistinguishable "spin-off."

The only limitation upon those provisions extending nonrecognition to spin-offs was contained in §203(h) and (i) defining reorganizations. The definition required that immediately after the transfer, the transferor or its stockholders or both be in control of the corporation to which the assets had been transferred, and "control" was defined as being the ownership of not less than eighty percent of the voting stock and eighty percent of the total number of shares of all other classes of stock.

With no restriction other than the requirement of control of the transferee, these provisions were a fertile source of tax avoidance schemes. By spinning-off liquid assets or all productive assets, they provided the means by which ordinary distributions of earnings could be cast in the form of a reorganization within their literal language.

The renowned case of Gregory v. Helvering, 293 U.S. 465, brought the problem to the Supreme Court. The taxpayer there owned all of the stock of United Mortgage Corporation which, in turn, owned 1000 shares of Monitor Securities Corporation. She wished to sell the Monitor stock and possess herself of the proceeds. If the sale were effected by United Mortgage, gain would be recognized to it, and its subsequent distribution of the net proceeds of the sale would have been a dividend to the taxpayer, taxable as ordinary income. If the Monitor stock were distributed to the taxpayer before sale, its full value would have been taxable to her as ordinary income. In order materially to reduce that tax cost, United Mortgage spun-off the Monitor stock to a new corporation, Averill, the stock of which was distributed to the taxpayer. Averill was then liquidated, and the taxpayer sold the Monitor stock. She contended that she was taxable only on the proceeds of the sale, reduced by an allocated part of her cost basis of United Mortgage, and at capital gain rates.

The Supreme Court found the transaction quite foreign to the congressional purpose. It limited the statute's definition of a reorganization to a reorganization of a corporate business or businesses motivated by a business purpose. It was never intended that Averill engage in any business, and it had not. Its creation, the distribution of its stock and its liquidation, the court concluded, was only a masquerade for the distribution of an ordinary dividend, as, of course, it was. . . .

Underlying such judicially developed rules limiting the scope of the nonrecognition provisions of the Code, was an acceptance of a general congressional purpose to facilitate the reorganization of businesses, not to exalt economically meaningless formalisms and diversions through corporate structures hastily created and as hastily demolished. Continuation of a business in altered corporate form was to be encouraged, but immunization of taxable transactions through the interposition of shortlived, empty, corporate entities was never intended and ought not to be allowed.

While these judicial principles were evolving and before the Supreme Court declared itself in Gregory v. Helvering, an alarmed Congress withdrew nonrecognition of gain to a stockholder receiving securities in a spin-off. It did so by omitting from the Revenue Act of 1934, a provision comparable to §203(c) of the Revenue Act of 1924.

Nonrecognition of gain to the stockholder in spin-off situations, however, was again extended by §317(a) of the Revenue Act of 1951, amending the 1939 Code by adding §112(b)(11). This time, the judicially developed restrictions upon the application of the earlier statutes were partially codified. Nonrecognition of gain was extended "unless it appears that (A) any corporation which is a party to such reorganization was not intended to continue the active conduct of a trade or business after such reorganization, or (B) the corporation whose stock is distributed was used principally as a device for the distribution of earnings and profits to the shareholders of any corporation a party to the reorganization."

If this transaction were governed by the 1939 Code, as amended in 1951, the Commissioner would have had the support of a literal reading of the A limitation, for it was not intended that American, in its then corporate form, should continue the active conduct of the banking business. From the prior history, however, it would appear that the intention of the A limitation was to withhold the statute's benefits from schemes of the Gregory v. Helvering type. It effectively reached those situations in which one of the parties to the reorganization was left only with liquid assets not intended for use in the acquisition of an active business or in which the early demise of one of the parties was contemplated, particularly, if its only office was a conduit for the transmission of title. The B limitation was an additional precaution intended to encompass any other possible use of the device for the masquerading of a dividend distribution.

The 1954 Code was the product of a careful attempt to codify the judicial limiting principles in a more particularized form. The congressional particularization extended the principles in some areas, as in the requirement that a business, to be considered an active one, must have been conducted for a period of at least five years ending on the distribution date and must not have been acquired in a taxable transaction during the five-year period. In other areas, it relaxed and ameliorated them, as in its express sanction of non-pro rata distributions. While there are such particularized variations, the 1954 Code is a legislative reexpression of generally established principles developed in response to definite classes of abuses which had manifested themselves many years earlier. The perversions of the general congressional purpose and the principles the courts had developed to thwart them, as revealed in the earlier cases, are still an enlightening history with which an interpretation of the reorganization sections of the 1954 Code should be approached.

Section 355(b) requires that the distributing corporation be engaged in the active conduct of a trade or business "immediately after the distribution." This is in contrast to the provisions of the 1951 Act, which, as we have noted, required an intention that the parent, as well as the other corporate parties to the reorganization, continue the conduct of an active business. It is in marked contrast to §355(b)'s highly particularized requirements respecting the duration of the active business prior to the reorganization and the methods by which it was acquired. These contrasts suggest a literal reading of the post-reorganization requirement and a holding that the Congress intended to restrict it to the situation existing "immediately after the distribution."

Such a reading is quite consistent with the prior history. It quite adequately meets the problem posed by the Gregory v. Helvering situation in which, immediately after the distribution, one of the corporations held only liquid or investment assets. It sufficiently serves the requirements of permanence and of continuity, for as long as an active business is being conducted immediately after the distribution, there is no substantial opportunity for the stockholders to sever their interest in the business except through a separable, taxable transaction. If the corporation proceeds to withdraw assets from the conduct of the active business and to abandon it, the Commissioner has recourse to the back-up provisions of §355(a)(1)(B) and to the limitations of the underlying principles. At the same time, the limitation, so construed, will not inhibit continued stockholder conduct of the active business through altered corporate form and with further changes in corporate structure, the very thing the reorganization sections were intended to facilitate.

Applied, to this case, there is no violation of any of the underlying limiting principles. There was no empty formalism, no utilization of empty corporate structures, no attempt to recast a taxable transaction in nontaxable form and no withdrawal of liquid assets. There is no question but that American's insurance and banking businesses met all of the active business requirements of §355(b)(2). It was intended that both businesses be continued indefinitely, and each has been. American's merger with Security, in no sense, was a discontinuance of American's banking business, which opened the day after the merger with the same employees, the same depositors and customers. . . . There was a strong business purpose for both the spin-off and the merger, and tax avoidance by American's stockholders was neither a predominant nor a subordinate purpose. In short, though both of the transactions be viewed together, there were none of the evils or misuses which the limiting principles and the statutory limitations were designed to exclude.

We are thus led to the conclusion that this carefully drawn statute should not be read more broadly than it was written to deny nonrecognition of gain to reorganizations of real businesses of the type which Congress clearly intended to facilitate by according to them nonrecognition of present gain.

The Commissioner, indeed, concedes that American's stockholders would have realized no gain had American not been merged into Security after, but substantially contemporaneously with, Agency's spin-off. Insofar as it is contended that §355(b)(1)(A) requires the distributing corporation to continue the conduct of an active business, recognition of gain to American's stockholders on their receipt of Agency's stock would depend upon the economically irrelevant technicality of the identity of the surviving corporation in the merger. Had American been the survivor, it would in every literal and substantive sense have continued the conduct of its banking business.

Surely, the Congress which drafted these comprehensive provisions did not intend the incidence of taxation to turn upon so insubstantial a technicality. Its differentiation on the basis of the economic substance of transactions is too evident to permit such a conclusion.

This, too, the Commissioner seems to recognize, at least conditionally, for he says that gain to the stockholders would have been recognized even if American had been the surviving corporation. This would necessitate our reading into §355(b)(1)(A) an implicit requirement that the distributing corporation, without undergoing any reorganization whatever, whether or not it resulted in a change in its corporate identity, continue the conduct of its active business.

We cannot read this broader limitation into the statute for the same reasons we cannot read into it the narrower one of maintenance of the same corporation identity. The congressional limitation of the post-distribution active business requirement to the situation existing "immediately after the distribution" was deliberate. Consistent with the general statutory scheme, it is quite inconsistent with the Commissioner's contention.

The requirement of §368(a)(1)(D) that the transferor or its stockholders be in control of the spun-off corporation immediately after the transfer is of no assistance to the Commissioner. It is directed solely to control of the transferee, and was fully met here. It contains no requirement of continuing control of the transferor. Though a subsequent sale of the transferor's stock, under some circumstances, might form the basis of a contention that the transaction was the equivalent of a dividend within the meaning of §355(a)(1)(B) and the underlying principles, the control requirements imply no limitation upon subsequent reorganizations of the transferor.

There is no distinction in the statute between subsequent amalgamating reorganizations in which the stockholders of the spin-off transferor would own 80% or more of the relevant classes of stock of the reorganized transferor, and those in which they would not. The statute draws no line between major and minor amalgamations in prospect at the time of the spin-off. Nothing of the sort is suggested by the detailed control-active business requirements in the five-year predistribution period, for there the distinction is between taxable and non-taxable acquisitions, and a tax free exchange within the five-year period does not violate the active business-control requirement whether it was a major or a minor acquisition. Reorganizations in which no gain or loss is recognized, sanctioned by the statute's control provision when occurring in the five years preceding the spin-off, are not prohibited in the postdistribution period. . . .

Nor can we find elsewhere in the Code any support for the Commissioner's suggestion of incompatibility between substantially contemporaneous divisive and amalgamating reorganizations. The 1954 Code contains no inkling of it; nor does its immediate legislative history. The difficulties encountered under the 1924 Code and its successors, in dealing with formalistic distortions of taxable transactions into the spin-off shape, contain no implication of any such incompatibility. Section 317 of the Revenue Act of 1951 . . . did require an intention that the distributing corporation continue the conduct of its active business, but that transitory requirement is of slight relevance to an interpretation of the very different provisions of the 1954 Code and is devoid of any implication of incompatibility. If that provision, during the years it was in effect, would have resulted in recognition of gain in a spin-off if the distributing corporation later, but substantially simultaneously, was a party to a merger in which it lost its identity, a question we do not decide, it would not inhibit successive reorganizations if the merger preceded the spin-off.

The Congress intended to encourage six types of reorganizations. They are defined in 368 and designated by the letters "A" through "F." The "A" merger, the "B" exchange of stock for stock and the "C" exchange of stock for substantially all of the properties of another are all amalgamating reorganizations. The "D" reorganization is the divisive spin-off, while the "E" and "F" reorganizations, recapitalizations and reincorporations, are neither amalgamating nor divisive. All are sanctioned equally, however. Recognition of gain is withheld from each and successively so. Merger may follow merger, and an "A" reorganization by which Y is merged into X corporation may proceed substantially simultaneously with a "C" reorganization by which X acquires substantially all of the properties of Z and with an "F" reorganization by which X is reincorporated in another state. The "D" reorganization has no lesser standing. It is on the same plane as the others and, provided all of the "D" requirements are met, is as available as the others in successive reorganizations. . . .

A decision of the Sixth Circuit appears to be at odds with our conclusion. In Curtis [v. United States, 336 F.2d 714 (6th Cir. 1964)], it appears that one corporation was merged into another after spinning-off a warehouse building which was an unwanted asset because the negotiators could not agree upon its value. The Court of Appeals for the Sixth Circuit affirmed a District Court judgment holding that the value of the warehouse company shares was taxable as ordinary income to the stockholders of the first corporation.

A possible distinction may lie between the spin-off of an asset unwanted by the acquiring corporation in an "A" reorganization solely because of disagreement as to its value and the preliminary spin-off of an active business which the acquiring corporation is prohibited by law from operating. We cannot stand upon so nebulous a distinction, however. We simply take a different view. The reliance in *Curtis* upon the Report of the Senate Committee explaining §317 of the Revenue Act of 1951, quite dissimilar to the 1954 Code, reinforces our appraisal of the relevant materials.

To the extent that our own decision in [Helvering v. Elkhorn Coal Co., 95 F.2d 732 (4th Cir. 1937)] is relevant, it tends to support our conclusion, not to militate against it.

Elkhorn was one of the interesting cases which contributed to the development of the judicial principles which served, as best they could, to confine pretensive arrangements in the early days long before adopting of the 1954 Code. Mill Creek Coal Company wanted to acquire for Mill Creek

stock one of the mining properties of Elkhorn. Had the bargain been
effectuated, directly, it would have been clearly a taxable transaction, for
Elkhorn had other mining properties. In an attempt to avoid the tax,
Elkhorn's other properties were spun-off to a new Elkhorn; old Elkhorn
conveyed its remaining properties to Mill Creek for stock and by successive
transactions, Elkhorn stockholders wound up owning stock in new Elkhorn
which owned all of old Elkhorn's mining properties, except the ones transferred to Mill Creek, and the Mill Creek stock received by old Elkhorn.
They were in precisely the same position as they would have been in if old
Elkhorn had transferred the Mill Creek properties to Mill Creek for stock.
It was an obviously transparent attempt to circumvent the requirement
that substantially all of the properties must be transferred to qualify for
nonrecognition in what would now be classified as a "C" reorganization.

The contention in *Elkhorn* was not that its stockholders realized gain
on the spin-off. The opinion denying a rehearing, particularly, suggests
the absence of recognizable gain as a result of the spin-off. It approved
the recognition of gain as a result of the subsequent "C" reorganization.

It is difficult now to envision any other result in *Elkhorn,* since the
stockholders' purpose of formalistic transformation of a clearly taxable
transaction into the form of a series of untaxable transactions was so bla-
tant. Nothing of the sort is represented here. Interestingly, however, *Elkhorn* would question the recognition of gain in the merger exchange here,
as to which the Commissioner wisely makes no contention under the 1954
Code, not recognition of gain at the earlier spin-off step. As to the first
step, the *Elkhorn* opinion appears to oppose the Commissioner's present
position.

For the reasons which we have canvassed, we think the Tax Court . . .
correctly decided that American's stockholders realized no recognizable
taxable gain upon their receipt in the "D" reorganization of the stock of
Agency.

Affirmed.

NOTES

1. Morris Trust *and* Elkhorn Coal. The court in *Morris Trust* argued
that its decision was supported by its prior opinion in *Elkhorn Coal,* in
which a divisive reorganization followed by a C reorganization was held
taxable. In *Morris Trust,* a divisive reorganization followed by an A reorganization was held tax free. Since a C reorganization is nothing but a de facto
merger (that is, a de facto A reorganization), can these two decisions be
squared?

In *Elkhorn Coal* the Commissioner sought to tax the shareholders on
the distribution made pursuant to the nominal C reorganization. In *Morris
Trust,* however, he sought to recharacterize the initial divisive reorganiza-

tion as a taxable transaction. Was that the Commissioner's fatal error in *Morris Trust*? Would the court in *Morris Trust* have sustained a challenge to the tax-free status of the merger of American into Security?

Congress has limited the C reorganization to acquisitions of "substantially all" the transferor corporation's assets. If a C reorganization could be preceded by a tax-free divisive D reorganization, the transferor could spin off any unwanted assets before transferring its remaining assets to the acquiring corporation, thereby circumventing the C reorganization's substantially-all requirement. *Elkhorn Coal* refused to permit the substantially-all limitation to be emasculated in this way. Would a contrary decision have been so bad? What abuse might the Commissioner fear?

2. *The statutory symmetries of §355.* The court in *Morris Trust* recognized that if the spin-off had been followed by a merger of the insurance company rather than of the bank, the spin-off would have failed to satisfy the requirement in §368(a)(1)(D) that the shareholders be in control of the spun-off company immediately after the transaction. The court said, however, that there is no similar requirement that the shareholders control the distributing corporation immediately after the transaction. Since a divisive D reorganization involves splitting one corporation into two, it would be peculiar for a control requirement to be imposed on the shareholders with respect to only one of the resulting corporations.

Section 368(a)(1)(D) requires that the shareholders control the spun-off corporation immediately after the transaction. There is no explicit requirement that they also control the distributing corporation for the simple reason that the shareholders, *by definition,* already control it — they are, after all, its shareholders. Simply put, a divisive reorganization contemplates that the shareholders of the spin-off corporation be former (and perhaps current) shareholders of the distributing corporation.

To be sure, the shareholders might sell or exchange their stock in the distributing corporation immediately after the transaction, but if they do so, the tax-free status of the transaction will be in jeopardy under the "device" language of §355(a)(1)(B). Indeed, the same statutory provision forbids the planned sale or exchange of the stock of either the distributing corporation or of the spun-off corporation. Thus, to meet the express requirement of a divisive D reorganization, former shareholders of the distributing corporation must control both corporations after the transaction.

The effect of following a divisive reorganization with an acquisitive reorganization is to introduce new shareholders into the transaction. If these new shareholders acquire a sufficient interest in one of the corporations so as to cause the former shareholders to lose "control," the transaction fails to meet the condition imposed on divisive reorganizations under §355(a)(1)(B). Yet the Treasury has promulgated a regulation under §355 stating that a planned exchange will not run afoul of the "device" language in §355(a)(1)(B) if the exchange is tax free under the reorganization provisions. Treas. Reg. §1.355-2(d)(2)(iii)(D). What weight does this proposed regulation give to the inner parenthetical in §355(a)(1)(B)? Where does this proposed regulation leave *Elkhorn Coal*? Does a tax-free exchange after a divisive reorganization present an opportunity for abuse?

3. *The statutory response to* Morris Trust. Section 355(e) was enacted in 1997 for two principle reasons: first, Congress believed "[i]n cases in which it is intended that new shareholders will acquire ownership of a business in connection with a spin off, the transaction more closely resembles a corporate level disposition of the portion of the business that is acquired." Second, rejecting the asymmetries in *Morris Trust,* Congress "believe[d] that the differences in treatment of certain transactions following a spin-off, depending upon whether the distributing or controlled corporation engages in the transaction, should be minimized."

Consider the following: *B* Corp., a state-chartered bank, has owned for many years all the stock of *I* Corp., an insurance company. The stock of *I* Corp. is distributed to the shareholders of *B* Corp., then *B* changes its charter to that of a national bank and raises new funds through a public offering. Assume that the spin-off of *I* Corp. was a necessary first-step in the public offering because national banks cannot own insurance companies.

Assuming the active trade or business requirement of §355(a)(1)(C) is met, the distribution by B of the I Corp. stock should satisfy all the requirements of §355(a)(1). Indeed, the device language of §355(a)(1)(C) should not be implicated because no stock of the distributing corporation (i.e., *B*) and no stock of the controlled corporation (i.e., *I*) is sold or exchanged as part of the transaction. However, if the post distribution public offering is sufficiently large, the distribution by *B* Corp. of the *I* Corp. stock will be taxable at the corporate level (though it will remain tax-free at the shareholder level) under §355(e).

Section 355(e) is triggered if an otherwise tax-free spin-off under §355 is part of a plan for one or more persons to acquire 50 percent or more control (by vote or value) of the distributing corporation or of the controlled corporation. Note that any transfer of control occurring less than two years before or after the spin-off presumptively is part of such a plan. §355(e)(2)(B). In the example above, if the public offering results in new shareholders acquiring 50 percent or more of the vote or value of *B* Corp. (see §355(f)(4)(A) incorporating §355(d)(4)), gain (but not loss) will be recognized to *B* on the spin-off as if *B* sold the *I* Corp. stock for its fair market value. And note that the same taxation would result if new shareholders acquired 50 percent or more control of the *I* Corp. rather than of *B* Corp.

The legislative history of §355(e) makes clear that no adjustment should be made to the basis of any corporate assets as a result of this taxation. This makes little sense and has the result of imposing a triple tax on corporate earnings: once under §355(e) on the distribution by the distributing corporation of the stock of the controlled corporation, a second time at the corporate level when the controlled corporation sells the appreciated assets or otherwise earns income from them, and a third time when the shareholders sell or exchange the distributed stock of the controlled corporation. One would expect that the controlled corporation would get a step-up in the basis of its assets if the distributing corporation is tax under §355(e), just as would occur if the assets had simply been sold in a taxable transaction. Indeed, such a basis step-up is mandated by statute in a similar context under §338(b)(1). Nonetheless, the effect of §355(e) apparently is to demand an eventual extra corporate level tax as the price for obtaining shareholder level deferral (under §355(a)) on the transaction.

Not all transfers of control will trigger taxation under §355(e). If the new shareholders acquiring control of the distributing or of the controlled corporation already had control of the other corporation, taxation under §355(e) is avoided. See §355(e)(3)(A)(iv). And, of course, the actual distribution under §355(a) works a transfer of control (from the distributing corporation to its shareholders), but that inevitable transfer of control is irrelevant under §355(e)(3)(A)(ii).

While §355(e) is triggered by the transfer of corporate control, certain asset acquisitions are treated as control transfers. Under §355(e)(3)(B), tax-free asset acquisitions (such as a tax-free merger or C reorganization) are equated to stock transfers for purposes of §355(e). Note that both taxable and tax-free stock transfers can trigger §355(e) but only tax-free assets transfers can have that effect. This rule makes sense because §355(e) imposes a corporate-level tax on the transaction, and if the assets were transferred in a taxable transaction, the corporate-level tax has already been incurred.

This example should make clear the §355(e) is both more and less than a congressional rejection of the *Morris Trust* case. *Morris Trust* held that a tax-free transfer of control in the distributing corporation is not a "device" within the meaning of §355(a)(1)(C), and that holding remains good law. On the other hand, taxation at the corporate level under §355(e) is triggered if post distribution control of the distributing corporation or of the controlled corporation is transferred in any manner. Thus, this rule applies to tax-free acquisitions (including tax-free asset transfers as occurred in *Morris Trust*) and to taxable transactions. Note, though, that nothing in §355(e) limits the device language in §355(a)(1)(C) so that a prearranged taxable transfer of control might invalidate the entire transaction under §355(a)(1)(C), thereby subjecting the transaction to taxation at both the corporate and individual levels.

Because §355(e) subjects the distributing corporation to taxation on any appreciation in the assets of the controlled corporation, at least one asymmetry remains. Suppose *P* Corp. owns two businesses, a toy business with assets having adjusted basis of $500,000 and fair market value of $900,000 and a software business with assets having adjusted basis and fair market value of $400,000. If *P* Corp. wishes to divide these two business under §355 and then transfer control of one of the two to new investors, it can do so without paying any toll under §355(e) by transferring the assets of the software business to a newly formed corporation and then distributing the stock of the newly formed corporation to its shareholders under §355. To be sure, when control of either business is relinquished, §355(e) will be implicated, but because the software assets were unappreciated, no taxation results. Had *P* Corp. instead spun off the assets of the toy business, §355(e) would have forced *P* to recognize a gain on the spinoff of $400,000.

4. *Some concluding thoughts on §355.* The corporate division problem is another example of some of the internal conflicts or strains of the present system of taxing corporations and their shareholders. If *A* forms two separate corporations and lets them grow independently, *A* is free to deal separately with them. But if *B* starts the same business activities in a single corporation, it will be difficult for *B* to separate them later without adverse tax consequences: A distribution from *B*'s corporation of one of its businesses, even in corporate form, resembles a dividend. *B* will argue that she should be allowed to achieve the same results as *A* so long as she keeps the business activities in "corporate solution," but unless the distribution passes the complicated tests of §355, it will not be tax free.

Confusion stems from the corporate system's allowing the retention of earnings without a direct tax on shareholders. If stock is sold, earnings to the extent reflected in the sale price are usually taxed at the shareholder level as capital gains. But if the earnings are distributed to the shareholder by an ongoing corporation, they are taxed as dividends. A tax-free division of a single corporation with retained earnings into two separate corporations gives the shareholder the potential to sell one at capital gains rates, the economic equivalent of a dividend distribution from the original corporation. Recall §302(b)(4) and the circumstances under which part of a business enterprise may be distributed at capital gains rates as a partial liquidation.

PROBLEMS

11-6. *X* Corp. has actively conducted two businesses for more than five years. Business 1 is worth $500,000 and *X*'s adjusted basis in the assets of business 1 of $400,000. Business 2 is also worth $500,000 and *X*'s adjusted basis in the assets of business 2 is $250,000. All of *X*'s outstanding stock is owned by *Y* with an adjusted basis of $600,000.

   a. Assume that *Y* purchased half of the shares of *X* Corp. three years ago for $450,000. *X* intends to create a new subsidiary, *S*, and then transfer one of the two businesses to *S*. As part of that transaction, X will then distribute all of the shares of S to Y. What are the tax consequences of this transaction to X, Y, and S, assuming that the assets of business 1 are transferred to S? How does your answer change if it is the assets of business 2 rather than of business 1 that are transferred to S?

b. Assume that Y has owned all of the X Corp. stock for more than five years. X will spin off one of the businesses as described in part (a) above and then merge the corporation owning business 1 (X or S) into a publicly traded corporation in an "A" reorganization. Does it matter which business is transferred to S? Why?

12

One-Party Reorganizations

A. RECAPITALIZATIONS

A recapitalization, in general, refers to a readjustment of the capital structure of a single, existing corporation. Because the term "recapitalization" is not defined in the Code, however, its scope is uncertain. Many types of conversions have been swept into its meaning by cases and rulings. As with other tax-free reorganizations, discussed in Chapters 10 and 11, the assumptions underlying nonrecognition are that the stock received in a recapitalization is a continuation of the old stock with a mere change in form and that gain or loss consequently should not be recognized, except as to boot received in the exchange.

The classic recapitalization occurs when a closely held family corporation has older owners close to retirement age who wish to transfer the opportunity for growth to younger managers, often their children. Typically, the recapitalization in such a case will involve an exchange of the older owners' common stock for preferred. This suits the estate planning needs of the retiring owners by keeping future equity appreciation out of their estates while retaining for them, in more secure form, their capital in the corporation. In addition, dividends on the preferred stock may provide the older owners with a stable retirement income. The recapitalization also suits the younger managers, who are eager to be rewarded for their efforts by the equity growth of the corporation but are unable to buy significant amounts of the old common stock. Risk of future loss also will be transferred to the new equityholders since the preferred stock has a preferred position over the common.

Another common type of recapitalization, filling a much different need and with a host of problems beyond the scope of this discussion, occurs with a financially distressed corporation. In such a case, the debtors and shareholders may together recapitalize the company's debt and equity structure, or they may contribute their debt and equity interests to a new corporation. See pages 445-448 supra.

If an exchange of stock for stock is treated as a tax-free recapitalization, then the substitute basis rules of §358 apply so that the basis of the stock received remains the same as the stock surrendered. In a recapitalization, the corporation usually retains all its tax attributes — e.g., no change in the basis of its assets, no effect on its earnings and profits. The corporation's tax existence, in other words, continues without interruption. No special provision for the carryover of tax attributes (such as a net operating loss) is needed, so the rules of §381 applicable to most reorganizations generally do not apply to recapitalizations.

Section 305(b) and (c) can make taxable certain disproportionate recapitalization exchanges when the effect of the transaction is a non-pro rata stock dividend. The Service does not, however, usually raise the §305(b) and (c) problems in the isolated recapitalization of a closely held corporation. See Rev. Rul. 75-93, 1975-1 C.B. 101, in which a disproportionate recapitalization exchange did not trigger §305(c) because it was not part of a plan to periodically increase equity interests. To the same effect, see Gen. Couns. Mem. 39088 (Dec. 7, 1983). See also Treas. Regs. §1.305-3(e) (examples 10, 11, and 12).

Recapitalizations can cover a variety of stock exchanges. For examples, see Treas. Regs. §1.368-2(e) as well as the following: common stock for preferred stock, Rev. Rul. 74-269, 1974-1 C.B. 87; and preferred stock for common stock, Rev. Rul. 77-238, 1977-2 C.B. 115. Recall from page 285 supra that an exchange of common stock for preferred stock may cause the preferred to be §306 stock under §306(c)(1)(B).

Recapitalizations also can include exchanges of bonds as well as of stock. The Service has ruled that convertible bonds may be exchanged for stock. See Rev. Rul. 72-265, 1972-1 C.B. 122. Bonds may be exchanged for bonds, and there is no original issue discount (see §1273) on a bond-for-bond and bond-for-stock recapitalization. See Rev. Rul. 77-415, 1977-2 C.B. 311. In Rev. Rul. 77-437, 1977-2 C.B. 28, the Service ruled that a debtor corporation recognized income from the cancellation of indebtedness on a bond exchange to the extent that the face value of the old bonds exceeded the face value of the new bonds.

A controversial problem in the recapitalization area has been the exchange of stock for bonds, as illustrated in *Bazley* below. It always has been clear that a distribution of its own debt securities by a corporation with earnings and profits is a taxable dividend. See page 136 supra. But the status of debt securities issued by a corporation in the course of a corporate recapitalization has been less clear. The 1939 Code provided (as does the "general rule" laid down in §354(a)(1) of the 1954 Code) that no gain or loss was to be recognized if stock or securities of a corporation that was a party to a "reorganization" were exchanged for stock and securities of the same corporation; the 1939 Code, like §368(a)(1)(E) of the current Code, defined a "reorganization" to include a recapitalization.

Suppose, then, that a corporation "recapitalized" by calling in its outstanding common stock and issuing in exchange other common stock (with a different par value or some other alteration of rights) plus bonds, debentures, or notes. Should the transaction be a tax-free exchange of the old stock for the new stock and bonds or other debt instruments? Should it be treated as a taxable sale or exchange? As a dividend of the debt instruments? *Bazley* considers this problem. For the effect of §354(a)(2) enacted in 1954, see the Notes following *Bazley*.

Bazley v. Commissioner _____
331 U.S. 737 (1947)

Mr. Justice FRANKFURTER delivered the opinion of the Court. . . .

[T]he Commissioner of Internal Revenue assessed an income tax deficiency against the taxpayer for the year 1939. Its validity depends on the legal significance of the recapitalization in that year of a family corporation in which the taxpayer and his wife owned all but one of the Company's one thousand shares. These had a par value of $100. Under the plan of reorganization the taxpayer, his wife, and the holder of the additional share were to turn in their old shares and receive in exchange for each old share five new shares of no par value, but of a stated value of $60, and new debenture bonds, having a total face value of $400,000, payable in ten years but callable at any time. Accordingly, the taxpayer received 3,990 shares of the new stock for the 798 shares of his old holding and debentures in the amount of $319,200. At the time of these transactions the earned surplus of the corporation was $855,783.82.

The Commissioner charged to the taxpayer as income the full value of the debentures. The Tax Court affirmed the Commissioner's determination, against the taxpayer's contention that as a "recapitalization" the transaction was a tax-free "reorganization" and that the debentures were "securities in a corporation a party to a reorganization," "exchanged solely for stock or securities in such corporation" "in pursuance of a plan of reorganization," and as such no gain is recognized for income tax purposes. [§§368(a)(1)(E) and 354(a)(1).*] The Tax Court found that the recapitalization had "no legitimate corporate business purpose" and was therefore not a "reorganization" within the statute. The distribution of debentures, it concluded, was a disguised dividend, taxable as earned income under [§§61(a) and 301]. 4 T.C. 897. The Circuit Court of Appeals

_____

*Section 354(a)(2), which limits greatly the general rule of §354(a)(1), was not enacted until 1954. — EDS.

for the Third Circuit, sitting en banc, affirmed, two judges dissenting. 155 F.2d 237.

Unless a transaction is a reorganization contemplated by [§368(a)], any exchange of "stock or securities" in connection with such transaction, cannot be "in pursuance of the plan of reorganization" under [§354]. While [§368(a)] informs us that "reorganization" means, among other things, "a recapitalization," it does not inform us what "recapitalization" means. "Recapitalization" in connection with the income tax has been part of the revenue laws since 1921. . . . Congress has never defined it and the Treasury Regulations shed only limited light. Treas. Reg. [§1.368-1(b)]. One thing is certain. Congress did not incorporate some technical concept, whether that of accountants or of other specialists, into [§368(a)], assuming that there is agreement among specialists as to the meaning of recapitalization. And so, recapitalization as used in [§368(a)] must draw its meaning from its function in that section. It is one of the forms of reorganization which obtains the privileges afforded by [§368(a)]. Therefore, "recapitalization" must be construed with reference to the presuppositions and purpose of [§368(a)]. It was not the purpose of the reorganization provision to exempt from payment of a tax what as a practical matter is realized gain. Normally, a distribution by a corporation, whatever form it takes, is a definite and rather unambiguous event. It furnishes the proper occasion for the determination and taxation of gain. But there are circumstances where a formal distribution, directly or through exchange of securities, represents merely a new form of the previous participation in an enterprise, involving no change of substance in the rights and relations of the interested parties one to another or to the corporate assets. As to these, Congress has said that they are not to be deemed significant occasions for determining taxable gain. . . .

In a series of cases this Court has withheld the benefits of the reorganization provision in situations which might have satisfied provisions of the section treated as inert language, because they were not reorganizations of the kind with which [§354], in its purpose and particulars, concerns itself. See Pinellas Ice & Cold Storage Co. v. Commissioner, 287 U.S. 462; Gregory v. Helvering, 293 U.S. 465; Le Tulle v. Scofield, 308 U.S. 415. . . .

Since a recapitalization within the scope of [§368] is an aspect of reorganization, nothing can be a recapitalization for this purpose unless it partakes of those characteristics of a reorganization which underlie the purpose of Congress in postponing the tax liability.

No doubt there was a recapitalization of the Bazley corporation in the sense that the symbols that represented its capital were changed, so that the fiscal basis of its operations would appear very differently on its books. . . . What is controlling is that a new arrangement intrinsically partake of the elements of reorganization which underlie the Congressional exemption and not merely give the appearance of it to accomplish a distribution of earnings. . . .

What have we here? No doubt, if the Bazley corporation had issued the debentures to Bazley and his wife without any recapitalization, it would have made a taxable distribution. Instead, these debentures were issued as part of a family arrangement, the only additional ingredient being an unrelated modification of the capital account. The debentures were found to be worth at least their principal amount, and they were virtually cash because they were callable at the will of the corporation which in this case was the will of the taxpayer. One does not have to pursue the motives behind actions, even in the more ascertainable forms of purpose, to find, as did the Tax Court, that the whole arrangement took this form instead of an outright distribution of cash or debentures, because the latter would undoubtedly have been taxable income whereas what was done could, with a show of reason, claim the shelter of the immunity of a recapitalization-reorganization. . . .

A "reorganization" which is merely a vehicle, however elaborate or elegant, for conveying earnings from accumulations to the stockholders is not a reorganization under [§368]. This disposes of the case as a matter of law, since the facts as found by the Tax Court bring them within it. And even if this transaction were deemed a reorganization, the facts would equally sustain the imposition of the tax on the debentures under [§356(a)(1) and (2)]. Commissioner v. Estate of Bedford, 325 U.S. 283. . . .

Other claims raised have been considered but their rejection does not call for discussion.

Judgments affirmed.

Mr. Justice Douglas and Mr. Justice Burton dissent in both cases for the reasons stated in the joint dissent of Judges Maris and Goodrich in the court below. Bazley v. Commissioner, 3 Cir., 155 F.2d 237, 244.

NOTES

1. *The 1954 changes in §354.* While the 1954 Code continued the general nonrecognition rule for shareholder exchanges incident to reorganizations, it added §354(a)(2) limiting nonrecognition to cases in which the principal amount of securities (debt instruments) received does not exceed the principal amount of debt instruments surrendered. By virtue of §354(a)(2), in conjunction with §356(a) and (d), the debentures in *Bazley* would have been taxed as boot even if the transaction had been held a reorganization since no debt instruments were surrendered.

Does §354(a)(2) render *Bazley* obsolete? Securities constituting boot received in a reorganization may be taxed under the installment sale provisions. See §453(f)(6) (last sentence). If such taxation is available, then gain will be deferred until payment on the securities is received. See §453(c). But if under *Bazley* an exchange is held to be a distribution taxable under §301 rather than a recapitalization, installment sale treatment is unavailable and the securities will be taxable on receipt. Accordingly, *Bazley* is still important for its gloss on the definition of a "recapitalization." Note that installment sale treatment will never be available with respect to securities that are "readily tradable." §453(f)(4)-(5).

Securities received as boot in a reorganization will not qualify for installment sale treatment under §453(f)(6) if receipt of the securities has the effect of a dividend. See §356(a)(2). Recall *Clark,* page 442 supra, . . . defining dividend equivalency.

2. *The effect of* Bedford. *Bedford,* cited by the Supreme Court in *Bazley,* involved these facts: Under a recapitalization plan, a shareholder exchanged 3,000 shares of cumulative preferred stock (par value $100) for 3,500 shares of cumulative preferred stock (par value $75), 1,500 shares of common stock (par value $1), and $45,240 of cash. The shareholder's gain (the difference between the adjusted basis of the shares given up and the value of the stock plus cash received) was $139,740. The corporation's earnings and profits were sufficient to cover the entire cash distribution. The government admitted that the transaction was a reorganization exchange, and the taxpayer admitted that the cash was property not permitted to be received tax free — i.e., boot. The only issue was whether under what is now §356(a)(1) and (2) the boot should be taxed as capital gain — like a sale of stock for cash — or as a dividend. The Court, conceding that the matter was not "wholly free from doubt," concluded that because the corporation had earnings and profits, the distribution of cash had "the effect of the distribution of a taxable dividend." The result of *Bedford* became generally known as the automatic dividend rule. That rule has now become discredited. See pages 441-443 supra.

3. *The "dividend limited to gain" rule of §356.* In citing §356 and *Bedford* as an alternative route to the same result reached by the "no reorganization" route, the Court in *Bazley* may have overlooked the fact that §356(a) requires boot to be treated as a dividend only if, and to the extent that, the taxpayer realizes a gain on the exchange itself. For example, suppose individual *A* owns the 100 outstanding shares of *X* Corp. with adjusted basis and fair market value of $100 per share. What are the tax consequences under §§354 and 356 if *A* exchanges all the stock for 50 shares of newly issued common stock worth $40 per share plus securities with a fair market value of $8,000, assuming that the exchange constitutes a "recapitalization" within the meaning of §368(a)(1)(E)? Since there is no gain (within the meaning of §1001(a)) on the exchange, *A* recognizes no income under §356 despite the presence of boot.

Turning to *Bazley,* the value of the stock and securities received may well have exceeded the taxpayer's basis for the stock surrendered, but the Tax Court made no finding to this effect. Even if there had been such a finding, the amount of the taxpayer's gain might have been less than the value of the distributed securities. Under the Supreme Court's holding in

Bazley, the taxpayer recognized the full value of the securities received as income without any offset for his basis in the stock turned in. Accordingly, even a taxpayer captured by the excess securities rule of §354(a)(2) may profit by arguing in favor of reorganization treatment for the exchange.

4. *Use of debt in a corporation's capital structure.* On incorporation, corporations often issue bonds or debentures to the incorporators, in addition to stock, so that the corporation can lay a foundation for the deduction of interest under §163. See pages 98-117 supra. Moreover, the bonds can be retired at the capital gain rate pursuant to §1271, whereas the redemption of stock would be open to the Pandora's box of §302. See Chapter 5 supra. In addition, an accumulation of surplus by the corporation to pay off the indebtedness, unlike an accumulation for the purpose of redeeming stock, may be permissible under §531, see pages 544-545 infra. *Bazley* and §354(a)(2) mean that a corporation that does not issue debt securities for these purposes to its shareholders at the time of incorporation will not find it easy to rectify its error in a tax-free manner later.

5. *Bankruptcy workouts and other debt restructurings.* When a corporation's financial health becomes impaired, the rights of creditors often are increased. For example, the failure of a corporation to make interest payments when due may entitle bondholders to take control of the company's board of directors. If the corporation's fortunes do not improve, the creditors may seek to restructure their interests in the enterprise; in the extreme case, the creditors may seek to oust the shareholders entirely.

Consider the situation in which a corporation replaces its outstanding debt with new debt having different terms. For example, short-term, low-interest notes might be replaced with long-term, higher-interest bonds. What are the tax consequences of such a debt swap?

Under Treas. Regs. §1.1001-3, "a significant modification of a debt instrument . . . is deemed to result in an exchange of the original instrument." Accordingly, gain or loss can be recognized by the debtholder. If, for example, the value of the debt received exceeds the holder's adjusted basis in the debt surrendered, gain will be recognized on the exchange. This might be the case when the corporation's distress has been reflected in the market price of its notes so that current holders of those notes may have paid significantly less than face value. What constitutes a "significant modification" is contained in Treas. Regs. §1.1001-3(e).

The transaction will also be taxable to the corporation, which raises the possibility of cancellation of indebtedness income to the corporation if it substitutes current low value debt for outstanding obligations initally issued for face value. Thus, if a corporation exchanges $1,100 face value bonds having a current fair market value of $800 for each $1,000 short-term note outstanding, the corporation will recognize $200 of cancellation of indebtedness income on each exchange. Unless the exchange occurs while the corporation is insolvent or in a bankruptcy proceeding, the can-

cellation of indebtedness income will be taxable immediately. See
§§61(a)(12), 108(a). If the insolvency exception applies, it is limited to
the extent of the debtor corporation's insolvency. §108(a)(3).

A corporation might also swap stock for debt. To the extent that the
value of such stock is less than the issue price of the surrendered debt,
once again the corporation will be faced with recognition of cancellation
of indebtedness income except to the extent §108 applies. Further, if
application of §108 to an insolvent or bankrupt corporation permits the
corporation to exclude some or all of its cancellation of indebtedness
income, the corporation will be forced to reduce its tax attributes (including its tax credits, NOL carryovers, and adjusted basis) as the tax "payment" for the exclusion. See §108(b).

B. REINCORPORATIONS

Suppose a corporation changes the state of its incorporation. Formally,
the shareholders must relinquish their old shares in exchange for new
ones. Should such an exchange be a taxable event? In a case that antedated
special statutory treatment for corporate reorganizations, the Supreme
Court held that the reincorporation of General Motors Corporation from
New Jersey to Delaware (coupled with a transfer of $5 million from the
corporation's earned surplus account to its capital account and minor
changes in the terms of the corporation's preferred stock) was a taxable
event to shareholders exchanging General Motors (New Jersey) common
stock for General Motors (Delaware) common stock. Marr v. United States,
268 U.S. 536 (1925).

The definition of a "reorganization" now includes such reincorporations and other changes in the identity or form of one corporation. See
§368(a)(1)(F). As with recapitalizations, the limitations applicable to the
carryover of tax attributes in a reorganization are generally not applicable
to reincorporations under §368(a)(1)(F). See, e.g., §381(b) and pages
504-506 infra. Until the Tax Equity and Fiscal Responsibility Act of 1982,
F reorganizations were not expressly limited to mere changes in the form,
identity, or place of incorporation of a *single* corporation, and case law
had treated the amalgamation of multiple corporations as an F reorganization so long as there was a sufficiently high percentage of common ownership. See, e.g., Davant v. Commissioner, 366 F.2d 874 (5th Cir. 1966); Reef
Corp. v. Commissioner, 368 F.2d 125 (5th Cir. 1966). The Conference
Report accompanying TEFRA of 1982 included the following: "This limitation [added to §368(a)(1)(F)] does not preclude the use of more than
one entity to consummate the transaction provided only one operating
company is involved. The reincorporation of an operating company in a
different State, for example, is an F reorganization that requires that more

than one corporation be involved." H.R. Conf. Rep. No. 760, 97th Cong., 2d Sess. 541 (1982). Accordingly, regardless of the extent of common ownership or control, the amalgamation of two or more corporations cannot be an F reorganization. See pages 417-429 supra for application of the D reorganization in such circumstances.

PROBLEMS

12-1. *X* Corp. has 100 shares of common stock outstanding, 80 owned by *A* and 20 by *B*. The fair market value of the *X* Corp. stock is $100 per share, and *X* Corp. has substantial earnings and profits. *A*'s basis in the *X* Corp. stock is $20 per share, while *B*'s basis in the *X* Corp. stock is $40 per share. What are the tax consequences to *A, B,* and *X* Corp. of the following alternative transactions?

    a. As part of a single transaction, *A* exchanges all her *X* Corp. stock for 800 shares of newly issued, nonvoting preferred stock (worth $10 per share) and *B* exchanges all his *X* Corp. stock for 100 shares of newly issued common stock.

    b. As part of a single transaction, *A* exchanges her *X* Corp. stock for 20 shares of a new class of common stock and long-term bonds with face amount and fair market value of $6,000. *B* exchanges his *X* Corp. stock for 20 shares of the newly issued common stock. How would your answer change if *A*'s basis in the *X* Corp. stock were $100 per share?

    c. How would your answers to (b) change if *B* were *A*'s son?

12-2. *Y* Corp., doing poorly but not yet insolvent, acquires $1 million face value of its outstanding, long-term bonds in exchange for 800 shares of newly issued preferred stock with par value of $1,000 per share. What are the tax consequences of the exchange to *Y* Corp.? How would your answer change if the exchange were made pursuant to a conversion privilege in the cancelled bonds?

12-3. *Z* Corp. has outstanding 20-year unsecured bonds with face value of $100,000 and fair market value of $70,000. What are the tax consequences to *Z* Corp. and to its bondholders if it exchanges these instruments for secured bonds bearing the same interest rate and maturity? What is the result if the new secured bonds have a face value and fair market value of $70,000?

13

Combining Tax Attributes: Net Operating Losses and Affiliated Corporations

A. CARRYOVER OF TAX ATTRIBUTES

In transactions covered by §§351, 355, and 368, the Code has specific provisions relating to the carryover of basis with respect to property transferred or stock exchanged. Thus, §358 provides, generally speaking, for a transfer of the adjusted basis of exchanging shareholders to the new stock or securities acquired by them. Similarly, §362 provides that property acquired by a corporation in connection with a §351 transaction or in connection with a reorganization shall, generally speaking, have the same basis as the property had in the hands of the transferor. See also §1223 relating to the holding period of property received in connection with such transactions.

Corporations have a great many more tax attributes than basis and holding periods of assets. Different corporations will employ different accounting methods, will have elected certain methods of depreciation with respect to property, will have positive or negative earnings and profits accounts, may or may not have foreign tax credits, and may or may not have unused investment tax credit carryovers or net operating loss carryovers. Consistent with the philosophy of the nonrecognition provisions such as §§351, 355, and the transactions to which §368 applies, these tax attributes should remain undisturbed after such transactions. One would also expect similar rules to apply in the case of those special mergers consisting of liquidations of controlled subsidiaries into their parents to which §§332, 337, and 334(b) apply.

Thus, if two corporations merge, one would expect that after the merger, in calculating whether distributions were made out of earnings and profits, one would look to the combined earnings and profits of the

503

two corporations. Section 381 (providing for carryover of tax attributes in certain tax-free exchanges) and other provisions of the Code generally carry out such expected results.

It should be noted, however, that when a corporation's existence is terminated by a purchase of all its assets, the attributes of the former corporation are obliterated by the transaction. Similarly, when a corporation makes an election under §338 to be treated as if it sold its assets to itself, the former corporation's attributes are obliterated. See pages 351-358 supra for a discussion of §338. Thus, in certain cases a §338 election will involve a trade-off between a step-up in basis and the loss of certain tax attributes. For example, if a corporation purchases stock of a subsidiary with appreciated assets and a large net operating loss, a §338 election may be inadvisable in some cases but not in others. By not making the election the purchaser would not be able to step up the bases of the subsidiary's assets, but the NOL would be preserved. On the other hand, if a §338 election were made, the gain that would be recognized on the deemed sale can be offset by an NOL, thereby providing a step-up in basis at no tax cost.

The foregoing simplified discussion has ignored the problems created over many decades by what some call the "traffic" in corporations having substantial net operating losses and corporations having other desirable tax attributes (for example, high-basis, low-value assets). Individuals having business deductions in excess of income can carry such losses back or forward as prescribed by §172 but cannot readily sell these tax benefits to others. When such net operating loss carryovers are lodged in a corporate entity, however, sale of the loss is no more difficult than the sale of the stock of the corporation — provided that the tax attributes are not reduced or eliminated by the transfer of the stock.

This "trafficking" in loss corporations has been resisted by the Treasury and the Congress for a number of decades, as described below.

1. Section 381

Section 381 provides for the carryover of tax attributes from a transferor corporation to an acquiring corporation in certain transactions. The transactions covered are (1) a liquidation of a controlled subsidiary and (2) A, C, or F tax-free reorganizations as well as certain nondivisive D reorganizations and G reorganizations involving bankruptcy. Note that in a §368(a)(1)(B) stock-for-stock reorganization, no need for the rules of §381 arises since the corporate existence of the acquired company continues even though an exchange occurs at the shareholder level. The same holds true for §368(a)(1)(E) recapitalizations. In other words, §381 deals, as its opening sentence states, with "the acquisition of assets of a corporation by another corporation." See Baicker v. Commissioner, 93 T.C. 316 (1989) (no carryovers in divisive reorganizations; not a §381 transaction).

The attributes inherited in a qualified transaction are subject to the operating rules of §381(b). It provides that the taxable year of the transferor shall close on the date of distribution or transfer, defined as the date when the distribution or transfer is completed or when substantially all the property has been transferred and the transferor ceases all activities other than liquidating activities. Treas. Regs. §1.381(b)-(1)(b). Section 381(b)(3) provides that the acquiring corporation may not carry back a postacquisition net operating loss or net capital loss to a preacquisition year of the transferor. Here the rules do not impinge on the carryover of the transferor's attributes to the transferee but instead block the transferee's use of its own losses — e.g., against income of a transferor corporation for a year prior to the merger. See also the discussion of CERTS at page 379 supra. Note that the rules of §381(b) do not apply to an F reorganization. See page 500 supra. Why is there no need to limit the carryback of postacquisition losses in an F reorganization?

Suppose Y Corp. with a wholly owned subsidiary, Sub Corp., acquires X Corp. in a forward triangular merger in which X Corp. merges into Sub Corp. and the former X Corp. shareholders receive Y Corp. stock. See page 429 supra. If Sub Corp. incurs a net operating loss after the acquisition, can that NOL be carried back, or does §381(b)(3) prevent the carryback? In Bercy Industries, Inc. v. Commissioner, 640 F.2d 1058 (9th Cir. 1981), the court permitted the carryback even though the reorganization was not a B, E, or F reorganization. See §381(b) and Treas. Regs. §1.381(a)-1(b)(3)(i). Notwithstanding what seems to be clear legislative language, the court had little difficulty reaching this result when Sub Corp. was merely a shell. Should a court reach the same result in a triangular merger if Sub Corp. is not a shell?

Section 381(c) lists numerous tax attributes of the transferor that carry over to the transferee. Of these the most prominent one that will be discussed in greatest detail is the net operating loss carryover of §381(c)(1). Note that while loss carryovers are transferred to the acquiring company, they can be used only against future income of the transferee. Other important inherited attributes include the transferor's earnings and profits. §381(c)(2). Under §381(c)(2)(A) the earnings and profits or deficit in earnings and profits of the transferor carry over to the transferee, but under §381(c)(2)(B) an inherited deficit in earnings and profits may be applied only against the transferee's posttransfer earnings and profits and not against the transferee's accumulated earnings and profits.

Under §381(c)(4) the acquiring corporation must continue to use the transferor's accounting method if both corporations have been using the same method. If different methods were used, the regulations specify the appropriate method to be used. See Treas. Regs. §1.381(c)(4)-(1)(c) and (d). Specific accounting provisions are provided under §381(c)(5) for inventories, under §381(c)(6) for depreciation allowance computation, under §381(c)(8) for installment obligations, and under §381(c)(16) for assumed expense liabilities.

2.   Section 382

Suppose in year 1 of its existence, X Corp. operates at a $100 loss (i.e., deductions exceed income by $100). In year 2, X Corp. produces $100 of income. Overall, X Corp. has $0 of income, and its tax consequences should reflect that. Strict adherence to the annual accounting concept would prevent X Corp. from offsetting income in year 2 with the loss in year 1. In fact, X Corp. is permitted to carry forward the year 1 loss to offset the income earned in year 2. §172. Similarly, if X Corp. had earned $100 of income in year 1 and had suffered a $100 loss in year 2, the year 2 loss could be carried back to offset the year 1 income (i.e., X Corp. would file an amended return for year 1). Under §172(b), a corporation can generally carry a loss back two years and forward 20 years if necessary, using up the loss in the earliest years in which income is sufficient to absorb the loss.

Now suppose X Corp. has a $100 loss in year 1 and Y Corp. has $100 of income in year 1. If X Corp. merges into Y Corp. and the X Corp. shareholders receive Y Corp. stock, should Y Corp. be able to use the $100 loss to offset the $100 of income? After all, if X Corp. could carry its losses back and forward, why should it not be permitted to carry its losses sideways to offset Y Corp.'s income? This situation gives rise to the concern that the merger of X into Y Corp. is motivated solely by the presence of the net operating losses. For example, suppose X Corp.'s assets at the time of the merger are worth $0. Even so, Y Corp., if it pays taxes at a 35 percent rate, may be willing to exchange up to $35 of Y Corp. stock for the X Corp. stock in the merger if the use of the X Corp. net operating loss will save $35 in taxes that Y Corp. would otherwise pay on its $100 of income.

While it is by no means clear that such a tax-motivated purchase is inefficient, Congress has since 1954 wrestled with the perceived problem of "trafficking" in net operating losses. On one hand, the carryover provisions perform an averaging function that allows corporations to overcome the limits of our annual accounting system. On the other hand, when NOLs are used to offset totally unrelated income (such as the acquisition of a corporation solely to obtain its NOLs), perhaps no legitimate averaging function is performed.

To address these concerns, §382 adopts the following approach: After a substantial ownership change, the earnings that can be offset by a net operating loss are limited, but the amount of the net operating loss that can be used by the acquiring corporation is not directly limited. The limitation-on-earnings approach is intended to approximate the results that would occur if a loss corporation's assets were combined with those of a profitable corporation in a partnership. In such a case, only the loss corporation's share of the partnership's income could be offset by the corporation's NOL carryforward See §704(c). Generally, the loss corporation's share of the partnership's income is limited to earnings generated by the assets contributed by the loss corporation. Section 382(f) prescribes an objective rate of return (the federal long-term tax-exempt rate) on the value of the corporation's net equity. The annual limitation, then, is the product of the prescribed rate and the value of the loss corporation's equity immediately before a specified ownership change. §382(b).

For example, suppose X Corp., a calendar year taxpayer, has $1 million of net operating loss carryforwards. On January 1, 1999, all the stock of X Corp. is sold in a transaction that triggers §382. On that date, the value of X Corp.'s stock was $500,000 and the applicable rate of return was 10 percent. In 1999 (and for each year thereafter), X Corp. could offset $50,000 (10 percent × $500,000) of income with the NOL carryforward. The same limitation would apply if X Corp. were merged into another corporation so long as an ownership change occurred as defined in §382(g). To the extent that X Corp. does not earn enough in 1999 (or in subsequent years) to absorb the $50,000 amount, the excess loss is carried forward to 2000 and is added to the $50,000 NOL limitation allowed in that year. §382(b)(2). The following Notes consider the details of §382.

The §382 limitation, although somewhat artificially determined, applies regardless of the actual performance of a loss company. For example, suppose all the stock of L Corp., a loss corporation, is sold by B to P in a transaction that triggers §382. After the acquisition, the amount of income that can be offset by the preacquisition NOLs is determined under §382 (i.e., the value of L Corp. multiplied by the federal long-term tax-exempt rate). This limitation applies even if L Corp. after the acquisition produces more income than the §382 limitation deems produced. Conversely, if L Corp. is merged into P Corp. in a transaction that triggers §382, P Corp. can offset income as determined under §382 even though the assets of the former L Corp. do not in fact produce that amount of income. Note that using the federal long-term tax-exempt rate as a proxy for the actual return on the assets may produce too large or too small a deduction. Once the §382 limitation is determined, however, it is used every year until the pre-change NOLs are used up or the 20-year carryforward limitation of §172 is reached.

For a thorough analysis of §382 and its legislative history, see Berry Petroleum Co. v. Commissioner, 104 T.C. 584 (1995).

NOTES

1. *Ownership changes.* New §382 applies if an "ownership change" occurs. §382(a), (j), (k)(3). An ownership change arises if the percentage of stock of the new loss corporation owned by one or more 5 percent

shareholders has increased by more than 50 percentage points as a result of an "owner shift" or an "equity structure shift." §382(g), (i). There are no substantive differences between an owner shift and an equity structure shift and no observable reason for the distinction. Treas. Regs. §1.382-2T(e)(2)(iii). Note that a series of unrelated transactions may be aggregated to constitute an "ownership change" but that all such transactions must have occurred during a single three-year testing period. §382(g), (i).

Notice that an ownership change occurs when there is a more than 50 percentage point change, not a more than 50 percent change. To illustrate, suppose A owns 20 percent of L Corp. If A acquires additional stock bringing A's ownership to 30+ percent, no ownership change has occurred even though A has increased his ownership of L Corp. by more than 50 percent. For an ownership change to occur, A would have to increase ownership in L Corp. to 70+ percent.

An owner shift includes any change in stock ownership by "5 percent shareholders" (those holding 5 percent or more in value of corporate stock before or after the change. For purposes of the 5 percent rule, all non-5 percent shareholders are aggregated as a single 5 percent shareholder. Owner shifts may occur in the following transactions: a purchase of stock from existing shareholders or the corporation; a §351 exchange; a redemption; exercise of stock conversion rights; or a combination of the foregoing.

For example, assume that the stock of L Corp. is publicly traded and that no shareholder owns 5 percent or more. No owner shift will occur so long as no person becomes a 5 percent shareholder. That is, random trading does not bring about an owner shift because the 5 percent shareholder (i.e., the aggregation of all of the non-5 percent shareholders) owns 100 percent before and after each trade. If, however, all the stock of widely held L Corp. is purchased by A, B, and C, none of whom were previous shareholders and each of whom acquires a one-third stock interest, a more than 50 percent owner shift occurs since their ownership has gone from 0 percent to 100 percent.

Similarly, if L Corp. — closely held by A, B, and C, each of whom is a one-third shareholder — makes a public offering so that 51 percent of the stock will be held by non-5 percent shareholders, a more than 50 percent owner shift will occur since all the stock owned by non-5 percent shareholders is treated as owned by one 5 percent shareholder, and that interest increases from 0 percent to 51 percent.

An "equity structure shift" includes any tax-free reorganization (other than a divisive D, an F, or a G reorganization). §382(g)(3). A more than 50 percent equity shift occurs if after the shift, the percentage of stock held by one or more of the new loss corporation's 5 percent shareholders is at least 50 percentage points more than the percentage of the old loss corporation's stock held by them during the testing period. The old loss corporation is the corporation with NOLs before the reorganization; the new loss corporation is the corporation entitled to use the NOLs after the reorganization. §382(k).

To illustrate an equity structure shift, suppose L Corp., a loss corporation, is merged into P Corp. in a tax-free transaction with P Corp. surviving. No shareholder of either corporation is a 5 percent shareholder. In the merger, the former L shareholders receive 49 percent of the stock of P, and the remaining stock of P is owned by P shareholders unrelated to the L shareholders. There has been a more than 50 percent equity structure change of L because the P shareholders (all of whom are non-5 percent shareholders and therefore lumped together as a single 5 percent shareholder) have gone from 0 percent owners of L to 51 percent shareholders of the new loss corporation. Had the former L shareholders received at least 50 percent of the P stock, there would have been no triggering equity structure change.

You may recall that in the context of an owner shift, all less-than-5 percent shareholders are aggregated and treated as a single 5 percent shareholder so that the constant buying and selling of a publicly traded corporation's stock does not cause problems under §382. In a reorganization (i.e., an equity structure shift), however, there may be two groups of less than 5 percent shareholders that are separately aggregated — the shareholders of the acquired and acquiring corporations. Each of these groups is treated separately for purposes of testing an ownership change. §382(g)(4)(B). Otherwise all reorganizations involving publicly held corporations would escape §382. Accordingly in the previous example, an ownership change occurs when the less than 5 percent shareholders of the acquiring corporation become 51 percent owners of the new loss corporation.

The relevant testing period used for determining whether an ownership change has occurred spans the three years preceding any owner shift or equity structure shift. §382(i)(1). Therefore, a series of unrelated transactions occurring during the testing period together may constitute an ownership change. If an ownership change has occurred earlier, the testing period for determining whether a second ownership change has occurred begins the day after the first exchange has occurred. §382(i)(2). In measuring whether an ownership change has occurred during the testing period, it is necessary to measure the difference between a 5 percent shareholder's highest and lowest percentage ownership during that period. For example, suppose X Corp. has 200 shares of common stock owned by A (100 shares), B (50 shares), and C (50 shares). On January 2 of year 1, A sells 60 shares to B. On January 1 of year 3, A purchases C's entire interest in X Corp. Overall, B, a 5 percent shareholder, has increased his interest by 30 percentage points (from a 25 percent owner to a 55 percent owner). A has decreased her ownership percentage from 50 percent to 45 percent; C has decreased his ownership from 30 percent to 0 percent. At first glance it appears that the 5 percent shareholders together have increased their ownership by only 30 percentage points, not the more than 50 percentage points necessary to trigger §382. *A*'s percentage ownership from his lowest ownership during the testing period, however, has increased from 20 percent after the sale to *B* to 45 percent after the purchase from *C*. This increase of 25 percentage points when added to the 30 percentage point increase for *B* now triggers the restrictions under §382. See Treas. Regs. §1.382-2T(c)(4).

For both owner shifts and equity structure changes, a series of transactions during the testing period may trigger the operation of §382. For example, suppose the following events occur in 1999: *B*, an individual, purchases 40 percent of the stock of *L*. *L* then is merged into *P* — which is wholly owned by *B* — in a tax-free transaction. In exchange for their stock in *L*, the *L* shareholders (none of whom was a 5 percent shareholder, other than *B*) receive stock with a value representing 60 percent of the *P* stock (*B* receives 24 percent, the other shareholders 36 percent). The merger is treated as a more than 50 percent equity structure change since immediately after the merger, *B* owned 64 percent of the combined entity (40 percent by virtue of *B*'s ownership prior to the merger plus 24 percent received in the merger), which is more than 50 percentage points over 0 percent, the lowest percentage in *L* owned by *B* during the testing period.

2. *Constructive ownership.* Suppose in case #1 that *B* owns all the stock of *L* Corp., a corporation with NOLs, and all the stock of *P* Corp. If *P* Corp. acquires all the *L* Corp. stock in a B reorganization, *P* Corp. has gone from a 0 percent shareholder in *L* Corp. to a 100 percent owner. Section 382 should not apply here, however, because there really has not been a change in ownership (i.e., *B* continues to own both corporations). Conversely, suppose in case #2 that *B* owns all the stock of *H* Corp., which in turn owns all the stock of *L* Corp. *P* Corp. is wholly owned by *C*, an individual who is unrelated to *B*. *B* sells the stock of *H* Corp. to *P*. Here, §382 should apply because of a change in ultimate ownership from *B* to *C* even though *H* Corp.'s direct ownership of *L* Corp. has remained at 100 percent.

Under §318(*l*)(3), the constructive ownership rules apply with modification in determining owner shifts and equity structure changes. Stock owned by entities (e.g., corporations, partnerships, trusts) are deemed owned by their shareholders or beneficiaries in proportion to their interests in the entity. It is only the stock of individuals that counts in determining ownership changes under §382. In case #1 above, because *B*, the ultimate beneficiary of *L* Corp.'s NOLs, remained a 100 percent shareholder of *L* Corp., §382 does not limit the carryover of *L* Corp.'s NOLs. Similarly, suppose the stock of *X* Corp., a publicly traded corporation, is not owned by any 5 percent shareholders. If *X* Corp. distributes to its shareholders all the stock of its wholly owned subsidiary, *Y* Corp., no ownership change occurs. Through the attribution rules, the shareholders of *X* Corp. owned 100 percent of *Y* Corp. before the transaction and 100 percent after. In case #2, when *P* purchases the stock of *H* Corp., which owns

L Corp., even though *H* Corp.'s direct ownership of *L* Corp. has not changed the ultimate beneficiary of *L* Corp.'s NOLs has changed. *C* has gone from a 0 percent owner of *L* Corp. to a 100 percent owner because *C* is deemed to own the *L* Corp. stock that *H* Corp. owns (i.e., *C* owns *P* Corp., which owns *H* Corp., which owns *L* Corp.).

For an illustration of the constructive ownership rules, see Treas. Regs. §1.382-2T(g)(4), (example 1).

3. *Definition of stock.* Certain preferred stock is not counted in determining ownership changes. §382(k)(6). Under this standard, the term "stock" does not include stock that is not entitled to vote, is limited and preferred as to dividends, does not participate in corporate growth to any significant extent, has redemption and liquidation rights that do not exceed the issue price (except for a reasonable redemption premium), and is not convertible. §1504(a)(4). Note that stock that may be labeled "common" stock may be treated as "preferred" stock, and stock labeled "preferred" stock may be treated as "common" stock for purposes of this rule. The Secretary has broad discretion in deciding what stock is counted in determining whether an ownership change has occurred. §382(k)(6). See Treas. Regs. §1.382-2T(f)(18)(ii) which contains a test for identifying when stock is not counted for purposes of §382. See also Treas. Regs. §1.382-2T(f)(18)(iii), which treats certain "debt" instruments as equity.

The preferred stock provision is intended legislatively to reverse the result in Maxwell Hardware Co. v. Commissioner, 343 F.2d 713 (9th Cir. 1965). In that case a loss corporation's old shareholders retained common stock representing more than 50 percent of the corporation's value, thereby avoiding the application of former §382. New shareholders, however, received special preferred stock that carried with it 90 percent participation in earnings attributable to newly contributed property. Section 382 would apply in *Maxwell Hardware* because the new shareholders went from 0 percent to 100 percent participating stock ownership even though the stock they received was called preferred stock.

4. *Options.* For the purpose of determining whether an ownership change has occurred, the stock of a loss corporation that is subject to an option may be treated as acquired by the option holder for purposes of testing whether *that holder* has undergone an ownership change. This may result in some options being considered as exercised while other options are ignored. For example, suppose *A* owns 100 shares (i.e., all the outstanding shares) of *X* Corp. *A* sells 40 shares to *B* and grants *B* an option to purchase the remaining 60 shares from *A*. At the same time, *A* has an option to purchase 100 new shares from *X* Corp. In testing whether *B* has triggered the §382 ownership test, only *B*'s option is assumed to have been exercised. Accordingly, *B* has gone from a 0 percent shareholder to a 100 percent shareholder, thereby triggering the limitation of §382. Treas. Regs. §1.382-2T(h)(4)(ii) (example 2). Note that if *A*'s option were also considered to be exercised, *B*'s percentage increase would be only 50 percent, not the more than 50 percent amount necessary to trigger §382.

You may recall that the IRS took a similarly selective approach to option exercise in the redemption area in *Patterson Trust,* page 196 supra. There, the court struck down the IRS attempt based on the language of the statute. Is Treas. Regs. §1.382-2T(h)(4)(ii) (example 2) valid?

Treas. Regs. §1.382-4(d)(2) provides that an option is treated as exercised if the option satisfies an ownership, control or income test. There is also a list of safe harbors that exclude some options from the deemed exercise rules. Treas. Regs. §1.382-4(d)(7).

5. *Continuity of business.* Following an ownership change, a loss corporation's NOL carryforwards (including applicable built-in losses) are disallowed unless during the two-year period following the ownership change the new loss corporation either (1) continues the old loss corporation's historic business or (2) uses a significant portion of the old loss corporation's assets in a business. §382(c). This continuity requirement is the same requirement that must be satisfied to qualify as a tax-free reorganization under §368. Treas. Regs. §1.368-1(d). See page 388 supra. The purpose of the requirement is to try to distinguish acquisitions motivated by NOLs from acquisitions motivated by the acquired corporation's assets or business. An extreme example of tax-motivated behavior is the subject of Alprosa Watch Corp. v. Commissioner, 11 T.C. 240 (1948). In that case a shareholder purchased the stock of a loss corporation, sold the assets back to the original shareholders, and infused the corporation with a new business. The court, prior to any version of §382, allowed the use of NOLs to offset postacquisition income. How would this situation be treated under §382?

6. *Section 382 limitation.* For any taxable year after the change date (that is, the date of a triggering ownership change), the amount of a loss corporation's taxable income for any year that can be offset by a prechange loss cannot exceed the §382 limitation. §382(a). The §382 limitation is an amount equal to the value of the loss corporation before the exchange multiplied by the federal long-term tax-exempt rate in effect on the change date. §382(b), (f). Once the §382 limitation is computed, it stays in effect regardless of fluctuations in the federal long-term tax-exempt rate.

The value of the corporation is the value of its stock. Because the ability to use NOLs increases when the value of the loss corporation increases, there may be an incentive for the shareholders of a loss corporation to increase the value of that corporation by contributing cash or other property immediately prior to an ownership change for which the shareholders would receive additional compensation from the acquiring party. Congress has discouraged this technique through an "anti-stuffing" rule under which the value of any prechange capital contribution is disregarded in determining the value of a corporation. §382(*l*)(1). Generally, any contribution received within two years of an ownership change is covered by the antistuffing rule if it does not contribute to the corporation's trade or business.

Congress was also concerned that the value of a loss corporation might be inflated because of investment assets held by the loss corporation to generate income to be offset by the corporation's business NOLs. See Berry Petroleum Co. v. Commissioner, 104 T.C. 584 (1995) (exploring what constitutes nonbusiness assets). The general aim of §382 is to limit the use of acquired NOLs to offset a hypothetical level of income generated by the loss corporation's business assets. To the extent that a loss corporation's investment assets inflate the use of the NOLs, §382's purpose is circumvented. Section 382(l)(4) provides, however, that if at least one-third of a loss corporation's assets consist of nonbusiness assets, the value of the corporation for purposes of the §382 limitation does not include the nonbusiness assets (reduced by any attributable indebtedness). In applying this one-third test, stock of a 50 percent or more owned subsidiary will not be considered a nonbusiness asset. Instead, §382(l)(6) adopts a look-through rule that considers the appropriate percentage of the subsidiary's assets deemed to be owned by the parent.

Just as Congress did not want nonbusiness assets to inflate the usable NOLs, it also did not want business assets to inflate the usable NOLs if those assets were going to be removed from the corporation. For example, assets used to redeem stock of the loss corporation are not counted in determining the §382 limitation. In general, the value of an old loss corporation is determined immediately prior to an ownership change. §382(e)(1). The value of the old loss corporation equals the value of its stock (including preferred stock). If, however, a redemption or other corporate contraction contributes to an ownership change, the value of the corporation is determined immediately after the ownership change. §382(e)(2). This will result in a lower value because corporate assets were used in the redemption. The effect of this special valuation rule is to discourage "bootstrap" acquisitions in which the purchasers finance the acquisition of a loss corporation with the corporation's own assets. See Berry Petroleum Co. v. Commissioner, 104 T.C. 584 (1995) (exploring the definition of what constitutes a "corporate contraction").

If a corporation is insolvent, its value may be $0, effectively eliminating all NOLs after an ownership change. Section 382(l)(5) provides a special rule that does not limit the use of NOLs for corporations involved in bankruptcy or similar proceedings if at least 50 percent of the loss corporation's stock immediately after the change is owned by former shareholders and certain long-term creditors. If a second ownership change occurs within two years after the initial change, however, the §382 loss limitation is reduced to zero. Special provisions prevent a purchaser from acquiring a loss corporation's debt immediately before initiating a bankruptcy proceeding, exchanging the debt for stock without triggering the §382 limitation, and then using the NOLs immediately and without limitation.

If the §382 limitation amount exceeds taxable income, the excess carries over. §382(b)(2). For example, suppose the §382 limitation amount for L Corp. with $1 million in NOLs is $100,000 per year. In the first year after an ownership change, the new loss corporation produces $70,000 of income, all of which is offset by the NOL carryover. In the second year, the new loss corporation can use $130,000 of the NOLs to offset income produced. In some situations, even though §382 does not directly result in the permanent loss of NOLs, the §382 limitation, combined with the 20-year carryforward limitation in §172, does result in a loss of NOLs. In the example above, if L Corp. had $3 million of NOLs and the §382 limitation is $100,000 per year, the new loss corporation will not be able to use $1 million of the NOLs to offset postownership change income.

Under §382, the federal long-term tax-exempt rate must be multiplied by the value of the loss corporation to determine whether NOLs are limited. By specifying that the long-term rate for federal obligations be used, Congress intended to provide a reasonable risk-free rate of return that a loss corporation could obtain in the absence of a change of ownership. Congress discounted the long-term *taxable* rate on federal obligations, however, by requiring the use of the long-term *tax-exempt* rate on federal obligations. This requirement was intended to take into account the fact that the purchase price of the loss corporation's stock reflects not only asset value but also the value of the NOLs themselves. Accordingly, Congress attempted to balance overvaluation of the worth of the loss corporation with undervaluation of the rate of return on the loss corporation's assets.

7. *Built-in gains.* The purpose of §382 is to limit the use of a loss corporation's NOLs to the income deemed to be produced by the loss corporation. The income that can be offset by the NOLs is not only the expected future income from operations but also any inherent gain in a loss corporation's appreciated assets. Section 382(h)(1)(A) allows a loss corporation with an "unrealized net built-in gain" to increase its §382 limitation by the "recognized built-in gain" for any taxable year within the five-year recognition period. See Notice 90-27, 1990-1 C.B. 336 (recognition period extended for an installment sale). A "net unrealized built-in gain" is defined as the amount by which the value of a corporation's assets exceeds the aggregate bases immediately before the ownership shift. A "recognized built-in gain" is defined as any gain recognized on the disposition of an asset during the recognition period if the taxpayer establishes that the asset was held by the loss corporation before the change date and that the gain is allocable to the period before the change date. The recognized built-in gain cannot exceed the net unrealized built-in gain reduced by the recognized built-in gains for prior years in the recognition period.

8. *Built-in losses.* The term "prechange loss" to which §382(a) applies includes NOL carryforwards arising prior to the change year, the allocable portion of a corporation's NOLs for the year in which the change occurs, and certain recognized built-in losses and deductions. §382(d), (h)(1)(B). The limitation on built-in losses and deductions reflects the fact that a corporation interested in purchasing a loss corporation with $1 million of

NOLs might also be interested in purchasing a corporation with no NOLs but having an asset with a basis of $1.1 million and a fair market value of $100,000. The purpose of the restrictions on built-in losses is to curtail trafficking in a corporation with assets (having built-in losses) that can be sold to offset the acquiring corporation's income from other sources. Under §382(h)(1)(B), if a loss corporation has a net unrealized built-in loss, any recognized built-in loss during the five-year recognition period is treated as a prechange loss and is therefore subject to the §382 limitation. Thus, if the ownership change occurs in 1999, and there is a net unrealized built-in loss, recognition of that loss in 2000 when the asset is sold will be subject to the §382 limitation along with prechange NOLs. A de minimis rule ignores a corporation's net unrealized built-in loss (or gain) if it does not exceed the lesser of (a) 15 percent of the fair market value of the assets of the corporation or (b) $10 million. §382(h)(3)(B).

"Net unrealized built-in loss" is defined as the amount by which the aggregate adjusted bases of a corporation's assets exceeds the fair market value of the assets immediately before the ownership change. A "recognized built-in loss" is any loss recognized on the disposition of an asset during the five-year recognition period except to the extent the taxpayer can prove either that the asset was not held by the loss corporation immediately prior to the exchange or that the loss was allocable to a period after the change date. §382(h)(2)(B).

Depreciation or amortization deductions during the five-year recognition period are treated as recognized built-in losses to the extent attributable to the excess of adjusted basis over fair market value. §382(h)(2)(B). Also, amounts that accrue before the change date but are allowable as deductions after such date (such as deductions deferred under §267, §465, or §469) are treated as built-in losses. §382(h)(6).

9. *Anti-abuse rules.* Section 382 does not alter the continuing application of §269, see pages 518-523 infra, or the separate return limitation year (SRLY) rules under the consolidated return regulations. See pages 525-533 infra. Moreover, §382(m) authorizes the Secretary to prescribe regulations to prevent avoidance of §382 through the use of related persons, pass-through entities, or other intermediaries. See, e.g., Treas. Regs. §1.382-2T(k)(4).

3. Section 383

Section 383(a) authorizes the Secretary to promulgate regulations that will limit capital loss carryforwards under §1212 to the taxable income of the loss corporation not exceeding the §382 limitation. Any capital loss carryforward used in a postchange year will reduce the §382 limitation that is applied to prechange losses. Similar rules are adopted for excess credits (e.g., the alternative minimum tax credit under §53 or the foreign tax credit under §901) and passive activity losses.

4. Section 384

Section 382 does not inhibit a loss corporation from acquiring a profitable corporation if there is no ownership change with respect to the loss corporation. In this situation, there is no trafficking in losses; rather, the loss corporation seeks to improve its economic performance through the acquisition. Accordingly, suppose L Corp., a loss corporation owned by B, acquires P Corp., a profitable corporation owned by C, for cash, and assume L Corp. and P Corp. report tax liability on a consolidated return. The ability of L Corp. to use its preacquisition NOLs to offset P Corp.'s postacquisition income is not inhibited by §382. The same is true if P Corp. merged into L Corp. so long as no ownership change in L Corp. takes place.

But suppose P Corp. is a "burnt-out" tax shelter — an entity that has produced depreciation deductions for its owners and that now has a large built-in gain because the bases of its assets have been adjusted downward under §1016 while the property's fair market value has not decreased correspondingly. For example, assume that after generating depreciation deductions P Corp. has depreciable assets with an aggregate basis of $50,000 and a fair market value of $300,000, subject to a $250,000 mortgage liability. If P Corp. sells the assets, the taxes on the $250,000 gain exceed the $50,000 of cash that P Corp. can expect to receive on an arm's-length sale.

Suppose the stock of P Corp. is acquired by L Corp., and either they file a consolidated return or P Corp. merges into L Corp. In the absence of a remedial provision, L Corp.'s preexisting NOLs can be used to offset gain generated by the postacquisition sale of the acquired assets. L Corp. may be happy to pay $50,000 in cash to acquire the appreciated assets. C, the ultimate seller of the tax shelter, may be happy to receive any cash or other property for C's interest in the burnt-out shelter. But Congress was unhappy with this technique of "laundering" the built-in gain from the sale of assets with preexisting NOLs.

Section 384 originated as an effort to deny the use of any preacquisition NOLs by a loss corporation to offset any built-in gains of an acquired corporation recognized during a five-year recognition period following an acquisition. But the provision was broadly drafted so that it also applies to a corporation with built-in gains that acquires a corporation with preacquisition NOLs. Even though §382 might permit the use of some NOLs by the acquiring corporation in this situation, §384 may apply to deny their use against recognized built-in gains of the acquiring corporation.

Section 384 applies if one corporation acquires control of another corporation and either corporation is a gain corporation (i.e., a corporation with net unrealized built-in gain at the time of acquisition). Control is defined as stock representing at least 80 percent of vote and value of the acquired corporation. §384(c)(5). Section 384 also applies to an asset acquisition if the acquisition qualifies as a tax-free A, C, or acquisitive D reorganization. If both the acquiring and the acquired corporations were part of the same control group under §1563 (using a 50 percent ownership test) during the previous five-year period (or the term of a corporation's existence, if shorter), §384 will not apply.

If §384 is applicable, the provision denies the use of any "preacquisition loss" of a loss corporation (but not of the gain corporation) to offset any "recognized built-in gain" of the gain corporation during the five-year recognition period. §384(a). In the examples above, L Corp.'s NOLs cannot be used to offset gain recognized on the sale of P Corp.'s appreciated assets. The term "preacquisition loss" includes NOLs and net unrealized built-in losses that are recognized during a five-year recognition period. §384(c)(3)(A). The term "recognized built-in gain" refers to any gain on the disposition of an asset during a five-year recognition period except to the extent that it can be established that the asset was not held by the gain corporation on the acquisition date. §384(c)(1)(A).

In some cases, §§382 and 384 overlap; in others, one or neither of the provisions applies. Suppose B owns all the stock of L Corp., a company with NOLs, and C owns all the stock of P Corp., a company with built-in gains. If L Corp. purchases all the stock of P Corp. and together they file a consolidated return, §382 will not prevent the use of L Corp.'s losses against P Corp.'s future income because there is no ownership change for L Corp. Section 384, however, will prevent the use of the NOLs to offset any built-in gains recognized by P Corp. during the five-year recognition period.

If, instead, L Corp. merges into P Corp. and C ends up with more than 50 percent of the surviving corporation, §382 will limit the use of L Corp.'s NOLs and §384 will also apply to limit any NOLs allowable under §382 that would otherwise be used to offset any of P Corp.'s recognized built-in gains. If P Corp. had no built-in gains prior to the merger, then only §382 would apply to limit the use of the NOLs. If, in the preceding example, L Corp. and P Corp. were both long-standing subsidiaries of H Corp., neither §382 nor §384 would apply to limit the use of the NOLs.

Suppose L Corp. and P Corp., which are unrelated, form a joint venture partnership, LP, which attempts to allocate income under the partnership agreement disproportionately to L Corp. As a technical matter, there has been no triggering event for purposes of §382 or §384. Nevertheless, Congress has given the Service authority to apply these loss limitation principles in abuse situations. §§382(m)(3), 384(f)(1).

5. Section 269

Enacted in 1943, §269 provides for the disallowance of tax benefits when
tax avoidance is the principal purpose for the acquisition of control of a
corporation or for transfers of property. Section 269, which can apply to
either an asset acquisition or a stock acquisition, provides the Service with
a powerful weapon because it is subjective in application: The provision can
apply when the acquirer (or persons controlling the acquirer) possesses a
"bad" state of mind. Under §269(a) the Service can disallow the deduction
of an NOL carryover if the control of a corporation or corporate assets
was acquired for the principal purpose of avoiding or evading federal
income tax by securing a deduction. To invoke §269, there are two requirements: (1) an acquisition and (2) a tax avoidance motive. The presence
of §§382-384 does not limit the application of §269. Treas. Regs. §1.269-
7. So it is possible that NOLs that would be allowed under §382 may
nevertheless be disallowed under §269.

On its face §269 seems to cover the acquisition by a profitable business
of a loss corporation with an NOL carryover. But does the provision apply
to an acquisition of a profitable business by a loss corporation?

Commissioner v. British Motor Car Distributors
278 F.2d 392 (9th Cir. 1960)

Before Pope, Hamlin and Merrill, Circuit Judges.
MERRILL, Circuit Judge.
The taxpayer corporation incurred losses while engaged in the business of selling home appliances. It disposed of all its assets and the corporate shares were then sold to new owners, who used the corporation to
operate a previously going automobile business. The question here presented is whether the taxpayer is entitled to carry over the losses incurred
in the old business, where it is clear that the principal purpose of the
acquisition of the taxpayer by the new owners was to avoid taxes.* The
Tax Court, five judges dissenting, ruled in the affirmative. . . .

British Motor Car Company was a partnership consisting of Kjell H.
Qvale, who had an 85 per cent interest, and his wife, who had a 15 per
cent interest. The partnership had existed from about May 1, 1948, and
engaged, in San Francisco, in the business of importing, distributing and
selling foreign automobiles and parts. On September 11, 1951, the partnership submitted an offer to counsel for the Empire Home Equipment Company, in which the former offered to buy the outstanding stock of the
corporation from its then owners for $21,250.00, upon the conditions,
inter alia, that the corporation would increase its authorized capital and

_____
*The tax years in question predate the enactment of §382. — EDS.

change its name. The offer was accepted. On November 2, 1951, Empire changed its name to British Motor Car Distributors, Ltd. On November 30, 1951, the partnership acquired all the outstanding shares of stock and immediately thereafter transferred its net assets (exclusive of the acquired shares) to the corporation in exchange for an additional 15,923 shares of stock. It is not claimed that there was any business purpose in the acquisition.

In the tax years ending October 31, 1952, and October 31, 1953, the corporation operated profitably in the automobile business. In its income and excess profits tax returns for those years, it carried forward the net operating losses that it had sustained in the appliance business in its fiscal years ending in 1949, 1950 and 1951. . . .

The Tax Court, in its construction of [§269(a)], adhered to its view as expressed in T.V.D. Company, 27 T.C. 879, 886, following the dictum in Alprosa Watch Company, 11 T.C. 240, to the effect that "it is manifest from the unambiguous terms of [§269] that it applies only to an acquiring corporation." The court points out that here the corporation is seeking to make use of its own previous loss; that it is the corporation, and not its new stockholders, which is securing the benefit of the deduction. *Alprosa Watch* is quoted to the effect that [§269(a)] "would seem to prohibit the use of a deduction, credit or allowance only by the acquiring person or corporation and not their use by the corporation whose control was acquired."

We do not read the language of the section, "securing the benefit of a deduction," as applying only to the actual taking of such deduction by the taxpayer. We should be closing our eyes to the realities of the situation were we to refuse to recognize that the persons who have acquired the corporation did so to secure *for themselves* a very real tax benefit to be realized by them *through* the acquired corporation and which they could not otherwise have realized.

This is not, as the corporation protests, a disregard of its corporate entity. Since [§269(a)] is expressly concerned with the persons acquiring control of a corporation, we must recognize such persons as, themselves, having a significant existence or entity apart from the corporation they have acquired. To ignore such independent entity simply because such persons are also the stockholders of their acquisition is to ignore the clear demands of [§269(a)]. It is not the fact that they are stockholders which subjects them to scrutiny. Rather, it is the fact that they are the persons specified by the section: those who have acquired control of the corporation. They may not escape the scrutiny which the section demands by attempting to merge their identity with that of their acquisition.

Section [§269(a)] contemplates that it shall not be limited to corporate acquirers. While Clause (2) is specifically limited to corporate acquirers, Clause (1) deals with "persons" as acquirers. That Clause (1) is to include noncorporate acquirers could not be more clearly implied. Nor do we find any sound reason, if this device for tax avoidance is to be struck down, for doing the job only when the tax avoider is a corporation. Legislative history indicates that a much broader construction was intended.[3]

To limit the effect of [§269(a)] to cases in which the taxpayer is seeking to deduct as its own a loss incurred by another would seem to limit Clause (1) to corporate acquirers. Who but a corporation could claim as its own a loss which had been incurred by an acquired corporation? Certainly an individual could not do so. The construction here contended for by the taxpayer corporation would then clearly frustrate legislative purpose. . . .

The corporation contends, as stated by the Tax Court, that the benefit to the stockholders (as distinguished from that to the corporate taxpayer) is too tenuous to bring the section into play. Tenuous or not, it is the benefit which actuated these persons in acquiring this corporation and is thus the very benefit with which this section is concerned. It is not for the courts to judge whether the benefit to the acquiring persons is sufficiently direct or substantial to be worth acquiring. That judgment was made by the acquirers. The judicial problem is whether the securing of the benefit was the principal purpose of the acquisition. If it was, the allowance of the deduction is forbidden.

Judgment reversed. The deductions claimed by the taxpayer are disallowed and judgment is entered for the Commissioner.

NOTES

1. *Acquisition requirement.* In *British Motor Car,* the stock of a floundering, inefficient corporation was sold, and the new owners changed the

---

3. H.R. No. 871, 78th Congress, First Session (1944 Cum. Bull. 901, 938):

> This section is designed to put an end promptly to any market for, or dealings in, interests in corporations or property which have as their objective the reduction through artifice of the income or excess profits tax liability.

> The crux of the devices which have come to the attention of your committee has been some form of acquisition on or after the effective date of the Second Revenue Act of 1940, but the devices take many forms. Thus, the acquisition may be an acquisition of the shares of a corporation, or it may be an acquisition which follows by operation of law in the case of a corporation resulting from a statutory merger or consolidation. The person, or persons, making the acquisition likewise vary, as do the forms or methods of utilization under which tax avoidance is sought. Likewise, the tax benefits sought may be one or more of several deductions or credits, including the utilization of excess profits credits, carry-overs and carry-backs of losses or unused excess profits credits, and anticipated expense of other deductions. In the light of these considerations, the section has not confined itself to a description of any particular methods for carrying out such tax avoidance schemes but has included within its scope these devices in whatever form they may appear. For similar reasons, the scope of the terms used in the section is to be found in the objective of the section, namely, to prevent the tax liability from being reduced through the distortion or perversion effected through tax avoidance devices. . . .

operation of the business to make it more efficient. Under these circumstances, should §269 come into play? Does the tax system create a disincentive for an inefficient business to become efficient, or does it simply remove tax benefits from consideration in a business decision, forcing the decision to rise or fall on its own merits?

It is now clear that §269 applies not only when NOL carryovers are acquired by a profitable business but also when the *benefits* of an NOL carryover are acquired by a loss corporation acquiring a profitable business. See also Vulcan Materials Co. v. United States, 446 F.2d 690, 698 (5th Cir. 1971). How would *British Motor Car* be decided under §382? Notice that the partnership that owned 0 percent of British Motor Car Distributors before the transaction in question owns 100 percent afterwards. Note that even if §382 would apply to this situation today, §269 might also apply to deny the use of the NOLs permitted by §382. Treas. Regs. §1.269-7.

If you conclude that both §§382 and 269 would apply in *British Motor Car* because of the ownership change, can §269 ever apply in a situation where §382 does not? Suppose *L* Corp., a loss corporation, acquires *P* Corp., a profitable corporation. If *L* Corp. and *P* Corp. file a consolidated return, the Service may in some circumstances argue that §269 prevents the use of *L* Corp.'s NOLs to offset *P* Corp.'s postacquisition income. For example, if the former shareholders of *P* Corp. continue to exercise real control over *P* Corp.'s governance even though *L* Corp. has acquired enough control to permit consolidated reporting, §269 may apply. See, e.g., Briarcliff Candy Corp. v. Commissioner, 54 T.C.M. 667 (1987).

The acquisition test under §269 is triggered by either of the following: (1) any person or persons acquiring sufficient stock to hold at least 50 percent of either the total combined voting power or total value of all shares (§269(a)(1)) or (2) a corporation acquiring property of another corporation with a carryover basis (§269(a)(2)). Section 269(a)(2) is used primarily to disallow NOL carryovers resulting from a corporate reorganization with an improper purpose involving unrelated corporations. Generally, an acquisitive reorganization would activate the carryover basis rule of §362 and would, in the absence of §269, enable the acquiring corporation to carry over the acquired corporation's tax attributes under §381. If the transferor is controlled directly or indirectly by the acquirer or its shareholders immediately before the acquisition, §269 does not apply. §269(a)(2). Accordingly, a merger between commonly controlled corporations will not result in the loss of any NOL carryovers. See Rev. Rul. 66-214, 1966-2 C.B. 98.

For a discussion of the acquisition requirement, see Hermes Consolidated, Inc. v. United States, 14 Cl. Ct. 398 (1988) (acquisition structured to avoid 50 percent threshold was successful).

2. *Tax avoidance motive.* The term "evasion or avoidance of tax," though not defined, is not restricted to behavior that would precipitate criminal or civil fraud penalties. Treas. Regs. §1.269-1(b). Acquiring an

NOL carryover that the acquirer would not otherwise enjoy will result in the avoidance of tax that would otherwise be paid on the profits of the acquirer. Note, however, that tax avoidance must be the "principal purpose" — the purpose that exceeds any other purpose in importance. Treas. Regs. §1.269-3(a). Determining the principal purpose is a question of fact. The regulations describe certain transactions that will ordinarily indicate the proscribed purpose. See, e.g., Treas. Regs. §1.269-3(b)(1), setting forth an example quite similar to the facts in *British Motor Car.*

Since tax reduction is often a motive behind an acquisition of a business with favorable tax attributes, what business purpose will suffice as a principal purpose of the acquisition? One typical business purpose for the acquisition of corporate control is the seller's insistence that the acquirer purchase stock rather than assets. See Glen Raven Mills v. Commissioner, 59 T.C. 1 (1972), a court-reviewed opinion in which the seller's insistence on a package deal in conjunction with some other factors was sufficient to constitute the principal purpose of the acquisition. What is the result if the *purchaser* insists on acquiring stock? For other business purposes, see American M.A.R.C., Inc. v. United States, 19 A.F.T.R.2d 929 (C.D. Cal. 1967) (a genuine belief that the acquired business could be turned around); Fairfield Communities Land Co. v. Commissioner, 47 T.C.M. (CCH) 1194 (1984) (acquisition of loss corporation to obtain cash and broaden the shareholder base); Clarksdale Rubber Co. v. Commissioner, 45 T.C. 234 (1965) (expansion of acquirer's business); Naeter Brothers Publishing Co. v. Commissioner, 42 T.C. 1 (1964) (combined operation favored by lenders).

Suppose an acquisition is 40 percent motivated by tax avoidance, 30 percent motivated by a desire for expansion, and 30 percent motivated by a desire to "go public" (which the acquisition would allow). Is tax avoidance the primary motive, or in making that determination, can a corporation combine all nontax motives? In U.S. Shelter Corp. v. United States, 13 Cl. Ct. 606 (1987), the court allowed the corporation to combine the nontax motives, concluding that §269 did not apply.

Authority is split with respect to whether §269 applies to losses incurred after an acquisition. Compare Borge v. Commissioner, 405 F.2d 673 (2d Cir. 1968) (§269 can apply to postacquisition losses), with Herculite Protective Fabrics Corp. v. Commissioner, 387 F.2d 475 (3d Cir. 1968) (postacquisition losses were true economic loss to acquirer and not subject to §269).

3. *Section 269(b).* Recall that pursuant to §§332 and 334(b) a parent liquidating a subsidiary generally recognizes no gain but inherits the subsidiary's basis in its assets. See pages 351-358 supra. Under §381(a)(1), a parent can succeed to the tax attributes of its liquidated subsidiary as well. If the parent has purchased the stock of a subsidiary, the parent can make an election under §338 to step up (or step down) the basis of the subsidiary's assets. See discussion at pages 314-329 supra. If the election is made,

the sale destroys the subsidiary's tax attributes, including any NOL carryovers (although the NOLs can offset any gain on the deemed §338 sale). If no election is made and the subsidiary is liquidated, the parent might succeed to the subsidiary's tax attributes.

Under §269(b)(1), the Service can disallow any deduction or other tax attribute that otherwise would be acquired if (1) there is a qualified stock purchase, (2) a §338 election is not made, (3) the acquired corporation is liquidated pursuant to a plan adopted within two years of acquisition, and (4) the principal purpose of the liquidation is tax avoidance. The liquidation of a newly purchased subsidiary ordinarily indicates that the principal purpose of the liquidation is tax avoidance, in the absence of evidence to the contrary. H.R. Rep. No. 432 (pt. II), 98th Cong., 2d Sess. 1623 (1984).

4. *Relationship between §§269 and 382.* Section 382 is triggered by objective criteria, §269 by subjective tax avoidance purpose. Because of its breadth, §269 can apply to disallow an NOL carryover that would not be disallowed under §382. Treas. Regs. §1.269-7. Indeed, deliberate avoidance of §382(a) may indicate that use of the NOL carryovers was the principal purpose for the acquisition. Luke v. Commissioner, 351 F.2d 568 (7th Cir. 1965). Conversely, the application of §382 may suggest the absence of a tax avoidance purpose.

PROBLEMS

13-1. *B* owns all the stock of *L* Corp., which has $2 million of NOL carryovers. *P* Corp. is a profitable business that earns approximately $300,000 a year. What effect does each of the following transactions have on the NOL carryovers?

a. *B* contributes sufficient cash to *L* Corp. to enable *L* Corp. to purchase the assets of *P* Corp.
b. *L* Corp. sells all its assets and uses the proceeds to purchase the assets of *P* Corp.
c. *L* Corp. acquires the stock of *P* Corp. for cash, *P* Corp. liquidates, and *L* Corp. continues to operate *P* Corp.'s profitable business.

13-2. Discuss the application of §382 in the following situations.

a. *L* Corp., a corporation with NOL carryforwards, is closely held by four unrelated individuals, *A, B, C,* and *D,* each of whom owns 25 percent of the *L* Corp. stock. There is a public offering of *L* Corp.'s stock. No person who purchases stock in the offering acquires 5 percent or more, and neither *A, B, C,* nor *D* acquires any additional stock. As a result of the offering the new shareholders own stock representing 60 percent of the outstanding *L* Corp. stock. Consider the restrictions, if any, on *L* Corp.'s use of the NOL carryforwards.

b. Suppose in (a) that *L* Corp. is publicly held, with no shareholder owning more than 2 percent of the outstanding stock.

c. Suppose *L* Corp. is wholly owned by *B*. *L* Corp. merges into *P* Corp., a publicly held corporation in which no shareholder owns more than a 2 percent interest. After the merger, *B* owns 60 percent of *P* Corp. Two years later, *P* Corp. sells additional stock to *C* equal to 50 percent of the stock value.

13-3. Determine the tax consequences in the following situations.

a. *X* Corp. is wholly owned by individual *A*, and its stock has a value of $3,000; *X* Corp. has NOL carryforwards of $10,000. *Y* Corp. is wholly owned by individual *B*, and its stock has a value of $9,000; *Y* Corp. has NOL carryforwards of $100. *Z* Corp. is owned by individual *C*, and its stock has a value of $18,000; *Z* Corp. has no NOL carryforwards. *X* Corp., *Y* Corp., and *Z* Corp. consolidate into *W* Corp. in a transaction that qualifies under §368(a)(1)(A). The applicable long-term tax-exempt rate on such date is 10 percent. As a result of the consolidation, *A* receives 10 percent of *W* stock, *B* receives 30 percent, and *C* receives 60 percent. *W*'s taxable income before any reduction for its NOLs is $1,400. Consider whether the NOLs can be used to offset *W*'s income.

b. Suppose in (a) that *X* Corp. holds an asset with a basis of $1,000 and a fair market value of $1,600 at the time of the consolidation. The asset is sold by *W* in year 1, thereby producing $600 of *W*'s $1,400 of taxable income.

c. Suppose in (a) that *X* Corp. holds an asset with a basis of $1,600 and a fair market value of $1,000 at the time of the consolidation. The asset is sold by *W*. Excluding this transaction and the use of any NOLs, *W* Corp. has taxable income of $2,000.

13-4. *L* Corp., a loss company with preacquisition losses, is wholly owned by *B*. *P* Corp., a profitable corporation with built-in gains, is wholly-owned by *C*. Consider whether §382 or §384 or both apply in the subparts below and what tax consequences follow.

a. *L* Corp. purchases all the *P* Corp. stock for cash and does not elect §338.

b. Suppose in (a) that *L* Corp. elects §338.

c. *P* Corp. purchases all the *L* Corp. stock for cash and does not elect §338.

    d. *L* Corp. merges into *P* Corp., and *B* ends up with 60 percent of the *P* Corp. stock.

    e. Suppose in (d) that *B* ends up with 40 percent of the *P* Corp. stock.

    f. Suppose *L* Corp. and *P* Corp. form *L-P,* a joint venture partnership. Under the *L-P* partnership agreement, much of the *L-P* income is allocated to *L* Corp.

B. AFFILIATED CORPORATIONS

In principle, every corporation reports its income and deductions separately from other corporations. Of course, the Service may seek exceptions to this principle if the corporate form is used to reallocate income. See pages 572-582 infra. The consolidated return provisions offer an opportunity for taxpayers to ignore this principle when several businesses are operated in several corporations rather than in only one. The use of multiple corporations might be the result of internal growth (i.e., new corporations formed via §351), purchase, or reorganization (i.e., a subsidiary acquisition through a B reorganization).

Why would individuals choose to operate a business or businesses through multiple corporations rather than through a single corporation? There may be a host of reasons — both nontax and tax motivated. Some of the nontax reasons for maintaining, acquiring, or forming multiple corporations include (1) minimizing potential tort liability (see Walkovszky v. Carlton, 18 N.Y.2d 414 (1966) (ownership of taxi fleet in many corporations, each owning only one or two cabs)); (2) regulatory restraints or benefits of combining businesses within a single corporation; (3) avoiding state law complications; (4) the existence of favorable, nonavailable contractual arrangements; (5) alleviation of labor problems; and (6) the existence of corporate goodwill.

Some of the tax advantages associated with multiple corporations include (1) the availability of differing accounting methods, table years, and other elections; (2) reallocation of income to avoid progressive tax rates; (3) the availability of multiple tax benefits, such as the accumulated earnings tax credit; (4) more favorable disposition of unwanted assets, e.g., through a tax-free spin-off (see Chapter 11 supra); and (5) greater flexibility with regard to earnings and profits and shareholder distributions. Many of these tax advantages have been limited. See Chapter 15.

Notwithstanding the tax advantages that sometimes attend multiple corporations, affiliated groups of corporations often find it desirable to file as though they constitute a single corporation. Under §§1501-1504, affiliated groups of corporations are given a privilege of making a single consolidated tax return that (roughly speaking) allows them to be treated as a single corporation for tax purposes. Only corporations controlled by a common parent corporation may make the election. Thus, if *B,* an individual, owns the stock of *X* Corp. and *Y* Corp., the two corporations may not file a consolidated return. If *B* owns the stock of *H* Corp., which owns the stock of *X* Corp. and *Y* Corp., then *X* Corp., *Y* Corp., and *H* Corp. can file a consolidated return.

Once the election is made for a taxable year, the corporations must continue to file on a consolidated basis unless the Commissioner consents to a termination or the common parent corporation is no longer in existence. Pursuant to a broad statutory grant (§1502), the Treasury has promulgated detailed regulations that often provide, for corporations filing consolidated returns, different rules than normally apply under the Code. These regulations constitute the "law" of consolidated returns. Under §1501, a group electing to file a consolidated return consents to these regulations.

NOTES

1. *Eligibility for filing.* A consolidated return may be filed by an "affiliated group" of corporations. Under §1504, that term means certain "includible" corporations linked through specified stock ownership requirements. Most corporations are includible, with certain exceptions such as tax-exempt corporations, insurance companies, certain foreign corporations, regulated investment companies, and S corporations. But see United States Padding Corp. v. Commissioner, 865 F.2d 750 (6th Cir. 1989) (subsidiary formed to comply with foreign government practice and policy was an includible corporation). The stock ownership provision of §1504 requires one or more chains of includible corporations connected to a common parent such that (a) stock with at least 80 percent of the voting power of all classes of stock and at least 80 percent of the value of each includible corporation (other than the common parent) must be owned directly by one or more of the other includible corporations, and (b) the common parent must also meet the 80 percent tests with respect to at least one of the other includible corporations. See Alumax, Inc. v. Commissioner, 109 T.C. 133 (1997) (court required to interpret the 80 perent voting control requirement of §1502(a)). Note that the direct ownership requirement rules out corporations owned by an individual or group of individuals or by a nonincludible corporation. If a consolidated return election is made by an affiliated group, all includible corporations in the group must file a consolidated return.

Under the stock ownership rules of §1504(a), "stock" does not include certain nonvoting preferred stock. §1504(a)(4). Accordingly, such stock is often used by members of an affiliated group to raise outside equity capital without destroying the right to file a consolidated return. Under §1504(a)(5), options are generally ignored in determining eligibility unless not treating the option as exercised would result in substantial federal tax savings and it is reasonably certain that the option will be exercised. Treas. Regs. §1.1504-4.

Even with a statutory definition of "affiliated group," some courts have denied the privilege of filing consolidated returns to a corporation that acquires another corporation solely to use its tax attributes on a consolidated return. For example, in Elko Realty Co. v. Commissioner, 29 T.C. 1012, aff'd per curiam, 260 F.2d 949 (3d Cir. 1958), a successful corporation acquired the stock of two other corporations that had been operating at a loss. Relying in part on the business purpose principle of Gregory v. Helvering, page 394 supra, the court denied the parent's right to file a consolidated return in the absence of a business purpose for the acquisition. See also R.P. Collins & Co. v. United States, 303 F.2d 142 (1st Cir. 1962) (§269 used to deny loss deductions on consolidated return). But see Zanesville Investment Co. v. Commissioner, 335 F.2d 507 (6th Cir. 1964) (consolidated returns permitted when postaffiliation losses of some members offset income from other members).

In light of the current regulations that restrict the use of preaffiliation and some postaffiliation net operating losses regardless of acquisition purpose, is the approach of the court in *Elko Realty* appropriate? See Treas. Regs. §§1.1502-15, 1.1502-21T, 1.1502-22T. Even when these restrictions apply, the regulations do not deny consolidated return treatment as did the court in *Elko Realty*.

2. *Election to file a consolidated return and other accounting considerations.* A consolidated return may be filed only if all affiliated corporations consent. §1502. Once an election is made, the affiliated group must continue to file on a consolidated basis unless the Commissioner grants permission to discontinue for "good cause." Treas. Regs. §1.1502-75(a)(2). Treas. Regs. §1502-20 (deconsolidation).

The taxable year for a consolidated return is based on the common parent's annual accounting period. In general, subsidiaries must adopt the parent's period. Treas. Regs. §1.1502-76(a)(1). But the subsidiaries are not required to adopt the accounting method of the common parent. Instead, each member of the group employs the method that would be used if it were filing a separate return. Treas. Regs. §1.1502-17(a).

Each member of an affiliated group is severally liable for the entire tax. This liability cannot be avoided or reduced by intercompany agreements but such agreements will be effective as between the parties and are frequently used by affiliated group members. See Rev. Rul. 73-605, 1973-2 CB 109 and Regs. §1.1502-6(c).

3. *Computation of a consolidated return: in general.* The basic concept underlying the treatment of a consolidated return is that the affiliated group is in effect a single taxable entity, notwithstanding the existence of multiple corporate forms. As such, the tax liability ought to be based on dealings with "outsiders" rather than dealings within the group. With this

"single taxpayer" approach in mind, consider the basic computational features.

The tax liability of an affiliated group filing a consolidated return is based on "consolidated taxable income." To determine the consolidated taxable income, the separate taxable income (or loss) of each group member is determined separately (subject to special rules relating to intercompany transactions and distributions, accounting methods, etc.). Treas. Regs. §1.1502-12. These separate incomes are then combined. In addition, each member's capital gains and losses, charitable contributions, §1231 transactions, and net operating losses are aggregated for purposes of applying the various statutory limitations. Treas. Regs. §1.1502-11. The gross consolidated tax liability is then computed in accordance with §§11, 541, 531, 1201, etc., on the consolidated taxable income. Finally, any consolidated investment credit or foreign tax credit is subtracted. Treas. Regs. §1.1502-2.

4. *Computation of a consolidated return: intercompany transactions.* One of the most significant aspects of the consolidated return regulations is the treatment of intercompany transfers. The regulations distinguish (a) deferred intercompany transactions, in which the purchaser must capitalize the expense, from (b) all other intercompany transactions for which payments are currently deductible. With respect to the latter category, the regulations require the payor and the payee to deduct and include the amounts within the same taxable year. The net effect is a "wash" so far as the group's consolidated taxable income is concerned.

The regulations' treatment of deferred intercompany transactions is more complicated. These transactions include sales or exchanges of property and the performance of services for which payments must be capitalized. The regulations adopt a "suspense account" concept. By deferring the "selling" corporation's gain or loss until the occurrence of certain specified events, the regulations attempt to match the inclusion of gain or the reporting of loss by the selling corporation with appropriate depreciation deductions by the purchasing corporation. Treas. Regs. §1.1502-13T. Thus, gain or loss is reported by the selling corporation at the same rate at which the asset is depreciated. In the case of inventory, Treas. Regs. §1.1502-18 generally taxes the gain on intercompany sales of inventory to the selling corporation, but only when the purchasing corporation sells the property to an outsider.

Events that trigger the recognition of the deferred gain or loss include the sale of property by the purchasing corporation to an outsider; the departure of the selling or purchasing member from the affiliated group prior to sale to an outsider; in some cases, the filing of separate returns by affiliated group members; and worthlessness, collection, or redemption of debt instruments used to purchase the property. If the acquired property is sold by the purchasing member on the installment method under §453, deferred gain is reported by the selling member as collections are made by the purchasing member. If the selling member is a dealer, however, sale by the purchasing member to an outside purchaser on the installment method must be reported by the selling member immediately. The selling member cannot defer gain on the purchasing member's resale. Treas. Regs. §1.1302-13T(m).

5. *Computation of a consolidated return: intercompany distributions.* Consistent with the theme that an affiliated group is a single taxable entity, dividend distributions between members of the group are eliminated from the computation of consolidated taxable income. Treas. Regs. §1.1502-13(f). The "investment basis adjustment" rules generally require that the parent's basis in the common stock of a subsidiary be reduced by the amount of intercompany dividend distributions, Treas. Regs. §1.1502-32. This reduction will increase the parent's gain (or decrease its loss) on any eventual sale of the stock. The theory behind this downward adjustment in basis is similar to that underlying the treatment of S corporations. See Chapter 16. Because the parent's stock basis is adjusted upward when a subsidiary earns income, the distribution from that subsidiary must decrease the basis. In keeping with that theory, there is no basis adjustment for distributions from years before 1966 or from post-1966 years in which no consolidated return was filed since for both of these situations there was no previous upward basis adjustment.

Nondividend distributions under §301(c)(2) and (3) also reduce basis and are tax free to the distributee. Distributions of property are governed by rules similar to those in §§301 and 311, except that any gain recognized by the distributing corporation is governed by the intercompany transaction rules discussed in Note 4 supra. Treas. Regs. §1.1502-13.

Distributions in liquidation are treated under the normal liquidation rules, see Chapter 7; Treas. Regs. §1.1502-13.

6. *Investment basis accounts and excess loss accounts.* In accordance with the single taxable entity concept, the consolidated return regulations attempt to avoid a duplicate recognition of investment gain (or loss) by a parent corporation that is attributable to earnings (or losses) of a subsidiary that have already been accounted for on the consolidated return. The "investment basis adjustment" (IBA) provisions of Treas. Regs. §1.1502-32 require a parent to make annual adjustments to its basis in the stock of the subsidiaries. The result is a fluctuating stock basis. In general, basis is increased for the "adjusted taxable income" of the subsidiary and for the subsidiary's share of any consolidated net operating (or capital) losses that were able to be carried back to a prior year. Basis is decreased by any utilized losses attributable to the subsidiary and by most distributions under §301. The regulations specifically set forth whether the additions and subtractions from basis apply to common or preferred (if any) stock. For an example of the adjustments required by Treas. Regs. §1.1502-32 with respect to depreciation deductions, see Woods Investment Co. v. Commissioner, 85 T.C. 274 (1985).

Basis adjustments are made in other contexts as well. See, e.g., §301(c)(2), discussed at page 120 supra, and §1367, discussed at page 162 infra, but in these situations basis cannot be reduced below zero. The IBA rules do permit a negative basis for the parent's stock in the subsidiary. This negative basis is defined by Treas. Regs. §1.1502-32(e)(1) as an "excess loss account" (ELA). The account will create income in the hands of the parent upon the occurrence of certain specified events. Treas. Regs. §1.1502-19. For example, assume *P* has a stock basis of $30 in the stock of *S,* its subsidiary, and that *P* and *S* file a consolidated return. If *S* suffers a $50 loss that is fully used to offset some of the group's consolidated taxable income, the ELA account will be $20. If *P* later sells the *S* stock for $20, a $40 gain must be recognized — the $20 sales proceeds plus the $20 ELA. The tax returns reporting loss deductions of $50 and gain of $40 will correspond to the economic result to *P* of its investment in *S* — $30 paid for the stock less $20 received on the sale.

7. *Limitations on consolidated reporting.* Congress and the Treasury have perceived a danger in consolidated reporting when a loss corporation is acquired to apply its net operating loss deductions (or other favorable tax attributes) against income of profitable affiliated group members. The problem here is the same as that raised in a reorganization or purchase context under §§381 and 382. See pages 504-515 supra. Indeed, when applicable, those provisions govern the treatment of affiliated group members. Members of a consolidated group are treated as a single entity (i.e., as if the group's subsidiaries were unincorporated). Treas. Regs. §1.1502-91T(a)(1). See generally Treas. Regs. §1.1502-91T to -99T.

The regulations also describe the parent change method, focusing on ownership changes with respect to a loss group's common parent stock. Treas. Regs. §1.1502-92(b)(1). For example, suppose *B* owns all the stock of *P* Corp., which files a consolidated return with its 80 percent owned subsidiary, Subco. Individual *C* owns the other 20 percent of Subco. During year 1, the *P* Corp. group incurs a $200 consolidated NOL, attributable entirely to Subco. In year 2, *B* sells 60 percent of *P* Corp. to *D,* an unrelated individual. *C* retains the 20 percent minority interest in Subco. Because the consolidated group is treated as a separate entity for purposes of §382, the sale of stock from *B* to *D* triggers §382 (i.e., *D*'s ownership in the *P* Corp. group has gone from 0 percent to 60 percent) even though *D*'s ownership in Subco would not trigger §382 (i.e., after the purchase *D* owns 60 percent × 80 percent, or 48 percent of Subco). Under §382, the *P* Corp. group's use of Subco's NOL will be limited. See page 506 supra.

The regulations also provide for an antiabuse rule (i.e., the modified parent change method), which in some cases counts the acquisition of a subsidiary's stock by a shareholder of the parent in testing for a §382(g) change of ownership in the parent. Treas. Regs. §1.1502-93T(b)(2). For example, suppose an existing shareholder of the parent owns 10 percent of the parent's stock. If that shareholder acquires an additional 35 percent of the parent's stock and 16 percent of the subsidiary's stock, an ownership change is triggered.

Special rules apply to new members entering or leaving a loss group. Treas. Regs. §§1.1502-94T (entering members), 1.1502-95T (departing members).

In calculating the §382 limitation, the value of the stock of each member of the loss group (other than stock owned directly or indirectly by another member) is multiplied by the federal long-term tax-exempt rate. For example, suppose *B* owns all the stock of *P* Corp., which owns 80 percent of the stock of *L* Corp. *C*, who is unrelated to *B*, owns the other 20 percent of the *L* Corp. stock. *P* Corp. and *L* Corp. file a consolidated return. *P* Corp.'s stock has a value of $1,000, and *L* Corp.'s stock has a value of $500. *L* Corp. has an NOL of $600 incurred while a member of the *P* Corp. group. *B* sells 100 percent of the *P* Corp. stock to *C*. The sale is an ownership change for the *P* Corp. group, triggering §382. The consolidated §382 limitation is the product of the long-term tax-exempt rate and $1,100, the sum of *P* Corp.'s $1,000 value and the $100 value of the *L* Corp. stock not owned by a member of the *P* Corp. group (i.e., *C*). If the long-term tax-exempt rate is 10 percent, then the *P* Corp. group can offset up to $110 of consolidated taxable income each year with *L* Corp.'s NOL.

Other rules under §382 generally apply in the consolidated group context to the entire group. For example, the ability to use an NOL is increased if a loss group has a net unrealized built-in gain that is recognized during the five-year recognition period. Treas. Regs. §1.1502-92(h). See page 514 supra. Also, the business continuity requirement of §382 is applied to the group as a whole. Treas. Regs. §1.1502-93T(d).

While §382 does apply to consolidated groups, the regulations impose an additional limitation on the group's ability to use the NOLs of one member to offset consolidated taxable income. This limitation is known as the "separate return limitation year," or SRLY. Treas. Regs. §1.1502-1(f). Generally, preaffiliation losses cannot be utilized to offset postaffiliation consolidated taxable income, except to the extent that the new member of the group contributes to the consolidated income. Treas. Regs. §1.1502-21T(c). A SRLY member's contribution to consolidated taxable income is determined on a cumulative basis over the period during which the SRLY member is a member of the consolidated group. Also, the SRLY limitation can be applied on a subgroup basis to SRLY members who were previously affiliated in another group and who continue to be affiliated in the new group. Similar rules exist for other tax attributes. See Treas. Regs. §1.1502-4T(f b) (foreign tax credit carryovers), §1.1502-22(c) (capital loss carryovers). The SRLY rule appears to duplicate the §382 limitation, but there are situations in which the SRLY rule applies while §382 does not.

For example, suppose *B*, an individual, and *P* Corp. each owns 50 percent of *L* Corp. stock. *L* Corp. has NOLs. If *P* Corp. purchases an additional 30 percent of the *L* Corp. stock from *B,* no ownership change has occurred under §382 because no shareholder of *P* Corp. has increased ownership in *L* Corp. by more than 50 percentage points. But even though §382 does not limit the use of *L* Corp.'s losses by the *P* Corp. group if it files a consolidated return, the SRLY rule limits the use of *L* Corp.'s preconsolidation NOLs by the *P* Corp. group. Under Treas. Regs. §1.1502-21T(c), the deduction of the SRLY loss by the *P* Corp. group is limited to the taxable income of the member with the SRLY loss (i.e., *L* Corp.). When the acquired corporation with a SRLY loss is part of a group of related corporations, the taxable income of this SRLY subgroup can be offset by the SRLY loss. Treas. Regs. §1.1502-21(c)(2).

If a corporation with a SRLY loss is acquired in a transaction that triggers a §382 ownership change, then §382 applies separately to the new loss member rather than on a consolidated basis. Suppose in the example above that *P* Corp. initially owns no stock of *L* Corp. but then acquires 100 percent of *L* Corp., which has a SRLY loss. This acquisition of *L* Corp. triggers §382 because the shareholders of *P* Corp., which owned 0 percent of *L* Corp. prior to the acquisition, own 100 percent after the acquisition. Although §382 applies, because *L* Corp. has a SRLY loss §382 does not apply on a consolidated basis. Instead, the §382 limitation applies to *L* Corp. separately. This separate §382 application is in addition to, and not in lieu of, the SRLY limitation. Accordingly, if the §382 limitation would allow the consolidated group to deduct a portion of *L* Corp.'s NOL but in fact *L* Corp. produces no consolidated taxable income under the SRLY rule, then no deduction is permitted.

Suppose a profitable corporation acquires another corporation, not because it has any net operating losses but rather because it has a large debt that is about to become worthless. Or perhaps the corporation to be acquired has assets that it is about to sell at a loss. The consolidated return regulations discourage the acquisition of a corporation with such "built-in" losses when the purpose of the acquisition is the use of those losses to offset postaffiliation income attributable to other members of the consolidated group. Treas. Regs. §1.1502-15T. The reach of these regulations can be significant. For example, normal operating expenses of a cash basis subsidiary that accrued in a preaffiliation year but were paid in a consolidated return year were held subject to the built-in deduction limitations. Rev. Rul. 79-279, 1979-2 C.B. 316.

The regulations define "built-in" deductions as those that are "economically accrued" by a corporation in a SRLY prior to acquisition but that are realized in a tax sense after the acquisition in a consolidated return year. These deductions are not disallowed by the regulations; instead, they are subject to the §382 and SRLY limitations on the carryover of preaffiliation losses. See §382(h). Some exceptions to these "built-in" loss limitations are made if the realization of the loss does not occur for at least five years or if the aggregate basis of the corporation's assets does not exceed the value of those assets by more than 15 percent. Finally, no restrictions are placed on the acquirer's own built-in deductions.

For the rules governing "outbound" transactions (i.e., those in which a corporation moves from a consolidated to a separate return), see generally Treas. Regs. §1.1502-20T(b).

8. *Advantages and disadvantages of consolidated reporting.* With the basic framework of the consolidated return regulations in mind, consider the advantages and disadvantages of consolidated reporting. The advantages include (a) using losses of an affiliate to offset income from another affiliate, (b) making tax-free intercorporate distributions, and (c) deferring gain (or loss) on intercompany transactions (e.g., sales).

Among the disadvantages of filing a consolidated return are (a) being subject to consistency requirements for election and accounting periods (although Treas. Regs. §1.1502-17(a) permits separate accounting methods for each member in accordance with §446); (b) sharing a single graduated tax rate, accumulated earnings tax credit, and other special exemptions and credits; (c) being subject to a binding election; and (d) complying with complex consolidated return regulations.

PROBLEMS

13-5. Forco, a foreign corporation that cannot make use of U.S. tax benefits, is planning a new U.S. venture to be operated through *L* Corp. It is expected that *L* Corp. will generate tax losses in its first several years. To make use of the expected losses, Forco finds a U.S. partner, *P* Corp., a profitable U.S. corporation. Forco and *P* Corp. form *L* Corp., with Forco receiving preferred stock with a fair market value of $800,000 and *P* Corp. receiving common stock with a fair market value of $200,000. The preferred stock is preferred as to dividends and on liquidation, but it has an adjustable rate feature whereby the level of dividends is set by reference to certain yields of U.S. Treasury obligations. In addition, this preferred stock is convertible into another class of preferred stock, identical in all respects to the outstanding preferred except that the adjustable rate feature references different U.S. Treasury obligations. Can *L* Corp. and *P* Corp. file a consolidated return allowing *P* Corp. to offset its profits with *L* Corp.'s losses? Consider §1504(a).

13-6. *P* Corp. has three wholly owned subsidiaries having the following items of income and loss:

	X	Y	Z
Ordinary business income (loss)	$300	($80)	$ 40
§1231 gains (loss)	80	40	(40)
Capital gains (loss)	20	40	(100)
§170 contributions	60		

What is the group's consolidated taxable income?

13-7. In Problem 13-6, what are the tax consequences of the following transactions?

    a. *P* Corp. leases computer software from *X* Corp., paying an annual $300 royalty.

    b. *P* Corp. pays interest of $60 to *Y* Corp. on an intercorporate loan.

    c. In year 1, *P* Corp. sells land with a basis of $300 and a fair market value of $400 to *Z* Corp. *Z* Corp. resells the land in year 2 to an unrelated party for $650.

    d. Suppose in (c) that *Z* Corp. sells the property on the installment method.

    e. Suppose in (c) that the property sold to *Z* Corp. is depreciable property that *Z* Corp. uses in its trade or business. *Z* Corp. depreciates the property using a straight-line method over 10 years.

13-8. Discuss the tax consequences of the following situations.

    a. *P* Corp. owns all the stock of *X* Corp., with which it files a consolidated return. *P* Corp.'s basis in the *X* Corp. stock is $100. In year 1, *X* Corp. earns $30 and makes no distribution. In year 2, *X* Corp. earns $20 and makes a $50 distribution to *P* Corp.

    b. Suppose in (a) that in year 1, *P* Corp. earns $200 and *X* Corp. has a net operating loss of $160. In year 2, *P* Corp. earns $100 and *X* Corp. suffers a $140 loss. *P* Corp. sells its *X* Corp. stock in year 3 for $80.

14

Penalty Provisions

The heart and soul of subchapter C is that distributed corporate earnings from operations should be taxed twice — once when the corporation earns them and again when they are distributed. Furthermore, it is Congress's intention that both taxes should be at ordinary income rates. The propriety or impropriety of these guiding principles has been explored in Chapter 8.

It is of course not true that Congress intended that all corporate earnings be taxed twice at ordinary income rates. For example, *X* Corp. might earn $10,000, which is taxed as ordinary income at corporate rates. Rather than distributing the earnings in the form of a dividend, *X* Corp. might accumulate the earnings, thereby increasing the value of the outstanding stock. Shareholder *A* might then sell stock, arrange for *X* Corp. to redeem stock under §302, or liquidate *X* Corp. under §331. All three of these possibilities would permit *A* to receive, directly or indirectly, the corporate earnings at capital gains rates. Notice that if any of these events is undertaken by *A*'s estate, there may be no gain recognized. Moreover, so long as *X* Corp. makes no distribution, the cash that otherwise would have been paid in taxes by a dividend-receiving shareholder can continue to earn income, thereby providing shareholders with the benefits of deferral.

Aware that subchapter C contains the seeds of its own circumvention, Congress has enacted various penalty provisions to keep taxpayers on the straight and narrow. In this chapter we will consider three: the accumulated earnings tax (§§531-537), the personal holding company tax (§§541-547), and the collapsible corporations provision (§341). The first two are taxes levied on the corporation in addition to normal corporate taxes (e.g., §§11 and 55). The collapsible corporations provision exacts its penalty by turning what would otherwise be a shareholder's capital gains income into ordinary income.

A. ACCUMULATED EARNINGS TAX

What tax pressures are there on corporations and their shareholders to accumulate income? Historically corporate tax rates have been lower than individual tax rates. Prior to 1982, the maximum rate for individuals was 70 percent, while corporations were taxed at a 46 percent maximum rate. This differential led some individuals to incorporate their businesses so as to accumulate earnings at the corporate level for eventual distribution at a time when the individual was in a lower tax bracket. During the period of accumulation, the taxpayer might gain access to the earnings through loans. Even with a 39.6 percent top rate for individuals and a 35 corporate rate, accumulation can be an attractive strategy. Once a corporation has earned and paid tax on income, the decision whether to distribute is only partially related to any differential between corporate and individual tax rates. The decision is also related to two factors — deferral and the capital gains/ordinary income differential. Accumulation allows the corporation to postpone payment of taxes that would be due on distribution, enabling it to invest the amount that would have been paid in taxes. For example, suppose a corporation has $1,000 available for distribution. Suppose further that the corporation will be taxed on income generated by the $1,000 at a 35 percent rate while the shareholder is taxable at a 31 percent rate. The fact that the individual rate is less than the corporate rate does not necessarily mean that the corporation should distribute the $1,000. If there is a distribution, the $1,000 itself is taxable to the shareholders (albeit at a 31 percent rate), resulting in only $690 available to generate income.

Compounding the incentive to avoid a shareholder-level tax on corporate earnings available for distribution is the capital gains/ordinary income differential (when it exists). A shareholder has an incentive to capture corporate earnings through transactions that will produce capital gains — sale, redemption, or liquidation — rather than through a distribution. In the example above, if the corporation does not distribute the $1,000, the value of the corporation's stock increases by $1,000, which can be realized by the shareholders at a capital gains rate upon eventual disposition. There may be no tax on the sale of the shareholder's stock following the shareholder's death. §1014.

The accumulated earnings tax is a penalty tax imposed by Congress to discourage the use of a corporation to accumulate earnings in order to shelter individual shareholders from receiving dividends taxable at the shareholder level. The motive triggering the tax is the accumulation of earnings beyond the reasonable needs of the business — a question of fact turning on subjective intent. The base of the accumulated earnings tax in any taxable year is the corporation's "accumulated taxable income" for that year, a term that must be distinguished from "earnings and profits" either of the current year or accumulated from prior years. Section 535 defines "accumulated taxable income" as taxable income less (1) the dividends-paid deduction of §561 and (2) the unused portion, if any, of the one-time accumulated earnings credit ($250,000 for most corporations). §535(c). The credit generally allows accumulation of $250,000 with impunity. Certain adjustments are made to taxable income under §535(b) to account for the fact that taxable income does not necessarily reflect dividend-paying capacity. Accordingly, taxable income is reduced by income taxes paid. Taxable income also is reduced by nondeductible charitable contributions, capital losses, net capital gain, and the taxes attributable thereto. Ignored in the computation of accumulated taxable income are intercorporate dividends-received deductions, net operating losses, partially tax-exempt interest, and capital loss carryovers since they merely affect the computation of tax liability but do not absorb cash available for dividends. Section 531 imposes a 39.6 percent tax on accumulated taxable income.

The accumulated earnings tax is essentially focused on cash available for distribution. Only cash that is not needed or used for the reasonable needs of the business is considered available for distribution. It follows that if cash is made unavailable for distribution to shareholders because it is invested in other assets not needed in the business, these unnecessary assets may be counted as unreasonably accumulated and available for distribution. Treas. Regs. §1.537-2. For example, the IRS is likely to maintain that cash used to make loans to shareholders or their relatives or to purchase a portfolio of stocks or properties unrelated to the corporation's business is the equivalent of cash on hand that could have and should have been paid out to shareholders. But if a corporation's earnings are used to buy a new business, to expand the present business, to meet working capital needs, to retire stock of a minority shareholder, or to pay off business debt, the corporation may be able to avoid imposition of the accumulated earnings tax. A thinly capitalized business with debt borrowed from outside sources may not have difficulty with the §531 tax since the repayment of debt is a reasonable business need. It has been held, however, that the §531 penalty cannot be imposed on a corporation that could have easily borrowed funds but chose instead to forgo dividends and build up cash to meet its business needs. See, e.g., Myron's Enterprises v. United States, 548 F.2d 331, 335 n.6 (9th Cir. 1977).

NOTES

1. *Unreasonable accumulations.* Section 532(a) imposes the accumulated earnings tax on corporations that accumulate to avoid taxes. Section 533 presumes that accumulation "beyond the reasonable needs of the business" reflects the improper tax avoidance motive. What constitutes the "reasonable needs of the business" is discussed in the Notes that follow. But even if we know the reasonable needs of the business, to determine

whether an accumulation is improper we need to know more than the earnings and profits account. When a corporation accumulates income in a year under scrutiny, it is not enough to compare reasonable business needs with earnings and profits to determine whether current accumulation is appropriate. The earnings and profits account may be misleadingly large or small. See Technalysis Corp. v. Commissioner, 101 T.C. 397(1993) (large accumulations evaluated in context of risky and highly competitive business).

In Ivan Allen Co. v. United States, 422 U.S. 617 (1975), the taxpayer, which engaged in the business of selling office furniture and supplies, was profitable during the years in question but paid dividends that were substantially less than taxable income. The parties agreed that taxpayer had reasonable business needs for operating capital. The parties further stipulated that if taxpayer's marketable securities were valued at cost, there was no unreasonable accumulation under §533(a). However, if the marketable securities were evaluated at fair market value, the taxpayer would be deemed to have accumulated earnings beyond the reasonable business needs.

The Court ruled that the securities should be evaluated at fair market value and so the taxpayer was guilty of unreasonable accumulation. While unrealized appreciation does not increase a corporation's accumulated taxable income under §§531 and 535 or its earnings and profits, the unrealized appreciation can serve as evidence that current accumulations of earnings and profits are unreasonable because the stock could be sold at fair market value to meet the needs of the business. The Court emphasizes the liquidity of the Xerox stock as the key factor. Should the result be different if the taxpayer had illiquid investment assets? Presumably, the valuation of the assets will reflect their illiquidity.

The Court rejected the taxpayer's argument, stating that looking at fair market value in effect violates the realization doctrine by forcing the taxpayer to sell the stock to meet the conceded business needs. The realization doctrine does not reach that far. The unrealized appreciation is used solely as a yardstick to determine if current accumulations are necessary. Moreover, the possibility of forced sale is too speculative because a taxpayer might not have to sell the property (e.g., the corporation might be able to borrow on the security of the property).

Finally, in dicta that are relevant in many areas of taxation, the Court was not bothered by the fact that its decision may conflict with standard accounting practice, noting: "The Court has not hesitated to apply the congressional policy underlying a revenue statute even when it does conflict with an established accounting practice."

Contrast *Ivan Allen* with Electric Regulator Corp. v. Commissioner, 336 F.2d 339 (2d Cir. 1964), in which earnings and profits at first glance seemed ample to meet business needs, but closer analysis revealed that prior earnings and profits had been reinvested in the corporation and that current accumulations were necessary to meet business needs. Indeed, as the court in *Electric Regulator* pointed out, had the corporation made the dividend distributions the IRS required, corporate assets would have been insufficient to meet reasonable business needs. In addition to focusing on accumulation of earnings and profits, it is equally important to consider what assets are on hand to meet the reasonable business needs.

2. *Burden of proof: presumptions.* Under §532, a corporation is subject to the accumulated earnings tax if it is "formed or availed of for the purpose of avoiding the income tax with respect to its shareholders . . . by permitting earnings and profits to accumulate instead of being divided or distributed." What is the relationship between this provision and the statutory presumptions — if that is what they are — of §533(a) (unreasonable accumulation shall be "determinative of the purpose to avoid the income tax with respect to shareholders" unless the corporation proves to the contrary by a preponderance of evidence) and §533(b) (if corporation is a mere holding company or investment company, this fact shall be "prima facie evidence of the purpose to avoid the income tax")?

Section 534 allows the taxpayer to shift the burden of proof to the government in Tax Court proceedings. Before mailing a notice of deficiency, the government may send a notification informing the taxpayer that the proposed notice of deficiency includes an amount imposed under §531. See Myco Industries v. Commissioner, 98 T.C. 270 (1992) (Commissioner's notice was not adequate to shift burden of proof to taxpayer because the notice failed to state the years for which the tax was asserted). The taxpayer may then submit a statement setting forth the grounds on which it will rely to prove it has not been accumulating unreasonably. The Tax Court will rule in advance on the sufficiency of the taxpayer's §534(c) statement (Rule 142 of Rules of Practice). If the statement is sufficient or if the notification has not been sent by the government, the burden is on the Service. Why is this procedure limited to Tax Court proceedings? For a §534(c) statement held insufficient because of vagueness, see Rutter v. Commissioner, 81 T.C. 937 (1983).

The purpose behind the notification procedure of §534 presumably is to encourage administrative resolution of accumulated earnings tax issues. We know that the burden of proof will be on the Commissioner for failure to notify the taxpayer of an impending deficiency notice based on §531. Where should the burden be placed if the Commissioner sends notification but then asserts a deficiency before the taxpayer has replied to the notification? See Manson Western Corp. v. Commissioner, 76 T.C. 1161 (1981).

In United States v. Donruss Co., 393 U.S. 297 (1969), the government argued that to rebut the presumption of §533(a) the taxpayer must establish by a preponderance of the evidence that tax avoidance was not "one of the purposes" for accumulating earnings beyond the reasonable needs of the business. In contrast, the taxpayer argued that the presumption could be rebutted by showing that tax avoidance was not the "dominant, controlling, or impelling" reason for the accumulation. The Court accepted the government's interpretation, saying that the taxpayer's interpretation "would exacerbate the problems that Congress was trying to avoid" by the statutory emphasis on the reasonableness of the accumulation rather than on the "vagaries of corporate motive." The taxpayer's construction "would allow taxpayers to escape the tax when it is proved that at least one other motive was equal to tax avoidance. We doubt that such a determination can be made with any accuracy, and it is certainly one which will depend almost exclusively on the interested testimony of corporate management." 393 U.S. at 308. In Technalysis Corp. v. Commissioner, 101 T.C. 397 (1993), the taxpayer won in spite of the court's finding that accumulation exceeded reasonable business needs because the court found no tax-avoidance purpose.

Will a finding of a shareholder deadlock be sufficient to rebut the §533 presumption of an improper purpose? In Atlantic Properties v. Commissioner, 519 F.2d 1233 (1st Cir. 1975), four of the five shareholders representing 75 percent of the vote wanted a dividend distribution, while one shareholder representing the other 25 percent wanted to accumulate. The corporate by-laws required an 80 percent vote for dividend distribution. The court found the corporation subject to the accumulated earnings tax. The same result was reached in Hedberg-Freidheim Contracting Co. v. Commissioner, 251 F.2d 839 (8th Cir. 1958), in which two shareholders were deadlocked. Cf. Casey v. Commissioner, 267 F.2d 26 (2d Cir. 1959), in which two shareholders were deadlocked but an unreasonable accumulation was not found.

3. *Reasonable needs of the business: anticipated needs.* Section 537(a)(1), providing that the term "reasonable needs of the business" includes the "reasonably anticipated needs of the business," was enacted in 1954. The Senate Report on the 1954 Code (page 318) says of §537:

> It is intended that this provision will make clear that there is no requirement that the accumulated earnings be invested immediately in the business so long as there is an indication that future needs of the business require such accumulation. In any case where there exists a definite plan for the investment of earnings and profits, such corporation need not necessarily consummate these plans in a relatively short period after the close of the taxable year. However, where the future needs of the business are uncertain or vague, or the plans for the future use of the accumulations are indefinite, the amendment does not prevent application of the accumulated earnings tax.

The Senate Report also states (pages 69-70):

> If the retention of earnings is justified as of the close of the taxable year, subsequent events should not be used for the purpose of showing that the

retention was unreasonable in such year. However, subsequent events may be considered to determine whether the corporation actually intended to consummate the plans for which the earnings were accumulated.

For cases in which §537(a)(1) has been construed, see Motor Fuel Carriers v. United States, 559 F.2d 1348 (5th Cir. 1977) (reversing Tax Court finding that plans too indefinite though later consummated); Cheyenne Newspapers v. Commissioner, 494 F.2d 429 (10th Cir. 1974) (accumulations prohibited for contingencies that were unreasonable); Bahan Textile Machinery Co. v. United States, 453 F.2d 1100 (4th Cir. 1972) (plans too vague and loans to shareholder's relatives indicate prohibited purpose); Sterling Distributors v. United States, 313 F.2d 803 (5th Cir. 1963) (plans sufficiently definite even though later abandoned); Vulcan Steam Forging Co. v. Commissioner, 35 T.C.M. (CCH) 110 (1976) (possible relocation of business justified accumulations for three years, but not for fourth year when relocation plans were abandoned). See also Myron's Enterprises v. United States, 548 F.2d 331 (9th Cir. 1977), in which taxpayer-lessee had made offers for six years to purchase property from lessor and had, during the six years, accumulated funds for the purchase and remodeling. The court of appeals found the plans were sufficiently definite and reversed the district court, which had held that reasonable needs must be reduced by the amount the sole shareholder would have been willing to lend the corporation.

In this era of high damage awards, can a corporation claim that accumulation is necessary to protect against liability? Treas. Regs. §1.537-1(f) sets forth a list of factors for determining whether an accumulation for anticipated product liability losses is reasonable. Some of the factors include (1) previous product liability experience, (2) the extent of commercial product liability insurance, (3) the income tax consequences of the taxpayer's product liability losses, and (4) the taxpayer's future potential liability in light of reasonable expansion plans.

4. *Reasonable needs of the business: working capital needs.* The cases of Bardahl Manufacturing Corp. v. Commissioner, 24 T.C.M. (CCH) 1030 (1965), and Bardahl International Corp. v. Commissioner, 25 T.C.M. (CCH) 935 (1966), created a statistical formula for determining the reasonably anticipated working capital needs of a business for an operating cycle. The operating cycle is the period of time required to convert cash into inventory, inventory into accounts receivable, and accounts receivable into cash. For example, if three months elapse from the purchase of the inventory to the receipt of payment in cash for the goods manufactured and sold, then the working capital needs are 25 percent of total annual operating costs and costs of goods sold. The length of the cycle depends on the type of business involved. In addition to the amount of working capital so determined, *Bardahl I* recognized the need for funds to pay for such items as the cost of plant expansion, the stockpiling of raw materials, and

notes and other liabilities payable in one year (including accrued income taxes). The *Bardahl* formula is now relied on as a guide to determine permissible accumulations, but it is not always rigidly applied, Thompson Engineering Co. v. Commissioner, 80 T.C. 672 (1983) (*Bardahl* formula inappropriate to measure business needs of mechanical contractor without routine operating cycle), rev'd, 751 F.2d 191 (6th Cir. 1985) (Tax Court impermissibly substituted its judgment for that of taxpayer). In Delaware Trucking Co. v. Commissioner, 32 T.C.M. (CCH) 105 (1973), the court found as reasonable the working capital needs for one cycle plus an additional 75 percent of that amount for anticipated increased labor costs and other costs resulting from inflation. See also Hughes, Inc. v. Commissioner, 90 T.C. 1 (1988) (working capital less than business needs; no accumulated earnings tax liability).

5. *Reasonable business needs: diversification.* What is "the" business, as this term is used in §533(a)? The regulations state that a corporation's business "is not merely that which it has previously carried on but includes, in general, any line of business which it may undertake." Treas. Regs. §1.537-3(a). Does this mean that a small grocery store may aspire to become a department store or a nationwide chain of stores — or to monopolize the manufacture and sale of widgets? The regulations under the 1939 Code, Treas. Regs. 118, §39.102-3(a), included the sentence just quoted but went on to warn that "a radical change of business when a considerable surplus has been accumulated may afford evidence of a purpose to avoid the surtax." This sentence was dropped in 1959. In defining "reasonable needs," the regulations speak favorably of an accumulation "to acquire a business enterprise through purchasing stock or assets" but disapprove of "investments in properties or securities which are unrelated to the activities of the business of the taxpayer corporation." Treas. Regs. §§1.537-2(b)(2), 1.537-2(c)(4).

If the business needs of another corporation can be taken into account, must the relationship between the corporations be that of parent-subsidiary, or will a brother-sister affiliation be sufficient? See Treas. Regs. §1.537-2(c)(3); Latchis Theaters v. Commissioner, 214 F.2d 834 (1st Cir. 1954) (accumulations to aid brother-sister corporation not sufficient reason). But compare Inland Terminals v. United States, 477 F.2d 836 (4th Cir. 1973), in which a subsidiary's accumulations to meet the business needs of its parent corporation were held to qualify as reasonable accumulations.

In Chaney & Hope, Inc. v. Commissioner, 80 T.C. 263 (1983), an individual, Mr. Hope, owned all the stock of brother-sister corporations. One corporation was engaged in the construction business; the other held large amounts of liquid assets. The brother-sister corporations were established for a variety of nontax business reasons. Both corporations agreed to indemnify the Travelers Indemnity Co., the company furnishing the bonding required on construction projects. Travelers insisted that both corporations sign the indemnity agreement. The court determined that the accumulations by one corporation to help the other corporation were unreasonable.

In *Chaney & Hope*, the court conceded that the total amount accumulated by the brother-sister corporations was reasonable in light of the bonding requirements. Why then should the taxpayer lose merely because of the nature of the corporate structure when if Mr. Hope had operated with one corporation the accumulation would have been reasonable? Note also that if the corporations had been parent-subsidiary, the accumulation would have been reasonable. Treas. Regs. §1.537-3(b). Through the attribution rules isn't every brother-sister relationship a parent-subsidiary relationship as well? See page 237 supra. Do the attribution rules apply to §531? In Hughes, Inc. v. Commissioner, 90 T.C. 1 (1988), the court held that a corporation is not liable for the accumulated earnings tax when earnings were accumulated to purchase the stock of an affiliated corporation, the taxpayer's primary customer, as part of a strategy to prevent a takeover of the purchased corporation.

6. *Reasonable business needs: payment of corporate debts.* In Helvering v. Chicago Stock Yards Co., 318 U.S. 693 (1943), involving a one-person corporation that was accumulating earnings for the purpose, among others, of paying off certain obligations of its subsidiaries, the Court suggested that the taxpayer's stockholder, had the taxpayer's surplus been distributed to him, could have equally well paid off the obligations in question. Does this suggest that despite a corporation's capital requirements, the §531 tax may be imposed if the earnings could have been distributed to the stockholders and reinvested by them in the corporation? What would this do to the reasonable business needs test in §535(c)? In Smoot Sand & Gravel Corp. v. Commissioner, 241 F.2d 197 (4th Cir. 1957), this suggestion was rejected on a showing that a distribution would have been subject to a tax rate of 89 percent in the shareholder's hands.

If at the time of organization the corporation issues both common stock and notes or bonds to its organizers, is accumulation for the retirement of the debt at or before maturity a reasonable need of the business? Note the reference in Treas. Regs. §1.537-2(b)(3) to a "sinking fund for the purpose of retiring bonds issued by the corporation." In *Chicago Stock Yards Co.*, there is a suggestion that the existence of long-term obligations might not be a satisfactory excuse for the accumulation of surplus if the obligations might be readily refinanced at the due date. Despite this suggestion, the payment of corporate debts is often regarded as a reasonable need of the business without regard to the possibility of refinancing the obligations. See, e.g., Gazette Telegraph Co. v. Commissioner, 19 T.C. 692 (1953), involving a corporation that on organization (a) issued common stock of a par value of $250,000 and 10-year promissory notes of a face amount of $250,000 to its organizers and (b) borrowed $400,000 from a bank, to acquire assets of a net value of about $900,000. Within about four years, both the notes and the bank loan were paid off. The court found that the notes were bona fide, that the capitalization was not too thin, and that the future intended repayment of the obligations was a reasonable need of the business that justified the accumulation of earnings.

7. *Reasonable needs of the business: redemptions.* In general, redemption of common or preferred stock will not be regarded as a proper reason for accumulating surplus. See Pelton Steel Casting Co. v. United States, 251 F.2d 278 (7th Cir. 1958) (accumulation to redeem majority interest shareholder not for reasonable needs of the business). Special circumstances, however, might justify an accumulation for the purpose of reducing shareholders' interests. See Technalysis Corp. v. Commissioner, 101 T.C. 397 (1993) (accumulation for purposes of funding stock buyback program to support market for taxpayer's stock was held reasonable business need); Gazette Publishing Co. v. Self, 103 F. Supp. 779 (E.D. Ark. 1952) (elimination of potentially disruptive minority stock interest); Mountain State Steel Foundries v. Commissioner, 284 F.2d 737 (4th Cir. 1960) (accumulation to redeem stock may be a reasonable business need). More recently, in Technalysis Corp. v. Commissioner, 101 T.C. 397 (1993), the court ruled that a corporation with accumulated earnings beyond its reasonable business needs was not subject to §531 when the accumulation was made to redeem shares at some future time in accordance with a general redemption plan.

See §537(a)(2) and (3) and §537(b) permitting accumulations to redeem stock under §303 (redemption to pay death taxes, etc., discussed at page 206 supra) and under the "excess business holdings" provisions applicable to tax-exempt private foundations.

Suppose X Corp. with accumulated earnings and profits earns $500,000 in year 5. That year X Corp. redeems all the stock of shareholder A. Assume the redemption reduces the current earnings and profits account to zero. See §312(n)(7). Prior to year 5, the accumulated earnings and profits were not deemed unreasonable. Can X Corp. face accumulated earnings tax liability for its year 5 activities if no earnings and profits accumulated in year 5? Recall that the base of the accumulated earnings tax is accumulated taxable income, §535, not earnings and profits for the year.

Even if the taxpayer manages to get rid of its earnings and profits for the year in question, apparently there may still be accumulated earnings tax liability. In GPD, Inc. v. Commissioner, 508 F.2d 1076 (6th Cir. 1974), the sole shareholder followed a pattern, over a period of years, of donating some of his shares of the corporation's stock to charity and later causing the corporation to redeem the stock from the charity. The redemptions in the tax year in question eliminated the corporation's current earnings and profits. The Tax Court held the accumulated earnings tax to be improper for the year. The circuit court reversed and assessed §531 liability. The court reasoned that normally, if there is no surplus cash on hand at the end of a year, there will be no accumulated earnings tax liability. Here, there was none, but there had been cash generated during that year that was found to be used for a nonbusiness purpose, i.e., the redemption of shares from the charity. Because there was accumulated taxable income for the year, the liability was imposed. A distribution of a dividend to shareholders reduces accumulated taxable income (and earnings and profits), §535(a), but a non-pro rata redemption as in *GPD, Inc.* does not reduce accumulated taxable income. See §§535(a), 561, and 562. For a case following *GPD, Inc.*, see Lamark Shipping Agency, Inc. v. Commissioner, 81 T.C.M. (CCH) 284 (1981). Notwithstanding the circuit court's reasoning in *GPD, Inc.*, it does seem odd to proclaim liability for accumulating income when the corporation has not accumulated any income for the year in question. See Doernberg, The Accumulated Earnings Tax: The Relationship between Earnings and Profits and Accumulated Taxable Income in a Redemption Transaction, 34 Fla. L. Rev. 715 (1982). Also, should accumulation for charitable purposes be treated as an impermissible purpose under the statute?

8. *The minimum accumulated earnings credit.* By virtue of §535(c)(2), a corporation may accumulate up to $250,000 of earnings and profits (overall, not annually) without being subject to the accumulated earnings tax. Of course, accumulation in excess of $250,000 is permitted if the taxpayer can show the accumulation is necessary to meet the reasonable needs of the business. Only the $250,000 minimum credit, however, is allowed to a corporation that is a "mere holding or investment company," §535(c)(3). Section 535(c)(1) does not allow these companies to accumulate based on the reasonable needs of the business. See Rev. Rul. 77-368, 1977-2 C.B. 201 (need for liquidity cannot be considered for investment or holding company).

When the Economic Recovery Tax Act of 1981 increased the minimum credit from $150,000 to $250,000, the $150,000 credit was retained for corporations whose "principal function . . . is the performance of services in the field of health, law, engineering, architecture, accounting, actuarial science, performing arts, or consulting." Why do these corporations receive a smaller credit than a mere investment corporation that has no business whatsoever?

To discourage the multiplication of corporate entities as a means of multiplying the allowable credit, §1551 was amended to apply to the accumulated earnings credit as well as to limit the use of the lower corporate rates. Moreover, if an affiliated group of corporations claims the 100 percent deduction for intracorporate dividends, the group is entitled to only one $250,000 minimum accumulated earnings credit. §243(b).

9. *Publicly held corporations and the accumulated earnings tax.* How likely is it that §531 will be applied to a publicly held corporation? See Trico Products Corp. v. Commissioner, 137 F.2d 424 (2d Cir. 1943), and Trico Products Corp. v. McGowan, 169 F.2d 343 (2d Cir. 1948), in which, al-

though there were more than 2,000 stockholders, six stockholders owned about two-thirds of the total shares. After the taxpayer paid a total of about $3.2 million in §531 surtaxes and interest, a minority stockholder brought a stockholder's derivative action against the directors for subjecting the corporation to the §531 penalty. The action was settled by a payment of about $2.5 million by the defendants to the corporation. See Mahler v. Trico Products Corp., 296 N.Y. 902, 72 N.E. 622 (1947).

See Golconda Mining Corp. v. Commissioner, 507 F.2d 594 (9th Cir. 1974), in which it was held that the accumulated earnings tax could not be applied to a publicly held company unless a small group of shareholders controlled at least 50 percent of its stock. The position of the IRS is that, in an appropriate case, there is no legal impediment in applying §531 to a publicly held corporation. See Rev. Rul. 75-305, 1975-2 C.B. 228. Apparently, Congress agreed with the IRS. In 1984 Congress enacted §532(c), which states that the accumulated earnings tax may be imposed on a corporation without regard to the number of shareholders. The Conference Report (at page 829) indicates, however, that it may be difficult to establish the requisite tax avoidance motive in the case of a widely held operating company in which no individual or group has legal or effective control.

In Techanalysis Corp. v. Commissioner, 101 T.C. 397 (1993), the court in dicta commented that widely held corporations can be subject to the accumulated earnings tax if the proscribed purposes exist. Technalysis itself had approximately 1,500 shareholders, and approximately 30 percent of the stock was held by the five members of the board of directors.

PROBLEMS

14-1. Does an individual shareholder ever have an incentive to accumulate income in a corporation if the shareholder's marginal tax rate is lower than the corporate marginal tax rate?

B. PERSONAL HOLDING COMPANY TAX

The personal holding company tax is another weapon that the Commissioner has, along with the accumulated earnings tax, to curtail the practice of accumulating profits in a corporation to avoid individual tax rates. The tax was enacted in 1934 to reach passive investment income and personal services earnings that are allowed to accumulate in a corporation. The personal holding company tax is a mechanical one, and tax avoidance motives are irrelevant or statutorily presumed. It therefore is possible to stumble unwittingly into being a personal holding company.

Two tests are applied to determine if income is personal holding company income: the stock ownership test and the income test. The tax generally applies to closely held corporations since, under the stock ownership test, more than 50 percent of the value of the stock must be owned directly or indirectly by five or fewer individuals. To make the ownership determination, the attribution rules of §544 apply. Under the income test at least 60 percent of "adjusted ordinary gross income" must be personal holding company income under §543(a), a term discussed in the following Notes.

The rate of tax imposed on undistributed personal holding company income is 39.6 percent. Because the purpose of the tax is not to raise revenue but to encourage dividend distributions from personal holding companies, relief is available under the dividends-paid deduction and the deficiency dividend provisions described in Note 4.

NOTES

1. *Sixty percent of adjusted gross income test.* Since 1964 the income test has required that at least 60 percent of the corporation's adjusted ordinary gross income for the taxable year be personal holding company income. Before 1964, the comparable requirement was 80 percent. To compute adjusted ordinary gross income, ordinary gross income is first defined by excluding from gross income the gains from the sale or other disposition of capital assets and §1231(b) assets. §543(b)(1). Then adjustments to ordinary gross income are made by subtracting depreciation, taxes, interest, and rent from rental income and mineral royalties. §543(b)(2). These adjustments are intended to determine whether the rental activities substantially contribute to the corporation's net income or constitute high gross/low net income activities, engaged in to minimize the importance of the corporation's other personal holding company income. Under §543(b)(2)(C) interest on condemnation awards, judgments, and tax refunds and interest earned by certain dealers in U.S. securities is also excluded. The following items are included in adjusted ordinary gross income: dividends, interest, royalties including special rules for mineral, oil, and gas royalties and copyright royalties, produced film rents, rental payments from a 25 percent or more shareholder, personal service contract payments, and income from trusts and estates.

Under §542(b), corporations filing consolidated returns are on a consolidated basis eliminating intragroup dividends and interest. Interest that is includible in adjusted ordinary gross income includes imputed interest under §483 and original issue discount, Treas. Regs. §§1.1232-3A(a), 1.1276(a)(4) and 1.279-2(b)(2).

2. *Personal holding company income.* Section 543(a) is the product of congressional efforts to distinguish the "tainted" personal holding com-

pany income from income that offers a "legitimate" reason to operate in corporate form.

In RAS of Sand River, Inc. v. Commissioner, 935 F.2d 270 (6th Cir. 1991), the taxpayer was wholly owned by a single individual. Although a written contract between the taxpayer and its customer for engineering services did not designate a particular person to perform the work or give the customer the right to designate who would perform the services, the court found that an oral agreement with the customer required the sole shareholder to perform the engineering services. The court was not influenced by the fact that the shareholder's services were not unique or irreplaceable.

Other categories of personal holding company income pose difficult interpretation problems as well. In Allied Industrial Cartage Co. v. Commissioner, 647 F.2d 713 (6th Cir. 1981), an individual owned all the stock in two corporations — one of which leased trucks and real estate to the other corporation. The Service argued that the rental income was personal holding company income under §543(a)(6). The court held that the use of the rental property could not be attributed to the individual because a business nexus existed for the corporate arrangement and no personal benefit accrued to the shareholder. See also Silverman & Sons Realty Trust v. Commissioner, 620 F.2d 314 (1st Cir. 1980).

In *Allied Industrial Cartage,* the contours of §543(a)(6) were at issue. That provision is aimed at rents paid by shareholders to a corporation for the use of an incorporated yacht, country home, or similar property. Can a shareholder avoid §543(a)(6) by arranging for a controlled corporation to rent the property? See the discussion of disguised dividends at page 144 supra.

Section 543(a)(2) treats certain other rental payments as personal holding company income. To distinguish an active rental business from passive rental receipts, the provision invokes a special formula. The adjusted income from rents is included as personal holding company income unless the rents amount to 50 percent or more of adjusted ordinary gross income (an "active" rental business) and the dividends paid at least equal the amount by which nonrent personal holding company income for the year exceeds 10 percent of its ordinary gross income. (Who dreams up these formulas?) If a taxpayer fails the numerical tests, can it still argue that the rental business is "active" by demonstrating a high level of services rendered in connection with the rental activities? See Eller v. Commissioner, 77 T.C. 934 (1981) (income from operation of commercial shopping center and mobile home park was personal holding company income despite level of services in which §543(a)(2) tests were not met; exhaustive review of the area).

Copyright royalties are considered personal holding company income under §543(a)(4). See Irving Berlin Music Corp. v. United States, 487 F.2d 540 (Cl. Ct. 1973), in which licensing receipts were found to be royalties for use of copyright property, subject to tax as personal holding company income, and not compensation for services. Cf. Rev. Rul. 75-202, 1975-1 C.B. 170, in which a transfer of the exclusive right to a copyright, subject to a contingent reversion, was held a sale and therefore did not give rise to personal holding company income.

Other categories of personal holding company income include dividends, interest, royalties (other than royalties from minerals, oil, gas, or copyrights), and annuities (§543(a)(1)); mineral, oil, and gas royalties (§543(a)(3)); produced film rents (§543(a)(5)); and income from trusts and estates (§543(a)(8)).

It is not always easy to distinguish royalties from other payments. In Dothan Coca-Cola Bottling Co. v. United States, 745 F.2d 1400 (11th Cir. 1984), the court held that amounts paid to the taxpayer by subbottlers constituted rent for the use of tangible real and personal property rather than royalties for the use of the taxpayer's franchise. The payments were 20 cents per gallon of Coke syrup sold by the taxpayer to the subbottlers. While adjusted income from rents can constitute personal holding company income, the Service conceded that the rents did not meet the personal holding company income requirements of §543(a)(2).

In this digital age, one area of importance concerns whether income received by a computer software company from licensing arrangements is personal holding company income. Section 543(a)(1) excepts certain software royalties if the corporation receiving the royalties: (1) is actively engaged in the business of developing computer software; (2) derives at least 50 percent of its gross income from such software; (3) incurs substantial trade or business expenses; and (4) distributes most of its passive income other than the royalties. See §543(a)(1) and (d).

3. *Stock ownership test.* Recall that in addition to the personal holding company income requirement, there is also a stock requirement — that at any time during the last half of the taxable year, more than 50 percent in value of the corporation's outstanding stock is owned, directly or indirectly, by or for not more than five individuals. §543(a)(2). Some trusts and tax-exempt organizations are considered "individuals" under §543(a)(2), presumably because they are susceptible to domination by the other corporate shareholders. Note that if fewer than 10 shareholders own a corporation, the stock ownership test is automatically satisfied.

The "directly or indirectly" language of §543(a)(2) is a dead giveaway that attribution rules apply. Section 544 provides the applicable rules that differ in some respects from §318. For example, there is attribution between siblings and no 50 percent threshold for attribution from corporations.

4. *Dividends-paid deduction; deficiency dividend procedure.* Under §545, the base for the tax is the corporation's taxable income with certain adjustments. The adjustments include decreasing taxable income by the amount of taxes paid, net capital gains reported, and the dividends-paid deduction

described in §561. That provision incorporates the dividends-paid deduction (the sum of dividends paid during the taxable year and within two and one-half months of the last day of the taxable year to a limited extent), consent dividends determined under §565, and the dividend carryover of §564. Dividends paid in property will qualify for a reduction under Treas. Regs. §1.562-1(a) to the extent of the property's adjusted basis at the time of distribution. This regulation was upheld in Fulman v. United States, 434 U.S. 528 (1978). Are *Fulman* and the regulation still sound law in light of the changes in §311 repealing *General Utilities?* If a corporation's taxable income is increased on the distribution of appreciated property, shouldn't the dividends-paid deduction be an amount equal to the adjusted basis plus any gain recognized to the corporation on the distribution? See §312(b). Otherwise the distribution of appreciated property may actually increase a corporation's personal holding company tax liability.

After the corporation's liability for personal holding company tax has been determined, it may mitigate or eliminate tax liability under the deficiency dividend procedure of §547, but the liability for interest and penalties is not eliminated by this procedure. Section 547 permits the corporation to make a dividend distribution to shareholders on which the shareholders are taxed currently, and the corporation may use this distribution to reduce its already determined past personal holding company liability. The deficiency dividend procedure can produce a dividend to a shareholder even on a liquidation. See §331(b) and §316(b)(2)(B).

5. *Foreign personal holding companies.* Foreign personal holding companies are dealt with by §§551-558. Because the corporation itself is thought to be beyond U.S. jurisdiction, each U.S. stockholder is taxed directly on his proportionate share of the corporation's undistributed income. Taxing the stockholder on undistributed income was held constitutional in Eder v. Commissioner, 138 F.2d 27 (2d Cir. 1943), despite the fact that the undistributed income was "blocked" and could not have been transferred to the United States. In 1962 this technique was used to tax some U.S. shareholders of so-called controlled foreign corporations on some of the corporation's undistributed income. §§951 et seq.

6. *Regulated investment companies, mutual funds, and real estate investment trusts.* Certain regulated investment companies (including mutual funds) may elect under subchapter M (§§851-855) to be subject to corporate taxation on only their undistributed income. These corporations, which must distribute currently at least 90 percent of their income, are treated as conduits through which the income from investments passes to their stockholders, and their long-term capital gains retain that character on distribution to the stockholders.

Sections 856-858 provide that certain real estate investment trusts (REITS) that distribute a specified percentage of current income shall be treated as corporations, with the important exception that distributed income is to be taxed to the beneficiaries rather than to the trust. The conduit concept is patterned on the treatment of regulated investment companies. The rules relating to and the treatments of investment companies and REITS differ in important ways from those corporations electing subchapter S, discussed in Chapter 16.

C. COLLAPSIBLE CORPORATIONS

To make sense of §341, the collapsible corporation provision, it is necessary to recall the tax laws existing prior to the Tax Reform Act of 1986. Recall, specifically, that under former §336, a liquidating corporation normally did not recognize gain on a liquidating distribution. Add to that the fact that there existed a substantial capital gains/ordinary income differential. Those two factors paved the way for a perceived misuse of corporate form to turn ordinary income into capital gains.

Suppose a film producer formed a corporation, exchanging $50,000 for all the corporate stock. The film was produced by the corporation and had a fair market value of $550,000. The exhibition profit would be taxed as ordinary income to the corporation, which is in the trade or business of producing motion pictures. The shareholder would have ordinary income on the distribution of proceeds. Suppose instead that the producer liquidates the corporation. Under §§331 and 334(a), the producer would recognize a $500,000 capital gain and take a $550,000 basis in the film. Under former §336, there was no gain to the liquidating corporation. By amortizing the basis in the film against the expected rentals, the producer could avoid any ordinary income recognition. Note that if this series of transactions were respected for tax purposes, the producer would have avoided ordinary income at the corporate level and again at the shareholder level, reporting only a single capital gain.

It was this conversion of ordinary income to capital gain that led to enactment of the collapsible corporation provision in 1958. The term "collapsible corporation" refers to a corporation used to convert ordinary income into capital gains, which having served this purpose is collapsed, i.e., liquidated.

Prior to the enactment of §341, use of collapsible corporations appealed to builders as well as motion picture producers. Suppose a builder formed a corporation with $50,000, and the corporation built a house with a fair market value of $250,000. Sale of the house by the corporation (or by an unincorporated builder) would produce ordinary income. Liquidation converted ordinary income into capital gains (§331) and provided a fair market value basis (§334) that offset the proceeds from the sale of the house by the builder following liquidation. Again under former §336, there was no gain to the liquidating corporation. As an alternative route to capital gains treatment, the builder would sell the stock to a purchaser who would then cause the corporation to liquidate. The builder would recognize a capital gain on the sale of the stock, while the purchaser would take a cost basis in the stock under §1012 that would result in no gain on an immediate liquidation. The purchaser of stock would take a fair market value basis in the house on liquidation under §334 and would recognize no income on an immediate sale of the house.

Section 341 requires that a shareholder's gain on the liquidation or sale of stock in a collapsible corporation be reported as ordinary income.

Ironically, the repeal of the *General Utilities* doctrine removed much of the tax avoidance potential that led to the enactment of §341. Now an individual cannot remove appreciated assets from a corporation without paying a corporate-level tax under either §311 (nonliquidating distribution) or §336 (liquidating distribution). In both examples above, the liquidating corporation would recognize gain on the distribution of property to its shareholders.

It is true that the taxpayer can still avoid that gain by selling the stock. The new purchaser, however, will then own a corporation that must recognize that gain, and presumably the purchase price will reflect that fact. With the repeal of the *General Utilities* rule it is impossible for a shareholder to obtain a step-up in basis of distributed property without a corporate-level tax.

Of course, there is still an incentive to turn what would otherwise be ordinary income potentially taxable at a 39.6 percent rate into a capital gain taxable at a 20 percent rate.

Finally, as noted at page 558 infra, §341(f) arms a taxpayer with the power to completely bypass §341 in many circumstances. To sum up, §341 makes little sense after the repeal of the *General Utilities* doctrine. Moreover, because it often can be bypassed, the provision serves only as a trap for the unwary. Nevertheless, because the tax laws have been known to change from time to time, it is appropriate to consider some of the intricacies of §341.

NOTES

1. *Definition of "collapsible corporation."* A "collapsible corporation," as the term is defined by §341(b)(1), must be formed or availed of:

   a. principally for the manufacture, construction, or production of property, for the purchase of certain categories of property (primarily property held for sale to customers in the ordinary course of its trade or business), or for the holding of stock in another corporation so formed or availed;
   b. with a view to (1) a sale or exchange of its stock, or a distribution to its shareholders, before it has realized two-thirds of the taxable

income to be derived from the manufactured or purchased property, and (2) a realization by the shareholders of gain attributable to the property.

For a thorough discussion of the requirements of §341, see King v. United States, 641 F.2d 253 (5th Cir. 1981).

Requirement (a) is satisfied by many corporations, especially since the concept of "manufacture, construction, or production of property" is defined very expansively. See Treas. Regs. §1.341-2(a)(5); Farber v. Commissioner, 312 F.2d 729 (2d Cir. 1963) (predevelopment activity of filing applications for building permits and paying fees and deposits constituted construction); Manassas Airport Industrial Park v. Commissioner, 66 T.C. 566 (1976), aff'd per curiam, 557 F.2d 1113 (4th Cir. 1977) (postliquidation obligation to build access road found to be evidence of uncompleted construction); cf. Rev. Rul. 77-306, 1977-2 C.B. 103 (lessor's lease of additional land to lessee and continuing right to approve changes to building not construction modifying Rev. Rul. 69-378, 1969-2 C.B. 49, which reached the opposite result because there lessor also participated in the financing by subordinating its mortgage and participated in success of venture by receiving a percentage of gross rentals collected). See also Rev. Rul. 72-422, 1972-2 C.B. 211, stating that the dollar amount expended is irrelevant in determining whether taxpayer has engaged in construction under §341.

Query: Can a personal service firm be considered a collapsible corporation on the ground that it was formed or availed of for the "production of property" or goodwill? See Computer Sciences Corp. v. Commissioner, 63 T.C. 327 (1974) (proprietary computer program and interview forms held to be produced property); F.T.S. Associates v. Commissioner, 58 T.C. 207 (1972) (marketing rights to secret process is produced property).

Much litigation concerning the definition of "collapsible corporation" has turned on whether requirement (b) was satisfied, i.e., whether the shareholders had the requisite "view" at the proper time.

With the repeal of the *General Utilities* doctrine, all appreciated corporate assets will eventually produce gain at the corporate level. How then can there be a requisite view to avoid tax on the appreciation? It is true that a shareholder can dispose of stock before that corporate-level gain is recognized, but won't the amount paid for the stock reflect the impending tax? Suppose you could buy stock of two corporations that were identical except that one corporation held appreciated assets that would result in a corporate-level tax on sale or distribution while the other held appreciated assets that would yield no corporate-level tax. Would you pay the same amount for the stock of each corporation?

The regulations speak of a "view" that exists before the manufacture, construction, production, or purchase of property is completed and are willing to overlook a subsequently conceived "view," at least in ordinary circumstances. Treas. Regs. §1.341-2(a)(3). This approach has led to a few shareholder victories. See Jacobson v. Commissioner, 281 F.2d 703 (3d Cir. 1960) (sale not contemplated until after construction was completed; held, not collapsible); Temkin v. Commissioner, 35 T.C. 906 (1961) (sale attributable to ill health of a principal shareholder, arising after construction was completed; held, not collapsible); *F.T.S. Associates,* supra (following *Temkin,* decision to sell after operations ceased and taxpayer insolvent); *Computer Sciences Corp.,* supra (view to sell formulated after production of computer program reduced to commercial value). See Crowe v. Commissioner, 62 T.C. 121 (1974), in which the prohibited view was not found to exist; the taxpayer had no freedom of choice in the sale of stock because of a unilateral option held and exercised by the other shareholder to buy him out in the event of a disagreement. Presumably the purchasing shareholder in *Crowe* cannot liquidate without addressing the potential collapsibility problem.

When §341 was first enacted, commentators engaged in a lively debate over the reference of the adverb "principally" in §341(b)(1). In Weil v. Commissioner, 252 F.2d 805 (2d Cir. 1958), the court said that "principally" modifies only "manufacture, construction," etc., and that the "view" need not be "the principal corporate objective." Although the *Weil* decision has gained a large measure of support, no court has as yet worked out the implications of the statement in the regulations that the "view" requirement is satisfied even if a sale, liquidation, etc., is no more than "a recognized possibility." Treas. Regs. §1.341-2(a)(2).

Because a finding of the prohibited view is a factual one, taxpayers must always consider the possibility that the Service will argue for collapsibility whenever a corporation's shareholder sells its stock or causes it to liquidate.

Under Rev. Proc. 89-3, 1989-1 C.B. 761, the Service will issue rulings that a corporation has not been formed or availed of with a view to the action stated in §341(b) when the enterprise has been in existence for at least 20 years with substantially the same owners and has been conducting substantially the same trade or business.

2. *Realization of two-thirds of taxable income.* Prior to the Deficit Reduction Act of 1984, §341(b) imposed a "substantial part" test in lieu of the "two-thirds" requirement. The former language led to some confusion and ultimately a restrictive view of §341's applicability. Under the former language, it was not clear whether a corporation was collapsible if it had realized a substantial part of the income to be derived from the collapsible property before the liquidation or sale, even though a substantial amount remained to be realized thereafter. A major exception to a finding of collapsibility was provided in Rev. Rul. 72-48, 1972-1 C.B. 102, in which the IRS announced that a realization of one-third of the taxable income took an asset outside the reach of §341. In keeping with the ruling the Service substituted an acquiescence for its prior nonacquiescence in Com-

missioner v. Kelley, 293 F.2d 904 (5th Cir. 1961), in which a corporation that realized 33 percent of potential income was held noncollapsible.

Under the current language, it is now clear that to avoid §341 a corporation must realize at least two-thirds, rather than one-third, of the potential income. Unquestionably this legislative change has broadened the reach of §341 to many unsuspecting corporations and their shareholders.

3. *The operative effects of §341.* If a corporation is collapsible, the shareholders (subject to certain exceptions) must report as ordinary income any gain from a sale or exchange of the stock, a distribution in partial or complete liquidation, or a nondividend distribution under §301(c)(3)(A) that would otherwise be reported as long-term capital gain. Although §341(a) does not explicitly mention gain on a redemption of shares, it must be assumed that redemptions are covered. Indeed, a redemption qualifying under §302(b) is characterized as an "exchange," thereby falling within the purview of §341(a).

As a result of the Tax Reform Act of 1986, §341 transforms short-term capital gain into ordinary income. Consider the outcome when a shareholder has capital losses that normally can be offset against short-term capital gain realized on a sale or liquidation of a collapsible corporation. Note that §341 has no impact if the shareholder incurs a loss on the transaction.

4. *Minority shareholders.* In determining whether the forbidden view exists, the regulations look to "those persons in a position to determine the policies of the corporation, whether by reason of their owning a majority of the voting stock of the corporation or not," Treas. Regs. §1.341-2(a)(2). Since the punitive rules of §341(a) apply to all shareholders of a collapsible corporation, a minority shareholder cannot escape by showing that she did not share in the forbidden view. But if she is the only shareholder who sells her stock, the corporation may not be collapsible because the dominant shareholders did not intend to sell *their* shares before a substantial part of the income was realized by the corporation. See Goodwin v. United States, 320 F.2d 356 (Cl. Ct. 1963), holding the collapsible provision inapplicable when the stock of a minority shareholder is redeemed and the majority shareholders continue to run the corporation.

Regardless of his view, however, a person who owns (directly and constructively) no more than 5 percent of the collapsible corporation's stock may be able to avail himself of the exception of §341(d)(1).

5. *The limitations of §341(d).* By virtue of §341(d), §341 does not apply to gain realized more than three years after the construction, etc., is completed or to gain recognized during a taxable year unless more than 70 percent of it was attributable to the collapsible property or, if certain conditions are satisfied, to persons owning not more than 5 percent of the corporation's stock. The three-year rule is difficult to satisfy in view of the broad meaning given to "manufacture, construction, or production," and the 5 percent rule is limited in its usefulness because of the constructive

ownership rules of §341(d) (last sentence). The 70 percent rule may be significant if the corporation holds both collapsible and noncollapsible property; if enough of the gain is attributable to the latter category, the gain attributable to the collapsible property slips through unscathed by §341. When the corporation's principal or only asset is real estate on which it has constructed a building, however, shareholders have not been very successful in establishing that 30 percent or more of their gain was of the noncollapsible variety. See, e.g., Farber v. Commissioner, 312 F.2d 729 (2d Cir. 1963), and cases cited therein.

In order to qualify for the 70 percent exception, a shareholder must meet the two-thirds requirement of §341(b)(1)(A). For example, suppose a corporation has completed one of two projects for sale to customers (§1221), and the sole shareholder liquidates, realizing a $100,000 gain, $40,000 attributable to the completed project and $60,000 attributable to the uncompleted project. Sections 341(d)(2) and (b)(1) combine to force ordinary income treatment for the entire gain since the corporation has not realized two-thirds of the ordinary income; therefore, all the gain is attributable to collapsible assets.

6. *Distributions of "excess" mortgage proceeds by collapsible corporation.* Much of the §341 litigation has concerned corporations that constructed apartment houses or other buildings under the Federal Housing Act and were able to borrow, on federally insured mortgages, more than the cost of construction. This excess of the mortgage loan over the corporation's cost might be attributable to construction economies, to inflation in the value of previously acquired land, to overly generous appraisals by the federal authorities, or to the uncompensated personal efforts of the shareholders.

Before 1954, it was common for such excess mortgage proceeds to be distributed to shareholders before the corporation had any earnings and profits (so the distribution would not be a taxable dividend). In Commissioner v. Gross, 236 F.2d 612 (2d Cir. 1956), the court held that such a distribution was to be applied against the shareholder's basis for his stock and that any excess over his basis was capital gain under §301(c)(3)(A). This result was changed by the enactment in 1954 of what is now §312(i), under which a distribution creates earnings and profits if the corporation's assets are subject to a loan that was made, guaranteed, or insured by the United States and that exceeds the adjusted basis of the mortgaged property. A distribution in these circumstances, therefore, will be a taxable dividend to the shareholders.

Section 312(i) does not make §341 unnecessary as to such construction companies, however, because §312(i) does not apply if the shareholders benefited from the excess mortgage money by selling their stock rather than by causing the corporation to distribute the funds to them. See also Zorn v. Commissioner, 35 T.C.M. (CCH) 1048 (1976), in which excess mortgage proceeds obtained from a private lender and distributed to shareholders led to a factual finding of the prohibited view and therefore collapsibility.

7. *The amnesty of §341(e)*. In Braunstein v. Commissioner, 374 U.S. 65 (1963), the Supreme Court refused to grant judicial relief to a corporation that held rental property that would have been a capital asset in the shareholder's hands, despite the absence of a tax avoidance motive. Section 341(e), inapplicable to the taxable year before the Supreme Court in *Braunstein* (1950), was enacted in 1958 in recognition of the fact that §341 not only prevents some taxpayers from transmuting potential ordinary income into capital gain but also forces others to report as ordinary income a gain that would have been taxed as capital gain if realized without the intervention of a corporation. But §341(e) accomplishes its intended purpose in remarkably labyrinthine fashion, and its involutions are not easily summarized.[1]

Roughly speaking, its underlying theory is that the collapsible corporation provisions should not be applied if the net unrealized appreciation in the corporation's "subsection (e) assets" (property that would produce ordinary income if sold by the corporation or by its principal shareholders) amounts to less than 15 percent of the corporation's net worth, defined in §341(e)(7). As the *Braunstein* opinion indicates, in determining whether property constitutes a "subsection (e) asset," §341(e) looks not only to the corporation's trade or business but also to the trade or business of the corporation's principal shareholders (those owning, directly or constructively, more than 20 percent — sometimes 5 percent — of the stock); sometimes §341(e) takes account of a hypothetical trade or business that is imputed to a shareholder because of the activities of other corporations in which the shareholder owned stock, directly or constructively, in the past. See Diecks v. Commissioner, 65 T.C. 117 (1975), in which no taint was found to exist for a 20 percent shareholder since his other businesses were unrelated; furthermore, because the corporation had no appreciated §341(e) assets, a stock sale qualified for §341(e). Under §341(e)(12) and Treas. Regs. §1.341-6(b)(2)(iii), in determining whether gain from the sale or exchange of property will be considered as ordinary income, recapture amounts, e.g., under §1245, are disregarded.

Because two of the principal shareholders in *Braunstein* had been engaged in the real estate construction business for many years, directly or through other corporations (36 T.C. 22, 23 (1961)), they might not have qualified for relief under §341(e) even if it had been in force in 1950. If they had been investors in real estate, with no interests in other

---

1. As an aside, it is interesting to note that the taxpayer's attorney in *Braunstein,* who unsuccessfully argued against the literal language of §341 and in favor of the spirit of the provision, also argued for the taxpayer in *Chamberlin,* page 269 supra. There, he scored a stunning victory by arguing that the preferred stock bailout was not addressed by any language in the Code and was, therefore, not subject to recharacterization, despite the fact that the transaction violated the spirit of the dividend provisions.

corporations, however, and if the buildings were held by the corporation for rental purposes, then §341(e)(1) would have applied, the buildings would not be "subsection (e) assets," and hence none of the corporation's net worth would have been attributable to unrealized appreciation in such assets — with the result that the corporation (regardless of the shareholders' "view") would not be collapsible.

8. *Consents under §341(f).* Another escape hatch for the shareholders of a collapsible corporation is offered in §341(f), under which the shareholders can sell their stock on the normal capital gain basis, provided the corporation agrees to recognize gain (if any) on its "subsection (f) assets" (primarily real estate and noncapital assets) when, as, and if it disposes of them in a transaction that would otherwise qualify for nonrecognition of gain. Such a consent ensures that all the unrealized gain on most collapsible property (and more) will be recognized at the corporate level regardless of the mode employed by the corporation to dispose of the property (e.g., on a distribution in liquidation). An exception is also provided for certain transfers (e.g., in corporate reorganizations, §351 transfers, and §332 liquidations of a subsidiary), provided the transferee files a similar consent.

Consider the §341(f) election in light of the *General Utilities* doctrine. Now every corporation, regardless of a §341(f) election, will recognize gain on the sale or distribution of all appreciated assets. (A §341 election would cause recognition on an involuntary conversion, but that is a small exception.) Accordingly, there is virtually no cost in making a §341(f) election because the corporation is electing treatment that would happen anyway under §§1001, 311, and 336. By making the election, a corporation at no cost will enable its shareholders to avoid recharacterization under §341(a).

PROBLEMS

14-2. In view of the repeal of the *General Utilities* rule by the Tax Reform Act of 1986, is there any justification for maintaining §341? Does §341(f) render §341 totally impotent? Consider §341(f)(5).

15

The Corporation as a Separate Taxable Entity

A. DEFINITION OF A CORPORATION

1. *Morrissey v. Commissioner*

In Morrissey v. Commissioner, 296 U.S. 344 (1935), the petitioners set up a trust to develop some tracts of land and to construct and operate a golf course. The trustees were authorized to buy, sell, lease, and operate the land owned by the trust; to construct and operate the golf course and club house; to make loans and investments; and to manage the property as if they were the owners. The trustees had no power to bind the beneficiaries. Beneficial interests in the trust were evidenced by transferable certificates. The trust was to continue for 25 years and was not terminated by the death of a trustee or beneficiary. During the years before the court, the trust developed the land, sold some of the lots, and constructed a golf course and club house, which were transferred to a corporation in exchange for its stock. The trustees leased and operated the golf facilities from the corporation for a period of time, but later their activities were confined to the collection of installments on the lots that were sold, the receipt of dividends from the incorporated golf facilities, and distributions to beneficiaries.

The Supreme Court held that the corporate income tax was properly imposed on the trust, which was deemed an "association" for tax purposes. See §7701(a)(3), which defines "corporation" to include "association." The characteristics necessary to tax a business enterprise as an association were set forth by the Court as follows: (a) associates, (b) an objective to carry on a trade or business, (c) continuity of life of the enterprise, (d) centralized management representing the owners, (e) limited liability for the owners, and (f) free transferability of ownership interests.

2. Professional Corporations

The Service was successful in arguing for association status in *Morrissey*. Subsequent to the *Morrissey* decision, however, certain taxpayers sought the sanctuary of association status for tax purposes even though such classification carried with it the possibility of a corporate-level tax. Doctors and other professionals practicing in unincorporated associations or partnerships wanted association status to take advantage of qualified pension and profit-sharing plans, then only available to corporate employees. Since most states prohibited the incorporation of professionals, many professionals formed associations adhering to the *Morrissey* characteristics. In this setting, the Service found itself arguing against association status. In Kintner v. United States, 216 F.2d 418 (9th Cir. 1954), the Ninth Circuit ruled that a professional medical service association was a corporation for federal tax purposes even though a state law prohibited the practice of medicine by corporations. For a good review of the history of professional corporations, see Richland Medical Association v. Commissioner, 953 F.2d 639 (4th Cir. 1992).

3. The Association Regulations

In 1960 the Service reacted to defeats in *Kintner* and other cases by enacting Treas. Regs. §301.7701-2, which codified the basic characteristics of an association described in *Morrissey*. These regulations set forth two prerequisites to association status: (1) an objective to carry on business for profit and (2) associates, although associates may be ignored in the one-person corporation or sole proprietorship situation. In lieu of an uncertain weighing of the various *Morrissey* factors, the regulations further provided a mechanical numbers test. An unincorporated organization would not be classified as an association unless such organization had three of four listed corporate characteristics: continuity of life, centralization of management, limited liability, and free transferability of ownership interests. These characteristics were defined in a manner stacked against corporate classification.

In light of the strict federal regulations, professionals lobbied state legislatures to enact professional corporation statutes permitting operation in corporate form. The Service's reaction to this turn of events was to issue specific regulations in 1965 intended to ignore the professional corporation statutes for federal tax purposes. The 1965 regulations were struck down as arbitrary, legislative in nature, and discriminatory by all courts that considered them. See, e.g., Kurzner v. United States, 413 F.2d 97 (5th Cir. 1969); O'Neill v. United States, 410 F.2d 888 (6th Cir. 1969); United States v. Empey, 406 F.2d 157 (10th Cir. 1969). When the solicitor general decided not to apply for certiorari in *Kurzner*, the IRS announced that it would no longer contest this issue. See Rev. Rul. 70-101, 1970-1 C.B. 278, listing the state statutes that will be recognized as conferring corporate status on professional service organizations. Subsequent rulings have added state statutes as they are enacted to the list set out in Rev. Rul. 70-101. In 1977, the 1965 regulations were revoked.

Despite recognition as a corporation, the personal service corporation and its shareholder-employees may be subject to a reallocation of income under principles developed in cases such as Lucas v. Earl. See Sargent v. Commissioner, 93 T.C. 572 (1989). See also page 582 infra.

4. Larson *and Limited Partnerships*

While the Service was still waging war to make federal corporate status unavailable for professionals, it found itself fighting to impose corporate status on certain noncorporate enterprises — limited partnerships. Reliance on the restrictive association regulations allowed limited partnerships operating much like corporations easily to escape that classification. These limited partnerships were used to market "tax shelters" to individual investors who might not otherwise be able to make such investments on their own. The partnership form was ideal since it allowed limited partners to take their pro rata shares of partnership losses or credits, which could then be used to offset income from other sources and thereby shelter income. Often the losses in the early years of a partnership exceeded a partner's actual cash investment in the partnership.[1] Faced with these proliferating "tax shelter" cases, the Service argued that a limited partnership should be taxed as a corporation under some circumstances, in which case the entity's losses would not pass through to the partners but could be used only by the entity.

In the absence of congressional guidance, courts faced a difficult task in determining the tax treatment of limited partnerships. Compare Zuckman v. United States, 524 F.2d 729 (Cl. Ct. 1975), holding a limited partnership not an association, with Larson v. Commissioner, 65 T.C. No. 10 (1975) (*Larson I*), holding a fairly typical California limited partnership an association. Even though the *Larson I* opinion was withdrawn for recon-

---

1. The ability of a partner to take loss deductions stems in part from the *Crane* doctrine, which allows purchase indebtedness to be included in basis, thereby increasing depreciation deductions. See Crane v. Commissioner, 331 U.S. 1 (1949). While there may be a day of reckoning for the partner who receives large loss deductions in the early years, there has been no shortage of genius in finding ways to postpone or avoid that day or at least make it less painful by qualifying for capital gains treatment on any recapture.

sideration within a month after its issuance, it created a near panic among some real estate groups. *Larson II* (Larson v. Commissioner 66 T.C. 159 (1976)), however, came as a relief to many taxpayers. In *Larson II*, the court applied the four-factor test of the regulations rigidly and without giving greater weight to any one factor over any other.

In holding for the petitioner, the court did not find more corporate than noncorporate characteristics. In an apparent response to *Larson II*, the Treasury in 1977 proposed and in the ensuing clamor immediately thereafter withdrew new regulations that would have classified most limited partnerships as associations. Several days after withdrawal, then-Secretary William Simon announced that regulations would not be reproposed. In April 1979 the Treasury agreed to follow *Larson II*.

The *Zuckman* and *Larson* opinions reflected a judicial policy of unwillingness to become involved in the recharacterization battle, when the taxpayers managed to satisfy the existing regulations on a technical or literal level. Such an approach was close to saying that "form is form," i.e., if a state adopted the UPA or the ULPA and the partnership agreement adhered to either act, the partnership form would be acknowledged for tax purposes. The result was that taxpayers and their counsel were usually be able to arrange the transaction to get the desired results, i.e., association or partnership status.

5. The "Check-the-Box" Regulations

In 1996 the Service withdrew from the business entity classification battle by issuing new regulations that permit eligible business entities to elect in many cases the type of classification they desire. Treas. Regs. §301.7701-3(a). The new regulations do, however, leave in place the prior regulations determining treatment of certain "business" trusts as associations. Treas. Regs. §301.7701-4(a). Under the new regulations, an eligible business entity is a business entity that is unincorporated and is not an association (i.e. businesses that previously elected to be taxed under Treas. Regs. §301.7701-3), trust, insurance company, bank, political/governmental entity or otherwise subject to special treatment under the Code. Additionally, partnerships whose interests are publicly traded or for which there is a secondary market are ineligible for the election. The regulations also provide a list of specific foreign entities that are deemed "per se" corporations and therefore precluded from electing out of corporate classification. See Treas. Regs. §301.7701-2(b)(8).

The regulations recognize two alternative classifications to corporate treatment. An eligible entity with two or more members can elect to be treated as either a corporation or a partnership for federal tax purposes and an eligible entity with a single owner can elect to be treated as a corporation or a disregarded entity (i.e., treated as transparent like a sole proprietorship, or branch or division of the owner). Treas. Regs. §301.7701-2(c), Treas. Regs. §301.7701-3(a). Entities that are disregarded are sometimes referred to as "tax nothings."

If an eligible entity does not make an election under Treas. Regs. §301.7701-3(c), then the regulations provide default rules. Absent an election, the default rules classify a domestic entity having two or more members as a partnership and entities having a single owner are disregarded for tax purposes. The default rules for foreign eligible entities are much more complicated as they are determined by the liability exposure of the organization's members. Treas. Regs. §301.7701-3(b)(2).

Once a business entity has elected to change its classification there is a prohibition on that entity changing its classification again for the following 60 months. This prohibition does not apply to the initial classification of a new entity since the initial classification is not a change. Additionally, this restriction does not apply to an entity formed prior to the effective date of the new regulations (January 1, 1997) that first elected to change its classification as of January 1, 1997. Although this is a change, the regulations have recognized an exception. Treas. Regs.§301.7701-3(c)(1)(iv). If an entity undergoes a more than 50 percent ownership change during the 60 month period, the IRS may allow a change in classification. Prop. Treas. Regs. §301.7701-3(c)(1)(iv). Note, however, that the more than 50 percent new owners must not have owned any interests in the entity on the filing date or the effective date of the prior election.

Because a reclassification may involve a taxable conversion, the advantages of reclassification must be weighed against the potential tax consequences. Under proposed regulations, a partnership that has elected to be treated as a corporation for tax purposes is deemed to have distributed all its assets and liabilities to the corporation in exchange for stock which it thereafter is deemed to have distributed to its partners. Prop. Treas. Regs. §301.7701-3(g)(i). A corporation that elects to be treated as a partnership is deemed to distribute all its assets and liabilities to its shareholders in liquidation, followed by deemed contribution by the shareholders to the newly formed partnership. Prop. Treas. Regs. §301.7701-3(g)(ii). A corporation with a single owner electing to be disregarded is deemed to have distributed all its assets and liabilities in liquidation to its single owner. Prop. Treas. Regs. §301.7701-3(g)(iii). A disregarded entity electing to be treated as a corporation is deemed to have contributed all its assets and liabilities to the corporation in exchange for stock. Prop. Treas. Regs. §301.7701-3(g)(iv).

The new regulations are relatively clear and concise by modern standards and have simplified the classification problem greatly. In the past any knowledgeable financial planner could choose the desired business classification by jumping through the requisite hoops set by the old regulations. The new regulations have simply made the choice of classification available without requiring the observation of the prior formalities.

However, the ease of choosing to operate as a transparent (e.g., partnership or disregarded entity) or nontransparent (e.g., corporation) entity from the point of view of Treasury may provide too much freedom, particularly in the international context where taxpayers may be able take tax advantage of entities classified one way for U.S. tax purposes and a different way for foreign tax purposes. An entity that is transparent for U.S. tax purposes and nontransparent for foreign tax purposes is sometimes referred to as a "hybrid entity." An entity that is nontransparent for U.S. tax purposes and transparent for foreign tax purposes is sometimes referred to as a "reverse hybrid."

6. Limited Liability Companies

A limited liability company (LLC) is a hybrid entity combining the corporate benefit of limited liability for the owners and, unless otherwise elected under the check-the-box regulations, the partnership's tax advantage of pass-through treatment for income tax purposes. To form an LLC, articles of organization (not incorporation) must be filed with the appropriate state authority. An LLC is owned by "members" rather than by shareholders or partners. In some cases, an LLC must have at least two members, but many states permit single-entity LLCs. A corporation, partnership, LLC, trust, estate, or other entity, as well as individuals, may be members. Contributions to an LLC in exchange for a membership interest may be made in the form of cash, property, the use of property, services, or any other valuable consideration. In some states, contributions may also be made in the form of a promissory note or other binding obligation.

Generally, an LLC is not required to have an operating agreement. Some states, however, require the adoption of an operating agreement and specify certain mandatory provisions. In the absence of an operating agreement, an LLC is governed by its articles and state law. Provisions with respect to an LLC's affairs generally may be included in an operating agreement to the extent that they are not inconsistent with state law or the LLC's articles. Typically, LLC statutes often rely on "default rules," or statutory provisions that apply unless an LLC's articles or operating agreement specifies otherwise. Default rules allow an LLC to be customized to suit the needs of its members.

Members of an LLC are usually permitted under state law to customize both distribution of cash and property and allocation of profits and losses to the members through the operating agreement or the articles. In the absence of any financial provisions in the operating agreement or in the articles, distributions are generally made and profits and losses are allocated on a proportional basis in accordance with the members' respective contributions. In most states, unless otherwise provided in the articles or operating agreement, a member has the right to withdraw on six months' notice. A withdrawing member is entitled to fair value of the membership interest.

One of the major advantages of an LLC is that it provides limited liability to all its members and managers. The typical state act provides that an individual or entity does not have any personal obligation for the liabilities of an LLC solely by reason of being a member, manager, or other agent of the LLC. Some states permit a member to waive limited liability. The ability to insulate an LLC member from personal liability as a member, regardless of management activities, is one of the primary distinctions between an LLC and a limited partnership. For example, under the Revised Uniform Limited Partnership Act (RULPA), a limited partner who participates in the partnership's management can become personally liable for partnership obligations.

Unless an operating agreement or the articles provide to the contrary, a membership interest is assignable in whole or in part. The assignment of a membership interest enables the assignee only to receive, to the extent assigned, the distributions from the LLC to which the assignor would otherwise be entitled. For the assignee to participate in the management and affairs of the LLC and to exercise other membership rights, in most states the remaining members must unanimously consent to the assignee's admission as a member.

B. DUMMY CORPORATIONS

The check-the-box regulations do not formally permit a corporation to choose to be taxed as a transparent entity. But can a taxpayer that has chosen to operate in corporate form under applicable state law nevertheless ignore that form for federal tax purposes?

Commissioner v. Bollinger _____
485 U.S. 340 (1988)

Justice SCALIA delivered the opinion of the Court.

Petitioner the Commissioner of Internal Revenue challenges a decision by the United States Court of Appeals for the Sixth Circuit holding that a corporation which held record title to real property as agent for the corporation's shareholders was not the owner of the property for purposes of federal income taxation. 807 F.2d 65 (1986). We granted certiorari . . . to resolve a conflict in the courts of appeals over the tax treatment of corporations purporting to be agents for their shareholders. . . .

I

Respondent Jesse C. Bollinger, Jr., developed, either individually or in partnership with some or all of the other respondents, eight apartment complexes in Lexington, Kentucky. (For convenience we will refer to all the ventures as "partnerships.") Bollinger initiated development of the first apartment complex, Creekside North Apartments, in 1968. The Massachusetts Mutual Life Insurance Company agreed to provide permanent financing by lending $1,075,000 to "the corporate nominee of Jesse C. Bollinger, Jr." at an annual interest rate of eight percent, secured by a mortgage on the property and a personal guaranty from Bollinger. The loan commitment was structured in this fashion because Kentucky's usury law at the time limited the annual interest rate for noncorporate borrowers to seven percent. Ky. Rev. Stat. §§360.010, 360.025 (1972). Lenders willing to provide money only at higher rates required the nominal debtor and record title holder of mortgaged property to be a corporate nominee of the true owner and borrower. On October 14, 1968, Bollinger incorporated Creekside, Inc., under the laws of Kentucky; he was the only stockholder. The next day, Bollinger and Creekside, Inc., entered into a written agreement which provided that the corporation would hold title to the apartment complex as Bollinger's agent for the sole purpose of securing financing, and would convey, assign, or encumber the property and disburse the proceeds thereof only as directed by Bollinger; that Creekside, Inc., had no obligation to maintain the property or assume any liability by reason of the execution of promissory notes or otherwise; and that Bollinger would indemnify and hold the corporation harmless from any liability it might sustain as his agent and nominee.

Having secured the commitment for permanent financing, Bollinger, acting through Creekside, Inc., borrowed the construction funds for the apartment complex from Citizens Fidelity Bank and Trust Company. Creekside, Inc., executed all necessary loan documents including the promissory note and mortgage, and transferred all loan proceeds to Bollinger's individual construction account. Bollinger acted as general contractor for the construction, hired the necessary employees, and paid the expenses out of the construction account. When construction was completed, Bollinger obtained, again through Creekside, Inc., permanent financing from Massachusetts Mutual Life in accordance with the earlier loan commitment. These loan proceeds were used to pay off the Citizens Fidelity construction loan. Bollinger hired a resident manager to rent the apartments, execute leases with tenants, collect and deposit the rents, and maintain operating records. The manager deposited all rental receipts into, and paid all operating expenses from, an operating account, which was first opened in the name of Creekside, Inc., but was later changed to "Creekside Apartments, a partnership." The operation of Creekside North Apartments generated losses for the taxable years 1969, 1971, 1972, 1973, and 1974, and ordinary income for the years 1970, 1975, 1976, and 1977. Throughout, the income and losses were reported by Bollinger on his individual income tax returns.

Following a substantially identical pattern, seven other apartment complexes were developed by respondents through seven separate partnerships. For each venture, a partnership executed a nominee agreement with Creekside, Inc., to obtain financing. (For one of the ventures, a different Kentucky corporation, Cloisters, Inc., in which Bollinger had a 50 percent interest, acted as the borrower and titleholder. For convenience, we will refer to both Creekside and Cloisters as "the corporation.") The corporation transferred the construction loan proceeds to the partnership's construction account, and the partnership hired a construction supervisor who oversaw construction. Upon completion of construction, each partnership actively managed its apartment complex, depositing all rental receipts into, and paying all expenses from, a separate partnership account for each apartment complex. The corporation had no assets, liabilities, employees, or bank accounts. In every case, the lenders regarded the partnership as the owner of the apartments and were aware that the corporation was acting as agent of the partnership in holding record title. The partnerships reported the income and losses generated by the apartment complexes on their partnership tax returns, and respondents reported their distributive share of the partnership income and losses on their individual tax returns.

The Commissioner of Internal Revenue disallowed the losses reported by respondents, on the ground that the standards set out in National Carbide Corp. v. Commissioner, 336 U.S. 422 (1949), were not met. The Commissioner contended that *National Carbide* required a corporation to have an arm's-length relationship with its shareholders before it could be recognized as their agent. Although not all respondents were shareholders of the corporation, the Commissioner took the position that the funds the partnerships disbursed to pay expenses should be deemed contributions to the corporation's capital, thereby making all respondents constructive stockholders. Since, in the Commissioner's view, the corporation rather than its shareholders owned the real estate, any losses sustained by the ventures were attributable to the corporation and not respondents. Respondents sought a redetermination in the United States Tax Court. The Tax Court held that the corporations were the agents of the partnerships and should be disregarded for tax purposes. Bollinger v. Commissioner, 48 T.C.M. 1443 (1984), ¶84,560 P-H Memo T.C. On appeal, the United States Court of Appeals for the Sixth Circuit affirmed. 807 F.2d 65 (1986). We granted the Commissioner's petition for certiorari.

II

For federal income tax purposes, gain or loss from the sale or use of property is attributable to the owner of the property. See Helvering v.

Horst, 311 U.S. 112, 116-117 (1940); Blair v. Commissioner, 300 U.S. 5, 12 (1937); see also Commissioner v. Sunnen, 333 U.S. 591, 604 (1948). The problem we face here is that two different taxpayers can plausibly be regarded as the owner. Neither the Internal Revenue Code nor the regulations promulgated by the Secretary of the Treasury provide significant guidance as to which should be selected. It is common ground between the parties, however, that if a corporation holds title to property as agent for a partnership, then for tax purposes the partnership and not the corporation is the owner. Given agreement on that premise, one would suppose that there would be agreement upon the conclusion as well. For each of respondents' apartment complexes, an agency agreement expressly provided that the corporation would "hold such property as nominee and agent for" the partnership, App. to Pet. for Cert. 21a, n.4, and that the partnership would have sole control of and responsibility for the apartment complex. The partnership in each instance was identified as the principal and owner of the property during financing, construction, and operation. The lenders, contractors, managers, employees, and tenants — all who had contact with the development — knew that the corporation was merely the agent of the partnership, if they knew of the existence of the corporation at all. In each instance the relationship between the corporation and the partnership was, in both form and substance, an agency with the partnership as principal.

The Commissioner contends, however, that the normal indicia of agency cannot suffice for tax purposes when, as here, the alleged principals are the controlling shareholders of the alleged agent corporation. That, it asserts, would undermine the principle of Moline Properties v. Commissioner, 319 U.S. 436 (1943), which held that a corporation is a separate taxable entity even if it has only one shareholder who exercises total control over its affairs. Obviously, *Moline*'s separate-entity principle would be significantly compromised if shareholders of closely held corporations could, by clothing the corporation with some attributes of agency with respect to particular assets, leave themselves free at the end of the tax year to make a claim — perhaps even a good-faith claim — of either agent or owner status, depending upon which choice turns out to minimize their tax liability. The Commissioner does not have the resources to audit and litigate the many cases in which agency status could be thought debatable. Hence, the Commissioner argues, in this shareholder context he can reasonably demand that the taxpayer meet a prophylactically clear test of agency.

We agree with that principle, but the question remains whether the test the Commissioner proposes is appropriate. The parties have debated at length the significance of our opinion in National Carbide Corp. v. Commissioner, supra. In that case, three corporations that were wholly owned subsidiaries of another corporation agreed to operate their production plants as "agents" for the parent, transferring to it all profits except for a nominal sum. The subsidiaries reported as gross income only this sum, but the Commissioner concluded that they should be taxed on the entirety of the profits because they were not really agents. We agreed, reasoning first, that the mere fact of the parent's control over the subsidiaries did not establish the existence of an agency, since such control is typical of all shareholder-corporation relationships, id., at 429-434; and second, that the agreements to pay the parent all profits above a nominal amount were not determinative since income must be taxed to those who actually earn it without regard to anticipatory assignment, id., at 435-436. We acknowledged, however, that there was such a thing as "a true corporate agent . . . of an owner-principal," id., at 437, and proceeded to set forth four indicia and two requirements of such status, the sum of which has become known in the lore of federal income tax law as the "six *National Carbide* factors":

> [1] Whether the corporation operates in the name and for the account of the principal, [2] binds the principal by its actions, [3] transmits money received to the principal, and [4] whether receipt of income is attributable to the services of employees of the principal and to assets belonging to the principal are some of the relevant considerations in determining whether a true agency exists. [5] If the corporation is a true agent, its relations with its principal must not be dependent upon the fact that it is owned by the principal, if such is the case. [6] Its business purpose must be the carrying on of the normal duties of an agent.

Id., at 47 (footnotes omitted).

We readily discerned that these factors led to a conclusion of non-agency in *National Carbide* itself. There each subsidiary had represented to its customers that it (not the parent) was the company manufacturing and selling its products; each had sought to shield the parent from service of legal process; and the operations had used thousands of the subsidiaries' employees and nearly $20 million worth of property and equipment listed as assets on the subsidiaries' books. Id., at 425, 434, 438, and n.21.

The Commissioner contends that the last two *National Carbide* factors are not satisfied in the present case. To take the last first: The Commissioner argues that here the corporation's business purpose with respect to the property at issue was not "the carrying on of the normal duties of an agent," since it was acting not as the agent but rather as the owner of the property for purposes of Kentucky's usury laws. We do not agree. It assuredly was not acting as the owner in fact, since respondents represented themselves as the principals to all parties concerned with the loans. Indeed, it was the lenders themselves who required the use of a corporate nominee. Nor does it make any sense to adopt a contrary-to-fact legal presumption that the corporation was the principal, imposing a federal tax sanction for the apparent evasion of Kentucky's usury law. To begin with, the Commissioner has not established that these transactions were an evasion. Respondents assert without contradiction that use of agency arrangements in order to permit higher interest was common practice, and it is by no means clear that the practice violated the spirit of the Kentucky law, much less its letter. It might well be thought that the borrower does not generally require usury protection in a transaction sophisticated enough to employ a corporate agent — assuredly not the normal modus operandi of the loan shark. That the statute positively envisioned corporate nominees is suggested by a provision which forbids charging the higher corporate interest rates "to a corporation, the principal asset of which shall be the ownership of a one (1) or two (2) family or (2) family dwelling," Ky. Rev. Stat. §360.025(2) (1987) — which would seem to prevent use of the nominee device for ordinary home-mortgage loans. In any event, even if the transaction did run afoul of the usury law, Kentucky, like most States, regards only the lender as the usurer, and the borrower as the victim. See Ky. Rev. Stat. §360.020 (1987) (lender liable to borrower for civil penalty), section 360.990 (lender guilty of misdemeanor). Since the Kentucky statute imposed no penalties upon the borrower for allowing himself to be victimized, nor treated him as in pari delictu, but to the contrary enabled him to pay back the principal without any interest, and to sue for double the amount of interest already paid (plus attorney's fees), see Ky. Rev. Stat. section 360.020 (1972), the United States would hardly be vindicating Kentucky law by depriving the usury victim of tax advantages he would otherwise enjoy. In sum, we see no basis in either fact or policy for holding that the corporation was the principal because of the nature of its participation in the loans.

Of more general importance is the Commissioner's contention that the arrangements here violate the fifth *National Carbide* factor — that the corporate agent's "relations with its principal must not be dependent upon the fact that it is owned by the principal." The Commissioner asserts that this cannot be satisfied unless the corporate agent and its shareholder principal have an "arm's-length relationship" that includes the payment of a fee for agency services. The meaning of *National Carbide*'s fifth factor is, at the risk of understatement, not entirely clear. Ultimately, the relations between a corporate agent and its owner-principal are always dependent upon the fact of ownership, in that the owner can cause the relations to be altered or terminated at any time. Plainly that is not what was meant, since on that interpretation all subsidiary-parent agencies would be invalid for tax purposes, a position which the *National Carbide* opinion specifically disavowed. We think the fifth *National Carbide* factor — so much more abstract than the others — was no more and no less than a generalized statement of the concern, expressed earlier in our own discussion, that the separate-entity doctrine of *Moline* not be subverted.

In any case, we decline to parse the text of *National Carbide* as though that were itself the governing statute. As noted earlier, it is uncontested that the law attributes tax consequences of property held by a genuine agent to the principal; and we agree that it is reasonable for the Commissioner to demand unequivocal evidence of genuineness in the corporation-shareholder context, in order to prevent evasion of *Moline*. We see no basis, however, for holding that unequivocal evidence can only consist of the rigid requirements (arm's-length dealing plus agency fee) that the Commissioner suggests. Neither of those is demanded by the law of agency, which permits agents to be unpaid family members, friends, or associates. See Restatement (Second) of Agency §§16, 21, 22 (1958). It seems to us that the genuineness of the agency relationship is adequately assured, and tax-avoiding manipulation adequately avoided, when the fact that the corporation is acting as agent for its shareholders with respect to a particular asset is set forth in a written agreement at the time the asset is acquired, the corporation functions as agent and not principal with respect to the asset for all purposes, and the corporation is held out as the agent and not principal in all dealings with third parties relating to the asset. Since these requirements were met here, the judgment of the Court of Appeals is affirmed.

Justice Kennedy took no part in the consideration or decision of this case.

NOTES

Justice Scalia's opinion is refreshing in its unwillingness to submerge the Court in an abstract test or a game of words involving the fifth *National Carbide* factor. Instead, the opinion finds a genuine principal-agent relationship in the existence of a written agreement when the property was acquired, in the fact that the corporation functioned as an agent for all purposes, and in the fact that the corporation held itself out as an agent in all third-party dealings.

Why wasn't the Court bothered by the argument that the decision was furthering evasion of state usury laws? Did Kentucky mean to prohibit the type of arrangements made by the taxpayers, or did the law have a more limited purpose?

Not all cases involving the agency issue concern corporations formed for the purpose of circumventing state usury limitations. See, e.g., Elot H. Raffety Farms v. United States, 511 F.2d 1234 (8th Cir. 1975) (the court of appeals recognized a corporation even though it was used only to avoid a foreign law requirement prohibiting conduct of a business by aliens). In Interstate Transit Lines v. Commissioner, 319 U.S. 590 (1943), a parent corporation was denied a deduction under §162(a) for a payment to its wholly owned subsidiary to defray the subsidiary's operating deficit for the taxable year, despite the fact that by contract it was entitled to the subsidiary's profits and was obliged to reimburse the subsidiary for its losses. The Court held that the subsidiary's operating deficit was not an expense of the parent's business. The case was complicated by the fact that the subsidiary was organized to engage in operations (intrastate transportation in California) that were forbidden to the parent because it was a foreign corporation. The Court was not called on to decide whether the parent's payments should be treated as an additional investment in the subsidiary.

PROBLEMS

15-1. Management Corp. is in the business of managing real estate investments made by limited partnerships in which it serves as the general partner. The limited partnerships are organized by Management Corp., which is compensated for both its management and organizational services. For a variety of reasons, banks making mortgage loans to the partnerships generally prefer that title to the property be held by a corporation. Management Corp. performs that function for the partnerships, which in turn compensate the corporation for its role. When Management Corp. performs this function, it represents to everyone it deals with that it is serving as an agent for the partnership. What else do you need to know to determine whether the corporation or the partnership is entitled to any deductions arising from the real estate activities?

C. REALLOCATION OF INCOME AND RELATED ISSUES

With corporate tax rates lower than the top individual tax rates, individuals have incentives to allocate income to corporations they control. Moreover, historically corporations have offered pension incentives to owner-employees not available to individual entrepreneurs. For example, prior to 1982 the pension opportunities available to employees of corporations far exceeded those available to the self-employed. In response to this disparity, professionals such as doctors and lawyers created wholly owned professional service corporations for which they would work. These corporations would be in the business of hiring out their sole employee (the doctor or lawyer) to his prior employer. The income that the corporation received was paid to its sole employee partly in cash and partly in the form of a lucrative pension plan. Thus, the professional service corporation often was used solely to obtain greater pension benefits.

Personal service corporations also offer income-splitting opportunities. For example, an architect might work exclusively for her professional service corporation for a salary far less than the fees received by the corporation for her services. Since the corporation will deduct the architect's salary under §162 as an ordinary and necessary business expense, the corporation's taxable income will be only that proportion of its receipts that it retains. The architect's taxable income, on the other hand, will equal her salary. By dividing receipts between herself and her corporation, no income goes untaxed, but the architect's compensation is taxed between two taxpayers, thereby taking advantage of the progressive rates of the income tax to reduce the total tax liability.

The allocation of income phenomenon is not restricted to shareholders trying to shift income to controlled corporations; it is a dominant issue for intercorporate allocations as well. In many cases U.S. corporations subject to U.S. taxation have an incentive to shift income to a related foreign corporation that may not be subject to U.S. taxation and is often subject to little foreign taxation. For example, suppose a U.S. corporation with a foreign subsidiary in a low tax jurisdiction manufactures thermostats at a cost of $100 that it sells to the subsidiary, which resells the thermostats to unrelated purchasers in the subsidiary's jurisdiction at a price of $500. If the U.S. parent charges the subsidiary $140 for the thermostats, it will have $40 subject to U.S. taxation. The $360 gain the subsidiary realizes on the resale is typically not subject to U.S. taxation. Often the Service in this type of situation will attempt to reallocate some of the subsidiary's income to the U.S. parent.

1. Section 482 in General

Section 482 authorizes the IRS to allocate gross income, deductions, and credits among related taxpayers to the extent necessary to prevent evasion of taxes or to reflect clearly the income of related taxpayers. The regulations implementing §482 are based on the principle that transactions between related parties should be evaluated on an "arm's length" basis — that is, how unrelated parties would structure the transaction.

Section 482 can apply whenever two taxpayers are "owned or controlled directly or indirectly by the same interests." In determining control, the IRS focuses on the realities of the situation rather than on whether there is formal legal control. Treas. Regs. §1.482-1(b)(3). Section 482 can apply to domestic and foreign corporations, but because of the steep graduation in §11 there is little to be gained by assigning income to a related U.S. corporation. In the international context, §482 is often applied to allocate income from a foreign subsidiary to a U.S. parent. The provision also applies, however, in the converse situation to allocate income from a foreign parent to a U.S. subsidiary or between commonly owned corporations, one foreign and one domestic.

The arm's-length character of a transaction between related parties (i.e., a controlled transaction) is best tested by comparing the results of the transaction in question with the results of unrelated taxpayers engaged in comparable transactions under comparable circumstances (i.e., uncontrolled transactions). The use of comparables is important in all the arm's-length methods described below. For two transactions to be considered comparable, an uncontrolled transaction need not be identical. When necessary, a reasonable number of adjustments may be made to account for material differences between a controlled and an uncontrolled transaction.

Comparability of two transactions can be established by looking at the following factors: functions, risks, contractual terms, economic conditions, and property or services. Treas. Regs. §1.482-1(d)(1). For two transactions to be comparable, the parties normally should perform the same functions (e.g., research and development, product design, assembly, marketing, warranty administration, transportation, and warehousing) with respect to the transactions. Also, the risks borne by the parties to each transaction should be similar. In comparing prices, the contractual terms (e.g., quantity, duration, warranty) of the two transactions should be comparable. For purposes of comparison, the economic conditions surrounding the two transactions (e.g., market alternatives for buyers and sellers, geographic markets, market size, and composition) should be similar. Finally, the nature of the property or services transferred should be comparable in both transactions.

The reallocation principles of §482 are best understood in the context of specific types of transactions. What follows is a summary of the principles that can apply to some of the more basic transactions addressed by the regulations. In any situation involving §482, the result is heavily dependent on the facts. Taxpayers receive little guidance from the decided cases. The regulations attempt to provide more certainty in reallocating income, but uncertainty still abounds. This uncertainty has made reallocation of income one of the most pervasive tax problems faced by multinational corporations.

a. Sales

When Parentco, a U.S. corporation, sells goods to Subco, a foreign subsidiary, which then resells the goods to unrelated purchasers, the gain that must be recognized by Parentco on the sale to Subco for U.S. tax purposes is determined in accordance with the arm's-length price that an unrelated purchaser would have paid under the same circumstances. The same is true if Parentco is a foreign parent corporation that sells goods to Subco, its wholly owned U.S. subsidiary, which resells to unrelated purchasers in the United States or if the foreign and U.S. corporations have a common parent corporation. The regulations detail the following pricing methods: the comparable uncontrolled price method, the resale price method, the cost plus method, and the comparable profits method. Treas. Regs. §1.482-3. Under some circumstances other methods are also permitted.

In a world with perfect information available at no cost, all methods would generate the identical allocation between parent and subsidiary corporation. A comparable transaction involving unrelated parties transacting at an arm's-length price is the best method of allocation. If that information is not available, working backward from the ultimate price charged by Subco to an unrelated purchaser may produce an arm's-length price for the sale from Parentco to Subco (i.e., the resale price method). If that information is not available, perhaps an arm's-length price can be determined by working forward from the actual manufacturing cost incurred by Parentco (i.e., cost plus method).

Under the "best method rule" of the regulations, the arm's-length price for a particular transaction should be determined using the method that provides the most accurate measure of an arm's-length result — hardly a shocking rule. Treas. Regs. §1.482-1(c). Use of the resale price method is generally appropriate when a manufacturer sells products to a controlled distributor that, without further processing or the use of significant intangibles, resells the products in uncontrolled transactions. Use of the cost plus method ordinarily is appropriate when a manufacturer sells products to a controlled taxpayer that resells after further processing or the use of significant intangibles. The comparable uncontrolled price method, if data are available, usually provides the most accurate measure of an arm's-length price.

Comparable uncontrolled price method. Under the comparable uncontrolled price method, the price for tax purposes deemed paid by Subco to Parentco is determined on the basis of "uncontrolled sales" made by Parentco to unrelated buyers. Treas. Regs. §1.482-3(b). An uncontrolled sale might include a sale made by Parentco to an unrelated purchaser if, like Subco, the purchaser is not an end-user. Also, comparable sales of the same product between two unrelated parties would provide information. In determining comparability, differences in the product or the circumstances surrounding the sale (e.g., volume discounts, whether the purchaser is a wholesaler or retail customer) are taken into account. For unique products or products in which the seller has a virtual monopoly, there may not be comparable uncontrolled prices.

Resale price method. If the comparable uncontrolled price method is unavailable (e.g., lack of comparables), the regulations then permit use of the resale price method, particularly when the related purchaser does not add significant value to the product (e.g., if the purchaser is a distributor) or does not use significant intangibles. Treas. Regs. §1.482-3(c). The resale price method is intended to measure the value of the distribution function performed by a related purchaser. Starting with the applicable resale price charged to unrelated purchasers, the resale price method determines an appropriate gross profit that is subtracted to determine the deemed transfer price on the sale between the related corporations. An appropriate gross profit is determined by multiplying the applicable resale price by an appropriate gross profit margin, which is essentially profit as a percentage of gross sales in uncontrolled transactions.

Cost plus method. The cost plus method is most appropriate when there are no comparable unrelated sales and the related purchaser does more than mere distribution (e.g., the subsidiary adds substantial value to the product) or uses significant intangibles. Treas. Regs. §1.482-3(d). Under this method, the costs of the company selling to the related party are determined and an appropriate gross profit markup is applied to determine the deemed sales price paid by the related party. Treas. Regs. §1.482-3(d).

Comparable profits method. The comparable profits method is based on the principle that similarly situated taxpayers will tend to earn similar returns over a reasonable period of time. The comparable profits method determines arm's-length consideration for a controlled transfer of property by referring to objective measures of profitability (profit-level indicators) derived from uncontrolled taxpayers that engage in similar activities with other uncontrolled taxpayers. An arm's-length range of constructive operating profits is determined by applying the profit-level indicators to the tested party. A controlled transaction will be considered arm's length if the tested party's actual operating profits are within the arm's-length range of the constructive operating profits. The tested party can be either party to a controlled transaction — generally the one that provides the simplest, and therefore the most easily compared, operations. In the case of the license of an intangible, the licensee will normally be the tested party.

Profit-level indicators are financial ratios that measure the relationships among profits, costs incurred, and resources employed. For example, the rate of return on capital employed is the ratio of operating profit to operating assets. This measure may provide an acceptable profit-level indicator if the tested party has substantial fixed assets or working capital. The regulations also provide a number of financial ratios, such as the ratio of operating profit to sales and the ratio of gross profit to operating expenses, that may serve as profit-level indicators. For a comparable uncontrolled company that has gross profits of $140 and operating expenses of $100, for example, the ratio of gross profits to operating expenses is 1.4. If the tested party has operating expenses of $50, then one point in the arm's-length range of constructive operating profits is $70.

In an example taken from the regulations, the comparable profit method is used to determine the transfer price for an intercompany sale of goods. Treas. Regs. §1.482-5(e). Foreign Parent (FP) manufactures consumer products. A U.S. subsidiary (USSub) purchases these products for distribution in the United States. Similar products are produced by other companies but none of them is sold to uncontrolled taxpayers. Because no comparable uncontrolled transactions exist and because there is insufficient data for use of either the cost plus or resale price methods, the comparable profits method is used by the IRS to verify the price paid by USSub to FP for the tangible property purchased in 1996.

USSub is selected as the tested party because of the availability of reliable data. USSub has the following financial profile:

	1994	1995	1996	Average
Sales	500,000	560,000	500,000	520,000
Cost of goods sold	393,000	412,400	400,000	401,800
Operating expenses	80,000	110,000	106,600	98,200
Operating profit	27,000	37,600	(4,600)	20,000

To test the transfer price paid by USSub to FP for the consumer products, the IRS would identify comparable parties to USSub (i.e., wholesale distributors in the same industry segment that perform similar functions and assume similar risks). Because working capital plays a significant role in generating operating profit, the IRS might choose the rate of return on capital as a profit-level indicator. Calculating the average ratio of operating profits to operating assets for each of the uncontrolled distributors and multiplying that ratio by the average operating assets of USSub for the three-year testing period leads to the following constructive operating profits (COP) for USSub:

Unrelated Distributor	OP/OA	USSub COP
A	1.7%	$ 8,840
B	3.1	16,120
C	3.8	19,760
D	4.5	23,400
E	4.7	24,440
F	4.8	24,960
G	4.9	25,480
H	6.7	34,840
I	9.9	51,480
J	10.5	54,600

If the IRS determines that the products sold by the distributors are not similar enough to allow the use of all the constructive operating profits, top and bottom constructive operating profits will be lopped off and the "interquartile" range (i.e., the 25th to the 75th percentile) of results will be used. In this example, the interquartile range is $19,760 to $34,840. Because USSub's reported average operating income of $20,000 falls within this range, the 1996 transfer pricing used by USSub will be accepted by the IRS even though there is an operating loss for 1996. If USSub's average operating income for the three-year period were $0, the IRS would determine a transfer price that increases USSub's operating profit to the median of the arm's-length range for 1996.

Other methods. All the methods just described and those described below relating to transactions other than sales depend in part on the availability of comparable transactions. Comparables are often difficult to locate, whether in the context of sales, services, or rentals of tangible property or licenses of intangible property. Moreover, product sales often are interrelated to the licensing of intangibles (e.g., manufacturing patents) used to produce the products. The difficulty in determining arm's-length prices for interrelated items has led to the development of alternative income allocation approaches used for determining the price of intercompany sales of inventory as well as royalty rates on intercompany licenses. Treas. Regs. §1.482-3(e). An appropriate method might include an allocation of overall profit based on an acceptable rate of return on invested capital or on a comparison of rates of return to operating costs.

b. Services

When one corporation performs services for or on behalf of a related corporation, the corporation purchasing the services is deemed to pay an arm's-length price to the corporation performing the services. The arm's-length price is deemed to equal the direct and indirect costs incurred in connection with the services performed; the regulations do not generally require the allocation of a profit for services performed between related parties if the services are incidental to the business function of the corporation. Treas. Regs. §1.482-2(b)(2).

c. Rentals of Tangible Property

When a taxpayer leases tangible property (e.g., machinery, equipment, real estate) to a related taxpayer, the regulations deem the user to have paid an arm's-length rental if the lease does not so provide. Treas. Regs. §1.482-2(c). An arm's-length rental is the amount that would have been charged on a transaction between unrelated parties. If the owner of a lease makes the property available to a related entity through a sublease, the arm's-length price is an amount equal to the owner's deductions (i.e., rent, maintenance, utilities, etc.). There is no deemed profit in the sublease situation.

d. Licenses of Intangible Property

Payments to a related party for a license or transfer of an intangible may be reallocated by the IRS if the payments are not deemed to be at arm's length. Intangible property for purposes of §482 is defined as including any patent, invention, formula, process design, pattern, know-how, copyright, trademark, franchise, license, or contract. §936(h)(3)(B). Methods for determining an arm's-length price for the transfer of an intangible include the comparable uncontrolled transaction (CUT) method, the comparable profits method (CPM), the profit split method (PSM), and the "other" method. Treas. Regs. §1.482-4(a). Generally, the comparable uncontrolled transaction method likely is the best method for determining an arm's-length price.

The comparable uncontrolled transaction method. Under the comparable uncontrolled transaction method, the arm's-length consideration for a controlled transfer of intangible property (i.e., transactions between related parties) is equal to the consideration charged in a comparable uncontrolled transaction (i.e., transactions between unrelated parties). Treas. Regs. §1.482-4(c). An uncontrolled transaction is considered comparable to a controlled transaction if the intangibles to be compared are in the same class of intangibles, relate to the same type of products within the same general industry, and have substantially the same profit potential (i.e., net present value). The regulations identify six classes of intangibles. Treas. Regs. §1.482-4(b). For example, patents, inventions, formulas, processes, designs, patterns, and know-how are in the same class; trademarks, trade names, and brand names are in the same class. These rules are intended to ensure that the circumstances surrounding the controlled and uncontrolled transactions are comparable.

The comparable profit method. Under this method, no adjustment is made to the operating income of a taxpayer if the income falls within the arm's-length range of results, which is a range of operating incomes for similar taxpayers. If the operating income does not fall within the arm's-length range, adjustments may be made in a taxpayer's transfer price to place the taxpayer within the arm's-length range.

The profit split method. Under this method, whether the allocation of the combined operating profit or loss attributable to one or more controlled transactions is arm's length is determined by reference to the relative value of each controlled taxpayer's contribution to that combined operating profit or loss. The relative value of each controlled taxpayer's contribution to the success of the relevant business activity is determined in a manner that reflects the functions performed, risks assumed, and resources employed by each participant in the relevant business activity. This method also calculates any residual profit splits based on the determined contribution values of each controlled taxpayer.

Periodic adjustments. Payments to a related party for a license or transfer of an intangible must be "commensurate with the income" attributable to the intangible. §482 (second sentence). The practical effect of the "commensurate with" language is that royalty arrangements between related parties can be periodically adjusted by the IRS to reflect changing market conditions. For example, royalty payments deemed received by a U.S. corporation from intangible property licensed to its foreign subsidiary might be adjusted periodically to reflect how the property actually performs in the hands of the licensee. If five or 10 years after the original license the intangible becomes extremely valuable, that increase in value (i.e., increased sublicensing royalties or increased sales of property incorporating the intangible) may be taxable to the licensor even if the royalty rates at the time of the original license were reasonable under the facts known at that time. This provision represents an extraordinary view of what an arm's-length transaction is — substituting an ex post determination for an ex ante determination. The fact that a royalty agreement at the time it was concluded provided for arm's-length payments does not guarantee that an adjustment will not be made in a subsequent year. Treas. Regs. §1.482-4(f)(2).

e. Loans

Like other transactions between related parties, a loan from one corporation to a related corporation must be made at arm's length; otherwise, the IRS may reallocate interest income between the parties. If U.S. Co. makes a loan to Subco, its foreign subsidiary, and charges inadequate interest, U.S. Co. has effectively transferred the earning of interest beyond U.S. tax jurisdiction. Conversely if Subco lends money to U.S. Co. and charges an artificially high interest rate, the interest deduction otherwise available to U.S. Co. diverts income to Subco. To prevent this assignment of income, the IRS generally imposes an arm's-length interest rate.

2. The Interplay of §482 and Foreign Law

The purpose of §482 is to force taxpayers for tax purposes to deal at arm's length with related parties. Suppose, however, that related parties are prohibited from setting an arm's-length price because of a foreign government law or regulation. For U.S. tax purposes, should §482 apply notwithstanding the impossibility of paying an arm's-length price?

In Procter & Gamble Co. v. Commissioner, 961 F.2d 1255 (6th Cir. 1992), Procter and Gamble (hereinafter P&G) owned all the stock of Procter and Gamble A.G. (hereinafter AG), a Swiss corporation engaged in marketing P&G's products in countries where P&G did not have a marketing subsidiary. AG licensed and paid royalties to P&G for the use of P&G's patents, trademarks, tradenames, knowledge, and assistance. AG, in turn, sublicensed the patents, etc., to its subsidiaries throughout Europe and the Middle East. The income earned by AG from its sublicensing activities was taxable directly to P&G under the controlled foreign corporation provisions (§§951-959). AG organized a Spanish subsidiary, Gamble

Espana, S.A. (hereinafter Espana) to manufacture and sell its consumer and industrial products in Spain. The Tax Court found that during the years in question, Spain prohibited the payment of royalties from Espana to AG.

Notwithstanding the Spanish prohibition against royalty payments to a parent corporation, the IRS determined that a royalty equal to 2 percent of Espana's net sales should be allocated to AG (and therefore be taxable to P&G). The IRS reasoned that no taxpayer would give away the right to use property in an arm's-length transaction. The only reason AG was willing to forgo a royalty payment from Espana was that, as a parent corporation, AG would reap the benefit of Espana's use of the royalty property in the form of increased stock value. A nonshareholder-licensor would not agree to license the use of its property unless it received royalty payments in exchange; otherwise, the income produced by the transferred property would inure to the benefit of the licensee's shareholders. Indeed, Spanish law recognized this fact by permitting the payment of royalties to unrelated licensors. Accordingly, there can be little doubt that it was the relationship of AG to Espana that gave rise to the uncompensated use of P&G's property.

Although the relationship of AG to Espana made the transaction possible, it was the existence of Spanish law that made the royalty payment impossible. Relying on the Supreme Court holding in Commissioner v. First Security Bank of Utah, 405 U.S. 394 (1972) (income shifted from a bank to a captive insurance company could not be allocated under §482 because receipt of insurance commissions by the bank would have violated U.S. banking laws), the Tax Court in *Procter & Gamble* ruled that the Service could not allocate income between related corporations when the purported misallocation was caused by foreign law. As a result of the Tax Court's decision, Procter & Gamble did not have to report royalty income deemed received by AG. See Texaco v. Commissioner, 98 F.3rd 825 (5th Cir. 1996).

A danger arises in allowing foreign law to impede the application of §482. It is not difficult to imagine that some taxpayers may actually encourage (and be willing to pay for) foreign governments to prevent certain arm's-length payments between related taxpayers so as to lower U.S. taxes. Should the United States allow foreign law to govern what is taxable in the United States when under the arm's-length principle of §482 the United States considers income to be subject to U.S. taxation?

PROBLEMS

15-2. USCO, a large U.S. oil company doing business in Saudi Arabia, is prohibited under Saudi law from selling any oil for more than $12 a barrel. The prohibition does not extend to resale by any purchaser from

USCO. USCO's costs of exploration are $9 a barrel. USCO sells the oil at $12 a barrel to Subco, a wholly owned subsidiary located in Finland, a low tax jurisdiction. Subco then resells the oil to independent purchasers at a price of $20 a barrel. Can the IRS reallocate any of Subco's profits to USCO? Consider Commissioner v. First Security Bank of Utah, 405 U.S. 394 (1972). Should *First Security* apply in an international context?

3. Income Shifting and the Assignment of Income Doctrine

Historically, the use of personal service corporations, discussed at page 560 supra, was motivated in part by the opportunities to lower income by dividing profits between a corporation and owner-employees. In Rubin v. Commissioner, 429 F.2d 650 (2d Cir. 1970), the Tax Court's application of the assignment of income doctrine to a taxpayer and his personal service corporation was reversed. Despite this reversal, the Tax Court continued to sustain assignment of income challenges to personal service corporations. The Tax Court was reversed again in Foglesong v. Commissioner, 621 F.2d 865 (7th Cir. 1980) (*Foglesong I*) (a chemical engineer owned 98 percent of a personal services corporation), and it finally conceded in Keller v. Commissioner, 77 T.C. 1014 (1981), that the assignment of income doctrine cannot be used to reallocate income away from a corporation to its employee-shareholder so long as the corporation is a viable entity. In *Keller* and in *Foglesong I,* the Tax Court observed that since §482 could apply to a taxpayer who worked as an employee for his controlled corporation, application of the assignment of income doctrine would be redundant.

In *Foglesong I* the circuit court gave the following explanation for why the assignment of income doctrine could not be used to reattribute income reported by Foglesong's corporation to Foglesong.

> Personal service corporation tax cases reveal a tension between "the principle of a graduated income tax . . . and the policy of recognizing the corporation as a taxable entity distinct from its shareholders in all but extreme cases." Rubin v. Commissioner, 429 F.2d 650, 652 (2d Cir. 1970). The impact of the graduated income tax is eroded when income is split artificially among several entities or over several tax years. The assignment of income doctrine under Section 61 (as formulated by Lucas v. Earl) seeks to recognize "economic reality" by cumulating income diffused among several recipients through "artificial" legal arrangements. The attribution of income to its "true earner" is simply a species of recognizing "substance" over "form."
>
> But, if the issue is one of attributing the income of a corporation to its sole stockholder-employee who "really" earned it, we encounter the important legal policy of the law favoring recognition of the corporation as a legal person and economic actor. . . .

Under the circumstances of this case, we think it inappropriate to attempt to weigh "business purpose" against "tax avoidance motives" in a determination whether the assignment of income doctrine of Lucas v. Earl should apply, in effect, to substantially disregard the corporate form. [T]o apply Lucas v. Earl in this fashion under the circumstances present here is effectively (and more realistically) to nullify the determination that the Corporation is a viable, taxable entity and not a sham. . . .

Do you agree with the majority in *Foglesong I* that application of the assignment of income doctrine would have been tantamount to disregard of the corporate entity? Recall that Foglesong was not the sole shareholder of the corporation. If the corporation had been held a sham, would all the income have been includible by Foglesong? In his dissenting opinion in *Keller*, Judge Wilbur wrote, 77 T.C. at 1042: "Mere existence — either of Mrs. Earl or petitioner's corporation — does not carry automatic immunity from the assignment of income doctrine." If Foglesong had signed the same employment documents with his sister rather than with the corporation, could the assignment of income doctrine have been applied? Suppose his sister owned a large chemical engineering firm?

In Sargent v. Commissioner, 93 T.C. 572 (1989), the court ruled that hockey players were employees of their hockey teams notwithstanding the fact that they had formed personal service corporations that contracted with the teams. *Keller* was distinguished on the ground that there was no issue as to who was the employer.

Foglesong I held out the promise that §482 could apply to allocate income between a personal services corporation and an employee-owner. But in Foglesong v. Commissioner, 691 F.2d 848 (7th Cir. 1982) (*Foglesong II*), the court ruled that §482 did not apply where an owner-employee worked exclusively for the corporation because the owner-employee under these circumstances did not operate a separate trade or business to which income could be allocated under §482. But see Haag v. Commissioner, 855 F.2d 855 (8th Cir. 1988) (rejecting *Foglesong II* and allocating much of the income of a corporation performing medical services to the owner-employee doctor). See also Rev. Rul. 88-38, 1988-1 C.B. 246 (IRS will not follow *Foglesong* on the separate business issue).

PROBLEMS

15-3. Rock Star earns between $500,000 and $1 million in royalties and salary under a contract with Recording Co. To defer recognition of most of this income until after Rock Star's greatness fades, Rock Star agrees to work exclusively for Deferral Corp., a wholly owned corporation of Rock Star's tax lawyer. Assume Deferral Corp. is located in the Cayman Islands, and its income is not subject to any U.S. or foreign income taxation.

Deferral Corp. agrees to pay Rock Star annual compensation of $750,000 in the form of a lifetime, $75,000 per year annuity. Thus, after one year, Rock Star will receive $75,000 for life, after two years, Rock Star will receive $150,000 for life, etc. The contract between Rock Star and Deferral Corp. can be canceled at the beginning of each year by either party.

    a. How should Rock Star and Deferral Corp. be taxed if Deferral Corp. enters into a new contract with Recording Co. after the old contract expires, obligating Rock Star to record and perform for Recording Co. on the same terms as before?

    b. Suppose Recording Co. refuses to sign with anyone other than Rock Star. Rock Star accordingly signs with Recording Co. and then assigns all his rights and obligations under the Recording Co. contract to Deferral Corp. in exchange for the lifetime annuity. How should Rock Star and Deferral Corp. be taxed?

4. Denial of Tax Benefits under §269A

Although Congress in 1982 substantially equalized the pension benefits available to employees and the self-employed, thereby removing a major incentive to form a personal services corporation, it also enacted §269A. That section resembles §482 by providing for income and deduction reallocations rather than tax benefit denial. But it is triggered by forming or acquiring control of a corporation with a principal purpose of avoiding tax or obtaining benefits otherwise unobtainable. The Conference Committee wrote of §269A: "The conferees intend that the provisions [of §269A] overturn the results reached in cases like Keller v. Commissioner, 77 T.C. 1014 (1981), where the corporation served no meaningful purpose other than to secure tax benefits which would not otherwise be available." H.R. Rep. No. 760, 97th Cong., 2d Sess. (1986).

    Suppose a husband, H, and wife, W, simultaneously graduate from law school. They form WH Corp., for which each works and in which each is a 50 percent shareholder. The corporation then hires out its two employees to two separate law firms for $50,000 per year. The corporation pays H and W only $35,000 each and retains (and pays taxes on) $30,000. Will this device reduce H and W's overall tax liability? Can the Commissioner wage a successful challenge to the scheme under §269A?

5. The "Graduated Bracket Amount" and §1561(a)

For some corporations, the corporate income tax rates are progressive. See page 87 supra. Just as individual taxpayers might seek to assign income to family members in lower tax brackets, so too might affiliated corporations seek to divide profits among several related entities so as to take advantage of the graduated corporate rates available to low-profit corporations. In §1561(a), Congress has provided that the "component members" of a "control group" must share a single run through the corporate progressive rates. A "control group" consists of a parent and its controlled subsidiary, §1563(a)(1); a brother-sister pair, §1563(a)(2); or three or more corporations, each of which is a member of a parent-subsidiary group or a brother-sister group and one of which is a common parent corporation, §1563(a)(3). The "component members" of controlled groups are defined in §1563(b). See §1561. Suppose *A* owns 40 percent and *B* owns 60 percent of the stock of *X* Corp. *A* owns all the stock of *Y* Corp. Are *X* Corp. and *Y* Corp. a brother-sister controlled group, or must there be a commonality of control? See United States v. Vogel Fertilizer Co., 455 U.S. 16 (1982).

II

SUBCHAPTER S CORPORATIONS

16

S Corporations: Overview

A. INTRODUCTION

In this chapter we begin our study of S corporations. Most corporations, called C corporations, see §1361(a)(2), are treated as taxpayers independent of their shareholders. Some corporations, called S corporations, see §1361(a)(1), file an informational return but do not (with some exceptions) pay income taxes. Instead, an S corporation's items of income and deduction are passed-through to its shareholders who report these items directly on their individual income tax returns. This chapter and the two following it are concerned exclusively with the taxation of such S corporations.

Subchapter C of the Internal Revenue Code, §§301-385, provides most of the provisions governing the taxation of *all* corporations, C corporations and S corporations alike. Subchapter S, §§1361-1378, adds those provisions specially applicable to S corporations. One important aspect of the taxation of S corporations is the coordination of the rules in these two subchapters. Indeed, §1371(a)(1) provides: "Except as otherwise provided in this title, and except to the extent inconsistent with this subchapter, subchapter C shall apply to an S corporation and its shareholders." Accordingly, we will examine sections in both Subchapters C and S, but when examining a provision in Subchapter C, our emphasis will be on its application to S corporations.

There are two basic models upon which pass-through taxation can be designed: the entity model and the aggregate model. Under a pure entity model, the entity computes its taxable income without reference to any tax attributes of its beneficial owners. That is, the entity's basis in its assets is independent of any asset basis of its shareholders or partners, the entity has a taxable year and method of accounting independent of the taxable years and accounting methods of its owners, etc. Once the entity's taxable income or loss is computed, it is passed through to its owners.

Under a pure aggregate model, the entity has no tax attributes of its own and does not compute a taxable income. Instead, the entity is treated as no more than an aggregate of its owners, so that, for example, it has no independent basis in its assets but instead uses the aggregate of its owners' bases. Thus, a separate depreciation schedule must be maintained for each owner's interest in each entity asset, each owner may have a distinct holding period for each asset, etc. While a pure aggregate approach to pass-through taxation is possible, in practice it would be very cumbersome to implement.

Subchapter K constructs a modified entity model for the taxation of partnerships and their partners. Computationally, we treat a partnership as an entity separate from its partners having its own tax attributes including basis, taxable year, and accounting method. However, much of Subchapter K is devoted to injecting some of the aggregate model into the mixture.

For example, §§722-723 ensure that initial aggregate inside basis equals initial aggregate outside basis. Further, the rules of §§705 and 752 struggle to preserve this equality. Indeed, the optional basis adjustments of §§734(b) and 743(b) can ensure that the equality between aggregate inside and aggregate outside bases is maintained despite excess distributions and dispositions of partnership interests. Equality of aggregate inside and outside bases minimizes the impact of the partnership on the taxation of its partners.[1]

Similarly, distributions from a partnership to a partner as well as contributions from a partner to a partnership usually are not taxable events. Thus, transfers of partnership property generally are taxable only when a nonpartner is involved. See §§721, 731; but see §§702(a)(2), 704(c)(1)(B), 737. Once again the rules of Subchapter K seek to make a partnership transparent to taxation of its partners.

The taxation of S corporations is much closer to a pure entity model. While aggregate inside basis will begin equal to aggregate outside basis, that equality will be broken once the S corporation incurs debt. There is, in other words, no corporate analog to §752. Distributions of property from a corporation to a shareholder are generally taxable to the entity (and through it, to its shareholders), and contributions to a corporation can be taxable depending on the ownership interests of the contributing shareholders. There are no optional basis adjustments akin to §§734(b) and 743(b). In fact, even the assignment of income doctrine gives way to the relatively pure entity model of Subchapter S in that precontribution unrealized gain and loss in contributed assets is shifted away from the

1. See page 665 infra.

contributing shareholder and to the other shareholders: There is no provision equivalent to §704(c). Finally, the flexibility for which partnership taxation is most noted is absent from Subchapter S because there are no special allocations of corporate-level income and deductions. Thus, Subchapter S is very different from Subchapter K.

But there are also similarities because each Subchapter implements a form of pass-through taxation. Pass-through taxation requires that distributive share of income (by whatever name) must increase outside basis while distributive share of loss must have the opposite effect. This is true in Subchapter K, and because it *must* be true if entity-level income and loss is to be recognized once and only once, it also is found in Subchapter S. Thus, our inspection of Subchapter S will reveal the corporate analogs of partnership outside basis, distributive shares, and outside basis adjustments. The remainder of this chapter presents an overview of the taxation of S corporations, emphasizing the similarities to and differences from the taxation of partnerships.

But before that overview begins, one more detail must be mentioned. A corporation can be a C corporation at some times and an S corporation at other times. To be sure, most corporations begin and end as one type or the other without any mid-life changes. But a C corporation is permitted to file an S corporation election and an S corporation's election may terminate, and in either event transition issues arise. This chapter as well as the next consider only S corporations wholly lacking all C corporation history. In Chapter 18 we look at the problems faced by existing C corporations filing an S corporation election as well as the problems of S corporations whose elections terminate.

B.   THE S CORPORATION ELECTION

Kean v. Commissioner _____
469 F.2d 1183 (9th Cir. 1972)

BYRNE, JR., District Judge:

Appellants, petitioners in the Tax Court, were shareholders in Ocean Shores Bowl, Inc., hereinafter referred to as Bowl, a Washington corporation. They appeal from a judgment of the Tax Court, 51 T.C. 337, invalidating Bowl's election under Subchapter S, . . . and disallowing petitioners' deductions on their personal tax returns of their pro rata shares of Bowl's 1962 and 1963 net operating losses.

Bowl was formed on March 20, 1962 and had only one class of stock issued and outstanding. On October 30, 1962 Bowl filed a timely election to be taxed as a small business corporation pursuant to [§1362] of the Internal Revenue Code of 1954. Consents to such election were contemporaneously filed by all of the shareholders of record and their wives. As a result of the election, Bowl's net operating losses of $15,316 for the short taxable year 1962 and $56,638.28 for 1963 were deducted in pro rata shares by petitioners on their 1962 and 1963 personal income tax returns.

Some Bowl debentures and 125 shares of Bowl stock were held in the name of petitioner, William MacPherson. He and his brother, petitioner Murdock MacPherson, were engaged in the real estate business in a company called MacPhersons, Inc. Each brother owned 45% of the stock of MacPhersons, Inc. with the remaining 10% being held by their mother. William and Murdock MacPherson had many joint investments which were conducted without any written agreement. Whoever initiated the investment would normally be responsible for its management. Neither held a power of attorney for the other. The books and records of MacPhersons, Inc. were maintained by its employee, Donald Minkler.

On their 1962 joint income tax return William MacPherson and his wife deducted the net operating loss of Bowl accruing to the 125 shares in William's name. In 1963 William MacPherson and his wife deducted one half of the net operating loss for that year attributed to said shares while Murdock MacPherson and his wife deducted the other one half on their joint return. In 1964 the William MacPhersons and the Murdock MacPhersons each reported the sale of one half of the 125 shares of Bowl stock and one half of the Bowl debentures. All of these returns were prepared by Donald Minkler.

A 1965 Internal Revenue Service audit disclosed that the 125 shares of Bowl stock and Bowl debentures, issued to William MacPherson in 1962, were purchased with a MacPhersons, Inc. check. The cost of the purchase was charged on the books of MacPhersons, Inc. equally against the drawing accounts of William and Murdock. Murdock MacPherson has never been repaid by William MacPherson for the amounts taken out of his drawing account to pay for the stock and debentures.

Murdock MacPherson was not a shareholder of record of Bowl. Neither he nor his wife were mentioned in the Subchapter S election filed with the Internal Revenue Service in October, 1962; nor did they file a consent to the election. None of the other shareholders knew that Murdock MacPherson was involved in any way with Bowl until the 1965 audit.

The Tax Court held that Bowl's Subchapter S election was invalid because Murdock MacPherson, as a beneficial owner of Bowl stock, was a shareholder within the meaning of [§1362] and had not consented to the corporation's election. Based on this finding, the court disallowed petitioners' deduction of their pro rata shares of the corporation's net operating losses.

Subchapter S of the Internal Revenue Code of 1954 allows a small business corporation, as defined by [§1361], to elect to be exempt from corporate income taxes with the consequence that its shareholders are taxed directly on the corporation's earnings or may deduct the corporation's losses. Section [1362(a)(2)] provides that the corporation's election is "valid only if all persons who are shareholders . . . consent to such election."

Petitioners contend that since Murdock MacPherson was not a shareholder of record and was not able to exercise any rights as a shareholder under Washington law, he was not a "shareholder" under [§1362]. We disagree. The question of who is a shareholder as the term is used in Subchapter S must be determined by federal rather than state law. . . . Treasury Regulation §1.1371-1(d)(1), implementing Subchapter S, states that "Ordinarily, the persons who would have to include in gross income dividends distributed with respect to the stock of the corporation are considered to be shareholders of the corporation."*

Petitioners challenge the validity of this regulation on the ground that it has no statutory basis and is in conflict with the legislative history. They rely on a portion of the report of the Senate Finance Committee discussing Subchapter S which stated:

> An election may be made to supply the tax treatment provided by this new subchapter only if all of the shareholders consent to this election. For this purpose the shareholders are those of record as of the first day of the taxable year in question, or if the election is made after that time, shareholders of record when the election is made.

S. Rep. No. 1900, 85th Cong., 2nd Sess., p. 87.

The Tax Court in Alfred N. Hoffman, 47 T.C. 218, 235 (1966), aff'd sub nom. Hoffman v. Commissioner of Internal Revenue, 391 F.2d 930 (5th Cir. 1968), in considering the contention that a shareholder of record rather than the beneficial owner of the stock must consent to the Subchapter S election, discussed the report of the Senate Finance Committee as follows:

> While this use of the words "of record" furnishes some support for petitioner's position, it is entirely inconsistent with the basic congressional purpose to tax the undistributed corporate income only to the persons who are accountable for dividends paid by the corporation, and those persons are the real owners of the stock whether or not they are the shareholders "of record." In the circumstances, we must rely upon the all pervasive legislative purpose and not upon the foregoing fragmentary phrase in the committee report.

Subchapter S allows shareholders of a small business corporation to elect alternative tax consequences resulting from stock ownership. Without a Subchapter S election the corporation is liable for corporate taxes, the

---

* This regulation has been withdrawn and more specific guidance is now provided. See Treas. Regs. §1.1362-6(b). — Eds.

shareholders cannot deduct corporate losses, and only distributed dividends are subject to the personal income tax. If the election is made, the corporation is exempt from corporate taxes and the shareholders may deduct corporate net operating losses but must pay personal income tax on all corporate income whether distributed or not. The desirability of a Subchapter S election depends upon the individual tax considerations of each shareholder. The final determination of whether there is to be an election should be made by those who would suffer the tax consequences of it. . . .

A treasury regulation which supplies the definition that Congress omitted must be sustained unless unreasonable and obviously inconsistent with the statute. Bingler v. Johnson, 394 U.S. 741, 89 S. Ct. 1439, 22 L. Ed. 2d 695 (1969); Commissioner of Internal Revenue v. South Texas Lumber Co., 333 U.S. 496. Treasury Regulation §1.1371-1(d)(1) is consistent with the basic purpose of Subchapter S and reasonably implements the legislative mandate.

We conclude, as did the Tax Court, that William and Murdock MacPherson jointly invested in the 125 shares of Bowl stock issued to William MacPherson. Murdock MacPherson was the beneficial owner of one half of that stock in William MacPherson's name and must be considered a "shareholder" for the purpose of [§1362]. Murdock MacPherson's failure to file a consent invalidates Bowl's Subchapter S election. Therefore, petitioners were not entitled to deduct their pro rata shares of Bowl's net operating loss for 1962 and 1963. . . .

Finally, petitioners contend that the District Director abused the discretion reposed in him by Treas. Reg. §1.1372-3(c)* and that the Tax Court erred in refusing to review the exercise of the District Director's discretion.

After the judgment of the Tax Court finding that Bowl's Subchapter S election was invalid due to Murdock MacPherson's failure to consent, petitioners requested of the District Director an extension of time, pursuant to Treas. Reg. §1.1372-3(c), in which to file consents. All the petitioners offered to file new consents for the years 1962 and 1963.

The District Director denied the request. Petitioners then filed a motion in the Tax Court for retrial, further trial or reconsideration, seeking a review of the discretion exercised by the District Director. The Tax Court denied the motion.

The District Director advised petitioners that he was rejecting the request for an extension because the Tax Court had "issued an opinion in these cases . . . and because we do not feel the circumstances of this matter meet the requirements of Regs. §1.1372-3(c)."

The fact that the Tax Court had issued an opinion invalidating Bowl's Subchapter S election was not a basis for refusing to allow petitioners an

---

* Treas. Regs. §1.1372-3(c) is now reissued as Treas. Regs. §1.1362-6(b)(3)(iii). — EDS.

extension of time to file consents. At the time the opinion was filed, no request had been made to the District Director and nothing in the opinion precluded him from granting a subsequent request for extension.

Additionally, there is no valid basis for the District Director's determination that the requirements of Treas. Reg. §1.1372-3(c) had not been met. Under the regulation the failure to file a consent will not invalidate the Subchapter S election and an extension of time to file new consents should be granted if it is shown to the satisfaction of the District Director that: (1) there was reasonable cause for the failure to file such consent, and (2) the government interest will not be jeopardized by treating the Subchapter S election as valid. There was reasonable cause for Murdock MacPherson's failure to file a timely consent. Murdock MacPherson was not a shareholder of record. He believed that whatever ownership interest he had in the shares did not necessitate his consent to Bowl's election. When the Internal Revenue Service disagreed with this position, the petitioners sought a judicial determination. Until the Tax Court issued its opinion, Murdock MacPherson did not know that his consent was required to consummate Bowl's election under [§1362]. Furthermore, there is nothing to indicate that any government interest is jeopardized by now validating the Subchapter S election.

At the time of the Subchapter S election, petitioners, other than possibly the MacPhersons, did not know or have reason to suspect that Murdock MacPherson had any ownership interest in Bowl's stock. The District Director's failure to exercise his discretion so as to allow petitioners to file their consents deprives eight taxpayers of deductions taken in good faith ten years earlier and saddles each taxpayer with a substantial liability for back taxes. It is apparent that Treas. Reg. §1.1372-3(c) was promulgated to prevent the harsh result reached in cases of this kind.

The District Director abused his discretion by arbitrarily refusing to allow petitioners an extension of time in which to file their consent to Bowl's Subchapter S election. Mensik v. C.I.R., 328 F.2d 147 (7th Cir. 1964); Bookwalter v. Mayer, 345 F.2d 476 (8th Cir. 1965).

We affirm the opinion of the Tax Court, except with regard to its refusal to review the exercise of the District Director's discretion, and order the District Director to grant petitioners an extension of time to file the consents pursuant to Treas. Reg. §1.1372-3(c).

Rev. Rul. 86-110

1986-2 C.B. 150

ISSUE

If a corporation's election to be an S corporation is automatically terminated because the corporation inadvertently had one or more ineligible shareholders for a limited period of time before discovery and correction, is the corporation treated as continuing to be an S corporation under section 1362(f) of the Internal Revenue Code during the period when it had one or more ineligible shareholders?

FACTS

X corporation is an electing small business corporation. *A*, the majority shareholder of *X*, on advice of counsel, transferred shares of *X* stock to two irrevocable trusts for the benefit of *A*'s minor children. Neither trust was an eligible shareholder under section 1361(c)(2) or section 1361(d)(3) of the Code because neither trust was treated by sections 671 through 679 as entirely owned by an individual that is a citizen or resident of the United States and because each trust had more than one income beneficiary. Thus, under section 1362(d)(2), the transfer of stock to the trusts resulted in an automatic termination of the S corporation election.

It was not *A*'s desire or expectation to terminate the election when the transfer of the stock was made to the trusts. *A* acted on the advice of counsel that such transfers would not jeopardize the Subchapter S election, and *A* would not have made the transfers but for this advice. *X* and its shareholders continued to file returns and report income in a manner consistent with their belief that the election was still in effect.

Within a reasonable period of time after discovery of the termination, *A* took steps to correct the problem so that *X* once more qualified as a small business corporation. In addition *X*, and each shareholder of *X*, agreed to make any adjustments required by the Service with respect to such period as the Service might specify.

LAW AND ANALYSIS

Section 1361(a) of the Code provides that the term "S corporation" means, with respect to any tax year, a small business corporation for which an election under section 1362(a) is in effect.

Section 1361(b)(1) of the Code defines a "small business corporation" as a domestic corporation that is not an ineligible corporation and does not (A) have more than 35 shareholders, (B) have as a shareholder, a person (other than an estate and other than a trust described in section 1361(c)(2)) that is not an individual, (C) have a nonresident alien as a shareholder, and (D) have more than one class of stock.

Section 1361(c)(2) of the Code provides that four types of domestic trusts may be shareholders of an S corporation: a trust that is treated as owned by an individual who is a citizen or resident of the United States;

a trust that was treated as owned by an individual who was a citizen or resident of the United States immediately before the death of the deemed owner and that continues in existence after such death, but only for the 60-day period (or 2-year period if the entire corpus of the trust is includible in the gross estate of the deemed owner) beginning on the day of the deemed owner's death; a trust with respect to stock transferred to it pursuant to the terms of a will, but only for the 60-day period beginning on the day on which such stock is transferred to it; and a trust created primarily to exercise the voting power of stock transferred to it.

Section 1361(d) of the Code provides that a qualified subchapter S trust can be treated as a trust described in section 1361(c)(2) if a beneficiary of the trust makes an election for such treatment. A qualified subchapter S trust is a trust the terms of which require that (i) during the life of the current income beneficiary, there shall be only one income beneficiary of the trust; (ii) any corpus distributed during the life of the current income beneficiary may be distributed only to such beneficiary; (iii) the income interest of the current income beneficiary in the trust shall terminate on the life of the current income beneficiary, the trust shall distribute all of its assets to such beneficiary. In addition, all the income of the trust must be distributed (or required to be distributed) currently to one individual who is a citizen or resident of the United States.

Section 1362(d)(2) of the Code provides that an election under section 1362(a) will be terminated whenever (at any time on or after the first day of the first taxable year for which the corporation is an S corporation) the corporation ceases to be a small business corporation.

Section 1362(f) of the Code provides that if (1) an election by any corporation is terminated under section 1362(d)(2) or (3) of the Code, (2) the Secretary determines that the termination was inadvertent, (3) no later than a reasonable period of time after discovery of the terminating event, steps are taken so that the corporation is once more a small business corporation, and (4) the corporation, and each person who was a shareholder during the period specified under section 1362(f), agree to make such adjustments (consistent with the treatment of the corporation as an S corporation) as may be required by the Secretary with respect to that period, then, notwithstanding the terminating event, such corporation will be treated as continuing to be an S corporation during the period specified by the Secretary.

S. Rep. No. 97-640, 97th Cong., 2d Sess. 12 (1982), 1982-2 C.B. 718, 723, discusses section 1362(f) of the Code. It states in part:

> If the Internal Revenue Service determines that a corporation's subchapter S election is inadvertently terminated, the Service can waive the effect of the terminating event for any period if the corporation timely corrects the event and if the corporation and the shareholders agree to be treated as if the election has been in effect for such period.

Under the facts presented, since *A* transferred stock to trusts that are ineligible shareholders under section 1361(b)(1) of the Code, *X* ceased to be a small business corporation, thereby terminating its S corporation election. However, the termination was inadvertent. *A* acted on advice of counsel and would not have made the transfers but for this advice. Further, *A* took the necessary steps to correct the problem within a reasonable time after discovery of the termination and *X* and its shareholders agreed to make such adjustments as may be required by the Secretary.

HOLDING

The S corporation is treated as continuing to be an S corporation under section 1362(f) of the Code for the period specified by the Service during which it had one or more ineligible shareholders.

NOTES

1. *Eligibility.* For a corporation to be taxed as an S corporation, it must be a "small business corporation" as defined in §1361(b) and it must file an election pursuant to §1362(a). Despite the name, the definition of a small business corporation is not based in any way on the size of the corporation's business. "Small" in this context refers to the number of shareholders: a "small business corporation" under §1361(b) cannot have more than 75 shareholders, although for this purpose a husband and wife are treated as a single shareholder, §1361(c)(1). Other requirements are: (1) the corporation must be domestic; (2) all shareholders must be individuals, estates, certain qualifying trusts, see §1361(c)(2)), pension, profit-sharing or stock bonus plans qualifying under §401, or charitable organizations, see §1361(c)(7); (3) no nonresident alien may be a shareholder; and (4) the corporation may have only one class of stock outstanding. In addition, the corporation must not be an insurance or financial company, or be any one of several other special types of corporations. See §1361(b)(2).

If a corporation satisfies these requirements, it may file an election to be taxed as an S corporation. Every shareholder must consent to this election, §1362(a)(2), although once made, the election need not be ratified by new shareholders who acquire stock after the election is filed. Because the effect of an S corporation election is to pass-through and tax shareholders on the corporation's income, requiring unanimous shareholder consent eliminates any possible argument that taxing a shareholder on the corporation's income violates the Constitution.

If an S corporation election is filed during the first 2½ months of the corporation's taxable year, the election can be effective for the current year or for the subsequent year, whichever the corporation prefers. If the election is filed after more than 2½ months into the current taxable year, it automatically becomes effective for the subsequent year. §1362(b). Once filed, an election continues until it is revoked or the corporation ceases to be a "small business corporation." And once an S corporation's Subchapter S election terminates, the corporation is prohibited from filing a new election for five taxable year years. §1362(g).

2. *Revocation and termination.* An S corporation may file a revocation of its election so long as shareholders holding more than one-half of its shares agree. §1362(d)(1). Note that this does *not* require consent by a majority of the shareholders: if, for example, one shareholder owns 51 of the 100 outstanding shares of the corporation, then that shareholder alone has the ability to terminate the S corporation election and the remaining shareholders have no say in the matter. The revocation may specify a prospective date, although, like the election itself, a revocation can be effective for the current taxable year if filed within the first 2½ months of the year.

If an eligible corporation makes a late election or makes no election at all for the current year, the corporation may nevertheless be treated as an S corporation if the Secretary of the Treasury determines that the failure to make a timely election was due to reasonable cause. §1362(b)(5). The Service has adopted a surprisingly generous interpretation of its authority under this provision. See Rev. Proc. 98-55, 1998-46 I.R.B. 27.

An S corporation election will be terminated without regard to its shareholders' desires if the corporation fails to satisfy the requirements of a small business corporation. For example, if one shareholder sells her shares to several others, the total number of shareholders may exceed 75, immediately terminating the S corporation election. Similarly, a shareholder could sell her stock to an impermissible trust or to a nonresident alien, and again the S corporation election would be terminated.

It might be the case that the corporation accidently terminates its S corporation election under §1362(d)(2). If the corporation can convince the Internal Revenue Service that the termination was inadvertent, S corporation status can be restored without legal interruption. §1362(f). However, the Service may require of the corporation and of its shareholders any adjustments the Service deems appropriate.

Note that the provisions governing the S corporation election plainly contemplate the possibility that a corporation will spend part of its existence as a C corporation and part as an S corporation. In this and the next chapter, we will consider only those corporations electing to be taxed as S corporations throughout their existence; the taxation of an S corporation having a C corporation history is substantially more complex. For example, such S corporations can terminate their S corporation election by having too much passive income. §1362(d)(3).

PROBLEMS

16-1. *S* Corp. is an S corporation having 76 shareholders including *H* and *W,* a married couple. *H* and *W* are about to become divorced from one another. Will their divorce have any impact on the other S Corp. shareholders and, if so, is there any way *H* and *W* can minimize this impact?

C.   FORMATION

There are no special rules governing the formation of an S corporation. Accordingly, we look to the general rules of subchapter C for the applicable provisions. Under §351, the transfer of property to a corporation in exchange for shares of the corporation is tax-free to the transferor-shareholder. However, unlike partnerships in which a similar rule is unconditional, the rule of §351 imposes an additional requirement: For the transfer to be tax-free to the shareholder (or shareholders), the transferor (or transferors) must be "in control" of the corporation immediately after the exchange. For this purpose, "in control" means ownership of stock possessing 80 percent of the vote as well as ownership of 80 percent of the shares of each class of nonvoting stock. See §§351(a), 368(c).

If several persons transfer property to one corporation in a single transaction, the control requirement will be satisfied so long as the group of transferors is in control of the corporation immediately after the transfer. Note that we count all the shares of all the transferors including shares owned prior to the transfer. For example, suppose S Corp. has 100 shares outstanding, 25 owned by individual *X* and 75 by individual *Y.* If *Y* and individual *Z* contribute property to the corporation in exchange for 25 shares each, the transaction falls within §351 because the transferor group (individuals *Y* and *Z*) owns 125 of the 150 outstanding shares (over 83 percent) immediately after the exchange.

When a transaction falls within §351, the transferor-shareholders take a carryover basis in the shares received. §358(a)(1). This should come as no surprise: Because no gain or loss is recognized on the exchange, basis cannot change. Accordingly, asset basis is transformed into stock basis for no net change. This rule corresponds to §722 in the partnership context.

If a transfer falls outside of §351 (because either the transferor group lacks control of the corporation after the exchange or the transfer consists of services rather than property), the exchange is fully taxable to the transferor-shareholder(s). That means the transferor-shareholder recognizes gain or loss on the exchange and takes a fair market value basis in the shares received. The effect of this rule is to increase the shareholder's net basis by the amount of gain (or reduced by the amount of loss) recognized on the transaction.

A corporation does not recognize gain or loss on the exchange of its stock for property (or for services) without regard to whether the transaction falls within §351. See §1032. Given the double tax regime implemented by subchapter C, this rule makes sense: Because the corporation has not engaged in any productive activity simply by receiving property for its stock, it should not yet be taxed on any income. This rule also makes sense in the pass-through context of subchapter S: There is no need to tax transactions between a pass-through entity and its owners; taxation can (but need not) wait until there occurs a transaction between the entity or its owners and a third party.[2]

Although the corporation's immediate tax consequences are independent of the application of §351, the corporation's basis in the assets acquired from the shareholder are not. If the transfer is tax-free to the transferor-shareholder under §351, the corporation carries over the shareholder's basis in the assets. §362(a). However, if the transaction falls outside of §351, the corporation takes a fair market value basis in the assets. These rules ensure that the corporation's asset basis and the shareholder's stock basis begin equal. In other words, initial aggregate inside basis will equal initial aggregate outside basis even if some or all of the transferor-shareholders fail to qualify under §351 (because, for example, they contribute services rather than property).

For purposes of §351, "property" does not include services. §351(d)(1). Some property, notably patents, copyrights, and accounts receivable, can owe most of their value to services. When such property is contributed to a corporation in exchange for stock, the question arises whether §351(a) should apply to the transaction. For the most part, the courts have construed broadly the term "property" in §351. See, e.g., Hempt Brothers, Inc. v. United States, 490 F.2d 1172 (3d Cir. 1974) (accounts receivable constitute "property").

D. PASS-THROUGH OF CORPORATE INCOME AND DEDUCTION

An S corporation is not a taxpayer.[3] Like a partnership, an S corporation computes its taxable income and then passes that income through to its

---

2. See page 663 infra.
3. An S corporation with a C corporation history can be a taxpayer. See Chapter 18 infra.

owners. Here, those owners are its shareholders, and each shareholder reports a proportion of the corporation's income based on the shareholder's relative ownership of the corporation's outstanding shares. For example, if shareholder X owns 15 of the 100 outstanding shares of S Corp.'s outstanding stock, then X reports 15 percent of S Corp.'s taxable income or loss. If a shareholder's percentage of stock ownership changes during the year, the corporation's income is allocated ratably to each day of the year and then passed through to each shareholder in proportion to the shareholder's ownership interest on each day. §1377(a).

As in the partnership context, the character of items of income and deduction recognized by the corporation and passed through to its shareholders is preserved. For example, capital gain recognized by the corporation will be reported as capital gain by the shareholders, and charitable contributions made by the corporation will be treated as charitable deductions of the shareholders. §1366(a)-(b); cf. §702(a)-(b).

The allocation of corporate income among the shareholders in proportion to stock ownership is mandatory and cannot be varied. In the partnership context, items of income and deduction can be allocated among the partners almost any way they desire, limited only by the requirement that allocations have "substantial economic effect."[4] This flexibility is wholly missing from subchapter S. In fact, the rule that corporate income be apportioned according to stock interests does not give way even in the face of assignment of income concerns.

For example, suppose individuals X and Y form S Corp., with X contributing cash of $10,000 and Y contributing inventory with adjusted basis of $6,000 and fair market value of $10,000. Each receives 50 shares of S Corp. stock, so that when the inventory is sold, each will report half of the $4,000 gain realized on the sale. In the partnership arena and consonant with assignment of income concerns, precontribution appreciation in the contributed assets must be allocated to the contributing partner under §704(c). Thus, in the partnership context Y would be taxable on the entire gain of $4,000. In subchapter S, however, the gain is allocated between X and Y in proportion to relative stock ownership.

Recognition of pass-through income by a shareholder must increase outside (i.e., stock) basis so that the income will not be taxed twice.[5] Similarly, recognition of pass-through loss must decrease outside basis so that loss will not be recognized twice. This is in fact the case under §1367(a), and this section fully parallels §705 including provisions treating tax-exempt income like taxable income and nondeductible, noncapitalizable expenses such as illegal bribes and kickbacks like deductions.[6]

An S corporation's items of income and deduction are passed-thru to its shareholders on the last day of the corporation's taxable year.

---

4. See Chapter 20 infra.
5. See page 661 infra.
6. Id.

§1366(a)(1). Accordingly, shareholders whose taxable years do not coincide with that of the corporation will enjoy some deferral, with the greatest deferral enjoyed by those shareholders whose taxable years end just prior to the close of the corporation's taxable year.[7]

Under §1378, an S corporation is not free to choose its taxable year. Unless the S corporation can convince the Service that it has a sufficient business purpose to justify some other taxable year, an S corporation must use the calendar year as its taxable year. While this rule eliminates deferral opportunities for calendar year taxpayers, it mandates deferral for fiscal-year taxpayers beyond that enjoyed by most taxpayers. Of course, because shareholders of S corporations must be individuals[8] and individuals invariably are calendar-year taxpayers, restricting S corporation's use of fiscal years should present little real opportunity for deferral.

Pass-through of corporate loss is limited to a shareholder's outside basis. §1366(d). However, in this situation outside basis includes not only the shareholder's stock basis but also her basis in certain corporate debt. While the limitation of §1366(d) operates much like §704(d) limiting the pass-through of partnership loss to the partner's outside basis, the §1366(d) concept of debt basis makes the S corporation limitation considerably more complex. This complexity is deferred until the next chapter.[9]

PROBLEMS

16-2. Individuals X, Y, and Z form XYZ Corp., an S corporation. X contributes Blackacre with adjusted basis of $600 and fair market value of $1,000 in exchange for 100 shares of XYZ Corp. Y contributes inventory with adjusted basis of $2,000 and fair market value of $1,000 in exchange for 100 shares of XYZ Corp. Z contributes cash of $100 and services worth $900 in exchange for 100 shares of XYZ Corp.

    a. How are X, Y, and Z taxed on their contributions?

    b. What are the tax consequences to the corporation and to each shareholder if the corporation sells each of the contributed assets sometime during the corporation's first taxable year, assuming the corporation has no income or loss other than from disposition of the contributed property?

E. NONLIQUIDATING DISTRIBUTIONS

The entity-level taxation of nonliquidating distributions made by S corporations to its shareholders could not be more different from the partner-

---

7. See page 906 infra.
8. With some exceptions, see §1361(c)(2)-(3) and page 737 infra.
9. See page 740 infra.

ship scheme implemented by §§731-733. In general, a distribution of appreciated property by an S corporation is taxed to the corporation as if it sold the property to a third-party for fair market value. That is, the corporation is taxed on the appreciation in the property at the time of distribution. §311(a)-(b)(1). This corporate gain, like all corporate income, is then passed through to the corporation's shareholders at the close of the taxable year. Note, though, that no loss can be recognized on a nonliquidating distribution, and so any loss realized on such a distribution is gone forever.

The distribution can also produce gain to the distributee-shareholder, but only if the value of the property distributed exceeds the shareholder's stock basis. §1368(b). This rule is analogous to that in §731(a)(1) providing that a partner is taxable on a distribution of cash only to the extent the amount of cash distributed exceeds the partner's outside basis. Note, though, that §1368(b) applies to distributions of property as well as distributions of cash, so that nonliquidating distributions of property from an S corporation, in contradistinction to distributions of property from a partnership, can produce recognition of income to the distributee if her outside (stock) basis is insufficient to absorb the distribution. Consistent with this rule, the distributee reduces stock basis by the value of the property distributed[10] and takes a fair market value basis in any property distributed.

Because a distribution of appreciated property will produce gain to the corporation, gain that will pass through to the shareholders and will increase their stock bases, one might reasonably ask whether any such basis increase is available to reduce gain recognized by the distributee. For example, suppose individual X owns 50 percent of the outstanding stock of S Corp. with an adjusted basis of $10,000 in that stock. What are the tax consequences to X if S Corp. distributes Blackacre to X when Blackacre is worth $12,000 and has an adjusted basis to S Corp. of $8,000?

One might conclude that X recognizes $2,000 on the distribution as distributee (because the value ($12,000) of Blackacre exceeds X's $10,000 stock basis by $2,000) and is taxed on an additional $2,000 of corporate-level income (because S Corp. is taxed on the $4,000 appreciation in Blackacre, and X's share of that appreciation is $2,000). However, might it not be the case that X reports the $2,000 of pass-through income *first*, so that X's stock basis is adjusted upwards by $2,000 before computing the tax consequences of the distribution to X as distributee. If true, X's stock basis of $12,000 can fully absorb the $12,000 fair market value of Blackacre, so that by this reasoning X recognizes no income beyond the $2,000 passed through from the corporation.

10. If the distributee recognizes income on the distribution because her stock basis is insufficient to absorb the full amount of the distribution, stock basis is reduced only by so much of the value of the property as was *not* recognized as income, §1367(a)(2)(A), thereby reducing stock basis to (but not below) zero.

This ordering is supported by §1368(d)(1), which provides that taxation of a distributee "shall be applied by taking into account (to the extent proper) . . . the adjustments to the basis of the [distributee] shareholder's stock described in §1367." We know from §1366(a) that corporate-level items are passed through to the shareholders on the last day of the corporation's taxable year. Since the corporate-level gain recognized on the distribution of property therefore is passed through on the last day of the corporation's taxable year, application of §1368(d)(1) seems to imply that the shareholder-level tax consequences of a distribution are not determined until the close of the corporation's taxable year.

Regulations make clear, as indicated above, that the shareholder-level tax consequences of a distribution cannot be determined until the close of the corporation's tax year. As a consequence, taxable activities of the corporation can affect the shareholder's tax treatment of a mid-year distribution. Consider the following example taken from the Reg. §1.1368-3 (example 1):

> A, an individual, owns all 10 outstanding shares of S Corp. with adjusted basis of $1 per share. S Corp. is a calendar-year S corporation. On March 1, S makes a distribution of $38 in cash to A. For the entire year, S has net taxable income of $24. As a result of the distribution, A recognizes $4 of income computed as follows: income on the distribution equals the excess of the amount distributed [$38] over the sum of A's prior stock basis [$10] + pass-through income from the current taxable year [$24]. Of course, A's stock basis must be reduced to zero as well. §1367(a)(2)(A).

This treatment is very different from that of subchapter K. Under §731(a), a distribution of cash to a partner is taxable to the partner to the extent the amount of cash distributed exceeds the partner's *predistribution* outside basis. In subchapter S, we use the shareholder's *year-end* outside (i.e., stock) basis adjusted first for the shareholder's pass-through items of income and loss.

Reconsider the example above but assume that the distribution consists of property having an adjusted basis to the corporation of $10 and a fair market value of $38. Now, the distribution will not result in any recognition to A because A's year-end stock basis, after adjustment for pass-through income and loss, is $62,[11] and that amount is sufficient to absorb the entire $38 value of the distribution. A's stock basis will end up at $24, reflecting an increase of $52 for pass-through income and a decrease of $38 for the distribution. See §1367(a)(1)(A), (2)(A).

A distribution of property in excess of the distributee-shareholder's stock basis will break the equality of aggregate inside basis and aggregate outside basis. In subchapter K, this equality also can be broken by a distribu-

---

11. Prior stock basis of $10 + pass-through income of ($24 + $28), for a total of $62.

tion (but only of cash), though it will be reestablished if the partnership has a §754 election in effect.[12] Because S corporation distributions of property as well as of cash can break the equality, and because there is no subchapter S equivalent to §754, the inside/outside bases equality is more likely to disappear for S corporations than it is for partnerships.

Despite the more general language in §1368(d)(1), the final sentence of §1368(d) makes clear that gain from the distribution in excess of stock basis is determined before adjusting stock basis downward for pass-through of loss pursuant to §1367(a)(2). Thus, positive basis adjustments are made prior to computing the tax consequences of a distribution even though negative adjustments are made after the computation. This ordering rule minimizes the likelihood that a taxpayer will be forced to recognize income by reason of a distribution in a year in which the S corporation loses money.

For example, suppose individual X owns one share of stock in an S corporation with an adjusted basis of $10 as of the beginning of the year. If the corporation has no income or deductions for the year, then a distribution of $10 or less to X will be tax-free, §1368(b)(1), while a distribution in excess of that amount will produce income to X in the amount of the excess. §1368(b)(2).

But what if the corporation has net income or loss for the year? If the corporation distributes $12 to X during the year and X's share of the corporation's net earnings is $3 for the year, then X will recognize no income because the §1367(a)(1) positive stock basis adjustment for X's share of the earnings is made *prior to* determining the tax consequences to X of the distribution. §1368(d) (final sentence). Conversely, if the corporation distributes only $9 to X and X's share of the corporation net loss for the year is $2, X has no income on the distribution because the §1367(a)(2) negative stock basis adjustment is only made after determination of the tax consequences of the distribution. That is, the distribution reduces X's stock basis to $1, so that X can report only $1 of her share of the corporation's loss and the remaining $2 is deferred under §1366(d). Of course, if X has some debt basis in the S corporation, the $2 of loss not be deferred because debt basis, like stock basis, can be used to absorb pass-through of loss. §§1366(d)(1), 1367(b)(2).

PROBLEMS

16-3. What are the tax consequences to the three shareholders and to the corporation if *XYZ* in Problem 16-2(b) above distributes cash of $6.00 per share to each shareholder halfway into the corporation's first taxable year?

---

12. See Chapter 26 infra.

F. DISPOSITIONS OF SHARES AND LIQUIDATING DISTRIBUTIONS

1. Disposition of Stock Not in Redemption

The disposition of stock in an S corporation is taxed just like the disposition of stock in a C corporation. That is, gain or loss is recognized on each share based on the difference between the amount realized as compared with the shareholder's adjusted basis in the stock. See §1001. However, disposition of stock in an S corporation is more complex than disposition of stock in a C corporation because (1) the disposition affects the pass-through of corporate-level tax items, (2) the disposition can affect the taxation of distributions made to the selling shareholder, and (3) distributions as well as pass-through of corporate level items of income and deduction affect stock basis, so that a shareholder who sells stock of an S corporation cannot determine the amount of gain or loss on the sale until the close of the corporation's taxable year.

Disposition of shares in an S corporation will affect taxation of the corporate-level items because such items are passed-through in proportion to relative stock ownership on a day-by-day basis. §1377(a)(1). For example, suppose individual A owns 50 of the 100 outstanding shares of S Corp., an S corporation using the calendar year as its taxable year. On June 30, A sells 25 of those shares to individual B. If the corporation has net taxable income for the year of $2,000, A must report $750 on her individual return: $500 for six months ownership of 50 percent of S Corp. and $250 for six months ownership of 25 percent of S Corp.[13]

Suppose that A had sold all 50 of her shares in S Corp. on June 30. Now, A reports only $500 of S Corp.'s income, that being half the income for half the year. Note that it does not matter *when* S Corp. earned the income. Thus, A reports the same $500 whether S Corp. earned $1,000 in each half year or if S Corp. lost $1,000 in the first six months and then earned $3,000 in the last six months. Because corporate tax items are ratably allocated to each day of the corporation's taxable year, it does not matter when during the year the corporation accrued or received any particular item.

A shareholder who sells her entire interest in an S corporation during the middle of the corporation's taxable year might prefer that her share of the corporation's tax items not depend on corporate activities occurring after the shareholder terminates her interest in the activity. If the buyer and seller agree, they may elect to treat the corporation's taxable year as ending on the date of sale, with a new taxable year beginning on the following day. §1377(a)(2). If such an election is filed, the outgoing shareholder will be taxable on her share of corporate activities occurring only

---

13. For ease of computation, assume that June 30 is exactly one-half of the year.

on or prior to the day she terminates her interest in the S corporation. Similarly, the incoming shareholder will be taxable on her share of corporate activities occurring after the sale.

Disposition of some or all of a shareholder's stock in an S corporation also affects the taxation of distributions made to the selling shareholder prior to the sale of the stock. Recall that distributions of cash or property are tax-free to the distributee-shareholder to the extent that the amount of the distribution does not exceed the distributee-shareholder's stock basis. §1368(b)(1). Recall also that it is the shareholder's stock basis as of the close of the corporation's taxable year which is used in this comparison, so that the shareholder's stock basis is adjusted for pass-through items of income and deduction.

If a shareholder sells some or all of her shares during the taxable year, §1367(a) adjustments to the basis of the transferred shares for pass-through items of income and deduction as well as the downward basis adjustments for all prior distributions are effective immediately prior to the stock transfer. Treas. Reg. §1.1367-1(d)(1). To understand what this means, assume that individual A owns 40 of the 100 outstanding shares of S Corp., an S corporation using the calendar year as its taxable year. As of January 1, A owns these 40 shares with an adjusted basis of $10 per share. On June 30, A sells 15 of his 40 shares to individual C for $15 per share. During the entire calendar year, S Corp. earns $200.

To compute A's gain on the sale of the 15 shares, we must know A's adjusted basis in those shares. We begin with A's adjusted basis of $10 per share as of the beginning of the calendar year. We then increase that adjusted basis for A's share of the corporation's income. Treating June 30 as the mid-point of the year, $100 of the corporation's gain is allocated to the period from January 1 through June 30 and the remaining $100 is allocated to July 1 through December 31. Accordingly, each of the 100 outstanding shares is allocated $1 for the first half of the year, so that A's stock basis as of June 30 is increased to $11 per share. Thus, the sale of 15 shares for $15 per share yields a taxable gain of $4 per share, or $60 total gain. In addition, A must report $65 of pass-through income for the year.

Add now to this example the additional fact that A received a distribution of $80 sometime during the first half of the year. Now, we must adjust the basis of the transferred shares not only for the pass-through income allocable to the pretransfer period but also for the distribution. The tax effect of the $80 distribution is to reduce A's stock basis by $80 total, or $2 per share. Accordingly, A's adjusted basis in the shares as of the date of sale is now $9,[14] producing a taxable gain of $6 per share or $90 total.

---

14. This $9 per share adjusted basis is computed as follows: initial basis of $10 plus pass-through income of $1 less distribution of $2 equals $9.

Individual *A* still reports pass-through income of $65 on his individual return.

To make this example even more complicated, assume that *A* uses a fiscal year ending August 31 as her taxable year. This wrinkle means that *A* must report his gain from the sale of the 15 shares in one taxable year and his share of the pass-through income in the next taxable year. Further, *A* cannot compute his gain from the stock sale until the close of the corporation's taxable year (i.e., until sometime after December 31), which is after *A*'s individual tax return is due! *A* must estimate his stock gain and pay his taxes based on that estimate. If (as is likely) his estimate was not perfect, he must file an amended return showing additional income or seeking a refund.

PROBLEMS

16-4. How does your answer to problem 16-3 above change if shareholder *X* sells 35 of her shares to shareholder *Y* and 35 of her shares to shareholder *Z* one-quarter of the way into the year? What if the sale takes place three-quarters of the way into the year? Assume in each case that the sale price is $12 per share.

16-5. *S* Corp. is an S corporation using the calendar year as its taxable year. As of January 1, 2002, individual *I* owns all 100 outstanding shares of *S* Corp. with an adjusted basis of $10 per share. On March 1, 2002, *S* Corp. distributes Blackacre to *I*. At the time of the distribution, *S* Corp. has an adjusted basis in Blackacre of $5,000 and Blackacre is worth $17,000. What are the tax consequences of this distribution, assuming that in addition to the distribution:

    a. *S* Corp. recognizes taxable income for the year of $3,000?
    b. *S* Corp. recognizes a net loss for the year of $2,000?
    c. *S* Corp. recognizes taxable income for the year of $3,000, and *S* Corp. redeems half of *I*'s shares for $15 per share on July 1, 2002?

16-6. How does your answer to Problem 16-5(a) above change if the corporation's adjusted basis in Blackacre immediately prior to the distribution is $20,000?

2. Redemptions of Stock

A sale of stock from a shareholder back to the issuing corporation is called a "redemption" of stock. §317(b). The effect of a redemption on the shareholder is dependent on the shareholder's ownership interest in the corporation. At one extreme, consider the case of a shareholder holding all 100 outstanding shares of X Corp. If this shareholder sells, for example, 10 of the shares back to the corporation, the shareholder's relationship to the corporation is essentially unchanged: Both before and after the transaction, the shareholder owns 100 percent of the corporation. Accordingly, one would expect this redemption to be taxed like a distribution of property from the corporation to the shareholder (i.e., the stock transfer would be ignored), and that (usually) is the case.[15]

At the other extreme, consider the case of a shareholder selling every share she owns back to the corporation in exchange for cash. Once the redemption is complete, the shareholder has no further relationship with the corporation. From the shareholder's perspective, this transaction is identical to a sale of the shares to some third party, and the shareholder in this case usually is taxed as if the sale had been made to a third party. See §302(b)(1).

As an intermediate case, consider a shareholder D owning 60 of 120 outstanding shares in X Corp. If D sells 30 shares back to the corporation (i.e., if the corporation redeems 30 shares), then D's interest in the corporation drops from one-half (60 of 120) to one-third (30 of 90). This redemption resembles both a distribution and a sale in some respects. Had the sale been to a third party, D's interest would have dropped from one-half to one-fourth (30 of 120). Thus, the redemption reduced D's proportionate share of corporate control *less than* an equivalent sale would have reduced it. However, a straight distribution without the tender of any shares would have left D's interest at one-half, so that this redemption had more effect on D's ownership of the corporation than that of a simple distribution. In other words, when some but not all of the stock of a partial owner of a corporation is redeemed, the effect of the redemption on the shareholder's interest in the corporation is less than that of a sale but more than that of a distribution.

The taxation of redemptions is governed by §302.[16] Under §302(a), a shareholder whose stock is redeemed will be taxed as if the stock had been sold to a third party *if* the transaction is described in §302(b)(1)-(4). If the redemption is not described in §302(b), the shareholder is taxed as if the redeemed shares had been contributed to the corporation and then a distribution of the redemption proceeds followed; that is, the shareholder will get distribution treatment rather than exchange treatment. See §302(d).

---

15. Under some circumstances, the taxation of a redemption does not turn on the effect of the transaction on the shareholder's interest in the corporation. See §§302(b)(4) (partial liquidations), 303 (redemptions to pay death taxes). In such cases, even a distribution to a sole shareholder can receive exchange treatment.

16. Some distributions are taxed under §303.

Before looking at the rules of §302(b), it is worthwhile to restate the effect of §302(a). If the redemption falls within §302(b), the shareholder will be taxed as if the shares had been sold to a third party. We have looked at that taxation already: Gain or loss is based on a comparison of the amount realized with the shareholder's adjusted basis in the redeemed shares, and the transaction can affect the taxation of distributions to the shareholder and will be affected by the shareholder's allocable portion of pass through income and loss.

If the transaction does *not* fall within §302(b), then the shareholder is taxed as if the redemption proceeds had been received in a straight distribution. We have looked at the taxation of this transaction as well: So long as the shareholder's stock basis (all the stock, not just the redeemed shares) can absorb the amount of the distribution, no gain or loss is recognized. If the amount of the distribution exceeds the shareholder's stock basis, gain will be recognized to the extent of the excess. One additional aspect of a redemption taxed as a distribution is that the redeemed shares are treated as contributed to the corporation so that the shareholder's adjusted basis in the redeemed shares flows into his remaining shares. Treas. Reg. §1.302-2(c).

Internal Revenue Code §302(b) (and §302(c), which is incorporated in §302(b) by reference) is a very complicated provision fully covered in Chapter 5. What follows is an overview of the major aspects of §302(b).

Look first at §302(b)(3). This section provides that a redemption will be taxed as an exchange if the transaction terminates the shareholder's entire interest in the corporation. Usually, this means that the corporation redeems every share of stock held by the shareholder. However, a transaction in which a shareholder sells some of his shares to a third party and has the remaining shares redeemed by the corporation includes within it an actual sale as well as a redemption *taxed as a sale* pursuant to §§302(b)(3) and 302(a).

Look next at §302(b)(2). This section imposes a two-part test on the shareholder's *postredemption* relationship to the corporation. First, the shareholder must own less than 50 percent of the outstanding shares of the corporation after the redemption. Second, the shareholder's ownership percentage of the outstanding shares must be less than 80 percent of his preredemption ownership interest.[17] To see how these tests work, reconsider the case of shareholder *D* whose stock interest drops from 60 of 120 shares to 30 of 90 shares.[18]

Because *D*'s ownership interest in the corporation after the redemption is less than 50 percent (i.e., less than 45 of the outstanding shares),

---

17. Technically, these tests are applied to the shareholder's ownership of voting stock only. Because an S corporation can have only one class of stock outstanding, this aspect of §302(b)(2) usually plays no role in redemptions by S corporations. See page 615 infra.
18. See page 610 supra.

D passes the first test of §302(b)(2). The second test requires that we compare D's preredemption ownership percentage (60 of 120 shares, or 50 percent), with D's postredemption ownership percentage (30 of 90 shares, or 33.33 percent). Because 80 percent of D's preredemption ownership percentage is 40 percent (i.e., 80 percent of 50 percent is 40 percent), D passes the second test of §302(b)(2) as well as the first test. Accordingly, the redemption is described in §302(b)(2) and so is taxed as a sale to D under §302(a).

Reconsider this example but assume that only 20 of D's shares have been redeemed, so that D's ownership interest drops from 60 of 120 to 40 of 100. Once again D passes the first test under §302(b)(2) (because D owns less than 50 of the 100 outstanding shares after the redemption), but now D fails the second test. D's ownership percentage of the corporation prior to the redemption was 50 percent (i.e., 60 of 120 shares), and D's ownership percentage after the redemption is 40 percent (i.e., 40 of 100 shares). Because 40 percent is not *less than* 80 percent of the prior 50 percent (it is exactly 80 percent of 50 percent), D fails the second test of §302(b)(2). Accordingly, the redemption may be taxed as a distribution rather than as an exchange. See §302(d).

One point worth making in this connection is that the second test of §302(b)(2) is *not* satisfied by a redemption of 20 percent of a shareholder's stock. In the example above, the redemption of 20 of D's 60 shares is a redemption of 33.33% of D's shares, yet D fails to qualify under §302(b)(2). The comparison mandated by §302(b)(2) is D's ownership percentage in the corporation prior to the redemption as compared with D's ownership percentage in the corporation after the redemption. You should not try to restate this test in some other way.

Section 302(b)(1) plays a minor role in the taxation of redemptions, in large part due to a Supreme Court case limiting it to redemptions effecting a "meaningful reduction" in the shareholder's ownership of the corporation. United States v. Davis, 397 U.S. 301 (1970). As it now stands, §302(b)(1) has very little application outside of redemptions of preferred stock, transactions not arising in subchapter S by virtue of the one class of stock limitation. And §302(b)(4), applicable only to "partial liquidations," requires a corporate contraction under the narrow terms of §302(e). Of all four provisions in §302(b), only §302(b)(4) does *not* turn on the effect that the redemption has on the shareholder's ownership interest in the corporation.

The role played by §302(b) in the context of S corporations is very different from its role in the context of C corporations. Individuals owning shares of stock in a C corporation generally seek exchange treatment when shares are redeemed because recovery of basis followed by capital gain usually is more favorable to them than dividend income. If, though, the redeeming corporation is an S corporation, dividend treatment is generally more favorable: while exchange treatment still produces recovery of basis followed by capital gain, only the basis in the shares redeemed is available to offset the amount of the distribution. Dividends from an S corporation, on the other hand, can be absorbed by a shareholder's entire stock basis.[19]

The effect of a redemption on the redeeming corporation does not turn on application of §302 — that section governs only the shareholder's taxation. To the corporation, a distribution in redemption of stock is simply a distribution, so that the corporation will be taxed on any gain (but not loss) in the distributed property. Of course, any gain so recognized will be passed through to the shareholders in proportion to their stock interests on a day-by-day basis.

PROBLEMS

16-7. Individual H owns all 100 outstanding shares of X Corp., an S Corporation, with an adjusted basis of $10.00 per share. X Corp. distributes $300 to H in redemption of 25 of the shares held by H. Assuming X Corp. has no items of income or deduction for the taxable year, what are the tax consequences to H if the redemption is taxed as a distribution pursuant to §302(d)? How does the taxation change if the redemption is taxed as an exchange pursuant to §§302(a) and 302(b)(4)?

3.   Liquidating Distributions

When a corporation liquidates — that is, when it distributes all of its assets to its shareholders in exchange for all of its outstanding shares — the transaction technically is a distribution in redemption of stock. That technical description nicely indicates how the transaction is taxed: For the corporation it is taxed pretty much like a nonliquidating distribution while for the shareholder it is taxed as a redemption.

Consider first the corporation. Recall that nonliquidating distributions of appreciated property produce recognition of income to the distributing corporation as if the property had been sold to a third party. This taxation continues in the context of liquidating distributions, and it reflects an important difference between subchapter S and subchapter K. In subchapter K, contributions and distributions generally are not taxable. Rather, taxation waits until property is transferred outside of the partnership family. For most purposes, the partnership is transparent to taxable transactions.

---

19. Because of the dividends-received deduction available to corporate shareholders, see §243, redemptions from an S corporation are in some ways like dividends from a C corporation to corporate shareholders.

C corporations are taxpayers independent of their shareholders, and a transaction between a C corporation and one or more of its shareholders usually is a taxable event. While S corporations avoid the double tax of C corporations, they retain the independent status upon which the corporate double tax is founded. Thus, for most purposes an S corporation's shareholders are treated like unrelated parties, so that, for example, a distribution of property from the corporation to a shareholder is taxed like a sale of the property by the corporation to an unrelated individual. Recall that a nonliquidating distribution is not taxed precisely equivalent to a sale because the corporation cannot recognize loss on a nonliquidating distribution. A liquidating distribution is taxed more closely to that of a sale because the corporation often (but not always) can recognize a loss on the liquidating distribution of property having adjusted basis in excess of fair market value. Of course, any corporate gain or loss recognized on the distribution will flow through to the shareholders, producing pass-through income or loss as well as stock basis adjustments.

In general, an S corporation recognizes gain or loss on a liquidating distribution as if the property were sold for its fair market value. §336(a). However, loss will not be recognized if the distribution is made to a 50 percent or greater shareholder and either (1) is not pro rata or (2) consists of property acquired by the corporation in a tax-free transaction less than five years prior to the liquidating distribution. §336(d)(1). In addition, loss on property can be lost if the property was acquired by the S corporation in a tax-free transaction and it was acquired for the purpose of recognizing a corporate loss on the property. §336(d)(2).[20]

To the shareholders, a liquidating distribution will be treated as a taxable exchange of their shares for assets distributed in the complete liquidation. Recall that §302(b)(3) provides exchange treatment (via §302(a)) for distributions resulting in a complete termination of a shareholder's interest in the corporation. Since a liquidating distribution results in a complete termination of every shareholder's interest within the meaning of §302(b)(3), exchange treatment should be available and the shareholders should take the distributed assets with fair market value bases. This is in fact the result. §331(a).

---

20. This last limitation applies only to the extent of the loss built into the property at the time of acquisition by the corporation. See §336(d)(2)(A).

17

S Corporations: Selected Topics

A. ONE CLASS OF STOCK

Every system of pass-through taxation needs a mechanism for allocating the entity's income and loss among its owners. In the partnership context, that mechanism is §704. Most partnership income can be allocated among the partners as they see fit, subject only to the "substantial economic effect" test of §704(b). However, to protect assignment of income concerns, partnership gain and loss arising from a variation between property basis and fair market value at the time of contribution must be allocated to the contributing partner pursuant to §704(c). As you may know, much of the flexibility and complexity of subchapter K has its origins in these two provisions.

The "one class of stock" requirement in §1361(b)(1)(D) is the mechanism for allocating income among owners of an S corporation. It thus is the analog of §704(b)-(c), albeit without the flexibility or complexity. Because an S corporation can have only a single class of stock, the corporation's income and loss can be allocated in proportion to stock ownership. Were there two or more classes of stock outstanding, each shareholder's proportionate ownership of the corporation would be difficult to define.

After much debate, regulations have been issued interpreting the "one class of stock" limitation in §1361(b)(1)(D). These regulations provide that a corporation is not treated as having more than one class of stock if "all outstanding shares of stock [of the corporation] confer identical rights to distribution and liquidation proceeds." Treas. Regs. §1.1361-1(*l*)(2)(i). In particular, different shares may have different voting rights without violating the one class of stock requirement. §1361(c)(4).

NOTES

1. *Shareholder agreements.* Especially in closely held corporations, shareholders often sign agreements restricting their rights to transfer their stock. For example, an employee may be required to sell her stock to another shareholder or back to the corporation if she terminates her employment. Sale and redemption agreements triggered by death, bankruptcy, and divorce also are common. If a shareholder signs such an agreement, do the restrictions transform the shareholder's stock into a second, impermissible class of stock?

In general, the answer is no. Under the regulations, "[t]he determination of whether all outstanding shares of stock confer identical rights to distribution and liquidation proceeds is made based on the corporate charter, . . . applicable state law, and binding agreements relating to distribution and liquidation proceeds." Treas. Regs. §1.1361-1(*l*)(2)(i). The regulations specifically provide that these "governing instruments" do not include buy-sell agreements, agreements restricting the transferability of shares, and similar arrangements unless (1) a principal purpose of the agreement is to circumvent the one class of stock requirement and (2) the agreement establishes a purchase price that, at the time the agreement is entered into, is significantly in excess of or significantly below the fair market value of the stock. Treas. Regs. §1.1361-1(*l*)(2)(iii)(A).[1] Further, bona fide agreements to redeem or purchase shares at death, divorce, disability, or termination of employment are disregarded without further showing. Treas. Regs. §1.1361-1(*l*)(2)(iii)(B).

The regulations offer several examples applying these rules. For example, suppose an S corporation enters into an agreement providing that distributions to its shareholders will be made in such proportions as to ensure that each shareholder will receive the same amount after taking into account state tax burdens. Thus, shareholders residing in Texas (which imposes no state income tax) will receive $100 per share, while shareholders in Georgia (which imposes a state income tax of as much as 6 percent) receive $106.38 per share.[2]

In this example, the corporation will be treated as having *more than* one class of stock outstanding because a binding agreement relating to distribution proceeds is a "governing instrument" and this governing instrument alters distribution rights such that those rights are not identical among all outstanding shares. An opposite result would be reached if the corporation declared equal distributions but then withheld differing

1. These regulations further provide that agreements that provide for the purchase or redemption of stock at book value or at a price between book value and fair market value will not be considered as establishing a price significantly in excess of or below the fair market value of the stock.

2. A 6 percent tax imposed on $106.38 equals $6.38, so that the after-tax amount equals $100.00.

amounts in accordance with differing state withholding laws: In this latter circumstance, the amounts withheld would constitute constructive distributions so that the total actual plus constructive dividend amount would be equal for all shareholders. Compare examples (6) and (7) of Treas. Regs. §1.1361-1(*l*)(2)(v).

As a second example, suppose an S corporation distributes 50 percent of its taxable income within three months of the close of its taxable year, and suppose further that this distribution must be made in the same proportion as the corporation's taxable income is reported. If individual *A* owned all 100 outstanding shares of the corporation at the beginning of the corporation's taxable year and sold 50 of those shares half way through the year to individual *B,* the distribution would be made 75 percent to *A* and 25 percent to *B.*

Does this arrangement create a second class of stock? Note that the corporate distribution is *not* made in proportion to stock ownership *as of the date of the distribution.* Although one might think that the outstanding shares do not have identical rights with respect to distributions and therefore constitute more than a single class of stock, the regulations specifically permit distributions to be made in proportion to varying stock ownership during the year so long as such distributions are made "within a reasonable time after the close of the taxable year in which the varying interests occur." Treas. Regs. §1.1361-1(*l*)(2)(iv).

2. *Corporate debt as a second class of stock.* You may know that shareholder investment in the form of debt often offers tax advantages over investment in the form of equity. For example, periodic returns on debt (i.e., interest) are deductible to the corporation while periodic returns on equity (i.e., dividends) are not. Similarly, payments in retirement of corporate debt qualify for exchange treatment (i.e., recovery of basis followed by capital gain), while payments in retirement of corporate equity must pass the hurdles of §302(b) to avoid taxation as dividends.

Ever seeking to protect the federal fisc, the Commissioner often asserts that shareholder debt should be reclassified (and taxed) as equity. In the context of subchapter S, the usual advantages of debt over equity disappear. Nonetheless, the Commissioner might seek to reclassify nominal debt as equity so as to challenge the very validity of the corporation's subchapter S election: If nominal debt is reclassified as equity, might it not be treated as a second class of stock which then terminates the S corporation election?

One important aspect of the one class of stock regulations is that a corporate instrument not nominally classified as equity (i.e., debt, call options, and other financial instruments) will not violate the one class of stock requirement unless (1) the instrument is reclassified as equity under general principles of tax law, and (2) a principal purpose of issuing the instrument is to circumvent the rights to distribution or liquidation conferred on the corporation's outstanding shares by the governing instruments or to circumvent the limitation on eligible shareholders. Further,

debt instruments owned only by the corporation's shareholders in proportion to their stock holdings (and for that reason likely to be reclassified as
equity) are not treated as a second class of stock under these regulations.
As a corollary, no debt held by the sole owner of an S corporation can
violate the one class of stock rule. Treas. Regs. §1.1361-1(l)(4)(ii)(B)(2).

Even corporate debt failing these standards can still avoid being classified as a second class of stock if it is a written unconditional promise to
pay a sum certain on demand or on a specific due date if (1) the interest
due on the debt is not contingent on the corporation's profits, the payment
of dividends, or the borrower's discretion, (2) the debt is not convertible
into corporate equity, and (3) the debt is held only by an individual (other
than a nonresident alien) or a trust or estate allowed to be a shareholder
of an S corporation under §1361(c)(2). Treas. Regs. §1.1361-1(l)(5)(i).
This safe harbor for "straight debt" is available even to debt subordinated
to other debt of the corporation. Treas. Regs. §1.1361-1(l)(5)(ii). In addition, the safe harbor for such "straight debt" in §1361(c)(5) is also available to indebtedness held by "a person which is actively and regularly
engaged in the business of lending money"; that is, "straight debt" can
be held by financial institutions even though financial institutions are not
eligible to be shareholders of an S corporation.

PROBLEMS

17-1. Does an S corporation have more than one class of stock (a)
if all employee-shareholders are required to sell their stock back to the
corporation at book value upon termination of employment; (b) if all
married couples who purchase stock must provide upon purchase a buy-
sell agreement (upon whatever terms they desire) automatically effective
upon divorce and separation; (c) if, should the corporation miss two consecutive interest payments on its long-term debt, holders of that debt
automatically receive voting, preferred stock (none of which is outstanding
currently); (d) if highly compensated employees receive bonuses in the
form of "phantom stock," that being the nontransferable right to receive
additional salary as dividends are paid in proportion to those dividends
and the right to receive, upon termination of employment, a lump sum
equal to the increase (if any) in the value of the corporation's stock from
the time the phantom stock was issued until termination of employment;
or (e) if any employee-shareholder who is fired for cause must sell her
stock to the corporation at cost?

B. QUALIFIED SUBCHAPTER S SUBSIDIARIES

An S corporation can own 100 percent of the stock of a "qualified subchapter S subsidiary," defined in §1361(b)(3)(B) to mean a corporation that

is otherwise eligible to be an S corporation but whose stock is owned by an electing S corporation. If the S corporation elects for its subsidiary to be treated as a qualified subchapter S subsidiary (sometimes called a "Q-Sub"), then for tax purposes the Q-Sub loses its independent status; instead, all of its assets are treated as owned directly by its parent S corporation. §1361(b)(3)(A). Q-Subs can offer substantial flexibility to S corporation shareholders without imposing a second layer of taxation.

For example, suppose an S corporation has an active but risky active business as well as substantial investment assets. If the business and investment assets are held by a single corporation, the investment assets are potentially available to creditors of the risky business. If, though, the risky business is placed in a Q-Sub, the investment assets are protected from such claims. Note that placing the *investment assets* in the Q-Sub would not be effective because the stock of the Q-Sub, as an asset of the parent S corporation, would still be available to satisfy claims arising out of the conduct of the risky business. As this example demonstrates, the hybrid nature of a Q-Sub — transparent for tax purposes but respected for state law purposes — provides a fertile field of opportunity.

NOTES

1. *Election, revocation, and termination.* Unless filed within the first 2½ months of the corporation's taxable year, an election to be taxed as an S corporation will not be effective until the corporation's next taxable year. §1362(b). A Q-Sub has more flexibility: An election can be made at any time, and it can be effective immediately. Prop. Treas. Regs. §1.1361-3(a)(2)-(3). Indeed, if shareholders of an existing C corporation wish to elect S corporation in the middle of the year, they can transfer their C corporation stock to an S corporation and then cause the (now subsidiary) C corporation to become a Q-Sub. See the example in Prop. Treas. Regs. §1.1361-3(a)(4). Of course, if the S corporation is formed solely for this purpose, the Commissioner might challenge the transaction under §269 or the general business purpose doctrine. See Prop. Treas. Regs. §1.1361-4(a)(2). For administrative relief granted to inadvertently late elections, see Rev. Proc. 98-55, 1998-46 I.R.B. 27.

The S corporation parent of a Q-Sub can revoke the Q-Sub election at any time. Prop. Treas. Regs. §1.1361-3(b)(1). It also can revoke the election up to 2½ months retroactively. Prop. Treas. Regs. §1.1361-3(b)(2). This presents the Q-Sub with a window of opportunity that has no counterpart for the S corporation parent.

A Q-Sub election will be terminated if the corporation ceases to be an eligible entity. §1361(b)(3)(C). This has a parallel for the S corporation parent. §1362(d)(2). Indeed, if the S corporation parent ceases to be an S corporation, the Q-Sub will immediately lose its status as a Q-Sub. See

§1361(b)(3)(B)(i). Perhaps more importantly, the Q-Sub will lose its status as a Q-Sub if a single share if its stock is transferred from the parent S corporation to any person or entity. *Id.* In all cases, the effect of a termination is to cause the assets owned by the former Q-Sub to be treated as if transferred to a new corporation in exchange for its stock. §1361(b)(3)(C).

  2. *Conversion from C corporation to Q-Sub.* If the S Corporation parent of an existing C corporation elects to treat the C corporation as a Q-Sub, the C corporation is treated as distributing all of its assets to its S corporation parent in a liquidating distribution. In general, this deemed distribution will be tax-free to both the (deemed liquidating) C corporation as well as to its S corporation parent under §§332 and 337. Prop. Treas. Regs. §1.1361-4(a)(2). However, the regulations add that "[t]he tax treatment of the liquidation or of a larger transaction that includes the liquidation will be determined under the Internal Revenue Code and general principles of tax law, including the step-transaction doctrine." *Id.*

  For example, the regulations provide that a deemed liquidation of an *insolvent* subsidiary pursuant to a Q-Sub election is a taxable event, Prop. Treas. Regs. §1.1361-4(d) (example 5), consistent with general corporate law that a transaction cannot be described in §§332 and 337 unless there is a distribution of property to the corporation's shareholders. Note that an attempt to shore up the assets of the insolvent subsidiary immediately prior to the Q-Sub election may not work. Rev. Rul. 68-602, 1968-2 C.B. 135.

  3. *Planning opportunities.* S Corp. runs two businesses, risky business and secure business. The shareholders of S Corp. would like to insulate the assets of secure business from those of risky business. However, the assets of risky business are encumbered by loans that do not permit transfer of the risky business assets until the loan is fully repaid. How can the shareholders of the S corporation accomplish their purpose?

  Transfer of the assets of secure business to a Q-Sub will not work because that will leave the assets of secure business (in the form of the Q-Sub stock) at risk. Transfer of the assets of the risky business would work but cannot be accomplished under the terms of the loan agreement. However, the shareholders of S Corp. can form a new S corporation and then transfer their stock of the existing S corporation to the newly formed corporation. Thus, the operating corporation becomes the subsidiary, and a Q-Sub election is immediately filed. Finally, the assets of secure business are transferred to the Q-Sub's parent (that is, to the newly-formed S corporation) in a state-law dividend. For tax purpose, though, this final step has no effect because the Q-Sub's assets are treated as owned directly by its S corporation parent. Thus, the state law dividend is a nontransaction for tax purposes and has the non-tax effect of protecting the assets of secure business from the risks associated with risky business. For a wealth of planning opportunities using Q-Subs, see Michael S. Lux & Scot A. McLean, The IRS Clears the Air on S Corporation Subsidiaries — Proposed Regulations Under Code Sec. 1361(b)(3), J. Passthrough Entities (July-August 1998), at 29.

PROBLEMS

17-2. *S* Corp., an electing S corporation, owns all the outstanding stock of two C corporations, Brother Corp. and Sister Corp. Brother and Sister each own half of the outstanding shares of Child Corp., also a C corporation. Can *S* Corp. file a Q-Sub election for Brother, Sister, and Child?

C. STOCK AND DEBT BASIS

Suppose Debtor borrows $100 from Lender. To Lender, the loan is an asset. As with any asset, we can sensibly ask what the owners's basis in the asset is. Basis, of course, is the amount of cash the asset holder can receive in exchange for the asset without recognizing gain. See §1001(a). Here, Lender can receive the $100 principal amount of the debt back from Debtor without recognizing income. Accordingly, Lender's basis in the debt must be $100. Indeed, if Lender receives less than $100 back from Debtor, Lender will be entitled to claim a deduction for a bad debt. See §166(a)(2), a result fully consistent with ascribing a $100 basis to Lender's debt.

When Debtor uses the borrowed proceeds to purchase property, Debtor will take a cost basis in the property acquired. Thus, the effect of the loan is to give $100 of basis to both Lender and to Debtor; for Lender, basis is in the right to repayment; for Debtor, basis is in the borrowed proceeds or in property acquired with those proceeds. A borrowing transaction thus produces a doubling of total basis.[3]

For determining the extent to which pass-through losses may be claimed on an S corporation shareholder's individual return, the shareholder may use both equity and debt basis to absorb such losses. Equity basis is nothing but stock basis. Debt basis in this context means the shareholder's basis, if any, in loans made to the corporation. That is, debt basis refers to basis enjoyed by the shareholder not in the capacity as shareholder

---

3. More accurately, no doubling of basis occurs because Debtor has a negative basis in the debt itself. That is, Debtor will have to repay the principal amount of the debt without receiving a deduction for the payment or increase the basis of any asset. Debtor sometimes is said to have a $100 "sisab" (backward basis) in the repayment obligation to make clear that Debtor's tax relationship to the loan transaction is the inverse of Lender's relationship. For the remainder of this discussion, we will ignore Debtor's inverse basis (sisab) in the loan.

but rather in the capacity as lender. Of course, if the shareholder has made no loans to the corporation, debt basis will be zero.

If an S corporation shareholder lends funds to the S corporation and then sells the note, the shareholder may recognize income on the sale even if the third party pays less than face value for the note. For example, if the lending shareholder has used the note's basis to absorb pass-through loss, that basis is not available to offset sale proceeds from disposition of the note. There is, then, no doubling of basis but only a shifting of basis.

Do not forget that this shifting basis is available *only* for absorbing pass-through loss and not for absorbing distributions. An S corporation shareholder who receives a distribution of cash or property in excess of stock basis must report the excess as gain,[4] and in this context only true stock basis is counted. Debt basis is simply irrelevant in computing a shareholder's income from a distribution.

We know that pass-through of corporate income must increase outside basis: outside basis adjustments arising from the pass-through of income and deduction are the linchpin of pass-through taxation.[5] Because there are two distinct outside bases per shareholder (one equity and one debt), we must determine how pass-through of corporate income affects each. Subchapter S provides a simple ordering rule: If pass-through losses have been absorbed by debt basis, subsequent pass-through income will increase debt basis before equity basis until the debt basis has been fully restored. §1367(b)(2).

For example, suppose individual A forms S Corp. by contributing $10,000 in exchange for 100 shares of S Corp. stock. In addition, A loans $40,000 to S Corp., and assume the loan is respected for tax purposes (i.e., the loan is not treated as equity). If the corporation distributes $15,000 to A, A must report $5,000 of income because the amount of the distribution exceeds A's stock basis by that amount. Of course, A will reduce her stock basis to zero.

Suppose that the corporation invests its remaining cash of $35,000 in some activity, and suppose further that this activity produces a loss of $5,000 the following year. Although A's stock basis is zero, this $5,000 may pass-through to A because it can be absorbed by A's debt basis. That is, A will report the $5,000 loss on her individual return and will reduce her debt basis to $35,000.

If the corporation recognizes $8,000 of income the following year, that income will pass-through to A and will increase outside basis. Because debt basis is restored before equity basis, the first $5,000 of pass-through income increases A's debt basis from its current value of $35,000 back to its initial value of $40,000. §1367(b)(2)(B). The remaining $3,000 of basis

4. See page 604 supra.
5. See page 602 supra.

increase is applied to A's stock, increasing its basis from zero to $3,000. Any future pass-through of income will increase A's stock basis *only* unless A's debt basis subsequently is reduced: Debt basis can never be increased under §1367(b)(2)(B) beyond its original value.

As this example makes clear, debt basis is important despite the absence of a provision like §752. Shareholders, then, will fight for recognition of debt basis even in circumstances when it is less than clear that the statute authorizes it. In particular, shareholders often seek debt basis when they are not lenders but only guarantors of third party debt. Should such guarantors be treated as lenders for purposes of §1366(d)?

Estate of Leavitt v. Commissioner _____
875 F.2d 420 (4th Cir. 1989)

MURNAGHAN, Circuit Judge:
    The appellants, Anthony D. and Marjorie F. Cuzzocrea and the Estate of Daniel Leavitt, Deceased, et al., appeal the Tax Court's decision holding them liable for tax deficiencies for the tax years 1979, 1980 and 1981. Finding the appellants' arguments unpersuasive, we affirm the Tax Court.

I

As shareholders of VAFLA Corporation, a subchapter S corporation during the years at issue, the appellants claimed deductions under §1374 of the Internal Revenue Code of 1954 to reflect the corporation's operating losses during the three years in question. The Commissioner disallowed deductions above the $10,000 bases each appellant had from their original investments.

The appellants contend, however, that the adjusted bases in their stock should be increased to reflect a $300,000 loan which VAFLA obtained from the Bank of Virginia ("Bank") on September 12, 1979, after the appellants, along with five other shareholders ("Shareholders-Guarantors"), had signed guarantee agreements whereby each agreed to be jointly and severally liable for all indebtedness of the corporation to the Bank. At the time of the loan, VAFLA's liability exceeded its assets, it could not meet its cash flow requirements and it had virtually no assets to use as collateral. The appellants assert that the Bank would not have lent the $300,000 without their personal guarantees.

VAFLA's financial statements and tax returns indicated that the bank loan was a loan from the Shareholders-Guarantors. Despite the representation to that effect, VAFLA made all of the loan payments, principal and interest, to the Bank. The appellants made no such payments. In addition, neither VAFLA nor the Shareholders-Guarantors treated the corporate payments on the loan as constructive income taxable to the Shareholders-Guarantors.

The appellants present the question whether the $300,000 bank loan is really, despite its form as a borrowing from the Bank, a capital contribution from the appellants to VAFLA. They contend that if the bank loan is characterized as equity, they are entitled to add a *pro rata* share of the $300,000 bank loan to their adjusted bases, thereby increasing the size of their operating loss deductions. Implicit in the appellants' characterization of the bank loan as equity in VAFLA is a determination that the Bank lent the $300,000 to the Shareholders-Guarantors who then contributed the funds to the corporation. The appellants' approach fails to realize that the $300,000 transaction, regardless of whether it is equity or debt, would permit them to adjust the bases in their stock if, indeed, the appellants, and not the Bank, had advanced VAFLA the money. The more precise question, which the appellants fail initially to ask, is whether the guaranteed loan from the Bank to VAFLA is an economic outlay of any kind by the Shareholders-Guarantors. To decide this question, we must determine whether the transaction involving the $300,000 was a loan from the Bank to VAFLA or was it instead a loan to the Shareholders-Guarantors who then gave it to VAFLA, as either a loan or a capital contribution.

Finding no economic outlay, we need not address the question, which is extensively addressed in the briefs, of whether the characterization of the $300,000 was debt or equity.

II

To increase the basis in the stock of a subchapter S corporation, there must be an economic outlay on the part of the shareholder. See Brown v. Commissioner, 706 F.2d 755, 756 (6th Cir. 1983), affg. T.C. Memo 1981-608 (1981) ("In similar cases, the courts have consistently required some economic outlay by the guarantor in order to convert a mere loan guarantee into an investment."); Blum v. Commissioner, 59 T.C. 436, 440 (1972) (bank expected repayment of its loan from the corporation and not the taxpayers, i.e., no economic outlay from taxpayers).[7]

A guarantee, in and of itself, cannot fulfill that requirement. The guarantee is merely a promise to pay in the future if certain unfortunate events should occur. At the present time, the appellants have experienced

7. Even the Eleventh Circuit case on which the appellants heavily rely applies this first step. See Selfe v. United States, 778 F.2d 769, 772 (11th Cir. 1985) ("We agree with *Brown* inasmuch as that court reaffirms that economic outlay is required before a stockholder in a Subchapter S corporation may increase her basis.").

no such call as guarantors, have engaged in no economic outlay, and have suffered no cost.

The situation would be different if VAFLA had defaulted on the loan payments and the Shareholders-Guarantors had made actual disbursements on the corporate indebtedness. Those payments would represent corporate indebtedness to the shareholders which would increase their bases for the purpose of deducting net operating losses under §1374(c)(2)(B). *Brown*, 706 F.2d at 757. See also Raynor v. Commissioner, 50 T.C. 762, 770-71 (1968) ("No form of indirect borrowing, be it guaranty, surety, accommodation, comaking or otherwise, gives rise to indebtedness from the corporation to the shareholders until and unless the shareholders pay part or all of the obligation.").

The appellants accuse the Tax Court of not recognizing the critical distinction between §1374(c)(2)-(A) (adjusted basis in stock) and §1374(c)(2)(B) (adjusted basis in indebtedness of corporation to shareholder). They argue that the "loan" is not really a loan, but is a capital contribution (equity). Therefore, they conclude, §1374(c)(2)(A) applies and §1374(c)(2)(B) is irrelevant. However, the appellants once again fail to distinguish between the initial question of economic outlay and the secondary issue of debt or equity. Only if the first question had an affirmative answer, would the second arise.

The majority opinion of the Tax Court, focusing on the first issue of economic outlay, determined that a guarantee, in and of itself, is not an event for which basis can be adjusted. It distinguished the situation presented to it from one where the guarantee is triggered *and actual payments are made*. In the latter scenario, the first question of economic outlay is answered affirmatively (and the second issue is apparent on its face, i.e., the payments represent indebtedness from the corporation to the shareholder as opposed to capital contribution from the shareholder to the corporation). To the contrary is the situation presented here. The Tax Court, far from confusing the issue by discussing irrelevant matters, was comprehensively explaining why the transaction before it could not represent any kind of economic outlay by the appellants.

The Tax Court correctly determined that the appellants' guarantees, unaccompanied by further acts, in and of themselves, have not constituted contributions of cash or other property which might increase the bases of the appellants' stock in the corporation.

The appellants, while they do not disagree with the Tax Court that the guarantees, standing alone, cannot adjust their bases in the stock, nevertheless argue that the "loan" to VAFLA was in its "true sense" a loan to the Shareholders-Guarantors who then theoretically advanced the $300,000 to the corporation as a capital contribution. The Tax Court declined the invitation to treat a loan and its uncalled-on security, the guarantee, as identical and to adopt the appellants' view of the "substance" of the transaction over the "form" of the transaction they took. The Tax Court did not err in doing so.

Generally, taxpayers are liable for the tax consequences of the transaction they actually execute and may not reap the benefit of recasting the transaction into another one substantially different in economic effect that they might have made. They are bound by the "form" of their transaction and may not argue that the "substance" of their transaction triggers different tax consequences. Don E. Williams Co. v. Commissioner, 429 U.S. 569, 579-80 (1977); Commissioner v. National Alfalfa Dehydrating & Milling Co., 417 U.S. 134, 149 (1974).[9] In the situation of guaranteed corporate debt, where the form of the transaction may not be so clear, courts have permitted the taxpayer to argue that the substance of the transaction was in actuality a loan to the shareholder. See *Blum*, 59 T.C. at 440. However, the burden is on the taxpayer and it has been a difficult one to meet. That is especially so where, as here, the transaction is cast in sufficiently ambiguous terms to permit an argument either way depending on which is subsequently advantageous from a tax point of view.

It is important to note that those cases did not involve the question posed here of whether an economic outlay existed because it clearly did. Actual payments were made. The only question was what was the nature of the payments, debt or equity.

In the case before us, the Tax Court found that the "form" and "substance" of the transaction was a loan from the Bank to VAFLA and not to the appellants:

> The Bank of Virginia loaned the money to the corporation and not to petitioners. The proceeds of the loan were to be used in the operation of the corporation's business. Petitioners submitted no evidence that they were free to dispose of the proceeds of the loan as they wished. Nor were the payments on the loan reported as constructive dividends on the corporation's Federal income tax returns or on the petitioners' Federal income tax returns during the years in issue. Accordingly, we find that the transaction was in fact a loan by the bank to the corporation guaranteed by the shareholders.

---

9. On the other hand, the Commissioner is not so bound and may recharacterize the nature of the transaction according to its substance while overlooking the form selected by the taxpayer. Higgins v. Smith, 308 U.S. 473, 477 (1940). In doing so, the Commissioner usually applies debt-equity principles to determine the true *nature* of the transaction. As the *Selfe* court noted:

> This principle is particularly evident where characterization of capital as debt or equity will have different tax consequences. Thus in *Plantation Patterns* the court held that interest payments by a corporation on debentures were constructive stockholder dividends and could not be deducted by the corporation as interest payments. There, the former Fifth Circuit recharacterized debt as equity at the insistence of the Commissioner.

Selfe, 778 F.2d at 773.

Whether the $300,000 was lent to the corporation or to the Shareholders/ Guarantors is a factual issue which should not be disturbed unless clearly erroneous. Finding no error, we affirm.

It must be borne in mind that we do not merely encounter naive taxpayers caught in a complex trap for the unwary. They sought to claim deductions because the corporation lost money. If, however, VAFLA had been profitable, they would be arguing that the loan was in reality from the Bank to the corporation, and not to them, for that would then lessen their taxes. [Is this true? — ED.] Under that description of the transaction, the loan repayments made by VAFLA would not be on the appellants' behalf, and, consequently, would not be taxed as constructive income to them. See Old Colony Trust Co. v. Commissioner, 279 U.S. 716 (1929) (payment by a corporation of a personal expense or debt of a shareholder is considered as the receipt of a taxable benefit). It came down in effect to an ambiguity as to which way the appellants would jump, an effort to play both ends against the middle, until it should be determined whether VAFLA was a profitable or money-losing proposition. At that point, the appellants attempted to treat the transaction as cloaked in the guise having the more beneficial tax consequences for them.

Finally, the appellants complain that the Tax Court erred by failing to apply debt-equity principles[11] to determine the "form" of the loan. We believe that the Tax Court correctly refused to apply debt-equity principles here, a methodology which is only relevant, if at all,[12] to resolution of the second inquiry — what is the nature of the economic outlay. Of course, the second inquiry cannot be reached unless the first question concerning whether an economic outlay exists is answered affirmatively. Here it is not.

11. . . . The appellants correctly state that the First, Fifth and Ninth Circuits have all applied traditional debt-equity principles in determining whether a shareholder's guarantee of a corporate debt was in substance a capital contribution. See Casco Bank & Trust Co. v. United States, 544 F.2d 528 (1st Cir. 1976), cert. denied, 430 U.S. 907 (1977); Plantation Patterns v. Commissioner, 462 F.2d 712 (5th Cir. 1971), cert. denied, 409 U.S. 1076 (1972); Murphy Logging Co. v. United States, 378 F.2d 222 (9th Cir. 1967). What the appellants fail to point out, however, is that those cases each involved activated guarantees, i.e., actual advances or payments on defaults. Therefore, the issue in those cases was not whether the taxpayer had made an "investment" — an economic outlay — in the corporation. The investment was admitted. The issue in those cases asked what was the nature of the investment — equity or debt. None of those cases involved the disallowance of deductions claimed by a shareholder pursuant to §1374 for his or her share of an electing corporation's operating losses where there had simply been no economic outlay by the shareholder under the guarantee.

12. In a §1374 subchapter S corporation case, the inquiry whether or not the economic outlay, assuming there is one, is debt or equity appears not to matter since the economic outlay, regardless of its characterization as debt or equity, will increase the adjusted basis. . . . There are no different tax consequences from the point of view of the taxpayer on the narrow issue of what amount of net operating losses may be deducted. Therefore, application of debt-equity principles in a case such as this one appears to be a red herring. However, we do not reach that issue because the Tax Court's factual finding that the appellants have shown no economic outlay on their part is not clearly erroneous.

The appellants, in effect, attempt to collapse a two-step analysis into a one-step inquiry which would eliminate the initial determination of economic outlay by first concluding that the proceeds were a capital contribution (equity). Obviously, a capital contribution is an economic outlay so the basis in the stock would be adjusted accordingly. But such an approach simply ignores the factual determination by the Tax Court that the Bank lent the $300,000 to the corporation and not to the Shareholders-Guarantors.

The appellants rely on Blum v. Commissioner, 59 T.C. 436 (1972), and Selfe v. United States, 778 F.2d 769 (11th Cir. 1985), to support their position. However, the appellants have misread those cases. In *Blum,* the Tax Court declined to apply debt-equity principles to determine whether the taxpayer's guarantee of a loan from a bank to a corporation was an indirect capital contribution. The Tax Court held that the taxpayer had failed to carry his burden of proving that the transaction was in "substance" a loan from the bank to the shareholder rather than a loan to the corporation. The *Blum* court found dispositive the fact that "the bank expected repayment of its loan from the corporation and not the petitioner." *Blum,* 59 T.C. at 440.

With regard to *Selfe,* the Tax Court stated:

> [T]he Eleventh Circuit applied a debt-equity analysis and held that a shareholder's guarantee of a loan made to a subchapter S corporation may be treated for tax purposes as an equity investment in the corporation where the lender looks to the shareholder as the primary obligor. We respectfully disagree with the Eleventh Circuit and hold that a shareholder's guarantee of a loan to a subchapter S corporation may not be treated as an equity investment in the corporation absent an economic outlay by the shareholder.

The Tax Court then distinguished *Plantation Patterns,* 462 F.2d 712 (5th Cir. 1972), relied on by *Selfe,* because that case involved a C corporation, reasoning that the application of debt-equity principles to subchapter S corporations would defeat Congress' intent to limit a shareholder's pass-through deduction to the amount he or she has actually invested in the corporation.

The Tax Court also distinguished In re Lane, 742 F.2d 1311 (11th Cir. 1984), relied on by the *Selfe* court, on the basis that the shareholder had actually paid the amounts he had guaranteed, i.e., there was an economic outlay. In *Lane,* which involved a subchapter S corporation, the issue was "whether advances made by a shareholder to a corporation constitute debt or equity. . . ." Id. at 1313. If the advances were debt, then Lane could deduct them as bad debts. On the other hand, if the advances were capital, no bad debt deduction would be permitted. Thus, the issue of adjusted basis for purposes of flow-through deductions from net operating losses of the corporation was not at issue. There was no question of whether there had been an economic outlay.

Although *Selfe* does refer to debt-equity principles, the specific issue before it was whether any material facts existed making summary judgment inappropriate. The Eleventh Circuit said:

> At issue here, however, is not whether the taxpayer's contribution was either a loan to or an equity investment in Jane Simon, Inc. The issue is whether the taxpayer's guarantee of the corporate loan was in itself a contribution to the corporation [as opposed to a loan from the bank] sufficient to increase the taxpayer's basis in the corporation.

The *Selfe* court found that there was evidence that the bank primarily looked to the taxpayer and not the corporation for repayment of the loan.[17] Therefore, it remanded for "a determination of whether or not the bank primarily looked to Jane Selfe [taxpayer] for repayment [the first inquiry] and for the court to apply the factors set out in *In re Lane* and section 385 to determine if the taxpayer's guarantee amounted to either an equity investment in or shareholder loan to Jane Simon, Inc. [the second inquiry]." Id. at 775. The implications are that there is still a two-step analysis and that the debt-equity principles apply only to the determination of the characterization of the economic outlay, once one is found.

This particular situation is not before us and we decline to address the question of whether a guarantee can be an economic outlay when accompanied by pledged collateral.

Granted, that conclusion is clouded by the next and final statement of the *Selfe* court: "In short, we remand for the district court to apply *Plantation Patterns* and determine if the bank loan to Jane Simon, Inc. was in reality a loan to the taxpayer." Id. To the degree that the *Selfe* court agreed with *Brown* that an economic outlay is required before a shareholder may increase her basis in a subchapter S corporation, *Selfe* does not contradict current law or our resolution of the case before us. Furthermore, to the extent that the *Selfe* court remanded because material facts existed by which the taxpayer could show that the bank actually lent the money to her rather than the corporation, we are still able to agree. It is because of the *Selfe* court's suggestion that debt-equity principles must be applied to resolve the question of whether the bank actually lent the money to the taxpayer/shareholder or the corporation, that we must part company with the Eleventh Circuit for the reasons stated above.

17. The loan officer so stated during deposition testimony. Furthermore, the bank originally extended a credit line to the taxpayer in consideration of her pledge of 4500 shares of stock in another corporation. When her business was later incorporated, the bank converted the loans made on the existing credit line to corporate loans, accompanied by taxpayer's agreement guaranteeing the corporation's indebtedness to the bank. The Eleventh Circuit noted that "a guarantor who has pledged stock to secure a loan has experienced an economic outlay to the extent that that pledged stock is not available as collateral for other investments." Id. at 772 n.7. Thus, upon remand, the district court could determine that there was an economic outlay on that basis alone, before deciding whether the form of the loan was to the taxpayer or to the corporation.

In conclusion, the Tax Court correctly focused on the initial inquiry of whether an economic outlay existed. Finding none, the issue of whether debt-equity principles ought to apply to determine the nature of the economic outlay was not before the Tax Court. The Tax Court is
Affirmed.

NOTES

1. *The rights of guarantors and lenders.* The *Leavitt* court recognized that the issue before it was a difficult one. A guarantor of corporate debt is liable on the debt in the sense that such a guarantor will be called upon to pay the debt if the corporation is unable to do so. Thus, if the corporation cannot repay the loan, the guarantor will be poorer by the amount of the debt. In this sense, such a guarantor is in the same economic position as a shareholder who makes a loan to the same corporation: If the corporation is unable to pay the debt, the lending shareholder will suffer the loss of repayment without an ability to pass that loss on to anyone else. The statute explicitly gives debt basis to such a shareholder-lender, and because a shareholder-guarantor is in a virtually identical economic position, the shareholder's claim to debt basis for the guarantee is strong.

However, there *are* differences between a guarantor and a lender which go unstated by the shareholder's argument. As we have discussed, a shareholder-lender has basis in the debt, basis which can be shifted by operation of §1366(d) into the shareholder's stock. A shareholder-guarantor, though, has no such basis. Accordingly, there is no basis to shift into equity basis for the guarantor.

2. *Implications of the taxpayer's argument.* Suppose a shareholder-guarantor were given debt basis for the guarantee, and suppose further that this debt basis were then used by the shareholder to absorb passed-through corporate loss under §1366(d). If the corporation then repays the debt (that is, makes full payment to the lender, not to the shareholder-guarantor), it must be the case that the guarantor recognizes income. That is, we will be forced to treat extinguishment of the guarantee as income to the extent that the shareholder received and used debt basis under §1366(d). While this certainly could be done, we usually do not think of debtor repayment as a taxable event to a guarantor.[7]

3. *Analysis of the government's argument.* As we have seen, there is little economic difference between a shareholder-lender and a shareholder-guarantor. The court in *Leavitt* nonetheless held that a shareholder-

---

7. Although if a guarantor is called upon to make good on the guarantee and then receives payment from the debtor, such payment will be taxable to the extent the guarantor deducted the initial payment. Use of the guarantee to absorb passed-through corporate loss would thus play the same role as did the deduction arising from payments made by the guarantor.

guarantor is unable to exploit the debt basis advantage of §1366(d) explicitly made available to shareholder-lenders. The court distinguished lenders from guarantors by observing that lenders make an actual outlay corresponding to their economic risk of loss while guarantors, although bearing the same risk of loss, make no such outlay.

This distinction by the *Leavitt* court is *at best* paper thin. In many cases the shareholder-lender obtains the cash loaned to the corporation by borrowing from a third party. Indeed, in such transactions it often is the case that the third-party lender makes the loan proceeds check payable directly to the corporation. In such circumstances the court's distinction between the nominal shareholder-lender and a shareholder-guarantor, based upon actual outlay, is meaningless. Indeed, if the shareholder guarantor substitutes his own note for that of the S corporation, shareholder basis is obtained without any significant alteration in legal relationships.

Indeed, tax law rarely turns on physical outlay although it often turns on economic reality. To be sure, for cash-basis taxpayers actual cash flow is crucial in determining the timing of income and deduction. But cash-basis accounting is an anomaly, a concession to simplify accounting for individuals and small businesses. Usually, tax consequences are independent of cash flow. For example, a taxpayer's basis in purchased property is "cost" under §1012, where cost includes not only actual outlays but also promises to make outlays in the future; that is, purchase money debt goes into basis. If tax consequences should follow economic reality unless Congress explicitly directs otherwise, how should *Leavitt* have come out?

Two arguments in favor of allowing a shareholder-guarantor to increase debt basis by reason of the guarantee often are advanced. The first is that a loan from a third party to an S corporation should be treated as made to a shareholder guarantor *if* the third-party lender looks primarily to the shareholder-guarantor for repayment. Indeed, the *Selfe* court seemed to adopt this view, and the *Leavitt* court disagreed with *Selfe* for just this reason.

On this theory, a court should seek to determine whether the loan, nominally made to the corporation, would not have been made but for the guarantee by one or more shareholders. Yet what if the loan would have been made without the guarantee but not on the same terms? For example, what if the effect of a guarantee is to allow the corporation to borrow at a lower interest rate? So long as the corporation has any assets whatsoever, the lender can look to some extent to the corporation for repayment. Presumably a lender who makes a loan to a corporation and then obtains a shareholder guarantee can and will look to both the corporation and the guarantor for repayment, and it is unrealistic to focus on one to the exclusion of the other.

4. *Partnership analogies.* The second argument advanced for allowing shareholder-guarantors to obtain debt basis for their guarantees is based on subchapter K's treatment of debt. Under §752, partnership debt in-

creases outside basis of the partners as they share economic risk of loss. If this rule were to apply to S corporation debt guaranteed by a shareholder, such debt would be allocated to the guarantor-shareholder.[8]

Yet this analogy understates the dissimilarities between the treatment of entity debt in subchapters K and S. In subchapter K, §752 provides that *all* entity debt must increase outside basis. Given that mandate in §752, the regulations then provide that recourse partnership debt is allocated among the partners as they share economic risk of loss. Nonrecourse partnership debt is allocated differently, generally in accordance with partnership profits interests.[9] The structural aspect of §752 is not that partnership debt is allocated as the partners share risk — the sharing of recourse debt proves that assertion false — but rather that *all* partnership debt, recourse and nonrecourse alike, increases outside basis.

This basic feature of §752 — not how partnership debt is allocated among the partners but rather that *all* debt must be allocated somehow — reinforces the transparency metaphor upon which subchapter K is based. As a general rule, partnership aggregate inside basis equals aggregate outside basis. To be sure, there can be exceptions to this rule, especially if a §754 election is not in place.[10] But for the most part this equality holds true, and it ensures that existence of the partnership will not affect the timing of income and deduction to the partners. For example, the equality of aggregate inside and outside basis means that sufficient outside basis will exist to absorb all pass-through partnership level deductions. Absent §752, partnership losses from leveraged property would be unavailable to the partners because of §704(d).

Subchapter S follows no transparency metaphor, and an S corporation's aggregate inside basis will not, in general, equal aggregate outside basis. Because there is no provision in subchapter S analogous to §752, it is a mistake to read into subchapter S any of the incidental allocation rules following from application of §752. That is, because there is no general rule in subchapter S providing that entity level borrowing increases outside basis, it is a mistake to read into subchapter S the partnership allocation rule that entity debt is allocated as partners share risk.

5. *A final note on* Leavitt. We still have no good answer to the question at issue in *Leavitt*. Internal Revenue Code §1366(d) allows a shareholder of an S corporation to deduct pass-through losses to the extent of the shareholder's equity and debt basis. This provision makes no mention of shareholder guarantees, and because it functions wholly different from §752, analogizing to subchapter K is inappropriate. But, as discussed above, a

8. Because no shareholder is liable on corporate debt absent a guarantee, a shareholder guarantee of corporate debt is equivalent to a partner's guarantee of a nonrecourse debt. Under the rules of §752, partnership nonrecourse debt guaranteed by a partner is allocated to the guarantor-partner. See page 737 infra.

9. See page 740 infra.

10. See Chapter 27 supra.

shareholder guarantee of corporate third-party debt is in many ways the equivalent of a direct loan from the shareholder-guarantor. So should the guarantee contribute to the shareholder's debt basis for purposes of §1366(d)?

The premise of §1366(d) seems to be that a shareholder of an S corporation should be permitted to deduct her share of pass-through losses to the extent of the shareholder's investment in the corporation. By explicitly including both equity and debt investment in §1366(d), Congress has taken the welcome if unusual step of recognizing that equity and debt are but two bands in a single spectrum. That is, investing in corporate equity and investing in corporate debt both reflect a shareholder's decision to seek profit from the corporation's business activity, with the difference between equity and debt largely being a greater or lesser risk of nonpayment and a greater or lesser possible profit.

From this perspective, a shareholder guarantee of corporate debt is similar to both equity and debt investments in that the guarantee represents a shareholder decision to place capital at risk in the venture. However, the guarantee is unusual in that it offers no opportunity for profit: Unless the shareholder-guarantor is compensated for the guarantee, the best that the shareholder-guarantor can hope for is that the guarantee will prove unnecessary. Of course, such uncompensated guarantees usually are not made out of disinterested generosity but instead are made to improve the prospects of the shareholder's equity (and debt, if any) investment in the corporation.

Economically, then, a shareholder guarantee of an S corporation's third-party debt is an additional investment of the shareholder in the corporate activity made to maintain or improve the shareholder's existing investment. Whether an investment is made with the shareholder's own funds, directly borrowed funds, or implicitly borrowed funds (i.e., by guaranteeing third-party debt) should be substantively irrelevant. By including both debt and equity investments within its embrace, §1366(d) represents a triumph of substance over form. The *Leavitt* court unfortunately emphasized just the reverse, and so the decision seems wrong.

PROBLEMS

17-3. Individual *X* forms *S* Corp., an S corporation, by contributing cash of $10,000 in exchange for 100 shares of *S* Corp. common stock. In addition, *X* contributes $15,000 to the corporation in exchange for a bond. During its first year, *S* Corp. borrows $75,000 from Big Bank, and this debt is guaranteed by *X.* Also during that year, it distributes $20,000 to *X.* For the entire year, *S* Corp. recognizes a taxable loss of $12,000. What are the tax consequences to *X* of the distribution, and how much of the corporation's loss can *X* claim on her individual return? How might *X* have improved her tax position without significantly changing the transactions?

D.   ASSIGNMENT OF INCOME CONCERNS

1.   *Precontribution Appreciation and Related Problems*

While the one class of stock rule ensures that an S corporation's income
and loss will be allocated among its shareholder's in proportion to ownership interests, it plays havoc with assignment of income concerns. For
example, suppose individuals X and Y form XY Corp., an S corporation,
with X contributing cash of $10,000 and Y contributing Blackacre with fair
market value of $10,000 and adjusted basis of $6,000. If each shareholder
receives ten shares of XY stock in exchange for the contribution, they will
each report one-half of the corporation's earnings. Accordingly, if the
corporation's only taxable activity is a sale of Blackacre for its current
value of $10,000, each shareholder will report $2,000 of income on the
shareholder's individual return and will increase outside basis by the same
amount. By contributing Blackacre to the corporation in anticipation of
sale, Y is able to shift half of the tax to X. In the partnership context, Y
would be taxable on the full $4,000 of gain under §704(c).

Assume that the corporation invests its $20,000 in Whiteacre, and that
when Whiteacre increases in value to $30,000, Y sells her shares of stock
to Z. Because Z is acquiring one-half of a corporation now worth $30,000,
presumably Z will pay $15,000 for the shares sold by Y. If Whiteacre is
subsequently sold, half of the gain will be includible to Z even though no
corporate asset has appreciated since Z bought in to the enterprise. The
sale of shares from Y to Z did not so much work a shift of income as a
doubling: Y was taxed implicitly on her share of the increase in value of
Whiteacre when she sold her stock to Z, and Z is taxed again on that
increase in value when Whiteacre is sold to a third party and the gain is
passed-through to the shareholders. Of course, this income will adjust Z's
stock basis upward from $15,000 to $20,000, so Z will enjoy an offsetting
loss should he sell her stock immediately thereafter. But because Y's share
of gain from Whiteacre is taxed to Z upon disposition of the property by
the corporation and the offsetting loss is deferred until Z sells his shares,
Z loses the time value of money on that taxable gain. In the partnership
context, this timing problem could be avoided by the partnership filing
an election under §754 so that Z's purchase of Y's interest in the venture
would trigger an optional basis adjustment under §743(b).

2.   *Family Ownership and Section 1366(e)*

Suppose Mother forms *S* Corp., an S corporation, by contributing cash of
$10,000 in exchange for 100 shares. As the corporation begins to turn a
profit, Mother gives some or all of the shares to her children. Because

the corporation's income is taxed to its shareholders, the effect of the stock transfer is to shift some or all of the corporation's income from Mother to her children. Does this run afoul of the assignment of income doctrine?

In general, the answer is no. Recall that income from property can be shifted by a transfer of the income-producing property. See, e.g., Blair v. Commissioner, 300 U.S. 579 (1941). The corporation's profit is just one form of income from property, and transfer of the stock is the transfer of the income-producing property. Transfer of the corporation's stock is, in general, no more abusive than a transfer of the initial $10,000 cash.

But what if the corporation's profit is derived in part from Mother's labor? For example, suppose that S Corp. is in the business of accounting, and it provides accounting services to its customer by hiring Mother, a public accountant. If Mother is paid only a small salary for her efforts, much of the value of Mother's services will be reported as corporate profit and will be passed through and taxed to the children.

In such circumstances, the Commissioner may reallocate some of the corporation's income back to Mother to more accurately reflect her contribution to the enterprise. §1366(e). Indeed, if Mother has transferred all of her shares so that she is no longer a shareholder, the Commissioner may tax some of the corporation's profit directly to Mother to approximate a fair salary for her services. Section 1366(e) broadly authorizes the Commissioner to reallocate income if one member of a family is undercompensated for services or the use of capital used by an S corporation owned in whole or in part by other family members. This section is similar to, but far broader than, §704(e)(2), a section targeted at family partnerships.

PROBLEMS

17-4. Individuals A and B form Z Corp., an S corporation, with A contributing a copyright with adjusted basis of $0 (because A wrote the manuscript) and a fair market value of $5,000 and B contributing depreciable machinery with adjusted basis of $3,000 and fair market value of $5,000. In return, each individual receives 50 shares of Z Corp. common stock. Assume the machinery is depreciable over five years on a straight-line basis.

a. If the corporation sells the machinery immediately for $5,000, how is the $2,000 gain allocated between A and B?
b. If B cleans and repairs the machinery so that its value increases to $6,000 and the corporation then sells it for that amount, how is the gain allocated between A and B?
c. If the corporation is entitled to a $600 depreciation deduction for its first taxable year, how is that deduction allocated between A and B?

E. SALES OF STOCK AND THE SECTION 338(h)(10) ELECTION

If the shareholders of an S corporation sell 80 percent or more of their stock to a corporate buyer in a qualified stock purchase (as defined in §338(h)(3)), the shareholders can jointly file an election to have the transaction treated as an asset sale rather than as the actual stock sale. That is, the S corporation is treated as if it sold its assets and then liquidated, distributing the sales proceeds to the selling shareholders. This artifice permits the purchasing corporation to take a cost basis in the S corporation's assets, a result that eliminates a third layer of tax once the S corporation becomes a controlled subsidiary of the corporate purchaser (and thus ceases to be an S corporation because it has an ineligible shareholder). Because this election can produce a tax benefit to the purchasing corporation, presumably the selling shareholders will be able to exact a greater sales price.

Because the S corporation is treated as selling its assets, all the rules applicable to assets sales are implicated. These rules include the tax on built-in gains under §1374 (discussed in the following chapter) and the depreciation recapture rules of §§1245 and 1250. Of course, if the S corporation owns some ordinary income assets, one disadvantageous effect of the §338(h)(10) election is that some of the sales gain will be includible as ordinary income.

The §338(h)(10) election can play an important role in the sale of an S corporation. What is surprising is that there is no statutory basis for permitting the shareholders of an S corporation to make such an election: By the explicit language of the statute, the election is available only if the stock sold is that of a corporation which is part of an consolidated group, a definition that precludes application of the statute to S corporations.

PROBLEMS

17-5.   Individual *B* owns all the outstanding shares of *S* Corp., an electing S corporation. *B* agrees to sell the stock of *S* Corp. to Acquiring Corp. for $1,000,000, payable half down and half in the form of an interest bearing installment obligation payable in two years. *B*'s adjusted basis in her *S* Corp. shares is $400,000, and that is *S* Corp.'s adjusted basis in its assets. If *B* files an election under §338(h)(10), how much gain does *B* report in the year of sale?

18

Transition Issues

A. FROM C CORPORATION TO S CORPORATION

An existing C corporation can elect S corporation status so long as it satisfies the requirements set forth in §1361(b) relating to maximum number of shareholders (75), maximum number of classes of shares outstanding (1), etc. As discussed above,[1] an election under §1362 will be effective for the corporation's next taxable year unless the corporation wishes the election to be effective for its current taxable year and the election is filed within the first two and one-half months of the year. Once the election becomes effective, the corporation becomes subject to the provisions of subchapter S and is taxed as described previously. However, because the corporation has a C corporation history, it is subject also to some special Subchapter S rules.

1. Shareholder Taxation of Distributions

In general, profits earned by a C corporation are taxed twice, once when earned by the corporation and a second time when distributed to the corporation's shareholders. However, not all distributions from a C corporation to its shareholders are taxable dividends: Distributions exceeding the corporation's earnings are treated as a return of the shareholder's capital to the extent of the shareholder's stock basis, with any excess taxed as gain from the sale or exchange of shares of stock. §301(c). Every C corporation must maintain an "earnings and profits" account, and distributions will be taxed as dividends only to the extent of this account.

---

1. See page 599 supra.

When an existing C corporation having a positive earnings and profits account elects S corporation status, there is the potential for tax avoidance. Distributions of postelection earnings should be passed through tax-free to the shareholder-distributees, but distributions out of the corporation's pre-election earnings and profits account should be taxable as dividends under subchapter C's regime. Section 1368(c) adopts a pro-taxpayer rule: Distributions are, in general, assumed to be out of postelection earnings to the extent of such earnings; only after all postelection earnings have been exhausted are distributions treated as coming from pre-election earnings and profits. To keep track of the corporation's postelection earnings, the statute defines an "accumulated adjustments" account (often called the "AA" account, or simply the "AAA"), which must be maintained by each S corporation having a positive C corporation earnings and profits account. See §1368(e)(1). This AA account reflects, with one modification, the corporation's postelection undistributed earnings.

Recall that distributions of S corporations having no C corporation history are taxed to the distributee-shareholders under §1368(b). Under this provision, the distribution is tax-free to the extent of the shareholder's stock basis, with any excess taxed as gain from the sale or exchange of shares. This same provision applies to S corporations having a C corporation history only if the corporation has no C corporation earnings and profits. As discussed above, if the corporation has positive C corporation earnings and profits, distributions are taxed to its shareholder-distributees under §1368(c).

Look closely at the three tiers of §1368(c). Tier 1, §1368(c)(1), provides that distributions to the extent of the corporation's accumulated adjustments account are taxed under§1368(b); that is, such distributions are taxed like all distributions made by S corporations lacking C corporation earnings and profits. Tier 2, §1368(c)(2), provides that distributions in excess of a corporation's accumulated adjustments account are taxed as dividends to the extent of the corporation's C corporation earnings and profits account. Tier 3, §1368(c)(3), applicable to distributions to the extent they exceed *both* the corporation's accumulated adjustments account *and* the corporation's earnings and profits account, provides precisely the same rule as tier 1, namely taxation under §1368(b) as if the distribution had been made by a corporation having no earnings and profits.

Consider the following example. X Corp. files an S corporation election effective January 1, 1995. As of that date, X Corp. has C corporation earnings and profits of $10,000. All outstanding shares of X Corp. are owned by individual J with aggregate stock basis of $12,000. During 1995, X Corp. recognizes $6,000 of taxable income and makes distributions totaling $30,000.

First, the $6,000 of postelection earnings pass through to shareholder J and increase her stock basis to $18,000. Second, of the $30,000 distributed to J, $6,000 is received tax-free under §§1368(c)(1) and 1368(b), reducing

J's stock basis back to $12,000. Of the remaining $24,000 distributed to *J*, $10,000 is taxed as a dividend under §1368(c)(2), reducing X Corp.'s earnings and profits to $0 and leaving *J*'s stock basis at $12,000. The remaining $14,000 is taxed under §§1368(c)(3) and 1368(b), so that $12,000 is received tax-free and $2,000 is taxed as gain from the sale or exchange of *J*'s shares, with *J*'s stock basis reduced to $0.

If X Corp. should recognize, say, $2,000 of income in 1996, it can then distribute up to that amount tax-free under §1368(c)(1) because recognition of income increases the corporation's accumulated adjustments account. Indeed, if X Corp. earns $2,000 in 1996 and distributes less than $2,000 in that year, X Corp.'s accumulated adjustments account will remain positive and can absorb distributions in subsequent years.

An S corporation's accumulated adjustments account can be reduced below zero by corporate losses. For example, suppose Y Corp. has earnings and profits of $10,000 and accumulated adjustments of $7,000. If the corporation distributes $5,000, that amount is treated as a distribution of pass-through income under §1368(c)(1) and reduces Y Corp.'s accumulated adjustment account down to $2,000. If the corporation recognizes a taxable loss of $5,000 in the next year, the accumulated adjustments account is reduced to negative $3,000, so that any distribution during this year will be taxed as a dividend to the extent of the corporation's $10,000 earnings and profits. Further, if the corporation earns only $1,000 in the following year, the accumulated adjustments account remains negative (i.e., negative $2,000), so again tier 1 is unavailable to shelter distributions. That is, if the corporation distributes $1,000 during that year, the full $1,000 will be taxed as a dividend. Even though the corporation distributes no more than it earns during the year, the distribution will be taxable to its shareholder-distributees.

Recall that tax-exempt income of an S corporation increases its share-holders' stock bases so that tax exempt income will not be taxable when distributed or upon disposition of the shares. Despite this, tax-exempt income does *not* increase an S corporation's accumulated adjustments account. To understand what this means, consider the following example.

Z Corp. files an S corporation election effective January 1, 1996. As of that date, Z Corp. has earnings and profits of $5,000. All of the outstanding shares of Z Corp. are owned by individual M with aggregate adjusted basis of $12,000. During 1996, Z Corp. recognizes no taxable income or loss but receives tax-exempt income of $1,000. In addition, Z Corp. distributes $500 to M.

Under §1367(a)(1)(A), the tax-exempt income increases M's stock basis to $13,000. However, the tax-exempt income does not increase Z Corp.'s accumulated adjustments account, so that account remains at $0. Thus, the entire distribution is taxed under §1368(c)(2) (i.e., under tier 2) as a dividend to Z and reduces the corporation's earnings and profits account to $4,500. M's stock basis remains at $13,000.

Do not conclude from this example that the tax-exempt income received by the corporation will be taxed as a dividend to M. It will not be: All postelection income of the corporation will be received by M tax-free under the pass-through/basis adjustment mechanism of §§1367(a)(2)(A) and 1368(b)(1). When a corporation has both pre-election earnings and profits as well as postelection income, an ordering rule must be used to determine if distributions are deemed to come first out of the pre- or postelection accounts. Section 1368(c) provides that ordering rule.

Recall that the effect of the three tiers in §1368(c) is to provide that distributions are assumed to come first out of the accumulated adjustments account and only after that account is exhausted out of pre-election earnings and profits. Because postelection tax-exempt income does not go into the corporation's accumulated adjustments account, distributions will be deemed to come out of pre-election earnings and profits before they are assumed to come out of postelection tax-exempt income. Distributions out of postelection tax-exempt income still come out tax-free to the shareholders but under tier 3 rather than under tier 1 as does postelection taxable income. That is, distributions out of postelection tax-exempt income get the same treatment to the shareholders as does postelection taxable income, but such distributions are deemed to be made *last*, after the accumulated adjustments account and the earnings and profits account are depleted. Because postelection tax-exempt income does not increase the corporation's earnings and profits account, its distribution will not result in additional dividend income.

If the shareholders of an S corporation having C corporation earnings and profits desire, the ordering rule of §1368(c)(1)-(2) can be reversed, so that distributions are assumed to come out of earnings and profits before the accumulated adjustments account. This election can be made on an annual basis and requires the consent of all shareholders receiving a distribution during the year. §1368(e)(3). Because the effect of such an election is to accelerate dividend income to the shareholders, it rarely is made. However, certain disabilities sometimes are imposed on an S corporation that has C corporation earnings and profits, and these disabilities can be avoided by distributing out the corporation's earnings and profits. These disabilities are discussed below in section (A)(3).

PROBLEMS

18-1.   *X* Corp., a C corporation using the calendar year as its taxable year, elects S corporation status effective January 1, 2000. As of that day, the corporation has earnings and profits of $8,000. During 2000, the corporation recognizes net taxable income of $6,000 and net tax-exempt income of $4,000. Also during that year, the corporation distributes $20,000 to its shareholders at the rate of $5,000 per calendar quarter (distributed February 14, May 15, August 15, and November 15, $2,500 to each of its two shareholders). As of January 1, 2000, shareholder *P* owns 50 shares with adjusted basis of $20 per share and shareholder owns 50 shares with adjusted basis of $100 per share. What are the tax consequences of these distributions to each shareholder?

2. Corporate-Level Tax on Built-In Gains

Suppose a C corporation owns substantially appreciated property. If this corporation sells the property and then distributes the proceeds, two taxes will be owed: One on the corporate-level gain and a second on the shareholder-level dividend. If the corporation sells the property and then files an S corporation election, both taxes are still incurred: The first as a C corporation and the second upon eventual distribution because of §1368(c)(2). But suppose the corporation files an S corporation election before selling the property. So long as the election is effective *prior to* sale of the property, the corporation's gain will not increase its C corporation earnings and profits account because the gain will be recognized *after* the corporation's earnings and profits account is closed by the election.

To inhibit corporations from electing S corporation status only to avoid the double tax on appreciated property, Congress enacted §1374. This section, applicable during the first 10 years of the corporation's S corporation existence, §1374(d)(7), imposes an annual tax equal to the corporation's "net recognized built-in gain" for the year times the highest corporate income tax rate (currently 34 percent). This tax can be understood only by working though the definitions in §1374(d).

Look first at §1374(d)(1). A corporation's "net unrealized built-in gain" equals the excess of the fair market value over the adjusted basis of all corporate assets owned by the corporation when its S corporation election becomes effective. "Net unrealized built-in gain" is thus fixed in amount once the election becomes effective and need not be recomputed each year.

As the corporation sells or exchanges the assets it held when its S corporation election became effective, its built-in unrealized gain becomes realized and recognized. During each of the corporation's first 10 taxable years as an S corporation, we compute the excess, if any, of its recognized built-in gains for the year over its recognized built-in losses, and this excess is called its "net recognized built-in gain." As you might expect, postelection appreciation does not contribute to the computation of "built-in gain," see §1374(d)(3), and postelection reduction in value does not add to "built-in loss," see §1374(d)(4). These amounts, adjusted for certain items of income and loss, are then netted to form the corporation's "net recognized built-in gain" for the year.

The §1374 tax is then imposed on this amount, subject to the limitation that if the corporation's total taxable income for the year is less than its "net recognized built-in gain" for the year, the tax is imposed only on the corporation's total taxable income. This limitation should come into play only if the corporation recognizes a net loss for the year, excluding recognition of its built-in gains and losses. However, if this limitation applies, the amount of the corporation's "net recognized built-in gains" which escape the §1374 tax is carried forward to the next year.[2] Thus, all of the corporation's built-in unrealized gain should eventually be subject to the §1374 tax unless the corporation holds property for more than 10 years after its S corporation election becomes effective.

If an S corporation is subject to the §1374 tax on built-in gains, the amount of the tax so imposed is treated as a loss of the corporation for the year in which the tax is imposed. §1366(f)(2). As a result, the amount of the tax is passed through to the corporation's shareholders like any other corporate loss, with the character of the loss determined by reference to the built-in gains upon which the §1374 tax was imposed.

PROBLEMS

18-2.   *Y* Corp., a C corporation using the calendar year as its taxable year, owns four capital assets with adjusted basis and fair market values as follows:

Asset	Adjusted Basis	Fair Market Value
Asset 1	$5,000	$8,000
Asset 2	5,000	3,000
Asset 3	5,000	2,000
Asset 4	5,000	9,000

Y Corp. elects S corporation status effective January 1, 2001. During 2001, *Y* Corp. sells assets 1 and 2 for $6,000 and $3,000. During 2002, *Y* Corp. sells asset 3 for $2,000. During 2003, *Y* Corp. sells asset 4 for $10,000. Compute the corporation's tax under §1374 for 2001-2003.

3.   *Disabilities Associated with Passive Investment Income*

Consider the case of a C corporation having substantial earnings and profits when its S corporation election becomes effective. Because of the ordering rule of §1368(c), the shareholder-level tax on those earnings will be deferred until all postelection taxable income has been distributed.

---

2. See §1374(d)(2)(B).

Congress apparently feels this deferral is inappropriate if the corporation amounts to no more than an incorporated pocketbook: If the corporation invests too much of its funds in passive investment income, it will be subject to a special corporate level tax and can even lose its status as an S corporation. Note, though, that these passive investment income rules apply only to S corporations having C corporation earnings and profits so that they can be avoided by distributing out the earnings and profits before or after the election is effective. Of course, if the earnings are not fully distributed before the S corporation election becomes effective, the disabilities imposed on excess passive investment income can be applicable until the earnings and profits are fully removed. To expedite distributions of its earnings and profits, an S corporation can elect under §1368(e)(3) to treat its distributions as coming first out of its earnings and profits rather than out of its accumulated adjustments account.[3]

NOTES

1. *Corporate tax on excessive passive income.* Internal Revenue Code §1375 imposes a tax on an S corporation having C corporation earnings and profits if its "net passive income" exceeds 25 percent of its gross receipts for the year. The definition of "net passive income" is in §§1375(b)(2)-(3) and 1362(d)(3)(D) and includes, in general, the corporation's gross receipts from royalties, rents, dividends, and annuities as well as gains from the dispositions of capital assets less any deductions properly allocable to these items. "Excess net passive income" is then defined by reference to a complicated formula in §1375(b)(1).

Consider the following example. Z Corp. is an S corporation having C corporation earnings and profits. During the current taxable year, the corporation has passive income of $50,000, deductions attributable to passive income of $10,000, and total taxable gross receipts of $100,000. (Assuming the corporation has no other deductions, its taxable income thus equals $90,000, although we do not need to know the corporation's taxable income to compute the tax under §1375.)

Under §1375(b)(1)(A), we have:

$$\frac{\text{excess net passive income}}{\text{net passive income}} = \frac{\text{excess passive income}}{\text{passive income}}$$

where "passive income" and "net passive income" have already been defined and "excess passive income" (a term not used in the Code) means the extent to which the corporation's passive income exceeds 25 percent of the corporation's gross receipts. Here, passive income equals $50,000,

3. See page 640 supra.

net passive income equals $50,000 minus $10,000, or $40,000, and excess passive income equals $50,000 minus 25 percent of $100,000, or $25,000. Accordingly, we have:

$$\frac{\text{excess net passive income}}{\$40,000} = \frac{\$25,000}{\$50,000}$$

Therefore, the "excess net passive income" in this example equals $40,000 times one-half, or $20,000. The tax under §1375 is then imposed on this amount at the highest corporate income tax rate (currently 34 percent), for a total tax of $6,800.[4]

Once again, recall that this tax is not imposed unless the corporation has positive C corporation earnings and profits. Suppose the shareholders of an S corporation believe their corporation lacks earnings and profits and so they allow the corporation to invest most or all of its funds in passive-income producing assets. Suppose the IRS then audits the corporation with respect to a taxable year prior to the effective date of the corporation's Subchapter S election. If this audit should yield so much as one dollar of additional corporate income for that earlier year, the shareholders will discover their corporation is now subject to the §1375 tax. To be sure, had they known of the additional Subchapter C earnings, they would have distributed them out of the corporation. But not knowing of these earnings until much later, they now find themselves trapped.

Section 1375(d) responds to the unfairness of this situation. If the shareholders cause the corporation to distribute out the unanticipated C corporation earnings and profits within a "reasonable" time after the unanticipated earnings and profits are discovered, the government can waive the §1375 tax. Of course, if the corporation has a positive accumulated adjustments account, an election under §1368(e)(3) may be necessary[5] and the shareholders' prior determination that the corporation lacked C corporation earnings and profits must have been made in good faith. If the §1375 tax is not waived, it reduces the amount of the corporation's passive investment income passed through to the corporation's shareholders. §1366(f)(3).

2. *Forced termination of S corporation status.* While the corporate-level tax imposed by §1375 on excessive passive investment income received by S corporations having Subchapter C earnings and profits should encourage most such corporations to distribute out their earnings and profits or reduce their receipt of passive investment income, those corporations will-

---

4. The corporation's excess net passive income under §1375 cannot exceed the corporation's taxable income, §1375(b)(1)(B), although for this purpose the corporation's taxable income is computed without allowance for any net operating loss deduction under §172 and the deductions in §§241-250 (excluding the deduction in §248 for organizational expenditures).

5. See page 640 supra.

ing to pay the §1375 tax face an even greater burden. Under §1362(d)(3), if an S corporation having Subchapter C earnings and profits has passive investment income exceeding 25 percent of its gross receipts for three consecutive years, the corporation's election as an S corporation is terminated. As with §1375, "passive investment income" is defined to mean gross receipts from "royalties, rents, dividends, interest, annuities, and sales and exchanges of stock and securities," §1362(d)(3)(D)(i), with some exceptions, see §1362(d)(3)(D)(ii)-(iv).

Because the forced termination in §1362(d)(3) is so easy to avoid, it rarely is operational. However, because its impact is so severe, one should be certain to avoid it. As with the corporate-level tax in §1375, the forced termination under §1362(d)(3) applies only to corporations having C corporation earnings and profits. Accordingly, S corporations lacking a C corporation past can simply ignore §1362(d)(3), and S corporations having a C corporation past may be able to avoid §1362(d)(3) by electing under §1368(e)(3) to treat its distributions as coming first out of its C corporation earnings and profits.

PROBLEMS

18-3. *M* Corp. is an S corporation having $100 in C corporation earnings and profits. In 2005, *M* Corp. has gross receipts of $160,000, of which half are from active business operations and half are royalty income. *M* Corp. also has $60,000 of deductions, of which $40,000 are allocable to the business operations and $20,000 are allocable to the royalty income. Compute *M* Corp.'s tax liability under §1375 as well as its taxable income for the year.

4. No Carryover from C Year to S Year

If a C corporation incurs capital losses in excess of its capital gains, the excess may not be deducted but instead is carried back or forward to a taxable year or years in which excess capital gains are recognized. §§1211(a), 1212(a). Similarly, if a C corporation incurs operating deductions in excess of taxable income, the excess is carried backward or forward as a net operating loss deduction. See §172. However, in no event may an excess capital loss, a net operating loss, or any other carryover, be carried from a year in which a corporation is a C corporation to a year in which the corporation is an S corporation. §1371(b)(1). Note that no carryover of any kind can originate in any year when the corporation is an S corporation. §1371(b)(2). As a result, there are no carryovers from S years to C years or from S years to other S years. Unused corporate losses may be available for shareholder use under §1366(d)(3).[6]

6. See page 647 infra.

B. FROM S CORPORATION TO C CORPORATION

A corporation's status as an S corporation can terminate by revocation under §1362(d)(1), by the corporation failing to meet the standards of §1361(b), see §1362(d)(2), or by receipt of excessive passive investment income if the corporation has C corporation earnings and profits, see §1362(d)(3). Regardless of the method of termination, the results are the same: If the termination is effective on a date other than the last day of the corporation's taxable year, the taxable year is divided into two short taxable years.[7] The first short taxable year ends on the day preceding the date of termination of the S corporation's election, §1362(e)(1)(A), and the second short taxable year begins on the following day, §1362(e)(1)(B). By this mechanism there is no taxable year during which the corporation is sometimes an S corporation and sometimes a C corporation. The two short years together are sometimes referred to as the "S termination year." §1362(e)(4).

Recall that when a corporation having subchapter C earnings and profits becomes an S corporation, distributions out of pre-S corporation earnings and profits are taxed as dividends while distributions out of post-S corporation earnings are taxed as a return of basis. See §1368(c). When an S election terminates, a similar issue arises because distribution of pre-termination earnings should be taxed as basis recovery while posttermination distributions should be taxed as dividends. Unfortunately, the rule is not so simple.

Under §1371(e)(1), posttermination cash distributions will be treated as made out of pretermination S corporation earnings to the extent of the corporation's accumulated adjustments account. All other distributions will be taxed under §301, the provision generally applicable to distributions from C corporations. However, an important limitation on §1371(e)(1) is that its benefits extend only to cash distributions made during the corporation's "posttermination transition period," and that usually extends one year from the effective date of the corporation's termination of its S corporation status. See §1377(b). Distributions made after the close of the posttermination transition period will be subject to §301 even if the corporation's accumulated adjustments account has not been fully depleted, so that if the corporation has (or generates) sufficient earnings and profits, the eventual distribution of profits made during the corporation's S period will nevertheless be taxed under subchapter C's regime.

Note that posttermination gains and losses will not affect the corporation's accumulated adjustments account. In addition, posttermination dis-

---

7. A termination under §1362(d)(3) for excessive passive investment income necessarily is effective on the first day of the corporation's taxable years. §1362(d)(3)(A)(ii). Terminations under §1362(d)(1) by revocation and under §1362(d)(2) by ceasing to be a small business corporation can be effective on any day of the corporation's taxable year. See §§1362(d)(1)(C), 1362(d)(2)(B).

tributions of property (i.e., of anything other than cash) are taxed under §301 even though the property may have been acquired or may have appreciated while the corporation was an S corporation. Accordingly, if a corporation is contemplating changing from an S corporation to a C corporation, the early disposition of appreciated property may be warranted if sale of the property in the near future is anticipated.

Finally, recall that tax-exempt income of an S corporation does not add to its accumulated adjustments account. §1368(e)(1)(A). In the context of a transition from a C corporation to an S corporation, this peculiarity affects the order in which corporate distributions are deemed to be out of C corporation earnings and profits or out of S corporation earnings.[8] When the transition is the other way, though, the exclusion of tax-exempt income from the corporation's accumulated adjustments account has a more dramatic impact: Posttermination distribution of the tax-exempt income will always be taxed under subchapter C's §301. This arises because the relief offered by §1371(e)(1) to posttermination distributions of S earnings extends only to the extent of the corporation's accumulated adjustments account. Because tax-exempt income does not go into the accumulated adjustments account, its distributions are unprotected by §1371(e)(1).

While the transition from S to C status brings little tax relief, there is one positive aspect. If the corporation had a prior C history, and if there is a surviving net operating loss from that earlier C period, it can be used by the corporation in its reincarnation as a C corporation. While §1371(b)(1) prohibits carryovers from C years to S years, there is no prohibition on carryovers from C years to C years, even if several S years are sandwiched in between. However, those S years count for determining if the carryover has expired. §1371(b)(3).

While S corporation losses generally pass through to the shareholders, §1366(d)(1) limits the pass through to the extent of a shareholder's stock and debt basis. If a corporation's status as an S corporation terminates, any losses suspended by application of §1366(d)(1) can be claimed by the affected shareholders in the following year, subject to the limitation that such losses cannot exceed their stock basis then. §1366(d)(3). Of course, any losses so claimed must reduce stock basis, §1366(d)(3)(C), just as they would were Subchapter S applicable in full. See §1367(a)(2)(B).

---

8. See page 639 supra.

III

SUBCHAPTER K PARTNERSHIPS

19

The Structure of Partnership Taxation

In this chapter we will look at the taxation of the four basic transactions in the life of a partnership: formation, daily business activity, nonliquidating distributions, and final disposition of the investment (liquidation of the partnership and sales of partnership interests). Those factual patterns that complicate understanding of the basic rules — encumbered property or the acquisition of partnership debt, for example — will be deferred. Having seen how the basic pieces fit together in simple circumstances, you will be better able to appreciate the nuances of Subchapter K's treatment of the more complex transactions.

A. A NOTE ON LIMITED LIABILITY COMPANIES

The rules of subchapter K apply to those entities falling within the definition of a "partnership" in §761(a). While a full examination of this definition is better postponed until later, it is worth noting at this point that a "partnership" for tax purposes can include many entities not classified as a "partnership" under relevant local law. And while incorporated entities are explicitly excluded from the §761(a) definition of a "partnership," there is no statutory requirement that a partnership include even a single member whose liability for debts of the entity is unlimited. That is, the statutory language of §761(a) includes the possibility of partnerships consisting exclusively of owners insulated from obligations of the entity.

Such organizations are called "limited liability companies," or LLCs for short. LLCs offer investors the non-tax advantage of limited liability equivalent to the better-known corporate veil. They also offer investors the tax advantages of pass-through taxation available under subchapter K. While the precise requirements of an LLC vary state-by-state, most states permit the investors in an LLC (usually called "members" rather than shareholders or partners) substantial flexibility in structuring management of the organization. For example, one LLC might be run by majority vote of its members, much like a general partnership, while another LLC might be run by a manager or management company as is common for corporations and limited partnerships.

For a tax lawyer, the name given to an organization is relatively unimportant as compared with its tax status under federal law. That does not mean, though, that a tax lawyer can ignore the state law distinctions between general partnerships, limited partnerships, LLCs, and similar organizations even though all are taxable as partnerships under subchapter K. For example, the partnership tax rules for allocating entity-level debt among partners is influenced by the extent of each partner's potential liability for repayment of such debts. Thus, for this purpose members of an LLC are treated like limited partners. Note that members of LLCs are treated like limited partners in this context not because they are (or are not) called "limited partners" but rather because they have the same substantive rights and obligations as limited partners with respect to entity-level debt.

There is at least one area of the Code in which the name given to a partner may determine the tax consequences of a transaction. Under §736(b)(3)(B), special rules generally favorable to the partnership apply to certain retirement payments made to a "general" partner. Because this provision of the Code has no particular relationship to entity debt, it is unclear if the specification of a "general" partner in §736(b)(3)(B) should be understood as requiring unlimited liability for entity-level obligations, participation in day-to-day management of the entity's activities, or some other characteristic usually part of a "general" partnership interest under state law. We will return to an examination of §736 later, but as you read various provisions of subchapter K and the regulations interpreting it, keep in mind that not all entities taxed as partnerships will have members who neatly fall under the traditional labels of general and limited partner.

B. THE PASS-THROUGH OF PARTNERSHIP INCOME

The most basic rule of subchapter K is in §701 which reads: "A partnership as such shall not be subject to the income tax imposed. . . . Persons carrying on business as partners shall be liable for income tax only in their separate or individual capacities." Despite this absolute rule of nontaxation, it does make sense to speak of a partnership's income. Consistent with the entity model of pass-through taxation, under §703 a partnership computes its taxable income *as if* it were a taxable entity. For example, if a partnership owned rental real estate, it might include rents and deduct maintenance, interest, and depreciation.

Once the partnership's taxable income is computed, that income is allocated among the various partners for inclusion on their individual returns. A partner's share of partnership income is called her "distributive" share. See §§702, 704. The term "distributive share" is one of the great misnomers in the Internal Revenue Code because a partner's distributive share is what is *included* on the partner's individual return and bears no necessary relation to any amount actually *distributed* to the partner.

For example, a partnership agreement might provide that no funds will be distributed to any partner during the first five years of the partnership. Thus, the first five years will see no partnership *distributions*. Nevertheless, there will be *distributive shares* each year because, as the partnership earns (or loses) income, the partners must include (or deduct) it on their individual returns. Do not confuse distributive shares with actual distributions or anything else of the sort. To be sure, it would have been easier if distributive shares had been called "allocative shares" or something similar. "Distributive share" is the statutory term, though, and so "distributive share" is the term we use.

Partnership taxation, then, is a two-step dance. In step 1, we compute the entity's taxable income. In step 2, we allocate that income among the partners. And nowhere is the independence of the two steps more clearly set out than in the Supreme Court's opinion in *United States v. Basye.*

United States v. Basye ————————————————————
410 U.S. 441 (1973)

MR. JUSTICE POWELL delivered the opinion of the Court.

I

Respondents, each of whom is a physician, are partners in a limited partnership known as Permanente Medical Group, which was organized in California in 1949. Associated with the partnership are over 200 partner physicians, as well as numerous nonpartner physicians and other employees. In 1959, Permanente entered into an agreement with Kaiser Foundation Health Plan, Inc., a nonprofit corporation providing prepaid medical care and hospital services to its dues-paying members.

Pursuant to the terms of the agreement, Permanente agreed to supply medical services for the 390,000 member-families, or about 900,000 individuals, in Kaiser's Northern California Region which covers primarily the San Francisco Bay area. In exchange for those services, Kaiser agreed to pay the partnership a "base compensation" composed of two elements.

First, Kaiser undertook to pay directly to the partnership a sum each month computed on the basis of the total number of members enrolled in the health program. That number was multiplied by a stated fee, which originally was set at a little over $2.60. The second item of compensation — and the one that has occasioned the present dispute — called for the creation of a program, funded entirely by Kaiser, to pay retirement benefits to Permanente's partner and non-partner physicians.

The pertinent compensation provision of the agreement did not itself establish the details of the retirement program; it simply obligated Kaiser to make contributions to such a program in the event that the parties might thereafter agree to adopt one. As might be expected, a separate trust agreement establishing the contemplated plan soon was executed by Permanente, Kaiser, and the Bank of America Trust and Savings Association, acting as trustee. Under this agreement Kaiser agreed to make payments to the trust at a predetermined rate, initially pegged at 12 cents per health plan member per month. Additionally, Kaiser made a flat payment of $200,000 to start the fund and agreed that its pro rata payment obligation would be retroactive to the date of the signing of the medical service agreement.

The beneficiaries of the trust were all partner and nonpartner physicians who had completed at least two years of continuous service with the partnership and who elected to participate. The trust maintained a separate tentative account for each beneficiary. As periodic payments were received from Kaiser, the funds were allocated among these accounts pursuant to a complicated formula designed to take into consideration on a relative basis each participant's compensation level, length of service, and age. No physician was eligible to receive the amounts in his tentative account prior to retirement, and retirement established entitlement only if the participant had rendered at least 15 years of continuous service or 10 years of continuous service and had attained age 65. Prior to such time, however, the trust agreement explicitly provided that no interest in any tentative account was to be regarded as having vested in any particular beneficiary. The agreement also provided for the forfeiture of any physician's interest and its redistribution among the remaining participants if he were to terminate his relationship with Permanente prior to retirement. A similar forfeiture and redistribution also would occur if, after retirement, a physician were to render professional services for any hospital or health plan other than one operated by Kaiser. The trust agreement further stipulated that a retired physician's right to receive benefits would cease if he were to refuse any reasonable request to render consultative services to any Kaiser-operated health plan.

The agreement provided that the plan would continue irrespective either of changes in the partnership's personnel or of alterations in its organizational structure. The plan would survive any reorganization of the partnership so long as at least 50% of the plan's participants remained associated with the reorganized entity. In the event of dissolution or of a nonqualifying reorganization, all of the amounts in the trust were to be divided among the participants entitled thereto in amounts governed by each participant's tentative account. Under no circumstances, however, could payments from Kaiser to the trust be recouped by Kaiser: once compensation was paid into the trust it was thereafter committed exclusively to the benefit of Permanente's participating physicians. . . .

During the years from the plan's inception until its discontinuance in 1963, Kaiser paid a total of more than $2,000,000 into the trust. Permanente, however, did not report these payments as income in its partnership returns. Nor did the individual partners include these payments in the computations of their distributive shares of the partnership's taxable income. The Commissioner assessed deficiencies against each partner-respondent for his distributive share of the amount paid by Kaiser. . . .

The Commissioner premised his assessment on the conclusion that Kaiser's payments to the trust constituted a form of compensation to the partnership for the services it rendered and therefore was income to the partnership. And, notwithstanding the deflection of those payments to the retirement trust and their current unavailability to the partners, the partners were still taxable on their distributive shares of that compensation. Both the District Court and the Court of Appeals disagreed. They held that the payments to the fund were not income to the partnership because it did not receive them and never had a "right to receive" them. They reasoned that the partnership, as an entity, should be disregarded and that each partner should be treated simply as a potential beneficiary of his tentative share of the retirement fund. Viewed in this light, no presently taxable income could be attributed to these cash basis taxpayers because of the contingent and forfeitable nature of the fund allocations.

We hold that the courts below erred and that respondents were properly taxable on the partnership's retirement fund income. This conclusion rests on two familiar principles of income taxation, first, that income is taxed to the party who earns it and that liability may not be avoided through an anticipatory assignment of that income, and, second, that partners are taxable on their distributive or proportionate shares of current partnership income irrespective of whether that income is actually distributed to them. The ensuing discussion is simply an application of those principles to the facts of the present case.

II

Section 703 of the Internal Revenue Code of 1954, insofar as pertinent here, prescribes that "[t]he taxable income of a partnership shall be computed in the same manner as in the case of an individual." Thus, while the partnership itself pays no taxes, §701, it must report the income it generates and such income must be calculated in largely the same manner as an individual computes his personal income. For this purpose, then, the partnership is regarded as an independently recognizable entity apart from the aggregate of its partners. Once its income is ascertained and reported, its existence may be disregarded since each partner must pay tax on a portion of the total income as if the partnership were merely an agent or conduit through which the income passed.[8]

In determining any partner's income, it is first necessary to compute the gross income of the partnership. One of the major sources of gross income, as defined in §61(a)(1) of the Code, is "[c]ompensation for services, including fees, commissions, and similar items." There can be no question that Kaiser's payments to the retirement trust were compensation for services rendered by the partnership under the medical service agreement. These payments constituted an integral part of the employment arrangement. The agreement itself called for two forms of "base compensation" to be paid in exchange for services rendered — direct per-member, per-month payments to the partnership and other, similarly computed, payments to the trust. . . .

Yet the courts below, focusing on the fact that the retirement fund payments were never actually received by the partnership but were contributed directly to the trust, found that the payments were not includable as income in the partnership's returns. The view of tax accountability upon which this conclusion rests is incompatible with a foundational rule, which this Court has described as "the first principle of income taxation: that income must be taxed to him who earns it." *Commissioner v. Culbertson*, 337 U.S. 733, 739-740 (1949). The entity earning the income — whether a partnership or an individual taxpayer — cannot avoid taxation by entering into a contractual arrangement whereby that income is diverted to some other person or entity. . . .

Permanente's agreement with Kaiser, whereby a portion of the partnership compensation was deflected to the retirement fund, is certainly within the ambit of *Lucas v. Earl.* The partnership earned the income and, as a result of arms'-length bargaining with Kaiser, was responsible for its diversion into the trust fund. The Court of Appeals found the *Lucas* principle inapplicable because Permanente "never had the right itself to receive the payments made into the trust as current income." 450 F.2d at 114. In support of this assertion, the court relied on language in the agreed state-

___

8. There has been a great deal of discussion in the briefs and in the lower court opinions with respect to whether a partnership is to be viewed as an "entity" or as a "conduit." We find ourselves in agreement with the Solicitor General's remark during oral argument when he suggested that "[i]t seems odd that we should still be discussing such things in 1972." The legislative history indicates, and the commentators agree, that partnerships are entities for purposes of calculating and filing informational returns but that they are conduits through which the taxpaying obligation passes to the individual partners in accord with their distributive shares. . . .

ment of facts stipulating that "[t]he payments . . . were paid solely to fund the retirement plan, and were not otherwise available to [Permanente]. . . ." Ibid. Emphasizing that the fund was created to serve Kaiser's interest in a stable source of qualified, experienced physicians, the court found that Permanente could not have received that income except in the form in which it was received.

The court's reasoning seems to be that, before the partnership could be found to have received income, there must be proof that "Permanente agreed to accept less direct compensation from Kaiser in exchange for the retirement plan payments." Apart from the inherent difficulty of adducing such evidence, we know of no authority imposing this burden upon the Government. . . .

III

Since the retirement fund payments should have been reported as income to the partnership, along with other income received from Kaiser, the individual partners should have included their shares of that income in their individual returns. §§61(a)(13), 702, 704. For it is axiomatic that each partner must pay taxes on his distributive share of the partnership's income without regard to whether that amount is actually distributed to him. . . .

The courts below reasoned to the contrary, holding that the partners here were not properly taxable on the amounts contributed to the retirement fund. This view, apparently, was based on the assumption that each partner's distributive share prior to retirement was too contingent and unascertainable to constitute presently recognizable income. It is true that no partner knew with certainty exactly how much he would ultimately receive or whether he would in fact be entitled to receive anything. But the existence of conditions upon the actual receipt by a partner of income fully earned by the partnership is irrelevant in determining the amount of tax due from him. The fact that the courts below placed such emphasis on this factor suggests the basic misapprehension under which they labored in this case. Rather than being viewed as responsible contributors to the partnership's total income, respondent-partners were seen only as contingent beneficiaries of the trust. In some measure, this misplaced focus on the considerations of uncertainty and forfeitability may be a consequence of the erroneous manner in which the Commissioner originally assessed the partners' deficiencies. The Commissioner divided Kaiser's trust fund payments into two categories: (1) payments earmarked for the tentative accounts of nonpartner physicians; and (2) those allotted to partner physicians. The payments to the trust for the former category of nonpartner physicians were correctly counted as income to the partners in accord with the distributive-share formula as established in the partnership agreement.[16] The latter payments to the tentative accounts of the individual partners, however, were improperly allocated to each partner pursuant to the complex formula in the retirement plan itself, just as if that agreement operated as an amendment to the partnership agreement.

The Solicitor General, alluding to this miscomputation during oral argument, suggested that this error "may be what threw the court below off the track." It should be clear that the contingent and unascertainable nature of each partner's share under the retirement trust is irrelevant to the computation of his distributive share. The partnership had received as income a definite sum which was not subject to diminution or forfeiture. Only its ultimate disposition among the employees and partners remained uncertain. For purposes of income tax computation it made no difference that some partners might have elected not to participate in the retirement program or that, for any number of reasons, they might not ultimately receive any of the trust's benefits. Indeed, as the Government suggests, the result would be quite the same if the "potential beneficiaries included no partners at all, but were children, relatives, or other objects of the partnership's largesse." The sole operative consideration is that the income had been received by the partnership, not what disposition might have been effected once the funds were received.

IV

In summary, we find this case controlled by familiar and long-settled principles of income and partnership taxation. There being no doubt about the character of the payments as compensation, or about their actual receipt, the partnership was obligated to report them as income presently received. Likewise, each partner was responsible for his distributive share of that income. We, therefore, reverse the judgments and remand the case with directions that judgments be entered for the United States.

It is so ordered.

MR. JUSTICE DOUGLAS dissents.

In theory, once a partnership's income is computed there are two ways in which it can be allocated among the partners. For example, if X is a one-third partner in the XYZ partnership, we could allocate to X one-third of each item of income, deduction, credit and loss *or* we could allocate to X one-third of some net figure combining all of these items. It is easiest to think of the allocation item-by-item. Thus, X might be allocated $10,000 of the partnership's $30,000 of income, $5,000 of the partnership's $15,000

---

16. These amounts would be divided equally among the partners pursuant to the partnership agreement's stipulation that all income above each partner's drawing account "shall be distributed equally."

of interest expense, etc. In fact, though, the code uses a slightly different method, passing some items through to the partners as individual items and others combined into one net figure.

In general, we net together all partnership level items whose tax status does not depend on non-partnership tax items appearing on a partner's individual return. For example, a partnership might make a "charitable contribution" within the meaning of §170(c) to a qualified educational institution. Such contributions generally are deductible up to 50% of a taxpayer's adjusted gross income. See §§170(b)(1)(A), 170(b)(1)(F). Accordingly, we cannot know the extent to which the partnership's contribution is deductible without knowing each partner's adjusted gross income as well as all other charitable contributions made by (or allocable to) each partner. We do not net the charitable contribution against the partnership's taxable income but rather allocate it as a distinct item among the partners. In the language of §703(a)(1), charitable contributions are "separately stated" items.

As a second example, suppose a partnership has $20,000 of ordinary income, $6,000 of (ordinary) deduction, and $10,000 of long-term capital loss. If this partnership has two equal partners, individuals A and B, how should the partners account for the partnership's items of income and loss?

If the $10,000 of capital loss had been an ordinary deduction, we would simply net the partnership items together to produce $4,000 of partnership taxable income. Our co-partners would then report $2,000 apiece. However, because the loss is capital, we cannot simply net it against the partnership's ordinary income: with certain limitations, capital loss cannot offset ordinary income. See §§1211-1212. Accordingly, the tax effect of the partnership capital loss will depend on each partner's individual tax status. For example, if partner A has some additional capital gain to be reported on her individual return, A's share of the partnership's capital loss can offset that gain. Capital gain and loss, therefore, are separately stated items (see §702(a)(1)-(2)), so that partners A and B will each report $7,000 of partnership income from the nonseparately-stated items and $5,000 of long-term capital loss.

PROBLEMS

19-1. Individuals X and Y form the XY partnership to perform charitable work in local hospitals. A good-hearted citizen transfers a 30-year treasury bond to the partnership to help it pay for its activities. The terms of the transfer provide, however, that all of the bond interest must be used for charitable purposes or the bond automatically reverts to its prior owner. At the end of the year, X and Y report no income from XY on their individual returns even though the bond paid interest. X and Y attach a statement to their returns saying: "We have no bond income this year for two reasons. First, the partnership owns the bond, not us. We have never owned it and will never own it. Therefore, we have no income from it. Second, all the bond interest will go to charitable uses. Because none of it will be used personally, we should not have to report any income." What do you think of these arguments?

C.   FORMATION AND OPERATION OF THE PARTNERSHIP

The rules governing partnership formation are in §§721, 722, and 723. They provide that the contribution of property to a partnership in exchange for a partnership interest is not a taxable event to the partnership or to the contributing partner. Further, they provide for a double carryover basis: The partnership carries over the contributing partner's basis in the asset and the partner carries over the asset basis into her partnership interest. Be sure to note that these rules apply not only to contributions forming the partnership but also to subsequent contributions (so-called midstream contributions) made by new or continuing partners.

Consider the following example. *P, Q,* and *R* form the PQR partnership by making the following contributions:

	Property	*Adjusted Basis*	*Fair Market Value*
P	Blackacre	$10,000	$10,000
Q	Whiteacre	8,000	10,000
R	Greenacre	15,000	10,000

In a financial sense, the partners have made equivalent contributions of property worth $10,000 apiece. In a tax sense, though, the contributions are quite distinct: *Q* has contributed appreciated property while R has contributed loss property. *P*'s basis in her partnership interest (her "outside" basis) will be $10,000, while *Q*'s basis will be $8,000 and *R*'s will be $15,000. Of course, the partnership will have a combined asset basis (the partnership's combined "inside" basis) of $33,000.

One effect of this double carryover basis rule is that any appreciation or loss in contributed property existing at the time of contribution will be built into the contributing partner's outside basis. For example, if *Q* sells her partnership interest for $10,000 shortly after acquiring it, she will recognize a gain of $2,000. Recognition of that gain is appropriate because *Q* has, in effect, simply sold Whiteacre for $10,000, and had that sale been effected directly, *Q* would have recognized a gain of $2,000.

While §722 gives us each partner's initial basis in her partnership interest, §705 informs us that these bases will change as the partnership makes or loses money. Suppose, for example, that Blackacre increases in value and is then sold by the partnership for $25,000. Assuming this is the only taxable event of the year, the partnership will have taxable income of $15,000 (amount realized of $25,000 less adjusted basis of $10,000) and each partner's distributive share will be $5,000. Accordingly, each partner will report $5,000 on her individual return and, pursuant to §705(a)(1)(A), each partner will increase her outside basis by the same amount. This basis adjustment is needed to ensure that partnership gains and losses are not recognized twice, once when recognized by the partnership and a second time upon disposition by the partner of her partnership interest.

For example, suppose partner P sells her interest in the year after Blackacre is sold but before any funds have been distributed. Because the fair market value of the partnership's assets now total $45,000 ($25,000 in cash, $10,000 worth of Whiteacre and $10,000 worth of Greenacre), P's one-third interest should sell for $15,000. Should P recognize gain on the sale of her partnership interest for its fair market value of $15,000?

The answer is no, and the easiest way to see that is to look at P's cash flow over the life of the partnership. P contributed property with an adjusted basis of $10,000. She received no distributions from the partnership and then received $15,000 upon disposition of her interest. Thus, her inflow of receipts exceeded the adjusted basis of her contribution by $5,000, and so P should recognize $5,000 of income over the life of the partnership. Because she already recognized that amount of income, there should be no further gain or loss when she sells her partnership interest.

This cash-flow analysis tells us that P's outside basis must be $15,000 when she sells her partnership interest. How do we reach that result under the code? Section 705(a)(1)(A) provides for a basis increase equal to the partner's distributive share of taxable income. For every dollar of partnership income the partner reports on her individual return, the partner's outside basis goes up by the same amount. This basis adjustment ensures that income taxed to the partner when earned by the partnership will not be taxed a second time upon disposition of the partnership interest.

Should there be an outside basis adjustment for a partner's distributive share of tax exempt income? Suppose individuals A and B form the AB partnership by contributing $5,000 apiece. The partnership invests its $10,000 in a municipal, tax-exempt bond paying 10 percent interest per year. In the first year, the partnership receives interest of $1,000. What effect should this have on the partners' outside bases?

The partnership is now worth $11,000, so that each partner's half interest is worth $5,500. If A sells her partnership interest for that amount, she will recognize gain of $500 unless she is entitled to a basis increase for her share of the partnership's tax-exempt income. If we do not provide such a basis increase, the tax-exempt interest will in fact be taxable to A, albeit not when earned by the partnership but only when *A* sells her interest. To keep the interest entirely tax-exempt, *A* is given an upward basis adjustment for her share of tax-exempt interest just as for taxable income. See §705(a)(1)(B). In the case of taxable income, this basis adjustment eliminates a second tax on the income; in the case of tax-exempt income, the basis adjustment eliminates a first tax on the income.

Just as outside basis is adjusted upward for distributive share of taxable income, so, too, outside basis is adjusted downward for distributive share of taxable losses (and all other deductions). §705(a)(2)(A). Similarly, the counterpart of tax-exempt income, nondeductible, noncapitalizable expenses (such as illegal bribes and kickbacks) also produce a downward basis adjustment. These downward basis adjustments can never produce a negative outside basis, see §705(a)(2) (parenthetical), because a partner's distributive share of losses cannot exceed his outside basis. §704(d).

PROBLEMS

19-2. Return to the *XY* charitable partnership of problem 19-1 above. Assuming the transfer of the bond is properly treated as a gift under §102, what tax consequences, if any, should there be to *X, Y,* and *XY* as a result of this gift of the bond? What if the donor's adjusted basis in the bond was $800 and the fair market value of the bond was $1,000?

D. NONLIQUIDATING DISTRIBUTIONS

Nonliquidating distributions (also sometimes called current distributions) are, in general, nontaxable to the distributee partner. §731(a). Because the rules applicable to cash distributions and property distributions differ somewhat, we will consider first a nonliquidating distribution of (noncash) property.

Suppose *X* is a member of the *XYZ* partnership with an outside basis of $10,000. Further, suppose that the partnership distributes Purpleacre to *X* when Purpleacre has a basis in the partnership's hands of $6,000 and a fair market value of $7,500.

Under §731(a)(1)-(2), *X* will not recognize gain or loss on the distribution. Indeed, loss can never be recognized on a nonliquidating distribution and gain can be recognized only if the distribution includes cash. Because the distribution is not a taxable event to *X,* it cannot increase or decrease her basis. However, because *X* now owns two assets (Purpleacre and her partnership interest) when before she owned only one (the partnership interest), *X*'s predistribution outside basis of $10,000 is allocated between the two assets.

Under §732(a)(1), X carries over the partnership's $6,000 basis in Purpleacre. And under §733(2), X reduces her outside basis by that $6,000 down to $4,000. The effect of these rules is not to change X's overall basis amount (it remains at $10,000) but simply to divide it between the partnership interest and the newly-acquired Purpleacre.

What if Purpleacre had had a basis to the partnership of $12,000? If we gave X a carryover basis of $12,000 in Purpleacre, we would have to give X a negative $2,000 outside basis to preserve the $10,000 total. Outside basis can never go negative, so we adopt a different allocation scheme. X takes a basis in Purpleacre of only $10,000, see §732(a)(2), and reduces her outside basis to zero. Note that the transaction remains tax-free; the only thing that changes is the allocation of X's predistribution outside basis between the postdistribution partnership interest and the distributed asset (Purpleacre). You should also note that the fair market value of Purpleacre plays no role in the taxation of X (at least until X sells or exchanges it in a taxable transaction).

We can restate the rules of §§731-733 as they apply to nonliquidating distributions of property (not cash!) as follows: No gain or loss is recognized and the distributee partner allocates her predistribution outside basis to the asset up to the partnership's predistribution basis in the asset. Any outside basis left over remains as outside basis. The effect of these rules is to preserve any gain or loss inherent in the property despite the distribution. If we gave the distributee partner a basis higher than carryover, recognition of income could be deferred by distributing an appreciated asset in anticipation of sale. If the distributee partner is given a basis lower than carryover (as is done when the distributee partner's outside basis cannot absorb the full carryover), recognition of income is accelerated.

The rules applicable to current distributions of cash work almost identically. Suppose X receives $6,000 of cash. Under §731(a) no gain or loss is recognized, and under §733(1), X reduces her outside basis by the $6,000 down to $4,000. Recognizing that cash implicitly always has a basis equal to face (or fair market) value, X is taxed just as if she received property with adjusted basis to the partnership of $6,000.

But what if X receives cash of $12,000? Had the cash been other property, we would simply give it a lower than carryover basis of $10,000 and reduce X's outside basis to zero. But because cash cannot have a lower than face-value basis, this technique will not work when X receives the cash. We could give X a negative $2,000 outside basis, but the code eschews negative basis. Accordingly, we force X to recognize $2,000 of income and reduce X's outside basis only to zero. Recognition of income replaces the negative basis.

Thus, the difference between the rules governing nonliquidating distributions of property and those governing nonliquidating distributions of cash is that the distribution of property with a basis exceeding the distributee partner's outside basis results in a basis adjustment to the distributed property. See §732(a)(2). In the case of a distribution of cash in excess of the distributee partner's outside basis, recognition of income substitutes for the basis adjustment. See §731(a)(1).

The effect of these rules is to preserve, as much as possible, the equality of aggregate inside basis with that of aggregate outside basis. The equality begins with the double carryover basis rule of §§722-723: Both outside basis and inside basis are initially set equal to the adjusted basis of contributed property. This equality continues with the basis adjustment rules of §705: Recognition of partnership income (taxable or tax exempt) occurs when inside basis goes up and causes, by reason of §705(a)(1)(A), outside basis to go up dollar for dollar. Similarly, recognition of partnership loss (taxable or tax exempt) occurs when inside basis goes down and causes, by reason of §705(a)(2)(A), outside basis to go down. Accordingly, the initial equality of aggregate inside and outside bases continues as the partnership engages in its day-to-day business activities.

For example, suppose X and Y form the XY general partnership by contributing $10,000 apiece. Aggregate inside basis begins at $20,000 (treating cash as having basis equal to face) as does aggregate outside basis ($10,000 per partner). If the partnership earns $1,000 during its first year, that amount will pass through to the partners presumably 50/50 (or $500 apiece) and will increase aggregate outside basis to $21,000. Inside basis is now $21,000 (the initial inside basis of $20,000 plus the $1,000 earned during the year), so aggregate inside and outside bases are equal.

The distribution rules of §§731-733 continue this equality, albeit with some exceptions. When property is distributed by the partnership to a partner, partnership inside basis decreases by the adjusted basis of the distributed property because the partnership no longer owns the property. And under the rule of §732(a)(1), that asset basis continues in the hands of the distributee partner and, under §733(2), it also reduces outside basis by the same amount. Thus, the reduction to inside basis equals the §733(2) reduction in outside basis so equality is preserved. If cash is distributed, the same result obtains under §733(1).

For example, suppose XY distributes $1,000 to X. No gain or loss is recognized by X, §731(a), and X reduces her outside basis from $10,500 to $9,500. Thus, aggregate outside basis totals $20,000 (X's outside basis of $9,500 plus Y's outside basis of $10,500). Inside basis also equals $20,000, since that was the initial value of the inside basis and all current earnings have been distributed.

However, the equality of aggregate inside and outside bases is not preserved if property is distributed having an adjusted basis in the hands of the partnership in excess of the distributee partner's predistribution outside basis. Recall that in such circumstances the distributee partner takes a basis in the property equal to her predistribution outside basis and outside basis is reduced to zero. §§732(a)(2), 733(2). Thus, inside basis is reduced by the adjusted basis of the asset in the hands of the partnership (because the asset no longer is owned by the partnership) while aggregate outside basis is reduced only by the distributee partner's predistribution outside basis.

For example, suppose the *XY* partnership invests $15,000 of its remaining $20,000 (after the distribution to *X*) in stock of company C. If that C stock is then distributed to partner *Y,* inside basis will decline from $20,000 to $5,000 (because the stock is no longer owned by the partnership). Under §732(a)(2), *Y* will take a basis in that stock of $10,500 and will reduce her basis to zero. See §733(2). Outside basis will then stand at $9,500 ($9,500 for *X* and $0 for *Y*) which is $4,500 higher than inside basis.

The same problem occurs if cash is distributed to a partner in an amount sufficient to trigger recognition of income under §731(a)(1). Recall that a distribution of cash will produce income to the distributee partner only if the partner receives cash in excess of her predistribution outside basis. In such circumstances, the distribution reduces aggregate inside basis by the amount of the cash distributed while outside basis is reduced only by the distributee partner's predistribution outside basis (because outside basis cannot be reduced below zero). In short, the only time a distribution will break the equality between aggregate inside and outside bases is when the distributee partner's outside basis is too small to absorb the partnership's basis in the distributed property.

Why is the equality between aggregate inside and outside bases important? If one or more individuals own some property, gain or loss on disposition of the property is determined by comparing the amount realized on the disposition with the owner's (or owners') adjusted basis in the property. If this same piece of property is contributed to a partnership, the double carry-over basis rule of §§722-723 ensures that disposition by the partnership will have the same tax consequences as would disposition of the property outside the partnership. The equality between aggregate inside and outside bases, in short, gives to the entity model of pass-through taxation much of the feel of the aggregate model without losing the simplifying structure of the entity.

If the partnership were given a basis in the property lower than its former basis in the hands of the contributing partner, more gain would be recognized upon disposition by the partnership than would have been recognized directly by the contributing partner. Conversely, if the partnership were given a basis in the property higher than its former basis in the hands of the contributing partner, less gain would be realized by a partnership disposition than by disposition directly by the partner. In short, the double carryover basis rule of §§722-723 ensures that contribution of property to a partnership is as transparent (to the tax system) as possible.

The double carryover basis rule of §§722-723 further ensures that an individual does not profit (or lose) by contributing property to a partnership shortly before selling the partnership interest. Indeed, the amount of gain or loss realized by all partners if they sold all their partnership interests is precisely equal to the gain realized by the partnership if it sold all its assets, so long as aggregate inside and outside bases are equal. If we think of the partners as each having undivided interests in the mass of partnership assets, then each partner's individual outside basis is simply her share of the partnership's aggregate inside (asset) basis.

As we have seen, the equality between aggregate inside and aggregate outside bases occasionally can be broken. This should suggest that the equality is not an essential feature of pass-through entity taxation. That is correct: Inside basis rules affect only the timing of recognition of income and loss and so can be varied without great penalty. For example, the relationship between aggregate inside basis and aggregate outside basis is much more attenuated under Subchapter S than under Subchapter K.

Recognition of income by a partnership has both good and bad tax effects for the partners. The bad effect is that the partners must report that income on their individual returns in proportion to their distributive shares. The good effect is that this recognition increases the partners' outside bases so that future recognition of income is reduced (or future recognition of loss is increased). Because partnership recognition of income and loss is determined by inside basis, any change to inside basis will have offsetting effects, one immediate and one deferred.

For example, suppose assets contributed to a partnership were given a basis equal to fair market value rather than carryover. For appreciated assets, this rule would produce less gain (or more depreciation) to the partnership and through it to the partners. Thus, the partners would report less income in the short run.

However, reporting less income now means reporting more income later because of the basis rules of §705. Recognition of pass-through income results in an outside basis increase, so that a fair market value basis rule for contributed, appreciated assets would leave the partners with lower outside bases, lower outside bases that ultimately will produce additional gain. The gain that was not recognized by the partnership on disposition of the asset, in other words, will be recognized by the partners on disposition of their partnership interests. Thus, a disparity between aggregate inside and outside bases does not mean that income will be counted twice (or lost) but that income will be accelerated or deferred.

While the inside basis rules could be changed without affecting the total amount of income recognized by a partner over the life of the partnership, the same is not true of the outside basis rules. When property is contributed to a partnership, the contributing partner carries the asset basis into her partnership interest. This is an essential structural rule of taxation: Because the partner does not recognize gain or loss on the partnership formation, the partner's asset basis must be preserved in the interest acquired.

For example, recall the *PQR* partnership formed as follows:

	Property	Adjusted Basis	Fair Market Value
P	Blackacre	$10,000	$10,000
Q	Whiteacre	8,000	10,000
R	Greenacre	15,000	10,000

As a result of the carryover outside basis rule in §722, if *Q* sells her partnership interest for its fair market value of $10,000 shortly after formation of the partnership, she will recognize a gain of $2,000. Recognition of $2,000 of gain is appropriate because *Q* has, in effect, sold Whiteacre for $10,000.

Any rule other than carryover would result in too much or too little income to *Q*. For example, giving *Q* a fair market value basis in her partnership interest would permanently exclude all precontribution asset appreciation (and loss) from the tax base.

Consider the following example. *P* and *Q* co-own Blackacre with adjusted total basis of $10,000 and fair market value of $14,000. They contribute Blackacre to the newly formed *PQ* partnership and become equal partners. *If P and Q are given initial outside bases equal to the fair market value of the property contributed* (i.e., of $7,000 each instead of $5,000 under §722), will the $4,000 precontribution asset appreciation permanently escape taxation?

Suppose the partnership sells Blackacre for its fair market value of $14,000. The partnership will recognize $4,000 of income (because its basis in the property was carryover, see §723), and that income will pass-through to (i.e., be reported by) the partners. Accordingly, *P* and *Q* will each report $2,000 of income from the sale of Blackacre.

In addition, *P* and *Q* will each increase their outside bases by the gain recognized. §705(a)(1). Since we assumed (contrary to §722) that each partner began with an outside basis of $7,000, that means each partner's outside basis will equal $9,000 once Blackacre is sold. However, the partnership has but $14,000 in cash (that being the sale proceeds), so that each partnership interest is worth $7,000. In other words, each partner has a $9,000 adjusted basis in a partnership interest worth $7,000.

As a result, a sale by *P* or *Q* of her partnership interest will produce a taxable loss of $2,000. This loss just offsets the prior income recognized by each partner when Blackacre was sold by the partnership. The net effect, then, is a wash: For each partner, $2,000 of income is reported when Blackacre is sold by the partnership and $2,000 of loss is reported when the partnership interest is sold by the partner. Thus, over the life of the partnership the precontribution appreciation of $4,000 is exempted from tax.

PROBLEMS

19-3. Ten individuals form the P partnership as co-equals by contributing $10,000 apiece. P uses this $100,000 to purchase some commercial real estate. During the first year, P turns an operating profit of $30,000. Half of this is distributed pro rata to the partners, and the other half is retained as a reserve. If one of the partners then sells her 10 percent interest in P for $15,000, how much gain should she report on the sale?

19-4. Individual C is a one-quarter partner in the $CDEF$ partnership. C receives a current distribution of property worth $20,000 and with adjusted basis to the partnership of $14,000. What are the tax consequences to C of this distribution if C's outside basis equals

a. $35,000?
b. $15,000?
c. $10,000?
d. How would your answers change if the distribution consisted of $20,000 in cash?

19-5. Individual H has a $10,000 outside basis in her interest in the PQ partnership. The partnership owns Blackacre with an adjusted basis of $12,000 and a fair market value of $18,000. The partnership will distribute Blackacre to H as well as cash of $6,000. How will H be taxed if

a. Blackacre and the cash are distributed as two separate distributions, with the cash first?
b. Blackacre and the cash are distributed in two separate distributions, with Blackacre first?
c. Blackacre and the cash are distributed as part of a single transaction?
d. From these problems, would you characterize the distribution rules as cash-first or cash-last? Which is most favorable to taxpayers?

E. LIQUIDATING DISTRIBUTIONS AND SALES OF PARTNERSHIP INTERESTS

Few special provisions apply to the sale of a partnership interest: Gain or loss is computed by comparing the amount realized by the selling partner with her adjusted basis. The character of that gain or loss as ordinary or capital will turn on the character of the assets held by the partnership. See §751(a), with some minor exceptions. To properly tax the selling partner on her share of the partnership's unrealized cash-basis items accruing prior to the sale, the selling partner's distributive share of those items is computed and includible by the selling partner. See §706(d)(2).

A liquidating distribution is conceptually a sale of the partnership interest back to the partnership (and through it to the other partners). Despite this, a liquidating distribution is taxed more like a current distribution than a sale. Thus, gain or loss generally are not recognized on a liquidating distribution even if the value of the property received by the terminating partner exceeds her outside basis. Rather, any gain or loss realized on the liquidating distribution is deferred and built into the basis of the property distributed. See §§731(a), 732(b). Because the anti-abuse rules in this context provide some extremely counter-intuitive results, we will defer further consideration of the liquidating distribution rules.

20

Determining Distributive Shares

Each partner reports her "distributive" share of the partnership's income and loss on her individual return. §702. Under §704(a), each partner's distributive share is determined by reference to the partnership agreement. Further, this section provides that a partner's distributive share may be specified item by item, so that partner X might have a 30 percent share of rents, a 25 percent share of royalties, and a 50 percent share of losses. Thus, §704(a) gives the partners great flexibility in allocating the partnership's tax items among themselves.

The term "partnership agreement" is defined in §761(c) to include all amendments made by the partners and specifically allows the partners to allocate the partnership tax items with hindsight: They may modify their agreement up to the time that the partnership tax return is due to be filed. Thus, distributive shares need not be defined until the partnership's income and loss is known and the nonpartnership tax status of the partners is determined. This definition, when combined with the rule of §704(a), seemingly encourages the partners to allocate partnership tax items in ways guaranteed to minimize the partners' aggregate tax liability.

Section 704(a) is unusual in that it expressly allows the partners, through amendment of the partnership agreement, to manipulate tax items. Usually, taxpayers adjust nontax items such as property rights, rental agreements, and sale terms, and then the tax consequences follow from these nontax arrangements. Here, though, the partners are given the power to say which partner reports how much of each tax item in a way that seemingly has nothing to do with any economic reality: Recall that distributive shares are not defined by reference to amounts distributed or to anything similar.

As should be expected, there are limitations. The partners' distributive shares as reflected in the partnership agreement will not be given effect if they lack "substantial economic effect." §704(b). The "substantial economic effect" test was first articulated by the Tax Court in Orrisch v. Commissioner, 55 T.C. 395 (1970), aff'd, 31 A.F.T.R.2d ¶73-1069 (9th Cir. 1973), and it has come to stand for the proposition that allocations must be consistent with the underlying economic arrangements of the partners (the economic effect requirement, see Treas. Regs. §1.704-1(b)(2)(ii)(a)) and must affect the dollar amounts to be received by the partners from the partnership independent of tax consequences (the substantiality requirement, see Treas. Regs. §1.704-1(b)(2)(iii)(a)).

The Treasury Department has promulgated a voluminous regulation (Treas. Regs. §1.704-1(b)) covering the substantial economic effect test, continuing and expanding the analysis in *Orrisch*. That regulation divides the test into two separate components: an economic effect test and a substantiality test. You may have heard that mastery of the substantial economic effect test is one of the most difficult parts of the tax law, and rightly so. Nevertheless, if looked at properly, drafting allocation provisions can become almost mechanical. In fact, drafting allocation provisions which pass tax muster is remarkably straight-forward. What causes much of the difficulty is drafting provisions that reflect the economic arrangements desired by the partners.

The term "special allocation" is used (although it is not defined in the Code or regulations) to describe any tax allocation other than one corresponding to the partner's general interest in the partnership. For example, if two partners agree to allocate all tax items equally between them except that depreciation deductions will be allocated exclusively to one partner, we say that the depreciation deductions have been specially allocated.

While the term "special allocation" is generally accepted, you should try to refrain from using it because it is premised on the naive notion that partners *have* a general interest in the partnership. If partner X is allocated 15 percent of the partnership's ordinary income, 20 percent of the partnership's capital gain, and 30 percent of the partnership's losses, there is no way to describe X's interest in the partnership by some general percentage. We will see that many provisions of subchapter K and the early regulations implicitly assume that each partner has some determinable general interest in the partnership. Yet there is nothing to prevent a partnership from allocating each item separately on a year-by-year basis.

A "bottom line" allocation is an allocation of the partnership's net income or loss. See Treas. Regs. §1.704-1(b)(1)(vii). Thus, rather than allocate the partnership's income and deductions item-by-item, bottom line allocations divide the net total. Such bottom line allocations are specifically authorized by §704(b) and represent nothing more than a short-form way of stating more common item allocations. For example, a bottom line allocation of 10 percent to partner *X* is equivalent to an allocation of 10 percent of each item of income and deduction to partner *X*.

A. BASIC MAINTENANCE OF CAPITAL ACCOUNTS

A "capital account" must be maintained for each partner according to the rules set forth in Treas. Regs. §1.704-1(b)(2)(iv). The capital account maintenance rules help enforce the substantial economic effect limitation on partnership allocations. If these rules are not followed, tax allocations specified in the partnership agreement may be disregarded by the Service. Treas. Regs. §1.704-1(b)(2)(iv)(a). Note in particular that each partner has a single capital account even if the partner owns several interests in the partnership. Treas. Regs. §1.704-1(b)(2)(iv)(b).

Just like a partner's outside basis, a partner's capital account begins with the partner's contribution to the partnership and is adjusted for distributions and further contributions of property as well as distributive share of income and loss. Treas. Regs. §1.704-1(b)(2)(iv)(b). However, while initial outside basis equals the adjusted basis of contributed property, initial capital accounts begin at the *fair market value* of contributed property. Treas. Regs. §1.704-1(b)(2)(iv)(d). Thus, the capital account balances measure the economic (rather than tax) relationship between the partners.

Booking in property at fair market value ensures that the contributing partner gets full credit for the value of her contribution. For example, suppose *A* and *B* form the *AB* general partnership with *A* contributing cash of $10,000 and *B* contributing Blackacre with fair market value of $10,000 but adjusted basis of only $6,000. *B* surely expects to be an equal partner with *A* because they have each contributed $10,000 in value to the partnership. *B*'s capital account is credited with the full value of Blackacre, and so the two partners begin with equal capital accounts reflecting their equality.

Of course, if Blackacre increases in value, say to $12,000, while held by the partnership, neither *A*'s nor *B*'s capital account will reflect the true value of the partner's interest in the partnership. As with outside basis, capital accounts are not adjusted simply because property appreciates (or depreciates) in value. Accordingly, partnership capital accounts reflect the *book* value of partnership property and do not (in general) reflect any unrealized appreciation or loss accruing after the property was acquired by the partnership.

There are, however, occasions when the partners must take into account the current fair market value of some or all partnership assets, and when they do so, the assets will be booked up (or down) to current fair market value. For example, if the partnership distributes property to one of its partners, the distributee partner's capital account must be reduced by

the full fair market value of the distributed property. Treas. Regs. §1.704-
1(b)(2)(iv)(e)(1). Accordingly, the distributed property is booked to current value immediately prior to the distribution. *Id.*

There are additional rules governing capital account maintenance, see
generally Treas. Regs. §1.704-1(b)(2)(iv), and there are other differences
between capital accounts and outside bases, see Treas. Regs. §§1.704-
1(b)(2)(iv)(c) (treatment of liabilities), 1.704-1(b)(2)(iv)(f) (revaluations
of property), 1.704-3 (contributed property). But to understand the basics
of the substantial economic effect test, we have all that we need. We will
return to capital account maintenance throughout these materials as we
cover specific transactions.

PROBLEMS

20-1. 1. *B* and *W* form the *BW* general partnership. *B* contributes
Blackacre with adjusted basis of $20,000 and fair market value of $25,000.
W contributes Whiteacre with adjusted basis of $28,000 and fair market
value of $25,000. *B* and *W* agree to allocate all items of gain or loss equally.
During the first year, BW earns $10,000 from renting Blackacre but loses
$6,000 from the operation of Whiteacre. The partnership makes no distri-
butions. What are the partners' capital accounts after the first year?

B. ECONOMIC EFFECT I: THE GENERAL TEST

The substantial economic effect test is divided under the regulations into
two components: the economic effect test and the substantiality test. Treas.
Regs. §1.704-1(b)(2)(i). We will postpone until section G an examination
of the second (substantiality) of these two tests, see Treas. Regs. §1.704-
1(b)(2)(iii). Remember, though, that partnership allocations will not be
valid unless they pass both tests.

Under the *general test for economic effect,* see Treas. Regs. §1.704-
1(b)(2)(ii)(b), allocations have economic effect if three conditions are
met. First, capital accounts must be properly maintained. Treas. Regs.
§1.704-1(b)(2)(ii)(b)(1). Second, liquidation proceeds must be distributed in accordance with final capital account balances. Treas. Regs. §1.704-
1(b)(2)(ii)(b)(2). And third, any partner with a capital account deficit at
time of liquidation of her partnership interest must have an unqualified
obligation to restore the amount of that deficit (within 90 days of liquidation of the interest) for distribution to creditors of the partnership or to
other partners. Treas. Regs. §1.704-1(b)(2)(ii)(b)(3). This deficit restoration obligation may arise from the partnership agreement or otherwise.
For example, state law may impose such an obligation on the partners.

Note that this regulation ties "distributive share" (i.e., partnership
allocation of income and deductions) to liquidating distributions. Further,

because nonliquidating distributions affect capital account balances, Treas. Regs. §1.704-1(b)(2)(iv)(b), nonliquidating distributions influence partnership allocations as well. What underlies these rules is an attempt to relate partnership allocations to the economic arrangements among the partners.

In order for an allocation to have economic effect, it must be consistent with the underlying economic arrangement of the partners. That is, in the event there is an economic benefit or economic burden that corresponds to an allocation, the partner to whom the allocation is made must receive such economic benefit or bear such economic burden. Treas. Regs. §1.704-1(b)(2)(ii)(a).

What does this mean? Suppose that a partnership earns $100 of income, and suppose further that this item of income is allocated under the partnership agreement to partner P. If capital accounts are maintained properly, this allocation will result in a $100 increase in P's capital account. And if liquidation proceeds will be distributed in accordance with final capital accounts, then P will receive 100 more dollars at liquidation (if not before) by reason of the allocation. The upward capital account adjustment, in other words, ensures that the economic benefit (receipt of more dollars) follows the tax allocation (inclusion of more income).

Consider the following partnership agreement. A and B each contribute $100 to the AB partnership. The partnership will purchase business equipment for $200, and assume that this equipment is depreciable at the rate of $40 per year for five years. A and B will equally share all income, but B will be allocated all depreciation deductions. If the partnership has rental income of $60 per year, what will the partnership books look like after five years?

At formation, the partnership capital accounts will equal $100 for each partner. The first year's activities produce taxable income of $60 and a depreciation deduction of $40. Allocating the income 50/50 between A and B while allocating the depreciation entirely to B produces capital accounts of $130 for A and $90 for B:

A	B	
$100	$100	Starting values
30	30	Distributive share of income
0	(40)	Distributive share of depreciation
$130	$ 90	Totals

After five years, the partnership capital accounts will be $250 for A and $50 for B:

A	B	
$130	$ 90	Carryover
120	120	Distributive share of income
0	(160)	Distributive share of depreciation
$250	$ 50	Totals

B was allocated all depreciation deductions. The economic burden associated with depreciation is risk of diminution in value of the depreciable property. Thus, economic effect requires that *B* bear that economic risk. Has this happened? Assume that the property has declined in value as it has been depreciated. That is, assume the equipment has declined to zero value. The partnership now holds cash of $300 ($60 per year received times five years) and nothing else of value. Liquidation proceeds can thus be distributed to the partners in accordance with final capital account balances: A will be entitled to $250 and *B* will be entitled to $50.

Have the tax consequences worked out? Each year of the five years, *A* included $30 of income. Over five years, *A* thus included $150 of income. Upon liquidation, *A* received $250 in cash, and that is precisely $150 more than *A* invested. Thus, *A* can and does receive the liquidating distribution with no further tax consequences, ultimately receiving one dollar of cash for every dollar of partnership income allocated to her.

As to *B*, each year *B* included $30 of income and deducted $40 of depreciation. Thus, *B*'s net result was $10 of deduction per year. Over the five years, then, *B* deducted a total of $50 which is the precise amount of money *B* lost in the venture ($100 invested less $50 received upon liquidation). Thus, *B*'s liquidating distribution properly has no tax consequences to *B*: the economic effect of the tax allocations ensured that the tax consequences were felt as the income was earned (and as the depreciation was claimed) over time.

Consider for a moment what would happen if the partners had allocated all tax items the same way but had provided (in violation of the general test for economic effect) that liquidation proceeds were to be distributed equally to *A* and to *B* regardless of final capital account balances. In this case, each partner would receive $150 in cash upon liquidation. As to *A*, such a liquidation would produce a taxable loss of $100 because the amount of money received is less than *A*'s preliquidation outside basis. The reverse would be true as to *B*: the distribution would produce a taxable gain of $100 because the cash distributed exceeds *B*'s preliquidation outside basis.

Absence of economic effect means, in other words, that the distribution of liquidation proceeds will result in gain or loss to the partners. A partner recognizing income on a liquidating distribution would (like *B*) have been allocated too little income (or too much loss) during the life of the partnership. Note that the absence of economic effect does not result in phantom income or loss *over the life of the partnership:* the outside basis rules in §705 ensure that whatever economic effect is lacking during the life of the partnership will be made up upon liquidation. Economic effect, in other words, is about the timing of partnership tax items. From another perspective, economic effect is about the amount each partner will receive upon liquidation: so long as capital accounts are properly maintained and liquidation proceeds are properly distributed, *any* set of partnership allocations will have economic effect under the general test.

Reconsider the last *AB* example but assume that the partnership recognizes no income in any year. Thus, the only tax item is a deduction of $40 per year for five years. At the end of that time, the partnership capital accounts will stand at $100 for A and negative $100 for *B:*

A	B	
$100	$100	Contributions
0	(200)	Distributive share of depreciation
$100	($100)	Totals

Assuming once again that the equipment declines in value to zero, the partnership will have no assets. Liquidation proceeds must be distributed in accordance with final capital account balances, but where is the $100 due A to come from? From *B*, of course, because a capital account deficit must be restored at liquidation under the rules of the general test for economic effect. Note that B deducted $40 per year times five years, or $200 total. B lost her entire investment of $100 and, because of the capital account deficit restoration obligation, B will lose another $100 upon liquidation. A, on the other hand, will have lost nothing and will receive $100 — precisely the amount initially invested — at liquidation.

You should now have a feel for what the regulations mean when they say that the partner given a tax allocation must also receive the associated economic benefit or burden. The benefit associated with an allocation of income is the right to receive more funds, while the burden associated with a deduction is risk of loss of funds. By reflecting tax allocations in properly maintained capital accounts, economic benefits and burdens follow tax allocations.

Although economic benefits and burdens must follow tax allocations, it sometimes happens that anticipated burdens do not materialize. In particular, the economic burden associated with depreciation deductions is the risk of diminution in value of the property. Often, depreciable property does not decline in value as quickly as its depreciation schedule suggests. In such cases, careful drafting of the partnership agreement can ensure that no partner bears an economic burden in excess of that actually incurred by the partnership.

For example, suppose that A and B form the AB partnership by contributing $5,000 each. The partnership will invest its $10,000 in depreciable property, and all depreciation deductions will be allocated to A. All other tax items will be allocated equally between A and B.

Assume that the partnership has no income or loss each year other than a $2,000 depreciation deduction. After two years, the capital accounts will be $1,000 for A and $5,000 for *B:*

A	B	
$5,000	$5,000	Cash contributions
(2,000)	0	Year 1 depreciation
(2,000)	0	Year 2 depreciation
$1,000	$5,000	Totals

Suppose the partnership now sells its property for $9,000 in anticipation of liquidation. As a result of the sale, the partnership recognizes a gain of $3,000, allocable under the partnership agreement equally between the partners. Accordingly, final capital accounts will be $2,500 for A and $6,500 for B:

A	B	
$1,000	$5,000	Carryover
1,500	1,500	Distributive share of gain
$2,500	$6,500	Totals

A has reported $4,000 of deduction and $1,500 of income for a net loss of $2,500, and that is the correct measure of A's economic loss. However, the partnership lost only $1,000 on the property; after all, it purchased the property for $10,000 and subsequently sold it for $9,000. Why is A losing $2,500 when the partnership lost but $1,000?

A's excess loss arises because the $3,000 dispositional gain was allocated 50/50 while the depreciation deductions were allocated entirely to A. Note that the taxable gain from disposition of the property is not the result of an increase in the value of the property. Rather, it represents a tax payback of the amount of depreciation claimed ($4,000) in excess of the true decline in value of the property ($1,000). To avoid this unfairness to A, the partnership agreement should allocate the entire gain back to A, resulting in final capital accounts of $4,000 for A and $5,000 for B:

A	B	
$1,000	$5,000	Carryover
3,000	0	Chargeback of gain
$4,000	$5,000	Totals

By this *gain chargeback*, we ensure that A suffers no loss beyond that suffered by the partnership. In this example, A suffers an economic loss of $1,000 over the life of the partnership. That loss is appropriate, however, because the partnership's property declined in value by that amount and, because A was specially allocated all depreciation deductions, A must bear that loss.

Consider the following arrangement. P and Q form the PQ partnership with P contributing cash of $25,000 and Q contributing cash of $75,000. The partnership uses its cash of $100,000 to purchase depreciable business property. The partnership agreement provides: (1) all cost recovery deductions (i.e., depreciation) will be allocated to Q; (2) all operating income and loss (excluding cost recovery deductions) will be allocated 25 percent to P and 75 percent to Q; and (3) all gain or loss from the eventual sale of the business property will be allocated 50 percent to P and 50 percent to Q. Assume that the cost of the business property is recovered at a rate of $10,000 per year for 10 years and that the partnership has income each year (excluding the cost recovery deduction) of $12,000.

At the start of the partnership, the capital accounts begin at $25,000 for *P* and $75,000 for *Q.* As a result of the activities in year one, *P*'s distributive share will include $3,000 of income while *Q*'s distributive share will include $9,000 of income and $10,000 of deduction. Accordingly, the capital accounts will become $28,000 for *P* and $74,000 for *Q*:

P	*Q*	
$25,000	$75,000	Cash contributions
3,000	9,000	Distributive share of income
0	(10,000)	Distributive share of depreciation
$28,000	$74,000	Totals

The partnership now owns business property with adjusted basis of $90,000 as well as cash of $12,000. If the partners wish to distribute that cash in a nonliquidating distribution, how much must go to *P*? The answer, and this is important, is that the tax allocations do not specify or restrict how nonliquidating distributions are to be made. The partners could choose to distribute as much or as little of the $12,000 cash as they see fit, and if they choose to distribute it all, for example, they can do so to *P* and *Q* in any proportions. *Tax allocations ("distributive shares") do not determine current distributions.*

Assume the partners decide to distribute the entire $12,000 in the same proportion as that income was allocated. In that case, $3,000 will be distributed to *P* and $9,000 will be distributed to *Q.* As a result of these distributions, the books will become $25,000 for *P* and $65,000 for *Q*:

P	*Q*	
$28,000	$74,000	Carryover
(3,000)	(9,000)	Distribution
$25,000	$65,000	Totals

Suppose the partnership sells its business property immediately at the beginning of year 2 for its initial cost of $100,000. As a result of that sale, the partnership will recognize a gain of $10,000, allocable under the partnership agreement $5,000 to *P* and $5,000 to *Q.* If the partnership now liquidates, the final (preliquidation) capital account balances will be $30,000 for *P* and $70,000 for *Q*:

P	*Q*	
$25,000	$65,000	Carryover
5,000	5,000	Distributive share of gain
$30,000	$70,000	Totals

It should come as no surprise that final capital account balances precisely equal the cash available for distribution: If the partnership owns nothing but cash, the requirement that liquidating proceeds be distributed in accordance with final capital account balances is premised on this equality. But consider the following: Has Q been treated fairly?

From one perspective Q has been treated fairly: Over the life of the partnership, Q included (net) $4,000 of income and made an economic profit of the same amount. To see this, recall that Q reported $9,000 of income and $10,000 of deduction at the end of the first year and reports $5,000 at the end of the second year as a result of the preliquidation sale. The net effect of these transactions is income of $4,000.

As to the economic profit, Q invested $75,000. Q received back $9,000 at the end of year one and $70,000 upon liquidation of the partnership, producing a net economic profit of $4,000. Thus, Q has been treated fairly in the sense that Q's tax situation properly reflects his economic situation.

But ignore taxes for a moment and look at what happened to Q. The partnership agreement provides that Q will be allocated three-quarters of all operating profit. The partnership in fact made $12,000 of operating profit, yet Q comes away from the partnership with only $4,000. What went wrong?

By allocating all cost recovery deductions to Q, Q was forced to bear the risk that the business property would decline in value. The property did not decline in value, though, instead producing a tax gain (but no economic gain) at disposition. Allocating Q all depreciation but only half of the resulting gain, Q's capital account suffered a net decline of $5,000 (that is, $10,000 decrease from the cost recovery deduction less $5,000 from Q's half of the dispositional gain).

By allocating all the depreciation deductions to Q, Q was forced to bear the economic risk of diminution in value of the business property: had it gone down in value, the loss would have been borne by Q. That risk of loss was reflected in Q's capital account by a downward adjustment of $10,000. When that loss did not mature, Q should have received an upward adjustment of the same amount. However, because the partnership agreement did not include the appropriate gain chargeback, Q's capital account received only half of the upward adjustment. Had there been a gain chargeback provision in the agreement, Q would have paid for his excess depreciation deductions by including an offsetting amount of income. Without the gain chargeback, Q pays for the depreciation by actually losing money.

How should this partnership agreement have been written? The easy answer is: However the partners want it. Unfortunately, determining exactly what the partners have in mind often is difficult. For example, partners rarely will request a gain chargeback provision directly. However, the same partners when shown an example demonstrating the effect of a gain chargeback often will agree that such a provision is needed to effectuate their intentions. The most effective way to ascertain the partners' intentions is to present them with a series of hypotheticals (losses followed by gains, gains followed by losses, extreme losses, extreme gains, refinancing of the partnership property, etc.) and ask them to decide what nontax results they desire. Once those desires are known, drafting the corresponding tax allocations should be relatively straight forward.

This brings up another important point in drafting the tax provisions of a partnership agreement. The tax allocations in a partnership agreement divide the partnership's profit and loss among the partners: What is allocated to one partner is unavailable to the others. Thus, the allocations form the rules of a zero-sum game, and like any such game, not all players can be winners at the same time. For example, if you suggest a gain chargeback provision to *P* and *Q* in the example above, you are helping *Q* but hurting *P*. Which partner is your client? If the partner*ship* is your client, why are you helping one partner over another?

There is nothing wrong with being the partnership's lawyer in its dealing with persons outside the partnership, but you cannot represent more than one partner in preparing a partnership agreement without a conflict of interest. At a minimum, you must thoroughly explain the conflict to each of the partners in writing and advise them to seek independent counsel. This is best done in the initial representation and fee agreement letter sent to and signed by all parties. Such advice, though, often will be taken as a lawyer's attempt to multiply fees needlessly. Whether you insist on independent representation (and thereby risk losing the transaction to some lawyer less concerned with ethical considerations) or agree to represent all partners as best you can (and thereby face the risk of future recriminations and lawsuits) is one of the great difficulties in the practice of partnership tax law. Even great lawyers have made mistakes in this area. Most clients, though, will appreciate your professionalism.

Let us recap the general test for economic effect. First, capital accounts must be properly maintained. See Treas. Regs. §1.704-1(b)(2)(ii)(b)(1), 1.704-1(b)(2)(iv). The easiest way to ensure that capital accounts are maintained properly in partnership agreements you write is *not* to provide detailed maintenance rules in the agreement. Rather, you should incorporate the regulations by reference, writing "Capital accounts will be maintained in accordance with the rules in Treasury Regulation section 1.704-1(b)" or something similar.

Second, upon liquidation of the partnership (or of any partner's interest), proceeds must be distributed in accordance with final capital account balances. Treas. Regs. §1.704-1(b)(2)(ii)(b)(2). Once again, detailed rules are not needed in the partnership agreement itself. Rather, include a sentence such as "Upon liquidation of one or more interests in the partnership, liquidation proceeds will be distributed in proportion to final capital account balances as adjusted for the distribution." The "as adjusted" language refers to adjustments made reflect any disparities between book value and tax basis. See Treas. Regs. §1.704-1(b)(2)(iv)(f)(5)(ii).

Third, each partner must have an unqualified obligation to restore a capital account deficit upon liquidation of her interest. Treas. Regs. §1.704-1(b)(2)(ii)(b)(3). While this obligation need not arise directly from the partnership agreement (e.g., state law may impose such an obligation on general partners), it is a good practice to explicitly declare the obligation in the partnership agreement. By making the deficit restoration obligation specific, there is less chance that incoming partners will be misled. In addition, you will avoid arguing the niceties of state law with an aggressive revenue agent auditing the partnership.

PROBLEMS

20-2. *P* and *Q* form the *PQ* partnership. They agree on a set of bottom-line allocations: (1) if there is a net loss for the year, it will be allocated 60 percent to *P* and 40 percent to *Q*; and (2) if there is net income for the year, it will be allocated 50 percent to *P* and 50 percent to *Q*. Are the partners' capital accounts *time dependent* in the sense that they turn on not only how much income and loss the partnership recognizes but also on the year in which items of income and loss are recognized?

20-3. *X* and *Y* form the *XY* Travel Agency, a general partnership, by contributing $10,000 each. They agree to split losses equally but, because *X* is a more experienced travel agent than *Y*, they agree to allocate 60 percent of the profits to *X* and 40 percent to *Y*. Assuming that these allocations should apply to economic gains and losses, write the tax allocation provisions for the *XY* partnership. (*Hint:* Make sure your provisions work properly if there is loss in year 1 and profit in year 2, then consider what happens if there is profit in year 1 and loss in year 2.)

C. ECONOMIC EFFECT II: THE ALTERNATE TEST

While the general test for economic effect is satisfactory for many partnerships, its deficit restoration obligation will be unacceptable to some partners, especially to limited partners (and to members of limited liability companies) for whom liability is statutorily limited. A limited partner makes an initial contribution to the partnership and agrees to make further contributions up to a stated maximum. That maximum can be as little as zero or as much as the partners agree, but whatever the amount, the existence of any limitation on a partner's obligation to contribute additional funds to the partnership is inconsistent with the deficit restoration requirement of the general test for economic effect. Allocations to limited partners, then, can never satisfy the general test for economic effect.

Revenue Ruling 97-38 _____
1997-38 I.R.B. 14

ISSUE

If a partner is treated as having a limited deficit restoration obligation under §1.704-1(b)(2)(ii)(c) of the Income Tax Regulations by reason of the partner's liability to the partnership's creditors, how is the amount of that obligation calculated?

FACTS

In year 1, *GP* and *LP*, general partner and limited partner, each contribute $100x$ to form limited partnership *LPRS*. In general, *GP* and *LP* share *LPRS*'s income and loss 50 percent each. However, *LPRS* allocates to GP all depreciation deductions and gain from the sale of depreciable assets up to the amount of those deductions. *LPRS* maintains capital accounts according to the rules set forth in §1.704-1(b)(2)(iv), and the partners agree to liquidate according to positive capital account balances under the rules of §1.704-1(b)(2)(ii)(b)(2).

Under applicable state law, *GP* is liable to creditors for all partnership recourse liabilities, but *LP* has no personal liability. *GP* and *LP* do not agree to unconditional deficit restoration obligations as described in §1.704-1(b)(2)(ii)(b)(3) (in general, a deficit restoration obligation requires a partner to restore any deficit capital account balance following the liquidation of the partner's interest in the partnership); *GP* is obligated to restore a deficit capital account only to the extent necessary to pay creditors. Thus, if *LPRS* were to liquidate after paying all creditors and *LP* had a positive capital account balance, *GP* would not be required to restore *GP*'s deficit capital account to permit a liquidating distribution to *LP*. In addition, GP and LP agree to a qualified income offset, thus satisfying the requirements of the alternate test for economic effect of §1.704-1(b)(2)(ii)(d). *GP* and *LP* also agree that no allocation will be made that causes or increases a deficit balance in any partner's capital account in excess of the partner's obligation to restore the deficit.

LPRS purchases depreciable property for $1,000x$ from an unrelated seller, paying $200x$ in cash and borrowing the $800x$ balance from an unrelated bank that is not the seller of the property. The note is recourse to *LPRS*. The principal of the loan is due in 6 years; interest is payable semi-annually at the applicable federal rate. *GP* bears the entire economic risk of loss for *LPRS*'s recourse liability, and *GP*'s basis in *LPRS* (outside basis) is increased by $800x$. See §1.752-2.

In each of years 1 through 5, the property generates $200x$ of depreciation. All other partnership deductions and losses exactly equal income, so that in each of years 1 through 5 *LPRS* has a net loss of $200x$.

LAW AND ANALYSIS

. . . To come within the safe harbor for establishing economic effect in §1.704-1(b)(2)(ii), partners must agree to maintain capital accounts under the rules of §1.704-1(b)(2)(iv), liquidate according to positive capital account balances, and agree to an unconditional deficit restoration obligation for any partner with a deficit in that partner's capital account, as described in §1.704-1(b)(2)(ii)(b)(3). Alternatively, the partnership may satisfy the requirements of the alternate test for economic effect provided in §1.704-1(b)(2)(ii)(d). *LPRS*'s partnership agreement complies with the alternate test for economic effect.

The alternate test for economic effect requires the partners to agree to a qualified income offset in lieu of an unconditional deficit restoration obligation. If the partners so agree, allocations will have economic effect to the extent that they do not create a deficit capital account for any partner (in excess of any limited deficit restoration obligation of that partner) as of the end of the partnership taxable year to which the allocation relates. §1.704-1(b)(2)(ii)(d)(3) (flush language).

A partner is treated as having a limited deficit restoration obligation to the extent of (1) the outstanding principal balance of any promissory note contributed to the partnership by the partner and (2) the amount of any unconditional obligation of the partner (whether imposed by the partnership agreement or by state or local law) to make subsequent contributions to the partnership. §1.704-1(b)(2)(ii)(c).

LP has no obligation under the partnership agreement or state or local law to make additional contributions to the partnership and, therefore, has no deficit restoration obligation. Under applicable state law, *GP* may have to make additional contributions to the partnership to pay creditors. However, *GP*'s obligation only arises to the extent that the amount of *LPRS*'s liabilities exceeds the value of *LPRS*'s assets available to satisfy the liabilities. Thus, the amount of *GP*'s limited deficit restoration obligation each year is equal to the difference between the amount of the partnership's recourse liabilities at the end of the year and the value of the partnership's assets available to satisfy the liabilities at the end of the year.

To ensure consistency with the other requirements of the regulations under §704(b), where a partner's obligation to make additional contributions to the partnership is dependent on the value of the partnership's assets, the partner's deficit restoration obligation must be computed by reference to the rules for determining the value of partnership property contained in the regulations under section 704(b). Consequently, in computing *GP*'s limited deficit restoration obligation, the value of the partnership's assets is conclusively presumed to equal the book basis of those assets under the capital account maintenance rules of §1.704-1(b)(2)(iv). See §1.704-1(b)(2)(ii)(d) (value equals basis presumption applies for purposes of determining expected allocations and distributions under the alternate test for economic effect); §1.704-1(b)(2)(iii) (value equals basis presumption applies for purposes of the substantiality test); §1.704-1(b)(3)(iii) (value equals basis presumption applies for purposes of the partner's interest in the partnership test); §1.704-2(d) (value equals basis presumption applies in computing partnership minimum gain).

The *LPRS* agreement allocates all depreciation deductions and gain on the sale of depreciable property to the extent of those deductions to *GP*. Because *LPRS*'s partnership agreement satisfies the alternate test for economic effect, the allocations of depreciation deductions to *GP* will have economic effect to the extent that they do not create a deficit capital account for *GP* in excess of *GP*'s obligation to restore the deficit balance. At the end of year 1, the basis of the depreciable property has been reduced to $800x. If *LPRS* liquidated at the beginning of year 2, selling its depreciable property for its basis of $800x, the proceeds would be used to repay the $800x principal on *LPRS*'s recourse liability. All of *LPRS*'s creditors would be satisfied and *GP* would have no obligation to contribute to pay them. Thus, at the end of year 1, *GP* has no obligation to restore a deficit in its capital account.

Because *GP* has no obligation to restore a deficit balance in its capital account at the end of year 1, an allocation that reduces *GP*'s capital account below $0 is not permitted under the partnership agreement and would not satisfy the alternate test for economic effect. An allocation of $200x of depreciation deductions to *GP* would reduce *GP*'s capital account to negative $100x. Because the allocation would result in a deficit capital account balance in excess of *GP*'s obligation to restore, the allocation is not permitted under the partnership agreement, and would not satisfy the safe harbor under the alternate test for economic effect. Therefore, the deductions for year 1 must be allocated $100x each to *GP* and *LP* (which is in accordance with their interests in the partnership).

The allocation of depreciation of $200x to *GP* in year 2 has economic effect. Although the allocation reduces *GP*'s capital account to negative $200x, while *LP*'s capital account remains $0, the allocation to *GP* does not create a deficit capital account in excess of *GP*'s limited deficit restoration obligation. If *LPRS* liquidated at the beginning of year 3, selling the depreciable property for its basis of $600x, the proceeds would be applied toward the $800x LPRS liability. Because *GP* is obligated to restore a deficit capital account to the extent necessary to pay creditors, *GP* would be required to contribute $200x to LPRS to satisfy the outstanding liability. Thus, at the end of year 2, *GP* has a deficit restoration obligation of $200*x*, and the allocation of depreciation to *GP* does not reduce *GP*'s capital account below its obligation to restore a deficit capital account.

This analysis also applies to the allocation of $200*x* of depreciation to *GP* in years 3 through 5. At the beginning of year 6, when the property is fully depreciated, the $800*x* principal amount of the partnership liability is due. The partners' capital accounts at the beginning of year 6 will equal negative $800*x* and $0, respectively, for *GP* and *LP*. Because value is conclusively presumed to equal basis, the depreciable property would be worthless and could not be used to satisfy *LPRS*'s $800*x* liability. As a result, *GP* is deemed to be required to contribute $800*x* to *LPRS*. A contribution by *GP* to satisfy this limited deficit restoration obligation would increase *GP*'s capital account balance to $0.

HOLDING

When a partner is treated as having a limited deficit restoration obligation by reason of the partner's liability to the partnership's creditors, the amount of that obligation is the amount of money that the partner would be required to contribute to the partnership to satisfy partnership liabilities if all partnership property were sold for the amount of the partnership's book basis in the property.

NOTES

1. *The alternate test and economic effect.* For partners who do not have an unlimited capital account deficit restoration obligation, the regulations offer an alternate test for economic effect. Treas. Regs. §1.704-1(b)(2)(ii)(d). In lieu of the capital account deficit restoration obligation imposed by the general test, the alternate test imposes three new requirements: (1) an allocation may drive the partner's capital account negative only to the extent that the partner can be required to make further capital contributions; (2) future events that would reduce a partner's capital account when they occur must be entered into the partner's capital account as soon as they reasonably can be anticipated (the look-ahead requirement); and (3) if the partner's capital account becomes negative in an amount beyond the maximum amount that the partner can be required to contribute to the partnership, partnership income must be allocated to the partner as quickly as possible to bring her capital account back up (the qualified income offset provision).

To understand the alternate test for economic effect, consider the following example. *G* and *L* form the *GL* limited partnership with *G* the general partner and *L* the limited partner who cannot be required to make further contributions to the partnership. The partners each contribute cash of $5,000, and the partnership agreement provides that losses will be allocated 70 percent to L and 30 percent to G. If the partnership incurs $8,000 of deductible expenses in its first year, how will the capital accounts stand?

Each partner's capital account will begin at $5,000. The first year's deduction of $8,000 is allocated $5,600 to L and $2,400 to G under the partnership agreement. Accordingly, L's capital account will show a deficit of $600 while G's capital account will stand at positive $2,600. Is there anything wrong?

If $8,000 is lost during the partnership's first year, only $2,000 of value remains within the partnership. If the partnership were to liquidate immediately after the conclusion of its first year, there would be only $2,000 to distribute but G's capital account balance would be $2,600. Assuming we distribute the entire $2,000 to G, G still ends up $600 short: Although G deducted only $2,400 during the life of the partnership, G will have suffered an economic loss of $3,000. This disparity between the *tax loss reported* by G and the *economic loss borne* by G is the touchstone of a lack of economic effect.[1]

We see the same lack of economic effect if we look at L. During the life of the partnership, L deducted $5,600. But L's economic loss is only $5,000 because that was the amount of L's initial investment and L cannot be required to contribute additional funds. The goal of the alternate test of economic effect is to ensure that L cannot deduct more than her maximum possible economic loss.

When one partner's capital account is negative while another's is positive, an immediate liquidation will force one partner to reimburse the other. If the partner with a negative capital account balance has no unconditional deficit restoration obligation, full reimbursement may be impossible. This is the situation that the alternate test for economic effect tries to avoid. Note that we cannot say with certainty that G will bear some of the loss allocated to L. If, for example, the partnership turns a profit in subsequent years, L's capital account may become positive and so G would not bear any of the loss allocated to L.

But we cannot know that L's capital account will increase in the future, and without that knowledge, G might bear some of L's loss. This possibility violates the regulation's standard of economic effect, see generally Treas. Regs. §1.704-1(b)(2)(ii), and so the tax allocations, as reflected in the

---

1. If these allocations were upheld despite their lack of economic effect, we would force L to recognize a gain of $600 on liquidation of the partnership, and we would allow G to recognize a loss of the same amount. Once again, absence of economic effect means only that a liquidating distribution of cash will produce gain or loss to the partners. See page 676 supra. Economic effect is about the *timing* of income and deductions; it is not about the total amount of income and deductions recognized over the life of the partnership (including the tax consequences of the liquidation).

partnership agreement, are not fully valid. To the extent that economic effect is lacking, the partners' distributive shares will be redetermined to correspond with the economics of the transaction.

This does not mean that the partnership agreement is wholly inoperative. As to the first $5,000 of loss allocated to L, economic effect is present. It is only as to the last $600 of loss — that is, as to the loss that makes L's capital account negative despite her lack of any obligation to make further contributions to the partnership — that economic effect is lacking. Thus, only the last $600 of loss will be reallocated to G. As the regulations make clear, allocations that are in part valid and in part invalid will be set aside only as to the invalid component. See, e.g., Treas. Regs. §1.704-1(b)(5) (ex. 1(iv)).

2. *The look-ahead requirement.* To appreciate the significance of the look-ahead requirement of the alternate test, consider what happens if the partnership distributes half of its cash (i.e., $1,000) at the beginning of its second year. Assume that the first year's deduction of $8,000 has been allocated $5,000 to L and $3,000 to G to preserve economic effect. If the $1,000 is distributed, for example, 70 percent to L and 30 percent to G, the effect of the distribution will be to reduce L's capital account to negative $700 and to reduce G's capital account to positive $1,700.

Once again L's capital account has become negative, and because L cannot be required to restore a capital account deficit, this means that something has gone wrong. L's net contribution to the partnership has been $4,300 (initial contribution of $5,000 less cash distributed to L of $700), yet L has deducted $5,000 of partnership losses. L's share of partnership deductions has thus exceeded the maximum economic loss L can be forced to bear.

Yet we made no allocations (to L or to G) in the second year: What caused the problem was the $700 reduction in L's capital account resulting from the distribution, not from an allocation of loss. Does that mean that the Commissioner can challenge the cash distribution as lacking economic effect?

Certainly not! The substantial economic effect test of §704(b) applies only to distributive shares — that is, to tax allocations — and not to anything else. The Commissioner has no authority to challenge a partnership's distributions or any other nontax aspect of its business. Accordingly, the Commissioner is helpless in year 2 and must hope that L's capital account deficit is increased prior to actual liquidation of L's interest in the partnership.

The look-ahead provision of the alternate test, see Treas. Regs. §1.704-1(b)(2)(ii)(d)(4), seeks to avoid this situation where a partner lacking an unlimited capital account deficit restoration obligation suffers a capital account reduction from a nontax item (such as from a cash distribution). The look-ahead provision requires that L's capital account be adjusted downward immediately once it is known with reasonable certainty that an event in the future will cause a capital account reduction. Thus, if we knew upon formation of the partnership that $700 would be distributed to L in year 2, we would start L's capital account at L's contribution of $5,000 less the future $700 reduction, or at $4,300. The effect of this reduction is to limit L's maximum share of the deduction in year 1 to $4,300. That is, by looking ahead to future events, we limit L's share of tax losses so that her capital account will be sufficient to absorb those future events when they occur.

What events must be anticipated in this way? Although you might think that all future distributions would be subject to the look-ahead provision, in fact that is not the case. Most partnerships only distribute cash as it is earned, and in such cases the capital account reduction from the distribution is precisely offset by the capital account increase from the distributive share of earnings. Only distributions in excess of distributive share of income — such as a distribution from a refinancing of partnership property — will cause a net reduction in capital accounts. Accordingly, only distributions in excess of distributive shares must be anticipated under the look-ahead provision, and a failure to anticipate such a distribution will violate the alternate test for economic effect if the distribution was reasonably expected to be made. There are other nontax activities of the partnership that can cause a net reduction in a partner's capital account, see generally Treas. Regs. §1.704-1(b)(2)(iv)(f), but they are too unusual or complex to be considered here.

By limiting tax allocations of losses and requiring immediate downward adjustments for future events that will decrease capital accounts, the alternate test for economic effect avoids, as much as possible, the situation in which a partner's capital account deficit exceeds her obligation to make future contributions to the partnership. Nevertheless, such a situation might occur. For example, an *unanticipated* distribution of cash in excess of distributive share of income might occur. In such circumstances, the regulations require that the limited partner be allocated income as soon as possible to bring her capital account back up. The provision in the partnership agreement providing for such an allocation of income is called a "qualified income offset" provision, a mandatory aspect of any partnership agreement if one or more partners does not have an unqualified obligation to restore a capital account deficit upon liquidation.

3. *Conditional deficit restoration obligations and cancellation of indebtedness income.* In Rev. Rul. 97-38 above, the general partner's capital account deficit restoration obligation was limited to repaying amounts owed to nonpartner creditors. As a result, the general partner's conditional restoration obligation was limited to the excess, if any, of the outstanding debt over the book value of the partnership's property. Thus, if the debt is repaid or forgiven, the partner's deficit restoration obligation drops to zero.

If the debt is forgiven, the partnership will recognize income from the discharge of indebtedness income under §61(a)(12). This income must be allocated in accordance with economic effect, and because neither partner will have a deficit restoration obligation at that time, the income will be subject to allocation under the partnership's minimum gain chargeback provision, at least to the extent of the general partner's negative capital account balance immediately before the debt discharge. See Rev. Rul. 92-97, 1992 C.B. 124. (*Note*: The partnership cannot exclude any of the income under §108(a) because that section is applied at the partner level. §108(d)(6)).

PROBLEMS

20-4.   *G* and *L* form the *GL* limited partnership with *G* the general partner and *L* the limited partner. *G* contributes cash of $60,000 and *L* contributes cash of $60,000. The partnership uses its initial cash of $120,000 to open an art gallery. The partnership agreement provides that *L* cannot be required to contribute additional funds to the partnership for three years. After then, *L*'s maximum contribution is $10,000. The partnership allocates income and losses 20 percent to *G* and 80 percent to *L*. If the partnership loses $30,000 per year for each of its first four years, how much of each year's loss is properly allocated to *G*? What are the capital account balances after four years?

20-5.   *X* and *Y* form the *XY* general partnership, with *X* contributing cash of $100 and *Y* contributing cash of $900. Each partner is liable to restore a capital account deficit only in favor of third-party creditors. The partnership borrows $9,000 and uses its cash of $10,000 to purchase depreciable; each year for five years, the property generates $2,000 of depreciation. The partners agree to allocate all items of loss and deduction 10 percent to *X* and 90 percent to *Y* and all items of income 50 percent to *X* and 50 percent to *Y*. The partners also agree to a minimum gain chargeback. After four years, the debt is forgiven. How should the income of $1,000 be allocated between *X* and *Y*?

D.   FAILURE TO SATISFY THE ECONOMIC EFFECT TEST

What happens if some tax allocation fails to satisfy the general test as well as the alternate test for economic effect? As we have already seen, an allocation in the partnership agreement lacking substantial economic effect will be disregarded. However, Treas. Regs. §1.704-1(b)(2)(ii)(*i*) provides an "economic effect equivalence" test:

> Allocations made to a partner that do not otherwise have economic effect
> . . . shall nevertheless be deemed to have economic effect, provided that as

of the end of each partnership taxable year a liquidation of the partnership at the end of such year or at the end of any future year would produce the same economic results to the partners as would occur if [the general or alternate tests] had been satisfied, regardless of the economic performance of the partnership.

As a first example, consider a two-person partnership in which it is agreed that all distributions, including liquidating distributions, will be made equally to each partner. Regardless of any tax allocations in the partnership agreement, each partner's distributive share of all partnership tax items must be 50 percent. No other allocation would reflect the partners' economic sharing of benefits and burdens.

Consider next the *GL* partnership in which *G* is the sole general partner and *L* is the sole limited partner having no obligation to make further contributions to the partnership. Each partner contributes cash of $5,000, and the partnership agreement provides that capital accounts will be maintained properly for each partner and that liquidation proceeds will be distributed in accordance with final capital account balances. The general partner, *G*, has an unconditional obligation to restore any capital account deficit upon liquidation. *L* has no such obligation, but the partnership agreement provides that no allocation will be made to *L* that would drive *L*'s capital account below zero. Further, *L*'s capital account will be maintained in accordance with a look-ahead provision that reduces *L*'s account once it is reasonably foreseeable that some future event will result in a net capital account decrease to *L*.

This limited partnership agreement meets all requirements of the general test as to *G* and meets all the requirements of the alternate test as to *L except that* there is no qualified income offset provision in the partnership agreement. If in the first year there is a depreciation deduction of $1,000 allocated 50/50 under the partnership agreement, does this allocation satisfy the economic effect equivalence test as to *L*?

The allocation of $500 of loss to *L* reduces her capital account from its starting value of $5,000 down to $4,500. This allocation has economic effect in the sense that liquidation proceeds can be distributed in accordance with positive capital account balances in the current year. Indeed, so long as *L*'s capital account is not negative, economic effect is guaranteed.

However, we cannot say that a liquidation in any future year will have economic effect. Suppose, for example, that *L*'s capital account goes negative in some future year because of an unanticipated distribution of loan proceeds. Suppose further that there is sufficient income in that future year to bring *L*'s capital account up to zero but, under the partnership agreement, only half of the year's income is then allocated to *L*. Had there been a qualified income offset provision in the partnership agreement, *L* would have been allocated sufficient income to eliminate the capital account deficit. Without the qualified income offset provision, *L*'s capital account deficit is reduced but not fully eliminated. A liquidation at the end of this future year thus would leave L with a deficit capital account but no restoration obligation, and that situation would not have obtained had there been a qualified income offset provision in the partnership agreement.

To be sure, these hypothetical future facts are unlikely. Nonetheless, the economic equivalence test requires that "a liquidation of the partnership . . . at the end of any future year would produce the same economic results to the partners as would occur if [the general or alternate tests] had been satisfied, regardless of the economic performance of the partnership." Treas. Regs. §1.704-1(b)(2)(i). The "regardless of the economic performance" language presumably allows the Commissioner to test the partnership agreement annually against *any* hypothetical future events. If so, this agreement seems to fail not only the actual economic effect test but the economic equivalence test as well.

So what is each partner's distributive share of the depreciation? Under §704(b), distributive shares are determined "in accordance with the partner's interest in the partnership" if "the allocation to a partner under the agreement . . . does not have substantial economic effect." The regulations list four nonexclusive factors that will be considered in determining a partner's "interest in the partnership," including (1) the partners' relative contributions to the partnership, (2) the interests of the partners in economic profits and losses, (3) the interests of the partners in cash-flow and other nonliquidating distributions, and (4) the rights of the partners to distributions of capital upon liquidation. Treas. Regs. §1.704-1(b)(3)(ii). This regulation also states as a general principle that

> a partner's interest in the partnership [means] the manner in which the partners have agreed to share the economic benefit or burden (if any) corresponding to the income, gain, loss, deduction, or credit . . . that is allocated. Treas. Regs. §1.704-1(b)(3)(i).

This statement in the regulations certainly invalidates, for example, an allocation of loss to a limited partner that drives the limited partner's capital account below the limited partner's obligation (if any) to make further contributions to the partnership. But what does this tell us with respect to the *GL* partnership lacking a qualified income offset provision? Because the allocation of depreciation to L reduces L's capital account, L will bear the economic burden associated with the depreciation. Thus, the allocation to L should stand.

Does this mean that the qualified income offset requirement of the alternate test is unenforceable? Far from it. Should L's capital account become negative because of some unforeseen distribution or similar event, an immediate liquidation would shift a loss to G although it had been allocated to L. Under the regulations, this possibility means that L's share of all subsequent income must be increased to eliminate the problem as quickly as possible. Treas. Regs. §1.704-1(b)(3)(i). That is, the regulations impose a qualified income offset on the partnership even if the partnership agreement does not contain one.

The Code includes a number of tax credits, such as general business credit in §38 and the low-income housing credit in §42. These tax credits often can be claimed by a partnership. How should tax credits be allocated under §704(b)? The regulations take the position that tax credits have no economic effect and therefore allocations of tax credits can never satisfy the general or alternate tests for economic effect. Thus, the regulations conclude that tax credits must be allocated "in accordance with the partners' interests in the partnership as of the time the tax credit or credit recapture arises." Treas. Regs. §1.704-1(b)(4)(ii).

This conclusion is hardly inescapable. A tax credit is simply an alternative specification of tax-exempt income. See generally Yoseph Edrey & Howard Abrams, Equitable Implementation of Tax Expenditures, 9 Va. Tax Rev. 109 (1989). Accordingly, allocation of a tax credit might be seen as an allocation of exempt income coupled with a distribution of cash in the same amount. From this perspective, partners should have complete freedom to allocate tax credits. Nevertheless, the regulations adopt the opposite approach.

E. ALLOCATIONS WITH RESPECT TO CONTRIBUTED PROPERTY

1. Allocations to the Contributing Partner under §704(c)(1)(A)

For clarity of presentation, all the examples in this section involve the contribution of appreciated or loss property as part of the formation of a partnership. The rules of §704(c)(1)(A) apply, however, whenever appreciated or loss property is contributed under §721.

Suppose P and Q form the PQ general partnership. P contributes cash of $10,000 and Q contributes property with fair market value of $10,000 but adjusted basis of only $6,000. As you already know, the opening books of the partnership read:

P		Q		
CA	OB	CA	OB	
$10,000	$10,000	$10,000	$6,000	Contributions

Under the rule of §704(c)(1)(A), the built-in gain of $4,000 must be allocated to Q. For example, if the property is subsequently sold for

$12,000, the first $4,000 of gain must be allocated to Q (under §704(c)(1)(A)) and the remaining $2,000 of gain may be allocated however the partners agree (under §704(b)). Assume that the partners agree to split equally all gain and loss (including any gain resulting from post-contribution appreciation of the property), except as required otherwise by §704(c)(1)(A). How will the partnership books read after sale of the property for $12,000?

There is a tax gain of $6,000, of which the first $4,000 is allocated entirely to Q and the remaining $2,000 of gain is allocated $1,000 to P and $1,000 to Q. In total, then, $1,000 is allocated to P and $5,000 is allocated to Q. Under §705, these allocations of gain affect the partners' outside bases, bringing each partner's outside basis to $11,000. However, there is book gain of only $2,000 (remember that the property was booked in at its fair market value at time of contribution), allocable $1,000 to P and $1,000 to Q. When book gain or loss differs from tax gain or loss, capital accounts are adjusted by the amount of *book gain or loss*. See Treas. Regs. §1.704-3(b). Accordingly, each partner's capital account is increased by $1,000 to $11,000. (If we had increased Q's capital account by her share of the tax gain, she would have received capital account credit for the precontribution appreciation twice, once when the property was contributed and a second time on sale.)

A similar analysis would be followed if the property had had a built-in loss when it was contributed to the partnership. For example, suppose the property contributed by Q had a fair market value of $10,000 but an adjusted basis of $14,000. The opening books of the partnership will read:

P		Q		
CA	OB	CA	OB	
$10,000	$10,000	$10,000	$14,000	Contributions

If the property is immediately sold by the partnership for its fair market value of $10,000, there will be a tax loss of $4,000, allocable entirely to Q under §704(c). However, there will be no book gain or loss, so neither partner's capital account is adjusted by reason of the sale. Thus, following the sale the partnership will have $20,000 in cash and each partner's outside basis and capital account will equal $10,000.

If the §704(c)(1)(A) property is depreciable, an additional level of complexity is introduced. Assume once again that P contributes cash of $10,000 and that Q contributes property with fair market value of $10,000 but adjusted basis of only $6,000. Assume in addition that the property is depreciable using the straight-line method over five years, so that the partnership is entitled to a depreciation deduction of $1,200 per year for five years.

To determine the proper allocation of this $1,200 per year, we first must determine the proper allocation of the partnership's "book depreciation." Treas. Regs. §1.704-1(b)(2)(iv)(g)(3) provides that "book depreciation . . . with respect to an item of partnership property is the amount that bears the same relationship to the book value of such property as the depreciation . . . computed for tax purposes . . . bears to the adjusted tax basis of such property." Therefore, because tax depreciation is $1,200 per year, book depreciation is $2,000 per year. That is, had the property's tax basis been equal to its fair market value at time of contribution, the partnership would be entitled to a depreciation deduction of $2,000 per year.

We allocate this book depreciation to the partners as they have agreed to allocate tax depreciation under §704(b); thus, in this case we allocate it 50/50, or $1,000 to each partner. Next, we allocate to the *noncontributing* partner as much tax depreciation as equals her share of the book depreciation. This allocation of $1,000 to *P* is reasonable: After all, it is not *P*'s fault that the tax basis is below its book basis. Lastly, we allocate the remaining tax depreciation — in this case, $200 per year — to *Q*, the contributing partner. See Treas. Regs. §1.704-1(c)(2)(i) (ex. 1).

Look at what happens to the partnership's books. At formation, the books stand as follows:

P		Q		
CA	OB	CA	OB	
$10,000	$10,000	$10,000	$6,000	Contributions

After one year (assuming there is no partnership income or loss other than the depreciation deduction), the books read:

P		Q		
CA	OB	CA	OB	
$10,000	$10,000	$10,000	$6,000	Contributions
(1,000)	(1,000)	(1,000)	(200)	Depreciation
$ 9,000	$ 9,000	$ 9,000	$5,800	Totals

After the second year (again assuming that there is no partnership income or loss other than the depreciation deduction), the books read:

P		Q		
CA	OB	CA	OB	
$9,000	$9,000	$9,000	$5,800	Carryover
(1,000)	(1,000)	(1,000)	(200)	Depreciation
$8,000	$8,000	$8,000	$5,600	Totals

Note that *Q*'s book/tax disparity began at $4,000 and is reduced by $800 per year. Accordingly, after five years the property will be fully depreciated and the book/tax disparity will be eliminated. At that time, the books will read:

P		Q		
CA	OB	CA	OB	
$8,000	$8,000	$8,000	$5,600	Carryover
(3,000)	(3,000)	(3,000)	(600)	Years 3-5 depreciation
$5,000	$5,000	$5,000	$5,000	Totals

Despite the complexity of these rules, the basic scheme should be apparent. The noncontributing partner is (or partners are) allocated as much tax depreciation as he would receive had there been no §704(c)(1)(A) problem at contribution. Whatever depreciation is left over is then allocated to the contributing partner.

To make sure you understand how this rule works, consider the following variation. Once again P contributes cash of $10,000 and Q contributes property worth $10,000. However, this time the property has an adjusted basis of $20,000 thus representing a built-in loss. Assuming that the property is depreciable over five years using the straight-line method, how should the depreciation be allocated?

The tax depreciation to be allocated is $4,000 per year for five years. Had there been no §704(c)(1)(A) problem, there would have been tax depreciation of $2,000 per year divided equally between the partners under the terms of the partnership agreement. We allocate to P, the noncontributing partner, what she would have received had there been no §704(c)(1)(A) problem. Accordingly, we allocate $1,000 of tax depreciation to P each year.

Q, the contributing partner, is allocated the remaining $3,000 of tax depreciation each year. Thus, Q's outside basis declines by $3,000 by reason of the depreciation. However, because we reduce capital accounts not by allocations of *tax* depreciation but only by allocations of *book* depreciation, we reduce Q's capital account by only $1,000 each year.

The opening books of the partnership will read:

P		Q		
CA	OB	CA	OB	
$10,000	$10,000	$10,000	$20,000	Contributions

After one year, the books will read:

P		Q		
CA	OB	CA	OB	
$10,000	$10,000	$10,000	$20,000	Contributions
(1,000)	(1,000)	(1,000)	(3,000)	Depreciation
$ 9,000	$ 9,000	$ 9,000	$17,000	Totals

After five years, the book will read:

P		Q		
CA	OB	CA	OB	
$9,000	$9,000	$9,000	$17,000	Carryover
(4,000)	(4,000)	(4,000)	(12,000)	Years 2-5 depreciation
$5,000	$5,000	$5,000	$ 5,000	Totals

Once again, we eliminate the book/tax disparity by treating the noncontributing partner as if there were no §704(c)(1)(A) problem and by allocating whatever is left over to the contributing partner.

PROBLEMS

20-6.   Reconsider the §704(c) problem at page 693. Try to combine the dispositional approach and the depreciation approach by answering the following question: What would be the tax consequences to the *PQ* partnership if the property, contributed with a fair market value of $10,000 and an adjusted basis of $6,000 and depreciable using the straight-line method over five years, were sold for $8,000 after it had been depreciated for two years?

Let us return to nondepreciable §704(c) property, and consider what happens if the property turns around in value. For example, suppose that *P* contributes cash of $10,000 to the *PQ* partnership and *Q* contributes property with fair market value of $10,000 and adjusted basis of $6,000. What are the tax consequences to *P* and *Q* if the property is subsequently sold by the partnership for $7,000?

Q's capital account begins at $10,000 to reflect not only *Q*'s investment in the property ($6,000) but also the precontribution appreciation ($4,000). The property then declines in value postcontribution, and the partners have agreed to share partnership losses equally. The partnership agreement requires that each partner be allocated one-half of the book loss, reducing each capital account to $8,500. But how do we allocate the tax gain of $1,000? Even if we allocate all of the tax gain to *Q*, there will be a book/tax disparity for both partners, because the final books will be:

P		Q		
CA	OB	CA	OB	
$10,000	$10,000	$10,000	$6,000	Contributions
(1,500)	0	(1,500)	0	Book loss from sale
0	0	0	1,000	Tax gain from sale
$ 8,500	$10,000	$ 8,500	$7,000	Totals

With $17,000 of cash now in the partnership, these books show that *P* and *Q* are equal partners (each will receive $8,500 on liquidation) and that each suffered an economic loss of $1,500. However, because outside bases do not equal capital accounts, tax aspects of the partnership have not followed economic aspects. What caused the book/tax disparities was the sale that produced a *book loss* but a *tax gain*. Without any tax loss to match the book loss, tax allocations in the year of sale could not correspond to the book allocations. The only way to eliminate the book/tax disparity is to make up equal and offsetting tax allocations for *P* and *Q:* If we gave *P* a tax allocation of $1,500 of loss and *Q* an additional $1,500 of gain, the books would be in balance.

Historically, the regulations have imposed a "ceiling" limitation on allocations under §704(c)(1)(A) such that the partners cannot be allocated more tax income or loss than is recognized by the partnership. See generally Treas. Regs. §1.704-3(b). In the example above, when the property is sold for $7,000, the tax gain recognized by the partnership equals $1,000. Accordingly, application of the ceiling limitation means that the partnership must allocate only that amount of tax gain and no more between the partners. In particular, they cannot allocate an extra $1,500 of gain to contributing partner *Q*. Further, because no tax loss is recognized by the partnership, no tax loss can be allocated to any partner.

Regulations promulgated under §704(c) provide three alternatives that can be used to respond to the problems caused by the ceiling limitation: (1) the *traditional method,* Treas. Regs. §1.704-3(b); (2) the *traditional method with curative allocations,* Treas. Regs. §1.704-3(c); and (3) *the remedial allocation method,* Treas. Regs. §1.704-3(d). The traditional method is the simplest: When the ceiling limitation is encountered, do nothing. Thus, in the example immediately above in which property is contributed to the partnership with a fair market value of $10,000 and then is sold for $7,000, the book/tax disparities for *P* and *Q* will remain until the partnership is liquidated.

The traditional method with curative allocations uses other tax income or deductions of the partnership to eliminate any book/tax disparity caused by the ceiling limitation. For example, suppose in the *PQ* example above that the partnership recognizes additional income of $3,000 in the year it disposes of the property contributed by *Q*. Consistent with the partnership agreement, allocation of this gain should be $1,500 to *P* and $1,500 to *Q*, both for book purposes and for tax purposes. However, if we allocate this gain equally for book purposes but entirely to *Q* for tax purposes, this disparate book/tax allocation will just offset the book/tax disparity caused by the ceiling limitation; thus, it cures the book/tax disparity caused by the ceiling limitation. Putting this curative allocation into the partnership's books produces:

P		Q		
CA	OB	CA	OB	
$10,000	$10,000	$10,000	$ 6,000	Contributions
(1,500)	0	(1,500)	1,000	Sale of property
1,500	0	1,500	3,000	Curative allocation
$10,000	$10,000	$10,000	$10,000	Totals

Just as we used unrelated partnership income to form the curative allocation, we can use unrelated partnership loss to the same effect. For example, suppose the partnership had an unrelated loss of $3,000 in the year that the partnership sold the property contributed by Q. We could allocate this loss equally between the partners for book purposes but entirely to P for tax purposes and thereby eliminate the book/tax disparities. Such a curative allocation of loss would leave the partnership books at:

P		Q		
CA	OB	CA	OB	
$10,000	$10,000	$10,000	$6,000	Contributions
(1,500)	0	(1,500)	1,000	Sale of property
(1,500)	(3,000)	(1,500)	0	Curative allocations
$ 7,000	$ 7,000	$ 7,000	$7,000	Totals

Indeed, any combination of unrelated income and loss totaling $3,000 can cure the book/tax disparity caused by application of the ceiling limitation, and the proposed regulations do not express a preference for income over loss or vice versa. Of course, the proposed regulations do not authorize curative allocations in any amount greater than that needed to eliminate the book/tax disparities. Treas. Regs. §1.704-3(c)(3)(i); see also Treas. Regs. §1.704-3(c)(4) (ex. 1(iii)). In particular, even if there is insufficient income and loss to cure a book/tax disparity caused by depreciation in one year, a curative allocation may not be made in a subsequent year. Treas. Regs. §1.704-3(c)(3)(i). Note also that "[a] partnership may limit its curative allocations to allocations of one or more particular tax items (e.g., only depreciation from a specific property or properties) even if the allocation of those available items does not offset fully the effect of the ceiling rule." Treas. Regs. §1.704-3(c)(1).

The ceiling limitation can rear its head in surprising circumstances. Suppose that the adjusted basis of Q's contributed property is only $4,000, and once again assume that this property is depreciable over five years using the straight-line method. The partnership is entitled to an annual depreciation deduction of $800 per year although book depreciation equals $2,000 per year.

Because the partnership agreement makes *P* and *Q* equal partners, for book purposes each partner must be allocated one-half of the book depreciation each year. That is, each partner's capital account must be reduced by $1,000 annually. For tax purposes, §704(c)(1)(A) requires that we allocate depreciation so as to take account of the variance between the property's value and basis at time of contribution. As we have seen, that means we should allocate tax depreciation to the noncontributing partner in an amount equal to her share of the book depreciation. Any tax depreciation remaining should then be allocated to the contributing partner. Because the noncontributing partner is *P*, this means that we should allocate tax depreciation to *P* of $1,000. However, the partnership's total depreciation for the year is only $800, and application of the ceiling limitation means that we cannot allocate more depreciation to *P* than the partnership recognizes. Accordingly, after one year the partnership's books will read:

P		Q		
CA	OB	CA	OB	
$10,000	$10,000	$10,000	$4,000	Contributions
(1,000)	(800)	(1,000)	0	Depreciation
$ 9,000	$ 9,200	$ 9,000	$4,000	Totals

The effect of the ceiling limitation in year 1 is to create a permanent book/tax disparity of $200 for each partner. If this continues for the remaining four years of the property's depreciable life, the partnership's books will be:

P		Q		
CA	OB	CA	OB	
$9,000	$9,200	$9,000	$4,000	Carryover
(4,000)	(3,200)	(4,000)	0	Years 2-5 depreciation
$5,000	$6,000	$5,000	$4,000	Totals

Once again, the regulations permit this to happen, so that the partners can have permanent book/tax disparities that will trigger recognition of income (to *Q*) and loss (to *P*) upon disposition of their partnership interests. Partner *P*, though, presumably would prefer that the book/tax disparity be eliminated by means of annual curative allocations, and the proposed regulations allow this. That is, if the partnership has unrelated income of $400 each year of the appropriate character, the partners may agree to allocate that income entirely to *Q* for tax purposes even though it is allocated equally between the partners for book purposes. Treas. Regs. §1.704-3(c)(3)(iii). Similarly, the partners should be permitted to make annual curative allocations of loss, allocating $400 of loss each year to *P* for tax purposes while allocating it equally between *P* and *Q* for book purposes. Note, though, that the partners must be consistent year to year, Treas. Regs. §1.704-3(c)(2), so that if curative allocations are eschewed in the first year they cannot be made in subsequent years.

In addition to the traditional method and this traditional method with curative allocations, the regulations offer a third alternative for handling book/tax disparities under §704(c)(1)(A): The remedial allocation method. Under this method, appreciated property contributed to a partnership in exchange for a partnership interest is divided into two components, one unappreciated and one with zero basis. For example, if depreciated property is contributed with adjusted basis of $4,000 and fair market value of $10,000, the remedial allocation method acts as if two properties had been contributed, one with adjusted basis and fair market value of $4,000 and a second with adjusted basis of $0 and fair market value of $6,000. Further, this second, zero basis property is treated as if purchased by the partnership, so that its depreciation schedule does not carry over from the contributing partner but instead starts fresh. See Treas. Regs. §1.704-3(d)(2).

In any year in which the ceiling limitation causes a book/tax disparity, the partners cure the disparity by manufacturing tax allocations to cure. Treas. Regs. §1.704-3(d)(1). These tax allocations will net to zero among all the partners, because the ceiling limitation always causes offsetting book/tax disparities. For example, assume *P* and *Q* form the *PQ* general partnership as equal partners, with *P* contributing cash of $10,000 and *Q* contributing depreciable property with adjusted basis of $4,000 and fair market value of $10,000. *P* and *Q* have agreed to use the remedial allocation method to eliminate any book/tax disparities caused by the ceiling limitation. Assume the depreciable property has a remaining useful life of five years, and assume also that the partners have agreed to recover the excess book depreciation (i.e., the $6,000 excess of fair market value over adjusted basis) using the straight-line method. Finally, assume that the property has a statutory recovery period of 10 years.

In the first year, there is $800 of tax depreciation. The book depreciation, though, equals $1,400: The partnership recovers $4,000 of book value over the five years remaining on the contributing partner's depreciation schedule, and it recovers $6,000 of the book value over a fresh, 10-year statutory recovery period using (by assumption in this example) the straight-line method. Thus, book depreciation in the first year equals $800 plus $600, or $1,400, allocated $700 per partner according to the partnership agreement. Accordingly, tax depreciation must be allocated $700 to *P* and $100 to *Q*, and there is no ceiling limitation problem caused in year 1.

The analysis in years 2 through 5 is the same as in year 1. Thus, after five years the partnership books stand as follows:

P		Q		
CA	OB	CA	OB	
$10,000	$10,000	$10,000	$4,000	Carryover
(700)	(700)	(700)	(100)	First year depreciation
(2,800)	(2,800)	(2,800)	(400)	Years 2-5 depreciation
$ 6,500	$ 6,500	$ 6,500	$3,500	Totals

In years 6 through 10, there is no tax depreciation but there is book depreciation of $600 per year. This book depreciation is allocated equally between P and Q according to the partnership agreement, and thus it creates a $300 per year book/tax disparity for each partner. Under the remedial allocation method, each partner reports an offsetting remedial tax allocation which cures the book/tax disparity without regard to other partnership income. Thus, assuming the partnership has no taxable activity in years 6 through 10, P includes a remedial allocation of $300 per year of deduction and Q reports $300 of ordinary income. This continues for each of years 7 through 10, fully eliminating the book/tax disparity.

P		Q		
CA	OB	CA	OB	
$6,500	$6,500	$6,500	$3,500	Start of year 6
(300)	0	(300)	0	Year 6 book depreciation
0	(300)	0	300	Remedial allocation
(1,200)	(1,200)	(1,200)	1,200	Years 7-10
$5,000	$5,000	$5,000	$5,000	Totals

Because the remedial allocation method violates the ceiling limitation, it arguably is inconsistent with Code section 704(c)(1)(A). Perhaps in recognition of this, the regulations provide that the Commissioner cannot require any partnership to use the remedial allocation method even if the method adopted by the partnership is unreasonable within the meaning of the antiabuse rule in Regulation §1.704-3(a)(10). See Treas. Regs. §1.704-3(d)(5)(ii).

PROBLEMS

20-7.   J and K form the JK general partnership, agreeing to be equal partners except as required by §704(c). J contributes cash of $24,000, and K contributes property with fair market value of $24,000 and adjusted basis of $8,000. This property is depreciable using the straight-line method over 10 years; at the time of its contribution by K, it has only four years remaining to its depreciable life. Compute the books of the partnership for its first 10 years of existence assuming (a) the partnership has no income or loss for any year other than depreciation from the contributed property; (b) the partnership has income of $2,000 each year in addition to its depreciation from the contributed property; and (c) the partnership has no income or deduction other than depreciation from the contributed property for its first two years and $1,000 of deduction each year thereafter. In each case, consider the traditional method, the traditional method with curative allocations, and the remedial allocation method for addressing the ceiling limitation.

2. Reverse §704(c) Allocations to the Existing Partners

Suppose the *XY* partnership owns a single asset with adjusted basis of $50,000 and fair market value of $80,000. If *Z* wants to join the partnership on an equal footing with *X* and *Y*, how much should *Z* be required to contribute to the partnership?

Prior to the admission of *Z*, each 50 percent interest in the partnership is worth $40,000. To avoid dilution of their interests, *X* and *Y* should insist that *Z* contribute an equal amount. Assuming *Z* contributes $40,000 to become a one-third partner, the partnership will have total assets worth $120,000, and each partner's interest will be worth $40,000. If the difference between the current fair market value and adjusted basis of the partnership's asset is entirely postcontribution appreciation, *X* and *Y* should each have an outside basis and capital account of $25,000 immediately prior to the admission of *Z*.

If we simply admit *Z* and do not make any changes to the books, *Z*'s capital account will be $40,000 (the value of her contribution) while the capital accounts of *X* and *Y* will remain at $25,000. This is not right: After all, the three partners each have a one-third interest in the partnership.

The regulations provide that assets may be revalued and capital accounts may be restated to reflect fair market values upon the admission of a new partner to the partnership. Treas. Regs. §1.704-1(b)(2)(iv)(f). In other words, we increase *X*'s and *Y*'s capital accounts to their fair market value of $40,000 when we admit *Z*. However, we do *not* make any adjustment to their outside bases. The effect of the restatement, then, is to create a book/tax disparity for *X* and *Y* equal to the preadmission appreciation in the partnership's assets. This book/tax disparity should be eliminated by allocating gain disproportionately to *X* and *Y*, by allocating depreciation deductions disproportionately away from *X* and *Y*, or by an alternative allocation just as if the disparity were caused by the contribution of appreciated property. For example, the next $90,000 of partnership income could be allocated equally among *X*, *Y*, and *Z* for book purposes (i.e., $30,000 each) but divided between only *X* and *Y* for tax purposes (i.e, $45,000 each).

Note that we are *not* dealing with a true §704(c) problem because the book/tax disparity is not caused by the contribution of appreciated or loss property — the contribution of *any property* by the incoming partner causes the need to restate capital accounts. Thus, technically, we address the book/tax disparity with special allocations under §704(b) rather than with an allocation under §704(c)(1). Aside from this technicality, though, the issue is just the same as under §704(c), and the regulations under §704(b) incorporate the §704(c) analysis by reference. See Treas. Regs. §1.704-1(b)(4)(i). Allocations under Treas. Regs. §1.704-1(b)(4)(i) based on §704(c) principles are called "reverse §704(c) allocations." Treas. Regs. §1.704-3(e)(3)(i). See also Treas. Regs. §1.704-3(a)(6).

Note, though, that while application of §704(c)(1)(A) to any book/tax disparity in property contributed to the partnership is mandatory, restating partnership assets to fair market value upon the admission of a new partner (and then applying §704(c)(1)(A) principles to any resulting book/tax disparities) nominally is optional. See Treas. Regs. §1.704-(1)(b)(2)(iv)(f). Failure to revalue partnership assets in such circumstances (or to otherwise follow §704(c)(1)(A) principles, see Treas. Regs. §1.704-1(b)(5) (ex. 14(iv))), though, might be treated as a gift between the partners. See the final sentence of Treas. Regs. §1.704-1(b)(2)(iv)(f).

If a partnership owns many assets having unrealized appreciation and loss, properly tracking all reverse §704(c) allocations on an asset-by-asset basis can be expensive and time-consuming. Nevertheless, the rules of §704(c) generally apply on an asset-by-asset basis. Treas. Regs. §1.704-3(a)(2). However, a "securities partnership" is permitted to aggregate unrealized gains and losses from "qualified financial assets" in making reverse §704(c) allocations. Treas. Regs. §1.704-3(e)(3). For the definition of a "securities partnership," see Treas. Regs. §1.704-3(e)(3)(iii). For the definition of "qualified financial assets," see Treas. Regs. §1.704-3(e)(3)(ii).

PROBLEMS

20-8.   *A* and *B* are equal partners in the *AB* general partnership. Each partner has an outside basis and capital account of $40,000. The partnership owns Purpleacre with adjusted basis of $80,000 and fair market value of $100,000. *C* is admitted to the partnership as a one-third partner, and *A* and *B* each reduce their interests from one-half to one-third. *C* contributes accounts receivable of $65,000 and accounts payable of $15,000 from her cash-basis business in exchange for her partnership interest. (a) What are the outside bases and capital accounts once *C* is admitted? How do the capital accounts and outside bases change if (b) the partnership receives payment on the receivables, (c) the partnership pays the payables, and (d) the partnership sells Purpleacre for $160,000?

F. ALLOCATIONS OF DEDUCTIONS ATTRIBUTABLE TO NONRECOURSE DEBT

Ensuring that partnership allocations have economic effect requires no more than satisfying the general or alternate test of economic effect under the §704(b) regulations. See Treas. Regs. §1.704-1(b)(2)(ii). However, if the partnership has incurred any nonrecourse debt, special rules under Treas. Regs. §1.704-2 can apply. In this section, we will examine those special rules to determine when they apply and how they apply. But before looking at these rules, it is helpful to master a few definitions. These definitions as well as the rules themselves can be found in Treas. Regs. §1.704-2.

1. Definitions

a. Nonrecourse Liability

For purposes of §704(b), a "nonrecourse liability" is one as to which no partner bears ultimate responsibility for repayment to any extent. Treas. Regs. §1.704-2(b)(3). In general, it is the partnership as an entity that is expected to repay partnership loans, with the funds coming from partnership activities or from capital contributions. But if the partnership is unable to make its loan payments as they come due, the lender may seek payment from the partners or may force a sale of partnership assets to satisfy the debt. Absent an agreement to the contrary, general partners bear ultimate responsibility for payment of all partnership obligations. That is, most partnership loans are recourse loans. But if the lender is willing, the loan agreement may provide that the lender will not seek repayment from any partner, and it is this contractual provision in a loan agreement that makes the loan nonrecourse. Equivalently, the entity (such as a limited liability company) might not have any partners generally liable for the entity's debts, making all of the entity's debts nonrecourse in this sense absent some special contractual agreement to the contrary.

Depending on the terms of the loan agreement, a lender may or may not have the right to proceed against all of the partnership's assets for repayment of the loan. If the lender has the right to go after all partnership assets without limitation, we sometimes say that the loan is "recourse as against the partnership." But for purposes of §704(b) and the regulations thereunder, the extent of the lender's rights against partnership assets is irrelevant. If the lender has rights against one or more partners, the loan is recourse. Treas. Regs. §1.752-1(a)(1). If the lender has rights only against partnership assets, the loan is nonrecourse. Thus, a partnership loan is a "nonrecourse liability" if and only if no partner bears ultimate responsibility for repayment, Treas. Regs. §1.752-1(a)(2), and the lender's rights against partnership assets are irrelevant.

b. Minimum Gain

Recall that the Supreme Court in Commissioner v. Tufts, 461 U.S. 300 (1983), held that the amount realized from disposition of property includes the amount of any outstanding nonrecourse debt encumbering the property. Thus, even if the mortgage is foreclosed and the owner of the property receives nothing, the amount realized will be greater than zero because of the nonrecourse debt. Indeed, if the owner's adjusted basis is less than the outstanding nonrecourse debt, disposition of the property (by foreclosure or otherwise) will produce gain at least equal to the excess of the nonrecourse debt over the property's adjusted basis.

Because we are defining minimum gain for use in the definition of economic effect, and because economic effect is defined by reference to a capital account analysis, the regulations define minimum gain by reference to asset *book value* rather than by reference to adjusted basis. Treas. Regs. §1.704-2(d)(3). Accordingly, for any piece of partnership property encumbered by nonrecourse debt, the term "minimum gain" means the excess of the nonrecourse debt over the property's book value: Disposition of the property will produce book gain at least equal to the "minimum gain" as defined in this way.

Total partnership minimum gain equals the aggregate of the minimum gain from all the partnership's property. Treas. Regs. §1.704-2(d)(1). Note that there is no such thing as negative gain or minimum loss: If the partnership's book value in a piece of property exceeds the outstanding nonrecourse encumbrance, there simply is no minimum gain with respect to that property. In addition, minimum gain is computed property by property: there is no offset of gain by built-in loss unless debts are cross-collateralized. *Id.;* see also Treas. Regs. §1.704-2(d)(2).

Consider the following example. X and Y form the XY general partnership by contributing $50 apiece. The partnership acquires depreciable property for $1,000, paying $100 down and signing a nonrecourse note for the remaining $900, pledging the depreciable property as security for the debt. Assume that the property generates a depreciation deduction of $100 per year, and assume that the partnership's annual income is just sufficient to pay its annual expenses (including interest on its debt). If the partnership is not required to make any principal payments on the debt in the early years, then the partnership will have no cash flow and will report a taxable loss of $100 each year.

There is no minimum gain at the beginning of the first year because the partnership has a book value (and adjusted basis) of $1,000 in the property while the outstanding debt is only $900. At the end of the first year, there is still no minimum gain because the nonrecourse debt does not *exceed* the book value of the property: they are equal (and $900). But one year later, minimum gain appears because depreciation lowers the book value to $800 while the outstanding nonrecourse debt remains at

$900. Accordingly, there is $100 of partnership minimum gain after the partnership's second year.

As this example demonstrates, partnership minimum gain can increase (and decrease) over time. As the partnership incurs nonrecourse debt, minimum gain will go up. Similarly, as the partnership repays its nonrecourse obligations, partnership minimum gain will decrease. Increases in the partnership's book value of its assets (for example, if capital improvements are made) will decrease minimum gain while decreases in book value (e.g., caused by depreciation allowed or allowable) will result in an increase in partnership minimum gain. The regulations require that each partnership compute its net increase or decrease in partnership minimum gain each year. Treas. Regs. §1.704-2(b)(4).

c. Nonrecourse Deductions

Whenever partnership minimum gain increases, we must identify those deductions causing the increase. Invariably, they will be depreciation deductions, although the regulations provide a set of rules for identifying the nonrecourse deductions when there is insufficient depreciation to cover the increase in minimum gain. See Treas. Regs. §1.704-2(c). These deductions, called "nonrecourse deductions" in the regulations, equal the increase (if any) in the partnership's minimum gain. See Treas. Regs. §1.704-2(c). All other deductions (including any additional depreciation deductions) are *not* "nonrecourse deductions." Thus, in the example above the depreciation deductions in year 2 (but not those in year 1) are nonrecourse deductions. The definition of nonrecourse deductions is important because it is these and only these deductions that are subject to the special rules of Treas. Regs. §1.704-2. Allocations of all other deductions and other partnership tax items are subject to the substantial economic effect rules we have already considered.

The key to understanding the rules governing the allocation of nonrecourse deductions lies in the Supreme Court's decision in Commissioner v. Tufts, 61 U.S. 300 (1983). Under *Tufts*, the amount realized from the disposition of property includes the amount of nonrecourse debt encumbering the property. And now you know why the nonrecourse regulations under §704(b) define "minimum gain" to mean the excess of encumbering debt over the encumbered property's book value: The "minimum gain" with respect to any piece of property is the book gain that would be recognized under *Tufts* if the property were immediately sold for no consideration other than satisfaction of the nonrecourse debt.

As explained above, nonrecourse deductions give rise to partnership minimum gain. Minimum gain gives rise to recognition of book income upon disposition of the property. Even though nonrecourse deductions have no associated partnership *economic* burden (because it is the lender who bears risk of diminution in value of the property associated with nonrecourse deductions), there is a *tax* burden associated with nonrecourse deductions: minimum gain. That is, whenever nonrecourse deductions are claimed, minimum gain is created. The existence of minimum gain means that there will be income (but not necessarily any cash) upon disposition of the property. Recognition of, and paying tax on, the eventual recognition of minimum gain is the tax burden associated with nonrecourse deductions, and the regulations require that the partners who enjoy the nonrecourse deductions must also suffer the tax burden of the recognition of minimum gain. There is more to the nonrecourse regulations, but this aspect is the conceptual key.

It is helpful to have a term for partnership deductions *other than* nonrecourse deductions. One might call them "recourse" deductions but that is misleading because it suggests that such deductions only arise in connection with partnership borrowing on a recourse basis: In fact, of course, such deductions can arise in the absence of any partnership borrowing. The term "non-nonrecourse" deductions is possible but it seems a bit unwieldy. We will use the term "economic" deductions for all deductions other than nonrecourse deductions to remind ourselves that such deductions correspond with economic benefits and burdens and are subject to the economic effect tests.

2.   General Principles

The touchstone of economic effect under the §704(b) regulations is that tax benefits and burdens must track economic benefits and burdens. Treas. Regs. §1.704-1(b)(2)(ii)(a). In the case of allocations of income, this requires that the partner who is allocated a dollar of income must eventually receive an equivalent dollar in distributions. And in the case of allocations of deductions, the partner who is allocated a dollar of loss must bear the economic risk of loss associated with that allocation. Properly maintaining partnership capital accounts, and distributing liquidation proceeds in accordance with final capital account balances, ensures that partnership allocations have economic effect within the meaning of these regulations. See generally Treas. Regs. §1.704-1(b)(2)(ii)(b).

The economic burden associated with depreciation deductions is risk of diminution in value of the depreciable asset. For example, suppose a partnership purchases depreciable equipment for $1,000. As depreciation is claimed by the partnership and allocated among the partners, asset basis goes down. If the asset actually declines in value as it was depreciated, there will be an economic loss (but not a tax loss) realized when the property is sold. That economic loss has already been allocated among the partners in the form of the deprecation deductions: As each partner claimed her distributive share of depreciation, her capital account decreased. If the property is eventually sold for its adjusted basis (that is, if its economic value decreases as the depreciation is claimed), there will be no tax gain or loss and so the sale will not affect partnership capital accounts. Thus, those partners who were allocated large percentages of the depreciation will have had their capital accounts significantly lowered, and they will receive pro tanto less at liquidation.

But what if the purchase was funded with nonrecourse debt? As the property declines in value, it is the lender and not the partnership that faces an economic loss: after all, the partnership can simply walk away from the investment. When property is secured by nonrecourse debt, the partnership's economic loss on the property is limited to the value of the property above the amount of the debt; that is, to the partnership's equity in the property. Once that equity is consumed (i.e., once the value of the property drops below the nonrecourse encumbrance), it is the lender who bears the risk of diminution of the property.

If it is the lender who bears the economic risk of diminution in value once the partnership's equity is gone, there is no economic risk borne by the partnership connected with depreciation deductions reducing adjusted basis below the amount of a nonrecourse encumbrance. Stated differently, allocations of depreciation deductions reducing book value below the amount of the nonrecourse encumbrance cannot have economic effect because there is no economic risk of loss (borne by the partnership) associated with such deductions. Treas. Regs. §1.704-2(b)(1).

Depreciation deductions reducing book value below the amount of a nonrecourse encumbrance are precisely the "nonrecourse deductions" defined above. There are special rules for the allocation of nonrecourse deductions because the standard rules cannot apply: Allocations of nonrecourse deductions never have substantial economic effect because they never have economic effect at all. However, while there is no economic burden associated with nonrecourse deductions, there *is* a tax burden, and the nonrecourse rules require that the benefits of nonrecourse deductions be enjoyed by those partners who will also bear the associated tax burden.

What is this tax burden? Nonrecourse deductions by definition increase partnership minimum gain. Treas. Regs. §1.704-2(c). That means that these deductions will generate partnership book income upon disposition of the property. Treas. Regs. §1.704-2(b)(2). As these nonrecourse deductions are allocated among the partners, each partner's share of the partner's minimum gain increase *pro tanto*. Treas. Regs. §1.704-2(g)(1)(i). And as the partnership's minimum gain decreases (by disposition of the property, partial or full repayment of the nonrecourse loan, or otherwise), the partners must be allocated partnership income in proportion to their shares of the minimum gain. Treas. Regs. §1.704-2(b)(2). Such a "minimum gain chargeback" provision is required by the nonrecourse regulations. See Treas. Regs. §1.704-2(f). As you would expect, a minimum gain chargeback allocation is not required as to a partner who contributes capital to the partnership which is then used to pay down the nonrecourse debt, Treas. Regs. §1.704-2(f)(3), or if the partner becomes personally liable for some or all of the debt, Treas. Regs. §1.704-2(f)(2).

Technically, the nonrecourse regulations impose a three-part requirement on allocations of nonrecourse deductions. Treas. Regs. §1.704-2(e). First, the partnership agreement must satisfy the general or alternate economic effect test with respect to its allocations of tax items *other than* nonrecourse deductions. Treas. Regs. §1.704-2(e)(1). Second, allocations of nonrecourse deductions must be made "in a manner that is reasonably consistent with allocations that have substantial economic effect of some other significant partnership item attributable to the property securing the nonrecourse liabilities." Treas. Regs. §1.704-2(e)(2). Third, the partnership agreement must contain a "minimum gain chargeback provision." Treas. Regs. §1.704-2(e)(3).[2]

The apparent ambiguity of the "reasonably consistent" language is removed by one of the examples in the nonrecourse regulations. See Treas. Regs. §1.704-2(m) (example 1(ii)). Suppose *P* and *Q* form the *PQ* partnership to acquire and develop certain depreciable real estate. Suppose further that all income and loss will be allocated 90 percent to *P* and 10 percent to *Q* for the first five years, and all tax items will be allocated equally thereafter. The nonrecourse regulations provide that allocating 90 percent of the nonrecourse deductions to *P* satisfies the "reasonably consistent" requirement as does an allocation of 50 percent. Indeed, the regulations further provide that any percentage between 90 percent and 50 percent to *P* is satisfactory.

From this example, we see that a partnership's ability to allocate nonrecourse deductions can be quite broad. The nonrecourse deductions that can be allocated to any one partner can be as small as that partner's lowest share of economic deductions, and they can be as large as that partner's greatest share of economic deductions. Any share within this range should qualify as "reasonably consistent" with the allocation of some substantial tax item from the property other than nonrecourse deductions as required by the regulations.

The partnership agreement must also include a "minimum gain chargeback" provision. Treas. Regs. §1.704-2(e)(3). Such a provision must provide that "[i]f there is a net decrease in partnership minimum gain for a partnership taxable year . . . each partner must be allocated items of partnership income and gain for that year equal to that partner's share of the net decrease in partnership minimum gain." Treas. Regs. §1.704-2(f)(1). Upon disposition of the property, this provision will trigger recognition of income to each partner who was allocated nonrecourse deduc-

---

2. If one partnership (the "upper tier" partnership) owns an interest in a second partnership (the "lower tier" partnership), nonrecourse indebtedness of the lower tier partnership will create partnership minimum gain for the upper tier partnership and its partners. Treas. Regs. §1.704-2(k).

tions in an amount precisely equal to those deductions. Any additional gain can then be allocated among the partners however they wish, subject only to the familiar tests of substantial economic effect. See generally Treas. Regs. §1.704-1(b)(2)(ii).

Consider the following example. *G* and *L* form the *GL* limited partnership, with *G* (the general partner) contributing cash of $10,000 and *L* (the limited partner) contributing cash of $40,000. The *GL* partnership agreement specifically provides that *L* cannot be required to contribute additional funds to the enterprise.

On January 1, 1995, the partnership acquires an apartment building for $1,000,000, paying cash of $50,000 and signing a nonrecourse note for the remaining $950,000. Assume that the partnership (1) makes an interest payment of 10 percent of the outstanding loan balance each December 31, (2) pays deductible expenses of $15,000 each December 31, (3) makes a principal payment of $20,000 each January 1 (i.e., beginning the second year), and (4) receives rents each December 31 equal to its cash flow (i.e., equal to its interest, expense, and principal payments). Assume also that the partnership is entitled to a depreciation deduction of $40,000 per year. Finally, assume that the *GL* partnership agreement provides that depreciation deductions will be allocated 90 percent to *L* and 10 percent to *G*, while all other items of income and deduction will be allocated 80 percent to *L* and 20 percent to *G*.

For 1995, these assumptions tell us that the partnership makes an interest payment of $95,000 and pays expenses of $15,000 out of its rent receipts of $110,000. Despite having a zero cash flow, the partnership shows a taxable loss of $40,000 for the year. This loss arises as follows: Income equals $110,000 while deductions equal $95,000 [interest] + $15,000 [expenses] + $40,000 [depreciation], for $150,000 total deductions. Under the terms of the partnership agreement, these items of income and deduction affect the capital accounts as follows:

G	L	
$10,000	$40,000	Initial balance
22,000	88,000	Rent receipts
(19,000)	(76,000)	Interest
(3,000)	(12,000)	Expenses
(4,000)	(36,000)	Depreciation
$ 6,000	$ 4,000	Totals

As of the end of 1995, the partnership has an adjusted basis and book value in its apartment building of $960,000 and the property is subject to a nonrecourse debt of $950,000. Because this book value exceeds the amount of the outstanding debt, there is no partnership minimum gain. Accordingly, there are no nonrecourse deductions in 1995, so the validity of the partnership's allocations must be tested under the familiar general and alternate tests of economic effect. Assuming the partnership agreement provides that liquidating distributions will be made in accordance with ending capital account balances, these allocations should have economic effect. Note, though, that because *L* is a limited partner without any obligation to contribute additional funds to the partnership, the alternate test for economic effect will not permit *L*'s capital account to become negative.

Now consider 1996. Under our assumptions, *GL* makes its first principal payment of $20,000. That payment reduces the partnership's year-end interest payment to $93,000. Assuming the partnership's other expenses remain at $15,000, our assumption of zero cash flow means that the partnership receives rental income of $128,000. Putting these figures into the partnership's capital accounts produces:

G	L	
$ 6,000	$ 4,000	Initial balance
25,600	102,400	Rent receipts
(18,600)	(74,400)	Interest
(3,000)	(12,000)	Expenses
(4,000)	(36,000)	Depreciation
$ 6,000	($ 16,000)	Totals

At the close of 1996, the partnership's adjusted basis and book value in its property equals $920,000 while the amount of the outstanding debt is now $930,000. Accordingly, there is $10,000 of partnership minimum gain, and that means there is $10,000 of nonrecourse deductions for the current year. Under the nonrecourse regulations, the nonrecourse deductions for the current year are assumed to consist of $10,000 of the depreciation. The remaining $138,000 of deductions ($93,000 of interest, $15,000 of expenses, and the remaining $30,000 of depreciation) are not nonrecourse deductions and so must be tested by the usual economic effect tests.

To determine whether the partnership's allocations of the economic deductions have economic effect, we recompute the partner's capital accounts with the nonrecourse deductions removed. Eliminating $10,000 of the depreciation produces:

G	L	
$ 6,000	$ 4,000	Initial balance
25,600	102,400	Rent receipts
(18,600)	(74,400)	Interest
(3,000)	(12,000)	Expenses
(3,000)	(27,000)	Economic depreciation
$ 7,000	($ 7,000)	Totals

These ending capital account balances are inconsistent with the requirement of economic effect because *L*'s capital account is negative while *L* has no unconditional obligation to restore a capital account deficit upon liquidation of her partnership interest. Accordingly, we must reallocate $7,000 of the deductions for the current year to *G* and away from *L*. Note that this reallocation has nothing to do with the partnership's nonrecourse deductions for the current year — we will turn to those in a moment.

Allocating an additional $7,000 of deductions to *G* produces the following capital accounts:

G	*L*	
$ 6,000	$ 4,000	Initial balance
25,600	102,400	Rent receipts
(18,600)	(74,400)	Interest
(3,000)	(12,000)	Expenses
(10,000)	(20,000)	Reallocated depreciation
$ 0	$ 0	Totals

These capital accounts ensure economic effect by keeping the limited partner's capital account nonnegative. Once we have established that the partnership's allocation of "economic" deductions satisfies the economic effect test, we determine whether the partnership's allocation of its nonrecourse deductions satisfies the nonrecourse regulations. There is $10,000 of nonrecourse deductions for the current year, and the partnership agreement allocates this amount $9,000 to *L* and $1,000 to *G*. Accordingly, the capital accounts become:

G	*L*	
$ 0	$ 0	Initial balance
(1,000)	(9,000)	Nonrecourse depreciation
($1,000)	($9,000)	Totals

It might seem that these ending capital account balances are invalid because *L*'s capital account is negative. However, the limitation that a partner's capital account cannot be more negative than the amount the partner can be required to contribute to the partnership is part of the economic effect requirement, while what causes *L*'s capital account to go negative here is the allocation of nonrecourse deductions. The nonrecourse regulations specifically provide that a limited partner's capital account may go negative not only by the maximum amount the partner can be forced to contribute to the partnership (if any) but also by the amount of the partner's share of the partnership's nonrecourse deductions. Treas. Regs. §1.704-2(g)(1). Here, *L*'s share of the partnership's nonrecourse deductions is $9,000, so *L*'s capital account deficit is allowed.

Recall the reason for the prohibition in the alternate test for economic effect on a limited partner's capital account becoming negative: If the partnership liquidates, each partner is supposed to receive her ending capital account balance or restore her ending capital account deficit. Treas. Regs. §1.704-1(b)(2)(ii)(b)(2). Because *L* cannot be required to restore a capital account deficit, the alternate test for economic effect seeks to avoid the creation of a deficit in the first place. See the "look ahead" requirement in Treas. Regs. §1.704-1(b)(2)(ii)(d)(4).

Here, *L*'s capital account deficit *necessarily* is temporary because *L*'s share of the partnership's minimum gain is $9,000. Therefore, upon disposition of the property, *L*'s capital account balance will be eliminated by operation of the minimum gain chargeback. The nonrecourse regulations permit a limited partner to have a negative capital account balance up to, and only up to, the amount of the limited partner's share of minimum gain because a deficit of that amount is necessarily temporary. Treas. Regs. §1.704-2(g)(1).

It is worth saying this one more time. *A partner's capital account may go negative to the extent of the sum of (1) the maximum amount the partner can be required to contribute to the partnership to cover a capital account deficit upon liquidation of her partnership interest plus (2) the partner's share of the partnership's minimum gain.* A partner's share of partnership minimum gain equals the net amount of partnership nonrecourse deductions allocated to the partner.

Continue this example for one more year. Once again, the partnership makes a principal payment of $20,000, reducing the partnership's year-end interest payment to $91,000. With assumed expenses of $15,000 and depreciation of $40,000, our assumption of zero cash flow means that the partnership receives rental income of $126,000. In addition, the principal payment reduces the outstanding debt to $910,000, and the depreciation deduction reduces the partnership's adjusted basis in its property down to $880,000. Accordingly, the partnership's minimum gain equals $30,000, an increase of $20,000 over the prior year.

We first check the validity of the partnership's allocations of the economic deductions by subtracting out the current year's nonrecourse deductions and then checking the partnership capital accounts. This produces:

G	L	
($ 1,000)	($ 9,000)	Initial balance
25,200	100,800	Rent receipts
(18,200)	(72,800)	Interest
(3,000)	(12,000)	Expenses
(2,000)	(18,000)	Depreciation
$ 1,000	($ 11,000)	Totals

Once again the partnership's allocation of its "economic" deductions fails to satisfy the economic effect test because *L*'s ending capital account is too negative. *L* has no obligation to contribute additional funds, and *L*'s share of the partnership's minimum gain (before taking into account the current year's increase) is $9,000. Accordingly, L's capital account is $2,000 below its minimum level so that $2,000 of the partnership's "economic" deductions must be reallocated to G. We thus replace the capital account analysis above with the following:

G	L	
($ 1,000)	($ 9,000)	Initial balance
25,200	100,800	Rent receipts
(18,200)	(72,800)	Interest
(3,000)	(12,000)	Expenses
(4,000)	(16,000)	Depreciation
$ 1,000	$ 9,000	Totals

We now put the current year's nonrecourse deductions into the partnership's capital accounts. The partnership agreement allocated depreciation 10 percent to G and 90 percent to L, so that the $20,000 of current nonrecourse deductions are allocated $2,000 to G and $18,000 to L. Putting these allocations into the capital accounts yields the following ending values:

G	L	
($1,000)	($ 9,000)	Initial balance
(2,000)	(18,000)	Nonrecourse depreciation
($3,000)	($27,000)	Totals

Total partnership minimum gain is $30,000, and of that amount, $27,000 is properly allocable to L ($9,000 from 1996 and $18,000 from 1997). Accordingly, if the partnership were to sell or otherwise dispose of the property immediately, the first $30,000 of gain would be allocated $3,000 to G and $27,000 to L under the partnership's minimum gain chargeback provision.

3. Distribution of Refinancing Proceeds

A partner's share of partnership minimum gain includes the amount of nonrecourse deductions that have been allocated to her. Treas. Regs. §1.704-2(g)(1). Allocating minimum gain in this way makes sense when the minimum gain arises from partnership deductions, usually depreciation. Recall that partnership minimum gain is the excess of the partnership's nonrecourse debts over the book value of the property securing those debts. Treas. Regs. §1.704-2(d)(1). In any one year, partnership minimum gain can increase in either of two ways. First, the partnership's adjusted basis in its assets may decline because of allowable depreciation deductions. Second, the debt may increase by reason of additional borrowing. If the partnership borrows on a nonrecourse basis and does not invest the proceeds in the security, the partnership's nonrecourse liabilities will increase without a concomitant increase in book value. Once again, partnership minimum gain will increase.

For example, suppose the *XY* partnership owns property with book value and adjusted basis of $100,000 and fair market value of $250,000. If the partnership borrows $120,000 against its property, the borrowing will create $20,000 of partnership minimum gain. If $20,000 of the loan proceeds is distributed to partner *X*, *X*'s capital account will decrease.

If the lender immediately forecloses on the partnership's property, there will be a taxable gain of $20,000 under the *Tufts* case. How should this taxable gain be allocated? The nonrecourse borrowing and foreclosure has the same effect as a sale of the property for $120,000, and that is precisely how the transaction is taxed. Who enjoyed the sale gain? *X* did when she was distributed the debt proceeds in excess of the partnership's adjusted basis. Accordingly, *X* should be allocated the gain from the foreclosure.

What this example demonstrates is that distribution of nonrecourse proceeds which causes an increase in partnership minimum gain should bring with it a dollar for dollar allocation of partnership minimum gain. Of course, if the partnership has cash in the bank when it incurs the nonrecourse debt, it will be impossible to determine the extent to which the subsequent distribution consists of nonrecourse proceeds as opposed to the bank funds. Under the nonrecourse regulations, "[a] partnership may use any reasonable method to determine whether a distribution by the partnership to one or more partners is allocable to proceeds of a nonrecourse liability." Treas. Regs. §1.704-2(h)(2).

4. Book/Tax Disparities

Recall that there can be a disparity between the adjusted basis of partnership property and its book value. Such a disparity will arise when property is contributed to the partnership having unrealized gain or loss. In addition, revaluations of partnership property — triggered by the admission of a partner or by the withdrawal of a partner — also can cause such book/tax disparities. The nonrecourse regulations provide for the computation of minimum gain in such circumstances by comparing the amount of the outstanding nonrecourse debt with the *book* value of the encumbered property. Because depreciation deductions attributable to partnership property having a book value different from its adjusted basis must be allocated in such a way as to take account of the property's book/tax disparity, adding nonrecourse debt to the partnership introduces a second layer of complexity beyond the scope of this discussion. The nonrecourse regulations provide an example of this difficult issue. See Treas. Regs. §1.704-2(m) (example 3). In addition, a special rule applies in the year partnership property is revalued to ensure that the revaluation does not trigger any immediate reallocation of income under the partnership's minimum gain chargeback provision. See Treas. Regs. §1.704-2(d)(4).

5. Partner Nonrecourse Debt

Suppose a partnership incurs a nonrecourse obligation that is guaranteed by one of its partners. While the debt nominally is nonrecourse, economic risk of loss for the debt is borne by the guarantor/partner. As you might expect, such an obligation is treated under §752 as a recourse obligation of the partnership and is subject to the §752 rules applicable to all partnership recourse loans. Treas. Regs. §1.752-2(b)(3)(i). Similarly, if a nonrecourse loan is made to a partnership by one of its partners, economic risk of loss is borne by the lender/partner. Once again, §752 treats the obligation as a partnership recourse loan subject to its general treatment applicable to all partnership recourse obligations. Treas. Regs. §1.752-2(c)(1).

The nonrecourse regulations are not so simple. When a debt is nonrecourse to the partnership but risk of loss is borne by one or more of its partners, the loan is called a "partner nonrecourse liability" in the nonrecourse regulations and such liabilities are subject to special rules. Treas. Regs. §§1.704-2(b)(4), 1.704-2(i).These rules provide that nonrecourse deductions arising from a partner nonrecourse liability must be allocated to the partner (or partners) who bear the risk of economic loss. Treas. Regs. §1.704-2(i)(1). Similarly, these rules provide that a net decrease in partner nonrecourse minimum gain must trigger a minimum gain chargeback provision allocating partnership income equal to the partner (or partners) having been allocated partner nonrecourse liability deductions. Treas. Regs. §1.704-2(i)(4). Finally, a distribution of the proceeds allocable to a partner nonrecourse liability must be treated in a manner consistent with the general rules governing the distribution of nonrecourse financing proceeds. See Treas. Regs. §1.704-2(i)(6).

PROBLEMS

20-9. L and G form the LG limited partnership, with limited partner L contributing cash of $90,000 and general partner G contributing cash of $10,000. The partnership constructs an apartment building for $1,500,000, using its cash of $100,000 as well as $1,400,000 of the proceeds of a $1,500,000 nonrecourse loan. Under the terms of the partnership agreement, all losses and the first $200,000 of profit will be allocated 90 percent to L and 10 percent to G. Profits in excess of $200,000 will be allocated 50 percent to each partner. Assume (1) the apartments generate rents of $150,000 per year, (2) the property generates a depreciation deduction of $90,000 each year, and (3) the partnership makes an interest payment of $140,000 each year. Because the construction costs did not fully consume the loan, the partnership distributes $90,000 to *L* and $10,000 to *G* during its second year. After four years, *LG* sells the property for $2,000,000, pays off the outstanding loan of $1,500,000, and distributes its remaining cash to the partners in liquidation of their interests. Discuss the tax consequences for each of the years.

G. SUBSTANTIALITY UNDER §704(b)

Under §704(b), distributive shares are determined by the partnership agreement unless those shares lack "substantial economic effect." So far, we have looked only at the definition of "economic effect" under the regulations. However, substantial economic effect is a two-part test: "First, the allocation must have economic effect. . . . Second, the economic effect of the allocation must be substantial. . . ." Treas. Regs. §1.704-1(b)(2)(i). The regulations further provide that an allocation is substantial if

> there is a reasonable possibility that the allocation (or allocations) will affect substantially the dollar amounts to be received by the partners from the partnership, independent of tax consequences. Notwithstanding the preceding sentence, the economic effect of an allocation (or allocations) is not substantial if, at the time the allocation becomes part of the partnership agreement, (1) the after-tax economic consequences of at least one partner may, in present value terms, be enhanced compared to such consequences if the allocation (or allocations) were not contained in the partnership agreement, and (2) there is a strong likelihood that the after-tax economic consequences of no partner will, in present value terms, be substantially diminished compared to such consequences if the allocation (or allocations) was not contained in the partnership agreement.

Treas. Regs. §1.704-1(b)(2)(iii)(a).

Consider the following example. *P* and *Q* form the *PQ* general partnership by contributing $100,000 each, and they agree to allocate all tax items 50/50. The partnership invests in both taxable and tax-free securities. In a year in which *P* is in a low tax bracket and *Q* is in a high tax bracket, the partners amend the partnership agreement as follows:

> Tax-exempt income is allocated to *Q* in an amount equal to the lesser of the partnership's tax-exempt income for the year and the partnership's taxable income for the year. Taxable income is allocated to *P* in an amount equal to the lesser of the partnership's tax-exempt income for the year and the partnership's taxable income for the year. Any remaining income (tax-exempt or taxable) not already allocated is divided equally between the partners.

Suppose the partnership has tax-exempt income of $10,000 and taxable income of $12,000. Under the partnership agreement, all $10,000 of the tax-exempt income is allocated to Q (the high-bracket partner) and an equal amount ($10,000) of taxable income is allocated to P (the low-bracket partner). The remaining $2,000 of taxable income is divided between the partners, so that each partner ends up with an allocation of $11,000 over all. The effect of the special agreements, in other words, is to continue the prior 50/50 in dollar terms but to allocate income by character to minimize the partners' collective tax liability.

Although these special allocations have economic effect (assuming capital accounts are maintained properly and liquidation proceeds will be distributed in accordance with final capital account balances), they will not be upheld because that economic effect is *insubstantial.* That is, the special allocations differ from the partners' general interests in the partnership only in a tax sense. Because the effect of the allocation is to allocate to each partner the same number of dollars as under the earlier, 50/50 sharing, the allocations lack substantiality because they will not affect the total number of dollars to be received by any partner. In the language of the regulations, these special allocations produce only *shifting* tax consequences. See Treas. Regs. §1.704-1(b)(2)(iii)(b).

While these special allocations probably ought not be upheld, it is surprisingly difficult to articulate a satisfactory basis for that result. It might be reasonable for the regulations to challenge all allocations by character (tax-exempt vs. taxable income, ordinary income vs. capital gain, etc.) as lacking economic effect. After all, dollars are fungible regardless of tax character. However, the regulations do not take such an all-encompassing approach.

For example, suppose the partnership agreement provided that all tax-exempt income would be allocable to Q and all taxable income would be allocated to P. The regulations would seem to uphold these allocations so long as the relative amounts of taxable and tax-exempt income to be earned by the partnership are uncertain. See Treas. Regs. §1.704-1(b)(5) (example 7(i)). Is it reasonable for the regulations to distinguish between character allocations in which the dollar amounts are reasonably certain and those in which they are not?

Congress has explicitly given its imprimatur to allocations made after the close of the taxable year in its definition of the "partnership agreement" in §761(c). Yet it is precisely such allocations (that is, allocations by character made with hindsight) that are rejected as "shifting" under the substantiality regulations. See Treas. Regs. §1.704-1(b)(5) (example 7(i)). Do these regulations define "substantial economic effect" in a way inconsistent with the flexibility of subchapter K? And if they do, are they invalid?

On the other hand, when allocations are made by character without knowing the precise amounts of income to be received by the partnership, the character of the partnership's income is being used as a measuring rod for allocating *amounts* of income. Once the partnership's income is known with relative certainty, however, allocations by character function only to control tax results: The same economic results could be obtained by allocating explicitly by amount.

For example, suppose the *XY* partnership invests in both taxable and tax-exempt securities. If the partners agree to allocate all taxable income to *X* and all tax-exempt income to *Y* at the beginning of the year before the partnership's income is known, the allocations will affect the dollar amounts to be received by the partners independent of tax consequences. That is, *X* may end up with a greater or lesser share of the partnership's income than *Y*.

Once it is known, say, that the partnership has $4,000 of taxable income and $6,000 of tax-exempt income, the same allocations to *X* and *Y* represent a complex method of making *X* and *Y* 40/60 partners. While there is nothing wrong with complex allocations per se, when the complexity is caused by using character allocations rather than percentages (i.e., 40 percent of all income to *X* and 60 percent of all income to *Y*), the complexity affects tax consequences without apparent justification. In such circumstances it seems appropriate to condemn the character allocations as having insufficient economic effect to support their legitimacy.

A second class of allocations lacking substantiality are those characterized by the regulations as *transitory*. Treas. Regs. §1.704-1(b)(2)(iii)(c). For example, suppose one member of a partnership with an expiring loss carryforward is allocated a disproportionate share of partnership income on condition that an offsetting amount of partnership loss be allocated to her in the future. While the allocation of a disproportionate share of income has economic effect in the first year, that effect is negated by the subsequent allocation of loss. Thus, the combined allocations lack economic effect and are properly condemned in the regulations. See Treas. Regs. §1.704-1(b)(5)(5) (example 8).

Is an allocation of depreciation transitory if combined with a gain chargeback? No: Because it is uncertain if the gain chargeback will ever be triggered — the regulations adopt the peculiar (but pro-taxpayer) position that depreciable property actually declines in value as it is depreciated — so there may be no gain at disposition. Treas. Regs. §1.704-1(b)(5) (example 1(xi)). Under the regulations, the economic effect of a set of allocations will be invalid as transitory only if there is a "strong likelihood" that one allocation will offset the other. Treas. Regs. §1.704-1(b)(2)(iii)(c).

When a depreciable capital asset is sold by a partnership, the depreciation recapture will be ordinary income under §1245 while the remainder of the gain will be capital. Whether the partnership agreement includes a gain chargeback or not, each partner must recognize ordinary income from the recapture in proportion to the depreciation deductions previously allocated to her, but in no event will any partner recognize more depreciation recapture than the amount of gain allocated to that partner from disposition of the property. See Treas. Regs. §1.1245-1(e).

PROBLEMS

20-10.   *L* and *M* form the *LM* general partnership by contributing cash of $10,000 each. The partnership uses its $20,000 to purchase depreciable machinery. Assume the cost of this machinery is recoverable over five years using straight-line depreciation and the gain from the disposition of this machinery is subject to depreciation recapture under §1245. The partnership holds the machinery for two years and has operating income of $3,000 per year. After two years, the machinery is sold for $28,000. The partnership agreement provides that all income and loss is to be allocated equally between the partners except that all cost recovery deductions are allocated exclusively to *L*. In addition, the partnership agreement includes a gain chargeback provision, allocating gain from the disposition of the machinery entirely to *L* up to the amount of the prior depreciation.

   a.   What are the partners' capital accounts after sale of the machinery, and how much capital gain and ordinary income did each partner report from that sale?
   b.   What if the partnership agreement does *not* include a gain chargeback provision and the property is sold for only $22,000?
   c.   If acquisition of the machinery had entitled the partnership to a tax credit of $1,000 (which did not affect the partnership's basis in the machinery), how should that tax credit be allocated?

H.   PROHIBITIONS ON RETROACTIVE ALLOCATIONS

In §706(c)-(d), Congress has prohibited retroactive allocations. In this context, "retroactive" allocations do not refer to allocations made after the close of the taxable year (which are explicitly authorized by §761(c)) but rather allocations of items of partnership income and loss to persons who were not partners when the items accrued.

For example, suppose that individual *J* joins the *P* partnership on December 15 by contributing cash of $15,000. Suppose further that the partnership has an interest deduction for the year of $15,000. Can that entire interest deduction be allocated to *J*?

Under §706(d)(2), *J* can be allocated only so much of the interest deduction as accrues on or after December 15, the date of *J*'s admission to the partnership. Note that this rule applies regardless of the accounting method used by the partnership and is independent of when the interest is actually paid. In particular, if the interest is paid on December 20, and even if the partnership uses the cash receipts and disbursements method of accounting (so that none of the interest expense is recognized by the partnership prior to actual payment), J can be allocated no more than 1/24th (one-half of one month) of the interest expense.

The retroactive limitation in §§706(c)-(d) predates the current version of §704(c)(1)(A). Regulations promulgated under §704(b) now require that partnership assets be revalued upon the admission of a new partner and that any disparity between the fair market value and book value of partnership assets at the time of a revaluation be allocated among the existing partners as they have agreed to share gain and loss from such assets. See Treas. Regs. §1.704-3(a)(6). Further, accrued but unrecognized accounts payable are subject to this rule. Treas. Regs. §1.704-3(a)(4). Thus, application of §§704(c)-(d) to unrealized cash-basis items triggered by admission of a new partner is superfluous given the current understanding of §704(c)(1)(A).

Suppose that J had joined the partnership on July 1 as a 50 percent partner. While the partners could not allocate to J any of the interest expense accruing between January 1 and June 30, they are free under §704(b) to allocate as much of the interest accruing on or after July 1 to J. For example, an allocation of all the interest accruing after June 30 would be valid even though the effect of such an allocation is the same as allocating half of the entire year's interest expense to J. Yet this latter allocation would run afoul of the rules in §706(d)(2). Astute lawyers, in other words, can accomplish by means of special allocations much of what seemingly is prohibited by the anti-retroactive rules.

Note that §§706(c)(2)(B) and 706(d)(1) refer to a partner's changing interest in the partnership. For example, the admission of a new, equal partner to a two-person partnership reduces the interests of the continuing partners from one-half to one-third each. The anti-retroactive rules seem to require in such a situation that the continuing partners be allocated only one-third of the relevant "cash basis items" accruing after admission of the new partner (see §706(d)(2)(B)).

Yet you should understand by now that such a rule is premised on an overly naive conception of a partner's interest in a partnership under subchapter K. The two members of a partnership can be equal partners one year and unequal the next without running afoul of the §704(b) substantial economic effect test. Thus, to say that the continuing partners become one-third partners when a new member is admitted assumes (1) that the partners were each one-half partners prior to admission of the new partner and (2) that the partners must continue to allocate all partnership items in accordance with some fixed percentage.

We know that it makes no sense to say that the continuing partners were each one-half partners for that part of the year prior to admission of the new partner because distributive shares are not determinable until the partnership agreement is no longer subject to modification; that is, until the "time prescribed by law for the filing of the partnership return for the taxable year." §761(c). Until that date, there simply *are no* distributive shares in any meaningful sense. If we could allocate as much or as little of any partnership tax item to one of the continuing partners had *J* not joined the partnership, why should the admission of *J* restrict the partners' flexibility?

Can the anti-retroactive rules be applied in any coherent sense to partners who were members of the partnership during the period when the relevant tax items accrued to the partnership? No, although the Tax Court has written an opinion to the contrary. Lipke v. Commissioner, 81 T.C. 689 (1983), aff'd, 751 F.2d 369 (2d Cir. 1984). This opinion, like §§706(c)-(d) that it interpreted, predates the current understanding of §704(c)(1)(A). Although no case has disapproved of such a broad interpretation of the anti-retroactive limitations in §§706(c)-(d), likely no case will follow it either.

PROBLEMS

20-11.   The *PQRS* partnership has for many years owned a commercial office building. As of January 1, 1995, the building has an adjusted basis to the partnership of $240,000, is worth $800,000, and is subject to a recourse debt of $600,000. Each partner has an outside basis of $60,000 and a capital account of negative $90,000. Each month the building generates rents of $8,000 but costs $6,000 for utilities to run. On December 31, 1995, an interest payment of $60,000 will be due, and the partners have no more cash to contribute to the venture. Accordingly, the partnership on December 1, 1995, admits *T* as a new, 20 percent partner and the existing partners each reduce their interests from 25 percent to 20 percent. In exchange for her partnership interest, *T* contributes cash of $50,000. Because *T*'s money is used to make the interest payment, the partners agree to specially allocate the interest deduction to *T*. Otherwise, *T* is to be allocated one-fifth of the partnerships's income and deductions for the current year. Can they do this? How best can the partners accomplish their goal?

21

A Partner's Outside Basis

A. BASIC PRINCIPLES UNDER §705

A partner may acquire her partnership interest in any of four ways: (1) in exchange for property contributed to the partnership, (2) by purchase, (3) by gift, or (4) through the estate of a decedent. If the interest is acquired by contribution, the partner's initial outside basis is the adjusted basis of the contributed property. §722. If the interest is acquired otherwise, §742 provides that usual rules apply: cost for purchases, §1012; carryover for gifts, §1015; and fair market value for devises and bequests, §1014. If multiple interests in a single partnership are acquired, either simultaneously or at different times, it is the Service's position that the partner has only a single, undifferentiated outside basis in all interests combined, Rev. Rul. 84-53, 1984-1 C.B. 159, which is consistent with the rule that a partner having multiple interests in a partnership has a single, unified capital account. Treas. Regs. §1.704-1(b)(2)(iv)(b).

The jargon term for a partner's adjusted basis in her partnership interest is "outside basis" to distinguish it from the partnership's "inside basis" in the partnership's assets. Regardless of the method of acquisition of the partnership interest, a partner's outside basis is adjusted under §705(a) for subsequent contributions, distributive share of income and loss, and distributions of cash and property. These adjustments generally ensure that partnership-level transactions affecting the entity's adjusted basis in its assets will be mirrored in adjustments to the partners' outside bases. Because aggregate inside basis and aggregate outside basis begin equal, see §§722 and 723, as a general rule (subject to some notable exceptions to which §§734(b) and 743(b) speak), aggregate inside and outside bases should remain equal throughout the life of the partnership.

There are a variety of situations when a taxpayer realizes income but is entitled to defer recognition of that income until some subsequent event occurs. For example, a taxpayer enjoys such deferral when it engages in a like-kind exchange of appreciated property, contributes appreciated property to a corporation in a §351 transaction, or receives restricted property (within the meaning of §83) in connection with the performance of services. If it is not a taxpayer but instead a partnership that engages in such a transaction, should the partners increase their outside bases when the income is realized or only subsequently when the income is recognized?

The language of §705(a)(1)(A) referring to "taxable" income of the partnership makes clear that the basis adjustments must wait until the income is recognized. Indeed, if a basis adjustment were made for income realized but deferred, the plain language of §705(a)(1)(A) would mandate a second adjustment for the same income when the deferral ended. While the statutory language applicable to deferred deductions and losses of the partnership is less clear (note the absence of the word "taxable" in §705(a)(2)(A)), it hardly seems likely that Congress intended for there to be one rule for deferred income and a second rule for deferred deductions.

The reasoning must be quite different, though, if a partnership realizes income that is forever exempt from taxation. In such circumstances a basis adjustment must be made immediately because there is no subsequent opportunity to do so, and if no basis adjustment is made, the income nominally exempted from taxation will in fact be taxable to the partners when they sell their partnership interests. Thus, the statute makes clear, see §705(a)(1)(B), that a partner is entitled to increase outside basis for her distributive share of partnership-level exempt income (and equivalently must reduce outside basis for her share of nondeductible, noncapitalizable expenditures (i.e., the equivalent of tax-exempt deductions) such as illegal bribes and kickbacks. §705(a)(2)(B)).

For purposes of §§705(a)(1)(B) and (a)(2)(B), the concept of tax-exempt income and deduction should be read broadly. For example, suppose a partnership receives property as a devise. The partnership will take such property without recognition of income under §102(a), and it will have a fair market value basis in such property under the general rule of §1014. Unless the partners share an equivalent outside basis adjustment under §705(a)(1)(B), the exemption provided by §§102(a) and 1014 will be lost, with mere deferral substituted in its place. Accordingly, it seems clear that the partners should share an outside basis increase equal to the fair market value of the property pursuant to §705(a)(1)(B).

What if the property had been gifted to the partnership rather than devised? In such circumstances the partnership's basis in the property is not fair market value but rather is carried over from the donor. §1015. Assuming the donor's adjusted basis in the property was less than the property's fair market value, the effect of §§102 and 1015 is to give the partnership exempt income as to the amount of the carryover basis and deferral as to the amount of unrealized appreciation in the property. Following the reasoning used above, this means that the partners should share an outside basis increase under §705(a)(1)(B) equal only to the carryover basis that the partnership takes in the gifted property.

Suppose that a partnership makes a contribution to a charity. Technically, a partnership is not entitled to claim a charitable deduction under §170. See §703(a)(2)(C). Instead, each partner's distributive share of the charitable contribution is reported directly by the partners (that is, the charitable deduction is a separately stated item, §702(a)(4)), subject to the various limitations applicable to charitable contributions generally. Even though the charitable deduction is not a deduction to the partnership, it must produce a downward outside basis adjustment else the partners will get a double benefit from the contribution, once as a separately stated item and again when the partnership interests are sold. The downward adjustment presumably is made under §705(a)(2)(B) for nondeductible, noncapitalizable expenditures of the partnership. Rev. Rul. 96-11, 1996-1 C.B. 140. More generally, any transaction having a permanent downward adjustment on the partnership's asset basis should have an equivalent effect on the partners' aggregate outside bases. See Treas. Regs. §1.701-2(f) (ex. 2) (requiring §705(a)(2)(B) basis adjustment for stock basis reductions under §1059 from receipt of an extraordinary dividend).

B. PARTNERSHIP INDEBTEDNESS AND OUTSIDE BASIS

When a partnership borrows money, inside basis increases automatically. If the general equality between aggregate inside and outside bases is to be maintained, such partnership borrowing must also increase aggregate outside basis. This is accomplished by operation of §752(a), which treats an increase in a partner's share of partnership debt as a cash contribution by the partner. This rule, when coupled with §722, means that an increase in a partner's share of partnership debt results in a dollar for dollar increase in outside basis. Similarly, §752(b) provides that a decrease in a partner's share of partnership debt is treated as a cash distribution to the partner.

A §752(a) increase in outside basis is useful in two ways. First, it allows the partner to report a larger distributive share of partnership losses. To ensure that outside basis never becomes negative, §704(d) suspends a partner's distributive share of loss in excess of the partner's outside basis. For example, if a partner with outside basis of $800 is allocated $1,000 of partnership loss, the partner will be entitled to report only $800 of that distributive share on her individual return. The remaining loss of $200 will be suspended until her outside basis is sufficiently positive to absorb it. Treas. Regs. §1.704-1(d)(1). By increasing a partner's outside basis by her share of the partnership's liabilities, §752(a) permits the partner to receive a greater allocation of deductions before triggering the loss suspension rule of §704(d).

Second, a §752(a) increase in outside basis allows the partner to receive a greater cash distribution without recognizing gain. Recall that §731(a)(1) provides that no gain is recognized on a partnership distribution except to the extent that any cash distributed exceeds the distributee partner's outside basis. Accordingly, a partner whose outside basis was increased by a share of partnership debt can receive more cash before triggering recognition of income under §731(a)(1).

You might think that a third benefit of a §752(a) increase in outside basis is a reduction of gain (or increase in loss) recognized on disposition of the partnership interest. However, because disposition of a partnership interest invariably involves a complete reduction in the partner's share of partnership liabilities, a selling partner obtains no benefit from the rule in §752(a). Indeed, the rule of Commissioner v. Tufts, 461 U.S. 300 (1983), applies to a selling partner, possibly forcing recognition of gain by reason of the release of a liability on disposition of the partnership interest.

1. History and Basic Principles

Traditionally, recourse partnership debt was allocated among the partners as they shared partnership losses and nonrecourse partnership debt was shared according to profits interests. Treas. Regs. §1.752-1(e) (repealed 1989). While the regulations gave no justification for these rules, it was generally understood that recourse debt was allocated in proportion to loss interests because the partners would share repayment of the debt in that proportion if called upon to pay it. Nonrecourse debt, on the other hand, was allocated according to profits interests presumably on the theory that if the debt was to be repaid at all, repayment would come out of partnership profits.

These simple rules provided little guidance in allocating partnership indebtedness in complex transactions. For example, how should debt be allocated if it is nonrecourse by its terms but repayment is guaranteed by one of the partners? Because the guarantor partner would bear the entire burden of repayment if the partnership failed to meet its obligation, one might expect that the debt would be allocated entirely to the guarantor partner. However, the Claims Court in Raphan v. United States, 3 Cl. Ct. 457 (1983), aff'd in part, rev'd in part, 759 F.2d 879 (Fed. Cir. 1985), interpreted old regulation §1.752-1(e) as allocating partnership debt according to "the partners' rights and responsibilities *as partners*" (emphasis supplied), and so because the guarantee was not part of the partnership agreement, the court treated the liability as one for which no partner was liable.

In §79 of the Tax Reform Act of 1984, Pub. L. No. 98-369, §79, 98 Stat. 494, 597 (1984), Congress expressed its disapproval of this holding in *Raphan* and instructed the Treasury to issue new regulations "relating to liabilities including the treatment of guarantees, assumptions, indemnity agreements, and similar arrangements." The new regulations were to allocate partnership debt according to "the manner in which the partners . . . share the economic risk of loss with respect to [the] debt." H.R. Rep. No. 861, 98th Cong., 2d Sess. 868, 869 (1984). Although new regulations were not promulgated for five years, the courts followed the new congressional mandate immediately.

Abramson v. Commissioner
86 T.C. 360 (1986)

WHITAKER, Judge: This consolidated case includes 10 different petitioners. . . . Each of the petitions includes, among other issues, the common issue of the tax consequences of the investment by the individual general partner and by all of the limited partners in a New Jersey limited partnership known as Surhill Company (Surhill). In the statutory notice, respondent disallowed each partner's share of the partnership losses, which included current expense and depreciation deductions. Issues related to this matter were severed and consolidated for the purposes of trial, briefing, and opinion. The issues arise out of the acquisition in 1976 and the exploitation of a movie originally entitled "Scandal" or "Scandello" and retitled "Submission" (Submission).

The issues as framed by respondent may be summarized as . . . whether petitioners may include in basis the amount of a nonrecourse note evidencing the unpaid portion of the purchase price due the seller of Submission. . . .

FINDINGS OF FACT

. . . Surhill was formed as a limited partnership under the laws of the State of New Jersey on December 10, 1976 by Edwin D. Abramson (Abramson). He and his wholly owned corporation, Creative Film Enterprises, Inc. (Creative), were the general partners of Surhill. The remaining petitioners were limited partners. . . . Surhill was organized for the purpose of purchasing the United States' rights to Submission. Creative was incorporated under the laws of the State of New Jersey by Abramson for the purpose of locating movies for acquisition by limited partnerships similar to Surhill and to become a general partner in such limited partnerships. The general partners together contributed $3,333 to Surhill and are entitled to 1 percent of the profit or loss. The limited partners together contributed the sum of $330,000 and are entitled to 99 percent of the profit or loss. . . .

In early 1976, Submission was brought to the attention of Joseph Brenner (Brenner), the principal officer of Joseph Brenner Associates, Inc. (Associates). . . . He negotiated with Walter Bedogni, an officer of Rizzoli Company, S.P.A., the owner of the film, which led to a proposal to contract with Associates for the distribution rights for an advance payment of $150,000 in cash plus a percentage of distributor film rentals. Negotiations ceased because the cash payment was more than Associates could afford to pay.

Thereafter, the film was presented to Abramson and Ziffer, with the information that Associates was interested in the distribution rights. . . .

The initial asking price for Submission was $1 million in cash plus a percentage of film rentals. The agreed upon price for the right to exploit Submission in the United States was $1,750,000, payable, $225,000 in cash and $1,525,000 evidenced by a nonnegotiable nonrecourse promissory note with interest. The note was due in 10 years, but was also payable out of one-half of the revenues received by Surhill from the film's distribution. As discussed below, payment of the purchase price was guaranteed by the partners. . . .

The closing documents consisted of the purchase agreement between Surhill and the seller of Submission, the promissory note, a copy of which was attached to the purchase agreement, a security agreement, a copy of which was attached to the promissory note, and the guarantee referred to in, and a copy attached to, the promissory note. . . .

The most critical document in this case is the so-called guarantee agreement[1] entered into by each of the limited partners and by the general partners. . . . The documents were drafted so as to respond to the requirements of the seller of the film that each partner would have personal liability for payment of a pro rata share of the note when due, but to provide the limited partners with the benefit of limited partner status

---

1. We have adopted petitioners' use of the terms "guarantee" and guarantor," though neither term is used in its conventional sense. A guarantee is a collateral promise or undertaking by one person to answer for payment of some debt in case of default of another who is liable for such payment in the first instance. Thus, by right of subrogation, a guarantor has a rememdy against the principal obligor to recover any amounts he has to pay to the creditor. See Brand v. Commissioner, 81 T.C. 821, 828 (1983).

As guarantors of an otherwise nonrecouse note, however, petitioners have incurred personal liability where the partnership has only limited liability. Therefore, petitioners and their assets are both primarily and ultimately liable to the sells in the event of default. They are primarily liable because neither the partnership nor any of its assets (other than the film) is subject to the nonrecourse obligation. They are ultimately liable, because there is no primary obligor against whom they have a right of subrogation. See Smith v. Commissioner, 84 T.C. 889, 908 (1985). Thus, on these facts, we use the terms "guarantee" and "guarantor" as including both primary and ultimate liability.

under New Jersey law and to preclude any partner, limited or general, from acquiring joint liability, that is, from being responsible to the seller of Submission for more than that partner's pro rata share of the promissory note. The pertinent part of the guarantee agreement reads as follows:

Guarantee Agreement

The undersigned hereby guarantees and promises to pay to Transcontinental Films Anstalt that percentage of the unpaid balance due Transcontinental Films Anstalt pursuant to a certain Promissory Note of even date in the principal sum of $1,525,000 issued to it by Surhill Company in payment of such note, set forth opposite his name below. . . .

Under no circumstances shall any of the undersigned persons have any liability under this guarantee or the Promissory Note issued to Transcontinental Films Anstalt in any amount greater than the percentage set forth opposite the undersigned's name above, multiplied by the outstanding balance due under the Promissory Note issued by Surhill Company to Transcontinental Films Anstalt at the time of default thereunder, after reduction for any amounts payable to Transcontinental Films Anstalt pursuant to the exercise of its rights under a certain Security Agreement of even date. Pertinent extracts from the subscription agreement, the promissory note, and the private placement memorandum are set forth in Appendix B attached hereto.

. . . The private placement memorandum fully summarizes the transaction, including the required execution of the guarantee agreement, a copy of which is attached together with copies of the other agreements requiring execution by the limited partners. The subscription agreement also emphasizes the personal liability to be assumed under the guarantee agreement. While the acquisition agreement describes the note as a "nonnegotiable, recourse promissory note," the note is actually a nonrecourse note in that it expressly provides that neither the general partners nor the limited partners will have any personal liability of any kind or nature on the note except as provided in the guarantee agreement. The so-called guarantee agreement, executed by each partner (general and limited) in his capacity as a partner, obligates each person to pay to the seller that percentage of the unpaid balance due the seller in the event of a default which is equal to the partner's percentage interest. A default occurs upon nonpayment of the balance due on the $1,525,000 on December 20, 1986. At that point, the seller must foreclose on the film and it may then look to each partner for that partner's share of the unpaid balance of the indebtedness. . . .

OPINION

. . . The next issue for decision is whether the petitioners may increase their bases in Surhill as a result of their guaranteeing the note given by Surhill to the seller of the film. . . .

As a result of the direct obligation undertaken by each petitioner qua partner to pay to the seller a portion of Surhill's debt pursuant to the so-called guarantee, each partner in Surhill increase his share of Surhill's liabilities. Thus, pursuant to section 752(a) and 722, each partner's basis in Surhill is increased as a result of this additional personal obligation as to which each partner is ultimately liable. See Smith v. Commissioner, 84 T.C. 889, 908 (1985).

The guarantee of an otherwise nonrecourse note places each guaranteeing partner in an economic position indistinguishable from that of a general partner with liability under a recourse note — except that the guaranteeing partner's liability is limited to the amount guaranteed. While recognizing that under state law there may be differences between the obligation of a general partner and those of a limited partner guarantor, such differences should not be controlling for Federal tax purposes. Each is obligated to use his personal assets to satisfy pro rata the partnership liability. In effect, the limited partners are the equivalent of general partners to the extent of their pro rata guarantees especially since, as to this obligation, the liability of the general partners is limited. Economic reality dictates that they be treated equally, and we so hold. Consequently, both general and limited partners will be entitled to include such liabilities in their basis to the extent of their pro rata guarantees. The $1,525,000 liability is apportioned to them in accordance with their loss ratios under the partnership agreement.

This holding is consistent with, and foretold by, our decision in Smith v. Commissioner, supra. In the *Smith* case, one of the partners executed and contributed to the partnership an assumption agreement as to a nonrecourse partnership liability. We held that the partner's basis was increased by the amount of the debt assumed, saying:

> Where, as here, the partner becomes ultimately liable to pay the debt, it is irrelevant for purposes of section 752(a) that the partnership of its property remains liable to the mortgagee. . . . By taking on ultimate and unconditional liability, petitioner constructively contributed the amount of the indebtedness to the partnership, and was thus entitled to increase his basis.

Smith v. Commissioner, 84 T.C. at 980.

Our facts are different in that the property, i.e, Submission, was still liable for the indebtedness and Surhill as obligated to pay the seller of the film one-half of its film rentals. We do not believe that these differences alter the result. In this partnership transaction, each partner is directly and ultimately liable for a pro rata portion of the obligation. The fact that the obligation might be paid in part by application of film rentals to which each partner otherwise would be entitled does not preclude the acquisition of basis. . . .

Based upon the foregoing,

Appropriate orders will be issued.

Reviewed by the Court.

Sterrett, Goffe, Chabot, Parker, Shields, Cohen, Swift, Jacobs, Wright, Parr, and Williams, JJ., agree with the majority opinion.

Nims, Korner, and Hamblen, JJ., agree with the result only.

Simpson, Wilbur, and Gerber, JJ., did not participate in the consideration of this case.

SWIFT, J., concurring: I agree with the result reached by the majority opinion but wish to comment on one aspect of the partnership's obligation under the loan. The majority correctly concludes that the $1,525,000 promissory note is nonrecourse as to the general and limited partners. Under the relevant loan documents, however, as I read them, it appears that the $1,525,000 promissory note is recourse as to the partnership itself (namely, Surhill). If so, the creditor, Rizzoli Company, is entitled to seek full recourse against all of Surhill's available assets if a default on the note occurs.

The apparent recourse nature of the promissory note as to Surhill, however, does not make the obligations of the general and limited partners secondary to Surhill's obligation. For Federal tax purposes, the fact that none of the partners has personal liability on the promissory note elevates the obligations of the partners under the guarantee agreements to primary obligations.

With the clarification that the promissory note appears to be recourse as to Surhill, I agree with the majority's conclusion that Brand v. Commissioner, 81 T.C. 821 (1983), is not applicable to the partners' obligations because the partners have no other person or partner to whom to look for reimbursement should they be required to make payments under the guarantee agreements.

[Dissenting opinion omitted.]

In Smith v. Commissioner, 84 T.C. 889 (1985), the Tax Court held that a partner who assumed a partnership's nonrecourse liability must be allocated that liability under §752. The Tax Court in *Abramson* similarly held that a partner who guaranteed part of a partnership's nonrecourse liability must be allocated the liability up to the amount of the guarantee. The court in *Abramson* distinguished an earlier loan guarantee case, Brand v. Commissioner, 81 T.C. 821 (1983). In that case, a partner had guaranteed a partnership's recourse liability, and the court determined that the guarantor did not bear the economic risk of nonpayment despite the guarantee. The court observed that when the liability is recourse as to the partnership, the guarantor partner has the right to seek reimbursement from the general partners if called upon to pay the debt. Ultimate liability for repayment, accordingly, remains with the general partners despite the guarantee. However, had the loan been nonrecourse as to the partnership, the guarantor partner would have no rights against the other partners if called upon to pay the debt. Thus, only in the case of a nonrecourse loan does a guarantee place ultimate risk of loss on the guarantor partner. When the loan is recourse as to the partnership, the guarantor partner's potential rights of subrogation leave ultimate risk of nonpayment on the partnership's general partners, and so the debt in this case should be allocated among those partners.

The facts of *Abramson* were unusual: By the terms of the loan agreement, the loan was recourse as to the partnership but the lender could not look through the partnership to its general partners for repayment. In effect, the court treated the loan under §752 as if it had been fully nonrecourse. In determining which partners bear ultimate liability for a partnership's debt, we must determine which partners will be called upon to pay the debt, assuming the partnership is unable to do so. If partner *A* can be forced to pay the lender but then has rights against partner *B,* there is no ultimate liability in *A*. However, if *A* has no rights against any partner but *A* has rights against the partnership, *A does* have ultimate liability for the debt: In allocating debt among the partners, the court in *Abramson* recognized that rights of reimbursement against the *partnership* are irrelevant.

These principles can be extended to cover loans from partners to the partnership. For example, suppose limited partner *L* makes a loan to the *P* partnership, and assume that the loan is without recourse so that no partner can be forced to make good on the partnership's obligation. As with any *nonrecourse* loan, if the partnership is unable to repay the debt the economic loss will fall on the lender. Here, that lender is *L*, the limited partner. Accordingly, the debt should be allocated entirely to *L* because *L* bears the economic risk of repayment. To be sure, *L* bears this risk in her capacity as lender rather than as partner, but as Congress made clear when it disapproved of *Raphan,* partnership debts should be allocated among the partners in accordance with economic realities, taking account of all guarantees and other loss-allocation arrangements. Of course, partnership indebtedness as to which no partner is liable for repayment in any capacity must be allocated in some other manner. See Treas. Regs. §1.752-4.

The Treasury Department promulgated temporary regulations under §752 in 1989 and 1990, and final regulations were issued in 1991. These regulations are discussed in the next section. Prior to these regulations, the allocation of partnership debt was covered by the following brief language in Regulation §1.752-1(e):

> A partner's share of partnership liabilities shall be determined in accordance with his ratio for sharing losses under the partnership agreement. In the

case of a limited partnership, a limited partner's share of partnership liabilities shall not exceed the difference between his actual contribution credited to him by the partnership and the total contribution which he is obligated to make under the limited partnership agreement. However, where none of the partners have any personal liability with respect to a partnership liability . . . then all partners, including limited partners, shall be considered as sharing such liability under §752(c) in the same proportion as they share the profits.

As you read the §752 regulations, ask yourself whether they better allocate partnership debt than did these simple rules as interpreted by *Abramson, Smith,* and *Brand.*

2.   Allocations under the Regulations

The regulations continue to allocate recourse and nonrecourse liabilities according to different rules. A "recourse liability" is defined as "[any] partnership liability . . . to the extent that any partner or related person bears the economic risk of loss for th[e] liability. . . ." Treas. Regs. §1.752-1(a)(1). A "nonrecourse liability" is any partnership liability "to the extent that no partner or related person bears the economic risk of loss." Treas. Regs. §1.752-1(a)(2). For application of these definitions, a "related person" includes family members (but not brothers and sisters), controlled entities, and commonly controlled entities. See Treas. Regs. §1.752-4(b)(1) (incorporating definitions (with modifications) from §§267(b) and 707(b)). Broadly speaking, the new regulations continue the tradition of allocating recourse liabilities according to loss interests and nonrecourse liabilities according to profits interests.

For purposes of §752, a liability of the partnership includes any obligation to the extent that incurring the obligation created or increased the basis to the partnership of any of its assets. Rev. Rul. 88-77, 1988-2 C.B. 129. For example, a short sale of stock creates a liability for purposes of §752, Rev. Rul. 95-26, 1995-1 C.B. 131, although the contribution of an account payable by a cash-basis partner does not constitute a liability for purposes of §752 but rather is treated as loss property under §704(c)(1)(A). Treas. Regs. §1.704-3(a)(4).

a.   Recourse Liabilities

i.   The Regulatory Scheme

Congress instructed the Treasury to issue regulations under §752 allocating partnership recourse liabilities in accordance with economic risk of loss, and that is what the regulations try to do. Under the regulations, a partner bears the economic risk of loss of a partnership liability to the extent the partner would be forced to make a payment to any person (including a contribution to the partnership) as the result of a constructive zero-value liquidation of the partnership. See Treas. Regs. §1.752-2(b)(1). In this context a zero-value liquidation means a liquidation of the partnership after all of its assets (including cash) have become worthless and are transferred for zero consideration in a fully taxable transaction. *Id.* The effect of a zero-value constructive liquidation is to determine how the capital account balances will stand if the partnership should lose all of its investments when the partnership's debts become due.

For example, suppose *A* contributes $600 and *B* contributes $400 to form the *AB* general partnership. The partnership agreement provides that capital accounts will be properly maintained for each partner, that liquidating proceeds will be distributed in accordance with final capital account balances, and that each partner has an obligation to restore a deficit capital account if one exists upon liquidation. In addition, assume that *A* is allocated 50 percent of partnership profits and 60 percent of partnership losses. *AB* borrows $9,000 on a fully recourse basis. The $10,000 cash is then used by the partnership to purchase Blackacre. How should the $9,000 indebtedness be allocated?

First, assume that all the partnership's assets (in this case, just Blackacre) become worthless and are sold for $0. This hypothetical sale is important because it means that the $10,000 hypothetical loss realized on Blackacre is recognized and adjusts the partners' capital accounts. Accordingly, after the hypothetical sale *A*'s capital account stands at minus $5,400 ($600 less 60 percent of $10,000) while *B*'s stands at minus $3,600 ($400 less 40 percent of $10,000). Thus, if the partnership liquidates immediately, *A* must contribute $5,400 while *B* must contribute $3,600. These final figures define the sharing ratios of the partnership liability: $5,400 to *A* and $3,600 to *B*. See examples 1 and 2 of Treas. Treas. Regs. §1.752-2(f).

One point worth making explicit is that we adjust the partners' capital accounts by the book (and not tax) loss realized on the hypothetical zero-value sale. This distinction will be important whenever a partnership owns an asset having a book value different from its tax basis. Such book/tax disparities can arise when appreciated or loss property is contributed to the partnership (see Treas. Regs. §1.704-1(b)(2)(iv)(d)(1)), as well as when partnership assets are revalued for book purposes such as when new partners join an existing partnership owning appreciated or loss property. See Treas. Regs. §1.704-1(b)(2)(iv)(f)-(g).

This example demonstrates a point latent in the new definitions: Under the §752 regulations, recourse debt allocations are influenced not only by the way in which the partners share losses but also by existing capital accounts. Anything that affects capital account balances potentially affects loss sharing ratios as well. In particular, annual distributive shares of gain and loss will affect capital account balances each year, so that the regulations seemingly contemplate a reallocation of partnership debt at least annually even in the absence of a change in the partnership's debt. Also worth noting is the implicit incorporation of the §704(b) allocation rules via the hypothetical sale and liquidation.

Reconsider the example above but assume (1) that B is a limited partner who cannot be required to make additional contributions to the partnership and (2) that B gives the lender a personal guarantee for the $9,000 debt. Once again the hypothetical sale and liquidation produces a taxable loss of $10,000, but now that loss is allocated $9,600 to A and $400 to B because B has no obligation to restore a capital account deficit upon liquidation. Thus, the final capital accounts stand at minus $9,000 for A and $0 for B, and so the loan is allocated entirely to A.

But what if the lender enforces the guarantee by collecting $9,000 directly from B? If so, none of the $9,000 deficit in A's capital account is needed to pay the lender. However, B as guarantor will be entitled to seek reimbursement from the partnership as principal debtor, and so A will still be required to contribute $9,000 to the partnership, although in this case for distribution to B rather than to the lender. In any event, A bears the ultimate economic liability associated with the debt despite B's personal guarantee so it is proper that the debt be allocated entirely to A. See Treas. Regs. §1.752-2(b)(5); see also Treas. Regs. §1.752-2(f) (examples. 3-4); Proesel v. Commissioner, 77 T.C. 992, 1004 (1981).

The outcome would be very different, though, if the loan had been nonrecourse with respect to the partnership. If the loan is nonrecourse (excluding B's guarantee), the partnership's loss on the hypothetical sale will be only $1,000 because the amount of the outstanding debt, $9,000, is included in the partnership's amount realized under *Tufts* in computing loss on the hypothetical sale. Under the terms of the AB partnership agreement, this loss will be allocated $600 to A and $400 to B. Each partner's capital account ends up at zero, so that ending capital account balances cannot be used to allocate the debt.

This indeterminacy is appropriate because the loan is nonrecourse as to the partnership. The capital account analysis employed by the regulations determines the extent to which each partner is liable for partnership debt in his or her capacity as a partner. In this case, neither A nor B is liable as a partner.

However, B is liable for the debt as a result of the personal guarantee. Further, if B is forced to pay off the loan pursuant to the guarantee, B will have no rights against A: Because the loan is nonrecourse with respect to the principal debtor (the partnership), B, like the lender, has recourse only against the property securing the debt. Thus, B bears the ultimate burden of repayment of the loan, and so the loan is treated as a recourse loan to B as to this amount. B accordingly is allocated the entire $9,000 loan. Smith v. Commissioner, 84 T.C. 889, 908 n.18 (1985).

Other portions of the regulations worth noting include those governing persons related to a partner, Treas. Regs. §1.752-2(c), arrangements tantamount to a guarantee, Treas. Regs. §1.752-2(j)(2), and the general anti-abuse provision in Treas. Regs. §1.752-2(j). In addition, the legislative history of the 1984 Act indicates that accrued but unpaid expenses and accounts payable of a cash-basis partnership should not be treated as partnership liabilities under §752. See also Rev. Rul. 88-77, 1988-2 C.B. 129. Note that if deductible expenses are contributed to a partnership by a cash-basis partner, §704(c) will be implicated. Treas. Regs. §1.704-3(a)(4).

PROBLEMS

21-1. *E* and *F* form the *EF* general partnership by contributing $20,000 each. The partnership purchases property for $100,000, paying $40,000 in cash and the remainder in the form of a $60,000 recourse note. Determine whether the debt is treated as recourse and, if so, how it is allocated if

a. the partnership agreement provides that losses will be divided equally between the partners.
b. the partnership agreement provides that losses will be allocated 90 percent to *E* and 10 percent to *F*.
c. the partnership agreement allocates losses equally between the partners, but *F* is a limited partner who cannot be required to contribute more than an additional $10,000 to the partnership.
d. both partners are general partners, losses are allocated equally between the partners, but *E* personally guarantees repayment of $60,000 of the debt.
e. both partners are general partners, losses are all allocated equally between the partners, *E* personally guarantees the debt, and the debt is nonrecourse as to the partnership.

21-2. *A* and *B* form the *AB* general partnership by contributing $10,000 apiece. The partnership agreement provides that losses will be allocated equally between the partners. The partnership borrows $80,000 from *R*. Is the debt recourse and, if so, how is it debt allocated if

a. the debt is fully recourse, and *R* is a corporation wholly owned by *B*?
b. the debt is nonrecourse, and *R* is a corporation wholly owned by *B*?
c. the debt is nonrecourse, and *R* is a corporation owned 25 percent by *A* and 75 percent by *B*?

ii. Some Questions

Having seen how the regulations work, it is time to ask whether they work properly. Although the regulations have their supporters, it seems undeniable that they are fundamentally flawed. See generally Howard E. Abrams, Long-Awaited Regulations Under Section 752 Provide Wrong Answers, 44 Tax L. Rev. 627 (1989). Consider example 1 of Regulation §1.752-2(f). *A* and *B* form the *AB* partnership by contributing $100 each. The partnership agreement provides that capital accounts will be maintained properly, that liquidating proceeds will be distributed in accordance with final account balances, and that any partner with a final capital account deficit will contribute the amount of the deficit to the partnership. In addition, losses are to be allocated 90 percent to *A* and 10 percent to *B*.

If the *AB* partnership borrows $800 on a fully recourse basis, the regulations conclude that the indebtedness is allocable entirely to *A*. Under the regulations, the constructive liquidation will produce a taxable loss of $1,000, allocable under the partnership agreement $900 to *A* and $100 to *B*. Accordingly, final account balances will stand at negative $800 for *A* and zero for *B*. Thus, *A*'s deficit account restoration obligation is triggered, so that *A* must make a contribution to the partnership of $800 for distribution to the lender. Only *A* makes a net contribution as a result of the constructive liquidation, and so the regulations allocate the entire $800 debt to *A*.

Yet the debt should be allocated partially to *A* and partially to *B*. Prior to the borrowing, a constructive liquidation as defined in the regulations would produce a taxable loss of $200, allocable $180 to *A* and $20 to *B*. Such a liquidation would leave final capital accounts at negative $80 for *A* and positive $80 for *B*. Thus, *A* would be required to contribute $80 for distribution to *B*.

Comparing this constructive liquidation with that of one occurring after the partnership borrowing, we see that the effect of the debt is to increase *A*'s net contribution by $720 (from $80 to $800) and to decrease *B*'s final capital account balance by $80 (from $80 to $0). Accordingly, the $800 debt potentially makes *A* worse off by $720 and *B* worse off by $80, and if it is to be allocated according to economic risk of loss (as mandated by Congress in the 1984 Tax Act), the debt should be allocated $720 to *A* and $80 to *B*.

The regulations err because of the tacit assumption that all net contributions following a constructive liquidation arise from partnership indebtedness. That simply is not true: If losses are allocated other than in proportion to capital account balances, a constructive liquidation can produce a net contribution which in part reflects the disparity between preliquidation capital accounts and loss sharing ratios. For example, the first $80 of *A*'s $800 net contribution in example 1 is merely a payback of *B*'s initial capital contribution, an obligation that arose immediately upon formation of the partnership and not upon acquisition of the partnership debt.

It is no coincidence that the $800 debt in example 1 is properly allocable 90 percent to *A* and 10 percent to *B;* that is, according to their loss-sharing ratios. If the partners' loss-sharing ratios equal their capital account ratios (and assuming no §704(c) problems), a constructive liquidation under the regulations will reduce all capital account balances to zero (caused by assuming all assets become worthless) and then will produce capital account deficits to all partners in proportion to loss ratios (summing to the amount of outstanding partnership debt). If loss-sharing and capital account ratios differ from one another, ending capital deficits will not be in proportion to loss ratios, but that is precisely what causes the problem in the §752 regulations. In such circumstances the difference between final capital account balances and loss ratios should *not* affect allocation of the debt.

b. Nonrecourse Liabilities

Under the regulations, partnership nonrecourse liabilities (i.e., liabilities as to which no partner is liable, see Treas. Regs. §1.752-1(a)(2)) are allocated in three tiers. Treas. Regs. §1.752-3(a). Under the first tier, nonrecourse liabilities are allocated to each partner in an amount equal to each partner's share of partnership minimum gain (i.e., in the same proportions as prior nonrecourse deductions were allocated). Reg §1.752-3(a)(1). Under the second tier, the remaining nonrecourse liabilities are allocated to each partner in an amount equal to the partner's §704(c) gain (including reverse §704(c) gain arising from the revaluation of partnership property) that would be recognized if the property were sold for the outstanding liability and no other consideration. Treas. Regs. §1.752-3(a)(2). Finally, all remaining nonrecourse liabilities are allocated among the partners in proportion to their profits interests. Treas. Regs. §1.752-3(a)(3). Tier 3 allocations may be made in accordance with the partners' general profits interests, in a manner reasonably consistent with the allocation of some tax item having economic effect, or in the manner in which the partners will share the nonrecourse deductions from the property. Treas. Regs. §1.752-3(a)(3).

While the three tiers may seem to speak to different concerns, in actuality all three seek to allocate the nonrecourse liabilities in accordance with profits interests. First consider tier 1. Minimum gain is the least book gain that will be recognized by the partnership upon a disposition of the property, Treas. Regs. §1.704-2(d)(1), and minimum gain resulting from the disposition of property subject to a nonrecourse liability must be allocated to the partners as they were allocated the nonrecourse deductions, Treas. Regs. §1.704-2(f). Thus, by allocating partnership nonrecourse liabilities according to each partner's share of minimum gain, tier 1 simply allocates the liability according to partner profits interests over which the partners have no allocative discretion.

Now consider tier 2. This tier allocates nonrecourse liabilities to each partner in an amount equal to the partner's share of §704(c) income. In determining the amount of §704(c) income allocable under tier 2, you assume that the property is transferred in satisfaction of the nonrecourse debt and for no other consideration. Treas. Regs. §1.752-3(a)(2); see also Rev. Rul. 95-41, 1995-1 C.B. 132. Income arising under §704(c) is attributable to the excess (if any) of the value of contributed property over the adjusted basis of the property at the time of contribution. See Treas. Regs. §1.704-3(a)(3)(ii). Section 704(c)(1) requires that such precontribution appreciation be allocated to the contributing partner. Thus, tier 2 allocates partnership nonrecourse liabilities in accordance with partner profits interests over which the partners have no allocative discretion, just like tier 1. Tier 3 then allocates the remainder of the nonrecourse liability in accordance with the allocation of gain over which the partners *do have* allocative discretion.

Consider how a partnership allocates gain from the disposition of an asset. If the asset is encumbered by a nonrecourse liability and the amount of that liability exceeds the partnership's adjusted basis, then there is partnership minimum gain, which, under the §704(b) regulations, must be allocated to the partners as they shared the nonrecourse deductions. Treas. Regs. §1.704-2(f). The gain, in other words, must be allocated as was the liability under tier 1.

Next, if the property's book value exceeds its adjusted basis, then the difference has been booked into one or more partners' capital accounts under §704(c) (or in accordance with §704(c) principles upon the revaluation of partnership assets under §704(b), see Treas. Regs. §1.704-1(b)(2)(iv)(f)(4)) and that difference must be allocated to those partners whose capital accounts include the excess book value. Treas. Regs. §1.704-3(a)(1). That is, the gain must be allocated as was the liability under tier 2. Any remaining gain may be allocated as the partners agree (subject to the general limitation of substantial economic effect under §704(b)), and this is how the remainder of the liability is allocated under tier 3.

As explained above, tier 1 allocates nonrecourse liabilities in accordance with the partners' profits interests properly considered. But it does more: Tier 1 backstops the provisions governing the allocation of nonrecourse deductions under §704(b) by ensuring that a partner properly allocated nonrecourse deductions will have sufficient outside basis to exploit them.

For example, assume *X* contributes $30,000 and *Y* contributes $10,000 to form the *XY* general partnership. The partnership then purchases depreciable property for $100,000, paying $40,000 in cash and signing a nonrecourse note for the remaining $60,000. Assume that the partnership

agreement provides that all profits and losses will be divided equally between X and Y except that depreciation will be allocated 75 percent to X
and 25 percent to Y.

If the partnership is entitled to claim a depreciation deduction each
year of $10,000, the partners' equity will be fully consumed after four years
(assuming the partnership has no other items of income or deduction,
and assuming also that there are no distributions or further borrowings).
After the fourth year, each partner's capital account should stand at zero.
Because there has so far been no nonrecourse deductions and there is no
§704(c) gain, the liability is allocated under tier 3 according to their profits
interests (where the definition "profits interests" offers the partners some
discretion. See Treas. Regs. §1.752-3(a)(3)). Accordingly, X's outside basis
should equal $30,000 and Y's outside basis should equal $30,000.

In year 5, the depreciation deduction of $10,000 is allocated $7,500
to X and $2,500 to Y. Assuming this allocation is deemed to satisfy the
substantial economic effect test of §704(b), it lowers X's capital account
to negative $7,500 and lowers Y's capital account to negative $2,500. The
depreciation in year 5 is a nonrecourse deduction (because it lowers the
basis of the property below that of the outstanding nonrecourse loan),
and so it triggers a reallocation of the partnership debt. Under tier 1, X
must be allocated $7,500 of the debt and Y must be allocated $2,500 of
the debt. The remaining $50,000 continues to be allocated in accordance
with partnership profits, or $25,000 to each partner. Thus, at the end of
the fifth year each partner has an outside basis of $25,000, computed as
follows: For X, prior year's outside basis of $30,000, less $7,500 distributable
share of depreciation deduction, and plus $2,500 increase in share of debt;
for Y, prior year's outside basis of $30,000, less $2,500 distributable share
of depreciation deduction, and less $2,500 reduction in share of debt.

If we continue this analysis through the tenth year when the property
is fully depreciated, we see that X's capital account will stand at negative
$45,000 and Y's capital account will be negative $15,000. The entire debt
now is allocated under tier 1, so that it goes 75 percent (or $45,000) to X
and 25 percent (or $15,000) to Y. Accordingly, X's outside basis is zero
(X's share of the debt of $45,000 plus contributed capital of $30,000 less
distributed share of depreciation of $75,000) as is Y's outside basis. Thus,
each partner had precisely enough outside basis to absorb the nonrecourse
deductions. In essence, then, the rules governing the allocation of nonrecourse deductions under §752 ensure that they do not pose a second
hurdle to the allocation of nonrecourse deductions. If the allocation of
such deductions pass muster under §704(b), there should be adequate
outside basis under §§752 and 704(d) to use them on the partners' individual returns.

If property encumbered by a nonrecourse debt has a §704(c) or reverse §704(c) book/tax disparity, the analysis becomes more complicated.
Consider the following example taken from Revenue Ruling 95-41. A and B
form the AB general partnership, with A contributing depreciable property

having adjusted basis of $4,000, fair market value of $10,000, and subject to a nonrecourse liability of $6,000, while B contributes cash of $4,000. How is the liability initially allocated, assuming that A and B agree to divide profits and losses equally except as required by §704(c)?

A and B each begin with a capital account of $4,000, and ignoring any reallocation of the debt, each partner has an outside basis of $4,000 as well. To the extent any of the debt is allocated to B, A's outside basis will decline and B's outside basis will increase. In fact, if more than $4,000 of the debt is allocated to B, A will recognize income on the reallocation. Of course, reallocation of the debt has no effect on the partners' capital accounts.

Under tier 1, the debt is allocated to the partners as they share minimum gain from the secured property, where minimum gain equals the excess of the debt over the book value of the property. Because the property was booked into the partnership at its current fair market value of $10,000, there is no minimum gain. Accordingly, there is no allocation of the debt under tier 1.

Under tier 2, the debt is allocated to the partners as they would share gain under §704(c)(1)(A) if the property were sold for the amount of the outstanding debt and for no other consideration. Here, that means we ask how much §704(c)(1)(A) gain there would be if the property were sold for $6,000. Because the adjusted basis of the property is $4,000, sale for $6,000 would yield a tax gain of $2,000 but a book loss of $4,000.

If the partners agree to use either the traditional method or the traditional method with curative allocations to address ceiling limitations problems, disposition of the property for $6,000 would produce a tax gain to A of $2,000 and no further tax allocations. Because this gain would be allocable to A under §704(c)(1), there is a $2,000 tier 2 allocation of the debt to A *if* the partnership uses the traditional method or the traditional method with curative allocations to address ceiling limitation issues arising under §704(c). Revenue Ruling 95-41 specifically provides that the possibility of curative allocations is ignored in determining the allocation of nonrecourse liabilities under tier two.

If the partnership uses the remedial allocation method to address ceiling limitation problems arising under §704(c)(1)(A), allocation of the debt under tier 2 is more complicated. Because a sale of the property for the amount of the debt (that is, a sale for $6,000) would yield a tax gain of $2,000 but a book loss of $4,000, the partnership would be required to make a remedial allocation of $2,000 of tax loss to B and an offsetting $2,000 remedial allocation of tax gain to A. Accordingly, the total allocation of gain to A from the hypothetical sale would be $4,000, and so this is the amount of the debt allocable to A under tier 2 *if* the partnership uses the remedial allocation method to address ceiling limitation problems.

Under tier 3, the remainder of the debt is allocated between the partners as they share profits. Actually, the partners have three choices under this tier. First, they may agree to allocate the remainder of the debt in accordance with their general profits interest. Second, they may agree to allocate the remainder of the debt in any way that is reasonably consistent with some other allocation having economic effect. Third, they may agree to allocate the remainder of the debt in accordance with the way in which they will allocate the nonrecourse deductions from the property. Reg §1.752-3(a)(3).

In summary, there is no allocation of the debt under tier 1. If the partnership uses the traditional method or the traditional method with curative allocations to address ceiling problems arising from the property, the debt is allocated $2,000 to A and $0 to B under tier 2; if the partners use the remedial allocation method, the tier 2 allocation is $4,000 to A and $0 to B. Finally, the remainder of the debt (which may be $4,000 or $2,000) is either divided equally between A and B or allocated entirely to B at the partnership's option.

PROBLEMS

21-3. *P* and *Q* form the PQ general partnership, agreeing that *P* will be allocated 40 percent and *Q* 60 percent of all tax items except that depreciation deductions will be divided equally. *P* contributes depreciable property subject to a nonrecourse liability of $6,000, with an adjusted basis of $4,000 and a fair market value of $10,000. *Q* contributes $6,000 cash.

    a.   What are the initial capital accounts and outside bases?

    b.   If the property contributed by *P* has five years remaining on its depreciable life (although a new depreciable life would be 10 years), what are the partners' capital accounts and outside bases after one year, assuming there is no other income or loss to the partnership and that the property is depreciated using the straight-line method?

21-4. *X* and *Y* are equal partners in the *XY* general partnership with capital accounts and outside basis of $3,000 each. *Z* joins by contributing machinery to the partnership in exchange for a 25 percent interest in profits and losses. At the time of *Z*'s admission, the machinery has an adjusted basis to *Z* of $15,000 and a fair market value of $20,000, and it is encumbered by an $18,000 nonrecourse debt. The partnership's only other asset is $6,000 in cash. In the first taxable year after *Z* joins, the partnership is entitled to a $6,000 depreciation deduction from the machinery. What are the partners' outside bases?

C.   WHY §752?

Having examined how §752 does (and possibly should) operate, it is time to ask why partnership borrowing has any effect on outside basis. In fact, because there is no provision in subchapter S equivalent to §752, the possibility of using §752 to exploit entity-level borrowing can be one reason for using a partnership instead of an S corporation.

Consider first partnership recourse indebtedness. As we have seen, such debt is to be allocated among the partners as they share economic risk of repayment. An increase in outside basis provides tax advantages for the partners, so that if section 752(a) did not provide the partners with a basis increase, they would seek to accomplish the same tax result some other way. Could they do it?

Yes. Rather than cause the partnership to incur the debt, the partners themselves could borrow the same amount and then contribute the borrowed proceeds to the partnership. Such actual contributions of cash would produce the outside basis increase under §722 as is obtained under §752(a) when the partnership incurs the debt directly. Of course, if the partnership distributed cash to the partners so that they could pay off their debt, these actual distributions would have the same effect as a reduction of partnership debt has under §752(b). At least with respect to recourse debt, then, §752 can be justified as giving the partners directly what they could obtain without §752 indirectly.

From a more structural perspective, the effect of §752 is to continue the equality of aggregate inside and outside bases started by the double carryover basis rules of §§722 and 723 and continued by the basis adjustment rules of §705. When the partnership borrows funds, inside basis goes up by the amount of the debt, either implicitly in the form of cash or explicitly in the basis of the assets acquired with the loan proceeds. Under §752(a), aggregate outside basis increases by the same amount. Similarly, repayment by the partnership of the loan reduces inside basis by the amount of the repayment. By maintaining the equality of aggregate inside and outside bases, §752 helps minimize the disruptions caused by the entity model of partnership taxation: Inside basis and outside basis should simply be two different ways to dividing the partners' aggregate investment in the enterprise, either asset-by-asset (inside basis) or partner-by-partner (outside basis).

This last justification for §752 applies with equal force to nonrecourse partnership debt: Because nonrecourse debt increases inside basis, it should also increase outside basis if aggregate inside and outside bases are to remain equal. If an individual purchases property subject to a nonrecourse loan, the property's adjusted basis is increased by the amount of the debt. If partnership nonrecourse loans did not increase outside basis, the partners would stand in a worse tax position by reason of the partnership than they would if they owned the property directly.

22

Nonliquidating Distributions

A. DISTRIBUTIONS NOT SUBJECT TO §751(b)

1. Basic Taxation Rules

a. Recognition of Gain and Loss

The basic principle underlying the tax treatment of partnership distributions is that the distribution should be tax-free to the partnership and to the distributee partner if possible. Under §731(a), loss is not recognized on a current distribution and gain is recognized by the distributee partner only if and to the extent that the amount of cash distributed exceeds the distributee partner's predistribution outside basis, such gain being capital because of the final sentence in §731(a) combined with §741. This is consistent with the basic paradigm underlying subchapter K that transactions between a partner and the partnership should not be taxable; instead, taxation generally waits until the partnership or one of its partners engages in a transaction with someone outside the partnership. However, the relative simplicity of §731(a) can be overruled by application of §751(b).

b. Basis of Distributed Property and Outside Basis

Most distributions described in §731(a) are tax-free, and those that are tax-free have no net effect on the distributee partner's overall basis. In general, §732 provides that the distributee partner carries over the partnership's adjusted basis in the distributed assets, and whatever basis is so allocated to the distributed property is subtracted from the distributee partner's outside basis under §733. Accordingly, the effect of a distribution tax-free under §731 is to reallocate the distributee partner's predistribution outside basis between the distributed property and the partner's post-distribution outside basis. Of course, to the extent the distribution includes cash as well as property, the distributee partner's outside basis is first reduced by the amount of the cash distributed, §733(1).

When the distributee partner's predistribution outside basis is less than the partnership's basis in the distributed assets, asset basis cannot carry over without producing a negative outside basis. Because outside basis can never become less than zero, see §733, when the distributee partner's predistribution outside basis is less than the partnership's basis in the distributed assets, the partner's outside basis drops to zero as a result of the distribution and the partner's entire predistribution outside basis is allocated to the distributed property. See §732(a)(2). Once again, though, if the distribution includes cash as well as property, the partner's pre-distribution outside basis is first used to absorb the cash and only the excess is allocated to the distributed property.

Consider the following example. Individual X is a member of the P partnership. P distributes cash of $7,000, inventory with adjusted basis of $6,000 and fair market value of $10,000, and a capital asset with adjusted basis of $24,000 and fair market value of $29,000, to X in a transaction described in §731. At the time of the distribution, X's outside basis equals $32,000.

Because the cash distributed does not exceed X's predistribution outside basis, there is no gain on the distribution. §731(a)(1). Under §732(a)(2), X's basis in the distributed assets equals $25,000, that being X's predistribution outside basis of $32,000 less the $7,000 cash distributed. Of that $25,000 basis, $6,000 is first allocated to the inventory pursuant to §732(c)(1)(A)(i) and the remaining $19,000 is allocated to the capital asset under §§732(c)(1)(B) and 732(c)(3)(B). X's outside basis is reduced to $0 under §733(1)-(2).

Reconsider this example, assuming that instead of receiving inventory and a capital asset, X receives two capital assets, asset A having adjusted basis to the partnership of $6,000 and fair market value of $10,000 and asset B having adjusted basis to the partnership of $24,000 and fair market value of $29,000. Once again assume that X also receives cash of $7,000 and that X's predistribution outside basis equals $32,000.

As before, X recognizes no gain because the cash distributed is less than X's predistribution outside basis. Similarly, X's basis in the distributed assets again totals $25,000. Because both assets are now assumed to be capital assets, there is no allocation under §732(c)(1)(A)(i). Instead, each capital asset is allocated under §732(c)(1)(B)(i) a carryover basis taken from the partnership (i.e., asset A is allocated a basis of $6,000 and asset B is allocated a basis of $24,000), but because the basis so allocated exceeds the $25,000 total provided by §732(a)(2), the basis of the capital assets is then decreased pursuant to §§732(c)(1)(B)(ii) and 732(c)(3).

This decrease is computed in three steps. First, we must determine the total amount of the basis decrease. Here, that is $5,000 because giving each capital asset a carryover basis yields a combined basis of $30,000 while the total basis to be allocated under §732(a)(2) equals only $25,000. Second, we allocate this $5,000 basis decrease to those capital assets having adjusted basis to the partnership in excess of fair market value (i.e., to those distributed capital assets having unrealized loss). §732(c)(3)(A). In this example, there is no allocation under this second step because both capital assets are appreciated. Third, we allocate any remaining basis decrease to the distributed capital assets in proportion to their adjusted bases (as adjusted under step two). §732(c)(3)(B). Thus, of the $5,000 basis decrease, $1,000 is allocated to capital asset A and $4,000 is allocated to capital asset B. Accordingly, X takes asset A with a basis of $5,000 and asset B with a basis of $20,000. X's outside basis is reduced to $0 under §733(1)-(2).

Note that the way in which §732(c) is written ensures that ordinary income assets (that is, unrealized receivables and inventory) will be given a carryover basis before any basis is given to capital assets, thereby minimizing the likelihood that a distribution will increase the amount of ordinary income recognized upon disposition of the distributed assets. Still, if a combined carryover basis for the distributed ordinary income assets exceeds the distributee partner's predistribution outside basis (reduced by any cash received in the distribution), because outside basis cannot go negative, the ordinary income assets will have a basis in the hands of the distributee partner lower than the adjusted basis of those assets in the hands of the partnership.

c. The Timing of Taxation

A loan from the partnership to a partner is not a distribution subject to §§731-733, at least unless and until the loan is forgiven by the partnership. This explains the rule that a draw against partnership share is not treated as a partnership distribution until the last day of the partnership taxable year, because until that day the partner's distributive share is uncertain and the partner may be required to repay some or all of the draw. See Treas. Regs. §1.731-1(a)(1)(ii).

At least one group of commentators has interpreted this rule to mean that the tax consequences of all partnership distributions are determined as of the close of the partnership taxable year, thereby permitting the partners to use the current year's income to absorb distributed cash. 2 A. Willis, J. Pennell & P. Postlewaite, Partnership Taxation ¶13.02 (6th ed. 1997). Such a reading of Treas. Regs. §1.731-1(a)(1)(ii) seems inconsistent with the words of the statute and does not appear to be the Service's understanding of the issue. See, e.g., sources cited in W. McKee, W. Nelson & R. Whitmire, Federal Taxation of Partnerships and Partners ¶19.03[2], at 19-25 n.93 (3d ed. 1996). Indeed, in Rev. Rul. 94-4, 1994-1 C.B. 195, the Service ruled that constructive distributions caused by a reduction in the share of partnership liabilities are treated as draws until the close of the taxable year, but in so ruling the Service took pains to explain why treating constructive distributions as falling within Treas. Regs. §1.731-1(a)(1)(ii) was consistent with the statute. If all distributions fell within this regulation, the Service would have had no need to justify constructive distributions as a special case. While there is no published revenue ruling in which the Service has ruled that a distribution described in §731 is not a "draw or advance" within the meaning of Treas. Regs. §1.731-1(a)(1)(ii), at least one ruling expressly recognizes that the tax consequences of a distribution are determined by reference to the distributee-partner's outside basis immediately prior to the distribution and that only "certain" distributions fall with the "draw or advance" exception. Rev. Rul. 92-97, 1992-2 C.B. 124.

2. *Distributions and Capital Accounts*

a. **Excess Cash**

Distributions reduce the outside basis of the distributee-partner. See §733. Because capital accounts and outside basis move up and down together (excluding the effect of partnership debt on outside basis), distributions of cash and property must also reduce capital accounts. That in fact is the rule, although the amount of the capital account adjustment under Treas. Regs. §1.704-1(b)(2)(iv)(e)(1) is somewhat different from the outside basis adjustment under §733.

Consider first a distribution of cash in amount sufficient to trigger recognition of income under §731(a)(1). For example, suppose P receives a distribution of $10,000 from the PQ partnership when P's outside basis and capital account are only $8,000. Under §731(a)(1), P recognizes income of $2,000 (which is capital gain under the last sentence of §731(a) combined with §741). In addition, P reduces her outside basis to $0 under §733(1). However, P's capital account is reduced by the full amount of the distribution, leaving P's capital account at negative $2,000.

This distribution is taxable to P because P's outside basis is not large enough to absorb the distribution. Recall that for a distribution to be tax-free, the distributee-partner must allocate her predistribution outside basis between the distributed property and her continuing interest in the partnership. Because cash must always be allocated a basis equal to face value, a tax-free distribution to P of $10,000 would leave P's outside basis at negative $2,000. To avoid this negative basis, P recognizes income of $2,000 and raises her outside basis to zero.

This trade-off of income recognition for outside basis is not possible with respect to *P*'s capital account. Capital accounts measure a partner's share of the partnership's book value. If a partner takes out of the partnership more than she has put in, her capital account must be negative. That she may have recognized income over the life of the partnership is irrelevant: Capital accounts reflect the partners' economic relationship and are unaffected by any partner's particular tax circumstances. Accordingly, *the distributee-partner's capital account is reduced by the full amount of the distribution even if outside basis is reduced by less under the "not below zero" language of §733.* Treas. Regs. §1.704-1(b)(2)(iv)(b).

Whenever a distribution of cash forces the distributee partner to recognize income under §731(a)(1), the distribution will also cause a book/tax disparity for the distributee partner. To see this, note that the effect of the distribution will be to reduce the distributee partner's capital account by the amount of cash distributed while the partner's outside basis will, when gain is recognized on the distribution, be reduced by less. This book/tax disparity does not correspond to a book/tax disparity in some partnership asset and so will not be cured by the disposition of any partnership asset. Thus, it is not like a book/tax disparity caused by the contribution of appreciated or loss property (or like the book/tax disparity caused by revaluations of partnership property). In addition, because a distribution of excess cash does not create an offsetting book/tax disparity for some nondistributee partner, the distributee partner's book/tax disparity cannot be cured by curative allocations as described in Treas. Regs. §1.704-3(c) or by remedial allocations as described in Treas. Regs. §1.704-3(d). Accordingly, any book/tax disparity created by the distribution of excess cash is permanent and will be resolved only when the distributee partner's interest in the partnership is liquidated unless the partnership has an election under §754 in effect.

b. Appreciated and Loss Property

When property is distributed, the distributee partner's outside basis is reduced by whatever basis is allocated to the distributed property. §733(2). That amount usually is the predistribution adjusted basis of the property in the hands of the partnership, §732(a)(1), although if the distributee-partner's outside basis is insufficient to absorb this amount, we use instead the partner's lesser, predistribution outside basis, §732(a)(2). This basis rule is consistent with the tax-free status of the distribution in that total basis to the distributee-partner is neither raised nor lowered: Her predistribution outside basis is allocated between the distributed asset and her continuing interest in the partnership. Note, though, that a distribution of appreciated property can also trigger recognition of income under §737 if the distributee-partner contributed appreciated property in the past.

How does a distribution of property affect the partnership capital accounts? Consistent with the treatment of booking-in contributed property at fair market value, Treas. Regs. §1.704-1(b)(2)(iv)(e)(1) provides:

> [A] partner's capital account [must] be decreased by the fair market value of property distributed by the partnership . . . to such partner. . . . To satisfy this requirement, the capital accounts of the partners first must be adjusted to reflect the manner in which the unrealized income, gain, loss and deduction inherent in such property (that has not been reflected in the capital accounts previously) would be allocated among the partners if there were a taxable disposition of such property . . . on the date of distribution.

For example, suppose P and Q are equal partners in the PQ partnership, each having a capital account and outside basis of $8,000. Assume that Blackacre is distributed to P when Blackacre has an adjusted basis and book value in the hands of the partnership of $6,000 and a current fair market value of $16,000. Assume further that the partners have agreed to allocate gain from the disposition of Blackacre 60 percent to P and 40 percent to Q. The effect of the distribution on the partners' capital accounts is:

P	Q	
$ 8,000	$ 8,000	Initial balance
6,000	4,000	Unrealized book appreciation in Blackacre
(16,000)	0	Fair market value of Blackacre
($ 2,000)	$12,000	Totals

i.   Predistribution Book/Tax Disparities

Whenever a distributed asset is revalued incident to a distribution, it is the unrealized *book* gain or loss and not the unrealized *tax* gain or loss that must be allocated among the partners. Treas. Regs. §1.704-1(b)(2)(iv)(e). For example, suppose X and Y form the XY general partnership by X contributing cash of $10,000 and Y contributing nondepreciable property with adjusted basis of $7,000 and fair market value of $10,000. X and Y agree to allocate all gain and loss equally except as otherwise required under §704(c). If the property contributed by Y is subsequently distributed to X when it has a fair market value of $12,000 (and ignoring the impact of §704(c)(1)(B)), the capital accounts will be:

X	Y	
$10,000	$10,000	Initial contributions
1,000	1,000	Book unrealized appreciation
(12,000)	0	Fair market value of property
($ 1,000)	$11,000	Totals

By allocating only the book unrealized appreciation between X and Y as a consequence of the distribution, we thereby ensure that the precontribution tax unrealized appreciation is not entered into the capital accounts twice: When the property was booked in at $10,000, Y's capital account was thereby credited with the $3,000 of tax precontribution appreciation. Accordingly, on the distribution we adjust the partners' capital accounts by the amount that their capital accounts would be adjusted had the property been sold for fair market value; that is, we adjust the capital accounts for any *book* unrealized appreciation or loss in the distributed property.

ii. Book/Tax Disparity Caused by Asset Revaluation

Reconsider the PQ example from page 752 above. In that example, a capital asset having an adjusted basis and book value of $6,000 and fair market value of $16,000 was distributed to P. At the time of the distribution, each partner had a capital account and outside basis of $8,000, and the partners agreed to allocate gain from disposition of the distributed property 60 percent to P and 40 percent to Q. As a result of the distribution, the partnership's books become:

	P		Q	
CA	*OB*	*CA*	*OB*	
$ 8,000	$8,000	$ 8,000	$8,000	Formation
6,000	0	4,000	0	Revaluation of asset
(16,000)	(6,000)	0	0	Distribution
($ 2,000)	$2,000	$12,000	$8,000	Totals

Does this result create a book/tax disparity for any of the partners? Consider first the nondistributee partner, Q. As a result of the distribution, Q's capital account is booked up by Q's share of the unrealized appreciation in Blackacre. However, the distribution works no change to Q's outside basis. Accordingly, the distribution *does* create a book/tax disparity for the nondistributee partner (unless all unrealized appreciation in the distributed asset is allocated to the distributee partner).

And what of the distributee partner? The effect of the distribution on the distributee partner's capital account is twofold: There is an increase for the partner's share of the unrealized appreciation in the distributed asset and a decrease for the fair market value of the asset. Outside basis will, in general, be reduced by the partnership's predistribution adjusted basis in the asset. Only if the distributee partner is allocated the entire unrealized gain or loss in the asset will the capital asset adjustments offset; otherwise, a book tax/tax disparity will be created for the distributee partner.

To see this, reconsider partner P above. P's capital account is reduced from $8,000 to negative $2,000 by reason of the distribution, for a net reduction of $10,000. P's outside basis, though, is reduced only from $8,000 to positive $2,000 under §733(2), so that the outside basis reduction is but $6,000, or $4,000 less than P's capital account reduction. Q also has a $4,000 book/tax disparity because the distribution to P increases Q's capital account by $4,000 yet leaves Q's outside basis unchanged.

Suppose, though, that the partners had agreed that all the gain from disposition of the distributed asset was allocable to P. Now the distribution has no capital account *or* outside basis effect on Q. P, on the other hand, sees her capital account and outside basis decrease from $8,000 to positive $2,000, so that there is no book/tax disparity to P or to Q as a result of the distributions. What this boils down to is the following: Distribution of an appreciated or loss asset will create a book/tax disparity for both the distributee and nondistributee partners in equal but opposite amounts if any of the unrealized appreciation or loss in the distributed property is allocable to the nondistributee partner. There is no net partnership book/ tax disparity by reason of the distribution — the partners' book/tax dispari- ties cancel each other out so that aggregate capital accounts continue to equal aggregate outside bases — but there is a book/tax disparity for each of the partners allocated some of the book unrealized appreciation in the distributed asset.

iii. Book/Tax Disparity Caused by Insufficient Outside Basis

The book/tax disparities caused by revaluations of distributed assets, like all book/tax disparities caused by revaluation of partnership assets, must under §704(b) be addressed in accordance with §704(c)(1)(A) prin- ciples. Treas. Regs. §1.704-1(b)(2)(iv)(g). However, some distributions of property can cause book/tax disparities unrelated to revaluations of partnership assets, and these book/tax disparities are permanent and can- not be cured by application of §704(c)(1)(A) principles.

Consider the distribution of an asset having adjusted basis, book value, and fair market value of $10,000 to a partner having an outside basis of only $8,000. This distribution is tax-free under §731(a)(1), and under §732(a)(2), the distributee partner takes a basis in the distributed asset of $8,000. Finally, under §733(2), the distributee partner's outside basis is reduced to $0.

This distribution causes a book/tax disparity for the distributee part- ner because the outside basis reduction of $8,000 is not equal to the capital account reduction of $10,000. As when cash is distributed in an amount sufficient to trigger recognition of income, see §731(a)(1), the distribution of property with inside basis sufficiently high to implicate the basis limita- tion in §732(a)(a) causes a book/tax disparity that cannot be eliminated with curative or remedial allocations because there is no offsetting book/ tax disparity for some other partner.

3. Distributions of Encumbered Property

When encumbered property is distributed by a partnership, the debt allocation rules of §752 are triggered. As to the nondistributee partners, the
effect is a constructive distribution equal to the share of debt eliminated.
As to the distributee-partner, though, the effect of the debt is twofold:
The distributee loses her share of the debt *qua* partner but acquires the
entire debt as an individual. These two effects are netted to produce a
single, net increase in share of debt. See Treas. Regs. §1.752-1(f); Rev.
Rul. 79-205, 1979-2 C.B. 255.

Revenue Ruling 79-205 _____
1979-2 C.B. 255

. . . FACTS

A and *B* are general partners in *M*, a general partnership, which was formed
for the purposes of owning and operating shopping centers.

On December 31, 1977, *M* made nonliquidating distributions in a
single transaction of a portion of its property to *A* and *B*. *A* and *B* are
equal partners in *M*. *M*, *A* and *B* are calendar year taxpayers. No assets of
the type described in section 751(a) of the Internal Revenue Code of 1954
were distributed by *M* to either *A* or *B*.

Immediately prior to the distribution *A* had an adjusted basis for *A*'s
interest in M of 1,000*x* dollars, and *B* had an adjusted basis for *B*'s interest
in M of 1,500*x* dollars. The property distributed to *A* had an adjusted basis
to *M* of 2,000*x* dollars, and was subject to liabilities of 1,600*x* dollars. The
property distributed to *B* had an adjusted basis to *M* of 3,200*x* dollars and
was subject to liabilities of 2,800*x* dollars. *A*'s individual liabilities increased
by 1,600*x* dollars by reason of the distribution to *A*. *B*'s individual liabilities
increased by 2,800*x* dollars by reason of the distribution to *B*. *A*'s share
and *B*'s share of the liabilities of M each decreased by 2,200*x* dollars (1/2
of 1,600*x* + 1/2 of 2,800*x* dollars) by reason of the distributions. The basis
and fair market value of the properties distributed were greater than the
liabilities to which they were subject.

LAW

Section 705(a) of the Code provides, in part, that the adjusted basis of a
partner's interest in a partnership shall be the basis of such interest determined under section 722 decreased (but not below zero) by partnership
distributions as provided in section 733.

Section 722 of the Code provides, in part, that the basis of a partnership interest acquired by a contribution of money shall be the amount of such money.

Section 731(a)(1) of the Code provides that in the case of a distribution by a partnership to a partner gain shall not be recognized to such partner, except to the extent that any money distributed exceeds the adjusted basis of such partner's interest in the partnership immediately before the distribution.

Section 732(a)(1) of the Code provides that the basis of property (other than money) distributed by a partnership to a partner other than in liquidation of the partner's interest shall, except as provided in section 732(a)(2), be its adjusted basis to the partnership immediately before such distribution.

Section 732(a)(2) of the Code provides that the basis to the distributee partner of property to which section 732(a)(1) is applicable shall not exceed the adjusted basis of such partner's interest in the partnership reduced by any money distributed in the same transaction.

Section 733 of the Code provides that in the case of a distribution by a partnership to a partner other than in liquidation of a partner's interest, the adjusted basis to such partner of the interest in the partnership shall be reduced (but not below zero) by the amount of any money distributed to such partner and the amount of the basis to such partner of distributed property other than money, as determined under section 732.

Section 752(a) of the Code provides that any increase in a partner's share of the liabilities of a partnership, or any increase in a partner's individual liabilities by reason of the assumption by such partner of partnership liabilities, shall be considered as a contribution of money by such partner to the partnership.

Section 752(b) of the Code provides that any decrease in a partner's share of the liabilities of a partnership, or any decrease in a partner's individual liabilities by reason of the assumption by the partnership of such individual liabilities, shall be considered as a distribution of money to the partner by the partnership.

Section 752(c) of the Code provides that for purposes of section 752 a liability to which property is subject shall, to the extent of the fair market value of such property, be considered as a liability of the owner of the property.

ANALYSIS AND HOLDING

In general, partnership distributions are taxable under section 731(a)(1) of the Code only to the extent that the amount of money distributed exceeds the distributee partner's basis for the partner's partnership interest. This rule reflects the Congressional intent to limit narrowly the area in which gain or loss is recognized upon a distribution so as to remove deterrents to property being moved in and out of partnerships as business reasons dictate. See S. Rep. No. 1622, 83rd Cong., 2nd Sess., page 96 (1954). Here, since partner liabilities are both increasing and decreasing in the same transaction offsetting the increases and decreases tends to limit recognition of gain, thereby giving effect to the Congressional intent. Consequently, in a distribution of encumbered property, the resulting liability adjustments will be treated as occurring simultaneously, rather than occurring in a particular order. Therefore, on a distribution of encumbered property, the amount of money considered distributed to a partner for purposes of section 731(a)(1) is the amount (if any) by which the decrease in the partner's share of the liabilities of the partnership under section 752(b) exceeds the increase in the partner's individual liabilities under section 752(a). The amount of money considered contributed by a partner for purposes of section 722 is the amount (if any) by which the increase in the partner's individual liabilities under section 752(a) exceeds the decrease in the partner's share of the liabilities of the partnership under section 752(b). The increase in the partner's individual liabilities occurs by reason of the assumption by the partner of partnership liabilities, or by reason of a distribution of property subject to a liability, to the extent of the fair market value of such property.

Because the distribution was part of a single transaction, the two properties are treated as having been distributed simultaneously to A and B. Therefore, all resulting liability adjustments relating to the distribution of the two properties will be treated as occurring simultaneously, rather than occurring in a particular order.

TREATMENT OF PARTNER A

A will be deemed to have received a net distribution of 600x dollars in money, that is, the amount by which the amount of money considered distributed to A (2,200x dollars) exceeds the amount of money considered contributed by A (1,600x dollars). Since 600x dollars does not exceed A's basis for A's interest in M immediately before the distribution (1,000x dollars), no gain is recognized to A.

Under section 732(a) of the Code, the basis of A of the property distributed to A is the lesser of (i) the adjusted basis of the property to the partnership (2,000x dollars), or (ii) the adjusted basis of A's partnership interest (1,000x dollars) reduced by the amount of money deemed distributed to A (600x dollars). Therefore, the basis of the property in A's hands is 400x dollars. Under section 733, the adjusted basis of A's partnership interest (1,000x dollars) is reduced by the amount of money deemed distributed to A (600x dollars) and by the basis to A of the distributed property (400x dollars). The adjusted basis of A's partnership interest is therefore reduced to zero.

TREATMENT OF PARTNER B

B will be deemed to have made a net contribution of $600x$ dollars, that is, the amount by which the amount of money considered contributed by B ($2,800x$ dollars) exceeds the amount of money considered distributed to B ($2,200x$ dollars). In applying sections 732(a) and 733 of the Code to B, the adjustment to B's basis in B's partnership interest attributable to the liability adjustments resulting from the distributions will be treated as occurring first, and the distribution of property to B as occurring second. By so doing, B's basis for the distributed property is increased and B's basis in B's partnership interest is decreased. This allocation gives greater effect to the general rule of section 732(a)(1), which provides for the partner to have the same basis in distributed property as the partnership had for that property.

Therefore, the first step is that B's basis for B's partnership interest ($1,500x$ dollars) is increased under sections 722 and 705(a) by the amount of the net contribution deemed made by B ($600x$ dollars), and is equal to $2,100x$ dollars. Next, under section 732(a) of the Code, the basis to B of the property distributed to B is the lesser of (i) the adjusted basis of the property to the partnership ($3,200x$ dollars), or (ii) the adjusted basis of B's partnership interest ($2,100x$ dollars) reduced by the amount of money deemed distributed to B (zero). Therefore, the basis of the property in B's hands is $2,100x$ dollars. Under section 733, the adjusted basis of B's partnership interest ($2,100x$ dollars) is reduced by the amount of money deemed distributed to B (zero) and by the basis to B of the distributed property ($2,100x$ dollars). The adjusted basis of B's partnership interest is therefore zero.

To make certain you understand this Revenue Ruling, consider the following example. Suppose K and L are equal members of the KL partnership, with each partner having a capital account of $10,000 and an outside basis of $13,000. Assume that the partnership has cash of $18,000 and Whiteacre with adjusted basis and fair market value of $8,000, subject to a debt of $6,000. What are the tax effects to K and to L if Whiteacre is distributed to K?

First, there is a change in partnership debt under §752. Prior to the distribution, each partner shared one-half of the partnership's $6,000 debt. After the distribution, the partnership debt is gone. However, the debt is now entirely allocable to K because K now owns the encumbered property. See §§752(a), 752(c). Accordingly, the distribution reduces L's share of the liability from $3,000 to $0 and increases K's share of the liability from $3,000 to $6,000. Applying §752(b) to L and §752(a) to K, we see that the effect of the liability shift is to decrease L's outside basis by $3,000 (under

§733(1)) and to increase *K*'s outside basis by the same amount (under §722). Of course, these changes in shares of partnership liabilities have no effect on the partners' capital accounts.

Second, there are the rules of §§731-733 with which to contend. Because this is a nonliquidating distribution of property, no gain or loss is recognized. §731(a). *K* takes the property with a carryover basis of $8,000, §732(a)(1), and reduces her outside basis by the same amount, §733(2). Third, *K* reduces her capital account by the $2,000 fair market value of the property distributed net of liabilities. Treas. Regs. §1.704-1(b)(2)(iv)(b). To summarize:

K		L		
CA	OB	CA	OB	
$10,000	$13,000	$10,000	$13,000	Start
0	3,000	0	(3,000)	§752
0	(8,000)	0	0	§733(2)
(2,000)	0	0	0	Net distribution
$ 8,000	$ 8,000	$10,000	$10,000	Ending balances

The distribution of Whiteacre was tax-free, and the hallmark of a tax-free transaction is a carryover of basis without increase or reduction. Prior to the distribution, *K* and *L* each had outside bases of $13,000, for a total outside basis of $26,000. After the transaction, *K* has an outside basis of $8,000 and *L* has an outside basis of $10,000, for a total outside basis of $18,000. In addition, *K* now owns Whiteacre with a basis of $8,000 under §732(a)(1), so that total basis after the distribution is $26,000, the same as before the distribution.

As a second check, look at the partners' capital accounts. Prior to the distribution, each partner had a capital account of $10,000. The effect of the distribution is to give *K* $2,000 in value, so that *K*'s capital account should be reduced by $2,000 and *L*'s capital account should remain unchanged. And that is precisely how the ending capital account balances read.

PROBLEMS

22-1. *A*'s outside basis and capital account is $22,000 prior to receiving a nonliquidating distribution consisting of the following:

	Adjusted Basis	Fair Market Value
Cash	$ 2,000	$ 2,000
Receivables	0	6,000
Inventory	2,000	5,000
Capital Asset 1	8,000	7,000
Capital Asset 2	14,000	21,000

Assuming §751 does not apply to this transaction, what are the tax consequences to *A* and what basis does *A* take in each of the distributed assets? If *A* had a one-third interest in the profits and losses of the partnership, what effect should this distribution have on A's capital account assuming that each distributed asset has book value equal to inside basis? To what extent does this distribution create a book/tax disparity for *A*? Of that book/tax disparity, how much should be addressed by resort to §704(c) principles and how much is permanent and so cannot be eliminated by curative or remedial allocations?

22-2. The *ABC* partnership owns ordinary income asset *X* and capital assets *Y* and *Z* with adjusted bases and fair market values as indicated:

	Adjusted Basis	Book Value	Fair Market Value
X	$10,000	$10,000	$30,000
Y	10,000	10,000	18,000
Z	25,000	25,000	15,000

C, a one-third partner, has an outside basis and capital account of $15,000. Assuming that §751 does not apply to the following distributions, what are the tax consequences to *C* if (a) she receives asset *X* in a nonliquidating distribution; (b) she receives asset *Z* in a nonliquidating distribution; or (c) she receives asset *Z,* subject to the partnership's only debt (fully recourse) of $6,000, assuming *C*'s capital account immediately prior to the distribution was $13,000 and *C*'s share of the debt was $2,000?

4. Distribution of Marketable Securities

Under §731(c)(1), a distribution of marketable securities may be taxed as a distribution of cash rather than as a distribution of property, with the result that gain will be recognized if the value of the securities (plus any cash actually distributed) exceeds the distributee's predistribution outside basis. See §731(a)(1). The term "marketable securities" in this context includes stocks, bonds, other financial instruments broadly defined, §731(c)(2)(C), and other property whose value is determined by such securities, see §731(c)(2)(B), but only if such securities are actively traded, §731(c)(2)(A). However, even such marketable securities generally will be treated as property if they were previously contributed to the partnership by the distributee partner. §732(c)(3)(A)(i).

The marketable securities treated as cash rather than as property are reduced by the excess, if any, of the distributee partner's distributive share of the unrealized appreciation in all marketable securities held by the partnership immediately prior to the distribution over the distributee partner's share of the unrealized appreciation in the marketable securities held by the partnership immediately after the distribution. §731(c)(3)(B).

Thus, the greater the unrealized appreciation in the securities distributed, the less such securities will be treated as cash rather than as property. This rule reflects the recognition that appreciated securities are less like cash substitutes and more like other property. Note that for §731(c)(3)(B) to apply, all marketable securities held by the partnership are treated as being of the same class and issuer. Treas. Regs. §1.731-2(b)(1).

Despite treating the securities as cash for purposes of recognition of income, they are treated as property for determining basis. Accordingly, the basis to the distributee of any marketable securities taxed as cash under §731(c) is determined under §732, increased by any gain recognized by the distributee by reason of treating the securities as cash. §731(c)(4). And the distributee's outside basis is adjusted under §733 as if no gain were recognized on the distribution. §731(c)(5).

These rules do not apply to most distributions from investment partnerships as defined in §731(c)(3)(C). See §§731(c)(3)(A)(iii), 731(c)(3)(C)(iii). However, when these rules do apply, the marketable securities are taken into account at their fair market values. §731(c)(1)(B). A distribution of marketable securities can trigger taxation under §§731(c), 704(c)(1)(B), and 737. For ordering rules, see Treas. Regs. §1.731-2(g).

5. Disposition of Distributed Assets

Suppose individual X is a partner in the P partnership. The P partnership is a dealer in real estate and distributes Purpleacre, a piece of its real estate inventory, to X. Assume that X's basis in Purpleacre becomes $10,000 under §732(a)(1). If X subsequently sells Purpleacre for $15,000, what are the tax consequences to X?

Under §1001(a), X realizes a gain of $5,000. Assuming no nonrecognition provision applies, X must recognize (i.e., report) this amount. But is it reportable as capital gain or ordinary income? Assuming that X is not a dealer in real estate, you would expect that the gain would be capital. However, that may not be the case.

As a general principle, the character of gain from the disposition of distributed property is determined by reference to the use of the property in the hands of the distributee. Because X is not a dealer in real estate, application of this principle means that X's income of $5,000 would be capital gain. However, §735(a) provides that ordinary income assets of the partnership will produce ordinary income (or loss) to the distributee partner regardless of other considerations. Thus, X's gain might be ordinary income by virtue of §735(a)(2).

The ordinary income assets of a partnership are divided into two groups: "unrealized receivables" and "inventory items." Although we will defer examining the definitions of unrealized receivables and inventory items until later, for now it suffices to think of unrealized receivables as including earned but uncollected fees for services and dispositions of noncapital assets, but only if the partnership uses the cash receipts and disbursements method of accounting. Inventory, for the most part, means those noncapital assets of the partnership described in §1221(1). Note, though, that some partnership assets can be both unrealized receivables *and* inventory items. See §751(d)(2)(B).

Section 735 treats unrealized receivables and inventory items differently. The ordinary income taint of §735(a) lasts forever as to unrealized receivables but only for five years as to inventory. Accordingly, distributed inventory can qualify for capital gain treatment if held by the distributee partner for more than five years. Of course, if the distributed inventory is not a capital asset in the hands of the distributee partner (e.g., if it is also inventory within the meaning of §1221(1) as to the distributee partner), then the §735(a) taint is redundant and disposition of the inventory will produce ordinary income to the distributee partner whenever sold. Finally, assets that are both unrealized receivables and inventory items will keep the §735(a) taint forever by the simultaneous application of §735(a)(1) and (2).

The operation of §735(a) can be summarized as follows: Property distributed by a partnership to a partner will produce ordinary income or loss upon disposition by the distributee partner if (1) the property is not a capital asset (or §1231 asset) in the hands of the distributee partner, (2) the property was an unrealized receivable to the partnership, or (3) the property was inventory to the partnership and the distributee partner sold or exchanged the property within five years of the distribution.

PROBLEMS

22-3. The *P* partnership distributes assets to *X* in a nonliquidating distribution. Prior to the distribution, the assets have an adjusted basis to the partnership of $12,000 and a fair market value of $15,000. At the time of the distribution, *X*'s outside basis equals $12,000. What are the tax consequences to *X* if she sells the assets

    a.   for $20,000 three years later, and the assets were inventory to the partnership and are capital assets to her?

    b.   for $20,000 three years later, and the assets were capital assets to the partnership and are inventory to her?

    c.   for $10,000 three years later, and the assets were inventory to the partnership and are capital assets to her?

    d.   for $20,000 three years later, and the assets were unrealized receivables to the partnership and are capital assets to her?

B.   Distributions Subject to §751(b)

Under §751(b), distributions that rearrange the partners' interests in ordinary income assets may be taxed as a sale or exchange between the distributee-partner and the partnership. As a result, either the partner or the partnership may recognize gain on the recharacterized transaction. Technically, §751(b) is triggered by a distribution that shifts interests in those ordinary income assets of the partnership falling within the definitions of "unrealized receivables" and "substantially appreciated inventory." Thus, before looking at the operation of §751(b), we need to consider the terms "unrealized receivables" and "substantially appreciated inventory." Note that cash is not §751 property. Treas. Regs. §1.751-1(e).

1.   The Definition of Unrealized Receivables

The term "unrealized receivables" includes a variety of ordinary income assets including (but not limited to) uncollected receivables of a cash-method partnership for services performed or to be performed and dispositions of inventory and other noncapital assets. In addition, the second and third sentences of §751(c) have grown as Congress has carved more exceptions to the general definition of a capital asset in §1221. In particular, disposition of some assets — notably depreciable property subject to depreciation recapture under §§1245 or 1250 and market discount bonds as defined in §1278 — produce both capital gain and ordinary income, and the definition of unrealized receivables includes the ordinary income component of such assets. A partnership's unrealized receivables often are called its "hot assets," but as to these part capital, part noncapital assets, only the noncapital part constitutes a hot asset.

   For example, suppose a partnership owns some depreciable equipment. Assume that the partnership has an adjusted basis in equipment of $10,000, that the fair market value of the equipment is $60,000, and that the equipment is subject to depreciation recapture under §1245 of $15,000. Because the equipment is §1231 property, it is not (in general) §751 property. However, the depreciation recapture is included within the definition of unrealized receivables in §751(c). Accordingly, the equipment is treated as if it were two assets: Non-§751 property with adjusted basis of $10,000 and fair market value of $45,000 as well as an unrealized receivable with adjusted basis of $0 and fair market value of $15,000.

   Because of this expansive definition of the term "unrealized receivables," even accrual method partnerships can have §751(c) hot assets. Such partnerships will not have unrealized receivables in the common sense — because the partnership accrues its items of income as well as of expense, its business receivables should all be realized despite any lack of collection — but they can easily have *unaccrued* contract rights for services to be performed and goods to be delivered as well as the various ordinary income assets (and parts of assets) listed in the final sentences of §751(c).

2.   *The Definition of Substantially Appreciated Inventory*

The ordinary income partnership assets to which §751(b) speaks include not only unrealized receivables but also "substantially appreciated inventory." As provided in §751(b)(3), the determination whether a partnership's inventory is "substantially appreciated" is made by looking at the inventory as a whole. If the inventory as a whole meets the definition of substantial appreciation, every item of the inventory is treated as substantially appreciated. On the other hand, if the inventory as a whole does not qualify as substantially appreciated, then no item of inventory is substantially appreciated. In particular, you *cannot* determine whether one item of the partnership's inventory is substantially appreciated without looking at the inventory as a group.

a.   Partnership Inventory Items

The definition of inventory items in §751(d) includes not only what you would expect to be there (inventory as defined in §1221(1)) but also "any other property of the partnership which, on sale or exchange by the partnership, would be considered property other than a capital asset and other than property described in §1231." This definition seems all encompassing even to the point of swallowing up the unrealized receivables defined in §751(c). Could Congress really have intended that "inventory" be defined so broadly?

The regulations explicitly provide that inventory items include all unrealized receivables, Treas. Regs. §1.751-1(d)(2)(ii), as well as all realized receivables, *see* Treas. Regs. §1.751-1(g)(ex. 2(b)). Despite this reading of §751(d), not all of a partnership's hot assets under §751(c) constitute inventory. For example, a capital asset subject to depreciation recapture under §1245 should not constitute inventory because the asset will produce capital gain (albeit not only capital gain) on disposition. Presumably all unrealized receivables within the definition of §751(c) having both capital gain and ordinary income parts fall without even the most expansive definition of partnership inventory. Accordingly, it must be the case that "unrealized receivables" as used in the definition of "inventory" means "receivables" in the common, nontechnical sense.

b.   Substantial Appreciation

A partnership's inventory items are "substantially appreciated" if the inventory's aggregate fair market value exceeds 120 percent of its aggregate adjusted basis. Because this test applies only to the inventory as a whole, either all inventory items will be treated as "substantially appreciated" or none of them will be. If the inventory is "substantially appreciated," then it will constitute §751 property along with the unrealized receivables (if any); if the inventory is not "substantially appreciated," then the inventory items are not §751 property except for those inventory items which also happen to be unrealized receivables.

For example, consider the *P* partnership owning the following assets:

	Adjusted Basis	Fair Market Value
Cash	$60,000	$60,000
Receivables	0	30,000
Inventory	15,000	21,000
Land	30,000	45,000

The fair market value of the inventory items (which includes the unrealized receivables) is $51,000 while the adjusted basis of the inventory items is $15,000. Because 120 percent of this adjusted basis figure is $18,000, the inventory items pass the appreciation test and so the partnership's inventory items are "substantially appreciated" within the meaning of §751(d). Thus, both the "inventory" and the "receivables" are §751 property.

Now reconsider this example but assume that the partnership uses an accrual method of accounting so that its receivables are realized:

	Adjusted Basis	Fair Market Value
Cash	$60,000	$60,000
Receivables	30,000	30,000
Inventory	15,000	21,000
Land	30,000	45,000

Now that the receivables are realized, the aggregate basis of the partnership's inventory items (again including the receivables) is $45,000, and 120 percent of this amount is $54,000. The aggregate fair market value of the inventory items is only $51,000, so that the inventory items fail the appreciation test of §751(d)(1)(A) and are not considered to be substantially appreciated. Of course, the receivables also are *not* §751 property because they are fully realized.

Note that the inventory alone (that is, without the receivables) *would* satisfy the substantial appreciation test. The effect of including the partnership's receivables in this case is thus to allow the partnership to avoid characterizing its inventory as substantially appreciated. We can make the following generalization about including a partnership's receivables in the definition of inventory items: if unrealized, the receivables will make satisfaction of the appreciation test more likely, while if realized, the receivables will make satisfaction of the appreciation test less likely.

It is worthwhile making the following point explicit: Even if a partnership's inventory items are not substantially appreciated, the partnership's *unrealized* receivables are subject to §751(b) including those receivables classified as inventory items under the broad definition of that term in §751(d). That is, a partnership asset is classified as §751 property if it falls within the definition of an unrealized receivable or an inventory item (or both).

3. Operation of §751(b)

Section 751(b) applies only to those distributions that rearrange the partners' shares of §751 property. To determine whether a distribution has this effect, we compare the distributee partner's predistribution interest in §751 and non-§751 property with her interests postdistribution. Prior to distribution, the partner's interest in each class of property is determined by multiplying the amount of each class of property owned by the partnership times the partner's interest in the property. After distribution, however, the partner's interest in each class of property is composed of two elements: (1) the partner's share of the partnership's property and (2) whatever property was actually distributed.

For example, assume that partner *C* agrees to reduce her interest in the *ABC* partnership from one-third to one-fifth in exchange for a distribution of $6,500 in cash and $4,000 of receivables. Prior to the distribution, the partnership books stand as follows:

Assets

	Adjusted Basis	Fair Market Value
Cash	$15,000	$15,000
Receivables	0	39,000
Land	9,000	9,000

Liabilities and Capital

	Adjusted Basis	Fair Market Value
A	$8,000	$21,000
B	8,000	21,000
C	8,000	21,000

Before the distribution, *C*'s share of the §751 property was worth $13,000 (one-third of the value of the receivables), and her share of the non-§751 property was worth $8,000 (one-third of the cash and land). After the distribution, *C*'s shares of the §751 and non-§751 property each consist of two components: Her share *received in the distribution* and her share *as a continuing partner*. *C*'s postdistribution share of the §751 property includes $4,000 received in the distribution and $7,000 as a continuing partner (one-fifth of $35,000), for a total of $11,000. Similarly, C's postdistribution share of the non-§751 property includes $6,500 received in the distribution plus $3,500 as a continuing partner (one-fifth of $17,500).

The effect of the distribution is to reduce C's interest in §751 property by $2,000 (from $13,000 to $11,000), and C's share of the non-§751 property increases by the same amount (from $8,000 to $10,000). Accordingly, the distribution has the effect of rearranging the partners' interests in §751 property, and so the distribution is subject to the recharacterization rules of §751(b).

In applying §751(b) to this or any other distribution, keep in mind that §751(b) recharacterizes but does not directly tax the distribution. That is, operation of §751(b) requires that we tax the distribution as if other transactions occurred. In taxing these hypothetical transactions, we apply familiar rules (such as §§731-733) without modification.

The recharacterization under §751(b) consists of three steps. First, we construct a hypothetical distribution of the property that was not, but proportionately should have been, actually distributed. This hypothetical distribution is subject to the usual §§731-733 distribution provisions. In this first example, the effect of the *actual* distribution is to reduce C's interest in §751 property by $2,000, and so the *hypothetical* distribution consists of $2,000 of receivables. Had the distribution had the effect of increasing C's interest in §751 property, the hypothetical distribution would consist of non-§751 property.

Second, this hypothetically distributed property is deemed sold back to the partnership for the excess property that was, but proportionately should not have been, actually distributed. In this case, that means that C is treated as selling the $2,000 worth of receivables back to the partnership in exchange for $2,000 cash. The partnership is treated as buying these receivables for $2,000 cash, which will have basis consequences for the partnership. Third, the remainder of the property actually distributed is taxed under the usual distribution rules of §§731-733. Here, that remainder consists of cash of $4,500 as well as $4,000 of receivables.

Actually working though the details, we first treat C as receiving a distribution of $2,000 worth of receivables. Under §731, C does not recognize any gain or loss. Under §732(a), C takes a zero carryover basis in the receivables, and under §733(2) C's outside basis remains at $8,000 as a result of this hypothetical distribution.

Step two is the hypothetical sale of these receivables back to the partnership. Under §1001, C recognizes a gain on this sale, taxable as ordinary income under §735(a). The partnership's basis in these receivables is its $2,000 cost under §1012. This hypothetical sale restores all the receivables to the partnership with an increased basis of $2,000.

Step three consists of a distribution of cash of $4,500 plus receivables of $4,000. Under §§731-733, this distribution is tax-free to C and causes C to reduce her outside basis by the amount of the cash received and by the partnership's zero basis in the distributed receivables. Accordingly, *C*'s postdistribution outside basis is $3,500. The final partnership books read:

Assets

	Adjusted Basis	Fair Market Value
Cash	$8,500	$ 8,500
Receivables	2,000	35,000
Land	9,000	9,000

Liabilities and Capital

	Adjusted Basis	Fair Market Value
A	$8,000	$21,000
B	8,000	21,000
C	3,500	10,500

Here is one more example. Once again assume that *C* agrees to reduce her partnership share from one-third to one-fifth in exchange for a distribution of $6,500 in cash plus $4,000 of receivables. However, assume that the predistribution partnership books read:

Assets

	Adjusted Basis	Fair Market Value
Cash	$15,000	$15,000
Land	9,000	9,000
Receivables	0	9,000
Inventory	21,000	30,000

Liabilities and Capital

	Adjusted Basis	Fair Market Value
A	$15,000	$21,000
B	15,000	21,000
C	15,000	21,000

As before, the effect of the hypothetical distribution is to reduce *C*'s interest in §751 property by $2,000 (from $13,000 down to $11,000). Accordingly, step 1 does not change: *C* is deemed to have received $2,000 of §751 property. Here, though, this hypothetical distribution could consist of receivables, inventory, or a combination of both. Does it matter what we choose?

Yes. Remember that step 2 consists of a deemed sale of the hypothetically distributed property back to the partnership. If we assume that *C* receives $2,000 of receivables as before, then *C* will again recognize $2,000 of income in step 2. However, if we assume that the hypothetical distribution consists of $2,000 of inventory, then *C*'s income in step 2 will equal $2,000 less the partnership's basis in that inventory. For example, if the $2,000 of inventory has an adjusted basis to the partnership of $1,400, the deemed distribution in step 1 will reduce *C*'s outside basis by $1,400 (to

$13,600) under §733(2), and C will take a $1,400 basis in that property under §732(a). Then when C is deemed to sell this inventory back to the partnership, C will recognize only $600 of income.

How should we decide which property is hypothetically distributed to C? Surely not by looking to the substance of the transaction, for there is no substance: The distribution is fictional. To avoid manipulation by the partners, we might assume a proportionate amount of all §751 property is distributed to C. The regulations seem to adopt this approach, although they also suggest that this allocation can be modified by agreement of the partners. See Treas. Regs. §§1.751-1(g)(example 3 (c)); 1.751-1(g)(example 5(c)).

To finish this example, assume that the hypothetical distribution consists of $2,000 worth of partnership inventory. The partnership's inventory has an adjusted basis equal to 70 percent of fair market value. Assuming this proportion holds true for each item of inventory separately, the $2,000 worth of inventory deemed distributed to C has an adjusted basis to the partnership of $1,400. Accordingly, the effect of the hypothetical distribution to C is a reduction in C's outside basis by $1,400 down to $13,600. In addition, the partnership now owns only $37,000 of inventory with adjusted basis of $19,600.

The $2,000 of inventory hypothetically distributed to C is then deemed sold back to the partnership for $2,000 of the cash actually distributed. As a result, C recognizes a gain of $600, ordinary under §735. In addition, the partnership now regains ownership of the entire $39,000 of inventory, and its adjusted basis in this inventory now equals $21,600.

Finally, the remainder of the actual distribution — $4,500 of cash and receivables worth $4,000 — is deemed distributed to C. Under §731, no gain or loss is recognized by C. C takes a carryover zero basis in the receivables, §732(a)(1), and C reduces her outside basis by that zero amount, §733(2), as well as by the $4,500 cash, §733(1). Accordingly, C's outside basis ends up at $9,100.

Section 751(b) can apply to §752(b) deemed distributions. For example, suppose the ABC partnership owns capital assets worth $147 and an unrealized receivable worth $48. In addition, the partnership has a recourse liability of $120. D is admitted as a one-fourth partner in exchange for a cash contribution of $25. Prior to D's admission, A, B, and C were equal one-third partners.

As a result of the admission of D, each continuing partner's share of the partnership's liability decreases from $40 (one-third of $120) to $30 (one-fourth of $120). Accordingly, each of the continuing partners has a constructive distribution of $10. See §752(b). Similarly, the receivables must now be divided among four partners, so that the continuing partners' shares drop from $16 each to $12 each.

The constructive distribution of $10 to A, B and C would be tax-free under §731(a) so long as their outside bases could absorb the amount of the distribution. However, §731 does not apply to a distribution to the extent that §751(b) covers the transaction. Here, the transaction results in a net reduction of $4 in *A*'s, *B*'s, and *C*'s interest in the partnership's §751 property. Accordingly, $4 of the $10 constructive distribution received by each partner is treated as an exchange for partnership receivables. See Rev. Rul. 84-102, 1984-2 C.B. 119. *A, B,* and *C* will therefore recognize $4 of ordinary income apiece, and the partnership will increase its adjusted basis in its receivables by $12.

This example raises one question. As a result of the admission of *D,* the partnership should revalue its assets (including the receivables) and restate the capital accounts to reflect the fair market value of those assets. Treas. Regs. §§1.704-1(b)(2)(iv)(f)(5)(i); 1.704-3(a)(6). Accordingly, all of the tax unrealized appreciation in the receivables must then be allocated to *A, B,* and *C* under a reverse §704(c) allocation. Does this mean that there is no shift of the receivables to *D?* Although such a conclusion makes sense, the only analysis is contrary. See Rev. Rul. 84-102.

Note that §751(b) does not apply to *D* in this situation because there is no distribution, constructive or otherwise, to the newly admitted partner. Because *D*'s share of the partnership's liabilities increases from $0 to $30, *D* makes a constructive contribution to the partnership under §752(a). In the absence of a distribution to *D,* §751(b) can have no application.

PROBLEMS

22-4. *X* and *Y* are equal partners in the *XY* partnership, each having an outside basis and capital account of $40,000. The books of the partnership are as follows:

Assets

	Adjusted Basis	Fair Market Value
Cash	$60,000	$60,000
Receivables	0	80,000
Inventory	20,000	40,000

Liabilities and Capital

	Adjusted Basis	Fair Market Value
X	$40,000	$90,000
Y	40,000	90,000

X agrees to reduce her interest in the partnership from one-half to one-fourth in exchange for a distribution of $60,000.

    a. What are the tax consequences to *X* and to *XY* if *X* receives $60,000 in cash?

    b. What are the tax consequences to *X* and to *XY* if *X* receives $60,000 in receivables?

 c. What are the tax consequences to X and to XY if X receives $40,000 in inventory and $20,000 in cash?

4. Does §751(b) Make Sense?

Now that you have been introduced to the complexities of §751(b), you should be wondering what justifies its existence. The goal of §751(b) is to ensure that each partner reports her share of the partnership's ordinary income. Note that §751(b) does not speak to any sort of transaction in which ordinary income is transformed into capital gain. Rather, the concern of §751(b) is that too much of the partnership's ordinary income might be reported by one partner and too little by another. Even when the difference between ordinary income and capital gain was great, one must wonder whether this relatively minor concern can support such an enormous structure.

 What is worse, though, is that §751(b) fails to accomplish even its limited goal. Under §751(b), partners' shares of §751 property are determined by reference to the *fair market value* of the §751 property. For example, a distribution that reduces a partner's share of unrealized receivables to zero will not trigger application of §751(b) if the partner's share of the substantially appreciated inventory increases by an equal amount.

 Does this makes sense? Assume that the partner's predistribution share of the unrealized receivables was $50,000, and assume that the partnership's adjusted basis in its inventory is equal to 80 percent of fair market value. If the effect of the distribution is to swap receivables for inventory, then the partner avoids $50,000 of ordinary income (because unrealized receivables have a zero basis) by picking up only $10,000 of income from the inventory (because $50,000 of inventory has an adjusted basis of $40,000). Even though the distribution does not affect the partner's share of the partnership's §751 property, it does affect the partner's share of the partnership's ordinary income.

 The flaw in §751(b) is its focus on the fair market value of the partnership's §751 property rather than on the appreciation in such property. If we want to be certain that the partners do not rearrange their interests in the partnership's ordinary income assets, we should recharacterize as an exchange any distribution that increases or reduces the distributee partner's share of the partnership's ordinary income (fair market value less adjusted basis) rather than the distributee partner's share of the ordinary income assets (just fair market value).

C. DISTRIBUTIONS AND THE DYNAMIC NATURE OF RECOURSE DEBT

We saw in Chapter 4 that the allocation of partnership recourse debt among the partners is dependent on the partners' relative capital accounts.

Thus, anything that affects those capital accounts potentially affects debt sharing. In particular, because distributions described in §731 reduce the distributee partner's capital account, such distributions can rearrange debt sharing among the partners.

Debt reallocation caused by distributions can be surprising in its effects. The following examples all involve distributions of cash from a general partnerships whose only asset consist of cash. No partnership will have any special allocations of income or deduction, and no §704(c) or reverse §704(c) problems will be present. In such circumstances one might expect the tax consequences of distributions to be simple. You be the judge.

Consider first the *PQ* general partnership, in which *P* and *Q* each contribute $30 for a one-half interest in profits and losses. Because capital accounts and outside basis are credited with the amount of cash contributed by the partners to the partnership,[1] each partner's capital account and outside basis equals $30. The partnership then borrows $40 on a fully recourse basis, and under §752(a) this partnership-level borrowing must increase the partners' outside basis dollar for dollar. Thus, aggregate partnership outside basis increases from its preborrowing value of $60 to $100.

The regulations promulgated under §752 provide that this outside basis increase of $40 is apportioned between *P* and *Q* by reference to a hypothetical zero-value sale and liquidation. See Treas. Regs. §1.752-2(b). That is, the partnership is assumed to sell all its assets (including cash) for an assumed fair market value of $0, the losses incurred on this sale are booked into the partners' capital accounts, and then the partnership is liquidated, triggering capital account deficit restoration obligations for all partners having negative capital account balances. The point of this hypothetical sale and liquidation is to determine how the partners have agreed to share the partnership's repayment obligations if the partnership's assets are insufficient to satisfy its debts.

Applying this analysis to the facts of our *PQ* partnership, the zero-value sale produces a book loss of $100 (because both the contributed capital of $60 and the borrowed funds of $40 are assumed to decline in value to $0), allocated equally between P and Q under the terms of the partnership agreement. Thus, the hypothetical zero-value sale produces partnership books reading:

P		Q		
CA	*OB*	*CA*	*OB*	
$30	$30	$30	$30	Initial values
(50)	- - - -	(50)	- - - -	Zero-value sale
($20)	- - - -	($20)	- - - -	Ending values

1. For capital accounts, see Treas. Regs. §1.704-1(b)(2)(iv)(d)(1); for outside basis, see Treas. Regs. §§1.722-1, 1.705-1(a)(2).

Thus, if the partnership were to liquidate at this point, each partner would have an obligation to contribute $20 to the partnership for payment to its lender. Under the §752 regulations, the partnership's debt is allocated between P and Q in the same proportion as these potential contributions would arise, so that the debt is allocated equally between P and Q. That means the partnership books (remembering that the zero-value sale and liquidation were only hypothetical) stand after the borrowing as:

P		Q		
CA	*OB*	*CA*	*OB*	
$30	$50	$30	$50	Postborrowing values

Suppose the partnership now distributes cash of $40 to partner P. The rules of §§731 and 733 are clear: No gain or loss is recognized by P or by Q, and P reduces her outside basis by the $40 distributed. The regulations providing for the maintenance of capital accounts are equally clear that P reduces her capital account by the same $40. Treas. Regs. §1.704-1(b)(2)(iv)(e)(1). Accordingly, application of these rules produces partnership books as follows:

P		Q		
CA	*OB*	*CA*	*OB*	
$30	$50	$30	$50	Current values
(40)	(40)	0	0	Distribution to P
($10)	$10	$30	$50	Ending values

However, we have not yet considered the possibility that the distribution reallocates the partnership's indebtedness between P and Q. Prior to the distribution, the debt was allocated equally between P and Q, or $20 each. To determine how the debt is allocated after the distribution, we again consider the effects of a hypothetical zero-value sale and liquidation.

A zero-value sale produces a book loss of $60 (because of the $100 formerly owned by the partnership, only $60 remains in its hands, the other $40 having been distributed), allocated equally between the partners under the terms of the partnership agreement. Thus, the effect of the zero-value sale is:

P		Q		
CA	*OB*	*CA*	*OB*	
($10)	$10	$30	$50	Current values
(30)	- - - -	(30)	- - - -	Zero-value sale
($40)	- - - -	$ 0	- - - -	Ending values

Because only *P* has a capital account deficit, the entire indebtedness of $40 is now allocated to *P*. That is an increase in *P*'s share of the debt of $20 (from $20 to $40) and a decrease in *Q*'s share of the same amount (from $20 to $0). A $20 increase in *P*'s share of the debt is treated as a contribution of $20 by *P* to the partnership, §752(a); Treas. Regs. §1.752-1(b), increasing *P*'s outside basis (but not her capital account) by that amount. Treas. Regs. §1.704-1(b)(2)(iv)(c). Similarly, the $20 decrease in *Q*'s share of the debt is treated as a distribution of cash to *Q*, §752(b); Treas. Regs. §1.752-1(c), decreasing *Q*'s outside basis (but not her capital account) by the same amount. Treas. Regs. §1.704-1(b)(2)(iv)(c). Thus, the books of the partnership agreement now read as follows:

P		Q		
CA	*OB*	*CA*	*OB*	
($10)	$10	$30	$50	Current values
0	20	0	(20)	Reallocation of debt
($10)	$30	$30	$30	Ending values

This example shows what should be a counter-intuitive result: Even though the distribution was made only to partner *P* in an otherwise perfectly symmetrical partnership, the outside bases of the partners go down together and equally. Put another way, the debt reallocation following a distribution gives extra outside basis to the distributee partner and takes outside basis from the nondistributee partner. The following examples show that these consequences of the debt allocation rules can produce some surprising results.

Reconsider the *PQ* partnership's initial books, with capital accounts of $30 and outside basis of $50 per partner. How much cash can be distributed to one partner without the recognition of income? The rule of §731(a)(1) seems to specify the maximum amount as $50, and indeed that is the most that can be distributed *in a single distribution* without the recognition of income. But suppose we distribute more than that, say $52, to P in two separate distributions of $26 each. After the first distribution but before considering the possibility of a debt reallocation, the partnership books stand as follows:

P		Q		
CA	*OB*	*CA*	*OB*	
$30	$50	$30	$50	Current values
(26)	(26)	(0)	(0)	Distribution
$ 4	$24	$30	$50	Ending values

A zero-value sale will produce a book loss of $74, allocated equally between *P* and *Q* under the partnership agreement. Thus, after the hypothetical zero-value sale the books read:

	P		Q		
CA	*OB*	*CA*	*OB*		
$ 4	$24	$30	$50		Current values
(37)	----	(37)	----		Distribution
($33)	----	($ 7)	----		Ending values

Because the capital account deficits have changed, the debt is reallocated. P's share increases from $20 to $33, for an increase of $13. Q's share of the debt decreases by the same amount, from $20 to $7. Therefore, the actual partnership books following the distribution and taking account of the debt reallocation are:

	P		Q	
CA	*OB*	*CA*	*OB*	
$4	$24	$30	$50	Before debt reallocation
0	13	0	(13)	Debt reallocation
$4	$37	$30	$37	Ending values

It should be clear from these books that the second distribution of $26 to P will not exceed P's predistribution outside basis and therefore will not force P to recognize income. In fact, the effect of the second distribution on the partnership books is:

	P		Q		
CA	*OB*	*CA*	*OB*		
$ 4	$37	$30	$37		Current values
(26)	(26)	0	0		Distribution
0	7	0	(7)		Reallocation of debt
($22)	$18	$30	$30		Ending values

What is the maximum amount that can be distributed to P (in a series of distributions) without the imposition of any tax? Reconsider the starting books of the PQ partnership, and assume that P receives a series of distributions always equal in value to P's predistribution outside basis. Thus, P first receives a distribution of $50, with the following consequences:

	P		Q		
CA	*OB*	*CA*	*OB*		
$30	$50	$30	$50		Current values
(50)	(50)	0	0		Distribution
0	20	0	(20)		Reallocation of debt
($20)	$20	$30	$30		Ending values

Second, P receives a distribution of $20, and because the debt already is allocated entirely to P, this distribution works no reallocation of the debt, so that the partnership's books become:

P		Q		
CA	*OB*	*CA*	*OB*	
($20)	$20	$30	$30	Current values
(20)	(20)	0	0	Distribution
($40)	$ 0	$30	$30	Ending values

By this technique, P was able to receive his initial capital contribution of $30 as well as the entire debt of $40 — that is, a total of $70 — without recognizing income on the distributions. To be sure, a taxpayer who receives a series of distributions may face a Service challenge that the distributions should be taxed as a single transaction, but that is a fight most practitioners are well prepared to handle. Surely, though, no one involved in the drafting of the distributions rules of subchapter K possibly intended that two cash distributions of $50 and $20 should have a different combined tax consequence than a single distribution of $70, all other things being equal. Yet that is precisely the situation under current law. Such a rule represents either a trap for the unwary or an 'abuse for the well-advised and cannot be defended under either interpretation.

If one plays the preceding example backwards, it demonstrates an additional surprise for the ill-advised. Suppose you represent individual P whose capital account is negative 40 and whose outside basis is $0 as set forth in the table above. If P contributes $20 in cash to the partnership, P's capital account and outside basis will increase by the full amount of the cash contribution. But if P were to contribute not $20 but $70, her outside basis will increase only to $50: The $70 P's contributes to the partnership will increase aggregate outside basis by that amount, but only $50 of the increase will be enjoyed by P and the remaining $20 will increase the outside basis of partner Q. Accordingly, one must be very careful before advising a client on the tax consequences of even the simplest contributions to a partnership if there is any outstanding entity-level debt.

For an even more surprising outcome, assume that X, Y, and Z form the XYZ general partnership with X contributing cash of $10 and Y and Z contributing cash of $100. Each partner receives a one-third share of all profits and losses, and the partnership immediately borrows $60. Because a zero-value sale and liquidation allocates the entire debt to X,[2] the partnership books at this point are:

---

2. A zero-value sale will produce a book loss of $270, allocated equally among the partners. Thus, A's capital account will be reduced to negative $80 while the capital accounts of Y and Z will be reduced to positive $10 each.

X		Y		Z		
CA	*OB*	*CA*	*OB*	*CA*	*OB*	
$10	$10	$100	$100	$100	$100	Initial capital
0	60	0	0	0	0	Debt allocation
$10	$70	$100	$100	$100	$100	Ending values

Assume that the partnership now distributes $70 to X. Because the debt was allocated entirely to X prior to this distribution, there is no debt reallocation.[3] Therefore, the books become:

X		Y		Z		
CA	*OB*	*CA*	*OB*	*CA*	*OB*	
$10	$70	$100	$100	$100	$100	Current values
(70)	(70)	0	0	0	0	Distribution to X
($60)	$ 0	$100	$100	$100	$100	Ending values

Now suppose that the partnership distributes $80 to Y. As a result of this distribution but prior to any debt reallocation, the books of the partnership become:

X		Y		Z		
CA	*OB*	*CA*	*OB*	*CA*	*OB*	
($60)	$70	$100	$100	$100	$100	Current values
0	(70)	(80)	(80)	0	0	Distribution to Y
($60)	$ 0	$ 20	$ 20	$100	$100	Ending values

To determine the effect of this distribution on the allocation of the partnership's debt, we consider the consequences of a hypothetical zero-value sale and liquidation. A zero-value sale will produce a book loss of $120, reducing X's capital account to negative $110, Y's capital account to negative $10, and Z's capital account to positive $70. Thus, the distribution works a reallocation of the debt, with Y's share increasing from $0 to $12 and X's share decreasing from $60 to $48.[4] As a result, X recognizes gain of

---

3. That is, a zero-value sale and liquidation at this point will trigger a capital account deficit restoration obligation only as to X, and so the entire debt continues to be allocated to X.

4. The regulations do not explicitly provide for the allocation of partnership recourse indebtedness among the partners when a zero-value sale and liquidation yields capital account deficit restoration obligations exceeding the total outstanding debt, but presumably the debt in such circumstances should be allocated among the partners in proportion to the deficit restoration obligations, a rule that was explicit in the initial temporary regulations, Temp. Treas. Regs. §1.752-1T(d)(3)(i), but inexplicably removed from the final regulations.

$12 and the partnership's books are:

X		Y		Z		
CA	OB	CA	OB	CA	OB	
($60)	$0	$100	$100	$100	$100	Current values
0	0	(80)	(80)	0	0	Distribution to Y
0	0	0	12	0	0	Debt reallocation
($60)	$0	$ 20	$ 32	$100	$100	Ending values

What should be surprising about this result is that the distribution *to Y* forced income recognition *to X.* The operation of §731 seems to impose gain recognition *only* when a partner removes from the partnership more than she has contributed. While we might argue about precisely how much X contributed (taking into account the partnership's debt), the taxable event to X was a distribution made entirely to Y; that is, X is taxed under application of §731 on a transaction in which it seems plain that X is removing nothing from the partnership. To be sure, complex arrangements can yield complex outcomes. But this partnership has no great complexity: all its assets are capital assets, and there are no special allocations. The simple rule of §731(a)(1) has somehow been twisted to produce what surely appears to be a bizarre outcome.

23

A Partner's Transactions with the Partnership

A. GUARANTEED AND SIMILAR PAYMENTS

Suppose partner X performs services for the XYZ partnership in exchange for a fixed salary. If the salary is treated as a distribution described in §731, there will be no gain or loss to the partnership or to X (assuming X's outside basis can absorb the distribution) but rather a reduction in X's outside basis. §733. If, though, the same payment had been made to a nonpartner, the recipient would have compensation income on the transaction and the partnership might be entitled to a business expense deduction under §162. Is it appropriate to allow X to defer recognition of what amounts to compensation income simply because of the happenstance that X is a partner in, as well as a service provider to, the XYZ partnership?

In §707(a)(1), Congress has provided that when a partner engages in a transaction with her partnership as would a nonpartner, the transaction should be taxed *as if* between the partnership and a nonpartner. In the example above, that means that X would have compensation income and the partnership would either deduct the expense under §162 or capitalize it under §263. Section 707(a)(1) also encompasses sales of property from a partner to the partnership and sales of property from the partnership to a partner.

Suppose the XYZ partnership agrees to pay $10,000 to partner X to manage the partnership. Such a payment might fall within §707(a)(1) if the compensation is equivalent to what a nonpartner would be paid for equivalent services. But what if the partnership agreement requires that the partnership be managed by a partner? In such circumstances it is hard to characterize X as acting other than in her capacity as a partner, and so §707(a)(1) arguably does not apply. Nevertheless, X should still have compensation income, and the partnership also should continue to enjoy a deduction, and those are precisely the effects of §707(c). Under §707(c), fixed payments (called "guaranteed" payments) made to a partner will be taxed as if made to a nonpartner even if the transaction does not fall within §707(a)(1). Accordingly, *X* will still be forced to recognize the distribution as compensation income and the partnership should be entitled to claim an equivalent deduction (because management expenses are ordinary and necessary business expenses).

In Pratt v. Commissioner, 64 T.C. 203 (1975), aff'd in part, rev'd in part, 550 F.2d 1023 (5th Cir. 1977), the Tax Court narrowly construed §§707(a)(1) and 707(c). At issue were payments to a partner for ongoing management duties as well as interest payments on loans from a partner to the partnership. The management fees were set at a fixed percentage of the partnership's gross rental income, and the court held these fees were not described in §707(a)(1) or in §707(c).

The court rejected the §707(a)(1) characterization on two grounds. First, the court wrote that

> Section 707(a)[1] refers to "transactions" between a partner and a partnership and is susceptible of being interpreted as covering only those services rendered by a partner to the partnership in a specific transaction as distinguished from continuing services of the partner which would either fall within section 707(c) or be in effect a partner's withdrawal of partnership profits.

Second, the court felt that the partners were "to receive the management fees for performing services within the normal scope of their duties as general partners and pursuant to the partnership agreement." The court acknowledged that the fees were reasonable in amount and would have been paid to a third-party if the general partner had not managed the partnership's rental activities. To the extent that the court's holding turned on the partnership agreement requiring the general partner to manage the partnership, perhaps the court was correct. To the extent that the court was saying that payments to a general partner for taking an interest in the partnership's affairs always fall outside of §707(a)(1), it seems to be reading §707(a)(1) for less than it is worth.

The court rejected the §707(c) characterization on the ground that payments based on the *gross income* of the partnership are "determined with respect to the income of the partnership" within the meaning of §707(c). Yet, the role of §707(c) (and §707(a)(1)) is to distinguish proprietary returns from compensation payments. Because the management fees were not based on the *net* income of the partnership, they did not resemble the return of a proprietor. Indeed, the managing partner would be entitled to be paid even if the partnership reported a net loss for the year. Unfortunately, the court interpreted the language of §707(c) by resort to the dictionary rather than to the section's underlying purpose.

As to the interest payments, the court concluded that §707(c), not §707(a)(1), applied. Market interest on an enforceable debt would seem to be the paradigmatic §707(a)(1) payment. You should wonder, though, why it matters which section applies because both require the recipient partner to report the payment as income and both allow the partnership to deduct the payment if it constitutes an ordinary and necessary business expense or other deductible expenditure (such as interest).

In *Pratt*, the partnership was an accrual taxpayer and the partners were cash basis individuals. Interest on the loan was accrued but not paid by the partnership. Ordinarily, an accrual basis taxpayer accrues deductions without regard to actual payment. Following this principle the partnership would deduct the interest under §163 during the current taxable year. The recipient partner, though, as a cash basis taxpayer would not be required to include the interest in income until actually received. This timing whipsaw whereby the payment is deducted but not included is disallowed by §267(a)(2), a provision generally applicable to payments between related taxpayers.

When §267(a)(2) applies, an accrual payor of an otherwise deductible payment may not accrue the deduction until the recipient includes it in income. Section 267(a)(2) applies to a transaction whenever the payor and recipient are "related" within the meaning of §267(b). By reason of §267(e)(1)(B), each partner (owning a capital interest, a profits interest, or both) is treated as related to the partnership. Accordingly, the matching of income and deduction mandated by §267(a)(2) applies to payments described in §707(a)(1). In our example, this means that the partnership will not be entitled to accrue the interest deduction until the recipient partner includes it as income, and that, presumably, will occur in the year of payment. The effect of §267(a)(2), in other words, is to put the payor partnership on the same method of accounting as the recipient partner.

However, if the payment is described not by §707(a)(1) but rather by §707(c), a different matching rule applies. Under Treas. Regs. §1.707-1(c), a partner must report a guaranteed payment received from an accrual basis partnership in the year in which the partnership accrues it. That is, income and deduction once again are matched, but this time in accordance with the partnership's (i.e., the payor's) method of accounting. In *Pratt*, then, characterization under §707(c) required the recipient partner to include the interest income in the year in which it was due and payable even though actual receipt did not occur.

The interpretations given to §§707(a)(1) and (c) by the Tax Court in *Pratt* seem erroneous, and the Service apparently agrees. In the following two Revenue Rulings, the Service states its current understanding of §§707(a)(1) and (c), an understanding inconsistent with the holdings in *Pratt*.

Revenue Ruling 81-300

1981-2 C.B. 143

FACTS

The taxpayers are the general partners in a limited partnership formed to purchase, develop and operate a shopping center. The partnership agreement specifies the taxpayers' shares of the profit and loss of the partnership. The general partners have a ten percent interest in each item of partnership income, gain, loss, deduction, or credit. In addition, the partnership agreement provides that the general partners must contribute their time, managerial abilities and best efforts to the partnership and that in return for their managerial services each will receive a fee of 5 percent of the gross rentals received by the partnership. These amounts will be paid to the general partners in all events.

Pursuant to the partnership agreement, the taxpayers carried out their duties as general partners and provided the management services required in the operation of the shopping center. The management fees of 5 percent of gross rentals were reasonable in amount for the services rendered.

LAW AND ANALYSIS

. . . In Pratt v. Commissioner, 64 T.C. 203 (1975), aff'd in part, rev'd in part, 550 F.2d 1023 (5th Cir. 1977), under substantially similar facts to those in this case, both the United States Tax Court and the United States Court of Appeals for the Fifth Circuit held that management fees based on a percentage of gross rentals were not payments described in section 707(a)[1] of the Code. The courts found that the terms of the partnership agreement and the actions of the parties indicated that the taxpayers were performing the management services in their capacities as general partners. . . .

When a determination is made that a partner is performing services in the capacity of a partner, a question arises whether the compensation for the services is a guaranteed payment under section 707(c) of the Code or a distributive share of partnership income under section 704. In Pratt, the Tax Court held that the management fees were not guaranteed payments because they were computed as a percentage of gross rental income received by the partnership. The court reasoned that the gross rental income was "income" of the partnership and, thus, the statutory test for a guaranteed payment, that it be "determined without regard to the income of the partnership," was not satisfied. On appeal, the taxpayer's argument was limited to the section 707(a)[1] issue and the Fifth Circuit found it unnecessary to consider the application of section 707(c).

The legislative history of the Internal Revenue Code of 1954 indicates the intent of Congress to treat partnerships as entities in the case of certain transactions between partners and their partnerships. See S. Rep. No. 1622, 83d Cong., 2d Sess. 92 (1954). The Internal Revenue Code of 1939 and prior Revenue Acts contain no comparable provision and the courts had split on the question of whether a partner could deal with the partnership as an outsider. . . . This resulted both in uncertainty and in substantial computational problems when an aggregate theory was applied and the payment to a partner exceeded the partnership income. In such situations, the fixed salary was treated as a withdrawal of capital, taxable to the salaried partner to the extent that the withdrawal was made from the capital of other partners. . . . Terming such treatment as unrealistic and unnecessarily complicated, Congress enacted section 707(a)[1] and (c) of the Code of 1954. Under section 707(a)[1] the partnership is considered an unrelated entity for all purposes. Under section 707(c), the partnership is considered an unrelated entity for purposes of sections 61 and 162 to the extent that it makes a guaranteed payment for services or for the use of capital.

Although a fixed amount is the most obvious form of guaranteed payment, there are situations in which compensation for services is determined by reference to an item of gross income. For example, it is not unusual to compensate a manager of real property by reference to the gross rental income that the property produces. Such compensation arrangements do not give the provider of the service a share in the profits of the enterprise, but are designed to accurately measure the value of the services that are provided.

Thus, and in view of the legislative history and the purpose underlying section 707 of the Code, the term "guaranteed payment" should not be limited to fixed amounts. A payment for services determined by reference to an item of gross income will be a guaranteed payment if, on the basis of all of the facts and circumstances, the payment is compensation rather than a share of partnership profits. Relevant facts would include the reasonableness of the payment for the services provided and whether the method used to determine the amount of the payment would have been used to compensate an unrelated party for the services.

It is the position of the Internal Revenue Service that in *Pratt* the management fees were guaranteed payments under section 707(c) of the Code. On the facts presented, the payments were not disguised distributions of partnership net income, but were compensation for services payable without regard to partnership income.

HOLDING

The management fees are guaranteed payments under section 707(c) of the Code.

Revenue Ruling 81-301
11981-2 C.B. 144

FACTS

ABC is a partnership formed in accordance with the Uniform Limited Partnership Act of a state and is registered with the Securities and Exchange Commission as an open-end diversified management company pursuant to the Investment Company Act of 1940, as amended. Under the partnership agreement, *ABC*'s assets must consist only of municipal bonds, certain readily marketable temporary investments, and cash. The agreement provides for two classes of general partners: (1) "director general partners" (directors) who are individuals and (2) one "adviser general partner" (adviser) that is a corporate investment adviser registered as such in accordance with the Investment Advisers Act of 1940, 15 U.S.C.A., section 80b-5 (1971).

Under the partnership agreement, the directors are compensated and have complete and exclusive control over the management, conduct, and operation of *ABC*'s activities. The directors are authorized to appoint agents and employees to perform duties on behalf of *ABC* and these agents may be, but need not be, general partners. Under the partnership agreement, the adviser has no rights, powers, or authority as a general partner, except that, subject to the supervision of the directors, the adviser is authorized to manage the investment and reinvestment of *ABC*'s assets. The adviser is responsible for payment of any expenses incurred in the performance of its investment advisory duties, including those for office space and facilities, equipment, and any of its personnel used to service and administer *ABC*'s investments. The adviser is not personally liable to the other partners for any losses incurred in the investment and reinvestment of *ABC*'s assets.

The nature of the adviser's services are substantially the same as those it renders as an independent contractor or agent for persons other than *ABC* and, under the agreement, the adviser is not precluded from engaging in such transactions with others.

Each general partner, including the adviser general partner, is required to contribute sufficient cash to *ABC* to acquire at least a one percent interest in the partnership. The agreement requires an allocation of 10 percent of *ABC*'s daily gross income to the adviser. After reduction by the compensation allocable to the directors and the adviser, *ABC*'s items of income, gain, loss, deduction, and credit are divided according to the percentage interests held by each partner.

The adviser's right to 10 percent of *ABC*'s daily gross income for managing *ABC*'s investment must be approved at least annually by a majority vote of the directors or a majority vote of all the partnership interests. Furthermore, the directors may remove the adviser as investment manager at any time on 60 days' written notice to the adviser. The adviser can terminate its investment manager status by giving 60 days' written notice to the directors. The agreement provides that the adviser will no longer be a general partner after removal or withdrawal as investment manager, but will continue to participate as a limited partner in the income, gains, losses, deductions, and credits attributable to the percentage interest that it holds.

LAW AND ANALYSIS

. . . Although the adviser is identified in the agreement as an "adviser general partner," the adviser provides similar services to others as part of its regular trade or business, and its management of the investment and reinvestment of *ABC*'s assets is supervised by the directors. Also it can be relieved of its duties and right to compensation at any time (with 60 days' notice) by a majority vote of the directors. Further, the adviser pays its own expenses and is not personally liable to the other partners for any losses incurred in the investment and reinvestment of *ABC*'s assets. The services performed by the adviser are, in substance, not performed in the capacity of a general partner, but are performed in the capacity of a person who is not a partner.

The 10 percent daily gross income allocation paid to the adviser is paid to the adviser in its capacity other than as a partner. Therefore, the gross income allocation is not a part of the adviser's distributive share of partnership income under section 702(a) of the Code or a guaranteed payment under section 707(c).

HOLDING

The 10 percent daily gross income allocation paid to the adviser is subject to section 707(a)[1] of the Code and taxable to the adviser under section 61 as compensation for services rendered. The amount paid is deductible by the partnership under section 162, subject to the provisions of section 265.

Why should a partnership care if a distribution is characterized as a §707(a)(1) (or §707(c)) payment? At least if the payment would be deductible, characterization under §707(a)(1) or as a guaranteed payment offers the partnership more flexibility than characterization as a distribution taxable under §§731-733. If the payment is taxed under §§731-733, there will be no tax consequences to the partnership and the partner will defer recognition of income so long as her outside basis can absorb the distribution. That result is precisely the same as would be obtained under §707(a)(1) (or under §707(c)) if the deduction were allocated to the recipient partner. Thus, at least in the case of a deductible payment, the partnership can obtain the equivalent of §§731-733 treatment simply by specially allocating the deduction. In addition, the partnership can allocate the deduction in any other way it desires, thus giving it added flexibility as compared with the §§731-733 route.

If the amount of a guaranteed payment is defined by reference to the partnership's net income, computation of the guaranteed payment may become circular. Suppose the managing partner of the *P* partnership is guaranteed to receive a payment of 10 percent of the partnership's net income, or $10,000, whichever is greater. If the partnership's income is $200,000 for the year (ignoring any deduction arising from the payment to the managing partner), the managing partner will be entitled to a payment of $20,000, no part of which is a guaranteed payment under Treas. Regs. §1.707-1(c) (example 2). However, if the partnership's net income had been only $80,000, the managing partner would be entitled to receive a distribution of $10,000, and this regulation provides that $2,000 of this amount would be a guaranteed payment under §707(c).

According to this regulation, 10 percent ($8,000) of the partnership's income is the managing partner's distributive share and the remaining $2,000 is a guaranteed payment. This characterization of the distribution cannot be correct because the partner's distributive share is *not* determined by reference to her current distributions. Distributive share, you should recall, is determined by reference to the partnership agreement and bears no necessary relationship to distributions of cash or property. Presumably the drafters of the regulation were trying to say that $8,000 of the distribution should be taxed under §§731-733, and the remainder is taxed as a guaranteed payment.

Even if we can understand what the regulation means, we still should be confused by its approach. Assuming that management fees constitute ordinary and necessary business expenses for the partnership, the guaranteed payment portion of the distribution should be deductible. Accordingly, if we follow the approach of the regulation, the partnership has taxable income of $78,000 ($80,000 less the $2,000 deduction for the guaranteed payment), so that the distribution should be recharacterized as a $7,800 distribution of distributive share and $2,200 of guaranteed payment. That is, the formula in the regulation for determining the amount of the guaranteed payment is circular.

A better approach would be to consider any amount guaranteed to be distributed — that is, any amount payable in all events — to be taxable under §707(c). Because such amounts are not tied to the economic well-being of the partnership, they ought not be taxed under §§731-733. Sections 731-733 offer a basis-first recovery to the distributee, just as §1001(a) offers basis-first recovery on the disposition of property. Payments closer to compensation or to interest than to proprietary returns should not be taxed so favorably, and §707(c) provides the appropriate mechanism for forcing the immediate recognition of income. Accordingly, the managing partner in the example above should treat the first $10,000 of distribution as a guaranteed payment regardless of the amount of the partnership's net income.

PROBLEMS

23-1.   A and B each have a 50 percent interest in the profits and losses of AB, an accrual basis partnership. A, however, is entitled to an annual distribution of $10,000 in addition to his share of profits. This payment is for services rendered annually to the partnership, and the payment would be deductible to the partnership if paid to a third party.

    a.   If AB has taxable income (excluding any deduction arising out of its obligation to A) of $100,000, how are A and B taxed? What if the income is entirely long-term capital gain?

    b.   If AB has no taxable income or loss for the year (excluding any deduction arising out of its obligation to A), how are A and B taxed? What if the payment to A is not made until the middle of the following year?

    c.   In case (a), how do your answers change if the deduction arising out of A's guaranteed payment is allocated solely to A?

23-2.   E and F each contribute $60 to the EF partnership. EF purchases a capital asset for $20. During the taxable year, the asset appreciates in value to $100 and then is distributed to E in satisfaction of a guaranteed payment obligation. The partnership has no income or loss and liquidates, distributing its cash of $100. How should that cash be divided between E and F, and what are the tax consequences to each partner?

B.   DISGUISED SALES AND RELATED PROBLEMS

Two individuals agree to form a partnership for the purpose of constructing federally supported, low-cost housing. Individual A contributes real estate to the partnership having an adjusted basis of $40,000 and a fair market value of $100,000. Individual B makes only a nominal contribution of cash. The partners agree that they will divide all profits and losses equally. In addition, they agree that $100,000 will be distributed to A once the construction loan is obtained.

In effect, A has agreed to sell the real estate to the partnership, with the sale proceeds to come out of the partnership's debt. Had it been explicitly structured in that manner, A would recognize a gain on the transaction of $60,000, that being the excess of A's amount realized for the real estate ($100,000) over A's adjusted basis in the real estate ($40,000). If A takes the position that the contribution and subsequent distribution should be taxed as two separate transactions, the first described in §721 and the second described in §731, should A prevail over the Commissioner's §707(a)(1) challenge? In Otey v. Commissioner, 70 T.C. 312 (1978), aff'd per curiam, 80-2 U.S.T.C. ¶9816 (8th Cir. 1980), the Tax Court sustained the taxpayer's position. Unhappy with this result, Congress responded with §707(a)(2)(B). And to close perceived loopholes in §707(a)(2)(B), Congress then enacted §§704(c)(1)(B) and 737.

1. Disguised Sales under §707(a)(2)(B)

Section 707(a)(2)(B) is the disguised sale provision, responding to *Otey* and cases like it in which a contribution of appreciated property is followed by a distribution of cash to the contributing partner. For example, when individual A in the example above contributes the real estate to the partnership, there has been a direct transfer of property to the partnership within the meaning of §707(a)(2)(B)(i). When the partnership subsequently distributes some of its borrowed funds to A, there is a direct transfer of money from the partnership to A within the meaning of §707(a)(2)(B)(ii). Accordingly, if these two transfers are recharacterized under §707(a)(2)(B)(iii), A will be taxed under §707(a)(1) as if she sold the real estate to the partnership. As a result, A will recognize gain on the transfer and the partnership will take a cost basis under §1012.

Note, though, that not all transfers of property from a partnership followed by a distribution to the contributing partner are taxed as sales under §707(a)(2)(B): Before the transaction is treated as a sale, the two transfers "when viewed together, [must] properly be characterized as a sale of property" under §707(a)(2)(B)(iii). What §707(a)(2)(B) leaves open, unfortunately, is determining when two transfers are properly viewed together as a sale.

Regulations provide that a transfer of property to a partnership by a partner followed by a distribution from the partnership to the partner will be treated as a disguised sale if the distribution to the partner would not have been made but for the partner's transfer of property and, if the two transactions are not simultaneous, the subsequent transaction is not dependent on the entrepreneurial risks of the partnership. Treas. Regs. §1.707-3(b)(1). This determination, so the regulations tell us, is made based on all the facts and circumstances in each case. Treas. Regs. §1.707-3(b)(2). However, these regulations also provide that if a transfer to the partnership and a distribution to the transferee partner are made within two years, the two transactions are presumed to constitute a sale. Treas. Regs. §1.707-3(c)(1) Conversely, contributions and distributions separated by more than two years are presumed not to constitute a sale. Treas. Regs. §1.707-3(d). In either situation, though, the particular facts surrounding the transactions can overcome the presumption. In particular, distributions of operating cash flow generally will not be recharacterized as part of a disguised sale. Treas. Regs. §1.707-4(b).

Consider the following example from Treas. Regs. §1.707-3(f) (example 1). E and F are equal partners in the EF general partnership. The partnership owns two pieces of unimproved real estate. Parcel 1 has a fair market value and adjusted basis of $500,000 while parcel 2 has a fair market value and adjusted basis of $1,500,000. E transfers parcel 3, also unimproved real estate, to the partnership in exchange for an increased interest in profits and losses: After the contribution of parcel 3, E's interest in the partnership is increased to two-thirds while F's interest is decreased to one-third. At the time of the contribution, parcel 3 has a fair market value of $1,000,000 and an adjusted basis of $900,000. Immediately after E contributes parcel 3, the partnership sells parcel 1 for $500,000 and distributes the proceeds to the partners in accordance with their new interests in the partnership; that is, $333,333 is distributed to E and $166,667 is distributed to F.

Because E's transfer of parcel 3 occurs within two years of the distribution by the partnership of the proceeds from the sale of parcel 1, the contribution and distribution are presumed to constitute a sale. However, part of that presumption is rebutted by the facts surrounding the transaction. Had E not contributed parcel 3, E would have had a one-half interest in the partnership and so presumably would have been entitled to receive half of the sale proceeds from the partnership's disposition of parcel 1. Accordingly, of the $333,333 actually distributed to E, only $83,333 (that being the excess of the actual distribution (i.e., $333,333) over what would have been distributed had E not contributed parcel 3 (i.e., $250,000)) was dependent on E's contribution of parcel 3. Thus, only $83,333 is treated as sale proceeds to E from the disguised sale of parcel 3. That is, E is treated as selling 8.33 percent of parcel 3 to the partnership in exchange for $83,333 and as contributing 91.67 percent of parcel 3 in exchange for the increased partnership interest. Because 8.33 percent of E's $900,000 adjusted basis in parcel 3 equals $74,970, E must recognize a gain on the deemed sale of $8,363. Consistent with this sale treatment, E should increase his outside basis by the gain recognized under §707(a)(2)(B) and the partnership should increase its basis in parcel 3 by the same amount.

Disguised sales from a partner to the partnership are but one of many transactions to which §707(a)(2)(B) speaks. A contribution of money by a partner to the partnership followed by a distribution of appreciated property to that partner could, under §707(a)(2)(B), be recharacterized as a disguised sale of the property by the partnership to the partner. Finally, §707(a)(2)(B) can address more complex transactions in which a contribution and distribution might closely resemble a partial sale to another partner, followed by mutual contributions to the partnership.

These more complex transactions can appear in unexpected settings. As you might expect, guaranteed payments to a partner for the use of capital are unlikely to be recharacterized under §707(a)(2)(B) as part of a disguised sale because they are taxable to the distributee under §707(c). However, the regulations provide that amounts classified as guaranteed payments by the partnership may be reclassified as constituting part of a disguised sale to the extent such payments are unreasonably large. See Treas. Regs. §1.707-4(a)(1)(iii). In addition, the regulations provide that "payments . . . designed to liquidate all or a part of [a] partner's interest in property contributed to the partnership rather than to provide the partner with a return on an investment in the partnership" will be treated as part of a disguised sale rather than as a guaranteed payment. Treas. Regs. §1.707-4(a)(1)(i).

Consider the following example taken from Treas. Regs. §1.707-4(a)(4) (example 2). C and D form a general partnership. C contributes property with adjusted basis of $20,000 and fair market value of $100,000 while D contributes no property but agrees to be responsible for the day-to-day management of the partnership's operations. The partners agree that all tax items will be allocated 75 percent to C and 25 percent to D. They also agree that all cash flow will be distributed in the same portion except that C will receive a guaranteed payment of $8,333 per year for the first four years. By the terms of the partnership agreement, the guaranteed payment will come out of D's cash flow only, and if the partnership does not generate sufficient revenue to meet its guaranteed payment obligation to C, D will contribute sufficient funds to meet that obligation.

Even if $8,333 is a reasonable annual payment for the use of C's contributed capital, the regulations provide that C's preferential distributions will be treated as part of a disguised sale. Note that if the form of the guaranteed payments is respected, the partnership will be entitled to an interest deduction of $8,333 each year for the first four years, or $33,332 total. Because C is allocated 75 percent of all partnership deductions, C will be allocated an interest deduction equal to 75 percent of $33,332, or $24,999. Thus, one effect of the nominal guaranteed payments is that C's capital account will be reduced by $24,999.

By reason of C's contribution of property to the partnership, C's capital account begins at $100,000. By reason of the nominal guaranteed payments, C's capital account is reduced by approximately 25 percent of its value. Thus, the net effect of the contribution and distributions is to credit C's capital account with about $75,000, which is precisely C's general percentage in partnership tax items and distributions of cash flow. Because the economic costs of *C*'s preferential distributions are borne entirely by *D*, the regulations conclude that *C* should be treated as having sold one-quarter of the property to *D*. Further, had *D* borrowed $25,000 from *C* repayable over four years, the annual loan payment (principle plus interest) would be approximately the amount of the nominal guaranteed payments. Thus, the transaction is recharacterized as if *C* had sold to *D* a one-quarter interest in the contributed property immediately prior to the formation of the partnership. The nominal guaranteed payments made to *C* will be reclassified as §731 distributions made to *D* and then paid over to *C* as repayment by *D* of the $25,000 loan.

If a partner contributes encumbered property to a partnership, the effect of the transfer may be to shift some of the encumbrance away from the contributing partner and to the other partners. See, e.g., Rev. Rul. 84-102, 1984-2 C.B. 119. Under §752(b), the reduction in the contributing partner's share of the encumbrance is treated as a distribution of cash, so that the transaction is treated to the contributing partner as a contribution and simultaneous distribution, thereby implicating the disguised sale rules of §707(a)(2)(B). Because of their complexity, the detailed rules governing pre-existing liabilities under §707(a)(2)(B) are beyond the scope of this book. See generally Treas. Regs. §1.707-5. As you might expect, though, liabilities incurred less than two years prior to the transaction are more likely to be captured by §707(a)(2)(B) than are liabilities incurred earlier. Treas. Regs. §1.707-5(a)(7).

PROBLEMS

23-3. Individual *Z* joins the *XY* general partnership by contributing property with fair market value of $100,000 and adjusted basis of $60,000 to the partnership. One day later, the partnership distributes cash of $50,000 to *Z*.

   a. What are the tax consequences to *Z* of these events, and what are *Z*'s outside basis and capital account? What is the partnership's adjusted basis in the property contributed by *Z*?
   b. Without doing any calculations, what differences would arise if the distribution were made one year after *Z*'s admission to the partnership?

2. Distributions of Contributed Property

Suppose *X* and *Y* form the *XY* partnership by *X* contributing Blackacre with fair market value of $50,000 and adjusted basis of $40,000 while *Y* contributes cash of $100,000. How will the partnership books stand if Blackacre is distributed to *Y* in a distribution falling within §731?

X		*Y*		
CA	*OB*	*CA*	*OB*	
$50,000	$40,000	$100,000	$100,000	Formation
0	0	(50,000)	(40,000)	Distribution
$50,000	$40,000	$ 50,000	$ 60,000	Ending balances

The precontribution appreciation in Blackacre has benefitted partner *X* in two ways. First, *X*'s capital account was credited with the full fair market value of Blackacre, thereby giving *X* credit for both his after-tax investment in Blackacre and its precontribution appreciation. Second, when Blackacre was distributed to *Y*, *Y*'s capital account was decreased by the full fair market value of Blackacre. Treas. Regs. §1.704-1(b)(2)(iv)(e)(1). That decrease redounds to *X*'s advantage in the sense that *X*'s ownership interest in the partnership is defined by the partners' relative capital accounts, so that as *Y*'s capital account goes down, *X*'s relative ownership interest in the partnership goes up. Thus, because *Y*'s capital account is reduced by the full value of Blackacre, *X* and *Y* end up with equal capital in the partnership.

The effect of the formation of *XY*, coupled with the distribution of Blackacre to *Y*, is a sale of Blackacre from *X* to *Y*. Had the sale been done explicitly prior to formation of the partnership, *X* would have recognized a gain of $10,000 and would have had $50,000 in cash to contribute to the partnership. *Y* also would have $50,000 remaining to contribute to the partnership, so that the partnership would end up with $100,000 in cash, as it in fact did after the actual formation and distribution. Indeed, the principle differences between the implicit sale via the partnership and an explicit sale outside the partnership are the avoidance of income recognition and lower outside basis to *X*.

Section 704(c)(1)(B) provides that if contributed property is distributed by the partnership within seven years, gain or loss must be recognized by the contributing partner in an amount equal to the gain that would be allocable to the contributing partner under §704(c)(1)(A) (that is, excluding any gain allocable under §704(b)) if the property were sold to a third party for its current fair market value. In our example above, this means that *X* will recognize gain of $10,000 when Blackacre is distributed to *Y*. Note that, because of the parenthetical in §704(c)(1)(B), the rule of §704(c)(1)(B) does not apply if the property is distributed back to the contributing partner (in our example, §704(c)(1)(B) does not apply if Blackacre is distributed to *X*). In addition, §704(c)(1)(B) does not apply if the transaction has the effect of a like-kind exchange. §704(c)(2).

Consistent with treating the distribution to *Y* as an implicit sale by *X*, appropriate basis adjustments are made to outside bases and to *Y*'s postdistribution basis in Blackacre. §704(c)(1)(B)(iii). That is, we recompute *X*'s contribution as if *X* had recognized gain on the contribution, and then we recompute the distribution to *Y* based on the first recomputation. Thus, *X* takes an initial outside basis of $50,000, and the partnership takes an inside basis in Blackacre of the same amount. Accordingly, when Blackacre is distributed to *Y*, *Y* takes a basis in Blackacre of $50,000 under §732(a)(1) and reduces her outside basis by that amount to $50,000 under §733(2). Section 704(c)(2) limits application of the rule in §704(c)(1)(B) when the overall effect of the transaction is that of a like-kind exchange between two partners, an exchange generally tax-free under §1031. For the relationship of §731(c) to §704(c)(1)(B), see Treas. Regs. §1.731-2(g)(1).

PROBLEMS

23-4. *P* and *Q* form the *PQ* general partnership, with *P* contributing depreciable property having an adjusted basis of $6,000 and fair market value of $10,000 and *Q* contributing cash of $10,000. *P* and *Q* are equal partners except as required by §704(c). Assume that the basis of the property contributed by *P* is recovered ratably over five years.

a. What are the tax consequences if the partnership distributes the property to *Q* after one year when the property has a fair market value of $8,000?

b. What are the tax consequences if the partnership distributes the property to *Q* after one year when the property has a fair market value of $10,000? Explain why there is a book/tax disparity for each partner.

3. Swap Transactions under §737

Suppose individual *X* contributes Blackacre with an adjusted basis of $60 and a fair market value of $100 to the *P* partnership in exchange for a partnership interest. Subsequently, the partnership distributes other property (with adjusted basis and fair market value of $100) to *X*. Under §§731-732, this distribution is tax-free to *X*, and *X* takes a carryover basis of $60 in the distributed property. Of course, *X* reduces her outside basis to $0 as a result of the distribution. §733(2).

Note what has happened: Without the imposition of any tax, *X* has managed to exchange one piece of property (what she contributed, namely Blackacre) for another (what she received) in the distribution. Of course, if the two pieces of property are like-kind within the meaning of §1031, a tax-free exchange is appropriate. But if the properties are dissimilar, X has managed to avoid taxation by running the exchange through the partnership.

Congress has ensured that partnerships cannot be used in this way. Section 737 is triggered by the distribution of property to a partner who contributed appreciated property in the past. In such circumstances, the distributee will recognize gain equal to the *lesser* of (1) the excess of the fair market value of the property distributed over the distributee's outside basis immediately prior to the distribution (but reduced by any cash received in the distribution, §737(a)(1)) or (2) the amount of the precontribution appreciation in the *contributed* property (i.e., the precontribution appreciation in Blackacre). In the example above, that means that X will recognize a gain of $40 on the distribution, gain which is treated as realized from the sale or exchange of the contributed property. §737(a) (final sentence). Consistent with taxing X on the appreciation in the contributed asset, §737(c) provides for a basis increase to the partner's outside basis as well as to the partnership's inside basis in the contributed asset. This basis provision plays the same role as that in §704(c)(1)(B)(iii).

Section 737 will not force the recognition of income on a distribution of cash because the amount defined in §737(a)(1) will equal zero. Recall that a distribution of cash triggers recognition of income under §731(a)(1) to the extent the cash distributed exceeds the distributee's outside basis. Thus, application of §737 would be redundant because the measure of recognition in §731(a)(1) is the same measure employed by §737(a)(1).

A partner's "net precontribution gain" is defined in §737(b) to include only the precontribution appreciation in property contributed by the partner within the last seven years and still held by the partnership. This seven-year limitation presumably is based on the notion that if the contribution and distribution are separated by more than seven years, it is inappropriate to treat them as related. The limitation that the property continue to be owned by the partnership co-ordinates §737 with §704(c)(1). Under §704(c)(1)(A), the precontribution gain will be allocated to the contributing partner upon disposition of the asset. Under §704(c)(1)(B), the precontribution gain will be taxed to the contributing partner upon distribution of the asset to some other partner. Thus, the precontribution appreciation will already have been taxed to the contributing partner except in the case when the contributed asset is still held by the partnership. And this last situation is precisely when §737 applies.

Section 737 explicitly limits its application to the amount of precontribution appreciation that would be taxed to the contributing partner if the property were distributed to some other partner. See §737(b). That is, §737 cannot tax a partner more harshly than would §704(c)(1)(B). In particular, the effect of §737 will be mitigated or eliminated entirely if the contributing partner has managed to eliminate the prior §704(c) book/

tax disparity by some means. For example, if the contributed property is depreciable by the partnership, the §704(c) book/tax disparity may be eliminated over time by differing allocations of book and tax depreciation. See, e.g., Treas. Regs. §1.704-3(b)(2) (example 1(ii)).

Section 737 provides an exception for property distributed to the partner who originally contributed the property to the partnership. §737(d)(1). And by referencing §704(c)(1)(B) in the definition of "net precontribution gain," §737 implicitly includes an exception for swap transactions that have the effect of a like-kind exchange. See §704(c)(2). Note also that the gain recognized under §737 is in addition to any gain recognized under §731(a)(1) if the distribution consists of cash as well as of property and that application of §737 defers to application of §751(b) should they both apply to the same transaction. §737(a). In addition, if distributed marketable securities are treated as cash under §731(c), then they are treated as cash for purposes of §737. Treas. Regs. §1.731-2(g)(1)(iii)(A).

PROBLEMS

23-5.   Reconsider the facts of part (a) in problem 23-4 above. How would *Q* be taxed under §737 if she had contributed unimproved real estate with adjusted basis of $2,000 and fair market value of $10,000 instead of cash? What if this property had an adjusted basis of $9,000 rather than $2,000?

4. *Capitalization Avoidance and §707(a)(2)(A)*

Sections 707(a)(2)(A) and 707(a)(2)(B) are similar in that both are triggered by a transfer to the partnership and a related distribution from the partnership to a partner. What distinguishes §707(a)(2)(A) from §707(a)(2)(B) is the requirement in §707(a)(2)(A)(ii) that the contributing/distributee partner receive *an allocation of income* to go along with the distribution of money or property. By reason of this allocation requirement, the contributing/distributee partner will recognize income on the transaction, and so transactions described in §707(a)(2)(A) cannot represent attempts to reduce the tax burden imposed on the contributing/distributee partner. Rather, such transactions may represent an attempt by the partnership to avoid the capitalization requirement of §263.

For example, suppose the *P* partnership constructs a commercial office building. The architect, whose normal fee is $40,000, contributes cash for a 25 percent interest in the partnership and receives in addition a gross income allocation of $20,000 per year for the first two years of the partnership. Further, the partnership agreement provides that the architect will be distributed $20,000 of cash in each of the first two years in addition to her share as partner. For ease of illustration, assume that the partnership generates rental income each year of $120,000.

This gross income allocation and distribution produces the same tax consequences to the architect as a salary of $40,000: The architect must report $40,000 of income over the first two years in addition to her 25 percent distributive share and the architect's outside basis and capital account each enjoy a net increase equal to her general 25 percent interest in the partnership. That is, after two years the architect will have included $40,000 by reason of the special gross income allocation as well as $50,000 (25 percent of the remaining $100,000 each year) as distributive share of partnership taxable income. In addition, the architect's outside basis will have increased by $90,000 by reason of the special allocations and one-quarter distributive shares and will have decreased by $40,000 by reason of the distributions, for a net increase of $50,000.

But consider the effect of the gross income allocation on the partnership generally. Had the architect been paid a straight salary, that salary would have been capitalizable as part of the cost of the building. Treas. Regs. §1.263(a)-2(d). As a result, the architect would have reported $40,000 of compensation income and the partnership would have had $120,000 of income to be allocated among its partners (of which $30,000 would have been the architect's distributive share). Because the architect was compensated indirectly with the special gross income allocation and distribution, though, the partnership has only $100,000 per year to allocate among its members. The money used to pay the architect's fee thus is not reported by the partners in their distributive shares, and that is the equivalent of including those funds and then deducting the fee. *In other words, allocating income to one partner and thus away from the others is equivalent to paying the same amount of income as a deductible expense.*

Of course, not all allocations are subject to recharacterization under §707(a)(2)(A). The legislative history of §707(a)(2)(A) indicates that a partner is acting as a third party to the extent that the partner's profit from a transaction is assured without regard to the success or failure of the joint undertaking. An allocation of *net* partnership income ordinarily should not fall within the scope of §707(a)(2)(A) because net income is dependent on the economic success of the partnership venture. Allocations of *gross* partnership income do not share this element of entrepreneurial risk and so are more liable to challenge under §707(a)(2)(A). Indeed, from this perspective the effect of §707(a)(2)(A) is to identify those allocations and distributions that together constitute disguised guaranteed payments.

Congress identified several specific factors that should be considered under §707(a)(2)(A). S. Rep. No. 169, 98th Cong., 2d Sess. at 227-28 (1984). The most important factor is the extent to which the distribution is subject to appreciable risk. Even an allocation of net income can be virtually risk-free as to both fact or payment and amount if the partnership's income stream is assured. For example, if the partnership owns property rented on a long-term lease to a credit-worthy lessee, an allocation of a fixed percentage of the partnership's net income might be tantamount to a risk-free allocation of a specific dollar sum. Capped allocations (i.e., allocations equal to the lesser of a percentage of the partnership's net income or a fixed annual sum) should easily be classified as falling within §707(a)(2)(A).

The second factor to be considered is the duration of the distributee partner's status as a partner. If the distributee's status as a partner is transitory, the allocation and distribution are more likely to be recharacterized as a fee for services or property. Even if the distributee's status as a partner is not transitory, if the distributee's continuing interest in the partnership is small as compared with the special allocation and distribution, the transaction is likely to fall within §707(a)(2)(A). Indeed, the legislative history indicates that this factor is particularly important if the special allocation lasts for only a short period of time. Thus, a special allocation of $25,000 for one year is ripe for recharacterization if the value of the partner's continuing profits interest is substantially less than $25,000 annually. Of course, no recharacterization is possible unless there is a related transfer of property or services to the partnership, payment for which would be capitalizable in full or in part.

Other factors identified by the legislative history include the proximity in time of the contribution of services or property and the distribution, the effect of the transaction on providing tax benefits to the partnership, and whether the contribution was booked in at less than fair market value.

PROBLEMS

23-6. *X* Corp. owns a business worth between $10,000,000 and $12,000,000. *Y* Corp. is willing to invest cash of $12,000,000 for a 50 percent interest in a partnership to be formed with *X*. The parties agree to credit *X* with a $10,000,000 initial capital account. While each partner will have a 50 percent interests in profits and losses, the partnership agreement provides for a gross income allocation to *X* of up to $1,000,000 in each of the first two years if the partnership attains certain profitability goals. Is this gross income allocation valid? If *X* anticipates exiting from the partnership after a few years, what net effect will this gross income allocation have had on *X* and on *Y*?

C. LIMITATIONS APPLICABLE TO CONTROLLED PARTNERSHIPS

Section 707(b) imposes two limits on a controlling partner's ability to exploit her position in the partnership for tax advantages. In this context, a controlling partner is one who owns (directly or indirectly) more than 50 percent of the capital or profits of the partnership. While determining a partner's share of capital should be purely mechanical, determining a partner's share of profits is more problematic in any complex partnership which specially allocates some profit items. This aspect of §707(b) is one more example of how some parts of Subchapter K reflect a surprising ignorance of the workings of partnership taxation. Be sure to note that a partner's share of both capital and profits include the capital and profits interests of all related parties, where related parties are defined in §267(c). See §707(b)(3).

1. Disallowed Losses

The loss disallowance rule in §707(b)(1) can apply to sales of property from partnerships to a related party as well as to sales of property to partnerships from a related party. Consider first the sale of loss property from a partnership to a related property.

The *AB* general partnership has two partners, *A* and *B*. Partner *A* has a capital account and outside basis of $25,000 while partner *B* has a capital account and outside basis of $75,000; assume the partnership agreement allocates all tax items 25 percent to *A* and 75 percent to *B*, and the partnership owns Blackacre with adjusted basis and book value of $40,000 as well as cash of $60,000. If the partnership sells Blackacre to *B* for its current fair market value of $30,000, what are the tax consequences to the partners?

The sale produces a book loss to the partnership of $10,000, and under the partnership agreement that loss is allocated $2,500 to *A* and $7,500 to *B*. Accordingly, *A*'s capital account is reduced to $22,500 and *B*'s capital account is reduced to $67,500. While the partnership realizes a tax loss of $10,000 on the sale, that loss is disallowed by application of §707(b)(1) because the purchaser (*B*) is in control of the selling partnership.

Despite the absence of a recognized tax loss, the partners must reduce their outside bases by their shares of the realized but unrecognized tax loss. Because the operation of §707(b)(1) is not to defer the loss but instead to disallow it entirely, the loss is properly treated as falling with §705(a)(2)(B) as a nondeductible, noncapitalizable expenditure. Or, in the words of Rev. Rul. 96-10, 1996-1 C.B. 138, this item falls within §705(a)(2)(B) because it "has a permanent effect on the partnership's basis in its assets, without a corresponding current or future effect on its taxable income." Thus, *A*'s outside basis is reduced to $22,500 and *B*'s outside basis is reduced to $67,500.

B's basis in Blackacre is its cost to *B* of $30,000. However, if *B* subsequently sells Blackacre at a gain, *B* may use the loss disallowed to the partnership to offset any gain realized on the sale. For example, if *B* eventually sells Blackacre for $45,000, *B*'s recognized gain will be only $5,000. The effect of this rule is to permit *B* to use not only that part of the loss denied to *B* under §707(b)(1) but also to use the remaining portion of the loss denied to *A* under that section as well.

Now consider the reverse transaction in which a controlling partner sells loss property to the partnership. For example, suppose partner *B* in the example above sells Whiteacre to the partnership for its fair market value of $8,000 when Whiteacre has an adjusted basis of $10,000 in *B*'s hands. Assume that at the time of the sale *A*'s outside basis and capital account equal $22,500 while *B*'s outside basis and capital account equal $67,500.

By virtue of §707(b)(1), the loss of $2,000 realized by *B* on the sale goes unrecognized, and the partnership takes a cost basis of $8,000 in Whiteacre. As before, if Whiteacre is subsequently sold at a gain, only so much of the gain as exceeds the disallowed loss must be recognized. Thus, if the partnership subsequently sells Whiteacre to a third party for its then fair market value of $14,000, the partnership realizes a book gain of $6,000 over its acquisition cost of $8,000. However, the partnership recognizes only $4,000 of tax gain by virtue of the penultimate sentence in §707(b)(1). How should this gain be allocated among the partners?

In the absence of any special allocation, *B* will be allocated 75 percent of the $4,000 tax gain, or $3,000. However, the partnership's tax gain is only $4,000 rather than $6,000 because of the prior tax loss that *B* sustained but was not allowed to deduct. Accordingly, when that disallowed loss reappears in the form of an income offset to the partnership, arguably it should benefit the partner who generated it; in other words, it should benefit *B*. Thus, *B* should be taxed on her share of the book gain (that is, on 75 percent of $6,000, or $4,500) less that $2,000 income offset, for a net share of $2,500. The remaining $1,500 tax gain recognized by the partnership would then be allocable to *A*. Note that the effect of this approach is to tax *A* as she would be taxed had *B*'s loss not been disallowed: The $1,500 tax gain allocated to *B* is precisely 25 percent of the partnership's book gain on the subsequent sale.

Put another way, the disposition of Whiteacre by the partnership for $14,000 produces book income of $6,000, taxable gain of $4,000, and tax-exempt income of $2,000. Should the partners be permitted (perhaps even required) to allocate all the exempt income to *B* because it was *B*'s disallowed loss that generated it? Assuming the partners in fact agree to allocate all the exempt income as well as $2,500 of the taxable income to *B* and the remaining $1,500 of taxable income to *A*, do these allocations lack substantiality because they do not affect the actual dollars either partner will receive but only affect the partners' tax positions? While there is no direct authority on this point, it would seem that allocating to *B* the tax benefit of the income offset generated by *B*'s prior disallowed loss should be permissible.

2. *Capital Gains*

Under §707(b)(2), gains from sales and exchanges between a partnership and its controlling partner (or between commonly controlled partnerships) are taxable as ordinary income if the transferred property is not a capital asset in the hands of the transferee. The same result obtains if the property is depreciable in the hands of the transferee by reason of the more general rule in §1239(a), see §1239(c)(1)(B). These two provisions deny capital gains benefits to dispositions that work little actual change in control over the transferred asset. Note that these rules apply only to gains and not to losses, so they will never operate to convert a capital loss into an ordinary deduction.

PROBLEMS

23-7. *M* has an 80 percent interest in the capital, profits and losses of the *MNOP* partnership. *M* sells unimproved real estate to *MNOP* for its fair market value of $16,000 although *M* has an adjusted basis in the real estate of $20,000 at the time of the transaction. *MNOP* subsequently sells the real estate for $18,000.

    a.   How much gain or loss should the partnership report on this sale, and of that gain or loss, how much should be allocated to *M*?

    b.   What is the net effect on *M*'s capital account and outside basis as a result of these transactions?

    c.   How would your answers to part (a) change if the subsequent sale was for $30,000 instead of $18,000?

23-8. *H* has a 40 percent interest in the capital and profits of the *P* partnership. *H* sells Blackacre to *P* for its current fair market value of $10,000 while *H*'s adjusted basis in Blackacre is $12,000.

    a.   What part of *H*'s loss may be recognized? What if *H*'s interest in the partnership had been 60 percent?

    b.   For each possibility in (a), what are the tax consequences to the partnership if it subsequently sells Blackacre for $15,000? For $9,000? For $11,000?

    c.   Do your answers to part (a) change if the sale is made by *W*, *H*'s spouse?

24

Acquisitions of Partnership Interests

A. CONTRIBUTIONS OF PROPERTY

Partnership interests may be acquired in different ways and at different times. At formation of the partnership, each of the partners will contribute property (possibly including cash) or services to the partnership in exchange for a partnership interest. Subsequently, new partners may be admitted in exchange for additional contributions, existing partners may make further contributions, or a nonpartner may join the enterprise by buying a partnership interest, receiving a partnership interest as a gift, or receiving a partnership interest through the estate of a decedent.

1. Basic Principles

In general, no gain or loss is recognized by the partnership or by any partner (including the contributing partner). §721(a). The contributing partner's adjusted basis in the property is carried over into the hands of the partnership, §723, as well as into the contributing partner's partnership interest, §722. We also have seen that the contributing partner's capital account is credited with the *fair market value* of the contributed property. Treas. Regs. §1.704-1(b)(2)(iv)(d)(1).

Capital accounts, more so than outside bases, reflect the partners' share of the partnership's value. When property is contributed to a partnership in exchange for a partnership interest, presumably the interest so created reflects the fair market value of the contributed property at the time of contribution. Crediting the contributing partner's capital account with the fair market value of the contributed property ensures that whatever value is recognized by the partners also is reflected in the capital accounts.

However, the partnership interest received by the contributing partner should reflect the fair market value of the contributed property as compared with the fair market value of the partnership's current assets. For example, suppose the *AB* partnership owns assets worth $100. If *C* is admitted to the partnership in exchange for a contribution of property worth $50, *C*'s capital account will properly reflect a one-third interest only if *C*'s interest is set equal to $50 (as it is) *and* the capital accounts of *A* and *B* total $100. That is, the capital accounts of *A* and *B* must reflect asset values as of the admission of the new partner, *C*. Accordingly, if we are to reflect all aspects of the contribution in the capital accounts, we should adjust each capital account by taking into account the current value of all partnership assets. The regulations specifically permit a partnership to revalue its assets and adjust capital accounts when property is contributed by a new (or continuing) partner. Treas. Regs. §1.704-1(b)(2)(iv)(f)(5)(i).

As a second example, suppose the *XY* partnership owns a single asset with book value and adjusted basis of $100 and fair market value of $140 when *Z* is admitted as a one-third partner in exchange for a cash contribution of $70. Assuming *X* and *Y* were equal partners prior to the admission of *Z*, we should increase the capital accounts of *X* and *Y* from $50 to $70 to reflect the value of the partnership as of the admission of *Z*. Thus, each one-third partner will have a capital account of $70 after the admission of *Z*. The $40 of unrealized appreciation in the partnership's asset should be allocable only to *X* and *Y* under principles similar to those applicable to §704(c) transactions. Treas. Regs. §1.704-1(b)(2)(iv)(d)(3).

These rules apply to contributions of "property," where property includes cash but does not include services. See Treas. Regs. §1.721-1(b)(1). Some kinds of property, notably copyrights and patents, have a strong service flavor, yet the courts have been willing to treat such property as falling within the ambit of §721. There is a similar "property" limitation applicable to the formation of a corporation, see §351(a), and courts will look to cases in that context for guidance under §721.

For example, in United States v. Stafford, 727 F.2d 1043 (11th Cir. 1984), a taxpayer contributed a letter of intent to a partnership in exchange for a 5 percent partnership interest. This letter of intent recited that the taxpayer and an insurance company had begun negotiations to finance and construct a hotel, with the insurance company providing a favorable loan and ground lease. The taxpayer contributed the letter of intent to the partnership and agreed to continue negotiations. Relying heavily on §351 cases and rulings, the court held that the letter of intent was "property" within the meaning of §721 even though it gave no enforceable rights to the partnership. The court likened the letter of intent to the goodwill of a sole proprietorship. See also Rev. Rul. 64-56, 1964-1 C.B. (pt.

1) 133, and Rev. Rul. 71-564, 1971-2 C.B. 179, for guidelines distinguishing between industrial know-how and services.

The rules in §§721 and 722 apply not only when a partnership is formed but also subsequently if property is transferred to the partnership in exchange for a partnership interest. Treas. Regs. §1.721-1. In fact, they also apply to transfers of property by an existing partner even if nothing is received in return. Rev. Rul. 78-357, 1978-2 C.B. 227. However, the Treasury has been instructed to promulgate regulations providing that nonrecognition under §721 will not be available if application of §721 would permit income to escape taxation by shifting it offshore.

2. Encumbered Property

When encumbered property is contributed to a partnership in exchange for a partnership interest, the partnership debt rules of §752 are implicated. As to the contributing partner, the effect of the transaction is a reduction of share of the debt from 100 percent (prior to the contribution) to a lesser percentage based on the debt allocation rules provided in the §752 regulations. With respect to the noncontributing partners, the effect is precisely the opposite. Accordingly, the contributing partner will be treated as receiving a distribution of cash under §752(b) while the noncontributing partners will be treated as making contributions of cash under §752(a).

For example, suppose that the XY partnership owns one asset with fair market value and adjusted basis of $200, and assume also that the partnership has no debt. X has a 75 percent interest in the profits and losses of the partnership while Y has the remaining 25 percent interest. Assume that the partnership's books stand as follows:

X		Y	
CA	OB	CA	OB
$150	$150	$50	$50

Z is admitted as a new partner in exchange for a contribution of Blackacre. Z's adjusted basis in Blackacre is $50. Blackacre is worth $160 and is encumbered by a debt of $60 which the partnership agrees to assume. After the admission of Z, X's interest in the partnership drops to one-half, Y's interest drops to one-sixth, and Z's interest becomes one-third. The partnership's books after the admission of Z are as follows:

X		Y		Z	
CA	OB	CA	OB	CA	OB
$150	$180	$50	$60	$100	$10

To understand this table, look first at the capital accounts. The capital accounts of the noncontributing partners (i.e., of X and Y) remain unchanged. Technically, the partnership assets should be revalued as a result of the admission of Z, and the capital accounts of X and Y should be adjusted to reflect any unrealized appreciation or loss in the partnership's assets. Treas. Regs. §1.704-1(b)(2)(iv)(e). However, because there was no unrealized appreciation or loss in the partnership's assets, no adjustments to the noncontributing partners' capital accounts are made. Z's capital account is equal to the value of Blackacre, net of its encumbrance. Because Blackacre is worth $160 and is subject to a debt of $60, its net value is $100, and that is the amount of Z's initial capital account. Treas. Regs. §1.704-1(b)(2)(iv)(b).

The ending outside bases are best understood via a two-step process. In step 1, Blackacre is contributed without regard for the possible debt reallocation under §752. Under §722, Z takes an initial outside basis of $50 because that was Z's adjusted basis in Blackacre. X and Y continue their outside bases of $150 and $50 because nothing has occurred to warrant a change.

In step 2, we consider the effects of §752. Prior to the contribution of Blackacre, Z's share of the $60 debt was the entire $60. After the contribution, Z's interest in the debt must be determined by reference to a hypothetical zero-value sale and liquidation. Treas. Regs. §1.752-2(b)(1). A zero-value liquidation would produce a book loss of $360, allocable $180 to X, $60 to Y and $120 to Z. Accordingly, final capital account balances will be negative $30 for X, negative $10 for Y, and negative $20 for Z. Each partner will be required to contribute her final capital account deficit to the partnership for distribution to the lender, and so these final capital account deficits determine the allocation of the debt: $30 for X, $10 for Y, and $20 for Z. Treas. Regs. §1.752-2(b)(1).

Thus, as a result of Z's admission to the partnership, Z's interest in the debt drops from $60 to $20. Accordingly, Z is deemed to receive a cash distribution of $40 under §752(b). Under §731, this deemed distribution does not produce any gain to Z because Z's outside basis is able to absorb it, and under §733(1), Z reduces her outside basis by $40 from $50 to $10.

As to X and Y, they are treated under §752(a) as making cash contributions equal to their increases in their shares of the partnership's debt. Prior to the admission of Z, there was no partnership debt so that each partner's share was zero. After the admission of Z, the partnership's debt equals $60, see §752(c), and X and Y are allocated $30 and $10 of that amount. Accordingly, X increases her outside basis by $30 and Y increases her outside basis by $10, in each case under §722.

Reconsider this example but assume Blackacre has a fair market value of $220 and is encumbered by a debt of $120. Once again Z's net contribution is $100, so the capital accounts will end up as before. However, there will be a difference in outside bases because of the greater debt. Once Z transfers Blackacre to the partnership, Z's share of the debt decreases from $120 to $40 while X's share increases from $0 to $60 and Y's increases from $0 to $20.

As to Z, there is a deemed distribution of $80 under §752(b), which means that Z recognizes $30 of income under §731(a)(1) and takes an initial outside basis of $0. X enjoys an increase in outside basis of $60 pursuant to §§752(a) and 722, while Y's outside basis enjoys a similar increase of $20. Accordingly, the partnership books will read:

X		Y		Z	
CA	OB	CA	OB	CA	OB
$150	$210	$50	$70	$100	$0

Consider one more variation on this theme. Assume again that Blackacre has a fair market value of $220 and is encumbered by a debt of $120, but assume this time that the debt is fully nonrecourse. As a result, the debt will be allocated among X, Y, and Z in three tiers: (1) first, in proportion to partnership minimum gain; (2) second, as the partners would share gain under §704(c)(1)(A), assuming the property were sold for the amount of the liability and for no other consideration; and (3) third, according to profits interests. Treas. Regs. §1.752-3(a).

There is no partnership minimum gain because the book value of Blackacre ($220) exceeds the debt ($120), Treas. Regs. §1.704-2(d)(1), so there is no tier one allocation. Treas. Regs. §1.752-3(a)(1). Under tier two, Z is allocated up to $70 of the debt, assuming the partners agree to address ceiling limitations with respect to the property contributed by Z by using the traditional method or the traditional method with curative allocations. Treas. Regs. §1.752-3(a)(2). The $50 remainder of the debt is allocated among the partners as they will share profits, so X's share is $25.00, Y's share is $8.33, and Z's share under tier three is $16.67. Treas. Regs. §1.752-3(a)(3). Accordingly, Z's total share of the debt is $86.67, which means that Z is treated as receiving a deemed distribution of $33.33, X is treated as contributing cash of $25.00, and Y is treated as contributing cash of $8.33. Thus, rounding all capital accounts to whole dollar amounts, the partnership books will read:

X		Y		Z	
CA	OB	CA	OB	CA	OB
$150	$175	$50	$58	$100	$17

PROBLEMS

24-1. A and B agree to form the AB general partnership. A will have a 25 percent interest in profits and losses while B will have a 75 percent interest in profits and losses. *A* agrees to contribute Whiteacre with adjusted basis of $60, fair market value of $120, and subject to a recourse debt of $20. *B* agrees to contribute Blackacre with adjusted basis of $25, fair market value of $260, and subject to a recourse debt of $160. What are the partners' initial capital accounts and outside bases?

3. Payables and Receivables

When an ongoing business is transferred to a partnership, it is inevitable that the transfer will include accounts payable as well as accounts receivable. Receipt of the receivables presents no unusual problems. If the transferor was a cash-basis taxpayer, the receivables will have a zero basis and will trigger application of §704(c), while if the transferor had accrued the receivables, they will enter the partnership as unappreciated property.

Payables are more difficult. Unaccrued accounts payable contributed to a partnership by a cash-basis transferor do not fall within the scope of §752. Rather, such payables are to be treated in accordance with §704(c) principles. Treas. Regs. §1.704-3(a)(4). To simplify the discussion as much as possible, consider the contribution of nothing but cash and accounts payable by a cash-basis partner.

Assume that *C* joins the *AB* partnership by contributing cash of $150 and payables of $50. The net value of *C*'s contribution is $100, and so that becomes the initial value of *C*'s capital account. *C*'s outside basis, on the other hand, begins at $150 under §722.

When the partnership pays the payables, the resulting deduction should be allocable to *C* under §704(c). This allocation will reduce *C*'s outside basis by $50 pursuant to §705(a)(2)(A). No reduction should be made to *C*'s capital account, though, because the (negative) value of the payables was taken into account when *C* was admitted to the partnership and given an initial capital account of only $100. If the payables had been accrued by *C* prior to the transfer, the analysis would be slightly different. Accrued payables are treated as liabilities of the partnership and are accounted for under §752. Accordingly, *C*'s initial basis will start at $150 less the amount of the payables properly allocable to *A* and *B*. When the payables are subsequently paid by the partnership, each partner will have a deemed distribution under §752(b). Because the payables are treated as liabilities of the partnership, no §704(c) problem is created when they are transferred to the partnership.

PROBLEMS

24-2. *X, Y,* and *Z* form the *XYZ* general partnership. *X,* a cash-basis taxpayer, contributes accounts receivable of $150 (with adjusted basis of

$0) and accounts payable of $50 in exchange for a 25 percent interest in profits and losses. Y contributes unimproved real estate with adjusted basis of $120 and fair market value of $100 in exchange for a 25 percent interest in profits and losses. Z contributes inventory with adjusted basis of $40, fair market value of $300 and encumbered by a debt of $100, in exchange for a 50 percent interest in profits and losses.

  a. Assuming both the contributed real estate and inventory are capital assets in the hands of the partnership, what are the outside bases and capital accounts of the partners if the receivables are collected, the payables are paid, and all the property is sold for its fair market value?
  b. What is the character of the partnership's income and loss?
  c. Was the partnership entitled to tack the contributing partner's holding period to its own with respect to the real estate and Z's inventory?

4. Promissory Notes

If a taxpayer contributes her own promissory note (other than a readily tradeable one) to a partnership, her capital account is not increased until there is a taxable disposition of the note by the partnership or as principal payments are made by the partner on the note. Treas. Regs. §1.70-1(b)(2)(iv)(d)(2). However, because such a note represents a promise by the partner to contribute additional funds to the partnership, contribution of such a note by a limited partner will permit that partner's capital account to go negative by the amount remaining unpaid on the note. See Treas. Regs. §1.704-1(b)(2)(ii)(d). A partner's outside basis is not increased by the contribution of such a note, Oden v. Commissioner, T.C. Memo 1981-184, aff'd in unpublished opinion, 679 F.2d 885 (4th Cir. 1982), although any plausible rationale for that result is lacking.

5. Holding Periods

Section 1223 provides various tacking rules applicable to tax-free exchanges. For example, §1223(2) provides that the holding period of property acquired in a carryover basis transaction includes the holding period of the transferor. Under this rule, the holding period of property acquired by a partnership in exchange for a partnership interest includes the holding period of the transferor partner. Thus, if property is held for more than one year before it is contributed to a partnership and then is disposed of immediately by the partnership, any gain or loss on the disposition will be long term to the partnership by reason of §1223(2).

The tacking rule applicable to the contributing partner is found in §1223(1), and it is slightly more complex. Under §1223(1), the contributing partner may tack her holding period of the contributed property onto that of her partnership interest if the contributed property was a capital or §1231 asset. As a result, tacking is not available if the contributed property was an ordinary income asset in the hands of the contributing partner. Note that it is irrelevant for application of §1223(1) whether the contributed property is a capital asset in the hands of the partnership once contributed. If a partner contributes properties with different holding periods, or if a partner acquires portions of his partnership interest at different times, the partner can have multiple holding periods in his single partnership interest. Prop. Treas. Regs. §1.1223-3(a).

6. Disposition of Contributed Property

Ordinary income assets distributed by a partnership to a partner will be subject to an ordinary income taint under §735(a). Section 724 provides a similar rule for property contributed to a partnership. However, §724 is broader than §735(a) in that it speaks not only to the conversion of ordinary income into capital gain but also to the conversion of capital loss into ordinary loss. Further, this aspect of §724 operates in a more complex manner than do the ordinary income provisions of §§724 and 735(a).

Under §724(a), disposition of contributed property by a partnership will produce ordinary income if the property was an unrealized receivable in the hands of the contributing partner. Under §724(b), a similar result obtains if the property was an inventory item in the hands of the contributing partner, but only if the disposition by the partnership occurs within five years of contribution of the property to the partnership. As under §735(a), the definitions of "unrealized receivables" and "inventory items" are found in §751(c)-(d). See §724(d).

Under §724(c), the contribution of capital loss property will taint subsequent loss on disposition by the partnership up to the amount of the built-in loss at contribution. For example, suppose partner P contributes property to the partnership having fair market value of $100 and adjusted basis of $120, and assume further that the property is a capital asset in the hands of P but constitutes an inventory item in the hands of the partnership. If the partnership subsequently sells the property for $75, it will recognize a loss of $45 on the sale. Of this loss, $20 will be capital under §724(c).

What if the property had been sold by the partnership for $105? In this case the loss recognized by the partnership is only $15, and the entire amount of that loss is capital under §724(c). Section 724(c), in other words, does not affect the amount of the loss but only its character as ordinary or capital.

As a last example, what if the property were sold by the partnership for $150? In this case there is a gain to the partnership of $30. Because the property is sold at a gain, §724(c) does not apply. Because the property was a capital asset to the contributing partner, §724(a)-(b) does not apply. Accordingly, no special recharacterization rules apply to this sale so that the gain of $30 is ordinary to the partnership because the property is an ordinary income asset in the hands of the partnership.

PROBLEMS

24-3.   The chart below describes various property contributed to the *P* partnership by its partners. For each piece of property, determine the tax consequences to the partnership if the property is sold for the indicated price.

Basis to partner	Value at contribution	Sale price	Character to partner	Character to partnership
$6,000	$8,000	$10,000	Inventory	Capital
6,000	8,000	7,500	Inventory	Capital
6,000	4,000	7,000	Inventory	Capital
6,000	4,000	7,000	Capital	Inventory
6,000	4,000	3,000	Capital	Inventory
6,000	8,000	5,000	Capital	Inventory

7.   *Contributions to Investment Companies*

The general rule of nonrecognition for transfers of property to a partnership in exchange for a partnership interest does not apply if the partnership, would be treated as an investment company were it incorporated. §721(b). This rule parallels the rule for transfers to corporations, see §351(e)(1), and both are intended to deny the benefits of deferral to business entities offering little more than diversification to its investors. See Treas. Regs. §1.351-1(c)(1). For the definition of "diversification" in this context, see Treas. Regs. §1.351-1(c)(5). Note that §721(b) provides for recognition of gain but not loss while §351(e)(1) provides for recognition of gain and loss.

B.   CONTRIBUTIONS OF SERVICES

A partner might be admitted to a partnership in exchange for future or past services. Does §721 apply to such an exchange? By its terms, §721 only applies to a contribution of "property." A long-standing regulation provides that

> [t]o the extent that any of the partners gives up any part of his right to be repaid his contributions (as distinguished from a share in partnership profits) in favor of another partner as compensation for services . . . section

721 does not apply. The value of an interest in such partnership capital so transferred to a partner as compensation for services constitutes income to the partner under section 61. Treas. Regs. §1.721-1(b)(1).

See also Prop. Treas. Regs. §1.721-1(b)(1) (proposed June 3, 1971). This regulation apparently draws a distinction between a service partner who receives an interest in the current value of the partnership (i.e., a "capital" interest) and one who receives an interest only in future profits (i.e., a "profits" interest). Does it make sense to distinguish between a capital interest and a profits interest?

A capital interest presumably is easier to value: The service partner receiving an interest in the current value of the partnership presumably should be taxed on the value of the capital interest acquired, measured by the current liquidation value of that partnership interest.

Valuing a profits interest is more difficult. If the partnership liquidated immediately after the service partner was given her profits interest, presumably the service partner would receive nothing. That the immediate liquidation value of the profits interest is zero does not, however, necessarily indicate that the profits interest has no value.

For example, suppose the *XY* partnership owns a single asset rented out to a credit-worthy lessee on a long-term lease. If *Z* performs services for the partnership in exchange for an interest in future profits — that is, in exchange for a share of future rent receipts — surely the profits interest has an immediate value equal to the discounted value of the expected rental income stream. While in the typical case the partnership's income stream will be more difficult to value than this one, it remains true that the right to share in a partnership's future profits has an immediate non-zero value.

And what of the partnership? Recall that §721 provides nonrecognition for both the contributing partner and for the partnership. If §721 does not cover a contribution of services, should the partnership recognize gain or loss on the transaction? If we follow an aggregate model of taxation, presumably the partnership should be treated as if it transferred a percentage of its assets to the service partner in a taxable exchange. On the other hand, if we follow an entity model of taxation, we might characterize the exchange as services for an unappreciated partnership interest akin to the taxation of corporations issuing stock for services under §1032.

1. Taxation of the Contributing Partner

Until 1971, most commentators assumed that the contribution of services to a partnership in exchange for a partnership interest was taxable only if the service partner received an immediate interest in partnership capital. That assumption was shattered in Diamond v. Commissioner, 492 F.2d 286

(7th Cir. 1974), aff'g 56 T.C. 530 (1971), where it was held that the fair market value of a partnership interest received in exchange for past services is taxable compensation. *Diamond* presented unusually simple facts because the service partner sold his partnership interest almost immediately after receipt, enabling the Commissioner to use the subsequent sale price to value the partnership interest. Indeed, all that was at issue in *Diamond* was whether the partner's income should be taxable as ordinary income (as compensation) or as short-term capital gain (from the sale of a partnership interest).

Despite its victory in *Diamond,* for two decades the Service did not actively seek to tax most partners who received only a profits interest in exchange for a contribution of services. However, the Service successfully argued in 1990 before the Tax Court that the *Diamond* holding should be reaffirmed. Campbell v. Commissioner, 59 T.C.M. 236 (1990), rev'd, 943 F.2d 815 (8th Cir. 1991). This revitalization of the *Diamond* doctrine was short lived, however, as the Court of Appeals for the Eighth Circuit reversed the Tax Court's decision in a very peculiar opinion.

Campbell v. Commissioner
943 F.2d 815 (8th Cir. 1991)

BEAM, Circuit Judge:
William and Norma Campbell appeal from the tax court's decision affirming, in part, the Commissioner's assessment of deficiencies in their federal income tax for the years 1979 and 1980. The Campbells challenge the tax court's finding that partnership profits interests received by Mr. Campbell constitute income. We affirm in part and reverse in part.

I. BACKGROUND

Prior to and during the years in issue, William Campbell was employed by Summa T. Group, a collection of business entities involved in the formation and syndication of limited partnerships. Campbell served as vice president and director for most members of the Summa T. Group, including Summa T. Realty, Inc., a real estate brokerage and consulting firm. He also served as vice president of Realty Properties Company, another member of Summa T. Group. Most of Campbell's services during these years were performed for Summa T. Realty. . . .

In partnership with Jim Nettles, another Summa T. Realty employee, Campbell packaged and sold interests in transactions on behalf of Summa T. Realty. Nettles left Summa T. Realty in 1979, and Campbell became responsible "for locating suitable properties for Summa T. Realty, negotiating the acquisition of those properties, obtaining the financing necessary to acquire the properties, organizing the partnerships which would eventually acquire those properties, and assisting in the preparation of offering materials in connection with the syndication of those partnerships." Following Nettles's departure, Campbell negotiated a new compensation agreement under which he received fifteen percent of the proceeds from each syndication and, for his services, special limited partnership interests (profits interests) in the partnerships that he helped form and finance. Campbell sought these interests because of the immediate tax benefits he would receive and the residual value they might have. Based on consultation with two tax attorneys, he believed that the receipt of these interests in exchange for services would not be taxable events, at the time of acquisition.

Relevant to this appeal, Campbell performed services in the formation and syndication of three limited partnerships. In 1979, he received a two percent special limited partnership interest in Phillips House Associates, Ltd. Realty Properties was the sole general partner in Phillips House, and David Kane, president of Realty Properties, was also a special limited partner. Phillips House was formed to purchase, renovate and operate a hotel in downtown Kansas City, Missouri. The offering memorandum, which was provided to potential investors in the thirty-five Class A limited partner units available for sale, predicted losses for tax purposes from 1979 to 1985, ninety-four percent allocated to the limited partners and two percent allocated to each special limited partner and the general partner. However, the memorandum warned that an Internal Revenue Service audit was likely. And, it was predicted that the IRS probably would disallow some or all of the deductions and allocations.

Twenty Class A interests were sold by December 31, 1979, and the remaining fifteen were sold by December 31, 1980. Each unit sold for $99,250. Resale of partnership units was subject to approval by the general partner, which could withhold approval arbitrarily. The partnership did not anticipate cash distributions to the Class A limited partners until 1982 and to the special limited partners and the general partner until 1984. Once cash became available for distribution, the Class A limited partners were given priority. They were also entitled to return of their capital investment upon the sale or refinancing of the hotel. The first $30,000 of any additional proceeds from such a transaction were allocated to the general partner as return of capital. The special limited partners were each entitled to a share of any remaining proceeds.

Diversified Financial Services, a member of Summa T. Group, received three percent of the Phillips House offering proceeds as reimbursement for expenses incurred in the offering. Realty Properties, and other members of the group, received 42.5 percent of the proceeds for "expense allowances, consulting fees, and management fees." Campbell provided services in the formation and syndication of the partnership. However, the record does not reveal what part of these fees were paid to Summa T.

Group for services actually performed by Campbell, nor does it reveal what part of Campbell's partnership interest, if any, was received as compensation for services for which his employer was compensated.

The other two limited partnerships at issue here were formed under similar agreements. Campbell received a one percent interest in The Grand partnership, which was formed in 1980 to purchase and operate the Howard Johnson's Motor Lodge in Myrtle Beach, South Carolina. Also in 1980, the Airport partnership was formed to purchase and operate the Northwest Airport Inn in St. Louis County, Missouri. Campbell received a one percent interest in Airport. As in Phillips House, Realty Properties was the general partner, Campbell and Kane were special limited partners, and thirty-five Class A limited partnerships were sold in both The Grand and Airport. Id. at 241-42, 244. Realty Properties and its affiliates, including Diversified Financial Services and Summa T. Realty, received 30.2 percent of the proceeds of The Grand's offering of limited partnership interests and 38.5 percent of the proceeds of Airport's offering. These payments were made for expense allowances, consulting fees, management fees and financing fees. Again, Campbell provided some of these services, and the record does not reveal the capacity in which he performed them. The offering memoranda for The Grand and Airport projected taxable losses for the first several years of operations. As with Phillips House, however, the memoranda warned that any of the deductions and credits might be disallowed by the Internal Revenue Service.

On May 10, 1983, the Commissioner issued a notice of deficiency for the tax years 1979 and 1980, alleging that Campbell should have included the value of his interests in these partnerships in ordinary income. The Commissioner valued Campbell's interests in Phillips House, The Grand and Airport at $42,084, $16,968 and $20,683, respectively. . . .

The tax court upheld, in part, the Commissioner's assessment of deficiency and addition to tax. The court agreed that the fair market value of the profits interests should have been included in Campbell's income. The court, however, did not fully agree with the Commissioner's valuation of the interests. Upon revaluation, the court sustained the Commissioner's deficiency in regard to The Grand. The court valued Campbell's interest in Airport at $ 15,000 and his interest in Phillips House at $25,000 and entered an order accordingly.

II. DISCUSSION

Campbell argues on appeal, as he did unsuccessfully in the tax court, that a service partner (i.e., a partner who receives his partnership interest in exchange for services provided to the partnership) who receives a profits interest (i.e., a right to share in profits and losses only, as opposed to an interest in the capital assets of a partnership) in a partnership does not realize income upon receipt of that interest, and, therefore, no taxable event occurs. In the alternative, he argues that the interests he received had no value at the time he received them and, thus, he should not have been taxed. . . .

B.   TAXING PROFITS INTERESTS

Although the Commissioner concedes the tax court's error in taxing a service partner's profits interest, the tax court's holding is not without support. In fact, the only circuit court to address the issue arrived at the same conclusion. See *Diamond,* 492 F.2d 286. However, Campbell and several amici curiae strongly argue that the tax court's decision does substantial damage to established principles of partnership tax law. In addition, several commentators have recently analyzed the issue and have come to a variety of conclusions. . . . Thus, we are reluctant to accept the Commissioner's concession without substantive review.

The tax court rejected Campbell's contention that the regulations promulgated under section 721 of the Internal Revenue Code and the general principles of partnership taxation exempt from taxation profits interests received in exchange for services. The court reaffirmed its holding that section 721 and its regulations are "inapplicable where, as in the *Diamond* case and the instant case, a partner receives his partnership interest in exchange for services he has rendered to the partnership." Section 721 relates to contributions of property to partnerships, but not to contributions of services, which are not property within the meaning of that section. Section 721 was enacted to allow the contribution of property to a partnership without recognition of gain or loss. The rationale for nonrecognition is that no disposition of property has occurred. Rather, the partnership interest represents a change in form of the asset. In the present case, the court held that the receipt of profits interests represented compensation for services, not change in form of assets.

The court also noted the inconsistency in imposing immediate taxation upon a service partner who receives a capital interest and not upon a service partner who receives a profits interest, as section 721 makes no distinction between the two. Further, the section 721 regulations do not expand the scope of the statute to provide nonrecognition of income to partners who contribute services in exchange for a partnership interest. Thus, the tax court found no authority to support different treatment for capital and profits interests received in exchange for services and held that Campbell received ordinary income upon receipt of the profits interests.

After finding that Campbell's receipt of the profits interests were taxable events, the court applied section 83 to determine when the income should have been recognized. Section 83 provides rules governing when property received in connection with the performance of services must be recognized as income. I.R.C. §83(a). The regulations define property to "include[] real and personal property other than either money or an unfunded and unsecured promise to pay money or property in the future." Treas. Treas. Regs. §1.83-3(e) (1985). The tax court had no doubt that a profits interest is property rather than a promise to pay money or property in the future. Further, the court found no substantial risk of forfeiture. Thus, the interests were taxable upon receipt.

The tax court's holding was based principally on *Diamond,* and that case is analogous. However, to fully understand the concerns raised, we must review several prior cases and the underlying statutory provisions. When a service partner receives an interest in partnership capital, the cases clearly hold that a taxable event has occurred. The receipt of the capital interest must be included in the service partner's income. See, e.g., United States v. Frazell, 335 F.2d 487, 489 (5th Cir. 1964). See also W. McKee, supra, para. 5.01, at 5-2 (transfer of capital interest is taxable). As an interest in intangible personal property, the receipt of a capital interest appears to be taxable under the authority of section 83 of the Internal Revenue Code.[6] There is little, if any, dispute that such a transaction involves the recognition of income.

As noted, however, when the service partner receives solely a profits interest, the tax consequences are unclear. In contrast to *Diamond,* the tax court has held, and the Commissioner has conceded in some cases, that receipt of a profits interest by a service partner creates no tax liability. See National Oil Co. v. Commissioner, T.C. Memo 1986-596, 52 T.C.M. (CCH) 1223, 1228 (1986) (Commissioner conceded that if taxpayer received only profits interest, no taxable event had occurred); Kenroy, Inc. v. Commissioner, T.C. Memo 1984-232, 47 T.C.M. (CCH) 1749, 1756-59 (1984) (profits interest had no fair market value, thus no tax liability upon receipt); Hale v. Commissioner, T.C. Memo 1965-274, 24 T.C.M. (CCH) 1497, 1502 n.3 (1965) ("Under the regulations, the mere receipt of a partnership interest in future profits does not create any tax liability. Sec. 1.721-(1)(b), Income Tax Regs.").

The Code does not expressly exempt from taxation a service partner's receipt of a profits interest, and the courts that have held that it is not taxed upon receipt do not appear to have closely analyzed the issue. However, commentators have developed three interrelated theories in support of the proposition that it is not a taxable event: (1) based upon regulation 1.721-1(b), a profits interest is not property for purposes of sections 61 and 83; (2) a profits interest may have no fair market value; and (3) the nonrealization concepts governing transactions between partner and partnership preclude taxation. . . .

---

6. A proposed amendment to the treasury regulations provides: "(i) If the partnership interest is transferred after June 30, 1969 . . . then the transfer of such interest in partnership capital shall be treated as a transfer of property to which section 83 and the regulations thereunder applies." Proposed Treas. Regs. §1.721-1(b)(1)(i) (1971).

The tax court and the Seventh Circuit rejected at least the first two of these theories in *Diamond*.[7] The tax court found that Diamond's receipt of a partnership profits interest in exchange for services was taxable as ordinary income, did not come within the scope of section 721 and had a readily ascertainable fair market value. The Seventh Circuit affirmed. *Diamond*, 492 F.2d at 286-87, 291. The facts in *Diamond* are very similar to those before us, except in regard to the issue of value. Diamond had arranged the financing of a land purchase in exchange for a profits interest in the partnership that was to hold title to the land. Id. at 286-87. Diamond arranged the financing and received his partnership profits interest and then, three weeks later, sold his interest to a third party for $40,000. Id. at 287. Diamond treated the sale proceeds as short-term capital gain, which he offset by short-term capital loss. Id.

The Seventh Circuit rejected Diamond's argument that regulation 1.721-1(b)(1), because it distinguishes between receipt of a capital interest and a profits interest and specifically states only that a service partner who receives a capital interest must recognize income, implies that a service partner who receives a profits interest does not recognize income. Id. at 288-89. The court noted that section 721 applies only to those partners who contribute property to the partnership and that the application of the regulation could also be so limited. Id. at 288. After considering other published views on the matter, the court declined to interpret the regulation as Diamond proposed. Id. at 289-91. Although it affirmed the tax court, the Seventh Circuit noted the presence of strong views to the contrary, id. at 289, and recognized the limitations of its holding:

> There must be wide variation in the degree to which a profit-share created in favor of a partner who has or will render service has determinable market value at the moment of creation. Surely in many if not the typical situations it will have only speculative value, if any.

Id. at 290.

The commentators generally agree that the nonrecognition principles of section 721 do not apply to a service partner because a service partner does not contribute property in exchange for his partnership interest. See, e.g., W. McKee, supra, para. 5.01, at 5-2. We also agree. However, the

7. Because section 83 had not been enacted at the time of the *Diamond* transfer, the court's holding was limited to finding that a service partner's receipt of a profits interest was governed by section 61. Although the language of the statute is clear, some question exists as to the applicability of section 83 to a service partner's receipt of a profits interest. . . . A proposed regulation under section 721 states: "If the partnership interest is transferred after June 30, 1969 . . . then the transfer of such interest *in partnership capital* shall be treated as a transfer of property to which section 83 and the regulations thereunder applies." Proposed Treas. Treas. Regs. 1.721-1(b)(1)(i) (1971) (emphasis added). Arguably, the section 1.721-1(b)(1) distinction between capital and profits interests and the regulations under section 83 create the implication that a profits interest is not property subject to section 83. . . . Regulation 1.83-3(e), however, includes all personal property within the definition of property for purposes of section 83.

section 721 regulations are relied upon to tax a service partner's receipt of a capital interest. And, as with a profits interest, a service partner who receives a capital interest has not contributed property in exchange for his partnership interest. Thus, the section 721 regulations provide some guidance when reviewing whether general principles of partnership taxation provide for nonrealization in this case.

Section 721 codified the rule that a partner who contributes property to a partnership recognizes no income. And, regulation 1.721-1(b)(1) simply clarified that the nonrecognition principles no longer apply when the right to return of that capital asset is given up by transferring it to another partner. At that time, the property has been disposed of and gain or loss, if realized, must be recognized. As a corollary, [regulation] section 1.721-1(b)(1) outlines the tax treatment of the partner who receives that capital interest. A substantial distinction, however, exists between a service partner who receives a capital interest and one who receives a profits interest. When one receives a capital interest in exchange for services performed, a shift in capital occurs between the service provider and the individual partners. The same is not true when a service partner receives a profits interest. In the latter situation, prior contributions of capital are not transferred from existing partners' capital accounts to the service provider's capital account. Receipt of a profits interest does not create the same concerns because no transfer of capital assets is involved. That is, the receipt of a profits interest never affects the nonrecognition principles of section 721. Thus, some justification exists for treating service partners who receive profits interests differently than those who receive capital interests.

Probably more relevant to our analysis, however, is section 707 of the Internal Revenue Code, which supports Campbell's argument. See I.R.C. §707. Generally, a partner receives a distributive share of income instead of compensation from his partnership. . . . Except under certain circumstances, "the general statutory policy for treating partnerships for tax purposes contemplated that the income of a partnership would flow through to the individual partners." *Pratt,* 550 F.2d at 1026. Only when the transaction is treated as one between the partnership and a partner acting in a nonpartner capacity is the payment received by the partner not considered a distributive share. See id. at 1026-27; I.R.C. §707(a)(2)(A). Section 707 created an exception to the general rule.

Section 707 provides that when a partner engages in a transaction with a partnership in a nonpartner capacity that transaction will be treated as between the partnership and one who is not a partner. I.R.C. §707(a)(1). When a partner receives payment for services performed for the partnership, that transaction falls under section 707(a)(1) if "the performance of such services . . . and the allocation and distribution, when viewed together, are properly characterized as a transaction occurring between the partnership and a partner acting other than in his capacity as a member of the partnership." Id. §707(a)(2)(A)(iii). This exception was enacted to prevent partnerships from using direct allocations of income to individuals, disguised as service partners, to avoid the requirement that certain expenses be capitalized. However, it was not intended to apply when a service provider acts within his capacity as a partner. See §707(a)(2)(A)(iii). Arguably, section 707(a) would be unnecessary if compensatory transfers of profits interests were taxable upon receipt because, if so, every such transfer would be taxed without this section.

In *Diamond,* where the service provider became a partner solely to avoid receiving ordinary income, we have no doubt that the receipt of the profits interest was for services provided other than in a partner capacity. That is, Diamond was likely to (and in fact did) receive money equal to the value of his services and apparently did not intend to function as or remain a partner. Thus, the receipt of his partnership profits interest was properly taxable as easily calculable compensation for services performed. Campbell's case, however, is not so clear. Campbell's interests were not transferable and were not likely to provide immediate returns. Thus, we doubt that the tax court correctly held that Campbell's profits interests were taxable upon receipt.

More troubling, however, is Campbell's argument that the profits interests he received had only speculative, if any, value. We fully agree with this contention and we reverse the tax court. As noted by the tax court, "fair market value is 'the price at which property would change hands in a transaction between a willing buyer and a willing seller, neither being under compulsion to buy nor to sell and both being informed' of all the relevant circumstances." See Palmer v. Commissioner, 523 F.2d 1308, 1310 (8th Cir. 1975) (quoting Hamm v. Commissioner, 325 F.2d 934, 937 (8th Cir. 1963)). And, while we review de novo the basis of a fair market value determination, the ultimate question of value is one of fact.

Campbell's expert testified that the values of the partnership interests were speculative and not in excess of $1,000. His opinion was based on the present values of the cash distributions projected in the offering memoranda. He discounted these values because of the restrictions on transferability and the lack of participation rights in management of the partnerships. He attached no present value to the projected tax benefits because of the substantial risk of disallowance upon likely audits. The Commissioner used the same basic method of valuation, except that he included the present value of the tax benefits in his calculations and used a much lower discount rate resulting in higher present values.

The tax court accepted the method of valuation proposed by the parties, with some modifications. The court rejected Campbell's expert's opinion that the tax benefits were so speculative that they had no value and rejected the Commissioner's determination of the appropriate discount rate. Then, based on the present value of the tax benefits and future cash payments, reduced by the speculative nature of the Phillips House interest, the court valued the interests as indicated above. Recognizing that the tax court's determination of value is a factual finding subject to clearly erroneous review, and that the tax court does not have to accept an expert's opinion as to value, see *Palmer*, 523 F.2d at 1310, we are, nonetheless, left with the firm belief that the court's valuation was erroneous.

The tax court relied too heavily on the fact that Class A limited partners were willing to pay substantial sums for their interests at the same time Campbell received his interest. Because of the difference in the nature of the investments, we believe that this fact is not relevant. The Class A limited partners had superior rights to cash distributions and return of capital, as well as some rights of participation. Further, the court should not have disregarded the expert's belief that the tax benefits were speculative in nature. The partnerships were taking untested positions in regard to deductions and all of them were likely to be challenged and disallowed by the IRS. In fact, many of the deductions were ultimately disallowed. Further, the predictions contained in the offering memoranda were just that — predictions. The partnerships had no track record. Any predictions as to the ultimate success of the operations were speculative. Thus, we hold that Campbell's profits interests in Phillips House, The Grand and Airport were without fair market value at the time he received them and should not have been included in his income for the years in issue.

III. Conclusion

The decision of the tax court holding that the Campbells should have included the receipt of profits interests in Phillips House, The Grand and Airport in ordinary income in the year of receipt is reversed. The remainder of the decision, in which Campbell alleges no error in this appeal, is affirmed.

Revenue Procedure 93-27 _____
1993-2 C.B. 343

Section 1. Purpose

This revenue procedure provides guidance on the treatment of the receipt of a partnership profits interest for services provided to or for the benefit of the partnership.

Section 2. Definitions

The following definitions apply for purposes of this revenue procedure.

.01   A capital interest is an interest that would give the holder a share of the proceeds if the partnership's assets were sold at fair market value and then the proceeds were distributed in a complete liquidation of the partnership. This determination generally is made at the time of receipt of the partnership interest.

.02 A profits interest is a partnership interest other than a capital interest.

SECTION 3. BACKGROUND

Under section 1.721-1(b)(1) of the Income Tax Regulations, the receipt of a partnership capital interest for services provided to or for the benefit of the partnership is taxable as compensation. On the other hand, the issue of whether the receipt of a partnership profits interest for services is taxable has been the subject of litigation. Most recently, in Campbell v. Commissioner, 943 F.2d 815 (8th Cir. 1991), the Eighth Circuit in dictum suggested that the taxpayer's receipt of a partnership profits interest received for services was not taxable, but decided the case on valuation. Other courts have determined that in certain circumstances the receipt of a partnership profits interest for services is a taxable event under section 83 of the Internal Revenue Code. See, e.g., Campbell v. Commissioner, T.C.M. 1990-236, rev'd, 943 F.2d 815 (8th Cir. 1991); St. John v. United States, No. 82-1134 (C.D. Ill. Nov. 16, 1983). The courts have also found that typically the profits interest received has speculative or no determinable value at the time of receipt. See Campbell, 943 F.2d at 823; St. John. In Diamond v. Commissioner, 56 T.C. 530 (1971), aff'd, 492 F.2d 286 (7th Cir. 1974), however, the court assumed that the interest received by the taxpayer was a partnership profits interest and found the value of the interest was readily determinable. In that case, the interest was sold soon after receipt.

SECTION 4. APPLICATION

.01 Other than as provided below, if a person receives a profits interest for the provision of services to or for the benefit of a partnership in a partner capacity or in anticipation of being a partner, the Internal Revenue Service will not treat the receipt of such an interest as a taxable event for the partner or the partnership.

.02 This revenue procedure does not apply:

(1) If the profits interest relates to a substantially certain and predictable stream of income from partnership assets, such as income from high-quality debt securities or a high-quality net lease;

(2) If within two years of receipt, the partner disposes of the profits interest; or

(3) If the profits interest is a limited partnership interest in a "publicly traded partnership" within the meaning of section 7704(b) of the Internal Revenue Code.

NOTES

1. *Application of §707(a)(2)(A).* The Circuit Court's decision arguable rested on the factual (and highly taxpayer specific) ground that the value of the partnership interest received in *Campbell* "had only speculative, if any value." See also United States v. Pacheco, 912 F.2d 297 (9th Cir. 1990). However, the court advanced a novel theory that the decision in *Diamond* was inconsistent with application of §707. The court wrote:

> [Section 707(a)(2)(A)] was enacted to prevent partnerships from using direct allocations of income to individuals, disguised as service partners, to avoid the requirement that certain expenses be capitalized. However, it was not intended to apply when a service provider acts within his capacity as a partner. See §707(a)(2)(A)(iii). Arguably, section 707(a) would be unnecessary if compensatory transfers of profits interests were taxable upon receipt because, if so, every transfer would be taxed without this section.

This reasoning is faulty for two reasons. First, while §707 does speak in part to transfers of property to a partner in exchange for services, it is unlikely that a partnership interest was intended to be "property" within the meaning of §707: Nothing in the legislative history of that section supports the *Campbell* court's reading. In addition, §707(a)(2)(A) should only apply to services the cost of which must be capitalized and in return for which the service partner is given a nonproprietary return; that is, by its explicit terms §707(a) is about transactions between a partnership and a partner *acting as a nonpartner,* and the contribution of services for a *bona fide* partnership interest simply has nothing to do with any part §707(a).

While the Circuit Court's *Campbell* opinion is far from persuasive, most commentators agree that taxing service partners on the receipt of a profits-only interest is unwise. In many situations the service partner will be required to render future services in exchange for the partnership interest. In such cases the partnership interest likely will not be transferable, at least until the services are fully performed. Section 83, a provision of the code having application far beyond that of subchapter K, allows a taxpayer to defer recognition of compensation income when the compensation takes the form of property that is not transferable and is subject to a substantial risk of forfeiture.

2. *Application of §83.* Section 83 applies whenever property is received "in connection with the performance of services." §83(a). In such circumstances, the fair market value of the property is includible in the recipient's gross income whenever the property becomes transferable or the property is no longer subject to a substantial risk of forfeiture. §83(a). In this context, a "substantial risk of forfeiture" includes property conditioned upon the future performance of substantial services. §83(c)(1). Thus, the service partner whose partnership interest cannot be transferred and who must

perform future services can defer recognition of income which would otherwise be immediately includible under *Diamond*.

There is, though, a cost for this deferral: When the partnership interest becomes transferable or is no longer conditioned on the performance of future services, the service partner must include the then-current fair market value of the interest as ordinary income. Treas. Regs. §1.83-1(a)(1). Thus, if the partnership interest appreciates, the entire appreciation will eventually be taxed as ordinary income.

Under Treas. Regs. §1.83-1(a)(1), property covered by §83(a) is not treated as transferred until the recipient is taxed. Thus, this regulation seems to be saying that the service partner protected from immediate recognition of income under §83(a) is not a partner. If true, the service partner's interest in partnership profits and losses must be reallocated to the other partners and amounts distributed to the service partner cannot be taxed under §§731-733 but must be recharacterized as payments to a nonpartner. If all the partners fall within §83(a) (as might be the case in a service-intensive partnership such as a law firm), does this regulation mean that no partnership exists? These problems indicate that the application of §83(a) to service partners requires some rethinking.

Of course, these problems do not arise if the partnership interest is transferable or is not subject to a substantial risk of forfeiture. In addition, the problems associated with §83(a) can be avoided by electing out of its grasp. If the service partner files an election as provided for in §83(b), receipt of the partnership interest is taxable immediately as under *Diamond*. In such cases the service partner must include the value of the partnership interest, valued without regard for restrictions on transferability that someday will lapse. §83(b)(1)(A).

If the service partner is taxed on receipt of the partnership interest, either under *Diamond* or under §83(b), a new problem arises. In this circumstance the service partner has been taxed on the present value of her profits interest, but when those profits are actually earned by the partnership, the service partner will be taxed again under §702(a). Will the service partner then be double taxed?

Before we can answer this question, we need to determine the service partner's initial outside basis. If the exchange of services for a partnership interest is tax-free to the service partner, presumably the service partner's initial outside basis is zero. Taxing the service partner should produce a nonzero outside basis, but how do we arrive at that conclusion?

Suppose the partnership had paid for the services with cash rather than with a partnership interest. If the service partner then contributed this cash in exchange for a partnership interest, the service partner's initial outside basis would equal the amount of cash contributed under §722. Under this reasoning, the service partner's initial outside basis should equal the fair market value of the service partner's partnership interest, because that is the value contributed to the partnership by the service partner.

Thus, the service partner's outside basis will start out positive and will increase as the service partner includes her distributive share of partnership income. Over the life of the partnership, the service partner presumably will include as distributive share the same income stream that caused her to be taxed on admission to the partnership. In one sense, then, she will be taxed on the same income twice. However, there is no overall extra taxation because her outside basis increases for every dollar of includible income, and that outside basis eventually will be used by the service partner to absorb a distribution, to absorb an allocation of loss, or otherwise to offset future income.

3. *Administrative relief.* In the two decades between *Diamond* and *Campbell,* the law applying to service partners was relatively settled, if only because the Service did not seek to enforce its victory in *Diamond.* With the Circuit Court's conflicting opinion in *Campbell,* the law became unsettled. Rather than resolve this conflict in the courts, the Service in 1993 repudiated most of its victory in *Diamond.* In Revenue Procedure 93-27, the Service ruled that it will not attempt to tax the contribution of services in exchange for a profits interest in most circumstances.

Is it appropriate for the Service to provide such relief? In its *Diamond* opinion, the Seventh Circuit held that the statute requires immediate taxation of a partner contributing services to a partnership in exchange for a partnership interest. Is Revenue Procedure 93-27 good law in the Seventh Circuit? Might the Service be estopped from arguing contrary to its published position?

PROBLEMS

24-4.   *A* and *B* are equal partners in the *AB* general partnership. The partnership's only asset is a racehorse with adjusted basis of $80,000 to the partnership. When the horse is worth $160,000, *C* is admitted to the partnership, receiving one-fourth of all future profits in exchange for training the horse. At the time of *C*'s admission to the partnership, *A* and *B* each have an outside basis and capital account of $40,000, and the partnership is free of debts.

a.   What are the tax consequences to all parties of *C*'s admission to the partnership?

b.   How would your answer change if *C* had contributed cash of $40,000 as well as future services?

c.   In either case, should *C* make an election under §83(b)?

d.   Reconsider the questions above, assuming that *C* is given an immediate one-quarter interest in partnership and capital immediately upon her admission to the partnership.

2.   Taxation of the Partnership

If a partner contributes services to a partnership in exchange for an interest in partnership capital, the partner is taxed on the transaction. Treas. Regs. §1.721-1(b)(1). Should the partnership be taxed as well? At first blush the answer seems to be that it should. After all, taxation of the service partner presumably is justified on the theory that services and a partnership interest are so dissimilar that the exchange should not be tax-free. And if that is true for the service partner, it ought to be equally true for the partnership.

Under this theory, we would tax the partnership as if it exchanged a pro rata portion of its assets to the service partner in exchange for the services, and the partnership would be taxed on the unrealized appreciation or loss in that portion of its assets. These assets would then be deemed recontributed back to the partnership in exchange for the service partner's partnership interest. Thus, the partnership's adjusted basis in its assets would be increased by the gain (or decreased by the loss) it recognizes on the admission of the service partner.

At closer examination, however, the argument for taxing the partnership cannot hold up. Although the partnership should be taxed if it exchanges its assets for dissimilar property, no such exchange has occurred by reason of the admission of the service partner. The service partner has *not* received an interest in the partnership's assets. Rather, the service partner has received an interest in the business venture, and as to that exchange §1001 cannot apply because a business enterprise cannot have a basis in itself.

A corporation does not realize income when it exchanges its own stock for money, other property, or for services. That result is mandated by §1032, which provides an absolute bar to recognition of income or loss on the exchange. No similar provision exists in subchapter K, and the lack of a partnership analog to §1032 sometimes is used to suggest that the contribution of property or services to a partnership is taxable to the partnership except to the extent that some section (i.e., §721) provides otherwise.

That suggestion is misguided, however, because it misappreciates the role of §1032. Prior to enactment of §1032, corporations issued stock for property without the recognition of income or loss because the Service conceded that the basis concept could not be applied to newly issued stock. However, the Service took the position that if a corporation acquired some of its own stock in the market, held it in treasury, and then reissued it for property, the corporation would be taxed on the reissuance on an amount equal to the excess of the value of the property received over the corporation's cost basis in the stock.

As you might expect, treating the reissuance of treasury stock as taxable while exempting the issuance of fresh stock caused corporations to reissue treasury stock only when the transaction would produce a taxable loss to the corporation — if the value of the property received would exceed the corporation's cost basis in its treasury stock, fresh stock would be used. Section 1032 was enacted to put treasury stock on a par with unissued stock.

Partnerships have no need of a provision akin to §1032 because a partnership interest cannot be held in treasury. Accordingly, issuance of a partnership interest, like issuance of unissued stock, cannot be taxable under §1001 because the basis concept cannot be applied to the exchange. Section 1032 is simply irrelevant to the problem.

Further, if a partnership *were* taxed on the issuance of a partnership interest in exchange for services, that taxation could be avoided whenever desired by the partnership. All the partnership need do is pay the service partner in cash for the services rendered, and then the service partner can recontribute the cash for her partnership interest. If the partnership does not have available cash, it easily could be borrowed and the loan can be repaid the following day once the cash is recontributed to the partnership by the service partner.

Having determined that a partnership should not be taxed on issuance of a partnership interest in exchange for services, are there any tax consequences of the transaction to the partnership? If the partnership had purchased the services for cash, the partnership would either deduct the expense or capitalize it depending on whether the expense was ordinary and necessary. This should be equally true if the services are acquired for a partnership interest: Either the nonservice partners should be entitled to a deduction or some partnership asset (possibly including goodwill) should show an increase in adjusted basis. Of course, this assumes that the partner is taxed on the contribution either because it involves a capital shift or falls without the bounds of Rev. Proc. 93-27.

This rule preserves the equality of aggregate inside and outside bases. When the service partner is admitted to the partnership in a taxable transaction, her outside basis should equal the fair market value of her partnership interest. Because no new assets are added to the partnership by reason of admission of the service partner, aggregate outside basis will rise above aggregate inside basis unless the admission of the service partner either reduces the nonservice partners' outside basis or increases the inside basis of some asset. Giving the partnership a deduction reduces the nonservice partners' outside bases while capitalizing the value of the services raises aggregate inside basis. Thus the overall equality of aggregate inside and outside bases is preserved.

C. NONCONTRIBUTION ACQUISITIONS

Partnership interests can be acquired in ways other than by contribution. Like other property, partnership interests can be bought, received as a gift, or received from the estate of a decedent. In each case the initial outside basis of the transferee is determined by the usual, non-subchapter K rules, see §742, as modified by §752 to account for partnership debt. Vis-à-vis the partnership, though, the transferee steps into the shoes of the transferor. In particular, the transferee assumes the capital account of the transferor, Treas. Regs. §1.704-1(b)(2)(iv)(*l*), and the capital accounts are *not* adjusted to reflect the current value of the partnership's assets. See Treas. Regs. §1.704-1(b)(2)(iv)(f).

This last rule, that the partnership's assets are not revalued for book purposes, seems to be a flaw in the regulations. Had the transferor's interest been liquidated and then the transferee admitted as a new partner, the partnership assets would be revalued. See Treas. Regs. §1.704-1(b)(2)(iv)(f). This regulation seems to be based on the notion that partnership assets should be booked up to fair market value whenever some transaction dependent on the value of the assets has occurred. Surely by this standard the sale or exchange of a partnership interest ought to trigger an asset revaluation because the price that the transferee is willing to pay is dependent on the current value of the partnership's assets.

Suppose *N* sells her limited partnership interest in the *LMN* partnership to *O* for $10,000. At the time of the sale, the partnership owns a single asset with adjusted basis of $21,000 and fair market value of $30,000, and assume *N* had a one-third interest in the capital and profits of the partnership. Assuming *N* had an outside basis and capital account of $7,000 at the time of the sale, *N* will recognize a gain of $3,000 and *O* will start with *N*'s capital account of $7,000.

Because *O* has acquired a limited partnership interest, *O* cannot be allocated deductions in excess of her positive capital account balance. Treas. Regs. §1.704-1(b)(2)(ii)(d). Accordingly, *O* cannot be allocated more than $7,000 of partnership losses. But *O*'s investment in the partnership is $10,000, and there is no obvious reason why an allocation of loss to *O* in excess of $7,000 but not exceeding $10,000 should be improper. Had *O*'s capital account been booked to fair market value, this problem would not arise.

PROBLEMS

24-5.   *D* has a 10 percent interest in the profits and losses of the *P* partnership. *D*'s outside basis equals $25,000 and her capital account stands at negative $10,000. In order to acquire her partnership interest, *D* borrowed $20,000 from the *B* bank, and *D* pledged her partnership interest as security for this loan. *D* defaults on the loan, and the *B* bank forecloses on the partnership interest.

   a.   What is the bank's basis in the partnership interest?
   b.   What is the bank's capital account in the partnership (assuming the bank is recognized by the partnership as a partner)?

25

Dispositions of Partnership Interests

Like any other asset, a partnership interest may be sold, exchanged, gifted, or devised. In addition, a partnership interest can be retired in exchange for a liquidating distribution. While the taxation of liquidating distributions is subject to specific and highly unusual rules of subchapter K, sales, exchanges and other dispositions of a partnership interest are taxed, in general, under the usual nonpartnership rules that cover sales and exchanges of property. For example, the sale or exchange of a partnership interest will produce gain or loss to the transferor while the gift or devise of a partnership interest will not. Furthermore, §742 specifically provides that the basis of a transferred interest in the hands of the transferee is determined under the familiar basis rules (§1011 et seq.) generally applicable to transfers of property. This chapter will focus on those rules specially applicable to the transfer of partnership interests with the understanding that such rules apply against the backdrop of the more general disposition of property rules.

A. DISTRIBUTIONS IN LIQUIDATION OF A PARTNERSHIP INTEREST

Payments made in liquidation of a partner's interest are taxed pursuant to §736, see §731(c), where §761(d) defines "liquidation of a partner's interest" to be "the termination of a partner's entire interest in a partnership by means of a distribution, or a series of distributions, to the partner by the partnership." Note that this definition of a liquidation includes not only distributions to all partners when the full partnership is dissolved but also distributions to one or more retiring partners from a continuing partnership. However, a distribution in retirement of one partnership interest (e.g., an interest as a limited partner) is not considered a liquidating distribution under §761(d) if the distributee continues to hold a separate partnership interest (e.g., a continuing interest as a general partner). See Treas. Regs. §1.761-1(d).

Although the logical starting point for an analysis of a liquidating distribution is §736, we will begin with the taxation of liquidating distributions under §§731-732. Section 736 is not itself a taxing provision. Rather, it provides that some distributions are to be taxed under the usual distribution rule of §§731-732 (see §736(b)) while other distributions are taxed under §704 or §707 (see §736(a)). The actual rules of taxation are found only in these other provisions of Subchapter K. However, the application of §§731-732 to liquidating distributions can be very different from its application to nonliquidating distributions, and so we turn first to these familiar code sections to discover their unfamiliar and unusual rules governing distributions in liquidation of a partnership interest.

1. A Note on §§731-732

The basic provisions covering the taxation of all partnership distributions are §§731, 732 and 733. Section 731 specifies when and to what extent a distribution is taxable to the distributee partner. (A distribution under §731 is never taxable to the distributing partnership, §731(b), except to the extent §751 may apply to the transaction, §731(c).) Sections 732 and 733 are basis provisions, with §732 addressing the basis of distributed property in the hands of the distributee partner, while §733 speaks to the effect, if any, on the distributee partner's outside basis. In the context of liquidating distributions, §733 plays no role because the distributee partner necessarily has no outside basis (because she has no partnership interest) after the transaction.

Most nonliquidating distributions are nontaxable because gain is not recognized unless the amount of cash distributed exceeds the distributee partner's predistribution outside basis. §731(a). Because the hallmark of a tax-free transaction is a continuation of basis, when a nonliquidating distribution is nontaxable there can be no net change in the tax basis available to the distributee partner. Accordingly, the basis effect of a nontaxable nonliquidating distribution is to divide the distributee partner's predistribution outside basis between her postdistribution outside basis and the distributed property. See §§732-733. This basic scheme is continued in the context of liquidating distributions with the added wrinkle that the distributee partner's postdistribution outside basis always is zero, so that the distributee partner's predistribution outside basis must be allocated entirely to the distributed property. §732(b).

Consider the following example. *P* receives a distribution of Blackacre in retirement of her partnership interest. At the time of the distribution, *P*'s outside basis was $10,000. Blackacre had an inside basis to the partnership of $8,000 and was worth $13,000 at the time of its distribution. Under §§732(b) and 732(c)(1)(B)(i), we see that *P* takes a basis of $10,000 in Blackacre, for no net change in *P*'s overall basis. Consistent with this basis result, the distribution is tax-free to *P* under §731. Indeed, no net change in basis invariably is coupled with a tax-free transaction; basis increase results from recognition of income, while basis decrease comes from a recognition of loss (or other deduction).

In this example, *P realizes* a gain of $3,000 under §1001(a) because that is the excess of the amount realized (the fair market value of Blackacre, or $13,000) over *P*'s adjusted basis in her partnership interest (i.e., her outside basis, or $10,000). No gain is *recognized* by virtue of §731(a), and the basis rule of §732(b) ensures that this unrecognized gain is deferred rather than exempted: Because Blackacre takes a basis in *P*'s hands of $3,000 less than fair market value, the realized but unrecognized gain will reappear upon disposition of Blackacre by *P*.

To appreciate why all liquidating distributions cannot be taxed so simply, reconsider the example but assume that *P* receives cash of $13,000 in lieu of Blackacre. In this circumstance we cannot defer recognition of *P*'s income without giving *P* a low basis in the cash received. Because cash always takes an implicit basis equal to face value, the effect of the transaction is to increase *P*'s tax basis from $10,000 (in the form of *P*'s predistribution outside basis) to $13,000 (in the form of *P*'s postdistribution cash), for a net increase of $3,000. Accordingly, it must be the case that *P* recognizes $3,000 of income, and that is precisely the rule of §731(a)(1): as in the context of nonliquidating distributions, a liquidating distribution of cash in excess of the distributee-partner's outside basis produces gain equal to that excess. Here, that excess is $3,000.

But what if the amount of the cash distribution had been only $7,500? Once again, cash must take an implicit basis equal to face value so that the effect of the transaction is a net reduction of $2,500 in *P*'s tax basis. Accordingly, *P* should be able to report a loss on the transaction of $2,500, and that is the rule of §731(a)(2). See also Treas. Regs. §1.732-1(c)(3). Indeed, note that the amount of loss allowed in §731(a)(2) is defined, as it should be, by reference to the distributee partner's predistribution outside basis as compared with the distributee partner's postdistribution basis in distributed property (see §731(a)(2)(B)) plus the basis implicit in any cash distributed (see §731(a)(2)(A)).

There is but one last wrinkle to the taxation of liquidating distributions under §§731-732, and it concerns distributions consisting *only* of ordinary income assets and cash. Consider once again a liquidating distribution to *P*, but assume now that *P* receives inventory of the partnership having inside basis of $8,000 and fair market value of $13,000. *If* we treated the inventory just like we treated Blackacre, the distribution would be tax-free to *P*, and *P* would take the inventory with a basis of $10,000.

Note, though, that prior to the distribution there was ordinary income of $5,000 to be had from disposition of the inventory because the partnership's predistribution basis in the inventory was $8,000 while fair market value was $13,000. If we followed the rule of §732(b) and allowed *P* to inject her entire outside basis into the inventory, there would be ordinary income of only $3,000 when *P* sells the inventory. While there is nothing inherently wrong with this approach, Congress is unwilling to allow a partnership distribution to reduce the amount of ordinary income to be recognized. Accordingly, ordinary income assets can take a basis no higher than carryover when received in a partnership distribution. See §732(c)(1)(A)(i). In particular, note that the allocation of additional basis under §732(c)(2) applies only to nonordinary income assets because it applies by its express language only to increases mandated by application of §732(c)(1)(B).

If the liquidating distribution includes one or more capital assets as well as ordinary income assets and cash, excess outside basis can be allocated to the nonordinary income assets pursuant to §732(c)(2). For example, suppose *P* with an outside basis of $10,000 receives a liquidating distribution consisting of cash of $5,000, inventory with inside basis of $1,000 and fair market value of $6,000, and a capital asset with inside basis and fair market value $2,000. If this distribution is tax-free to *P*, *P* must carry over her outside basis into the assets distributed. §732(b). The cash takes an implicit basis of $5,000, the inventory can take a basis of no more than $1,000 under §732(c)(1)(A)(i), and that leaves $4,000 for the capital asset. Under §§732(b)-(c), this is exactly how *P*'s outside basis is allocated among the distributed assets. In particular, *P*'s basis in the capital asset can exceed the partnership's former adjusted basis in that asset, §732(c)(2)(A), and can even exceed the asset's fair market value, §732(c)(2)(B).

But what if there had been no capital asset? For example, reconsider the possibility that the inventory has an adjusted basis of $8,000 and a fair market value of $13,000, and the liquidating distribution consists only of this inventory. Section 732(b) certainly seems to say that *P*'s predistribution outside basis of $10,000 goes into the basis of the property distributed. However, §732(c)(1)(A) specifies that the inventory may take a basis of no more than carryover; that is, of no more than $8,000. If we have $10,000 of basis to allocate under §732(b) but only $8,000 of that basis is allocated under §732(c), where does the remaining $2,000 of basis go? Note that §732(c)(2) is not applicable because there is no basis increase required under paragraph §732(c)(1)(B).

Surprisingly, the additional $2,000 of basis goes nowhere! Although §732(b) purports to specify the amount of basis to be allocated among the distributed properties, in reality it specifies only the *maximum* amount of basis to be allocated. If less basis is allocated under §732(c)(1)(A)(i), *and if there are no non-§751 assets to be allocated basis under §732(c)(2)*, then the basis rule of §732(b) — although unconditional on its face — is ignored. In such circumstances, the important basis rule is contained in §732(c)(1)(A)(i), with §732(b) defining only the maximum possible basis of the ordinary income assets.

Can this be true? If basis is lost by P, it must be the case that P recognizes a loss on the transaction. That in fact is what happens under §731(a)(2) where loss can be recognized only on a liquidating distribution consisting entirely of cash and §751 property. In such cases there is no property that can absorb basis in excess of carryover. Accordingly, in such circumstances the distributee partner loses tax basis and a loss is recognized precisely equal to the amount of the basis so lost.

We can summarize the rule covering the taxation of liquidating distributions under §§731-732 as follows: (1) Gain is recognized only if the amount of cash distributed exceeds the distributee partner's outside basis; (2) loss is recognized only if the distribution consists of cash and §751 assets, and the inside basis of the distributed property, plus the amount of the distributed cash, is less than the distributee partner's outside basis; (3) if no loss is recognized on the distribution, the distributee partner's outside basis, less the amount of cash received, will be allocated among the properties distributed (first to the §751 properties by reason of §732(c)(1)(A)); and (4) if loss is recognized on the distribution, the distributee partner will take a basis in each distributed asset equal to its predistribution basis in the hands of the partnership. In each of the three following examples, assume that Q receives a liquidating distribution taxable under §§731-732, and assume that Q's outside basis immediately prior to the distribution equals $20,000.

Example 1: Suppose Q receives cash of $10,000 plus inventory with adjusted basis and fair market value of $8,000. No gain is recognized by Q because the amount of the cash distributed does not exceed Q's outside basis. To determine whether Q recognizes a loss, we must first determine Q's basis in the distributed inventory. Under §732(b), the maximum amount of basis to be allocated under §732(c) equals $10,000. Under §732(c)(1)(A)(i), $8,000 of that amount is allocated to the inventory. Further, because only cash and §751 assets were distributed to Q, the remainder of Q's outside basis goes unallocated. Then, under §731(a)(2), Q recognizes a loss of $2,000, a loss that is capital by reason of the final sentence in §731(a) coupled with §741.

Example 2: Suppose once again that Q receives cash of $10,000 plus inventory with adjusted basis of $8,000, but now assume that the inventory has a fair market value of $15,000. Once again, gain is not recognized because the amount of the cash distributed does not exceed Q's outside basis. Also once again, Q takes a basis in the inventory of $8,000 under §732(c)(1). Thus, there is once again a capital loss of $2,000 under

§731(a)(2). The tax consequences to Q in example two are precisely the same as in example 1.

But notice what is different about example 2. In example 1, Q realized (and recognized) a loss on the distribution of $2,000, where that realized loss, computed under §1001, is the excess of Q's outside basis over the value of the property (and cash) distributed. In example 2, however, Q realizes a gain on the distribution yet recognizes a loss! That is correct: *Recognition* of a loss under §731(a)(2) is independent of any gain or loss *realized* on the transaction. Indeed, if you go back and look closely at the rules governing liquidating distributions in §§731-732, you will see that the *value* of the distributed property plays no role in determining the extent to which the distributee partner recognizes gain or loss on the liquidating distribution. To be sure, the *inside basis* of distributed property can be important (under §732(c)(1)), but its value — so important in calculating realized gains and losses under §1001 — is simply irrelevant. Accordingly, in a liquidating distribution taxable under §§731-732, the distributee partner can recognize a loss even though she realizes a gain.

Example 3: Q receives a liquidating distribution consisting of cash of $11,000, inventory with adjusted basis of $8,000 and fair market value of $12,000, and an unrealized receivable with adjusted basis of $4,000 and fair market value of $10,000. Under §732(b), there is a maximum basis of $9,000 to be allocated between the inventory and the receivable. Under §732(c)(1)(A)(i), the inventory is allocated a carryover basis of $8,000 and the receivable is allocated a carryover basis of $4,000. However, because these basis allocations total more than the $9,000 maximum as specified by §732(b), we adjust these bases downward pursuant to §§732(c)(1)(ii) and 732(c)(3). In particular, under §732(c)(3)(B) there is a total negative adjustment of $3,000, of which $2,000 is allocated to the inventory and $1,000 is allocated to the receivable. Thus, the inventory takes an adjusted basis of $6,000 and the receivable takes an adjusted basis of $3,000.

2. Application of §736

a. A First Note on the Application of §736

In the absence of §736, the taxation of liquidating distributions would be controlled by §§731-732, discussed above, as well as by §751(b), a provision that can overrule the application of §731, see §731(c). Like §751(b), §736 also trumps the application of §731 by virtue of an explicit statement in §731(c). Accordingly, we need to determine precisely when §736 applies.

By its terms, §736(a) applies to "payments" made in liquidation of a partnership interest. A liquidating distribution of cash certainly falls within the scope of §736, but does a distribution of noncash partnership property also fall within it? Arguably, the term "payment" is narrower than the term "distribution" to which §§731-732 apply.

Does §736 apply to noncash distributions? Surprisingly, there is no definitive answer. The regulations under §736 do not speak to this issue, and every example in those regulations considers only cash distributions. The leading commentators quite clearly assume that §736 can apply to noncash distributions, but they give no indication of having considered any alternative.

Look closely at §736(b)(1). Under certain conditions, a "payment" to which §736 speaks "shall be considered a distribution by the partnership and not as a distributive share or guaranteed payment." If the term "payment" was intended to be synonymous with "distribution," then this section would be saying that a distribution shall be considered as a distribution. While it is not impossible that is what Congress intended (the Code is full of truisms), surely it is at least possible that what was intended was something more informative.

The regulations promulgated under §751 cast a murky light on this problem. In example 2 of Treas. Regs. §1.751-1(g), a liquidating distribution of noncash property is explicitly assumed to be taxed under §736. However, because the partnership has no unrealized receivables and no goodwill, the entire distribution is taxed under §736(b) and through it to §§731-732. Thus, §736 has no impact, and that might help explain why the application of §736 goes unexplained.

In example 6 of that same regulation, another liquidating distribution of noncash property is considered. Here, though, the partnership owns unrealized receivables so that application of §736 to the liquidating distribution is germane. Unfortunately, no mention of §736 is to be found, and the analysis presented by the regulations seems to tacitly assume that the distribution is taxed directly under §§731-732 (except to the extent §751(b) overrules §731). No explanation for the inconsistency between examples 2 and 6 is offered.

Fortunately, this issue is largely irrelevant because most liquidating distributions will be taxed the same whether §736 applies or not. However, that is not always the case, and at the end of this Section we will return to this issue to pinpoint its implications.

b. Classification of Payments under §736

All payments made in liquidation of a partnership interest are divided into two groups: the §736(a) payments and the §736(b) payments. Payments made in exchange for a partner's interest in "partnership property" are classified as §736(b) payments, and all other payments are classified as §736(a) payments. In general, all payments are treated as payments for "partnership property," see §§736(b)(2), 736(b)(3). However, when the liquidating distribution is made to a general partner and capital is not a material income producing factor in the partnership (i.e., the distribution is made by a service-oriented partnership), a special rule applies. In this case, §736(b)(2)provides that "partnership property" does not include unrealized receivables.[1] Accordingly, liquidating distributions from a service partnership to a general partner made in exchange for the partner's share of unrealized receivables are classified as §736(a) payments. In addition, if this partner receives payments for her share of the partnership's goodwill, these payments also are taxed as §736(a) payments. However, under §736(b)(2)(B), the partnership agreement may elect to have payments for partnership goodwill taxed under §736(b) instead. Thus, there is an elective component to §736 that applies only to payments for partnership goodwill. Of course, none of this is relevant unless capital is not a material income-producing factor in the partnership *and* the liquidating distribution is made to a general partner.

If a liquidating distribution can contain a §736(a) component because capital is not a material income-producing factor in the partnership and the distribution is in liquidation of a general partnership interest, determining the current value of partnership goodwill can be important. For example, suppose general partner P receives a liquidating payment of $20,000 in exchange for her one-fourth interest in the service-oriented *PQRS* partnership. If the partnership owns only receivables with aggregate fair market value of $80,000, then the entire payment is classified as a §736(a) payment because it is received by P in exchange for her share of the receivables. But what if the partnership's receivables are not worth $80,000, so that some of the $20,000 distributed to P is for P's share of the partnership's goodwill. If the partnership agreement provides that liquidating payments for goodwill are taxable under §736(b), then that portion of the $20,000 properly allocable to partnership goodwill is taxable under §736(b) and, through it, under §§731-732. The regulations provide: "Generally, the valuation placed by the partners upon a partner's interest in partnership property in an arm's length agreement will be regarded as correct." Treas. Regs. §1.736-1(b)(1).

When a liquidating distribution is made to a general partner from a service-oriented partnership, two details must be kept in mind. First, if the partnership agreement is silent as to the taxation of liquidating distributions received in exchange for goodwill, then such payments fall within §736(a). Smith v. Commissioner, 313 F.2d 16, 21 (10th Cir. 1962). In addition, to the extent partnership goodwill appears on the partnership books with a positive basis (as in the case of purchased goodwill), this goodwill is treated as "partnership property," and payments to a retiring

---

1. For purposes of §736, the term "unrealized receivable" includes only traditional receivables as defined in §751(c)(1)-(2) (note the parentheticals in the flush language following §736(c)(2)).

partner for her share of such purchased goodwill are taxed under §736(b). See Treas. Regs. §1.736-1(b)(3).

An entity can be taxed as a partnership even though it is not a "partnership" under relevant state law. For example, the members of a limited liability company usually can elect partnership or corporate taxation.[2] If the members of a service-oriented limited liability company elect to be taxed as partners, will payments made to a retiring member in exchange for a share of the entity's unrealized receivables be described in §736(a)? Recall that §736(a) usually applies only to payments made to *general* partners. While a member of a limited liability company may have rights to participate in the management of the entity similar to those of a general partner, the member lacks the general liability for entity obligations associated with general partner status. Assuming the retiring member performed substantial services for the entity (recall that it must be a service-oriented entity for §736(a) to apply), presumably the member will be treated as a "general" partner for purposes of §736(a).

c. Taxation of Payments in Liquidation of a General Partnership Interest When Capital Is Not a Material Income-Producing Factor

Those payments classified as §736(a) payments (which can only include payments for unrealized receivables and, unless the partnership agreement provides otherwise, payments for goodwill) must be further divided into two groups: (1) those §736(a) payments taxed as the distributee partner's distributive share, and (2) those §736(a) payments taxed to the distributee partner as a guaranteed payment. Under §736(a), payments are taxed as distributive share if determined *with regard* to the income of the partnership. If the amount of a §736(a) payment is determined *without regard* to the income of the partnership, it is taxed as a guaranteed payment.

For example, suppose Q is a one-third general partner in the service-oriented *PQR* partnership. Suppose further that *PQR* owns cash of $30,000 plus receivables worth $60,000. If Q receives a liquidating distribution of $30,000 in cash, one-third of the distribution (i.e., $10,000) will be taxed under §736(b) and the remaining two-thirds (i.e., $20,000) will be characterized as a §736(a) payment. If the partnership also agrees to distribute 5 percent of its net income to Q during each of the next three years, these additional payments will be characterized as §736(a) payments unless the partnership agreement provides to the contrary. Assuming these additional payments fall within §736(a), they will be taxed as distributive share to Q because they are determined with regard to the partnership's income. If, though, Q were to receive a fixed amount each year instead of the 5

---

2. See page 900 infra.

percent of income, the additional payments would be taxed as guaranteed payments.

Saying that Q's additional payments are taxed as distributive share means that (1) Q must report the amount in her gross income, as all partners must do with respect to distributive share and (2) the character of that income to Q is dependent on its character to the partnership. If the payments were taxed as guaranteed payments, they would be includible to Q as ordinary income: Guaranteed payments always are includible as ordinary income. Treas. Regs. §1.707-1(c); see also Treas. Regs. §1.736-1(a)(4). Further, the regulations provide that any §736(a) payment taxed to the recipient as a guaranteed payment is deductible to the partnership. Treas. Regs. §1.736-1(a)(4).

Is there a significant difference between those §736(a) payments taxed as distributive share and those taxed as guaranteed payments? Not really: While the guaranteed payments can be deducted by the partnership, taxing income as a distributive share to the retiring partner has the effect of excluding the income from all other partners. Similarly, the distributee partner must include the payment regardless of the characterization. Thus, only the character of the income is affected: Distributive share can be capital gain while guaranteed payments always are ordinary.

A distribution in liquidation of a general partnership interest from a service partnership can include both §736(a) and §736(b) components. However, the §736(b) component represents that portion of the liquidating distribution received in exchange for partnership property (excluding unrealized receivables), and since there can be *no* §736(a) component unless capital is not a material income-producing factor,[3] it is unlikely that the §736(b) component will be substantial. Nonetheless, even a service partnership can own some assets and certainly can have zero-basis goodwill.

Consider the following example. Individual D is a one-quarter partner in the *ABCD* general partnership. The partnership owns capital assets with adjusted basis of $12,000 and fair market value of $16,000 as well as unrealized receivable of $80,000 and self-generated goodwill with adjusted basis of $0 and fair market value of $20,000. If $29,000 is distributed to D in liquidation of her partnership interest (assume the distributed cash represents loan proceeds obtained to liquidate D's partnership interest), $20,000 will be taxable under §736(a)(2) as a guaranteed payment, $4,000 will be taxable under §736(b) as in exchange for partnership property, and $5,000 will be taxable under §736(a)(2) or §736(b) depending on

3. If the amount of the payments to the retiring partner exceeds the fair market value of the retiring partner's interest in the venture, then that excess might be described in §736(a). However, the regulations promulgated under §704(b) require the partnership agreement to provide that a retiring partner will receive only the positive balance, if any, of her capital account. Treas. Regs. §1.704-1(b)(2)(ii)(b)(2). Accordingly, there should be no such excess.

what the partnership agreement says concerning partnership goodwill. Assuming D's outside basis at the time of the distribution equals $3,000 and that the partnership agreement says nothing about partnership goodwill, D will have ordinary income of $25,000 under §736(a)(2) and a capital gain of $1,000 under §§736(b)(1) and 731(a)(1).

There is one more complexity to taxation under §736(a). As discussed above, liquidating distributions made to a general partner from a partnership in which capital is not a material income-producing factor will be classified as §736(a) payments if made for the distributee partner's share of unrealized receivables. For application of §736, the definition of an "unrealized receivable" is narrower than usual. See the parenthetical in the first sentence of §751(c) following subsection (2).

d. Taxation of Payments under §736(b)

Most liquidating payments made by a partnership including all partnerships in which capital *is* a material income-producing factor as well as all liquidating distributions to *limited* partners are classified as §736(b) payments, and such payments are then taxed under §§731, 732, and 751(b). Formally, application of §751(b) to liquidating distributions is the same as for nonliquidating distributions. However, if the distribution consists exclusively of cash, it necessarily is the case that the distributee partner's postdistribution share of the partner's §751 assets is zero, and so the distribution has the effect of exchanging the partner's share of §751 assets for cash, and so §751(b) is triggered.

For example, suppose A is a one-quarter partner in the $ABCD$ partnership when the partnership books stand as follows:

Assets

	Adjusted basis	Fair market value
Capital Asset	$12,000	$20,000
Receivables	0	12,000
Inventory	8,000	16,000
Cash	20,000	20,000

Liabilities and Capital

	Adjusted basis	Fair market value
A	$10,000	$17,000
B	10,000	17,000
C	10,000	17,000
D	10,000	17,000

If A receives cash of $17,000 in liquidation of her partnership interest, what are the tax consequences to A and to the partnership? Because capital is a material income-producing factor in this partnership, the entire $17,000 received by A in liquidation of her partnership interest is treated as a §736(b) payment, see §736(b)(2), and under §736(b)(1), taxation is determined under §§731 and 751. Prior to the liquidating distribution, A's share of the partnership's §751 property was $3,000 of the receivables with $0 adjusted basis and $4,000 of the inventory with $2,000 adjusted basis. Accordingly, the effect of the liquidating distribution is to reduce A's interest in the §751 assets from $7,000 to $0.

Under §751(b), there is a hypothetical nonliquidating distribution of A's share of the §751 property, see generally Treas. Regs. §1.751-1(b)(3), so that A is deemed to received $3,000 of the receivables with a basis of $0 and $4,000 of the inventory with a basis of $2,000, see §732(a), and no gain or loss is recognized, §731. Under §733(2), A reduces her outside basis by $2,000, down to $8,000. Next, A is treated as selling both the receivables and the inventory back to the partnership, producing ordinary income to A of $3,000 on the receivables and $2,000 on the inventory. Because the partnership takes a cost basis in the property of is treated as buying from A, the partnership's adjusted basis in the receivables becomes $3,000 and its adjusted basis in the inventory becomes $10,000.

Finally, A is treated as receiving the remainder of the cash ($17,000 less $7,000, or $10,000) in a liquidating distribution taxable under §731. This produces a capital gain of $2,000. Thus, A has recognized total income of $7,000, of which $5,000 is ordinary and $2,000 is capital. The partnership increases its basis in its ordinary income by $5,000.

In this example, A recognizes income of $7,000 whether or not §751(b) applies. The effect of §751(b) is to convert part of that gain (in this case $5,000 of the gain) into ordinary income. A's recognition of ordinary income reflects her share of the appreciation in the partnership's inventory: Prior to the distribution, the partnership owned inventory and unrealized receivables with adjusted basis of $8,000 and value of $28,000, so that A's one-quarter share of the appreciation was $5,000. After the transaction the partnership's basis in the inventory and receivables is increased by the ordinary income recognized by A. This makes sense because A's share of the appreciation has already been taxed; the basis increase to the partnership ensures that A's share of the appreciation will not be taxed again.

e.   Deferred Payments under §736

Payments made to a retiring partner in liquidation of her partnership interest can be made over time. For example, the partnership might agree to pay a fixed amount of money or a fixed percent of its profits each year for some fixed number of years. In such circumstances the tax consequences of the §736 payments spread out over several years. Regulations under §736 give substantial flexibility in allocating the partner's outside basis to the §736(b) payments received over time and, in the rare occasion when the deferred payments include both §736(a) and §736(b) components, similar flexibility in allocating each payment between §736(a) and §736(b) (although the total amount allocated to each section over all years must reflect the value of the retiring partner's interest in the various assets of the partnership). Treas. Regs. §1.736-1(b)(4)-(7).

Consider the following example. X retires from the XYZ partnership when the partnership books stand as follows. In liquidation of her partnership interest, X receives cash of $10,000 and will receive four additional annual distributions in the same amount.

Assets

	Adjusted basis	Fair market value
Cash	$45,000	$45,000
Receivables	0	45,000
Capital asset	12,000	15,000
Goodwill	0	45,000

Liabilities and Capital

	Adjusted basis	Fair market value
X	$19,000	$50,000
Y	19,000	50,000
Z	19,000	50,000

Because capital is a material income-producing factor in the partnership, the entire $50,000 to be distributed to X is described in §736(b) and so is taxable under §§731 and 751(b). Prior to the distribution, X's interest in the partnership's §751(b) assets consisted of $15,000 of the receivables with adjusted basis of $0. Putting the timing issue aside, X is treated as receiving a nonliquidating distribution of $15,000 of the receivables, tax-free under §731 and with a carryover basis of $0 under §732. Because the receivables take a $0 basis in X's hands, there is no reduction to X's outside basis under §733(2).

X is then treated as selling these receivables back to the partnership, producing ordinary income to X of $15,000 and the partnership takes a cost basis in the receivables deemed purchased, so the partnership increases its adjusted basis in its receivables to $15,000. Finally, the remainder of the cash, namely $35,000, is taxed to X under §731, yielding a capital gain of $16,000. Thus, X recognizes ordinary income of $15,000 and capital gain of $16,000 on the liquidating distribution, and the partnership can increase the basis of its receivables by $15,000.

Taking the installment nature of the payments into account, we first observe under Treas. Regs. §1.736-1(b)(5) that there is no §736(a) component to any of the payments. The regulation further seems to provide that X may elect to treat the payments as a recovery of basis first or under the installment method. If X makes no election to the contrary, the first payment will be tax-free and the second will be taxable only to the extent of $1,000, while the third, fourth, and fifth payments will be taxable in full. To the extent any payment is taxable, presumably X will recognize 15/31's of the income as ordinary and 16/31's as capital.

X may elect to recognize a portion of the $31,000 income with each payment. If X so elects, 31/50's of each payment will be taxable while 19/50's of each payment will be treated as a recovery of basis. Thus, X will have income of $3,100 from each payment. Of that $3,100, presumably 15/31's (or $1,500) will be ordinary while 16/31's (or $1,600) will be capital. Certainly it is possible that the Service will seek to require X to report the ordinary income first and the capital gain last.

f. Section 736, Partnership Goodwill, and the §704(b) Regulations

Payments in liquidation of a general partnership interest when capital is not a material income-producing factor can be divided into three groups: (1) payments for the distributee's share of unrealized receivables, taxed under §736(a); (2) payments for the distributee's share of all other partnership property, taxed under §736(b); and (3) payments for goodwill, taxed under §736(a) or under §736(b) depending on the partnership's election. See §736(b)(2)(B). Under long standing regulations, goodwill of the partnership in this context includes "an arrangement among the partners in the nature of mutual insurance." Treas. Regs. §1.736-1(a)(2). Is this broad interpretation of "goodwill" consistent with the §704(b) regulations?

In general, the goodwill of a business means its value as a going concern in excess of its asset value; that is, a business has goodwill to the extent that its reputation is valuable. Investments in advertising, quality control, customer service and other intangibles all help to increase the value of a company's goodwill. Goodwill within the meaning of §736(b)(2)(B) certainly includes this traditional concept of the term, but in this sense the goodwill is like any other asset of the business.

Recall that special allocations of partnership income, deduction, credit, and loss will be allowed only if they have substantial economic effect within the meaning of §704(b)(2). Under the §704(b) regulations, a partnership will fail the substantial economic effect test if liquidating distributions are made other than in accordance with final capital account balances after adjustment is made for all unrealized appreciation and loss in partnership assets. Treas. Regs. §1.704-1(b)(2)(ii)(b)(2). Partnership goodwill in the traditional sense will be reflected in such adjusted capital account balances, so that distributions in liquidation of a partnership interest may (indeed, must) include amounts for the distributee's share of partnership goodwill *in the traditional sense*.

But what of the "arrangement[s] among the partners in the nature of mutual insurance" allowed by the §736 regulations? Such arrangements reflect a shifting of value from the remaining partners to the retiring partner (or to the beneficiaries of a deceased partner) unrelated to any economic event of the partnership. Accordingly, payments in the nature of mutual insurance are unrelated to the partners' capital accounts and so fail to meet the standards of the §704(b) regulations. Treas. Regs. §1.704-1(b)(2)(ii)(b)(2). These regulations do not, of course, prohibit partnerships from providing for liquidating distributions in the nature of mutual insurance — such a prohibition would go well beyond the authority of §704 — but they do seem to say that the tax allocations of such a partnership are subject to challenge. Treas. Regs. §1.704-1(b)(1)(i). If you write a partnership agreement that provides for some mutual insurance among the partners, be sure to think carefully if the risks are worth it and, even more importantly, be certain to explain the risks to your clients.

g. A Final Note on the Application of §736

As discussed above, §736 unambiguously applies to liquidating distributions of cash, but its application to distributions of property is less than clear. If §736 does *not* apply to distributions of property, then such distributions will be taxable directly under §§731-732. These same provisions apply even if §736 *is* applicable, at least as to distributions in exchange for the partner's share of partnership property as defined in §736(b). Application of §736, therefore, can make a difference only as to distributions *not* in exchange for the partner's interest in partnership property; that is, to distributions for a general partner's share of partnership unrealized receivables and goodwill from a partnership in which capital is not a material income-producing factor.

Let us first focus on property received by the retiring partner in exchange for her share of the partnership's receivables. Under §736(a), the retiring partner will recognize ordinary income equal to the value of this property, assuming §736 can apply to such distributions. If §736 does not apply, then the distribution will be taxed under §§731-732 and §751(b), and precisely the same result will obtain under §751(b) because unrealized receivables have a zero basis to the partnership, so long as the retiring partner's share of the receivables drops to zero. Thus, if the distributed property does not include any §751 property, the possible application of

§736 is irrelevant to the retiring partner. As to the partnership, application of §736 will provide a deduction while application of §751(b) will produce a basis increase in the receivables. Thus, all else being equal the continuing partners would prefer that §736 apply.

However, if the liquidating distribution includes some §751 property, possible application of §736 becomes important. If §736 applies to the distribution, the retiring partner recognizes income under §736 and the partnership enjoys a corresponding deduction. Treas. Regs. §1.736-1(a)(4). However, if §736 does not apply, the retiring partner might avoid recognition of income because the distribution might have little or no effect on the partner's interest in §751 property: There will be a re-arrangement of interests in §751 property to which §751(b) speaks *only if* the distribution contains less than the retiring partner's full share of §751 property. Treas. Regs. §1.751-1(b)(1)(ii). As to the remaining partners, to the extent that the retiring partner avoids recognition of income, the partnership receives no deduction or inside basis increase.

For example, suppose the service-oriented *MNOP* general partnership owns unrealized receivables with adjusted basis of $0 and fair market value of $20,000, and assume that each partner has an outside basis of $0. If the partnership liquidates by distributing one-quarter of the receivables to each partner, what are the tax consequences to the partners? If the distributions are not subject to §736 because they are not "payments," then each partner takes a carryover basis of $0 in the receivables under §732(b) and there is no gain or loss under §§731(a) and 751(b). If, though, §736 applies to these distributions, each partner has a guaranteed payment of $5,000 under §736(a)(2), producing $5,000 income to each partner under §707(c) as well as $20,000 of income (under §1001(a)) and a $20,000 deduction (under Treas. Regs. §1.736-1(a)(4)) to the partnership.

Application of §736 to liquidating distributions of property again can be important with respect to partnership goodwill. If §736 applies to distributions of property, election by the partnership under §736(b)(2)(B) to treat payments for goodwill under §736(b) causes such payments to be taxed under §§731-732. In such circumstances, the possible application of §736 is irrelevant because the same sections — §§731-732 and 751(b) — apply to the distribution. However, if no election under §736(b)(2)(B) is made, taxation under §736 produces ordinary income to the partner and a deduction (under §736(a)(1)) to the partnership while taxation under §§731-732 produces no income to the partner and no deduction to the partnership.

PROBLEMS

25-1. *A* retires from the *ABC* partnership when the partnership books stand as indicated below. *A* receives a cash payment of $40,000 and will receive four additional payments in the same amount.

Assets

	Adjusted basis	Fair market value
Capital asset	$30,000	$ 60,000
Receivables	0	240,000
Inventory	30,000	90,000
Cash	90,000	90,000
Goodwill	0	120,000

Liabilities and Capital

	Adjusted basis	Fair market value
A	$50,000	$200,000
B	50,000	200,000
C	50,000	200,000

Assuming that each partner's capital account equals that partner's outside basis, how is A taxed under §736?

B. DISPOSITION OF A PARTNERSHIP INTEREST

We now turn to the transfer of a partnership interest *other than* in exchange for a liquidating distribution. When *any* asset is transferred, certain questions should leap to mind. First, is the transferor taxable on the transaction? Second, if gain or loss is recognized, how is the asset's holding period computed and, more generally, is any gain or loss characterized as ordinary or capital? Third and finally, how does the transferee compute her basis in the newly acquired asset? With respect to the transfer of a partnership interest, the difficult issues usually arise in connection with the second question.

1. Basic Rules

Under §741, the sale or exchange of a partnership interest produces gain or loss to the transferor. The amount of the gain or loss is determined simply by comparing the transferor partner's amount realized on the transaction with her outside basis in her partnership interest. Note that, except as modified by §751(a), this gain or loss is taxable as capital gain or loss. §741.

While computing the amount of gain or loss on the disposition of a partnership interest is not difficult, one aspect of the computation is easy to forget. Under §752(d), the amount realized in exchange for a partnership interest includes the transferor partner's share of the partnership's liabilities. For example, if *P* is a one-half partner in the *PQ* partnership, which owns Blackacre worth $1,000,000 and subject to a debt of $600,000, *P*'s amount realized should she sell her partnership interest will include not only what she actually receives for her interest (presumably $200,000) but also an additional $300,000 as her one-half share of the partnership's liability. Including the transferor's share of partnership liabilities in amount realized makes sense for the same reason that liabilities contribute to amount realized in a nonpartnership setting: What goes into basis must be reflected either in an out-of-pocket expenditure or in an adjustment to amount realized. Commissioner v. Tufts, 461 U.S. 300 (1983)

The general capital gain (or loss) rule in §741 is modified by application of §751(a). Under §751(a), we divide the gain or loss realized on the sale into ordinary income and capital gain components. Note, though, that the following rule always holds true: *The net gain (or loss) recognized by the transferor partner under §751(a) will always equal the gain or loss computed under §741 without regard to §751(a).* That is, the effect of §751(a) is only to bifurcate the overall gain or loss between ordinary and capital components. It may be the case, however, that one of the components is positive (an ordinary or capital gain) while the other is negative (an ordinary or capital loss).

Capital gain recognized on the sale of a partnership interest might be attributable to collectibles held by the partnership or to §1250 capital gain arising from depreciable real estate. Because such gains are taxed at rates higher than that applicable to general long-term capital gain, see §1(h), capital gain recognized on the sale or exchange of a partnership interest must be divided into the various classes of capital gains according to the assets held by the partnership. See §1(h)(5)(B) and §1(h)(11). For detailed rules on making the allocations, see Prop. Treas. Regs. §1.1(h)-1. Note that no similar allocations need be made upon receipt of a liquidating distribution even when such a distribution produces capital gain to the exiting partner.

2. Application of §751(a)

Under regulations promulgated in December of 1999, application of §751(a) is computed in three steps. Prop. Treas. Regs. §1.751-1(a)(2). In step 1, the selling partner determines how much ordinary income or loss would be includible as distributive share if, instead of selling her partnership interest, the partnership sold its assets for fair market value. This first step is computed by taking into account all provisions that affect the selling partner's distributive share including curative and remedial allocations under §704(c)(1)(A) and in connection with reverse §704(c) adjustments. This is the amount of ordinary income (or loss) the selling partner reports under §751(a). In step 2, the partner determines the gain or loss that is realized on the sale of her partnership interest, computed by ignoring the application of §751(a). This is the selling partner's net income or loss from the sale. And in step 3, the selling partner determines the capital gain or loss from the sale by subtracting from the net income or loss as determined in step 2 the amount of ordinary income computed in step 1.

Consider the following example. X is a one-third partner in the XYZ general partnership with partnership books as follows:

Assets

	Adjusted basis	Fair market value
Inventory	$7,500	$ 9,000
Receivables	0	18,000
Land	9,000	12,000

Liabilities and Capital

	Adjusted basis	Fair market value
X	$5,500	$13,000
Y	5,500	13,000
Z	5,500	13,000

If partner X sells her partnership interest for its fair market value of $13,000, X will recognize ordinary income of $6,500 because that is the amount of ordinary income that X would report if the partnership sold all its assets for their current fair market values. Because the gain realized on the sale is $7,500 (computed as amount realized of $13,000 less adjusted basis of $5,500), the capital gain on the sale is $7,500 less $6,500, or $1,000. Note that in this case the amount of capital gain recognized on the sale equals X's share of the unrealized appreciation in the partnership's capital asset.

Reconsider this example but assume that X's outside basis is $8,000 rather than $5,500 (perhaps because X acquired her partnership interest by purchase at a time when the partnership owned appreciated assets). If X again sells her one-third interest in the partnership for $13,000, X again reports ordinary income of $6,500 because that figure is determined by the fair market value of the partnership's assets as compared with the partnership's basis in those assets: the selling partner's outside basis has no relevance to the computation of the ordinary income component under §751(a). Now, though, the net income realized on the sale is only $5,000 (amount realized of $13,000 less outside basis of $8,000), and so X recognizes a capital loss of $1,500 on the sale.

As this second example demonstrates, the capital gain or loss component on the sale of a partnership interest will not necessarily equal the selling partner's share of the unrealized gain or loss in the partnership's assets. In this example, X reports a capital loss even though all the partnership's assets are appreciated. Note also that in computing the ordinary income component of the sale, all aspects of the selling partner's distributive share are relevant including, if the partnership owns assets with adjusted basis more or less than book value, §704(c) considerations.

PROBLEMS

25-2. Reconsider the facts of problems 27-1 above. How would A be taxed if she sold her partnership interest to B and C?

25-3. G has a 50 percent interest in the losses of the GH partnership and a 75 percent interest in its profits. What are the tax consequences to G if she sells her partnership interest for $98,000 when the partnership books stand as follows?

Assets

	Adjusted basis	Fair market value
Capital asset	$30,000	$50,000
Receivables	0	40,000
Inventory	60,000	64,000
Cash	10,000	10,000

Liabilities and Capital

	Adjusted basis	Fair market value
G	$50,000	$98,000
H	50,000	66,000

25-4. XYZ, an accrual partnership, has the following assets:

Assets

	Adjusted basis	Fair market value
Capital asset	$30,000	$45,000
Receivables	30,000	30,000
Inventory	15,000	21,000
Cash	60,000	60,000

X, a one-third partner in XYZ for the past five years, would like to exit the partnership. X, Y, and Z decide to adopt one of the two following plans. Plan A is for X to receive cash of $52,000 in liquidation of her partnership interest. Plan B is for X to receive a liquidating distribution consisting of an undivided one-third interest in all partnership assets, followed by a sale of that undivided interest to Y and Z for $52,000. X's adjusted basis in her partnership interest equals $45,000. Determine the tax consequences of each plan to X, Y, Z, and the partnership.

25-5.   How do your answers in problem 27-4 above change if the partnership uses the cash receipts and disbursements method of accounting so that the partnership books stand as follows and X's outside basis equals $35,000?

Assets

	Adjusted basis	Fair market value
Capital asset	$30,000	$45,000
Receivables	0	30,000
Inventory	15,000	21,000
Cash	60,000	60,000

25-6.   Reconsider your answers to problem 27-4 above, assuming that the capital asset is subject to a liability of $12,000 so that each partnership interest is worth only $48,000. Now, Plan A is for X to receive cash of $48,000 while Plan B is for X to receive an unencumbered one-third interest in each asset, followed by a sale to Y and Z for $48,000.

25-7. P and Q form the PQ general partnership by contributing cash of $800,000 apiece. The partnership uses its cash of $1,600,000 to purchase depreciable equipment. The partnership leases this equipment to a third party and gives that third party the right to purchase the equipment for the partnership's adjusted basis anytime after the fifth year of the lease. Assume that this option is exercised when the partnership has an adjusted basis in the property of $1,000,000 and the property is worth $1,400,000. How will the partners be taxed if they (a) sell the asset to the third party for $1,000,000 or (b) sell their partnership interests to the third party for $500,000 each? Recall that depreciable property is subject to depreciation recapture under §1245.

3.   Non-Sale Dispositions

If a partnership interest is exchanged for other property, the transaction is taxed as a sale. §1001(a). This is true even if the other property is itself a partnership interest because an exchange of partnership interests cannot qualify for like-kind treatment under §1031. See §1031(a)(2)(D). If a partnership interest is abandoned, the loss will be ordinary because of the lack of sale or exchange unless the abandonment works a reduction in the partner's share of partnership debt; in such a case, reduction of debt is treated as a constructive distribution under §731 and so there is capital gain or loss except to the extent that §751(b) applies to the transaction. Rev. Rul. 93-80, 1993-2 C.B. 239.

4.   Closing of the Taxable Year

In general, a partnership's taxable year does not close as a result of the disposition of a partner's interest. §706(c)(1). However, the partnership's taxable year *does* terminate with respect to the exiting partner. §706(c)(2)(A). Thus, the exiting partner will report her distributive share of the partnership's income and deduction up to the time of her exit. The partnership may close its books as of the date of the partner's exit (called an interim closing of the books) or it can wait until the close of its taxable year and then apportion year-end totals to the periods before and after the partner's exit. See Treas. Regs. §1.706-1(c)(2)(ii). It is worth noting that the partnership year closes with respect to a partner who dies as well as to an exiting partner, whether the partner exits by selling her interest or by having the interest liquidated. §706(c)(2)(A).

A cash-basis partnership is forced to accrue most deductions under §706(d) whenever partnership interests change during the year. See §706(d)(2). Thus, when a partner exits the partnership during the partnership's taxable year, the exiting partner will include her distributive share of accrued partnership deductions regardless of the partnership's method of accounting. However, the exiting partner will not include accrued but unreceived income of the partnership unless the partnership uses an accrual method of accounting or the partnership apportions year-end totals in lieu of an interim closing of the books.

5.   Termination of the Partnership

If a partnership terminates, there is a liquidating distribution to all the partners. Under §708(b)(1), a partnership can terminate in either of two ways. First, a partnership terminates if "no part of any business . . . continues to be carried on by any of its partners in a partnership." §708(b)(1)(A). Second, a partnership terminates if "within a 12-month period there is a sale or exchange of 50 percent or more of the total interest in partnership capital and profits." §708(b)(1)(B). Only sales and exchanges of partnership interests are relevant to termination under §708(b)(1)(B), so that transfers by gift and devise are ignored, as are liquidations of partnership interests. See Treas. Regs. §1.708-1(b)(1)(ii). Note, though, that even a tax-free exchange of a partnership interest can trigger a termination under §708(b)(1)(B). This second type of partnership termination often is called a "technical termination."

A ceasing to conduct business termination can arise not only if the partnership goes out of business but also if all but one of the partners quits the partnership. The definition of a "partnership" in §761(a) includes only groups of investors, so that a partnership cannot exist with but a single partner. As a consequence, a two-person partnership necessarily terminates if one partner buys out the other or if one partner's interest in the partnership is liquidated. See Treas. Regs. §1.708-1(b)(1)(i).

When a partnership terminates, its taxable year ends and a liquidating distribution is made to its partners. In the case of a technical termination triggered by the sale of a partnership interest, the liquidating distribution is made to the continuing partners and to the *purchasing* partner. That is, the liquidation is deemed to occur immediately *after* the sale triggering the termination. Treas. Regs. §1.708-1(b)(1)(iv).

Because a technical termination under §708(b)(1)(B) does not terminate the partnership's activity under state law, a technical termination invariably is followed by a reformation of the partnership. Indeed, such a reformation often is invisible to the partners and to the world in general because nothing (aside from tax consequences) changes. Technically, however, the terminating partnership is deemed to contribute all of its assets to a new partnership in exchange for all of the interests in this new partnership, and then the terminating partnership is deemed to distribute those interests in the new partnerships to its members in liquidation of the terminating partnership. Treas. Regs. §1.708-1(b)(1)(iv).

Although an actual partnership termination and reformation would affect the partners' capital accounts and introduce new §704(c)(1) problems, no such complexity results from a technical termination under §708(b)(1)(B) because a technical termination does not affect the partners' capital accounts. Treas. Regs. §1.704-1(b)(2)(iv)(*l*). In addition, a technical termination does not trigger recognition of income under §704(c)(1)(B), Treas. Regs. §1.704-4(c)(3) or under §737, Treas. Regs. §1.737-2(a). And while property in the newly formed partnership will be treated as §704(c) property only if it was §704(c) property in the hands of the predecessor partnership, Treas. Regs. §1.704-3(a)(3)(i), the newly formed partnership is *not* required to use the same method for addressing ceiling limitations as did the predecessor partnership, Treas. Regs. §1.704-3(a)(2). See Treas. Regs. §1.708-1(b)(1)(iv) for additional guidance. The most significant drawback of a technical termination is that any depreciable property owned by the partnership must be treated as newly placed in service, see §168(i)(B) (final sentence), thereby lengthening the period over which the partnership will recover its remaining basis in its property.

If all but one of the partners wish to dispose of their interests in the venture, the partnership will terminate because a partnership requires at least two partners. Treas. Regs. §301.7701-3(a). Transfer of the business into the hands of the sole remaining member can be accomplished in different ways, and the particular form selected can affect the tax consequences of the transaction.

For example, suppose individuals *X*, *Y* and *Z* are equal one-third partners in the *XYZ* general partnership having outside bases and capital accounts of $14,000. Assume that the partnership's assets consists of cash of $24,000 as well as inventory with adjusted basis to the partnership of $18,000 and fair market value of $12,000, so that each partner's interest in the venture is worth $12,000. The partnership could terminate, distributing the inventory to X and $12,000 of cash to Y and Z. Equivalently, X could purchase the interests of Y and Z for cash of $12,000 each, and then the partnership would terminate automatically, distributing its cash and the inventory to X in a liquidating distribution. Whichever route is taken, X ends up with the inventory and Y and Z each get $12,000 in cash.

If the first route is taken, the distribution will produce a loss of $2,000 to Y and to Z, capital under §§731(a) (final sentence) and 741 except to the extent recharacterized under §751(b). On these facts, though, §751(b) will not apply because the inventory has declined in value and application of §751(b) is limited to "substantially appreciated" inventory. X will receive the inventory tax-free under §731 and will take a $14,000 basis in the $12,000 worth of inventory, see §732(b), so that if X sells the inventory there will be a loss of $2,000, ordinary under §735(a)(2) if the sale is made within five years of the liquidating distribution. Thus, of the $6,000 loss on the inventory, only X's share will qualify for ordinary loss treatment, with Y and Z saddled with $2,000 of capital loss apiece.

But if the second route is taken, Y and Z will each recognize a loss of $2,000 on the sale of her partnership interest to X. That sale will be subject to §751(a) and so the loss will be ordinary because §751(a), unlike §751(b), applies to all partnership inventory whether substantially appreciated or not. The liquidating distribution will again give X a $14,000 basis in the inventory worth $12,000, so as before X can enjoy an ordinary loss by selling the inventory within five years. Thus, by taking the second route rather than the first, the partners have preserved the entire ordinary loss in the partnership's inventory.

Next, consider the two-person PQ general partnership holding an appreciated capital asset with adjusted basis of $50,000 and fair market value $80,000. Assume that each partner has a capital account and outside basis of $25,000 and that partnership has held its asset and the partners have held their partnership interests for more than a year. Thus, there is unrealized appreciation of $30,000 in the partnership, and that unrealized appreciation and any subsequent appreciation should eventually produce a long-term capital gain.

If P wants to buy out Q's interest in the property, P might simply pay cash of $40,000 to Q for Q's partnership interest. This would produce a capital gain of $15,000 to Q, and then the partnership would liquidate, distributing the asset to Q in a liquidating distribution. P's outside basis in her partnership interest immediately prior to the distribution would be $65,000 ($25,000 in half the partnership and cost of $40,000 in the other half), so that P's basis in the distributed property would be $65,000 under §732(b). Suppose P subsequently sells the property for $90,000. P clearly recognizes a capital gain of $25,000 under §1001(a), but is all of that gain long-term?

Under §735(b), a partner's holding period in distributed property includes the holding period of the distributing partnership. Thus, on these facts the statute clearly says that P's holding period exceeds one year immediately after the distribution because P is entitled to tack the partnership's holding period to her own. As a result, the gain should be entirely long-term.

In McCauslen v. Commissioner, 45 T.C. 588 (1966), the Tax Court held that some of the gain (here, $5,000 of the gain) would be short-term because P may not tack the partnership's holding period to that portion of the asset attributable to the partnership interest purchased from Q. In effect, the Court rewrote §735(b) to tack not the partnership's holding period in the distributed asset but rather the partner's holding period in her partnership interest. The Court's holding in *McCauslen* was essentially unreasoned and quite clearly indefensible; no court ever followed it (though no court ever expressly disavowed it, either).

McCauslen was one of those cases consigned to the junk-heap of history until January of 1999, at which time the Service issued a revenue ruling expressly following the peculiar holding of *McCauslen*. Rev. Rul. 99-6, 1999-6 I.R.B. 6 (1999). This Ruling concludes that a sale by one partner in a two-person partnership of her interest in the venture to the other partner is taxable to the selling partner under §741 but that for determining the purchasing partner's holding period in distributed assets the transaction should be recast as if the partnership made a liquidating distribution to the two partners, followed by a sale of half the assets from one partner to the other. By recasting the transaction in this way, the purchasing partner loses the tacking benefit of §735(b) because half the assets are deemed acquired by purchase and not be distribution.

This ruling makes little sense. First, it is internally inconsistent: The same transaction is treated as a sale to the selling partner yet as a presale distribution to the purchasing partner. Second, it is inconsistent with the structure of subchapter K: A capital asset held by a partnership for more than one year will produce long-term capital gain to all the partners without regard for the length of period these partners have held their partnership interests. See, e.g., Podell v. Commissioner, 55 T.C. 429 (1970); Madison Gas & Elec. Co. v. Commissioner, 72 T.C. 521 (1979); Treas. Regs. §1.702-1(a)(2). There is no reason why the benefit of long-term capital gain treatment should be lost simply because the partnership distributes its assets in liquidation of the partnership. After all, such a distribution generally is tax-free and the partners essentially step into the shoes of the partnership. See §§731(a), 732(b), 735(b). Hopefully this ruling will be dismissed by the courts; its long-term effect on the credibility of the Service cannot help but be negative.

Under some circumstances, partners may wish to convert their partnership into a different but related form. For example, the partners may wish to convert a general partnership into a limited partnership or convert a limited or general partnership into a limited liability company (electing to be taxable as a partnership). Such a conversion is not treated as a liquidation of the partnership nor as a sale or exchange of the partnership interests. Accordingly, the only tax consequences of such a conversion would be deemed contributions and deemed distributions under §752(a)-(b) if the conversion worked a change in the partners' share of partnership debt. See Rev. Rul. 95-37, 1995-1 C.B. 130; Rev. Rul. 84-52, 1984-1 C.B. 157. If the partnership elects to be taxable as a corporation, see Treas. Regs. §301.7701-3(g)(1).

PROBLEMS

25-8.   *A, B,* and *C* are each one-third partners in the *ABC* partnership. On February 1, 2008, *C* sells her partnership interest to *D*. On March 1, 1998, *D* sells her partnership interest to *E*. On April 1, 1998, *A* sells her interest to *F*. On May 1, 2008, *B* sells her interest to *G*. When does the partnership terminate and to whom are liquidating distributions made?

6.   *Death of a Partner*

In general, property received from the estate of a decedent takes a fair market value basis in the hands of the transferee. §1014. However, this basis rule does not apply to income in respect of a decedent ("IRD") as defined in §691. In general, IRD within the meaning of §691 includes those items of income which would have been includible to the decedent had the decedent been an accrual taxpayer. In other words, IRD includes all accrued but unrealized items of income received by the estate or the decedent's successor.

If a partner dies, does the partnership interest qualify for a full step-up in basis under §1014 regardless of the assets held by the partnership? In a related context, the Tax Court has held that no basis step-up is appropriate with respect to the decedent partner's share of partnership unrealized receivables on the theory that if such receivables had been held directly by the decedent they would constitute IRD. Quick Trust v. Commissioner, 54 T.C. 1336 (1970), aff'd per curiam, 444 F.2d 90 (8th Cir. 1971); see also Woodhall v. Commissioner, 454 F.2d 226 (9th Cir. 1972). Such an approach is overbroad, however, because much of what constitutes an unrealized receivable under §751(c) (such as depreciation recapture) does not constitute IRD if held directly. See §691(a)(1). Note that §736(a) payments received by a decedent's successor are always treated as IRD by reason of §753.

26

Loss Limitations

Under §702(a) (especially §702(a)(8)), a partner includes her distributive share of partnership tax items in her individual gross income. Each partner's distributive share is determined under §704, and through it (usually) by the partnership agreement. Thus, partnership items of income, deduction, credit, and loss cannot be claimed by a partner except to the extent of her distributive share of each item.

Does that mean a partner includes all items of distributive share on her individual return? Absolutely not! With respect to distributive share of partnership loss, a variety of limitations must be overcome before the tax benefit of such losses can flow through to the partner's return. For example, capital losses cannot, in general, offset ordinary income. See §1211(b). In this chapter we will look at four similar loss limitations: The first, §704(d), applies exclusively to distributive share of partnership loss, while the others, §§465, 469, and 163(d), apply to all losses including but not limited to partnership distributive shares.

A. SECTION 704(d): THE OUTSIDE BASIS LIMITATION

Under §704(d), a partner's distributive share of partnership loss can be claimed on the partner's individual tax return only to the extent of the partner's outside basis. Although neither the Code nor the regulations promulgated under §704(d) specifically say so, the term "loss" in this context includes all partnership deductions. The limitation of §704(d) only arises at the conclusion of each partnership taxable year (because that is when distributive share is determined), and in applying the §704(d) limitation, the regulations specifically provide that the partner's outside basis is first adjusted upward for distributive share of partnership income. Reg. §1.704-1(d)(2). The partner's outside basis is also adjusted downward for distributive share of nondeductible, noncapitalizable partnership expenses (such as illegal bribes and kickbacks).

Losses disallowed under §704(d) are not lost forever. Rather, they are deferred until the partner's year-end outside basis is able to absorb them. For example, suppose partner *X* has an outside basis of $60 and a distributive share of partnership loss equal to $100. By reason of §704(d), *X* will be allowed to claim only $60 of the partnership's loss on her individual return. The remainder of the loss will be suspended. If *X*'s outside basis the following year exceeds next year's distributive share of loss by $40 or more, all of the suspended loss will be allowed at that time. If, though, *X*'s outside basis next year is $50 while her share of distributive loss is $40, only $10 of the suspended loss will be allowed then and the remaining $30 will continue to be suspended to the following year, or later.

Although §704(d) seems to suspend a loss until additional funds are contributed to the partnership (note the use of the word "repaid" in the final sentence of §704(d)), the regulations make clear that any year-end positive outside basis can revive a suspended loss. Treas. Regs. §§1.704-1(d)(1), 1.704-1(d)(4) (example 1). Accordingly, not only contributions but also distributive share of partnership income can trigger recognition of a suspended loss.

A partner's capital account, like outside basis, is adjusted downward to reflect the partner's distributive share of partnership loss. If some of the partner's distributive share is disallowed by reason of §704(d), should the partner's capital account be adjusted only for that portion of the loss allowed? Recall that capital accounts reflect the economic relationships among the partners. Capital accounts are not, therefore, adjusted for tax aspects of partnership transactions per se. Distributive shares of partnership income and loss affect capital accounts not because such shares are includible on the partners' individual income tax returns but because such shares correspond to how the partners have agreed to allocate economic gain and loss. For example, distributive shares of tax-exempt income increase capital accounts just as do distributive shares of taxable income even though tax-exempt income has no effect on the partners' individual tax returns. Accordingly, distributive share of partnership loss reduces capital accounts pro tanto without regard to the impact, if any, of §704(d).

1.   The Relation of §704(d) to §704(c)

Consider the following example. *A* and *B* form the *AB* general partnership as equal partners, with *A* contributing cash of $500 and *B* contributing property worth $500 but having an adjusted basis of $100. In its first year of operation, the partnership sustains a taxable loss of $300. As equal partners, A and B are each allocated half of the partnership's loss. But for application of §704(d), each partner would report a loss of $150 on her individual return as her distributive share. But because of §704(d), B can report only $100 of that loss, with the remaining $50 of loss suspended until B's year-end outside basis is sufficient to absorb it.

B's distributive share of partnership loss is disallowed presumably because it is inappropriate for B to recognize a loss from the partnership's activity in excess of B's after-tax investment in the partnership. B's book share of the loss equals $150 because B's capital account was credited with the *value* of the property B contributed to the venture. But until the precontribution unrealized appreciation in that property is taxed, B's investment has consisted primarily of pretax dollars.

In general, only after-tax investments can generate deductions. For example, suppose individual C owns property with a value of $500 and an adjusted basis of $100. If the entire investment is lost, C's deduction cannot exceed $100: Losing the $400 of unrealized appreciation cannot produce a deduction because it is the loss of basis, not of value, which produces a tax deduction. Recall the definition of "loss" in §1001(a).

Further, allowing a partner to recognize distributive share of loss in excess of outside basis would force the partner to take a negative basis in her partnership interest. As we have seen, recognition of distributive share of partnership loss must be coupled with an outside basis decrease if the loss is not to be recognized twice, once as distributive share and a second time upon disposition of the partnership interest.

There is, of course, a way to increase investment basis without making a contribution of after-tax dollars: promise to make an after-tax contribution in the future. In the case of a nonpartnership investment, this means borrowing and incorporating the debt proceeds in the investment. In a partnership context, debt could be introduced in either of two ways: (1) have the partner borrow directly (outside debt) or (2) have the partnership borrow and attribute the debt to the partner under §752 (inside debt). We will consider the impact of debt on the application of §704(d) in section C below.

2. Transfers of Partnership Interests

Suppose P transfers her partnership interest after some prior distributive share of partnership loss had been suspended under §704(d). Should P be entitled to claim the suspended loss upon disposition of the interest? Should the suspended loss be available to the transferee of P's partnership interest? Under §704(d), a suspended loss is never available to a transferee, although the loss may be available to the transferor if the transfer of the partnership interest is a taxable disposition.

Reconsider the *AB* general partnership in which *A* contributed cash of $500 and *B* contributed property with value of $500 and adjusted basis of $100. As discussed above, if the partnership sustains a taxable loss of $300, allocable equally to *A* and *B*, only $100 of *B*'s share will be allowable and the remaining $50 of distributive share of loss will be suspended under §704(d). If *B* sells her partnership interest for $400 in the middle of the next year, can *B* claim any of the suspended $50 of loss?

It depends. Disposition of a partnership interest closes the partnership's taxable year with respect to the transferor partner. §706(c)(2)(A). Accordingly, the sale forces *B* to recognize her share of the partnership's income and loss as of the date of sale, computed either by an interim closing of the partnership's books or by apportionment of the partnership's year-end totals. See Treas. Regs. §1.706-1(c)(2)(ii). If *B*'s distributive share of partnership income for this short partnership year exceeds *B*'s distributive share of loss, then *B*'s year-end outside basis will be positive and *B* will be entitled to reclaim some or all of the suspended loss. For example, if *B*'s share of income for the short partnership taxable year equals $140 and *B*'s share of loss equals $100, *B* will be entitled to claim $40 of the $50 suspended loss. Of course, if *B* made a contribution to the partnership during this same period, the outside basis increase resulting from such a contribution would also allow *B* to claim some or all of the suspended loss, depending on the extent of the outside basis increase resulting from the contribution.

If, in the example above, only $40 of *B*'s suspended loss is allowable to *B* as a result of *B*'s sale of her partnership interest, what happens to the remaining $10 of suspended loss? It is lost forever, and that is the appropriate result. Recall that §704(d) requires a partner to trade loss recognition for outside basis: In the absence of §704(d), excess distributive share of loss would be recognized but outside basis would become negative. When a partner sells her partnership interest, the §704(d) suspended loss is gone forever but the dispositional gain on sale of the interest is computed with reference to a zero (not negative) outside basis. The transferee is not entitled to the suspended loss because the transferor in effect used it on disposition of the partnership interest by reporting less gain.

Note that §704(d) is a *timing* provision: A loss is suspended until outside basis can absorb it or until a taxable disposition has, in effect, consumed it. But what if a partner with a suspended §704(d) loss makes a gift of her partnership interest? Should the suspended loss be available to the donee if her year-end outside basis can absorb it?

The answer seems to be that the donee should be able to reclaim the suspended loss of her donor when her year-end outside basis becomes positive. Of course, the issue still is one of timing: if the donee can claim the suspended loss, her outside basis will decrease pro tanto and so there will be more gain (or less loss) upon disposition of her partnership interest. Nonetheless, since the partnership did sustain a loss in the past that was not, by reason of §704(d), claimed on any partner's individual tax return, it seems appropriate that the donee should be able to claim the donor's suspended loss if the transfer was by gift. Unfortunately, there appears to be no authority for the transfer of a §704(d) suspended loss to a donee. Compare Reg. §1.1366-2(a)(5) specifically prohibiting the transfer of a suspended loss in the context of S corporations.

PROBLEMS

26-1. *J* is a partner in the *JKL* partnership having a 10 percent interest in profits and losses. Both *J* and the partnership use the calendar year as their taxable year and each uses the cash receipts and disbursements method of accounting. As of December 30, 1995, *J* has an outside basis and capital account of $10,000. For the year ending December 31, 1995, the partnership reports a net loss of $250,000. On June 30, 1996, *J* sells her partnership interest to Buyer for $15,000. Between January 1, 1996, and June 30, 1996, the partnership incurs $300,000 in losses. Between July 1, 1996, and December 31, 1996, the partnership recognizes $400,000 of income in excess of deductions.

   a. How much of the 1995 loss can *J* claim?
   b. How much of the 1996 loss can *J* claim, assuming the partnership uses an interim closing of the books to determine *J*'s distributive share for 1996? How does your answer change if the partnership allocates its year-end totals ratably over the year?
   c. *J* makes a payment to the partnership in December of 1996 equal to her closing capital account deficit. Does this payment allow *J* to claim an additional share of partnership losses? If not, what are the tax consequences of the payment?

B. SECTION 465: THE AT-RISK LIMITATIONS

1. *An Overview of §465*

Section 465 disallows deductions from an activity to the extent such deductions exceed the investor's "at-risk" investment in the activity, with such disallowed deductions deferred until that time, if ever, when the taxpayer's at-risk investment increases. Section 465 thus is similar to §704(d), with the taxpayer's at-risk investment in §465 standing in for outside basis in §704(d). Section 465, though, is broader in scope than §704(d) in that

§465 can apply to any investment activity whether conducted in a partnership or otherwise. However, because §465 applies only to individuals (including individuals who invest in an activity as partners or S corporation shareholders), it does not, in general, apply to C corporations. See §465(a)(1).

The general rule of disallowance in §465 is contained in §465(a)(1). By reason of §465(a)(2), losses disallowed under §465(a)(1) are suspended only until the taxpayer's at-risk investment in the activity increases or income from the activity is includible. In general, this will occur no later than when the taxpayer disposes of her interest in the activity in a taxable transaction. An example will help make this clear, but before we can understand an example we must look at some of the defined terms in §465.

A taxpayer's amount "at risk" in an activity is defined in §465(b) to include all cash invested, the adjusted basis of all property contributed, and most borrowed amounts as to which the taxpayer is personally responsible for repayment. Thus, a taxpayer's amount at risk in an investment is similar to the taxpayer's adjusted basis in the property with the major difference being that nonrecourse loans can add to basis but will not, in general, increase a taxpayer's amount at risk. However, some nonrecourse loans are treated as at-risk contributions in real estate investments, see §465(b)(6), while some fully recourse loans are excluded, see §465(b)(3). We will return to these details in the definition of "at risk" later.

Section 465(a)(1) broadly disallows "loss[es]" in excess of at-risk investment, and "loss" is defined in §465(d) to include "the excess of the deductions . . . allocable to an activity . . . over the income . . . from such activity." Thus, the term "loss" is given a much greater scope than is usual under §1001(a). Under §465(d), *all* deductions including ordinary and necessary business expenses and depreciation can be losses subject to the loss limitation rule of §465(a)(1). On the other hand, no deduction is a §465 "loss" except to the extent it exceeds the taxpayer's income from the activity. Thus, the loss limitation rule of §465(a)(1) applies only to deductions from an activity in excess of the taxpayer's income from the activity, and so the at-risk limitation of §465 is an anti-shelter rule just like §704(d), the passive activity loss rules of §469, and the investment interest limitation of §163(d).

Section 465(a)(1) by its terms only applies to certain specified activities. This was once an important constraint on the application of §465 because only the investment activities specified in §465(c)(1) were covered. However, §465 has applied to all investment activities since 1979, see §465(c)(3). Section 465(c)(3) by its language includes any activity engaged in by the taxpayer in carrying on a trade or business or for the production of income.

One thing that has not changed since §465 was first enacted in 1976 is that it generally applies on an activity-by-activity basis. More than one activity may be aggregated only under two circumstances. First, aggregation is allowed if the activities constitute a trade or business and the taxpayer actively participates in management of the trade or business. Second, aggregation is allowed if the activities constitute a trade or business carried on by a partnership or S corporation and 65 percent of the losses for the taxable year are allocable to persons who actively participate in the management of the trade or business. If neither situation exists, the activities are treated separately.

This is an important aspect of §465 because, as an anti-shelter provision, §465 only limits losses in excess of income. Application on an activity-by-activity basis means that income from one venture cannot be offset by a loss (in excess of amounts at risk) from another. In contradistinction, §704(d) applies to all investments of a single partnership and the passive-loss rules of §469 allow income from one passive investment to be offset by a loss from almost any other passive investment.

It is time to consider an example. Individual *X* purchases an apartment complex for $1,000,000, paying $100,000 down and signing a nonrecourse note for the remaining $900,000. Assume that the apartments generate income of $30,000, deductible expenses of $20,000, and a depreciation deduction of $50,000 per year. Finally, assume that the special rule in §465(b)(6) applicable to certain real estate financing does not apply.

We know that *X* must include the $30,000 in income, but may *X* also claim the deductions of $70,000? The first $30,000 of deductions are not subject to limitation under §465 because of the definition of "loss" in §465(d): Only deductions *in excess of* the investment's income are losses under §465. As to the remaining $40,000 of deductions, they are losses under §465 (and thus are subject to §465), but they are not disallowed by §465(a) because *X*'s amount at risk equals $100,000. Remember that losses under §465(d) are disallowed only to the extent that they exceed the taxpayer's amount at risk.

After this first year, *X*'s deduction of $40,000 of §465 "losses" will cause *X*'s amount at risk to decrease from $100,000 down to $60,000, and *X*'s adjusted basis in the property will decline from $1,000,000 to $950,000 (because of the depreciation deduction of $50,000). Year 2 mirrors year 1, with *X* including $30,000 and deducting $70,000 (of which $50,000 is depreciation), so *X*'s amount at risk will further decline to $20,000 and *X*'s adjusted basis in the property will drop to $900,000.

Year 3 of the investment triggers §465(a). In year 3, there is $30,000 of income and $70,000 of deduction. Once again, the first $30,000 of deductions are not subject to §465 because they do not exceed the activity's income and so are not "losses" under §465(d). The remaining $40,000 of deductions are subject to §465, and because the taxpayer's amount at-risk equals only $20,000, only $20,000 of deductions are allowable. The remaining $20,000 is disallowed under §465(a)(1), and these deductions will be treated as deductions in the next year pursuant to §465(a)(2).

Before considering year 4 of the investment, we must determine *X*'s adjusted basis in the property. Prior to year 3, *X*'s adjusted basis in the property was $900,000. In year 3, the property generated $50,000 of depreciation. Thus, in the absence of §465 X's adjusted basis in the property would be $850,000.

That analysis does not change in the presence of §465: The basis of the property becomes $850,000 after year 3 even though some of the depreciation deduction was disallowed by reason of §465(a)(1). This rule may seem peculiar to you: Why should basis go down if the depreciation deduction was disallowed? The answer is that the depreciation deduction was not disallowed but merely suspended: Under §465(a)(2), the deduction will reappear in some subsequent year. Follow the example for two more years and everything will become clear.

In the next year there again is income of $30,000, all of which is taxable to X. In addition, there is $90,000 of deductions, $70,000 arising this year and $20,000 carried forward from the prior year under §465(a)(2). Of these deductions, $30,000 are not "losses" under §465 and so are allowable and the remaining $60,000 of deductions are disallowed under §465(a)(1). Note that if there had been rental income of $90,000 or more, all the deductions would have been allowable because they would not be "losses" within the meaning of §465(d). Further, the deductions would have been allowable even without additional rental income had X made an additional at-risk investment.

At the end of year 4, X's adjusted basis in the property is $800,000, X's at-risk investment is $0, and $60,000 of deductions is in suspension. Suppose X now defaults on the mortgage and loses the property. As a result of the foreclosure, X realizes income of $100,000 under the *Tufts* doctrine. The suspended deductions are now allowable because the dispositional income ensures that the suspended deductions do not exceed the investment's income for the year. That is, in the year of disposition the suspended deductions will not be §465(d) losses because they do not exceed the dispositional income. And because they are not §465(d) losses, they are not disallowed by operation of §465(a)(1).

2. The §465 Proposed Regulations

Proposed more than 13 years ago, the regulations under §465 have yet to be either adopted in final form or withdrawn. Consequently, their status is uncertain. Nevertheless, they can help develop an understanding of the more subtle applications of §465. For example, loss that exceeds the taxpayer's amount at risk cannot drive the amount at risk negative but instead must be suspended. Proposed regulation §1.465-3(b), however, explains that amount at risk may be reduced below zero in some cases. This can occur when a taxpayer receives a distribution from an activity an amount in excess of the taxpayer's amount at risk. For example, if a taxpayer's amount at risk in an activity is $90 and the taxpayer is distributed $110 from the activity, the taxpayer's amount at risk is reduced to negative $20.

Similarly, if a recourse loan of $110 is converted to nonrecourse the amount at risk will also be reduced to negative $20.

Another aspect of the proposed regulations is the treatment of repayments based on the occurrence of a contingency. The nature of the contingent liability determines the effect on the taxpayer's amount at risk. If the likelihood of the contingency occurring is such that the taxpayer is effectively protected against loss then the amount is not treated as being at-risk. Conversely, amounts will be considered at risk where the likelihood of the contingency occurring is not such that the taxpayer is effectively protected from risk or the protection does not cover all likely possibilities. Specifically, the regulations contemplate the purchasing of hazard insurance protection for contributed assets. Hazard insurance protection will not cause a taxpayer to be considered "not at risk." See Prop. Regs. §1.465-4(c).

The proposed regulations also illustrate an instance in which a taxpayer's amount at risk will be increased even though the taxpayer is not personally liable for a borrowed amount. Where an amount used in an activity covered by §465 is secured by property not used in the activity, the net fair market value of the secured property will equal the increase in amount at risk. See Prop. Regs. §1.465-25(a)(1). If the net fair market value of the secured property changes, the amount at risk in the activity will be adjusted to reflect the change in net fair market value. Note, however, that any amounts paid on the loan must first be applied to that portion of the loan, if any, that exceeds the net fair market value of the secured property. Consequently, those amounts will not increase amount at risk but will be considered repayment of a nonrecourse loan secured by property used in the activity. See Prop. Regs. §1.465-25(a)(2). If the property used as security is later contributed to the activity, the amount at risk attributed to the property will be adjusted as if the net fair market value of the property was reduced to zero. Prop. Regs. §1.465-25(a)(3).

3.   Application of §465 to Partners and Partnerships

Section 465 does not apply to partnerships but only to their partners. Because §465 applies on an activity-by-activity basis, a partner's distributive share of losses otherwise allowable can be claimed on a partner's individual return only to the extent of the partner's distributive share of income plus the partner's at-risk investment in the partnership. Because §704(d) is applied before §465, deductions in excess of a partner's outside basis will never reach the disallowance rule of §465(a)(1). Accordingly, the impact of §465 is limited to distributive share of partnership loss *less than* a partner's outside basis but *more than* the partner's at-risk investment in the partnership.

How can such a situation arise? Because contributions to the partnership of cash and property increase outside basis and at-risk investment equally, only deductions in excess of the adjusted basis of contributed property (plus contributed cash) can be subject to §465. Partnership debt — more specifically, nonrecourse partnership debt, which increases outside basis but which does not qualify as an at-risk amount — is what presents the possibility of application of §465(a)(1).

For example, suppose *A* and *B* form the *AB* general partnership as equal partners by contributing cash of $500 each. If the partnership then purchases a computer for $10,000 by paying $1,000 down and signing a nonrecourse note for $9,000, each partner's outside basis will equal $5,000. However, because borrowed funds only constitute at-risk funds to the extent the partners are personally liable for repayment, §465(b)(2)(A), each partner's at-risk investment remains at $500 apiece. Accordingly, neither *A* nor *B* will be entitled to claim a distributive share of partnership loss in excess of $500 unless further contributions are made, partnership income is recognized but not distributed, or the loan is converted to a recourse basis. And if a loan starts out as recourse and then is converted to a nonrecourse obligation, the conversion may trigger income recognition under §465(e).

A second way in which §465 can apply to a partnership investment is by outside nonrecourse borrowing. Suppose individual *X* borrows $10,000 to contribute to partnership *P*, and suppose further that this loan is nonrecourse and secured only by *X*'s partnership interest. While *X* will have an outside basis of $10,000 under §722, *X* should have no at-risk investment because *P* is not personally liable for repayment of the loan.

Not all nonrecourse partnership borrowing is disqualified under §465(b)(2). The real estate industry successfully lobbied for §465(b)(6) providing that nonrecourse borrowing against a real estate investment *is* treated as an at-risk amount so long as the lender is a government instrumentality, see §465(b)(6)(B)(ii), or is a qualified person as defined in §465(b)(6)(D). Combining the rules of §§752, 704(d), and 465, we see that only nonrecourse funding of a real estate investment can provide limited partners with deductions in excess of contributions: Recourse financing will not provide *limited* partners with outside basis, while nonrecourse financing will not provide an at-risk increase except as to real estate investments.

Just as real estate provides the one exception to the rule that nonrecourse financing will not satisfy §465, there is also one situation in which fully recourse financing will not qualify as at risk. Under §§465(b)(3) and 465(c)(3)(D), borrowed funds will not be treated as at risk even if the borrower is fully liable for repayment if the lender is "any person who has an interest in [the] activity," where the definition of an "interest in [the] activity" is left undefined except that being only a creditor is *not* a tainted interest. See §465(b)(3)(B)(i). The legislative history of §465 fails to explain why a fully recourse loan should be treated as nonrecourse if made from one involved in the activity, but presumably Congress was afraid that loans between involved parties are easy to fabricate and often unenforced. This aspect of §465 finds a surprising resonance in application of §704(d).

Suppose a partner guarantees a nonrecourse loan of the partnership. For allocating the debt under §752, the debt is treated as recourse to the guarantor partner because the guarantor partner has no ability to seek reimbursement from any other partner.[1] Should such a guarantee also increase the guarantor partner's "at-risk" amount. Clearly it should, although the regulations seem to take the opposite view. See Prop. Regs. §1.465-6(d). For a cogent analysis of this regulation and its failings, see Richard W. Harris & Louis H. Moran, Guaranteed LLC Debt: Does the Guarantor-Member Receive At-Risk Basis, 91 J. Taxation 16 (1999).

PROBLEMS

26-2.   Individual *K* invests $10,000 in the *KLM* partnership. The partnership purchases real estate for $1,000,000, paying $100,000 in cash and signing a note for the remaining $900,000. Assume that *K*'s share of the debt is $25,000 under §752. If *K*'s distributive share of loss for each of the first two years is $20,000 (and *K* has no distributive share of income during those years), how much partnership loss can *K* claim on her individual return for the first two years and what is *K*'s outside basis at the end of the second year? If *K* has $40,000 distributive share of income for the partnership's third year, what does *K* put on her individual return from the partnership's activities?

C.   A REEXAMINATION OF SECTION 704(d) AND ITS RELATION TO SECTION 704(b)

1.   Misallocations of Loss

Consider the following example. *X* and *Y* form the *XY* general partnership by contributing cash of $10,000 each. The partnership incurs no debt, and it generates deductions of $12,000 in its first year. What are the tax consequences to *X* and *Y* if this entire deduction is allocated to *X*?

So long as the partnership maintains proper capital accounts, provides that liquidating proceeds will be distributed in accordance with final capital account balances, and each partner has a deficit restoration obligation, this allocation is valid under §704(b) because it has substantial economic effect. To be sure, the allocation drives *X*'s capital account negative, but that is irrelevant in light of *X*'s deficit restoration obligation. The only relevance of *X*'s negative capital account is that if *X*'s partnership interest

1. See page 737 supra.

liquidates before X's capital account becomes positive, X will be obligated to restore the amount of her capital account deficit to the partnership for distribution to creditors or to Y. For example, if the partnership liquidates immediately after its first year, X will be required to contribute $2,000 for distribution to Y.

Even though the allocation of the partnership's $12,000 deduction to X satisfies the substantial economic effect test of §704(b), X will not be entitled to claim the full $12,000 deduction on her individual return because of §704(d). Prior to the allocation, X's outside basis totals $10,000. Under §704(d), distributive share of loss is suspended to the extent it exceeds outside basis. Accordingly, X may claim only $10,000 of her $12,000 distributive share of loss.

Why? The problem is *not* that X will bear the economic burden of the loss only to the extent of $10,000: Satisfaction of the substantial economic effect test ensures that the economic benefits and burdens associated with tax allocations follow the allocations. Treas. Regs. §1.704-1(b)(2)(ii)(a). Section 704(d) plainly is about something *other than* economic effect, but it is less than obvious just what that might be.

In this example, the §704(d) problem could have been avoided by allocating no more than $10,000 of the loss to X so that the remaining loss could be absorbed by Y's outside basis. In general, §704(d) problems always can be avoided in this way because the aggregate of all partners' outside bases should be sufficient to cover their partnership's total loss. A partnership's total loss (deductible and nondeductible combined) should never exceed its total inside basis — recovery of basis, after all, is what a loss (or other deduction) represents. Further, the aggregate outside basis will almost always equal aggregate inside basis. Thus, if total partnership loss will not exceed aggregate inside basis, it will not exceed aggregate outside basis, and that means that all losses can be claimed without implicating §704(d) if the losses are allocated properly.

In one sense, then, §704(d) is not about excess deductions but about misallocation of deductions. Except in very limited circumstances, a partnership can avoid triggering §704(d) by allocating its losses properly. Of course, the substantiality requirement of §704(b) imposes some limitations on the partnership's ability to manipulate subsequent allocations of income and loss to offset earlier allocations. Still, suspended losses under §704(d) should be avoidable by careful planning and tailored special allocations.

If the partnership has no §704(c) problems, and putting aside the possibility of partnership debt, outside bases should equal capital accounts. A distributive share of loss that would implicate §704(d) — that is, a distributive share of loss in excess of outside basis — also would drive the partner's capital account negative. Negative capital accounts present no difficulties (as to general partners) under the substantial economic effect test of §704(b), but §704(d) is not satisfied. Why?

The reason that general partners can have negative capital accounts without violating the economic effect test is that they are subject to a capital account deficit restoration obligation. Reconsider the *XY* example above, with *X* being allocated the entire $12,000 first year loss. This allocation reduces *X*'s capital account to negative $2,000, so that if the partnership were to liquidate immediately, *X* would owe $2,000 to *Y*.

In effect, *X* has borrowed $2,000 from *Y*. Twelve thousand dollars of the partners' capital was lost in the first year, which means that if the entire loss is allocated to *X*, we are treating *X* as losing everything she contributed to the partnership plus $2,000 more. This additional $2,000 came from *Y*, and *X*'s capital account deficit restoration obligation ensures that *X* cannot leave the partnership without repaying the debt. That is, in the absence of partnership indebtedness a deficit capital account means that one partner has borrowed from another.

Indeed, partners *X* and *Y* could have avoided the §704(d) problem entirely by making their borrowing explicit. Suppose that *Y* had loaned *X* $2,000, and then the partnership had been formed by *X* contributing cash of $12,000 (her original $10,000 plus the borrowed $2,000) and *Y* contributing cash of $8,000. Again, there is $20,000 invested in the partnership, but now the first year's loss of $12,000 can be allocated to *X* without implicating §704(d) because *X*'s outside basis can absorb the entire $12,000 distributive share of loss. By substituting explicit borrowing outside the partnership for the implicit borrowing within the partnership created by a negative capital account, *X* and *Y* can avoid the limitation of §704(d).

But *X* still cannot claim more than $10,000 of partnership loss on her individual return! Having escaped the clutches of §704(d), the partners have landed squarely within the confines of §465 because *X*'s amount at-risk is only $10,000. To be sure, *X* has contributed a full $12,000 to the partnership, but of that amount, $2,000 was borrowed. Further, although *X* is fully responsible for repayment of her debt to *Y*, the borrowed proceeds are not treated as "at risk" because *Y* has an interest in the partnership. Recall that even fully recourse loans do not contribute to a taxpayer's at-risk amount if the lender "has an interest in [the] activity" other than as a creditor. See §465(b)(3).

At least in the context of a partnership without debt (and assuming no §704(c) problems), the effect of §704(d) is to ensure that the partners cannot avoid the related party rules of §465 by implicitly borrowing within the partnership. This cannot have been the rationale for enactment of §704(d) — §704(d) was enacted decades before §465 — but it does provide some support for §704(d) as part of the current Code.

Now let us add some partnership borrowing to the example. Once again, suppose *X* and *Y* each contribute $10,000 to the *XY* general partnership. Once again, assume that the partnership loses $12,000 during its first year. We will again try to allocate the entire loss to partner *X*, but now assume that the partnership has borrowed $10,000 from some third-party lender on a fully recourse basis. Can *X* now claim the entire $12,000 loss?

X can claim the entire loss without limitation under §704(d) because *X*'s outside basis is increased to $15,000 under §752(a) by reason of the partnership debt. In the absence of the partnership's borrowing, X cannot claim more than $10,000 of partnership loss on her individual return because of §704(d). Existence of the debt, though, allows X to claim up to $15,000 of losses because partnership indebtedness increases outside basis. This miraculous effect of the partnership debt on X's ability to claim distributive share of loss in excess of actual contributions should cause you pause, though, because the partnership debt has had no real effect on X's economic position. Recall that, even in the absence of any partnership borrowing, X's distributive share of loss in excess of her capital contribution (implicitly) resulted in a loan from X to Y of $2,000. Whether the partnership incurs any liability or not, the excess allocation of loss to X imposes a repayment obligation on X. Why should the happenstance of a third-party lender be relevant?

Once again, recall §465. Under that section, borrowed funds contribute to a taxpayer's amount at risk so long as the taxpayer is responsible for repayment of the loan *and* the lender does not have an interest in the investment activity. Sections 752(a) and 704(d) seem to echo this rule by increasing outside basis for a partner's share of partnership debt but not for inside borrowing implicitly occurring whenever one partner's capital account goes negative.

However, the existence of third-party debt ought to be irrelevant to the application of §704(d). Once again, reconsider the XY example, and look at the partnership books following the partners' contributions and the borrowing by the partnership of $10,000. The partnership has $30,000 of cash, each partner has an initial capital account of $10,000, and the partnership owes $10,000. Once $12,000 is lost, the partnership's assets have declined to $18,000 and X's capital account has dropped to negative $2,000; Y's capital account remains at $10,000.

If the partnership liquidates immediately, X will be required to contribute $2,000 to the partnership by reason of her capital account deficit restoration obligation. That $2,000 will not, though, be distributed to the third-party lender. After all, the partnership's indebtedness is only $10,000, and the partnership has assets of $18,000 even without X's contribution arising from her capital account deficit restoration obligation. The $2,000 that X must contribute is for distribution to Y, and the existence of the third-party loan is an economic irrelevancy. Because the third-party lender must be paid before Y is entitled to receive her partnership capital, X's negative capital account represents a loan from Y and not from the third-party lender.

If §704(d) were to backstop §465 properly, distributive share of partnership loss would be disallowed only to the extent it reflects an implicit loan from one partner to another. Such an implicit loan arises whenever one partner's distributive share of loss forces the partner's capital account negative while the aggregate of all capital accounts remains positive. Distributive share of loss causing a negative capital account should not be disallowed when the sum of all partners' capital accounts is negative, for it is at that point that the capital account deficit restoration obligations reflect obligations to third-party lenders and not to other partners.

PROBLEMS

26-3. *X, Y,* and *Z* form the *XYZ* general partnership, with *X* contributing cash of $10 and *Y* and *Z* contributing cash of $100 each. The partnership borrows $60, and profits and losses are generally allocated one-third to each partner except as follows. In year 1, the partnership loses $70, and this loss is allocated entirely to *X*. In year 2, the partnership loses $80, and this loss is allocated entirely to *Y*. What are the tax consequences of these transactions, and how do the partnership books stand at the close of year 2?

2. *Contributions of Notes*

Suppose a taxpayer joins a partnership by contributing a promise to pay a sum certain, plus fair interest, in exchange for a partnership interest. That is, suppose the partner contributes her own note to the partnership. What are the tax consequences of the contribution, and what happens when the note is paid?

Outside the partnership context, we know that acquisition indebtedness is treated like cash. That is, a taxpayer who purchases a building for $1,000,000 takes a basis in the building equal to the full cost whether she pays with cash, a note, or cash plus a note. In essence, all taxpayers accrue their debt obligations, even those otherwise using the cash method of accounting. Consistent with this approach, payment of the note has no tax consequences and release of the debt yields income (*Kirby Lumber* income) to the debtor.

Should a rule for the purchase of a partnership interest be any different? Surprisingly, the courts have said that it should be. In *Oden v. Commissioner,*[2] the Tax Court held that a taxpayer transferring his own note to a partnership in exchange for a partnership interest acquired a zero-basis in his partnership interest under §722. According to the court, the taxpayer's basis in the note was zero because the taxpayer paid nothing for it. Thus, the court reasoned, the substitute basis rule of §722 gives the taxpayer the same zero basis in the partnership interest.

What little merit this overly technical interpretation of §722[3] possesses is more than outweighed by the disastrous implications of giving the con-

---

2. T.C. Memo 1981-184, aff'd in unpublished opinion, 679 F.2d 885 (4th Cir. 1982).

3. Indeed, the Court's conclusion that the taxpayer has a zero basis in his own note because he paid nothing for it is inaccurate. If a taxpayer's basis in property is the value the taxpayer can receive in exchange for the property tax-free, see §1001(a), then a taxpayer's basis in his own note is fair market value (i.e., face value if the note pays fair interest).

tributing partner a zero outside basis. If the court is correct that the taxpayer takes an initial outside basis of zero under §722, then it must be the case that the partnership takes a zero basis in the note under §723. Accordingly, if the partnership sells the note, it will recognize income equal to the entire amount realized on the sale. Yet, had the partner simply borrowed the same amount from a third party and then contributed the cash to the partnership ab initio, the partnership would have the cash and the third-party lender would own the note without there being any income to the partnership.

In fact, if the partnership takes a zero basis in the note, does it have income when the contributing partner makes principle payments? That result would seem to follow from the *Oden* decision, but it plainly makes no sense. Is the contributing partner entitled to claim a deduction as payments are made, or do such payments result in outside basis when, and as, made? Consider the possibility that the principle payments on the note might be made after the contributing partner withdraws from the partnership.

As we know, contributed property is booked into capital accounts at fair market value rather than at adjusted basis. Presumably a partner who contributes her own note should then increase her capital account by the value of the note. Not so: The regulations specifically (and surprisingly) provide that the contributing partner's capital account is increased only when principle payments are made on the note or the note is transferred by the partnership in a taxable disposition. Treas. Regs. §1.704-1(b)(2)(iv)(d)(2). However, to ensure that the contributing partner is properly credited for the value of the note upon liquidation, the same regulation provides that the note will be deemed satisfied to the extent of its fair market value upon liquidation of the contributing partner's partnership interest.

This zero-basis problem also arises in the context of subchapter C when a taxpayer contributes her own note to a corporation in exchange for stock in a transaction to which §351(a) applies. See the discussion of *Peracchi* above.[4]

D.   SECTION 469: THE PASSIVE LOSS LIMITATIONS

The passive loss limitations of §469 represent the newest and most successful attack on tax shelters. Section 469 represents a congressional concern that excess deductions from investments have allowed taxpayers to shelter unrelated taxable income. Somewhat surprisingly, the congressional response was not to reduce or eliminate the deductions felt to be excessive. Instead, §469 prevents losses from most investments from offsetting unre-

4. See page 37 supra.

lated income. Thus, §469 does not eliminate the tax advantages of investments which produce economic profit without the recognition of current income such as can be obtained by exploiting generous deductions for research, see §174, machinery, see §168, and farming, see e.g., §180.

Under §469(a), net deductions and credits from a taxpayer's passive activities are disallowed and carried over to the following year. Like the at-risk rules of §465, the passive loss limitations of §469 disallow *excess* deductions: Passive losses may offset passive income without limitation under §469. Any losses suspended by operation of §469(a) are allowable when the taxpayer disposes of her investment in the passive activity in a fully taxable transaction, see §469(g). This is another similarity with §465. However, §469 applies only to the aggregate of all passive losses over all passive income, thereby allowing losses from one passive activity to offset income from an unrelated passive activity. The at-risk rules, in contradistinction, generally operate on an activity-by-activity basis. §465(c)(2).

The definition of "passive activity" in §469 is surprising. Under §469(c), a passive activity is any activity "which involves the conduct of any trade or business, and in which the taxpayer does not materially participate." This definition requires that the activity be an active trade or business for some taxpayer but not for the particular taxpayer in question. See §§469(c)(6), 469(h). Under this definition, holding stocks and bonds is *not* a passive activity because the holding of financial assets by one taxpayer is not a trade or business for some other taxpayer. Portfolio income such as interest and dividends accordingly cannot be offset by passive losses. See §469(e)(1)(A)(i).

Section 469 specifically provides that all rental activity is passive. §469(c)(2). However, special rules apply to the rental of real estate. For taxpayers who "actively participate" in renting real estate (and "active participation" is less than material participation, compare §469(i)(6) with §469(h)), the first $25,000 of net loss is not treated as passive and so can offset active income (such as salary) and portfolio income. §469(i). However, this $25,000 advantage for rental real estate is phased out for taxpayers with adjusted gross income in excess of $100,000. §469(i)(3).

Two special rules apply only to partners. First, a limited partnership interest never constitutes material participation in the partnership's activity. §469(h)(2). This rule ensures that distributive income and loss of a limited partner is passive if the partnership actively conducts a trade or business. Second, passive loss from publicly traded partnerships (as defined in §469(k)(2)) cannot offset passive income from any other activity. See §469(k)(1). In essence, then, income from publicly traded partnerships is treated as portfolio income while loss is treated as passive, the worst of both worlds.

It might seem that there is some redundancy between §§465 and 469 since both are tax shelter provisions and §465 has such broad application. However, they speak to different issues: §469 will disallow "losses" from activities even if the taxpayer has substantial funds at risk while §465 can disallow "losses" even if the taxpayer actively participates in the activity. Thus, most losses must pass both hurdles. Nevertheless, many tax scholars agree that with the enactment of §469, §465 should either be eliminated entirely or limited to seller-financed debt.

Section 469 applies to investments made long before its enactment. For many taxpayers, the effect of §469 is to render worthless and nonmarketable many of their prior investments. Such taxpayers cannot get out of their tax shelters and cannot use the excess losses produced by these shelters to offset other income. For such taxpayers, what is needed are new investment vehicles producing passive income. Such investments could then be purchased and the income they produce would be sheltered by the taxpayer's existing tax shelter vehicles. Such investments — affectionately called PIGs (for passive income generators) — are highly desirable under current law.

E. SECTION 163(d): THE INVESTMENT INTEREST LIMITATION

The investment interest limitation of §163(d) is one congressional response to the deferral opportunities presented by the realization doctrine. As you know, while the realization doctrine nominally defers recognition of both gains and losses, in practice it defers only gains because taxpayers are free to sell their loss properties while holding on to the appreciating assets. Indeed, it is precisely this potential manipulation of the realization doctrine that explains §1211 limiting a taxpayer's recognition of capital losses to the extent of realized capital gains (plus up to $3,000 for noncorporate taxpayers).

Just as a taxpayer might try to accelerate recognition of capital losses while deferring recognition of capital gains, a taxpayer might try to accelerate recognition of interest expenses while deferring the recognition of appreciation in an asset purchased with borrowed funds. For example, consider a taxpayer who can invest in young wine at an initial cost of $1,000,000. Assume that the wine increases in value as it ages; in fact, assume that it increases in value at a rate of 10 percent per year. What is the taxpayer's net return on the investment if she borrows the entire purchase price of $1,000,000 at an interest rate of 10 percent per year, assuming the taxpayer holds the wine for three years?

It is obvious that the taxpayer has no pretax gain or loss from the investment: Borrowing at 10 percent to invest at 10 percent is a wash transaction. However, if the interest is paid annually and is deductible against other income as paid, the investment produces a positive after-tax return. Let us assume the taxpayer is in the 40 percent tax bracket and compute the taxpayer's after-tax gain.

The cost of the investment includes three interest payments of $100,000 apiece as well as a principle payment of $1,000,000. Assuming interest is deductible as paid, the after-tax cost of each interest payment is $60,000. To compute the present value of the cost of the investment, we discount each payment for the time value of money until the payment is due. Using an after-tax discount rate of 6 percent (which corresponds to a pretax interest rate of 10 percent, the same rate at which the wine investment appreciates), the present cost of the investment is $1,000,000.00.

We compare that present cost to the present value of the expected return. The taxpayer will receive $1,331,000 in three years. Of that amount, $331,000 will be taxable, producing a tax liability of $132,400. Accordingly, the net after-tax return to the taxpayer will be $1,198,600, and the present value of that return is $1,006,367.67, for an after-tax profit of $6,367.67. By deducting the interest currently but reporting the appreciation only at the end of the investment, the taxpayer is able to turn a profit without making any real investment. Application of §163(d), though, would defer the interest deduction until the taxpayer sold the wine, reducing the taxpayer's after-tax profit to $0.00. Of course, because interest expenses often fall within the reach of the passive loss limitation in §469, the importance of §163(d) is now small.

PROBLEMS

26-4. Reconsider problem 26-2 taking the possible application of §469 into account.

26-5. The partnership agreement of the *XYZ* partnership provides that each of 10 limited partners must contribute $100,000 initially and an additional $25,000 per year for four years. Individual *X* is one such limited partner, and after two years in the partnership, *X* resigns and receives the amount she has contributed — $150,000 — in liquidation of her partnership interest. Assuming *X*'s capital account and outside basis equaled $150,000 as of the date *X*'s interest was liquidated, does *X* have any tax consequences as a result of the liquidation? In particular, must *X* report any income from the cancellation of indebtedness because she no longer is obligated to contribute to the partnership $25,000 per year for two more years?

26-6. Individual *C* invests $10,000 to acquire a 10 percent limited interest in the *P* partnership. During each of its first two taxable years, the partnership recognizes $20,000 of taxable interest income as well as a loss of $100,000 from its ownership of a professional football team. How much of *C*'s distributive share of loss may *C* claim on her individual return? How do your answers change if *C* also invested $5,000 to acquire a 5 percent general partnership interest as well as the limited interest?

27

Optional Basis Adjustments

Aggregate outside basis equals aggregate inside basis when a partnership is formed. §§722-723. Because outside basis is adjusted for inside recognition of income and loss as well as for inside borrowing, §§705, 752, aggregate outside basis should remain equal to aggregate inside basis throughout the life of the partnership. Similarly, the double basis adjustments in §§704(c)(1)(B)(iii) and 737(c) further ensure that aggregate inside and outside bases remain equal.

However, some partnership distributions and most dispositions of partnership interests can disturb this equality of inside and outside bases. Yet, it is the equality of aggregate inside and outside bases which supports the fundamental transparency metaphor underlying subchapter K: So long as total inside basis equals total outside basis, the partners essentially are treated as an aggregate of co-owners. If this equality is broken, existence of the partnership can produce timing disparities for the partners. Nonetheless, absent an election by the partnership, neither a partnership distribution nor the disposition of a partnership interest will generate an adjustment to the basis of the partnership's assets to restore the equality. §§734(a), 743(a). If, though, an election under §754 has been made by the partnership, the partnership's basis in its assets will be adjusted to correct the imbalance. §§734(b), 743(b).

Note that while there are *two* basis adjustment provisions, §§734(b) and 743(b), there is only a *single* election, §754. This one election applies to both §734(b) and to §743(b), so that a partnership must elect to take both or neither: there is no way to elect the §734(b) adjustment without the §743(b) adjustment, or vice versa. Treas. Regs. §1.754-1(a). In addition, there is no provision for revoking a §754 election. Without the consent of the government, an election under §754 is permanent, lasting until the dissolution of the partnership. Treas. Regs. §1.754-1(c).

While the basis adjustments of §§734(b) and 743(b) are triggered by the same election, they have their differences. The optional basis adjustment under §734(b) arises upon the occurrence of certain partnership distributions (note that §734 immediately follows the provisions governing the taxation of partnership distributions, §§731-733). The optional basis adjustment under §743(b) arises upon the taxable disposition of a partnership interest or upon the death of a partner (taxation of dispositions of partnership interests are covered by §§741-742). The most significant difference between the operation of §734(b) and §743(b) is that the inside basis adjustment under §734(b) applies to all partners equally while the inside basis adjustment under §743(b) applies only to the transferee partner.

A. THE OPTIONAL BASIS ADJUSTMENT UNDER §734(b)

1. Distributions Triggering the Optional Basis Adjustment

a. Nonliquidating Distributions of Excess Cash

Suppose cash is distributed to a partner in a nonliquidating transaction covered by §731. The effect of this distribution on the partnership's inside basis is to reduce that inside basis by the amount of cash distributed: When *any* property is distributed by a partnership, the partnership's inside basis is reduced by the amount of the partnership's basis in the distributed property for the simple reason that the partnership no longer owns the property. Because cash always has an implicit basis equal to face value, a distribution of cash reduces inside basis by the amount of cash distributed.

What is the effect of this distribution on the partners' aggregate outside basis? It depends on whether the distributee partner recognizes income under §731 by reason of the distribution. For example, suppose the distributee-partner has an outside basis of $10,000 immediately before the distribution. If the distribution consists of $7,000, the distributee takes the cash tax-free and reduces her outside basis to $3,000 under the rules of §731(a)(1) and §733(1). Outside basis thus is reduced by the amount of cash distributed, so that the effect of the distribution is to reduce aggregate inside and outside bases equivalently. That is, a distribution of cash fully absorbed by the distributee partner's outside basis preserves the equality of inside and outside bases.

But what if the distribution consists of $12,000? In this case the distributee partner must recognize $2,000 of income because her outside basis is insufficient to absorb the entire distribution. §731(a)(1). By reason of the parenthetical language in §733, she reduces her outside basis by $10,000. Accordingly, the distribution reduces aggregate outside basis by only $10,000 while aggregate inside basis is reduced by the full $12,000 (because the $12,000 is no longer owned by the partnership). This distribution breaks the equality of aggregate inside and outside bases: Aggregate inside basis will be lower than aggregate outside basis after the distribution. Further, the amount of the disparity is precisely equal to the gain recognized by the distributee-partner on the distribution.

b. Nonliquidating Distributions of High-Basis Property

A nonliquidating distribution of property is tax-free to the distributee under §731. The inside basis effect of such a distribution is clear: Once the property is distributed, aggregate inside basis is reduced by the partnership's adjusted basis in the distributed property because it no longer owns the property. As with distributions of cash, the distribution of property *may* disturb the equality of aggregate inside and outside bases depending on the predistribution outside basis of the distributee partner.

For example, suppose the partnership distributes Blackacre to partner X having an outside basis of $10,000. Assume the partnership has an inside basis in Blackacre of $7,000 immediately prior to the distribution. Assuming §751(b) does not apply to this distribution, the outside basis consequences to X are determined by application of §§732-733.

Under §732(a)(1), X takes Blackacre with a carryover basis of $7,000. Under §733(2), X reduces her outside basis by that same $7,000. Accordingly, the effect of the distribution in this case is to reduce both aggregate inside basis and aggregate outside basis by the partnership's predistribution adjusted basis in the property distributed. The distribution therefore does not disturb the equality of aggregate inside and outside bases.

But now reconsider the distribution, assuming the property has a predistribution adjusted basis to the partnership of $12,000. The distribution remains tax-free to X under §731, but now X's basis in Blackacre is *not* carried-over from the partnership. Instead, X takes a basis of only $10,000 in Blackacre under the limitation of §732(a)(2). And under §733(2), X reduces her outside basis to zero (the parenthetical language of §733 is not implicated in this case). Accordingly, aggregate outside basis is reduced only by $10,000 although inside basis is reduced by the full $12,000. More generally, whenever a nonliquidating distribution of property triggers the basis limitation rule of §732(a)(2), the distribution will reduce inside basis more than outside basis, with the difference equal to the excess of the partnership's predistribution adjusted basis in the distributed property over the distributee partner's predistribution outside basis. A distribution of high-basis property, like a distribution of excess cash, will thus cause aggregate inside basis to be low relative to aggregate outside basis.

c.   Liquidating Distributions

When a partnership makes a liquidating distribution, inside basis is lost because partnership property is removed from the partnership and outside basis is reduced because the distributee ceases to be a member of the partnership. While both aggregate inside basis and aggregate outside basis are thus reduced, the amount of the reductions will not be equal unless the predistribution inside basis of the property distributed (including any cash distributed) happens to equal the distributee partner's predistribution outside basis. In the absence of such a coincidence, the equality of aggregate inside basis and outside basis will be broken, and without knowing more, we cannot predict which will be greater.

For example, suppose individual X is a partner in the XYZ partnership, and assume the partnership distributes Blackacre, with an adjusted basis of $7,000 to the partnership, to X in complete liquidation of X's partnership interest. Assuming this distribution is taxed to X under §§731-732, X will not recognize any gain or loss on the transaction. If X had an outside basis of $10,000 immediately before the distribution, the effect of the distribution is to reduce aggregate inside basis by $7,000 (because the partnership no longer owns Blackacre) and to reduce aggregate outside basis by $10,000 (because X no longer is a partner). Thus, aggregate inside basis will now exceed aggregate outside basis by the $3,000 difference.

But suppose that the partnership had a $12,000 adjusted basis in Blackacre prior to the distribution. X still recognizes no gain or loss, but now aggregate inside basis is reduced by $12,000 while aggregate outside basis is reduced by only $10,000. Thus, aggregate inside basis will now be less than aggregate outside basis by $2,000. In short, a distribution in liquidation of a partner's interest in the partnership can cause the post-distribution aggregate inside basis to be greater than or less than the post-distribution aggregate outside basis. Liquidating distributions producing taxable gain or loss to the exiting partner under §731(a) also can affect inside and outside basis unequally.

2.   The Amount of the Adjustment under §734(b)

If a partnership has a §754 election in effect, no distribution can disturb the equality between aggregate inside and aggregate outside bases. More accurately, no distribution can affect the relationship between aggregate inside and aggregate outside bases: If they were equal prior to a distribution or disposition, they will be equal afterward. If they were unequal before, they will continue unequal after.

How could aggregate outside and aggregate inside bases be unequal? Because the §734(b) and §743(b) basis adjustments are optional, a partnership can operate without them. If such a partnership makes a distribution that breaks the equality, or if a partner disposes of her partnership interest in such a manner as to break the equality, a subsequent §754 election will ensure that future distributions preserve the discontinuity caused by the pre-election distribution or disposition. That is, the effect of the optional basis adjustment in §734(b) is to preserve the absolute difference between aggregate inside basis and aggregate outside basis. If that absolute difference is zero when the election is made (i.e., if they are equal), it will remain zero. If that difference is positive, it will remain positive.

Consider the following example. A and B form the AB general partnership by contributing cash of $10,000 each. During its first year, the partnership distributes $15,000 to A. During its second year, the partnership distributes an additional $1,000 to A. Assume that the partnership has no taxable income at any point and that it incurs no indebtedness. Finally, assume that a §754 election is filed by the partnership effective on the first day of the partnership's second taxable year.

The effect of the first distribution on A is to reduce her outside basis to zero, see §733(1), and to cause her to recognize $5,000 of income, see §731(a)(1). As a result of the distribution, aggregate inside basis decreases to $5,000 and aggregate outside basis drops to $10,000. Because no §754 election is in effect when the distribution occurs, a disparity between aggregate inside and aggregate outside bases arises.

When the second distribution is made, A recognizes an additional $1,000 of income under §731(a)(1). Because A's outside basis is zero, the distribution does not reduce A's outside basis. Thus, the effect of the distribution is to decrease aggregate inside basis to $4,000 while leaving aggregate outside basis at $10,000.

However, because a §754 election is now in place, the distribution triggers a basis adjustment under §734(b)(1)(A) of $1,000. This is a positive inside basis adjustment, increasing aggregate inside basis back to $5,000. Accordingly, the second distribution does not change the relationship between aggregate inside and outside bases: Aggregate outside basis exceeds aggregate inside basis by $5,000 both before and after the distribution.

Under some circumstances, the basis adjustments mandated by §734(b) are deferred. See Treas. Regs. §1.755-1(c)(4). When such deferral occurs, the relationship between aggregate inside and outside bases will be upset by the amount of the deferred adjustment. Once the deferral terminates, the proper relationship will be restored.

3. Allocating the §734(b) Adjustment under §755

While §§734(b) and 743(b) specify the *net amount* of the optional basis adjustments, the actual allocation of those amounts to specific partnership assets is governed by §755. One feature of the §755 regulations is that they provide one set of rules for basis adjustments arising under §734(b) and a separate set of rules for basis adjustments arising under §743(b).

Before allocating a §734(b) basis adjustment to the partnership's remaining assets, those assets must be divided into two classes: One class consists of the partnership's ordinary income assets while the other class consists of the partnership's cash, capital assets, and assets described in §1231. If a §734(b) basis adjustment is triggered by the distribution of an ordinary income asset, the basis adjustment may be made only to any remaining ordinary income assets of the partnership. Treas. Regs. §1.755-1(c)(1)(i). Similarly, if the distribution consists of cash, capital assets, or assets described in §1231, any resulting §734(b) adjustment will be limited to the partnership's remaining capital assets. Treas. Regs. §1.755-1(c)(1)(i)-(ii). If an adjustment arising from application of §734(b) cannot be made because the partnership lacks assets of the appropriate class (ordinary or capital), then the adjustment is deferred until the partnership acquires property of the appropriate class. Treas. Regs. §1.755-1(c)(4).

a.   Allocation of Positive §734(b) Adjustments

Assuming a partnership owns assets of the proper class, a *positive* adjustment under §734(b) is allocated among those *appreciated* assets of the property class in proportion to their unrealized appreciation. If the amount of the increase exceeds the total unrealized appreciation in the assets of the proper class, the excess of the adjustment is then allocated among all assets of the proper class in proportion to their fair market values. Treas. Regs. §1.755-1(c)(2)(i).

Consider the following problem. The *ABC* partnership owns ordinary income asset W and capital assets *X, Y,* and *Z* with adjusted bases and fair market values as follows:

Asset	Adjusted Basis	Fair Market Value
Ordinary asset W	$ 4,000	$30,000
Capital asset X	30,000	24,000
Capital asset Y	15,000	24,000
Capital asset Z	50,000	12,000

C, a one-third partner, receives asset *Z* in a nonliquidating distribution. At the time of this distribution, *C* has an outside basis and a capital account of $33,000. Assume that §751(b) does not apply to this transaction.

Because this is a nonliquidating distribution of property, *C* recognizes no gain or loss. See §731. Because the adjusted basis of the distributed property in the hands of the partnership exceeds *C*'s predistribution outside basis, *C* does not take a carryover basis in the asset. Instead, *C* transfers her entire outside basis into asset Z and reduces her outside basis to zero. See §§732(a)(2), 733(2). Assuming the partnership has a §754 election in effect, the partnership is entitled to an optional basis adjustment of positive $17,000 pursuant to §734(b).

Because the distributed property was a capital asset, the §734(b) adjustment can be made only to the remaining capital assets of the partnership, that is, to assets X and Y. Because the basis adjustment is positive, it is made first to asset Y to the extent of the unrealized appreciation in that asset. Thus, of the $17,000 basis adjustment, $9,000 is first made to asset Y.

The remaining $8,000 of basis adjustment is allocated to all partnership capital assets (that is, to assets X and Y) in proportion to relative fair market values. Treas. Regs. §1.755-1(c)(2)(i). Because assets X and Y have equal fair market values, the remaining $8,000 of basis adjustment is divided between them, leaving the postadjustment books of the partnership as follows:

Asset	Adjusted Basis	Fair Market Value
Ordinary asset W	$ 4,000	$30,000
Capital asset X	34,000	24,000
Capital asset Y	28,000	24,000

Strategic distribution of a high-basis asset in anticipation of sale of some low-basis asset can effect a *basis strip*. Consider the case of a partnership owning two capital assets, one high-basis and the other low-basis. For example, suppose that asset X has an inside basis of $0 while asset Y has an inside basis of $100, with each asset having a fair market value of $100. What are the tax consequences of a nonliquidating distribution of asset Y to a partner having a zero outside basis in her partnership interest immediately prior to the distribution?

The partner recognizes no gain or loss by reason of the distribution, and the distributee partner takes a basis in Y of $0 under §732(a)(2). Assuming the partnership has an election under §754 in effect at the time of the election, the distribution triggers an upward basis adjustment under §734(b) of $100, allocable to asset X. That is, the effect of the distribution is to strip basis from asset Y and transfer it to asset X. Assuming the partnership anticipates selling asset X in the near future and the distributee-partner anticipates holding asset Y for some time, this shifting of inside basis allows the partners to defer recognition of $100 of income.

b. Allocation of Negative §734(b) Adjustments

If the §734(b) basis adjustment is *negative,* the adjustment is allocated a little differently. It remains the case that the basis adjustment must be made only to assets of the proper class, and when the adjustment is negative, it is allocated first to partnership assets of the proper class having unrealized loss, to the extent of such loss. Any additional negative basis adjustment is made to assets of the proper class in proportion to their adjusted bases (taking into account any adjustments made with respect to unrealized loss), Treas. Regs. §1.755-1(c)(2)(ii), but in no event is any basis reduced below zero, Treas. Regs. §1.755-1(c)(3). If the partnership does not have assets of the proper class with sufficient adjusted basis to absorb a negative §734(b) basis adjustment, the unallocated portion of the adjustment is suspended until the partnership acquires assets of the proper class that can absorb the negative basis adjustment. Treas. Regs. §1.755-1(c)(4).

For example, suppose partner N has an outside basis of $30,000 and receives a liquidating distribution consisting of $20,000 in cash when the books of the partnership read:

Asset	Adjusted Basis	Fair Market Value
Cash	$30,000	$30,000
Ordinary asset W	51,000	21,000
Capital asset X	7,000	4,000
Capital asset Y	2,000	5,000

The amount of the basis adjustment is negative $10,000 under §734(b)(2)(A), allocable only to partnership capital assets because the distribution consisted only of cash. See Prop. Treas. Regs. §1.755-3(c)(1)(ii). Of the $10,000 total adjustment, $3,000 is first allocated to asset X because that asset has an unrealized loss to the partnership of that amount. Of the remaining $7,000, $4,000 is allocated to asset X and $2,000 is allocated to asset $Y,$ reducing the basis of each asset to zero. Because the partnership now has no capital asset with a positive adjusted basis, the remaining $1,000 of negative basis adjustment must be suspended until the partnership acquires a capital asset having a positive adjusted basis.

c. Allocation of §734(b) Adjustments to Depreciable Property

When a §734(b) basis adjustment is made to depreciable property, there is an additional issue: Should the basis adjustment be recovered over the remaining recovery period of the depreciable property or over a new (and therefore longer), fresh recovery period? The partners generally would prefer that upward adjustments be recovered over the existing property's remaining recovery period (i.e., over a relatively short period) and that downward adjustments be recovered over some longer period.

But the regulations adopt just the reverse approach. Treas. Regs. §1.734-1(e). For example, if a positive §734(b) basis adjustment of $55,000 is allocable to some residential real estate (such as an apartment complex) having a statutory recovery period 27.5 years, see §168(c)(1), that adjustment will produce additional depreciation of $2,000 per year for 27.5 years[1] even if the underlying property has been depreciated for many years. Conversely, if the adjustment is negative $55,000, that adjustment will reduce the partnership's depreciation over the remaining recovery term of the underlying property. Thus, if the real estate has only 11 years remaining to its depreciable life, then the depreciation will be reduced by $5,000 for each of those years.

PROBLEMS

27-1. The *ABC* partnership owns assets as set forth in the chart below:

Asset	Inside Basis	Fair Market Value
Inventory	$33,000	$45,000
Receivable #1	0	15,000
Receivable #2	0	45,000
Land	9,000	6,000
Building	9,000	18,000
Securities	30,000	6,000

A, B, and *C* are each a one-third partner having a capital account and outside basis of $27,000. *Ignoring the possible impact of §751(b),* what basis adjustments are appropriate under §§734(b) and 755 if the partnership has an election under §754 in effect and (a) C receives the inventory in a nonliquidating distribution, or (b) C receives the securities in a nonliquidating distribution, or (c) C receives receivable #2 in a liquidating distribution?

27-2. Suppose in problem 1(b) that the partnership sells the building after the distribution. How much income does each partner report?

B. THE OPTIONAL BASIS ADJUSTMENT UNDER §743(b)

Consider the basis effects of a sale or exchange of a partnership interest. Inside basis is unaffected by the transaction, §743(a) and the purchaser of the partnership interest will take a cost basis in the partnership interest. §742. Unless the selling partner's outside basis happens to equal the sale price, the net effect of the sale is to change aggregate outside basis without

---

1. Assuming the depreciation must be taken using the straight-line method, see §168(b)(3), and ignoring the mid-month convention. See §168(d)(2).

affecting inside basis. If the selling partner realizes a gain, aggregate outside basis increases, while if the selling partner realizes a loss, aggregate outside basis decreases. In either circumstance, the equality between aggregate inside and outside basis will be broken by the sale. Note that the same problem will arise whenever a partner dies, because the transferee of a partnership interest passing through the estate of a decedent takes a basis in the interest equal to fair market value, just as if the interest had been purchased. See §1014.

For example, suppose *P, Q,* and *R* are equal partners in the successful *PQR* general partnership. Assume each partner has an outside basis and capital account of $10,000, and assume also that the partnership owns assets with aggregate adjusted basis of $30,000 and aggregate fair market value of $90,000. If the partnership has no outstanding debt, each partner's interest should be worth $30,000.

Suppose *R* wishes to sell her partnership interest to *S* for its current value of $30,000. R will realize and recognize a taxable gain of $20,000 on the sale, and depending on the makeup of the partnership's assets, some or all of that gain may be ordinary income under §751(a). Of course, *S* will take an initial outside basis equal to her cost of $30,000. §§742 and 1012. However, *S* acquires *R*'s capital account without regard to the amount paid by *S* for the partnership interest. Treas. Regs. §1.704-1(b)(2)(iv)(*l*).

If no §754 election is in place when *S* buys into the partnership, a sale by the partnership of its assets for $90,000 forces the partnership to recognize a gain of $60,000. This gain will be allocated among the partners in accordance with the partnership agreement, which presumably means that each partner will recognize gain of $20,000. Indeed, *P* and *Q* should be unaffected by *R*'s sale to *S,* so recognition of $20,000 apiece for *P* and *Q* is appropriate. Because the partnership recognizes a total gain of $60,000 on the sale of its assets, that leaves $20,000 of gain for *S* (just as if *R* never sold her interest).

Thus, *S* must report $20,000 of income even though *S*'s partnership interest has not increased in value. This phantom income will be offset by a phantom loss when S sells her partnership interest, because *S*'s outside basis is increased to $50,000 under §705(a)(1)(A) while its value remains at $30,000 (a one-third interest in $90,000 of cash). In effect, *R*'s share of the unrealized appreciation is taxed twice: Once to *R* on the sale of her interest and a second time when the partnership sells its assets and *R*'s share of the gain is includible by *S.* Because *S*'s cost basis in her outside basis did not flow through the partnership into the partnership's assets, *S* reports phantom income during the life of the partnership and an offsetting phantom loss at its end. In addition, if the partnership owns ordinary income assets, the phantom income will include an ordinary income component without any guarantee that the dispositional loss will include a similar amount of noncapital loss. Not a good deal for *S.*

1. *Two-Way Adjustments under §743(b)*

In general, the effect of the optional basis adjustment under §743(b) is to preserve the equality between aggregate inside and outside bases following the taxable disposition of a partnership or after the death of a partner. However, if an election under §754 is not filed until after this equality is broken, determining the amount of a §743(b) election is considerably more difficult. Under current regulations, the effect of a §743(b) adjustment is, in general, to give the purchasing partner a cost basis in her share of the each of the partnership's assets. While that result ensures that the purchasing partner will not be allocated any phantom income or deductions from operation of the partnership, it can require that a single §743(b) adjustment give rise to both positive and negative basis adjustments, a result finding precious little support in the statute.

For example, suppose the *LMNO* partnership owns two assets, inventory with adjusted basis of $800 and fair market value of $1,000 as well as a capital asset with adjusted basis of $1,600 and fair market value of $1,400. Assume each partner has an outside basis and capital account of $600 and that each partner's interest is worth the same amount. Thus, the books of the partnership are:

Asset	Book Value	Inside Basis	Fair Market Value
Inventory	$ 800	$1,000	$1,000
Capital Asset	1,600	1,400	1,400
	$2,400	$2,400	$2,400

	Capital Account	Outside Basis	Fair Market Value
L	$ 600	$ 600	$ 600
M	600	600	600
N	600	600	600
O	600	600	600
	$2,400	$2,400	$2,400

If partner *L* sells her partnership interest for $600, it is clear that the amount of the §743(b) basis adjustment is $0, and the proposed regulations come to that conclusion. See Treas. Regs. §1.743-1(b). However, the §755 proposed regulations mandate not zero but two basis adjustments: a positive basis adjustment of $50 to the purchasing partner's share of the inventory as well as a negative $50 basis adjustment to the purchasing partner's share of the capital asset. These two basis adjustments always net to the amount defined by §743(b) (here, they net to $0), but as this example demonstrates either can in magnitude exceed that amount.

Technically, the proposed regulations provide that the net amount of a §743(b) basis adjustment is equal to the difference between (1) the transferee's outside basis immediately after the transfer and (2) the transferee's share of the adjusted basis of the partnership's property. Treas. Regs. §1.743-1(b). The first of these two values is easy to determine: When a partnership interest is sold or exchanged, the transferee's outside basis will be the purchasing partner's cost of the partnership interest, while if the partnership interest is transferred as a result of the death of a partner, the transferee's outside basis generally will be fair market value as of the date of death. In each case, the proposed regulations make clear that the transferee's outside basis includes the transferee's share, if any, of partnership indebtedness as provided for under §752.

The second of the two values — the transferee's share of the adjusted basis of the partnership's property — is somewhat more complex. The regulations provide that the transferee's "share of the partnership's adjusted basis in the partnership's assets" is equal to the sum of (1) the transferee's share of "previously-taxed capital" plus (2) the transferee's share of partnership liabilities. The transferee's share of "previously taxed capital" is then defined to equal the amount of cash that the transferee would receive if the partnership immediately sold all its assets and then liquidated, but increased by the transferee's distributive share of tax loss from that hypothetical sale of assets and decreased by the transferee's distributive share of tax gain. Treas. Regs. §1.743-1(d)(1). Note that this computation provides for an *increase* for distributive share of loss and a *decrease* for distributive share of gain, adjustments that might at first glance seem reversed.

Consider the following example. A and B each have a 25 percent interest in the capital, profits and losses of the ABC general partnership, and C has the remaining 50 percent interest. When the partnership's books stand as follows, A sells her partnership interest to D for its current fair market value of $7,000.

Asset	Book Value	Inside Basis	Fair Market Value
Capital Asset X	$10,000	$10,000	$18,000
Capital Asset Y	6,000	6,000	10,000
	$16,000	$16,000	$28,000

	Capital Account	Outside Basis	Fair Market Value
A	$ 4,000	$ 4,000	$ 7,000
B	4,000	4,000	7,000
C	8,000	8,000	14,000
	$16,000	$16,000	$28,000

On the sale from A to D, A realizes a gain of $3,000. Absent an election under §754, the effect of the sale would be to increase aggregate outside basis from $16,000 to $19,000 without any offsetting effect on aggregate inside basis. §743(a). If, though, such an election has been filed, then the partnership is entitled to adjust the inside basis of its assets by $3,000 under §743(b) (benefitting only D), computed as follows.

When D purchases A's partnership interest, D assumes A's capital account without adjustment. Treas. Regs. §1.704-1(b)(2)(iv)(*l*). If all the assets of the partnership were sold in a fully taxable transaction, D would be allocated one-quarter of the $12,000 gain, increasing D's capital account from $4,000 to $7,000. Thus, if the partnership were immediately liquidated, D would be entitled to receive $7,000 in cash.

D's share of the partnership's previously-taxed capital thus equals $7,000 less the $3,000 gain allocated to D on the sale, or $4,000. Because D's outside basis is D's cost of $7,000, the §743(b) adjustment equals $7,000 minus $4,000, or $3,000. Note that this adjustment to the partnership's basis in its assets restores the equality of aggregate inside and outside bases broken by the sale of A's partnership interest.

Reconsider this example, but assume that capital asset Y has a book value and an adjusted basis to the partnership of $10,000 but is subject to a recourse liability of $4,000. Now, taking into account the liability under §752, the partnership's books become:

Asset	Book Value	Inside Basis	Fair Market Value
Capital asset X	$10,000	$10,000	$18,000
Capital asset Y	10,000	10,000	10,000
	$20,000	$20,000	$28,000

	Capital Account	Outside Basis	Fair Market Value
Liability	$ 4,000	$- - - - - -	$ 4,000
A	4,000	5,000	6,000
B	4,000	5,000	6,000
C	8,000	10,000	12,000
	$20,000	$20,000	$28,000

If partner A now sells her partnership interest to D for its current fair market value of $6,000 while an election under §754 is in effect, there is an inside basis adjustment of $2,000 under §743(b), computed as follows. D's share of the partnership's previously taxed capital remains at $4,000,[2] but now D's share of the liabilities equals $1,000. Accordingly, D's "proportionate share of the adjusted basis of the partnership's property" equals $5,000, and because D's initial outside basis equals $7,000 (purchase price of $6,000 plus D's $1,000 share of the partnership's liabilities), the adjustment equals $7,000 less $5,000, or $2,000. Note once again that this adjustment to the partnership's basis in its assets restores the equality of aggregate inside and outside bases broken by the sale of A's partnership interest.

---

2. Final capital account balance of $5,000 less $1,000 distributive share of gain equals $4,000.

It can be the case that a partner's share of the partnership's inside basis as defined by the regulations is negative, although there is no evidence that the drafters of the §743 regulations appreciated this possibility. For example, suppose X and Y form the XY general partnership, with X contributing cash of $300 in exchange for a 75 percent interest in profits and losses and Y contributing a capital asset with adjusted basis and fair market value of $100 in exchange for the remaining 25 percent interest in profits and losses. When an election under §754 is not in effect, the partnership distributes $200 in cash to Y. This distribution forces Y to recognize income of $100 under §731(a)(1) and reduces Y's outside basis to $0 under §733(2). Assume that the capital asset appreciates to $900, so that the books of the partnership stand as follows:

Asset	Book Value	Inside Basis	Fair Market Value
Cash	$100	$100	$ 100
Capital Asset	100	100	900
	$200	$200	$1,000

	Capital Account	Outside Basis	Fair Market Value
X	$300	$300	$ 900
Y	(100)	0	100
	$200	$300	$1,000

Because no election under §754 was in effect when the distribution of cash was made to Y, the distribution did not result in an adjustment to the partnership's inside basis. §734(a). Thus, one effect of the distribution was to break the equality between aggregate inside basis (now equal to $200) and aggregate outside basis (now equal to $300). If Y sells her partnership interest to Z for its current value of $100, the §743(b) adjustment equals $200. This value arises by comparing the Z's cost basis of $100 with Z's share of inside basis as defined in the regulations. Under that definition, Z's share of inside basis equals negative $100 (current capital account balance) plus $200 (capital account increase if all partnership assets sold) less $200 (distributive share of gain from hypothetical sale of assets), for a net value of negative $100! Note that this produces a §743(b) basis adjustment of $200, and that basis adjustment restores the equality of aggregate outside basis to aggregate inside basis.

Suppose that it is X rather than Y who sells her partnership interest, this time for its current value of $900. Now, the §743(b) basis adjustment equals $600. This adjustment equals the excess of the price paid by Z for the partnership interest (i.e., $900) over Z's share of the partnership's inside basis. Z's share of inside basis equals the amount of cash Z would receive in liquidation of the partnership if all the assets were sold in a fully taxable transaction, or $900, less distributive share of gain on the hypothetical sale of asset, or $600, for a net value of $300. Note that under this definition Z's share of the partnership's inside basis ($300) exceeds the partnership's *total* inside basis ($200). The §743(b) adjustment is then $900 less $300, or $600. *This time the adjustment does not restore the equality between aggregate inside and outside bases.*

To help understand the convoluted definition of a partner's share of "previously taxed capital," consider the following two examples. The *CDE* partnership owns three assets: *X*, a capital asset; *Y*, a capital asset; and *Z*, inventory. *C*, a one-third partner in capital, profits, and losses, has a capital account and outside basis of $700. *C* sells her interest in *CDE* for $1,000 while the partnership has a §754 election in effect and the partnership books stand as follows:

Asset	Book Value	Inside Basis	Fair Market Value
X	$ 600	$ 600	$1,500
Y	900	900	600
Z	600	600	900
	$2,100	$2,100	$3,000

	Capital Account	Outside Basis	Fair Market Value
Purchaser	$ 700	$1,000	$1,000
D	700	700	1,000
E	700	700	1,000
	$2,100	$2,400	$3,000

The purchaser's outside basis immediately after the purchase equals cost of $1,000 because there are no partnership liabilities. The purchaser's share of previously taxed capital equals $700 because a fair market value sale of all the partnership assets would produce a gain of $1,200 (on assets *X* and *Z*) and a loss of $300 (on asset *Y*). Thus, the result of this hypothetical sale is to increase the purchaser's capital account from $700 (taken from *C*) to $1,000 (one-third of the gain (or $400) less one-third of the loss (or $100), for a net distributive share of positive $300). From this, the purchaser's share of previously taxed capital equals $1,000 (final capital account balance) less $400 (distributive share of gain from the hypothetical sale) plus $100 (distributive share of loss from the hypothetical sale), for a net total of $700. From these two computations we can determine that the amount of the §743(b) adjustment is $300, that being the excess of the purchaser's initial outside basis of $1,000 over the purchaser's share of previously taxed capital of $700. This inside basis adjustment of $300 will cause aggregate outside basis to equal aggregate inside basis, restoring the equality that existed prior to the sale by *C*.

In this example the transferee's share of previously taxed capital equals the transferee's capital account. The reason that the definition of a partner's share of previously taxed capital (sometimes called the partner's share of inside basis) is more complex can be explained by the need to account for §704(c)(1)(A) and reverse-§704(c) allocations, that is, by allocations accounting for a variance between the book value of an asset and its adjusted basis to the partnership. If there are no such variations, then a partner's share of inside basis equals her capital account plus her share of the partnership's liabilities. If, though, the partner's capital account has been increased for appreciation that has not yet been recognized by the partnership, then the partner's capital account must be reduced by that appreciation to properly measure the partner's share of *previously* taxed capital. Similarly, if a partner's capital account has been reduced by some element of unrealized loss in partnership assets, then that partner's capital account must be increased by that unrealized loss to equal the partner's share of *previously* taxed capital.

For example, reconsider the example above but assume that partner *C* initially contributed asset *X* to the partnership when it had an adjusted basis of only $300 and a fair market value of $600. Making this change, once *C* sells her interest the books of the partnership will read:

Asset	*Book Value*	*Inside Basis*	*Fair Market Value*
X	$ 600	$ 300	$1,500
Y	900	900	600
Z	600	600	900
	$2,100	$1,800	$3,000

	Capital Account	*Outside Basis*	*Fair Market Value*
Purchaser	$ 700	$1,000	$1,000
D	700	700	1,000
E	700	700	1,000
	$2,100	$2,400	$3,000

Once again the purchaser's initial outside basis equals $1,000, but the purchaser's share of inside basis is only $400. This figure is computed as follows: If the partnership sold its assets for fair market value, the purchaser's distributive share of gain (i.e., of *tax* gain) would be $800 ($700 from asset *X* and $100 from asset *Z*) as well as distributive share of tax loss of $100 (from asset *Y*). Of the tax gain, only $500 would increase the purchaser's capital account (because §704(c)(1)(A) gain does not increase capital account), so that the purchaser's final capital account balance would be $1,100. We subtract from that figure the purchaser's distributive share of *tax* gain (i.e., $800) and add to that the purchaser's distributive share of *tax* loss (i.e., $100), for a net reduction of $700, making the purchaser's share of the partnership's inside basis $400. Accordingly, the §743(b) adjustment is $1,000 less $400, or $600. In short, a partner's share of "previously taxed capital" is defined the way it is to take into account the possibility that a sale of the partnership's assets would affect capital accounts by one set of numbers (book gain and loss) and outside bases by another set of numbers (tax gain and loss).

2. Allocating the §743(b) Adjustment under §755

a. Basic Rules

When a partnership interest is sold, exchanged, or passes through the estate of a decedent, the transferee will take what amounts to a fair market value basis in the partnership interest. If an election under §754 is in effect at the time of the transaction, current regulations provide, in general, that an optional basis adjustment will be made to each partnership asset in an amount that reflects the transferee's share of the unrealized appreciation or loss in that asset. In contradistinction to the basis adjustment arising from distributions under §734(b), this basis adjustment triggered by application of §743(b) affects the transferee partner only and so has no effect on the partnership's common basis.

Because optional basis adjustments under §743(b) affect the inside transferee partner only, the partnership must now keep two sets of partnership books, one unadjusted by §743(b) for the entire partnership and one reflecting the §743(b) adjustment for the transferee partner. Indeed, once an election under §754 is filed, the partnership must open an additional set of books every time a partnership interest is sold or exchanged, or when a partner dies.

Technically, a §743(b) adjustment is computed under §755 in two steps. In step 1, the adjustment for each class of property is determined, where one class consists of the partnership's ordinary income assets and the other class consists of the partnership's capital assets, §1231 assets, and cash. In step 2, the basis adjustment for each class is allocated among the partnership's assets within each class.

Consider the following example. The *ABC* partnership owns ordinary income asset *W* and capital assets *X, Y,* and *Z* with adjusted bases and fair market values as follows:

Asset	Adjusted Basis	Fair Market Value
W (ordinary)	$ 3,000	$30,000
X (capital)	30,000	24,000
Y (capital)	15,000	24,000
Z (capital)	51,000	12,000

C, a one-third partner with a capital account and outside basis of $33,000, sells her interest to *D* for its fair market value of $30,000 when an election under §754 is in effect. Under §743(b), the amount of the adjustment equals negative $3,000, that being the excess of *D*'s purchase price over

D's share of the "previously taxed capital" of the partnership. The partnership's class of ordinary income assets consists of asset W alone, while the class of capital assets includes assets *X, Y*, and *Z*.

The §743(b) basis adjustment is divided between the two classes as follows. First, it must be determined what *D*'s share of the partnership's ordinary income would be if the partnership sold it assets for fair market value. Here, that would be a sale of asset W for $30,000, producing a taxable gain to the partnership of $27,000 of which *D*'s share as a one-third partner would be $9,000. Thus, the §743(b) basis adjustment to the class of ordinary income assets (i.e., to asset W in this example) is $9,000. Treas. Regs. §1.755-1(b)(2)(i). The §743(b) basis adjustment allocated to the class of capital assets (i.e., to assets *X, Y*, and *Z* in this example) is that amount which, when added to the adjustment allocated to the ordinary income assets, yields the total adjustment as defined by §743(b). Because the total §743(b) adjustment is negative $3,000, the §743(b) adjustment allocated to the class of capital assets is negative $12,000. Treas. Regs. §1.755-1(b)(2)(i)(A)-(B).

The negative $12,000 basis adjustment allocated to the class of capital assets must then be divided into adjustments for each capital asset; here, that means the negative $12,000 basis adjustment must be allocated among assets *X, Y*, and *Z* in proportion to *D*'s share of the unrealized appreciation or loss in each asset. Accordingly, the negative $12,000 basis adjustment is allocated as follows: negative $2,000 to asset *X*, positive $3,000 to asset *Y*, and negative $13,000 to asset *Z*.[3] In tabular form:

Asset	Adjusted Basis	Fair Market Value	Adjustment
W (ordinary)	$ 3,000	$30,000	$ 9,000
X (capital)	30,000	24,000	(2,000)
Y (capital)	15,000	24,000	3,000
Z (capital)	51,000	12,000	(13,000)

b.   Allocation of §743(b) Adjustments to Depreciable Property

If an adjustment is made to depreciable property, the proper recovery applicable to the adjustment must be determined. As in the case of adjustments arising under §734(b), the general rule here is the negative basis adjustments are recovered over the remaining depreciable life of the asset while positive basis adjustments are recovered over a new depreciable life as if the asset were newly placed in service. Treas. Regs. §1.743-1(j)(4)(B)(1).

3. If *D*'s share of the net unrealized appreciation or loss in the capital assets did not exactly equal *D*'s basis adjustment allocable to the class of capital assets, then the adjustment to each capital asset must be adjusted for the difference. See Treas. Regs. §1.755-1(b)(3)(ii)(B).

However, if there is a §743(b) positive basis adjustment allocable to property having §704(c)(1)(A) built-in gain, then there is an exception to this general rule *if* the partnership has elected to use the remedial allocation method with respect to the appreciated property. In such circumstances, any positive §743(b) basis adjustment is recovered over the remaining depreciable period applicable to the built-in gain, Treas. Regs. §1.743-1(j)(4)(B)(2), that being a useful life determined not by reference to the depreciable life of the property in the hands of the partner who contributed the property but a new depreciable life as of the date of the property's contribution to the partnership. See Treas. Regs. §1.704-3(d)(2) (final sentence). Surprisingly, the proposed regulations do not expressly make this rule applicable to reverse §704(c) allocations.

c.   Partnership Disposition of Adjusted Property

Reconsider the problem discussed on page 889 whose solution is summarized on the chart on page 890. That chart, reproduced below, sets forth the partnership's common basis for each of its assets as well as the §743(b) adjustment allocable to partner *D* who purchased a one-third interest in the partnership for $90,000 when an election under §755 was in effect.

Asset	Adjusted Basis	Fair Market Value	Adjustment
W (ordinary)	$ 3,000	$30,000	$ 9,000
X (capital)	30,000	24,000	(2,000)
Y (capital)	15,000	24,000	3,000
Z (capital)	51,000	12,000	(13,000)

If the partnership should subsequently sell asset *W* for $27,000, how will partner *D* be taxed? The regulations make clear that the partnership first determines *D*'s distributive share of gain or loss by reference to the partnership's common basis in the property and then that amount is decreased by any positive adjustment or increased by any negative adjustment allocable to the property. Thus, when asset *W* is sold for $27,000, the partnership recognizes a taxable gain of $24,000, of which $8,000 (i.e., one-third) is allocable to *D*. Because *D*'s §743(b) basis adjustment is positive $9,000, *D* reports her $8,000 distributive share of income less her $9,000 basis adjustment; that is, *D* recognizes a $1,000 loss. See Treas. Regs. §1.743-1(j).

It is worth mentioning that a substantial part of what someone pays for a partnership interest might represent the value of the partnership's good will. Goodwill, like any other partnership asset, can be allocated inside basis under §§743(b) and 755. Unfortunately, inside basis allocated to partnership goodwill is unlikely to be recovered until the partnership is liquidated or a partnership interest is sold.

3. Distribution of Property Subject to a §743(b) Basis Adjustment

If a partnership distributes property subject to a basis adjustment under §743(b), the partner who is entitled to benefit from the adjustment will lose that benefit. If the distribution happens to be to that partner, we can give her an equivalent benefit by increasing her basis in the distributed property. That is, we can add the basis adjustment benefitting the distributee partner to the asset's inside basis and then follow the standard rules governing the distribution of property in §§731-733.

For example, once again reconsider the problem discussed on page 889 whose solution is summarized on the chart on page 890. That chart, reproduced below, sets for the partnership's common basis for each of its assets as well as the §743(b) adjustment allocable to partner D who purchased a one-third interest in the partnership for $90,000 when an election under §755 was in effect.

Asset	Adjusted Basis	Fair Market Value	Adjustment
W (ordinary)	$ 3,000	$30,000	$ 9,000
X (capital)	30,000	24,000	(2,000)
Y (capital)	15,000	24,000	3,000
Z (capital)	51,000	12,000	(13,000)

If asset Y is distributed to partner D in a nonliquidating distribution, D's adjusted basis in the property under §732(a)(1) will not be the partnership's common basis of $15,000 but rather the partnership's common basis as adjusted by D's §743(b) basis adjustment, or $15,000 plus $3,000 for a total of $18,000. Treas. Regs. §1.743-1(g)(1)(i). As a consequence, D must reduce her outside basis by that same amount, leaving D with an outside basis of $72,000.

Note that the basis adjustment given to asset Y is, in effect, taken away from distributee partner's outside basis under §733(2). This should not be surprising: By adjusting only *inside* basis, the optional basis adjustments affect only timing of income, not ultimate amount of income. Giving additional basis to the distributed asset and taking it from the distributee partner's outside basis changes the timing of recognition of income: Less income is recognized when the asset is sold while more will be recognized when the partnership interest is sold. If the optional basis adjustment were given to the asset *without* taking it from outside basis, an inside adjustment affecting timing would be converted into an outside adjustment affecting the total amount of income to be recognized.

If the asset is distributed to some partner *other than* the purchasing partner, we can preserve the optional basis adjustment only by reallocating it to some other asset of the partnership. Treas. Regs. §1.743-1(g)(2)(ii).

For example, if asset *Y* above were distributed to partner *A* or *B*, we would reallocate *D*'s $3,000 §743(b) basis adjustment formerly allocated to asset *Y* to some other partnership asset. The regulations provide that such an adjustment should be made to the remaining partnership assets pursuant to the rules generally applicable to §734(b) adjustments. Treas. Regs. §1.743-1(g)(2)(ii).

If a partnership terminates because of sales or exchanges of interests totaling more than 50 percent of partnership profits and capital, see §708(b)(1)(B), the partnership is deemed to transfer all of its assets to a new partnership in exchange for all interests in that new partnership, and then these interests in the new partnership are deemed distributed by the terminating partnership to its members, Treas. Regs. §1.708-1(b)(1)(iv). The basis to the new partnership will include any optional basis adjustment to partnership property arising under §743(b). Treas. Regs. §1.743-1(h)(1); see Treas. Regs. §1.708-1(b)(1)(v). A much more complicated rule applies to transfers of property subject to a §743(b) adjustment in a §351 transaction. See Treas. Reg. §1.743-1(h)(2).

PROBLEMS

27-3. Suppose on the facts of problem 27-1 that no distribution is made but instead *C* sells her partnership interest to *D* for its fair market value of $45,000.

    a.   What basis adjustments are appropriate under §§743 and 755?
    b.   How does this affect the partnership's computation of depreciation from the building?
    c.   If the partnership then sells all of its assets, how much gain or loss does each partner report and what is each partner's capital account?

27-4. Ignoring the possible application of §751(b):

    a.   Using the facts of problem 27-3(a), what basis adjustments must be made if the partnership distributes receivable #1 to partner *A*?
    b.   Using the facts of problem 27-3(a), what is *D*'s basis in receivable #2 if that receivable is distributed to *D* in complete liquidation of her partnership interest?

C. MECHANICS OF THE ELECTION

An election under §754 must be filed by the partnership (not by each partner separately), and it must be filed along with the partnership's tax return. Under some circumstances, a partnership is not required to file a partnership return. Nonetheless, if such a partnership wishes to file a §754 election, it must file a return and attach the §754 election to it.

Does it make sense for a partnership to file a §754 election? In general, basis adjustments under §734(b) are much less common than adjustments under §743(b), so the issue boils down to this: Who profits and who loses when a §743(b) basis adjustment is generated? Since most partners antici-pate that the partnership will make rather than lose money, most partners anticipate eventually selling their interests at a gain. Recall that disposition of a partnership interest for more than the selling partner's outside basis results in a *positive* basis adjustment under §743(b).

A positive basis adjustment under §743(b) will benefit the purchaser of a partnership interest by allowing the purchaser to recognize less gain when the partnership sells its appreciated assets, albeit at the cost of addi-tional gain (or less loss) upon a subsequent disposition of the partnership interest. Thus, the *nominal* beneficiary of the optional basis adjustment is a prospective purchaser of a partnership interest.

Accordingly, the purchaser should be willing to pay more for an ap-preciated partnership interest if there is an election under §754 in effect, so that some of the value of the §754 election should be captured by the selling partner in the form of a higher sale price. Because the selling partner will profit from the election and the other partners seemingly are unaffected by it, one might think that §754 elections are commonplace and noncontroversial.

Nothing could be further from the truth. Because an adjustment un-der §743(b) affects only the purchasing partner, each transfer of a partner-ship interest forces the partnership to open a new set of books reflecting the inside basis of all partnership assets as adjusted under §§743(b) and 755. Opening and maintaining a new set of books increases the partner-ship's accounting costs, accounting costs that will be borne for the indefi-nite future by every partner *other than* the selling partner. That is, the benefit of the §743(b) basis adjustment flows to one partner and its costs remain with the others. As you can imagine, the propriety of filing a §754 election can be controversial within a partnership.

In the case of a widely held partnership, the costs associated with repeated sales of small partnership interests by hundreds or even thou-sands of partners far exceed the benefits of the optional basis adjustments, and so the partnership agreements for such partnerships invariably provide that no §754 election will be filed. For smaller partnerships, the costs associated with §754 election are lower, and so the election might be worth its costs. But these smaller partnerships should follow the teachings of their larger brethren in at least one respect: *The mechanism for determining whether a §754 election will be made should be spelled out in the partnership agreement.*

For example, the partnership agreement could provide that any partner holding more than 30 percent (or 50 percent, or 12 percent, or any other percentage) has an absolute right to insist that a §754 election be filed by the partnership. Conversely, the partnership agreement could provide that no election will be filed unless every partner agrees, or unless three-quarters of the partners agree. What is important is that the partners' right to force or veto a prospective §754 election be defined in the partnership agreement well *before* a conflict arises. There are a variety of tax elections which a partnership must make, and a well-drafted partnership agreement should specify how these elections will be made or, alternatively, who will decide when the time arises.

D. OPTIONAL BASIS ADJUSTMENTS AND CAPITAL ACCOUNTS

The regulations promulgated under §704(b) provide specific rules governing the effects of the optional basis adjustments on partners' capital accounts. Treas. Regs. §1.704-1(b)(2)(iv)(m). Despite the statutory similarity of the §§734(b) and 743(b) optional basis adjustments, the capital account consequences of these two basis adjustments differ substantially. Under these rules, the optional basis adjustment under §734(b) triggered by the distribution of property produces capital account adjustments to all the partners while the §743(b) adjustment arising upon the taxable disposition of a partnership interest produces no capital account adjustment to the purchaser or to any other partner.

As we know, the optional basis adjustment under §734(b) affects the partnership's common basis in its assets; that is, the basis adjustment benefits all the partners in the partnership by reducing the gain (or increasing the loss) recognized by the partnership upon disposition of the adjusted property. Under the regulations, a §734(b) basis adjustment affects the partners' capital accounts precisely the same as the basis adjustment from the adjusted property is shared. Treas. Regs. §1.704-1(b)(2)(iv)(m)(4).

For example, suppose A has a 25 percent interest in the profits of the AB partnership while B owns the remaining 75 percent interest. If a distribution to one of the partners triggers an optional basis adjustment of $1,000 to some partnership asset, then A should receive a $250 capital account increase and B should receive a $750 capital account increase. Note, however, that the capital account adjustment is made when the basis adjustment is made. Therefore, if the basis adjustment is suspended because the partnership does not own property that can absorb the basis adjustment, the capital account adjustment is likewise suspended *en passant.* Treas. Regs. §1.704-1(b)(2)(iv)(m)(5).

Surprisingly, the optional basis adjustment under §743(b) does not yield a similar rule. The regulations make clear that, in general, no capital account adjustment is allowed when partnership assets are adjusted under §743(b). Treas. Regs. §1.704-1(b)(2)(iv)(m)(2); see Treas. Regs. §1.704-1(b)(5) (ex. 13(iii)). Recall that the basis adjustment under §743(b) affects the purchasing partner only, so one might suspect that a §743(b) basis adjustment would produce a capital account adjustment for the incoming partner only. But that is not the case, and this rule can lead to some surprises.

For example, suppose *Z* purchases *Y*'s limited partnership interest in the *XY* limited partnership. Assume that *Y*'s capital account balance at the time of the sale was $10,000, and assume also that because partnership assets have appreciated, *Z* pays $15,000 for the partnership interest. Even if the partnership has a §754 election in effect at the time of the sale, *Z* takes *Y*'s capital account without an increase for the premium paid by *Z* to *Y*. As a consequence, unless *Z* can be required to make additional contributions to the partnership (which is uncommon for limited partners), *Z* cannot be allocated more than $10,000 of partnership deductions for the current year even though *Z* has sufficient basis to absorb up to $15,000 of losses.

E. BASIS ADJUSTMENTS UNDER §732(d)

Even if an election under §754 is not filed by a partnership, the distribution of property can trigger the equivalent of a §743(b) basis adjustment. If a partner acquires her partnership interest by purchase, taxable exchange, or devise and no §754 election is in effect at the time the partnership interest is acquired, then this partner may elect to have the equivalent of a §743(b) basis adjustment applied to any property distributed by the partnership to her within two years of the acquisition of her partnership interest. §732(d).

The effect of a §732(d) basis adjustment should be a basis swap between the distributed property and the distributee partner's outside basis. For example, consider the case of the *ABC* general partnership owning cash of $300 and property with adjusted basis of §1,500 and fair market value of $2,100. Individuals *A, B,* and *C* are each one-third partners in *ABC,* and assume that partner *C* sells her partnership interest to *D* for its fair market value of $800 when an election under §754 is not in effect. At the time of the sale, *C*'s outside basis and capital account equal $600.

Because no §754 election is in effect when *D* purchases *C*'s partnership interest, this purchase has no effect on the partnership's inside basis.

§743(a). If the partnership then distributes one-third of the property to *D* in a nonliquidating distribution, *D* will recognize no gain or loss on the distribution and, absent a basis adjustment under §732(d), *D* will take a carryover basis in the distributed property of $500. §732(a)(1). *D*'s outside basis will decline from $800 to $300. §733(2).

If *D* elects to have an optional basis adjustment under §732(d), then we recompute the basis consequences of the distribution as if the distributed property had been subject to a basis adjustment under §743(b) when *D* purchased an interest in the partnership. Such a basis adjustment would have resulted in a $200 basis increase in the property, benefiting only *D*. As a consequence, *D*'s basis in the distributed property now is $700, §732(a)(1), and *D*'s outside basis is reduced to $100, §733(1). As compared with the same transaction lacking a §732(d) basis adjustment, we see that the effect of the election is to shift $200 of basis from *D*'s partnership interest into the distributed property. Accordingly, a §732(d) basis adjustment can be a strategic tool with respect to property the partnership holds and intends to sell: Gain from the sale can be reduced by distributing to new partners their share of the property that they (rather than the partnership) will then sell.

This optional application of §732(d) has three requirements: (1) no §754 election is in effect when the distributee acquired her partnership interest, (2) property is distributed within two years of acquisition of the partnership, and (3) the distributee partner files an appropriate election. Under some circumstances, even if the distribution occurs more than two years following the distributee partner's acquisition of her partnership interest, the basis adjustment provided by §732(d) is mandatory. Under Treas. Regs. §1.732-1(d)(4), the basis adjustment under §732(d) is mandatory if (1) a partner acquires her partnership interest by purchase, taxable exchange, or devise when a §754 election is not in effect; (2) at the time of acquisition, the fair market value of all partnership property (excluding money) exceeds 110 percent of the partnership's adjusted basis in its property; (3) if the acquiring partner's interest in the partnership were liquidated immediately after the acquisition, the effect of the basis allocation rules in §732(c) would be to shift basis from nondepreciable property to depreciable property; and (4) the effect of applying §732(d) would be to avoid such a basis shift.

In general, the basis allocation rules of §732(c) prevent a distribution of property from shifting basis of capital assets (sometimes called "cold" assets) into the basis of ordinary income assets (often called "hot" assets). Such a basis shift is not permitted because Congress is unwilling to exchange taxation of ordinary income for taxation of capital gain. If depreciable capital assets are not quite "hot," they are also not quite "cold": Additional basis given to a depreciable capital asset likely will produce an increase in the distributee partner's depreciation deductions, deductions that will offset ordinary income. Thus, it might be fair to classify deprecia-

ble capital assets as "lukewarm": hotter than nondepreciable capital assets
yet cooler than unrealized receivables and inventory. The mandatory operation of §732(d) was designed to ensure that a strategic failure to file a
§754 election cannot be used to move basis from cold assets to lukewarm
ones. See, e.g., Rudd v. Commissioner, 79 T.C. 225 (1982).

As part of the of the Taxpayer Relief Act of 1997, the basis allocation
rules of §732(c) were modified. While these modifications responded to
criticisms having little to do with §732(d), see generally William D. An-
drews, Inside Basis Adjustments and Hot Asset Exchanges in Partnership
Distributions, 47 Tax L. Rev. 3 (1991); Noël B. Cunningham, Needed
Reform: Tending the Sick Rose, 47 Tax L. Rev. 77 (1991), one effect seems
to be that mandatory application of §732(d) can no longer arise because
requirement (4) (that the effect of applying §732(d) would be to avoid an
impermissible basis shift) will never be satisfied. The Treasury, however,
continues to believe that strategic failure to file a §754 election may result
in a basis shift that can be thwarted by the mandatory application of
§732(d), and so the §732(d) regulations have not been withdrawn.

28

Partnership-Level Issues

A. CLASSIFICATION AS A PARTNERSHIP

"Partnership" is a defined term; in fact, it is *twice* defined. Under §761(a), a partnership is any profit-seeking organization other than a corporation, trust or estate. A similar definition is provided in §7701(a)(2). Because each of these definitions define the term "partnership" by exclusion (that is, as everything *other than* corporations, trusts and estates), it really is the definition of "corporation" in §7701(a)(3) that sets the contours of the partnership definition. Note, though, that §761(a) specifically limits partnerships to unincorporated entities: If an organization is incorporated under applicable state law, it cannot be taxed as a partnership. In addition, the statute plainly contemplates the existence of certain noncorporate "associations" taxable as corporations.

Not all organizations are *business* organizations. A joint undertaking to share expenses (say, by a group of homeowners agreeing to care for common property) does not constitute a partnership under subchapter K. Treas. Regs. §301.7701-1(a)(2). In Madison Gas & Elec. Co. v. Commissioner, 72 T.C. 521 (1979), aff'd, 633 F.2d 512 (5th Cir. 1980), a group of power companies joined together to construct a nuclear power plant that would deliver power to the joint venturers for resale. At issue was the deductibility of various construction expenses: The power companies argued that these costs were ordinary and necessary expenses incurred in their existing business, while the Service argued that they were nondeductible start-up costs of a newly formed partnership. See §195. The taxpayer argued that the arrangement among the power companies was no more than an agreement to share expenses without any profit-seeking motive, but the court held that the in-kind distribution of electricity constituted a sharing of economic profit sufficient to support partnership status.

As to those organizations that are undoubtedly business organizations, for several decades the regulations tried to distinguish entities taxable as partnerships from associations taxable as corporations by reference to certain supposed "corporate characteristics" such as continuity of life, centralization of management, limited liability, and free transferability of interests. Treas. Regs. §301.7701-2(a)(1) (repealed 1996). While these regulations were not by their terms elective, taxpayers usually could structure their unincorporated business organizations to be taxed as partnerships or as corporations as they preferred by manipulating relatively insignificant aspects of the organization.

In the late 1980s and early 1990s, most states enacted limited liability company statutes, thereby permitting businesses to have all the nontax characteristics of corporations (including limited liability for all investors) while technically not being corporations. Thus, the organizer of a limited liability company files articles of organization and an operating agreement instead of articles of incorporation and corporate by-laws, investors contribute cash or property to the limited liability company and receive membership certificates instead of shares, and these investors are called "members" instead of "shareholders." Somewhat surprisingly, courts and the Service were willing to treat such corporate look-alikes as unincorporated entities, and so limited liability companies could then qualify for taxation as partnerships by manipulating their various "corporate characteristics."

As the efficacy of the old association regulations was declining, Congress enacted §7704 providing that publicly traded partnerships (including limited liability companies and similar business organizations otherwise taxable as partnerships) would be taxed as corporations if their interests were traded on an established securities market or for which their was a secondary market making the interests readily tradeable. These two factors — the increasing failure of the meaningless "corporate characteristics" in the association regulations and the more objective standard imposed by §7704 — ultimately convinced the Treasury to repeal the old association regulations and replace them with an explicitly elective regime for distinguishing entities taxable as partnerships from associations taxable as corporations. However, because the statutory term "partnership" explicitly excludes all corporations, the regulations continue to provide that incorporated entities may not be taxed as partnerships.

1. Elective Classification

Under Treas. Regs. §301.7701-2(b)(1)-(8) (excluding (2)), a variety of business organizations are denied elective classification and must instead be taxed as corporations. These entities include all incorporated entities, heavily regulated entities such as insurance companies and banks, entities wholly owned by a state or municipality, and a variety of foreign business entities traditionally treated as corporations under domestic and foreign laws. All other business organizations are classified as "eligible" entities, see Treas. Regs. §301.7701-3(a), and such organizations can elect to be taxed as a partnerships or as a corporations, with the default rule generally favoring partnership treatment. See Treas. Regs. §301.7701-3(b)(1)(i). However, if an eligible entity has a single owner and elects not to be taxed as a corporation, the electing entity is ignored for tax purposes and so will be treated as a division if its parent is a corporation or a partnership or as a sole proprietorship if its parent is an individual. Treas. Regs. §301.7701-3(b)(1)(ii). Once an eligible entity makes its election (other than accepting its default status, usually that of a partnership), it may not change its election for 60 months. Treas. Regs. §301.7701-3(c)((1)(iv). Thereafter, the entity need only file a new election if it is changing its status. Treas. Regs. §301.7701-3(c)(1)(i).

While the current regulations (often called the "check-the-box" regulations) generally have been well received, they do leave many questions unanswered. For example, suppose LX and LY form the XY general partnership, with LX and LY each being a single-owner limited liability company owned by individuals X and Y respectively. If LX and LY each elect to be taxed as corporations and XY elects to be taxed as a partnership, any debt incurred by XY on a fully recourse basis will be allocated under §752 between LX any LY based on their potential liability to repay that debt. Under current regulations, that will turn on their relative partnership capital account deficits following a hypothetical zero-value sale and liquidation, Treas. Regs. §1.752-2(b)(1), which essentially means that it depends on the partnership loss sharing ratios and the partners' relative capital accounts. See, e.g., Treas. Regs. §1.752-2(f) (example 1); Howard E. Abrams, Long-Awaited Regulations under Section 752 Provide Wrong Answers, 44 Tax L. Rev. 627 (1989).

But what if LX or LY (or both) elects not to be taxed as a corporation? While such an election works no change in the legal relationships among the parties (because the election is effective only as to the taxation of LX vis-à-vis owner X and LY vis-à-vis Y), it arguably rearranges the debt shares. For exampe, if LY elects not to be taxed as a corporation, then because LY has a single owner, LY is ignored for tax purposes and Y is deemed to be one of the two partners in the XY partnership (along with LX still being taxed as a corporation). And while the debt remains fully recourse as to XY, individual Y has no personal liability for the debt (and no obligation to restore any capital account deficit) because of the limited liability offered by LY, which though ignored for federal tax purposes is still very much alive for all other purposes including (especially) protecting Y from creditors of the XY partnership. Y's lack of personal liability on the partnership's debt seems to eliminate any allocation of the debt to *Y*. See Treas. Regs. §1.752-2(b)(3)(i). Ironically, the sharing of the debt changes because under the regulations ultimate responsibility for repayment is altered, see Treas. Regs. §1.752-2(a), *even though the election has worked no change in anyone's liability on the debt.*

Most foreign business organizations are not eligible entities. See Treas. Regs. §301.7701-2(b)(8). For example, a Naamloze Vennootschap (NV) formed in the Netherlands is always taxable as a corporation. Treas. Regs. §301.7701-2(b)(8)(i). If in response to our current elective classification regime the Netherlands creates a new form of business organization (say, an NNV) with all the attributes of an NV but with a new name, will such an entity be eligible for elective classification or will the Treasury amend its list of ineligible foreign entities? If we have truly moved to elective classification, then presumably foreign governments will be able to exploit elective classification by creating their own versions of limited liability companies.

2. Publicly Traded Partnerships

In §7704(a), Congress has provided that certain publicly traded partnerships will be taxed as corporations. For this purpose, a "publicly traded partnership" is one whose partnership interests (1) are traded on an established securities market or (2) are readily traded on a secondary market.§7704(b). This provision was enacted as part of the Revenue Act of 1987 in response to the growth of "master limited partnerships," huge entities having thousands of partners and assets worth tens (or hundreds) of millions of dollars.

Note, though, that if the income of a partnership consists of 90 percent or more of investment income as defined in §7704(d), the partnership will avoid the clutches of §7704(a). The legislative history of this provision explains that no corporate-level tax need be imposed because a corporate-level tax was imposed on the underlying income-producing investment. The definition of "qualifying income" in §7704(d), however, imposes no requirement that the passive-type income come from a corporate taxpayer.

3. Recognizing Partner Status

a. General Principles

In Commissioner v. Culbertson, 337 U.S. 733 (1949), the Supreme Court held that a partnership consists of two or more persons who have proprietary interests in the profits of their joint venture. An agreement to divide profits is strong evidence that an arrangement is a partnership and that the parties are partners. On the other hand, one whose compensation from the organization is fixed in amount or otherwise independent of the success of the venture (e.g., one whose compensation is based on net receipts) is likely to be treated as an employee or independent contractor.

Whether someone is recognized for tax purposes as a partner turns on the application of federal law, although a court might conclude that in this area federal law should be informed by state law definitions of partnership status. Yet the Service has on occasion ignored state definitions to take an expansive view of partnership status. In Rev. Rul. 77-137, 1977-1 C.B. 178, the Service ruled that an assignee of a partnership interest will be taxed as a partner if she acquires substantially all dominion and control over a limited partnership interest even if the assignee fails to satisfy conditions imposed by the partnership agreement. And in Rev. Rul. 77-332, 1977-2 C.B. 484, the Service ruled that non-CPA members of a CPA firm with the rights and liabilities of partners must be taxed as partners despite local law prohibiting them from being partners because they were not CPAs.

b. Family Partnerships

As you know, the existence of progressive tax rates encourages taxpayers to structure their affairs so that taxable income is reported by low-bracket taxpayers. In Lucas v. Earl, 281 U.S. 111 (1930), the Supreme Court held that earned income is taxable to the income earner without regard to contractual assignments of the right to receive the income. On the other hand, in Blair v. Commissioner, 300 U.S. 5 (1937), the Court held that the incidence of taxation on income from property can be shifted by an assignment of the property (but not by assignment of only the income from property) from one taxpayer to another.

You can imagine that a partnership might offer substantial assignment of income opportunities to an aggressive taxpayer. For example, a highly compensated professional might form a partnership with her child, with the child contributing little of value in exchange for a substantial partnership share. The parent could then enter into an employer/employee relationship with the partnership, and the partnership will report as its net income the excess of what it receives for the parent's services from third parties in excess of what it pays the parent as salary. Accordingly, if the salary paid to the parent is small, the partnership will have large earnings. These earnings will then be passed through to the partners in accordance with their distributive shares, allowing the child to report (at low tax rates) what amounts to some of the parent's income. An extreme example of taxpayer initiative is Tinkoff v. Commissioner, 120 F.2d 564 (7th Cir. 1941), where an accountant took his son into his accounting firm on the day the son was born.

Congress has in §704(e) attempted to address the assignment-of-income possibilities consistent with the two-pronged assignment of income doctrine articulated in *Earl* and *Blair*. Under §704(e)(1), the donee of a partnership interest will be recognized as the true owner *if* capital is a material income-producing factor in the partnership. If capital is *not* a material income producing factor in the partnership, then presumably the partnership's income is attributable to the labor of its partners, and the incidence of taxation on income from labor cannot be shifted under *Earl*. On the other hand, if capital *is* a material income-producing factor, the *Blair* prong of the assignment-of-income doctrine militates in favor of recognizing the donee as a partner for tax purposes.

Consider, though, the case of a partnership in which both labor and capital are material income-producing factors. If one partner received her partnership interest as a gift from another partner, there remains the possibility of an impermissible assignment of earned income if the donor partner receives an inadequate salary. To combat this possibility, §704(e)(2) provides that the donee partner will be treated as the true owner of her interest only if the donor partner received reasonable compensation for services rendered to the partnership.

In addition, §704(e)(2) speaks to attempted assignments of income lacking a full transfer of the underlying income-producing property. For example, suppose the donor-partner transfers one-tenth of the partnership's capital to the donee partner but the partnership agreement allocates one-half of all partnership income to the donee. While such an allocation should pass the substantial economic effect test of §704(b), it fails to satisfy the *Blair* prong of the assignment-of-income doctrine that taxation of income from property income can be shifted only by a transfer of the income-producing property. See, e.g., Helvering v. Horst, 311 U.S. 112 (1940). In this example, the donor has transferred one-tenth of the property yet seeks to shift one-half of the taxation.

Under §704(e)(2), special allocations of income to a donee partner are invalid to the extent they allocate disproportionately more income to the donee partner than to the donor partner, as measured by relative capital shares. Note that for this section as well as for §704(e)(1), a donee partner includes any partner who acquires a partnership interest from a family member (as defined in the final sentence of §704(e)(3)) even if the acquisition was fully paid. For purposes of §704(e), in other words, even sales of partnership interests between family members are considered gifts.

In Carriage Square, Inc. v. Commissioner, 69 T.C. 119 (1977), Arthur Condiotti was the president and controlling shareholder of Carriage Square, Inc. That corporation and several trusts each benefiting an immediate member of Condiotti's family formed a limited partnership, and at issue was the extent to which the interests of the trusts in the partnership should be respected for tax purposes. The partnership engaged in the business of developing real estate, and each partner made a minor capital contribution to the venture. In fact, substantially all of the funds used in the enterprise came as borrowed funds from a third-party lender, and Condiotti guaranteed repayment of the loans to permit the partnership to obtain favorable interest rates.

In a reviewed opinion, the Tax Court held that the trusts' interests in the partnership had to be ignored despite §704(e)(1) because capital was not a "material income producing factor" in the partnership within the meaning of §704(e)(1). While it seems plain that all of the partnership's profits came from capital and not from labor, the court held that for purposes of §704(e)(1), only capital contributed by the partners can be considered, relying on language in Treas. Regs. §1.704-1(e)(1)(i).

The majority opinion held that capital was not a material income-producing factor in the partnership's business because the business assets were purchased with borrowed capital. Yet §704(e)(1) limits its application to partnerships in which capital is a material income-producing factor to preserve the *Earl* prong of the assignment of income doctrine, namely that the incidence of taxation on income from labor cannot be shifted. Certainly it cannot be said that the partnership's business was primarily a service business; after all, the partnership was in the business of developing real estate. Dissenting in part and concurring in part, Judge Tannenwald observed that the regulations under §704(e) emphasize the function capital serves for the partnership, not the source from which it is obtained.

How can a business lacking any significant capital investment turn a profit? In *Carriage Square*, the partnership entered into a risky enterprise, with the prospect of high returns compensating for the significant risk of partial or even total loss. The activity was funded by a commercial bank which accepted a more certain and more limited return on its investment. What allowed the partnership to make a profit in this case was the willingness of Carriage Square, Inc., as general partner (and of the sole shareholder of the general partner in the capacity as guarantor) to accept a risk of loss in exchange for the possibility of gain.

What motivated the bank to fund the partnership's activity was its substantial certainty of repayment, certainty based upon the capital of the partnership's general partner as well as that of Condiotti, its sole shareholder (in his capacity as guarantor). Judge Tannenwald imputed Condiotti's capital to his corporation and then relied on §704(e)(2) and its emphasis on the relative partnership capital of donor and donee to allocate most of the income to the Carriage Square, Inc. But should Condiotti's capital be imputed to his corporation?

If the motivation for the guarantee was to benefit Condiotti by increasing his corporation's net worth, then imputation of Condiotti's capital to the corporation should be appropriate. But recall the circumstances of the partnership's formation: The sole general partner was a corporation controlled by Condiotti, and each of the limited partners was a trust created for the benefit of Condiotti or one of his near relatives. In guaranteeing the partnership's debt, Condiotti presumably was intending to benefit himself and his loved ones. The intended beneficiary of the guarantee most likely was Condiotti's family rather than his corporation. If so, should the taxpayer have won this case by relying on Judge Tannenwald's analysis and §704(e)(2)?

However, under the unearned income prong of the assignment-of-income doctrine, the incidence of taxation on income from capital can be shifted only by a transfer of the underlying capital; a mere assignment of the income unaccompanied by the capital will not suffice. Helvering v. Horst, 311 U.S. 112 (1940). By guaranteeing the partnership's debt, Condiotti sought to generate income for the trusts without an actual transfer of significant capital. This attempt should fail, not because of §704(e) but because of the more general assignment of income doctrine. To the extent the partnership's income was generated by its ability to borrow at an interest rate lower than it could have obtained without the guarantee, the income should be taxable to Condiotti as guarantor. However, the courts to date have been unable to articulate a consistent approach to the taxation of gratuitous guarantees, both for the income tax and for the transfer (gift, estate and generation-skipping) taxes. *Carriage Square* was one more opportunity forgone.

PROBLEMS

28-1.   *X* and *Y* form the *XY* general partnership, with *X* contributing cash of $100,000 and *Y* contributing unimproved real estate with adjusted basis of $20,000 and fair market value of $100,000. *X* and *Y* agree to be equal partners. One year after *XY* is formed, the partnership distributes $100,000 to *Y*. Assume that this distribution is treated as a disguised sale under §707(a)(2)(B). Is there a partnership? When was it formed?

B. PARTNERSHIP ELECTIONS

Any taxpayer can be faced with a variety of elections: taxable year, methods of accounting (including installment method treatment), and depreciation methods for depreciable assets, just to name a few. A partnership is faced with these same elections as well as some special ones such as the optional basis election under §754. Specifying who has the authority to make these elections is an important part of any partnership agreement.

1. Taxable Year

The general provisions governing taxable years are in §§441-443. For partnerships, two more specific provisions also apply: §§706 and 446. These two provisions place substantial restrictions on a partnership's freedom to choose its taxable year. To understand why these restrictions are imposed, we must recall how and when partnership income is includible on each partner's individual tax return.

Under §706(a), a partner's distributive share of partnership income and deduction is includible "for any taxable year of the partnership ending within or with the taxable year of the partner." In effect, this means that the partner's distributive share is recognized by the partner on the last day of the *partnership's* taxable year. For example, consider the case of a partnership using a fiscal year ending January 31 of each year and an individual partner using the calendar year as her taxable year.

Each January 31, the partner includes her distributive share of the partnership's income for the prior 12 months. In particular, on January 31, 1994, she includes her share of the partnership's activities from February 1, 1993, through January 31, 1994. Because this partner uses the calendar year as her taxable year, her tax return for 1994 will be due on April 15, 1995. Although 11/12's of the partnership's activity was conducted in 1993, the partner will owe no tax on it until April 1995, producing deferral up to 26½ months (from February of 1993 until April 15, 1995). For individual taxpayers not including partnership distributive share on their returns, maximum deferral should be no more than 15½ months (from January of one year until April 15 of the following year). The mismatch of partner and partnership taxable years, in other words, produced added deferral of 11 months.

Now suppose that the partnership's taxable year ended November 30 instead of January 31. Now, the partner's individual return for 1994 (due April 15, 1995) will include her distributive share for the partnership's activities from December 1, 1993 through November 30, 1994. Maximum deferral is now reduced to 16½ months, only one month more than that available to all taxpayers under our system of annual accounting. If the partnership's taxable year had coincided with the partner's taxable year, there would be no additional deferral.

The rules of §706(b) seek to minimize the deferral by limiting the mismatch between the partnership's taxable year and that of its partners. Section 706(b) creates three rules for determining a partnership's taxable year. Under rule 1, if any group of partners having a combined interest in partnership capital and profits exceeding 50 percent share a common taxable year, then the partnership must adopt that common taxable year (called the "majority interest taxable year" in §706(b)(1)(B)(i)) as its taxable year.

If no group satisfies this test, then under rule 2 the partnership must adopt the taxable year shared by its "principal" partners, if they in fact share a common taxable year. §706(b)(1)(B)(ii). For this purpose, a "principal" partner is any partner owning 5 percent or more of partnership capital or profits. §706(b)(3). If the principal partners do not share a common taxable year (or if there are no principal partners), then under rule 3 the partnership must adopt the calendar year as its taxable year or another taxable year prescribed by regulations. §706(b)(1)(B)(iii). Regulations now require partnerships whose taxable years are not determined under rules 1 and 2 to adopt that taxable year which results in the least aggregate deferral of income to the partners, Treas. Regs. §1.706-1T(a)(1), taking into account each partner's particular taxable year and the partners' relative interests in the partnership, Treas. Regs. §1.706-1T(a)(2).

Consider the following example. The P partnership is formed by X corporation and 90 individuals. X corporation has a 10 percent interest in the capital and profits of P and uses a fiscal year ending March 31 as its taxable year. Each individual owns 1 percent of P's capital and profits and uses the calendar year as her taxable year. The partnership must adopt the calendar year as its taxable year under rule 1: Any 51 of the individual partners hold more than 50 percent of the partnership's capital and profits and they share the calendar year as their taxable year. Under §706(b)(1)(B)(i), the partnership must adopt that common year as its taxable year.

Suppose, however, that the 1 percent interests were held by 90 separate corporations all using different fiscal years as their taxable years. P would now be required to use X's fiscal year as its taxable year because there is no "majority interest taxable year" under rule 1, and X is the only "principal" partner for purposes of rule 2. And if X's interest amounted to only 4 percent of the partnership (with six more small owners), the partnership would be required to follow the regulations in determining its taxable year under rule 3.

There are two exceptions to these rules. A partnership may adopt any taxable year without regard to the rules of §706(b)(1) *if* it can convince the government that it has an adequate business purpose for its selection. §706(b)(1)(C). Also, a partnership may adopt a taxable year beginning up to three months *earlier* than the required taxable year as determined under the rules of §706(b) (i.e., one producing up to three months deferral) simply by electing to do so under §444. However, any partnership electing to take advantage of §444 is required to prepay to the Treasury the value of the deferral so obtained. See §7519.

PROBLEMS

28-2.   Corporations X, Y, and Z form the XYZ general partnership, with X and Y each having a 40 percent interest in partnership capital, profits and losses and Z having the remaining 20 percent interest. X uses a fiscal year ending January 31, Y uses a fiscal year ending July 31, and Z uses a fiscal year ending November 30. What taxable year must the partnership adopt?

2.   *Method of Accounting*

A partnership, like any taxpayer, must adopt a method of accounting. Under §446(a), a taxpayer's method of accounting for tax purposes must be kept using the same method used for financial purposes. Under §446(b), a taxpayer's method of accounting must clearly reflect the taxpayer's income. In addition, a taxpayer having two or more businesses may use separate methods of accounting for each business. §446(d).

Most businesses use an accrual method of accounting. The cash method is unavailable to most corporations and to most partnerships having a corporate taxpayer, see §448(a), and any business involved in the production, purchase or sale of merchandise must use an inventory method of accounting. See Treas. Regs. §1.446-1(a)(4)(i).

Recall that many taxpayers may elect to expense some of the cost of up to tangible business property in lieu of depreciation under §179, subject to certain income limitations, see §179(b)(2), (3). While it is the partnership that makes the §179 election, §703(b), the maximum dollar limitation applies at both the partnership *and* the partner level. §179(d)(8); Treas. Regs. §1.179-1(f)(2). This means that the partnership may file a §179 election with respect to no more than that permitted by §179 of partnership property without regard to the number of partners in the partnership. In addition, no individual may claim more than that permitted by §179 including any distributive share of a §179 deduction.

C.   SPECIAL ISSUES

1.   *The Anti-Abuse Rules*

Various provisions in subchapter K respond to congressionally-perceived abuses of the more structural aspects of partnership taxation. For example, the possibility that contributions and distributions can be used to achieve inappropriate deferral led to enactment of the disguised sale provision in §707(a)(2)(B) as well as the anti-mixing bowl provisions of §§704(c)(1)(B) and 737. Similarly, that allocations of gross income might be used to convert capital expenses into the equivalent of deductible expenditures led to §707(a)(2)(A). In contrast to these targeted anti-abuse provisions enacted by Congress, the Department of Treasury has promulgated under §701 two broad anti-abuse rules potentially applying to *all* partnership transactions. While these rules seek to prevent taxpayers from using the partnership form to reduce income taxes, the rules explicitly have no relevance to partnerships used to minimize the estate, gift, or generation-skipping taxes. Treas. Regs. §1.701-2(i).

a. The General Anti-Abuse Rule

Under the general anti-abuse rule of Treas. Regs. §1.701-2(b), any inappropriate use of the rules of partnership taxation can lead to the following remedies: (1) the partnership will not be treated as a separate entity; (2) one or more of the partners will not be treated as a partner; (3) the method of accounting used by the partnership will be adjusted to more clearly reflect income; (4) partnership-level items of income, gain, loss, deduction, or credit will be reallocated; and (5) the claimed tax treatment will be adjusted or modified. In this context, inappropriate use of the rules of partnership taxation means that "a partnership is formed or availed of in connection with a transaction a principal purpose of which is to reduce substantially the present value of the partners' aggregate federal tax liability in a manner that is inconsistent with the intent of Subchapter K, in light of the applicable statutory and regulatory provisions and the pertinent facts and circumstances." Treas. Regs. §1.701-2(b).

This regulation is troublesome because of its reference to the "intent of Subchapter K." A definition of the intent of Subchapter K is provided in Treas. Regs. §1.701-2(a). According to this regulation, the purpose of Subchapter K is to allow "taxpayers to conduct joint business activities through a flexible economic arrangement without incurring an entity-level tax." However, the regulation further provides that three requirements are encompassed within this definition: (1) a partnership must be bona fide, and all transactions must have a substantial business purpose; (2) the form of transactions must be respected under substance over form principles; and (3) tax consequences under Subchapter K must be an accurate reflection of economic reality unless a contrary result is clearly contemplated by the provision being utilized.

Suppose a transaction complies with all the requirements of Subchapter K yet produces significant tax advantages to the participants. For example, suppose appreciated property is contributed to a partnership and then distributed to some other partner more than seven years after the contribution. Such a distribution does not trigger income to the contributing partner under §704(c)(1)(B) because that provision has only a seven-year reach. In such circumstances can the Service invoke the general anti-abuse rule, effectively extending application of §704(c)(1)(B)?

Or consider the following. A partnership is formed and the partners deliberately do not file an election under §754, thereby eschewing the optional basis adjustments of §§734(b) and 743(b). Because these optional basis adjustments are not made, aggregate inside basis eventually exceeds aggregate outside basis, thereby permitting the partners to enjoy some deferral of income until they exit the partnership. Can the Service invoke the general anti-abuse rule to treat the partners as if a §754 election had been filed, even though such an election is expressly optional? Surprisingly, the Treasury believes that such administrative discretion is allowable. See Treas. Regs. §1.701-2(d) (example 8).

Application of the general anti-abuse rule has two threshold requirements: (1) a principal purpose of reducing tax liability (2) in a manner inconsistent with the intent of Subchapter K. The first requirement may be the most troubling aspect of the general anti-abuse provision because it appears to require that the subjective intentions of the partners' entering into a questionable transaction be carefully examined. If a transaction is otherwise unchallengeable, why should the motives of the taxpayer affect the tax consequences? Conversely, if a transaction is otherwise questionable, can a taxpayer avoid application of the general anti-abuse rule by proving that her motives were pure?

In the example in the regulations involving the alleged improper failure to make an optional basis adjustment, the regulations provide: "On these facts, any purported business purpose for the transaction is insignificant in comparison to the tax benefits that would result if the transaction were respected for federal tax purposes." §1.701-2(d) (example 8). This example suggests that taxpayer motivation is a one-way street: improper motive may condemn an otherwise legitimate transaction but pure motives cannot save an overly beneficial one.

The New York State Bar Association, in a report on the general anti-abuse regulation prior to its final adoption, stated the opinion that the regulations should make clear that the general anti-abuse rule does not apply to transactions which have passed muster under more specific anti-abuse rules found in subchapter K. New York State Bar Association Tax Section, Report on The Proposed Partnership Antiabuse Rule, Tax Notes Today, July 11, 1994, at 233-52. For example, if a transaction is not characterized as a disguised sale under §707(a)(2)(B) (say, because there was more than two years between the transfers) it should not be recharacterized under the general anti-abuse rule in §1.701-2(b). That is, if §1.707-3(d) provides for a presumption that a transfer made after more than two years is not a sale, should not a taxpayer be entitled to that presumption? Unfortunately, no such statement was included in the final regulations.

b. The Abuse of Entity Rule

Treas. Regs. §1.701-2(e) provides a separate "abuse of entity" rule. This rule provides that "[t]he Commissioner can treat a partnership as an aggregate of its partners in whole or in part as appropriate to carry out the purpose of any provision of the Internal Revenue Code or the regulations promulgated thereunder." However, this rule exempts provisions that clearly contemplate entity treatment of a partnership, as long as the tax results of the transaction are explicitly contemplated by the provision in question.

The abuse of entity rule seems to be directed at little more than one type of violation of the more general anti-abuse rule, albeit without imposing on the Service any obligation to find that a principal purpose of the transaction was tax avoidance. For example, suppose two corporations are engaged in legitimate business activities through a partnership. The partnership issues a certain type of high yield discount obligations to a third party. Section 163(e)(5) limits the interest deductions which a corporation may take on this type of obligation. In this circumstance, the regulations provide that the partnership must be treated as an aggregate of its partners to give effect to §163(e)(5). Treas. Regs. §1.701-2(d) (ex. 1). Compare this supposedly abusive use of the partnership form with a partnership formed by an S corporation and a nonresident alien (who could not own stock in the S corporation directly without terminating the corporation's subchapter S status). Here, the regulations provide that no abuse exists. Treas. Regs. §1.701-2(d) (example 2).

2. Treatment of Organization and Syndication Expenses

A partnership often is formed by an individual as a device to raise needed capital. For example, D may own unimproved real estate which could be improved by constructing apartments or an office building. To raise the needed capital, D proposes to form a partnership with D as the sole general partner and 35 limited partners. D will contribute the real estate in exchange for her general partnership interest and each limited partner will be required to contribute cash of $30,000. If the development needs an equity investment of about $1,000,000, this partnership will provide adequate funding if and only if all the limited partnership interests can be sold.

D will have a lawyer draft the proposed partnership agreement as well as documents explaining the venture to prospective investors. These documents are usually referred to as the prospectus or offering statement for the investment. Depending on the anticipated financial sophistication and number of prospective investors, these documents might have to be filed with federal or state regulators.

D will then try to sell the project to various investors. Because the project cannot succeed unless all limited partnership interests are purchased, the partnership agreement will include a provision specifying that capital contributions of limited partners will be placed in a special escrow account. If all limited interests have been sold by a specified date, the escrowed funds will be distributed to the partnership and the activity will begin. If some interests remain unsold, the escrowed accounts will be returned to the investors and the partnership will never form.

The process of selling interests to investors is called syndication, and it can be an expensive process. Lawyer's fees will be incurred in drafting the prospectus, and most likely accountant's fees will arise as well. The promoter of the investment might be entitled to reimbursement of some filing fees, registration fees, and even selling costs, all depending on the terms of the partnership agreement.

Under §709(a), a partnership is forbidden from deducting organization and syndication expenses. However, organization expenses (as defined in §709(b)(2)) can be amortized by the partnership over a period not less than 60 months. Because it makes little sense to defer recognition of deductions, partnerships invariably elect the shortest period, namely 60 months. Accordingly, a partnership making such an election will be entitled to deduct just under 2 percent of its organization costs over each of its first 60 months. Note that if the partnership is formed other than in January, the partnership's first 60 months will be spread over six (not five) calendar years. Note also that the amortization rule of §709(b)(1) applies only to "organization" expenses. "Syndication" expenses cannot be deducted by reason of §709(a) and cannot be amortized under §709(b); syndication expenses, in other words, will never be recovered at the entity level. While these nonamortizable syndication costs are treated as capital expenditures for accounting purposes, for proper maintenance of capital accounts the regulations surprisingly treat syndication costs as nondeductible, noncapitalizable expenses under §705(a)(2)(B) so that syndication costs must reduce the partners' capital accounts (but not outside bases) when incurred. Treas. Regs. §1.704-1(b)(2)(iv)(i)(2).

PROBLEMS

28-3. *R*, an individual, owns unimproved real estate worth $100,000. In order to develop this property, *R* forms *R* Group, a limited partnership comprised of *R* and 10 investors. *R* spends $10,000 on legal and accounting fees developing the *R* Group offering circular, $5,000 in legal fees to ensure that the *R* Group is properly formed and registered with the state, $1,000 in transfer fees to transfer title to the property from *R* to the partnership, and $2,500 in miscellaneous expenses such as the cost of opening the partnership checking account and purchasing liability insurance for the partnership's officers. The partnership reimburses *R* for these costs. What are the tax consequences to *R* and to the partnership of the payment by *R* of these expenses and of *R*'s reimbursement?

3. *Cancellation of Indebtedness Income and §108*

If a partnership acquires its outstanding debt for less than the debt's principal amount, the partnership will realize cancellation of indebtedness income just as any other taxpayer would in the same circumstances. Such income is subject to the relief provisions in §108, but that section has a peculiar application to partners and partnerships. Although income resulting from a discharge of a partnership debt is partnership-level income, §108(d)(6) specifically provides that the basic relief provisions of §108 (i.e., §§108(a), (b), and (g)) apply only at the partner level.

Section 108(a) allows a taxpayer to exclude cancellation of indebtedness (COI) income if the taxpayer is involved in a bankruptcy proceeding, §108(a)(1)(a), or, even in the absence of a formal bankruptcy proceeding, to the extent that the taxpayer is insolvent, §§108(a)(1)(B), 108(a)(3). Because these sections apply only at the partner level, §108(d)(6), partnership COI income is includible in each partner's distributive share without regard to partnership bankruptcy or insolvency. The exclusion provided by §108(a) can apply to such income, but only to the extent that an individual partner is involved in a bankruptcy proceeding or is insolvent. In short, partnership COI income is includible to the partnership without regard to the possible application of §108.

Because only §§108(a), (b), and (g) are explicitly made applicable at the partner level, an implication arises that the other parts of §108 are applicable at the entity level. In particular, it seems that application of §108(e)(5) is limited to the entity level. And that can cause a problem.

Section 108(e)(5) codifies the purchase-price reduction exception to the *Kirby Lumber* rules: No COI income results from the mere reduction in price (paid over time) of property purchased by the taxpayer. Because of the limited scope of §108(d)(6), this provision applies when the *partnership* enjoys a price reduction on property it purchased. That makes sense: If the partnership purchases property and the price is then reduced, there should be no COI income to the partnership or to any partner. Thus, limiting application of §108(e)(5) to the entity level seems to work.

However, by its terms the purchase-price reduction exception in §108(e)(5) is limited to cases *other than* when the purchaser is in bankruptcy or is insolvent. This limitation seems to be no more than an ordering rule: If the taxpayer is bankrupt, exclusion under §108(a) will be available even in a purchase-price reduction situation, while if the taxpayer is solvent, exclusion under §108(e)(5) still obtains. Consider, though, the case of a partnership which is insolvent while its partners are financially sound. For example, suppose *X* partnership was formed to operate an apartment complex, and *X* is owned by doctors, lawyers, and other professionals. If real estate prices fall, the partnership's property might fall in value to less than the amount of its outstanding mortgage on the property. If so, the partnership is insolvent.

Now consider the tax consequences of the seller of the property, holding the mortgage on the partnership's property, agreeing to reduce the outstanding debt down to the current value of the property. Such a debt reduction has become common since real estate prices fell in the late 1980s, and these types of transactions continue to occur today.

Reduction of the debt triggers COI income to the partnership. Can this COI income be excluded under §108? For any other taxpayer, the answer is clearly yes. But for the partnership and its partners, the statutory answer is no.

To see this, note first that §108(a) cannot apply here because its application is limited to bankrupt and insolvent taxpayers and, because it applies only at the partner level, the various partners rather than the partnership would have to be in financial difficulty. Does §108(e)(5) exclude the COI income? It cannot apply at the partnership level because by its terms it only applies when the debt reduction occurs *other than* in connection with a Title 11 bankruptcy case or insolvency of *the purchaser*. Since the purchaser (i.e., the partnership) is insolvent, §108(e)(5) should not apply.

Can §108(e)(5) apply to protect each individual partner? Presumably not, because it seems to be the case that §108(e)(5) applies only at the entity level. Recall that §108(d)(6) specifies which parts of §108 apply at the partner level, and §108(e)(5) is not in that list. Thus, there seems to be no exclusion of COI income resulting from a price reduction of partnership property when the partnership itself is involved in a bankruptcy proceeding or is insolvent. There is no indication that Congress intended this result, but the statute apparently demands it. Fortunately, the Service has ruled announced that in such circumstances each partner may apply §108(e)(5) at the partner level despite the lack of statutory support for its application. Rev. Proc. 92-92, 1992-2 C.B. 505. No statutory authority for this largess is given.

D.   MERGERS AND DIVISIONS

Under certain circumstances, a partnership resulting from the merger of two or more partnerships will be treated as the continuation of one of the merging entities. This avoids for the continuing partnership the liquidating distribution usually incident to termination. In addition, the surviving partnership will continue to use the taxable year, accounting methods, and other tax incidents (including the optional basis adjustments under §§734 and 743 if an election under §754 was filed) of its predecessor.

Under §708(b)(2)(A), a partnership formed by the merger of two or more partnerships will "be considered the continuation of any merging or consolidating partnership whose members own an interest of more than

50 percent in the capital and profits of the resulting partnership." This provision is troublesome because it permits the possibility that the resulting partnership will be treated as the continuation of *more than one* of the merging partnerships.

For example, suppose partnership X is owned by individuals A, B, and C, while partnership Y is owned by individuals B, C, and D. If X and Y consolidate into XY with A, B, C, and D each getting a one-quarter interest, under the terms of §708(b)(2)(A), XY should be treated as the continuation of both prior partnerships. That cannot be correct, though, because there is no reason to believe that X and Y had identical taxable years, used the same methods of accounting, or had filed the same elections. Under the regulations, "if the resulting partnership can . . . be considered a continuation of more than one of the merging or consolidating partnerships, it shall . . . be considered the continuation of that partnership which is credited with the contribution of the greatest dollar value of assets to the resulting partnership." Treas. Regs. §1.708-1(b)(2)(i). In our example, we would have to know the dollar value of assets transferred by X and Y to XY to know which partnership will be treated as surviving the consolidation.

If a partnership divides into two or more partnerships, one or more of the resulting partnerships may be treated as a continuation of the initial entity. The test for divisions mirrors that for mergers and consolidations: Each of the resulting partnerships whose partners owned 50 percent or more of the capital and profits of the initial partnership is treated as a continuation of the initial partnership. §708(b)(2)(B). Once again there may be several partnerships qualifying for continuation under this rule, but here there is no difficulty with multiple continuations. For example, if our $ABCD$ partnership split back into the ABC and BCD partnerships, both ABC and BCD would be treated as a continuation of $ABCD$.

PROBLEMS

28-4.   Individual M, a partner in the KLM partnership, sells her partnership interest to individual O. Assume that this sale forces a technical termination of the partnership under §708(b)(1)(B). The remaining partners and individual O continue to operate the business in partnership form. Is this new partnership a continuation of KLM by virtue of §708(b)(2)?

Table of Cases

Table of Revenue Rulings and Procedures and Other Miscellaneous IRS Pronouncements

Principal rulings are in italics.

Index